International Conference on Recent Advances in Natural Language Processing 2011

(RANLP 2011)

Hissar, Bulgaria
12-14 September 2011

Editors:

Galia Angelova
Ruslan Mitkov
Kalina Bontcheva
Nikolai Nikolov

ISBN: 978-1-62276-511-9

Printed from e-media with permission by:

Curran Associates, Inc.
57 Morehouse Lane
Red Hook, NY 12571

Some format issues inherent in the e-media version may also appear in this print version.

Printed by Curran Associates, Inc. (2013)

Association for Computational Linguistics
209 N. Eighth Street
Stroudsburg, Pennsylvania 18360

Phone: 1-570-476-8006
Fax: 1-570-476-0860

acl@aclweb.org

Additional copies of this publication are available from:

Curran Associates, Inc.
57 Morehouse Lane
Red Hook, NY 12571 USA
Phone: 845-758-0400
Fax: 845-758-2634
Email: curran@proceedings.com
Web: www.proceedings.com

Preface

Welcome to the 8th International Conference on "Recent Advances in Natural Language Processing" (RANLP 2011) in Hissar, Bulgaria, 12–14 September 2011. The main objective of the conference is to give researchers the opportunity to present new results in Natural Language Processing (NLP) based on modern theories and methodologies.

The conference is preceded by two days of tutorials (10-11 September 2011) and the lecturers are:

- Kevin Bretonnel Cohen (University of Colorado School of Medicine)
- Patrick Hanks (University of the West of England, Bristol and University of Wolverhampton)
- Erhard Hinrichs (University of Tuebingen)
- Zornitsa Kozareva (Information Sciences Institute, University of Southern California) and Preslav Nakov (National University of Singapore)
- Inderjeet Mani (Children's Organization of Southeast Asia)
- Lucia Specia and Wilker Aziz (University of Wolverhampton)

The conference keynote speakers are:

- Ido Dagan, Bar Ilan University
- Patrick Hanks, University of the West of England and University of Wolverhampton
- Inderjeet Mani, Children's Organization of Southeast Asia
- Roberto Navigli, Sapienza University of Rome
- Pierre-Paul Sondag, European Commission, DG INFSO
- Hans Uszkoreit, University of Saarland

This year 29 regular papers, 38 short papers, 48 posters and 2 demos have been accepted for presentation at the conference. RANLP'2011 also hosts 6 workshops (one of which student workshop) on influential NLP topics, such as unsupervised and semi-supervised NLP methods, information extraction and knowledge acquisition, language technologies for digital humanities and cultural heritage, biomedical NLP, and parallel corpora.

The proceedings cover a wide variety of NLP topics: datasets, annotation, treebanks, parallel corpora, information extraction, parsing, word sense disambiguation, translation, indexing, ontologies, question answering, document similarity, document classification, anaphora resolution, referring expressions generation, textual entailment, latent semantic analysis, summarization, rhetorical relations, etc.

We would like to thank all members of the Programme Committee and all reviewers. Together they have ensured that the best papers were included in the proceedings and have provided invaluable comments for the authors.

Finally, special thanks go to the University of Wolverhampton, the Bulgarian Academy of Sciences, Ontotext, and the Association for Computational Linguistics – Bulgaria for their generous and continuing support for RANLP.

Welcome to Hissar and we hope that you enjoy the conference!

The RANLP 2011 Organisers

The International Conference RANLP–2011 is organised by:

Research Group in Computational Linguistics, University of Wolverhampton, UK

Linguistic Modelling Department,
Institute of Information and Communication Technologies,
Bulgarian Academy of Sciences, Bulgaria

Association for Computational Linguistics - Bulgaria

RANLP–2011 is partially supported by:

The University of Wolverhampton, UK

The Institute of Information and Communication Technologies,
Bulgarian Academy of Sciences, Bulgaria

Ontotext AD

Association for Computational Linguistics - Bulgaria

Programme Committee Chair:

Ruslan Mitkov, University of Wolverhampton

Organising Committee Chair:

Galia Angelova, Bulgarian Academy of Sciences

Workshop Coordinator:

Kiril Simov, Bulgarian Academy of Sciences

Publication Chair:

Kalina Bontcheva, University of Sheffield

Proceedings Printing:

Nikolai Nikolov, INCOMA Ltd., Shoumen

Programme Committee Coordinators:

Ivelina Nikolova, Bulgarian Academy of Sciences
Irina Temnikova, University of Wolverhampton
Natalia Konstantinova, University of Wolverhampton
Preslav Nakov, National University of Singapore, Singapore

Program Committee:

Guadalupe Aguado de Cea (Polytechnic University Madrid, Spain)
Elisabeth André (University of Augsburg, Germany)
Galia Angelova (Bulgarian Academy of Sciences, Bulgaria)
Silvia Bernardini (University of Bologna, Italy)
Kalina Bontcheva (University of Sheffield, UK)
António Branco (University of Lisbon, Portugal)
Kevin Bretonnel Cohen (University of Colorado School of Medicine, USA)
Nicoletta Calzolari (Institute of Computational Linguistics CNR, Italy)
Dan Cristea ("Al. I. Cuza" University of Iasi, Romania)
Gloria Corpas (University of Malaga, Spain)
András Csomai (University of North Texas, USA)
Walter Daelemans (University of Antwerp, Belgium)
Arantza Díaz de Ilarraza (University of Basque Country, Spain)
Alexander Gelbukh (National Polytechnic Institute, Mexico)
Pablo Gervás (Complutense University of Madrid, Spain)
Ralph Grishman (New York University, USA)
Catalina Hallett (University of Wolverhampton, UK)
Graeme Hirst (University of Toronto, Canada)
Véronique Hoste (University College Ghent, Belgium)
Diana Inkpen (University of Ottawa, Canada)
Frances Johnson (Manchester Metropolitan Univ., UK)
Alma Kharrat (Microsoft, USA)
Richard Kittredge (CoGenTex, Inc., USA)
Steven Krauwer (University of Utrecht, The Netherlands)
Hristo Krushkov (Plovdiv University "P. Hilendrski", Bulgaria)
Lori Lamel (LIMSI - CNRS, France)
Ricardo Mairal Usón (National University of Distance Education, Spain)
Manuel J. Mana Lopez (University of Huelva, Spain)
Yuji Matsumoto (NAIST, Japan)
Irina Matveeva (Dieselpoint Inc., USA)
Diana Maynard (University of Sheffield, UK)
Rada Mihalcea (University of North Texas, USA)
Andrei Mikheev (Infogistics Ltd & Daxtra Tech. Ltd, UK)
Ruslan Mitkov (University of Wolverhampton, UK)
Johanna Monti (University of Salerno, Italy)
Andrés Montoyo (University of Alicante, Spain)
Rafael Muñoz Guillena (University of Alicante, Spain)
Preslav Nakov (National University of Singapore, Singapore)
Roberto Navigli (University di Roma La Sapienza, Italy)
Ani Nenkova (University of Pennsylvania, USA)
Kemal Oflazer (Carnegie Mellon University, Qatar)
Constantin Orasan (University of Wolverhampton, UK)

Manuel Palomar (University of Alicante, Spain)
Javier Perez Guerra (University of Vigo, Spain)
Stelios Piperidis (ILSP, Greece)
John Prager (IBM, USA)
Gábor Prószéky (MorphoLogic, Hungary)
Stephen Pulman (Oxford University, UK)
Marta Recasens (Stanford University, USA)
Allan Ramsay (University of Manchester, UK)
Horacio Rodriguez (Technical University of Catalonia, Spain)
Horacio Saggion (Universitat Pompeu Fabra, Spain)
Murat Saraclar (Bogazici University, Turkey)
Frederique Segond (Xerox Research Centre Europe, France)
Khaled Shaalan (British University in Dubai, United Arab Emirates)
Khalil Sima'an (University of Amsterdam, The Netherlands)
Kiril Simov (Bulgarian Academy of Sciences, Bulgaria)
Lucia Specia (University of Wolverhampton, UK)
Keh-Yih Su (Behavior Design Corporation, Taiwan)
Maite Taboada (Simon Fraser University, Canada)
George Totkov (Plovdiv University "P. Hilendrski", Bulgaria)
Kristina Toutanova (Microsoft, USA)
Dan Tufiş (Research Institute for AI, Romania)
L. Alfonso Urena Lopez (University of Jaen, Spain)
Karin Verspoor (University of Colorado Denver, USA)
Manuel Vilares Ferro (University of Corunna, Spain)
Piek Vossen (VU University Amsterdam, The Netherlands)
Yorick Wilks (University of Sheffield, UK)

Reviewers:

Rao Muhammad Adeel Nawab (University of Sheffield, UK)
Naveed Afzal (University of Wolverhampton, UK)
Hanady Ahmed (Qatar University, Qatar)
Itziar Aldabe (University of the Basque Country, Spain)
Ahmet Aker (University of Sheffield, UK)
Wilker Aziz (University of Wolverhampton, UK)
Pedro Paulo Balage Filho (University of Wolverhampton, UK)
Alexandra Balahur (University of Alicante, Spain)
Verginica Barbu (Romanian Academy, Romania)
Elena Bárcena Madera (National University of Distance Education, Spain)
Dimitar Blagoev (Plovdiv University "P. Hilendrski", Bulgaria)
Ester Boldrini (University of Alicante, Spain)
Svetla Boytcheva (State University of Library Studies and Information Technologies, Bulgaria)
María del Carmen Guarddon Anelo (National University of Distance Education, Spain)
José Guilherme Camargo de (Bruno Kessler Foundation, Italy)
Sheila Castilho (University of Wolverhampton, UK)
Atanas Chanev (University of Pisa, Italy)
Miranda Chong (University of Wolverhampton, UK)
Iria da Cunha (Universitat Pompeu Fabra, Spain)
Noa Cruz Díaz (University of Huelva, Spain)
Iustin Dornescu (University of Wolverhampton, UK)
Isabel Duran (University of Malaga, Spain)
Maud Ehrmann (European Commission - Joint Research Centre, Italy)
Óscar Ferrández Escamez (University of Utah, USA)
Joey Frazee (University of Texas, USA)
Kallirroi Georgila (University of Southern California, USA)
Richard Gil Herrera(University Simon Bolivar, Venezuela and University of Granada, Spain)
Margarita Goded-Rambaud (National University of Distance Education, Spain)
José M. Gómez (University of Alicante, Spain)
Le An Ha (University of Wolverhampton, UK)
Najeh Hajlaoui (University of Wolverhampton, UK)
Laura Hasler (University of Strathclyde, UK)
Iris Hendrickx (University of Lisbon, Portugal)
Adrian Iftene (Al. I. Cuza University of Iasi, Romania)
Iustina Ilisei (University of Wolverhampton, UK)
Radu Ion (Romanian Academy, Romania)
Rubén Izquierdo Beviá (University of Alicante, Spain)
Heng Ji (New York University, USA)
Alice Kaiser-Schatzlein (University of Wolverhampton, UK)
Jason Kessler (Indiana University, USA)
Natalia Konstantinova (University of Wolverhampton, UK)
Ioannis Korkontzelos (University of Manchester, UK)
Milen Kouylekov (CELI Language & Information Technology, Italy)
Elena Lloret (University of Alicante, Spain)
María Victoria López (Public University of Navarre, Spain)
Annie Louis (University of Pennsylvania, USA)
Wolfgang Maier (University of Düsseldorf, Germany)
Arturo Montejo-Ráez (University of Jaén, Spain)
Paul Morarescu (SRI International, USA)
Paloma Moreda (University of Alicante, Spain)

Ivelina Nikolova (Bulgarian Academy of Sciences, Bulgaria)
Michael Oakes (University of Sunderland, UK)
Shiyan Ou (Nanjing University, China)
Ionut Pistol ("Al.I.Cuza" University of Iasi, Romania)
Emily Pitler (University of Pennsylvania, USA)
Paul Piwek (The Open University, UK)
Natalia Ponomareva (University of Wolverhampton, UK)
Jelena Prokic (Ludwig-Maximilians-Universität, Germany)
Prokopis Prokopidis (Institute for Language and Speech Processing, Greece)
Georgiana Puscasu (University of Wolverhampton, UK)
Luz Rello (Universitat Pompeu Fabra, Spain)
Miguel Angel Rios Gaona (University of Wolverhampton, UK)
Ana Rull (National University of Distance Education, Spain)
Estela S. Boro (University of Alicante, Spain)
Armando S. Cueto (University of Alicante, Spain)
Doaa Samy (Cairo University, Egypt)
Miriam Seghiri (University of Malaga, Spain)
Violeta Seretan (University of Edinburgh, UK)
Smriti Singh (Indian Institute of Technology Patna, India)
Yvonne Skalban (University of Wolverhampton, UK)
Sanja Stajner (University of Wolverhampton, UK)
Ekaterina Stambolieva (University of Wolverhampton, UK)
Veselin Stoyanov (Johns Hopkins University, USA)
Ang Sun (New York University, USA)
Irina Temnikova (University of Wolverhampton, UK)
Diana Trandabat ("Al.I.Cuza" University of Iasi, Romania)
Sonia Vázquez (University of Alicante, Spain)
Cristina Vertan (University of Hamburg, Germany)
Manuel de la Villa (University of Huelva, Spain)
Sandra Williams (The Open University, UK)
Alistair Willis (The Open University, UK)
Shumin Wu (University of Colorado at Boulder, USA)
Anssi Yli-Jyra (University of Helsinki, Finland)
Jakub Zavrel (Textkernel BV, The Netherlands)
Kalliopi Zervanou (University Of Tilburg, The Netherlands)
Imed Zitouni (IBM Research, NY, USA)

Invited Speakers:

Ido Dagan, Bar Ilan University
Patrick Hanks, University of the West of England and University of Wolverhampton
Inderjeet Mani, Children's Organization of Southeast Asia
Roberto Navigli, Sapienza University of Rome
Pierre-Paul Sondag, European Commission, DG INFSO
Hans Uszkoreit, University of Saarland

Table of Contents

Conference Programme

Monday, 12 September, 2011

8:50–9:00 Opening

9:00–10:00 Invited Talk: Pierre-Paul Sondag "Language Technologies: A broad EU overview"

Hall 1: Event Extraction

10:00–10:30 *Extracting STRIPS Representations of Actions and Events*
Avirup Sil and Alexander Yates

10:30–11:00 *Acquiring Topic Features to improve Event Extraction: in Pre-selected and Balanced Collections*
Shasha Liao and Ralph Grishman

Hall 2: Relation Extraction

10:00–10:30 *Minimally Supervised Rule Learning for the Extraction of Biographic Information from Various Social Domains*
Hong Li, Feiyu Xu and Hans Uszkoreit

10:30–11:00 *Extracting Relations Within and Across Sentences*
Kumutha Swampillai and Mark Stevenson

Hall 3: POS Tagging and Parsing

10:00–10:30 *Knowledge-Poor Approach to Shallow Parsing: Contribution of Unsupervised Part-of-Speech Induction*
Marie Guégan and Claude de Loupy

10:30–11:00 *Fast Domain Adaptation for Part of Speech Tagging for Dialogues*
Sandra Kübler and Eric Baucom

11:00–11:30 Coffee break and Posters (Lobby)

Monday, 12 September, 2011 (continued)

Hall 1: POS Tagging, Parsing and Grammars

Hall 2: Summarisation, Generation and Machine Translation

Monday, 12 September, 2011 (continued)

Hall 3: Resources

11:30–11:50 *JRC-NAMES: A Freely Available, Highly Multilingual Named Entity Resource*
Ralf Steinberger, Bruno Pouliquen, Mijail Kabadjov, Jenya Belyaeva and Erik van der Goot

11:50–12:10 *MDL-based Models for Alignment of Etymological Data*
Hannes Wettig, Suvi Hiltunen and Roman Yangarber

12:10–12:30 *Building a Multilingual Named Entity-Annotated Corpus Using Annotation Projection*
Maud Ehrmann, Marco Turchi and Ralf Steinberger

12:30–12:50 *Bilingual lexicon extraction from comparable corpora for closely related languages*
Darja Fišer and Nikola Ljubešić

12:50–14:30 Lunch

14:30–15:30 Invited Talk: Patrick Hanks "How People Use Words to Make Meanings"

Hall 1: Sentiment Analysis

15:30–16:00 *Sentiments and Opinions in Health-related Web messages*
Marina Sokolova and Victoria Bobicev

16:00–16:30 *An Exploration into the Use of Contextual Document Clustering for Cluster Sentiment Analysis*
Niall Rooney, Hui Wang, Fiona Browne, Fergal Monaghan, Jann Müller, Alan Sergeant, Zhiwei Lin, Philip Taylor and Vladimir Dobrynin

Monday, 12 September, 2011 (continued)

Hall 2: Text and Discourse Segmentation

15:30–16:00 *Pause and Stop Labeling for Chinese Sentence Boundary Detection*
Hen-Hsen Huang and Hsin-Hsi Chen

16:00–16:30 *Multilabel Tagging of Discourse Relations in Ambiguous Temporal Connectives*
Yannick Versley

Hall 3: Named Entity Recognition

15:30–16:00 *Noun Compound and Named Entity Recognition and their Usability in Keyphrase Extraction*
István Nagy T., Gábor Berend and Veronika Vincze

16:00–16:30 *A Named Entity Recognition Method using Rules Acquired from Unlabeled Data*
Tomoya Iwakura

16:30–18:30 Coffee Break and Poster Session 1 (Lobby)

Tuesday, 13 September, 2011

9:00–10:00 Invited Talk: Inderjeet Mani "Getting Oriented: Spatial Prepositions, Frames of Reference, and Spatial Reasoning"

Hall 1: Coreference Resolution

10:00–10:30 *An Incremental Entity-Mention Model for Coreference Resolution with Restrictive Antecedent Accessibility*
Manfred Klenner and Don Tuggener

10:30–11:00 *Cross-Domain Dutch Coreference Resolution*
Orphée De Clercq, Véronique Hoste and Iris Hendrickx

Tuesday, 13 September, 2011 (continued)

Hall 2: Summarisation

10:00–10:30 *Finding the Best Approach for Multi-lingual Text Summarisation: A Comparative Analysis*
Elena Lloret and Manuel Palomar

10:30–11:00 *Automatically Creating General-Purpose Opinion Summaries from Text*
Veselin Stoyanov and Claire Cardie

Hall 3: Event and Temporal Relation Extraction

10:00–10:30 *Exploring the Usefulness of Cross-lingual Information Fusion for Refining Real-time News Event Extraction: A Preliminary Study*
Jakub Piskorski, Jenya Belayeva and Martin Atkinson

10:30–11:00 *Temporal Relation Extraction Using Expectation Maximization*
Seyed Abolghasem Mirroshandel and Gholamreza Ghassem-Sani

11:00–11:30 Coffee Break and Student Posters (Lobby)

Hall 1: Semantic Processing and Applications

11:30–11:50 *Improving Chunk-based Semantic Role Labeling with Lexical Features*
Wilker Aziz, Miguel Rios and Lucia Specia

11:50–12:10 *Improving WSD using ISR-WN with Relevant Semantic Trees and SemCor Senses Frequency*
Yoan Gutiérrez, Sonia Vázquez and Andrés Montoyo

12:10–12:30 *Investigating Advanced Techniques for Document Content Similarity Applied to External Plagiarism Analysis*
Daniel Micol, Rafael Muñoz and Óscar Ferrández

12:30–12:50 *Using Cognates in a French-Romanian Lexical Alignment System: A Comparative Study*
Mirabela Navlea and Amalia Todirașcu

Hall 2: Coreference Resolution, Discourse, Annotation

11:30–11:50 *Highly Multilingual Coreference Resolution Exploiting a Mature Entity Repository*
Josef Steinberger, Jenya Belyaeva, Jonathan Crawley, Leonida Della-Rocca, Mohamed Ebrahim, Maud Ehrmann, Mijail Kabadjov, Ralf Steinberger and Erik Van-der-Goot

11:50–12:10 *Singletons and Coreference Resolution Evaluation*
Sandra Kübler and Desislava Zhekova

12:10–12:30 *Modelling Entity Instantiations*
Andrew McKinlay and Katja Markert

12:30–12:50 *A New Scheme for Annotating Semantic Relations between Named Entities in Corpora*
Mani Ezzat and Thierry Poibeau

Hall 3: Student Workshop

12:50–14:30 Lunch

14:30–15:30 Invited Talk: Hans Uzskoreit "Research Results and Technology Visions for Multilingual Europe"

Hall 1: Information Extraction-Related Tasks

15:30–15:50 *Prototypical Opinion Holders: What We can Learn from Experts and Analysts*
Michael Wiegand and Dietrich Klakow

15:50–16:10 *Multiword Expressions and Named Entities in the Wiki50 Corpus*
Veronika Vincze, István Nagy T. and Gábor Berend

Tuesday, 13 September, 2011 (continued)

Hall 2: Building Resources

15:30–15:50 *Towards the Automatic Merging of Lexical Resources: Automatic Mapping*
Muntsa Padró, Núria Bel and Silvia Necsulescu

15:50–16:10 *Unsupervised Learning for Persian WordNet Construction*
Mortaza Montazery and Heshaam Faili

Hall 3: Authorship Attribution and Autoreferentiality Detection

15:30–15:50 *Domain Independent Authorship Attribution without Domain Adaptation*
Rohith Menon and Yejin Choi

15:50–16:10 *Cultural Configuration of Wikipedia: measuring Autoreferentiality in Different Languages*
Marc Miquel Ribé and Horacio Rodríguez

16:10–16:50 Coffee Break and Student Poster Session

Wednesday, 14 September, 2011

9:00–10:00 Invited Talk: Roberto Navigli "Is it Just a Waste of Time? Word Sense Disambiguation for the Skeptic"

Hall 1: Semantic Processing

10:00–10:30 *Combining Relational and Attributional Similarity for Semantic Relation Classification*
Preslav Nakov and Zornitsa Kozareva

10:30–11:00 *In Search of Missing Arguments: A Linguistic Approach*
Josef Ruppenhofer, Philip Gorinski and Caroline Sporleder

Wednesday, 14 September, 2011 (continued)

Hall 2: Dictionary and Terminology

10:00–10:30 *Enlarging Monolingual Dictionaries for Machine Translation with Active Learning and Non-Expert Users*
Miquel Esplà-Gomis, Víctor M. Sánchez-Cartagena and Juan Antonio Pérez-Ortiz

10:30–11:00 *Morphological Analysis of Biomedical Terminology with Analogy-Based Alignment*
Vincent Claveau and Ewa Kijak

Hall 3: Grammars

10:00–10:30 *Adaptability of Lexical Acquisition for Large-scale Grammars*
Kostadin Cholakov, Gertjan van Noord, Valia Kordoni and Yi Zhang

10:30–11:00 *Integration of Data from a Syntactic Lexicon into Generative and Discriminative Probabilistic Parsers*
Anthony Sigogne, Matthieu Constant and Éric Laporte

11:00–11:30 Coffee Break and Posters (Lobby)

Hall 1: Information Extraction-Related Tasks

11:30–11:50 *Pattern Learning for Event Extraction using Monolingual Statistical Machine Translation*
Marco Turchi, Vanni Zavarella and Hristo Tanev

11:50–12:10 *META-DARE: Monitoring the Minimally Supervised ML of Relation Extraction Rules*
Hong Li, Feiyu Xu and Hans Uszkoreit

12:10–12:30 *Mining Transliterations from Wikipedia using Dynamic Bayesian Networks*
Peter Nabende

12:30–12:50 *Detecting Opinions Using Deep Syntactic Analysis*
Caroline Brun

Wednesday, 14 September, 2011 (continued)

Hall 2: Knowledge Acquisition / Resources

11:30–11:50 *Using Visual Information to Predict Lexical Preference*
Shane Bergsma and Randy Goebel

11:50–12:10 *Systematic Knowledge Acquisition for Question Analysis*
Dat Quoc Nguyen, Dai Quoc Nguyen and Son Bao Pham

12:10–12:30 *A Semi-Automatic, Iterative Method for Creating a Domain-Specific Treebank*
Corina Dima and Erhard Hinrichs

12:30–12:50 *Determining Immediate Constituents of Compounds in GermaNet*
Verena Henrich and Erhard Hinrichs

Hall 3: Genre Analysis, Polarity Classification, Language Learning, Arabic Language Processing

11:30–11:50 *Segmentation and Clustering of Textual Sequences: a Typological Approach*
Christelle Cocco, Raphaël Pittier, François Bavaud and Aris Xanthos

11:50–12:10 *A Contextual Classification Strategy for Polarity Analysis of Direct Quotations from Financial News*
Brett Drury, Gaël Dias and Luís Torgo

12:10–12:30 *On the Contribution of MWE-based Features to a Readability Formula for French as a Foreign Language*
Thomas François and Patrick Watrin

12:30–12:50 *Exploiting Hidden Morphophonemic Constraints for Finding the Underlying Forms of 'weak' Arabic Verbs*
Allan Ramsay and Hanady Mansour

12:50–14:30 Lunch

Wednesday, 14 September, 2011 (continued)

14:30–15:00 Invited Talk: Ido Dagan "Let Computers Think in Human Language"

Hall 1: Textual Entailment/Knowledge Acquisition

15:00–15:30 *A Confidence Model for Syntactically-Motivated Entailment Proofs*
Asher Stern and Ido Dagan

15:30–16:00 *Learning Script Participants from Unlabeled Data*
Michaela Regneri, Alexander Koller, Josef Ruppenhofer and Manfred Pinkal

Hall 2: Parsing and Discourse

15:00–15:30 *Towards Minimal Recursion Semantics over Bulgarian Dependency Parsing*
Kiril Simov and Petya Osenova

15:30–16:00 *Discourse Structures to Reduce Discourse Incoherence in Blog Summarization*
Shamima Mithun and Leila Kosseim

Hall 3: Formal aspects of Language Processing

15:00–15:30 *Parallel Suffix Arrays for Linguistic Pattern Search*
Johannes Goller

15:30–16:00 *A Mechanism to Restrict the Scope of Clause-Bounded Quantifiers in 'Continuation' Semantics*
Anca Dinu

16:30–18:30 Coffee and Poster Session 2

18:30–18:40 Closing

Poster and Demo Session 1, 12 September, 16:30–18:30

Poster and Demo Session 1, 12 September, 16:30–18:30 (continued)

Poster and Demo Session 1, 12 September, 16:30–18:30 (continued)

Studying Translationese at the Character Level
Marius Popescu

Linear Transduction Grammars and Zipper Finite-State Transducers
Markus Saers and Dekai Wu

Finding Negative Key Phrases for Internet Advertising Campaigns using Wikipedia
Martin Scaiano and Diana Inkpen

Establishing Implementation Priorities in Aiding Writers of Controlled Crisis Management Texts
Irina Temnikova

Poster and Demo Session 2, 14 September, 16:40–18:30

Demo

TechWatchTool: Innovation and Trend Monitoring
Hong Li, Feiyu Xu and Hans Uszkoreit

Posters

"Yes we can?": Subjectivity Annotation and Tagging for the Health Domain
Muhammad Abdul-Mageed, Mohammed Korayem and Ahmed YoussefAgha

Wordnets: State of the Art and Perspectives. Case Study: the Romanian Wordnet
Verginica Barbu Mititelu

Creation and Development of the Romanian Lexical Resources
Elena Boian, Constantin Ciubotaru, Svetlana Cojocaru, Alexandru Colesnicov, Ludmila Malahov and Mircea Petic

Analyses Tools for Non-head Structures
Sirine Boukedi and Kais Haddar

Visualization for Coreference Annotation
Andre Burkovski and Gunther Heidemann

Poster and Demo Session 2, 14 September, 16:40–18:30 (continued)

The RST Spanish Treebank On-line Interface
Iria da Cunha, Juan-Manuel Torres-Moreno, Gerardo Sierra, Luis Adrián Cabrera-Diego, Brenda Gabriela Castro Rolón and Juan Miguel Rolland Bartilotti

Lexical Generalisation for Word-level Matching in Plagiarism Detection
Miranda Chong and Lucia Specia

Multiple Evidence for Term Extraction in Broad Domains
Boris Dobrov and Natalia Loukachevitch

Language Modeling for Document Selection in Question Answering
Nicolas Foucault, Gilles Adda and Sophie Rosset

Evaluating Various Linguistic Features on Semantic Relation Extraction
Marcos Garcia and Pablo Gamallo

Automatic titling of Articles Using Position and Statistical Information
Cédric Lopez, Violaine Prince and Mathieu Roche

Unsupervised Domain Adaptation based on Text Relatedness
Georgios Petasis

Bilingual Experiments with an Arabic-English Corpus for Opinion Mining
Mohammed Rushdi-Saleh, M. Teresa Martín-Valdivia, L. Alfonso Ureña-López and José M. Perea-Ortega

Experiments on Term Extraction using Noun Phrase Subclassifications
Merley da Silva Conrado, Walter Koza, Josuka Díaz-Labrador, Joseba Abaitua, Solange Oliveira Rezende, Thiago Pardo and Zulema Solana

Adaptive Feedback Message Generation for Second Language Learners of Arabic
Khaled Shaalan and Marwa Magdy

Building a Patient-based Ontology for User-written Web Messages
Marina Sokolova and David Schramm

Recognition and Classification of Numerical Entities in Basque
Ander Soraluze, Iñaki Alegria, Olatz Ansa, Olatz Arregi and Xabier Arregi

Poster and Demo Session 2, 14 September, 16:40–18:30 (continued)

Extracting STRIPS Representations of Actions and Events

Avirup Sil and **Alexander Yates**
Center for Data Analytics and Biomedical Informatics
Temple University
Broad St. and Montgomery Ave.
Philadelphia, PA 19122
{avirup.sil, yates}@temple.edu

Abstract

Knowledge about how the world changes over time is a vital component of common-sense knowledge for Artificial Intelligence (AI) and natural language understanding. Actions and events are fundamental components to any knowledge about changes in the state of the world: the states before and after an event differ in regular and predictable ways. We describe a novel system that tackles the problem of extracting knowledge from text about how actions and events change the world over time. We leverage standard language-processing tools, like semantic role labelers and coreference resolvers, as well as large-corpus statistics like pointwise mutual information, to identify STRIPS representations of actions and events, a type of representation commonly used in AI planning systems. In experiments on Web text, our extractor's Area under the Curve (AUC) improves by more than 31% over the closest system from the literature for identifying the preconditions and add effects of actions. In addition, we also extract significant aspects of STRIPS representations that are missing from previous work, including delete effects and arguments.

1 Introduction

Common-sense knowledge about the changes in the state of the world over time is one of the most crucial forms of knowledge for an intelligent agent, since it informs an agent of the ways in which it can act upon the world. A recent survey of the common-sense knowledge involved in the recognizing textual entailment task demonstrates that knowledge about action and event semantics, in particular, constitutes a major component of the knowledge involved in understanding natural language (LoBue and Yates, 2011). This knowledge is also vital for central AI tasks like planning, plan recognition (Kautz, 1991; Geib and Steedman, 2007), and dialogue processing (Carberry, 1990; Litman and Allen, 1987).

In this paper we explore text mining approaches to extracting common-sense knowledge about action and event semantics. Our previous approach (Sil et al., 2010) (henceforth, S10) identifies the preconditions and effects of actions. We describe how we extend S10's approach by identifying additional kinds of effects; by connecting this knowledge to an external ontology and generalizing the preconditions and effects; and by identifying argument variables for each predicate. Our experiments show that our novel extractor can identify the fully-formed STRIPS representations of actions with precision 0.73 and recall 0.72, and it improves on S10's AUC for tasks that both systems can handle by over 31%.

The next section discusses previous work. Section 3 introduces STRIPS representation and the challenges involved in extracting such representations. Section 4 details our extraction techniques. Section 5 presents our experiments. Section 6 concludes and discusses future work.

2 Previous Work

The most closely related work has investigated how to extract "scripts" or "narrative event schemas" (Chambers and Jurafsky, 2009) — sets of events that often occur together. Schank and Abelson's (1977) famous example of a restaurant script includes events such as sitting down, ordering, eating, and paying the bill. Script knowledge is distinct from STRIPS representations in that a script relates one event e to a subsequent event e', whereas STRIPS relates an event e to a state of the world s before or after e. Our extracted knowledge could complement the standard restaurant script, for example, with knowledge that `is hungry(diner)` is true before the diner eats, and $\neg$`is hungry(diner)` is true afterwards. Neither of these statements constitutes an event in a script, but they do fall into the STRIPS paradigm.

Other research into extracting the relationships between events has investigated causal relationships (Girju, 2003) and, more generally, paraphrases, such as in the DIRT system (Lin and Pantel, 2001). Such systems typically do not distinguish between event-event relationships that appear in scripts — *e.g.*, a flooding event e_2 can follow a raining event e_1 — and event-state relationships — *e.g.*, `is wet(grass)` follows a raining event e_1. Our system is focused only on the latter: we are concerned how the state of the world changes with the occurrence of an event rather than how one event influences another event. Furthermore, existing systems do not consider precondition relationships, which are neither causal nor paraphrases, and which are central to AI representations of actions and events.

Extracting and representing selectional preferences has attracted significant attention recently, especially using latent-variable probabilistic models like Latent Dirichlet Allocation (Ritter et al., 2010). Preconditions are a more general type of restriction on the arguments to actions than selectional preferences — *e.g.* asleep(x) is a precondition to `awaken`, but would not be considered a selectional preference because it does not constitute a class or type, but rather a property, of x.

3 STRIPS Representations

3.1 Background and Terminology

We define *actions* as observable phenomena, or *events*, that are brought about by rational agents. Because actions and events are central to AI, there is a long history of work in representing their semantics. One of the best-known, and still widely used, representations for action semantics is the STRIPS representation (Fikes and Nilsson, 1971); two examples of STRIPS representations are given in Figure 1. We use STRIPS to represent both actions and events. Formally, a STRIPS representation is a 5-tuple $(a, args, pre, add, del)$ consisting of the action name a, a list $args$ of argument variables that range over the set of objects in the world, and three sets of predicates that reference the argument variables. The first, the *precondition* list pre, is a set of conditions

		awaken	insert
STRIPS	**args:**	x	o, p
	pre:	$asleep(x)$	$object\#1(o)$, $opening\#1(p)$, $\neg\text{in}(o,p)$
	add:	$awake(x)$	$\text{in}(o,p)$
	del:	$asleep(x)$	$\neg\text{in}(o,p)$
S10	**pre:**	$asleep$	$person$, $slot$
	add:	$awake$	in

Figure 1: Two example STRIPS representations (above), and corresponding examples of the representation extracted in our prior work, S10 (below). In contrast with S10, the STRIPS representations require extracting delete effects and resolving coreference relationships among arguments to predicates. Also, our version of STRIPS uses WordNet synsets to unambiguously specify predicate names.

that must be met in order for the action to be allowed to take place. For instance, in order for someone to *awaken*, she or he must first be *asleep*. The other two sets of conditions specify how the world changes when the action takes place: the add list describes the set of new conditions that must be true afterwards (*e.g.*, after the event `insert(pencil24,sharpener3)`, `in(pencil24,sharpener3)` holds true), and the del list specifies the conditions that were true before the action happened but are no longer true. These add and del conditions are sometimes collectively referred to as *effects* or *postconditions*.

Formally, the precondition, add, and delete lists correspond to a set of rules describing the logical consequences of observing an event. To describe these rules, we assume a representation of the world grounded in a logical form, such as situation logic (Barwise, 1989) or episodic logic (Schubert and Hwang, 2000). For simplicity, we represent the passage of time by discrete time points t, together with a temporal-ordering relation *after*(t_1, t_2). This is the same notion of time traditionally adopted by AI planning systems, although recent work has gone into elaborating this representation (Bresina et al., 2002; Younes et al., 2003). A set of constants identify the *objects* that exist in the world, and at each time point, a set of logical *predicates* describes the *state* of the world at that time, for instance $\texttt{on(book1, shelf4,} t_9\texttt{)}$.

Let t_1 be the time point immediately preceding an event e with arguments **args**, t_2 the time of event e, and t_3 the time immediately following e. For each precondition p, each add effect a, and each delete effect d, the following rules hold:

$$\forall_{\mathbf{args}} e(\mathbf{args}, t_2) \Rightarrow p(\mathbf{args}_p, t_1)$$
$$\forall_{\mathbf{args}} e(\mathbf{args}, t_2) \Rightarrow a(\mathbf{args}_a, t_3)$$
$$\forall_{\mathbf{args}} e(\mathbf{args}, t_2) \Rightarrow \neg d(\mathbf{args}_d, t_3)$$

where $\mathbf{args}_x$ represents the subset of the arguments to which the predicate x applies. Finally, we assume a second-order *frame axiom* that states that unless explicitly updated by an event's effects, predicates that were true (false) before an event remain true (false) afterwards.

3.2 Problem Formulation: STRIPS Extraction

The STRIPS extraction task takes as input a word or phrase e naming a type of event, like `insert`, and a large collection D of documents that mention the action at least once. As output, systems produce a STRIPS representation of the event: the argument list for the event; three sets of predicates representing the preconditions, add effects, and delete effects; and for each predicate, the list of variables that the predicate applies to.

This problem formulation is a first step towards extracting knowledge of dynamics, although it certainly does not cover the full scope of the problem. For instance, we do not attempt to extract representations for durative or repetitive events, or actions like `escalate` or `accelerate` that change quantities or numerical attributes. Furthermore, we restrict our attention in this paper to extracting predicates with only a single argument. Despite the restrictions from the full problem of extracting knowledge of dynamics, our problem formulation involves a number of difficult technical challenges which together constitute a substantial extraction problem.

3.3 Challenges

Word sense ambiguity, synonyms, and syntactic ambiguity plague our system, as they do all extraction systems, but in contrast to S10 we expect our extractor to identify sense-disambiguated entries in an ontology for predicates, rather than ambiguous terms. Hence, we want to extract *liquid#3* (fluid matter having no fixed shape but a fixed volume) in Wordnet (Fellbaum, 1998) as a precondition for action *boil* as opposed to *liquid#4* (a frictionless continuant that is not a nasal consonant). Like the KNOWITALL system and related Web IE systems (Etzioni et al., 2005; Downey et al., 2005), we rely on the redundancy inherent in large document collections to help address these issues. In addition, we face these challenges:

Lack of Explicitly Stated Knowledge: Commonsense knowledge, like preconditions and postconditions of events, is often taken for granted by the author and reader, and thus does not need to be stated explicitly. Our biggest challenge is to create a system that can extract this knowledge even though it is never stated explicitly.

Temporality: Our patterns must distinguish between implications that are true before an event vs. after an event.

Generalization: The most common example of a `cut` event in text may be of a scissors cutting paper, but we do not want to conclude from these examples that scissors and paper are preconditions for cutting. Instead, some larger class of objects, like the set of sharp objects, is a better description of the precondition for the cutting instrument. Unlike S10, we expect a STRIPS extractor to extract appropriately-generalized predicates.

Rule Extraction: Like the DIRT system (Lin and Pantel, 2001), a STRIPS extraction system must identify rules rather than grounded facts. Instead of discovering `asleep(person1)`, we want to discover patterns like $\forall_{x,t_1,t_2} \texttt{awaken}(x, t_2) \wedge \texttt{after}(t_2, t_1) \Rightarrow \texttt{asleep}(x, t_1)$. In contrast, S10 does not identify predicate arguments, which enable the use of preconditions and effects as inference rules.

4 Extraction Methods

4.1 Extracting Preconditions and Add Effects

Our previous system, S10 identifies the names of preconditions and add effects. We briefly review S10's approach here.

Given a corpus where each document contains an event e, S10 begins by identifying relations and arguments in a large text corpus using an open-domain semantic role labeler (Huang and Yates, 2010) and OpenNLP's noun-phrase coreference resolution system[1]. Taking a set of candidate predicate words, we then define different features of the labeled corpus that measure the proximity in the annotated corpus between a candidate word and the action word. Using a small sample of labeled action words with their correct preconditions and effects, we then train an RBF-kernel Support Vector Machine (SVM) to rank the candidate predicate words by their proximity to the action word.

S10 use three different types of features for measuring proximity: first, we compute the pointwise mutual information (PMI) (Turney, 2002) between the event e and the candidate word c using the document set D. For any set of words W, let D_W represent the set of documents containing all words in W.

$$PMI(e,c) = \log \frac{|D_{\{e,c\}}|}{|D_{\{e\}}||D_{\{c\}}|} \quad (1)$$

Second, we compute the three-way PMI between e, c, and *discriminator features* f:

$$PMI(e,c,f) = \log \frac{|D_{\{e,c,f\}}|}{|D_{\{e\}}||D_{\{c\}}||D_{\{f\}}|} \quad (2)$$

By using discriminator features f like `before` and `requires`, these three-way PMI features can measure if e and c relate to one another in a way that is indicative of preconditions, in particular. Likewise, discriminator features like `after` and `causes`, can measure whether c relates to e in the manner of an effect. In practice, approximately 200 discriminator features for preconditions and 200 for add effects are selected using greedy, χ^2 feature selection.

The third kind of feature for measuring proximity between e and c relies on semantic role and coreference annotations. For instance, one such measure counts how often c occurs as an argument to a predicate e, as indicated by the semantic role annotations. Another feature counts how often c corefers with an argument to a predicate e, and another counts how often c appears within a window of text near a predicate e. See S10 for full details on these features.

4.2 Connecting Extractions to an Ontology

One obvious shortcoming of the S10 system is that it fails to generalize adequately. For instance,

[1]http://opennlp.sourceforge.net

s	CW_s
`nurse#1`	{nurse}
`doctor#1`	{doctor,allergist}
`health_prof.#1`	{doctor,nurse,allergist}
`person#1`	{doctor,nurse,poet,...}

Table 1: Sample candidate preconditions from CS for action 'heal', together with the set of words in the corpus for 'heal' that have the candidate synset as a hypernym.

the system extracts `hammer` as a precondition for the action `crush`. While it is true that if one has a hammer, then one can crush things, this is too strict of a precondition. Using this incorrect knowledge, a system might conclude from the text "Jane crushed the soda can with her hands" that *hands* are a kind of *hammer*.

Our first extension to the baseline S10 system is to give it the capacity to generalize the predicates it finds, by giving it more general candidate predicates. Let synsets(w) denote the set of WordNet synsets for a word w, and let CW be the set of candidate words used by S10. For each $c \in CW$, we add each $s \in$ synsets(c) to a new candidate predicate list of synsets CS; if c does not appear in WordNet, we add c itself to CS. We then add all direct and indirect hypernyms of the synsets in CS to CS. In Table 1, we show a sample of the candidate preconditions s from CS for action `heal`. We also show the subset CW_s of words from CW that have s as a hypernym.

Our second extension to S10 is to modify the definition of our features so that they apply to the synsets in CS rather than the words in CW. To compute the PMI-based features, we set $|D_{\{s\}}|$ to $|D_{CW_s}|$, and $|D_{\{e,s,f\}}|$ to be $|D_{\{e,f\}} \cap D_{CW_s}|$. For semantic role-based features, let $F(e,c)$ denote one of the counts we compute for candidate word c and event e. For hypernyms, we change this to $F(e,s) = \sum_{c \in CW_s} F(e,c)$. We refer to S10 with the new candidates CS and the modified features as S10$'$.

Correctly ranking the elements of CS is significantly harder than ranking CW (the problem for S10), because the new list has far more elements — multiple synsets and hypernyms for each element of CW. The feature set in the S10$'$ system is unable to handle these new challenges. In particular, S10$'$ tends to choose overly

feature	description
root-dist	1. $\max_{r \in R} d(s,r)$ 2. $\min_{r \in R} d(s,r)$ 3. $\frac{\sum_{r \in R} d(s,r)}{\lvert R \rvert}$
max-dist	$\max_{c \in CW_s} \min_{s' \in synsets(c)} d(s,s')$
avg-dist	$\frac{\sum_{s' \in synsets(c) \lvert c \in CW_s} d(s,s')}{\lvert CW_s \rvert}$
weighted dist	$\frac{\sum_{c \in CW_s, s' \in synsets(c)} d(s,s')C(c)}{\sum_{c \in CW_s} C(c)}$

Table 2: Features added to S10′ to create HYPER.

feature	description
prefix	1 if p = {un-,im-,in-} concatenated with an add effect
loose count	a separate feature $\lvert D_{\{neg,p,f\}} \rvert$ for each $neg \in$ {"no", "not"} and each $f \in$ {"after", "during", "as", "before"}
strict count	for each neg and f, $\lvert D_{\{\text{“}neg\ p\ f\text{”}\}} \rvert$
simple PMI	for each neg, $PMI(neg, p)$ and $PMI(\text{“}neg\ p\text{”}, e)$
ratio PMI	for each neg, $\frac{PMI(\text{“}neg\ p\text{”}, e)}{PMI(p,e)}$

Table 3: Features for classifying whether a precondition predicate p is a delete effect of an event e.

general hypernyms far too often. For example, synsets like `physical_entity#1` tend to rank highly as preconditions and add effects according to S10′, as many words in CW are hyponyms of `physical_entity#1`, and thus this synset has high scores for count and PMI-based features.

To compensate, we include several new features that measure the generality of hypernyms. Table 2 lists the new features we add to S10′ to create our new extractor, which we call the HYPER model. Here, $d(s, s')$ is the distance between s and s', or the number of hyponym relationships separating s and s'; R is the set of root nodes in the WordNet hierarchy; and $C(w)$ is the frequency of word w in our corpus. The first three features calculate the maximum, minimum and average distance separating s and any root node of the WordNet hierarchy. The second and third features find the maximum and average distance between s and the terms in CW_s. The final feature computes a weighted distance between s and the elements $c \in CW_s$, where each weight is the frequencies of c. Each of these features helps to differentiate between very general synsets and more specific synsets (or synsets for terms appearing frequently in the corpus). Adding these features to HYPER allows the SVM to balance between candidate synsets that score highly on the standard S10′ features and candidate synsets that are less general.

4.3 Detecting Delete Effects

S10′ and HYPER can identify preconditions and add effects, but they do not handle delete effects. We extend the system with a separate extractor for delete effects. By far the most common kind of delete effect is one that falsifies a precondition predicate: *e.g.*, before someone puts a book down, they are holding the book, and afterwards they are not. So far, we have restricted our attention to this common case, although more general extractors are possible for conditional delete effects, which falsify a predicate only on the condition that the predicate was true before the event.

We create a binary SVM classifier that predicts for each precondition predicate whether or not the precondition turns false after the event. For each precondition predicate p, we construct features that measure how strongly p is associated with negation in the context of the event e. We include a mix of orthographic features, count features, and PMI-based features. The full set of our features for this classifier is listed in Table 3.

As an example of the delete effects classifier in action, consider the event `maim`. HYPER can extract `unhurt` as a precondition and `hurt` as an add effect. In general, whenever we see an add effect that contradicts a precondition, we expect to delete the precondition. The `prefix` feature in Table 3 for `maim` flags `unhurt` as a possible precondition to be deleted because it matches 'un' + add effect `hurt`.

4.4 Determining Arguments

The last subtask for our STRIPS extractor is to "relation-ify" our extracted representation by assigning arguments to the event e and each predicate. S10 makes no attempt to identify arguments to extracted predicates. As a result, for action awaken, the S10 representation does not distinguish between a case where one entity x is asleep and another entity y wakes up, and the case where x is asleep and then x awakens.

This is a complex, structured-prediction problem involving coreference resolution between the arguments to extracted relationships. As a first attempt, we resort to an effective heuristic solution. We use the argument role labels supplied by our propbank-style semantic role labeler as candidate variables for our representation. For an extracted predicate p for e, we assign arguments to p based on the semantic role label or labels with which it is most commonly associated in the annotated corpus. That is, for each possible semantic role r, we count how often p occurs in a phrase that is an argument to e and is annotated with role r. We also count how often p occurs as part of any phrase that is annotated with role r. Let $score(e, r, p)$ denote the sum of these two counts. We choose an argument variable $r* = \arg\max_r score(e, r, p)$, and write p as the predicate $p(r*)$. Finally, we set the arguments of e to be the set of unique arguments chosen for all of its extracted predicates.

Figure 2 shows an example of this technique and two baselines. The input to each system is a STRIPS representation without arguments and the output adds arguments. For action maim, the semantic role heuristic finds that person#1 and unhurt#1 occur most often in phrases marked with a propbank A1 role. Hence, it concludes that they both should have the same argument label. object#1 occurs more in phrases with A2 roles, and is given a separate argument variable as a result. These two roles then constitute the argument set for event maim.

	action	pre	add
S10′:	maim	person#1 unhurt object#1	hurt
Distinct var. baseline:	maim(a,b,c,d)	person#1(a) unhurt(b) object#1(c)	hurt(d)
Same var. baseline:	maim(a)	person#1(a) unhurt(a) object#1(a)	hurt(a)
Semantic Role heuristic:	maim(A1,A2)	person#1(A1) unhurt(A1) object#1(A2)	hurt(A1)

Figure 2: Addition of arguments to predicates for action 'maim'.

5 Experiments

5.1 Experimental Setup

We use the same experimental setup as in S10: we use the dataset of 40 actions from the lexical units in the frames that inherit from the Transitive_action frame in FrameNet(Johnson et al., 2003). We use the same document collection of 15,088 documents that we downloaded from the Web for these 40 action words. For each action word, candidate predicates for precondition and add effect extraction were the top 500 words ranked by PMI with the action word. This list was augmented with the superclasses from WordNet, as described above. For each action word, we hand-constructed a STRIPS representation (we did not use S10's labeled data because it did not include the WordNet superclasses as candidate words, or as part of its hand-constructed representations). On average, our labeled data had 2.6 preconditions, 0.8 add effects, 0.5 delete effects, and 3 argument variables per action word. In all of our extraction experiments, we take care to test the extractors on different action words from the ones on which they are trained (for any components that require training), so that results should generalize to new action words beyond the ones in our current collection.

5.2 Results and Discussion

Our first experiment compared predicate extraction (preconditions and add effects) between S10′ and HYPER. We use 5-fold cross-validation, with each run training on 32 action words and testing on the remaining 8. The training data consists of action words, candidate words, feature values, and a +1 label for candidates matching our hand-constructed representation, and -1 for those that did not match. We train a regression model, so that our SVMs produce real-valued predictions for (action word, candidate word) pairs. We construct a list of all such pairs and rank them according to the SVM output. Figure 3 shows our results. The area under the curve (AUC) for both preconditions and add effects is significantly higher (0.34 improvement in AUC for preconditions, 0.17 for add effects) for the full model, largely because the S10′ model ranks very general WordNet classes, like physical_entity, very highly for most action words, simply because they appear so often as the

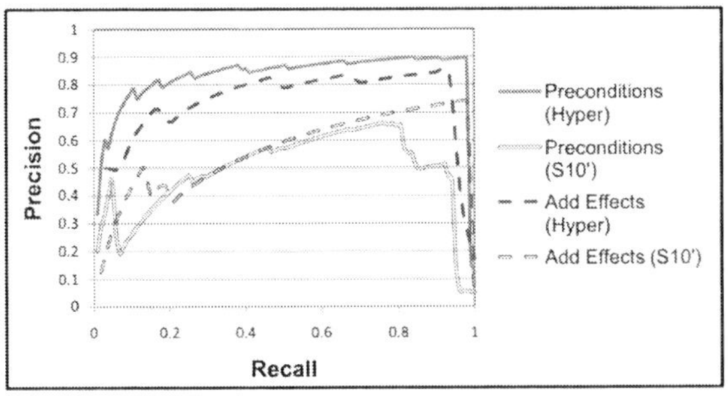

Figure 3: Precision-Recall curves for extracting preconditions and add effects.

superclasses of words in the documents. By incorporating the features that measure the generality of classes, the full extraction model can learn to rank these very general classes much lower, except when strongly supported by evidence from the documents. The absolute performance of the full extractor is quite strong, with AUC 0.82 for preconditions and 0.72 for add effects, compared with AUCs for S10′ of 0.48 for preconditions and 0.52 for add effects.

We measured the performance of our delete effect extractor using the same 5-fold cross-validation setup. Recall that our delete classifier predicts which preconditions become false after the action. To separate the evaluation of this classifier's performance from our precondition extractor, we use gold-standard preconditions as input to the classifier. As before, we construct train and test sets consisting of the action word, the precondition, values for our features, and a label of +1 if the precondition is in fact a delete effect, and -1 otherwise. We train an SVM classifier, and measure its precision and recall on detecting true delete effects for each of the five folds. Table 4 shows the results for extracting this kind of knowledge. The average precision across the folds was 72.2%, and recall was 52.6%, for an F1 of 60.8. In contrast, a baseline that predicts all preconditions are also delete effects achieves an F1 of 41.3 (26% precision, 100% recall), and other baselines (random, no preconditions are delete effects) performed worse. Thus, the delete effect classifier is able to reliably detect negative knowledge, which is rarely stated explicitly, using co-occurrence statistics and other simple features.

For argument matching, we measured performance by the overall quality of the extracted STRIPS representations, including arguments. We first computed a maximal matching

Technique	Prec.	Recall	F1
All pre. are deleted	26	90	40.3
No pre. are deleted	100	10	18.2
SVM trained model	**72.2**	**52.6**	**60.8**

Table 4: Precision and recall for our system which extracts delete effects. The final SVM trained model has gold standard preconditions as input to the classifier. For an action with no delete effects, if the system predicts no delete effects, we judged precision and recall to be 100%, which is why the recall of the second baseline is nonzero. Precision and recall numbers are macro-averaged across actions.

between the argument variables selected by our method and the argument variables in the hand-constructed STRIPS representation. After computing the matching, we substituted the variables from the gold standard representation into the automatically-produced variables. We then measured the quality of our automatically-generated full STRIPS representation by measuring how many of the predicted predicates match exactly a predicate in the gold standard (precision), and how many of the gold standard predicates were found exactly in the automatically-generated representations (recall). For the purposes of this calculation, we used the top 3 automatically-generated preconditions and top 1 automatically-generated add effect per action word according to the HYPER extractor, regardless of the numeric scores for each predicate. (We found that recall increased but precision dropped more when we included a second add effect per action word.) We did not include delete effects in this experiment. We compared our heuristic technique to two baselines, one which predicts that all extracted predicates for an action share the same variable, and one which treats every argument as a distinct variable. Table 5 shows our results. The semantic role labeling heuristic improves dramatically over the closest baseline by 25 points in F1. Overall, our complete extraction system found precondition and add effect predicates and arguments for STRIPS representations with an F1 of 0.72, using only statistics over a small corpus collected from the Web and a small set of hand-labeled examples.

Technique	Prec.	Recall	F1
All preds. have same var.	32	33	32
Each pred. has distinct var.	56	58	57
Semantic role heuristic	**73**	**72**	**72**

Table 5: Precision and recall of our complete representation with extracted predicates and arguments.

6 Conclusion and Future Work

We have presented a system for extracting a complete STRIPS representation of 40 common actions from text, with an overall F1 of 0.72. We demonstrate that our system significantly outperforms the closest comparable one from the literature and extracts richer representations. Future directions include extracting more sophisticated representations of action semantics, especially multi-argument predicates and logical connectives between predicates, and extracting representations for more complex actions, like durative or repetitive actions.

References

Jon Barwise. 1989. *The Situation in Logic*. CSLI.

John Bresina, Richard Dearden, Nicolas Meuleau, David Smith, and Rich Washington. 2002. Planning under continuous time and resource uncertainty: A challenge for AI. In *Proc. of the 18th Conference on Uncertainty in Artificial Intelligence*.

Sandra Carberry. 1990. *Plan Recognition in Natural Language Dialogue*. MIT Press, Cambridge, MA, USA.

Nathanael Chambers and Dan Jurafsky. 2009. Unsupervised learning of narrative schemas and their participants. In *Proceedings of ACL-IJCNLP 2009*.

Doug Downey, Oren Etzioni, and Stephen Soderland. 2005. A Probabilistic Model of Redundancy in Information Extraction. In *IJCAI*.

O. Etzioni, M. Cafarella, D. Downey, S. Kok, A. Popescu, T. Shaked, S. Soderland, D. Weld, and A. Yates. 2005. Unsupervised named-entity extraction from the web: An experimental study. *Artificial Intelligence*, 165(1):91–134.

Christiane Fellbaum, editor. 1998. *WordNet: An Electronic Lexical Database*. Bradford Books.

R. Fikes and N. Nilsson. 1971. STRIPS: A new approach to the application of theorem proving to problem solving. *Artificial Intelligence*, 2(3/4):189–208.

Christopher W. Geib and Mark Steedman. 2007. On natural language processing and plan recognition. In *IJCAI*, pages 1612–1617.

Roxana Girju. 2003. Automatic detection of causal relations for question answering. In *Proceedings of the ACL 2003 workshop on Multilingual summarization and question answering*, pages 76–83, Morristown, NJ, USA.

Fei Huang and Alexander Yates. 2010. Open-domain semantic role labeling by modeling word spans. In *ACL*.

Christopher Johnson, Miriam Petruck, Collin Baker, Michael Ellsworth, Josef Ruppenhofer, and Charles Fillmore. 2003. *FrameNet: Theory and practice*.

Henry A. Kautz. 1991. A formal theory of plan recognition and its implementation. In *Reasoning about plans*, pages 69–124. Morgan Kaufmann Publishers Inc., San Francisco, CA, USA.

D. Lin and P. Pantel. 2001. DIRT – Discovery of Inference Rules from Text. In *KDD*.

Diane J. Litman and James F. Allen. 1987. A plan recognition model for subdialogues in conversations. *Cognitive Science*, 11(2):163 – 200.

Peter LoBue and Alexander Yates. 2011. Types of common-sense knowledge needed for recognizing textual entailment. In *ACL*.

A. Ritter, Mausam, and Oren Etzioni. 2010. A latent dirichlet allocation method for selectional preferences. In *ACL*.

R.C. Schank and R.P. Abelson. 1977. *Scripts, plans, goals and understanding: an inquiry into human knowledge structures*. Erlbaum.

Lenhart K. Schubert and Chung Hee Hwang. 2000. Episodic Logic meets Little Red Riding Hood: A comprehensive natural representation for language understanding. In Lucja Iwanska and Stuart C. Shapiro, editors, *Natural Language Processing and Knowledge Representation: Language for Knowledge and Knowledge for Language*, pages 111–174. MIT/AAAI Press.

Avirup Sil, Fei Huang, and Alexander Yates. 2010. Extracting action and event semantics from web text. In *AAAI Fall Symposium on Common-Sense Knowledge (CSK)*.

P. D. Turney. 2002. Thumbs up or thumbs down? semantic orientation applied to unsupervised classification of reviews. In *Procs. of ACL*, pages 417–424.

Håkan L. S. Younes, David J. Musliner, and Reid G. Simmons. 2003. A framework for planning in continuous-time stochastic domains. In *AAAI*.

Acquiring Topic Features to Improve Event Extraction: in Pre-selected and Balanced Collections

Shasha Liao
Computer Science Department
New York University
liaoss@cs.nyu.edu

Ralph Grishman
Computer Science Department
New York University
grishman@cs.nyu.edu

Abstract

Event extraction is a particularly challenging type of information extraction (IE) that may require inferences from the whole article. However, most current event extraction systems rely on local information at the phrase or sentence level, and do not consider the article as a whole, thus limiting extraction performance. Moreover, most annotated corpora are artificially enriched to include enough positive samples of the events of interest; event identification on a more balanced collection, such as unfiltered newswire, may perform much worse. In this paper, we investigate the use of unsupervised topic models to extract topic features to improve event extraction both on test data similar to training data, and on more balanced collections. We compare this unsupervised approach to a supervised multi-label text classifier, and show that unsupervised topic modeling can get better results for both collections, and especially for a more balanced collection. We show that the unsupervised topic model can improve trigger, argument and role labeling by 3.5%, 6.9% and 6% respectively on a pre-selected corpus, and by 16.8%, 12.5% and 12.7% on a balanced corpus.

1 Introduction

The goal of event extraction is to identify instances of a class of events in free text, along with their arguments. In this paper, we focus on the ACE 2005 event extraction task, which involved a set of 33 generic event types and subtypes appearing frequently in the news. It generally expresses the core arguments plus place and time information of a single event, like *Attack*, *Marry* or *Arrest*.

In general, identifying an ACE event can be quite difficult. Given a narrow scope of information, even a human cannot make a confident decision. For example, for the sentence:

(1) So he returned to combat ...

it is hard to tell whether it is an *Attack* event, which is defined as a violent physical act causing harm or damage, or whether it refers to a more innocent endeavor such as a tennis match. A broader field of view is often helpful to understand how facts tie together. If we read the whole article, and find it to be a terrorist story, it is easy to tag this as an *Attack* event; however, if it is in a tennis report, we probably won't tag it as an *Attack* event.

The problem of event identification is exacerbated if we shift to corpora with a topic distribution different from the training and official test corpus. In general, an effort is made to have the test corpora be representative of the sort of texts to which the NLP process is intended to be applied. In the case of the event extraction, this has generally been news sources such as newswires or broadcast news transcripts. However, a particular event type is likely to occur infrequently in the general news, which might contain many different topics, only a few of which are likely to include mentions of this event type. As a result, a typical evaluation corpus (a few hundred hand-annotated documents), if selected at random, would contain only a few events, which is not sufficient for training. To avoid this, these annotated corpora are artificially enriched through a combination of topic classification and manual review, so that they contain a high concentration of the events of interest. For example, in the MUC-3/4 test corpora, about 60% of the documents include relevant events, and in the ACE 2005 training corpus 48% include *Attack* events.

If we train and test the event extraction system on ACE annotated corpora, the problem epitomized by (1) is not significant because there are very few sports articles in the ACE evaluation: 74% of the instances of the word "combat" indicate an *Attack* event. However, if you extend the evaluation to a more balanced collection, for example, the un-filtered New York Times (NYT) newswire, you will find that there are a lot of sports articles and an event extractor will mistakenly tag lots of sports events as *Attack* events. Grishman (2010) drew attention to this phenomenon, pointing out that only about 17% of articles from the contemporaneous sample of The NYT newswire contained attack events, compared to 48% in the ACE evaluation. In this situation, if we apply the event extractor trained on the ACE corpus to the balanced NYT newswire, the performance may be significantly degraded.

Clearly, the topic of the document is a good predictor of particular event types. For example, a reference to "war" inside a business article might refer to a financial competition; while "war" inside a military article would be more likely to refer to a physical attack event. Text classification is used here to identify document topic, and the final decision can be made based on both local evidence and document relevance (Grishman 2010). However, this method has three disadvantages:

First, the event type and document topic are not always strongly connected, and it depends significantly on what kind of event we are going to explore. If the events are related to the main category of the article, only knowing the article category is enough. But if they are not, treating each document as a single topic is not enough. For example, *Die* events might appear in military, financial, political or even sports articles. And most of the time, it is not the main event reported by the article. The article may focus more on the reason for the death, the biography of the person, or the effect of the death.

Second, when the article talks about more than one scenario, simple text classification will basically ignore the secondary scenario. For example, if a sports article that reported the results of a football game also mentions a fight between the fans of two teams, the topic of the document might be "sports", which is irrelevant to *Attack* events; however, there is an *Attack* event, which appears in the secondary scenario of the document.

Third, the category or relevance depends on the annotated data, and a classifier may be unable to deal with articles whose topics were rarely seen in the training data. Thus, if the category distribution of the evaluation data is different from the training data, a text classifier might have poor performance.

To solve the first two problems, we need to treat each document as a mixture of several topics instead of one; to solve the third problem, we want to see if unsupervised methods can give us some guidance which a supervised method cannot. These two goals are easily connected to a topic model, for example, Latent Dirichlet Allocation.

2 ACE Event Extraction

In this section, we will describe the ACE event extraction task and explain why it is difficult.

2.1 Task Description

ACE defines an event as a specific occurrence involving participants[1], and it annotates 8 types and 33 subtypes of events. In this task, an *event mention* is a phrase or sentence within which an event is described, including trigger and arguments. An event mention must have one and only one trigger, and can have an arbitrary number of arguments. The *event trigger* is the main word that most clearly expresses an event occurrence. The *event mention arguments (roles)*[2] are the entity mentions that are involved in an event mention, and their relation to the event. For example, an event "attack" might include participants like "attacker" or "target", or attributes like "time within" and "place". Arguments will be taggable only when they occur within the scope of the corresponding event, typically the same sentence.

Here is an example:

(4) Three ***murders*** *occurred in* ***France today****, including the senseless* ***slaying of Bob***

[1] See http://projects.ldc.upenn.edu/ace/docs/English-Events-Guidelines_v5.4.3.pdf for a description of this task.

[2] Note that we do not deal with event mention coreference in this paper, so each event mention is treated as a separate event.

*Cole. **Bob** was on his way home when **he** was **attacked**...*

There are two *Die* events, which share the same *Place* and *Time* roles, with different *Victim* roles. And there is one *Attack* event sharing the same *Place* and *Time* roles with the *Die* events.

Event type	Trigger	Role		
		Place	**Victim**	**Time**
Die	murder	France		today
Die	slaying	France	Bob Cole	today
Event type	**Trigger**	**Role**		
		Place	**Target**	**Time**
Attack	attack	France	Bob	today

Table 1. An example of event trigger and roles

2.2 Problems

Identifying the trigger – the word most clearly expressing the event - is essential for event extraction. Usually, the trigger itself is the most important clue in detecting and classifying the type of an event. For example, the word "attack" is very likely to represent an *Attack* event while the word "meet" is not. However, this is not always enough. If we collect all the words that serve as an event trigger at least once, and plot their probability of triggering an event (Figure 1), we see that the probabilities are widely scattered. Some words always trigger an event (probability = 1.0), but most are ambiguous.

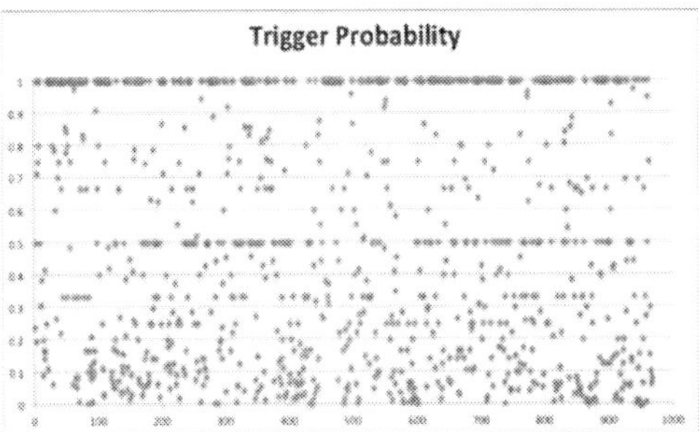

Figure1. Distribution of trigger probability (X axis represents the words in alphabetical order)

Why is identifying an event so difficult? First of all, a word may be ambiguous and have several senses, only some of which correspond to a particular event type. Moreover, identifying the correct sense is not enough: several different senses of a word might refer to the same event type, and the same sense does not guarantee the occurrence of the specific event: the arguments need to be considered as well. Take the word "shoot", for example; the senses "hit with a missile from a weapon" and "fire a shot" might both predicate an *Attack* event, but to guarantee that, we need to not only identify its sense is, for example, "fire a shot", not "record on photographic film", but also identify that its target is a person, organization, Geo-Political Entity (GPE), weapon or facility, not an animal. Hunting-related or shooting-contest-related activities should not be tagged as *Attack* events.

Thus, the identification of the trigger and the arguments interact: the relation between the trigger and the argument is one essential factor to identify both the trigger and the role of the argument. For example, if we know that the object of the word "shoot" is a person and it has the "fire a shot" sense, we can confidently identify the person as the *Target* role, and tag "shoot" as the trigger of an *Attack* event.

As a result, most current event extraction systems consider trigger and argument information together to tag a reportable event (see the baseline system in section 5.1).

3 Related Work

To the best of our knowledge, we are the first to use unsupervised topic models in event extraction. However, there are some similar approaches that consider the relevance of the document to the specific scenario or event type. For scenario extraction in MUC-3/4, Riloff (1996) initiated this approach and claimed that if a corpus can be divided into documents involving a certain event type and those not involving that type, patterns can be evaluated based on their frequency in relevant and irrelevant documents. Yangarber et al. (2000) incorporated Riloff's metric into a bootstrapping procedure. Patwardhan and Riloff (2007) presented an information extraction system that finds relevant regions of text and applies extraction patterns within those regions. Liao and Grishman (2010b) also pointed out that the pre-selection of the bootstrapping corpus (based on document topic) is quite essential to this approach. Although their approach involved bootstrapping, it gives the intuition that the event/scenario and the document topic are strongly connected.

For ACE event extraction, most current systems focus on processing one sentence at a time (Grishman et al., 2005; Ahn, 2006; Hardy et al. 2006). However, there have been several studies using high-level information at the document level. Finkel et al. (2005) used Gibbs sampling, a simple Monte Carlo method used to perform approximate inference in factored probabilistic models. By using simulated annealing in place of Viterbi decoding in sequence models such as HMMs, CMMs, and CRFs, it is possible to incorporate non-local structure while preserving tractable inference. They used this technique to augment an information extraction system with long-distance dependency models, enforcing label consistency and extraction template consistency constraints. Ji and Grishman (2008) extended the scope from a single document to a cluster of topic-related documents and employed a rule-based approach to propagate consistent trigger classification and event arguments across sentences and documents. Liao and Grishman (2010a) extended this consistency within each event type to a distribution among different event types, and obtained an appreciable improvement in both event and event argument identification.

There is not as much work on evaluation on a more balanced collection when the training corpus has a different distribution. Grishman (2010) first pointed out that understanding the characteristics of the corpus is an inherent parts of the event extraction task. He gave a small example of the effect of applying an event extractor to a more balanced corpus, and used a document classifier to reduce the spurious errors.

4 Topic Features in Event Extraction

Most previous studies that acquire wider scope information use preselected corpora, like (Riloff 1996); or are rule-based, like Ji and Grishman (2008); or involve supervised learning from the same training data, like Finkel et al. (2005), Liao and Grishman (2010a). We are more interested in using a topic model to provide such information.

A topic model, like Latent Dirichlet Allocation (LDA), is a generative model that allows sets of observations to be explained by unobserved groups. For example, if the observations are words collected into documents, it posits that each document is a mixture of a small number of topics and that each word is attributable to one of the document's topics. For event extraction, there is a similar assumption that each document consists of various events, and each event is presented by one or several snippets in the document. We want to know if these two can be somehow connected and how one can improve the other.

In this paper, we are more interested in an unsupervised approach from a large untagged corpus. In this way, we can avoid the data bias that may be introduced by an unrepresentative training collection, thus providing better high-level information than previous approaches, especially when applied to the final target application instead of a specially selected development or evaluation corpus.

4.1 Features from Unsupervised Topic Model (LDA)

Latent Dirichlet Allocation (LDA) tries to group words into "topics", where each word is generated from a single topic, and different words in a document may be generated from different topics. Thus, each document is represented as a list of mixing proportions for these mixture components and thereby reduced to a probability distribution on a fixed set of topics. In LDA, each document may be viewed as a mixture of various topics. A document is generated by picking a distribution over topics, and given this distribution, picking the topic of each specific word to be generated. Then words are generated given their topics. Words are considered to be independent given the topics; this is a standard bag of words model assumption where individual words are exchangeable.

Unlike supervised classification, there are no explicit labels, like "finance" or "war", in unsupervised LDA. Instead, we can imagine each topic as "a cluster of words that refers to an implicit topic". For example, if a document contains words like "company", "financial", and "market", we assume it contains a "financial topic" and are more confident to find events like *Start-Position, End-Position,* while a document that contains "war", "combat", "fire", and "force" will be assumed to contain the "war topic", which is more likely to contain *Attack*, *Die*, or *Injure* events.

4.2 Features from Multi-label Text Classifier

As the event extraction system uses a supervised model, it is natural to ask whether supervised topic features are better than unsupervised ones. There are several possible approaches. For example, we can first run a topic classification filter to predict whether or not a document is likely to contain a specific type of event. However, because of the limited precision of a simple classifier such as a bag-of-words MaxEnt classifier (for *Attack* events, the precision is around 69% in ACE data), using it as a pre-filter will lead to event recall or precision errors. Instead, we decide to use the topic information as features within the event extraction system. As one document might contain several event types, we tag each document with labels indicating the presence of one or more events of a given type, which is a multi-label text classification problem. In this section, we build a supervised multi-label text classifier to compare to the unsupervised topic model.

The basic idea for a multi-label classifier comes from the *credit attribution* problem in social bookmarking websites, where pages have multiple tags, but the tags do not always apply with equal specificity across the whole page (Ramage et al. 2009). This relation between tag and page is quite similar to that between event and document, because one document might also have multiple events of differing specificity. For example, an *Attack* event may be more related to the main topic of the document than a *Meet* event.

We use Labeled LDA (L-LDA) to build the multi-label text classifier, which is reported (Ramage et al. 2009) to outperform SVMs when extracting tag-specific document snippets, and is competitive with SVMs on a variety of datasets. L-LDA associates each label with one topic in direct correspondence, and is a natural extension of both LDA and multinomial Naïve Bayes. In our experiment, each document can have several labels, each corresponding to one of the 33 ACE event types. In this way, we can easily map the goal of predicting the possible events in a document into a multi-label classification problem.

5 Experiment

We set up two experiments to investigate the effect of topic information.

First, we did a 5-fold cross-validation on the whole ACE 2005 corpus. We report the overall Precision (P), Recall (R), and F-Measure (F).

Second, we did an experiment to address the crucial issue of mismatch in topic distribution between training and test corpora. In this experiment, the whole ACE 2005 corpus is used as the training data, and unfiltered New York Times newswire data (NYT) is used for testing. The NYT corpus comes from the same epoch (June 2003) as the ACE corpus, but there is no pre-selection. This test data contains 75 consecutive articles. We annotated the test data for the three most common event types in ACE – *Attack*, *Die*, and *Meet* – and evaluated this balanced corpus on these three events.

5.1 Event Extraction Baseline System

We use a state-of-the-art English IE system as our baseline [Grishman et al. 2005]. This system extracts events independently for each sentence, because the definition of event mention argument constrains them to appear in the same sentence. The system combines pattern matching with statistical models. In the training process, for every event mention in the ACE training corpus, patterns are constructed based on the sequences of constituent heads separating the trigger and arguments. A set of Maximum Entropy based classifiers are also trained:

- **Argument Classifier:** to distinguish arguments of a potential trigger from non-arguments; uses local features like the event type of the potential trigger, path from the mention to the trigger, mention type, head word of the mention, etc.
- **Role Classifier:** to classify arguments by argument role; uses similar features as the argument classifier
- **Trigger Classifier:** Given local evidence, like the potential trigger word, the event type, and a set of arguments, to determine whether this is a reportable event mention.

In the test procedure, each document is scanned for instances of triggers from the training corpus. When an instance is found, the system tries to match the environment of the trigger against the set of patterns associated with that trigger. This pattern-matching process, if successful, will assign some of the mentions in the sentence as arguments of a potential event mention.

The argument classifier is applied to the remaining mentions in the sentence; for any argument passing that classifier, the role classifier is used to assign a role to it. Finally, once all arguments have been assigned, the trigger classifier is applied to the potential event mention; if the result is successful, this event mention is reported[3].

[3] Note that argument / role recall is rather low, because it is dependent on the correct recognition and classification of entity mentions, whose F measure (with our system) is about 81% for named mentions and lower for nominal and prenominal mentions.

5.2 Topic Features

Encoding topic features into the baseline system is straightforward: as the occurrence of an event is decided in the final classifier – the trigger classifier – we add topic features to this final classifier. Although the argument / role classifiers have already been applied, we can still improve the argument / role classification, because only when a word is tagged as a trigger will all the arguments/roles related to it be reported.

The unsupervised LDA was trained on the entire 2003 NYT newswire except for June to avoid overlap with the test data, a total of 27,827 articles; we choose K= 30, which means we treat the whole corpus as a combination of 30 latent topics[4].

The multi-label text classifier was trained on the same ACE training data as the event extraction, where each label corresponds to one event type, and there is an extra "none" tag when there are no events in the document. Thus, there are in total 34 labels.

For inference, we use the posterior Dirichlet parameters $\gamma^*(w)$ associated with the document (Blei 2003) as our topic features, which is a fixed set of real-values. Thus, using the multi-label text classifier, there are 34 newly-added features; while using unsupervised LDA, there are 30 newly-added features. Stanford topic modeling software is used for both the multi-label text classifier and unsupervised LDA.

For preprocessing, we remove all words on a stop word list. Also, to reduce data sparseness, all inflected words are changed to their root form (e.g. "attackers"→"attacker").

5.3 Evaluation on ACE data

We might expect supervised topic features to outperform unsupervised topic features, when the distribution of training and testing data are the same, because its correlation to event type is clearer and explicit. However, this turns out not to be true in our experiment (Table 2): the unsupervised features work better than the supervised features. This is understandable given that there are only hundreds of training documents for the supervised topic model, and the precision of the document classification is not very good, as we mentioned before in section 4.2. For unsupervised topics, we have a much larger corpus, and the topics extracted, although they may not correspond directly to each event type, predicate a scenario where a specific event might occur.

5.4 Evaluation on NYT data

From the ACE evaluation, we can see that the unsupervised LDA works better than a supervised classifier, which indicates that even if the training and testing data are from the same distribution, the unsupervised topic features are more helpful. In our second evaluation, we evaluate on a more balanced newswire corpus, with no pre-selection.

First, we implement Grishman (2010)'s solution (Simple Combination) to combine the document event classifier (a bag-of-words maximum-entropy model) with local evidence used in the baseline system. The basic idea is that if a document is classified as not related to a specific event, it should not contain any such events; while if it is related, there should be such events. Thus, an event will be reported if

$$\sqrt{P(reportable\_event) \times P(relevant\_document)} > \tau$$

where P(reportable_event) is the confidence score from the baseline system, while P(relevant_document) is computed from the document classifier.

Table 3 shows that the simple combination method (geometric mean of probabilities) performs a little better than baseline. However, we find that the gains are unevenly spread across different events. For *Attack* events, it provides some benefit (from 57.9% to 59.6% F score for trigger labeling), whereas for *Die* and *Meet* events it does not improve much. This might be because *Attack* events are closely tied to a document's main topic, and using only the main topic can give a good prediction. But *Die and Meet* events are not closely tied to the document main topic, and so the simple combination does not help much.

Unsupervised LDA performs best of all, which indicates that the real distribution in the balanced corpus can provide useful guidance for event extraction, while supervised features might not provide enough information, especially when testing on a balanced corpus.

---

[4] We tested some other values of K, and found K =30 works best, although we did not systematically explore alternative values.

Performance / System	Trigger Classification			Argument Classification			Role Classification		
	P	R	F	P	R	F	P	R	F
Baseline system	64.3	51.1	56.9	69.4	21.8	33.2	62.8	19.7	30.0
Multi-label classifier	66.8	50.0	57.2	54.4	25.5	34.7	48.9	22.9	31.1
Unsupervised LDA	63.9	59.7	**61.7**	71.1	27.0	**39.1**	64.6	24.5	**35.5**

Table 2. Overall performance on ACE test data

Performance / System	Trigger Classification			Argument Classification			Role Classification		
	P	R	F	P	R	F	P	R	F
Baseline system	53.8	51.1	52.4	41.4	19.7	26.7	39.4	18.8	25.4
Simple Combination	63.1	47.4	54.2	41.4	19.7	26.7	39.4	18.8	25.4
Multi-label classifier	60.8	65.7	63.2	35.6	27.9	31.3	31.9	25.0	28.0
Unsupervised LDA	60.3	81.0	**69.2**	45.3	34.6	**39.2**	44.0	33.7	**38.1**

Table 3. Performance on NYT collection

5.5 NYT Data Analysis

Here, we give some examples to show why topic information helps. First, we give an example where the supervised topics method does not work but unsupervised does. In our baseline system, many verbs in sports or other articles will be incorrectly tagged as *Attack* events. In such cases, as there are very few sports articles in ACE training data, and there is no event type related to sport, the supervised classifier might not capture this feature, and prefer to connect a sports article to an *Attack* event in the testing phase, because there are a lot of words like "shot", "fight". However, as there are a lot of sports articles in NYT data, the unsupervised LDA can capture this topic. Here is an example:

(2) His only two ***shots*** *of the game came in overtime and the goal was just his second of the playoffs, but it couldn't have been bigger.*

In the ACE training data, "shot" is tagged 67.5% of the time as an *Attack* event. We checked the data and found that there are very few sports articles in the ACE corpus, and the word "shot" never appears in these documents. Thus, a supervised classifier will prefer to tag a document containing the word "shot" as containing an *Attack* event. However, because a sports topic can be explicitly extracted from an unannotated corpus that contains a reasonable portion of sports articles, the unsupervised model would be able to build a latent topic *T* which contains sports-related words like "racket", "tennis", "score" etc. Thus, most training documents which contain "shot" will have a low value of *T*; while the sports documents (although very few), will have a high value of *T*. Thus, the system will see both a positive feature value (the word is "shot"), and a negative feature value (*T's* value is high), and still has the chance to correctly tag this "shot" as *not-an-event*, while in the baseline system, the system will incorrectly tag it as an *Attack* event because there are only positive feature values.

The topic features can also help other event types. For *Die* events, consider:

(3) A woman lay unconscious and ***dying*** *at Suburban Hospital in Bethesda, Md.*

The word "dying" only appears 45.5% as a *Die* event in the training data, and is not tagged as a *Die* event by the baseline system. The reason is that there are a lot of metaphors that do not represent true *Die* events, like "dying nation", "dying business", "dying regime". However, when connected to the latent topic features, we know that for some topics, we can confidently tag it as a *Die* event.

For *Meet* events, we also find cases where topic features help:

(4) President Bush ***meets*** *Tuesday with Arab leaders in Egypt and the next day with the Israeli and Palestinian prime ministers in Jordan,….*

The baseline system misses this *Meet* event. The word "meets" only appears 25% of the time as a *Meet* event in the training data, because there are phrases like "meets the requirement", "meets the standard" which are not *Meet* events. However, adding topic features, we can correct this and similar event detection errors.

6 Conclusion

We proposed to use a topic model (LDA) to provide document level topic information for event trigger classification. The advantage of LDA for text classification or clustering is that it treats each document as a mixture of several topics instead of one, providing a more natural connection to the event extraction task. Both supervised and unsupervised LDA were applied. We evaluated the influence on two sets: one with the same distribution as the training data; the other a more balanced newswire collection without pre-selection.

Our experiments indicated that an unsupervised document-level topic model trained on a large corpus yields substantial improvements in extraction performance and is considerably more effective than a supervised topic model trained on a smaller annotated corpus.

References

David Ahn. 2006. *The stages of event extraction*. Proc. COLING/ACL 2006 Workshop on Annotating and Reasoning about Time and Events. Sydney, Australia.

David Blei, Andrew Ng, and Michael Jordan. 2003. "Latent Dirichlet Allocation". Journal of Machine Learning Research 3: pp. 993–1022

J. Finkel, T. Grenager, and C. Manning. 2005. Incorporating Non-local Information into Information Extraction Systems by Gibbs Sampling. In *Proceedings of the 43rd Annual Meeting of the Association for Computational Linguistics*, pages 363–370, Ann Arbor, MI, June.

Thomas Griffiths and Mark Steyvers. 2004. Finding scientific topics. *Proceedings of the National Academy of Sciences 101 (Suppl. 1): 5228–5235. doi:10.1073/pnas.0307752101. PMID 14872004*

Ralph Grishman, David Westbrook and Adam Meyers. 2005. NYU's English ACE 2005 System Description. *In Proc. ACE 2005 Evaluation Workshop, Gaithersburg, MD.*

Ralph Grishman. 2010. The impact of task and corpus on Event Extraction Systems. *In Proceedings of LREC 2010*

Heng Ji and Ralph Grishman. 2008. *Refining Event Extraction through Cross-Document Inference.* In Proceedings of ACL-08: HLT, pages 254–262, Columbus, OH, June.

Shasha Liao and Ralph Grishman. 2010b. Filtered Ranking for Bootstrapping in Event Extraction. *In Proceedings of COLING 2010.*

Shasha Liao and Ralph Grishman. 2010a. Using Document Level Cross-Event Inference to Improve Event Extraction. *In Proceedings of ACL 2010*

M. Maslennikov and T. Chua. 2007. *A Multi resolution Framework for Information Extraction from Free Text.* In Proceedings of the 45th Annual Meeting of the Association of Computational Linguistics, pages 592–599, Prague, Czech Republic, June.

S. Patwardhan and E. Riloff. 2007. *Effective Information Extraction with Semantic Affinity Patterns and Relevant Regions.* In Proceedings of the 2007 Joint Conference on Empirical Methods in Natural Language Processing and Computational Natural Language Learning, pages 717–727, Prague, Czech Republic, June.

Ellen Riloff. 1996. Automatically Generating Extraction Patterns from Untagged Text. *In Proc. Thirteenth National Conference on Artificial Intelligence (AAAI-96), 1996, pp. 1044-1049.*

Daniel Ramage, David Hall, Ramesh Nallapati, Christopher D. Manning 2009. Labeled LDA: a supervised topic model for credit attribution in multi-labeled corpora. *In Proceedings of the 2009 Conference on Empirical Methods in Natural Language Processing*

Minimally Supervised Rule Learning for the Extraction of Biographic Information from Various Social Domains

Hong Li **Feiyu Xu** **Hans Uszkoreit**

German Research Center for Artificial Intelligence (DFKI), LT-Lab
Alt-Moabit 91c, 10559 Berlin, Germany
{lihong,feiyu,uszkoreit}@dfki.de
http://www.dfki.de/lt/

Abstract

This paper investigates the application of an existing seed-based minimally supervised learning algorithm to different social domains exhibiting different properties of the available data. A systematic analysis studies the respective data properties of the three domains including the distribution of the semantic arguments and their combinations. The experimental results confirm that data properties have a strong influence on the performance of the learning system. The main results are insights about: (i) the effects of data properties such as redundancy and frequency of argument mentions on coverage and precision (ii) the positive effects of negative examples if used effectively (iii) the different effects of negative examples depending on the domain data properties and (iv) the potential of reusing rules from one domain for improving the relation extraction performance in another domain.

1 Introduction

Domain adaptation is very important for information extraction (IE) systems. IE systems in the real world are often required to work for new domains and new tasks within a limited adaptation or tuning time. Thus, automatic learning of relation extraction rules for a new domain or a new task has been established as a relevant subarea in IE research and development (Muslea, 1999; Tsujii, 2000; Uszkoreit, 2011), in particular for minimally supervised or semi-supervised bootstrapping approaches (e.g., (Brin, 1998; Agichtein and Gravano, 2000; Yangarber, 2001; Sudo et al., 2003; Bunescu and Mooney, 2005; McDonald et al., 2005; Greenwood and Stevenson, 2006; Jones, 2005; Xu et al., 2007; Xu, 2007; Kozareva and Hovy, 2010a; Kozareva and Hovy, 2010b)). The advantage of the minimally supervised approaches for IE rule learning is that only initial seed knowledge is needed. Therefore the adaptation might be limited to substituting the seed examples. However, different domains/corpora exhibit rather different properties of their learning/extraction data with respect to the learning algorithm. Depending on the domain, the need for improving precision by utilizing negative examples may differ. An important research goal is the exploitation of more benign domains for improving extraction in less suitable domains.

Xu et al. (2007) and Xu (2007) present a minimally supervised learning system for relation extraction, initialized by a so-called semantic seed, i.e., examples of the target relations. We dub our system DARE for Domain Adaptive Relation Extraction. The system supports the domain adaptation with a compositional rule representation and a bottom-up rule discovery strategy. In this way, DARE can handle target relations of various complexities and arities. Relying on a few examples of a target relation as semantic seed dispenses with the costly acquisition of domain knowledge through experts or specialized resources.

In practice, this does not work equally well for any given domain. Xu (2007) and Uszkoreit et al. (2009) concede that DARE's performance strongly depends on the specific type of relation and domain. In our experiments, we apply DARE to the extraction of two different 4-ary relations from different domains (Nobel Prize awards and MUC-6 management succession events (Grishman and Sundheim, 1996)). In the data set of the first domain, the connectivity between relation instances and linguistic patterns (rules) approximates the small world property (Amaral et al., 2005). In MUC-6 data on the other hand, the redundancy of both mentions of instances and patterns as well as their connectivity are very low.

DARE achieves good performance with the first data set even with a singleton seed, but cannot deal nearly as well with the MUC-6 data.

A systematic comparative analyses was not possible since the two experiments differ in several dimensions: domain, relation, size of data sets, origin of data sets and the respective distribution of mentions in the data. In this paper, a much more systematic analysis is performed in order to understand the differences between domains represented by their respective data sets. We decide to use DARE because of its domain-adaptive design and because of its utilization of negative examples for improving precision (Uszkoreit et al., 2009). At the same time, this is the first study comparing the effects of the DARE utilization of negative examples relative to different domains. In order to secure the significance of the results, we restrict our experiments to one simple symmetric binary relation, i.e. the biographic relation "married to", a single text sort, i.e., Wikipedia articles, and three biographic domains exhibiting different data properties, i.e., entertainers, politicians and business people.

The three data sets are compared with respect to relation extraction performance with and without negative examples in relation to certain data properties. Furthermore, the potential for porting rules from one domain to another and the effects of merging domains are investigated. Our data analysis and experiments give us interesting insights into the relationship between the distribution of biographic information in various social domains and its influence on the learning and extraction task. Given the same target relation "married to", the entertainment domain contains most mentions and owns better data properties for learning than others. But, in the parallel, there are often multiple relations reporting about the same married couples in the entertainment domain, leading to the learning of spurious rules and finally bad precision.

The remainder of the paper is organized as follows: Section 2 explains the DARE system. In section 3, we represent our research idea and our experiments and evaluations. In section 4, we close off with summary and conclusion.

2 DARE

DARE is a minimally supervised machine learning system for relation extraction on free texts, consisting of two parts: 1) rule learning and 2) relation extraction (RE). Rule learning and RE feed each other in a bootstrapping framework. The bootstrapping starts from so-called "semantic seeds", which is a small set of instances of the target relation. The rules are extracted from sentences automatically annotated with semantic entity types and parsing results (e.g., dependency structures), which match with the seeds. RE applies acquired rules to texts in order to discover more relation instances, which in turn are employed as seed for further iterations. The core system architecture of DARE is depicted in Figure 1. The entire bootstrapping stops when no new rules or new instances can be detected. Relying entirely on semantic seeds as domain knowledge, DARE can accommodate new relation types and domains with minimal effort.

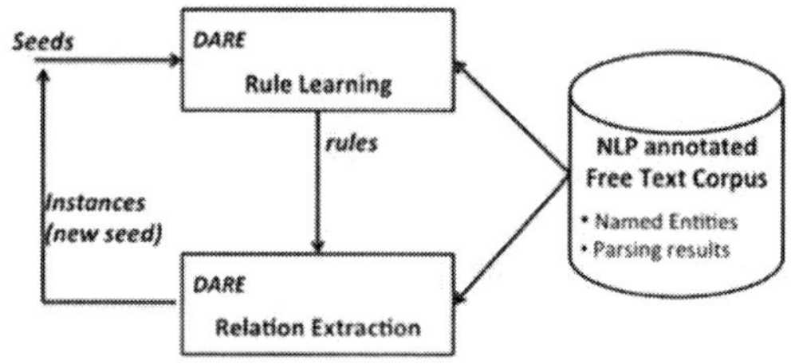

Figure 1: DARE core architecture

DARE can handle target relations of varying arity through a compositional and recursive rule representation and a bottom-up rule discovery strategy. A DARE rule for an n-ary relation can be composed of rules for its projections, namely, rules that extract a subset of the n arguments.

Let us consider an example target relation from (Xu, 2007). It contains prize award events at which a person or an organization wins a particular prize in a certain area and year. The relation can be presented as follows:

(1) *<recipient, prize, area, year>*

(2) is an example relation instance of (1), referring to an event mentioned in the sentence (3).

(2) *<Mohamed ElBaradei, Nobel, Peace, 2005>*

(3) *Mohamed ElBaradei won the 2005 Nobel Prize for Peace on Friday for his efforts to limit the spread of atomic weapons.*

(4) is a simplified dependency tree of the parsing result of (3).

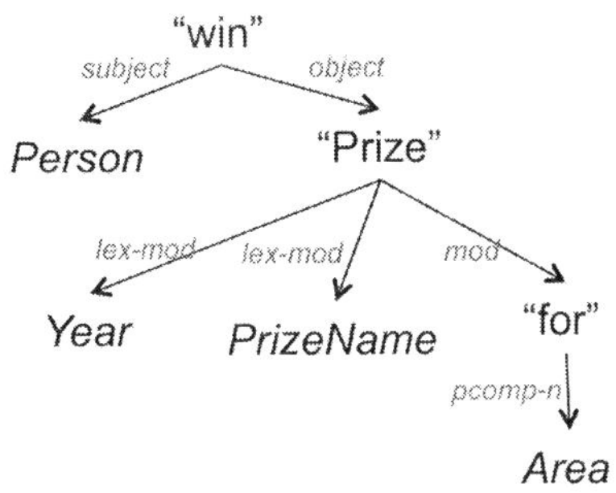

(4)

From the tree in (4), DARE learns three rules in a bottom-up way. The first rule is dominated by the preposition "for", exacting the argument *Area*. The second rule is dominated by the noun "Prize", extracting the arguments *Year* and *PrizeName*, and calling the first rule for the argument *Area*. (5) and (6) show the first and second DARE rules.

(5) extracts the semantic argument *Area* from the prepositional phrase headed by the preposition "for", while (6) extracts the three arguments *Year*, *Prize* and *Area* from the complex noun phrase and calls the rule (5) for the semantic argument *Area*.

(5)

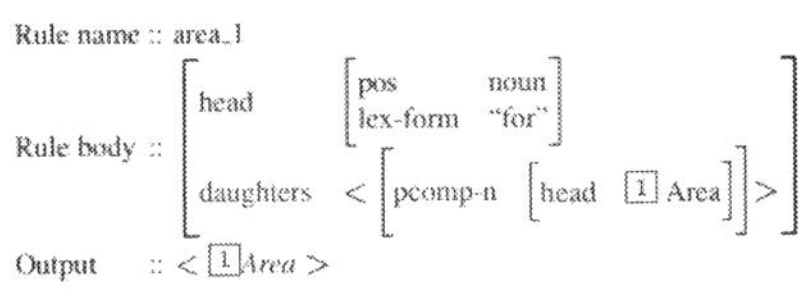

(6)

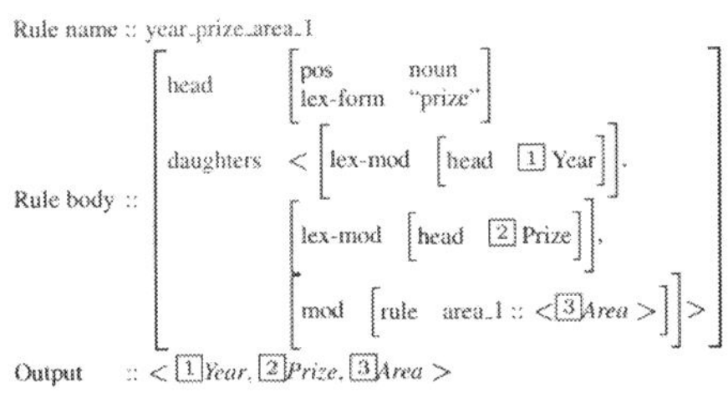

(7) is the third rule that extracts all four arguments from the verb phrase dominated by the verb "win" and calls the second rule to handle the arguments embedded in the linguistic argument "object".

(7)

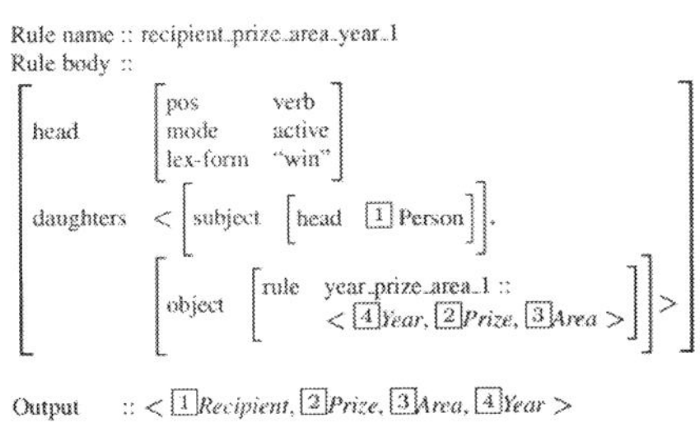

During the bootstrapping, the confidence values of the newly acquired rules and instances are calculated by DARE in the spirit of the "Duality principle" (Brin, 1998; Yangarber, 2001; Agichtein and Gravano, 2000), i.e., the confidence values of the rules are dependent on the truth value of their extracted instances and on the seed instances from which they stem. The confidence value of an extracted instance makes use of the confidence value of its ancestor seed instances. DARE employs two NLP modules: a named-entity recognizer SProUT (Drozdzynski et al., 2004) and a parser (De Marneffe et al., 2006). SProUT is adapted to new domains by adding rules for new NE types and extending the gazetteers.

3 Learning a General Relation from Single and Multiple Domains

The motivation of this work is to learn as many extraction rules as possible for extracting instances of the marriage relation between two persons, to fill, for instance, a biographic database about popular persons from different social domains. We employ DARE to learn the extraction rules from texts for three social categories: entertainment, politicians and business people.

3.1 Data Set and Data Properties

For each domain, we collect 300 Wikipedia documents, each document about one person. For the entertainment domain, we choose pages about actors or actresses of the Oscar academy awards and grammy winners. Pages about the US presidents and other political leaders are selected for the politician domain. American chief executives covered by the Wikipedia are candidates for the business people corpus. In Table 1, we show the distribution of persons, their occurrences and sentences referring to two persons. We immediately observe that the business texts mention much fewer persons or relationships between persons than the texts on politicians. Most mentions of persons and relationships can be found in the entertainment texts so that we can expect to find more extraction rules there than in the other domains.

3.2 Challenges without Gold Standard

Uszkoreit et al. (2009) discussed the challenge of seed selection and its influence on performance in a minimally supervised learning system, e.g., one randomly selected seed is sufficient to find most mentions in the Nobel Prize corpus, but many seeds cannot improve the performance for the MUC-6 corpus. Although we are aware of this problem, we still have to live with the situation

Domain	Entertainer	Politician	Business Person
Number of documents	300	300	300
Size (MB)	4.8	6.8	1.6
Number of person occurrences	61450	63015	9441
Number of person entities	9054	6537	1652
Sentences containing person-person-relations	9876	11111	1174

Table 1: Data Properties of the three Domain Corpora

that all three corpora selected here are unlabeled free texts and their data properties for learning are unknown to us. Furthermore, as pointed out by Agichtein and Gravano (2000), without annotated data, the calculation of recall is infeasible. Therefore, our evaluation can only provide the precision value and the number of the correctly extracted instances.

3.3 Experiments

In the first experiment, we begin by learning from each domain separately starting with positive examples from the domain. Then we merge the seeds and learn from the merged data of all three domains. The performance and the quality of the top ranked rules lead us to the second experiment, where we add negative seed in order to improve the ranking of the good rules. In the third experiment, we apply the good rules from the most fertile domain, i.e. entertainment, to the other two domains in order to find more relation instances in these texts.

3.3.1 Positive Seed

We decide to run 10 experiments, initialized each time with one positive example of a marriage instance for each respective domain, in order to obtain a more objective evaluation than only one experiment with a randomly selected seed. In order to operationalize this obvious and straightforward strategy, we first selected ten prominent married persons from the three sets of 300 persons featured in our Wikipedia articles. For finding the most prominent persons we simply took the length of their Wikipedia article as a crude indication. However, these heuristics are not essential for our experiments, since an increase of the seed set will normally substitute for any informed choice. For the runs with one example, the figures are the rounded averages over the ten runs with different seeds. For the merged corpus only one run was executed based on the three best seeds merged from the three domains.

Table 2 presents all figures for precision and number of correctly extracted instances for each domain and merged domains. The average precision of the business person domain is the highest, while the entertainment domain extracts the most correct instances but with the lowest precision. The politician domain has neither good precision nor good extraction gain.

Single domain	1 positive seed (each)	
	Precision	Correct Instances
Entertainer	5.9%	206
Politician	16.19%	159
Business Person	70.45%	31
Multiple domains	3 positive seed (merged)	
	Precision	Correct instances
merged corpus	8.91%	499

Table 2: Average values of 10 runs for each domain and 1 run for the merged corpus with best seeds

As expected, the distribution of the learned rules and their rankings behave differently in each domain. We got 907 rules from the entertainment domain, 669 from the politician domain, but only 7 from the business person domain. For illustration we only present the top-ranked rules from each domain cutting off after rank 15. The rules are extracted from the trees generated by the Stanford Dependency Parser for the candidate sentences of our corpora (De Marneffe et al., 2006). Here, we present the rules in a simplified form. The first elements in the rules are *head*, followed by their daughters. *A* and *B* are the two person arguments for the target relation. The good rules are highlighted as bold.

- **Top 15 rules in the entertainment domain:**
  1. <person>: dep(A), dep(B)
  2. ("meet", VB): obj(A), subj(B)
  3. **("divorce", VB): subj(A, dep(B))**
  4. **("wife", N): mod(A), mod(B)**
  5. **("marry", VB): dep(A), nsubj(B), aux("be",VB)**
  6. ("star", VB): dep(A), subj(B)
  7. **("husband",N): mod(A), mod(B)**
  8. <position>: dep(A), dep(B)

9. ("attraction", N): mod(A), mod(B)
10. <person>: mod(A), mod(A)
11. ("include", VB): obj(A , dep(B))
12. **("marry", VB): obj(A), subj(B)**
13. ("star", VB): obj(A , dep(B))
14. <person>: dep(A, dep(B))
15. **("marriage", N): dep(A), mod(B)**

- **Top 15 rules in the politician domain:**
  1. <person>: dep(A), dep(B)
  2. ("children", N): dep(A, dep(B))
  3. **("wife", N): mod(A), mod(B)**
  4. **("marry", VB): obj(A), subj(B)**
  5. ("son", N): mod(A), mod(B)
  6. <position>: mod(A), mod(B)
  7. ("include", VB): obj(A , dep(B))
  8. <person>: mod(A), mod(B)
  9. <person>: dep(A), mod(B)
  10. ("defeat", VB): obj(A), subj(B)
  11. ("successor", N): mod(A), mod(B)
  12. ("lose", VB): subj(A), dep(B)
  13. ("with", IN): obj(A, dep(B))
  14. ("father", NN): mod(A), mod(B)
  15. ("appoint", VB): nsubj(A), dep(B), aux("be", VB)

- **Top rules in the business-person domain**
  1. ("children", N): dep(A), dep(B)
  2. ("have", VB): subj(A, dep(B))
  3. ("give", VB): subj(A), obj(B)
  4. ("date", VB): subj(A), obj(B)
  5. (A): dep(("wife", NN), mod(B))
  6. ("student", N): dep(A , dep(B))
  7. **("marry", VB): obj(A), subj(B)**

- **Top 15 rules in the merged corpus:**
  1. <person>: dep(A), dep(B)
  2. **("wife", N): mod(A), mod(B)**
  3. ("son", N), mod(A): mod(B)
  4. **("marry", VB): obj(A), subj(B)**
  5. ("meet", VB), obj(A): subj(B)
  6. ("include", VB): obj(A), dep(B)
  7. <position>: mod(A), mod(B)
  8. ("children", N): dep(A), dep(B)
  9. <person>: dep(A , mod(B))
  10. <person>: dep(A), mod(B)
  11. **("marry", VB): dep(A), nsubj(B), aux("be",VB)**
  12. ("father", N): dep(A), dep(B)
  13. ("tell", VB): obj(A), subj(B)
  14. **("husband",N): mod(A), mod(B)**
  15. <person>: mod(A), mod(B)

In all experiments, the good rules are not ranked highest. Although many good rules can be learned from the entertainment domain, several dangerous rules (such as the rule extracting instances of the "meet"-relation) are ranked higher because they are mentioned more frequently and often match with a seed person pair standing in marriage relation. In this domain, the married persons are often mentioned together in connection with other popular activities. This overlap of marriage with other relations causes many wrong rules. For example, the top ranked rule is learned from the following sentence (8) matching the seed (*Charles Laughton, Elsa Lanchester*).

(8) In total, he (Billy Wilder) directed fourteen different actors in Oscar-nominated performances: Barbara Stanwyck, . . . , Audrey Hepburn, Charles Laughton, Elsa Lanchester, Jack Lemmon, . . .

Many couples are mentioned in such coordination constructions. Therefore, this rule has a high connectivity and produces more than 2000 relation instances, boosting the rank of the rule to the top. Yet most instances extracted by this rule are incorrect. Several rules of similar type are the reason for the low precision in the entertainer and the politician domains. On the other hand, all three domains share the good rule:

(9) **("marry", VB): obj(A), subj(B)**

The extraction results from the merged corpus are comparable to the entertainment domain: low precision and high gain of instances. The increase of the data size supports higher recall.

Driven by our scientific curiosity, we increase the number of our positive seed to 10 with 10 runs too. Table 3 shows that the average precision for entertainer and politician domains do not improve significantly. All three domains yield a higher recall because more good rules could be learned from the larger seed.

Single domain domain	10 positive seed (each)	
	Precision	Correct instances
Entertainer	6.12%	264
Politician	17.32%	185
Business Person	78.95%	60
Multiple domains	30 positive seed (merged)	
	Precision	Correct instances
merged corpus	8.93%	513

Table 3: Experiments with 10 positive seeds for every corpus and 30 seeds for the merged corpus

But enlarged seeds could not help in finding more highly ranked good rules. On the contrary, some good rules disappear from the top positions. The reason is that different seeds produce different good rules but sometimes share the same bad rules, thus unfortunately boosting these bad rules in rank. Bad rules are rules which extract wrong instances.

It is interesting to observe that the merged corpus in both experiments extracts more correct instances than the sum of the single domains together, in particular, in the one seed experiment, 499 (merged) vs. 396 (the sum of the single domains). In the case of the 10 seed experiment, the merged corpus extracted 513 correct instances while the single domains together 509. This indicates that both the enlargements of seeds and corpus size raise recall.

3.3.2 Negative Seed for Learning Negative Rules

Next we improve precision by accounting for other relations in which married couples are frequently mentioned:

1. Laurence Olivier saw Vivien Leigh in The Mask of Virtue.
2. Olivier and Leigh began an affair after acting as lovers in Fire Over England .
3. In the June 2006 Ladies' Home Journal, she said she (Nicole Kidman) still loved Cruise.
4. She (Nicole Kidman) became romantically involved with actor Tom Cruise on . . ..
5. He (Tom Cruise) and Kidman adopted two children.

Table 4 shows the average number of different relations reported about the extracted couples involved in the three domains. Thus, given a person pair as seed, DARE also learns rules which mention other relationships, especially in the entertainment domain.

Entertainer	Politician	Business Person
5.10	2.85	1.59

Table 4: Average number of various relations reported about the extracted couples

There are several approaches to negative samples for rule learning. Most of them ((Etzioni et al., 2005), (Lin et al., 2003), (Yangarber, 2003) and (Uszkoreit et al., 2009)) use the instances of other target relations as their negative examples or negative seed. Inspired by them, we employ negative seed examples to weed out dangerous rules. The dangerous rules are rules which extract incorrect instances in addition to the correct instances. We apply the negative seed to learn so-called negative rules and hope that the negative rules will cover the dangerous rules learned by the positive

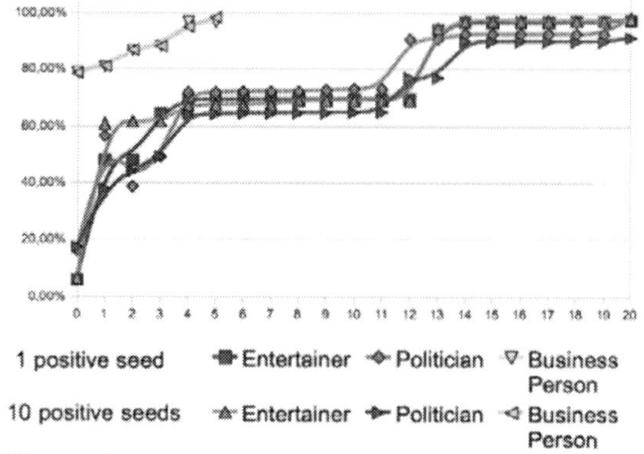

Figure 2: Average precision of experiments in 3 domains with 1 or 10 positive seeds and 1 to 20 negative seeds: *x axis* for negative seed, *y axis* for precision

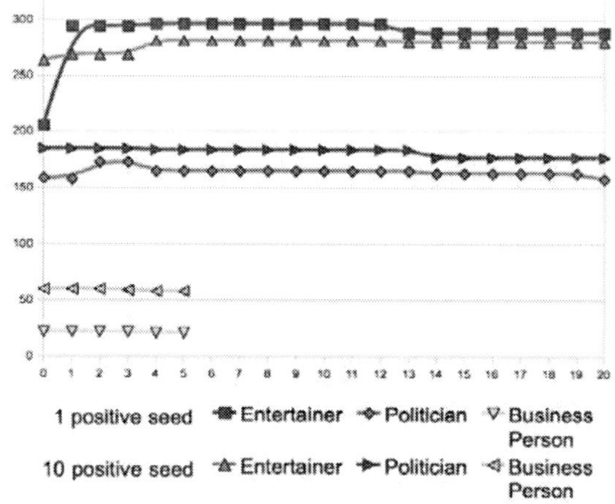

Figure 3: Correct instances of experiments in 3 domains with 1 or 10 positive seeds and 1 to 20 negative seeds: *x axis* for negative seed, *y axis* for number of extracted correct instances

seed. For the negative seed construction, we develop a new approach. Negative seed for our target relation contains person pairs who do not stand in a marriage relation, but who are extracted by the top 20 ranked rules produced from positive seed. The learning of the negative rules works just like the learning of the positive ones, but without any iterations. Once we have obtained rules from negative examples, we only use them for subtracting any identical rules from the rule set learned from positive seed.

Figure 2 shows the improvement of precision after the utilization of negative seed for 1 positive and 10 positive seed situations, while Figure 3 depicts the development of the extracted corrected instances. It appears that the number of the positive seeds does not make a significant difference of the performance development. For the business person domain, only a few negative seeds suffice for getting 100% precision. For both entertainment and politician domains, the negative seeds considerably improve precision. There are several jumps in the curves. In the entertainment domain, the first negative seed removes the strongest bad rule. As a side-effect some good rules move upwards so that both precision and recall increase significantly and at the same time some other bad rules move downwards which are connected to subsequent negative seeds. Therefore, the second negative seed does not lead to big jump in the performance. Similar phenomena can be observed by analysing other flat portions of the curve.

In the following, we show only the top 10 rules learned from the entertainment domain with 1 positive seed and 20 negative seeds because of the limit of space.

(10) *top 10 rules learned from the entertainment domain:*

1. **("wife", N): mod(A), mod(B)**
2. **("divorce", VB): subj(A, dep(B))**
3. **("marry", VB): obj(A), subj(B)**
4. **("husband",N): mod(A), mod(B)**
5. **("marry", VB): dep(A), nsubj(B), aux("be",VB)**
6. **("marriage", N): dep(A), mod(B)**
7. ("appear", VB): dep(A), subj(B)
8. <person>: dep(A), mod(B)
9. <position>: mod(A), mod(B)
10. ("friend", N): mod(A), mod(B)

The entertainment domain has taken the biggest advantage of the negative seed strategy. The top 6 rules are all good rules. The other two domains contain only a subset of rules.

3.3.3 Exploitation of Beneficial Domains for Other Domains

The above experiments show us that the entertainment domain provides a much better resource for learning rules than the other two domains. As it will often happen that relevant application domains are not supported by beneficial data sets, we finally investigate the exploitation of data from a more popular domain for RE in a less beneficial domain. We apply rules learned from entertainment domain to the politician and business person domains. Table 5 shows that applying the top six rules in (10) learned from the entertainment domain discover many additional correct instances from the other two domains.

	Precision	new instances
Politician	98.48%	27
Business person	96.72%	17

Table 5: Additional instances extracted by the learned top six rules from the entertainment domain

4 Summary and Conclusion

In this paper we provide new evidence for the successful application of a minimally supervised IE approach based on semantic seed and bottom-up rule extraction from dependency structures to new domains with varying data properties. The experiments confirm and illustrate some hypotheses on the role of data properties on the learning process. A new approach to gathering and exploiting negative seed has been presented that considerably improves precision for individual and merged domains. Some positive effects of merging domains could be demonstrated.

An important observation is the successful exploitation of data from a related but different domain for a domain that does not possess suitable learning data. Thus we can cautiously conclude that the underlying minimally supervised bootstrapping approach to IE is not necessarily doomed to failure for domains that do not possess beneficial data sets for learning. Just as Xu (2007) already observed when they were able to use extraction rules learned from Nobel Prize news to detecting instances of other award events, we could now obtain first evidence for the effective reusability of rules learned from a combination of positive and negative examples.

Future research will have to confirm that the observed improvements of RE, especially the gain of precision obtained by the new method for using negative examples will actually scale up to much larger data sets and to more complex relations. We have already successfully applied the learned rule sets for the detection of marriage instances to collecting biographical information from other web data. However because of the inherent problems associated to measuring precision and especially recall in web-based IR/IE tasks, a rigid evaluation of these extractions will only be possible after extensive and expensive hand labelling efforts.

Acknowledgements

This research was conducted in the context of the German DFG Cluster of Excellence on Multimodal Computing and Interaction (M2CI), projects Theseus Alexandria and Alexandria for Media (funded by the German Federal Ministry of Economy and Technology, contract 01MQ07016), and project TAKE (funded by the German Federal Ministry of Education and Research, contract 01IW08003).

References

Eugene Agichtein and Luis Gravano. 2000. Snowball: Extracting relations from large plain-text collections. In *Proceedings of the 5th ACM International Conference on Digital Libraries (DL'00)*, San Antonio, TX, June.

LAN Amaral, A. Scala, M. Barthélémy, and HE Stanley. 2005. Classes of small-world networks. *Proceedings of the National Academy of Sciences*, 102(30):10421–10426.

Sergey Brin. 1998. Extracting patterns and relations from the world wide web. In *WebDB Workshop at 6th International Conference on Extending Database Technology, EDBT'98.*

R. C. Bunescu and R.J Mooney. 2005. A shortest path dependency kernel for relation extraction. In *Proceedings of the Human Language Technology Conference and Conference on Empirical Methods in Natural Language Processing*, pages 724–731, Vancouver, B.C., October.

M.C. De Marneffe, B. MacCartney, and C.D. Manning. 2006. Generating typed dependency parses from phrase structure parses. In *LREC 2006.*

Witold Drozdzynski, Hans-Ulrich Krieger, Jakub Piskorski, Ulrich Schäfer, and Feiyu Xu. 2004. Shallow processing with unification and typed feature structures — foundations and applications. *Künstliche Intelligenz*, 1.

O. Etzioni, M. Cafarella, D. Downey, A.M. Popescu, T. Shaked, S. Soderland, D.S. Weld, and A. Yates. 2005. Unsupervised named-entity extraction from the web: An experimental study. *Artificial Intelligence*, 165(1).

Mark A. Greenwood and Mark Stevenson. 2006. Improving semi-supervised acquisition of relation extraction patterns. In *Proceedings of the Workshop on Information Extraction Beyond The Document.* Association for Computational Linguistics.

Ralph Grishman and Beth Sundheim. 1996. Message understanding conference - 6: A brief history. In *Proceedings of the 16th International Conference on Computational Linguistics*, Copenhagen, June.

R. Jones. 2005. *Learning to Extract Entities from Labeled and Unlabeled Text.* Ph.D. thesis, University of Utah.

Zornitsa Kozareva and Eduard Hovy. 2010a. Learning arguments and supertypes of semantic relations using recursive patterns. In *Proceedings of COLING 2010*, Uppsala, Sweden.

Zornitsa Kozareva and Eduard Hovy. 2010b. Not all seeds are equal: Measuring the quality of text mining seeds. In *Proceedings of HLT/NACL 2010*, Los Angeles, California.

W. Lin, R. Yangarber, and R. Grishman. 2003. Bootstrapped learning of semantic classes from positive and negative examples. In *Proceedings of ICML-2003 Workshop on The Continuum from Labeled to Unlabeled Data*, pages 103–111.

Ryan McDonald, Fernando Pereira, Seth Kulick, Scott Winters, Yang Jin, and Pete White. 2005. Simple algorithms for complex relation extraction with applications to biomedical IE. In *Proceedings of ACL 2005*. Association for Computational Linguistics.

Ion Muslea. 1999. Extraction patterns for information extraction tasks: A survey. In *AAAI Workshop on Machine Learning for Information Extraction*, Orlando, Florida, July.

K. Sudo, S. Sekine, and R. Grishman. 2003. An improved extraction pattern representation model for automatic IE pattern acquisition. *Proceedings of ACL 2003*, pages 224–231.

Junichi Tsujii. 2000. Generic nlp technologies: language, knowledge and information extraction. In *Proceedings of the 38th Annual Meeting on Association for Computational Linguistics (ACL).*

Hans Uszkoreit, Feiyu Xu, and Hong Li. 2009. Analysis and improvement of minimally supervised machine learning for relation extraction. In *14th International Conference on Applications of Natural Language to Information Systems.*

Hans Uszkoreit. 2011. Learning relation extraction grammars with minimal human intervention: Strategy, results, insights and plans. In Alexander Gelbukh, editor, *Computational Linguistics and Intelligent Text Processing*, volume 6609 of *Lecture Notes in Computer Science*. Springer Berlin / Heidelberg.

Feiyu Xu, Hans Uszkoreit, and Hong Li. 2007. A seed-driven bottom-up machine learning framework for extracting relations of various complexity. *Proceedings of ACL 2007*, pages 584–591.

Feiyu Xu. 2007. *Bootstrapping Relation Extraction from Semantic Seeds.* Phd-thesis, Saarland University.

Roman Yangarber. 2001. *Scenarion Customization for Information Extraction.* Dissertation, Department of Computer Science, Graduate School of Arts and Science, New York University, New York, USA.

R. Yangarber. 2003. Counter-training in discovery of semantic patterns. In *Proc. ACL-2003*. Association for Computational Linguistics.

Extracting Relations Within and Across Sentences

Kumutha Swampillai and **Mark Stevenson**
Department of Computer Science
Sheffield University
S1 4DP, UK
(k.swampillai|m.stevenson)@dcs.shef.ac.uk

Abstract

Previous work on relation extraction has focussed on identifying relationships between entities that occur in the same sentence (intra-sentential relations) rather than between entities in different sentences (inter-sentential relations) despite previous research having shown that inter-sentential relations commonly occur in information extraction corpora. This paper describes a SVM-based approach to relation extraction that is applied to both types. Adapted features and techniques for counter-acting bias in SVM models are used to deal with specific issues that arise in the inter-sentential case. It was found that the structured features used for intra-sentential relation extraction can be easily adapted for the inter-sentential case and provides comparable performance.

1 Introduction

Relation extraction is an established subfield of information extraction concerned with extracting related pairs of entities from text. The majority of research has been applied to extracting relations within single sentences (intra-sentential relations), examples include (Chieu and Ng, 2002; Culotta and Sorensen, 2004; Sekine, 2006; Banko and Etzioni, 2008). However, an analysis of the MUC6 corpus (Swampillai and Stevenson, 2010) showed that 28.5% of the relations occur between entities in different sentences (inter-sentential relations). This paper describes a SVM-based approach which is applied to the extraction of both inter- and intra-sentential relations.

A number of challenges are faced when extracting inter-sentential relations. The structured features, that are based on parse trees and have been successfully used for intra-sentential relation extraction, do not naturally apply over multiple sentences. The limited research published on inter-sentential relation extraction (Roberts et al., 2008; Hirano et al., 2010) does not employ parse tree features. We address this problem by introducing new structured features (see section 3.2) for the inter-sentential case.

There is also a greater data sparsity issue when learning extraction models for inter-sentential relations due in part to the smaller number of relations expressed inter-sententially. We investigate a learning approach called threshold adjustment (Shanahan and Roma, 2003) to counter-act the imbalance in the data.

The remainder of the paper is organised as follows: Section 2 discusses previous work on relation extraction. Section 3 describes a relation extraction system suitable for both inter- and intra-sentential relation extraction that uses both flat and structures features. The MUC6 relation extraction task is described in Section 4. Section 5 investigates whether the bias in the relation extraction SVM models can be mitigated using threshold adaption. Section 6 reports the results of the inter-sentential and intra-sentential relation extraction system described. Finally, Section 7 concludes the paper with a discussion of the effectiveness of a composite kernel approach to inter-sentential relation extraction.

2 Related Work

The majority of the work on relation extraction has focused on intra-sentential relations and there has been limited research on inter-sentential relation extraction. Roberts et al. (2008) applies

an SVM approach to identify inter-sentential relations in the biomedical domain where flat features are used to represent the relations. A low performance is achieved on the inter-sentential relations alone (f-measure < 0.19) but they were able to improve overall performance by combining their inter- and intra-sentential data sets.
In addition, Roberts et al. (2008) give a distribution of inter-sentential relations in their corpus where the number of inter-sentential relations occurring in a pair of sentences is inversely proportional to the number of intervening sentences with 42.9% of inter-sentential relations present in consecutive sentences.

More recently Hirano et al. (2010) have reported that 12% of the relations in their Japanese news corpus are inter-sentential. It learns extraction patterns using a bootstrapped classification algorithm. A novel feature is created for inter-sentential relations where a tree is constructed to represent a possible relation based on a *salient referent list*, i.e. a map of the references in the document. The tree contains the two entities and the proposed relation type which is augmented with entity class and POS. An f-measure of 51% is reported for inter-sentential relations.

Flat features commonly used for intra-sentential relation extraction (Mintz et al., 2009) include: a feature representing the entity that occurs first in the sentence; the sequence of lexical tokens and part-of-speech (POS) tags between the two entities, in the sentence; a sequence of lexical tokens and their POS tags on the left hand side of the first entity and on the right hand side of the second entity; a dependency path between the two entities and the verbs that occur between the entities. Composite kernels using flat and structured features have been successfully applied for intra-sentential relation extraction (Zelenko et al., 2003; Bunescu and Mooney, 2004; Culotta and Sorensen, 2004; Zhou et al., 2007). Culotta and Sorensen (2004) and Zhou et al. (2007) have shown that tree kernels combined with flat kernels are more effective for intra-sentential relation extraction than either kernel used alone. In experiments on the ACE corpus, Zhou et al. (2007) achieved f-measures of 0.741 using syntactic parse tree features which outperforms dependency trees. Zhang et al. (2006) further explored which portion of parse trees are most informative for intra-sentential relation extraction by testing seven different subtrees as features. The shortest path-enclosed tree performed the best where the shortest path-enclosed tree is the subtree that includes only the two entities participating in the relation and the intervening syntactic structure.

3 Relation Extraction System

We classify relations using SVMs, a standard approach that has been widely used in relation extraction (Agichtein and Gravano, 2000; Zelenko et al., 2003; Roberts et al., 2008; Ittoo and Bouma, 2010). The SVM^{light} implementation (Joachims, 2002) and Moschitti's tree kernel tools (Moschitti, 2006) are used. Each pair of entities that appears in the document and is of the correct named entity types is considered a *possible relation* for that relation type. Features are extracted from the text to represent each *possible relations* and these are classified using a binary SVM model. These features are adapted from the set of commonly used features for intra-sentential relation extraction and are based on both flat features and the structured features derived from parse trees. Experiments are also conducted combining the two types of features in composite kernels.

To our knowledge tree and composite kernels have not been applied to inter-sentential relation extraction.

3.1 Flat Features

The entities participating in an inter-sentential relation can occur in any two sentences in a document; therefore the sequence of tokens between the two entities can include a large number of tokens. We therefore use a windowing method to model context of the entities separately. This feature list is given below:

- A window of t tokens from the surrounding context of each entity.
- A window of t POS tags from the surrounding context of each entity
- The two nearest dominating verbs for each of the entities, identified in the parse tree structure.
- A distance feature, $dist$, which corresponds to the number of intervening sentences between e_1 and e_2.

The use of a window to select the token and POS tag features for each entity, instead of the sequence of tokens between two entities, avoids the situation where document length token sequence is used as a feature. In these experiments two window sizes are used: $t = 6$ and $t = 12$ which represent three and six tokens to the left-hand-side and right-hand-side of e_1 and e_2 respectively. The likelihood of a inter-sentential relation is inversely proportional to the distance between the two participating entities and the *dist* feature adds this information to the representation.

3.2 Structured Features

Structured features used for intra-sentential relation extraction are based on parse trees. As only entities occurring in the same sentence can be part of a intra-sentential relation, it can be assumed that related entities always appear in a single parse tree. However, this assumption does not hold for inter-sentential relations. We overcame this problem by joining parse trees for pairs of entities by adding a new node (ROOT) that connects the parses. Two new features were developed using this approach based on the shortest path-enclosed tree (Zhang et al., 2006):

- The shortest path tree (SPT) structure which only contains the shortest path between the two entities, that is the conjunction of the path from e_1 to the root and the path from e_2 to the root.

- The adapted shortest path-enclosed tree (SPET) consisting of a subtree containing the shortest path between the two participating entities and all intervening nodes and structure to provide context.

Examples are shown in Figure 1.

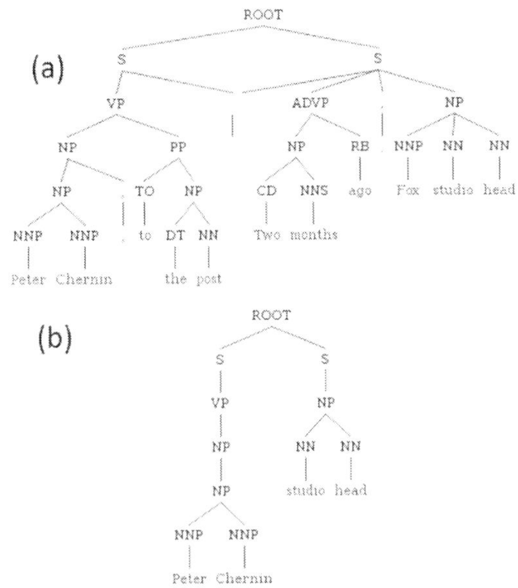

Figure 1: Examples of (a) shortest path-enclosed tree and (b) shortest path tree adapted for inter-sentential relation extraction.

4 Extraction Task

The MUC 6 management succession task identifies information about people entering or leaving management positions in organizations and has been shown to include both inter- and intra-sentential relations (Swampillai and Stevenson, 2010). The main entities participating in these events are the persons joining or leaving (*Per*), the positions they are taking up or vacating (*Post*) and the organizations in which the position exists (*Org*). A version of the MUC6 corpus that has been converted to binary relations is used (Swampillai and Stevenson, 2010), where the three relation types, *PerOrg*, *PerPost* and *PostOrg*, have been manually identified annotated.

For example, the following sentences include one intra-sentential relation, *PerPost(Vern Raburn, president)*, and two inter-sentential relations, *PerOrg(Vern Raburn, Paul Allen Group)* and *PostOrg(president, Paul Allen Group)*.

> "Paul G. Allen, the billionaire co-founder of Microsft Corp., has started a company and named longtime friend *Vern Raburn* its *president*.
>
> The company, to be called *Paul Allen Group* will be based in Bellevue, Wash., and will coordinate the overall strategy..."

Intuitively, inter-sentential relation extraction is related to co-reference resolution. However, whilst the resolution of anaphoric expressions can address a significant proportion of these relations, an analysis of the MUC6 corpus by Stevenson (2006) shows that many of these relations require inference across information contained in multiple sentences, possibly using discourse analysis and world knowledge. For example, the following sentences describe a *PerPost* relation where *Kenneth Newell* leaves the position of *senior vice president, Europe, Africa and Mediterranean*.

"David J. Bronczek, vice president and general manager of Federal Express Canada Ltd., was named *senior vice president, Europe, Africa and Mediterranean*, at this air-express concern.

Mr. Bronczek succeeds *Kenneth Newell*, 55, who was named to the new post of senior vice president, retail service operations."

This relation can only be inferred using the knowledge that when one executive replaces another they must leave the position they are currently holding. This paper proposes an approach that does not require the kind of complex linguistic understanding required for co-reference resolution and addresses all inter-sentential relations.

5 Data Sparsity

In the case of intra-sentential relations, possible relations are constrained to pairs of entities that occur within a sentence. Whereas for inter-sentential relations all pairs of entities that occur in a document are possible relations. This causes an explosion in the number of negative instances in the inter-sentential case compared to the intra-sentential case. This coupled with a smaller number of positive relations (only 28.5%) causes a highly unbalanced data set. The percentage of positive examples of relations in all cases is shown in Table 2. It should be noted that there are an extremely limited number of *PerPost* inter-sentential relations, only 64, present in the corpus. This level of imbalance in the data set can render classifiers ineffective (Wu and Chang, 2003).

Relation Type	Intra	Inter
PerOrg	14.99% (1568)	0.53% (29320)
PerPost	23.44% (1971)	0.25% (25697)
PostOrg	20.07% (1495)	0.79% (22475)

Table 1: The bias of the data is expressed here as the percentage of positive relation instances with the total number of instances for each relation type given in brackets.

Various approaches to learning with unbalanced data have been proposed. Undersampling the negative class prior to learning (Japkowicz, 2000) discards a large proportion of the data and the data used for learning no longer approximates the probability distribution of the target population. The other approach is to introduce a bias in the learning algorithm which compensates for the unbalanced training data without discarding information. Two established methods are cost-sensitive learning (Morik et al., 1999) and hyperplane adjustment (Shanahan and Roma, 2003) both of which have been applied to the relation extraction system. Experiments comparing the two techniques showed that cost-sensitive learning does not perform as well as hyperplane adjustment and these results are not reported here.

5.1 Threshold Adjustment

Threshold adjustment is a method for counteracting the bias in SVM models resulting from unbalanced data (Shanahan and Roma, 2003). In the case of unbalanced data the SVM hyperplane is biased towards the negative class, however the hyperplane can be offset so that it preserves the orientation of the original hyperplane but pushes it towards the negative class. The threshold, β, is used to adjust the hyperplane immediately training. Given a set of labelled training instances $\{x_i, y_i\}_{i=1...n}$ where input points x_i map to targets $y_i \in \pm 1$, the class prediction of a new test instance x is derived using

$$sign\left(\sum_{i=1}^{n} \alpha_i y_i K(x, x_i) + b - \beta\right) \quad (1)$$

where the bias b and coefficients α_i are found by SVM training and K is the kernel function. The constant β is added to bias in the model in favour of the positive instances. Inter-sentential relation extraction is carried out for various values of β, using a prototypical feature selection, including both the flat and structured features. Table2 gives results for the baseline, $\beta = 0$, and the results for the best performing model for each relation type where β maximizes the f-measure. These results show that adjusting the threshold for SVMs can achieve a statistically significant[1] improvement in f-measure over standard SVM models for both relation types.

6 Relation Extraction

The relation extraction system described in Section 3 was evaluated on both inter-sentential and intra-sentential relations in the MUC6 corpus. Training and testing was performed using 10-fold nested cross validation.

[1] Statistical significance is tested using the Mann-Whitney U test, $P < 0.05$.

Method	*PerOrg*			*PerPost*			*PostOrg*		
	R	P	F-Meas.	R	P	F-Meas.	R	P	F-Meas.
No Bias	0.284	1.000	0.443	0.000	0.000	0.000	0.422	1.000	0.594
Threshold Adaption	$\beta = -0.75$			$\beta = -1$			$\beta = -0.75$		
	0.561	0.920	**0.697**	0.541	0.076	**0.133**	0.668	0.992	**0.799**

Table 2: Maximum performance boost of cost-sensitive learning and threshold adjustment methods on the performance of inter-sentential relation extraction SVM models.

6.1 Nested Cross-Validation

Nested cross-validation (Scheffer, 1999) was used to automatically set the threshold parameter, β, by optimizing it empirically during training. This method also ensures that β is set independently from our testing data. This sub-divides the training data in each cross-validation fold into sub-folds which are used to identify the optimal value of the threshold for that particular training data. This threshold value is then used when evaluating the test data of the original cross-validation fold. The optimal threshold value of each cross-validation fold is identified in the sub-folds by training using a variety of threshold values and evaluating them on the sub-fold reserved for testing. The threshold with the highest average value across all sub-folds is then used. This nested cross-validation algorithm is described in Algorithm 1.

Algorithm 1 Procedure for carrying out nested cross-validation to determine the optimal threshold value, β^*, for the training data in each fold. This algorithm extends standard cross-validation by adding an inner loop to estimate the optimal threshold value by finding the maximum f-score for each threshold value , β.

```
thresholds = {0.25, ..., -1}
Split data, T, into 10 folds (t_1, t_2, ... t_10)
for i = 1 to 10 do
    test_set ← t_i
    training_set ← T − t_i
    Split training_set into 9 folds (v_1, v_2, ... v_9)
    for j = 1 to 9 do
        testing_validation_set ← v_j
        training_validation_set ← training_set − v_j
        Train SVM using the training_validation_set, evaluate
        on test_validation_set and record the predictions, pred(k).
        for all β ∈ thresholds do
            Calculate the f-measure of pred(j) with a threshold setting of β and
            record, F(pred(j))_β.
        end for all
    end for
    for all β ∈ thresholds do
        F_avg(β) ← (Σ_{j=1to9} F(pred(j))_β) / 9.
    end for all
    Determine the best threshold setting, β*, where β* = argmax F_avg(β).
    Train the SVM using training_set, evaluate on test_set with β* as threshold setting
    and record performance, P(i)
end for
performance ← (Σ_{i=1to10} P(i)) / 10
return performance
```

6.2 Results

The performance of various feature sets (kernels) is evaluated on both the inter-sentential (Table 3) and intra-sentential (Table 4) relation extraction task. The relation extraction system classifies possible relations from the corpus as one of the three relation types, *PerOrg*, *PerPost* or *PostOrg*. The recall, precision and f-measure metrics is reported after each classifier and kernel. The first three kernels in the tables contain flat features, where $Winn$ indicates the inclusion of n POS tags and tokens surrounding each entity. The SPT and $SPET$ kernels are the shortest path-enclosed tree and the shortest path tree kernels. The final two are composite kernels combining each tree kernel, SPT and $SPET$, with the overall best performing flat kernel, $Win12 + Dist + Verbs$.

The best performance is achieved using the composite SPT kernel for all relation types and for both the inter-sentential and intra-sentential tasks. However, in the case of inter-sentential relations there is no statistically significant difference[2] between the performance of the SPT kernel and the composite SPT kernel on both *PerOrg* and *Pos-*

[2] Statistical significance is tested using the Mann-Whitney U test, $P < 0.05$.

Kernel	*PerOrg*			*PerPost*			*PostOrg*		
	R	P	F-Meas.	R	P	F-Meas.	R	P	F-Meas.
Flat									
Win 6+Dist	0.117	0.730	0.201	0.015	0.200	0.029	0.336	0.809	0.475
Win 12+Dist	0.191	0.644	0.295	0.075	0.440	*0.128*	0.400	0.681	0.504
Win 12+Dist+Verbs	0.517	0.740	*0.608*	0.059	0.500	0.106	0.677	0.743	*0.708*
Tree									
SPT	0.467	0.798	*0.589*	0.000	0.000	0.000	0.524	0.814	*0.638*
SPET	0.314	0.608	0.414	0.035	0.167	*0.058*	0.475	0.656	0.551
Composite									
SPT and Win 12+Dist+Verbs	0.518	0.877	**0.651**	0.144	0.327	**0.200**	0.693	0.853	**0.765**
SPET and Win 12+Dist+Verbs	0.442	0.762	0.560	0.072	0.300	0.116	0.588	0.777	0.669

Table 3: Performance of *inter-sentential* relation extraction for flat, tree and composite kernels using threshold optimization.

Kernel	*PerOrg*			*PerPost*			*PostOrg*		
	R	P	F-Meas.	R	P	F-Meas.	R	P	F-Meas.
Flat									
Win 6	0.535	0.484	0.508	0.645	0.588	0.615	0.614	0.550	0.581
Win 12	0.628	0.441	0.519	0.654	0.561	0.604	0.521	0.503	0.512
Win 12+Verbs	0.589	0.459	0.516	0.660	0.571	0.612	0.415	0.596	0.489
Tree									
SPT	0.566	0.636	0.599	0.630	0.631	0.631	0.623	0.754	0.683
SPET	0.616	0.414	0.495	0.576	0.575	0.575	0.564	0.538	0.551
Composite									
SPT and Win 12+Verbs	0.757	0.649	**0.699**	0.682	0.624	**0.652**	0.759	0.741	**0.750**
SPET and Win 12+Verbs	0.568	0.560	0.564	0.595	0.628	0.611	0.685	0.668	0.677

Table 4: Performance of *intra-sentential* relation extraction for flat, tree and composite kernels using using threshold optimization.

tOrg relations. This shows the minimal contribution of flat features to the inter-sentential classification task, unlike the intra-sentential task where the addition of flat features makes a marked improvement.

For both tasks the relation type with the best f-measure is *PostOrg* at 0.809 and 0.750 for the inter- and intra-sentential relations respectively. The data set associated with this relation is the least skewed of the data sets. In contrast *PerPost*, the most unbalanced data set, has the worst f-measure for the intra-sentential relation extraction task at 0.652 and fails to make any impact on the inter-sentential relation extraction task with an f-measure of only 0.200. This suggests that bias still has an effect on performance despite the steps taken to mitigate against it.

Different behaviour is observed for inter- and intra-sentential relations when comparing the results of the experiments using the flat kernel. The use of a wider context feature window and surrounding verbs improves the overall f-measure scores for inter-sentential relations, substantially improving recall while slightly degrading precision. However, for the intra-sentential case adding context and verb features either maintains or degrades performance. Flat features alone achieve better performance for the inter-sentential task (0.608, 0.128 and 0.708) than for intra-sentential task (0.519, 0.615 and 0.581).

Results using tree and composite kernels show that the SPT tree representation is more effective than the SPET tree for both tasks. This may be because SPET subtrees are larger and potentially contain more noise. Tree kernels perform better than those created from flat features demonstrating that structured features are hugely informative for relation extraction.

Overall, the results show that the best performing kernel is the composite SPT kernel. This is inline with previous research into intra-sentential relation extraction (Zhou et al., 2007; Zhang et al., 2006) where the best results are achieved with a shortest path composite kernel. For inter-sentential relations f-measures of 0.651, 0.200 and 0.809 are achieved. The use of the composite kernel SVM approach to relation extraction gives comparable performance on the inter-sentential task except in the case of relations with extremely skewed training data.

7 Conclusions

This paper investigates whether state-of-the-art approaches to intra-sentential relation extraction can be effectively adapted for inter-sentential relation extraction. The results demonstrate that a composite kernel approach to inter-sentential relation extraction can achieve comparable results with intra-sentential relation extraction. We have also shown that the structured features used for intra-sentential relation extraction can be easily adapted for the inter-sentential case. The performance of structured features has been found to be superior to flat features which have previously been used for the inter-sentential relation extraction task (McDonald et al., 2005; Roberts et al., 2008).

Overall, composite kernels, that combine a larger context window with a SPT tree, were found to give better performance than either flat or structured features alone. Inter-sentential *PerPost* relations could not effectively be extracted using this approach, most likely due to the bias in the *PerPost* data set.

Threshold adaption, which was optimised using nested cross-validation, significantly improved the performance of SVM models for inter-sentential relation extraction. Average f-measure improved from 0.295 to 0.605, a significant improvement in performance over all kernel types.

References

Eugene Agichtein and Luis Gravano. 2000. Snowball: Extracting Relations from Large Plain-Text Collections. *In Proceedings of the 5th Association for Computing Machinery International Conference on Digital Libraries*, 85–94.

Michele Banko and Oren Etzioni. 2008. The Tradeoffs between Open and Traditional Relation Extraction. *In proceedings of the 46th Association for Computational Linguistics Annual Meeting and Human Language Technology Conference (ACL-08:HLT)*, 28–36.

Razvan Bunescu and Raymond J. Mooney. 2004. Collective Information Extraction with Relational Markov Networks. *In Proceedings of the 42nd Annual Meeting on Association for Computational Linguistics (ACL 2004)*, 438–446.

Hai Leong Chieu and Hwee Tou Ng. 2002. A Maximum Entropy Approach to Information Extraction from Semi-Structured and Free Text. *In Proceedingd of the Eighteenth International Conference on Artificial Intelligence (AAAI02)*, 768–791.

Aron Culotta and Jeffrey Sorensen. 2004. Dependency Tree Kernels for Relation Extraction. *In Proceedings of the 42nd Annual Meeting on Association for Computational Linguistics (ACL 2004)*, 423–430.

Toru Hirano, Hisako Asano, Yoshihiro Matsuo and Genichiro Kikui. 2010. Recognizing Relation Expression between Named Entities based on Inherent and Context-dependent Features of Relational words. *In Proceedings of the 23rd International Conference on Computational Linguistics (Coling 2010: Posters)*, 409–417.

Ashwin Ittoo and Gosse Bouma. 2010. On Learning Subtypes of the Part-Whole Relation: Do Not Mix Your Seeds. *In Proceedings of the 48th Annual Meeting on Association for Computational Linguistics (ACL 2010)*, 1328–1336.

Nathalie Japkowicz. 2000. The Class Imbalance Problem: Significance and Strategies. *In Proceedings of the 2000 International Conference on Artificial Intelligence (ICAI)*, 111–117.

Thorsten Joachims. 2002. *Learning to Classify Text using Support Vector Machines*. Kluwer Academic Publishers, Norwell, MA, USA.

Ryan McDonald, Fernando Pereira, Seth Kulick, Scott Winters, Yang Jin, and Pete White. 2005. Simple Algorithms for Complex Relation Extraction with Applications to Biomedical IE. *In Proceedings of the 43rd Annual Meeting on Association for Computational Linguistics (ACL '05)*, 491–498.

Tara McIntosh and James R. Curran. 2007. Challenges for Extracting Biomedical Knowledge from Full Text. *In Proceedings of the Workshop on Biological, Translational and Clinical Language Processing (BioNLP 2007)*, 171–178.

Mike Mintz, Steven Bills, Rion Snow and Daniel Jurafsky. 2009. Distant supervision for relation extraction without labeled data. *In Proceedings of the Joint Conference of the 47th Annual Meeting of the ACL and the 4th International Joint Conference on Natural Language Processing of the AFNLP*, 1003–1011.

Katharina Morik, Peter Brockhausen and Thorsten Joachims. 1999. Combining Statistical Learning with a Knowledge-Based Approach - A Case Study in Intensive Care Monitoring. *Proceedings of the Sixteenth International Conference on Machine Learning (ICML '99)*, 268–277.

Alessandro Moschitti. 2006. Making Tree Kernels Practical for Natural Language Learning. *In Proceedings of the 11st Conference of the European Chapter of the Association for Computational Linguistics (EACL 2006)*, 113–120.

Angus Roberts, Robert Gaizauskas and Mark Hepple. 2008. Extracting Clinical Relationships from Patient Narratives. *In Proceedings of the Workshop on Current Trends in Biomedical Natural Language Processing*, 10–18.

Tobias Scheffer. 1999. Error Estimation and Model Selection. *Technischen Universität Berlin, School of Computer Science.*

Satoshi Sekine. 2006. On-Demand Information Extraction. *In Proceedings of the COLING/ACL 2006 Main Conference Poster Sessions*, 731–738.

James G. Shanahan and Norbert Roma. 2003. Boosting Support Vector Machines for Text Classification through Parameter-free Threshold Relaxation. *In Proceedings of the 12th International Conference on Information and Knowledge Management (CIKM '03)*, 247–245.

Mark Stevenson. 2006. Fact Distribution in Information Extraction. *Journal of Language Resources and Evaluation*, 40:183–201.

Kumutha Swampillai and Mark Stevenson. 2010. Inter-sentential Relations in Information Extraction Corpora. *In Proceedings of the 7th International Conference on Language Resources and Evaluation (LREC-2010)*, 2637–2641.

Vladimir N. Vapnik. 1995. *The nature of statistical learning theory*. Springer-Verlag Inc., New York, USA.

Konstantinos Veropoulos, Colin Campbell and Nello Cristianini. 1999. Controlling the Sensitivity of Support Vector Machines. *Proceedings of the International Joint Conference on AI (IJCAI 1999)*, 55–60.

Gang Wu and Edward Y. Chang. 2003. Class-Boundary Alignment for Imbalences Dataset Learning. *In ICML 2003 Workshop on Learning from Imbalanced Datasets II, Washington, DC.*

Dmitry Zelenko, Chinatsu Aone and Anthony Richardella. 2003. Kernel methods for Relation Extraction. *Journal of Machine Learning Research*, 3:1083–1106.

Min Zhang, Jie Zhang, Jian Su and Guodong Zhou. 2006. A Composite Kernel to Extract Relations between Entities with both Flat and Structured Features. *In Proceedings of the 21st International Conference on Computational Linguistics (Coling) and the 44th annual meeting of the Association for Computational Linguistics (ACL)*, 825–832.

GuoDong Zhou, Min Zhang, DongHong Ji and QiaoMing Zhu. 2007. Tree Kernel-Based Relation Extraction with Context-Sensitive Structured Parse Tree Information. *In Proceedings of the 2007 Joint Conference on Empirical Methods in Natural Language Processing and Computational Natural Language Learning (EMNLP-CoNLL)*, 728–736.

Knowledge-Poor Approach to Shallow Parsing: Contribution of Unsupervised Part-of-Speech Induction

Marie Guégan
Syllabs
15, rue Jean-Baptiste Berlier
75013 Paris, France
guegan@syllabs.com

Claude de Loupy
Syllabs
15, rue Jean-Baptiste Berlier
75013 Paris, France
loupy@syllabs.com

Abstract

Natural language processing tasks often rely on part-of-speech (POS) tagging as a preprocessing step. However it is not clear how the absence of any part-of-speech tagger should hamper the development of other natural language processing tools. In this paper we investigate the contribution of fully unsupervised part-of-speech induction to a common natural language processing task. We focus on the supervised English shallow parsing task and compare systems relying either on POS induction, on POS tagging, or on lexical features only as a baseline. Our experiments on the English CoNLL'2000 dataset show a significant benefit from POS induction over the baseline, with performances close to those obtained with a traditional POS tagger. Results demonstrate a great potential of POS induction for shallow parsing which could be applied to resource-scarce languages.

1 Introduction

Shallow parsing is a specific type of phrase chunking which is often used for different Natural Language Processing (NLP) tasks like text mining or question answering. The goal of the task is to divide a text into syntactically related non-overlapping groups of words (Tjong Kim Sang and Buchholz, 2000). These include noun, verb, or adjective phrases. It usually requires a part-of-speech (POS) tagger and a training corpus annotated with shallow parsing tags.

Unfortunately, one is often constrained by the lack of resources, tools or language experts, for instance when dealing with resource-scarce languages. In particular, the elaboration of a POS tagger is a delicate issue. Without any linguistic expert, the only possible approaches are statistical. Training POS taggers requires the manual constitution of either a large annotated corpus or a large morphosyntactic lexicon. These resources are very costly, both in time and in terms of linguistic knowledge required from the annotator.

By contrast, we notice that the concept of shallow parsing is relatively easily understandable by native speakers, even if they are not linguists. Relative to POS tagging, its annotation does not require a prohibitive amount of time and effort[1]. This is especially the case when the full shallow parsing task is reduced to a certain chunk type, as noun phrases for instance. Hence we think the most difficult requirement for the task is the POS tagging preprocessing step.

This observation drew our attention to the following question: is the POS tagging step necessary to shallow parsing? In this paper we intend to show how shallow parsing may benefit from fully unsupervised POS induction methods, as an alternative to accurate POS tagging. Section 2 introduces related work. Despite the popularity of shallow parsing and POS induction, we found only one paper related to POS induction for shallow parsing. Section 3 describes the models, tools and corpora we used: an existing POS induction tool (Clark, 2003), an implementation of Conditional Random Fields (CRF++) and the CoNLL'2000 dataset. Experiments and results are presented in Section 4. POS induction greatly improves the baseline, with performances close to supervised POS tagging.

2 Related Work

Shallow parsing has become a common task in NLP. The originality of our method is to rely on part-of-speech induction rather than accurate POS tagging.

[1] The standard English shallow parsing corpus contains around 50 distinct POS tags and only 10 chunk types.

2.1 Shallow Parsing

Traditional approaches rely on preprocessing by an accurate POS tagger. Most work on shallow parsing is based on the English CoNLL'2000 shared task, which provided reference datasets for training and testing. The CoNLL dataset actually contains POS tags assigned by the Brill (1995) tagger. A number of approaches have been evaluated on these datasets, for general shallow parsing as well as for the simpler noun phrase chunking task: support vector machines (SVM) with polynomial kernels (Kudo and Matsumoto, 2001; Goldberg and Elhadad, 2009) and linear kernels (Lee and Wu, 2007), conditional random fields (Sha and Pereira, 2003), maximum likelihood trigram models (Shen and Sarkar, 2005), probabilistic finite-state automata (Araujo and Serrano, 2008), transformation-based learning or memory-based learning (Tjong Kim Sang, 2000). So far, SVM have achieved the best state-of-the-art performances.

To our knowledge, little work has considered other languages. Chunking corpora have been derived from the Arabic Treebank (Diab *et al.*, 2004) and the UPENN Chinese Treebank-4 (Chen *et al.*, 2006). Goldberg *et al.* (2006) showed that the traditional definition of base noun phrases as non-recursive noun phrases does not apply in Hebrew, and proposed an alternate definition. Nguyen *et al.* (2009) discuss on how to build annotated data for Vietnamese text chunking and how to apply discriminative sequence learning to Vietnamese text chunking. The lack of tools and annotated corpora in non-English languages is clearly an issue.

Following this observation and contrary to the approaches cited above, we make the assumption that no POS tagger is available. To compare our work with previous approaches and to allow extensive experiments, we evaluated our method on English using the standard CoNLL'2000 dataset. The lack of similar annotated corpora in other languages unfortunately constrained the scope of this article to English.

2.2 Part-of-Speech Induction

Unlike van den Bosch and Buchholz (2002) who studied shallow parsing on the basis of lexical features only, we choose to incorporate features related to the traditional notion of part of speech. In this work we apply part-of-speech induction techniques to acquire additional features. This task differs from semi-supervised part-of-speech tagging, where the tagger is trained on an untagged corpus but uses a morphosyntactic lexicon giving possible tags for each word (e.g. (Merialdo, 1994)). Part-of-speech induction is the task of clustering words into word classes (or *pseudo-POS*) in a completely unsupervised setting. No prior knowledge such as a morphosyntactic lexicon is required. The only resource needed is a relatively large training text corpus.

Christodoulopoulos *et al.* (2010) and (Biemann, 2010) compiled helpful surveys of the domain. Christodoulopoulos *et al.* (2010) evaluated seven POS induction systems spanning nearly 20 years of work: class-based n-grams (Brown *et al.*, 1992), class-based n-grams with morphology (Clark, 2003), Chinese Whispers graph clustering (Biemann, 2006), Bayesian HMM with Gibbs sampling (Goldwater and Griffiths, 2007), Bayesian HMM with variational Bayes (Johnson, 2007), sparsity posterior-regularization HMM (Graça *et al.*, 2009), and feature-based HMM (Berg-Kirkpatrick *et al.*, 2010). The performance measures were mainly based on mapping accuracies (with respect to a gold standard) and entropy coefficients.

Biemann *et al.* (2007) and Biemann (2010) succinctly tested their Chinese Whispers algorithm on the shallow parsing task with the English CoNLL'2000 dataset. They showed a significant improvement of the use of unsupervised pseudo part-of-speech tags over the baseline that discarded any POS information. However, their experiments covered several tasks and were not focused on shallow parsing. By contrast, in this article we use an alternate POS induction algorithm and propose a more in-depth evaluation of shallow parsing with POS induction.

3 Resources, Models and Tools

This section describes the tools and resources used in this work. Figure 1 depicts the global organization of our modules.

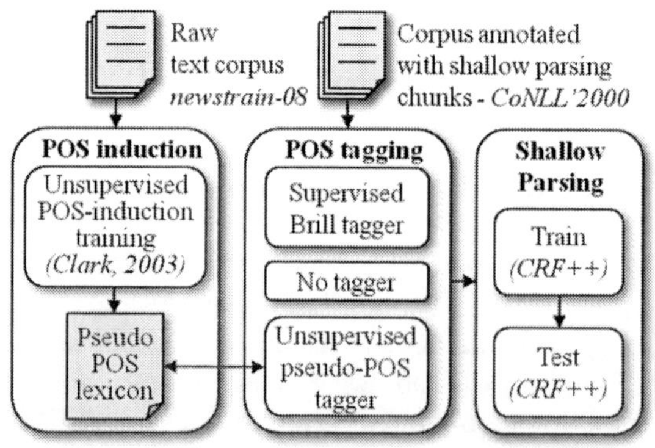

Figure 1. Overview of the system

On the left side of the figure, an unsupervised pseudo-POS tagger is learnt using POS induction techniques. This step requires a raw text corpus as input and produces a list of (word, cluster identifier) pairs which constitute the pseudo-POS lexicon. On the center, a POS tagger is optionally applied to the training and test corpora annotated with shallow parsing tags. Eventually, a supervised training of shallow parsing is conducted on the training set and evaluated on the test set (on the right).

The following sections describe the tools and corpora we used for the POS induction step and for the shallow parsing step. This information is summarized in Table 1.

3.1 Unsupervised POS Induction

Model and Tool

Based on Christodoulopoulos *et al.* (2010), we opted for Clark (2003)'s tool[2]. It was the best performing system in almost every language, and one of the fastest methods. It incorporates morphological information into a distributional clustering algorithm. To our knowledge, it has not yet been evaluated on the shallow parsing task.

The clustering algorithm is based on a cluster bigram model (Ney *et al.*, 1994). Assume we have of corpus of size N, composed of words $w_1 \dots w_N$. We note w_i^j the sequence of all words between i and j. We define a clustering function c that deterministically assigns a unique cluster identifier to each word form. The bigram model is a specific type of first-order hidden Markov model where each observation type (word form) is allowed to a single latent class. The model defines the probability of word w_i given history w_1^{i-1} and clustering c as:

$$P\left(w_i \middle| w_1^{i-1}, c\right) = P\left(w_i \middle| c(w_i)\right). P\left(c(w_i) \middle| c(w_{i-1})\right)$$

In our case, the deterministic nature of the clustering makes the likelihood of the model easy to express in terms of word and cluster occurrence counts in the corpus given the clustering. The likelihood is maximized using an exchange algorithm similar to the k-means algorithm. It converges locally until a stopping criterion is reached. It consists in iteratively increasing the likelihood of an initial clustering by moving words one after the other to better clusters.

The morphological component biases the clustering so as to cluster together morphologically similar words. Clark (2003) models the morphology of words belonging to a same cluster using letter Hidden Markov Models and uses it to define a prior for this cluster in the basic cluster bigram model. The final output consists of a large table giving a unique cluster identifier to each word token, followed by the conditional probability of the word given the cluster. The pseudo POS tagging itself hence comes down to a simple deterministic look-up into the table.

Unlike Biemann (2010), the number of pseudo-POS clusters should be provided as a parameter of the algorithm. In our experiments, we learnt several pseudo-POS taggers with a number of clusters varying from 10 to 200 (see Section 4.3). Another parameter for Clark's tool is the token cutoff frequency. This threshold assigns all words occurring less than the specified number of times to a particular cluster. This cluster is the one that will be used for tagging unknown words.

Corpus

The tool takes a tokenized corpus as input. The corpus chosen for our experiments is *newstrain-08*, an English monolingual language model training dataset which was provided for the WMT'09 translation task[3]. Its size is approximately 2.5 Gb and 500 million tokens. We set the token cutoff frequency to 50[4].

Such enormous corpora might not be available for some languages. However we believe that the approach remains valid on smaller corpora. We therefore experimented on a subset of the newstrain-08 corpus restricted to the first million tokens only. To avoid losing too much information, the cutoff frequency was then set to 1: only hapaxes were discarded.

Step	Tool	Corpus	Corpus Size
POS induction	*(Clark, 2003)*	newstrain-08 full	500M tokens
		newstrain-08 short	1M tokens
Shallow Parsing	CRF++	CoNLL'2000 train	211,727 tokens 8936 sentences
		CoNLL'2000 test	47,377 tokens 2012 sentences

Table 1. Tools and corpora used for POS induction and shallow parsing

[2] Available on Alexander Clark's Web page: http://www.cs.rhul.ac.uk/home/alexc/pos2.tar.gz

[3] The corpus is available at: http://statmt.org/wmt09/training-monolingual.tar

[4] Other parameter values are "-s 5" (number of HMM states) and "-i 20" (stopping criterion: maximum number of iterations)

3.2 CRFs for Shallow Parsing

Model and Tool

We follow Sha and Pereira (2003), who achieved near state-of-the-art results on the English shallow parsing task using Conditional Random Fields (CRFs) (Lafferty *et al.*, 2003). CRFs allow us to incorporate a large number of features in a flexible way. We used the CRF++ implementation[5], distributed under the GNU Lesser General Public License and new BSD License.

Our feature set is defined as follows. On a 5-token window centered on the current token to be classified, we included all lowercased form token unigrams and bigrams, as well as (pseudo) POS tag unigrams, bigrams and trigrams. We also incorporated phrase chunk label bigrams. These features are commonly used for shallow parsing. Finally, we added on the same 5-token window a feature indicating whether the forms begin with a capital, as well as features accounting for the form ending (3 characters) on a window of 3 tokens. The purpose of these features is to facilitate the classification of unknown words by incorporating morphological information into the model.

In some experiments (see Section 4.4), we tried several feature frequency cutoff values, varying from 1 occurrence in the training set to at least 100. The default is set to 1.

Corpus

The standard reference corpus for English shallow parsing is the CoNLL'2000 shared task dataset. The CoNLL dataset[6] was automatically derived from a subset of the Wall Street Journal (WSJ) portion of the Penn Treebank. It consists of partitions of the WSJ: sections 15-18 as training data (8936 sentences) and section 20 as test data (2012 sentences). It contains phrase boundaries in the IOB representation, as well as part-of-speech tags assigned by the Brill tagger[7]. The corpus contains 48 Brill tags.

A sentence extracted from the CoNLL training corpus is shown in Table 2. Here, chunk phrases are separated with horizontal dashed lines. Each chunk type has 2 types of chunk labels: prefix B indicates the beginning of the chunk phrase, and prefix I stands for *inside the chunk phrase*. Label O represents tokens that do not belong to any phrase.

Token	Brill Tag	Chunk Label
A.P.	NNP	B-NP
Green	NNP	I-NP
currently	RB	B-ADVP
has	VBZ	B-VP
2,664,098	CD	B-NP
shares	NNS	I-NP
outstanding	JJ	B-ADJP
.	.	O

Table 2. Example sentence from the CoNLL'2000 training corpus

In some experiments, we discarded all Brill tags. In our POS-induction-based experiments, we replaced them with pseudo-POS tags.

4 Experiments and Results

Our experiments have 4 goals: (i) estimate the gain of POS induction over a system that does not rely on any part-of-speech information; (ii) estimate performance variation depending on the size of the shallow parsing training corpus; (iii) study the influence of the number of pseudo-POS clusters; (iv) observe the system behavior with CRF feature pruning. Our results were evaluated using the Perl script provided by CoNLL[8].

4.1 The CoNLL Shallow Parsing Task

We first evaluated our system in the traditional setting. Our objective is to estimate the potential of POS induction for shallow parsing in the case where no POS tagger is available.

We conducted three runs using the same CRF feature template (Section 3.2), depending on whether the POS tags are the original Brill tags from the corpus (*Brill*), our pseudo-POS tags (*P50*), or no tag at all as a baseline (*NoPOS*). For this experiment, we used the CoNLL datasets for training and testing. The pseudo-POS tagger was learnt on the full newstrain-08 corpus. We set the number of pseudo-POS tags to 50, which is comparable to the number of Brill tags.

Detailed results are presented in Table 3. It shows precision, recall and F-measure for each chunk category. Precision p is the percentage of correct phrases over the total number of phrases annotated by the system. Recall r is the percentage of correct phrases over the total number of true phrases in the reference. The F-measure F_1 is defined as the harmonic mean of precision and recall[9].

[5] Available at http://crfpp.sourceforge.net/

[6] See http://www.clips.ua.ac.be/conll2000/chunking/

[7] The original manually annotated tags from WSJ were discarded in order to make the CoNLL task more realistic.

[8] http://www.cnts.ua.ac.be/conll2000/chunking/conlleval.txt

[9] $F_\beta = \frac{(1+\beta^2).p.r}{\beta^2.p+r}$ with $\beta = 1$

Chunk types	Baseline: NoPOS p	r	F_1	found	Unsupervised: P50 p	r	F_1	found	Supervised: Brill p	r	F_1	found
ADJP	80.00	59.36	68.15	325	79.05	68.04	73.13	377	81.27	76.26	78.68	411
ADVP	84.21	75.75	79.76	779	82.94	80.25	81.57	838	84.24	80.83	82.50	831
CONJP	38.46	55.56	45.45	13	55.56	55.56	55.56	9	50.00	55.56	52.63	10
INTJ	100	100	100	2	100	50.00	66.67	1	100	50.00	66.67	1
LST	0	0	0	0	0	0	0	0	0	0	0	0
NP	91.38	91.01	91.19	12372	94.09	93.87	93.98	12393	94.44	94.13	94.29	12381
PP	96.71	97.15	96.93	4833	96.47	98.17	97.31	4896	96.84	98.03	97.43	4870
PRT	76.79	81.13	78.9	112	77.68	82.08	79.82	112	78.85	77.36	78.10	104
SBAR	85.82	83.74	84.77	522	89.49	85.98	87.70	514	88.10	85.79	86.93	521
VP	91.64	90.58	91.10	4604	93.33	93.09	93.21	4646	93.78	94.18	93.98	4678
All	91.91	90.79	**91.34**	23562	93.61	93.35	**93.48**	23786	93.99	93.82	**93.90**	23807
Accuracy				94.61				95.84				96.12

Table 3. Detailed chunking results for the English shallow parsing task

Column *found* in Table 3 gives the total number of phrases annotated by the system (correct or incorrect). *Accuracy* is the percentage of correct guesses at the token level.

First, we recall that the state-of-the art system of Lee and Wu (2007) reached a 94.22% F-measure using Brill part-of-speech tags. Comparably, our system performs reasonably well when using the same tags (Brill: F-measure 93.90%), considering that it was not subject to any refinements. Without any POS information, the system already achieves a high F-measure (91.34%).

We observe a 2% overall gain of P50 (F-measure 93.48%) over NoPOS, and a drop from Brill inferior to 0.5%. P50 beats Brill on a few categories, although not substantially: conjunctions, particles, and subordinating conjunctions. Its performances are very close to Brill on the 4 most frequent chunk types: adverb phrases, noun phrases, prepositional phrases, and verb phrases. These results incidentally suggest a great potential of the approach for noun phrase chunking, for which state-of-the-art systems reach about 96.8% F-measure (Araujo and Serrano, 2008).

The category of adjective phrases is the most difficult. Although significantly improving the recall of NoPOS, the F-measure for P50 lies exactly between NoPOS and Brill.

Looking into the test corpus

We examined the output test corpus to explain the differences between the unsupervised approach (P50) and the supervised approach (Brill). The accuracies tell us that on 47,377 tokens, Brill correctly tagged 130 tokens more than P50. Looking specifically at the 2,808 tokens that were unknown to the pseudo-POS tagger, Brill correctly tagged 16 tokens more than P50. Unknown words thus only account for 12% of the 130-token advantage.

The major sources of disagreement on chunks are shown in Table 4. These account for more than half the 130-token difference. It shows for instance that in cases where Brill chose B-NP and P50 chose I-NP, Brill was correct for 15 tokens more than P50. We observe that P50 tends to annotate too long noun and verb phrases (P50: incorrect I-NP and I-VP). It also shows more difficulties finding the beginning of verb and adjective phrases (Brill: B-VP and B-ADJP).

Finally, we examined the Brill parts of speech of misclassified chunks on which Brill and P50 disagreed (see Table 5). P50 mostly fails on adjectives and adverbs. Yet it better classifies IN tokens (preposition, subordinating conjunction).

Brill	P50	Brill correct	P50 correct	Diff
B-NP	I-NP	79	64	15
B-VP	B-PP	21	9	12
B-ADJP	B-ADVP	17	6	11
B-ADJP	B-VP	11	0	11
B-ADVP	I-NP	11	2	9
B-VP	B-NP	26	17	9
B-VP	I-VP	20	11	9

Table 4. Disagreement between Brill and P50 on a few chunks

Brill POS	Brill correct	P50 correct	Diff
JJ	87	49	38
RB	74	46	28
TO	34	21	13
VBG	37	26	11
VB	22	13	9
CC	56	49	7
IN	39	53	-14

Table 5. Disagreement between Brill and P50 on a few parts of speech

4.2 Training Corpus Size

Corpora such as the CoNLL'2000 dataset are expensive to produce and not yet available for many languages. Therefore we were interested in the evolution of performances with the size of the training corpus. We repeated the experiments from previous section on corpus sizes ranging from 1% (approximately 90 sentences) to 100% (approximately 9000 sentences). All systems were tested on the CoNLL test set. Each experiment was run on 20 different splits of the training corpus (except for the full corpus).

In addition, we wanted to take into account the difficulty of compiling large monolingual corpora in some languages. We therefore also tested the method using a much smaller corpus for POS induction training. It contains a subset of 1 million words from the newstrain-08 corpus, as opposed to 500 million for the full corpus (see Section 3.1). In this experiment we also set the number of pseudo-POS clusters to 50.

Figure 2 shows the F-measures for varying sizes of the training corpus on the abscissa on a logarithmic scale. The four curves correspond to the following taggers: Brill, pseudo POS tagger trained on the full newstrain-08 corpus (P50), pseudo POS tagger trained on the smaller newstrain corpus (P50m), and no tagger (NoPOS). Each point denotes the mean of the 20 runs. To give an insight of the variation in F-measure across all runs, we added box plots on the P50 curve. Each box is centered on the median of the runs. Half the points lie between its lower and upper sides. The whiskers extend to the most extreme data point which is no more than 1.5 times the height of the box away from the box.

We observe a significant improvement of our POS-induction-based systems over the baseline (NoPOS), especially for smaller training corpora. For a 1% sample of the CoNLL corpus, the F-measures are approximately 65% only for the baseline (NoPOS), 78% for the unsupervised systems (P50 and P50m) and 83.5% in the supervised setting (Brill).

A 90% F-measure is achieved starting from 10% of the training corpus by Brill, and starting from 20% by P50. More generally, the unsupervised system needs a little more than twice as much annotated data as the supervised system to achieve a similar F-measure.

With less than 200 sentences (2% sample), the unsupervised system almost achieves 83% F-measure, which is only achieved by the baseline starting from 900 sentences (10% sample).

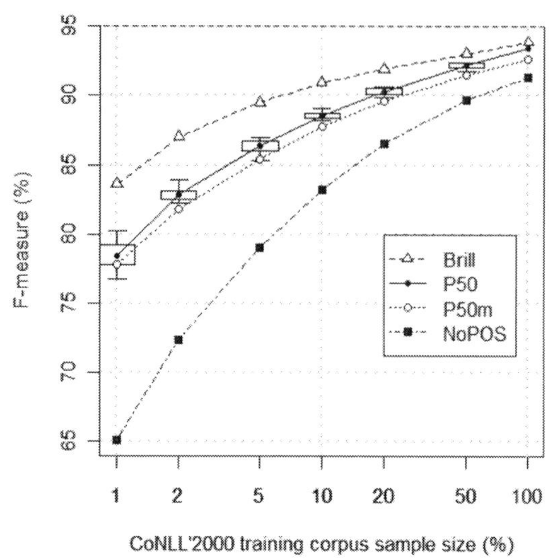

Figure 2. F-measure depending on the training corpus sample size and on the POS tagger

Finally, we notice that P50 and P50m get very close results, despite the fact that their pseudo POS taggers have been trained on 500M tokens and 1M tokens respectively. This result validates the approach for the case where only relatively small raw text corpora are available for training the pseudo POS tagger. This finding could be highly valuable for resource-scarce languages.

4.3 Number of pseudo-POS clusters

Some POS induction algorithms have the advantage over supervised POS tagging to easily adapt the number of word classes to the task.

Biemann (2010) conjectures for the same chunking task that results could be significantly improved with a smaller cluster number. To verify this hypothesis, we trained several pseudo-POS taggers with a cluster number between 10 and 200. Similarly to the experiments reported in the previous section, we evaluate the systems on varying sizes of the CoNLL training corpus[10].

Results are presented in Figure 3. From 10 to 50 clusters, performances increase with the number of clusters for all sizes of the training corpus. By contrast, P100 and P200 only improve over P50 for corpus sizes superior to 10%, which represents about 900 sentences. This can be attributed to the sparseness of pseudo POS tags in small training sets. We conclude that for small training corpus sizes, the number of pseudo-POS tags should be chosen carefully. On the whole, the F-measures vary in a 5.3% interval for a 1% sample, and in a 1.1% interval for the full corpus.

[10] Again, 20 runs for each size of the training corpus

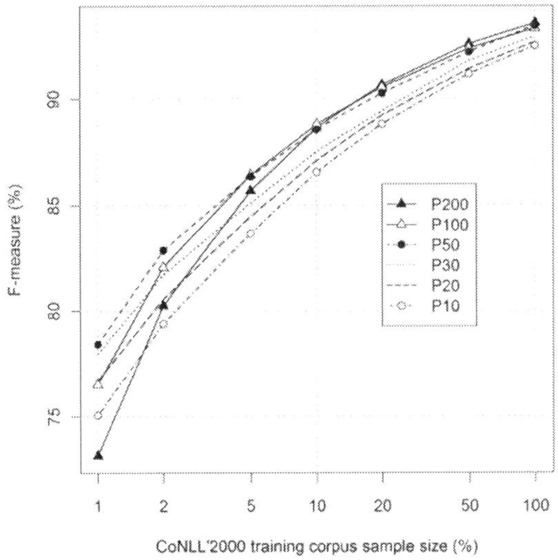

Figure 3. F-measure depending on the CoNLL'2000 training corpus sample size for a varying number of pseudo-POS clusters

The F-measures obtained using the full training dataset are: 93.6 (P200), 93.34 (P100), 93.48 (P50), 92.97 (P30), 92.72 (P20), and 92.53 (P10). They were 91.34 for the baseline and 93.9 for Brill (see Table 3): even 10 pseudo-POS clusters are sufficient to beat the baseline, and this is valid for all sizes of the training corpus.

4.4 CRF Feature Selection

In the last experiment we tested CRF feature pruning. The idea is to select the features appearing at least k times in the training corpus. This was motivated by Goldberg and Elhadad (2009), who explored the importance of lexical features in shallow parsing and other sequence labeling tasks. The performance of their anchored SVM system only decreased from 93.69% to 93.12% with heavy pruning ($k = 100$), while the baseline dropped from 93.73% to 91.83%. In addition, they showed comparable performances between heavily pruned models and full models when tested on out-of-domain data.

As in Goldberg and Elhadad (2009), we set the feature frequency threshold to values ranging from 1 to 100. Each experiment was run only once using the whole CoNLL training corpus.

Figure 4 shows that the supervised part-of-speech tagging system is the most robust to feature pruning. It loses less than 1% for $k = 100$. In comparison, the baseline NoPOS loses 4.3%. This indicates a strong dependency to the domain of the training corpus.

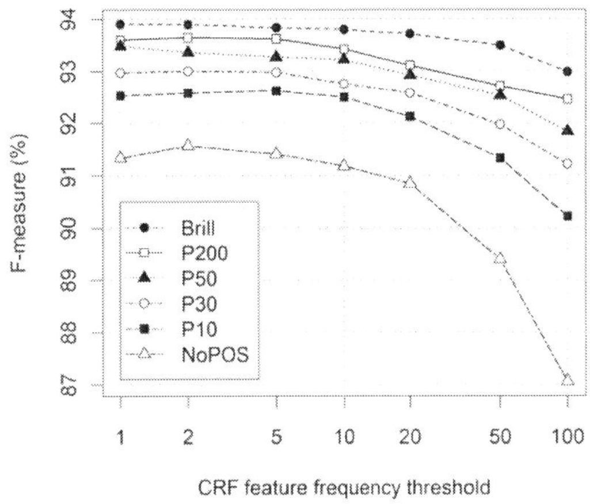

Figure 4. F-measure for various CRF feature pruning thresholds

The unsupervised systems resist quite well to feature pruning for $k < 20$, losing 1.1% and 1.6% F-measure for 200 and 50 clusters. P50 models have around 350,000 features for $k = 1$ and 5,100 features only for $k = 100$, while the baseline keeps from 270,000 to 2,200 features.

As in Goldberg and Elhadad (2009), it will be interesting to test the pruned models on out-of-domain corpora, and see how POS induction-based systems behave in comparison to systems relying on accurate part-of-speech information.

5 Conclusion and Future Work

In this paper, we study the contribution of part-of-speech induction to shallow parsing. The general context of our work is the automatic treatment of minority languages for which few linguistic resources are available, though we experimented on English only. Our constraint is the lack of any POS tagger. The experiments were carried out on the standard English CoNLL'2000 dataset, which allowed extensive experiments and explicit comparison to related work. We used Clark (2003)'s tool for the POS induction step and CRF++ for the shallow parsing train and test steps. Results show a significant advantage of POS-induction-based systems over a baseline which uses lexical features only.

In the future, we intend to apply these techniques to both shallow parsing and noun phrase chunking for minority languages. This will require the constitution of annotated corpora for training and testing. This paper shows that, for English, a corpus of 1 M words for POS induction, as well as a few hundred annotated sentences are enough to obtain interesting performances. If this could be proved on other languages, it could be a very interesting point to manage NLP for resource-scarce languages.

Acknowledgments

The research leading to these results has received funding from the European Community's Seventh Framework Programme (FP7/2007-2013) under Grant Agreement n° 248005[11].

References

Araujo, L., & Serrano, J. I. (2008). Highly accurate error-driven method for noun phrase detection. *Pattern Recognition Letters*, *29*(4), 547-557.

Berg-Kirkpatrick, T., Bouchard-Côté, A., DeNero, J., & Klein, D. (2010). Painless unsupervised learning with features. *Proceedings of HLT-NAACL 2010* (pp. 582-590).

Biemann, C. (2006). Unsupervised Part-of-Speech Tagging Employing Efficient Graph Clustering. *Proceedings of ACL-CoLing 2006 - Student Research Workshop* (pp. 7-12).

Biemann, C. (2010). Unsupervised Part-of-Speech Tagging in the Large. *Research on Language and Computation*, *7*(2-4), 101-135.

Biemann, C., Giuliano, C., & Gliozzo, A. (2007). Unsupervised Part of Speech Tagging Supporting Supervised Methods. *Proceedings of RANLP-07*.

van den Bosch, A., & Buchholz, S. (2001). Shallow parsing on the basis of words only. *Proceedings of ACL'02* (p. 433).

Brill, E. (1995). Transformation-based error-driven learning and natural language processing: a case study in part-of-speech tagging. *Computational Linguistics*, *21*(4), 543-565.

Brown, P. F., DeSouza, P. V., Mercer, R. L., Pietra, V. J. D., & Lai, J. C. (1992). Class-Based n-gram Models of Natural Language. *Computational Linguistics*, *18*(4), 467-479.

Chen, W., Zhang, Y., & Isahara, H. (2006). An Empirical Study of Chinese Chunking. *Proceedings of COLING/ACL 2006 Poster Sessions* (pp. 97-104).

Christodoulopoulos, C., Goldwater, S., & Steedman, M. (2010). Two decades of unsupervised POS induction: how far have we come? *Proceedings of EMNLP 2010* (pp. 575-584).

Clark, A. (2003). Combining distributional and morphological information for part of speech induction. *Proceedings of EACL 2003* (pp. 59-66).

Diab, M., Hacioglu, K., & Jurafsky, D. (2004). Automatic Tagging of Arabic Text: From Raw Text to Base Phrase Chunks. *Proceedings of HLT-NAACL 2004: Short Papers* (p. 149–152).

Goldberg, Y., Adler, M., & Elhadad, M. (2006). Noun phrase chunking in Hebrew: influence of lexical and morphological features. *Proceedings of ACL-CoLing 2006* (pp. 689-696).

Goldberg, Y., & Elhadad, M. (2009). On the role of lexical features in sequence labeling. *Proceedings of EMNLP 2009* (pp. 1142-1151).

Goldwater, S., & Griffiths, T. L. (2007). A fully Bayesian approach to unsupervised part-of-speech tagging. *Proceedings of ACL'07* (pp. 744-751).

Graça, J., Ganchev, K., Taskar, B., & Pereira, F. (2009). Posterior vs. Parameter Sparsity in Latent Variable Models. *Proc. of NIPS* (p. 664–672).

Johnson, M. (2007). Why Doesn't EM Find Good HMM POS-Taggers? *Proceedings of EMNLP-CoNLL 2007*.

Kudo, T., & Matsumoto, Y. (2001). Chunking with support vector machines. *Proceedings of NAACL 2001* (pp. 1-8).

Lafferty, J., McCallum, A., & Pereira, F. (2001). Conditional random fields: Probabilistic models for segmenting and labeling sequence data. *Proceedings of ICML'01* (pp. 282–289)

Lee, Y.-S., & Wu, Y.-C. (2007). A robust multilingual portable phrase chunking system. *Expert Systems with Applications*, *33*(3), 590-599.

Merialdo, B. (1994). Tagging English text with a probabilistic model. *Computational Linguistics*, *20*(2), 155--171. MIT Press.

Ney, H., Essen, U., & Kneser, R. (1994). On structuring probabilistic dependencies in stochastic language modelling. *Computer Speech and Language*, *8*(1), 1-38.

Nguyen, L. M., Nguyen, H. T., Nguyen, P. T., Ho, T. B., & Shimazu, A. (2009). An empirical study of Vietnamese noun phrase chunking with discriminative sequence models. *Proc. of the 7th Workshop on Asian Language Resources* (pp. 9-16).

Sha, F., & Pereira, F. (2003). Shallow parsing with conditional random fields. *Proceedings of NAACL 2003* (pp. 134-141).

Shen, H., & Sarkar, A. (2005). Voting Between Multiple Data Representations for Text Chunking. In *Advances in Artificial Intelligence* (Vol. 3501, pp. 389-400). Springer Berlin / Heidelberg.

Tjong Kim Sang, E. F. (2000). Noun Phrase Recognition by System Combination. *Proceedings of NAACL 2000* (p. 6).

Tjong Kim Sang, E. F., & Buchholz, S. (2000). Introduction to the CoNLL-2000 shared task. *Proceedings of CoNLL 2000 - LLL 2000* (pp. 127-132).

[11] http://www.ttc-project.eu

Fast Domain Adaptation for Part of Speech Tagging for Dialogues

Sandra Kübler, Eric Baucom
Indiana University
{skuebler,eabaucom}@indiana.edu

Abstract

Part of speech tagging accuracy deteriorates severely when a tagger is used out of domain. We investigate a fast method for domain adaptation, which provides additional in-domain training data from an unannotated data set by applying POS taggers with different biases to the unannotated data set and then choosing the set of sentences on which the taggers agree. We show that we improve the accuracy of a trigram tagger, TnT, from 85.77% to 86.10%. In order to improve performance on unknown words, we investigate using active learning for learning ambiguity classes of domain specific words, yielding an accuracy of 89.15% for TnT.

1 Introduction

Part of speech (POS) tagging for English is often considered a solved problem. There are well established approaches such as Markov model trigram taggers (Brants, 2000), maximum entropy taggers (Ratnaparkhi, 1996), or Support Vector Machine based taggers (Giménez and Màrquez, 2004), and accuracy reaches approximately 97%.

However, most experiments in POS tagging for English have concentrated on data from the Penn Treebank (Marcus et al., 1993). If POS taggers trained on the Penn Treebank are used to tag data from other domains, accuracy deteriorates significantly. Blitzer et al. (2006) apply structural correspondence learning for learning pivot features to increase accuracy in the target domain. However, their approach is restricted to discriminative approaches to POS tagging.

In this paper, we investigate a simple and fast method for domain adaptation that is usable with any POS tagger: selecting reliably tagged in-domain data to add to the training set. This method has been successful for domain adaptation for dependency parsing (Chen et al., 2008). We use a corpus of dialogues collected in a collaborative task as target domain, thus introducing the challenges of processing spontaneous speech: hesitations, corrections, false starts, and contractions. We assume that this domain is more challenging than a target domain of biomedical texts, which is often used for domain adaptation research. Spontaneous speech dialogues do not only differ in terminology, but also in the types of sentences. Dialogues, for example, contain a higher percentage of questions and imperatives than formal written language, such as news or scientific writings.

Our domain adaptation experiments concentrate on adding in-domain training data based on an ensemble of POS taggers. The experiments show that extending the training set generally improves POS tagging accuracy. However, it cannot provide information on the ambiguity classes for words that do not appear in the source domain. For this reason, we integrate an active learning strategy for adding ambiguity classes for words that are identified automatically as unlikely to be tagged correctly.

The remainder of the paper is structured as follows: In section 2, we provide an overview of domain adaptation techniques in POS tagging and parsing. Section 3 describes our approach to domain adaptation, and section 4 describes the experimental setup. In section 5, we discuss our findings for domain adaptation, and in section 6, we describe the active learning extension.

2 Related Work

Domain adaptation is a task that has received much attention in recent years, with different results, ranging from evaluations that it is "frustratingly easy" (Daume III, 2007) to "frustratingly hard" (Dredze et al., 2007). The main differentiating factor seems to be whether a small portion of annotated in-domain training data is available or only a large-size, unannotated data set. In our work, we concentrate on the second, more difficult, scenario.

Most work on domain adaptation has focused on parsing rather than on POS tagging (e.g. (McClosky et al., 2006; Yoshida et al., 2007; Chen et al., 2008; Rimell and Clark, 2008). Chen et al. (2008)) perform domain adaptation for a dependency parser. They show their best results are reached by adding only a selection of the information provided by a parser trained on out-of-domain data. Since short dependencies are more reliable than long ones, they select only the short, and thus reliable, ones and gain an increase in accuracy. Rimell and Clark (2008) adapt the Penn Treebank to parse grammatical relations in the biomedical domain. They report that the domains are similar structurally and that the lexicon is the main difference between the domains. Yoshida et al. (2007) investigate the influence of an external POS tagger on parsing accuracy in an HPSG parser. They show that the quality of the POS tagger has a significant influence even in-domain. The situation can be improved by allowing the POS tagger to output multiple, weighted POS tags from which the parser can choose. They show that allowing the tagger to output multiple POS tags improves parsing results both in-domain and out-of-domain.

Clark et al. (2003) use the results of one POS tagger on unannotated data to inform the training of another tagger in a semi-supervised setting using a co-training routine with a Markov model tagger and a maximum entropy tagger. The authors test both agreement-based co-training, where the sentences are added to training only if the taggers both agree, and naive co-training, where all sentences from one tagger are added to the training of the other, with no filter. For small sets of seed sentences, both types of co-training improve accuracy, with the higher quality, smaller training set from agreement-based co-training performing slightly better. The authors also report results for using naive co-training after the taggers were already trained on large amounts of manually annotated data. Naive co-training did not improve the taggers when trained in such a way (the authors leave agreement based co-training to future work).

Blitzer et al. (2006) investigate domain adaptation for POS tagging using the method of structural correspondence learning (SCL). SCL provides an informative feature-space for modeling the similarities between source and target domain by identifying *pivot* features. Pivot features behave similarly across domains, and if non-pivot features in the different domains correspond to many of the same pivot features, they are assumed to correlate. The machine learning algorithm is trained with the feature-space model from SCL on the source domain, with the idea that the trained model will now be informative for the unlabeled target domain as well. Blitzer et al. (2006) evaluate the SCL transfer of a POS tagger from the Penn Treebank to a corpus of biomedical abstracts (MEDLINE), reporting an improvement from 87.9% to 88.9%. The authors report that vocabulary is the main difference between the domains. However, SCL can only be applied to feature-based discriminative learning methods.

3 Domain Adaptation by Tagger Combination

For our experiments, we use the Wall Street Journal part of the Penn Treebank as source domain and dialogues in a collaborative task as target domain. In the target domain, we have access to a large unannotated corpus and a small annotated corpus, which we use for evaluation purposes. In order to adapt a POS tagger to the target domain, we extend the training set by sentences from the large unannotated corpus. Our hypothesis is that these sentences will provide the POS tagger with relevant information from the target domain. For assigning POS tags to the additional sentences from the target domain, we use three different POS taggers trained on the Penn Treebank. Then we select those sentences for which a majority of taggers agree on the POS tags. The method of using agreement between taggers was originally used by van Halteren et al. (2001) to improve tagger performance. We investigate the following questions: 1) How does the number of agreeing POS taggers influence the accuracy of the final tagger? 2) Should we select only complete sentences or add all trigrams on which the taggers agree? Lifting the restriction that the taggers agree on complete sentences will increase the size of the training set. 3) Do we need the full Penn Treebank training set, or does this large training set dominate the smaller training set from the target domain?

4 Experimental Setup

4.1 Data Sets

We use three corpora: the Penn Treebank for the source domain; the HCRC Map Task Corpus (Thompson et al., 1996) for additional training in the cooperative dialogue domain; and the CReST corpus (Eberhard et al., 2010) for evaluation in the target domain.

The HCRC Map Task Corpus (Thompson et al., 1996) is a multi-modal corpus composed of 18 hours of digital audio and 150 000 words of transcription, representing 128 two-person conversations. The conversations were obtained from a cooperative problem solving task, in which two participants were asked to help one another fill in a route on a map. HCRC is annotated for speaker and dialogue turn information, as well as for POS tags. However, we use only the actual transcriptions. This corpus serves as our unannotated, in-domain training corpus.

The CReST Corpus (Eberhard et al., 2010) is a multi-modal corpus consisting of 7 dialogues, comprising 11 317 words in 1 977 sentences. Similar in domain to the HCRC corpus, it represents cooperative dialogues, but is based on a slightly different task: one of the participants is located in a search environment, while the other is outside but has access to a map of the environment. The participants need to collaborate to fulfill their tasks (locating objects in the environment and placing objects on the map).

CReST is annotated for POS, syntactic dependency and constituency, disfluency, and dialogue structure. The POS tagset is a superset of the tagset for the Penn Treebank, with the additional tags representing features unique to natural dialogue.

Data Preparation. Due to differences between the transcriptions of HCRC and CReST, we made small, systematic changes to HCRC to make it more consistent with CReST. For instance, HCRC had various permutations of `mmhmm` which we changed to the standard `mhm` transcription in CReST. Since the Penn Treebank does not contain all tags used in CReST, we translated the additional CReST tags into tags of the original tagset for our experiments. E.g. the POS tag `VBI` (imperative verb) is translated into `VB` (verb in the base form).

4.2 POS Taggers

We use three POS taggers: TnT (Brants, 2000), MElt (Denis and Sagot, 2009), and SVMTool (Giménez and Màrquez, 2004). These taggers were chosen because they represent the state of the art for single-direction taggers and also because they use different approaches to POS tagging and thus have different biases. Our assumption is that the different biases will result in different types of POS tagging mistakes.

TnT (Brants, 2000) is a trigram Markov model POS tagger with state-of-the-art treatment of unknown words. TnT generates files containing lexical and transition frequencies and thus provides us with the option of including new trigrams directly into the trained model.

The Maximum-Entropy Lexicon-Enriched Tagger (MElt) (Denis and Sagot, 2009) is a conditional sequence maximum entropy POS tagger that uses a set of lexical and context features, which are a superset of the features used by Ratnaparkhi (1996) and Toutanova and Manning (2000).

SVMTool (Giménez and Màrquez, 2004) is a discriminative POS tagger based on support vector machines. The features and specifications used in training were taken from the SVMTool model for English, based on the Penn Treebank.

5 Experiments

We perform six experiments: The first experiment establishes a baseline by training the POS taggers out of domain on the Penn Treebank and then using them without adaptation on the target domain. In the second experiment, the training set is extended by those HCRC sentences on which all three taggers agree. In the third experiment, we investigate whether the accuracy of the adapted tagger deteriorates if we choose all sentences on which only two taggers agree. In the fourth experiment, we investigate the effect of adding trigram information on which all taggers agree to the TnT trained model. In the fifth experiment, we also add lexical information to the TnT model. In the final experiment, we investigate whether the large size of the Penn Treebank neutralizes effects from the additional training data, based on the experiment with sentences on which all three taggers agree.

Tagger	baseline	all3
MElt	83.91	84.32†
SVMTool	84.60	85.15†
TnT	**85.77**	85.70

Table 1: The results of the baseline and of selecting all sentences on which all taggers agree. Dags indicate a significant improvement over the baseline.

5.1 Agreement Among All POS Taggers

This experiment uses all three POS taggers, trained on the Penn Treebank, to tag all sentences from the HCRC corpus. Then all sentences are selected on which the taggers agree. These sentences are added to the Penn Treebank training set, and the taggers are retrained and evaluated on the CReST corpus. The results of the baseline and this experiment are shown in table 1.

The results show that both discriminative POS taggers, MElt and SVMTool, improve significantly over the baseline (McNemar, $p < 0.001$). TnT, in contrast, suffers a non-significant decrease in performance. However, TnT's baseline results are significantly higher than the two other taggers'. This can be explained by the state-of-the art module for guessing unknown words in TnT, which is based on suffix tries extracted from hapax legomena in the training data set. For the baseline, TnT reaches an accuracy of 16.64% on unknown words, MElt 11.65%, and SVMTool 10.32%.

In order to determine whether our initial low performance was due to within-domain tagging issues, such as "fuzzy" linguistic boundaries (Manning, 2011), or simply to the level of difference between our source and target domains, we conducted a brief analysis of the errors from this experiment. We found that the top three discrepancies in the `all3` condition for TnT, comprising 55.32% of the incorrect tags, were the result of mistakenly labeling a gold-tagged interjection (`UH`) with an adjective (`JJ`), noun (`NN`), or an adverb (`RB`) tag. The next most common mistake was labeling a gold-tagged `SYM` (incomplete or non-word) with `JJ` (5.32% of discrepancies). `SYM` and `UH` are much more common in a corpus of spoken dialogue transcriptions than in closely edited financial news. Thus, these top four mistakes represent errors arising from the dissimilarity of the domains (as opposed to the fifth mistake, mistaking `IN` (preposition) for `RB`, which is a more traditional within-domain tagging error, with "fuzzy" linguistic boundaries partially to blame).

Training	# of words
baseline	1 342 561
all3	1 391 238
me/svm	1 413 106
me/tnt	1 418 957
svm/tnt	1 412 917

Table 2: Number of words in the training set.

Tagger	me/svm	me/tnt	svm/tnt	all3
MElt	84.37†	84.28	84.59†	84.32†
SVM	84.98	85.30†	85.47†	85.15†
TnT	**85.94**	85.84	85.70	85.70

Table 3: Results of adding all sentences for which two taggers agree.

5.2 Agreement Between Two Taggers

The reason for requiring all three POS taggers to agree on full sentences is that the selected sentences will be reliable. However, the method also has the drawback that only a rather small number of sentences fulfill this criterion. The first 2 rows in table 2 show the number of words in the training data for the baseline experiment with only Penn Treebank data and for the `all3` experiment. They show that only a very small number of words is added: The number of words increases from approximately 1.34 million words to 1.39 million, i.e. only 50 000 words are added out of the 150 000 words in the HCRC corpus, an insignificant number when compared to the source domain data.

Thus, in order to provide more in-domain training data, we relax the constraint on the selection of sentences from the HCRC corpus and select all sentences for which two specific taggers agree. The results are shown in table 3. The last column in this table repeats the results from the previous experiment.

These results show that the additional data (cf. table 2) improves performance over the experiment requiring agreement between all three taggers. It is worth noting that MElt and TnT perform best with training where the common sentences are from the two *other* taggers. For SVMTool, including TnT improves accuracy, but there is no significant difference between the combination of MElt with TnT and the one with SVMTool and TnT. We assume that TnT has reached saturation on the Penn Treebank and cannot learn new information from additional data tagged with its own bias. Sentences from the other taggers, however, do present new information.

We had a closer look at the sentences that were added to TnT when MElt and SVMTool (me/svm) agree and when MElt and TnT (me/tnt) agree and found considerable differences in the distribution of POS tags. These differences can also be found in the test set tagged with TnT, based on the two training sets. In all data sets, the combination me/tnt seems to keep the lexical bias of the Penn Treebank more strongly than the combination me/svm. For example, the word `left` is consistently tagged as a noun when TnT uses the me/svm combination. In most instances, this is the correct decision. The me/tnt combination, in contrast, prefers a verb reading. For the word `back`, the me/svm combination selects the correct adverb reading over the verbal particle reading preferred by the me/tnt reading. Since the combination of SVMTool and TnT also keeps the bias, the innovation in the me/svm combination cannot be attributed to having SVMTool in the combination.

We also investigated whether using a union of sentences from different pairs of taggers would increase overall accuracy. This adds approximately 70 000 words to the training set. However, the results of this experiment proved to be not significantly different from those based on tagger pairs.

5.3 From Complete Sentences to n-grams

The results from the previous experiment show that adding more training data, even if it is less certain, improves the accuracy of the final tagger. One possibility to provide more training material consists in relaxing the constraint that the taggers need to agree on complete sentences. Instead, we extract either all longest matching n-grams or all trigrams on which the taggers agree. The n-grams are processed and added to the TnT model from the Penn Treebank. This is only possible because TnT stores its trained model in an accessible format. The discriminative POS taggers could not be used for this experiment since adding incomplete sentences as training data would have influenced their trained models negatively.

As before, all evaluations are performed on CReST. The results of this experiment are shown in table 4. The first 3 columns contain the results of merging n-grams or trigrams from 2 different taggers; the last column shows the results for merging all 3 taggers. The first row repeats the results from previous experiments using complete sentences that taggers agree upon. We restrict ourselves to adding only transition information here and merely use the lexicon from the Penn Treebank baseline. We will investigate adding both transition and lexical information in the next experiment. The results show that adding trigrams instead of complete sentences, based on MElt and SVMTool, results in approximately 25 000 additional trigram counts, and it improves the accuracy of the final tagger from 85.94% to 86.10%. Adding all n-grams, in contrast, adds around 33 000 trigram counts and results in slightly lower accuracies, demonstrating that in some cases, the sheer amount of data may be counteracted by substandard quality. Again, TnT profits most from in-domain sentences provided by a combination of MElt and SVMTool.

	me/svm	me/tnt	svm/tnt	all3
full	85.94	85.84	85.70	85.70
n	85.88	85.55	85.93	85.76
tri.	**86.10**	85.77	85.93	85.98

Table 4: Results of adding n-grams or trigrams to TnT's model.

5.4 Adding Lexical Information

A look at the words that are mistagged with the highest frequency in the previous experiment, in which we added trigram information, shows that they fall into two different categories: words such as `okay`, `um`, `gonna` that are typical for dialogues but do not occur frequently in the Penn Treebank; and words that have a different POS preference in the target domain. An example for this category is the word `left`, which tends to be a verb in the Penn Treebank and an adverb in CReST.

For this reason, we decided to add the lexical information from the trigrams to TnT's lexicon. The results of this experiment are shown in table 5. They show that adding lexical information results in lower accuracies: they decrease minimally from 86.10% (adding only trigram transition information) to 86.00% when adding both transition and lexical information. When adding n-grams and lexical information, the results improve over adding only n-grams, but they do not reach the

	me/svm	me/tnt	svm/tnt	all3
n	85.88	85.55	85.70	85.70
n+lex.	86.00	85.86	85.81	85.88
tri.	**86.10**	85.77	85.93	85.98
tri.+lex.	86.00	85.42	85.78	85.86

Table 5: Results of adding lexical information to TnT's model.

Tagger	baseline	red. base.	red.+all3
MElt	83.91	79.38	83.86
SVMTool	84.60	78.79	83.90
TnT	85.77	79.86	84.11

Table 6: The results of restricting the size of the out-of-domain training set.

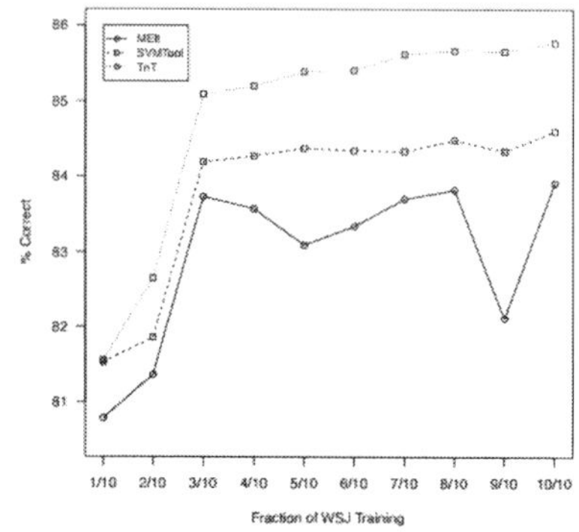

Figure 1: Accuracy as a function of amount of WSJ training

best trigram result.

Since this result did not meet our expectation, we analyzed the changes to the lexicon file and the tagging errors. The extended lexicon contains 326 additional words, but only 8 of them also occur in CReST (`ah`, `fifteen`, `forty-five`, `furthest`, `hmm`, `mhm`, `um`, `yeah`). `yeah` is by far the most common word in the test data. The small number of added words that actually occur in the test set severely restricts possible improvements on in-domain POS tagging.

A comparison of TnT's performance with and without the extended lexicon shows that there are 101 discrepancies (in 11 317 words) in which the POS tagger without additional lexical information makes the correct decision. Out of these discrepancies, the word `yeah` accounts for 45 errors. Here, the extended lexicon lists the tag `NN` instead of the tag `UH`. The reason lies in the fact that `yeah` does not occur in the Penn Treebank, and the three taggers trained on this treebank all (wrongly) tag `yeah` with the most frequent tag for unknown words.

From the error analysis, we can conclude that the added words do not correspond to the words that are needed in the test domain, which means that the HCRC map task corpus data are not similar enough to the CReST data. However, we can also conclude that even if there were a larger overlap, there is a high chance that those words would be mistagged by the ensemble of taggers so that adding the new words would result in a deterioration of the performance.

5.5 Decreasing Out-Of-Domain Training Data

In a final experiment, we investigate whether the difference in amounts of training data between source domain and target domain neutralizes the positive influence of adding in-domain information. Table 2 shows that the number of words added by our methods ranges between one third and half of the original data set. It is therefore possible that the added information does not change the transition probabilities enough to improve the behavior of the final tagger. For this reason, we restrict the size of the Penn Treebank training set to the number of words in the in-domain set, thus reducing the influence of the out-of-domain data. For this experiment, the in-domain training set is taken from the combination of all 3 taggers, as reported in table 1. The results of this experiment are shown in table 6.

The results show that training the POS tagger on only the reduced Penn Treebank containing 46 680 words results in a severe loss in accuracy, from approximately 84% to approximately 79%. Adding more training data from the Penn Treebank consistently increases the results, as shown in Figure 1, thus demonstrating that more data is more important than in-domain knowledge.

These experiments shows that even a fairly "easy" problem such as POS tagging requires a large training set. In the first experiment, combining the reduced Penn Treebank with the in-domain data set increases the accuracies of all POS taggers over the reduced baseline, but they do not reach the baseline based on the whole Penn Treebank. This experiment shows that the sheer size of the training set is more important than access to in-domain training data, at least when the quality of

	base	all3	me/svm	me/tnt	svm/tnt
trans.	85.77	86.10	85.77	85.93	85.98
active	89.04	89.13	**89.15**	89.03	**89.15**

Table 7: Results of adding an active learning lexicon to the training for TnT. All differences between the two experiments are significant.

this additional training set is not guaranteed.

6 Extending the Lexicon with Active Learning

The results of the previous sections show that adding information on which taggers trained out-of-domain agree is useful for moderately improving tagging accuracy and especially for reestimating transition probabilites. However, the method is unsuitable for finding the correct ambiguity sets for words that do not occur in the out-of-domain training set. Such words must be treated in the tagger's module for handling unknown words, which is often based on suffix information extracted from infrequent words in the training set. However, many of the unknown words in the CReST corpus are colloquial words and thus do not show the same morphological characteristics as words in the training set. The words `yeah` and `mhm` are good examples: it is rather unlikely that the tagger can guess their ambiguity set based on their bigram suffixes `ah` and `hm`. This problem is not unique to the domain of spontaneous speech. Biomedical terms, for example, also display atypical suffixes, which make them difficult to classify.

Since the training corpus cannot provide the required information, we decided to acquire minimal information from the target domain via active learning. This goal here is to automatically identify words that TnT was likely to tag incorrectly. These words are then presented to the user, who is asked to provide the ambiguity sets for the words. In our experiment, we simulated the user by looking up the words identified by our program in the CReST gold standard.

In order to determine which words would be difficult for TnT, we built a suffix trie similar to TnT's model for unknown words. For the sake of simplicity, we restricted the trie to a maximum suffix length of three letters. Then, each word in our CReST test corpus that did not occur in the Penn Treebank training lexicon was matched against the suffix trie. If the word's suffix was not present in the trie, the word was presented to the user and added to TnT's lexicon. The extended lexicon was used in combination with the extended transitions based on trigrams from section 5.3. In total, 74 ambiguity classes were added in the active learning lexicon.

The results in table 7 show that adding the active learning lexicon to the Penn Treebank baseline improves tagging accuracy to 89.04%, outperforming our best previous results (cf. table 4). The best results of 89.15% are based on combinations of the active learning lexicon and transition information from where just two taggers agree on HCRC trigrams. This illustrates that adding new words to the lexicon results in a higher improvement than adding new transition information. However, the best results are gained by a combination of the two methods. All active learning results are significantly higher than the previous best result of 86.10%.

For the Penn Treebank baseline, there were 176 word types that were wrongly tagged. In the active learning experiment, 71 types (40.34%) were added with their ambiguity classes, among them the prevalent word `yeah`. All of these words were unambiguous in the target domain.

7 Conclusion and Future Work

We investigated a generally applicable method of domain adaptation for POS tagging, which uses the consent of three POS taggers with different biases to add in-domain sentences to the training set. We show that we reach a slight but significant increase in accuracy from 85.77% to 86.10% when using all trigrams on which the POS taggers agree. Reducing the size of the out-of-domain training set has a detrimental effect on the quality of the POS tagger. The improvement from adding in-domain trigrams is due to more accurate transition probabilities. In contrast, the lexical additions from the in-domain data were detrimental. The active learning strategy of adding user-defined lexical information for difficult unknown words improves this accuracy to 89.15%. However, this accuracy is still far below an in-domain accuracy, which reaches 95.66%.

TnT's better performance on this task may be due to its superior handling of unknown words, but may also be a result of the fact that the feature sets used with MElt and SVMTool were designed specifically for the Penn Treebank. We may be able to improve results for those two taggers if we optimize the feature set for the target domain. However, this means modifying the implementation of the taggers since the feature extraction is not modular. For the future, we are planning to investigate whether structural correspondence learning (Blitzer et al., 2006) will reach higher accuracies, even though it cannot be used with our best performing POS tagger, TnT. We will also repeat these experiments with a biomedical target domain to see if our results transcend domains.

Acknowledgment

This work is based on research supported by the US Office of Naval Research (ONR) Grant #N00014-10-1-0140.

References

John Blitzer, Ryan McDonald, and Fernando Pereira. 2006. Domain adaptation with structural correspondence learning. In *Proceedings of the Conference on Empirical Methods in Natural Language Processing (EMNLP)*, Sydney, Australia.

Thorsten Brants. 2000. TnT–a statistical part-of-speech tagger. In *Proceedings of the ANLP-NAACL*, Seattle, WA.

Wenliang Chen, Youzheng Wu, and Hitoshi Isahara. 2008. Learning reliable information for dependency parsing adaptation. In *Proceedings of the 22nd International Conference on Computational Linguistics (COLING)*, Manchester, UK.

Stephen Clark, James Curran, and Miles Osborne. 2003. Bootstrapping POS-taggers using unlabelled data. In *Proceedings of the Seventh Conference on Natural Language Learning (CoNLL)*, Edmonton, Canada.

Hal Daume III. 2007. Frustratingly easy domain adaptation. In *Proceedings of the 45th Annual Meeting of the Association of Computational Linguistics*, Prague, Czech Republic.

Pascal Denis and Benoit Sagot. 2009. Coupling an annotated corpus and a morphosyntactic lexicon for state-of-the-art POS tagging with less human effort. In *Proceedings of the Pacific Asia Conference on Language, Information and Computation (PACLIC 23)*, Hong Kong, China.

Mark Dredze, John Blitzer, Partha Pratim Talukdar, Kuzman Ganchev, João Graca, and Fernando Pereira. 2007. Frustratingly hard domain adaptation for dependency parsing. In *Proceedings of the CoNLL Shared Task Session of EMNLP-CoNLL 2007*, Prague, Czech Republic.

Kathleen Eberhard, Hannele Nicholson, Sandra Kübler, Susan Gunderson, and Matthias Scheutz. 2010. The Indiana "Cooperative Remote Search Task" (CReST) Corpus. In *Proceedings of the Seventh International Conference on Language Resources and Evaluation (LREC)*, Valetta, Malta.

Jesús Giménez and Lluís Màrquez. 2004. SVMTool: A general POS tagger generator based on Support Vector Machines. In *Proceedings of LREC*, Lisbon, Portugal.

Christopher Manning. 2011. Part-of-speech tagging from 97% to 100%: Is it time for some linguistics? In *Proceedings of CICLing*, Tokyo, Japan.

Mitchell Marcus, Beatrice Santorini, and Mary Ann Marcinkiewicz. 1993. Building a large annotated corpus of English: The Penn Treebank. *Computational Linguistics*, 19(2):313–330.

David McClosky, Eugene Charniak, and Mark Johnson. 2006. Reranking and self-training for parser adaptation. In *Proceedings of COLING-ACL*, Sydney, Australia.

Adwait Ratnaparkhi. 1996. A maximum entropy model for part-of-speech tagging. In *Proceedings of EMNLP*, Philadelphia, PA.

Laura Rimell and Stephen Clark. 2008. Adapting a lexicalized-grammar parser to contrasting domains. In *Proceedings of EMNLP*, Honolulu, Hawaii.

Henry Thompson, Anne Anderson, Ellen Gurman Bard, Gwyneth Doherty-Sneddon, Alison Newlands, and Cathy Sotillo. 1996. The HCRC Map Task Corpus: Natural dialogue for speech recognition. In *Proceedings of the ARPA Human Language Technology Workshop*, Plainsboro, NJ.

Kristina Toutanova and Christopher D. Manning. 2000. Enriching the knowledge sources used in a maximum entropy part-of-speech tagger. In *Proceedings of EMNLP-VLC*, Hong Kong.

Hans van Halteren, Walter Daelemans, and Jakub Zavrel. 2001. Improving accuracy in word class tagging through the combination of machine learning systems. *Computational Linguistics*, 27(2):199–229.

Kazuhiro Yoshida, Yoshimasa Tsuruoka, Yusuke Miyao, and Jun'ichi Tsujii. 2007. Ambiguous part-of-speech tagging for improving accuracy and domain portability of syntactic parsers. In *IJCAI'07: Proceedings of the 20th International Joint Conference on Artifical intelligence*, Hyderabad, India.

Using a Morphological Database to Increase the Accuracy in POS Tagging

Hrafn Loftsson
School of Computer Science
Reykjavik University
hrafn@ru.is

Sigrún Helgadóttir
The Árni Magnússon Institute
for Icelandic Studies
sigruhel@hi.is

Eiríkur Rögnvaldsson
Department of Icelandic
University of Iceland
eirikur@hi.is

Abstract

We experiment with extending the dictionaries used by three open-source part-of-speech taggers, by using data from a large Icelandic morphological database. We show that the accuracy of the taggers can be improved significantly by using the database. The reason is that the unknown word ratio reduces dramatically when adding data from the database to the taggers' dictionaries. For the best performing tagger, the overall tagging accuracy increases from the base tagging result of 92.73% to 93.32%, when the unknown word ratio decreases from 6.8% to 1.1%. When we add reliable frequency information to the tag profiles for some of the words originating from the database, we are able to increase the accuracy further to 93.48% – this is equivalent to 10.3% error reduction compared to the base tagger.

1 Introduction

In general, part-of-speech (PoS) taggers can be catagorised into two types. First, *data-driven* taggers, i.e. taggers that are trained on pre-tagged corpora and are both language and tagset independent, e.g. (Brants, 2000; Toutanova et al., 2003; Shen et al., 2007). Second, *linguistic rule-based taggers*, which are developed "by hand" using linguistic knowledge, with the purpose of tagging a specific language using a particular tagset, e.g. (Karlsson et al., 1995; Loftsson, 2008).

All taggers use a particular tagset T and rely on a dictionary D containing the *tag profile* (ambiguity class) T_w for each word w. A tag profile T_w indicates which tags are assignable to w, thus $T_w \subset T$. Essentially, for each word w, a tagger disambiguates T_w by selecting (or removing all but) one tag from it with regard to context. The dictionary D is derived by a data-driven tagger during training, and derived or built during development of a linguistic rule-based tagger.

When tagging new text, PoS taggers frequently encounter words that are not in D, i.e. so-called *unknown words*. An unknown word u can be quite problematic for a tagger, because the tag profile for u needs to be guessed. In most cases, PoS taggers therefore contain a special module, called an *unknown word guesser*, to generate the tag profile for unknown words. Frequently, the guessing of the tag profile for unknown words is incorrect and therefore the tagging accuracy for these words is considerably lower than the tagging accuracy for known words. To increase the overall tagging accuracy of PoS taggers, one might therefore try to refine the underlying unknown word guessers. Another approach is simply to try to minimise the ratio of unknown words by extending the dictionaries used by the taggers.

In this paper, we use the latter approach. We experiment with extending the dictionaries used by three PoS taggers for Icelandic with data from a large morphological database (Bjarnadóttir, 2005). Our logical assumption is that the overall tagging accuracies of the taggers can be increased by this method, but we are also interested in how extended dictionaries affect the accuracy for unknown words and known words separately.

The three taggers used in our experiments are: i) the linguistic rule-based tagger *IceTagger* (Loftsson, 2008); ii) *TriTagger*, a re-implementation of the statistical tagger *TnT* by Brants (2000); and iii) a serial combination of the two (Loftsson et al., 2009).

The morphological database does not contain any frequency information for the tags in the tag profile for each word, but, nevertheless, we show that the tagging accuracy of the taggers can be improved significantly by using the database. The reason is that when we add most of the data from the database to the taggers' dictionaries the unknown word ratio decreases dramatically, from 6.8% to 1.1%. In that case, the overall tagging accuracy of the best performing tagger, the serial combination of IceTagger and TriTagger, increases from the base tagging result of 92.73% to 93.32%. When we add reliable frequency information, derived from a corpus, to the tag profiles for a part of the words originating from the database, we are able to increase the accuracy further to 93.48% – this is equivalent to 10.3% error reduction compared to the base tagger.

Interestingly, it seems that very few papers exist in the literature regarding extensions of the dictionaries used by PoS taggers. In (Rupnik et al., 2008), a dictionary derived from training is essentially extended by using a backup lexicon extracted from a large corpus (which is different from the training corpus). In contrast, we use a morphological database to extend a tagger's dictionary, but use a corpus for deriving frequency information for part of the dictionary entries. In (Tufis et al., 2008), an unknown word u, and its tag profile and lemma obtained by a tagger when tagging new texts, is used by a morphological generator to generate tag profiles for new word forms that are morphologically related to u. The dictionary is thus extended incrementally, each time new text is tagged. In contrast, since we have access to a large morphological database, we extend a tagger's dictionary once and for all.

2 The morphological database

At the Árni Magnússon Institute for Icelandic Studies, a comprehensive full form database of modern Icelandic inflections has been developed (Bjarnadóttir, 2005). Its Icelandic abbreviation is *BÍN* ("Beygingarlýsing íslensks nútímamáls"), and henceforth we use that term. BÍN contains about 280,000 paradigms, with over 5.8 million inflectional forms. The output from the database used in this project contains lemma, word form, word class, and morphological features for common nouns, proper nouns, adjectives, verbs, and adverbs. It is important to note that the database does, however, not contain any frequency information for the word forms.

A web interface for BÍN is available at `http://bin.arnastofnun.is`, from where a text file in the format used in this project can be downloaded. Below are 16 lines from the file, demonstrating entries for the lemma "hestur" 'horse':

```
hestur;6179;kk;alm;hestur;NFET
hestur;6179;kk;alm;hesturinn;NFETgr
hestur;6179;kk;alm;hest;ÞFET
hestur;6179;kk;alm;hestinn;ÞFETgr
hestur;6179;kk;alm;hesti;ÞGFET
hestur;6179;kk;alm;hestinum;ÞGFETgr
hestur;6179;kk;alm;hests;EFET
hestur;6179;kk;alm;hestsins;EFETgr
hestur;6179;kk;alm;hestar;NFFT
hestur;6179;kk;alm;hestarnir;NFFTgr
hestur;6179;kk;alm;hesta;ÞFFT
hestur;6179;kk;alm;hestana;ÞFFTgr
hestur;6179;kk;alm;hestum;ÞGFFT
hestur;6179;kk;alm;hestunum;ÞGFFTgr
hestur;6179;kk;alm;hesta;EFFT
hestur;6179;kk;alm;hestanna;EFFTgr
```

The exact meaning of the data in each column is not important for our discussion, but we point out that the lemma is in the first column, gender is in third column ("kk"=masculine), the word form is in the fifth column, and the morphological features case, number and definiteness are in the last column (for example, "NF"=nominative, "ET"=singular, "gr"=definite article).

3 The corpus and the taggers used

The Icelandic Frequency Dictionary (IFD) corpus (Pind et al., 1991) has been used to train and test taggers for Icelandic (Helgadóttir, 2005; Loftsson, 2008; Dredze and Wallenberg, 2008; Loftsson et al., 2009). The corpus contains about 590,000 tokens, and its underlying tagset about 700 tags, of which 639 tags actually appear in the corpus. The tags are character strings where each character has a particular function. The first character denotes the *word class*. For each word class there is a predefined number of additional characters (at most six), which describe morphological features, like *gender*, *number* and *case* for nouns; *degree* and *declension* for adjectives; *voice*, *mood* and *tense* for verbs, etc. To illustrate, consider the word form "hestur" 'horse'. The corresponding tag is "nken", denoting noun (*n*), masculine (*k*), singular (*e*), and nominative (*n*) case.

As mentioned in Section 1, we use one linguistic rule-based tagger (IceTagger), one data-driven tagger (TriTagger), and a serial combination of the two in our experiments. Both IceTagger and TriTagger are implemented in Java and are part of the open-source IceNLP toolkit[1].

IceTagger is reductionistic in nature, i.e. it removes inappropriate tags from the tag profile T_w

[1] IceNLP is available at `http://icenlp.sourceforge.net`

for a specific word w in a given context. IceTagger first applies local rules for initial disambiguation and then uses a set of heuristics (global rules) for further disambiguation. The tag profile for each word used by IceTagger is ordered by the frequency of the tags – the first tag listed is the most frequent one and the last tag is the least frequent one. If a word is still ambiguous after the application of the heuristics, the default heuristic is simply to choose the most frequent tag (the first tag) for the word. An important part of IceTagger is its unknown word guesser, *IceMorphy*. It guesses the tag profile for unknown words by applying morphological analysis and ending analysis. In addition, IceMorphy can fill in the *tag profile gaps*[2] in the dictionary for words belonging to certain morphological classes (Loftsson, 2008).

TriTagger is a re-implementation of the well known Hidden Markov Model (HMM) tagger TnT by Brants (2000)[3]. TriTagger uses a trigram model to find the sequence of tags for words in a sentence which maximises the product of contextual probabilities ($P(t_i|t_{i-2}, t_{i-1})$) and lexical probabilities ($P(w_i|t_i)$):

$$P(t_1)P(t_2|t_1) \prod_{i=3}^{n} P(t_i|t_{i-2}, t_{i-1}) \prod_{i=1}^{n} P(w_i|t_i) \quad (1)$$

In the above equation, w_i denotes word i in a sentence of length n ($1 \leq i \leq n$) and t_i denotes the tag for w_i. The probabilities are derived using maximum likelihood estimation based on the frequencies of tags found during training.

HMM taggers handle unknown words by setting tag probabilities according to words' suffixes. The term suffix is here defined as a final sequence of characters of a word. TnT, and thus TriTagger, generate probability distributions for suffixes of various lengths. The distribution for particular suffixes is based on words in the training data that share the same suffix. The reader is referred to (Brants, 2000) for the details of suffix handling.

[2]A tag profile gap for a word occurs when a tag is missing from the tag profile. This occurs, for example, if not all possible tags for a given word are encountered during training.

[3]The TnT tagger is extremely efficient – both training and testing are very fast. Unfortunately, TnT is closed source which limits its use when changes need to be carried out to its default behaviour. TriTagger is open-source and therefore its functionality can be changed or extended relatively easily. Moreover, our experiments have shown that its tagging accuracy is almost identical to the accuracy obtained by TnT. On the other hand, TriTagger has not been optimised for run-time efficiency.

Below, we exemplify the tag profiles stored in the dictionaries for IceTagger and TriTagger for a specific word "konu" 'woman':

```
konu nveþ nveo nvee
konu 122 nveþ 44 nveo 42 nvee 36
```

The first tag profile is stored in the dictionary for IceTagger. The possible tags are "nveþ", "nveo", and "nvee" (denoting noun, feminine, singular, dative/accusative/genetive), sorted by decreasing frequency. The second tag profile is stored in the dictionary for TriTagger. It contains similar information, but, additionally, frequency information is attached to both the word itself and each possible tag.

3.1 Base tagging results

We have previously shown (Loftsson et al., 2009) that a significant improvement in tagging accuracy is obtainable by running a serial combination of IceTagger and a HMM tagger (TriTagger). Specifically, the best result was obtained by making the HMM perform initial disambiguation only with regard to the word class (the first letter of a tag), then running IceTagger, and finally by making the HMM disambiguate words that IceTagger was not able to fully disambiguate. This tagger is called *HMM+Ice+HMM*.

In our current experiments, we use 10-fold cross-validation on the exact same training and test splits of the so-called *corrected version* of the IFD corpus used by Loftsson et al. (2009). Each test corpus contains about 10% of the tokens from the IFD, while the corresponding training corpus contains about 90% of the tokens. The average unknown word ratio using this data split is about 6.8%.

We use a version of the corrected IFD corpus in which type information for proper nouns (named-entity classification) has been removed, and additionally we only use one tag for numerical constants. The reason for these changes is to make the tagset of the corpus comparable to tagsets for other languages. These changes reduce the size of the tagset from about 700 tags to about 600 tags, and the number of tags actually appearing in the IFD reduces from 639 tags to 567.

Table 1 shows the average accuracy of the three taggers. In this table (and in all the ones that follow), the average accuracy is based on testing using the first nine test corpora, because the tenth one was used for developing IceTagger. We consider the accuracy figures in Table 1 as our base

Tagger	Unknown	Known	All
TriTagger	72.98	92.18	90.86
IceTagger	77.02	93.07	91.98
HMM+Ice+HMM	77.47	93.84	92.73

Table 1: Average base tagging accuracy (%). Average ratio of unknown words in testing is 6.8%.

Tagger	Unknown	Known	All
TriTagger	74.44	91.53	90.63
IceTagger	80.44	92.83	92.18
HMM+Ice+HMM	80.53	93.57	92.89

Table 2: Average tagging accuracy (%) using dictionaries extended with lemmata only from BÍN. Average ratio of unknown words in testing is about 5.3%.

tagging results – in the experiments described in the next section we try to improve on these figures.

4 The experiments

In this section, we describe the setup and results of two experiments. First, we extend the dictionaries used by the three taggers by using data from the morphological database BÍN. Second, we add reliable frequency information to some of the dictionary entries (tag profiles).

4.1 Extending the dictionaries

This part of our experiment is in two parts. First, we generate a file F_1 by extracting only lemmata from the database output described in Section 2. F_1 contains about 280,000 lemmata. To clarify, only the first line in the example output shown in Section 2 is then included in F_1. Second, we drop the lemmata condition and generate a file F_2 by selecting most of the word forms from the database output[4]. F_2 contains about 5.3 million rows.

To generate an extended dictionary for a tagger (classifier) C using data from F_1, we perform the following (the same procedure applies when using F_2):

1. Derive a dictionary from F_1, containing words and their corresponding tag profiles. Symbols denoting morphological features in F_1 are mapped to the symbols used in the IFD tagset. We call the resulting dictionary D_{BIN}.

2. Combine D_{BIN} with the dictionary D generated by a tagger C during training (the number of entries in D are about 55,000, on the average). The result is a new dictionary D_{EXT}. If a word exists in both D and D_{BIN} then only the entry from D appears in D_{EXT}.

3. Test tagger C using dictionary D_{EXT}.

[4]Because of memory issues with the taggers, we exclude proper nouns that are names of places.

The above description holds when generating an extended dictionary for IceTagger, a tagger which does not need frequency information in the tag profile for words. In the case of TriTagger, we simply assume a uniform distribution, i.e. we mark each tag in the tag profile T_w for word w with the frequency 1. Note that for TriTagger, extending the dictionary only affects the lexical probabilities from Equation 1 – the contextual probabilities remain unchanged.

Recall (from Section 3) that HMM taggers handle unknown words by generating probability distributions for suffixes of various lengths using the words in the training data. We want the generation of these probability distributions to be only dependent on the data from D (from the IFD corpus), but not as well from D_{BIN}. The reason is twofold. First, the IFD corpus is large enough for deriving reliable suffix probability distributions. Second, using all the words from a very large dictionary (like D_{EXT}) to generate the distributions significantly slows down the tagging process. This issue demonstrates the importance of having access to open-source software. We simply changed the loading module of TriTagger such that it does not use all dictionary entries for suffix handling. If the loading module finds a special entry in the dictionary (essentially a specially marked comment) it does not use the succeeding entries for suffix handling. We put the special entry into D_{EXT} after the last entry from D and thus before the first entry from D_{BIN}.

Let us first consider the case of using file F_1 for extending the dictionaries, i.e. when only extracting lemmata from the database output. In that case, the resulting D_{BIN} contains about 260,000 entries. Table 2 shows the accuracy of the taggers when using this version of the extended dictionary.

Comparing the results from Tables 2 and 1, we note the following:

- The average unknown word ratio decreases

by about 1.5% (from about 6.8% to about 5.3%).

- The accuracy for known words decreases in the three taggers. The most probable reason is that the tag profile for some of the lemmata entries coming from D_{BIN} contains gaps (see Section 3). This can be attributed to the fact that only a single line from the database output is selected when extracting the lemmata, but in many cases a lemma can have multiple analysis (tags). Note that this decrease in accuracy for known words is considerably higher in TriTagger (0.65 percentage points) than in IceTagger (0.24 percentage points). This is because the unknown word guesser IceMorphy, used by IceTagger, can fill into the tag profile gaps for certain morphological classes, as mentioned in Section 3.

- The accuracy for unknown words increases in all the three taggers – the highest gain (3.42 percentage points) is obtained by IceTagger. For the case of IceTagger the reason is that IceMorphy first applies morphological analysis to unknown words (before trying ending analysis). For an unknown word u, IceMorphy searches for a morphologically related word (a known word) to u in its dictionary, i.e. a word containing the same stem but a different morphological suffix. The added lemmata entries can thus serve as related words for unknown words and since the morphological analysis module of IceTagger is quite accurate (Loftsson, 2008), the added lemmata entries help to increase the tagging accuracy of unknown words.

- The accuracy for all words increases in both IceTagger and HMM+Ice+HMM, but only by 0.20 and 0.16 percentage points, respectively. Obviously, the decreased accuracy for known words "cut backs" the gain obtained in the accuracy for unknown words. TriTagger's relatively large reduction in accuracy for known words is to blame for the reduction in its accuracy for all words.

Let us now consider the second case, when using file F_2 for extending the dictionaries. F_2 contains most of the entries from the database and the resulting D_{BIN} contains about 2.6 million entries.

Tagger	Unknown	Known	All
TriTagger	65.82	91.96	91.66
IceTagger	63.38	92.86	92.53
HMM+Ice+HMM	60.41	93.69	93.32

Table 3: Average tagging accuracy (%) using dictionaries extended with most of the data from BÍN. Average ratio of unknown words in testing is 1.1%.

Table 3 shows the accuracy of the taggers when using this large version of the extended dictionary.

Comparing the results from Tables 3 and 1, we note the following:

- The average unknown word ratio drops down to 1.1%. Concurrently, the accuracy for unknown words decreases substantially in all the three taggers. This is because the unknown word ratio drops dramatically and only "hard" unknown words remain – mostly proper nouns and foreign words.

- The accuracy for known words decreases in the three taggers by 0.15-0.22 percentage points. This is a lower decrease than when using only lemmata entries from BÍN (see Table 2) and can be explained by the fact that in this case the added entries from BÍN should not contain tag profile gaps. Why do we then see a slight decrease in accuracy for known words? Recall that BÍN does not contain any frequency information and therefore, for the added dictionary entries, we had to: i) assume a uniform distribution of tags in the the tag profile for TriTagger, and ii) assume no specific order for the tags in the tag profile for IceTagger (see the discussion on the order of the tags in Section 3). This is the most probable reason for the slight reduction in the tagging accuracy of known words.

- The accuracy for all words increases significantly in all the three taggers, about 0.4-0.8 percentage points. This result confirms our logical assumption that the tagging accuracy can be increased by extending the dictionaries of taggers – even in the absence of reliable frequency information.

4.2 Adding frequency information

Recall from Section 3 that the tag profile in the dictionary used by IceTagger is assumed to be sorted. When a word cannot be fully disambiguated, this enables IceTagger to select the most frequent tag (the first tag) in the tag profile for the word. On the other hand, when frequency information is missing, as is the case for the BÍN data, the first tag of the remaining tags in the tag profile may or may not be the most frequent tag. Thus, when IceTagger applies the defult heuristic to choose the first tag that may be an arbitrary choice.

For a HMM tagger, the lack of reliable frequency information in a tag profile for a word can also cause problems. This follows directly from Equation 1, i.e. the term $P(w_i|t_i)$ stands for lexical probabilities which are computed using maximum likelihood estimation from a dictionary containing frequency information for each tag in the tag profiles for words.

In order to get reliable frequency information for the BÍN data, we use a tagged corpus named *MÍM* ("Mörkuð íslensk málheild"; `http://mim.hi.is`) which is being developed at the Árni Magnússon Institute for Icelandic Studies. The final size of the MÍM corpus will be 25 million tokens, but the version that we use contains about 17 million tokens.

Recall from Section 4.1 that D_{BIN} denotes a dictionary derived from BÍN. From the MÍM corpus, we derive a frequency dictionary D_{MIM}. We then create a new dictionary D_{NEW} (based on D_{BIN}) in which frequency information for some of its tag profiles comes from D_{MIM}. Specifically, we use the following procedure:

1. Each word w in D_{BIN} is looked up in D_{MIM}. If w is not found in D_{MIM}, then w and its tag profile is copied to D_{NEW}. Each tag in the tag profile for w is given the frequency 1 (i.e. a uniform distribution is assumed). If w is found in D_{MIM}, proceed to step 2.

2. Order the tags in the tag profile for w in D_{BIN}, according to the frequencies of the tags in the tag profile for w in D_{MIM}. If a tag t for a word w is found in D_{MIM} but not in D_{BIN}, then t does not become a part of the tag profile for w in D_{NEW}. The reason is that the dictionary D_{MIM} is derived from a tagged corpus which has not been manually inspected and thus contains tagging errors. In other words, the tag profile from D_{BIN} is considered more reliable than the one in D_{MIM}.

3. Combine the new dictionary D_{NEW} with the dictionary D used by a tagger C as explained in step 2 in Section 4.1.

Tagger	Unknown	Known	All
TriTagger	65.84	92.22	91.93
IceTagger	63.47	93.11	92.78
HMM+Ice+HMM	60.50	93.85	93.48

Table 4: Average tagging accuracy (%) using dictionaries extended with most of the data from BÍN and with arranged tag profiles for some of the words. Average ratio of unknown words in testing is 1.1%.

To illustrate, consider the following three tag profiles for the word "skögultennur" 'buckteeth':

```
skögultennur nvfn nvfo
skögultennur nvfo nken nvfn
skögultennur nvfo nvfn
```

The first tag profile appears in D_{BIN}. The tags "nvfn" and "nvfo" appear in alphabetic order. The second tag profile appears in D_{MIM} (shown here without the frequency numbers for each tag). The tag profile is sorted in ascending order of frequency of the tags. Note that the second tag profile contains the tag "nken" (resulting from a tagging error in MÍM) which does not appear in the first tag profile. When generating the resulting tag profile for D_{NEW} – the third line in the illustration above – the tag "nken" does thus not appear.

We used the procedure described above to generate extended dictionaries with frequency information for TriTagger and sorted tag profiles for IceTagger. Of the 2.6 million tag profiles in D_{BIN}, 250,000 were found in D_{MIM} (i.e. about 10%). This procedure thus "arranged" 250,000 of the tag profiles in D_{BIN}.

Table 4 shows the result of using the three taggers with extended dictionaries and with arranged tag profiles for some of the words. The accuracy of TriTagger improves from 91.66%, when using BÍN data without frequency information (see Table 3) to 91.93% (3.25% error reduction). The accuracy of IceTagger improves from 92.53% to 92.78% (3.5% error reduction), and the accuracy of HMM+Ice+HMM improves from 93.32% to 93.48% (2.4% error reduction). The error reduction between our HMM+Ice+HMM tagger, with an extended dictionary and arranged tag profiles, and the base version of HMM+Ice+HMM (see Table 1), is 10.3%.

5 Future work

In Section 4.2, we showed that the accuracies of the three taggers can be improved significantly by arranging the tag profiles of the taggers using frequency information from the MÍM corpus. We used about 17 million tokens from the corpus, but once it has been extended to its final size of 25 million tokens, we would like to repeat this part of the experiment, thus using more data, to see if the accuracy increases further.

Note that we have only been able to arrange part of the tag profiles (about 10%) in the extended dictionaries by using frequency information from MÍM. In future work, we would also like to experiment with arranging the remainder of the tag profiles according to unigram tag frequencies (for example, derived from the IFD corpus), i.e. tag frequenies that are not associated with individual words. We would then be seeking an answer to the question whether assigning unigram tag frequencies to the tag profiles of words, for which we do not have reliable frequency information, results in higher tagging accuracy compared to assigning a uniform distribution to the tag profiles (i.e. giving each tag the frequency 1 as we have done).

6 Conclusion

We have experimented with adding data from a large morphological database to the dictionaries used by three open-source PoS taggers for Icelandic. Our results show that the tagging accuracy improves significantly when extending the dictionaries, and even further improvement in accuracy can be obtained by adding frequency information to some of the dictionary entries (tag profiles).

Our best performing tagger, a serial combination of a linguistic rule-based tagger and a statistical tagger, obtains a state-of-the-art tagging accuracy of 93.48% when using extended dictionaries and added frequency information. This is equivalent to 10.3% error reduction compared to the best base tagger.

Acknowledgments

The work presented in this paper was partly supported by the Icelandic Research Fund, grant 070025023.

References

K. Bjarnadóttir. 2005. Modern Icelandic Inflections. In H. Holmboe, editor, *Nordisk Sprogteknologi 2005*. Museum Tusculanums Forlag, Copenhagen.

T. Brants. 2000. TnT: A statistical part-of-speech tagger. In *Proceedings of the* 6th *Conference on Applied Natural Language Processing*, Seattle, WA, USA.

M. Dredze and J. Wallenberg. 2008. Icelandic Data Driven Part of Speech Tagging. In *Proceedings of the* 46th *Annual Meeting of the Association for Computational Linguistics: Human Language Technologies*, Columbus, OH, USA.

S. Helgadóttir. 2005. Testing Data-Driven Learning Algorithms for PoS Tagging of Icelandic. In H. Holmboe, editor, *Nordisk Sprogteknologi 2004*. Museum Tusculanums Forlag, Copenhagen.

F. Karlsson, A. Voutilainen, J. Heikkilä, and A. Anttila. 1995. *Constraint Grammar: A Language-Independent System for Parsing Unrestricted Text*. Mouton de Gruyter, Berlin, Germany.

H. Loftsson, I. Kramarczyk, S. Helgadóttir, and E. Rögnvaldsson. 2009. Improving the PoS tagging accuracy of Icelandic text. In *Proceedings of the* 17th *Nordic Conference of Computational Linguistics (NODALIDA-2009)*, Odense, Denmark.

H. Loftsson. 2008. Tagging Icelandic text: A linguistic rule-based approach. *Nordic Journal of Linguistics*, 31(1):47–72.

J. Pind, F. Magnússon, and S. Briem. 1991. *Íslensk orðtíðnibók [The Icelandic Frequency Dictionary]*. The Institute of Lexicography, University of Iceland, Reykjavik, Iceland.

J. Rupnik, M. Grčar, and T. Erjavec. 2008. Improving Morphosyntactic Tagging of Slovene Language through Meta-tagging. *Informatica*, 32(4):437–444.

L. Shen, G. Satta, and A. Joshi. 2007. Guided learning for bidirectional sequence classification. In *Proceedings of the* 45th *Annual Meeting of the Association for Computational Linguistics*, Prague, Czech Republic.

K. Toutanova, D. Klein, C. D. Manning, and Y. Singer. 2003. Feature-rich part-of-speech tagging with a cyclic dependency network. In *Proceedings of HLT/NAACL 2003*, Edmonton, Canada.

D. Tufis, E. Irimia, R. Ion, and A. Ceausu. 2008. Unsupervised Lexical Acquisition for Part of Speech Tagging. In *Proceedings of the* 6th *International Conference on Language Resources and Evaluation (LREC 2008)*, Marrakech, Morocco.

Actions Speak Louder than Words: Evaluating Parsers in the Context of Natural Language Understanding Systems for Human-Robot Interaction

Sandra Kübler, Rachael Cantrell, Matthias Scheutz
Indiana University
{skuebler,rcantrel,mscheutz}@indiana.edu

Abstract

The standard ParsEval metrics alone are often not sufficient for evaluating parsers integrated in natural language understanding systems. We propose to augment intrinsic parser evaluations by extrinsic measures in the context of human-robot interaction using a corpus from a human cooperative search task. We compare a constituent with a dependency parser on both intrinsic and extrinsic measures and show that the conversion to semantics is feasible for different syntactic paradigms.

1 Introduction

Human-robot interactions (HRI) in *natural language* (Scheutz et al., 2007) pose many challenges for natural language understanding (NLU) systems, for humans expect robots to (1) generate quick responses to their request, which requires all processing to be done in real-time, (2) to rapidly integrate perceptions (e.g., to resolve referents (Brick and Scheutz, 2007)), and (3) to provide backchannel feedback indicating whether they understood an instruction, often before the end of an utterance. As a result, NLU systems on robots must operate *incrementally* to allow for the construction of meaning that can lead to robot action before an utterance is completed (e.g., a head-turn of the robot to check for an object referred to by the speaker). Hence, the question arises how one can best evaluate NLU components such as parsers for robotic NLU in the context of HRI.

In this paper, we argue that intrinsic parser evaluations, which evaluate parsers in isolation, are insufficient for determining their performance in HRI contexts where the ultimate goal of the NLU system is to generate the correct actions for the robot in a timely manner. For high performance of a parser with respect to intrisic measures does not imply that the parser will also work well with the other NLU components. A correct but overly complex parse passed to the semantic analysis unit, for example, may not result in the correct meaning interpretation and will thus fail to generate correct actions. Similarly, fragmented input from the speech recognizer may not lead to any parsable sequence of words, again likely resulting in incorrect robot behavior. Hence, we need an extrinsic evaluation to determine the utility and performance of a parser *in the context of other NLU components at the level of semantics and action execution.*

To this end, we introduce an evaluation architecture that can be used for extrinsic evaluations of NLU components and demonstrate its utility for parser evaluation using state-of-the-art parsers for each of the two main parsing paradigms: the Berkeley *constituent parser* (Petrov and Klein, 2007) and MaltParser (Nivre et al., 2007b), a *dependency parser*. The evaluation compares intrinsic and extrinsic measures on the *CReST corpus* (Eberhard et al., 2010), which is representative of a broad class of collaborative instruction-based tasks envisioned for future robots (e.g., in search and rescue missions). To our knowledge, no previous extrinsic parser evaluation used conversions to semantic/action representations, which can be performed for different parser types and are thus ideally suited for comparing parsing frameworks. Moreover, no previous work has presented a combined intrinsic-extrinsic evaluation where the extrinsic evaluation uses full-fledged semantic/action representations in an HRI context.

2 Previous Work

Evaluating different types of parsers is challenging for many reasons. For one, intrinsic evaluation measures are often specific to the type of parser. The ParsEval measures (precision and recall) are the standard for constituent parsers, attachment scores for dependency parsing. Yet, none of these measures is ideal: the ParsEval measures have been widely criticized because they favor flat annotation schemes and harshly punish attachment errors (Carroll et al., 1998). Additionally, there is no evaluation scheme that can compare the performance of constituent and dependency parsers, or parsers using different underlying grammars. Converting constituents into dependencies (Boyd and Meurers, 2008), evens out differences between underlying grammars. However, it is well known that the conversion into a different format is not straightforward. Clark and Curran (2007), who convert the CCGBank to DepBank, report an F-score of 68.7 for the conversion on gold data. Conversions into dependencies have been evaluated on the treebank side (Rehbein and van Genabith, 2007), but not on the parser side; yet, the latter is critical since parser errors result in unpredicted structures and thus conversion errors.

Intrinsic parsing quality has been shown to be insufficient for comparing parsers, and adding extrinsic measures to the evaluation can lead to inconclusive results, in comparing two dependency parsers (Mollá and Hutchinson, 2003), three constituent parsers (Preiss, 2002), and for a deep and a partial parser (Grover et al., 2005).

We propose to use intrinsic and extrinsic measures together to assess tradeoffs for parsers embedded in NLU systems (e.g., low-intrinsic/high-extrinsic quality is indicative of parsers that work well in challenging systems, while high-intrinsic/low-extrinsic quality is typical of high-performance parsers that are difficult to interface).

3 An Evaluation Framework for HRI

For evaluation, we propose the robotic `DIARC` architecture (Scheutz et al., 2007) which has been used successfully in many robotic applications. In addition to components for visual perception and action execution, `DIARC` consists of five NLU components. The first two components, a speech recognizer, and a disfluency filter which filters out common vocal distractors ("uh", "um", etc.) and common fillers ("well", "so", etc.) will not be used here. The third component optionally performs trigram-based part of speech (POS) tagging. The fourth component, the parser to be evaluated, which produces the constituent tree or dependency graph used by the fifth component, the λ converter, to produce formal semantic representations. If the semantic representation indicates that a command needs to be executed, the command is passed on to an action interpreter (which then retrieves an existing action script indexed by the command or, if no such script is found, forwards the request to a task planner, which will plan a sequence of actions to achieve it (Schermerhorn et al., 2009)).

The semantic conversion process makes use of combinatorial categorial grammar (CCG) tags associated with lexical items, which are essentially part-of-speech tags enriched with information about the word's arguments. Given a word and the appropriate CCG tag, the corresponding semantic representations are retrieved from a semantic lexicon. These representations are λ-expressions expressed in a fragment of first-order dynamic logic sufficiently rich to capture the language of (action) instructions from the corpus (c.f. e.g., (Goldblatt, 1992)). Expressions are repeatedly combined using β-reduction until all words are converted and (preferably) only one λ-free formula is left (Dzifcak et al., 2009).

For example, the sentence "do you see a blue box?" is translated as $\texttt{check-and-answer}(\exists x.see(\texttt{self}, x) \wedge box(x) \wedge blue(x))$. `check-and-answer` is an action that takes a formula as an argument, checks its truth (if possible), and causes the robot to reply with "yes" or "no" depending on the outcome of the check operation[1].

The conversion from dependency graphs to semantic representations is straightforward: When a dependent is attached to a head, the dependent is added to the CCG tag, resulting in a convenient format for semantic conversion. Then each node is looked up in the dictionary, and the definition is used to convert the node. For the example above, the parse graph indicates that "a" and "blue" are syntactic arguments of "box", "you" and "a blue box" are arguments of "see", and the clause "you see a blue box" is an argument of "do". Based on the lexical definitions, the phrase "a blue box" is combined into the expression $(\exists x.box(x) \wedge blue(x))$. As argument of the verb "see", it is then combined into the expression $(\exists x.see(\texttt{self}, x) \wedge box(x) \wedge blue(x))$, and ultimately $\texttt{check\&answer}(\exists x.see(\texttt{self}, x) \wedge box(x) \wedge blue(x))$.

The conversion for constituent trees is less straightforward since it is more difficult to automatically identify the head of a phrase, and to connect the arguments in the same way. We use a slightly different method: each node in the

[1] `self` is a deictic referent always denoting the robot.

tree is looked up in the dictionary for a suitable word/CCG tag combination given the words dominated by the node's daughters. The λ conversions are then performed for each sentence after the parser finishes producing a parse tree.

4 Experimental Setup

For parser evaluations, we use an HRI scenario where processing speed is critical (often more important even than accuracy) as humans expect timely responses of the robot. Moreover, a parser's ability to produce fragments of a sentence (instead of failing completely) is highly desirable since the robot can ask clarification questions (if it knows where the parse failed) as opposed to offline processing tasks as humans are typically willing to help. This is different from a corpus, where no clarification question can be asked. *Correctness* here is determined by correct semantic interpretations that can be generated in the semantic analysis based on the (partial) parses. While these aspects are often of secondary importance in many NLU systems, they are essential to a robotic NLU architecture. Since we experiment with a new corpus that has not been used in parsing research yet, we also present an intrinsic evaluation to give a reference point to put the parsers' performance into perspective with regard to previous work.

More specifically, we investigate two points: (1) Given that spoken commands to robots are considerably shorter and less complex than newspaper sentences, is it possible to use existing resources, i.e., the Penn Treebank (Marcus et al., 1993), for training the parsers without a major decrease in accuracy? And (2), are constituent or dependency parsers better suited for the NLU architecture described above, in terms of accuracy and speed?

To answer these questions, we carried out two experiments: (1) The intrinsic evaluation. This is split into two parts: one that compares constituent and dependency parsers on our test data when both parsers were trained on the Penn Treebank; and one that compares the parsers trained on a small in-domain set. (2) The extrinsic evaluation, which compares the two parsers in the NLU architecture, is also based on in-domain training data.

Intrinsic and extrinsic measures: For the first experiment we use standard intrinsic parsing measures: for the constituent parser, we report labeled precision (LP), labeled recall (LR), and labeled F-score (LF); for the dependency parser the labeled attachment score (LAS). The second experiment uses the accuracy of the logical forms and the correct action interpretation and execution as a measure of quality. For this experiment, we also report the processing time, i.e., how much time the complete system requires for processing the test set from the text input to the output of logical forms.

Data sets: For the intrinsic evaluation, we used the Penn Treebank. For the constituent experiments, we used the treebank with grammatical functions since the semantic construction requires this information. The only exception is the experiment using the Berkeley parser with the Penn Treebank: Because of memory restrictions, we could not use grammatical functions. For the dependency parser, we used a dependency version of the Penn Treebank created by *pennconverter* (Johansson and Nugues, 2007).

For the in-domain experiments (intrinsic and extrinsic), we used CReST (Eberhard et al., 2010), a corpus of natural language dialogues obtained from recordings of humans performing a *cooperative, remote search task*. The multi-modal corpus contains the speech signals and transcriptions of the dialogues, which are additionally annotated for dialogue structure, disfluencies, POS, and syntax. The syntactic annotation covers both constituent annotation based on the Penn Treebank annotation scheme and dependencies based on the dependency version of the Penn Treebank. The corpus consists of 7 dialogues, with 1,977 sentences overall. The sentences are fairly short; average sentence length is 6.7 words. We extracted all commands (such as "walk into the next room"), which our robot can handle, and used those 122 sentences as our test set. We performed a 7-fold cross validation, in which one fold consists of all test sentences (i.e. commands) from one of the 7 dialogues. All the other folds combined with the declarative sentences from all dialogues served as training data. The number of commands per dialogue varies so the evaluation was performed on the set of all test sentences rather than averaged over the 7 folds.

Parsers: We use both state-of-the-art constituent and dependency parsers: As constituent parser, we chose the Berkeley parser (Petrov and Klein, 2007), a parser that learns a refined PCFG grammar based on latent variables. We used grammars based on 6 split-merge cycles.

	Berkeley parser				MaltParser	
training data	POS acc.	LP	LR	LF	POS acc.	LAS
Penn	86.9	47.2	44.8	46.0	88.1	40.6
CReST	67.8	56.7	48.9	52.5	92.8	70.5

Table 1: The results of the intrinsic evaluation.

For the dependency parser, we used MaltParser (Nivre et al., 2007b), a pseudo-projective dependency parser, which has reached state-of-the-art results for all languages in the CONLL 2007 shared task (Nivre et al., 2007a). We decided to use version 1.1 of MaltParser, which allows the use of memory-based learning (MBL) in the implementation of TiMBL[2]. MBL has been shown to work well with small training sets (cf., (Banko and Brill, 2001)). MaltParser was used with the Nivre algorithm and the feature set that proved optimal for English (Nivre et al., 2007b). TiMBL parameters were optimized for each experiment in a non-exhaustive search. When trained on the Penn Treebank, the parser performed best using MVDM, 5 nearest neighbors, no feature weighting, and Inverse Distance class weighting. For the experiments on the dialogue corpus, the default settings proved optimal. Since MaltParser requires POS-tagged input, we used the Markov model tagger TnT (Brants, 1999) to tag the test sentences for dependency parsing; the Berkeley parser performs POS tagging in the parsing process.

For the experiment based on the complete NLU architecture, we used an incremental reimplementation of the Nivre algorithm called Mink (Cantrell, 2009) as dependency parser. Mink uses the WEKA implementation of the C4.5 decision tree classifier (Hall et al., 2009) as guide. The confidence threshold for pruning is 0.25, and the minimum number of instances per leaf is 2.

5 Results

The results of the **intrinsic parser evaluation** are shown in Table 1. The POS tagging results for TnT (for MaltParser) are unexpected: the small in-domain training set resulted in an increase of accuracy of 4.7 percent points. The result for the POS tagging accuracy of the Berkeley parser trained on CReST is artificially low because the parser did not parse 9 sentences, which resulted in missing POS tags for those sentences. All of the POS tagging results are lower than the TnT accuracy of 96.7%, reported for the Penn Treebank (Brants, 1999). This is due to either out-of-domain data or the small training set for the training with CReST.

When the parsers were trained on the Penn Treebank, the very low results for both parsers (46.0 F-score, 40.6 LAS) show clearly that pre-existing resources cannot be used for training. The low results are due to the fact that the test set consists almost exclusively of commands, a sentence type that, to our knowledge, does not occur in the Penn Treebank. A comparison between ParsEval measures and LAS is difficult. We refrained from converting the constituent parse to dependencies for evaluation because it is unclear how reliable the conversion for parser output is.

The results for the Berkeley parser trained on the dialogue data from CReST are better than the results trained on the Penn Treebank. However, even with training on in-domain data, the F-score of 52.5 is still considerably lower than state-of-the-art results for in-domain parsing of the Penn Treebank. This is partly due to our inclusion of grammatical functions in the parsing process as well as in the evaluation. Thus, the parsing task is more difficult than in other experiments. Another possible reason for the low performance is the size of the training set. We must assume that the Berkeley parser requires a larger training set to reach good results. This is corroborated by the fact that this parser did not find any parse for 9 sentences. The dependency parser performs equally badly when trained on the Penn Treebank (40.6 LAS). However, when it is trained on in-domain data, it reaches an LAS of 70.5, which corroborates the assumption that TiMBL performs well with small data sets.

An error analysis of the parser output based on the CReST training shows that one frequent type of error results from differing lexical preferences between the Penn Treebank and the CReST domain. The word "left", for example, is predominantly used as a verb in the Penn Treebank, but as an adverb or noun in the dialogue corpus, which results in frequent POS tagging errors and subse-

[2]`http://ilk.uvt.nl/timbl/`

((S (VP (VB hold) (PRT (RP on)) (S (VP (VB let) (S (NP (PRP me)) (VP (VB pick) (PRT (RP up)) (NP (DT those) (JJ green) (NNS boxes))))))))

Figure 1: Constituent parse for "hold on let me pick up those green boxes".

quent parsing errors.

For the **extrinsic evaluation** in the context of the NLU system, we report *exact match* accuracy for the logical forms. Since the semantic conversion fails on unexpected parser output, the quantitative semantic evaluation is based only on syntactically-correct sentences, although partially-correct parses are instructive examples, and thus are included in the discussion. More parses were *almost* correct than perfectly so: 27% were perfectly correct for the constituent parser, and 30% for the dependency parser.

Of these, 90% of dependency graphs were correctly semantically combined. while just 64% of constituent trees were correctly combined. Mink was also faster: Averaged over a range of sentence lengths and complexities, the NLU system using Mink was roughly twice as fast as the one with the Berkeley parser. Averaged over 5 runs of 100 sentences each, Mink required approx. 180 ms per sentence, the Berkeley parser approx. 270 ms.

The most egregious problem area involves a typical phenomenon of spontaneous speech that an utterance does not necessarily correspond to a sentence in the syntactic sense: Many utterances contain multiple, independent phrases or clauses, e.g., "hold on let me pick up those green boxes", as a single utterance. The ideal translation for this utterance is: $wait(listener); get(speaker, \{x|green(x) \wedge box(x)\})$ where ";" is the sequencing operator.

The constituent parse for the utterance is shown in Figure 1. This parse is partially correct, but the two commands are not treated as a conjunction of clauses; instead, the second command is treated as subordinate to the first one, This analysis results in the argument structure shown in Table 2, where each phrase takes its phrasal constituents as arguments. The semantic definitions and CCG tags are shown in Table 3. Some definitions do not have the same number of arguments as the CCG tags, in particular the verb "pick" with its raised subject, which will be applied by the semantics of the verb "let". The correspondence between the constituent parse and semantics output is shown in Table 4. The dependency parse is shown in Figure 2. The two commands are correctly analyzed as in-

Phr.:Head	Arguments
VP:hold	(PRT=on,S)
VP:let	(S)
S	(NP=me,VP)
VP:pick	(PRT=up,NP)
NP	(DT=those,JJ=green,NNS=boxes)

Table 2: The argument structure based on the constituent parse.

Token	Arg. Str.	Semantics
hold	S/RP	$\lambda x.wait(x)$
on	RP	on
let	S/NP/S	$\lambda x.\lambda X.X(x)$
me	NP	$speaker$
pick	S/RP/NP	$\lambda x.\lambda y.\lambda z.pick(x, y, z)$
up	RP	up
those	NP/NP	$\lambda X.\{x \| X(x)\}$
green	NP/NP	$\lambda X.\lambda x.green(x) \wedge X(x)$
boxes	NP	box

Table 3: Semantics for the example sentence.

Head	Dependents
HOLD	on
LET	me, pick
PICK	up, boxes
BOXES	those, green

Table 5: Syntactic head/dependent relationships.

dependent clauses.

The parse results in the syntactic head and dependent relationships and the semantic head and dependent relationships for the words in the utterance, constructed from the definitions in Table 5. In the semantic analysis, "pick" is similar to the syntactic analysis in that it takes a noun phrase and a particle as its arguments. This results in the following combination: $\lambda x.\lambda y.\lambda z.pick(up, z, y)$ (up) (those green boxes)[3]. The first application applies "up" to x, resulting in the analysis: $\lambda y.\lambda z.pick(up, z, y)$ (those green boxes) which in turn is converted into: $\lambda z.pick(up, z, those\_green\_boxes)$.

[3] Here, "those green boxes" is a human-convenient shorthand for its full semantic definition.

	Constituency	Semantic
1	NP_1:boxes (DT=those,JJ=green)	$\{x \| green(x) \wedge boxes(x)\}$
2	VP_1:pick (PRT=up,NP_1)	$\lambda z.pick(up, z, \{x \| green(x) \wedge box(x)\})$
3	S_1(NP_2=speaker,VP_1)	$pick(up, speaker, \{x \| green(x) \wedge box(x)\})$
4	VP_2:let (S_1)	$pick(up, speaker, \{x \| green(x) \wedge box(x)\})$
5	$S_2(VP_2)$	$pick(up, speaker, \{x \| green(x) \wedge box(x)\})$
6	VP_3:hold (PRT=on,S_2)	$wait(pick(up, speaker, \{x \| green(x) \wedge box(x)\}))$ ⇐ **error**
7	$S_4(VP_3)$	

Table 4: Correspondence between the constituent parse and the semantics output.

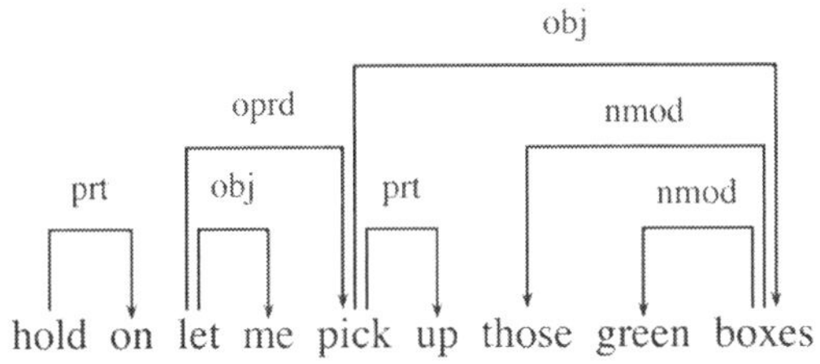

Figure 2: The dependency analysis.

Here we find a systematic difference between the syntactic analysis and the intended semantic one: While syntactically, the adjective "green" is dependent on the head "boxes", it is the opposite in the semantic analysis. The definition of "boxes" indicates that it is a predicate that takes as an argument an abstract entity "x", representing the real-world item that has the property of being a box. This predicate, $box(x)$, is itself then applied to the predicate "green", which has the definition $\lambda X.\lambda x.green(x) \wedge X(x)$. The variable X represents the concept that will be applied. This application produces $\lambda x.green(x) \wedge box(x))$. Thus a conversion rule reverses dependencies within noun phrases.

6 Discussion

The results show that a considerable number of sentences could be parsed but not converted correctly to logical form because of the way certain information is represented in the parses. Additionally, a small difference in the parsers' behavior, namely MaltParser's ability to provide partial parses, resulted in a large difference in the usability of the parsers' output – partial parses are not only better than parse failures, but may even be the expected outcome in an HRI settings, since they can be successfully translated to logical form.

While the same parser performed better under both intrinsic and extrinsic evaluation, this may not necessarily always be the case (see section 2). It is possible that one parser provides imperfect parses when evaluated intrinsically but the information is presented in a form that can be used by higher applications. This occurred in our experiment in the case of the dependency parser, whose partial parses could be converted in completely correct semantic representations. I.e., while the parse may not be completely correct with regard to the gold standard, it may still provide enough information to use for the higher component so that no information loss ensues.

One advantage of our extrinsic evaluation is that the conversion to semantics can be performed for a wide range of different syntactic annotations. While previous evaluations stayed within one parsing framework (e.g., dependency parsing), our evaluation included a constituent and a dependency parser (this evaluation can be extended to "deeper" parsers such as HPSG parsers). Additionally, the conversion to semantics involves a wide range of syntactic phenomena, thus providing a high granularity compared to extrinsic evaluations in information retrieval, where only specific sentence parts (e.g., noun phrases) are targeted.

7 Conclusions

We introduced a novel, semantics-based method for comparing the performance of different parsers in an HRI setting and evaluated our method on a test corpus collected in a human coordination task.

The experiments emphasize the importance of performing an extrinsic evaluation of parsers in typical application domains. While extrinsic evaluations may depend on the application domain, it is important to show that parsers cannot be used off-the-shelf based on intrinsic evaluations. To estimate the variance of parsers, it is important to establish a scenario of different applications in which parsers can be tested. An NLU component in an HRI setting is an obvious candidate since the conversion to semantics is possible for any syntactic paradigm, and the HRI setting requires evaluation metrics, such as the time behavior or the incrementality of the parser, which are typically not considered.

Acknowledgment

This work was in part supported by ONR grants #N00014-10-1-0140 and #N00014-07-1-1049.

References

Michele Banko and Eric Brill. 2001. Scaling to very very large corpora for natural language disambiguation. In *Proceedings of ACL-EACL'01*, pages 26–33, Toulouse, France.

Adriane Boyd and Detmar Meurers. 2008. Revisiting the impact of different annotation schemes on PCFG parsing: A grammatical dependency evaluation. In *Proceedings of the ACL Workshop on Parsing German*, Columbus, OH.

Thorsten Brants. 1999. *Tagging and Parsing with Cascaded Markov Models*. DFKI, Universität des Saarlandes.

Timothy Brick and Matthias Scheutz. 2007. Incremental natural language processing for HRI. In *Proceedings of the Second ACM IEEE International Conference on Human-Robot Interaction*, pages 263–270, Washington D.C.

Rachael Cantrell. 2009. Mink: An incremental data-driven dependency parser with integrated conversion to semantics. In *Student Workshop at RANLP*, Borovets, Bulgaria.

John Carroll, Ted Briscoe, and Antonio Sanfilippo. 1998. Parser evaluation: a survey and a new proposal. In *Proceedings of LREC 1998*, pages 447–454, Granada, Spain.

Stephen Clark and James Curran. 2007. Formalism-independent parser evaluation with CCG and DepBank. In *Proceedings of ACL 2007*, Prague, Czech Republic.

Juraj Dzifcak, Matthias Scheutz, and Chitta Baral. 2009. What to do and how to do it: Translating natural language directives into temporal and dynamic logic representation for goal management and action execution. In *Proceedings of the IEEE International Conference on Robotics and Automation (ICRA'09)*, Kobe, Japan.

Kathleen Eberhard, Hannele Nicholson, Sandra Kübler, Susan Gunderson, and Matthias Scheutz. 2010. The Indiana "Cooperative Remote Search Task" (CReST) Corpus. In *Proceedings of LREC-2010*, Valetta, Malta.

Robert Goldblatt. 1992. Parallel action: Concurrent dynamic logic with independent modalities. *Studia Logica*, 51(3/4):551–578.

Claire Grover, Mirella Lapata, and Alex Lascarides. 2005. A comparison of parsing technologies for the biomedical domain. *Natural Language Engineering*, 11:27–65.

Mark Hall, Eibe Frank, Geoffrey Holmes, Bernhard Pfahringer, Peter Reutemann, and Ian Witten. 2009. The WEKA data mining software: An update. *SIGKDD Explorations*, 11(1).

Richard Johansson and Pierre Nugues. 2007. Extended constituent-to-dependency conversion for English. In *Proceedings of NODALIDA 2007*, Tartu, Estonia.

Mitchell Marcus, Beatrice Santorini, and Mary Ann Marcinkiewicz. 1993. Building a large annotated corpus of English: The Penn Treebank. *Computational Linguistics*, 19(2):313–330.

Diego Mollá and Ben Hutchinson. 2003. Intrinsic versus extrinsic evaluations of parsing systems. In *Proceedings of the EACL 2003 Workshop on Evaluation Initiatives in Natural Language Processing*, pages 43–50, Budapest, Hungary.

Joakim Nivre, Johan Hall, Sandra Kübler, Ryan McDonald, Jens Nilsson, Sebastian Riedel, and Deniz Yuret. 2007a. The CoNLL 2007 shared task on dependency parsing. In *Proceedings of EMNLP-CoNLL 2007*, Prague, Czech Republic.

Joakim Nivre, Johan Hall, Jens Nilsson, Atanas Chanev, Gülşen Eryiğit, Sandra Kübler, Svetoslav Marinov, and Erwin Marsi. 2007b. MaltParser: A language-independent system for data-driven dependency parsing. *Natural Language Engineering*, 13(2):95–135.

Slav Petrov and Dan Klein. 2007. Improved inference for unlexicalized parsing. In *Proceedings of HLT-NAACL'07*, Rochester, NY.

Judita Preiss. 2002. Choosing a parser for anaphora resolution. In *Proceedings of DAARC*, Lisbon, Portugal.

Ines Rehbein and Josef van Genabith. 2007. Treebank annotation schemes and parser evaluation for German. In *Proceedings of EMNLP-CoNLL 2007*, pages 630–639, Prague, Czech Republic.

Paul Schermerhorn, J Benton, Matthias Scheutz, Kartik Talamadupula, and Rao Kambhampati. 2009. Finding and exploiting goal opportunities in real-time during plan execution. In *Proceedings of the 2009 IEEE/RSJ International Conference on Intelligent Robots and Systems*, St. Louis.

Matthias Scheutz, Paul Schermerhorn, James Kramer, and David Anderson. 2007. First steps toward natural human-like HRI. *Autonomous Robots*, 22(4):411–423.

Constructing Linguistically Motivated Structures from Statistical Grammars

Ali Basirat
NLP Lab, School of ECE,
College of Engineering,
University of Tehran, Tehran, Iran
a.basirat@srbiau.ac.ir

Heshaam Faili
NLP Lab, School of ECE,
College of Engineering,
University of Tehran, Tehran, Iran
hfaili@ut.ac.ir

Abstract

This paper discusses two Hidden Markov Models (HMM) for linking linguistically motivated XTAG grammar and the automatically extracted LTAG used by MICA parser. The former grammar is a detailed LTAG enriched with feature structures. And the latter one is a huge size LTAG that due to its statistical nature is well suited to be used in statistical approaches. Lack of an efficient parser and sparseness in the supertags set are the main obstacles in using XTAG and MICA grammars respectively. The models were trained by the standard HMM training algorithm, Baum-Welch. To converge the training algorithm to a better local optimum, the initial state of the models also were estimated using two semi-supervised EM-based algorithms. The resulting accuracy of the model (about 91%) shows that the models can provide a satisfactory way for linking these grammars to share their capabilities together.

1 Introduction

Tree Adjoining-Grammar (TAG) is a tree generating system that forms the object language by the set of derived trees (Joshi and Schabez, 1991). This formalism as a Mildly Context Sensitive Grammar is supposed to be powerful enough to model the natural languages (Joshi, 1985).

In the lexicalized case (LTAG), each lexical item of the object language is associated with at least one elementary structure of the grammar called *elementary tree*. Each elementary tree in LTAGs can be considered as a complex description of its anchor that provides a domain of locality over which the anchor can specify syntactic and semantic constraints(Bangalore and Joshi, 1999). Extended domain of locality and factoring of recursion from the domain of dependency are the main key properties of using these grammars (Bangalore and Joshi, 1999).

There are two ways for creating the set of elementary trees (Faili and Basirat, 2010). The first method is the manual crafting of the elementary trees as it was done in the XTAG project (XTAG-Group, 2001). And the alternate one is the automatically extraction of them from some annotated treebanks as it was done in (Xia, 2001; Chen, 2001). The result of the former method is a detailed LTAG that is enriched with semantic representation but suffers from the lack of statistical information. The output of the latter one on the other hand, is a huge size LTAG that suffers from the sparseness problem in the elementary trees set but contains enough statistical information that make it suitable to be used in statistical approaches. The relatively huge size of the automatically extracted elementary trees set is an obstacle in annotating these structures with semantic representation (Chen, 2001).

One of the negative aspects of using LTAGs is their high computational complexity of parsing algorithm, ($O(n^6)$) (Kallmeyer, 2010). Regarding the work presented in (Sarkar, 2007), the factors that affect the parsing complexity of such lexicalized grammars are the number of trees selected by the words in the input sentence and the clausal complexity of the sentence to be parsed. The first factor, named *Syntactic Lexical Ambiguity*, directly addresses *Supertagging*, proposed by Bangalore and Joshi (1999).

Supertagging is a robust partial parsing approach that can be applied for increasing up the speed of LTAG parsing algorithm (Bangalore and Joshi, 1999). In supertagging the flexibility of linguistically motivated lexical descriptions are integrated with the robustness of statistical approaches. The idea is based on extending the notion of '*tag*' from the standard *Part Of Speech* to a tag that represents a rich and complex syntactic structure, called *Supertag*. In the lexicalized grammars like LTAGs each elementary structure of the grammar can be considered as a supertag. Supertagging itself is the task of assigning the supertags to each word of the processing sentence. *After* supertagging the only thing that the LTAG parser should do is to attach these selected supertags for creating a forest of derived/derivation trees.

Supertagging as a search problem can be modeled by two major methods, *generative model* and *classification approach* (Bangalore et al., 2005). In the former method the problem is modeled by a *Hidden Markov Model* and in the latter one it is modeled by the discriminant approaches like *SVM* and *Maximum Entropy Estimation*. Applying each of these methods in supertagging is subject to the availability of enough statistical information about the problem. Hence, due to their statistical nature, the automatically extracted LTAGs are more suitable to be used by supertagging algorithm than the manually crafted LTAGs. This characteristic of automatically extracted LTAGs caused the emergence of some powerful statistical parsers like MICA (Bangalore et al., 2009) that works based on the supertagging approach.

The lack of an efficient LTAG parser for manually crafted LTAGs beside the weakness of the automatically extracted LTAGs in representing semantic representation, encouraged us to rectify these deficiencies by making an interface between these grammars. The interface was established between individual elementary trees of each grammars such that any elementary tree of the source LTAG could be mapped onto an elementary tree of the target LTAG. The idea is similar to the *Hidden TAG Model* (Chiang and Rambow, 2006) that links many spoken dialects of a language to benefit from sharing rich resources. Here by relating two different perspectives of a natural language presented in the form of two LTAGs, we are going to share their capabilities together.

The interface was modeled as a sequence tagger that deals with the problem of how to map each supertag sequence of the source LTAG onto a supertag sequence of the target LTAG given the local and non-local information of the source sequence. An unsupervised sequence tagger based on *Hidden Markov Model* (HMM) was proposed that produces a target supertag sequence given a source supertag sequence. The sequence tagger was trained using the standard HMM training algorithm called *Baum-Welch*. Due to this fact that the algorithm convergence is tightly depending on the HMM initial state, the initial state of the HMM also was trained intellectually using an EM-Based semi-supervised bootstrapping algorithm. The solution was applied on the manually crafted English XTAG grammar (XTAG-Group, 2001) as target LTAG and the automatically extracted LTAG used by MICA parser (Bangalore et al., 2009) as source LTAG.

The significance of this work is as follow. First, as a solution for enhancing the parsing efficiency of the XTAG grammar, as it was done by Faili (2009). Second, as a fully automated method for bridging between grammars in order to share their capabilities together.

2 Related Work

Bridging between grammars in order to share their capabilities is considered by some researchers. Improving the parsing quality in the resource-poor languages (Chiang and Rambow, 2006), enriching automatically extracted LTAGs with semantic representation (Chen, 2001; Faili and Basirat, 2010; Faili and Basirat, 2011), increasing the syntactic coverage of lexicalized resources (Dang et al., 2000; Kipper et al., 2000), and finding the overlap between two grammars (Xia and Palmer, 2000) are considered as the most important reasons for performing this task.

In general, the proposed methods for performing such a task could be classified into two major categories. The first category consists of the methods that try to link the grammars using the structural similarities of the grammar's elements regardless of the syntactic environments that the elements may be placed. The approaches proposed in (Chen, 2001), (Xia and Palmer, 2000), and (Ryant and Kipper, 2004) are classified in this category.

The second one consists of the methods that try to make the connection regarding the statistical information of the syntactic environments where the grammar's elements appear on. Chiang and Rambow (2006) by introducing a novel concept, namely *hidden TAG model*, proposed a model analogous to a HMM for linking a resource-rich language to a resource-poor language. In

(Faili and Basirat, 2010; Faili and Basirat, 2011) also a statistical approach based on HMM for linking the automatically extracted LTAG from Penn Treebank (Chen, 2001) and English XTAG grammar (XTAG-Group, 2001) was proposed. Here by introducing two statistical models, we have closely followed the approach presented in (Faili and Basirat, 2011).

3 HMM-based LTAG mapping

The task of mapping a MICA elementary tree sequence onto an appropriate XTAG elementary tree sequence could be formulated as below:

> *Given a sequence of MICA elementary trees* $T = (t_1, \ldots, t_n)$ *assigned to sentence* $S = (w_1, \ldots, w_n)$ *by MICA, tag each element of T with an elementary tree* $t'_i \in$ *XTAG Grammar such that the likelihood of* $T' = (t'_1, \ldots, t'_n)$ *given T and S be maximized.*

This problem directly addresses a Hidden Markov Model (HMM) that relates a MICA elementary tree sequence as an observation sequence to the most probable XTAG elementary tree sequence as a hidden state path. Given such a model, the *Viterbi* algorithm can be used for finding the most probable hidden state path that generates the observation sequence. The rest of this part deals with the problem modeling using HMM.

3.1 Problem Modeling Using HMM

Regarding the existence gap between XTAG and MICA grammars (Chen, 2001), two possible mapping models were proposed. The M-1 model simply ignores this gap. It assumes every syntactic structure in the MICA grammar has at least one corresponding element in the XTAG grammar. In this case, each hidden state is exactly corresponded to a XTAG elementary tree. The MICA supertags also are considered as the observation symbols. Given any XTAG elementary tree t'_i and t'_j, the state transition matrix ($A = [a_{i,j}]$) contains the probability of seeing t'_j after t'_i in a sequence of XTAG elementary trees. For each MICA elementary tree t_j and XTAG elementary tree t'_i the observation probability matrix ($B = [b_{i,j}]$) also contains the probability $P(t_j|t'_i)$.

On the other hand, the alternate model, M-2, tries to model the relation between the grammars with respect to the existence gap between them. In this model it is assumed that there are some syntactic structures in the MICA grammar that are not supported by the XTAG grammar. The main difference between M-1 and M-2 is in their hidden states. In addition to the hidden states used in M-1, a new symbolic state, namely *UNKNOWN*, is added to the M-2 hidden states set. This new state is the representative of all syntactic structures that are modeled by MICA grammar but not by XTAG grammar.

3.2 Training

Both of the M-1 and M-2 models were trained by the Baum-Welch algorithm. As the other HMM training algorithm, Baum-Welch algorithm also cannot find the global optimum of the search space. This weakness is inherited from the HMM in which does not provide any clear solution to use any extra information of the problem. In this case, the initial state of the training algorithm provides a way to use a part of environment's knowledge that can largely cover the mentioned weakness (Rabiner, 1989).

To lead the training algorithm to a better solution two methods was peoposed for estimating the initial state of the models. Next part, introduces these algorithms.

3.3 Initialization

The initial state of the models has been trained using two novel semi-supervised EM-based training algorithms. The algorithms work based on the available set of MICA and XTAG elementary tree sequences achieved from parsing a set of English sentences namely *Initialization Data Base (IDB)*.

In the M-1 model, IDB must be selected so that all of its sentences can be modeled in both of XTAG and MICA grammars. This constraint is due to the M-1 assumption about the problem.

In M-2 the only constraint over the IDB sentences is that the sentences must be modeled in the MICA's grammar. In this case, IDB can be partitioned into two parts. The sentences that can be modeled by XTAG grammar, *Parsable Initialization dataset (PI)*, and the sentences that cannot be modeled by the XTAG grammar, *NotParsable Initialization dataset (NPI)*. The partitioning enables the model to consider the existence gap between the grammars.

3.3.1 Initializing M-1

Let C and C' be two sets of elementary tree sequences achieved from parsing IDB using MICA and XTAG parsers, respectively. Due to the statistical nature of MICA parser, for any sentence $S_i \in$ IDB, C contains a set of scored elementary tree sequences. Nevertheless, C' contains an ambiguity set of elementary tree sequences without any clear way to disambiguate it.

Given C and C', the simplest and most intuitive way for estimating the initial values of the HMM is MLE. Nevertheless, performing this application is subject to disambiguating the output of the XTAG parser stored in C'. This problem addresses a function that assigns a real value to each member of C' as shown in eq. 1.

$$\omega : C' \rightarrow \mathbb{R} \tag{1}$$

Given such a weighting function ω, the probability of transition $(S_i \rightarrow S_j)$ in hidden states can be estimated by taking weighted count from all bigrams (S_i, S_j) in C' and normalizing by the sum of all bigrams (S_i, S_k) that share the same first elements. A similar method also can be used for computing the probabilities presented in the observation matrix (B) and Π.

Given $C" = \omega(C')$ and C, we define function Λ for generating the HMM λ using the aforementioned MLE (eq. 2).

$$\Lambda : C" \times C \rightarrow \lambda \tag{2}$$

The main problem here is to find an appropriate function ω. Function ω was estimated using a semi-supervised EM-based method. The algorithm takes the C and C' as input and attempts to estimate some values for function ω such that the objective function $\mathfrak{I}$ presented in eq. 3 is being maximized. Function $\mathfrak{I}$ shows the likelihood of observing C given the HMM λ achieved by Λ.

$$\mathfrak{I} = P(C|\lambda = \Lambda(C", C)) \tag{3}$$

In the EM formulation, the E-step was defined as the computing the value of λ using Λ. In M-step the algorithm attempts to update the ω regarding the earlier model resulted from E-step. Eq. 4 shows how to estimate the value of ω for a XTAG elementary tree sequences $T' \in C'$. In this equation, ξ shows the set of XTAG elementary tree sequences in C' that are generated from the sentence S, the generator of T'. $T_i \in C$ also represents the *ith* MICA elementary tree sequence in ξ. The index n shows the total number of sequences in C generated from S ($|\xi|$).

$$\omega(T') = \frac{\sum_{i=1}^{n} P(T_i)P(T_i, T'|\lambda)}{|\xi|} \tag{4}$$

3.3.2 Initializing M-2

In this part also for the sake of simplicity, C_{MP}, C_{XP} and C_{MNP} are used as the supertagging result of *PI* in MICA grammar, *PI* in XTAG grammar, and *NPI* in MICA grammar, respectively. Unlike the M-1 that uses all of the MICA elementary tree sequences resulted from parsing a sentence in IDB, here only the most probable MICA elementary tree sequence was used. So, related to each sentence in PI and NPI, we have a single MICA elementary tree sequence in C_{MP} and C_{MNP} respectively.

In this model, in addition to computing ω, applying MLE is subject to generating the set of elementary tree sequences for the sentences in dataset *NPI*. We name this set of elementary tree sequences C_{XNP}. Each sequence in C_{XNP} consists of XTAG elementary trees and have to contain at least one *UNKNOWN* symbol regarding this fact that NPI contains the sentences that couldn't be modeled in XTAG grammars. Given the paired sets (C_{MNP}, C_{XNP}) and (C_{MP}, C_{XP}) and an appropriate weighting function ω as shown in eq. 5, the initial values of HMM can be estimated using the mentioned MLE method.

$$\omega : C_{XNP} \cup C_{XP} \rightarrow \mathbb{R} \tag{5}$$

The ω was estimated using a *semi-supervised boot strapping EM-based* algorithm. Like the initialization algorithm proposed in sec. 3.3.1, this algorithm also has an iterative nature that tries to estimate some values for ω (hence for HMM parameters) in a greedy manner. The objective function in this phase is to maximize the likelihood of observing MICA supertag sequences in $C_{MNP} \cup C_{MP}$ (eq. 6). In the heart of the algorithm, the C_{XNP} is bootstrapped by applying a customized version of Viterbi algorithm on the C_{MNP} using the earlier value of HMM.

$$\mathfrak{I} = P(C_{MP} \cup C_{MNP} \mid \lambda) \tag{6}$$

The algorithm consists of four main stages as below:

1. *Pre Initializing*: Initializing the HMM parameters with out considering UNKNOWN hidden state.

2. *Bootstrapping*: Bootstrapping C_{XNP} by annotating C_{MNP} with hidden states labels.

3. *Updating*: Estimating the new value of HMM using Maximum Likelihood Estimation (MLE) on the paired sequences (C_{MNP}, C_{XNP}) and (C_{MP}, C_{XP})

4. *Termination*: Until the termination criterion is not satisfied go to step 2.

In the rest of this part we will express each phase in detail.

Pre Initializing: In this step, it tries to estimate the HMM parameters from the related sequences in (C_{MP}, C_{XP}) using the MLE. Applying the MLE over these sets gives some approximations about the probabilities presented in the HMM parameters except the probabilities related to UNKNOWN hidden state. The weighting function used in this phase gives a uniform distribution of probability to each member of C_{MP} that are generated from same sentence.

The probabilities related to UNKNOWN hidden states also could be estimated using some heuristics over the existence gap between the grammars. For instance, the amount of uncertainty involved in the HMM parameters resulted by the MLE is a criterion for estimating the probabilities related to the UNKNOWN.

Bootstrapping: In this phase it tries to annotate each MICA supertag sequence in C_{MNP} with a set of hidden state paths given the earlier value of HMM. To do this, a modified version of Viterbi algorithm, namely *Forced Viterbi*, was used. The algorithm looks for the hidden state paths that have the highest consistency with the earlier HMM and pass through UNKNOWN hidden state.

Before applying Forced Viterbi over C_{MNP}, we need some assumptions about the source elementary trees that are more likely to be corresponded to UNKNOWN. A simple solution for making such assumption is feasible via taking a differential between C_{MNP} and C_{MP}, and looking for the n-grams in the former that are not presented in the latter. The result of this process is a set of n-grams of MICA elementary trees, namely *Gap-set*, that their related n-gram in the original sentence couldn't be modeled in the XTAG grammar. For any n-gram in Gap-Set that is observed in a MICA elementary tree sequence member of C_{MNP}, by considering all conditions that the UNKNOWN can be assigned to the elementary trees of the observed n-gram, the Forced Viterbi algorithm will generate 2^n XTAG elementary tree sequences.

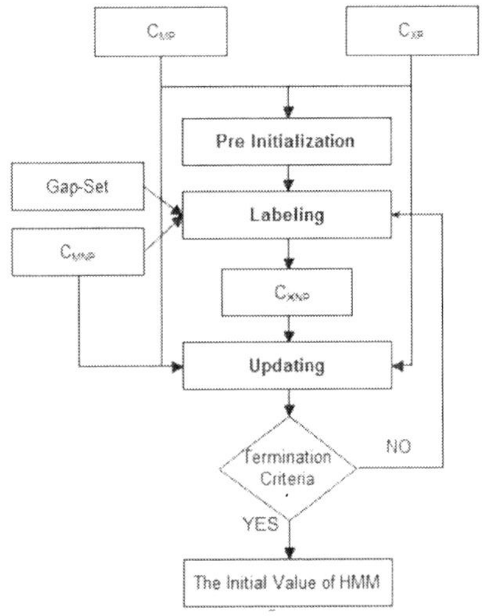

Figure 1: The HMM Initialization algorithm used in M-2

Updating: In this step, the HMM parameters will be updated regarding the paired sets (C_{MNP}, C_{XNP}) and (C_{MP}, C_{XP}). Having these paired sets and a scoring function ω, the HMM parameters can be updated using the mentioned MLE method.

For each XTAG elementary tree sequence $T' \in C_{XP} \cup C_{XNP}$ and its related MICA elementary tree sequence $T_i \in C_{MP} \cup C_{MNP}$, the scoring function ω can be defined as shown in eq. 7. ξ in this equation refers to the set of XTAG elementary trees that are generated from the same sentence and $T' \in \xi$.

$$\omega(T') = \frac{P(T', T \mid \lambda)}{\mid \xi \mid} \tag{7}$$

Fig. 1 gives an outline over the HMM initialization algorithm. Observing same values for the probability presented in eq. 6 or exceeding the predefined maximum number of iterations are two candidates to be used as termination criteria.

4 Numerical Results

4.1 Experiments Description

To evaluate the accuracy of the proposed models, the models have been initialized and trained with three real world data sets including ATIS , IBM Manual and Wall Street Journal (WSJ) corpora. Some parts of these datasets were randomly selected and divided into three distinct sections as initialization dataset (IDB), training dataset (TRDB) and testing dataset (TSDB). Table 4.1

No. Sentences				
	IDB_{M-1}	IDB_{M-2}	TRDB	TSDB
ATIS	904	991	1280	18
IBM	3463	4473	9742	102
WSJ	11913	16871	21709	197
No. words				
ATIS	7726	9734	16917	209
IBM	32840	46833	154668	1547
WSJ	102355	155879	221337	2029

Table 1: Statistical information about initialization, training and testing datasets used in M-1 and M-2

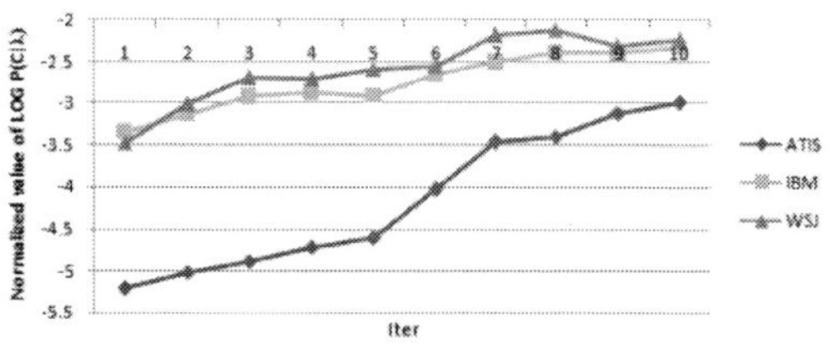

Figure 2: The values of the objective function presented in eq. 8 while initializing the M-1

shows some statistics about the datasets used in initialization, training and testing the models.

4.2 Initializing

The results of applying each of the initializing methods M-1 and M-2 over the IDBs are presented in figure 2 and 3 respectively. These figures show the value of Θ presented in eq. 8. 'O' in this equation refers to all MICA elementary tree sequences used in the algorithms. The observed progress in the likelihood of observing the MICA elementary tree sequences is an evidence on the successful of the algorithms.

$$\Theta = \frac{\sum_{T_i \in O} \log P(T_i \mid \lambda)}{\mid O \mid} \tag{8}$$

As these show, while the values resulted from M-2 are strictly ascending in a logarithmic manner, increasing in the values resulted from M-1 has no specific, predictable manner. It is due to the objective function shown in eq. 3 in which doesn't consider the score values of each MICA elementary tree sequences in C. In fact, related to any sentence in each IDB, C contains many scored MICA elementary tree sequences used in initializing algorithm but in the value of the objective function.

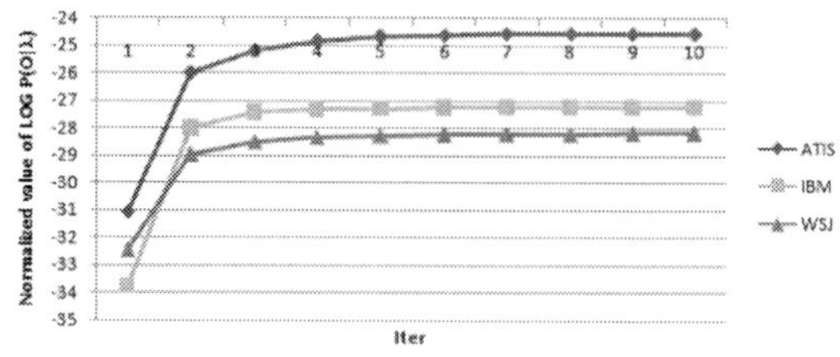

Figure 3: The values of the objective function presented in eq. 8 while initializing the M-2

	M-1	M-2	Base Line
ATIS	59.83%	80.00%	78.30%
IBM	79.55%	88.30%	88.70%
WSJ	87.75%	91.50%	88.96%

Table 2: The result of the tagging accuracy on the test sets

4.3 Models Evaluation

The models were evaluated in two ways, *tagging accuracy* and *parsed sequences*. The first criterion originally introduced in (Faili and Basirat, 2011), enables us to evaluate the models as XTAG supertaggers. The latter one also, provide a way to evaluate them when combining with a LTAG parser. In *parsed sequences* the main focus is on the number of resulted XTAG sequences that their constituents elementary trees can be attached to each other regarding the standard operations defined in TAG formalism, *Substitution* and *Adjunction*.

Due to the lack of a gold annotated corpus, the tagging accuracy has been done manually. Table 4.3 shows the result of the tagging accuracy over the mentioned test sets (TSDBs). The base line here is the result of tagging accuracy reported in (Faili and Basirat, 2011). As it can be seen, M-2 gives the best accuracy in comparison to the M-1 and the base line.

The result of the alternate criterion, parsed sentences, is given in table 4.3. As it shows, here also the M-2 gives a better response in compare to the M-1. An important point that should be noted is that, not all of the sentences in the test sets are covered by the XTAG grammar. In fact, our experiments showed that of all sentences in each of the ATIS-TSDB, IBM-TSDB, and WSJ-TSDB, all but 6%, 13% and 24% of them could be parsed by XTAG parser respectively.

	M-1	M-2
ATIS	5%	33%
IBM	12.74%	43.10%
WSJ	50.25%	57%

Table 3: Number of the parsed sentences

5 Conclusion

Two Hidden Markov Models (HMM) were proposed to make a bridge between the linguistic view of the English XTAG grammar and the statistical nature of the LTAG used by MICA parser (Bangalore et al., 2009). The models were trained by the standard HMM training algorithm, Baum-Welch. The initial state of the models also were estimated using two semi-supervised EM-based algorithms. The models can be used to combine the statistical approaches with the grammar engineering.

References

Srinivas Bangalore and Arvanid K. Joshi. 1999. Supertagging: An approach to almost parsing. *Computational Linguistics*, 25(2):237–266.

S. Bangalore, P. Haffner, and G. Emami. 2005. Factoring global inference by enriching local representations. Technical report, AT&T Labs - Reserach.

Srinivas Bangalore, P. Boulllier, A. Nasr, O. Rambow, and B. Sagot. 2009. Mica: A probabilistic dependency parser based on tree insertion grammar. *North American Chapter of the Association for Computational Linguistics (NAACL)*.

John Chen. 2001. *Toward Efficient Statistical Parsing Using Lexicalized Grammatical Information*. Ph.D. thesis, University of Delaware.

David Chiang and Owen Rambow. 2006. The hidden tag model: Synchronous grammars for parsing resource-poor languages. Proceedings of the 8th International Workshop on Tree Adjoining Grammar and Related Formalisms, July.

H. Dang, K. Kipper, and Martha Palmer. 2000. Integrating compositional semantic into a verb lexicon. In *In Proceedings of the Eighteenth International Conference on Computational Linguistic (COLING-2000)*.

Heshaam Faili and Ali Basirat. 2010. Augmenting the automated extracted tree adjoining grammars by semantic representation. In *6th IEEE International Conference on Natural Language Processing and Knowledge Engineering (IEEE NLP-KE'10)*, Beijing.

Heshaam Faili and Ali Basirat. 2011. An unsupervised approach for linking automatically extracted and manually crafted ltags. In *12th International conference on Intelligent Text Processing and Computational Linguistics (CICLing-2011)*, Tokyo, February.

Heshaam Faili. 2009. From partial toward full parsing. In *Recent Advances In Natural Language Processing (RANLP)*.

Arvanid K. Joshi and Yves Schabez. 1991. Tree adjoining grammars and lexicalized grammars. Technical Report MS-CIS 91–22, Department of Computer & Information Science, University of Pennsylvania.

Arvanid K. Joshi. 1985. How much context-sensitivity is necessary for characterizing structural descriptions? *Natural Language Processing: Theoretical, Computational, and Psychological Perspectives*, pages 206–250. New York, NY: Cambridge University Press.

Laura Kallmeyer. 2010. *Parsing Beyond Context-Free Grammars*, volume 0 of *Cognitive Technologies*. Springer.

K. Kipper, H. Dang, and Martha Palmer. 2000. Class-based construction of verb lexicon. In *In Proceedings of Seventh nation Conference on Artificial Intelligence (AAAI-2000)*.

Lawrence R. Rabiner. 1989. A tutorial on hidden markov models and selected applications in speech recognition. *Proceedings of the IEEE*, 77(2):257–286.

Neville Ryant and Karin Kipper. 2004. Assigning xtag trees to verbnet. TAG+7: Seventh International Workshop on Tree Adjoining Grammar and Related Formalisms, May 20-22.

Anoop Sarkar. 2007. Combining supertagging and lexicalized tree-adjoining grammar parsing. In Srinivas Bangalore and Aravind Joshi, editors, Complexity of Lexical Descriptions and its Relevance to Natural Language Processing: A Supertagging Approach.

Fia Xia and Martha Palmer. 2000. Evaluating the coverage of ltags on annotated corpora. the Workshop on Using Evaluation within HLT Programs: Results and Trends, May 30.

Fia Xia. 2001. *Automatic grammar generation from two different perspectives*. Ph.D. thesis, University of Pennsylvania.

XTAG-Group. 2001. A lexicalized tree adjoining grammar for english. Technical Report IRCS 01–03, Institute for Research in Cognitive Science, University of Pennsylvania.

An Open Source Punjabi Resource Grammar

Shafqat Mumtaz Virk University of Gothenburg, Sweden virk@chalmers.se

Muhammad Humayoun University of Savoie, France humayoun@gmail.com

Aarne Ranta University of Gothenburg, Sweden aarne@chalmers.se

Abstract

We describe an open source computational grammar for Punjabi; a resource-poor language. The grammar is developed in GF (Grammatical framework), which is a tool for multilingual grammar formalism. First, we explore different syntactic features of Punjabi and then we implement them in accordance with GF grammar requirements, to make Punjabi the 17th language in the GF resource grammar library.

1. Introduction

Grammatical Framework (Ranta, 2004) is a special-purpose programming language for multilingual grammar applications. It can be used to write multilingual *resource* or *application* grammars (two types of grammars in GF).

Multilingualism of the GF grammars is based on the principle that same grammatical categories (e.g. noun phrases and verb phrases) and syntax rules (e.g. predication) can appear in different languages (Ranta, 2009a). A collection of all such categories and rules, which are independent of any language, makes the abstract syntax of GF grammars (every GF grammar has two levels: abstract and concrete). More precisely, the abstract syntax defines semantic conditions to form abstract syntax trees. For example the rule that a common noun can be modified by an adjective is independent of any language and hence is defined in the abstract syntax, e.g.:

```
Very big blue house
fun[1] AdjCN : AP → CN → CN ;
```

However, the way this rule is implemented may vary from one language to another; as each language may have different word order and/or agreement rules. For this purpose, we have the concrete syntax, which is a set of linguistic objects (strings, inflection tables, records) providing rendering and parsing. We may have multiple parallel concrete syntaxes for one abstract syntax, which makes the GF grammars multilingual. Also, as each concrete syntax is independent from others, it becomes possible to model the rules accordingly (i.e. word order, word forms and agreement features are chosen according to language requirements).

Current state-of-the-art machine translation systems such as Systran, Google Translate, etc. provide huge coverage but sacrifice precision and accuracy of translations. On the contrary, domain-specific or controlled multilingual grammar based translation systems can provide a higher translation quality, on the expense of limited coverage. In GF, such controlled grammars are called *application grammars.*

Writing application grammars from scratch can be very expensive in terms of time, effort, expertise and money. GF provides a library called the *GF resource library* that can ease this task. It is a collection of linguistic oriented but general-purpose *resource grammars,* which try to cover the general aspects of different languages (Ranta, 2009a).

Instead of writing application grammars from scratch for different domains, one may use resource grammars as libraries (Ranta, 2009b)[2]. This method enables to create the application grammar much faster with a very limited linguistic knowledge.

The number of languages covered by GF resource library is growing (17 including Punjabi). Previously, GF and/or its libraries have been used to develop a number of multilingual as well as monolingual domain-

[1] In GF code, `cat` and `fun` belong to abstract syntax. On the contrary, `lincat` and `lin` belong to concrete syntax.

[2] This idea is influenced by programming language API tradition in which, a standard general-purpose library is supported by the language. It is then used by programmers to write specific applications.

specific application grammars (see GF homepage [3] for details on these application grammars).

In this paper, we describe the resource grammar development for Punjabi. Punjabi is an Indo-Aryan language widely spoken in Punjab regions of Pakistan and India. Punjabi is among one of the morphologically rich languages (others include Urdu, Hindi, Finish, etc) with SOV word order, partial ergative behavior, and verb compounding. In Pakistan it is written in *Shahmukhi,* and in India, it is written in *Gurmukhi* script (Humayoun, 2010). Language resources for Punjabi are very limited (especially for the one spoken in Pakistan). With the best of our knowledge this work is the first attempt of implementing a computational Punjabi grammar as open-source software, covering a fair enough part of Punjabi morphology and syntax.

2. Morphology

Every grammar in GF resource grammar library has a test lexicon, which is built through the lexical functions called the lexical paradigms; see (Bringert et el, 2011) for synopsis. These paradigms take lemma of a word and make finite inflection tables, containing different forms of the word, according to the lexical rules of that particular language. A suite of Punjabi resources including morphology and a big lexicon are reported by (Humayoun and Ranta, 2010). With minor required adjustments, we have reused morphology and a subset of that lexicon, as a test lexicon of about 450 words for our grammar implementation. However, the morphological details are beyond the scope of this paper and we refer to (Humayoun and Ranta, 2010) for more details on Punjabi morphology.

3. Syntax

While morphology is about types and formation of individual words (lexical categories), it is the syntax, which decides how these words are grouped together to make well-formed sentences. For this purpose, individual words, which belong to different lexical categories, are converted into richer syntactic categories, i.e. noun phrases (NP), verb phrases (VP), and adjectival phrases (AP), etc. With this up-cast the linguistic features such as word-forms, number & gender information, and agreements, etc, travel from individual words to the richer categories.

In this section, we explain this conversion from lexical to syntactic categories and afterwards, we demonstrate how to glue the individual pieces to make clauses. These are then can be used to make well-formed sentences in Punjabi. The following subsections explain various types of phrases.

3.1. Noun Phrases

A noun phrase (`NP`) is a single word or a group of words that does not have a subject and a predicate of its own, and does the work of a noun (Verma, 1974). Now we show the structure of noun phrase in our implementation, followed by the description of its different parts.

Structure: In GF, we represent the `NP` as a record with three fields, labeled as: 's' , 'a' and 'isPron':

```
NP: Type={s        : NPCase => Str ;
          a        : Agr  ;
          isPron   : Bool } ;
```

The label 's' is an inflection table from `NPCase` to string (`NPCase => Str`). `NPCase` has two constructs (`NPC Case`, and `NPErg`) as shown below:

```
NPCase = NPC Case | NPErg ;
Case   = Dir | Obl | Voc | Abl ;
```

The construct (`NPC Case`) stores the lexical cases (i.e. Direct, Oblique, Vocative and Ablative) of a noun[4]. As an example consider the following table for the noun "boy":

s	.NPC Dir	=>	mʊnɖɑ:	مُنڈا
s	.NPC Obl	=>	mʊnɖɛ	مُنڈے
s	.NPC Voc	=>	mʊnɖi:a	مُنڈیا
s	.NPC Abl	=>	mʊnɖɛo:ɳ	مُنڈیوں

Other than storing the lexical cases of a noun as shown in the above table, we also construct the ergative case (i.e. `NPErg` in the code above). We do it at the noun phrase level for the

[3] http://www.grammaticalframework.org/

[4] Punjabi nouns have four lexical cases.

following reason: In Urdu, the case markers that follow the nouns in the form of post-positions cannot be handled at lexical level through morphological suffixes and thus need to be handled at syntax level (Butt and King, 2002)[5]. It also applies to Punjabi. So we construct the ergative case of a noun by attaching ergative case marker 'nɛ' to the oblique case of the noun at `NP` level. For instance, the ergative form of our running example "boy" is:

```
s.NPErg => mʊnɖɛ nɛ_Erg منڈے نے
```

It is used for the subjects of perfective transitive verbs (see Section 3.5 for more details).

The label 'a' represents the agreement feature (`Agr`) and stores information about gender, number and person that will be used for agreement with other constituents. It is defined as follows:

```
Agr     = Ag Gender Number Person ;
```

In Punjabi, the gender can be *masculine* or *feminine*; number can be *singular* and *plural*; and person can be first, second casual, second with respect and third person near & far. These are defined as shown below:

```
Gender  =  Masc | Fem ;
Number  =  Sg | Pl ;
Person  =  Pers1 | Pers2_Casual |
           Pers2_Respect |
           Pers3_Near | Pers3_Far
```

Finally, the label '`isPron`' is a Boolean parameter, which shows whether `NP` is constructed from a pronoun. This information is important when dealing with the exceptions in ergative behavior of verbs for the first and second person pronouns in Punjabi. For example consider the following constructions:

mi:ɳ_I ro:ʈi:_bread kʰadi:_ate
میں روٹی کھادی
`I ate bread.`
tu:ɳ_you ru:ʈi:_bread kʰaɖi:_ate
توں روٹی کھادی
`You ate bread.`
au:nɛ:_He ru:ʈi:_bread kʰadi:_ate
اونے روٹی کھادی
`He ate bread.`

mʊnɖɛ:_boy nɛ:_ErgMarker ru:ʈi:_bread kʰadi:_ate
مُنڈے نے روٹی کھادی
`The boy ate bread.`

From the above examples, we can see that, when we have the first or second person pronoun as subject, the ergative case marker is not used (first two examples). On the contrary, it is used in all other cases. So for our running example, i.e. the noun (boy, mʊnɖa:), the label '`isPron`' is false.

Construction: First, the lexical category noun (N) is converted to an intermediate category, common noun (`CN`) through the `UseN` function.

```
fun UseN : N → CN ;       -- mʊnɖa:, boy
```

`CN` is a syntactic category, which is used to deal with the modifications of nouns by adjectives, determiners, etc. Then, the common noun is converted to the syntactic category, noun phrase (`NP`). Three main types of noun phrases are: (1) common nouns with determiners, (2) proper names, and (3) pronouns. We build these noun phrases through different noun phrase construction functions depending on the constituents of `NP`. As an example consider (1). We define it with a function DetCN given below:

```
Every boy, hər_every mʊnɖa: _boy
fun DetCN : Det → CN → NP ;
```

Here (`Det`) is a lexical category representing determiners. The above given function takes the determiner (`Det`) and the common noun (`CN`) as parameters and builds the `NP`, by combining appropriate forms of the determiner and the common noun agreeing with each other. For example if 'every' and 'boy' are the parameters for the above given function the result will be a `NP`: every boy, *hər mʊnɖa:*. Consider the linearization of `DetCN`:

```
lin DetCN det cn = {
 s=\\c => detcn2NP det cn c det.n;
 a = agrP3 cn.gdet.n ;
 isPron = False } ;
```

As we know from the structure of `NP` (given in the beginning of §3.1) 's' represents the inflection table used to store different forms of `NP` built by the following line from the above code:

```
s = \\c => detcn2NP det cn c det.n;
```

[5]This also explains the reason for `NPErg` to be separate from "`NPC Case`".

Notice that the operator ('\\') is used as shorthand to represent different rows of the inflection table 's'. An alternative but a verbose code segment for the above line will be:

```
s = table {
NPC Dir=>detcn2NP det cn Dir det.n;
NPC Obl=>detcn2NP det cn Obl det.n;
NPC Voc=>detcn2NP det cn Voc det.n;
NPC Abl=>detcn2NP det cn Abl det.n}
```

Where the helper function `detcn2NP` is defined as:

```
detcn2NP : Determiner → CN → NPCase
→ Number → Str =
\dt,cn,npc,n → case npc of {
  NPC c => dt.s  ++ cn.s!n!c ;
  NPErg => dt.s++cn.s!n!Obl++"nɛ"};
```

Also notice that the selection operator (the exclamation sign `!`) is used to select appropriate forms from the inflection tables (i.e. `cn.s!n!c`, which means the form of the common noun with number 'n' and case 'c' from the inflection table `cn.s`).

Other main types of noun phrases (2) and (3) are constructed through the following functions.

```
fun UsePN   : PN → NP ;   Ali, ali:
fun UsePron : Pron → NP ; he, ae:h
```

This covers only three main types of noun phrases, but there are other types of noun phrases as well, i.e. adverbial post-modified `NP`, adjectival modified common nouns etc. In order to cover them we have one function for each such construction. Few of these are given below; for full details we refer to (Bringert et el, 2011).

Paris today, $aj_{\_today}\ pi{:}ras_{\_Paris}$

```
fun AdvNP : NP → Adv → NP ;
```

Big house, $\upsilon adda{:}_{\_big}\ g^{h}\partial r_{\_house}$

```
fun AdjCN : AP → CN  → CN ;
```

3.2. Verb Phrases

A verb phrase (`VP`), as a syntactic category, is the most complex structure in our constructions. It carries the main verb and auxiliaries (such as adverb, object of the verb, type of the verb, agreement information, etc), which are then used in the construction of other categories and/or clauses.

Structure: In GF, we represent a verb phrase as a record, as shown below:

```
VPH : Type = {
    s:VPHForm => {fin, inf : Str};
    obj : {s : Str ; a : Agr} ;
    subj: VType ;
    comp: Agr =>Str;
    ad  : Str ;
    embComp : Str} ;
```

The label 's' represents an inflection table which keeps a record with two string values, i.e. `{fin, inf : Str}` for every value of `VPHForm`, which is defined as shown below:

```
VPHForm =
  VPTense VPPTense Agr|VPInf|VPStem ;
VPPTense=
  PPres|VPPast|VPFutr|VPPerf;
```

The structure of `VPHForm` makes sure that we preserve all inflectional forms of the verb. In it we have three cases: (1) Inflectional forms inflecting for tense (`VPPTense`) and number, gender, person with `Agr` defined on page 3. (2) The second constructor (`VPInf`) carries the infinitive form. (3) On the contrary, `VPStem` carries the root form. The reason for separating these three cases is that they cannot occur at the same time.

The label '`inf`' stores the required form of the verb in that corresponding tense, whereas 'fin' stores the copula (auxiliary verb).

The label '`obj`' on the other hand, stores the object of the verb and also the agreement information of the object. The label '`subj`' stores information about transitivity of the verb with `VType`, which include: intransitive, transitive or di-transitive:

```
VType = VIntrans|VTrans|VDiTrans ;
```

The label '`comp`' stores the complement of the verb. Notice that it also inflects in number, gender and person (with `Agr` defined on page 3), whereas the label '`ad`' stores the adverb.

Finally, '`embComp`' stores the embedded complement. It is used to deal with exceptions in the word order of Punjabi when making a clause. For instance, if a sentence or a question sentence is a complement of the verb then it takes a different position in the clause; i.e. it comes at very end of the clause as shown in the example with bold-face:

$oo_{\_she}$ $kehendi_{\_say}$ $ai_{\_Aux}$ $keh_{\_that}$ $main_{\_I}$ $roti_{\_bread}$ $khanda_{\_eat}$ $waN_{\_Aux}$

She says that I (masculine) eat bread.

On the contrary, if an adverb is used as a complement of verb then it comes before the main verb, as shown in the following example:

oo$_{\_she}$ *kehendi*$_{\_say}$ *ai*$_{\_Aux}$ *keh*$_{\_that}$ *oo*$_{\_she}$ *tez*$_{\_briskly}$ *chaldi*$_{\_walks}$ *ai*$_{\_Aux}$

She says that she walks briskly

Construction: Lexical category verb (V) is converted to syntactic category verb phrase (VP) through different VP construction functions. The simplest is:

```
fun UseV : V → VP ;
lin  UseV v = predV v ;
```

The function predV converts the lexical category V to the syntactic category VP:

```
predV : Verb → VPH = \verb -> {
s = \\vh => case vh of {
  VPTense VPPres (Ag g n p) => {
     fin =copula CPresent n p g;
     inf =verb.s!VF Imperf p n g} ;
  VPTense VPPast (Ag g n p) => {
   fin = [] ;
   inf =verb.s!VF Perf p n g};
  VPTense VPFutr (Ag g n p) => {
   fin = copula CFuture n p g ;
   inf =  verb.s ! VF Subj p n g };
  VPTense VPPerf (Ag g n p) => {
    fin = [] ;
    inf = verb.s!Root ++ cka g n} ;
  VPStem => { fin = [] ;
      inf =  verb.s ! Root };
  _ => {fin = [] ;
        inf = verb.s!Root}};
 obj = {s = [] ; a = defaultAgr} ;
 vType = VIntrans ; ad   = [] ;
 embComp = [] ; comp = \\_ => []};
```

The lexical category V has three forms (corresponding to perfective/imperfective aspects and subjunctive mood). These forms are then used to make four forms (VPPres, VPPast, VPFutr, VPPerf in the above code) at the VP level, which are used to cover different combinations of tense, aspect and mood of Punjabi at clause level.

As an example, consider the explanation of the above code in bold-face. It builds a part of the inflection table represented by 's' for VPPres and all possible combination of gender, number and person (Ag g n p). As shown above, the imperfective form of lexical category V (VF Imperf p n g) is used to make present tense at VP-level. The main verb is stored in the field labeled as 'inf' and the corresponding auxiliary verb (copula) is stored in the label 'fin'.

All other parts of VP are initialized to default or empty values in the above code. These parts will be used to enrich the VP with other constituents, e.g. adverb, complement etc. This is done in other VP construction functions including but not limited to:

Want to run, duɽna$_{\_run}$ *tʃahna*$_{\_want}$

```
ComplVV : VV → VP → VP;
```

Sleep here, ai:t̪ʰe:$_{\_here}$ *suna*$_{\_sleep}$

```
AdvVP         : VP → Adv → VP;
```

3.3. Adjectival Phrases

At morphological level, Punjabi adjectives inflect in number, gender and case (Humayoun and Ranta, 2010). At syntax level, they agree with the noun they modify using the agreement information of the NP. Adjectival phrase (AP) can be constructed simply from the lexical category adjective (A) through the following function:

PositA : A → AP ;   (*Warm, gərəm*)

Or from other categories such as:

Warmer than I, mi:re:$_{\_I}$ to:ɳ$_{than}$ gərəm$_{_warm}$

```
ComparA : A  → NP → AP ;
```

3.4. Adverbs and Closed Classes

The construction of Punjabi adverbs is very simple because "they are normally unmarked and don't inflect" (Humayoun and Ranta, 2010). We have different construction functions for Adverbs and other closed classes both at lexical and syntactical level. For instance, consider the construction of adverbs with two functions (but not limited to):

Warmly, gərəm dʒuxi:

```
fun PositAdvAdj : A → Adv ;
```

Very quickly, boht$_{\_very}$ *ti:zi*$_{\_quickly}$ *de nal*$_{\_coupla}$

```
fun AdAdv   : AdA → Adv → Adv ;
```

3.5. Clauses

While a phrase is a single word or group of words, which are grammatically linked to each other, a clause on the other hand, is a single phrase or group of phrases.

Different types of phrases (e.g. `NP`, `VP`, etc) are grouped together to make clauses[6]. Clauses are then used to make sentences. In GF tense system the difference between a clause and a sentence is: A clause has a variable tense while a sentence has a fixed tense.

We first construct clauses and then just fix their tense in order to make sentences. The most important construction of a clause is:

```
PredVP : NP → VP → Cl; -- Ali walks
```

The clause (Cl) has the following type:

```
Clause : Type =
   {s  :  VPHTense  =>  Polarity  =>
Order =>Str} ;
```

Where:

```
VPHTense = VPGenPres|VPImpPast
|VPFut|VPContPres|VPContPast
|VPContFut|VPPerfPres|VPPerfPast
|VPPerfFut|VPPerfPresCont|VPSubj
|VPPerfPastCon|VPPerfFutCont ;
Polarity = Pos | Neg
Order = ODir | OQuest
```

The tense system of GF resource library covers only eight combinations with four tenses (present, past, future and conditional) and two anteriorities (`Anter` and `Simul`). It does not cover the full tense system of Punjabi, which is structured around the aspect and the tense/mood.

We make sentences in twelve different tenses (`VPHTense` in the above given code) at clause level to get a maximum coverage of the Punjabi tense system. `Polarity` is used to construct positive and negative, while `Order` is used to construct direct and question clauses.

We ensure the SOV agreement by saving all needed features in `NP`. These are made accessible in the `PredVP` function.

A distinguishing feature of Punjabi SOV agreement is ergative behavior where transitive perfective verb may agree with the direct object instead of the subject. Ergativity is ensured by selecting the agreement features and noun-form accordingly. We demonstrate this in the following simplified code segment:

```
subj agr : NPCase * Agr =
case vt of {
VPImpPast  => case vp.subj of {
  VTrans     => <NPErg, vp.obj.a>;
  VDiTrans   => <NPErg, defaultAgr>;
  _            => <NPC Dir, np.a>}  ;
  _     => <NPC Dir, np.a>}
```

For perfective aspect (`VPImpPast`), if the verb is transitive then it agrees with the object and therefore the ergative case of `NP` is used (`VTrans` in the above code).

For `DiTransitive` (i.e. `VDiTrans` in the above code) the agreement is set to default but the ergative case is still needed.

In all other cases, specified with the wild card “_” above, the agreement is made with the subject (`np.a`), and we use the direct case (i.e. `NPC Dir`).

After selecting the appropriate forms of each constituent (according to the agreement features) they are grouped together to form the clause. For instance, consider the following simplified code segment combining different constituents of a Punjabi clause:

```
np.s!subj ++ vp.obj.s ++ vp.ad ++
vp.comp!np.a   ++ nahim ++ vps.inf
++ vps.fin ++ vp.embComp;
```

Where:

(1) `np.s!subj` is the subject; (2) `vp.obj.s` is the object (if any); (3) `vp.ad` is the adverb (if any); (4) `vp.comp!np.a` is verb's complement; (5) `nahim` is the negative clause constant; (6) `vps.inf` is the verb; (7) `vps.fin` is the auxiliary verb; (8) `vp.embComp` is an embedded complement.

4. Coverage and Limitations

The grammar we have developed consists of 40 categories and 190 syntax functions. It covers only a fair enough part of the language. The reason for this limitation is approach of the common abstract syntax defined for all the languages in the GF resource library. Indeed it is not possible to have an abstract syntax, which is common to, and covers all features of all languages. Consequently, the current grammar does not cover all aspects of Punjabi.

However, this does not put any limitation on the extension of a language resource. It can be extended by implementing language specific features as extra language-specific modules. However these features will not be accessible

[6] Verb phrases alone can also be used as clause some times.

through the common API, but can be accessed in the Punjabi application grammars.

5. Evaluation and Future Work

It is important to note that completeness is not the success criteria for this kind of grammar based resource but accuracy is (Ranta 2009b). Evaluating a resource grammar is just like evaluating a software library in general. However, this type of evaluation is different from evaluation of a natural language processing application in general, where testing is normally done against some corpus. To evaluate the accuracy, we use the Punjabi resource grammar to translate, and observe, a test suite of examples[7] from English to Punjabi and vice versa. We achieved an accuracy of 98.1%. The reason for not having 100% accuracy is that our current grammar does not cover all aspects of the language. One such aspect is compound verbs of Punjabi, formed by nouns and the auxiliary verb 'to be' (*hona:*). In this case, its gender must agree with the inherent gender of the noun. We have not yet covered this agreement for compound verbs and therefore, produce incorrect translations. An interesting (yet wrong) example would be:

bariʃ honda pe:a ae: (It is raining)

Instead of "hʊnda pi:a", it should be "hondi: pəi:"

Another such feature is the repetitive use of verb in Punjabi (e.g. mʊnɖa$_{_boy}$ ru:ndɛ:$_{\_weping}$ ru:ndɛ:$_{\_weping}$ su:ɳ$_{_slept}$ gi:a$_{_coupla}$, مُنڈا روندے روندے سوں گیا, the boy slept weeping). Coverage of such language specific details is one direction for the future work.

6. Related Work and Conclusion

In general language resources for Punjabi are very limited; especially for the one spoken in Pakistan and written in *Shahmukhi*. Furthermore, most of the applications related to Punjabi are designed only for the Punjabi, written and spoken in India; hence, only support the *Gurmukhi* script. A review of such applications is given in (Lehal, 2009).

There are some attempts to interchange between these scripts with transliteration systems. However, the current systems only seem to provide partial solutions, mainly because of the vocabulary differences (Humayoun and Ranta, 2010).

A transfer-based machine translation system reported in (Lehal, 2009) translates between Punjabi and Hindi only. On the contrary, the Punjabi resource grammar is based on Interlingua approach, which makes it possible to translate between seventeen languages in parallel. With the best of our knowledge this work is the first attempt to implement a computational Punjabi grammar as open source.

We have described the implementation of the computational grammar for Punjabi. It might be a useful resource, and may encourage other researchers to work in this direction.

As the resource grammar does not cover full features of Punjabi, although it is not possible to use it for parsing and translation of arbitrary text, it is best suited for building domain specific application grammars.

[7]See (Bringert et el, 2011) for this test suite of examples.

References

B. Bringert, T. Hallgren, A. Ranta. 2011. *GF Resource Grammar Library Synopsis*. www.grammaticalframework.org/lib/doc/synopsis.html.

M. Butt, H. Dyvik, T. H. King, H. Masuichi, C. Rohrer. 2002. *The Parallel Grammar Project*. In Proceedings of COLING-2002. Workshop on Grammar Engineering and Evaluation.

M. Humayoun and A. Ranta. 2010. *Developing Punjabi* Morphology, *Corpus and Lexicon*. The 24th Pacific Asia conference on Language, Information and Computation. pp: 163-172.

G. S. Lehal. 2009. *A Survey of the State of the Art in* Punjabi *Language Processing*, Language In India, Volume 9, No. 10, pp. 9-23.

A. Ranta. 2004. *Grammatical Framework: A Type*-Theoretical *Grammar Formalism*. Journal of Functional Programming, 14(2), pp. 145-189.

A. Ranta. 2009a. *Grammatical Framework: A Multilingual Grammar Formalism, Language and Linguistics Compass*, Vol. 3.

A. Ranta. 2009b. *Grammars as Software Libraries*. In Y. Bertot, G. Huet, J-J. Lévy, and G. Plotkin (eds.), *From Semantics to Computer Science*, Cambridge University Press, pp. 281-308.

M. K. Verma. 1974. *The Structure of the Noun Phrase in English and Hindi by Review* author(s): R. K. Barz, L. A. Schwarzschild Journal of the American Oriental Society, Vol. 94, No. 4, pp. 492-494.

Multi-Document Summarization by Capturing the Information Users are Interested in

Elena Lloret
University of Alicante
Apdo. de Correos 99
E-03080, Alicante, Spain
elloret@dlsi.ua.es

Laura Plaza
Universidad Complutense de Madrid
C/Prof. José García Santesmases, s/n
28040 Madrid, Spain
lplazam@fdi.ucm.es

Ahmet Aker
University of Sheffield
211 Portobello
Sheffield, S1 4DP, UK
a.aker@dcs.shef.ac.uk

Abstract

This paper proposes a method for automatically generating summaries taking into account the information in which users may be interested. Our approach relies on existing model summaries from tourist sites and captures from them the type of information humans use to describe places around the world. Relational patterns are first extracted and categorized by the type of information they encode. Then, we apply them to the collection of input documents to automatically extract the most relevant sentences and build the summaries. In order to evaluate the performance of our approach, we conduct two types of evaluation. On the one hand, we use ROUGE to assess the information contained in our summaries against existing human written summaries, whereas on the other hand, we carry out a human readability evaluation. Our results indicate that our approach achieves high performance both in ROUGE and manual evaluation.

1 Introduction

The amount of information currently available is growing at an exponential rate. Information presented in different formats (text, images, audio, video) needs to be carefully processed in order to allow users to manage it efficiently and effectively. Text summarization (TS) can provide many advantages to users, since TS systems are able to generate a brief summary of one or several documents by selection and/or generalization of what is important in the source (Spärck Jones, 2007).

However, TS is an especially challenging Natural Language Processing (NLP) task, since the generation of summaries depends on a wide range of issues, such as the summarization input, output or purpose. In particular, the type of text or domain we deal with is of great importance in TS, since each domain has its particular features, and they need to be treated accordingly. For instance, when summarizing newswire text, the reader is mainly concerned about the *who*, *what*, *when*, *where* and *why* of the fact reported in the news item; when summarizing a research paper, the reader is mostly interested in the *problem* being faced, the *method* proposed to solve it and the *results* achieved. Therefore, being capable of knowing what a user would like to read in a summary will allow the summaries to be biased towards such information. The order in which this information is shown in the source documents is also important (Barzilay et al., 2002), and thus this same order should be kept in the summary. Continuing with the newswire example, the information in news articles may be presented in chronological order, in a cause-effect manner, etc., so that this logical order ensures the coherence of the text.

In this paper, we suggest an approach to automatically generate extractive summaries from a set of documents. Our approach exploits the information in existing model summaries to capture what is salient regarding a certain document type or domain (in particular, documents describing tourist places such as a church, bridge, tower or a mountain). Then, this information is used to extract the most important sentences from the input documents. Moreover, our approach also takes into consideration the order in which the information is usually presented in the model summaries and reuse this information to order sentences in the automatic summary.

2 Related Work

A great number of techniques have been proven to be effective for generating summaries automatically. Such approaches include template creation (Oakes and Paice, 1999), statistical techniques (Teng et al., 2008; Lloret and Palomar, 2009), discourse analysis (Marcu, 1999; Teufel and Moens, 2002), graph-based methods (Mihalcea, 2004; Plaza et al., 2008), and machine learning algorithms (Fattah and Ren, 2008; Schilder and Kondadadi, 2008).

Moreover, new scenarios, such as the generation of summaries that can be used as image captions (Aker and Gaizauskas, 2009; Plaza et al., 2010; Aker and Gaizauskas, 2010a), have recently drawn special attention in recent years. In particular, this image caption generation task has been automatically approached by analyzing image-related text from the immediate context of the image, for instance, the surrounding text in HTML documents (Mori et al., 2000; Deschacht and Moens, 2007). In these approaches, named entities and other noun phrases in the image-related text are identified and assigned to the image as captions.

Similar to these approaches, our aim is to produce summaries capable of providing a brief description for an image of an object related to the tourist domain, for instance the *Eiffel Tower*. Instead of analyzing the text surrounding the image (which may be not available), we use documents obtained from the web using the place name as query. In order to achieve this goal, we rely on the corresponding human written descriptions or summaries to capture which information a user would be interested in when describing an object of the type shown in the image. This information is extracted in the form of dependency patterns, and next used for selecting from the web-documents the most suitable sentences to appear in the summary. To our knowledge, capturing the types of information people include in human summaries via dependency patterns, and applying them on the input documents to generate automated summaries has not been previously investigated.

3 Dependency Pattern Models

Knowing the types of information humans use to describe a specific topic can help automatic procedures to produce high quality summaries about that topic. Our topics are place or object names around the world, for instance Edinburgh Zoo (see Section 3.1). We use dependency relational patterns for capturing the types of information humans include when describing them. In Section 3.2 we describe the acquisition of these relational patterns and in Section 3.3 we highlight the strategy we followed to categorize those patterns by the type of information they encode.

3.1 Data

As corpus, we use the document's collection described in Aker and Gaizauskas (2010b). This collection contains 310 images with manually assigned place names. Each image has up to 4 model summaries (932 in total) which were created manually from the information in an online social site, *VirtualTourist.com*. The summaries contain a minimum of 190 and a maximum of 210 words and are expected to contain the type of information a user wants to know about an object.

Each image in the collection was associated to the top 30 web-documents that were gathered using the Yahoo! search engine[1] and the place names as queries. We use these web-documents to generate the automated image summaries/descriptions (see Section 4).

3.2 Dependency Patterns

The model summaries were used to learn models for capturing the types of information users include in descriptions of images. To construct them we adopted the dependency relational patterns extraction described by Aker and Gaizauskas (2010a). As a result, we build what we call a *Dependency Pattern Model (DpM)*. Our patterns are derived from dependency trees. The dependency trees are obtained using the Stanford parser.[2]

First, we pre-process each model summary by applying sentence splitting, named entity tagging[3] and replacing any occurrence of a string denoting the object type (e.g. *church, bridge*) by the term "OBJECTTYPE".[4] Next, we apply the Stanford parser to parse the sentences and extract patterns where each pattern is composed of a verb and two other words being in direct or indirect relation with the verb.

For illustration consider the sentence shown in Table 1. The first two rows of the table show the original sentence and its form after named entity tagging and replacing the string denoting the object type (*bridge*) with "OBJECTTYPE". The final two rows of the table show the output of the Stanford dependency parser and the relational patterns identified for this example. For each verb identified, we extracted two further words being

[1] http://search.yahoo.com/

[2] http://nlp.stanford.edu/software/lex-parser.shtml

[3] For performing shallow text analysis the OpenNLP tools (http://opennlp.sourceforge.net/) were used.

[4] There are in total 107 object types. This list is used as a lookup when processing the sentences.

Original sentence: The bridge was built in 1876 by W. W.	
Input to the parser: The OBJECTTYPE was built in DATE by W. W.	
Output of the parser: *det(OBJECTTYPE-2, The-1), nsubjpass(built-4, OBJECTTYPE-2), auxpass(built-4, was-3), prep-in(built-4, DATE-6), nn(W-10, W-8), agent(built-4, W-10)*	
Patterns: The OBJECTTYPE built, OBJECTTYPE was built, OBJECTTYPE built DATE, OBJECTTYPE built W, was built DATE, was built W	

Table 1: Example sentence for dependency pattern.

in direct or indirect relation to the current verb. Two words are directly related if they occur in the same relational term. The verb *built-4*, for instance, is directly related to *DATE-6* because they both are in the same relational term *prep-in (built-4, DATE-6)*. Two words are indirectly related if they occur in two different terms but are linked by a word that occurs in those two terms. The verb *was-3* is, for instance, indirectly related to *OBJECTTYPE-2* because they are both in different terms but linked with *built-4* that occurs in both terms. For instance, for the term *nsubjpass (built-4, OBJECTTYPE-2)* we use the verb *built* and extract patterns based on this. *OBJECTTYPE* is in direct relation to *built* and *The* is in indirect relation to *built* through *OBJECTTYPE*. So a pattern from these relations is *The OBJECTTYPE built*. The next pattern extracted from this term is *OBJECTTYPE was built*. This pattern is based on direct relations. The verb *built* is in direct relation to *OBJECTTYPE* and also to *was*. We continue this process until we cover all direct relations with *built* resulting in two more patterns (*OBJECTTYPE built DATE* and *OBJECTTYPE built W*).

3.3 Pattern Categorization

We next categorized the relational patterns by the type of information they encode. For doing this we first performed an analysis of the human written model summaries and recorded for each sentence the kind of information it contains about the object. Then, we manually categorized this information into the following categories:

- **type**: sentences containing the "type" information of the object such as *XXX* is a *bridge*.
- **year**: sentences containing information about, for instance, when the object was built, in case of mountains, for instance, when it was first climbed.
- **location**: sentences containing information about where the object is located.
- **background**: sentences containing some general information about the object (e.g., its history).
- **surrounding**: sentences containing information about what other objects are close to the main object.
- **visiting**: sentences containing information about, e.g., visiting times, prices, etc.

We then assigned each relational pattern to one of the above categories, provided the pattern occurred five or more times in the object type corpora. In total there were 800 relational patterns that satisfied this restriction. We used three people to assign these patterns to one of the categories described above. Finally, we selected those patterns in which the three humans agreed on the same category they should belong to (400 patterns in total).

4 Generating Summaries

The proposed approach for generating summaries takes as input the set of documents describing an image's location to be summarized and the query used to retrieve them. The summaries are created in a two step process: first, several features from the document sentences are extracted, and they are used to compute different scores for each sentence (Section 4.1). Second, the sentences are assigned to the categories their patterns are associated with and ranked according to their scores. This ranking is used to analyzed different strategies for building summaries, focusing on the type of information users may be more interested in (Section 4.2).

4.1 Feature Extraction and Sentence Scoring

In the first step of our summarization approach, we propose several features and functions for scoring sentences. Given the set of documents to summarize, we first obtain the dependency patterns for each sentence along with the frequency of these patterns in the model summaries (the so called *DpM*). This information is then used to build the two following vector representations for each sentence:

- ***Binary vector (BinVec):*** A vector of six positions, each position representing one of the pattern categories described in Section 3.3. Each position gets a binary score depending on whether or not a pattern from that category is found in the sentence.
- ***Frequency vector (FreqVec):*** Each category position is set to the number of pattern occurrences in the sentence belonging to that category.

For example, the sentence *"Karnak temple is the biggest temple in Egypt owing its monumental size to 1300 years of construction"* contains the patterns *[is the OBJECTTYPE, is biggest OBJECTTYPE, is OBJECTTYPE location]* as defined in the *DpM*. The two first patterns belong to the category "type", while the third one belongs to the "location" category. Thus, this sentence is represented by the binary vector *[1 0 1 0 0 0]* and the frequency vector *[2 0 1 0 0 0]*. We next extract the following features for scoring sentences:

- ***Pattern Frequency (PattFreq):*** is the sum of occurrence frequencies of dependency patterns in *DpM* detected also in the sentence *S*, as shown in Equation 1.

$$PattFreq(S) = \sum_{p \epsilon S} FreqDpM(p) \quad (1)$$

- ***Category Frequency (CatFreq):*** is computed by multiplying each category position in the frequency vector by the number of dependency patterns in the *DpM* belonging to that category and adding these partial results, as shown in Equation 2.

$$CatFreq(S) = \sum_{i=1}^{6} FreqVec(S,i) \times FreqDpM(Cat_i) \quad (2)$$

- ***Category Occurrence (CatOcc):*** is computed in a similar fashion to *CatFreq* but using the binary vector instead of the frequency vector, as shown in Equation 3.

$$CatFreq(S) = \sum_{i=1}^{6} BinVec(S,i) \times FreqDpM(Cat_i) \quad (3)$$

- ***Object Similarity (ObjSim):*** Sentence similarity to the object being described is derived from two further similarities: ***Query Similarity (QuerySim)*** and ***Object Type Similarity (ObjTypeSim)***. *QuerySim* is calculated as the normalized cosine similarity over the vector representation of the sentence and the query. *ObjTypeSim* is a binary value indicating the presence of the object type name (e.g., "temple", "church") in the sentence. We combine these two similarities so that if both are equal to '0', then *ObjSim* is set to '0'; if only one of these similarities is higher than '0', then *ObjSim* is set to the non-zero similarity value; otherwise, if both similarities are higher than '0', *ObjSim* is set to $QuerySim \times ObjTypeSim$.

Using the previous features, we compute three different scores for each sentence. We refer to these scores as ***Pattern Frequency Score (PattFreqScore)***, ***Category Frequency Score (CatFreqScore)*** and ***Category Occurrence Score (CatOccScore)***. To obtain these scores, we multiply, respectively, the sentence values for the *PattFreq*, *CatFreq* and *CatOcc* features by the *ObjSim* feature value.

4.2 Sentence Selection

The goal of this step is to select the most relevant sentences according to what users are interested in and ordering them to build the final summary. Since the dependency patterns are grouped into six different categories of information, we can select the sentences for the summary from these categories so that we ensure that the summary covers most relevant information while reducing redundancy. We first assign each sentence to the category its patterns are associated with. Since a sentence may contain patterns from more than one category, we test two strategies for assigning sentences to categories:

- The sentence is assigned to its most frequent category (as represented in its frequency vector). If several categories present the same frequency, then the sentence is assigned to all of them. We name this strategy the ***Most Frequent Category (MostFreqCat)***.
- The sentence is assigned to all categories for which a pattern has been found in it. We refer to this strategy as ***All Categories (AllCat)***.

Using these two strategies, we generate summaries by including the best scored sentence from the category "type", then "year", then "location", then "background", then "surrounding" and then "visiting". For the categories "background" and "visiting", respectively, the top three and two sentences are included. If the summary does not reach the desired summary length, we fill the summary with additional sentences from the "background" category. The reason why we fill in the summary with "background" sentences is that they provide general information about the topic, being useful when user are interesting in additional facts about the object to be summarized. Moreover, it is worth noting that we make sure not to add to the summary any sentence that is already part of it.

5 Evaluation

According to the two sentence selection strategies and the three scores computed for each sentence (Section 4), we generated 6 different types of 200-word summaries from the documents describing each image in the corpus. Table 2 shows two examples of summaries about the Vatican Museums. The one at the top is generated following the ***All Categories*** strategy for selecting sentences after computing the ***Category Frequency Score*** for each one, whereas the second one is an example of human made summary for the same object.

We next evaluated the automatic summaries both quantitatively and qualitatively.

5.1 Quantitative Evaluation

We use ROUGE (Lin, 2004) to assess the automatic summaries in comparison to the human written ones available in the image captioning corpus. ROUGE is a well-known evaluation method for summarization which is based on the common number of n-grams between a peer and one or several model summaries. The metrics taken into consideration for this evaluation are ROUGE-1 (R-1), ROUGE-2 (R-2) and ROUGE-SU4 (R-SU4). R-1 and R-2 compute the number of unigrams and bigrams, respectively, that coincide in the automatic and model summaries. R-SU4 measures the overlap of skip-bigrams between them allowing a skip distance of 4 words.

We first evaluate the automatic summaries in order to analyze which strategy and feature is capable of obtaining the best results. These results can be seen in Table 3. A paired t-test is used to account for the statistical significance of the results with a 95% confidence interval. Then, we select the best performing approach (***AllCat-CatFreqScore***) and we set up a comparative framework with current summarization approaches that have been tested on the same data. These results are shown in Table 4. In this framework, we establish an upper bound consisting of evaluating one human written summary against the remaining human written ones for the same place name. In addition, a semantic-graph based summarizer and a statistical-based one are also used for comparison because they have been successfully tested within the image captioning domain in previous research (Plaza et al., 2010).

Summarization Approach	R-1	R-2	R-SU4
AllCat-PattFreqScore	0.39960	0.09961	0.15463
AllCat-CatFreqScore	**0.40239**	**0.10045**	**0.15600**
AllCat-CatOccScore	0.40141	0.10041	0.15555
MostFreq-PattFreqScore	0.39982	0.09897	0.15371
MostFreq-CatFreqScore	0.40103	0.09976	0.15441
MostFreq-CatOccScore	0.39869	0.09742	0.15289

Table 3: ROUGE recall results for the summaries.

Summarization Approach	R-1	R-2	R-SU4
Human	0.42083	0.11191	0.16655
AllCat-CatFreqScore	0.40239	0.10045	0.15600
Semantic-graphs	0.37971	0.08950	0.14290
Statistical summarizer	0.35875	0.08551	0.13371

Table 4: Comparison of summarization approaches (automatic vs. human summaries).

5.2 Qualitative Evaluation

We also performed a manual readability assessment of a set of 50 randomly-selected summaries from our best approach (***AllCat-CatFreqScore***). We asked three people to evaluate the summaries according to the following criteria: grammaticality, redundancy, clarity, focus and coherence, following the evaluation guidelines in DUC conferences (Dang (2006)). Then, these values were mapped into a quantitative scale where the maximum value is 5 and the lowest is 1. The average scores for each criterion are shown in Table 5. For comparison we also show the readability scores for the human written summaries of the image descriptions reported in Aker and Gaizauskas (2010b).

Criterion	AllCat-CatFreqScore	Image Descriptions
Grammaticality	4.19	4.72
Redundancy	3.74	4.92
Clarity	4.41	4.90
Focus	3.81	4.88
Coherence	3.21	4.86

Table 5: Results for the readability evaluation.

AllCat-CatFreqScore summary: The Vatican Museums (Italian: Musei Vaticani), in Viale Vaticano in Rome, inside the Vatican City, are among the greatest museums in the world, since they display works from the immense collection built up by the Roman Catholic Church throughout the centuries. The building was used as a prison until 1870, but now houses a museum. It is easy to find located across the street from the entrance to the Vatican Museum and a short walk from St Peter&'s Basilica. The closest Metro stop to the museum entrance is Cipro-Musei Vaticani near Piazza Santa Maria delle Grazie, where there is also a parking garage. The most popular areas open to tourists are the Basilica of St. Peter and the Vatican Museums. This museum is named after Pope Pius VII (whose last name was Chiaramonti before his election as pope), who founded it in the early 1800s. [...]
Human written summary: Not everyone who visits the Vatican is aware that it is a sovereign state and has been since 1929. The Pope rules it as Europe's only absolute monarch! It includes St. Peter's Cathedral, The Vatican Gardens, The Vatican Museums, and the famed Sistine Chapel. All of these should be on your agenda for a visit, especially the Sistine Chapel. Go early because you will, no doubt, have to stand in line. The last person to enter is at 1:00 PM. So, it's better to see it first and then see the Cathedral. Michelangelo did the ceiling for Pope Julius II, and it shows the Creation of the World and The Fall of Man. It was restored in the 1980s. [...]

Table 2: Examples of an automatic and a model summary fragments.

5.3 Discussion

It can be seen from Table 3 that the best approach for automatically generating summaries is the one in which the score of a sentence is computed using the category frequency, and sentence selection involves considering all categories of information that the sentence includes (*AllCat-CatFreqScore*). This strategy obtains a recall value for R-1 of 0.40239. Moreover, this value is statistically significant with respect to the other approaches except for the *AllCat-CatOccScore*. Regarding R-2 and R-SU4, this approach also achieves the best results compared to the others but the results in these cases are not statistically significant, except for *MostFreqc-CatOccScore* for R-SU4.

Concerning the comparison with other systems, our approach significantly improves the results obtained by the semantic-graphs and statistical based summarizers for all ROUGE metrics.

On the other hand, it is important to stress upon the fact that the human written summaries were generated from external sources and written following an abstractive paradigm (i.e., they include material that is not explicitly present in the source documents), whereas our proposed method is an extractive one (i.e., it selects sentences from the source documents). As a consequence, the chances to have common sentences between our summaries and the human-made ones decrease, as well as the corresponding ROUGE scores.

Regarding the readability assessment, Table 5 showed that our approach obtains close results to the human performance in Aker and Gaizauskas (2010b). However, the coherence criteria is the poorest in performance and should be improved. We plan to face this problem in the future.

6 Conclusions and Future Work

This paper presented the analysis of several approaches to automatically generate summaries from a set of documents related to tourist sites. For generating such summaries, we took into account the type of information users reflect when writing summaries of this particular domain. Therefore, we analyzed a collection of model summaries in order to determine which information would be relevant to extract from the source documents. In this manner, we performed dependency pattern identification and categorization and then used this information to suggest three score schemes to represent the sentences in the source documents, as well as two strategies for automatically assigning each sentence to a category. In order to build the final summary, sentences pertaining to each of the categories were selected in turn, taking also into account the order in which such sentences are placed in the summary. We used ROUGE for evaluating all the proposed approaches, and we also compared the performance of our summaries with the human written ones. The results obtained are very encouraging, our summaries being comparable to the human written ones. We believe that the differences of the results between our summaries and the human written ones are partly due to the manner of generating summaries. While ours were produced following an extractive paradigm which selects sentences from documents, the human written models are in fact abstracts, and this means that some of the vocabulary in them may not appear in the source documents or has been paraphrased. Furthermore, the readability evaluation also shows that our approach performs well with respect to some criteria, such as grammaticality, clarity and focus, but we have to pay special attention to the coherence of the summaries.

In the short term, it would be interesting to use the same strategy to generate summaries in other domains and analyze whether it is feasible and appropriate. Furthermore, in the long term we plan to improve our best approach by automating the pattern categorization stage. Moreover, in order to overcome the lack of coherence of the generated summaries, the benefits of anaphora resolution over the documents, as well as sentence fusion or simplification should be analyzed in the future.

Acknowledgments

This research is funded by Generalitat Valenciana (projects PROMETEO/2009/119 and ACOMP/2011/001); the Spanish Government through the FPI and FPU programs and projects TEXT-MESS (TIN2006-15265-C06-01) and TIN2009-14659-C03-01; and by the TRIPOD project supported by the European Commission (Contract No. 045335).

References

Ahmet Aker and Robert Gaizauskas. 2009. Summary generation for toponym-referenced images using object type language models. In *Proc. of the International Conference RANLP-2009*, pages 6–11.

Ahmet. Aker and Robert Gaizauskas. 2010a. Generating image descriptions using dependency relational patterns. In *Proc. of the 48th Annual Meeting of the Association for Computational Linguistics*, pages 1250–1258.

Ahmet Aker and Robert Gaizauskas. 2010b. Model summaries for location-related images. In *Proceedings of LREC 2010*.

Regina Barzilay, Noemie Elhadad, and Kathleen R. McKeown. 2002. Inferring strategies for sentence ordering in multidocument news summarization. *Journal of Artificial Intelligent Research*, 17:35–55.

H.T. Dang. 2006. Overview of DUC 2006. *National Institute of Standards and Technology*.

K. Deschacht and M.F. Moens. 2007. Text Analysis for Automatic Image Annotation. *Proc. of the 45 th ACL*.

Mohamed Abdel Fattah and Fuji Ren. 2008. Probabilistic neural network based text summarization. In *Proc. of the International Conference on Natural Language Processing and Software Engineering*, pages 43–48.

Chin-Yew Lin. 2004. ROUGE: a package for automatic evaluation of summaries. In *Proc. of ACL Text Summarization Workshop*, pages 74–81.

Elena Lloret and Manuel Palomar. 2009. A Gradual Combination of Features for Building Automatic Summarisation Systems. In *Proc. of the 12th International Conference on Text, Speech and Dialogue (TSD)*, pages 16–23.

Daniel Marcu. 1999. Discourse trees are good indicators of importance in text. In *Inderjeet Mani and Mark Maybury, editors*, Advances in Automatic Text Summarization, pages 123–136. MIT Press.

Rada Mihalcea. 2004. Graph-based ranking algorithms for sentence extraction, applied to text summarization. In *Proc. of the ACL 2004 on Interactive poster and demonstration sessions*, page 20.

Y. Mori, H. Takahashi, and R. Oka. 2000. Automatic word assignment to images based on image division and vector quantization. In *Proc. of RIAO 2000: Content-Based Multimedia Information Access*.

Michael P. Oakes and Chris D. Paice. 1999. The automatic generation of templates for automatic abstracting. In *BCS-IRSG Annual Colloquium on IR Research*.

Laura Plaza, Alberto Díaz, and Pablo Gervás. 2008. Concept-graph based biomedical automatic summarization using ontologies. In *Proc. of the 3rd Textgraphs workshop on Graph-based Algorithms for NLP*, pages 53–56.

Laura Plaza, Elena Lloret, and Ahmet Aker. 2010. Improving automatic image captioning using text summarization techniques. In *Proc. of the 13th International Conference on Text, Speech and Dialogue*, pages 165–172.

Frank Schilder and Ravikumar Kondadadi. 2008. FastSum: Fast and accurate query-based multi-document summarization. In *Proceedings of ACL-08: HLT, Short Papers*, pages 205–208.

Karen Spärck Jones. 2007. Automatic summarising: The state of the art. *Information Processing & Management*, 43(6):1449–1481.

Zhi Teng, Ye Liu, Fuji Ren, Seiji Tsuchiya, and Fuji Ren. 2008. Single document summarization based on local topic identification and word frequency. In *Proc. of the 2008 Seventh Mexican International Conference on Artificial Intelligence*, pages 37–41.

Simone Teufel and Marc Moens. 2002. Summarizing scientific articles: experiments with relevance and rhetorical status. *Computational Linguistis*, 28(4):409–445.

Efficient Algorithm for Context Sensitive Aggregation in Natural Language Generation

Hemanth Sagar Bayyarapu
Language Technologies Research Center
International Institute of Information Technology
Hyderabad, AP, India - 500032
hemanth.sagar@research.iiit.ac.in

Abstract

Aggregation is a sub-task of Natural Language Generation (NLG) that improves the conciseness and readability of the text outputted by NLG systems. Till date, approaches towards the aggregation task have been predominantly manual (manual analysis of domain specific corpus and development of rules). In this paper, a new algorithm for aggregation in NLG is proposed, that learns context sensitive aggregation rules from a parallel corpus of multi-sentential texts and their underlying semantic representations. Additionally, the algorithm accepts external constraints and interacts with the surface realizer to generate the best output. Experiments show that the proposed context sensitive probablistic aggregation algorithm performs better than the deterministic hand crafted aggregation rules.

1 Introduction

Aggregation is the process in which two or more linguistic structures are merged to form a single sentence. It helps in generating concise and fluent text and hence is an essential component in any NLG system (Reiter and Dale 2000). Figure 1(a) presents an example of de-aggregated text while Figure 1(b) shows its aggregated counterpart. Clearly, the aggregated text is fluent while the de-aggregated text is artificial with lot of redundancy.

Reiter (1994) proposed a consensus pipeline architecture for NLG systems with three stages:

- Content-Determination: Selects the information (propositions) to be conveyed and organizes the information in a rhetorically coherent manner.
- Sentence-Planning: Generates referring expressions, combines multiple propositions, selects appropriate lexical items and syntactic structures for each (aggregated) proposition and adds cohesion devices (eg, discourse markers) to make the text flow smoothly.
- Surface-Realizer: Converts the lexicalized linguistic structure into a linearized string while ensuring grammaticality, proper punctuation, correct morphology.

Bacteria are prokaryotic.
Bacteria are unicellular.
Bacteria have a cell wall.
Bacteria have DNA.
The shape of the DNA is circular.
The DNA is inside cytoplasm.

(a) De-aggregated text

Bacteria are prokaryotic and unicellular.
They have a cell wall, a plasma membrane and a circular DNA within cytoplasm.

(b) Aggregated text

Figure 1: Example showing de-aggregated text and its equivalent aggregated text.

The input to the process of aggregation, a submodule of Sentence-Planning in the consensus architecture described above, is a set of propositions selected by Content-Determination module which are organized using rhetorical relations between the propositions. Typical NLG systems use a two-stage aggregation process (Wilkinson, 1995). In the first stage, i.e., *semantic grouping*, the input set of propositions are partitioned into multiple sets, each of which is realized as a sentence. In the second stage, decisions related to actual realization of each set partition are taken.

The essential idea behind semantic grouping is that the propositions that form a set and get realized as a meaningful sentence are related somehow. For example in Figure 1, the first two propositions (*Bacteria are unicellular. Bacteria are prokaryotic.*) are two assertive sentences about *Bacteria* and hence are aggregated. But it is not true that these two propositions will always be aggregated into a single sentence as shown in Figure 2.

Bacteria are unicellular while fungi can be either unicellular or multicellular.
Bacteria are prokaryotic and hence lack a cell nucleus.
On the other hand, fungi are eukaryotic and have a true cell nucleus bounded by a membrane.

Figure 2: Example answer from a corpus of QAs in Biology domain.

This shows that semantic grouping depends not only on the similarity between propositions, but also on the context (communicative goal of the text). The issue of context in semantic grouping gains importance especially in systems that present the same information in different views (Example: QA systems). For example, the two propositions (*Bacteria are unicellular. Bacteria are prokaryotic*) occur in examples shown in Figures 1 & 2. In the example in Figure 1, these propositions are aggregated while in the example in Figure 2 they are not. If we look at the context of these texts, the text in Figure 1 is *a short description about Bacteria*. On the other hand, the text in Figure 2 talks about *the fundamental difference between Bacteria and Fungi*.

The problem that is considered in this paper is as follows: Given a parallel corpus of multi-sentential texts and their underlying semantic representations along with the communicative goal of the text, can we learn semantic grouping rules automatically? The semantic representation assumed in this paper is a conceptual graph (Figure 3 shows an example of a conceptual graph), but the applicability of the approach is generic and can be customised to accomodate any semantic representation. A context-dependent discriminative model is learned which, given a proposition set and the context, estimates the probability of aggregation of the propositions. The problem of semantic grouping is modelled as a hypergraph partitioning problem that uses the probabilities outputted by the context-dependent discriminative model. To address the problem of hypergraph partioning, Multi-level Fiduccia-Mattheyses Framework (MLFM) is used (Karypis and Kumar, 1999).

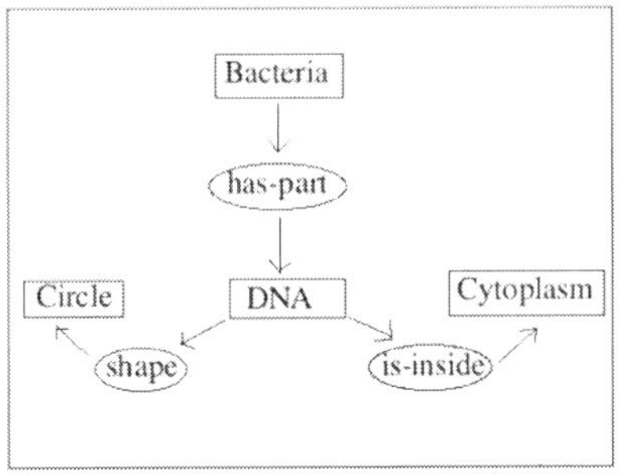

Figure 3: Example of a conceptual graph.

The approach is evaluated in the biology domain against two alternatives, namely handcrafted rules (HC) and a greedy clustering approach (GC) using the probabilities outputted by the context-dependent discriminative model. Additionally, we also test the impact of context by ignoring context while learning the discriminative model (Context-independent discriminative model).

An overview of related work is presented in Section 2. The corpus used in the experiments is discussed in Section 3. Then, in Section 4, the approach is discussed followed by Section 5 which presents the experiments done and their results. Finally, Section 6 concludes the paper with discussions and future work.

2 Related Work

Aggregation has been employed since the early NLG systems. In PROTEUS, a computer program that generates commentaries on a tic-tac-toe game, Davey (1979) used conjunctions to express SEQUENCE and CONTRASTIVE relations. Derr and McKeown (1984) showed how focus of attention helps in taking decisions related to choice between a sequence of simple sentences and a complex one. ANA (Kukich, 1983), used financial domain specific aggregation rules to generate complex sentences upto 34 words. Logical derivations were used to combine clauses and to remove easily inferrable clauses in (Mann and Moore, 1980).

Hand-crafted aggregation rules developed as a result of corpus analysis are employed by (Scott and de Souza, 1990; Hovy, 1990; Dalianis, 1999; Shaw, 1998). Walker et al. (2001) proposed a overgenerate-and-select approach in which the over-generate stage lists out large number of potential sentence plans while the ranking stage selects the top ranked sentence plan using rules that are learned automatically from the training data. Cheng and Mellish (2000) propose a genetic algorithm coupled with a preference function. Barzilay and Lapata (2006) view the problem of semantic grouping as a set partioning problem. They employ a local classifier that learns similarity between the propositions and then use ILP (Branch-and-bound algorithm) to infer a globally optimal partition.

This work is different from the earlier work in two aspects. We use contextual information to obtain better grouping that is applicable across different systems (even QA systems) while their work does not use the contextual information. Also, we assume a more generic hypergraph representation and use MLFM technique which works well even with large number of propositions.

What is the nucleolus?
The nucleolus is a small and optically dense region in the interior of the cell nucleus.
It is made of ribosomic RNA (rRNA) and proteins.

Context C = { Nucleolus }

Proposition set S = {

(Nucleolus is-region-of Cell-Nucleus)
(Nucleolus size small)
(Nucleolus density optically-dense)
(Nucleolus has-part RRNA)
(Nucleolus has-part Protein)

}

Figure 4: Example of a QA pair and its triple representation.

3 Corpus

A total of 717 QA pairs are collected from various sources in the biology domain. Concepts are extracted from the question which acts as contextual information. For example, when the question is *What is a binary fission?*, the concept *Binary-Fission* becomes the context. The answer is converted into sets of triples, each set corresponding to a sentence. Each triple consists of two concepts (or instances of concepts) connected by a relation. For example, the triple *(Mitosis next-event Cytokinesis)* contains two concepts namely *Mitosis* and *Cytokinesis* connected by the relation *next-event*. Figure 4 shows a QA pair and its triple representation. The context and sets of triples are extracted from each QA pair manually. The manual annotation process uses the component library described in (Barker et al., 2001).[1]

A total of 6337 triples are collected corresponding to 717 answers with each answer having 8.839 triples on an average. The highest number of triples for an answer is 46 while the lowest is 1. The total number of sentences in the answers is 1862, i.e., 2.596 sentences per an answer.

4 Approach

4.1 Hypergraphs

A hypergraph (H) is a generic graph wherein edges can connect any number of vertices and are called hyperedges. In other words, each edge is a set of vertices. It is formally represented by a pair (V,E) where V is the set of vertices and E is the set of hyperedges. Each edge $e_i \in$ E has associated weight w_i. An edge with zero weight means that the the edge does not exist.

4.2 k-way Hypergraph Partitioning problem

Let P be a k-tuple (p_0 , p_1, p_2...) where each p_i is a set of vertices from V such that $\cap_{i=0}^{i=k-1} p_i = \phi$ and $\cup_{i=0}^{i=k-1} p_i = V$. The k-way Hypergraph partitioning problem can be formulated as follows:

> Given a hypergraph H = (V,E), find a k-way partitionment $\delta : V \rightarrow P$ that maps each of the vertices of H to one of the k disjoint partitions such that some cost function $\gamma : P \rightarrow \mathbb{R}$ is minimized.

4.3 Modelling Aggregation as hypergraph partitioning problem

Relationships among the propositions are often complex than pairwise. Assuming this complex relationship as pairwise ones reduces the fluency

[1]The component library is available online at http://www.cs.utexas.edu/ mfkb/RKF/tree/

of the verbalized text in some cases. To deal with this complex relationship, it is better to directly use hypergraphs instead of pair-wise approximation.

We view the problem of aggregation as a hypergraph partioning problem guided by a data-driven context sensitive discriminative model. The input to the algorithm is a *conceptual graph* which can be alternatively represented as a set of propositions. The goal is to find optimal partitions of the set of propositions given context, where each partition represents an aggregated sentence. The set of propositions is viewed as a graph where each proposition represents a vertex as shown in Figure 5. Hyperedges are constructed on the graph obtained from propositions. Each hyperedge of this hypergraph connects one or more propositions. The weight w_i of each hyperedge is given by the context sensitive discriminative model discussed in section 4.4. The hypergraph along with edge weights is the input to the multi-level k-partitioning algorithm.

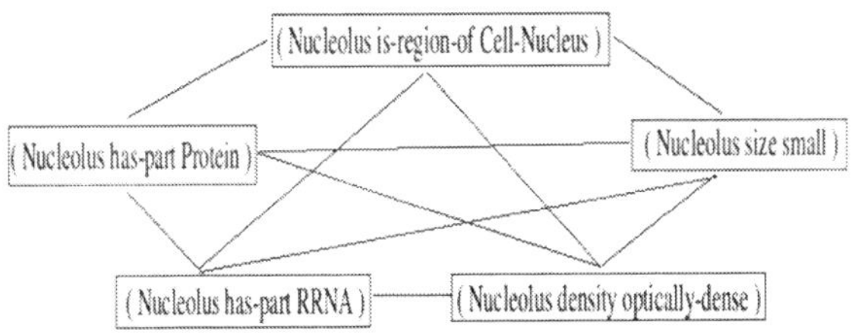

Figure 5: Example of a proposition set and its view as a graph

4.4 Context Sensitive Discriminative Model

The weight w_{iA} of a hyperedge (A) in the hypergraph formed from the inputs (S) is the probability of aggregation of propositions in A given contextual information (C) and S.

$$w_{iA} = p_A = P(A|C, S) \quad (1)$$

The contextual information include the communicative goal (the concepts in the question) The features that are used to predict the probability of aggregation of a proposition set are based on:

- *Cohesion of the proposition set* is the average score of similarities between each pair of propositions in A:

$$Coh_A = \frac{\sum_{i=1,j=1,i\neq j}^{i=|A|,j=|A|} sim(A_i, A_j)}{|A|} \quad (2)$$

  The similarity between each pair is the number of matches in the components of triples. For example, since the triples *(Mitosis subevent Prophase), (Mitosis subevent Anaphase)* match in two slots, the similarity score is 2/3.

- *Complexity of the realization* is a cumulative weighted score of number of words, number of relative clauses, number of connectives, etc. and this score depicts how difficult it is to interpret the sentence corresponding to the proposition set A (if it is generated using the surface realizer). The score value is ∞ if the propositions cannot be realized as a single sentence because the surface realizer cannot find suitable structure that accomodates all the propositions.

- *Dissimilarity with rest of the propositions* calculates how dissimilar the proposition set A is with the rest of the propositions (S-A). The maximum distance (or minimum similarity) of each proposition in S-A from A is calculated and averaged.

- *Similarity with context C* is the score of the extent of the cover of context by the triples. It is the ratio of number of concepts in the context C that occur in any of the triples in A to the total number of concepts in C.

A number of boolean features and their conjunctive features are generated using the above scores with score bounds. Such feature structures are generated for each hyperedge in the hypergraph formed from S. All the subsets of S which are in Z (the correct partitioning of S) are positive instances and rest are negative instances. A maximum entropy model is employed to predict the probabilities of aggregation of a set of propositions.

While using the maximum entropy model to predict the aggregation probability, we can also utilize pattern matching rules to group propositions as a pre-processing step. The pattern matching rules can include domain specific rules, inference rules, etc. The motivations for this grouping are: (1) propositions are a mere representation of complex texts, (2) when the number of propositons is very high, optimization on the level of propositions becomes intractable.

Any constraint on the output can be expressed as features in the discriminative model. Transitivity constraint on set of propositions is automatically captured in the usage of hyperedges. External constraints like complexity of sentence is expressed in the features of the discriminative model (Complexity of the realization).

5 Experiments

We use a n-fold cross validation on the corpus described in section II. We use two baselines for comparison: (1) Hand-Crafted rules (HC) and (2) Greedy clustering of hypergraph (GC). Hand-crafted rules are pattern matching rules on sets of propositions. An example rule is to aggregate two triples if they share atleast two slots. In the second baseline, i.e., the greedy clustering of hypergraph, the graph is clustered using the probability scores of hyperedges based on the context sensitive model. The top scoring hyperedges that are non-overlapping and cover the entire input set are outputted. Also, in order to test the impact of context, we build a context independent discriminative model but follow the same hypergraph partitioning approach (HGP).

5.1 Evaluation metrics

Let Y be the output partition of our approach and Z be the correct partitioning which is annotated manually. We use the following evaluation metrics:

- Precision: the ratio of correct pair-wise aggregations in Y and total pair-wise aggregations in Y
- Recall : the ratio of correct pair-wise aggregations in Y and total pair-wise aggregations in Z
- F-score: the harmonic mean of Precision and Recall

5.2 Results

The results are shown in Table 1. All the scores are average scores on a 5-fold cross validation. Hand-Crafted rules performed very poor because there are very few rules covering aggregation of more than five propositions while the corpus consisted of many such proposition sets. The effect of context is clear as the context dependent (HGPC) model outperforms context independent model by 7.15%. This proves that the usage of context is very important if the model has to be generic and adaptable to any kind of NLG system.

Model	Recall	Precision	F-Score
HC	32.5	21.6	25.9
GC	41.7	47.5	44.4
HGP	40.02	58.8	47.6
HGPC	49.6	61.1	54.75

Table 1: Results on pairwise aggregations; Comparison between Hand-Crafted rules (HC), Greedy clustering (GC), Hyper-graph partitioning model with context (HGPC) and without context (HGP)

6 Conclusions

The number of propositions in an answer in our corpus varied from 1 to as large as 46. We used an empirically proven scalable partitioning framework that works well when the number of propositions is huge. We presented a novel context sensitive aggregation algorithm for NLG systems. Also we presented a much natural hypergraph approach to semantic grouping than other methods that approximate the complicated relationships (among the entities that are checked for aggregation) with pair-wise approximations. The approach is adaptable to any domain and any representation. With a small corpus of 717 QA pairs, good results are obtained over the hand-crafted approaches.

In our future work, we would like to test the described approach for scalability. The MLFM technique used in this work is proven to be the best technique for partitioning a set of more than 200 propositions. Also, the evaluations in this paper have been conducted in partial isolation from the actual output of the surface realizer. In our future work, we would also like to consider the impact of aggregation on the final textual outputs.

References

Barker, Ken , Bruce Porter, and Peter Clark. 2001 A library of generic concepts for composing knowledge bases. In Proceedings of First International Conference on Knowledge Capture, 2001.

Barzilay, Regina and Mirella Lapata. 2006. Aggregation via Set Partitioning for Natural Language Generation. In Proc. of NAACL/HLT, 2006.

Cheng, Hua and Chris Mellish. 2000. Capturing the interaction between aggregation and text planning in two generation systems. In Proceedings of INLG-2000, Israel.

Dalianis, Hercules. 1999. Aggregation in Natural Language Generation. Journal of Computational Intelligence, Volume 15, Number 4, pp 384-414, November 1999. Abstract

Davey, Anthony C. 1979. Discourse Production. Edinburgh University Press, Edinburgh.

Derr, Marcia A. and Kathleen R. McKeown. 1984. Using focus to generate complex and simple sentences. In Proceedings of the Tenth International Conference on Computational Linguistics (COLING-84) and the 22nd Annual Meeting of the ACL, pages 319326, Stanford University, Stanford, CA.

Donia R. Scott and Clarisse S. de Souza. 1990. Getting the message across in RST-based text generation. In R. Dale, C. Mellish, and M. Zock, editors, Current Research in Natural Language Generation

Hovy, Eduard H. 1990. Unresolved issues in paragraph planning. In R. Dale, C. Mellish, M. Zock, eds., Current Research in Natural Language Generation, 1741. Academic Press, New York.

Karypis, G. and V. Kumar. 1999. Multilevel k-way hypergraph partitioning. In Proceedings of the Design and Automation Conference, 1999.

Kukich, Karen. 1983. Design of a knowledge-based report generator. In Proceedings of the 21st Annual Meeting of the ACL, pages 145150, Cambridge, MA, June 15-17,.

Mann, William C. and James A. Moore. 1980. Computer as author results and prospects. Technical Report RR-79-82, USC Information Science Institute, Marina del Rey, CA.

Reiter, Ehud and Robert Dale. 2000 Building Natural Language Generation Systems. Cambridge University Press, Cambridge.

Reiter, Ehud. 1994 Has a consensus NL generation architecture appeared, and is it psycholinguistically plausible? In Proceedings of the Seventh International Workshop on Natural Language Generation, pages 163170, Nonantum Inn, Kennebunkport, Maine.

Shaw, James. 1998. Clause aggregation using linguistic knowledge. In Proceedings of the 9th International Workshop on Natural Language Generation., pages 138147.

Wilkinson, John. 1995. Aggregation in natural language generation: Another look. Co-op work term report, Department of Computer Science, University of Waterloo, Septembe

Walker, Marilyn, Owen Rambow and Monica Rogati. 2001. Spot: A trainable sentence planner. In Proceedings of the second annual meeting of North American Chapter of Association for Computational Linguistics, 17-24, Pittsburgh, PA

Enriching a Statistical Machine Translation System Trained on Small Parallel Corpora with Rule-Based Bilingual Phrases

Víctor M. Sánchez-Cartagena, Felipe Sánchez-Martínez, Juan Antonio Pérez-Ortiz
Transducens Research Group
Departament de Llenguatges i Sistemes Informàtics
Universitat d'Alacant, E-03071, Alacant, Spain
{vmsanchez, fsanchez, japerez}@dlsi.ua.es

Abstract

In this paper, we present a new hybridisation approach consisting of enriching the phrase table of a phrase-based statistical machine translation system with bilingual phrase pairs matching structural transfer rules and dictionary entries from a shallow-transfer rule-based machine translation system. We have tested this approach on different small parallel corpora scenarios, where pure statistical machine translation systems suffer from data sparseness. The results obtained show an improvement in translation quality, specially when translating out-of-domain texts that are well covered by the shallow-transfer rule-based machine translation system we have used.

1 Introduction

Statistical machine translation (SMT) (Koehn, 2010) is currently the leading paradigm in machine translation research. SMT systems are very attractive because they may be built with little human effort when enough monolingual and bilingual corpora are available. However, bilingual corpora large enough to build competitive SMT systems are not always easy to harvest, and they may not even exist for some language pairs. On the contrary, rule-based machine translation systems (RBMT) may be built without any parallel corpus; however, they need an explicit representation of linguistic information whose coding by human experts requires a considerable amount of time.

When both parallel corpora and linguistic information exist, hybrid approaches (Thurmair, 2009) may be followed in order to make the most of such resources. We focus on alleviating the data sparseness problem suffered by phrase-based statistical machine translation (PBSMT) systems (Koehn, 2010, ch. 5) when trained on small parallel corpora. We present a new hybrid approach which enriches a PBSMT system with resources from shallow-transfer RBMT. Shallow-transfer RBMT systems, which are described in detail below, do not perform a complete syntactic analysis of the input sentences, but rather work with much simpler intermediate representations. Hybridisation between shallow-transfer RBMT and SMT has not yet been explored. Existing hybridisation strategies involve more complex RBMT systems (Eisele et al., 2008) which are usually treated as black boxes; in contrast, our approach directly uses the RBMT dictionaries and rules.

We provide an exhaustive evaluation of our hybridisation approach with two different language pairs: Breton–French and Spanish–English. While the first one suffers from actual resource scarceness, many different parallel corpora are available for the second one, which allows us to test our approach on different domains and check if it is able to improve the poor performance of PBSMT systems when translating texts from a domain not covered by the bilingual training data.

The rest of the paper is organised as follows. Next section overviews the two systems we combine in our approach. Then, section 3 outlines related hybrid approaches, whereas our approach is described in section 4. Sections 5 and 6 present the experiments conducted and discuss the results achieved, respectively. The paper ends with our conclusions and future research lines.

2 Translation Approaches

2.1 Phrase-Based Statistical Machine Translation

PBSMT systems (Koehn, 2010, ch. 5) translate sentences by maximising the translation probability as defined by the log-linear combination of a number of feature functions, whose weights are chosen to optimise translation quality (Och, 2003). A core component of every PBSMT system is the phrase table, which contains bilingual phrase pairs extracted from a bilingual corpus after word alignment (Och and Ney, 2003). The set of translations from which the most probable one is chosen is built by segmenting the source sentence in all possible ways and then combining the translation of the different source segments according to the phrase table. Common feature functions are: source-to-target and target-to-source phrase translation probabilities, source-to-target and target-to-source lexical weightings (calculated by using a probabilistic bilingual dictionary), reordering costs, number of words in the output (word penalty), number of phrase pairs used (phrase penalty), and likelihood of the output as given by a target-language model.

2.2 Shallow-Transfer Rule-Based Machine Translation

The RBMT process (Hutchins and Somers, 1992) can be split into three different steps: analysis of the source language (SL) text to build a SL intermediate representation; transfer from that SL intermediate representation to a target language (TL) intermediate representation; and generation of the final translation from the TL intermediate representation.

Shallow-transfer RBMT systems use relatively simple intermediate representations, which are based on lexical forms consisting of lemma, part of speech and morphological inflection information of the words in the input sentence, and simple shallow-transfer rules that operate on sequences of lexical forms: this kind of systems do not perform a complete syntactic analysis. Apertium (Forcada et al., 2011), the shallow-transfer RBMT platform used to evaluate our approach, splits the transfer stage into structural and lexical transfer. The lexical transfer is done by using a bilingual dictionary which, for each SL lexical form, provides a single TL lexical form; thus, no lexical selection is performed. It is worth noting that multi-word expressions, such as *on the other hand* (which acts as a single adverb), may be analysed to (or generated from) a single lexical form.

Structural transfer is done by applying a set of rules in a left-to-right, longest-match fashion to prevent the translation to be performed word for word in those cases in which this would result in an incorrect translation. Structural transfer rules process sequences of lexical forms by performing operations such as reorderings and gender and number agreements. For the translation between non-related language pairs, the structural transfer may be split into three levels in order to facilitate the writing of rules by linguists. The first level performs short-distance operations (such as gender and number agreement between nouns and adjectives) and groups word sequences into *chunks*; the second one performs inter *chunk* operations; and the third one generates a sequence of lexical forms from each *chunk*. Note that, although this multi-stage shallow transfer allows performing operations between words which are distant in the source sentence, shallow-transfer RBMT systems are less powerful that the ones which perform full parsing.

3 Related Work

Bilingual dictionaries are the most reused resource from RBMT. They have been added to SMT systems since its early days (Brown et al., 1993). One of the simplest strategies, which has already been put into practice with the Apertium bilingual dictionaries (Tyers, 2009), consists of adding the dictionary entries directly to the parallel corpus. In addition to the obvious increase in lexical coverage, Schwenk et al. (2009) state that the quality of the alignments obtained is also improved when the words in the bilingual dictionary appear in other sentences of the parallel corpus. However, it is not guaranteed that, following this strategy, multi-word expressions from the bilingual dictionary that appear in the SL sentences are translated as such by the SMT decoder because they may be split into smaller units by the phrase-extraction algorithm. Our strategy differs from these approaches in that we ensure the proper translation of multi-word expressions, but also add the dictionary entries to the training corpus with the aim of improving word alignment. Other approaches go beyond adding a dictionary to the parallel corpus: dictionary entries may constrain the decoding process (Langlais, 2002), or may be used in conjunction with handcrafted rules to reorder the SL sentences to match the structure of the TL (Popović and Ney, 2006).

Although RBMT transfer rules have also been reused in hybrid systems, they have been mostly used implicitly as part of a complete RBMT engine. For instance, Dugast et al. (2008) show how a PBSMT system can be bootstrapped using only monolingual data and an RBMT engine. Another remarkable study (Eisele et al., 2008) presents a strategy based on the augmentation of the phrase table to include information provided by an RBMT system. In this approach, the sentences to be translated by the hybrid system are first translated with an RBMT system and then a small phrase table is obtained from the resulting parallel corpus. Phrase pairs are extracted following the usual procedure (Koehn, 2010, sec. 5.2.3) which generates the set of all possible phrase pairs that are consistent with the word alignments. In order to obtain reliable word alignments, they are computed using an alignment model previously built from a large parallel corpus. Finally, the RBMT-generated phrase table is added to the original one. On the contrary, our approach directly generates phrase pairs which match either an entry in the bilingual dictionary or a structural transfer rule; thus preventing them from being split into smaller phrase pairs even if they would be consistent with the word alignments. In addition, our approach does not require a large parallel corpus from which to learn an alignment model. Preliminary experiments show that our hybrid approach outperforms Eisele et al.'s (2008) strategy when translating from Spanish to English.

Other strategies involving neither transfer rules nor bilingual dictionaries may alleviate the data sparseness problem in PBSMT. For example, paraphrases may be derived from a SL monolingual corpus (Marton et al., 2009) and verb forms may be substituted by their lemma when translating into highly-inflected languages (de Gispert et al., 2005).

4 Enhancing Phrase-Based SMT With Shallow-Transfer Linguistic Resources

Our hybridisation strategy modifies two elements of a standard PBSMT system: the word alignments and the phrase translation model.

4.1 Improving Word Alignment with RBMT Bilingual Dictionaries

As improving the quality of the word alignments in a PBSMT system could lead to improvements in translation performance (Lopez and Resnik, 2006), in our approach we add to the original corpus all the entries, after suitably inflecting them, from the Apertium bilingual dictionary, to help the word aligment process. Recall that some multi-word expressions are encoded as single lexical forms in the Apertium dictionaries; therefore, the entries generated from Apertium may contain multi-word parallel segments. Once word alignments have been computed and the probabilistic bilingual dictionary used to compute the lexical weightings of the phrase pairs has been learned, dictionary entries are ignored and no phrase pair are extracted from them. In contrast to Schwenk et al. (2009), we avoid extracting phrase pairs which do not preserve the translation of multi-word expressions as such by including the dictionary entries directly in the phrase table, as discussed next.

4.2 Enriching the Phrase Translation Model

As already mentioned, the Apertium structural transfer detects sequences of lexical forms which need to be translated together to prevent them from being translated word for word, which would result in an incorrect translation. Therefore, adding to the phrase table of a PBSMT system all the bilingual phrase pairs which either match one of these sequences of lexical forms in the structural transfer or an entry in the bilingual dictionary ensures that all the linguistic information of Apertium is encoded with the minimum amount of phrase pairs.

4.2.1 Phrase Pair Generation

Generating a phrase pair from every entry in the bilingual dictionary is straightforward: it only involves the inflection of source and target lexical forms. The generation of phrase pairs from the structural transfer rules is performed by finding sequences of SL words in the sentences to be translated that match a structural transfer rule. Each of these sequences constitute the SL side of a bilingual phrase pair; the corresponding TL phrase is obtained by translating the SL side with Apertium.

It is worth noting that the generation of bilingual phrase pairs from the shallow-transfer rules is guided by the test corpus. We decided to do it in this way in order to avoid meaningless phrases and also to make our approach computationally feasible. Consider, for instance, a rule which is triggered every time a determiner followed by a noun and an adjective is detected. Generating phrase pairs from this rule would involve combining all the determiners in the dictionary with all the nouns and all the adjectives, causing the generation of many meaningless phrases, such as *el niño inalámbrico – the wireless boy*. In addition, the number of combinations to deal with would become unmanageable as the length of the rule grows.

4.2.2 Scoring the New Phrase Pairs

State-of-the-art PBSMT systems usually attach 5 scores to every phrase pair in the translation table: source-to-target and target-to-source phrase translation probabilities, source-to-target and target-to-source lexical weightings, and phrase penalty.

To calculate the phrase translation probabilities of the new phrase pairs obtained from the shallow-transfer RBMT resources we simply add them once to the list of corpus-extracted phrase pairs, and then compute the probabilities by relative frequency as it is usually done (Koehn, 2010, sec. 5.2.5). In this regard, it is worth noting that as RBMT-generated phrase pairs are added only once, if one of them happens to share its source side with many other corpus-extracted phrase pairs, or even with a single, very frequent one, the RBMT-generated phrase pair will receive lower scores, which penalises its use. To alleviate this without adding the same phrase pair an arbitrary amount of times, we introduce an additional boolean score to flag phrase pairs obtained from the RBMT resources.

To calculate the lexical weightings (Koehn, 2010, sec. 5.3.3) of the RBMT-generated phrase pairs the alignments between the words in the source side and those in the target side are needed. They are computed by tracing the operations carried out in the different stages of the shallow-transfer RBMT system. Only those words which are neither split nor joint with other words by the RBMT engine are included in the alignments; thus, multi-word expressions are left unaligned. This is done for convenience since, in this way, the number of lexical probabilities to take into account is reduced, and, as a result, phrase pairs containing multi-word expressions receive higher scores.

5 Experimental Settings

We evaluated our RBMT–SMT hybridisation approach on two different language pairs, namely Breton–French and Spanish–English, and with different small training corpus sizes. While the Breton–French language pair suffers from actual resource scarceness (there are only around 30 000 parallel sentences available), Spanish–English was chosen because it has a wide range of parallel corpora available, which allows us to perform both in-domain and out-of-domain evaluations.

SMT systems for Spanish–English were trained from the Europarl v5 parallel corpus (Koehn, 2005), collected from the proceedings of the European Parliament. Its whole target side, except for the Q4/2000 portion, was used to train the TL model used in the experiments. We learned the translation model from corpora of different sizes; more precisely, we used fragments of the Europarl corpus consisting of 2 000, 5 000, 10 000, 20 000, 40 000 and 80 000 parallel sentences. The sentences in each training set were randomly chosen (avoiding the Q4/2000 portion) in such a way that larger corpora include the sentences in the smaller ones.

Regarding Breton–French, the translation model was built using the only freely-available parallel corpus for such language pair (Tyers, 2009), which contains short sentences from the tourism and computer localisation domains split in different sections for training, tuning and testing. We also used different training corpora sizes, namely 2 000, 5 000, 10 000, 20 000, and 26 835 parallel sentences, the last one corresponding to the whole training section of the corpus. As in the Spanish–English pair, sentences were randomly chosen and larger corpora include the sentences in the smaller ones. The TL model was learnt from a monolingual corpus built by concatenating the target side of the whole bilingual training corpus and the French monolingual data from the Europarl corpus provided for the WMT 2011 shared translation task.[1]

Corpus		Origin	Sentences
Language model		Europarl, Tyers (2009)	1 975 773
Training	$2k$	Tyers (2009)	2 000
	$5k$	Tyers (2009)	5 000
	$10k$	Tyers (2009)	10 000
	$20k$	Tyers (2009)	20 000
	$\approx 27k$	Tyers (2009)	26 835
In-domain tuning		Tyers (2009)	2 000
In-domain test		Tyers (2009)	2 000

Table 1: Description of the Breton–French parallel corpora used in the experiments.

The weights of the different feature functions were optimised by means of minimum error rate training (MERT; Och, 2003). Breton–French systems were tuned using the *tuning* section of the parallel corpus by Tyers (2009) and evaluated using the *devtest* section of the same corpus. Note that we can only perform in-domain evaluation for this language pair.

Regarding Spanish–English, we have carried out both in-domain and out-of-domain evaluations. The former was performed by tuning the systems with 2 000 parallel sentences randomly chosen from the Q4/2000 portion of Europarl v5 corpus (Koehn, 2005) and evaluating them with 2 000 random parallel sentences from the same corpus; special care was taken to avoid the overlapping between the test and development sets. The out-of-domain evaluation was performed by using the *newstest2008* set for tuning and the *newstest2010* test for testing; both sets belong to the news domain and are distributed as part of the WMT 2010 shared translation task.[2] Tables 1 and 2 summarise the data about the corpora used in the experiments.

We used the free/open-source PBSMT system Moses[3] (Koehn et al., 2007) together with the

[1] `http://www.statmt.org/wmt11/translation-task.html`

[2] `http://www.statmt.org/wmt10/translation-task.html`

[3] Revision 3739, downloaded from `https://mosesdecoder.svn.sourceforge.net/svnroot/mosesdecoder/trunk`.

Corpus		Origin	Sentences
Language model		Europarl	1 650 152
Training	$2k$	Europarl	2 000
	$5k$	Europarl	5 000
	$10k$	Europarl	10 000
	$20k$	Europarl	20 000
	$40k$	Europarl	40 000
	$80k$	Europarl	80 000
In-domain tuning		Europarl	2 000
In-domain test		Europarl	2 000
Out-of-domain tuning		WMT 2010	2 051
Out-of-domain test		WMT 2010	2 489

Table 2: Description of the Spanish–English parallel corpora used in the experiments.

SRILM language modeling toolkit (Stolcke, 2002), which was used to train a 5-gram language model using interpolated Kneser-Ney discounting (Goodman and Chen, 1998). Word alignments from the training parallel corpus were computed by means of GIZA++ (Och and Ney, 2003). The Apertium (Forcada et al., 2011) engine and the linguistic resources for Spanish–English and Breton–French were downloaded from the Apertium Subversion repository.[4] The Apertium linguistic data contains 326 228 entries in the bilingual dictionary, 106 first-level rules, 31 second-level rules, and 7 third-level rules for Spanish–English; and 21 593, 169, 79 and 6, respectively, for Breton–French (see section 2.2 for a description of the different rule levels).

We have tested the following configurations:

- a state-of-the-art PBSMT system with the feature functions discussed in section 2.1 (*baseline*);
- the Apertium shallow-transfer RBMT engine, from which the dictionaries and transfer rules have been taken (*Apertium*);
- the hybridisation approach described along this paper (*phrase-rules*) and a variation in which only dictionary-matching bilingual phrases are included in the phrase table (*phrase-dict*); and
- a reduced version of our approach in which the entries in the bilingual dictionary are only added to the training corpus for the computation of the word alignments and the probabilistic bilingual dictionary, as explained in section 4.1 (*alignment*).

6 Results and Discussion

Table 3 reports the translation performance as measured by BLEU (Papineni et al., 2002) for the different configurations and language pairs described in section 5. Statistical significance of the differences between systems has been computed by performing 1 000 iterations of paired bootstrap resampling (Zhang et al., 2004) with a p-level of 0.05. In addition, table 4 presents the optimal weight obtained with MERT for the feature function that flags whether a phrase pair has been obtained from the Apertium bilingual resources (dictionaries and rules). Table 5 shows the proportion of RBMT-generated phrases used to perform each translation.

The results show that our hybrid approach outperforms both pure RBMT and PBSMT systems in terms of BLEU. However, the difference is statistically significant only under certain circumstances. The in-domain evaluation shows that the statistical significance only holds in the smallest corpus scenarios (i.e., when the training corpus contains at most 40 000 sentences for Spanish–English, and for all the training corpus sizes except 20 000 for Breton–French[5]), and the difference between the baseline PBSMT system and our hybrid approach is reduced as the parallel training corpus grows. Apertium data has been developed bearing in mind the translation of general texts (mainly news) whereas the in-domain test sets come from the specialised domains of parliament speeches (Spanish–English) or tourism and computer localisation (Breton–French). Thus, as soon as the PBSMT system learns reliable information from the parallel corpus, Apertium phrases become useless. On the contrary, the out-of-domain Spanish–English tests, performed on a general (news) domain, show a statistically-significant improvement with all the training corpus sizes tested. In this case, Apertium-generated phrases, which contain hand-crafted knowledge from a general domain, cover more sequences of words in the input text which are not covered, or are sparsely found, in the original training corpora. The data reported in tables 4 and 5 support these hypotheses; in the in-domain evaluation, the proportion of phrases generated from Apertium included in the translations drops abruptly as the corpus grows. On the contrary, when evaluating the Spanish–English systems in a different domain, the proportion of Apertium-

[4]Revisions 24177, 22150 and 28674, respectively.

[5]Our results do not agree with those by Tyers (2009), who reported a substantial improvement in BLEU when adding dictionaries to the training corpus. In a personal communication, the author stated that in Tyers (2009) a baseline in which the feature weights were optimised with MERT was compared to a system enriched with the Apertium dictionaries using the default (not optimised) feature weights. Incidentally, not optimising the feature weights provided better results. If the feature weights are optimised in both cases the results obtained are in the line of those reported in this paper.

		In-domain							Out-of-domain						
		$2k$	$5k$	$10k$	$20k$	$\approx 27k$	$40k$	$80k$	$2k$	$5k$	$10k$	$20k$	$\approx 27k$	$40k$	$80k$
es-en	baseline	20.74	24.24	26.46	28.45	-	29.86	30.88	12.59	14.90	16.92	18.63	-	20.32	21.80
	alignment	19.31	23.71	25.89	28.10	-	29.73	30.83	12.06	14.55	16.88	18.66	-	20.34	21.68
	phrase-dict	**24.29**	**26.39**	**27.93**	**29.30**	-	**30.36**	31.14	19.76	20.48	**21.26**	**21.89**	-	**22.67**	**23.20**
	phrase-rules	**24.68**	**26.81**	**28.28**	**29.40**	-	**30.41**	31.02	**20.97**	**21.36**	**22.20**	**22.77**	-	**23.29**	**23.76**
	Apertium	18.00							20.30						
br-fr	baseline	18.86	24.17	28.26	33.17	34.69	-	-	-	-	-	-	-	-	-
	alignment	17.53	23.56	27.82	32.17	34.76	-	-	-	-	-	-	-	-	-
	phrase-dict	**21.57**	**26.39**	**29.66**	33.42	35.50	-	-	-	-	-	-	-	-	-
	phrase-rules	**22.67**	**26.42**	**29.60**	33.14	**35.83**	-	-	-	-	-	-	-	-	-
	Apertium	17.56							-						

Table 3: BLEU score achieved by the different configurations listed in section 5. Hybrid system scores in bold mean that they outperform both Apertium and the PBSMT baseline, and that the improvement is statistically significant. The score of the hybrid system built with the Apertium rules and dictionaries is underlined if it outperforms its dictionary-based counterpart by a statistically significant margin. The $\approx 27k$ corpus size is only tested with the Breton–French language pair because it corresponds to the full Breton–French training corpus size.

generated phrases is higher and falls smoothly, and the value of the feature function is higher than in the in-domain tests.

The inclusion of shallow-transfer rules provides a statistically-significant improvement over the dictionaries for all the training corpus sizes in the Spanish–English out-of-domain evaluation scenario and for the smallest ones in the in-domain tests. That is, shallow-transfer rules are effective when the decoder chooses a high proportion of Apertium-generated phrase pairs.

Finally, the addition of the bilingual dictionaries to the training corpus before the computation of the word alignments and the probabilistic bilingual dictionary results in a small performance drop. It remains to be studied whether the dictionaries improve alignments but not translation performance.

7 Conclusions and Future Work

In this paper we have described a new hybridisation approach consisting of enriching a PBSMT system by adding to its phrase table bilingual phrase pairs matching structural transfer rules and dictionaries from a shallow-transfer RBMT system. The experiments conducted show an improvement of the translation quality when only a small parallel corpus is available. Our approach also helps when training on larger parallel corpora and the texts to translate come from a general (news) domain that is well covered by the RBMT system; in this case, shallow-transfer rules have a greater impact on translation quality than dictionaries.

Our future plans include evaluating the presented hybridisation strategy with more language pairs and bigger training corpora, focusing on test corpora from the news domain, which seems to be the scenario in which our approach better fits. We also plan to further investigate the negative impact that adding the entries in the Apertium bilingual dictionary to the corpus has on translation performance.

Acknowledgments

Work funded by the Spanish Ministry of Science and Innovation through project TIN2009-14009-C02-01 and by Generalitat Valenciana through grant ACIF/2010/174 (VALi+d programme).

References

P. F. Brown, S. A. D. Pietra, V. J. D. Pietra, M. J. Goldsmith, J. Hajic, R. L. Mercer, and S. Mohanty. 1993. But dictionaries are data too. In *Proceedings of the workshop on Human Language Technology*, pages 202–205.

A. de Gispert, J.B. Mariño, and J.M. Crego. 2005. Improving statistical machine translation by classifying and generalizing inflected verb forms. In *Proceedings of the 9th European Conference on Speech Communication and Technology*, pages 3185–3188.

L. Dugast, J. Senellart, and P. Koehn. 2008. Can we Relearn an RBMT System? In *Proceedings of the 3rd Workshop on Statistical Machine Translation*, pages 175–178.

A. Eisele, C. Federmann, H. Saint-Amand, M. Jellinghaus, T. Herrmann, and Y. Chen. 2008. Using Moses to integrate multiple rule-based machine translation engines into a hybrid system. In *Proceedings of the 3rd Workshop on Statistical Machine Translation*, pages 179–182.

M. L. Forcada, M. Ginestí-Rosell, J. Nordfalk, J. O'Regan, S. Ortiz-Rojas, J. A. Pérez-Ortiz, F. Sánchez-Martnez, G. Ramírez-Sánchez, and F. M. Tyers. 2011. Apertium: a free/open-source platform for rule-based machine translation. *Machine Translation*. doi: 10.1007/s10590-011-9090-0.

		2k	5k	10k	20k	≈ 27k	40k	80k
es-en in-domain	phrase-dict	0.0025	0.0010	−0.0003	−0.0003	-	0.0007	0.0067
	phrase-rules	0.0029	−0.0061	0	−0.0023	-	−0.0054	−0.0094
es-en out-of-domain	phrase-dict	0.0202	0.0138	0.0073	0.0162	-	0.0211	0.0259
	phrase-rules	0.0227	0.0219	0.0288	0.0156	-	0.0092	0.0230
br-fr in-domain	phrase-dict	0.0106	0.0052	0.0098	0.0079	0.0115	-	-
	phrase-rules	0.0024	0.0103	0.0020	0.0044	0.0029	-	-

Table 4: Relative weights assigned to the binary feature function that flags whether a phrase pair has been obtained from the Apertium bilingual resources (dictionaries and rules) or from the training parallel corpus in the different evaluation set-ups. Weigths have been normalised by dividing them by the highest weight assigned to a feature of its corresponding set-up.

		2k	5k	10k	20k	≈ 27k	40k	80k
es-en in-domain	phrase-dict	0.194	0.120	0.100	0.062	-	0.046	0.026
	phrase-rules	0.172	0.105	0.083	0.047	-	0.033	0.019
es-en out-of-domain	phrase-dict	0.282	0.229	0.188	0.144	-	0.121	0.088
	phrase-rules	0.374	0.319	0.277	0.237	-	0.194	0.167
br-fr in-domain	phrase-dict	0.276	0.184	0.133	0.096	0.086	-	-
	phrase-rules	0.319	0.224	0.181	0.138	0.134	-	-

Table 5: Proportion of phrase pairs used in the translation of the test set that have been generated from the Apertium bilingual resources (dictionaries and rules).

J. Goodman and S. F. Chen. 1998. An empirical study of smoothing techniques for language modeling. Technical Report TR-10-98, Harvard University, August.

W. J. Hutchins and H. L. Somers. 1992. *An introduction to machine translation*, volume 362. Academic Press, New York.

P. Koehn, H. Hoang, A. Birch, C. Callison-Burch, M. Federico, N. Bertoldi, B. Cowan, C. Shen, W.and Moran, R. Zens, C. Dyer, O. Bojar, A. Constantin, and E. Herbst. 2007. Moses: Open Source Toolkit for Statistical Machine Translation. In *Proceedings of the 45th Annual Meeting of the Association for Computational Linguistics, demonstration session*, pages 177–180.

P. Koehn. 2005. Europarl: A parallel corpus for statistical machine translation. *MT summit*, 5:12–16.

P. Koehn. 2010. *Statistical Machine Translation*. Cambridge University Press.

P. Langlais. 2002. Improving a general-purpose Statistical Translation Engine by terminological lexicons. In *Second International Workshop on Computational Terminology*, pages 1–7.

A. Lopez and P. Resnik. 2006. Word-based alignment, phrase-based translation: Whats the link. In *Proceedings of the 7th Conference of the Association for Machine Translation in the Americas*, pages 90–99.

Y. Marton, C. Callison-Burch, and P. Resnik. 2009. Improved statistical machine translation using monolingually-derived paraphrases. In *Proceedings of the 2009 Conference on Empirical Methods in Natural Language Processing*, pages 381–390.

F. J. Och and H. Ney. 2003. A systematic comparison of various statistical alignment models. *Computational Linguistics*, 29:19–51, March.

F. J. Och. 2003. Minimum error rate training in statistical machine translation. In *Proceedings of the 41st Annual Meeting on Association for Computational Linguistics*, pages 160–167.

K. Papineni, S. Roukos, T. Ward, and W. Zhu. 2002. BLEU: a method for automatic evaluation of machine translation. In *Proceedings of the 40th Annual Meeting on Association for Computational Linguistics*, pages 311–318.

M. Popović and H. Ney. 2006. Statistical machine translation with a small amount of bilingual training data. In *LREC workshop on Minority Languages*, pages 25–29.

H. Schwenk, S. Abdul-Rauf, L. Barrault, and J. Senellart. 2009. SMT and SPE machine translation systems for WMT'09. In *Proceedings of the 4th Workshop on Statistical Machine Translation*, pages 130–134.

A. Stolcke. 2002. SRILM – an extensible language modeling toolkit. In *7th International Conference on Spoken Language Processing*, pages 901–904.

G. Thurmair. 2009. Comparing different architectures of hybrid Machine Translation systems. In *Proceedings MT Summit XII*.

F. M. Tyers. 2009. Rule-based augmentation of training data in Breton-French statistical machine translation. In *Proceedings of the 13th Annual Conference of the European Association for Machine Translation*, pages 213–217.

Y. Zhang, S. Vogel, and A. Waibel. 2004. Interpreting BLEU/NIST scores: How much improvement do we need to have a better system. In *Proceedings of the 4th International Conference on Language Resources and Evaluation*, pages 2051–2054.

Assessing the Post-Editing Effort for Automatic and Semi-Automatic Translations of DVD Subtitles

Sheila C. M. de Sousa, Wilker Aziz and **Lucia Specia**
Research Group in Computational Linguistics
University of Wolverhampton
Stafford Street, Wolverhampton, WV1 1SB, UK
{sheila.castilhomonteirodesousa, w.aziz, l.specia}@wlv.ac.uk

Abstract

With the increasing demand for fast and accurate audiovisual translation, subtitlers are starting to consider the use of translation technologies to support their work. An important issue that arises from the use of such technologies is measuring how much effort needs to be put in by the subtitler in post-editing (semi-)automatic translations. In this paper we present an objective way of measuring post-editing effort in terms of *time*. In experiments with English-Portuguese subtitles, we measure the post-editing effort of texts translated using machine translation and translation memory systems. We also contrast this effort against that of translating the texts without any tools. Results show that post-editing is on average 40% faster than translating subtitles from scratch. With our best system, more than 69% of the translations require little or no post-editing.

1 Introduction

Automatic and semi-automatic translation have become a potential help in the subtitling industry due to the increasing demand for translations and the short time professionals have to deliver them. Many attempts have been made to translate subtitles automatically by using different Machine Translation (MT) approaches such as Rule-Based (RBMT), Example-Based (EBMT), Statistical (SMT) and also Translation Memory (TM) systems. However, no previous work compares different approaches in terms of the effort that is required to post-edit the translations they produce. Additionally, the related work in the field does not provide an in-depth comparison between the effort needed to translate subtitles from scratch and the effort needed to post-edit a draft version produced using translation tools.

The ability to objectively assess translation technology tools according to their post-editing effort is essential for a well informed decision among the large variety of tools available, as well as to ensure that such tools produce translations that require less effort to post-edit (PE) than the effort that would be necessary to translate the same texts from scratch (HT).

In this paper we compile a corpus of English – Brazilian Portuguese subtitles and we compare two different MT approaches as well as a TM system using this corpus. The translations obtained are post-edited and the original sentences are also translated from scratch, both using a tool specially designed to gather objective and subjective effort indicators: time spent on performing the task and qualitative assessments. Results show that translators can greatly benefit from automatically obtained translations.

The rest of this paper is organized as follows: Section 2 gives an overview of prior work; Section 3 describes our parallel corpus of subtitles; Section 4 describes how the experiments were performed; Section 5 presents the results; and Section 6 concludes the paper and gives some directions for further research.

2 Related Work

Popowich et al. (2000) propose a number of preprocessing steps in order to improve the accuracy of an RBMT system for translating closed captions. Two native speakers assessed the translations, reporting 70% accuracy.

O'Hagan (2003) experiments with English-Japanese subtitles for the movie *The Lord of the Rings*. Subtitles from the first movie are used to feed a TM system and subtitles from the second movie are used for testing. Results are not encouraging, probably due to the poor TM coverage.

Armstrong et al. (2006) train an EBMT system in two scenarios: i) using a homogenous corpus compiled exclusively with DVD subtitles, and ii) using a heterogenous corpus compiled with a mix of subtitles and sentences from the Europarl (Koehn, 2005). The results show that a homogenous setting leads to better translations.

Flanagan (2009) extends the work of Armstrong et al. (2006) by using larger parallel corpora of subtitles from multiple genres. A subjective evaluation querying users who watched movies containing the translated subtitles in terms of intelligibility and acceptability was performed. Results show an average performance ($\sim$ 3 on a 1-6 scale).

Melero et al. (2006) combine a black-box MT system and a TM using a corpus of newspaper articles and United Nation texts to translate subtitles. They find that MT+TM performs significantly better than MT in terms of BLEU (Papineni et al., 2002) in an English-Spanish task. For English-Czech they compare HT against PE in terms of time. The comparison is somewhat inconclusive as the HT and PE were compared using different texts and a single human translator.

Volk (2008) uses a large proprietary corpus of subtitles (5 million sentences) to train an SMT system. The author reports BLEU: i) using a single reference, and ii) using the translations produced by six post-editors. The author finds that SMT outputs can still be acceptable translations even though they do not exactly match the HT as long as they lie within 5 keystrokes, distance from it.

Similarly to prior work we compile a corpus of DVD subtitles in order to perform in-domain subtitle translations. We train our own SMT model and compare it against other MT approaches and a TM. Our main goal is to demonstrate that, regardless of the MT/TM strategy, PE is faster than HT without a loss in quality. For that, we design a comprehensive evaluation: i) objectively in terms of time (Specia, 2011), ii) subjectively using well specified scoring guidelines (Specia, 2011), and iii) automatically in terms of BLEU using single and multiple references. As a by-product, a comparison between different translation approaches is performed.

3 Corpus

The corpus used in this research was compiled with subtitles from the American TV series "*X Files*" which were downloaded from the free subtitle websites "TVsubtitles.net"[1] , "All-subs.org"[2] and "Opensubtitles.org"[3], where fans of the series volunteer to transcribe and translate subtitles. The corpus presented several types of noise which had to be cleaned such as: i) spelling errors, ii) non-uniform character casing, iii) different encoding, and iv) XML-like tags.

Subsequently, the corpus was automatically aligned at the sentence level using heuristics aimed at maximizing the time overlap between the source and target subtitles. The sentence alignment was revised to guarantee the largest possible set of 1-1 correspondences and also to correct mistakes that resulted from the particularities of aligning subtitles. After the correction of the sentence alignment, four episodes were randomly chosen and kept aside as our *test data*. Statistics about the resulting sentence-aligned parallel corpus are reported in Table 1.

Corpus	Training	Test
en tokens	720,845	17,796
pt tokens	613,201	14,000
Sentence pairs	76,295	2,379

Table 1: Token and sentence numbers in the parallel corpus

4 Experiments

This section describes how the effort to translate subtitles from scratch was compared to the effort to post-edit translations automatically obtained through different tools.

4.1 Systems

We used three translation tools in this research: two MT systems and a TM system:

RBMT: we used the commercial RBMT system Systran SMTU[4] as a black-box tool.

TM: we used the TM system Trados Studio[5] with a translation memory built using the parallel corpus described in Section 3. To restrict human intervention at the PE stage, we used the *auto-translate* option available in the toolkit. This option ensures that all 100% source matches are automatically translated. As for

[1] http://www.tvsubtitles.net/
[2] http://www.allsubs.org/
[3] http://www.opensubtitles.org/
[4] http://wwwv5.systransoft.com/
[5] http://www.trados.com/en/sdl-trados/default.asp

the remaining segments, the first match retrieved respecting a 70% fuzzy match threshold is accepted without manual correction. When no match is found, the original sentence is copied in the output.

In-domain SMT: we used the parallel corpus (Section 3) to train an `en-pt` phrase-based SMT system using the Moses toolkit (Koehn et al., 2007). The training set was further divided into 74,295 sentence pairs for phrase extraction and the remaining 2,000 sentences pairs for tuning the parameters of the system. For language modeling, we used the Portuguese side of the parallel corpus, along with 262K additional out-of-domain sentences from the Lácio-Ref corpus (Aluisio et al., 2003).

Out-of-domain SMT: we used the SMT system Google Translate as a freely available wide-coverage black-box tool.

4.2 Post-editing Task

Eleven volunteers participated in our experiments: they are native speakers of Brazilian Portuguese and fluent speakers of English and have some experience with translation tasks. They were sent guidelines and asked to post-edit automatic Portuguese translations and to translate English subtitles from scratch.

In order to anticipate any problems the translators could have with both the tool's interface and the task guidelines, and to calculate the translators' agreement regarding the subjective PE assessments (Figure 1), a pilot test was performed. Six translators participated in the pilot test which lasted one week. Each translator post-edited and evaluated the same set of 30 sentences with 10 sentences repeated for intra-agreement computation. Using the Kappa index (Landis and Koch, 1977), an average inter-agreement rate of 0.48 (moderate) and an average intra-agreement rate of 0.69 (substantial) were obtained.

The main experiment was set to last two weeks (W1 and W2) and the translators were divided into two groups (G1 and G2). In W1, 125 English subtitles (sources) were randomly selected from the test set. For every source we produced 4 automatic translations (using Google, Systran, Moses and Trados) which were post-edited by every member of G1. At the same time, members of G2 translated the 125 original source sentences without the aid of any of the translation tools (they could use dictionaries, but no translation tools).

To prevent any bias in the time measurement towards HT or PE, G1 and G2 performed different tasks (translation or post-editing) in the experiment with the same test (source) sentences, and we never asked the same translator to post-edit the output of a source sentence that he/she had previously translated or vice-versa.

Since we were also interested in collecting evidence to compare the effort on post-editing the output of different MT/TM systems, we used the same PE task for pairwise system comparisons. For every source we combined the 4 systems' outputs in pairs, resulting in 6 pairs that were randomly assigned to the members of G1. To avoid assigning more than one comparison pair to a given translator, we had 6 translators performing the PE task. It is worth highlighting that the jobs were distributed during the week, so we could randomly distribute the two automatic translations being compared on different days, reducing the chances that a translator would notice the presence of source duplicates.

In W2 we selected another 125 source sentences and repeated the process swapping the roles of translators in G1 and G2. The purpose of having two weeks and swapping the roles of the groups was to gather effort indicators on HT and PE from the same human translators. Because there were 6 system combinations, the group performing the PE tasks in W2 also had to contain 6 translators. Since we only had 11 translators, one translator did not participate in the HT task and participated twice in the PE task.

We implemented a simple tool to aid the translators performing both tasks. The tool presents the source sentence and its recent context and, in the case of the PE task, the automatic translation. After the translation or post-editing of a sentence, the tool queries the translator for an assessment of the effort put into translating/post-editing the sentence. For the PE task, the translator answers the question '*How much post-editing effort did the translation require?*' and for the HT task, '*How hard was it to translate the source text?*'. The scales for PE and HT assessments are shown in Figures 1 and 2, respectively. Clear guidelines explaining these options were given to the translators.

Score	Description
1	Complete retranslation
2	A lot of post-editing but quicker than translation
3	A little post-editing
4	No modification performed

Figure 1: Scale for PE evaluation

Score	Description
1	Difficult
2	Moderate
3	Easy

Figure 2: Scale for translation evaluation

The PE tool logs the time spent to translate or post-edit individual sentences. Translators can therefore pause between sentences, but they were asked to avoid pausing when possible. Translators were asked to translate/post-edit the sentence literally when it lacked context. Additionally, for post-editing, they were asked to perform the minimum amount of editing necessary to make the translation ready for publishing.

5 Results

To compare different translation tools, we used the human assessments for PE effort collected using the PE tool, as well as BLEU, a standard automatic evaluation metric, computed here for the draft translations before their post-editing. We computed BLEU i) using a single reference translation, that is, the original fan-sub subtitles in Portuguese (ref_0) and ii) using multiple references collected as part of the HT/PE task (i.e. ref_0, five translations made from scratch ref_{1-5} and twelve post-edited translations ref_{6-17}). The aim was to measure how close to any manually obtained translation the MT and TM outputs were and what percentage of the draft translations was reutilized in the PE task. Table 2 compares the performance of the four systems according to BLEU.

References	Google	Moses	Systran	Trados
Single	21.51	**22.28**	13.90	09.22
Multiple	**92.24**	72.04	70.23	28.36

Table 2: BLEU scores using single and multiple (18) references

Overall, both SMT systems outperform the RBMT and TM tools. By comparing the scores one can observe that when BLEU is computed with ref_0 only, Moses has a slightly better performance than Google, even though Google is certainly trained using much larger corpora. This may be due to the fact that Moses was trained using in-domain data, i.e., the corpus with subtitles of the same series. As a consequence, it is more likely that Moses learns specific vocabulary from the series and that translations look more similar to those in the reference set. However, when BLEU is computed with multiple references, even though the translations from all systems may differ from what was originally expected (ref_0), they can still be valid alternative translations that often match the choices made by other translators (ref_{1-17}). This resulted in a different ranking where Google significantly outperforms all other systems. While Moses and Systran have very similar scores, the TM system still performs poorly.

It is worth noticing that TM systems are not meant to be used without human intervention, and therefore our settings tend to penalise Trados, particularly in terms of lexical matching metrics such as BLEU. In fact, unless a full match is possible, all options produced by the TM will contain some noise or words in the source language. Table 3 illustrates the percentage of matches of different types retrieved by Trados. Although BLEU is certainly not a good metric for Trados, it is interesting to compare the TM with Moses, since both are based on the same parallel corpus.

Test set	Full	Fuzzy	Untranslated
Average	1.79%	58.55%	38.66%

Table 3: Different types of matches retrieved by Trados with a 70% threshold for fuzzy matches

In addition to BLEU, the subjective human assessments for PE effort were also compiled. Table 4 shows the percentage of translations assigned different effort scores. More than 92% of the sentences translated by Google were scored as no or little post-editing needed (scores 3 and 4). Over 70% of Moses' and Systran's outputs were also scored 3 or 4. Trados required little or no post-editing for only 36% of its outputs. The MT systems had no more than 8% of the sentences requiring complete retranslation. Trados, however, had more than 47% of its outputs scored as 1. These results are very well aligned to those in Table 2, confirming the BLEU scores using multiple references.

System	1	2	3	4
Google	1.73%	6.00%	28.80%	63.47%
Moses	4.27%	18.40%	36.80%	40.53%
Systran	7.47%	17.73%	40.40%	34.40%
Trados	47.47%	15.87%	19.20%	17.47%

Table 4: How often post-editing a system output was scored 1, 2, 3 or 4

The comparison of translation tools according to the time needed to post-edit their outputs shows that the statistical systems produce translations that require less time to be post-edited. Table 5 illustrates the system comparison in terms of PE time.

System	Google	Moses	Systran	Trados
Google	-	139	161	187
Moses	69	-	122	164
Systran	69	106	-	145
Trados	48	67	89	-

Table 5: How many times the system in the first column produced an output that was more quickly post-edited than each of the other systems (other columns)

According to these time measurements, Google seems to produce the most outputs which can be post-edited in less time as compared to all other systems. Out of 250 cases, Moses was faster to post-edit than Google on 69 translations, while Google was faster than Moses on 139 translations. Although Moses seems to perform slightly better than Systran, both systems are very close: i) both were faster than Google on 69 sentences, ii) Moses was faster than Systran on 122 sentences against 106 for the rule-based, and finally iii) both outperform Trados.

When the systems are compared regarding PE effort assessments, as shown in Table 6, the results are similar to those using PE time, demonstrating a good correlation between objective and subjective effort indicators.

System	Google	Moses	Systran	Trados
Google	-	97	115	186
Moses	22	-	73	162
Systran	30	65	-	159
Trados	8	11	40	-

Table 6: How many times the system in the first column produced an output that was better scored than each of the other systems

To support our main claim in this paper that post-editing draft translations requires less effort than translating text from scratch, we compared the PE effort and HT effort in terms of time. Table 7 shows that post-editing the output of any system is faster than translating subtitles from scratch.

System	Faster than HT
Google	94%
Moses	86.8%
Systran	81.20%
Trados	72.40%

Table 7: How often post-editing a translation tool output is faster than translating the text from scratch

While Table 7 shows how frequently PE is faster than HT, Table 8 shows the actual difference in time. By comparing the average time each translator spent on translating and to post-editing sentences we reach an average ratio (PE/HT) of 0.5952 with a ± 0.098 standard deviation, that is, the time to perform PE represents on average about 60% of the time to perform HT. The small standard deviation supports the assumption that PE is 40% faster than HT, regardless of the translator and the source of automatic translations. In other words, translating from scratch consistently takes 70% longer (HT/PE) than post-editing the same sentence.

Annotator	HT (s)	PE (s)	HT/PE	PE/HT
Average	31.89	18.82	1.73	0.59
Deviation	9.99	6.79	0.26	0.09

Table 8: Comparing the time to translate from scratch (HT) with the time to post-edit MT (PE), in seconds

As an additional experiment to study the relation between sentence length and PE effort in terms of time and subjective scores, in Tables 9 and 10 we analyzed the data according to different categories of PE and HT effort scores. Table 9 summarizes the percentage of outputs scored 1-4, the average source length and the average time spent on post-editing, including standard deviation. Table 10 summarizes the same aspects for the sentences translated from scratch.

Score	Samples	Time		Length
		Average (s)	Deviation	
1	15.2%	32.19	29.95	8.503
2	14.0%	40.87	50.98	9.343
3	31.0%	18.92	20.63	7.924
4	38.9%	5.02	8.15	6.122

Table 9: Correlation between PE effort score and average input sentence length

Score	Samples	Time		Length
		Average (s)	Deviation	
1	7.04%	111.19	82.875	10
2	18.96%	53.21	38.875	9
3	74.0%	20.29	19.342	6.89

Table 10: Correlation between translation effort score and average input sentence length

In Table 9 we can see that sentences scored 4 took on average 5 seconds to be post-edited. This may be because the tool did not permit the translators to read a sentence before they started post-editing it, thus 5 seconds would be the average time the translators spent reading the source sentence and its suggested translation, to then decide that it did not needed any post-editing.

More than 38% of the sentences were scored 4 (no modification performed) and more than 69% were designated as little or no post-editing performed. Although Tables 9 and 10 provides a certain pattern regarding the length of sentences and the scores (shorter sentences seem to have higher scores); it is interesting to note that sentences scored 1 are surprisingly shorter than sentences scored 2. Our hypothesis is that sentences that are shorter and contain several errors are more likely to be deleted whereas longer sentences tend to be fixed because it saves time on typing. It seems to take less effort to erase and rewrite short sentences than to reorder them.

It is worth noticing that post-edited translations scored 1-2 in Table 9 and sentences translated from scratch scored 2 in Table 10 have a similar length, which allows us to compare them in terms of time. Table 9 shows that post-editing sentences scored 2 is a bit slower than sentences scored 1 (requires complete retranslation). Nevertheless it does not mean that post-editing those sentences is slower than translating their original sources from scratch. We can see in Table 9 that post-editing a sentence that requires complete retranslation (scores 1-2) is less time-consuming than translating the same sentence from scratch (score 2 in Table 10). This may be so because even when the sentence requires complete retranslation the translator may benefit from the translation of some terms even if he or she considers the translation inappropriate for the sentence. The output sentence may provide the translator with a gist of the translation whereas translating from scratch also involves the effort of considering several possibilities for translating the source.

Finally, we were concerned with the quality of the post-edited translations. Although the translators were asked to perform the minimum necessary operations while post-editing, they were instructed to produce translations that were "ready for publishing". We conducted an automatic evaluation comparing each of the 12 sets of post-edited translations to the 5 sets of translations made from scratch and the corpus-based reference (ref_{0-5}). We observed a high average BLEU score of 69.92 $\pm$ 4.86 (less than 7% standard deviation), which suggests that PE does not imply any loss in translation quality, as compared to standard translations. It is always important to highlight that post-edited translations that do not match a reference are not necessarily bad as they could still be valid paraphrases. A human evaluation of these aspects is yet to be performed.

6 Conclusions and Future Work

We presented experiments showing that automatic and semi-automatic translation of DVD subtitles may be of great help to subtitlers, since the pre-translated subtitles are proven to be less time-consuming to post-edit than translating from scratch. As expected, we found a high correlation between a subjective scoring of the post-editing effort and the actual time necessary to post-edit translations. In addition, we found a strong correlation between this scoring and sentence length: high scoring translations are usually those with short length. Nevertheless, Table 10 gives us an insight that short sentences that contain several errors are more likely to be completely discarded and translated from scratch.

Regarding the performance of the translators, Table 8 confirms that the average time spent to translate from scratch is more than 70% higher than the time to post-edit the same sentence. Further analysis has shown that all the translators had a better time performance when post-editing a pre-translated sentence. The number of times that PE was faster than HT (Table 7) is substantial proof of our hypothesis. Even the TM system, which often did not perform as well as the other MT systems, achieved a high performance when compared against translating from scratch. Translating with TM systems may be a way of ensuring consistency in the translation, that is, the TM system may help the translator to be consistent when translating the same sentence more than once.

We believe that by treating punctuation and character case and by having a larger corpus, the TM system would retrieve a greater number of high percentage matches. A larger corpus would obviously contribute to a better performance of the SMT Moses as well. The rule-based system could also have an improved performance if its linguistic resources were specific to the subtitle domain, maybe by extracting in-domain bilingual dictionaries from parallel corpora.

Despite the small size of the corpus, it became evident that automatic and semi-automatic translation of subtitles can be a real help for subtitlers by speeding up the translation process by 40% for most of the subtitles (from 72 to 94% depending on the translation engine). This can also mean in practical terms a cost reduction for subtitling companies.

In future work, to clarify some choices regarding scores the translators have made, a questionnaire will be developed in order to have a more detailed analysis of the output of the systems. We also want to evaluate the subtitles including the process of fitting the translation according to specific restrictions in the field: time and length. In addition, the post-edited subtitles could be evaluated by native speakers of the target language (regarding quality) in the role of real end-users watching the videos with subtitles.

Acknowledgments

This project was supported by the European Commission, Education & Training, Erasmus Mundus: EMMC 2008-0083, Erasmus Mundus Masters in NLP & HLT programme. We would like to thank Professor Dr. Jorge Baptista for his support and insights and all translators who participated in this experiment.

References

Sandra M. Aluisio, Gisele Pinheiro, Marcelo Finger, Maria G. V. Nunes, and Stella E. Tagnin. 2003. The lacio-web project: overview and issues in brazilian portuguese corpora creation. In *Corpus Linguistics*, pages 14–21, Lancaster, UK.

Stephen Armstrong, Colm Caffrey, and Marian Flanagan. 2006. Translating dvd subtitle from english-german and enlish-japanese using example-based machine translation. In *Audiovisual Translation Scenarios*, MuTra '06, pages 1–12, Copenhagen, Denmark.

Marian Flanagan. 2009. Using example-based machine translation to translate dvd subtitles. In *Proceedings of the 3rd Workshop on Example-Based Machine Translation*, pages 85–92, Dublin, Ireland.

Philipp Koehn, Hieu Hoang, Alexandra Birch, Chris Callison-Burch, Marcello Federico, Nicola Bertoldi, Brooke Cowan, Wade Shen, Christine Moran, Richard Zens, Chris Dyer, Ondřej Bojar, Alexandra Constantin, and Evan Herbst. 2007. Moses: open source toolkit for statistical machine translation. In *Proceedings of the 45th Annual Meeting of the ACL: Poster and Demonstration Sessions*, pages 177–180, Prague, Czech Republic.

Philipp Koehn. 2005. Europarl: A parallel corpus for statistical machine translation. In *MT Summit*.

J. Richard Landis and Gary G. Koch. 1977. The measurement of observer agreement for categorical data. *Biometrics*, 33:159–174.

Maite Melero, Antoni Oliver, and Toni Badia. 2006. Automatic multilingual subtitling in the etitle project. In *Proceedings of the Twenty-eighth International Conference on Translating and the Computer*, Aslib '06, London, UK.

Minako O'Hagan. 2003. Can languge technology respond to the subtitler's dilemma? - a preliminary study. In *Proceeding of the 25th International Conference on Translation and the Computer*, London, UK.

Kishore Papineni, Salim Roukos, Todd Ward, and Wei-Jing Zhu. 2002. Bleu: a method for automatic evaluation of machine translation. In *Proceedings of the 40th Annual Meeting on Association for Computational Linguistics*, ACL '02, pages 311–318, Philadelphia, Pennsylvania.

Fred Popowich, Paul Mcfetridge, Davide Turcato, and Janine Toole. 2000. Machine translation of closed captions. *Machine Translation*, 15:311–341.

Lucia Specia. 2011. Exploiting objective annotations for measuring translation post-editing effort. In *15th Annual Conference of the European Association for Machine Translation*, EAMT '11, Leuven, Belgium.

Martin Volk. 2008. The automatic translation of film subtitles. a machine translation success story? In *Resourceful Language Technology: Festschrift in Honor of Anna*, volume 7, Uppsala, Sweden.

JRC-NAMES: A Freely Available, Highly Multilingual Named Entity Resource

Ralf Steinberger, Bruno Pouliquen, Mijail Kabadjov, Jenya Belyaeva & Erik van der Goot
European Commission – Joint Research Centre
Via Enrico Fermi 2749, 21027 Ispra (VA), Italy
{Firstname.Lastname}@jrc.ec.europa.eu

Abstract

This paper describes a new, freely available, highly multilingual named entity resource for person and organisation names that has been compiled over seven years of large-scale multilingual news analysis combined with Wikipedia mining, resulting in 205,000 person and organisation names plus about the same number of spelling variants written in over 20 different scripts and in many more languages. This resource, produced as part of the *Europe Media Monitor* activity (EMM, http://emm.newsbrief.eu/overview.html), can be used for a number of purposes. These include improving name search in databases or on the internet, seeding machine learning systems to learn named entity recognition rules, improve machine translation results, and more. We describe here how this resource was created; we give statistics on its current size; we address the issue of morphological inflection; and we give details regarding its functionality. Updates to this resource will be made available daily.

1 Introduction

The release consists of named entity lists and Java-implemented software. The software performs two main functionalities: (1) It recognises known names in text of any language and returns the name as it was found, its position and length, the standard variant of the name and the unique numerical name identifier. (2) It allows exporting all known name variants so that users can exploit the resource in further ways.

JRC-Names is the result of a multi-year large-scale effort to recognise new person and organisation names in up to 100,000 news articles per day in up to 20 different languages[1], to automatically recognise which newly found names are variants of each other, to enhance the name list with additional information extracted from Wikipedia, and to manually improve the database entries for the most frequently found names. While the Named Entity Recognition (NER) module itself is not part of the release, updates to *JRC-Names* will be made available daily so that users will always have access to the latest named entity (NE) list.[2]

In the following sections, we describe possible uses of this resource (2), list other available NE resources (3), explain very briefly how the resource was built (4), give some statistics on the resource and provide technical details on the released software (5).

2 Uses of this named entity resource

The tool serves many purposes and addresses various problems, including the following:

(a) Proper names are a problem when searching databases, the internet and other repositories, because variants of searched names are often not found (Stern & Sagot 2010). This results in non-optimal use and exploitation of repositories for documents, images and audio-visual content. *JRC-Names* allows standardising the names and improving retrieval;

(b) Names are a known problem for machine translation as they should not be translated like other words (Babych & Hartley 2003); names can be extracted before the translation process and the foreign language variant can be re-inserted in the target language to solve this problem;

[1] EMM-NewsExplorer (http://emm.newsexplorer.eu/) currently extracts new names from news articles in Arabic, Bulgarian, Danish, Dutch, English, Estonian, Farsi, French, German, Italian, Norwegian, Polish, Portuguese, Romanian, Russian, Slovene, Spanish, Swahili, Swedish and Turkish.

[2] Accessible via http://langtech.jrc.ec.europa.eu/.

(c) Lists of names in two different scripts are often used to learn transliteration rules (e.g. Pouliquen 2009).
(d) Names can be recognised and marked up in text to use as seeds when training a machine learning NER system (e.g. Buchholz & van den Bosch 2000);
(e) Social networks are less biased by national viewpoints if produced using multi-national sources and entity lists;
(f) Recognition of names is useful as input to the tasks of opinion mining, co-reference resolution, summarisation, topic detection and tracking, cross-lingual linking of related documents across languages, etc.

JRC-Names is a resource that can be useful in all these scenarios. Potential beneficiaries of the tool are IT developers and researchers in the field of text mining and machine translation; news agencies, photo agencies and other media organisations; business intelligence, and possibly more.

3 Related work

In this section, we summarise previous efforts to compile multilingual name lists. Work on developing NER systems is abundant and shall not be discussed here. For an overview of the state-of-the-art in NER, see Nadeau & Sekine (2009).

Wentland et al. (2008) built a multilingual named entity dictionary by mining Wikipedia and exploiting various link types. They first built an English named entity repository of about 1.5 million names, by selecting all article headers and by assuming that these headers are named entities if at least 75% of these strings are more frequently found in uppercase than in lowercase (except at the beginning of a sentence). They then exploit the multilingual links, as well as the redirect and disambiguation pages to identify target language equivalences in altogether fifteen languages. This method produced 250,000 named entities for the most successful language German, and about 3,000 for the lesser-resourced language Swahili.

Toral et al. (2008) built the resource *Named Entity WordNet* by searching for NEs in WordNet and by combining information found in WordNet and in Wikipedia. The resource consists of 310,000 entities, including 278,000 persons. Name variants found in Wikipedia are included.

Stern & Sagot (2010) exploit Wikipedia and GeoNames to produce a French language-focused NE database which includes 263,000 person names and 883,000 variants, extracted from French Wikipedia entries by parsing the first sentence and the redirection pages.

Prolexbase (Maurel, 2008) is a mostly manually produced resource containing about 75,000 names for different entity types, built up over many years.

With the exception of Prolexbase, all of these person name resources are the result of exploiting Wikipedia. Wikipedia is strong at providing cross-lingual and cross-script variants, but it contains only few spelling variants within the same language and it does not contain information on morphological variants. In contrast, our resource is mostly built up by recognising name variants in real-life multilingual text, and it additionally contains Wikipedia variants, resulting in up to 400 spelling variations for a single name. Future releases of *JRC-Names* will also recognise morphological inflections of entity names.

4 How the NE resource was created

This section summarises the role of NER in EMM (Section 4.1), explains how the NE information in *JRC-Names* is extracted (4.2), how the tool automatically detects which name strings are variant spellings for the same entity (4.3), and how the NE database is enhanced through human moderation (4.4) and with Wikipedia (4.5), and how morphological variants are recognised (4.6). Due to space limitations, the sub-sections on NER (4.2) and on name variant merging (4.3) are very brief, but this work has been described in much detail in Steinberger & Pouliquen (2009).

4.1 Role of NER in EMM

The freely accessible *Europe Media Monitor* (EMM) family of applications gather a current average of 100,000 news articles per day in up to 50 languages from the internet, classify them into hundreds of categories, cluster related news, link news clusters over time and across languages, and – for twenty languages – perform entity recognition, classification and disambiguation for the entity types person, organisation and location. EMM also gathers information about entities from all news articles and displays it on over one million entity pages. For an overview of EMM, see Steinberger et al. (2009).

4.2 Multilingual NER from the news

NER in EMM is performed using manually constructed language-independent rules that make use of language-specific lists of titles and other

معمر القذافي; Mouammar Kadhafi; Muammar al-Gaddafi; Moammar Gadhafi; Muammar Gheddafi; Муамар Кадафи; Muammar Kadhafi; Muammar Kaddafi; Muammer Kaddafi; Muamar Gadafi; معمر قذافي; Moamerja Gadafija; Muammar Kadafi; Muammar el Gaddafi; Муамар Каддафи; Muamar el Gadafi; Moammar Gaddafi; Moamar Gaddafi; Moamer Kadhafi; Muammar Gadafi; Moamer Gadafi; Mouammar Khadafi; Moammar Kadhafi; Muammar Gadaffi; Muammar Khadaffi; Muammar Khaddafi; Muammar Qaddafi; Muhammar Gheddafi; Muammar al Gaddafi; Moammar Gadaffi; Muamar Kadafi; Муаммар Каддафи; Moamer Gathafi; Muammar Khadafi; Mouammar Kaddafi; Muamar Kadhafi; Muamar al Gadafi; Muammar el-Qaddafi; Muammar Gadafy; Muammar Kadaffi; Muammar Gadhafi; Moamer Gaddafi; Muammar al-Ghadhafi; Muamar Gaddafi; Muammar Ghaddafi; Muamar Khadafi; Muammar Ghadhafi; Muammar al-Gadafi; Muammar al-Qadhafi; Mouammar El Kadhafi; Muammar Qadhafi; Muammer Gadaffi; Moammar Gheddafi; Mouamar Kadhafi; Mouamar Khadafi; Moamer Kadaffi; Moammar al-Qadhafi; Moamer Qadhafi; Moamar Kadhafi; Moammar Khadafi; Moamar Gadafi; Moammar Qaddafi; Muammer Gaddafi; Muammar el-Gaddafi; Moeammar Kadhafi; Mummar Gaddafi; Muammar al-Qathafi; Muammar al-Kadhafi; Muammar Al-Kaddafi; Muammar Al-Qadhafi; Moammar Khadaffi; Muammar al-Qaddafi; Mouammar Al Kadhafi; Moammar Ghadafi; Muammar Al Gaddafi; Moammar Kaddafi; Moammar al-Kadhafi; Mouammar El-Kadhafi; Moammar Khaddafi; Moammar Qadhafi; Muammar al-Gathafi; Muammar Ghadaffi; Muhammar Gaddafi; Muammar Gaddaffi; Muammar el Gadafi; Muammar Abu Minyar al-Gaddafi; Muammar al-Kadafi; Muhamar Kadafi; Mouamar Kaddafi; Moammer Gaddafi; Muammar Al-Gaddafi; Muammar al-Khadafi; Mouammar El Khaddafi; Muammar Gadhaffi; Моамар Кадафи; Muamar Al Gadafi; Mouammar

Figure 1. Name variant spellings for Libyan leader Muammar Gaddafi, as found in multilingual media reports.

words and phrases that are typically found next to names, such as titles (*president*), professions or occupations (*tennis player, playboy*), references to countries, regions, ethnic or religious groups (*French, Bavarian, Berber, Muslim*), age expressions (*57-year-old*), verbal phrases (*deceased*), modifiers (*former*) and more. These pattern words, which we refer to as *trigger words*, can also occur in combination (*57-year-old former British Prime Minister*) and patterns can be nested to capture more complex titles (e.g. *current Chair of RANLP* Ruslan Mitkov). In order to be able to cover many different languages, no other dictionaries and no parsers or part-of-speech taggers are used. To avoid detecting strings such as *Monday Angela Merkel* as a name, non-name uppercase words (including *Monday*) from a *name stop word* list are excluded from the recognition. The trigger word files contain between a few hundred and a few thousand words and regular expressions per language (to deal with inflection and other variations). Trigger word lists are produced in a combination of a manual collection from various online sources, machine learning and bootstrapping. The trigger words found historically next to each name are stored in order to build up a frequency-ranked repository of common titles (and more) for each entity.

The method is relatively simple and may at first seem labour-intensive, compared to machine learning methods that learn recognition rules on the basis of examples. However, its main advantages are that it is light-weight (it does not require linguistic tools such as morphological analysers or part-of-speech taggers), it is modular (a new language can simply be plugged in by providing the language-specific trigger words, rules and trigger word lists can be manually verified and corrected so that the method allows high levels of control. Further details can be found in Steinberger & Pouliquen (2009).

Organisation name recognition is relatively weakly developed in EMM's media monitoring applications. Organisation names are recognised if one of the words of the name candidate is a typical organisation name part from a given list (*organisation, club, international, bank*, etc.). Additionally, a Bayesian classifier trained on lists of known person and organisation names decides on the type of a new entity. Due to our coarse entity type categorisation, other entity types are frequently included into the type *organisation*, such as *Belfast Agreement*, *Nobel Prize*, *Red Mosque* or *World War I*. The entity type *Organisation* should thus be interpreted as *Other Entities*.

4.3 Name variant matching

The NER tool identifies about 1,000 new names per day and the name database currently contains about 1.15 million different entities plus about 200,000 additional spelling variants (see **Figure 1** for an example of naturally occurring spelling variants). To identify which of the names newly found every day are new entities and which ones are merely variant spellings of entities already contained in the database, we apply a language-independent name similarity measure to decide which name variants should be automatically merged. This algorithm carries out the following steps, which are the same for all languages and scripts: (1) If the name is not written using the Roman script: Transliteration into the Roman script (using standard n-to-n character transliteration rules); all names are lower-cased; (2) name normalisation; (3) vowel removal to create a consonant signature; (4) for all names with the same consonant signature, calculate the overall similarity between each pair of names, based on the edit distance of two representations of both names: between the output of steps (1) and (2). If the overall similarity of two names is above the empirically defined threshold of 0.94, the two names are automatically merged. If the similarity lies below that value, they are kept as separate entities. This threshold was set to reach almost 100% precision and to avoid erroneously merging variants of different entities. Additional variants can be assigned to known names in a manual verification process (see 4.4).

The normalisation rules (see **Figure 2**) are hand-crafted, based on the observation of regular name spelling variations. The method for normalisation and variant mapping is the same for all languages and all rules apply to all languages.

4.4 Daily manual verification and improvement

The process described in the previous sections does not as such need manual intervention, but human control does help improve the quality of the database regarding a number of issues: (1) correct recognition mistakes such as *Genius Report* or *Opfer von Diskriminierung* (English: *Victim of Discrimination*) – such names will be kept to avoid their renewed recognition in the future; (2) tune the NER process (e.g. by adding newly found name stop words, such as *Report*); (3) merge name variants whose similarity lies below the merger threshold; (4) change the main name of an entity; (5) correct the entity type (person P, organisation O, toponym T); (6) launch an automatic Wikipedia mining process (see 4.5). Manual intervention is only carried out for the most frequently mentioned names, or for regular mistakes that affect large numbers of entities (e.g. weekdays being recognised as part of the name; or morphological inflections erroneously being recognised as regular name variants). Due to high user visibility, the manual process additionally focuses on entities involved in large events such as the Olympics, Oscar and Nobel Prize nominations, and similar. An average of one hour of human effort per day is currently dedicated to these tasks.

4.5 Wikipedia lookup to add name variants in more languages

An automatic routine allows the human moderator to retrieve from Wikipedia additional name variants, as well as a photograph for any given entity, if available. The tool checks – for all known name variants of an entity – whether a Wikipedia entry exists and, if successful, mines the cross-lingual links for additional multilingual name variants. It is due to this process that the database contains name variants in languages for which EMM's NER tool has not yet been developed (e.g. Chinese, Japanese and Hebrew). The Wikipedia mining process is not launched in batch mode to allow verifying the correctness of the photograph.

4.6 Morphological inflections of names

In many languages, proper names and other words are morphologically inflected. Adding inflected names to the database would be inefficient and untidy. At the same time, simple lookup procedures would miss inflected names when only searching for the base form. In order to capture at least a large part of the inflected names, inflections for names having been found in at least five different news clusters are pre-generated, separately for each language, for all known name variants. The rules for the morphological expansion are hand-crafted, following the major morphological patterns of a language (see **Figure 3**). They do not cover all exceptions, and they may over-generate, i.e. produce forms that do not actually exist in that language. However, they are very efficient and they allow to recognise a majority of name inflections in text and to return the base form for that name.

In addition to morphological variants, this method also produces other regular variants: For instance, non-hyphenated variants of

Latin normalisation:

- accented character → non-accented equivalent
- double consonant → single consonant
- ou → u
- 'al-' →
- wl (beginning of name) → vl
- ow (end of name) → ov
- ck → k
- ph → f
- ž → j
- š → sh
- x → ks

Remove vowels

Malik al-Saïdoullaïev
Malik al-Saidoullaiev
Malik al-Saidoulaiev
Malik al-Saidulaiev
Malik Saidulaiev
... **mlk sdlv**

Name	Normalised form
Mohammed Siad Barre, Mohamed Siad Barré, Мохаммед Сиад Барре, محمد سياد بري	**mhmd sd br** (mohamed siad bare)
Mahmoud Ahmadinejad, Mahmūd Ahmadīnežād	**mhmd hmdnjd** (mahmud ahmadinejad)

Figure 2. Selection of name normalisation rules and their result. The hand-crafted rules are based on empirical observations about regular spelling variations. They are purely pragmatically motivated and not intended to represent any linguistic reality.

```
Tony(a|o|u|om|em|m|ju|jem|ja)?\s+Blair(a|o|u|om|em|m|ju|jem|ja)
```

Figure 3. Regular expression for the automatic creation of Slovene inflection forms for the name of the former British Prime Minister *Tony Blair*.

hyphenated names are being pre-generated, and Arabic names without the name particles *al* or *el* when the full name contains them, etc. (e.g. *Mohammed al-Mahdi* --> *Mohammed Mahdi*).

5 Statistics and technical details

We will first give details about EMM's entire name database (Section 5.1) and then about the subset of data that is part of the *JRC-Names* distribution (5.2). The remaining sub-sections explain how to read the NE resource file (5.3), give details about the accompanying software (5.4) and discuss plans for future extensions of JRC-Names (5.5).

5.1 Some statistics on the name database

EMM's NE database currently contains 1.18 million person and 6,700 organisation names (status July 2011). Additionally, it contains about 200,000 person and 25,000 organisation name variants. The database grows by almost 1,000 name forms (names or variants) per day. The names in the database are written in 27 different scripts (See **Table 1** for the top of the frequency list, ranked by names including their variants). Latin includes all European Union languages except Greek and Bulgarian; the Arabic script also covers Farsi.

ISO15924	TEXT	Number Variants	Count Entities
Latn	Latin	1588622	1263969
Cyrl	Cyrillic	104107	88097
Arab	Arabic	17691	14513
Jpan	Japanese (Han+Hiragana+Katakana)	6995	6785
Hans	Han (Simplified variant)	4751	4512
Hebr	Hebrew	3811	3664
Kore	Korean (Hangul+Han)	2432	2354
Deva	Devanagari (Nagari)	1527	1043
Grek	Greek	1476	1410
Thai	Thai	1203	1140
Geor	Georgian (Mkhedruli)	1072	1021
Beng	Bengali	674	645
Taml	Tamil	639	618
Mlym	Malayalam	278	272
Armn	Armenian	195	188
Knda	Kannada	145	139
Telu	Telugu	128	126
Ethi	Ethiopic (Ge☒ez)	112	108

Table 1. Number of NEs and their variant spellings written in 18 out of the 27 different scripts contained in the NE database.

The question regarding the distribution of the names across different languages is not easy to answer as the news tends to mention names from around the world. The fact that a certain name is more often mentioned by the press in one country (or in combination with a certain country name) can be misleading. For instance, entity number 10101 (*European Union*) was the most frequently mentioned entity in German language news in 2010 (before *Angela Merkel*) and it was the second most frequently mentioned name in English language news (after *Barack Obama*). However, for look-up purposes in most European languages, it does not matter whether *Silvio Berlusconi* is an Italian, German or Romanian name, as long as it gets recognised in texts of that language.

5.2 Statistics on *JRC-Names*

JRC-Names does not contain the entire contents of our database. Instead, it contains the subset of names that satisfy at least one of the following conditions: (a) they have been found in at least five different news clusters; (b) they have been manually validated; (c) they have been retrieved from Wikipedia. The first condition helps to drastically cut down on wrongly identified names. Names thus need to be found repeatedly and in different contexts before they get accepted in the list of *known names*. Secondly, names that have been mentioned only once or twice in the course of many years (they are the majority), will be less useful for most users.

The released data contains about 205,000 distinct names and 204,000 additional variants (status July 2011). The dataset grows by about 230 new entities and an additional 430 new name variants per week. The data set contains relatively few organisations (3.2%). Out of this current total of 205,000 unique names, almost two thirds (63.76%) do not have name variants; 22.52% and 5.31% have two and three variants, respectively. There are 3760 names with ten or more variants, 242 with 50 or more, and 37 with more than 100 variants. The names with the most name variants are *Muammar Gaddafi* (413 variants, see **Figure 1**), *Mikhail Saakashvili* (256 name variants) and *Mahmoud Ahmadinejad* (246 variants).

Only an extremely small subset of these names and their variants has been manually verified (although manual moderation does focus on the most highly visible and the most frequently mentioned names). For this reason, the name list will contain a number of errors. We have identified the following types: (a) non-entities (e.g. *Red Piano* or *French Doctor*); (b) names with Wikipedia scope notes (e.g. *Vinci (construction)*); (c) names with a wrong name extent (e.g. *Even Obama*); (d) inflected names (e.g. *Tonyjem Blairom*); (e) wrong entity type (e.g. *Merlin Biosciences* as a Person; see the discussion in Section 4.2) and (f) non-unique organisation names (e.g. *Health Ministry*). However, we do not consider spelling mistakes found in media reports (e.g. *Condaleeza Rice* instead of the correct spelling *Condoleezza Rice*) as being errors in *JRC-Names* as they do occur in real-life texts, and knowing them helps identify intended references to entities. (g) It is unavoidable that several unique identifiers occasionally exist for the same entity (e.g. *Sergei Izvolskij* and *Sergey Izvolskiy*). (h) It is possible that different entities have been merged into one entity. (i) It is furthermore very likely that different persons sharing the same first and last name have the same identifier because no disambiguation mechanism is in place.

5.3 Reading the named entity resource file

The tool consists of Java-implemented software and a named entity resource file. Updates of the resource file will be made available for download daily so that users will always have the newest NE data. The resource file is a UTF8-encoded Java zip file. There is no need to open this file if the provided software is used, but we describe the file structure here in case users do want to access the file: Each line consists of four tab-separated columns containing: name ID; type; language; and name variant (see **Table 2**). *Name ID* is a unique numerical identifier for the entity. In this release, *Type* can only be Person (P) or Organisation (O). The column *Language* contains the ISO 639-2 two-digit code for the language if the name variant should only be looked up in that language. If a name can be looked up in all languages, which is the default, the value is *u* (undefined). The strings in the column *name variant* are the known spellings of the name, one per line. Multi-word strings are separated by the '+' sign (e.g. *United+Nations*). For all lines with the same name ID, the first line shows the main name, i.e. the variant that we chose to use for display purposes inside EMM. We usually choose it because it either is the name variant most frequently found in the news, or because it is the variant found on Wikipedia, or because it is a frequent Latin script version of a name originally written in another script.

While many name variants will only occur in some languages and not in others, it does not normally do any harm to search for the foreign language variants in a text. However, in some cases, a name variant may have a different meaning in other languages. In such cases, it is useful to restrict the lookup information to a subset of languages, or even to a single language, in order to avoid false positives. To give an example: the short name of the German insurance company *Allianz* is homographic with a common German noun (English *alliance*), so the simple word *Allianz* should not be recognised as the insurance company in German language texts. The multiword name variants *Versicherer Allianz*, *Allianz SE*, *Allianz-Konzern* and others will be recognised. Another example is the acronym 'FN', which stands for the political party *Front National* in French language text, while it stands for *Förenta nationerna* (*United Nations*) in Swedish. By restricting the lookup to specific languages, we can thus avoid mistakes. See **Table 2** for some sample entries.

3202	O	u	United+Nations
3202	O	u	Nations+Unies
3202	O	fr	ONU
3202	O	u	ಸಂಯುಕ್ತ+ರಾಷ್ಟ್ರ+ಸಂಸ್ಥೆ
3202	O	u	Ujedinjeni narodi
3202	O	sv	FN
13752	O	u	Front National
13752	O	fr	FN
13752	O	u	国民戦線
13752	O	u	Фронт Насионал

Table 2. Selected lines from the name resource file, showing the unique numerical identifier, the entity type, the language scope and the name variant.

5.4 Programming details / Usage of the tool

The NE resource file is accompanied by Java code. The code consists of a library that implements the actual text matching, and of a number of source files to demonstrate how to match entities in a text and how to extract the entity information from the NE resource file. This information can then also be used to produce the full list of name variants.

The matching software, after reading and analysing the NE resource file, searches for any of the known entities in multilingual text. For every entity found, the software will return the following values: (a) the numerical name identifier; (b) the main name for that entity; (c) the name string found (this can be any variant from the NE resource file); (d) the offset in the text; (e) the length of the name string found. The lookup process is case-sensitive: For languages distinguishing case, the uppercase letters in the NE resource file will only match if they are also spelt with uppercase in the text, while lowercase letters will match both upper and lower case.

The tool in principle searches for any of the name variants in texts of any language, with the exception of those cases where names are marked as being language-specific or their recognition is blocked for a specific language, as described in Section 5.3.

The lookup process is fast because the software uses finite state technology. It does not require large amounts of memory. It can be run effortlessly on a modern desktop computer. This tool has been in use for several years. It is robust and its output can be seen on EMM's web pages (see http://emm.newsbrief.eu/overview.html).

5.5 Further planned developments

This first release of *JRC-Names* does not recognise morphologically inflected variants of entity names. However, it is planned that future versions will include morphological variant recognition in one of two ways. Either morphological variants will be pre-generated (similar to the process described in Section 4.6) and added to the named entity resource file; or inflection variants will be dealt with as part of the lookup process performed by the software, for instance through the application of regular expressions. The recognition of other name spelling variants will also be included consistently, such as: hyphenated versus non-hyphenated name variants (e.g. *Yves Saint-Laurent* vs. *Yves Saint Laurent*); names with or without name infixes such as 'al' (*Khan al Khalil* vs. *Khan Khalil*); names with and without spaces in languages where space separation is optional (e.g. 巴拉克·歐巴馬 and 巴拉克歐巴馬), and more.

We also plan to make available frequency counts for names and their variants and, if possible, counts of the frequency per language. Furthermore, we may be able to publish the most frequent trigger words (titles and more, see Section 4.2) found next to each entity.

Acknowledgments

The *Europe Media Monitor* EMM is a multiannual group effort involving many tasks, of which some are much less visible to the outside world. We would thus like to thank all past and present OPTIMA team members for their help and dedication. We would also like to thank our Unit Head Delilah Al Khudhairy for her support.

References

Babych Bogdan, Anthony Hartley (2003). Improving machine translation quality with automatic named entity recognition. Proceedings of the 7th International EAMT workshop on MT and other Language Technology Tools – Improving MT through other Language Technology Tools: Resources and Tools for Building MT, Budapest, Hungary.

Buchholz Sabine & Antal van den Bosch (2000) Integrating seed names and ngrams for a name entity list classifier. In Proceedings of 2nd International Conference on Language Resources and Evaluation. LREC-2000, Athens, Greece.

Maurel Denis (2008). Prolexbase: A multilingual relational lexical database of proper names. In Proceedings of the 6th Conference on Language Resources and Evaluation. Marrakesh (Morocco).

Nadeau David & Satoshi Sekine (2009). A survey of entity recognition and classification. In: Satoshi Sekine & Elisabete Ranchhod (eds.): Named Entities – Recognition, classification and use. John Benjamins Publishing Company, Amsterdam/Philadelphia.

Pouliquen Bruno (2008). Similarity of names across scripts: Edit distance using learned costs of n-grams. In Proceedings of the 6th international Conference on Natural Language Processing (GoTal'2008). Göteborg, Sweden.

Steinberger Ralf & Bruno Pouliquen (2009). Cross-lingual Named Entity Recognition. In: Satoshi Sekine & Elisabete Ranchhod (eds.): Named Entities - Recognition, Classification and Use, Benjamins Current Topics, Volume 19, pp. 137-164.

Steinberger Ralf, Bruno Pouliquen & Erik van der Goot (2009). An introduction to the Europe Media Monitor family of applications. Proceedings of the SIGIR'2009 Workshop 'Information Access in a Multilingual World'. Boston, USA.

Stern Rosa & Benoît Sagot (2010). Resources for named entity recognition and resolution in news wires. Proceedings of the LREC 2010 Workshop on Resources and Evaluation for Identity Matching, Entity Resolution and Entity Management, Malta.

Toral Antonio, Rafael Muñoz, Monica Monachini (2008). Named Entity WordNet. In Proceedings of the 6th Conference on Language Resources and Evaluation. Marrakesh (Morocco).

Wentland Wolodja, Johannes Knopp, Carina Silberer, Matthias Hartung (2008). Building a Multilingual Lexical Resource for Named Entity Disambiguation, Translation and Transliteration. Proceedings of LREC 2006, Genoa, Italy.

MDL-based Models for Alignment of Etymological Data

Hannes Wettig, Suvi Hiltunen, Roman Yangarber
Department of Computer Science
University of Helsinki, Finland
First.Last@cs.helsinki.fi

Abstract

We introduce several models for alignment of etymological data, that is, for finding the best alignment, given a set of etymological data, at the sound or symbol level. This is intended to obtain a means of measuring the quality of the etymological data sets, in terms of their internal consistency. One of our main goals is to devise automatic methods for aligning the data that are as objective as possible, the models make no a priori assumptions—e.g., no preference for vowel-vowel or consonant-consonant alignments. We present a baseline model and several successive improvements, using data from the Uralic language family.

1 Introduction

We present work on induction of alignment rules for etymological data, in a project that studies genetic relationships among the Uralic language family. This is a continuation of previous work, reported in (Wettig and Yangarber, 2011), where the methods were introduced. In this paper, we extend the models reported earlier and give a more comprehensive evaluation of results. In addition to the attempt to induce alignment rules, we aim to derive measures of quality of data sets in terms of their internal consistency. More consistent dataset should receive a higher score in the evaluations. Currently our goal is to analyze *given*, existing etymological datasets, rather than to construct cognate sets from raw linguistic data. The question to be answered is whether a complete description of the correspondence rules can be discovered automatically. Can they be found directly from raw etymological data—sets of cognate words from languages within the language family? Are the alignment rules are "inherently encoded" in a dataset (the *corpus*) itself? We aim to develop methods that are as objective as possible, that rely only on the data, rather than on any prior assumptions about the data, the possible rules and alignments.

Computational etymology encompasses several problem areas, including: discovery of sets of genetically related words—*cognates*; determination of genetic relations among groups of languages, from raw or organized linguistic data; discovering *regular sound correspondences* across languages in a given language family; and reconstruction, either diachronic—i.e., reconstruction of proto-forms for a hypothetical parent language, from which the word-forms found in the daughter languages derive, or synchronic—i.e., of word forms that are missing from existing languages.

Several approaches to etymological alignment have emerged over the last decade. The problem of discovering cognates is addressed, e.g., in, e.g., (Bouchard-Côté et al., 2007; Kondrak, 2004; Kessler, 2001). In our work, we do not attempt to find cognate sets, but begin with given sets of etymological data for a language family, possibly different or even conflicting. We use the principle of *recurrent sound correspondence*, as in much of the literature, including the mentioned work, (Kondrak, 2002; Kondrak, 2003) and others. Modeling relationships within the language family arises in the process of evaluation of our alignment models. Phylogenetic reconstruction is studied extensively by, e.g.,(Nakhleh et al., 2005; Ringe et al., 2002; Barbancon et al., 2009); these work differ from ours in that they operate on pre-compiled sets of "characters", capturing divergent features of entire languages within the family, whereas we operate at the level of words or cognate sets. Other related work is further mentioned in the body of the paper.

We describe our datasets in the next section, present a statement of the etymology alignment problem in Section 3, cover our models in detail in Sections 4– 6, and discuss results and next steps in Section 7.

2 Data

We use two digital Uralic etymological resources, *SSA—Suomen Sanojen Alkuperä*, "The Origin of Finnish Words", (Itkonen and Kulonen, 2000), and the StarLing database, (Starostin, 2005). StarLing, originally based on (Rédei, 1988 1991), differs from SSA in several respects. StarLing has about 2000 Uralic cognate sets, compared with over 5000 in SSA, and does not explicitly indicate dubious etymologies. However, Uralic data in StarLing is more evenly distributed, because it is not Finnish-centric like SSA is—cognate sets in StarLing are not required to contain a member from Finnish. The Uralic language family has not been studied by computational means previously.

3 Aligning Pairs of Words

We begin with pairwise alignment: aligning a set of pairs of words from two related languages in our data set. The task of alignment means, for each word pair, finding which symbols correspond. We expect that some symbols will align with themselves, while others have undergone changes over the time when the two related languages have been evolving separately. The simplest form of such alignment at the symbol level is a pair $(\sigma : \tau) \in \Sigma \times T$, a single symbol σ from the *source alphabet* Σ with a symbol τ from the *target alphabet* T. We denote the sizes of the alphabets by $|\Sigma|$ and $|T|$, respectively.[1]

Clearly, with this type of 1x1 alignment alone we cannot align a source word $\boldsymbol{\sigma}$ of length $|\boldsymbol{\sigma}|$ with a target word $\boldsymbol{\tau}$ of length $|\boldsymbol{\tau}| \neq |\boldsymbol{\sigma}|$.[2] To model also *insertions* and *deletions*, we augment both alphabets with the empty symbol, denoted by a dot, and use $\Sigma_.$ and $T_.$ as augmented alphabets. We can then align word pairs such as *ien—ige*, meaning "gum" in Finnish and Established, for example, as:

$$\begin{array}{ccc} i & e & n \\ | & | & | \\ i & g & e \end{array} \qquad \begin{array}{cccc} i & . & e & n \\ | & | & | & | \\ i & g & e & . \end{array}$$

etc. The (historically correct) alignment on the right consists, e.g., of symbol pairs: (i:i), (.:g), (e:e), (n:.).

4 The Baseline Model

We wish to encode these aligned pairs as compactly as possible, following the Minimum Description Length Principle (MDL), see e.g. (Grünwald, 2007; Rissanen, 1978). Given a data corpus $D = (\boldsymbol{\sigma}_1, \boldsymbol{\tau}_1), \ldots, (\boldsymbol{\sigma}_N, \boldsymbol{\tau}_N)$ of N word pairs, we first choose an alignment of each word pair $(\boldsymbol{\sigma}_i, \boldsymbol{\tau}_i)$, which we then use to "transmit" the data, by simply listing the sequence of the atomic pairwise symbol alignments.[3] In order for the code to be uniquely decodable, we also need to encode the word boundaries. This can be done by transmitting a special symbol # that we use only at the end of a word.

Thus, we transmit objects, or *events*, e, in the event space E—which is in this case:

$$E = \Sigma_. \times T_. \cup \{(\# : \#)\}$$

We do this by means of Bayesian marginal likelihood, or *prequential* coding, see e.g., (Kontkanen et al., 1996), giving the total code length as:

$$L_{base}(D) = \tag{1}$$
$$-\sum_{e\in E} \log \Gamma(c(e) + \alpha(e)) + \sum_{e\in E} \log \Gamma(\alpha(e))$$
$$+ \log \Gamma\left[\sum_{e\in E} (c(e) + \alpha(e))\right] - \log \Gamma\left[\sum_{e\in E} \alpha(e)\right]$$

The *count* $c(e)$ is the number of times event e occurs in a complete alignment of the corpus; in particular, $c(\# : \#) = N$ occurs as many times as there are word pairs. The alignment counts are maintained in a corpus-global *count matrix* M, where $M(i,j) = c(i : j)$. The $\alpha(e)$ are the (Dirichlet) priors on the events. In the baseline algorithm, we set $\alpha(e) = 1$ for all e, the so-called uniform prior, which does not favor any distribution over E, *a priori*. Note that this choice nulls the second summation in equation 1.

Our baseline algorithm is simple: we first randomly align the entire corpus, then re-align one word pair at a time, greedily minimizing the total cost in Eq. 1, using dynamic programming.

In the matrix in Fig. 1, each cell corresponds to a partial alignment: reaching cell (i, j) means having read off i symbols of the source and j symbols of the target word. We iterate this process, *re-aligning* the word pairs, i.e., for the given word pair, we subtract the contribution of its current alignment from the global count matrix, then re-align the word pair, then add the newly aligned events back to the global count matrix. Re-alignment continues until convergence.

Re-alignment Step: align source word $\boldsymbol{\sigma}$ consisting of symbols $\boldsymbol{\sigma} = [\sigma_1 ... \sigma_n] \in \Sigma^*$ with target word $\boldsymbol{\tau} = [\tau_1 ... \tau_m]$. We use dynamic programming to fill in the matrix, e.g., top-to-bottom, left-to-right:[4]

Alignments of $\boldsymbol{\sigma}$ and $\boldsymbol{\tau}$ correspond in a 1-1 fashion to paths through the matrix, starting with cost equal to 0 in top-left cell and terminating in bottom-right cell, moving only downward or rightward.

Each cell stores the cost of the *most probable* path so far: the most probable way to have scanned $\boldsymbol{\sigma}$ up to symbol σ_i and $\boldsymbol{\tau}$ up to τ_j, marked X in the Figure:

$$V(\sigma_i, \tau_j) = \min \begin{cases} V(\sigma_i, \tau_{j-1}) & +L(. : \tau_j) \\ V(\sigma_{i-1}, \tau_j) & +L(\sigma_i : .) \\ V(\sigma_{i-1}, \tau_{j-1}) & +L(\sigma_i : \tau_j) \end{cases} \tag{2}$$

Each term $V(.,.)$ has been computed earlier by the dynamic programming; the term $L(.)$—the cost of align-

[1] We refer to "*source*" and "*target*" language for convenience only—our models are symmetric, as will become apparent.

[2] We use boldface to denote words, as vectors of symbols.

[3] By *atomic* we mean that the symbols are not analyzed—in terms of their phonetic features—and treated by the baseline algorithm as atoms. In particular, the model has no notion of identity of symbols *across* the languages!

[4] NB: in Fig. 1, the left column and the top row store the costs for symbol deletions *at the beginning* of the source and the target word, respectively.

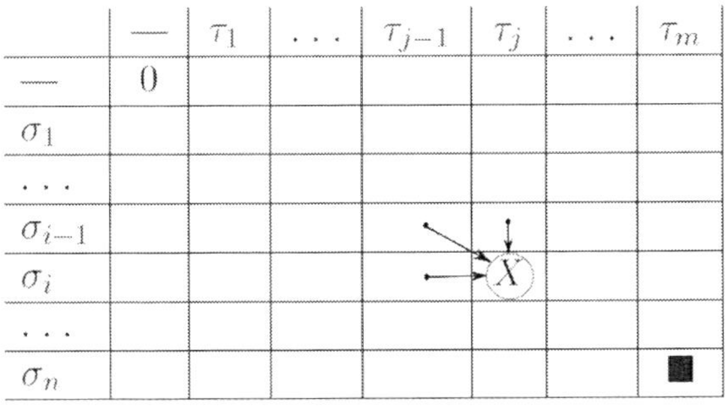

Figure 1: Re-alignment matrix: computes Dynamic Programming search for the most probable alignment.

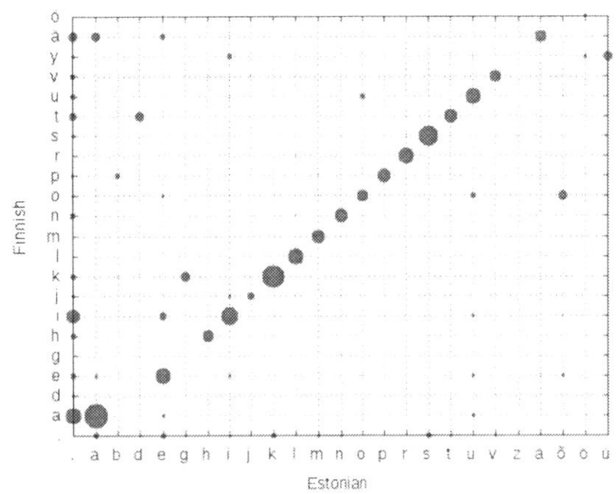

Figure 2: Global count matrix, using two-part model

ing the two symbols—is a parameter of the model, computed in equation (3).

The parameters $L(e)$, or $P(e)$, for every observed event e, are computed from the *change* in the total code-length—the change that corresponds to the cost of adjoining the new event e to the set of previously observed events E:

$$L(e) = \Delta_e L = L(E \cup \{e\}) - L(E)$$

$$P(e) = 2^{-\Delta_e L} = \frac{2^{-L\left(E\cup\{e\}\right)}}{2^{-L(E)}} \quad (3)$$

Combining eqs. 1 and 3 gives the probability:

$$P(e) = \frac{c(e)+1}{\sum_{e'} c(e') + |E|} \quad (4)$$

In particular, the cost of the most probable *complete* alignment of the two words will be stored in the bottom-right cell, $V(\sigma_n, \tau_m)$, marked ■. An example alignment count matrix is shown in Fig. 2.

4.1 The Two-Part Code

The baseline model revealed two problems. First, it seems to get stuck in local optima, and second, it produces many events with very low counts (occurring only once or twice).

To address the first problem we use simulated annealing with a sufficiently slow cooling schedule. This yields a reduction in the cost, and a better—more sparse—alignment count matrix.

The second problem is more substantial. Starting from a common ancestor language, the number of changes that occurred in either language should be small. We expect *sparse* data—that only a small proportion of all *possible* events in E will actually ever occur.

We incorporate this notion into the model by means of a two-part code. First we encode which events have occurred/have been observed: we send **a.** the number of events with non-zero counts—this costs $\log(|E|+1)$ bits, and **b.** specifically which subset $E^+ \subset E$ of the events have non-zero counts—this costs $\log \binom{|E|}{|E^+|}$ bits. This first part of the code is called the *codebook*. Given the codebook, we transmit the complete data, E^+, using Bayesian marginal likelihood. The code length becomes:

$$\begin{aligned} L_{tpc}(D) = &\log(|E|+1) + \log \binom{|E|}{|E^+|} \quad (5) \\ &- \sum_{e \in E^+} \log \Gamma\big(c(e)+1\big) \\ &+ \log \Gamma\Bigg(\sum_{e \in E^+} \big(c(e)+1\big)\Bigg) - \log \Gamma(|E^+|) \end{aligned}$$

where E^+ denotes the set of events with non-zero counts, and we have set all $\alpha(e)$'s to one. Optimizing the above function with simulated annealing yields much better alignments.

4.2 Aligning Multiple Symbols

Multiple symbols are aligned in (Bouchard-Côté et al., 2007; Kondrak, 2003). For example, Estonian and Finnish have frequent geminated consonants, which correspond to single symbols/sounds in other languages; diphthongs may align with single vowels; etc. We extend the baseline model to a 2x2 model, to allow correspondences of up to two symbols on both the source and the target side. The set of admissible *kinds* of events is then extended to include:

$$K = \left\{ \begin{array}{lll} (\# : \#), & (\sigma : .), & (\sigma\sigma' : .), \\ (. : \tau), & (\sigma : \tau), & (\sigma\sigma' : t), \\ (. : \tau\tau'), & (\sigma : \tau\tau'), & (\sigma\sigma' : \tau\tau') \end{array} \right\} \quad (6)$$

We expect correspondences of the different types to behave differently, so we encode the occurrences of different event kinds separately in the codebook:

$$L_{mult} = L(CB) + L(Data|CB) \quad (7)$$

$$L(CB) = \sum_{k \in K} \left[\log(N_k+1) + \log \binom{N_k}{M_k} \right] \quad (8)$$

$$L(D|CB) = -\sum_{e\in E} \log \Gamma\big(c(e)+1\big) \quad (9)$$
$$+ \log \Gamma \left[\sum_{e\in E} \big(c(e)+1\big)\right] - \log \Gamma(|E|)$$

where N_k is the number of possible events of kind k and M_k the corresponding number of such events actually observed in the alignment; $\sum_k M_k \equiv |E|$.

5 Three-Dimensional Alignment

The baseline models align languages pairwise. The alignment models allow us to learn 1-1 patterns of correspondence in the language family. This model is easily extended to *any* number of languages. The model in (Bouchard-Côté et al., 2007) also aligns more than two languages at a time. We extend the 2-D model to three dimensions as follows. We seek an alignment where symbols correspond to each other in a 1-1 fashion, as in the 2-D baseline. A three-dimensional alignment is a triplet of symbols $(\sigma : \tau : \xi) \in \Sigma_. \times T_. \times \Xi_.$. For example, the words meaning "9" in Finnish, Estonian and Mordva, can be aligned simultaneously as:

$$\begin{array}{ccccccccc} y & . & h & d & e & k & s & \ddot{a} & n \\ | & | & | & | & | & | & | & | & | \\ \ddot{u} & . & h & . & e & k & s & a & . \\ | & | & | & | & | & | & | & | & | \\ v & e & \chi & . & . & k & s & a & . \end{array}$$

In 3-D alignment, the input data contains all examples where words *in at least two* languages are present[5]—i.e., a word may be missing from one of the languages, (which allows us to utilize more of the data). Thus we have two types of examples: *complete*—where all three words present (as "9" above), and *incomplete*—containing words in only two languages. For example, for (*haamu:—:čama*)—"ghost" in Finnish and Mordva—the cognate Estonian word is missing.

We next extend the 2-D count matrix and the 2-D re-alignment algorithm to three dimensions. The 3-D re-alignment matrix is directly analogous to the 2-D version. For the alignment counts in 3-D, we handle complete and incomplete examples separately.

Our "marginal" 3-D alignment model aligns three languages simultaneously, using three marginal 2-D matrices, each storing a pairwise 2-D alignment. The marginal matrices for three languages are denoted $M_{\Sigma T}$, $M_{\Sigma\Xi}$ and $M_{T\Xi}$. The algorithm optimizes the total cost of the complete data, which is defined as the *sum* of the three 2-D costs obtained from applying prequential coding to the marginal alignment matrices.

When computing the cost for event $e = (\sigma, \tau, \xi)$, we consider complete and incomplete examples separately. In "incomplete" examples, we use the counts from the corresponding marginal matrix directly. E.g., for event count $c(e)$, where $e = (\sigma, -, \xi)$, and "$-$" denotes the missing word, the event count is given by: $M_{\Sigma\Xi}(\sigma, \xi)$,

[5]This was true by definition in the baseline 2-D algorithm.

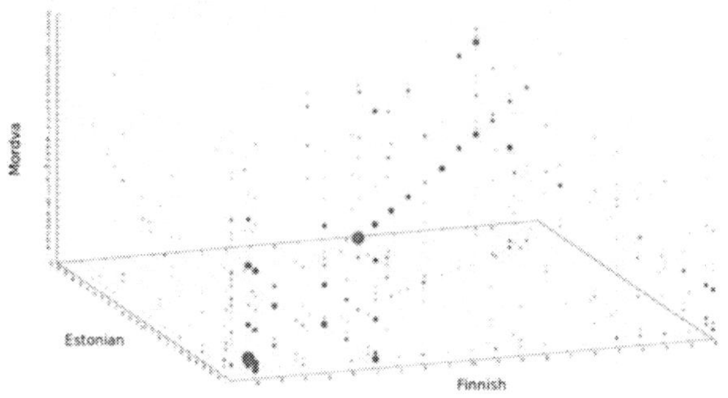

Figure 3: 3-dimensional alignment matrix.

and the cost of each alignment is computed as in the baseline model, directly in two dimensions.

In case when the data triplet is complete—fully observed—the alignment cost is computed as the *sum of the pairwise 2-D costs*, given by three marginal alignment count matrices:[6]

$$\begin{aligned} L(\sigma : \tau : \xi) &= L_{\Sigma T}(\sigma : \tau) \\ &+ L_{\Sigma\Xi}(\sigma : \xi) \\ &+ L_{T\Xi}(\tau : \xi) \end{aligned} \quad (10)$$

The cost of each pairwise alignment is computed using prequential two-part coding, as in sec. 4.1. Note that when we register a complete alignment (σ, τ, ξ), we register it in *each* of the base matrices—we increment each of the marginal counts: $M_{\Sigma T}(\sigma, \tau)$, $M_{\Sigma\Xi}(\sigma, \xi)$, and $M_{T\Xi}(\tau, \xi)$.

To calculate the transition costs in the Viterbi algorithm, we also have two cases, complete and incomplete. For incomplete examples, we perform Viterbi in 2-D, using the costs directly from the corresponding marginal matrix, equation (5).

3-D re-alignment phase: for complete examples in 3-D, is a direct analogue of the 2-D re-alignment—in the (i, j) plane—in eq. (2), extended to the third dimension, k. The cell $V(\sigma_i, \tau_j, \xi_k)$—the cost of the most probable path leading to the cell (i, j, k)—is calculated by Dynamic Programming, using the symbol-alignment costs $L(\sigma : \tau : \xi)$. In addition to the three source cells as in eq. (2), in plane k, there are four additional source cells from the previous plane, $k - 1$.

Visualization: We wish to visualize the distribution of counts in the final 3-D alignment, except that now we must deal with *expected counts*, rather than observed counts, because some of the examples are incomplete. We can form a 3-D *visualization matrix* M^* as follows:

- Compute $|D|$, the total number of alignments in the complete data (including the end-of-word alignments)

[6]Note that this results in an incomplete code, since every symbol is coded twice, but that does not affect the learning.

- For each cell (i, j, k) in M^*, the weight in that cell is given by $P(i : j : k) \cdot |D|$, where $P(i : j : k)$ is the probability of the alignment.

- The matrix of expected counts will have no zero-weight cells, since there are no zero-probability events—except $(. : . : .)$. To suppress visualizing events with very low expected counts, we don't show cells with counts below a threshold, say, 0.5.

A distribution of the expected counts in 3-D alignment is shown in figure 3. The three languages are Finnish, Estonian and Mordva. The area of each point in this figure is proportional to the expected count of the corresponding 3-way alignment.

6 Nuisance Suffixes

The existing etymological datasets are not always perfectly suited to the alignment task as we have defined it here. For example, the SSA contains mostly complete word-forms from all the languages, as they would appear in a dictionary. As a consequence, this frequently includes morphological material that is not relevant from the point of view of etymology or alignment. To illustrate this (in the Indo-European family), consider aligning English *maid* and German *mädchen*—in German, the word-form without the suffix has disappeared. Many instances with such suffixes are found in the SSA; StarLing presents *stemmed* data to a larger extent, though assuring that every form in the dataset is perfectly stemmed is a very difficult task. From the point of view of computational alignment, such "nuisance" suffixes present a problem, by confusing the model.

We extend the model to handle, or discover, the nuisance suffixes automatically, as follows. Consider, in the realignment matrix in Fig. 1, the cells (i, j) (marked X,) (i, m), and (j, n). We always end by transitioning from cell marked ■, to the terminal cell, via the special end-of-word alignment event $(\# : \#)$, whose cost is computed from N, the number of word pairs in the data (this final transition is not shown in the figure).

While previously, we could only reach the terminal cell from cell ■ via event $(\# : \#)$, we now also permit a *hyper-jump* from any cell in the matrix to the terminal cell, which is equivalent to treating the remainder of source and/or target word as a nuisance suffix. Thus, hyper-jump from cell marked X means that we code the remaining symbols $[\sigma_{i+1}...\sigma_n]$ in $\boldsymbol{\sigma}$ and $[\tau_{j+1}...\tau_m]$ in $\boldsymbol{\tau}$ separately, *not* using the global count matrix.

That is, to align $\boldsymbol{\sigma}$ and $\boldsymbol{\tau}$, we first code the symbols up to X jointly, prequentially, using the global count matrix. After X, we code a special event $(- : -)$, meaning an aligned *morpheme boundary*, similar to $(\# : \#)$ which says we have aligned the *word* boundaries. Then we code the rest of $[\sigma_{i+1}...\sigma_n]$, and the rest of $[\tau_{j+1}...\tau_m]$, both followed by $\#$.

If we hyper-jump from cell (i, m), rather than from X, then we code the event $(- : \#)$—empty suffix on target side, and then code the rest of $[\sigma_{i+1}...\sigma_n]$ in $\boldsymbol{\sigma}$ and $\#$. Symmetrically for the hyper-jump from (j, m).

	Two-part model	*Suffix model*
Fin-Est	21748.29	21445.01
Fin-Ugr	10987.98	10794.87

Table 1: Nuisance suffix models.

The cost of each symbol in the suffix can be coded, for example, according to: a uniform language model: each source symbol costs $-\log 1/(|\Sigma| + 1)$; a unigram model: for each source symbol σ (including $\#$), compute its frequency $p(\sigma)$ from the raw source data, and let $cost(\sigma) = -\log p(\sigma)$; a bigram model; etc.

Table 1 compares the code length between the original 1x1 two-part code model and a nuisance suffix model (for two language pairs). The code length is always lower in the nuisance suffix model.

Although it finds instances of true nuisance suffixes, the model may be fooled by certain phenomena. For example, when aligning Finnish and Estonian, the model decides that final vowels in Finnish which have disappeared in Estonian are suffixes, whereas that is historically not the case. To avoid such misinterpretation, the suffix detection feature should be used in conjunction with other model variants, including alignment of more than a pair of languages.

7 Results

One way to evaluate the presented models thoroughly would require a *gold-standard* aligned corpus; the models produce alignments, which would be compared to expected alignments. Given a gold-standard, we could measure performance quantitatively, e.g., in terms of accuracy. However, no gold-standard alignment for the Uralic data currently exists, and building one is very costly and slow.

Alignment: We can perform a qualitative evaluation, by checking how many correct sound correspondences a model finds—by inspecting the final alignment of the corpus and the alignment matrix. A matrix for a 2-D, 1x1 two-part model alignment of Finnish-Estonian is shown in figure 2. The size of each ball is proportional to the number of alignments in the corpus of the corresponding symbols.

Finnish and Estonian are closely related, and the alignment shows a close correspondence—the model finds the "diagonal," i.e., most sounds correspond to "themselves." We must note that this model has no *a priori* knowledge about the nature of the symbols, e.g., that Finnish *a* is identical to or has any relation to Estonian *a*. The languages are coded separately, and they may have different alphabets—as they do in general (we use transcribed data).

Rules of correspondence: One of our main goals is to model complex rules of correspondence among languages. We can evaluate the models based on how

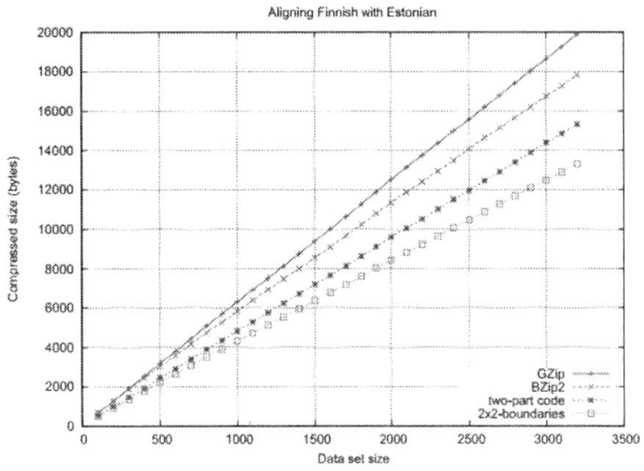

Figure 4: Comparison of compression power. Two-part code model refers to the 1x1 model that is described in section 4.1 and 2x2-boundaries model multiple symbol alignment model that is discussed in section 4.2.

well they discover rules, and how complex the rules are. In Fig. 2, the baseline model finds that Fin. *u* ~ Est. *u*, but sometimes to *o*—this entropy is left unexplained by this model. However, the more complex 2x2 model identifies the cause exactly—by discovering that Finnish diphthongs *uo, yö, ie* correspond to Estonian long vowels *oo, öö, ee*, which covers (i.e., explains!) all instances of (*u*:*o*).

The plot shows many Finnish-Estonian correspondences, which can be found in handbooks, e.g., (Lytkin, 1973; Sinor, 1997). For example, *ä*~*ä* vs. *ä*~*a* about evenly—reflecting the rule that original front vowels (*ä*) became back (*a*) in non-first syllables in Estonian; word-final vowels *a, i, ä*, preserved in Finnish are often deleted in Estonian; etc. These can be observed directly in the alignment matrix, and in the aligned corpus.

Compression: In figure 4, we compare the models against standard compressors, gzip and bzip, tested on over 3200 Finnish-Estonian word pairs from SSA. The data given to our models is processed by the compressors, one word per line. Of course, our models know that they should align pairs of consecutive lines. This shows that learning about the "vertical" correspondences achieves much better compression rates—extract regularity from the data.

Language distance: We can use alignment to measure inter-language distances. We align all languages in StarLing pairwise, e.g., using a two-part 1x1 model. We can then measure the *Normalized Compression Distance* (Cilibrasi and Vitanyi, 2005):

$$NCD(\mathbf{a}, \mathbf{b}) = \frac{C(\mathbf{a}, \mathbf{b}) - \min(C(\mathbf{a}, \mathbf{a}), C(\mathbf{b}, \mathbf{b}))}{\max(C(\mathbf{a}, \mathbf{a}), C(\mathbf{b}, \mathbf{b}))}$$

where $0 < NCD < 1$, and $C(\mathbf{a}, \mathbf{b})$ is the compression cost—i.e., the cost of the complete aligned data for languages $\mathbf{a}$ and $\mathbf{b}$. The pairwise compression distances

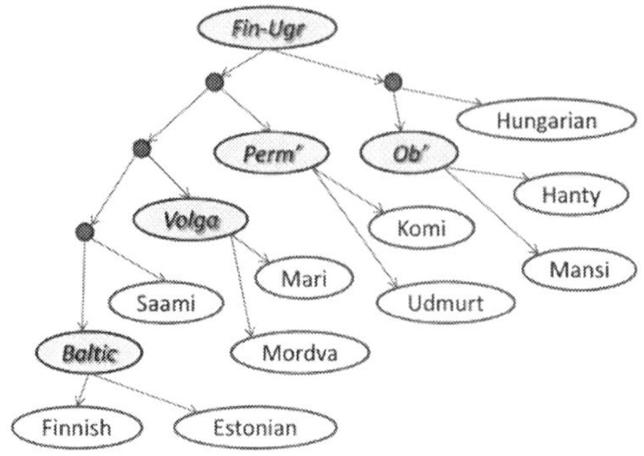

Figure 5: Finno-Ugric branch of the Uralic family

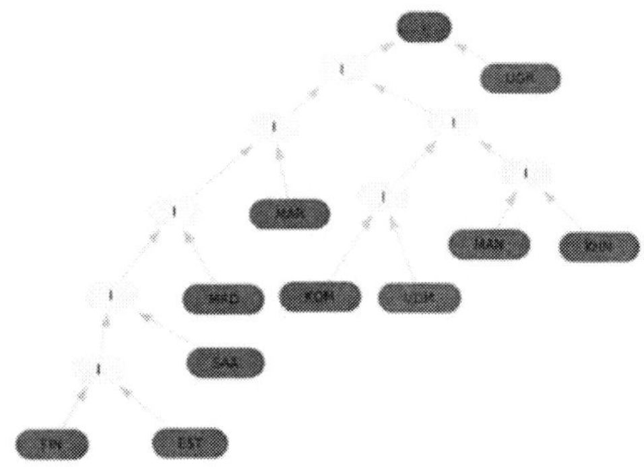

Figure 6: Finno-Ugric tree induced by NCD

are shown in table 2. We can then use these distances to draw phylogenetic trees, using hierarchical clustering methods. We used the UPGMA algorithm, (Murtagh, 1984), the resulting tree shown in Fig. 6. More sophisticated methods, such as the Fast Quartet method, CompLearn, (Cilibrasi and Vitanyi, 2011) may produce even more accurate trees. Even such a simple model as the 1x1 baseline shows emerging patterns that mirror the relationships in the Uralic family tree, shown in Fig. 5, adapted from (Anttila, 1989). For example, scanning the entries in the table corresponding to Finnish, the compression distances *grow* as the corresponding distance within the family tree grows. Sister languages (in bold) should be closest among all their relations. This confirms that the model is able to compress better—find *more regularity* in the data—between languages that are are more closely related.

8 Conclusions and Future Work

We have presented a baseline model for alignment, and several extensions. We have evaluated the models qualitatively, by examining the alignments and the rules of correspondence that they discover, and quantitatively by measuring compression cost and language distances. We trust that the methods presented here provide a good basis for further research.

We are developing methods that take *context*, or en-

	fin	*khn*	*kom*	*man*	*mar*	*mrd*	*saa*	*udm*	*ugr*
est	**.37**	.70	.70	.71	.70	.66	.58	.73	.77
fin		.73	.69	.75	.69	.63	.58	.69	.77
khn			.67	**.63**	.70	.71	.66	.71	.76
kom				.67	.65	.67	.70	**.41**	.70
man					.67	.71	.77	.68	.75
mar						**.64**	.67	.67	.73
mrd							.64	.70	.72
saa								.68	.76
udm									.75

Table 2: Pairwise normalized compression costs for Finno-Ugric sub-family of Uralic, in StarLing data.

vironment into account in modeling. The idea is to code sounds and environments as vectors of phonetic features and instead of aligning symbols, to align individual features of the symbols. The gain from introducing the context enables us to discover more complex rules of correspondence. We also plan to extend our models to diachronic reconstruction, which allows reconstruction of proto forms.

Acknowledgments

This research was supported by the Uralink Project of the Academy of Finland, grant 129185. We thank Teemu Roos for his suggestions, and Arto Vihavainen for his work on the implementation of the algorithms.

References

R. Anttila. 1989. *Historical and comparative linguistics*. John Benjamins.

F. Barbancon, T. Warnow, D. Ringe, S. Evans, and L. Nakhleh. 2009. An experimental study comparing linguistic phylogenetic reconstruction methods. In *Proc. Conf. on Languages and Genes*, UC Santa Barbara. Cambridge University Press.

A. Bouchard-Côté, P. Liang, T.Griffiths, and D. Klein. 2007. A probabilistic approach to diachronic phonology. In *Proc. EMNLP-CoNLL*, Prague.

R. Cilibrasi and P.M.B. Vitanyi. 2005. Clustering by compression. *IEEE Transactions on Information Theory*, 51(4).

R.L. Cilibrasi and P.M.B. Vitanyi. 2011. A fast quartet tree heuristic for hierarchical clustering. *Pattern Recognition*, 44(3):662–677.

P. Grünwald. 2007. *The Minimum Description Length Principle*. MIT Press.

E. Itkonen and U.-M. Kulonen. 2000. *Suomen Sanojen Alkuperä (The Origin of Finnish Words)*. Suomalaisen Kirjallisuuden Seura, Helsinki, Finland.

B. Kessler. 2001. *The Significance of Word Lists: Statistical Tests for Investigating Historical Connections Between Languages*. The University of Chicago Press, Stanford, CA.

G. Kondrak. 2002. Determining recurrent sound correspondences by inducing translation models. In *Proceedings of COLING 2002*, Taipei.

G. Kondrak. 2003. Identifying complex sound correspondences in bilingual wordlists. In *A. Gelbukh (Ed.) CICLing*, Mexico. Springer LNCS, No. 2588.

G. Kondrak. 2004. Combining evidence in cognate identification. In *Proceedings of Canadian-AI 2004*, London, ON. Springer-Verlag LNCS, No. 3060.

P. Kontkanen, P. Myllymäki, and H. Tirri. 1996. Constructing Bayesian finite mixture models by the EM algorithm. Technical Report NC-TR-97-003, ESPRIT Working Group on NeuroCOLT.

V. I. Lytkin. 1973. *Voprosy Finno-Ugorskogo Jazykoznanija (Issues in Finno-Ugric Linguistics)*, volume 1–3. Nauka, Moscow.

F. Murtagh. 1984. Complexities of hierarchic clustering algorithms: the state of the art. *Computational Statistics Quarterly*, 1.

L. Nakhleh, D. Ringe, and T. Warnow. 2005. Perfect phylogenetic networks: A new methodology for reconstructing the evolutionary history of natural languages. *Language*, 81(2).

K. Rédei. 1988–1991. *Uralisches etymologisches Wörterbuch*. Harrassowitz, Wiesbaden.

D. Ringe, T. Warnow, and A. Taylor. 2002. Indoeuropean and computational cladistics. *Transact. Philological Society*, 100(1).

J. Rissanen. 1978. Modeling by shortest data description. *Automatica*, 14(5).

Denis Sinor, editor. 1997. *The Uralic Languages: Description, History and Foreign Influences (Handbook of Uralic Studies)*. Brill Academic Publishers.

S. A. Starostin. 2005. Tower of babel: Etymological databases. http://newstar.rinet.ru/.

H. Wettig and R. Yangarber. 2011. Probabilistic models for alignment of etymological data. In *Proc. NODALIDA*, Riga, Latvia.

Building a Multilingual Named Entity-Annotated Corpus Using Annotation Projection

Maud Ehrmann, Marco Turchi, Ralf Steinberger
European Commission - Joint Research Centre (JRC), IPSC - GlobeSec
Via Fermi 2749, 21020 Ispra (VA) - Italy
name.surname@jrc.ec.europa.eu

Abstract

As developers of a highly multilingual named entity recognition (NER) system, we face an evaluation resource bottleneck problem: we need evaluation data in many languages, the annotation should not be too time-consuming, and the evaluation results across languages should be comparable. We solve the problem by automatically annotating the English version of a multi-parallel corpus and by projecting the annotations into all the other language versions. For the translation of English entities, we use a phrase-based statistical machine translation system as well as a lookup of known names from a multilingual name database. For the projection, we incrementally apply different methods: perfect string matching, perfect consonant signature matching and edit distance similarity. The resulting annotated parallel corpus will be made available for reuse.

1 Introduction

Named Entity recognition is a well-established task, acknowledged as fundamental to a wide variety of natural language processing (NLP) applications (Nadeau and Sekine, 2007). As for other text mining applications, annotated corpora constitute a crucial and constant need for named entity recognition (NER). Within a development or training framework, annotated corpora are used as models from which machine learning systems, or computational linguists, can infer rules and decision criteria; within an evaluation framework, they are used as a gold standard to assess systems' performances and help to guide their quality improvement, *e.g.* via non-regression tests.

During the last decade, several named entity (NE) annotated corpora were built, thanks to a large series of evaluation campaigns (Fort et al., 2009). However, most of these gold-standard data are available only for English or for a few languages. Even if unsupervised methods tried to overcome this difficulty, the shortage of annotated data for the large majority of the world's languages remains a problem. An obvious solution is to manually produce annotated corpora, but it is a complex and time-consuming task and it may be difficult to find experts in each specific language.

Beyond the scarcity of annotated corpora, another issue lies in the fact that annotation schemas or guidelines usually differ from one annotated corpus to another: named entity extents can be different (*e.g.* inclusion or not of the function in a person name), as well as entity types and granularity (*e.g.* some corpora may consider product names, whereas others will differentiate, within this category, vehicles, awards and documents, and others will not even consider product names). Such divergences should be expected, as annotated corpora are built according to different applications. However, they constitute a real issue, particularly when developing or evaluating multilingual NE recognition systems and the effort to reuse existing annotated data collections is big.

Our goal is to automatically build a set of multilingual named entity-annotated corpora, taking advantage of the existence of parallel corpora (bilingual or multiparallel). Traditionally used in the field of Machine Translation, parallel corpora have been exploited in recent years in various NLP tasks, including linguistic annotation, with the creation of annotated corpora. The underlining principle is *annotation projection*, where annotations available for a text in one language can be projected, thanks to the alignment, to the corresponding text in another language, creating herewith a newly annotated corpus for a new language.

This paper presents how we applied this method to named entity annotations, projecting automatically annotated English entities to, firstly, French, Spanish, German and Czech multiparallel corpora and, secondly, Russian parallel corpora. We experimented with several annotation projection techniques: starting from the baseline of simply searching for the English name string in foreign text, results improve gradually by adding new information and varying projection methods. Our objective is to make freely available named entity annotated-corpora in a large set of languages, with a quality similar to that of manually annotated data.

This method shows several advantages. Firstly it could be a way of overcoming the NE-annotated data shortage problem. Then, it could solve the non-harmonized annotation issue: if the projected annotations (on the target side) always come from the same automatic recognition system (on the source side), then we obtain annotated corpora in different languages, but with a common annotation schema. The use of multiparallel corpora also presents the benefit of ensuring the comparability of NER system results across languages; morever, as named entity recognition systems are domain-sensitive, it could be relevant to evaluate multilingual NER systems on equivalent tasks.

The remainder of the paper is organized as follows. We introduce related work (section 2), then present our NE projection method (section 3), report the results (section 4) and finally conclude and propose some elements for future work (section 5).

2 Related Work

Regarding the automatic acquisition of NE annotated corpora, some work investigates how to constitute monolingual annotated data (An et al., 2003; Nothman et al., 2008).

With respect to parallel corpora, their exploitation has been growing in recent years, showing their usefulness in various NLP tasks like word sense disambiguation or cross-lingual tagging (refer to the state of art presented by Bentivolgi and Pianta (2005)). With respect to cross-lingual knowledge induction, multiple work addressed the challenge of automatic parallel treebank building (Lavie et al., 2008; Hwa et al., 2005), whereas (Padó and Lapata, 2009; Bentivogli and Pianta, 2005) explored semantic information projection.

Several researchers investigated named entity annotation and parallel corpora exploitation. Yarowsky *et al.* (2001) carried out some pioneer experiments, investigating the feasibility of annotation projection over four NLP tasks, including named entity recognition. The goal was to automatically induce stand-alone text analysis tools via robust (and noisy) annotation projection. More recently, Ma (2010) applied a co-training algorithm on unlabelled bilingual data (English-Chinese), showing that NE taggers can complement and improve each other while working together on parallel corpora. Samy *et al.* (2005) developed a named entity recognizer for Arabic, leveraging an Arabic-Spanish parallel corpus aligned at sentence level and POS tagged. With a slightly different goal, Klementiev and Roth (2008) proposed an algorithm for cross-lingual multiword NE discovery in a bilingual weakly temporally aligned corpus. The work of Volk *et al.* (2010) on combining parallel treebanks and geo-tagging showed similar results to what we offer, with the difference that they focused on the location type only and worked with a bilingual French-German corpus. Finally, Shah *et al.* (2010) designed a Machine Translation-based approach to NER which includes a NE annotation projection phase based on word alignment.

These approaches aimed at developing/improving NER systems and parallel annotated corpora seemed to be a positive side-effect of these experiments. In comparison, our work differs from that mentioned here in that we aim at developing an annotated multilingual parallel corpus for evaluation purposes. Using a multilingual parallel corpus is beneficial over using a bilingual corpus in that we save more annotation time. More importantly, text type, entity type distribution, and entity annotation specifications are the same across all languages, resulting in a more useful evaluation resource. We will make this multi-parallel corpus freely available to other system developers.

3 Named Entity Annotation Projection

Given a multiparallel corpus and a monolingual NER system, our objective is to automatically provide NE annotations for each text of the aligned corpora. A possible solution to project a named entity between two aligned texts is to translate this entity; accordingly, our multilingual NE annotation projection method relies, for the most part, on the use of a statistical machine translation system.

We used a multiparallel corpus in English, French, Spanish, German and Czech (news texts coming from the WMT shared tasks (Callison-Burch et al., 2009)), hereafter *En-4*, and an English-Russian one (union of two news data sets (Klyueva and Bojar, 2008; Rafalovitch and Dale, 2009)), hereafter *En-Ru*. For each language, *En-4* has a training set of roughly 70,000 sentence pairs and a test set of 2,490 sentence pairs, against 160,000 and 2,700 respectively for *En-Ru*. We used the test sets for the annotation projection. The next sections detail each step of the NE annotation projection process.

3.1 Automatic annotation of Source Named Entities

The first step is to annotate NEs in one corpus in a given language. We chose to annotate English entities of type *Person* (including titles), *Location* and *Organisation* and tried to project them in the corresponding texts in other languages. As a matter of fact, English is a resource-rich language with already existing efficient tools, but one may choose another source language, according to his/her goals and constraints. We used an in-house NER system (Steinberger and Pouliquen, 2007; Crawley and Wagner, 2010) to process the English source side text (any NER system or even manual annotation could have been used at this stage). Obviously, the NER system's quality is a crucial element that determines the projection quality. In the English texts of the *En-4* and *En-Ru* corpora, the NER system annotated 826 unique entities (corresponding to 1,395 occurrences) and 674 (1,312 occurrences) respectively.

3.2 Source Named Entity Translation

The second step corresponds to the translation of the previously extracted entities into the target languages. We make use of two different NE translation sources: translations resulting from the application of a Phrase-Based Statistical Machine Translation system (PBSMT), and translations resulting from the exploitation of a multilingual Named Entity database.

3.2.1 PBSMT System

One of the most popular classes of statistical machine translation (SMT) systems is the Phrase-Based Model (Koehn, 2010). It is an extension of the noisy channel model, introduced by (Brown et al., 1994), using phrases rather than words. A source sentence f is segmented into a sequence of I phrases and the same is done for the target sentence e, where the notion of phrase is not related to any grammatical assumption: a phrase is an n-gram. The best translation e of f is obtained by maximizing the PBSMT model probability $p(e|f)$, relying on three components: the probability of translating a phrase e_i into a phrase f_i, the distance-based reordering model and the language model probability.

Phrases and probabilities are estimated processing the parallel data. Word to word alignment is firstly extracted running the IBM models (Brown et al., 1994), and then proximity rules are applied to obtain phrases, see (Koehn, 2010). Probabilities are estimated counting the frequency of the phrases in the parallel corpus. In this work, we used the open source PBSMT system Moses (Koehn et al., 2007).

Since Named Entities correspond most of the time to small sets of contiguous words (phrases), the phrase-based model appeared to be well-suited to translate this kind of units. Instead of running a whole SMT system, we could have used the word alignment only or done a simple phrase-table lookup. By choosing the first option, we would have been dependent on the NE alignment quality and, by choosing the second one, we would have lost another advantage of the PBSMT system: its decoder's capacities, which allows the reconstruction of the good target phrase even if spread over different phrases (a NE could be cut into different phrases during the phrase table extraction). These choices were confirmed by preliminary experiments.

Experimental framework We translate Named Entities in isolation and not the full sentences where they occur. Translating the full sentences would have implied finding again the entities in the output, which seemed quite complicated and time-consuming. Regarding the training phase, we chose a specific configuration that does not correspond to the classical idea of translation: we trained the PBSMT system using the training sets of the corpora *plus* the parallel sentences that we want to annotate, *i.e.* the test sets. It means that the translation system should know how to translate a source entity because it has seen it in the training data; this reduces the number of completely untranslated entities. Finally, with respect to the SMT output, we did not only consider the most probable translation but took into account the top

15 ranked translations according to $p(e|f)$.

Correction Phase Entity translations are not always correct because the PBSMT system tries to reproduce the most readable sentence driven by the language model; in this way, the translation system may add articles, prepositions or in some cases groups of words before or after the entity name. For example, the french translation of *Afghanistan* is *en Afghanistan* and the translation of *Germany* is *l' Allemagne*. In these cases, only *Afghanistan* and *Allemagne* should be projected, as prepositions and articles cannot be part of proper names in French. We could observe similar phenomena in other languages. To address this problem, we post-processed the translations in a simple way: applying stopword lists. This allowed us to correct a certain number of entities for each language, even if some wrong entities could remain in the translation list. Before projecting these "corrected" translated entities in the aligned corpora, we asked bilingual annotators to check the correctness of the translated entities, according to a set of evaluation categories that identifies possible translation errors. In all languages, the main problems seem to be the addition and subtraction of word(s) during the translation phase (En: *tariq ramadan* Fr: *peut-être tariq ramadan*). More details about this evaluation are reported in (Ehrmann and Turchi, 2010).

3.2.2 External Named Entity Resource

In addition to the SMT approach, we benefit from an external multilingual named entity database; it contains, among others, translations and transliterations of entity names in several languages. By querying this database, we retrieved, for each English entity, a list of translated entities (that may have different spellings) in a given language.[1]

The information coming from the external resource is quite reliable, because part of the entity names has been manually checked. However, it is not exhaustive. On the contrary, the SMT system provides translations almost every time, but they may be incorrect. In other words, information coming from the external resource and the SMT system can complement each other, the former boosting precision and the latter ensuring recall. For example, *Sakharov Prize for Freedom of Thought* is correctly translated by the SMT system for each language while the database does not contain this name.

3.3 Annotation Projection Methods

Once we have a list of possible translations (or candidates) for a given NE in an English sentence, we try to project it into the corresponding sentences of the aligned corpora. We incrementally apply different projection strategies.

String matching The first projection method we use is a strict string matching: the candidate is present or not in the translated sentence. With this method, we are able to project the entity *european parliament*[2] from the English sentence to the corresponding Spanish one in the following example:

English: recipients of the 2005 sakharov prize from the <organization>european parliament</organization>...
Candidate list: parlamento europeo, presidente del parlamento europeo, parlamento de europa, parlamento europea
Spanish: las "Damas de Blanco", galardonadas con el premio sajarov 2005 otorgado por el <organization> parlamento europeo </organization>, ...

This method is rigorous and does not allow to catch named entities showing different spellings or morphological variants that are not present in the candidate list. The following is an example where the entity (*tariq ramadan*) cannot be projected in the target Czech sentence:

English: with the possible exception of <person> tariq ramadan </person>...
Candidate list: tariq ramadan, ramadan tariq
Czech: nevyjímaje tarika ramadana

Consonant Signature matching If the string matching method does not retrieve any result, then we try to match candidates and potential NE over consonant signatures. The consonant signature of a token is obtained by first producing a "normalised" form and then by removing the vowels, as described in (Steinberger and Pouliquen, 2007). The normalised form is produced through the application of a small set of transformation rules based on empirically observed regularities between name variants (double to single consonant, *ck* to *k*, *ou* to *u* etc.). We compare the first candidate token to each sentence token and if there

[1]The database contains 134,046 en-fr NE translations, 157,442 en-es, 156,363 en-de, 2,807 en-cs and 65,916 en-ru.

[2]During the projection step we work on lower-case texts.

is an exact match between their consonant signatures, we continue the comparison with the next tokens until the end of the candidate unit. Considering again the *tarik ramadan* example and its consonant signature [trk - rmdn], this method allows to project its person tag onto the string *tarika ramadana* which, even if not present in the candidate list, has the same consonant signature.

Similarity Distance Finally, for cases where the consonant signature matching method fails, we attempt to project the NE by computing a similarity measure between the consonant groups. Reproducing the work done by (Pouliquen, 2008), we applied a cost-based Levenshtein edit distance, "*where the difference between two letters is not binary but depends on the distance between two letters*". This distance is learned from a set of existing named entity variants. By looking at several examples, we empirically determined the threshold of 0.7, above which the similarity shows good candidates for matching. With this third method, we succeed to project some more candidates, as illustrated by this example: the name *samantha geimer* can be projected from English to Czech, thanks to the calculation of the string similarity distance between the two groups [smnth - gmr] and [smnth - gmrv]:

English: the lawyer of samantha geimer, the victim...
Candidate list: samantha geimer, geimer samantha
Czech: právní zástupkyne obeti, samanthy geimerové

4 Results

4.1 Experimental settings

We ran several experiments according to various set-ups. First of all, we started from the baseline of simply searching for the English named entities in the foreign texts. Then, during the source NE annotation step, we noticed the presence of wrong English entities. We are not interested in evaluating the quality of the NER system that we used but we wondered how it can affect our projection performance. Therefore, we manually corrected the English entities of the *En-4* corpus; performance results are reported according to corrected and non-corrected source entities. Finally, we evaluate the performance of the projection combining different translation approaches. English entities are translated using: (1) external information: for each language pair, a list of English-Foreign entity associations is used as a look-up table (*DB* in Table 1), (2) machine translation system (*SMT*) and (3) external information and machine translation system together: a list of all possible translations is associated to each English entity[3](*ALL*). Moreover, with respect to the SMT approach (case 2), we consider two different SMT outputs: (2a) highest-ranking translation (*SMT-1*) and (2b) top 15 ranked translations (*SMT-15*). By considering the less probable translations up to 15, we expect to cover as much as possible morphological variations in inflected languages.

4.2 Results

As we do not have a reference corpus, we only compute projection Recall. In the future, we plan to manually annotate a part of the multilingual set to evaluate Precision.

Recall results are presented in Table 1. As said above, we combined several translation approaches and projection methods. First it should be noted that the baseline gives quite good results for target languages of the same alphabet (from 0.3 to 0.5 in the *En-4* corpus). Most of the successful English projections are for person names, but performance decreases with inflected languages. Adding external information (*DB*) brings some improvements but it all depends on the amount of translations available in the database, as shown by the difference in gains between French (+12 pts) and Czech (+5 pts). By taking into account the highest-ranking translation (SMT-1), recall improves quite significantly for each target language, although Czech and Russian show lower results. Merging of external and SMT-1 translations (*ALL with SMT-1*) produces small improvements.

Overall results improve even more considering more SMT translations (SMT-15) and varying projection methods. As evidenced by Figure 1, taking into account less probable translations emitted by the SMT system yields significant improvements, especially for inflected languages (+8pts for French, +24 for Czech and +37 for Russian). Then, applying different projection methods for the remaining non-projected entities increases again the results (+0.4 pts on average for all languages), consonant signature and similarity measure giving more or less the same contribution. Adding external information on top of this

[3]If more than one translation matches the target sentence, it is counted only one time.

Translation configurations	French	Spanish	German	Czech	Russian
Baseline	0.493	0.415	0.494	0.312	0.041
Baseline (corrNE)	0.508	0.431	0.516	0.323	0.041
DB	0.628	0.59	0.631	0.375	0.201
SMT-1	0.840	0.846	0.836	0.604	0.433
ALL (with SMT1)	0.869	0.852	0.857	0.594	-
SMT-15	0.929	0.917	0.921	0.837	0.803
SMT-15 + csnt	0.940	0.933	0.933	0.879	0.842
SMT-15 + cnst + sim	0.953	0.942	0.947	0.919	0.867
ALL (with SMT-15)	0.93	0.916	0.924	0.831	0.803
ALL (with SMT-15) + cnst + sim	0.954	0.943	0.95	0.918	0.867

Table 1: Projection Recall performance according to various translation configurations and projection methods. Recall is computed relative to the total number of English annotated entities in each corpus. *CorrNE* = corrected English Named Entities; *csnt* = consonant signature and *sim* = similarity measure. Apart from Baseline, all results are computed with corrected English entities.

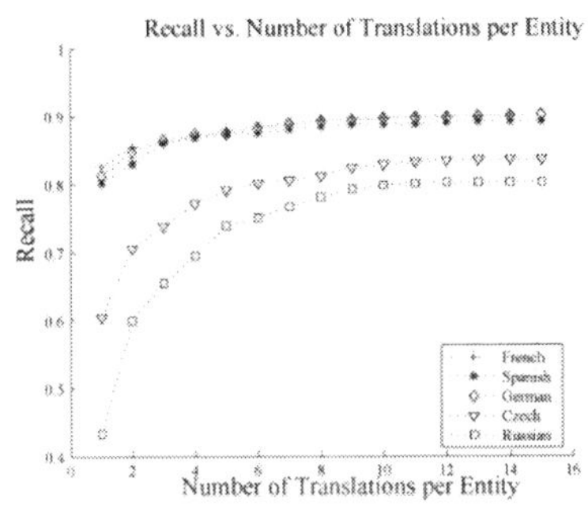

Figure 1: Recall projection performance according to the number of SMT translations (with string matching projection method).

configuration (SMT15 + csnt + sim + DB) brings only small improvements. At the end, best results range from 0.86 to 0.95, showing significant improvements over the baseline. Among the different approaches we tried out, the most beneficial ones are SMT-15 for the translation and the combination of three methods for the projection, particularly in the case of highly inflected languages.

4.3 Error Analysis

Non-projected entities are approximately the same across languages. We identified four main reasons of non-projection. First, as already pointed out, it happens that some English NEs are wrongly annotated, even when manually corrected. This can be illustrated with the following case: in the English entity *iraqi prime minister nouri al-maliki* only *prime minister nouri al-maliki* is annotated and, in consequence, it is not possible to project the Spanish translation *primer ministro nouri al-maliki* on the target *primer ministro iraquí nouri al-maliki*. Then, entity translations can be incorrect. We can report this example: the English entity *state secretary peter wichert* is wrongly translated by *secretario de estado peter wichert habría solicitado*, which make the projection impossible. Furthermore, human sentence translations across parallel texts are not always equivalent, which sometimes block the projection, even with correctly translated entities: *European Court of Justice* appears as *corte europeo* in the Spanish sentence, whereas we try to project *corte europea de justicia*. Finally, there are some hopeless cases combining all sorts of mistakes.

5 Conclusion and Future Work

This work showed how parallel corpora can support the automatic creation of multilingual NE annotated-corpora. By projecting NE annotations across aligned texts in different languages, we solved the evaluation resource bottleneck problem, saving annotation time and providing comparable annotated data. The resource will be made available http://langtech.jrc.it/. Our approach can be improved in several ways. In order to make the source language annotation step more "objective" and reliable, we intend to combine different NE recognition systems through a voting system. Then, we plan to evaluate the precision of the projection. In addition, it could be interesting to project more fine-grained information, considering NE sub-parts like functions, titles, etc. At last, we are currently working on Italian and Hungarian and we intend to reproduce this work on other parallel corpora, including for resource-poor languages.

References

An, J., Lee, S. and Lee, G. (2003) Automatic acquisition of named entity tagged corpus from world wide web. In *Proceedings of ACL (ACL'03)*, Sapporo.

Bentivogli, L. and Pianta, E. (2005) Exploiting parallel texts in the creation of multilingual semantically annotated resources: the MultiSemCor Corpus. In *Natural Language Engineering* pp. 247–261, Cambridge University Press.

Bering, C., Drozdzynski, W., Erbach, G., Guasch, C., Homola and others. (2003) Corpora and evaluation tools for multilingual NE grammar development. In *Proceedings of Multilingual Corpora - Linguistic Requirements and Technical Perspectives*, Lancaster.

Brown, P.F., Della Pietra, S., Della Pietra, V.J. and Mercer R.L.(1994). The Mathematic of Statistical Machine Translation: Parameter Estimation. In *Computational Linguistics*, 19(2):263–311.

Callison-Burch, C., Koehn, P., Monz, C. and Schroeder, J. (2009) Findings of the 2009 Workshop on Statistical Machine Translation. In *Proceedings of the Fourth WMT'09*, Athens.

Crawley, J. B. and Wagner, G. (2010). Desktop text mining for law enforcement. In *Proceedings of ISI'10*, Vancouver.

Ehrmann, M. and Turchi, M. (2010). Building Multilingual Named Entity Annotated Corpora Exploiting Parallel Corpora. In *Proceedings of AEPC*, Tartu, Estonia.

Fort, K., Ehrmann M. and Nazarenko, A. (2009) Towards a Methodology for Named Entities Annotation. In *Proceedings of LAWIII*, Singapore.

Hwa, R., Resnik, P., Weinberg, A., Cabezas, C. and Kolak, O. (2005). Bootstrapping parsers via syntactic projection across parallel texts. In *Natural Language Engineering*, 11(3).

Klementiev, A. and Roth, D. NE Transliteration and Discovery from Multilingual Corpora. (2008) In *Learning Machine Translation*. MIT Press.

Klyueva N. and Bojar O. UMC 0.1: Czech-Russian-English Multilingual Corpus. (2008) In *Proceedings of International Conference Corpus Linguistics*.

Koehn, P., Hoang, H., Birch, A., Callison-Burch, C., Federico, M., Bertoldi, N. and others (2007). Moses: Open source toolkit for statistical machine translation. ACL, 45(2), Columbus, Oh, USA.

Koehn, P. (2010). Statistical Machine Translation. Cambridge Univ. Press.

Lavie, A., Parlikar, A. and Ambati, V. (2008). Syntax-driven learning of sub-sentential translation equivalents and translation rules from parsed parallel corpora. In *Proceedings of theHLT-SSST-2 workshop*, Columbus, Ohio.

Paroubek, P., Chaudiron, S. and Hirschman, V. (2007). Principles of Evaluation in Natural Language Processing. In *TAL*, 48-1

Ma, X. (2010) Toward a Named Entity Aligned Bilingual Corpus. In *Proceedings of the Seventh LREC Conference*, Malta.

Nadeau, D., and Sekine, S. (2007) A survey of named entity recognition and classification. In *Linguisticae Investigaciones*, 30-1, pp. 3-26.

Nothman, J., Curran, J., and Murphy, T. (2008) Transforming Wikipedia into named entity training data. In *Proceedings of the ALTA Workshop*, Hobart.

Padó, S. and Lapata, M. (2009) Cross-linguistic projection of role-semantic information. In *Journal of Artificial Intelligence Research*, 36.

Pouliquen, B. (2008) Similarity of names across scripts: Edit distance using learned costs of n-grams In *Advances in Natural Language Processing*, Sringer.

Rafalovitch, A. and Dale, R.(2009) United Nations General Assembly Resolutions: A Six-Language Parallel Corpus. In *Proceedings of the MT Summit*

Samy, D., Moreno-Sandoval, A. and Guirao, J.M. (2005). A Proposal for an Arabic Named Entity Tagger Leveraging a Parallel Corpus (Spanish-Arabic). In *Proceedings of RANLP Conference*, Borovets, Bulgaria.

Shah R., Lin B., Gershman A. and Frederking R. (2010). SYNERGY: A Named Entity Recognition System for Resource-scarce Languages such as Swahili using Online Machine Translation. In *Proceedings of (AfLaT), LREC*, Valleta, Malta.

Steinberger, R. and Pouliquen B. (2007). Cross-lingual Named Entity Recognition. In *Named Entities - Recognition, Classification and Use*, Benjamins Current Topics, Vol. 19, pp. 137-164.

Turchi, M., DeBie, T. and Cristianini N. (2008). Learning Performance of a Machine Translation System: a Statistical and Computational Analysis. In *Proceedings of the Third WMT'08*, Columbus, Oh, USA.

Volk, M., Goehring, A. and Marek, T. (2010) Combining Parallel Treebanks and Geo-Tagging. In *Proceedings of The Fourth LAW Workshop*, Uppsala.

Yarowsky, D., Ngai, G. and Wicentowski, R. (2001) Inducing Multilingual Text Analysis Tools via Robust Projection across Aligned Corpora. In *Proceedings of HLT'01*, San Diego.

Bilingual Lexicon Extraction from Comparable Corpora for Closely Related Languages

Darja Fišer
Faculty of Arts,
Univeristy of Ljubljana
darja.fiser@ff.uni-lj.si

Nikola Ljubešić
Faculty of Humanities and Social Sciences,
University of Zagreb
nikola.ljubesic@ffzg.hr

Abstract

In this paper we present a knowledge-light approach to extract a bilingual lexicon for closely related languages from comparable corpora. While in most related work an existing dictionary is used to translate context vectors, we take advantage of the similarities between languages instead and build a seed lexicon from words that are identical in both languages and then further extend it with context-based cognates and translations of the most frequent words. We also use cognates for reranking translation candidates obtained via context similarity and extract translation equivalents for all content words, not just nouns as in most related work. The results are very encouraging, suggesting that other similar languages could benefit from the same approach. By enlarging the seed lexicon with cognates and translations of the most frequent words and by cognate-based reranking of translation candidates we were able to improve the average baseline precision from 0.592 to 0.797 on the mean reciprocal rank for the ten top-ranking translation candidates for nouns, verbs and adjectives with a 46% recall on the gold standard of 1000 random entries from a traditional dictionary.

1 Introduction

Most cross-lingual NLP applications require bilingual lexicons but their compilation is still a major bottleneck in computational linguistics. Automatic extraction of bilingual lexicons is typically performed on parallel corpora (Och and Ney, 2000) but they exist only for a limited number of language pairs and domains and it is often impractical or even impossible to build one from scratch.

This is why an alternative approach has become popular in recent years. It relies on texts in two languages which are not parallel but comparable (Fung, 1998; Rapp, 1999) and therefore easier to compile, especially from the increasingly rich web data (Xiao and McEnery, 2006). The approach relies on the assumption that the term and its translation appear in similar contexts (Fung, 1998; Rapp, 1999). This means that the translation of a source word can be found by identifying a target word which has the most similar context vector in a comparable corpus. However, a direct comparison of vectors in two different languages is not possible, which is why a dictionary is needed to first translate the features of source context vectors into the target language and compute similarity on those. But this step seems paradoxical: the very reason why we are applying the complex comparable corpus technique for extracting translation equivalents is the fact that we do not have a bilingual dictionary at our disposal in the first place. This issue has largely remained unaddressed in previous research, which is why we propose a knowledge-light approach that does not require any bilingual resource. Instead, it takes advantage of similarities between the source and the target language in order to obtain a seed lexicon used for translating features of context vectors.

The paper is structured as follows: in the following section we give an overview of related work. In Section 3 we present the construction of the resources used in the experiment. Section 4 describes the experimental setup and reports the results of automatic and manual evaluation. We conclude the paper with final remarks and ideas for future work.

2 Related Work

The seminal papers on bilingual lexicon extraction from non-parallel texts are (Fung, 1998) and (Rapp, 1999) whose main assumption is that the term and its translation share similar contexts. The method consists of two steps: first, contexts of words are modeled and then similarity between the source-language and target-language contexts are measured with the help of a dictionary. Most approaches represent contexts as weighted collections of words using log-likelihood (Ismail and Manandhar, 2010), TF-IDF (Fung, 1998) or PMI (Shezaf and Rappoport, 2010). After building context vectors for words in both languages, the similarity between a source word's context vector and all the context vectors in the target language is computed using a similarity measure, such as cosine (Fung, 1998), Jaccard (Otero and Campos, 2005) or Dice (Otero, 2007).

If we want to compare context vectors across languages, the translation of features in context vectors is required, which assumes that a dictionary is available. Alternative solutions for situations when this is not the case have not been explored to a great extent but (Koehn and Knight, 2002) show that it is possible to obtain a seed lexicon from identical and similarly spelled words that is directly extracted from the comparable corpus. Taking the idea one step further, (Al-Onaizan and Knight, 2002) and (Shao and Ng, 2004) use transliteration rules for Arabic and Chinese respectively to harvest translation candidates, which is especially efficient for named entities and new vocabulary not yet present in dictionaries. At the subword level, (Markó et al., 2005) defined a set of string substitution rules to obtain domain-specific Spanish-Portugese cognates. As an addition to the standard approach, (Saralegi et al., 2008) use string similarity as a reranking criterion of translation candidates obtained with context similarity measures.

Our approach most closely resembles (Koehn and Knight, 2002) in that, just like them, we use identical words as our seed lexicon. The difference is that we iterate the calculation of translation equivalents, extending the seed lexicon on every step with additional information, such as context-checked cognates and translation equivalents of most frequent words in the corpus. We also carry out a final cognate-based reranking of translation candidates similar to (Saralegi et al., 2008).

As opposed to (Koehn and Knight, 2002), we are working with much larger corpora and much closer languages, which is why our seed lexicon is much larger, yielding a higher recall as well as precision of the extracted translation equivalents that consequently results in a more usable resource in a real-world setting. And finally, we are not limiting our experiments to nouns, but are working with all content words.

3 Building Resources

In this section we present two resources we built for this experiment: the comparable corpus and the seed lexicon. Since our goal in the experiment reported in this paper is the extraction of translation equivalents for the general vocabulary, we built a Croatian-Slovene comparable news corpus from the 1 billion-word hrWaC and the 380 million-word slWaC that were constructed from the web by crawling the .hr and .si domains (Ljubešić and Erjavec, 2011). We extracted all documents from the domains jutranji.hr and delo.si, which are on-line editions of national daily newspapers with a high circulation and a similar target audience. The documents were already tokenized, PoS-tagged and lemmatized, resulting in 13.4 million tokens for Croatian and 15.8 million tokens for Slovene.

Unlike many language combinations with English, no machine-readable dictionary is available for Croatian and Slovene. Having said this, it is also true that Croatian and Slovene are very close languages. Namely, according to (Scannell, 2007), the cosine for 3-grams in Croatian and Slovene of is 74%, compared to only 34% for English and German that (Koehn and Knight, 2002) used, while a similar result as for Croatian and Slovene was obtained for Czech and Slovak (70%) and Spanish and Portuguese (76%). This means that the lack of dictionary resources for such language pairs can be compensated by exploiting the similarities between the languages. We therefore decided to build a seed lexicon from the comparable news corpus by extracting all identical lemmas that were tagged with the same part of speech in both languages.

As Table 1 shows, the seed lexicon contains about 33,500 entries, 77% of which are nouns. Manual evaluation of 100 random entries for each part of speech shows that nouns perform the best (88%) and that the average precision of the lexicon for all parts of speech is 84%.

The errors we observed in manual evaluation are mostly Croatian words that appeared in the Slovene part of the corpus. They probably orig-

PoS	Size	Precision
nouns	25,703	88%
adjectives	4,042	76%
verbs	3,315	69%
adverbs	435	54%
total	33,495	84%

Table 1: Analysis of the seed lexicon.

inated from readers' comments that are written in informal language which often contains Croatian expressions. Such errors could be avoided in the future by a stricter filtering of the corpus. However, more serious problems could be caused by some false friends that got into the seed lexicon (e.g. *"neslužben"* which means *"unofficial"* in Croatian but *"not part of sbd's job"* in Slovene) and should be addressed in our future work.

4 Extracting Translation Equivalents

In the experiment presented in this paper, our task is to extract a bilingual lexicon from a comparable corpus. The seed lexicon we use to translate features of context vectors was compiled automatically and contains words from the corpus which are identical in both languages. The translation equivalents obtained with this seed lexicon represent the baseline which we then try to beat by extending the seed lexicon with cognates and first translation candidates of the most frequent words in the corpus and a final reranking of the translation equivalents based on cognate clues.

4.1 Experimental Setup

Throughout the experiment we use best-performing settings for building and comparing context vectors from our previous research (see (Ljubešić et al., 2011)). We build context vectors for all content words in each language with a minimum frequency of 50 occurrences in the corpus. The co-occurrence window is 7 content words with encoded position of context words in that window, and log-likelihood as association measure. Vector features are then translated with the seed lexicon, after which Jensen-Shannon divergence is used as similarity measure.

Finally, ten top-ranking translation candidates are kept for automatic and manual evaluation. We try to improve the results by extending the seed lexicon with contextually confirmed cognates as well as with first translations of the most frequent words. In addition, we rerank the translation candidates of all content words obtained with this procedure by taking into account cognate clues among the candidates. The details of lexicon extension and reranking are described in the following sections.

4.2 Evaluation Framework

Automatic evaluation and comparison of the results is performed on a gold standard that contains 1000 randomly selected entries of nouns (618), adjectives (217) and verbs (165) from a traditional broad-coverage Croatian-Slovene dictionary which contains around 8,100 entries. Although we include adverbs in seed lexicon extensions based on their positive impact on this task, we do not include them in the gold standard for two reasons: (I) many tokens tagged as adverbs in the corpus are mistagged other parts of speech and (II) most adverbs in both Croatian and Slovene can be easily generated from adjectives and there is only a small amount of those for which this does not hold, and they can be considered a closed word class.

Mean reciprocal rank (Vorhees, 1999) on the ten top-ranking translation candidates is used for calculating precision. In this experimental setup, recall for nouns is always 45% because we always find translations for 278 of the 618 nouns from the gold standard that satisfy the frequency criterion (50) in the source corpus and have at least one translation in the target corpus that meets the same frequency criterion. For other parts of speech recall is also constant: 42% for adjectives and 56.4% for verbs. Overall recall is 46.2%. The baseline precision used for evaluating seed lexicon extensions of 0.592 was calculated by translating features in context vectors of nouns, verbs and adjectives with the seed lexicon of identical words using the settings described in the previous section. Baseline precision for individual parts of speech is 0.605 for nouns, 0.566 for adjectives and 0.579 for verbs. For a more qualitative insight into the results we also performed manual evaluation of each experimental setting on a sample of 100 random translation equivalents.

4.3 Extending the Seed Lexicon with Cognates

In order to beat the baseline we first extended the seed lexicon with cognates. We calculated them with BI-SIM, the longest common subsequence of bigrams with a space prefix added to the beginning of each word in order to punish the differences at the beginning of the words (Kondrak and Dorr, 2004). The threshold for cognates has been empirically set to 0.7.

In this step, translation equivalents were calculated as explained above for all content words (nouns, adjectives, verbs and adverbs), taking into account 20 top-ranking translations and analyzing them for cognate clues in that order.

If we found a translation equivalent that met the cognate threshold of 0.7, we added that pair to the lexicon. If the seed lexicon already contained a translation for a cognate we identified with this procedure, we replaced the existing lexicon entry with the new identified cognate pair. Replacing entries is a decision based on empirical results.

PoS	**Size**	**Precision**
nouns	1,560	84%
adjectives	779	92%
verbs	706	74%
adverbs	114	85%
total	3,159	84%

Table 2: Manual evaluation of cognates.

As Table 2 shows, we identified more than 3,000 contextually proven cognates, almost half of which are nouns. Manual evaluation of 100 random cognates for each part of speech shows that cognate extraction is most accurate for adjectives (92%), probably because of the regular patterns used to form adjectives in Croatian and Slovene (e.g. Cro. "*digital*an", Slo. "*digital*en", Eng. "*digital*").

Manual evaluation shows that the quality of the extracted cognates on all parts of speech but nouns is substantially higher than the quality of identical words used to generate the seed lexicon. These results can be explained by the different extraction methods for identical words and for cognates: while full string matching was the only criterion for extracting identical words, cognates had to meet an additional criterion – they had to appear in similar enough contexts (i.e. among the 20 top-ranking translation candidates calculated with the context similarity measure). Experimenting with a context similarity threshold as well as a minimum frequency criterion for identical words did not improve the results. On the other hand, we use context-dependent cognates because calculating cognates between all lemmata of specific parts of speech proved to be very noisy even on high cognate thresholds and it did not have a positive impact on this task. Nouns have a higher precision on identical words than on contextually proven cognates probably because of a high amount of proper nouns in the corpus.

Table 3 contains the results of automatic evaluation of bilingual lexicon extraction with the seed lexicon that was extended with cognates. Nouns and adjectives contribute to the task the most, although the amount of adjectives added to the lexicon is half the size of nouns. Adding all parts of speech to the lexicon improves the results for 0.061.

When taking into account specific parts of speech, nouns experience the biggest improvement (0.103) while, interestingly, adjectives show a decrease in precision. " Adjectives, however, show the biggest improvement if only nouns are added to the seed lexicon. The reason for that is probably the syntactic similarity of Croatian and Slovene because of which, since we encode the position in features as well, adjectives are precisely matched between languages if primarily nouns co-occuring with them are taken into account. A similar, but less strong improvement can be observed with verbs that obtain the highest results if only cognate adverbs are added to the seed lexicon.

lexicon	**N**	**A**	**V**	**all**
baseline	0.605	0.566	0.579	0.592
cognates-N	0.657	0.578	0.596	0.630
cognates-Adj	0.669	0.567	0.590	0.634
cognates-V	0.630	0.497	0.555	0.589
cognates-Adv	0.604	0.573	0.608	0.598
cognates-all	0.708	0.534	0.604	0.653

Table 3: Automatic evaluation of translation extraction with a seed lexicon including cognates.

4.4 Extending the Seed Lexicon with First Translations of the Most Frequent Words

We have shown that precision of the first translation candidates of highly frequent words in the corpus is especially high (Fišer et al., 2011). We therefore decided to add them to the seed lexicon as well and see if they can improve the quality of the task of bilingual lexicon extraction. We only took into account the first translation candidates for words that appear in the corpus at least 200 times. If the seed lexicon already contained an entry we were able to translate with this procedure, we again replaced the old pair with the new one.

PoS	Size	Precision	Cognates
nouns	2,510	71%	48%
adjectives	957	57%	38%
verbs	1,002	63%	30%
adverbs	325	59%	26%
total	4,794	62%	34%

Table 4: Manual evaluation of first translations of the most frequent words.

Overall, first translation candidates yielded 1,635 more entries for the seed lexicon than cognates but their quality is much lower (by 22% on average). More than 52% of the extracted first translation candidates are nouns, which are also of the highest quality (71%) according to manual evaluation performed on a random sample of 100 first translation equivalents for each part of speech. It is interesting that many of the manually evaluated first translation candidates were also cognates, especially among nouns (48%), further strengthening the argument for using cognates in bilingual lexicon extraction tasks for closely related languages. In 23% of the cases the incorrect translation candidates were semantically closely related words, such as hypernyms, co-hyponyms or opposites that are not correct themselves but probably still contribute to good modeling of contexts and thereby help bilingual lexicon extraction.

Table 5 gives the results of automatic evaluation of bilingual lexicon extraction with the seed lexicon that was extended with first translation candidates. As with cognates, nominal first translations have the most impact on the size of the extended lexicon (2,510 new entries), but share an almost identical precision gain with adjectives. Best performance, again, is achieved when adding all parts of speech to the seed lexicon improving the baseline results by 0.113, 85% more than in case of adding cognates to the seed lexicon. This shows a higher importance of adding high-frequency first translation candidates to the seed lexicon as opposed to adding contextually proven cognates.

When analyzing the precision on specific parts of speech, nouns again experience the largest precision increase of 0.152 (a 48% increase when compared to cognates). The situation with adjectives resembles the one observed when cognates were added to the seed lexicon. This time, adding all parts of speech did not decrease precision, but again, the highest precision is obtained when adding only first translation nouns to the seed lexicon (a 141% higher increase than when adding all parts of speech). This shows once again the importance and potential simplicity of adding syntactic information to the task by just weighting parts of speech on specific positions differently when extracting a specific part of speech.

lexicon	N	A	V	all
baseline	0.605	0.566	0.579	0.592
first-N	0.665	0.665	0.626	0.659
first-Adj	0.700	0.581	0.589	0.656
first-V	0.643	0.513	0.546	0.599
first-Adv	0.610	0.583	0.581	0.599
first-all	0.757	0.607	0.639	0.705

Table 5: Automatic evaluation of translation extraction with a seed lexicon including first translations.

4.5 Combining Cognates and First Translations of the Most Frequent Words to Extend the Seed Lexicon

In order to study the total impact of seed lexicon extension with new information that was extracted from the corpus automatically, we combine the cognates and first translation candidates in order to measure the gain of both information sources. Thereby the seed lexicon was extended with 2,303 new entries, amounting to 35,798 entries overall. When we start adding cognates and then add first translations of most frequent words (overwriting the existing lexicon entries with new information), we achieve precision of 0.731 while changing the order gives a slightly lower score of 0.723. This shows once again that first translations are more beneficial for the context vector translation for bilingual lexicon extraction.

Manual evaluation of a random sample of 100 translation equivalents we extracted from the best-performing extended seed lexicon shows that 88 entries contained the correct translation among the ten top-ranking translation candidates and that 64 of those were found in the first position while 24 were found in the remaining nine positions. This significantly outperforms our baseline of 0.592.

What is more, many lists of ten top-ranking

translation candidates contained not one but several correct translation variants. Also, as many as 59 of correct translation candidates were cognates and 41 of them appeared in the first position, suggesting that the results could be improved even more by a final reranking of translation candidates based on cognate clues which we describe in the following section.

4.6 Reranking of Translation Candidates with Cognate Clues

Once we obtained translation candidates ranked according to our similarity measure, the final reranking of 10 highest-ranking translation candidates was performed. The source word was compared by the previously described BI-SIM function with each of the ten translation candidates. Two lists were formed, one with words satisfying the 0.7 cognate threshold, and another one with the words not satisfying the criterion. Finally, the lists were merged by putting the cognate list of translation equivalents in front of the non-cognate list.

PoS	Baseline	Extended	Reranking
nouns	0.605	0.768	0.848
adjectives	0.566	0.605	0.698
verbs	0.579	0.658	0.735
all	0.592	0.713	0.797

Table 6: Automatic evaluation of translation extraction per part of speech with reranking.

Table 6 shows the baseline results for all parts of speech, the results obtained by using the extended seed lexicon, and the results of reranking the final translation candidates. As expected, the biggest gain through reranking is achieved for adjectives (15.4%), probably because of the regularity of patterns for forming adjectives in both languages. Nouns and verbs experience a similar precision boost (around 11%).

Regarding the final results, the best score is achieved for nouns with a total precision increase of 40%. Although adjectives experience the biggest boost by reranking, their extraction precision is still the lowest. The observations made about their sensitivity to parts of speech being encoded in their context vectors should therefore be exploited in further research. The overall improvement of the results for all parts of speech is 34.6%.

These figures confirm the positive impact of exploiting language similarity on knowledge-light extraction of bilingual lexicons from comparable corpora for closely related languages. Last but not least, the described method results in a fully automatically created resource the quality of which already makes it a useful resource for practical tasks.

5 Conclusions and Future Work

In this paper we presented a knowledge-light approach to bilingual lexicon extraction from comparable corpora of similar languages. When tested on a comparable news corpus for Croatian and Slovene, it outperforms related approaches both in terms of precision (0.797 for nouns, adjectives and verbs) and recall (46%). Unlike most related approaches it deals with all content words not just nouns, and enriches the seed lexicon used for translating context vectors from the results of the translation procedure itself, thereby experiencing a 35% precision increase on the lexicon extraction task. The proposed approach is directly applicable on a number of other similar language pairs for which there is a lack of bilingual lexica.

In the future, we plan to extend our approach to multi-word expressions as well because they are an important component for most HLT tasks. We plan to exploit the observed positive impact of preferring specific parts of speech when calculating translation equivalents of other parts of speech. Additionally, we wish to address polysemy by refining the translation procedure of context vectors as well as measuring similarity of contexts within and across languages.

Acknowledgments

Research reported in this paper has been supported by the ACCURAT project within the EU 7th Framework Programme (FP7/2007-2013), grant agreement no. 248347, and by the Slovenian Research Agency, grant no. Z6-3668.

References

Al-Onaizan, Y. and Knight, K. 2002. Translating Named Entities Using Monolingual and Bilingual Resources. In: *ACL'02*, pp. 400-408.

Fišer, D., Ljubešić, N., Vintar, Š and Pollak, S. 2011. Building and using comparable corpora for domain-specific bilingual lexicon extraction. In: *BUCC'11*.

Fung, P. 1998. A statistical view on bilingual lexicon extraction: From parallel corpora to nonparallel corpora. In: *AMTA'98*, pp. 1-17.

Ismail, A. and Manandhar, S. 2010. Bilingual lexicon extraction from comparable corpora using in-domain terms. In: *COLING'10*, pp. 481-489.

Koehn, P. and Knight, K. 2002. Learning a translation lexicon from monolingual corpora. In: *ULA'02*, pp. 9-16.

Kondrak, G. and Dorr, B. J. 2004. Identification of Confusable Drug Names: A New Approach and Evaluation Methodology. In: *COLING'04*.

Ljubešić, N., Fišer, D., Vintar, Š and Pollak, S. Bilingual Lexicon Extraction from Comparable Corpora: A Comparative Study. In: *WOLER'11*.

Ljubešić, N. and Erjavec, T. 2011. Compiling web corpora for Croatian and Slovene. In: *BSNLP'11*.

Markó, K., Schulz, S. and Hahn, U. 2005. Multilingual Lexical Acquisition by Bootstrapping Cognate Seed Lexicons. In: *RANLP'05*, pp. 301-307.

Och, F. J. and Ney, H. 2000. Improved Statistical Alignment Models. In: *ACL'00*, pp. 440-447.

Otero, P. G. and Campos J. R. P. 2005. An Approach to Acquire Word Translations from Non-parallel Texts. In: *EPIA'05*, pp. 600-610.

Otero, P. G. 2007. Learning Bilingual Lexicons from Comparable English and Spanish Corpora. In: *MTS'07*, pp. 191-198.

Rapp, R. 1999. Automatic Identification of Word Translations from Unrelated English and German Corpora. In: *ACL '99*, pp. 519-526.

Saralegi, X., San Vicente, I. and Gurrutxaga, A. 2008. Automatic Extraction of Bilingual Terms from Comparable Corpora in a Popular Science Domain. In: *BUCC'08*.

Scannell, K. P. 2007. Language Similarity Table http://borel.slu.edu/crubadan/table.html.

Shao, L. and Ng, H. T. 2004. Mining New Word Translations from Comparable Corpora. In: *COLING'04*.

Shezaf, D. and Rappoport, A. 2010. Bilingual Lexicon Generation Using Non-Aligned Signatures. In: *ACL'10*, pp. 98-107.

Vorhees, E.M. 1999. TREC-8 Question Answering Track Report. In: *TREC-8*, pp. 77-82.

Xiao, Z. and McEnery, A. 2006. Collocation, Semantic Prosody and Near Synonymy: A Cross-linguistic Perspective. In: *Applied Linguistics* 27(1): 103-129.

Sentiments and Opinions in Health-related Web Messages

Marina Sokolova
Faculty of Medicine, University of Ottawa
and
Electronic Health Information Lab,
CHEO Research Institute
sokolova@uottawa.ca

Victoria Bobicev
Department of Applied Informatics,
Faculty of Computers, Informatics
and Microelectronics,
Technical University of Moldova
vika@rol.md

Abstract

In this work, we analyze sentiments and opinions expressed in user-written Web messages. The messages discuss health-related topics: medications, treatment, illness and cure, etc. Recognition of sentiments and opinions is a challenging task for humans as well as an automated text analysis. In this work, we apply both the approaches. The paper presents the annotation model, discusses characteristics of subjectivity annotations in health-related messages, and reports the results of the annotation agreement. For external evaluation of the labeling results, we apply Machine Learning methods on the annotated data and present the obtained results.

1 Motivation

In recent years, Text Data Mining (TDM) and Natural Language Processing (NLP) intensively studied sentiments and opinions in user-written Web texts (e.g., tweets, blogs, messages). Researchers analyzed sentiments and opinions that appear in consumer-written product reviews, financial blogs, political discussions (Blitzer et al, 2007; Ferguson et al, 2009; Kim and Hovy, 2007). Health care and medical delivery service is another area where practitioners become interested in what users write in their Web posts. Importance of knowing user opinions had became evident during H1N1 pandemic, the first pandemic when Web discussions influenced the general public (Eysenbach, 2009); Figure 1 presents an example.[1]

The shift from contrived medical text to less rigorously written and edited user-written texts is a challenge for TDM and NLP methods. The current techniques were primarily designed to analyze medical publications in traditional media (e.g., journal articles) and organizational documents (e.g., hospital records) or task-dependent (e.g., information retrieval related to insurance claims)(Angelova, 2009; Cohen et al, 2010; Konovalov et al, 2010).

> Posted by Kristi: I really dont know why everyones freaking out about the H1N1 vaccine. I got it the first day it came out (about a week and a half ago) and so did 4 of my family members. None of us had any problems and were all really glad we got the vaccine.

Figure 1: A user post about H1N1 vaccination.

The goal of this work is to study sentiments and opinions in health-related Web messages. We start with building a data set of annotated sentences. We present an opinion and sentiment annotation scheme and its application to tag sentences harvested from the Web messages. We report evaluation of manual annotation agreement. Finally, machine learning methods are applied to automatically assess the sentence labeling.

2 Opinions and Sentiments

We are interested in the expressions of user *private state* which is not open to objective observation or verification (Quirk et al, 1985). These personal views are revealed through thoughts, perceptions and other subjective expressions that can be found in text (Wiebe, 1994).

We assume that the private states can be revealed by emotional statements, *sentiments*, and subjective statements that may not imply emotions, *opinions*. In this work, statements are considered within the sentence bounds; thus, sentences are the units of our language analysis. We agree with Lasersohn (2005) and Kim and Hovy (2007) that opinion can be expressed about a fact of matter, and should not be treated as identical to sentimental expression.

[1] http://www.gocoldflu.info/archives/, accessed April 25, 2011

We further sub-categorize sentiments into *positive* and *negative*, and opinions – into *positive*, *negative* and *neutral*. Sentences that do not bear opinions or sentiments are considered objective by default and are left for future studies.

3 Opinion and Sentiment Annotation

3.1 Annotation Model

Annotation of subjectivity can be centered either around perception of a reader/annotator (Strapparava and Mihalceal, 2008) or the author of a text (Balahur and Steinberger, 2009). Our model is author-centric. Our guidelines for annotators defined that a subjective statement contains information which has not been taken by the author from some external source but rather his/her personal thoughts (as defined in Section 2). We requested that annotators do not impose their own sentiments and attitudes towards information in the text (Balahur and Steinberger, 2009). Instead we suggested that an annotator imagined sentiments and attitudes that the author possibly had while writing.

Separation of good and bad news from the author attitude is important in the health-related analysis. We know that subjective expressions are highly reflective of the text content and context (Chen, 2008). Health-related messages are often written about illnesses and medical treatment. Users write about diseases, symptoms, sick relative and friends. This information is naturally distressing and may cause a negative attitude in annotators. We asked annotators not to mark descriptions of symptoms and diseases as subjective; only author's opinion or sentiment should be annotated. For example, "For a very long time I've had a problem with feeling really awful when I try to get up in the morning" is a description of some symptoms and should not be annotated as subjective. In contrast, "I don't know if that makes sense, it seems to me that the new drug which stimulates red blood cell production would be a more logical approach, erythropoiten (sp?)" exposes the author's thoughts and ideas. It should be annotated as an opinion though without an emotional attitude. Another example, "Alas, I didn't record the program, but wish I had" expresses the author's regret and should be annotated as a negative opinion about the action (i.e., not recording the program).

We considered essential to advise annotators not to agonize over the annotation and, if doubtful, leave the example un-annotated (Balahur and Steinberger, 2009). The rule is especially important for annotation of user-written texts, when annotators can be destructed and even annoyed by misspellings, simplified grammar and informal style and unfamiliar terminology specific to an individual user..

3.2 Schema

Our annotation schema is based on the following assumptions:

(a) annotation was performed on a sentence level; one sentence expressed only one assertion; this assumption held in a majority of cases;

(b) only author's subjective comments were marked as such; if the author conveyed opinions or sentiments of others, we did not mark it as subjective as the author was not the holder of these opinions or sentiments;

(c) we did not differentiate between the objects of comments; author's attitude towards a situation, an event, a person or an object were considered equally important.

Annotators were informed that the annotation was sentence-level and examples of annotated texts presented them were also with annotated sentences. Thus they tended to annotate sentences. If consecutive sentences were subjective, every one was marked. In some cases, only a subjective part of a sentence was tagged, whereas the other part, containing factual information was not included in the sentiment tag.

3.3 Mode

User-written messages usually have opening, body, and closure. Opening can be email subject, parameters of the message, body presents the main content, and closure can be signature or a link to a personal web site.

We used the markup tags HEADER, FOOTER and BODY (Figure 2). HEADER referred to the parameters of the message, FOOTER marked the closing part which started with the signature; this part was marked FOOTER regardless of its length and omitted from the processing. BODY marked the message between HEADER and FOOTER.

To comply with our annotation schema, we divide BODY into CITATION and TEXT. CITATION marked embedding of the previous messages in the current one, TEXT marked the text of the message written by the author. In the current study, we are interested in the TEXT part; other parts are left for future work. TEXT was divided in sentences and further analyzed for opinions and sentiments.

HEADER:
Path: cantaloupe.srv.cs.cmu.edu!das-news.harvard.edu!ogicse!emory!gatech!pitt.edu!pitt!geb
From: geb@cs.pitt.edu (Gordon Banks)
Newsgroups: sci.med
Subject: Re: vangus nerve (vagus nerve)
Message-ID: <19397@pitt.UUCP
Date: 5 Apr 93 14:27:13 GMT
Article-I.D.: pitt.19397
References: <52223@seismo.CSS.GOV
Sender: news@cs.pitt.edu
Reply-To: geb@cs.pitt.edu (Gordon Banks)
Organization: Univ. of Pittsburgh Computer Science
Lines: 16
BODY:
CITATION:
In article <52223@seismo.CSS.GOV bwb@seismo.CSS.GOV (Brian W. Barker) writes:
> mostly right. Is there a connection between vomiting
> and fainting that has something to do with the vagus nerve?
TEXT:
Stimulation of the vagus nerve slows the heart and drops the blood pressure.
FOOTER:

Gordon Banks N3JXP | "Skepticism is the chastity of geb@cadre.dsl.pitt.edu | the intellect, and it is shameful to surrender it too soon."

Figure 2: Example of a message.

4 Empirical Application

4.1 Data

For our empirical part, we used the sci.med texts of *20 Newsgroups* [2]. It is a benchmark data set of 20,000 messages, popular in applications of machine learning techniques, such as text classification and text clustering. There are 1000 sci.med messages. Most sci.med messages were posted by people who wanted to know something about an illness, drugs or treatment (e.g., questions on tuberculosis, haldol prescription to elderly). After the question appeared on the message board, other people could reply and add comments (Figure 2).

To group messages by their content, we merged the messages with the same topic. A script automatically placed all messages with the same Subject line in the file with the same title. Thus, we obtained 365 files named "Arrhythmia", "arthritis and diabetes", "Athletes Heart", etc. Essentially, a file stored the whole discussion thread on the title topic. Many files contained only one question and one or two answers. Several topics raised interest of many list members. Such files contained rather hot discussions (e.g., "Candidayeast Bloom"," MSG sensitivity", "Homeopathy"). In contrast, some files contained newsletters, conference announcements, other announcements that were considered objective (Section 2); these files were deleted from annotation. Finally, 357 files were left for the annotation.

4.2 Annotation results

10 undergraduate and 10 master students were involved in the process. A master student had 30 files to annotate. The results of the annotation were examined; students with better annotations received more files. An undergraduate student had 10 files to annotate; only students with the satisfactory quality annotations were given more files. Finally, the 357 files have been annotated by at least one annotator.

216 have been tagged by two annotators, and 21 have been tagged by three annotators. 120 files have been tagged by only one annotator. A majority of these files did not contain subjective information, e.g., a question and a factual answer . We have divided the final tags into 3 categories:[3]:

subjective sentences : both annotators identified them as subjective, sentiment or opinion, and marked either the same polarity or neutral;

weak subjective sentences : only one annotator identified them as subjective;

non-subjective and uncertain sentences : sentences that the annotators did not mark as subjective or marked with the opposite polarity.

[2] `http://kdd.ics.uci.edu/databases/20newsgroups/20newsgroups.html`

[3] The labelled sentences are posted on `www.ehealthinformation.ca/ap0/opendata.asp`

Subjective sentences		
1st annotator	2nd annotator	#
negative sentiment	negative sentiment	92
neutral opinion	neutral opinion	85
positive opinion	neutral opinion	57
negative opinion	neutral opinion	53
negative sentiment	negative opinion	48
negative opinion	negative opinion	43
positive sentiment	positive sentiment	41
negative sentiment	neutral opinion	41
positive opinion	positive opinion	27
positive sentiment	positive opinion	21
positive sentiment	neutral opinion	20
Weak subjective sentences		
1st annotator	2nd annotator	#
no annotation	neutral opinion	655
no annotation	negative sentiment	331
positive opinion	no annotation	212
negative opinion	no annotation	201
positive sentiment	no annotation	172
no annotation	unspecif. sentiment	12
Non-subjective and uncertain subjectivity		
1st annotator	2nd annotator	#
no annotation	no annotation	4190
positive sentiment	negative opinion	34
negative sentiment	positive sentiment	28
positive opinion	negative sentiment	9
positive opinion	negative opinion	9

Table 1: Annotation results for sentiment and opinion sentences in the sci.med texts.

Table 1 lists the results for the three sentence groups.

4.3 Discussion

6408 sentences were annotated in total. The majority – 4190 sentences – were considered non-subjective by both annotators. *Neutral opinion* was the most frequent subjective label, some persons asked questions and some replied in many cases expressing their own opinions. 85 sentences were marked *neutral opinion* by both annotators. In 655 cases, it was a weak subjectivity (i.e., identified by one annotator). The latter set contained ambiguous sentences, without clear indicators was the expressed statement author's thought or just information taken from some sources. We report some examples: "Symptoms can be drastically enhanced by food but not inflammation", "The low residue diet is appropriate for you if you still have obstructions", "Then they may be able to crowd out garbage genes"

Negative sentiment was another large set of the ambiguous annotation. In Section 3.1, we wrote that the texts were about diseases, so it was natural that sometimes annotators marked descriptions of symptoms or sickness as *negative sentiment*. Often *negative sentiment* was attributed to sentences that were interpreted as subjective only in the message context. For example, "I said that I PERSONALLY had other people order the EXACT SAME FOOD at TWO DIFFERENT TIMES from the SAME RESTAURANT" was marked *negative sentiment* in context of a very opinionated discussion. For the annotator, it was clear that the author of the text had been really angry, and the sentence did carry negative emotion even if it did not contain indicative words.

We have found that sarcasm was a strong factor for the polarity disagreement between annotators. "I'm forever in your debt" was marked as *positive sentiment* and *negative sentiment*, because it was positive as is but was used in a sarcastic answer to another message; one annotator took the whole context in consideration but another one did not. "Surprise surprise different people react differently to different things." and "Subject: Scientific Yawn" (denouncing an alternative medicine) are two other illustrations of opposite polarity labeling. Perhaps, a more complex set of sentiment annotation tags can help to capture such sentiments.

Content-wise, we found that several types of sentences created problems while annotation: advices, suggestions ("go and see a doctor"); courtesy ("thank you in advance", "I would greatly appreciate any reply", "good luck"); questions and indirect questions ("can somebody point me", "I am interested in", "I would like to find any information"). An appropriate remedy can be to divide subjective sentences into categories, e.g., reporting, advice, judgment and sentiment (Asher et al, 2009). Rhetorical relations formed another influential factor. However, correct identification of this phenomena requires a higher proficiency of annotations.

Additionally, annotators faced challenges intrinsic to the user-written text (Section 3.1). Indeed, syntactic rules were not strictly respected and there were mistypes and misspellings. Other challenges were recognitions of trade-mark and proprietary names ("itraconazole", "Oodles of Noodles"), public health and related services ("AMA", "FDA", "State Licensing Board", "ABFP") and medi-

Table 2: Concordance matrix.

	1st observer		
2nd observer	YES	NO	Totals
YES	a	b	g_1
NO	c	d	g_2
Totals	f_1	f_2	N

cal and scientific terms ("Candida", "sinusitis", "yeast bloom").

5 Empirical Evaluation

5.1 Concordance evaluation

To assess the quality of subjective labeling, we computed two types of measures. First, we separately assessed agreement between the annotator labeling of positive and negative sentiments and opinions. We opted for two, positive and negative, measures because annotators may agree on *what constitutes* a subjective label and disagree on *what does not*, e.g., their understanding of *positive* may be close and their understanding of *not positive* may be far apart. We find the two-dimensional values being more informative than the one-dimensional value (Bhowmick et al, 2008; Murakami et al, 2010).

We applied two measures introduced in (Cicchetti and Feinstein, 1990a):

$$p_{pos} = 2a/(f_1 + g_1) \quad (1)$$

$$p_{neg} = 2d/(N - (a - d)) \quad (2)$$

Next, we computed a commonly used *kappa* to evaluate a ratio between the chance-corrected observed agreement and the chance-corrected perfect agreement (Cicchetti and Feinstein, 1990a):

$$kappa = \frac{\frac{a+d}{N} - \frac{f_1 g_1 + f_2 g_2}{N^2}}{1 - \frac{f_1 g_1 + f_2 g_2}{N^2}} \quad (3)$$

Notations are presented in Table 2.

We report the assessment results in Table 3.

The reported results show that annotators find a common ground on sentences that *do not* belong to the categories. This mutual understanding holds across all the subjective categories. We interpret this as a possibility of correct identification of negative examples for all the categories. Annotators also agree on what belongs to positive and negative sentiments; for these two categories, we expect correct identification of positive and negative examples.

Annotation	p_{pos}	p_{neg}	*kappa*
Pos Sentiment	0.667	0.956	0.621
Neg Sentiment	0.674	0.886	0.562
Average	0.671	0.921	0.592
Assessment	p_{pos}	p_{neg}	*kappa*
Pos Opinion	0.409	0.892	0.350
Neg Opinion	0.460	0.884	0.365
Neut Opinion	0.497	0.761	0.280
Average	0.455	0.846	0.332

Table 3: Concordance assessment.

5.2 Statistical language analysis

To analyze the lexical indicators of subjectivity, we built N-gram models ($N = 1, 2, 3, 4$). The N-gram models estimate the probability of a word sequence $w_1 \dots w_n$ as a conditional probability of the word w_n appearing after the sequence of words $w_1 \dots w_{n-1}$:

$$P(w_n|w_1^{n-1}) \approx P(w_n|w_{n-N+1}^{n-1}) \quad (4)$$

The models were built for subjective sentences and weak subjective sentences (upper parts of Table 1). We analyzed most frequent words (occurrence $\geq$ 3) and word combinations output by the models. To make the task feasible, we deleted stop words (i.e., pronouns, prepositions, articles, determiners and auxiliary verbs).

Uni- and bi-gram outputs had shown that very few emotionally charged words appear among the most frequent words. Examples of such words are "good", "happy", "hard", "unfortunately"; "good", "happy", however, may indicate courtesy expressions more than sentiments. For instance, their most frequent bi-grams are "very good", "am happy". Tri- and quadri-gram outputs were very sparse (i.e., occurrences < 5), thus, not reliable for semantic generalization. Important to note that words listed in SentiWordNet (Denecke, 2008) and WordNet-Affect (Strapparava and Mihalceal, 2008) as a rule do not appear in our data .

We computed a significant relative frequency difference (Rayson and Garside, 2000) to find words and word combinations ($N = 2, 3, 4$) on which two sets of sentences differ. The difference was computed as follows:

$$LL(w) = 2(a \log \frac{a(a+b)}{c} + b \log \frac{b(a+b)}{d}) \quad (5)$$

where w – the word, a and b are the occurrences of w in sets A and B respectively, c and d – sizes of

A and B in words. We chose LL because the measure allows two-tailed comparison of w's position in sets A and B.

This method, too, output a few emotionally charged words: "trouble", "hard", "problem", "expensive" are content words that differentiate between positive and negative opinions; "bad", "problem", "hard", "better" appear among words that differentiate between positive and negative sentiments. Word combinations on which the sets differ do not contain emotionally charged words.

5.3 Machine Learning Experiments

Sentiment and opinion classification results are highly susceptible to the classification task, the data characteristics and selected text features. Consequently, the data characteristics affect the classification accuracy. We wished to assess how well algorithms discriminate between

(a) positive and negative sentiment sentences,

(b) positive and negative opinion sentences.

Our hypothesis was that if algorithms achieved a competitive accuracy of learning then it confirmed a good quality of labels.

5.4 Data

We used the labeled sentences without any additional pre-processing. As a result, two sentence sets have been built:

Sentiments 62 positive and 179 negative sentences;

Opinions 169 positive and 74 negative sentences.

We represented each set through all the words that appear in the set more than twice. Two types of attributes were used in experiments: bag of all the words (binary representation) and occurrences of all the words (numeric representation). The two representations provided similar results. We further report the numeric representation results, which were slightly better than binary.

5.5 Learning Results

We applied *Naive Bayes (NB)*, *Decision Trees (DT)*, *K-Nearest Neighbor (KNN)* and *Support Vector Machines (SVM)*. $Fscore$, $Precision(Pr)$, $Recall(R)$ and $BalancedAccuracy(ROC)$ were used to evaluate the performance.

Sentiments				
Algorithm	Pr	R	Fscore	ROC
NB	0.679	0.726	0.686	**0.611**
K-NN	0.649	0.705	0.664	0.578
SVM	**0.714**	**0.751**	**0.708**	0.574
DT	0.552	0.743	0.633	0.485
Baseline	0.552	0.743	0.633	0.485
Opinions				
Algorithm	Pr	R	Fscore	ROC
NB	0.791	0.790	0.767	**0.805**
K-NN	0.744	0.753	0.720	0.586
SVM	**0.850**	**0.848**	**0.839**	0.777
DT	0.734	0.741	0.737	0.682
Baseline	0.484	0.695	0.571	0.481

Table 4: Classification results for positive and negative sentence classification. The values are averaged for positive and negative classes. Best values are in **bold**. Baseline is calculated if all the sentences are into the majority class.

Table 4 reports the best results. For positive and negative sentiments, the reported results were obtained with the following parameters: *DT* – learning coefficient $\alpha = 0.15$, *NB* used kernel estimates; *K-NN* – 9 neighbors, Euclidean distance; *SVM* – complexity parameter C = 0.65, kernel polynomial = 0.52. For positive and negative opinions, the reported results were obtained with the following parameters: *DT* – learning coefficient $\alpha = 0.40$; *NB* – with kernel estimates; *K-NN* – 1 neighbor, Euclidean distance; *SVM* – complexity parameter C = 2.75, kernel polynomial K= 1.0.

Our results are competitive with previously obtained results. As reported in (Sokolova and Lapalme, 2011), opinion-bearing sentences are classified against facts with $Precision$ 80% – 90% (Yu and Hatzivassiloglou, 2003); for consumer reviews, opinion-bearing text segments are classified into positive and negative categories with $Precision$ 56% – 72%; for online debates, posts were classified as positive or negative with $F-score$ 39% –67%, $F-score$ increased to 53% – 75% when the posts were enriched with the Web information, . 90% $BalancedAccuracy(ROC)$ was obtained in opinion spam reviews versus genuine reviews classification. For positive and negative review classification, $Accuracy$ is 75.0% –81.8% when data sets are represented through all the uni- and bigrams.

6 Text Mining and Corpora Annotation in the Domain

Opinion mining and sentiment analysis have become a major research topic for Computational Linguistics. A high demand for knowledge sources prompted development of semantic resources SentiWordNet (Denecke, 2008), WordNet-Affect (Strapparava and Mihalceal, 2008), MicroWNOp (Balahur et al, 2010), as well as lists of affective words or collocations created ad-hoc (Whitelaw et al, 2005; Yu and Hatzivassiloglou, 2003) and even non-affective words (Sokolova and Lapalme, 2011). Sometimes positive and negative text rating was available and used in machine-learning experiments (Pang et al, 2002). At the same time, there are no available sources for sentiment and opinion analysis of user-written health discussions. We work to build such a source.

Sentiment and opinion analysis intensively studied consumer-written product reviews (Blitzer et al, 2007). Somewhat lesser attention was given to political discussion boards (Kim and Hovy, 2007). In (Ferguson et al, 2009), financial blogs were annotated on the document and paragraphs level with their sentiment towards the same topic using a five-point scale *Very Negative, Negative, Neutral, Positive, Very Positive*, in addition to the labels *mixed*, which indicates a mixture of positive and negative sentiment, and *not relevant*. It seemed intuitive that paragraph -level annotation should be useful in providing more accurate information which can be leveraged by a machine learning module. However, the results did not show any improvement. To the best of our knowledge there was only one corpus of blogs with fine-grained annotation of subjectivity (Boldrini et al, 2009). A multilingual corpus of blog posts on different topics of interest in three languages - Spanish, Italian and English was annotated using a fine-grained annotation schema in order to capture the different subjectivity/ objectivity, emotion/opinion/ attitude aspects.

Unlike the listed above work, we concentrate on discussions of health-related topics. There are few dedicated work on polarity of health and medical text. In (Niu et al., 2005; Niu et al., 2006), the authors analyzed textual expressions corresponding to *positive, negative, neural* clinical outcomes. In our work, however, clinical outcomes are set apart from user sentiments and opinions.

So far, experiments in corpora annotation attracted considerably less attention. In (Wiebe et al, 2005), the authors annotated articles at the word- and phrase-level by using fine-grained annotation scheme. Another experiment on news annotation was carried on for the SemEval 2007 Affective Text Task (Strapparava and Mihalceal, 2008). The subjectivity annotation of newspaper articles was discussed in (Balahur and Steinberger, 2009) and (Bhowmick et al, 2008). In the former, the researchers extracted 1592 quotes (reported speech) from newspaper articles and annotated for the sentiment on the target of the quotes. The annotation guidelines allowed increase of the inter-annotator agreement from $< 50\%$ up to 60%. In the latter, the authors collected 1000 affective sentences and categorized them into *direct* and *indirect* affect categories. Our work, instead, is focused on positive and negative sentiments and opinions in user-written Web messages.

7 Conclusion and Future Work

In this paper, we have presented a study of sentiments and opinions in user-written Web messages. We focused on messages posted on health discussion boards. In those messages, users discussed health and ailment, treatments and drugs, asked questions about possible cures. Without having precedents of subjectivity analysis in health discussions, we have designed an author-centric annotation model. The model shows how positive and negative sentiments and positive, negative and neutral opinions can be identified in health discussions.

We applied the annotation model to the sci.med messages of *20 NewsGroups*. We have evaluated concordance of the manual annotation by computing three measures : p_{pos}, p_{neg} and $kappa$. The results show that annotators better identify sentiments than opinions and stronger agree on what type of sentences do *not* belong to positive or negative subjective categories. Our Machine Learning results are comparable with previous results in the subjectivity domain.

Our future plans are to continue the annotation; the final aim is to have all texts annotated by at least five persons. We also plan to study objective, factual statements expressed by users in their messages.

Acknowledgements

The first author's work is in part funded by a Discovery grant of Natural Sciences and Engineering Research Council of Canada. The second author thanks the conference organizers for the RANLP grant.

References

Angelova, G. Ontological Approach to Terminology Learning. *Comptes rendus de l'Academie bulgare des Sciences*, **62**(10), pp. 1319–1326, 2009.

Asher N., Benamara F., Y. Y. Mathieu. Appraisal of opinion expressions in discourse, *Lingvisticae Investigationes*, **32**(2), 2009.

Balahur, A., R. Steinberger, M. Kabadjov, V. Zavarella, E. van der Goot, M. Halkia, B. Pouliquen, J. Belyaeva. Sentiment Analysis in the News, *Proceedings of the Seventh conference on International Language Resources and Evaluation*, 2010.

Balahur, A., R. Steinberger Rethinking Sentiment Analysis in the News: from Theory to Practice and back. *Proceedings of the 1st Workshop on Opionion Mining and Sentiment Analysis*, 2009

Bhowmick, P., P. Mitra, A. Basu. An Agreement Measure for Determining Inter-Annotator Reliability of Human Judgements on Affective Text, *Proceedings of Workshop on Human Judgements in Computational Linguistics*, COLING, p.p. 58–65, 2008.

Blitzer, J., M. Dredze, F. Pereira. Biographies, bollywood, boom-boxes and blenders: Domain adaptation for sentiment classification. *Proceedings of ACL*, 440–447, 2007

Boldrini, E., A. Balahur, P. Martnez-Barco, A. Montoyo EmotiBlog: a finer-grained and more precise learning of subjectivity expression models. In *Proceedings of LAW IV, ACL*, 2009

Chen, W. Dimensions of Subjectivity in Natural Language (Short Paper). In *Proceedings of ACL-HLT*, 2008.

Cicchetti, D., A. Feinstein. High Agreement but Low Kappa: The Problems of Two Paradoxes, *Journal of Clinical Epidemiology*, **43**(6),p.p. 543–549 and p p. 551–558, 1990.

Cohen, K., C. Roeder, W. Baumgartner Jr., L. Hunter, and K. Verspoor Test suite design for biomedical ontology concept recognition systems. *Proceedings of LREC*, pp. 441–446, 2010.

Denecke, K. Using SentiWordNet for multilingual sentiment analysis, *Data Engineering Workshop, IEEE 24th International Conference*, 2008.

Eysenbach, G. Infodemiology and infoveillance. *Journal of Medical Internet Research*, **11**(1), 2009.

Ferguson, P., O'Hare, N., Davy, M., Bermingham, A., Tattersall, S., Sheridan, P., Gurrin, C., Smeaton, A. Exploring the use of Paragraph-level Annotations for Sentiment Analysis of Financial Blogs. *WOMAS 2009 - Workshop on Opinion Mining and Sentiment Analysis*, 2009.

Kim, S.-M., E. Hovy. Crystal: Analyzing predictive opinions on the web. *Proceedings of the 2007 EMNLP-CoNLL*, pages 1056–1064, 2007.

Konovalov S, M. Scotch, L. Post, C. Brandt. Biomedical Informatics Techniques for Processing and Analyzing Web Blogs of Military Service Members, *Journal of Medical Internet Research*, **12**(4), 2010.

Lasersohn, P. Context Dependence, disagreement, and predicates of personal taste *Linguistics and Philosophy*, **28**, pages 643–686, 2005

Murakami, K., E. Nichols, J. Mizuno, Y.Watanabe, H. Goto, M. Ohki, S. Matsuyoshi, K. Inui, Y. Matsumoto. Automatic Classification of Semantic Relations between Facts and Opinions, *Proceedings of NLP Challenges in the Information Explosion Era*, COLING, p.p. 21–31,2010,

Niu, Y., X. Zhu, J. Li, G. Hirst. Analysis of polarity information in medical text, in *Proceedings of the AMIA Annual Symposium*, 2005, 500–574.

Niu, Y., X. D. Zhu, G. Hirst. Using outcome polarity in sentence extraction for medical question-answering. In *Proceedings of the AMIA Annual Symposium*, 2006, 599–603.

Pang, B., L. Lee, S. Vaithyanathan, Thumbs up? Sentiment Classification using Machine Learning Techniques *Proceedings of EMNLP'-02*, pages 79-86, 2002.

Quirk, R., S. Greenbaum, G. Leech, J. Svartvik *A Comprehensive Grammar of the English Language* Longman, 1985.

Rayson, P., R. Garside. Comparing corpora using frequency profiling. *Proceedings of Comparing Corpora Workshop, ACL*, p.p. 1–6, 2000.

Sokolova, M., G. Lapalme. Learning opinions in user-generated Web content. *Journal of Natural Language Engineering*, to appear.

Strapparava, C., R. Mihalcea Learning to Identify Emotions in Text, *Proceedings of the 2008 ACM symposium on Applied Computing* 2008

Whitelaw, C., N. Garg, S. Argamon Using Appraisal Groups for Sentiment Analysis. *Proceedings of the 14th ACM international conference on Information and knowledge management*, pp. 625 – 631, 2005.

Wiebe, J. Tracking point of view in narrative. *Computational Linguistics*, **20**, pp. 233–287, 1994

Wiebe, J., T. Wilson, C. Cardie Annotating Expressions of Opinions and Emotions in Language, *Language Resources and Evaluation*, **39** (2–3), pp. 165–210, 2005

Yu, H., V. Hatzivassiloglou Towards Answering Opinion Questions: Separating Facts from Opinions and Identifying the Polarity of Opinion Sentences. In *Proceedings of EMNLP-03*, 2003.

An Exploration into the Use of Contextual Document Clustering for Cluster Sentiment Analysis

Niall Rooney, Hui Wang
University of Ulster
{nf.rooney,h.wang}
@ulster.ac.uk

Fiona Browne
Queen's University,Belfast
f.browne@qub.ac.uk

Fergal Monaghan, Jann Müller, Alan Sergeant, Zhiwei Lin, Philip Taylor
SAP Research Belfast
{fergal.monaghan,
jann.mueller,
alan.sergeant,
zhiwei.lin,
philip.taylor}@sap.com

Vladimir Dobrynin
St Petersburg State University
v.dobrynin@bk.ru

Abstract

In this paper we consider whether the thematic document clustering approach of Contextual Document Clustering is able to capture the overall sentiment of a cluster of documents. We provide a novel mechanism to determine the sentiment of a cluster based on the latter approach and assess the approach on three data sets formed from the NY Times annotated corpus. We demonstrate that CDC does provide a strong tendency to capture the sentiment of a cluster.

1 Introduction

Sentiment analysis or opinion mining is a recent area of text classification research which tries to determine the opinion that a section of text expresses. Esuli & Sebastiani (2005) describes three subtasks:

- determining whether a given piece of text has a factual nature, neutral nature or whether it expresses an opinion on its material (the Subjective-Objective (SO) polarity of the text)
- determining whether a given piece of text expresses a positive or negative opinion on its subject matter orientation (the Positive-Negative (PN) polarity of the text)
- determining the strength of the subject matter orientation

Turney & Littman (2003) make no distinction between the latter two sub-tasks and propose a measure of semantic orientation which indicate both the direction and intensity of a text. To capture this, they focus on the semantic orientation of a word which they capture by measuring the strength of association with a set of seed words (with either absolute positive or negative polarity). They propose two measures for strength of association based on point-wise mutual information and latent semantic analysis estimated from given corpora. Other mechanisms for semantic orientation have focused on the linguistic constraints on the orientation of adjectives (e.g. the word "and" usually conjoins adjectives of the same orientation) (Hatzivassiloglou & McKeown, 1997) or that synonymous words have similar orientation

(Esuli & Sebastiani, 2005). The aforementioned mechanisms try to give an absolute value for the orientation of a word regardless of its context of use. Wilson et al.(2009) present a two stage classification approach to determine the contextual polarity of subjective clues (words which have been part of annotated subjective expressions) in a corpus. They based this on features primarily as a consequent of local dependency relationships (parent-child) in sentences (although they do use other features mainly at a sentence level). More recent directions in a sentiment analysis for text classification have focussed on the use of unsupervised modelling approaches for text classification. Much of this work has focussed on extending topic modelling approaches such as Probabilistic Latent Semantic Indexing (Mei et al., 2007) or Latent Dirchlet Allocation (Lin & He, 2009) to incorporate the use of sentiment as a variable.

To our knowledge, little work has focussed on determining the sentiment of a cluster rather than the individual documents. Dobrynin et al.(2004,2006,2008) proposed the unsupervised mechanism of Contextual Document Clustering (CDC) that by discovering distinct and relevant contexts, allows for the hard partitioning of documents in a corpus into theme based clusters. A "theme" is an implicit concept and can be considered as equivalent in intent to its lexical definition. CDC considers words in a corpus as any character sequence occurring between separators (either whitespace or punctuation marks) in any text in document. A term in a document is a constrained character sequence based on a regular expression, so in general the set of terms is a subset of the set of words. Also a word cannot be a stop word. A context is a probability distribution of co-occurring terms in documents given a context term. CDC's partitioning of documents, is based on information theoretic considerations of semantic similarity between a document and a context. There exists a logarithmic relationship between a context term's document frequency and the context's entropy. As such, the final choice of context terms and their respective contexts are based on the grouping of context words into a fixed number N_{dfg} of document frequency intervals, and the entropy of their associated context. Contexts are chosen from each interval in a round robin fashion in order of least entropy from each group. In total N_c are chosen. To allow for the fact that after this step, certain contexts may still be too similar based on a comparison of their distributions, merging steps are carried out to merge similar contexts.

In this paper we assess whether CDC by capturing theme related documents within a given cluster, also intrinsically captures the theme's sentiment and would allow for a categorization of a cluster based on sentiment. We hypothesis that if this is the case, an independent measure of a cluster's sentiment will show a high likelihood that a cluster to be either positive or negative in sentiment overall or be a mixture of positive and negative sentiments so that the overall sentiment is neutral. In the latter case this would allow for a further decomposition of sentiment analysis based on sub-regions of the cluster. In the small minority of cases will a cluster be composed solely as a mixture of neutral sentiments. In general, all clusters will contain a mixture of negative and positive sentiments, so we are assessing if the sum polarity tends to be mainly positive or negative i.e. a majority of clusters will either be positive or negative in sentiment.

2 Methodology

For each cluster formed by CDC, it is possible to derive a set of base concepts that provide tag descriptors of the cluster. These tags provide a semantic description of the cluster. Our assumption is that these descriptors also form the basis for determining the overall sentiment of a cluster by the additional use of lexicons of known positive and negative words. This allows a simpler determination of the cluster's sentiment. If it can be shown that for a majority of clusters, a cluster has either a positive or negative sentiment, this provides support for the hypothesis given in section 1.

Each cluster C has a cluster description consisting of a set of cluster tags T and the cluster contains a set of D_c documents. Each document, $d \in D_c$ consists of a set S_d of sentences where a sentence is determined by known boundaries such as punctuation marks. A tag is a contiguous sequence of two or three word phrases. Let Pos be the set of known positive words. These are words that exist in the original lexicon of positive words and exist in the corpus. Let Neg be the set of known negative words. These are words that exist in the original lexicon of negative words and exist in the corpus. Let N_{dc} be the number of documents in cluster C. Let df_w be the number of documents in the cluster for which the word frequency of a word w within a document is non-zero.

$$df_w = |\{d \in D_c : tf(w,d) > 0\}|$$

Let df_t be the number of documents in the cluster for which the tag frequency $pf(t,d)$ of the tag t within the document is non-zero:

$$df_t = |\{d \in D_c : pf(t,d) > 0\}|$$

The document frequency of documents $df_{t \wedge w}$ which contain both a tag t and word w within the same sentence (in the same *vicinity*), is defined as:

$$df_{t \wedge w} = |\{d \in D_c : \exists s \in S_d : tf(w,s).pf(t,s) > 0\}|$$

The cluster sentiment CS is calculated as follows based on Pointwise Mutual Information (PMI) between a word $w \in Pos$ or a word $w \in Neg$ and a tag t summed over all tags:

$$CS = \sum_{t \in T} TS(t)$$

$$TS(t) = \log_2\left(\frac{\prod_{w \in P} df_{t \wedge w}}{\prod_{w \in P} df_t.df_w}\right) - \log_2\left(\frac{\prod_{w \in N} df_{t \wedge w}}{\prod_{w \in N} df_t.df_w}\right)$$

In effect, cluster sentiment is the summation of the tag sentiments.
This formula is based on Turney & Littman study (2003) where we are replacing occurrences of a co-occurring word (with another word) with a co-occurring tag t. We only consider tags that do not contain either positive or negative words as part of their phrasal text.

We assume a cluster has positive sentiment if,

$$CS > Thres$$

neutral if,

$$Thres >= CS >= -Thres$$

and negative if,

$$CS < -Thres$$

Normally the threshold value is 0, however we allow an admittedly arbitrary greater value than 0 to indicate that weakly positive or negative cluster sentiment should be considered neutral. We refer to this calculation for clusters as **CS-standard**. A standard lexicon may also have a measure of the subjective strength of the word whether a word in most contexts is seen as strongly or weakly subjective.

To allow for this factor we modified $TS(t)$ to include a subjectivity factor for lexicon words, where words which are strongly subjective have a different factor to words that are weakly subjective.

$$TS(t) = \log_2\left(\frac{\prod_{w \in P} \alpha_w.df_{t \wedge w}}{\prod_{w \in P} df_t.df_w}\right) - \log_2\left(\frac{\prod_{w \in N} \alpha_w.df_{t \wedge w}}{\prod_{w \in N} df_t.df_w}\right)$$

We refer to this calculation for clusters as **CS-subj**. The factor, α_w was set to 2.0 for strongly subjective lexicon words and to 1.0 for weakly subjective.

CS-standard considers all tags to be of equal importance. Based on the tag document frequency within a cluster, it is possible to give each tag a weighting normalized by the tag frequency range:

$$CS = \sum_{t \in T} \lambda_t TS(t)$$

$$\lambda_t = 0.5 + \left(0.5 * \frac{df_t - \min_{tag \in T} df_{tag}}{\max_{tag \in T} df_{tag} - \min_{tag \in T} df_{tag}}\right)$$

We refer to this mechanism as **CS-rank**. This approach gives a weighting for each tag between 0.5 and 1.0, so that tags with higher document frequency have greater weighting.

3 Evaluation

The choice of data set was determined by two factors. Firstly, the data set had to contain sufficient documents to form a set of information-rich contexts and hence clusters. Secondly, the nature of the data set has a high likelihood of expressing a mixture of subjective opinions. For this purpose, we chose data from the NY Times annotated corpus (Sandhaus, 2008). We considered 3 subsets of data for the respective years of 2005 (Nyt-2005), 2006 (Nyt-2006) and 2007 (Nyt-2007) and ran the same evaluation for each corpus. We based each evaluation on the subjectivity lexicon provided by Wilson et al. (2005) which lists a set of words with either positive or negative polarity and a measure of subjective strength (either strong or weak). This latter feature was the basis for the setting of α_w in CS-subj. In total there are 2304 positive words and 4145 negative words. Not all words were present in each of the 3 corpora and such words were ignored. Table 1 summarizes the data characteristics for the three data sets and indicates that the parameters are stable for each evaluation, not surprisingly as there is no variation in the nature of the data. Nyt-2007 has fewer documents as data was only recorded up to April, 2007. The *Thres* value was set to 5.0 indicating that clusters with sentiment only weakly positive or weakly negative, we considered as neutral.

Data set	Number of documents	Number of clusters	Number of positive words in corpus	Number of negative words in corpus
Nyt-2005	89975	1363	2172	3796
Nyt-2006	87029	1339	2165	3785
Nyt-2007	39950	1396	2132	3675

Table 1 Data set characteristics

There appears to be an imbalance between the number of positive and negative words but this imbalance is less pronounced if we consider only words in the lexicon that occur in the vicinity of cluster tags (only such words contribute to the evaluation scores). This is shown in Table 2.

Data set	Number of positive words in vicinity of a given tag	Number of negative words in vicinity of a given tag
Nyt-2005	1790	2657
Nyt-2006	1912	3010
Nyt-2007	1912	3095

Table 2 Lexicon words used in Evaluations

As described in the Introduction, CDC requires an apriori setting of how many distinct contexts to select N_c and the number of document frequency intervals N_{dfg} (Rooney *et al.*, 2006). Note that there can be fewer contexts formed than requested due to merging of similar contexts and fewer clusters also due to non-assignment of documents to given contexts. In each evaluation, N_c was set to 2000 and N_{dfg} to 7, as previous work has shown these values to be appropriate settings for these sizes of data sets. We then calculate the number of positive, negative or neutral clusters and express the relative number of clusters as percentages. This process was carried out for each evaluation and results were averaged over the 3 years. The average of the evaluations is shown in Figure 1.

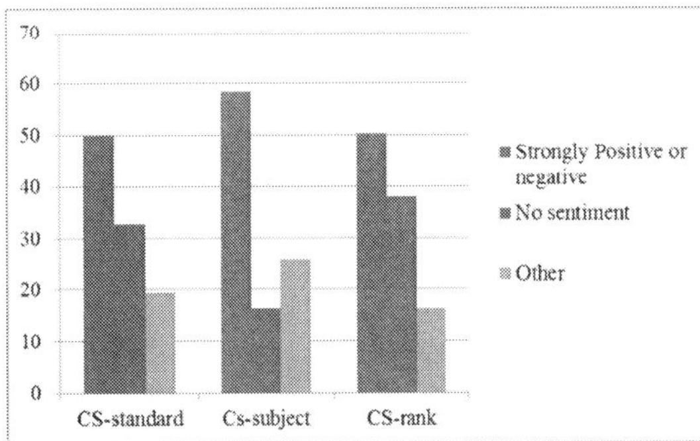

Figure 1: Cluster sentiment averaged over nyt_2005, nyt_2006,nyt_2007

Clearly there is a majority of clusters that are either positive or negative in sentiment in the case of both CS-standard and CS-subj so that our hypothesis is justified. There is very little to distinguish these two mechanisms with CS-subj returning a slightly elevated percentage of positive clusters and a similarly decreased percentage of negative sentiment clusters and this was reflected not only in the averages but in the individual evaluations. CS-rank shown a somewhat different profile with there still been a majority of clusters being identified as positive or negative, but a relative reduction in the percentage of positive clusters and a relative increases in the percentage of negative clusters. However investigation into each data set showed the consistent pattern of increasing the number of neutral clusters and we can consider this mechanism of 'smoothing' the individual contribution of each tag.

Further evidence is provided for our hypothesis when we examined clusters deemed as neutral. We consider each neutral cluster as belonging to one of two categories: *no sentiment* if in fact the overall sentiment is 0 which only happens if no sentiment value is calculated for given cluster tags and *sentiment* otherwise. Figure 2 shows the results of this categorization average over the 3 evaluations.

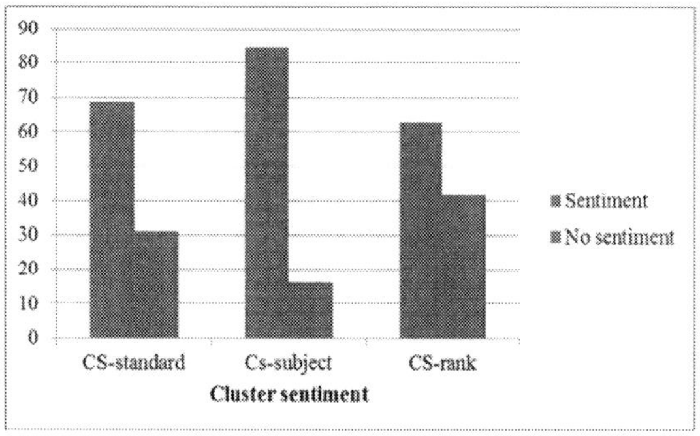

Figure 2: Neutral Cluster decomposition averages averaged over nyt_2005, nyt_2006, nyt_2007

Regardless of the cluster sentiment measure, only a minority of neutral clusters are truly neutral and show no tag sentiment. Of course in the other case the cluster would need to be decomposed into smaller regions to allow for the discovery of regions of either positive or negative sentiment, if we are not to regard the cluster as "neutral". CDC provides graph based mechanisms to structure the content of clusters whose use for sentiment analysis will be explored in future work.

It is not uncommon for CDC to form clusters based on themes which share tags, as tags are not a description of the intrinsic theme or context, but simply indicators of the cluster's content. As this is the case, it was of interest to consider whether clusters that have a high degree of similarity in their tags could have different cluster sentiment classification. We considered a pair of clusters that shared at least 70% of tags relative to the first cluster in a pairing as highly similar. Table 3 shows a summary of the outcome.

Clearly there is evidence that between 23 to 29 percent of cluster pairings have different sentiment, again highlighting the use of cluster tags as the basis for determining cluster sentiment. The tags by themselves do not give any indication of the overall cluster sentiment, but individually they are the basis for determining tag sentiment as contributors to overall cluster sentiment.

Data set	Number of highly similar clusters	Number of highly similar clusters with different cluster sentiment (Percentage)
Nyt-2005	449	130 (29%)
Nyt-2006	473	136 (29%)
Nyt-2007	336	78 (23%)

Table 3 Similar pairs of clusters and Number with differing cluster sentiment

We do not have an independent means of assessing the strength of our approach to tag sentiment and hence cluster sentiment - we would need human assessors to provide a qualitative evaluation, but we have seen a considerable number of examples whereby the tag sentiment for different clusters is clearly reflected the documents that contain these tags. By way of example, consider the following two highly similar clusters <13820,15095> drawn from the Nyt_2006 evaluation, where the clusters identifiers are as a result of the CDC process. The following table shows the tagging for cluster 13820.

Tag list for cluster
tom glavine
orlando hernández
omar minaya
pedro martínez
dominican republic
carlos delgado
willie randolph
shea stadium

Table 4 Cluster tags for cluster 13820

Clearly the cluster is topically related to "baseball". The tag list is much longer for 15095 with 7 of the tags from 13820, also occurring for 15095. 15095 is also topically related "baseball" – how they vary thematically is intrinsic to the context, which is hard for us to convey as they are probabilty distribution in words but clearly the themes have some level of similarity. If we consider the tag "pedro martínez", this has tag sentiment -15.78 in 15095 and 39.87 in 13820. The given tag occurs in 4 documents in 15095 and 2 in 13820. Table 4 shows the titles for these documents (the content of a document is a concatenation of both its title and its body of text) which demonstrates that the tag "pedro martínez" has a strong difference in sentiment for these two clusters, allowing for the fact that the judgment is based on titles only.

Cluster: 15095	Cluster: 13820
Randolph Lets Bygones Be Bygones Martinez May Have to Consider Retiring Martinez Takes It Step by Step, Gingerly Martinez on Hill, But Not in Shape	No News on Martinez, and Mets Say That's Good Martinez: Good Guy In Mets' Black Hat

Table 5 Document titles containing the same tag "pedro martínez" but different clusters

4 Conclusions

We have shown in this paper that for the given type of data, CDC is likely to form clusters reflecting an intrinsic polarity in sentiment. This may only be reflected in news articles where the expression of opinions is commonplace and we propose considering other data sets of a less opinionated nature to see how they compare. In future work, we aim to benchmark our approach against other approaches to document clustering to see if CDC is superior in this aspect.

References

Dobrynin, V. Patterson, D. Rooney, N. (2004): Contextual Document Clustering. ECIR 2004: 167-180

Esuli, A., & Sebastiani, F. (2005). Determining the semantic orientation of words through gloss analysis. *Proceedings of CIKM-05, 14th ACM International Conference on Information and Knowledge Management,* 617–624.

Hatzivassiloglou, V., & McKeown, K. R. (1997). Predicting the semantic orientation of adjectives. *Proceedings of the 35th Annual Meeting of the Association for Computational Linguistics and Eighth Conference of the European Chapter of the Association for Computational Linguistics,* 174-181.

Lin, C., & He, Y. (2009). Joint sentiment/topic model for sentiment analysis. *Proceeding of the 18th ACM Conference on Information and Knowledge Management,* 375-384.

Mei, Q., Ling, X., Wondra, M., Su, H., & Zhai, C. X. (2007). Topic sentiment mixture: Modeling facets and opinions in weblogs. *Proceedings of the 16th International Conference on World Wide Web,* 171-180.

Rooney, N., Patterson, D., Galushka, M., & Dobrynin, V. (2006). A scaleable document clustering approach for large document corpora. *Information Processing & Management, 42*(5), 1163-1175.

Rooney, N., Patterson, D., Galushka, M., Dobrynin, V., & Smirnova, E. (2008). An investigation into the stability of contextual document clustering. *Journal of the American Society for Information Science and Technology, 59*(2), 256-266.

Sandhaus, E (2008) *The New York Times Annotated Corpus.* Linguistic Data Consortium, Philadelphia.

Turney, P. D., & Littman, M. L. (2003). Measuring praise and criticism: Inference of semantic orientation from association. *ACM Transactions on Information Systems (TOIS),* 315-346.

Wilson, T., Wiebe & Paul Hoffmann, P.(2005). Recognizing Contextual Polarity in Phrase-Level Sentiment Analysis. Proceedings of HLT/EMNLP 2005,Vancouver, Canada.

Wilson, T., Wiebe, J., & Hoffmann, P. (2009). Recognizing contextual polarity: An exploration of features for phrase-level sentiment analysis. *Computational Linguistics, 35*(3), 399-433.

Pause and Stop Labeling for Chinese Sentence Boundary Detection

Hen-Hsen Huang
Department of Computer Science and Information Engineering,
National Taiwan University,
Taipei, Taiwan
hhhuang@nlg.csie.ntu.edu.tw

Hsin-Hsi Chen
Department of Computer Science and Information Engineering,
National Taiwan University,
Taipei, Taiwan
hhchen@csie.ntu.edu.tw

Abstract

The fuzziness of Chinese sentence boundary makes discourse analysis more challenging. Moreover, many articles posted on the Internet are even lack of punctuation marks. In this paper, we collect documents written by masters as a reference corpus and propose a model to label the punctuation marks for the given text. Conditional random field (CRF) models trained with the corpus determine the correct delimiter (a comma or a full-stop) between each pair of successive clauses. Different tagging schemes and various features from different linguistic levels are explored. The results show that our segmenter achieves an accuracy of 77.48% for plain text, which is close to the human performance 81.18%. For the rich formatted text, our segmenter achieves an even better accuracy of 82.93%.

1 Introduction

To resolve sentence boundary is a fundamental issue for human language understanding. In English, sentence boundary detection (SBD) focuses on the disambiguation of the usages of punctuation marks such as period to determine if they mark the end of sentences.

In Chinese, the concept of "sentences" is fuzzier and less-defined. Native Chinese writers seldom follow the usage guidelines of punctuation marks. They often decide where to place a pause (i.e., a comma) and where to place a stop (i.e., a full-stop) in the writing according to their individual subjectivity. People tend to concatenate many clauses with commas. As a result, a Chinese sentence is often very long. That makes a text hard to be understood by both humans and machines. For example, a real world sample sentence

"這是有點霸道，但也有道理，因為他們是上市公司，每一季要向美國證管會報告總公司、附屬公司及子公司的營運及財務狀況，帳都是照一套會計原則來做，所以很多時候他們的要求，是出自一種單純的需要，而並不是故意要來欺負我們。"

could be divided into three sentences such as

"這是有點霸道，但也有道理。" 'This is a little overbearing, but is also reasonable.'

"因為他們是上市公司，每一季要向美國證管會報告總公司、附屬公司及子公司的營運及財務狀況，帳都是照一套會計原則來做。" 'Because they are listed companies and should report a summary of operation and financial status of their corporation, subsidiaries, and affiliates to the U.S. Securities quarterly, the accounts are prepared in accordance with the same set of accounting principles.'

"所以很多時候他們的要求，是出自一種單純的需要，而並不是故意要來欺負我們。" 'For this reason, their requests are usually from the simple need, not to intentionally bully us.'

The meaning from the set of shorter sentences is more concentrated and more readable than from the single longer one.

An even serious issue of Chinese punctuation marking is raised from the massive informal writing on the Internet. The articles posted frequently lack of punctuation marks. Authors usually separate clauses by whitespaces and newline symbols, and the boundaries of sentences are partially or entirely missing. Splitting an entire document into sentences is indispensable. For example, the following text from the Internet

"父親在一條小徑裡找到一株相思樹 正結滿了一小粒一小粒的果實
我終於知道所謂「相思果」是什麼
剪下一兩條樹枝 上面都是纍纍的紅豆
慢慢的從山上走下來
天色也跟著漸漸的黑了"

could be divided into a number of sentences with proper punctuation marks:

"父親在一條小徑裡找到一株相思樹，正結滿了一小粒一小粒的果實。" 'My father found an acacia in a narrow path, which is covered with fruits.'

"我終於知道所謂「相思果」是什麼。" 'I eventually knew the so called "Acacia fruit" is.'

"剪下一兩條樹枝，上面都是纍纍的紅豆。" 'Cut a couple of branches, on which there are full of red beans.'

"慢慢的從山上走下來，天色也跟著漸漸的黑了" 'Slowly walked down from the hill, and the sky was getting dark.'

As well, the punctuation marked text becomes more structured and more readable. At present, numerous Chinese documents on the Internet are written without the punctuation marks. To deal with those informal written data, splitting the entire document into sentences is a fundamental task as important as the Chinese word segmentation does.

In this paper, we classify the delimiter type between each pair of successive clauses into "pause" (a comma) to indicate a short stop in a sentence, and "stop" (a full-stop, an exclamation mark, or a question mark) to indicate the end of a sentence. Conditional random fields (CRFs) (Lafferty et al., 2001) are used for such a sequential labeling task. Given a text which lacks of punctuation marks or is improperly marked, the proposed model will insert or modify the punctuation marks in the text, and determine the boundaries of sentences.

The rest of this paper is organized as follows. First, we review the related work in Section 2. In Section 3, two datasets and their characteristics are presented. The labeling scheme and a variety of features are introduced in Section 4. In Section 5, the experimental results are shown and discussed. Finally, Section 6 concludes the remarks.

2 Related Work

A typical SBD task in English is to distinguish the usages of a period, including full-stop, abbreviation, number point, and a part of ellipsis (...). Various approaches are applied in this task and achieve very high performance. A rule-based model manually encoded by experts achieves an error rate of 0.9% (Aberdeen et al., 1995). The best unsupervised method achieves an error rate of 1.41% without the need of the dictionary and the abbreviation list (Mikheev, 2002). By the supervised learning approach, a modern SVM-based model achieves an even lower error rate of 0.25% (Gillick, 2009).

In Classical Chinese, there are no space and punctuation marks in the writing. As a result, all the Chinese characters in a paragraph are successive (one by one) without word, clause, and sentence boundaries. Huang et al. (2010) propose a CRF model with various features including n-gram, jump, word class, and phonetic information to segment a Classical Chinese text into clauses and achieve an F-score of 83.34%.

In Modern Chinese, Jin et al (2004) propose a method to classify the roles of commas in Chinese long sentences to improve the performance of dependency parsing. Xu et al (2005) propose a method to split a long sentence into shorter pieces to improve the performance of Chinese-English translation task. Zong and Ren (2003), and Liu and Zong (2003) segment a spoken utterance into a set of pieces. The above works focus on segmenting long sentences into shorter units for certain applications. Different from their works, recovery of the missing punctuations, and resolutions of the usages of both commas and full-stops are the major contributions of this paper.

3 Datasets

For comparison with human labeling, we sample 36 articles from Sinica corpus (Chen et al., 1996) and label them with punctuation marks by 14 native Chinese readers. Articles in this Sinica dataset are sourced from newspapers and the Internet, in which the written style and the topics are largely diverse. An article is divided into a number of fragments split by a pause punctuation (i.e., a comma) or a stop punctuation (i.e., a full-stop, an exclamation mark, or a question mark).

Dataset	#articles	#fragments	#fragments ending with a pause	#fragments ending with a stop	Average length in a fragment	#pause/#stop
Sinica dataset	36	4,498	3,175	1,323	11.76	2.40
Master dataset	1,381	296,055	204,848	91,207	10.45	2.25

Table 1. Statistics of Sinica and Master Datasets

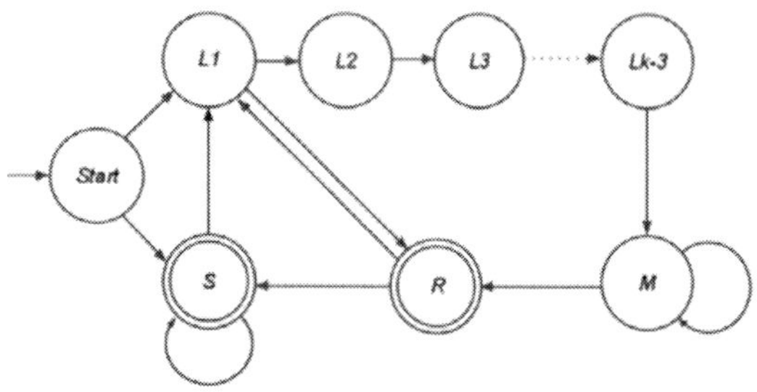

Figure 1. Markov Chain of the *k*-tag set tagging scheme

Each article is shown to three labelers without the punctuation marks, and the labelers have to label an appropriate punctuation mark at the end of each fragment. Among the 36 articles, there are 4,498 fragments in total to be labeled. The agreement between labelers is 0.554 in Fleiss' kappa, i.e., the category of moderate agreement. The mellow human agreement shows the ambiguity and the subjectivity inherent in the pause and stop labeling task.

The Sinica dataset is still not enough to be a moderate training dataset. Thus, we construct a larger Master dataset which is a collection of 1,381 articles written by Chinese masters. The masters include the modern Chinese pioneers such as Lu Xun (魯迅) and Zhu Ziqing (朱自清), the famous contemporary writers, and the professional columnists. These masters are not only the experts in Chinese writing, their writing styles are also the paradigm for Chinese learners. For this reason, the uses of punctuation marks by them can be considered as the expert-level annotation. In this way, the collection of their articles is a dataset naturally authoritative. Since the Master dataset is crawled from the Internet, the layout information like HTML tags and symbols are available in addition to the plain text. Some HTML tags such as line breaker and paragraph maker can be used as clues to sentence segmentation.

The statistics of the two datasets are shown in Table 1. The number of documents in Master dataset is 38.36 times larger than that in Sinica dataset. Besides, the number of fragments in the former dataset is 65.82 times larger than that in the latter one. The average length of a fragment in these two datasets is quite similar, i.e., 11.76 and 10.45 characters. Besides, the ratio of the number of pauses to stops is also similar, i.e., 2.40 and 2.25.

4 Labeling Method

To label the type of each delimiter between successive fragments, the sequential labeling model, CRFs, is applied. We experiment different tagging schemes and feature functions with CRF.

4.1 Tagging Scheme

The typical tagging scheme for text segmentation is 2-tag set in which two types of labels, "start" and "non-start", are used. As shown in Table 1, the ratios of the pauses to the stops are 2.40 in Sinica dataset and 2.25 in Master dataset. In other words, the classification between the class "start" and the class "non-start" is unbalanced. On average, a stop-ending clause appears after two to three pause-ending clauses.

Rather than the 2-tag set scheme, a longer tagging schemes, *k*-tag sets, are reported better in Chinese word segmentation (Xue, 2003; Zhao et al., 2006) and Classical Chinese sentence segmentation (Huang et al, 2010). We experiment different *k*-tag set schemes in pause and stop labeling. A fragment could be labeled with one of the following tags: L_1, L_2, …, $L_{k\text{-}3}$, R, M, and S.

L means *Left boundary*. The tag L_i ($1 \leq i \leq k\text{-}3$) labeled on fragment f denotes f is the i-th fragment of a sentence. The tag R, which means *Right boundary*, marks the last fragment of a sentence. The fragments between $L_{k\text{-}3}$ and R are labeled with the tag M (*Middle*). A single fragment forming a sentence is labeled with the tag S (*Single*). The Markov Chain of the *k*-tag set tagging scheme is shown in Figure 1. For example, the fragments in the first sample in Section 1 can be labeled in the 4-tag set scheme as follows:

"這是有點霸道，" (L_1)
"但也有道理。" (R)
"因為他們是上市公司，" (L_1)
"每一季要向美國證管會報告總公司、附屬公司及子公司的營運及財務狀況，" (M)

"帳都是照一套會計原則來做。" (*R*)
"所以很多時候他們的要求，" (L_1)
"是出自一種單純的需要，" (*M*)
"而並不是故意要來欺負我們。" (*R*)

In this paper, 2-tag set, 4-tag set, and 5-tag set are explored.

4.2 Linguistic Features

Several types of features are proposed as follows.

Phonetics Level (*P*): The features include the initials, finals, and tones of the first character and the last character in a fragment. The syllabic feature useful in the speech recognition is unavailable in the written text. In this study, we use the pronunciation of each Chinese character to capture the phonetics information. In our assumption, the pronunciation combination between the last character of a fragment and the first character of the next fragment is a clue to the type (a pause or a full-stop) of successive fragments. The phonetic system is based on Mandarin Phonetic Symbols (MPS), also known as Bopomofo, in which there are 21 types of initials, 36 types of finals, and 5 types of tones.

Character Level (*C*): The features include the leftmost and the rightmost Chinese character (Hanzi) unigrams, bigrams, and trigrams of a fragment, and the number of Chinese characters in a fragment. From the empirical statistics of the distribution of Chinese words by length, 79.52% of Chinese words are covered in unigrams, bigrams, and trigrams (Chen et at., 1997).

Word Level (*W*): The features include the leftmost and the rightmost word unigrams, bigrams, and trigrams of a fragment, and the number of words in a fragment. We perform Chinese word segmentation with the Stanford Chinese word segmenter (Chang et al., 2008). As shown in Table 1, the average lengths (in Characters) of a fragment are 11.76 and 10.45 in Sinica dataset and in Master dataset, respectively. The average length of Chinese words in these two datasets is 2.49 characters. For this reason, all the characters in most fragments are able to be captured within the leftmost and the rightmost trigrams.

Part-of-Speech Level (*POS*): The features include the leftmost and the rightmost POS unigrams, bigrams, and trigrams in a fragment. Besides, the presences or absences of certain POS tags in a fragment are also checked. These tags include noun, pronoun, verb, conjunction, particle, adverb, adjective, and their combinations.

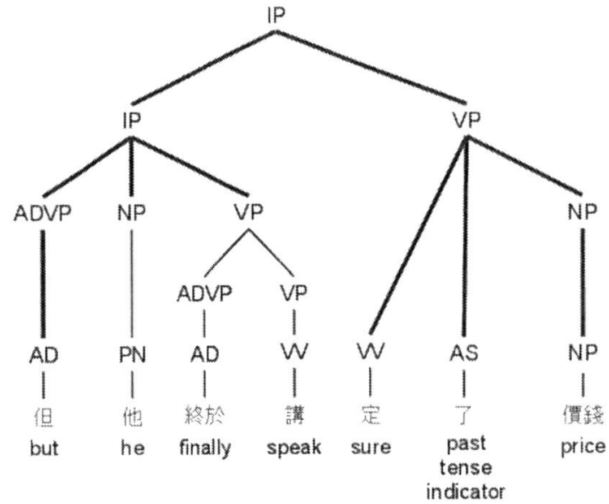

Figure 2. Extracting the top-level structure from the syntax tree

We perform POS tagging with the Stanford parser (Levy and Manning, 2003).

Syntactic Level (S): We get the syntactic tree of a fragment by the Stanford parser, and extract the structure of the upper three levels, which forms the fundamental composition of the fragment. In addition, the leftmost path and the rightmost path of the tree are also extracted. Figure 2 shows the upper three levels of the parsing tree, the leftmost path, and the rightmost path of the sample fragment in the bold edges. For instance, the structure of the upper three levels in Figure 2 formed in preorder format is IP(IP(ADVP NP VP) VP(VV AS NP)), the leftmost path is IP(IP(ADVP(AD))), and the rightmost path is IP(VP(NP(NP))).

Topic-Comment Structure (*TC*): A Chinese sentence is usually composed of a topic and several comments. The topic clause contains the topic of the sentence, and the comment clauses give more information on the topic, which is usually omitted in the comment clauses. Once a new topic appears in a clause to begin a new sentence, the sentence before the clause will be known to be complete in topic-comment structure. For example, the sentence

"我的心分外地寂寞。" 'My heart is especially lonely.'

is a single clause and is complete in the topic-comment structure. In this example, the topic is the noun phrase "我的心" ('My heart'), and the comment is "分外地寂寞" ('is especially lonely').

Consider another example:

"我從山下走下來，一路瀏覽兩旁的夜景，一路細數空中的星光。" 'I walked from the mountain, looked at both sides of scenarios, and gazed at the stars in the sky.'

The topic is the pronoun 'I', and the three verb phrases, 'Walked …', 'Looked at …', and 'Gazed at …', are all the comments. For a given text, if one can accurately classify each fragment as a topic or a comment, the boundaries of sentences are also resolved.

To detect the topic clause is difficult. In this study, we capture the cue for topic-comment structure from the surface information. We postulate that a topic-clause tends to be a noun phrase or a complete fragment consisting of both noun phrase and verb phrase, and the comment-clause tends to be a verb phrase. For this reason, a fragment is represented in one the four types, NP, VP, NP-VP, and OTHER. In addition, the core noun in the noun phrase and the core verb in the verb phrase are also extracted.

Discourse Connective (*DC*): Some word pairs are usually used between or within sentences. We prepare a discourse connective list that contains 33 inter-sentence connectives such as "最初 ... 目前" (originally … at present) and 348 intra-sentence connectives like "不但 … 而且" (not only … but also). The two words in a pair of inter-sentence connective are collocated across sentences. For example, the pair "最初 … 目前" is almost shown in two successive sentences respectively rather than shown in the fragments which belong to a single sentence. Therefore, this is a clear cue that a stop should be inserted between inter-sentence connectives. In the other hand, the two words in a pair of intra-sentence connective are collocated within a single sentence. In this case, no stop should be inserted between them.

For each fragment, we use four features, inter-forward, inter-backward, intra-forward, and intra-backward, to capture discourse connection between it and its preceding (successive) fragment. When fragments f_i and f_j ($i<j$) contain an inter-sentence connective, the inter-forward feature of f_i and the inter-backward feature of f_j will be increased by 1. We deal with the intra-sentence connective in the similar way. That is, the corresponding intra-forward and intra-backward features will be increased accordingly. In the current implementation, the window size is set to 2.

Collocated Word (*CW*): Rather than the connectives collected from dictionaries, numerous inter and intra sentence word pairs are automatically mined from the training data as supplements to Discourse Connective, which is relatively smaller. We collect the collocations that tend to appear between inter and intra sentences from the training data, and filter them with mutual information and classification confidence.

Layout Information (*LI*): The layout information such as whitespaces, tabs, and new-lines are usually available in the text. Moreover, the articles posted on the Internet are often embedded with a lot of HTML tags and special symbols that indicate the layout styles. Those tags includes the line breaker (*
), the paragraph marker (<p>*), the span (*<span>*), the block (*<div>*), the non-breaking space (* *), and so on. The types and the occurrences of the surrounding symbols and tags form the features to represent the layout information of a fragment.

The layout information is unavailable from Sinica dataset because it is comprised of plain text.

5 Experiments

There are three parts of experiments. In the first part, we evaluate the performances of different tagging schemes with the basic features. As results, the best tagging scheme will be utilized in the following experiments. In the second part, the performances of various features and their combinations are evaluated. The best combination of the features will be adopted in the last part of experiments. In the last part, we compare the performance of our best model with those of the labelers. All the evaluation results are reported using 5-fold cross-validation.

5.1 Evaluation Metrics

All the evaluation performances are reported in terms of accuracy, precision, recall, and F-score.

Accuracy, which measures how many pauses and stops are correctly predicted, is a metric for labeling. For evaluating sentence boundary detection, we define precision as the ratio of the predicted stops between sentences which are actually stops, recall as the ratio of the stops between sentences correctly detected as stops, and F-score as the harmonic mean of precision and recall. The last punctuation mark in an article is excluded from evaluation because it is always a stop.

Tag Set	Acc.	Precision	Recall	F-Score
2-tag set	73.84%	60.25%	44.33%	51.08%
4-tag set	**77.01%**	**65.08%**	**51.59%**	**57.55%**
5-tag set	75.75%	64.68%	46.90%	54.37%

Table 2. Comparison between tagging schemes

Features	Acc.	Precision	Recall	F-Score
P	70.76%	52.53%	33.30%	40.76%
C	77.01%	65.08%	**51.59%**	57.55%
W	76.95%	66.04%	48.79%	56.12%
POS	76.77%	68.22%	43.23%	52.92%
S	71.78%	53.80%	46.56%	49.92%
TC	71.66%	55.19%	32.90%	41.22%
DC	69.73%	47.73%	2.35%	4.48%
CW	69.69%	47.58%	3.40%	6.35%
P+C+W	77.09%	65.06%	52.15%	57.90%
P+C+W+ POS	78.09%	69.08%	49.71%	57.82%
P+C+W+ POS+S	78.25%	69.02%	50.80%	**58.53%**
P+C+W+ POS+S+ TC	**78.38%**	69.63%	50.42%	58.49%
P+C+W+ POS+S+ TC+DC	77.97%	**70.76%**	46.12%	55.84%
P+C+W+ POS+S+ TC+DC+ CW	77.64%	68.99%	47.16%	56.02%
LI	78.91%	**99.97%**	30.82%	47.12%
P+C+W+ POS+S+ LI	82.74%	78.15%	**59.50%**	67.56%
P+C+W+ POS+S+ TC+LI	**82.93%**	78.90%	59.38%	**67.76%**

Table 3. Comparison among features

5.2 Tagging Scheme

The 2-tag set, 4-tag set, and 5-tag set schemes are trained over the Master dataset with the feature set on Character Level (i.e., C feature type in Section 4.2). As a result, the 4-tag set scheme outperforms the others. In the following experiments, the tag scheme is fixed to the 4-tag set.

5.3 Features

We train the model with various features over the Master dataset, and the results are listed in Table 3. The abbreviation of each feature is shown in Section 4.2. Firstly, we focus on the results when the layout information is unavailable.

Among the individual features, Character Level (*C*) features achieve the highest accuracy of 77.01% in pause and stop labeling and F-score of 57.55% in sentence boundary detection. Discourse Connective (*DC*) and Collocated Word (*CW*) suffer from the rarely matched patterns, so that the performance is out of expectation. Since the word pairs in Collocated Word are mined from the training data, we can lower the filter threshold to increase the coverage of Collocated Word. However, by adding the lower confident word pairs, the overall performance gets decreased at all.

A word is a more meaningful unit than a character in Chinese. However, the features from Word Level (*W*) are slightly inferior to those from Character Level (*C*) in our experiments. After analyzing the wrongly classified examples, we found that the Chinese word segmentation errors propagate to sentence boundary detection task. In addition, many clue words such as "了" (paste tense indicator), "嗎" (interrogative particle), and "吧" (particle used after an imperative sentence) are single character words, hence Character Level (*C*) features cover these words as well. Part-of-speech not only has the highest precision among all the single feature set, but also improves the precision when it is combined with the other features.

Although the features from Character Level (*C*) play a crucial role in the experiments, they only capture the first three and the last three characters. All of the information in the middle of fragment is missing. We try to capture that information by Syntactic Level (*S*), Topic-Comment Structure (*TC*), Discourse Connective (*DC*), and Collocated Word (*CW*). The experimental results show the combination of features on Phonetics Level (*P*), Character Level (*C*), Word Level (*W*), Part-of-Speech Level (*POS*), Syntactic Level (*S*), and Topic-Comment Structure (*TC*) achieves the best accuracy of 78.38% in pause and stop labeling and the second highest F-score of 58.49% in sentence boundary detection for the plain text. This is a significant improvement over those models trained with the features on Character or Word levels.

Layout Information *(LI)* is a special feature that achieves an extremely high precision of 99.97% and a low recall of 30.82%. The layout tags almost appear between the paragraphs or between the text blocks. In most cases, the successive clauses across two paragraphs have be inserted a full-stop. Thus, Layout Information (*LI*) is a sharp clue to roughly segment the entire article into smaller units. Combining Layout Information (*LI*) with the best models for plain text segmentation, the performance is improved by 4.55% in accuracy and 9% in F-score. Finally, our model achieves an accuracy of 82.93% and an F-score of 67.76%.

5.4 Comparison with Human Labeling

The model trained on Master dataset is also tested on Sinica dataset to compare the performance with human labeling. Because Sinica dataset is comprised of plain text and no layout information is available, the best model for plain text is applied in this subsection.

The human performance is counted from 14 native Chinese readers' labels. The labeler who performs the best achieves an accuracy of 85.81% and an F-score of 72.15% when the author's labels are regarded as ground truth. The labeler who performs the worst has an accuracy of 77.92% and an F-score of 50.42%. The average accuracy and the F-score for all labelers are 81.18% and 67.51%, respectively. Table 4 shows the performance differences between native labelers and our model. Our model achieves 95.44% of human capability in pause and stop labeling, and 80.98% of human capability in the task of predicting sentence boundary. Overall, our model is inferior to the human average but out-perform some individuals in predicting sentence boundary.

The agreement between our model and the human labelers is 0.382 in Fleiss' kappa, and the agreements between each labeler and all the rest labelers are range from 0.363 to 0.657. This means that our model competes with native readers in this task.

Labeler	Acc.	Precision	Recall	F-score
Human Best	85.81%	70.26%	74.15%	72.15%
Huma Middle	81.15%	63.77%	72.54%	67.87%
Huma Worst	77.92%	87.97%	35.34%	50.42%
Human Average	81.18%	66.67%	68.38%	67.51%
Our Model	77.48%	65.16%	47.09%	54.67%

Table 4. Comparison between our model and the article authors

6 Conclusion

In this paper, we point out the importance of Chinese sentence boundary detection and the issue of informal writing on the Internet. To address this problem, an automatic punctuation mark label model is proposed. We test different tagging schemes and the feasibilities of various features with CRFs. For the plain text segmentation, our model with various useful linguistic features achieves accuracies of 78.38% and 77.48%, and F-scores of 58.49% and 54.67% in Master dataset and Sinica dataset, respectively. Moreover, our segmenter achieves an agreement of 0.382 compared with the human labelers. That is better than some native Chinese readers.

The best tagging scheme is 4-tag set, which outperforms the shorter and the longer tag sets in the experiments. The most useful single feature is Character (*C*), which achieves an accuracy of 77.01% and an F-score of 57.55%.

The articles ubiquitous on the Internet are usually not only plain text but embedded with layout information. For the rich formatted text, our model achieves an accuracy of 82.93% and an F-score of 67.76%. This result reveals that our model is useful to deal with the web data. Our model can be used in the application of web information extraction system, and also can be applied as the preprocessor for other tasks such as parsing and discourse boundary detection.

References

John Aberdeen, John Burger, David Day, Lynette Hirschman, Patricia Robinson, and Marc Vilain. 1995. MITRE: description of the Alembic system used for MUC-6. In *Proceedings of the 6th conference on Message understanding*, pages 141–155. Association for Computational Linguistics, Morristown, NJ, USA.

Pi-Chuan Chang, Michel Galley, and Chris Manning. 2008. Optimizing Chinese Word Segmentation for Machine Translation Performance. In *Proceedings of the Third Workshop on Statistical Machine Translation*, Prague, Czech Republic, June.

Aitao Chen, Jianzhang He, and Liangjie Xu. 1997. Chinese Text Retrieval Without Using a Dictionary. In *Proceedings of the 20th Annual International ACM SIGIR Conference on Research and Development in Information Retrieval*, pages 42-49, Philadelphia PA, USA.

Keh-Jiann Chen, Chu-Ren Huang, Li-Ping Chang and Hui-Li Hsu. 1996. SINICA CORPUS: Design Methodology for Balanced Corpora. In *Proceedings of PACLIC 11th Conference*, pages 167-176.

Dan Gillick. 2009. Sentence Boundary Detection and the Problem with the U.S. In Proceedings *of Human Language Technologies: The 2009 Annual Conference of the North American Chapter of the Association for Computational Linguistics (NAACL HLT)*, Short papers, pages 241-244, Boulder, Colorado, June. Association for Computational Linguistics.

Hen-Hsen Huang, Chuen-Tsai Sun, and Hsin-Hsi Chen. 2010. Classical Chinese Sentence Segmentation. In *Proceedings of CIPS-SIGHAN Joint Conference on Chinese Language Processing*, pages 15-22, Beijing, China, August.

Mei xun Jin, Mi-Yong Kim, Dongil Kim, and JongHyeok Lee. 2004. Segmentation of Chinese Long Sentences Using Commas. In *Proceedings of SIGHAN*, pages 1-8, Barcelona, Spain.

John Lafferty, Andrew McCallum, and Fernando Pereira. 2001. Conditional Random Fields: Probabilistic Models for Segmentation and Labeling Sequence Data. In *Proceedings of the 18th International Conference on Machine Learning*, pages 282-289.

Roger Levy and Christopher D. Manning. 2003. Is it harder to parse Chinese, or the Chinese Treebank? In *Proceedings of the 41st Annual Meeting on Association for Computational Linguistics*, pages 439-446.

Ding Liu and Chengqing Zong. 2003. Utterance Segmentation Using Combined Approach Based on Bi-directional N-gram and Maximum Entropy. In *Proceedings of the Second SIGHAN Workshop on Chinese Language Processing*, pages 16-23.

Andrei Mikheev. 2002. Periods, Capitalized Words, etc. *Computational Linguistics*, 28(3):289–318.

Jia Xu, Richard Zens, and Hermann Ney. 2005. Sentence Segmentation Using IBM Word Alignment Model 1. In *Proceedings of the European Association for Machine Translation (EAMT 2005)*, pages 280-287.

Nianwen Xue. 2003. Chinese Word Segmentation as Character Tagging. *Computational Linguistics and Chinese Language Processing*, 8(1):29-48.

Hai Zhao, Chang-Ning Huang, Mu Li, and Bao-Liang Lu. 2006. Effective Tag Set Selection in Chinese Word Segmentation via Conditional Random Field Modeling. In *Proceedings of the 20th Pacific Asia Conference on Language, Information and Computation (PACLIC-20)*, pages 87-94, Wuhan, China, November 1-3.

Chengqing Zong and Fuji Ren. 2003. Chinese Utterance Segmentation in Spoken Language translation. In *Proceedings of the 4th International Conference on Intelligent Text Processing and Computational Linguistics (CICLing)*, pages 516-525, Mexico, Feb 16-22.

Multilabel Tagging of Discourse Relations in Ambiguous Temporal Connectives

Yannick Versley
Collaborative Research Centre (SFB) 833
University of Tübingen
versley@sfs.uni-tuebingen.de

Abstract

Many annotation schemes for discourse relations allow combinations such as *temporal+cause* (for events that are temporally and causally related to each other) and *temporal+contrast* (for contrasts between subsequent time spans, or between events that are temporally coextensive). However, current approaches for the automatic classification of discourse relations are limited to producing only one relation and disregard the others.

We argue that the information contained in these 'additional' relations is indeed useful and present an approach to tag multiple fine-grained discourse relations in ambiguous connectives from the German TüBa-D/Z corpus. Using a rich feature set, we show that good accuracy is possible even for inferred relations that are not part of the connective's 'core' meaning.

1 Introduction

In order to account for the structure of text beyond the level of single clauses, it is common to postulate *discourse relations* holding between clauses or groups of clauses. Discourse relations are frequently marked by *connectives* such as *because*, *as* or *while*, which give an indication both of (syntactic or anaphoric) linking possibilities for the spans and of the possible relations.

Many connectives (such as *because* or *for instance*) always signal one specific discourse relation. This fact has, after initial successes in purely structural discourse parsing (Soricut and Marcu, 2003), led to decreased attention from researchers. Other connectives, however, are ambiguous between multiple readings and their disambiguation necessitates similar semantic information as implicit (connective-less) discourse relations.

Ambiguous temporal markers such as *after*, *as* or *while* usually occur with a purely temporal reading, but also with additional non-temporal discourse relations, such as causal and contrastive readings. When these non-temporal relations occur instead of, or in addition to, the temporal reading, they require similar similar inferences from the reader as in connective-less discourse relations, but may be easier to detect automatically. For our goal of accurate classification, multilabel classification becomes necessary when the non-temporal discourse relations co-occur with the temporal ones:

(1) a. As [$_{arg2}$ *individual investors have turned away from the stock market over the years*], [$_{arg1}$ *securities firms have scrambled to find new products that brokers find easy to sell*].

b. [$_{arg1}$ *"Forget it," he said*] as [$_{arg2}$*he handed her a paper*].

c. But as [$_{arg2}$ *the French embody a Zen-like state of blase when it comes to athletics*] (try finding a Nautilus machine in Paris), [$_{arg1}$ *my fellow conventioners were having none of it*].

In the examples from (1), the sentence in (b) is clearly temporal (and non-causal), and the one in (c) is clearly causal (and non-temporal), whereas in (a) the connective contributes both a causal and a temporal aspect to the coherence of the text.

In the Penn Discourse Treebank (Prasad et al., 2008), which uses multiple labels as a last resort when annotators cannot reach an agreement or feel that an instance is inherently ambiguous, 5.5% of discourse connectives are assigned multiple discourse relations. The proportion of multiple vs. single discourse relation varies from connective to connective, with a higher proportion in ambiguous temporal connectives, where it ranges from *after*'s 9% and *while*'s 12.7% over *as* (23.6%) and *when* (21%) to *meanwhile* with 70% of the instances that have multiple labels.

The annotation of discourse connectives in the TüBa-D/Z (Telljohann et al., 2009), which we used in our experiments, uses combinations of temporal and other relations to signal causation between successive events or a contrast between co-temporal events, yielding 64.6% of multilabel instances for *nachdem* (after/since), and 53.8% of multilabel instances for *während* (while).

Hence, it is necessary for accurate classification to identify *both* of the discourse relations holding in such a case, whereas most recent research, such as Pitler and Nenkova (2009) or Wellner (2009) has focused on single-relation classification.[1]

A notable exception is Bethard and Martin's (2008) work on instances of *and*, where the presence of a temporal or causal relation is classified independently of the other.

In terms of the features used in classification, the perception that most connectives are unambiguous has created a disparity in terms of features between approaches that target discourse relations signaled by a connective (so-called *explicit* relations) and those that are inferred between adjacent discourse segments in the absence of connectives (*implicit* relations).

Work on explicit (i.e., connective-bearing) relations has emphasized simpler features, such as the syntactic neighbourhood of the connective (Pitler and Nenkova, 2009) or features based on tense and mood of the argument clauses (Miltsakaki et al., 2005). In contrast, work targeting implicit discourse relations harnesses a larger variety of features, including word pairs (Marcu and Echihabi, 2002; Sporleder and Lascarides, 2008), structural properties of the argument clauses (Lin et al., 2009), semantic parallelism between arguments' main verbs' classes, emotive polarity, and other special word categories (Pitler et al., 2009).

In the remainder of this paper, we formulate the disambiguation of ambiguous temporal connectives as a multilabel classification task (where the system can, and should, assign more than one discourse relation). The results (sections 5, 6) show that a rich feature set - partly inspired by the state of the art for implicit relations - is instrumental in detecting the 'non-obvious' discourse relations in temporal connectives.

2 Annotating Ambiguous Temporal Connectives in the TüBa-D/Z

For our study on automatic classification, we use instances of two German temporal connectives that can also carry a non-temporal discourse relation, namely *während* and *nachdem*:

The default reading of *nachdem* (corresponding to English *after/as/since*) signals a *temporal* relation between subsequent events, which is also compatible with a *causal* discourse relation, or a *contrast* between two events or states. *Nachdem* is also used in contexts where it confers an argumentative relation between propositions (*evidence*), or between a licensing proposition and a question or imperative (*speech-act*). As seen in example (1), *rhetorical* relations such as 'evidence' and 'speech-act' can occur with arguments that would be incompatible with the temporal reading of *nachdem*:

(2) Und *nachdem* ja die vertraglichen Bindungen noch weiterlaufen, und zwar bis zum Jahre 2006, werden heuer und in den kommenden Jahren noch weitere 250 Millionen Euro zur Auszahlung gelangen.
And as the contractual obligations are still in force, and run up to 2006, this year and in the coming years a further EUR 250 million will be paid out.

Similar to its English counterpart *while*, German *während* has a *temporal* reading that locates the sub-clause in the phase of the matrix clause, but also allows a *contrast* reading where two propositions are contrasted with respect to a common integrator.

In a prototypical example such as (3), we find a parallel structure with one pair of entities being compared (*Mary* and *Peter*) and an attribute in which they differ (liking *bananas* versus prefering

[1]Both Pitler and Nenkova, and Wellner classify only the first relation. Pitler and Nenkova count the system response as correct when it includes any of the discourse relations in the gold standard, while Wellner counts a system-generated relation as correct if it reproduces the first of the two relations of a multi-relation instance.

Relations	*nachdem*	*während*
Temporal	93.9	76.7
Result	60.2	
├ situational	*53.4*	
│ ├ enable	*31.6*	
│ └ cause	*21.7*	
└ rhetorical	*6.4*	
├ evidence	*4.1*	
└ speech-act	*2.4*	
Comparison	10.5	76.7
├ parallel	*4.8*	
└ contrast	*5.8*	*76.7*

Percent of instances tagged with a given label (including subcategories); Numbers across top-level relations sum up to more than 100% because of multi-label instances.

Table 1: Discourse relation inventory

peaches).

(3) Während [Maria] [Bananen] mag, bevorzugt [Peter] [Pfirsiche].
While [*Mary*] *likes* [*bananas*], [*Peter*] *prefers* [*peaches*].

Such a structure, which we can describe using a common integrator such as "*People* like *fruits*", receives the *contrast* relation.

In cases where a contrast coincides with co-temporal states, or a temporal relation coincides with an inferred contrast, a secondary temporal or contrast relation is annotated to reflect the ambiguity.

Our data set – the connective occurrences from the current extent of the TüBa-D/Z plus additional texts that are scheduled for the inclusion in one of the next releases, totaling about 60 000 senteces – contains 294 instances of *nachdem* and 527 instances of *während*. Where available, we used the syntactic annotation from the treebank; in the remaining cases, we used a syntactic parser (Versley and Rehbein, 2009) to provide syntax trees for the feature extraction. Table 1 shows the full taxonomy of relations for the ambiguous connectives considered in the experiments.

3 Multilabel classification

Reproducing the connective annotation in the TüBa-D/Z presents a hierarchical multi-label classifcation task: more than one label may apply to a given instance, and labels are arranged in taxonomical categories.

As in classical multi-label tagging, the classifier should take into account the suitability of individual classification labels for a given example; however, the context of discourse relation classification shows stronger interdependence of labels (e.g., a non-temporal example is bound to have an evidence or contrast relation).

3.1 Evaluating multilabel classification

As multilabel classification goes beyond assigning exactly one atomic label, scoring whether the proposed label combination is identical to the gold standard (*equal* in the results table) fails to give partial credit to a system response that reproduces some, but not all of the correct discourse relations.

The *dice* evaluation measure accounts for the overlap between the gold standard label combination and the label combination in the system response, calculated as $\frac{2|A \cap B|}{|A|+|B|}$. Both *equal* and *dice* measure can be calculated at each level of the taxonomy, yielding values for $d = 1$ (the topmost level) up to $d = 3$ (the finest taxonomic level).

In addition, the assignment of any particular relation can be evaluated using the standard F-measure and precision/recall.

3.2 Greedy classification

One of the classical approaches to multilabel classification is to decompose the labeling decision into binary decisions for each possible label (one-vs-all reduction) and using confidence values to choose one or several labels among those that are most confidently classified as positive examples.

To yield the finer-grained distinctions from the taxonomy (such as *Comparison.contrast* vs. *Comparison.parallel*), the classifier makes an additional decision on the fine-grained class corresponding to the coarse-grained one, which is again realized through training separate classifiers for each fine-grained relation.

In our experiments, we use SVMperf, an SVM implementation that is able to train classifiers optimized for performance on positive instances (Joachims, 2005). To improve the separability of the data (SVMperf, like the AMIS package used for CRF training, uses linear classifiers), we use feature combinations up to degree 2.

3.3 A CRF-based approach

One disadvantage of the greedy decomposition into a sequence of binary decisions outlined above is that this variant is unable to model dependencies between the labels assigned by the system; similarly, the greedy decomposition is unable to use evidence for or against individual fine-grained relations in the decision regarding the coarse-grained relations.

As an alternative approach, we consider a classifier that directly ranks possible label combinations, considering all (fine-grained) labels at once. The model ranks all label combinations $Y \in \mathcal{Y}$ using a feature function Φ and the learned weight vector w:

$$\overline{Y} = \arg\max_{Y \in \mathcal{Y}} \langle w, \Phi(x, Y) \rangle$$

where $\mathcal{Y}$ contains all allowable label combinations and Φ extracts a *feature vector* containing the information about the problem instance (x) and the label combination under consideration (Y).

In order to describe each instance, we factor Φ as $\Phi(x, Y) := \Phi_{\text{lab}}(Y) \times \Phi_{\text{data}}(x)$ (i.e., assuming a label feature `Temporal` and a data feature `main-present`, Φ would contain the combined feature (`Temporal,main-present`)).

In our case, the label information from Φ_{lab} contains the set of coarse-grained relations assigned (e.g. `Temporal+Result`), as well as the fine-grained relations, individually (in the example, both `Temporal` and `Result.situational.enable`). It is easy to see that the problem size increases superlinearly with the number of possible relations, because the set $\mathcal{Y}$ of possible labelings can grow quadratically. Keeping the problem size in check provides a gain in efficiency that is already helpful at the current data size, and becomes crucial as the label set and amount of data grow with the addition of more connectives.

To mitigate this problem, we factor the actual feature vector into a *feature forest* (Miyao and Tsujii, 2002) that contains shared nodes for each element, which means that the necessary computations become linear in (*number of fine-grained relations+ number of coarse-grained relation combinations*).

Since the CRF approach optimizes for likelihood of the correct (fine-grained) solution, the results of the CRF classifier may not always give optimal results with respect to a given evaluation metric. To compensate for this, we introduce a *bias* parameter that is added to the score of candidate labelings with more than one label, which forces the classifier towards including (more) labels even when it is not completely certain about them.

4 Classification features

In contrast to newer work in this area, earlier approaches for explicit discourse relations, such as Miltsakaki et al. (2005), have mainly relied on linguistic features indicating the clause or event type, which allows to separate temporal from atemporal uses of a connective in some cases. For our classification experiments, we include a set of baseline features reflecting these linguistic properties as well as more specific features aiming at the differences between different types of argument clauses, but also features that target broader lexical information – in this case, those aimed at the semantics of each argument clause (by taking the head itself, or a characterization), but also co-taxonomic relations between the argument clauses as well as pairs of lemmas and (syntactic) productions.

A first set of *baseline features* include basic linguistic features, such as **clause order** (i.e., topicalization/fronting), as the non-temporal discourse relations are more likely to occur with fronted subclauses than with postposed ones; **tense** features include indicators for perfect, passives, and modal verbs as well as the tense of the finite verb in each clause; a binary **negation** feature indicates the presence of negating adverb (e.g., English *not*), determiners (*no*) or pronouns (*none*).

4.1 Clause type and status

Beyond the information from clause order and tense, **punctuation** after the sentence helps identify different types of sentences (since questions and imperatives can be an indication of the discourse-internal *speech act* relation).

For each clause, a number of **modifying adverbials** such as temporal, causal or concessive adverbials (excluding the *nachdem-* or *während-*clause), conjunctive focus adverbs (*also, as well*), and commentary adverbs (*doubtlessly, actually, probably...*). Additional temporal or causal adverbials, which fill the respective function for the main clause, make it less likely that the subordinate clause temporally locates or causally explains the main clause, whereas conjunctive focus adverbs often indicate a *parallel* relation. Finally commentary adverbs are indicative of discourse-internal relations since they indicate deviations from purely factual reporting.

In order to capture event contingency between clauses (which is typical for temporal and causal relations, but not for contrastive relations), we included both referential and lexico-semantical indicators: the **compatible subject pronoun** feature indicates that the subject of one clause is a compatible antecedent for the subject of the other clause (which, due to parallelism and subject preference, is a relatively robust indicator for the subjects being coreferential). In this context, morphological compatibility is relatively simple to derive from the morphological tags in the treebank (which include number and grammatical gender), but it would be expected that the same information can be reliably derived from the output of a morphological analyzer.

4.2 Shallow lexical-semantical features

In general, targeting specific linguistic properties of the clauses linked by the connective will provide crucial information in some cases (as, for example, the co-temporal reading of *während* can be excluded when tenses disagree), but is not sufficient when the choice of discourse relation is influenced by the kind of event that is denoted by the argument clauses, or more general aspects of their meaning.

Some predicates occur often enough to be used as a generalization, and often provide either linguistic hints (in the case of verbs that are typically individual-level, rather than stage-level predicates and would not be located or be used to locate temporally, e.g. *exist*) or are typically thought of as causer, or causee, of an event (as, e.g., *crash* is more likely to be the result or explanation to another event than *fly*). The **semantic head** feature includes the semantic head (i.e., main verb) of each clause, which can provide this kind of information where the main verb is informative and occurs often enough in the training data.

Since most predicates are not frequent enough to occur in a significant number, we need informative statistics that can uncover relevant aspects of their meaning. One such distributional statistic considers the type of (sub-)clauses in which verbs typically appear: verbs such as *require*, *suspect*, or *fear* often occur as part of a *because* clause, while *arrest*, *resign* or *conclude* often occur as part of a *after* adverbial clause. Bethard and Martin (2008), who use this strategy for the prediction

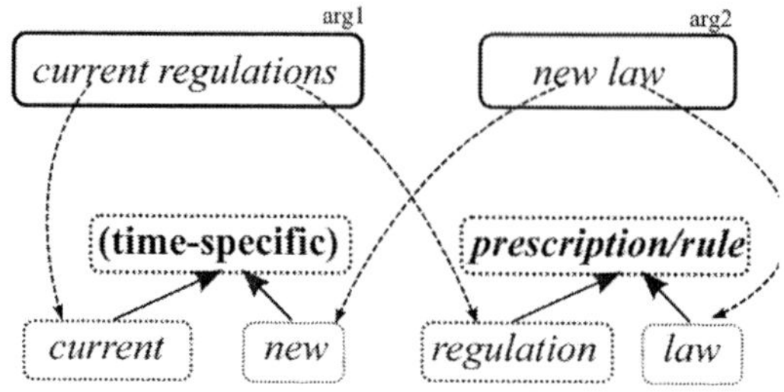

Figure 1: Lexical relation feature

of causal and temporal readings of *and*, are able to use n-gram search for such frequency statistics. In the case of German, morphological flexibility and the verb order in subclauses mean that it is necessary to consider a larger context. For the **association** feature in our experiments, we extracted counts from subclause occurrences in the DE-WaC corpus (Baroni and Kilgariff, 2006) using the subordinating conjunctions *bevor* (before), *nachdem* (after/as/since), *weil* (because) and *obwohl* (although). Using (local) pointwise mutual information (MI) scores, each pair of conjunction and verb lemma is assigned binary features indicating whether it has a negative score, or the quantile of lemmas for that connective, according to positive MI values.

The **lexical relation** feature targets pairs of words across both clauses that are taxonomically related and thus could form a contrast pair. As an example, consider *the current regulations* occurring in one clause and *the new law* in the other, which would yield a pair of time-related adjectives *current-new*, and a pair *regulation-law* of concepts that are both hyponyms of *prescription/rule* (cf. figure 1). To find these pairs of taxonomically related concepts, we use the hyperonymy hierarchy in GermaNet 5.0 (Kunze and Lemnitzer, 2002) to produce the least common subsumer of two terms plus two superordinate terms. For adjectives and verbs, requiring a least common subsumer always yields related pairs. In contrast, the upper levels of the noun hierarchy are very general, and we ensure that only related pairs are used by ignoring the upper three levels of the noun hierarchy for this feature.

Another, shallower way of representing the relation(s) between the words in each argument clause has proven to be effective in research on unlabeled relations: The **pairs of lemmas** feature extracts

All relations	dice	eq	contrast	Temp
contrast+Temporal	0.844	0.533	0.868	**0.868**
best (CRF)	0.823	0.552	0.874	0.823
best (CRF+bias)	0.855	**0.581**	0.893	0.853
best (SVMperf)	**0.857**	0.579	**0.897**	0.854
Only primary relation	Accuracy			
contrast	0.655			
baseline (CRF)	0.674			
best (CRF)	0.712			

Table 2: Results for *während*

pairs of lemmas occurring across the two argument clauses. On one hand, this feature can detect co-taxonomic pairs such as *current-new* or *rise-fall* (as well as nontaxonomic relations such as *accident-injured*) whenever these occur very frequently. On the othe hand, such a feature can also uncover the presence of a personal pronouns, or two definite articles, in each of both clauses, or particular adjectives.

Among all pairs of lemmas, we only select those that occur at least 5 times in the training data, and select the 500 most 'interesting' the by using overall entropy as a selection criterion. Using entropy in this way serves to exclude very frequent word pairs (which occur in – nearly – every pair of clauses that has been seen) as well as very infrequent ones.

4.3 Structural information

In order to account for structure, we include the **productions** feature, which is based on nonterminal and preterminal productions (e.g., `NX` → `ART ADJX NN` for an NP with a determiner, an adjective and a noun, or `ART` → `der` for *der* occurring as a determiner). Among those productions that occur in at least 500 of the clause pairs, the 500 with the highest entropy are used (filtering out those that are very rare, or frequent enough to appear in nearly *each* sentence).

5 Impact of Features

An overview on the evaluation results for *während* and *nachdem* is provided in tables 2 and 3, whereas table 4 contains more detail on the impact of each feature. In general, all of the evaluation metrics (cf. section 3.1) are improved by the rich set of features. Fine-grained accuracy (dice[2] and dice[3]) benefits more by the ranking-based CRF approach, and the best coarse-grained accuracy (eq[1] and dice[1]) is achieved by the greedy SVM classification.

Due to space reasons, we limited the feature analysis in table 4 to feature sets containing either (i) base features plus any single feature, or (ii) all but a single one of the features.

As can be seen in the table, the most difficult relations to identify are minority relations such as *contrast*, *parallel*, *evidence*, and *speech-act*. *Speech-act* is rare enough that no better-than-baseline feature set ever produces it. In contrast, the best feature set achieves F-measures of 0.41 (*contrast*), 0.39 (*parallel*) and 0.33 (*evidence*) on these relations, with precision values between 0.33 (*evidence*) and 0.36 (*contrast*), and recall values between 0.33 (*evidence*) and 0.47 (*contrast*). Considering that these relations are quite rare (the most frequent of them, *contrast*, occurs in 5.8% of the *nachdem* instances),

The feature that has most impact by itself is the presence of modifying adverbials (**mod.adv.**), especially for *parallel* and *cause* relations. The *association* feature (**assoc**) is the most effective in identifying *cause* and *evidence* relations, as it provides information on kinds of events that a verbs refers to. Co-occurrence of a verb in the sub- or main clause with the introducing or modifying connective can help to distinguish temporally-locating events (which can, e.g., occur in *before* subclauses), or states of affairs that can serve as a reason for something (which would occur in *because* or *although* subclauses).

Both of the shallow features, **productions** and lemma pairs (**wordpairs**) have a relatively broad effect and lead to successful identification of some of the minority relations (*cause*, *contrast*, *evidence*). However, they are noisy enough that overall performance drops below the baseline (in the case of word pairs, the dice measure for the finer taxonomy level and strict equality seem to improve, however).

In the reverse feature selection, however, we see that the noisy information brought in by the shallow lexical features (*productions* and *wordpairs*) is quite useful: performance drops very visibly without these features (0.844 to 0.835 for removing the *productions* feature, to 0.817 for *wordpairs*).

Looking at the learning curves (for the full feature set minus the *assoc* feature), in figure 2, we find that the identification of *cause* and *enable* relations seems to be relatively robust to sparse data problem, as the improvement from 20% of training data (i.e., randomly subsampling each train-

setting	dice[1]	dice[2]	dice[3]	eq[1]	Comparison	Result	Temporal	contrast	cause	evidence
random	0.742	0.707	0.627	0.415	0.065	0.610	0.938	0.000	0.231	0.083
Temporal+enable	0.829	0.789	0.680	0.541	0.000	0.752	0.968	0.000	0.000	0.000
baseline (CRF)	0.782	0.747	0.683	0.466	0.143	0.625	0.953	0.087	0.248	0.211
best (CRF)	0.823	0.806	**0.729**	0.548	0.341	0.678	**0.974**	0.333	0.355	**0.400**
best (CRF+bias)	0.845	**0.814**	0.710	0.595	0.348	0.764	0.972	0.286	0.347	0.286
baseline (SVMperf)	0.829	0.789	0.680	0.541	0.000	0.752	0.968	0.000	0.000	0.000
best (SVMperf)	**0.849**	0.811	0.718	**0.609**	**0.514**	**0.763**	0.970	**0.410**	**0.369**	0.333

Table 3: Results for *nachdem*

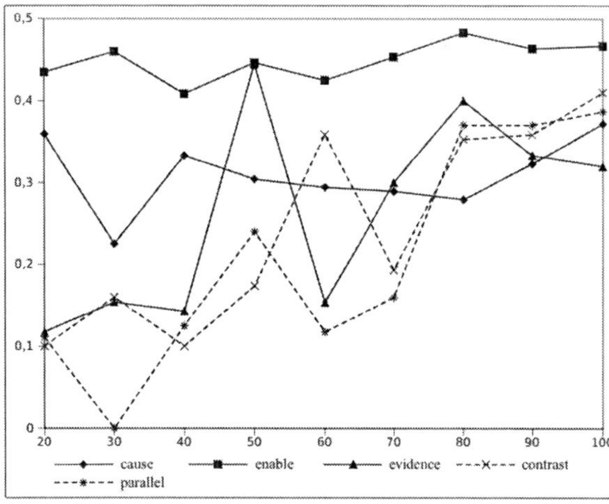

Figure 2: Learning curves for single relations (*nachdem* only)

ing fold to 20% of its size) to the complete data only yields limited improvement, whereas relations such as *evidence*, *contrast* and *parallel* seem to profit strongly from more data (which is understandable, however, since these relations are less frequent than the others).

Although the annotated instances stem from a relatively large corpus (slightly over one million words), it seems very plausible that larger training data would benefit the disambiguation results. For connective annotation on a fixed-size corpus (such as the TüBa-D/Z, or the Penn Treebank used for the Penn Discourse Treebank), combining the benefits of connective-specific and non-specific disambiguation would be especially relevant, as the former allows to model the specific connective meaning, whereas connective-independent models would be less sensitive to sparse data.

6 Summary

We carried out multilabel tagging experiments on two datasets: one containing occurrences of *nachdem* from the TüBa-D/Z corpus (shown in table 3), one containing occurrences of *während*, using 10-fold cross-validation on the training set. For both the CRF-based approach and the SVM-based one-versus-all reduction, the best-performing feature set we found contains all features minus the *association* feature.

For both *nachdem* and *während*, the most frequent sense (Temporal+enable, or Temporal+contrast) is by far predominant and yields a very strong baseline, which the CRF-based classifier only surpasses for *nachdem* with an appropriate setting for the bias parameter to prevent the classifier from under-labeling (i.e., assigning fewer relations than optimal). Both the biased CRF classifier and the greedy SVM-based approach outperform the most-frequent sense baseline for all aggregate measures, which is more difficult for the top level of the taxonomy where one single coarse-grained relation combination often accounts for over 50% of all instances.

To our knowledge, this study is the first successful study on disambiguating German connectives, after the results of (Bayerl, 2004) who studied the explicit connective *wenn* (if/when), which stay further below the most-frequent sense baseline. We take this to confirm the intuition that problems in large-scale discourse classification, including those thought to be unrewarding such as ambiguous explicit connectives, are best tackled with a combination of an annotation scheme that is appropriate to the task (i.e., focused on coherence relations rather than speaker intentions), informative features, and a machine learning approach that can make use of these features to reproduce all the distinctions that are present in the annotation.

We also hope that the general direction of (i) reproducing all of the information present in the gold annotation and (ii) using a rich set of features for the disambiguation of ambiguous explicit con-

	dice[1]	dice[2]	dice[3]	equal	Comp.	contr.	parallel	Result	cause	enable	evidence	sp.-act	Temp.
base (cl.order, tense, neg.)	0.829	0.789	0.678	0.541	0.000	0.000	0.000	0.752	0.054	0.485	0.000	0.000	0.968
base + assoc	0.809	0.768	0.676	0.507	0.075	0.000	0.067	0.728	**0.338**	0.477	**0.276**	0.000	0.968
base + csubj	0.829	0.789	0.678	0.541	0.000	0.000	0.000	0.751	0.073	**0.488**	0.000	0.000	0.968
base + sem.head	0.829	0.789	0.680	0.541	0.000	0.000	0.000	0.752	0.103	0.485	0.000	0.000	0.968
base + lexrel	0.829	0.789	0.678	0.541	0.000	0.000	0.000	0.752	0.133	0.485	0.000	0.000	0.968
base + mod.adv.	**0.832**	0.789	0.675	0.551	0.216	0.000	**0.222**	**0.753**	0.162	0.484	0.000	0.000	0.968
base + productions	0.782	0.731	0.645	0.480	**0.272**	0.159	0.150	0.700	0.331	0.429	0.105	**0.111**	0.949
base + punc	0.827	0.789	0.680	0.541	0.000	0.000	0.000	0.749	0.056	**0.488**	0.000	0.000	0.968
base + wordpairs	0.824	0.774	**0.683**	**0.551**	0.262	**0.294**	0.000	0.741	0.284	0.458	0.261	0.000	0.965
all	0.844	0.802	0.706	0.588	0.478	0.343	0.312	0.756	0.356	0.430	0.435	0.000	0.970
all w/o assoc	**0.849**	**0.811**	**0.718**	**0.609**	**0.514**	**0.410**	0.387	**0.763**	0.369	**0.463**	0.333	0.000	0.970
all w/o csubj	0.835	0.795	0.703	0.568	0.485	0.343	0.323	0.736	0.333	0.431	**0.455**	0.000	0.970
all w/o sem.head	0.844	0.802	0.701	0.588	0.478	0.333	0.323	0.758	0.338	0.423	0.381	0.000	0.968
all w/o lexrel	0.843	0.799	0.710	0.588	0.507	0.343	**0.389**	0.753	**0.385**	0.442	0.364	0.000	0.968
all w/o mod.adv.	0.840	0.803	0.699	0.585	0.386	0.375	0.160	0.754	0.333	0.419	0.435	0.000	0.968
all w/o productions	0.834	0.781	0.689	0.575	0.486	0.350	0.353	0.738	0.281	0.400	0.400	0.000	0.964
all w/o punc	0.842	0.800	0.706	0.585	0.478	0.343	0.312	0.754	0.365	0.432	0.435	0.000	0.968
all w/o wordpairs	0.817	0.769	0.676	0.541	0.465	0.302	0.242	0.721	0.362	0.408	0.244	0.000	0.953

Table 4: Impact of features (for *nachdem*, SVMperf)

nectives will be a fruitful direction for discourse relation disambiguation also in other languages than German.

References

Baroni, M. and Kilgariff, A. (2006). Large linguistically-processed web corpora for multiple languages. In *EACL 2006*.

Bayerl, P. S. (2004). Disambiguierung deutschsprachiger Diskursmarker: Eine Pilot-Studie. *Linguistik Online*, 18.

Bethard, S. and Martin, J. (2008). Learning semantic links from a corpus of parallel temporal and causal relations. In *ACL/HLT 2008*.

Joachims, T. (2005). A support vector method for multivariate performance measures. In *Proceedings of the International Conference on Machine Learning (ICML)*.

Kunze, C. and Lemnitzer, L. (2002). GermaNet – representation, visualization, application. In *Proceedings of LREC 2002*.

Lin, Z., Kan, M.-Y., and Ng, H. T. (2009). Recognizing implicit discourse relations in the Penn Discourse Treebank. In *EMNLP 2009*.

Marcu, D. and Echihabi, A. (2002). An unsupervised approach to recognizing discourse relations. In *ACL 2002*.

Miltsakaki, E., Dinesh, N., Prasad, R., Joshi, A., and Webber, B. (2005). Experiments on sense annotations and sense disambiguation of discourse connectives. In *TLT 2005*.

Miyao, Y. and Tsujii, J. (2002). Maximum entropy estimation for feature forests. In *HLT 2002*.

Pitler, E., Louis, A., and Nenkova, A. (2009). Automatic sense prediction for implicit discourse relations in text. In *ACL-IJCNLP 2009*.

Pitler, E. and Nenkova, A. (2009). Using syntax to disambiguate explicit discourse connectives in text. In *ACL 2009 short papers*.

Prasad, R., Dinesh, N., Lee, A., Miltsakaki, E., Robaldo, L., Joshi, A., and Webber, B. (2008). The Penn Discourse Treebank 2.0. In *Proceedings of LREC 2008*.

Soricut, R. and Marcu, D. (2003). Sentence level discourse parsing using syntactic and lexical information. In *Proc. HLT/NAACL-2003*.

Sporleder, C. and Lascarides, A. (2008). Using automatically labelled examples to classify rhetorical relations: An assessment. *Natural Language Engineering*, 14(3):369–416.

Telljohann, H., Hinrichs, E. W., Kübler, S., Zinsmeister, H., and Beck, K. (2009). Stylebook for the Tübingen Treebank of Written German (TüBa-D/Z). Technical report, Seminar für Sprachwissenschaft, Universität Tübingen.

Versley, Y. and Rehbein, I. (2009). Scalable discriminative parsing for German. In *Proc. IWPT 2009*.

Wellner, B. (2009). *Sequence Models and Ranking Methods for Discourse Parsing*. PhD thesis, Brandeis University.

Noun Compound and Named Entity Recognition and their Usability in Keyphrase Extraction

István Nagy T.[1], **Gábor Berend**[1] and **Veronika Vincze**[2]
[1]Department of Informatics, University of Szeged
{nistvan,berendg}@inf.u-szeged.hu
[2]Hungarian Academy of Sciences, Research Group on Artificial Intelligence
vinczev@inf.u-szeged.hu

Abstract

We investigate how the automatic identification of noun compounds and named entities can contribute to keyphrase extraction and we also show how previously identified noun compounds affect named entity recognition and vice versa, how noun compound detection is supported by identified named entities. Our experiments demonstrate that already known noun compounds yield better performance in named entity recognition and already known named entities enhance noun compound detection. The integration of noun compound and named entity related features into a keyphrase extractor also proves to be more effective than the model not including them. Our results indicate that the above features tend to be beneficial in several NLP-related tasks.

1 Introduction

In natural language processing, the proper treatment of multiword expressions (MWEs) is essential for many higher-level applications (e.g. information extraction or machine translation). Multiword expressions are lexical items that can be decomposed into single words and display idiosyncratic features (Sag et al., 2002), in other words, they are lexical items that contain space. They are frequent in language use and usually exhibit unique and idiosyncratic behavior, thus, they often pose a problem to NLP systems. Named entities (NEs) are another class of linguistic elements that require special treatment in many NLP systems ranging from information retrieval to machine translation.

In this paper, we demonstrate how the automatic identification of noun compounds and named entities can contribute to keyphrase extraction and we also investigate how previously identified noun compounds affect named entity recognition (NER) and vice versa, how noun compound detection is supported by identified named entities. We briefly describe our methods, then discuss our results in detail. We argue that previous knowledge of noun compounds can enhance keyphrase extraction and NER while previously identified NEs can contribute to noun compound identification. We believe that employing NE- and noun compound-related features in other higher-level applications will also enhance performance.

2 Noun compounds and named entities in NLP applications

A compound is a lexical unit that consists of two or more elements that exist on their own. Compounds can be classified as follows (Sag et al., 2002; Kim, 2008): nominal compounds (*bass player*), adjectival compounds (*dark skinned*), adverbial compounds (*all in all*), prepositional compounds (*in front of*), and multiword conjunctions (*in order that*).

Named entity recognition is another widely researched topic in NLP. There are several methods developed for many languages and domains (Grishman and Sundheim, 1995; Chinchor, 1998; Tjong Kim Sang, 2002; Tjong Kim Sang and De Meulder, 2003). Multiword named entities can be composed of any words or even characters and their meaning cannot be traced back to their parts. For instance, *Ford Focus* refers to a car and has nothing to do with the original meaning of *ford* or *focus*, thus, it is justifiable to treat the whole expression as one unit.

Multiword expressions and named entities usually need special treatment in NLP systems due to their idiosyncratic features. Named entities often consist of more than one word, i.e. they can be seen as a specific type of multiword expressions / noun compounds (Jackendoff, 1997). The distinction between noun compounds and multiword named entities is similar to that of between single-token common nouns and proper nouns. Although both noun compounds and multiword named entities consist of more than one word, they form one semantic unit and thus, they should be treated as one unit in NLP systems. Taking the example of POS-tagging, the linguistic behavior of compound nouns and multiword NEs is the same as that of single-word nouns, thus, they are preferably tagged as nouns (or proper nouns) even if the phrase itself does not contain any noun (e.g. *has-been* or *Die Hard*). Once identified as such, they can be treated similarly to single words in syntactic parsing for example.

However, the meaning of their parts and their connection alone cannot determine the semantics of the whole phrase, which yields that higher level applications need to pay special attention to them. For instance, in machine translation, it must be assured that the parts of a multiword expression are not translated separately, e.g. *racing car* should be translated to German as *Rennwagen*.

Noun compounds and multiword NEs behave similarly in language use in that both types function as one unit. It is this similarity that we would like to exploit when investigating the effect of already known NEs/noun compounds on the identification of the other type. On the other hand, our research focuses on the role of noun compounds and named entities in keyphrase extraction. In order to gain keyphrases from free texts, noun compounds might be of great help since once identified, they can be considered as one unit, i.e. like any other single word, which can be beneficial in e.g. frequency counts. Furthermore, the subject of texts is in many cases a named entity (in the Wiki50 corpus (Vincze et al., 2011), 39 articles are about a person, organization, location or another named entity), which fact underlines the importance of giving named entities a special treatment when identifying the topic of a text by keyphrases.

3 Experiments

For the evaluation of our models, we used Wiki50 (Vincze et al., 2011), in which several types of multiword expressions (including nominal compounds) and four classes of named entities were marked. Machine learning models were also evaluated on a 1000-sentence database from the British National Corpus that contains 345 noun compounds (Nicholson and Baldwin, 2008).

leave-one-out	R	P	F
MWE	58.07	69.86	63.42
MWE + NE	65.65	72.44	68.68
NE	85.58	86.02	85.81
NE + MWE	87.07	87.28	87.18

Table 1: Results of leave-one-out approaches in terms of precision (P), recall (R) and F-measure (F) in Wiki50. MWE: our CRF trained with basic feature set, which was extended with automatically collected MWE dictionary, MWE + NE: our CRF with MWE features extended with NEs as feature, NE: our CRF trained with basic feature set, NE + MWE: our CRF model with basic features extended with MWEs as feature.

3.1 Wikipedia based method for detecting noun compounds

For identifying noun compounds, we collected n-grams which occurred as links in English Wikipedia articles. Later, non-English terms, named entities and non-nominal compounds were automatically deleted from the list. We combined three methods: first, a noun compound candidate was marked if it occurred in the list. The second method involved the merge of two possible noun compounds: if a b and b c both occurred in the list, a b c was also accepted as a noun compound. Third, a noun compound candidate was marked if its POS-tag sequence matched one of the previously defined patterns. POS tags were determined by the Stanford POS Tagger (Toutanova and Manning, 2000). Results achieved by the combination of these methods are shown in the *DictCombined* row of Table 2.

3.2 Machine Learning approaches

In addition to the above-described approach, we defined another method for automatically identifying noun compounds. The Conditional Random Fields (CRF) classifier was used (MALLET implementations (McCallum, 2002)). The feature set includes the following categories (Szarvas et al., 2006):

orthographical features: capitalisation, word length, bit information about the word form (contains a digit or not, has uppercase character inside the word, etc.), character level bi/trigrams;

dictionaries of first names, company types, denominators of locations; noun compounds col-

lected from English Wikipedia (see 3.1);
frequency information: frequency of the token, the ratio of the token's capitalised and lowercase occurrences, the ratio of capitalised and sentence beginning frequencies of the token which was derived from the Gigaword dataset[1];
shallow linguistic information: part of speech;
contextual information: sentence position, trigger words (the most frequent and unambiguous tokens in a window around the word under investigation) from the train text, the word between quotes, etc.
To identify noun compounds we used the Wiki50 corpus to train CRF classification models (they were evaluated in a leave-one-document-out scheme). Results are shown in the *MWE* row of Table 1.

In order to use the Wiki50 corpus for testing only, we automatically generated a train database for the CRF trainer. The train set consists of 5,000 randomly selected Wikipedia pages and we ignored those containing lists, tables or other structured texts. Since this document set has not been manually annotated, dictionary based noun compound labeling was considered as the gold standard. As a result, we had a less accurate but much bigger training database. The CRF model was trained on the automatically generated train database with the above presented feature set. Results can be seen in *CRF* row of Table 2. However, the database included many sentences without any labeled noun compounds hence negative examples were overrepresented. Therefore, we thought it necessary to filter the sentences: only those with at least one noun compound label were retained in the database (*CRF + SF*). With this filtering methodology the CRF could build a better model. The above-described feature set was completed with the information that a token is a named entity or not. The *MWE + NE* row of Table 1 shows that this feature proved very effective in the leave-one-document-out scheme, so we used it in the automatically generated train database too. As shown in the *CRF + NE* row of Table 2, the CRF model which was trained on the automatic training set could achieve better results with this feature than the original *CRF*.

First, the Stanford NER model was used for identifying NEs. However, we assumed that a model trained on Wikipedia could more effectively identify NEs in Wikipedia (as it is the same domain). Therefore, we merged the four NE classes marked in Wiki50 into one NE class to train the CRF with common feature set described above. Results are shown in the *NE* row of Table 1. The *CRF + OwnNE + SF* row in Table 2 represents results achieved when we exploited as features the NEs that were identified by using the entire Wiki50 corpus as the training dataset. Although the *CRF + NE + SF* (when NEs were identified by the Stanford model) did not achieve better results than the *CRF + SF*, our Wikipedia based NE CRF model to identify NEs in the automatically generated training dataset (*CRF + OwnNE SF*) yielded better F-score than *CRF + SF*, which means that NE is a good feature in the identification of noun compounds. Since the sentence filtering yielded better results, in the following this approach will be used.

Sometimes it was not unequivocal to decide whether a multiword unit is a noun compound or a NE (e.g. *Attorney General*): some of the dissimilarities between the manual annotations were related to this problem. However, we assumed that a term can occur either as a NE or a noun compound. Therefore, if the dictionary method marked a particular word as noun compound and the NE model also marked it as NE, we had to decide which mark to delete. The *CRF + OwnNELeft + SF* row in Table 2 shows results we achieved if the NE labeling was selected as feature and the standard noun compound notation was removed, whereas the row *CRF + MWELeft + SF* refers to the scenario when the NE feature was deleted, and the standard noun compound notation remained.

We also wanted to see what results the above described approaches can achieve in another corpus. So we evaluated our methods on the BNC dataset too, these results are shown in Table 3. In Table 3 it can be seen that our approaches achieve worse results on the BNC dataset than on Wikipedia. This is largely due to the fact that our approaches rely heavily on Wikipedia. In addition, there are differences between the two corpora. For example, in the BNC dataset only compounds with two parts are marked while in the Wikipedia corpus noun compounds with 3 or more tokens can also occur. Due to this, the method of merging overlapping noun compounds could not even be used here. However, the difference between the CRF-

[1]Linguistic Data Consortium (LDC), catalogId: LDC2003T05

Approach	R	P	F	R	P	F
mwetoolkit	-	-	-	12.41	38.32	18.75
DictCombined	52.47	59.45	55.75	50.10	60.46	54.81
CRF	44.38	58.42	50.44	43.69	60.10	50.60
CRF + SF	53.39	56.66	54.98	52.94	57.57	55.15
CRF + NE	45.81	58.37	51.33	45.16	59.84	51.48
CRF + NE + SF	53.12	55.89	54.47	52.72	57.26	54.90
CRF + OwnNE + SF	53.29	57.60	55.36	52.84	59.8	56.13
CRF + OwnNELeft + SF	53.44	57.60	55.44	53.32	59.81	56.38
CRF + MWELeft + SF	53.53	58.74	56.02	53.01	59.67	56.14

Table 2: Results of different methods for noun compounds in terms of precision (P), recall (R) and F-measure (F) in Wikipedia corpus. mwetoolkit: the mwetoolkit system, DictCombined: combination of dictionary based methods, CRF: our CRF model trained on automatically generated database, SF: sentences without any MWE label filtered, NE: NEs marked by Stanford NER used as feature, OwnNE: NEs marked by our CRF model (trained on Wikipedia) used as feature, OwnNELeft: the NE labeling selected as feature and the standard noun compound notation removed, MWELeft: the NE feature deleted and the standard noun compound notation selected.

based and dictionary-based approaches is bigger in the BNC dataset. Furthermore, in this corpus too, CRF approaches enhanced with the NE feature performed best.

We found only one available other system to English noun compound recognition. This is the mwetoolkit system (Ramisch et al., 2010), a language-independent tool developed for collecting MWEs from texts (which is able to identify noun compounds). We evaluated it on these two corpora too. This system also relies heavily on POS tag features, therefore we completed the mwetoolkit POS tag rules with our POS rules. However, the mwetoolkit basically does not mark MWEs in the raw text, it just extracts noun compounds from the text, i.e. multiple occurrences of the same MWE are not taken into account. Therefore, in order to compare the results of our approaches to those of mwetoolkit, we assessed our methods similarly to the evaluation scheme used in the mwetoolkit. The results of mwetoolkit and our methods on the Wikipedia corpus can be seen on the right side in Table 2 and the BNC dataset on the right site in Table 3. As the tables show, with this evaluation method we achieve better F scores. This is probably due to that if a particular phrase occurs several times in the text and we cannot identify it, it counts as only one recall error in this evaluation, and in the other evaluation, each occurrence of the same MWE must be identified. The right handside of Tables 2 and 3 shows that we were able to achieve considerably better results than mwetoolkit. Again, in this type of evaluation, CRF models which used NEs as feature reached the best F-score. The mwetoolkit style evaluation is useful in e.g. collecting dictionary entries while the other type of evaluation is useful in e.g. information extraction or machine translation.

3.3 Named Entity Recognition with MWEs

As explained above, NEs are good features when we would like to extract noun compounds from texts. Therefore, we investigated the usability of noun compounds in named entity recognition. So we used the Wiki50 corpus to train CRF classification models with the basic feature set, which was extended with the feature noun compound MWE for NE recognition and they were evaluated in a leave-one-document-out scheme. Results of these approaches are shown in the *NE + MWE* row of Table 1. Comparing these results to those of the *NE* method (when the CRF was trained without the noun compound feature), noun compounds are also beneficial in NE detection.

4 Keyphrase extraction

Keyphrase extraction aims at the determination of the most important phrases of documents. The domain of keyphrase extraction most frequently involves scientific literature, but there have been other works that deal with other genres of texts as well (such as news articles as done in Farkas et al.

Approach	R	P	F	R	P	F
mwetoolkit	-	-	-	10.22	18.84	13.26
DictCombined	30.39	37.13	33.42	31.31	42.25	35.97
CRF	27.27	40.49	32.59	30.44	42.20	35.37
CRF + SF	34.91	39.48	37.06	39.11	41.33	40.19
CRF + NE	27.27	38.70	31.99	30.44	40.88	34.89
CRF + NE + SF	31.97	40.73	35.83	38.64	43.65	40.99
CRF + OwnNE + SF	36.78	36.10	36.43	41.22	37.93	39.50
CRF + NELeft	40.28	39.35	39.81	44.68	40.29	42.37
CRF + MWELeft	36.57	40.60	38.48	40.98	42.68	41.81

Table 3: Results of different methods for noun compounds in terms of precision (P), recall (R) and F-measure (F) in BNC dataset. mwetoolkit: the mwetoolkit system, DictCombined: combination of dictionary based methods, CRF: our CRF model trained on automatically generated database, SF: sentences without any MWE label filtered, NE: NEs marked by Stanford NER used as feature, OwnNE: NEs marked by our CRF model (trained on Wikipedia) used as feature, OwnNELeft: the NE labeling selected as feature and the standard noun compound notation removed, MWELeft: the NE feature deleted and the standard noun compound notation selected.

(2010)). Since keyphrases can be interpreted as the most important phrases of a document with respect to its content, their utilization in various NLP systems – ranging from document summarization to information retrieval or document classification – can be beneficial.

The fact that MWEs often prove to be proper keyphrases as well implies that the knowledge of MWEs in a given text can be exploited in the determination of the keyphrases of that document. However, we note that the two tasks (i.e. finding the MWEs and the keyphrases of documents) should be treated differently, since not all multiword expressions behave necessarily as keyphrases in all environments (e.g. although the phrase *research group* is definitely an MWE, its treatment as a keyphrase when it is present in the affiliations part of a scientific paper is not likely to be a valid choice for such a phrase that describes well the content of the document.)

In order to examine the possible utility of the usage of multiword expressions in the task of keyphrase extraction, we conducted experiments in this field. In our experiments we regarded the extraction of keyphrases from scientific documents as a supervised learning task, similarly to others (Frank et al., 1999; Turney, 2003; Witten et al., 1999). As for the dataset of our experiments, we used that of the shared task on keyphrase extraction of SemEval-2 (Kim et al., 2010).

The dataset is a subset of the ACM Digital Library and consists of 244 scientific publications of length ranging from 6 to 8 pages from four different research areas in computer science and economics. The documents were split into a training set of 144 documents and a test set of 100 documents by the organizers of the shared task. For training and testing our system, we used the keyphrases assigned to the documents coming from the readers of the papers of the dataset (similarly as it was done at the shared task).

4.1 Methodology

In our system we used the supervised learning approach for keyphrase extraction, in which the keyphrases of a document are determined by first identifying a set of potentially good phrases, then classifying its elements as either proper or non-proper keyphrases, based on the prediction of a machine learned model. We used the machine learning framework of MALLET (McCallum, 2002) for learning the proper keyphrases. Experiments using Maximum Entropy and Naïve Bayes classifiers were both conducted.

One key aspect in keyphrase extraction is the way keyphrase nominates are selected and represented. As the number of potentially extracted n-grams and that of genuine keyphrases among them shows high imbalancedness usually, keyphrase nominates are worth to be filtered, instead of using any successive n-grams. In our definition keyphrase candidates were n-grams that were not longer than 4 tokens and started with a non-stopword token having either a `noun`, `adjective` or `verb` POS-code. Finally, an n-gram to be regarded as a keyphrase aspirant was also required to end with a non-stopword token having a POS-code either `noun` or `adjective`. Some phrases that fulfilled the above mentioned criteria were still discarded, due to positional rules, e.g. no phrase was regarded as a keyphrase aspirant if it occurred only in the *References* part of an article. This way 39,838 phrases were extracted from the 144 documents of the training corpus, which served as our training examples.

Once we had the keyphrase candidates, they had to be brought to a normalized form. The normalization of an n-gram consisted of lowercasing and Porter-stemming each of the lemmatized forms of its tokens, then putting these stems into alphabetical order (while omitting the stems of stopword tokens). With this kind of representation it was then possible to handle two syntactically different, but semantically equivalent phrases, such as *diffusion of innovation* and *Innovation diffusion* in the same way. For the linguistic analysis of the articles (i.e. tokenizing, lemmatization, POS-tagging) we used the Stanford CoreNLP API [2].

As for a baseline for our systems, we tried out KEA (Witten et al., 1999) as one of the most cited supervised keyphrase extracting tool, and also implemented its features in our system, which has its own strategy for generating keyphrase aspirants but uses the same standard features as well and uses the machine learning framework of MALLET. The two basic features for the keyphrase extraction system in KEA are the **tf-idf** score for an n-gram and **its relative first occurrence** within its context (i.e. the quotient of the first position of a certain n-gram and the length of the whole containing document).

To show the added value of MWEs in the task of keyphrase extraction, we designed a feature that indicated whether a certain n-gram (1) is an MWE, (2) can be built up from more MWEs, or just simply is the (3) superstring of at least one MWE. In order to do this we constructed a wide list of MWEs from Wikipedia (dump file 2011-01-07): we gathered all the links and formatted (i.e. bold or italic) text on Wikipedia that was at least two tokens in length, started with lowercase letters and contained only English characters or some punctuation. Based on this list, an alignment of its elements and the corpus was carried out (taking care of linguistic alternations), regarding those n-grams as genuine MWEs that started and ended with tokens of either a `noun` or `adjective` POS-code and had no other (possibly zero) tokens in between them that were of POS-code either `noun`, `adjective`, `preposition` or `possessive ending`. Thus when deciding on the MWE-related features of a keyphrase aspirant, we only had to decide if it was (1) annotated by our automatic process (taking the MWE list extracted from Wikipedia and the POS-sequence of a candidate into account) as an MWE in its full length (e.g. *maximal social welfare ratio*); (2) said to be able to put together from two MWEs present in our list (e.g. *resource allocation problems*, where *resource allocation* and *allocation problems* were in our list separately, but not as one phrase); (3) said to be a superstring of at least one MWE (e.g. *general analysis remains*, due to the presence of *general analysis*). Results achieved by KEA and our system (with and without using the above mentioned MWE-feature) are present in Table 4.

Besides the utilization of MWEs in the keyphrase extraction task, we were also interested in the effect of using features involving named entities. In order to investigate this, we implemented a set of binary features that were related to the orthography and semantics of keyphrase aspirants, as NEs usually both have special orthographic characteristics and special semantic roles in their content. For the determination of these feature values, we assigned the NE annotation of Stanford CoreNLP to keyphrase aspirants in such a manner that the feature values set to be true also implied the positions of the tokens having a specific NE-class within the keyphrase candidate. The position of one token of an n-gram was incorporated into the feature space as follows: separate features were created to indicate if an n-gram contained a certain type of NE-class standing at the beginning (B), inside (I) or at the end (E) of a keyphrase candidate. We also reserved a symbol for single token (S) keyphrase aspirants. For instance, *Nash* got positive value for the feature *S-PER* whereas *Nash equilibrium* had the feature *B-PER* set as true (and S-PER as false, naturally).

Strange orthography also had its binary features for n-grams incorporating similarly the position

[2] http://nlp.stanford.edu/software/corenlp.shtml

	Naïve Bayes			Maximum Entropy		
	Top-5	Top-10	Top-15	Top-5	Top-10	Top-15
KEA	22.2/9.23/13.04	18.0/14.96/16.34	15.53/19.37/17.24	20.4/8.48/11.98	18.2/15.13/16.52	15.93/19.87/17.68
BL	9.6/4.0/5.64	8.9/7.4/8.08	8.3/10.4/9.25	11.8/4.9/6.93	9.6/8.0/8.72	8.7/10.8/9.62
NE	7.6/3.2/4.46	5.7/4.7/5.17	5.2/6.5/5.77	14.4/6.0/8.46	10.9/9.1/9.9	10.1/12.6/11.25
MWE	18.4/7.6/10.8	13.7/11.4/12.44	11.1/13.8/12.28	18.4/7.6/10.8	14.4/12.0/13.07	10.9/13.6/12.13
COM.	12.6/5.2/7.4	12.1/10.1/10.99	10.0/12.5/11.1	13.8/5.7/8.1	14.8/12.3/13.44	13.2/16.5/14.65
EXT.	8.8/3.7/5.17	7.6/6.3/6.9	6.7/8.3/7.4	25.4/10.6/14.91	20.8/17.3/18.88	18.2/22.7/20.2
BEST	18.4/7.6/10.8	15.1/12.6/13.71	13.3/16.6/14.8	25.8/10.7/15.15	20.4/17.0/18.52	18.4/22.9/20.42
BMWE	21.6/9.0/12.68	17.3/14.4/15.71	14.4/18.0/15.98	26.0/10.8/15.27	21.2/17.6/19.25	19.0/23.7/21.09

Table 4: Evaluation results of keyphrase extraction in form of Precision/Recall/F-score at the top 5, 10 and 15 keyphrase levels using Naïve Bayes and Maximum Entropy classifiers. KEA: KEA system, BL: our baseline system using the standard KEA features, NE: our baseline system extended with the NE-related features, MWE: our baseline system extended with the MWE-related features, COM.: our baseline system extended with both NE- and MWE-related features, EXT.: extended feature set, BEST: the best combination of features without MWE-related features, BMWE: the best combination of features with MWE-related features

of the tokens that induced the feature to be set to true, e.g. in *UDDI registries* the feature *B-ORTHOGRAPHY* feature was set to true. A token was regarded to have strange orthography if it contained any uppercase letter besides its initial letter, or if it had more than 2 occurrences of the same character right after each other in any of its tokens. Results of the NE and orthography involving features are present in Table 4. To conclude our experiments we also experimented with the extension of the feature set that contained e.g. character suffix features, positional features within the document, POS-code related features, etc.

4.2 Results

As can be seen in Table 4, the Maximum Entropy models overperform the Naïve Bayes models. Best results are achieved for the top 15 keywords in each scenario. Results also show that the inclusion of the NE and MWE features proved useful in keyphrase extraction. Regarding NEs, although Naïve Bayes results somewhat declines when including NEs, its positive effect on the Maximum Entropy model is obvious. The addition of the MWE-features yielded better F-scores in each scenario, and best results can be achieved if all the useful features are enhanced by MWE-features, which clearly underlines the beneficiary effect of using MWEs in keyphrase extraction.

5 Discussion

Our results demonstrate that previously known noun compounds are beneficial in NER and identified NEs enhance MWE detection. This may be related to the fact that multiword NEs and noun compounds are similar from a linguistic point of view as discussed above – moreover, in some cases, it is not easy to determine even for humans whether a given sequence of words is a NE or a MWE (capitalized names of positions such as *Prime Minister* or taxonomic names, e.g. *Torrey Pine*). In the test databases, no unit was annotated as NE and MWE at the same time, thus, it was necessary to disambiguate cases which could be labeled by both the MWE and the NE systems. By fixing the label of such cases, disambiguity is eliminated, that is, the training data are less noisy, which leads to better overall results.

In keyphrase extraction, MWEs proved to be useful as well. This may be related to the fact that in many cases, keyphrases consist of multi-word tokens, thus, being an MWE might be suggestive of being a keyword aspirant too. It must be mentioned that not all MWEs are proper keywords, however, and must be filtered by other features as well. As for the importance of named entities in keyphrase extraction, in certain domains, person names tend to be common keyphrases (e.g. news) while in others, they do not typically function as keyphrases (e.g. biological publications), which highlights the domain-specificity of the problem. However, the keyphrase extractor can still profit from already known NEs: in one case, they can be excluded from the set of keyphrase aspirants while in the other case, they are proper keyword candidates.

6 Conclusions

In this paper, we investigated how the automatic identification of noun compounds and named entities can contribute to keyphrase extraction and we also showed how previously identified noun compounds affect named entity recognition and vice versa, how noun compound detection is supported by identified named entities. Our experiments demonstrate that already known noun compounds yield better performance in NER and already known NEs enhance MWE detection. The integration of MWE- and NE-related features into a keyphrase extractor also proves to be more effective than the model not including them. Our results indicate that MWEs and NEs tend to be beneficial features in several NLP-related tasks. We firmly believe that our results in detecting noun compounds and named entities can be fruitfully applied in other higher-level applications as well in e.g. information extraction, document classification or machine translation.

Acknowledgments

This work was supported by the Project "TÁMOP-4.2.1/B-09/1/KONV-2010-0005 – Creating the Center of Excellence at the University of Szeged", supported by the European Union and co-financed by the European Regional Development Fund and by the project BELAMI financed by the National Innovation Office of the Hungarian government.

References

Nancy A. Chinchor. 1998. Overview of MUC-7/MET-2. In *Proceedings of MUC-7*.

Richárd Farkas, Gábor Berend, István Hegedűs, András Kárpáti, and Balázs Krich. 2010. Automatic free-text-tagging of online news archives. In *Proceeding of ECAI 2010*, pages 529–534, Amsterdam, The Netherlands. IOS Press.

Eibe Frank, Gordon W. Paynter, Ian H. Witten, Carl Gutwin, and Craig G. Nevill-Manning. 1999. Domain-specific keyphrase extraction. In *Proceeding of 16th IJCAI*, pages 668–673.

Ralph Grishman and Beth Sundheim. 1995. Design of the MUC-6 evaluation. In *Proceedings of the 6th Conference on Message Understanding*, pages 1–12, Stroudsburg, PA, USA. ACL.

Ray Jackendoff. 1997. *The Architecture of the Language Faculty*. MIT Press, Cambridge, MA.

Su Nam Kim, Olena Medelyan, Min-Yen Kan, and Timothy Baldwin. 2010. Semeval-2010 task 5: Automatic keyphrase extraction from scientific articles. In *Proceedings of SemEval'10*, pages 21–26, Morristown, NJ, USA. ACL.

Su Nam Kim. 2008. *Statistical Modeling of Multiword Expressions*. Ph.D. thesis, University of Melbourne, Melbourne.

Andrew Kachites McCallum. 2002. Mallet: A machine learning for language toolkit. http://mallet.cs.umass.edu.

Jeremy Nicholson and Timothy Baldwin. 2008. Interpreting Compound Nominalisations. In *LREC 2008 Workshop: Towards a Shared Task for Multiword Expressions (MWE 2008)*, pages 43–45, Marrakech, Morocco.

Carlos Ramisch, Aline Villavicencio, and Christian Boitet. 2010. Multiword Expressions in the wild? The mwetoolkit comes in handy. In *Coling 2010: Demonstrations*, pages 57–60, Beijing, China, August. Coling 2010 Organizing Committee.

Ivan A. Sag, Timothy Baldwin, Francis Bond, Ann Copestake, and Dan Flickinger. 2002. Multiword Expressions: A Pain in the Neck for NLP. In *Proceedings of CICLing-2002*, pages 1–15, Mexico City, Mexico.

György Szarvas, Richárd Farkas, and András Kocsor. 2006. A Multilingual Named Entity Recognition System Using Boosting and C4.5 Decision Tree Learning Algorithms. In *Discovery Science*, pages 267–278.

Erik F. Tjong Kim Sang and Fien De Meulder. 2003. Introduction to the CoNLL-2003 Shared Task: Language-Independent Named Entity Recognition. In Walter Daelemans and Miles Osborne, editors, *Proceedings of CoNLL-2003*, pages 142–147. Edmonton, Canada.

Erik F. Tjong Kim Sang. 2002. Introduction to the CoNLL-2002 Shared Task: Language-Independent Named Entity Recognition. In *Proceedings of CoNLL-2002*, pages 155–158. Taipei, Taiwan.

Kristina Toutanova and Christopher D. Manning. 2000. Enriching the knowledge sources used in a maximum entropy part-of-speech tagger. In *Proceedings of EMNLP 2000*, pages 63–70, Stroudsburg, PA, USA. ACL.

Peter Turney. 2003. Coherent keyphrase extraction via web mining. In *Proceedings of IJCAI '03*, pages 434–439.

Veronika Vincze, István Nagy T., and Gábor Berend. 2011. Multiword expressions and named entities in the Wiki50 corpus. In *Proceedings of RANLP 2011*, Hissar, Bulgaria.

Ian H. Witten, Gordon W. Paynter, Eibe Frank, Carl Gutwin, and Craig G. Nevill-Manning. 1999. Kea: Practical automatic keyphrase extraction. In *ACM DL*, pages 254–255.

A Named Entity Recognition Method using Rules Acquired from Unlabeled Data

Tomoya Iwakura
Fujitsu Laboratories Ltd.
1-1, Kamikodanaka 4-chome, Nakahara-ku, Kawasaki 211-8588, Japan
iwakura.tomoya@jp.fujitsu.com

Abstract

We propose a Named Entity (NE) recognition method using rules acquired from unlabeled data. Rules are acquired from automatically labeled data with an NE recognizer. These rules are used to identify NEs, the beginning of NEs, or the end of NEs. The application results of rules are used as features for machine learning based NE recognizers. In addition, we use word information acquired from unlabeled data as in a previous work. The word information includes the candidate NE classes of each word, the candidate NE classes of co-occurring words of each word, and so on. We evaluate our method with IREX data set for Japanese NE recognition and unlabeled data consisting of more than one billion words. The experimental results show that our method using rules and word information achieves the best accuracy on the GENERAL and ARREST tasks of IREX.

1 Introduction

Named Entity (NE) recognition aims to recognize proper nouns and numerical expressions in text, such as names of people, locations, organizations, dates, times, and so on. NE recognition is one of the basic technologies used in text processing such as Information Extraction and Question Answering.

To implement NE recognizers, semi-supervised-based methods have recently been widely applied. These methods use several different types of information obtained from unlabeled data, such as word clusters (Freitag, 2004; Miller et al., 2004), the clusters of multi-word nouns (Kazama and Torisawa, 2008), phrase clusters (Lin and Wu, 2009), hyponymy relations extracted from WikiPedia (Kazama and Torisawa, 2008), NE-related word information (Iwakura, 2010), and the outputs of classifiers or parsers created from unlabeled data (Ando and Zhang, 2005). These previous works have shown that features acquired from large sets of unlabeled data can contribute to improved accuracy. From the results of these previous works, we see that several types of features augmented with unlabeled data contribute to improved accuracy. Therefore, if we can incorporate new features augmented with unlabeled data, we expect more improved accuracy.

We propose a Named Entity recognition method using rules acquired from unlabeled data. Our method uses rules identifying not only whole NEs, but also the beginning of NEs or the end of NEs. Rules are acquired from automatically labeled data with an NE recognizer. The application results of rules are used as features for machine-learning based NE recognitions. Compared with previous works using rules identifying NEs acquired from manually labeled data (Isozaki, 2001), or lists of NEs acquired from unlabeled data (Talukdar et al., 2006), our method uses new features such as identification results of the beginning of NEs and the end of NEs. In addition, we use word information (Iwakura, 2010). The word information includes the candidate NE classes of each word, the candidate NE classes of co-occurring words of each word, and so on. The word information is also acquired from automatically labeled data with an NE recognizer.

We report experimental results with the IREX Japanese NE recognition data set (IREX, 1999). The experimental results show that our method using rules and word information achieves the best accuracy on the GENERAL and ARREST tasks. The experimental results also show that our method contributes to fast improvement of accuracy compared with only using manually labeled

Table 1: Basic character types

Hiragana (Japanese syllabary characters), Katakana, Kanji (Chinese letter), Capital alphabet, Lower alphabet, number and Others

training data.

2 Japanese Named Entity Recognition

This section describes our NE recognition method that combines both word-based and character-based NE recognitions.

2.1 Chunk Representation

Each NE consists of one or more words. To recognize NEs, we have to identify word chunks with their NE classes. We use Start/End (SE) representation (Uchimoto et al., 2000) because an SE representation-based NE recognizer shows the best performance among previous works (Sasano and Kurohashi, 2008). SE representation uses five tags which are S, B, I, E and O, for representing chunks. S means that the current word is a chunk consisting of only one word. B means the start of a chunk consisting of more than one word. E means the end of a chunk consisting of more than one word. I means the inside of a chunk consisting of more than two words. O means the outside of any chunk. We use the IREX Japanese NE recognition task for our evaluation. The task is to recognize the eight NE classes. The SE based NE label set for IREX task has $(8 \times 4) + 1 = 33$ labels such as B-PERSON, S-PERSON, and so on.

2.2 Word-based NE Recognition

We classify each word into one of the NE labels defined by the SE representation for recognizing NEs. Japanese has no word boundary marker. To segment words from Japanese texts, we use MeCab 0.98 with ipadic-2.7.0.[1]

Our NE recognizer uses features extracted from the current word, the preceding two words and the two succeeding words (5-word window). The basic features are the word surfaces, the last characters, the base-forms, the readings, the POS tags, and the character types of words within 5-word window size. The base-forms, the readings, and the POS tags are given by MeCab. Base-forms are representative expressions for conjugational words. If the base-form of each word is not equivalent to the word surface, we use the base-form as a feature. If a word consists of only one character, the character type is expressed by using the corresponding character types listed in Table 1. If a word consists of more than one character, the character type is expressed by a combination of the basic character types listed in Table 1, such as Kanji-Hiragana. MeCab uses the set of POS tags having at most four levels of subcategories. We use all the levels of POS tags as POS tag features.

We use outputs of rules to a current word and word information within 5-word window size as features. The rules and the word information are acquired from automatically labeled data with an NE recognizer. We describe rules in section 3. We use the following NE-related labels of words from unlabeled data as word information as in (Iwakura, 2010).

Candidate NE labels: We use NE labels assigned to each word more than or equal to 50 times as candidate NE labels of words.

Candidate co-occurring NE labels: We use NE labels assigned to co-occurring words of each word more than or equal to 50 times as candidate co-occurring NE labels of the word.

Frequency information of candidate NE labels and candidate co-occurring NE labels: These are the frequencies of the NE candidate labels of each word on the automatically labeled data. We categorize the frequencies of these NE-related labels by the frequency of each word n; $50 \leq n \leq 100$, $100 < n \leq 500$, $500 < n \leq 1000$, $1000 < n \leq 5000$, $5000 < n \leq 10000$, $10000 < n \leq 50000$, $50000 < n \leq 100000$, and $100000 < n$.

Ranking of candidate NE labels: This information is the ranking of candidate NE class labels for each word. Each ranking is decided according to the label frequencies.

For example, we obtain the following statistics from automatically labeled data with an NE recognizer for *Tanaka*: S-PERSON was assigned to *Tanaka* 10,000 times, B-PERSON was assigned to *Tanaka* 1,000 times, and I-PERSON was assigned to words appearing next to *Tanaka* 1,000 times. The following NE-related labels are acquired for *Tanaka*: Candidate NE labels are S-PERSON and B-ORGANIZATION. Frequency information of candidate NE labels are $5000 < n \leq 10000$ for S-PERSON, and $500 < n \leq 1000$ for B-ORGANIZATION. The ranking of candidate NE labels are the first for S-PERSON, and second for

[1] http://mecab.sourceforge.net/

B-ORGANIZATION. Candidate co-occurring NE labels at the next word position is I-PERSON. Frequency information of candidate co-occurring NE labels at the next word position is $500 < n \leq 1000$ for I-PERSON.

2.3 Character-based NE Recognition

Japanese NEs sometimes include partial words that form the beginning, the end of NE chunks or whole NEs.[2] To recognize Japanese NEs including partial words, we use a character-unit-chunking-based NE recognition algorithm (Asahara and Matsumoto, 2003; Nakano and Hirai, 2004) following word-based NE recognition as in (Iwakura, 2010).

Our character-based NE recognizer uses features extracted from the current character, the preceding two characters and the two succeeding characters (5-character window). The features extracted from each character within the window size are the followings; the character itself, the character type of the character listed in Table 1, and the NE labels of two preceding recognition results in the direction from the end to the beginning.

In addition, we use words including characters within the window size. The features of the words are the character types, the POS tags, and the NE labels assigned by a word-based NE recognizer.

As for words including characters, we extract features as follows. Let $W(c_i)$ be the word including the i-th character c_i and $P(c_i)$ be the identifier that indicates the position where c_i appears in $W(c_i)$. We combine $W(c_i)$ and $P(c_i)$ to create a feature. $P(c_i)$ is one of the followings: B for a character that is the beginning of a word, I for a character that is in the inside of a word, E for a character that is the end of a word, and S for a character that is a word. [3]

We use the POS tags of words including characters within 5-character window. Let $POS(W(c_i))$ be the POS tag of the word $W(c_i)$ including the i-th character c_i. We express these features with the position identifier $P(c_i)$ like $P(c_i)$-$POS(W(c_i))$. In addition, we use the character types of words including characters. To utilize outputs of a word-based NE recognizer, we use NE labels of words assigned by a word-unit NE recognizer. Each character is classified into one of the 33 NE labels provided by the SE representation.

2.4 Machine Learning Algorithm

We use a boosting-based learner that learns rules consisting of a feature, or rules represented by combinations of features consisting of more than one feature (Iwakura and Okamoto, 2008). The boosting algorithm achieves fast training speed by training a weak-learner that learns several rules from a small portion of candidate rules. Candidate rules are generated from a subset of features called bucket. The parameters for the boosting algorithm are as follows. We used the number of rules to be learned as R=100,000, the bucketing size for splitting features into subsets as $|B|$=1,000, the number of rules learned at each boosting iteration as ν =10, the number of candidate rules used to generate new combinations of features at each rule size as ω=10, and the maximum number of features in rules as ζ=2.

The boosting algorithm operates on binary classification problems. To extend the boosting to multi-class, we used the one-vs-the-rest method. To identify proper tag sequences, we use the Viterbi search. To apply the Viterbi search, we convert the confidence value of each classifier into the range of 0 to 1 with sigmoid function defined as $s(X) = 1/(1 + exp(-\beta X))$, where X is the output of a classifier to an input. We used β=1 in this experiment. Then we select a tag sequence which maximizes the sum of those log values.

To obtain a fast processing and training speed, we apply a technique to control the generation of combinations of features (Iwakura, 2009). This is because fast processing speed is required to obtain word information and rules from large unlabeled data. Using this technique, instead of manually specifying combinations of features to be used, features that are not used in combinations of features are specified as atomic features. The boosting algorithm learns rules consisting of more than one feature from the combinations of features generated from non-atomic features, and rules consisting of only a feature from the atomic and the non-atomic features. We can obtain faster training speed and processing speed because we can reduce the number of combinations of features

[2]For example, Japanese word "*houbei*" (visit U.S.) does not match with LOCATION "bei (U.S)".

[3]If "*Gaimusyouha*", is segmented as "*Gaimusyou (the Ministry of Foreign Affairs) / ha (particle)*", then words including characters are follows; *W(Gai) = Gaimusyou, W(mu) = Gaimusyou, W(syou) = Gaimusyou*, and *W(ha)=ha*. The identifiers that indicate positions where characters appear are follows; *P(Gai) =B, P(mu) = I, P(syou) = E*, and *P(ha)*=S.

to be examined by specifying part of features as atomic. We specify features based on word information and rules acquired from unlabeled data as the atomic features.

3 Rules Acquired from Unlabeled Data

This section describes rules and a method to acquire rules.

3.1 Rule Types

Previous works such as Isozaki (Isozaki, 2001), Talukdar et al., (Talukdar et al., 2006), use rules or lists of NEs for only identifying NEs. In addition to rules identifying NEs, we propose to use rules for identifying the beginning of NEs or the end of NEs to capture context information. To acquire rules, an automatically labeled data with an NE recognizer is used. The following types of rules are acquired.

Word N-gram rules for identifying NEs (*NE-W-rules*, for short): These are word N-grams corresponding to candidate NEs.

Word trigram rules for identifying the beginning of NEs (*NEB-W-rules*): Each rule for identifying the beginning of NEs is represented as a word trigram consisting of the two words preceding the beginning of an NE and the beginning of the NE.

Word trigram rules for identifying the end of NEs (*NEE-W-rules*): Each rule for identifying the end of NEs is represented as a word trigram consisting of the two words succeeding the end of an NE and the end of the NE.

In addition to word N-gram rules, we acquire Word/POS N-gram rules for achieving higher rule coverage. Word/POS N-gram rules are acquired from N-gram rules by replacing some words in N-gram rules with POS tags. We call *NE-W-rules*, *NEB-W-rules* and *NEE-W-rules* converted to Word/POS N-gram rules *NE-WP-rules*, *NEB-WP-rules* and *NEE-WP-rules*, respectively. Word/POS N-gram rules also identify NEs the beginning of NEs and the end of NEs

To acquire Word/POS rules, we replace words having one of the following POS tags with their POS tags as rule constituents: proper noun words, unknown words, and number words. This is because words having these POS tags are usually low frequency words.

3.2 Acquiring Rules

This section describes the method to acquire the rules used in this paper. The rule acquisition consists of three main steps: First, we create automatically labeled data. Second, seed rules are acquired. Finally the outputs of rules are decided.

The first step prepares an automatically labeled data with an NE recognizer. The NE recognizer recognizes NEs from unlabeled data and generates the automatically labeled data by annotating characters recognized as NEs with the NE labels.

The second step acquires seed rules from the automatically labeled data. The following is an automatically labeled sentence.
[Tanaka/\$PN mission/\$N party/\$N $]_{ORG}$ went/ \$V to/\$P [U.K / \$PN]$_{LOC}$ ..." ,
where \$PN (Proper Noun), \$N, \$V, and \$P following / are POS tags, and words between "[and]" were identified as NEs. ORG and LOC after "]" indicate NE types.

The following seed rules are acquired from the above sentence by following the procedures described in previous sections:
NE-W-rules: {*Tanaka mission party* → ORG},
NEB-W-rules: {*went to U.K* → LW=B-LOC},
NEE-W-rules: {*party went to* → FW=E-ORG},
NE-WP-rules: {*\$PN mission party* → ORG},
NEB-WP-rules: {*went to \$PN* → LW=B-LOC},
NEE-WP-rules: {*\$PN mission party* → LW=B-ORG},
where FW, LW, B-LOC, and E-ORG indicate the first words of word sequences that a rule is applied to, the last words of word sequences that a rule is applied to, the beginning word of a LOCATION NE, and the end word of an ORGANIZATION NE, respectively. The left of each → is the *rule condition* to apply a rule, and the right of each → is the seed output of a rule. If the output of a rule is only an NE type, this means the rule identifies an NE. Rules with outputs including = indicate rules for identifying the beginning of NEs or the end of NEs. The left of = indicates the positions of words where the beginning of NEs or the end of NEs exist in the identified word sequences by rules. For example, LW=B-LOC means that LW is B-LOC.

The final step decides the outputs of each rule. We count the outputs of the rule condition of each seed rule, and the final outputs of each rule are decided by using the frequency of each output. We use outputs assigned to each seed rule

more than or equal to 50 times.[4] For example, if LW=B-LOC are obtained 10,000 times, and LW=B-ORG are obtained 1,000 times, as the outputs for {*went to $PN*}, the followings are acquired as final outputs:
LW=B-LOC_RANK1, LW=B-ORG_RANK2, LW=B-LOC_FREQ-5000 $< n \leq$ 10000, and LW=B-ORG_FREQ-500 $< n \leq$ 1000.

The LW=B-LOC_RANK1 and the LW=B-ORG_RANK2 are the ranking of the outputs of rules. LW=B-LOC is 1st ranked output, and LW=B-ORG is 2nd ranked output. Each ranking is decided by the frequency of each output of each rule condition. The most frequent output of each rule is ranked as first.

LW=B-LOC_FREQ-5000 $< n \leq$ 10000 and LW=B-ORG_FREQ-500 $< n \leq$ 1000 are frequency information. To express the frequency of each rule output as binary features, we categorize the frequency of each rule output by the frequency of each rule output n; $50 \leq n \leq 100$, $100 < n \leq 500$, $500 < n \leq 1000$, $1000 < n \leq 5000$, $5000 < n \leq 10000$, $10000 < n \leq 50000$, $50000 < n \leq 100000$, and $100000 < n$.

3.3 Rule Application

We define the rule application by following the method for using phrase clusters in NER (Lin and Wu, 2009). The application of rules is allowed to overlap with or be nested in one another. If a rule is applied at positions b to e, we add the features combined with the outputs of the rule and matching positions to each word; outputs with *B*- (beginning) to b-th word, outputs with *E*- (end) to b-th word, outputs with *I*- (inside) within $b + 1$-th to $e - 1$-th words, outputs with *P*- (previous) to $b - 1$-th word, and outputs with *F*- (following) to $e + 1$-th word.

If a rule having the condition {*went to $PN*} is applied to {.... Ken/$PN went/$V to/$P Japan/ $PN for/$P ...}, the followings are captured as rule application results: b-th word is went, the word between b-th and e-th is to, e-th word is Japan, $b - 1$-th is Ken, and $e + 1$-th is for.

If the output of the rule is LW=B-LOC, the following features are added: B-LW=B-LOC for went, I-LW=B-LOC for to, E-LW=B-LOC for Japan, P-LW=B-LOC for Ken, and F-LW=B-LOC for for.

[4]We conducted experiments using word information and rules obtained from training data with different frequency threshold parameters. The parameters are 1, 3, 5, 10, 20, 30, 40, and 50. We select 50 as the threshold because the parameter shows the best result among the results obtained with these parameters on a pilot study.

3.4 Repeatedly Acquisition

We also apply a method to acquire word information (Iwakura, 2010) to the rule acquisition repeatedly. This is because the previous work reported that better accuracy was obtained by repeating the acquisition of NE-related labels of words. The collection method is as follows.

(1) Create an NE recognizer from training data.

(2) Acquire word information and rules from unlabeled data with the current NE recognizer.

(3) Create a new NE recognizer with the training data, word information and rules acquired at step (2). This NE recognizer is used for acquiring new word information and rules at the next iteration.

(4) Go back to step (2) if the termination criterion is not satisfied. The process (2) to (4) is repeated 4 times in this experiment.

4 Experiments

4.1 Experimental settings

The following data prepared for IREX (IREX, 1999) were used in our experiment. We used the CRL data for the training. CRL data has 18,677 NEs on 1,174 stories from Mainichi Newspaper. In addition, to investigate the effectiveness of unlabeled data and labeled data, we prepared another labeled 7,000 news stories including 143,598 NEs from Mainichi Shinbun between 2007 and 2008 according to IREX definition. We have, in total, 8,174 news stories including 162,859 NEs that are about 8 times of CRL data. To create the additional labeled 7,000 news stories, about 509 hours were required. The average time for creating a labeled news story is 260 seconds, which means only 14 labeled news stories are created in an hour.

For evaluation, we used formal-run data of IREX: GENERAL task including 1,581 NEs, and ARREST task including 389 NEs.

We compared performance of NE recognizers by using the F-measure (FM) defined as follows with Recall (RE) and Precision (PR);
FM = 2 × RE × PR / (RE + PR),
where,
RE = NUM / (the number of correct NEs),
PR = NUM / (the number of NEs extracted by an NE recognizer),

Table 2: Experimental Results: Each AV. indicates a micro average F-measure obtained with each NE recognizer. B., +W, +R, and +WR indicate the base line recognizer, using word information, using rules, and using word information and rules. Base indicates the base line NE recognizer not using word information and rules.

	B.	+ W	+ R	+WR
GENERAL	85.35	88.04	85.93	**88.43**
ARREST	85.64	89.35	87.39	**91.33**
AV.	85.40	88.56	86.22	89.00

and NUM is the number of NEs correctly identified by an NE recognizer.

The news stories from the Mainichi Shinbun between 1991 and 2008 and Japanese WikiPedia entries of July 13, 2009, were used as unlabeled data for acquiring word information and rules. The total number of words segmented by MeCab from these unlabeled data was 1,161,758,003, more than one billion words. [5]

4.2 Evaluation of Our Proposed Method

We evaluated the effectiveness of the combination of word information and rules. Table 2 shows experimental results obtained with an NE recognizer without any word information and rules (NER-BASE, for short), an NE recognizer using word information (NER-W for short), an NE recognizer using rules (NER-R, for short), and an NE recognizer using word information and rules (NER-WR, for short), which is based on our proposed method

We used word information and rules obtained with the NER-BASE, which was created from CRL data without word information and rules. We see that we obtain better accuracy by using word information and rules acquired from unlabeled data.

The NER-WR shows the best average F-measure (FM). The average FM of the NER-WR is 3.6 points higher than that of the NER-BASE. The average FM of the NER-WR is 0.44 points higher than that of NER-W, and 2.78 points higher than that of the NER-R. These results show that combination of word information and rules contributes to improved accuracy. We also evaluated the effectiveness of the combination of rules for identifying NEs, and rules for identifying beginning of NEs or end of NEs. The micro average FM values for an NE recognizer using rules for identifying NEs, an NE recognizer using rules for identifying beginning of NEs or end of NEs, and the NE recognizer using the both types of rules are 85.77, 84.19 and 86.22. This result shows using the two types of rules are effective.

Table 3: Experimental Results obtained with NE recognizers using word information and rules: G., A., and AV. indicate GENERAL, ARREST, and a micro average obtained with each NE recognizer at each iteration, respectively.

	1	2	3	4	5
G.	85.35	**88.43**	88.22	88.20	88.31
A.	85.64	91.33	91.52	91.49	**92.19**
AV.	85.40	89.00	88.88	88.85	**89.08**

Then we evaluate the effectiveness of the acquisition method described in section 3.4. Table 3 shows the accuracy obtained with each NE recognizer at each iteration. The results at iteration 1 is the results obtained with the base line NE recognizer not using word information and rules. We obtained the best average accuracy at iteration 5. The results obtained with the NE recognizer at iteration 5 shows 4.76 points higher average F-measure than that of the NE recognizer at iteration 1, and 0.37 points higher average F-measure than that of the NE recognizer at iteration 2.

Table 4 shows the results of the previous works using IREX Japanese NE recognition tasks. All the results were obtained with CRL data as manually labeled training data. Our results are F-measure values obtained with the NE recognizer at iteration 5 on Table 3.

We see that our NE recognizer shows the best F-measure values for GENERAL and ARREST. Compared with our method only using unlabeled data, most previous works use handcrafted resources, such as a set of NEs are used in (Uchimoto et al., 2000), and NTT GOI Taikei (Ikehara et al., 1999), which is a handcrafted thesaurus, is used in (Isozaki and Kazawa, 2002; Sasano and Kurohashi, 2008). These results indicate that word information and rules acquired from large unlabeled data are also useful as well as handcrafted resources. In addition, we see that our method with large labeled data show much better perfor-

[5]We used WikiPedia in addition to news stories because Suzuki and Isozaki (Suzuki and Isozaki, 2008) reported that the use of more unlabeled data in their learning algorithm can really lead to further improvements. We treated a successive numbers and alphabets as a word in this experiment.

Table 4: Comparison with previous works. GE and AR indicate GENERAL and ARREST.

	GE	AR
(Uchimoto et al., 2000)	80.17	85.75
(Takemoto et al., 2001)	83.86	-
(Utsuro et al., 2002)	84.07	-
(Isozaki and Kazawa, 2002)	85.77	-
(Sasano and Kurohashi, 2008)	87.72	-
(Iwakura, 2010)	87.34	91.95
This paper	**88.31**	**92.19**

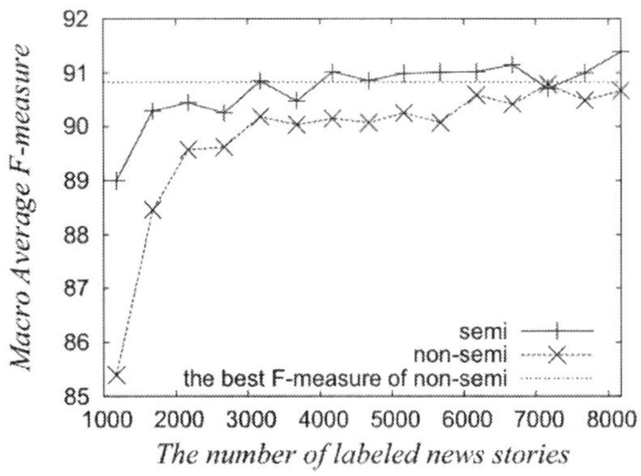

Figure 1: Experimental results obtained with different size of training data. Each point indicates the micro average F-measure of an NE recognizer.

mance than the other methods.

4.3 Evaluating Effectiveness of Our Method

This section describes the performances of NE recognizers trained with larger training data than CRL-data. Figure 1 shows the performance of each NE recognizer trained with different size of labeled training data. The leftmost points are the performance of the NE recognizers trained with CRL data (1,174 news stories). The other points are the performances of NE recognizers trained with training data larger than CRL data. The size of the additional training data is increased by 500 news stories.

We examined NE recognizers using our proposed method (semi), and NE recognizers not using our method (non-semi). In the following, semi-NER indicates NE recognizers using unlabeled data based on our method, and non-semi-NER indicates NE recognizers not using unlabeled data. Figure 1 shows that the semi-NER trained with CRL data shows competitive performance of the non-semi-NER trained with about 1.5 time larger training data consisting of CRL data and additional labeled 500 news stories. To create manually labeled 500 news stories, about 36 hours are required.[6] To achieve the competitive performance of the non-semi-NER trained with CRL data and the labeled 7,000 news stories, semi-NER requires only 2,000 news stories in addition to CRL data. This result shows that our proposed method significantly reduces the number of labeled data to achieve a competitive performance obtained with only using labeled data. Figure 1 also shows that our method contributes to improved accuracy when using the large labeled training data consisting of CRL data and 7,000 news stories. The accuracy is 90.47 for GENERAL, and 94.30 for ARREST. In contrast, when without word information and rules acquired from unlabeled data, the accuracy is 89.43 for GENERAL, and 93.44 for ARREST.

5 Related Work

To augment features, methods for using information obtained with clustering algorithms were proposed. These methods used word clusters (Freitag, 2004; Miller et al., 2004), the clusters of multi-word nouns (Kazama and Torisawa, 2008), or phrase clusters (Lin and Wu, 2009). In contrast, to collect rules, we use an automatically tagged data with an NE recognizer. Therefore, we expect to obtain more target-task-oriented information with our method than that of previous works. Although there are differences between our method and the previous works, our method and previous works are complementary .

To use rules in machine-learning-based NE recognitions, Isozaki proposed a Japanese NE recognition method based on a simple rule generator and decision tree learning. The method generates rules from supervised training data (Isozaki, 2001). Talukdar et al., proposed a method to use lists of NEs acquired from unlabeled data for NE recognition (Talukdar et al., 2006). Starting with a few NE seed examples, the method extends lists of NEs. These methods use rules or lists of NEs for identifying only NEs. Compared with these methods, our method uses rules for identifying the beginning of NEs and the end of NEs in addition

[6]We estimate the hours by using the average labeling time of a news story. The average time is 260 seconds per news story.

to rules identifying whole NEs. Therefore, our methods can use new features not used in previous works.

6 Conclusion

This paper proposed an NE recognition method using rules acquired from unlabeled data. Our method acquires rules for identifying NEs, the beginning of NEs, and the end of NEs from an automatically labeled data with an NE recognizer. In addition, we use word information including the candidate NE classes, and so on. We evaluated our method with IREX data set for Japanese NE recognition and unlabeled data consisting of more than one billion words. The experimental results showed that our method using rules and word information achieved the best accuracy on the GENERAL and ARREST tasks.

References

Rie Ando and Tong Zhang. 2005. A high-performance semi-supervised learning method for text chunking. In *Proc. of ACL 2005*, pages 1–9.

Masayuki Asahara and Yuji Matsumoto. 2003. Japanese named entity extraction with redundant morphological analysis. In *Proc. of HLT-NAACL 2003*, pages 8–15.

Dayne Freitag. 2004. Trained named entity recognition using distributional clusters. In *Proc. of EMNLP 2004*, pages 262–269.

Satoru Ikehara, Masahiro Miyazaki, Satoshi Shirai, Akio Yokoo, Hiromi Nakaiwa, Kentaro Ogura, Yoshifumi Ooyama, and Yoshihiki Hayashi. 1999. *Goi-Taikei -A Japanese Lexicon CDROM*. Iwanami Shoten.

Committee IREX. 1999. *Proc. of the IREX workshop*.

Hideki Isozaki and Hideto Kazawa. 2002. Speeding up named entity recognition based on Support Vector Machines (in Japanese). In *IPSJ SIG notes NL-149-1*, pages 1–8.

Hideki Isozaki. 2001. Japanese named entity recognition based on a simple rule generator and decision tree learning. In *Proc. of ACL 2001*, pages 314–321.

Tomoya Iwakura and Seishi Okamoto. 2008. A fast boosting-based learner for feature-rich tagging and chunking. In *Proc. of CoNLL 2008*, pages 17–24.

Tomoya Iwakura. 2009. Fast boosting-based part-of-speech tagging and text chunking with efficient rule representation for sequential labeling. In *Proc. of RANLP 2009*.

Tomoya Iwakura. 2010. A named entity extraction using word information repeatedly collected from unlabeled data. In *Proc. of CICLing 2010*, pages 212–223.

Jun'ichi Kazama and Kentaro Torisawa. 2008. Inducing gazetteers for named entity recognition by large-scale clustering of dependency relations. In *Proc. of ACL-08: HLT*, pages 407–415.

Dekang Lin and Xiaoyun Wu. 2009. Phrase clustering for discriminative learning. In *Proc. of ACL-IJCNLP 2009*, pages 1030–1038.

Scott Miller, Jethran Guinness, and Alex Zamanian. 2004. Name tagging with word clusters and discriminative training. In *Proc. of HLT-NAACL 2004*, pages 337–342.

Keigo Nakano and Yuzo Hirai. 2004. Japanese named entity extraction with bunsetsu features (in Japanese). In *IPSJ Journal, 45(3)*, pages 934–941.

Ryohei Sasano and Sadao Kurohashi. 2008. Japanese named entity recognition using structural natural language processing. In *Proc. of IJCNLP 2008*, pages 607–612.

Jun Suzuki and Hideki Isozaki. 2008. Semi-supervised sequential labeling and segmentation using giga-word scale unlabeled data. In *Proc. of ACL-08: HLT*, pages 665–673.

Yoshikazu Takemoto, Toshikazu Fukushima, and Hiroshi Yamada. 2001. A Japanese named entity extraction system based on building a large-scale and high quality dictionary and pattern-matching rules (in Japanese). 42(6):1580–1591.

Partha Pratim Talukdar, Thorsten Brants, Mark Liberman, and Fernando Pereira. 2006. A context pattern induction method for named entity extraction. In *Proc. of CoNLL 2006*, pages 141–148.

Kiyotaka Uchimoto, Qing Ma, Masaki Murata, Hiromi Ozaku, Masao Utiyama, and Hitoshi Isahara. 2000. Named entity extraction based on a maximum entropy model and transformati on rules. In *Proc. of the ACL 2000*, pages 326–335.

Takehito Utsuro, Manabu Sassano, and Kiyotaka Uchimoto. 2002. Combining outputs of multiple Japanese named entity chunkers by stacking. In *Proc. of EMNLP 2002*, pages 281–288.

An Incremental Entity-Mention Model for Coreference Resolution with Restrictive Antecedent Accessibility

Manfred Klenner
University of Zurich
Institute of Computational Linguistics
klenner@cl.uzh.ch

Don Tuggener
University of Zurich
Institute of Computational Linguistics
tuggener@cl.uzh.ch

Abstract

We introduce an incremental entity-mention model for coreference resolution. Our experiments show that it is superior to a non-incremental version in the same environment. The benefits of an incremental architecture are: a reduction of the number of candidate pairs, a means to overcome the problem of underspecified items in pairwise classification and the natural integration of global constraints such as transitivity. Additionally, we have defined a simple salience measure that - coupled with the incremental model - proved to establish a challenging baseline which seems to be on par with machine learning based systems of the 2010's SemEval shared task.

1 Introduction

With notable exceptions (Luo et al., 2004; Yang et al., 2004; Daume III and Marcu, 2005; Culotta et al., 2007; Rahman and Ng, 2009; Cai and Strube, 2010; Raghunathan et al., 2010) supervised approaches to coreference resolution are often realised by pairwise classification of anaphor-antecedent candidates. A popular and often reimplemented approach is presented in (Soon et al., 2001). As recently discussed in (Ng, 2010), the so called mention-pair model suffers from several design flaws which originate from the locally confined perspective of the model:

- Generation of (transitively) redundant pairs, as the formation of coreference sets (coreference clustering) is done after pairwise classification
- Skewed training sets based on pair generation mechanics which lead to classifiers biased towards negative classification
- No means to enforce global constraints such as transitivity
- Underspecification of antecedent candidates

Mention-pair systems operate in a non-incremental mode, i.e. all pairs are classified prior to the construction of the coreference sets. A clustering step is needed where, additionally, inconsistencies (e.g. transitively incompatible pairs) can be removed. This often is realised as an optimisation step, where scores derived from pairwise classification are used as weights in a decision taking process that incorporates linguistic constraints, e.g. (Finkel and Manning, 2008). Although this overcomes the limitations of the strictly local perspective of pairwise classifiers, it still suffers from the problem of unbalanced data (much more negative than positive examples are generated). The large number of candidate pairs, in general, is a problem, e.g. (Wunsch et al., 2009).

These problems can be remedied by an incremental entity-mention model, where candidate pairs are evaluated on the basis of emerging coreference sets. The amount of candidate pairs is reduced, since only one (virtual prototype) example of each coreference set needs to be compared to a new anaphor candidate[1]. Moreover, the problem of inconsistent decisions vanishes, since the virtual prototype of a coreference set bears all the known morphological and semantic information of the elements of the set. If an anaphor candidate is compatible with the prototype then it is compatible with each member of the coreference set. A clustering phase on top of the pairwise classifier no longer is needed.

[1]We are aware of the fact that, linguistically speaking, anaphoric expressions depend on previously mentioned entities (e.g. 'she' → 'Clinton'), whereas coreferent expressions do not always (e.g. 'Hillary Clinton' ... 'United States Secretary of State'). We use the terms 'anaphoric' and 'anaphora' to subsume both relations.

We have compared our incremental entity-mention model to a non-incremental mention-pair version. The memory-based learner TiMBL (Daelemans et al., 2007) was used for pairwise classification. To define a simple baseline, we adopted previous work on salience-based models for coreference resolution. It turns out that our salience measure coupled with the incremental model performs quite well, e.g. it outperformes the systems from the 2010's SemEval shared task on 'coreference resolution in multiple languages' in our own post-task evaluation.

Our system uses real preprocessing (i.e. the use of a parser (Schneider, 2008; Sennrich et al., 2009)) and extracts markables (nouns, named entities and pronouns) from the chunks based on POS tags delivered by the preprocessing pipeline.

We first introduce the incremental model, present constraints on buffer list access, discuss our filtering system and our approximation of the binding theory. We then turn to our simple salience measure initially used as a baseline. In the empirical section, the impact of the incremental entity-mention model on the number of candidate pairs is quantified and a comparison of the variants (incremental, non-incremental etc.) of our German system on the TüBa-D/Z (Naumann, 2006) is given. We also describe our post-task evaluation with the 2010's SemEval data, the results from the BioNLP shared task on coreference resolution in the biomedical domain and our results on the CoNLL 2011 shared task development set.

2 Our Incremental Entity-mention Model

Fig. 1 shows the base algorithm. Let I be the chronologically ordered list of markables, C the set of coreference sets (i.e. the coreference partition) and B a buffer where markables are stored, if they are not anaphoric (but might be valid antecedents). Furthermore, m_i is the current markable and $\oplus$ means concatenation of a list and a single item.

The algorithm proceeds as follows: a set of antecedent candidates is determined for each markable m_i (steps 1 to 7) from the coreference sets (r_j) and the buffer (b_k). A valid candidate r_j or b_k must be compatible with m_i. The definition of compatibility depends on the POS tags of the anaphor-antecedent pair (in order to be coreferent, e.g. two pronouns must agree in person, number and gender, while two nouns, at least in German, need not necessarily agree in gender).

If an antecedent candidate is already in a coreference set (r_j), m_i is compared to the virtual prototype of the set in order to reduce underspecification. The virtual prototype bears information accumulated from all elements of the coreference set. For instance, assume a candidate pair 'Clinton ... she'. Since the gender of 'Clinton' is unspecified, the pair might or might not be a good candidate. But if 'Clinton' is part of a coreference set, let's say: {'Hillary Clinton', 'she', 'her', 'Clinton'} then we can derive the gender from the other members and are more safe in our decision. The virtual prototype here would be: singular, feminine, human.

In languages such as German, where morphological information is much more discriminatory than in English and where at the same time underspecification appears quite often (e.g. the reflexive pronoun 'sich' might refer to any third person noun phrase, be it singular or plural, masculine, feminine or neutral), this is particularly helpful.

If no compatible antecedent candidates are found, m_i is added to the buffer (Step 8). If there are compatible candidates in the candidate list Cand, the most salient $ante_i \in$ Cand (or, in the machine learning setting, the most probable) is selected (step 10) and the coreference partition is augmented (step 11). If $ante_i$ comes from a coreference set, m_i is added to that set. Otherwise ($ante_i$ is from the buffer), a new set is formed, $\{ante_i, m_i\}$, and added to the set of coreference sets.

2.1 Restricted Accessibility of Antecedent Candidates

As already discussed, access to coreference sets is restricted to the virtual prototype - the concrete members are invisible. This reduces the number of considered pairs (from the cardinality of a set to 1).

Moreover, we restrict access to buffer elements: if an antecedent candidate, r_j, from a coreference set exists, then elements from the buffer, b_k, are only licensed if they are more recent than r_j.

Although this rule is heuristic and no evaluation of the impact of different versions of such a 'discourse model' have been carried out yet, we believe that 'accessibility' of antecedent candidates along these lines is a fruitful notion. It might

```
for i=1 to length(I)
    for j=1 to length(C)
        r_j := virtual prototype of coreference set C_j
        Cand := Cand ⊕ r_j if compatible(r_j, m_i)
    for k= length(B) to 1
        b_k:= the k-th licensed buffer element
        Cand := Cand ⊕ b_k if compatible(b_k, m_i)
if Cand = {} then B := B ⊕ m_i
if Cand ≠ {} then
    ante_i := most salient element of Cand
    C := augment(C,ante_i,m_i)
```

Figure 1: Incremental model: base algorithm

lead to cognitively adequate models for coreference resolution, where cognitive burden determines which antecedent candidates are valid at all. Clearly, future work must start with an evaluation of our current setting.

2.2 Filtering and Training Based on Anaphora Type

There is a number of conditions not shown in the basic algorithm in Fig. 1 that define compatibility of antecedent and anaphor candidates based on POS tags: Reflexive pronouns must be bound to the subject governed by the same verb. Relative pronouns are bound to the next NP in the left context. Personal and possessive pronouns are licensed to bind to morphologically compatible antecedent candidates (named entities, nouns[2] and pronouns) within a window of three sentences. Named entities must either match completely or the antecedent must be longer than one token and all tokens of the anaphor must be contained in the antecedent (e.g. 'Hillary Clinton' ... 'Clinton'). Demonstrative NPs are mapped to nominal NPs by matching their heads (e.g. 'The recent findings' ... 'these findings'). Definite NPs match with noun chunks that are longer than one token[3] and must be contained completely without the determiner (e.g. 'Recent events' ... 'the events'). To licence non-matching (bridging) nominal anaphora, we apply hyponymy and synonymy searches in WordNet (Fellbaum, 1998) and GermaNet (Hamp and Feldweg, 1997) respectively.

For the machine learning approaches we used the standard features of mention-pair models (e.g. (Soon et al., 2001)). We trained individual classifiers per anaphora type, i.e. for nominal anaphora, reflexive, possessive, relative and personal pronouns. We manually tuned the feature selection of each classifier. Both the mention-pair and the entity-mention model share these features and filters.

2.3 Binding Theory as a Filter

There is another principle that nicely combines with our incremental model and helps reducing the number of candidates even further: binding theory (e.g. (Büring, 2005)). We know that 'Clinton' and 'her' cannot be coreferent in the sentence 'Clinton met her'. Thus, the pair 'Clinton'-'her' need not be considered at all. Furthermore, all mentions of the 'Clinton' coreference set, say {'Hillary Clinton', she, her, 'Clinton'}, are transitively exclusive and can be discarded as antecedent candidates.

Actually, there are subtle restrictions to be captured here. We have not implemented a full-blown binding theory on top of our dependency parsers. Instead, we approximated binding restrictions by subclause detection. 'Clinton' and 'her' are in the same subclause (the main clause) and are, thus, exclusive. This is true for nouns and personal pronouns, only. Possessive and reflexive pronouns are allowed to be bound in the same subclause.

2.4 An Empirically-based Salience Measure

In the pioneer work of (Lappin and Leass, 1994), salience calculation included manually specified weights for grammatical functions (e.g. *subject* got the highest score). The distance between the candidates and other properties are

[2] To identify animacy and gender of NEs, we use a list of known first names annotated with gender information and look up Wikipedia categories to map NEs to WordNet/GermaNet synsets. To obtain animacy information for common nouns, we conduct a WordNet search.

[3] If we do not apply this restriction, too many false positives are produced - simple head matching appears to be very noisy.

also taken into account in order to determine salience. Such approaches suffered from a proper empirical justification[4]. Consequently, machine-learning approaches have replaced manually designed salience measures. Now it is the classifier that determines 'salience'.

Our salience measure is a variant of the one in (Lappin and Leass, 1994). Instead of manually specifying the weights, we derived them empirically on the basis of the coreference gold standard (for German, this is the coreference annotated treebank TüBa-D/Z ; for English, OntoNotes[5] was used). The salience of a dependency label, D, is estimated by the number of true mentions in the gold standard that bear D (i.e. are connected to their heads with D), divided by the total number of true mentions. The salience of the label *subject* is thus calculated by:

$$\frac{Number\ of\ true\ mentions\ bearing\ subject}{Total\ number\ of\ true\ mentions}$$

For a given dependency label, this fraction indicates how strong is the label a clue for bearing a true mention. We get a hierarchical ordering of the dependency labels (*subject* > *object* > *pobject* ...) according to which antecedent candidates are ranked.

Clearly, future work will have to establish a more elaborate calculation of salience to be used for classification without machine learning. To our surprise, however, this salience measure performed quite well together with our incremental architecture.

3 Evaluation

We evaluate our system in two languages (German and English) and in two domains (newswire text and abstracts from the biomedical domain). We directly compare our incremental entity mention model to the generative mention-pair model on the basis of the German TüBa-D/Z corpus in a 5-fold cross-validation. We also investigate the competitiveness of the incremental model compared to other systems in two tasks and languages: SemEval[6] (English and German) and BioNLP[7] (English). Results of the CoNLL 2011[8] shared task development data (English) are also provided.

[4]There are notable exceptions, e.g. (Ge et al., 1998), where salience calculation is combined with statistics.

[5]http://www.bbn.com/ontonotes/

[6]http://stel.ub.edu/semeval2010-coref/

[7]https://sites.google.com/site/bionlpst/home/protein-gene-coreference-task/

[8]http://conll.bbn.com/

3.1 Reducing the Number of Candidate Pairs

Anaphora Type	Pos	Neg
Mention-pair model (**171526 instances**)		
Nouns	5626	5144
Relative pronouns	1428	2459
Reflexive pronouns	1372	728
Possessive pronouns	**5346**	**21571**
Personal pronouns	**23025**	**104827**
Total	36797	134729
Entity-mention model (**40229 instances**)		
Nouns	1776	3787
Relative pronouns	1382	2330
Reflexive pronouns	462	530
Possessive pronouns	**1416**	**8156**
Personal pronouns	**4023**	**16367**
Total	9059	31170

Figure 2: Number of training instances per anaphora type of Fold 1 of the TüBa-D/Z

Fig. 2 shows the number of training instances of the first fold (about 5'000 sentences) from the TüBa-D/Z both for the incremental and the non-incremental algorithm. Overall a huge reduction by a factor of 4 (-131297 instances, -76.55 %) can be observed when moving from the non-incremental mention-pair to the incremental entity-mention model. As we use the same filter set in all runs, no true mentions are deleted in the incremental approach. The reduction in positives results from pairing an anaphor candidate with only one virtual prototype of the coreference set it belongs to as opposed to redundantly pairing it with all members of its set. As during testing only pairs consisting of the set's virtual prototype and the anaphor candidate are considered, this is sufficient and the additional pairs are not needed. The reduction in negatives results from the same mechanism. Instead of pairing the anaphor with all mentions of a set it does not belong to, only one negative pair with the prototype is generated. Additionally, some pairs are created with compatible members from the buffer list.

The reason for the relatively minor reduction in reflexive and relative pronouns is that the search for antecedents is limited to the same sentence or even a specific (sub-) clause. On the other hand, we allow for possessive and personal pronouns a window of three sentences wherein antecedent candidates may be found. In the latter two cases, the incremental approach to pair generation has a more drastic impact on the number of training instances (-64.44%, -84.05% resp.).

3.2 TüBa-D/Z Model Comparison

We can see from the results (Fig. 3) that the incremental entity-mention model outperforms the mention-pair model. The entity-mention model with the TiMBL classifier performed best by improving recall (+ 7.01%) and losing some precision (- 0.79%) compared to the mention-pair model. To our surprise, the simple salience approach performed quite well, losing only 0.85% precision and 1.88% recall compared to its machine learning variant. Given that bridging anaphora is not resolved in the salience mode, a reduction in recall was to be expected. It still outperforms the mention-pair model that implements machine learning.

Model	F1	P	R
Mention-pair (TiMBL + ILP)	49.35	53.67	45.69
Entity-mention (TiMBL)	52.79	52.88	52.70
Entity-mention (salience)	51.41	52.03	50.82

Figure 3: CEAF scores of the 5-fold TüBa-D/Z cross-validation

Overall the results of the TüBa-D/Z evaluation are low, indicating that end-to-end coreference resolution with real preprocessing is still a difficult problem. It is important to note that we implemented a version of the CEAF metric which does not account for singletons (i.e. coreference sets with only one mention) because we believe that finding singletons is not a crucial part of the coreference resolution task and that it improves results artificially. We can see the difference of evaluating with or without singletons if we compare these results with the ones from SemEval (Fig. 5), where singletons are considered in the evaluation process. The SemEval German task also uses data from the TüBa-D/Z , allowing an approximate comparison of the results to illustrate the effects of considering singletons in evaluation. The CEAF F1-measure of our incremental model reaches 76.8% on the SemEval data (Fig. 5), while without singletons, we reach 52.79% in the TüBa-D/Z evaluation (Fig. 3).

3.3 Error Analysis

We simulated perfect resolution of the individual classifiers of the best performing system (Entity-mention(TiMBL)) from the model comparison (Fig. 4). We ran the system on the first fold (ca. 5000 sentences) of the TüBa-D/Z , resolving one type of anaphora (e.g. nominal anaphora) using gold standard information per run, while the other anaphora types were resolved by the system.This gives us an indication of the upper bounds of the system: How good would our system be, if it resolved e.g. nominal anaphora perfectly?

with filters means that only pairs that pass the filters are resolved. In the *without filters* mode, all pairs of the corresponding anaphora type are resolved correctly, disregarding filter decisions. The other anaphora types are resolved by the system in both modes. The difference in performance between the *with* and *without filtering* mode indicates how good our filters are: the smaller the difference, the better the filters (compare values horizontally). The performance difference of the individual classifiers with perfect resolution compared to the overall system performance (right column, compare vertically) indicates the difficulty of resolving that anaphora type.

For example, in the first row that indicates resolution performances of nominal anaphora we can see that we roughly lose 10% in F1 measure due to our nominal filters (72.70% - 62.61%). Compared to the actual system performance in the last row in the right column (53.86%) we see that we lose an additional 9% in F1 measure because of imperfect resolution of nominal anaphora (62.61% - 53.86%). This sums up to a total loss of 19% in F1 measure compared to system performance with perfect resolution of nominal anaphora. Compared to the minor difference of 1.8% F1 measure between perfect and imperfect resolution of reflexive pronouns (-1.5% through filtering and -0.3% through imperfect classification) the difficulty of resolving nominal anaphora becomes obvious.

3.4 SemEval 2010, BioNLP 2011 and CoNLL 2011

To get an indication of the competitiveness of our incremental approach we carried out evaluations over recent shared task data sets. The SemEval coreference task (Recasens et al., 2010) focused on coreference resolution in multiple languages and comparing different evaluation metrics. The test data for German was composed of the TüBa-D/Z whereas the English data was gathered from the OntoNotes corpus.

The main goal of the BioNLP protein/gene coreference task was to resolve non-name-containing mentions in protein/gene-interactions to their appropriate name-containing antecedents

	Without filtering			With filtering		
	F1	Precision	Recall	F1	Precision	Recall
Nouns	**72.70**	69.53	76.17	**62.61**	63.70	61.55
Personal pronouns	60.42	62.05	58.88	58.86	60.64	57.19
Relative pronouns	56.25	57.91	54.68	55.97	57.65	54.39
Possessive pronouns	56.06	57.35	54.82	55.81	57.18	54.51
Reflexive pronouns	55.68	57.11	54.32	54.16	55.64	52.77
System	-	-	-	**53.86**	54.64	53.09

Figure 4: CEAF scores for the simulation of perfect classification (upper bounds) of the individual classifiers for the first 5000 sentences of the TüBa-D/Z .

and thereby improving overall recall of interaction extraction (i.e. the main task). The test data consists of abstracts gathered from PubMed.

As the SemEval training data for English and German were not available at the time of our post-task experiments, we were only able to evaluate the salience based classification.

The SemEval coreference task offers many different settings. Since we are interested in real end-to-end coreference resolution we evaluated the *open/regular* setting, meaning that real preprocessing components are used as opposed to perfect gold standard preprocessing data. Results of the SemEval task are given in Figure 5.

Except for the (recently questioned, e.g. (Luo, 2005; Cai and Strube, 2010)) MUC metric in the English evaluation, the incremental model (incr) achieved best results throughout the SemEval experiments in both languages. All other systems that competed in the task implemented a mention-pair model. Overall, an improvement can be observed compared to the other systems, mainly in precision.

The simple salience based measure is not suited for resolving bridging anaphora. Therefore, bridging anaphora was not resolved by the system in these experiments (but still included in the evaluation) which might be a reason for the relatively low recall.

More recently, we have adapted our salience-based incremental architecture to the biomedical domain. Our results in the recent BioNLP 2011 shared task are competitive as well (see Fig. 6).

The results of our evaluation over the CoNLL 2011 shared task development set are given in Fig. 7. CEAF and BCUB scores are considerably lower compared to the SemEval results. We believe these differences originate from the updated scoring algorithms for CEAF and BCUB. They were modified for the CoNLL scorer according to suggestions by (Cai and Strube, 2010). The CoNLL scorer has stricter mention boundary handling than the SemEval scorer. Moreover, singletons were not marked in the CoNLL data.

Team	R	P	F1
A	22.18	73.26	34.05
incr	21.48	55.45	30.96
B	19.37	63.22	29.65
C	14.44	67.21	23.77
D	3.17	3.47	3.31
E	0.70	0.25	0.37

Figure 6: BioNLP 2011 Protein/Gene Coreference Task Results

Metric	R	P	F1
CEAFM	51.08	51.08	51.08
CEAFE	44.35	39.93	42.03
BCUB	60.91	70.69	65.44
BLANC	63.63	72.58	66.81
MUC	45.18	49.83	47.39

Figure 7: CoNLL 2011 Development Set Results

4 Related Work

The work of (Soon et al., 2001) is a prototypical and often re-implemented (baseline) model that is based on pairwise classification and machine learning. Our non-incremental mention-pair model can be seen as an adaption of this system and its features. Coreference clustering is discussed e.g. in (Denis and Baldridge, 2009; Finkel and Manning, 2008). Our mention-pair model uses the Balas algorithm for clustering as discussed in (Klenner, 2007).

Direct empirical comparison of supervised mention-pair and entity-mention models can be found in e.g. (Luo et al., 2004; Yang et al., 2004; Rahman and Ng, 2009). Only in (Rahman and Ng, 2009) a clear improvement by the entity-mention model is observed. Other supervised entity-mention models such as (Daume III and Marcu, 2005; Culotta et al., 2007; Raghunathan et al., 2010) are not directly compared to

System	CEAF R	CEAF P	CEAF F1	MUC R	MUC P	MUC F1	BCUB R	BCUB P	BCUB F1	BLANC R	BLANC P	BLANC F1
German, open regular												
bart	61.4	61.2	61.3	**61.4**	36.1	45.5	75.3	58.3	65.7	**55.9**	60.3	57.3
incr	**76.8**	**70.4**	**73.4**	50.4	**47.1**	**48.7**	**81.7**	**75.6**	**78.5**	55	**72.6**	**57.8**
English, open regular												
bart	70.1	64.3	67.1	**62.8**	52.4	57.1	74.9	67.7	71.1	55.3	73.2	57.7
corry-b	70.4	67.4	68.9	55.0	54.2	54.6	73.7	74.1	73.9	57.1	75.7	60.6
corry-c	**70.9**	67.9	69.4	54.7	55.5	55.1	73.8	73.1	73.5	57.4	63.8	59.4
corry-m	66.3	63.5	64.8	61.5	53.4	**57.2**	**76.8**	66.5	71.3	**58.5**	56.2	57.1
incr	67.6	**73**	**70.2**	34	**62.5**	44.1	66.7	**86**	**75.1**	57.1	**78.4**	**61.1**

Figure 5: Our SemEval 2010 post-task evaluation results

mention-pair models. Also, in the recent SemEval 2010 and BioNLP 2011 shared tasks no entity-mention models participated.

Our work differs from the research mentioned above as it focuses on using an incremental entity-mention architecture to impose constraints on candidate pair generation as opposed to generating cluster-level features for (machine learning-based) classification. Our hypothesis, also for future work, is that progress is possible by not only improving classifier performance but by improving other steps of the coreference resolution pipeline that lead up to the classifier, namely pair generation and antecedent candidate accessibility.

5 Conclusions

We have introduced an incremental entity-mention algorithm for coreference resolution and evaluated its impact on pair generation and the performance of architectural variants. A performance comparison of our model to systems from different shared tasks produced good results. We also discussed a simple and very fast salience-based approach that performed quite well, i.e. it outperformed all systems of the 2010's SemEval shared task.

The benefits of an incremental model are:

- due to the restricted access to potential antecedent candidates, the number of generated candidate pairs can be reduced drastically
- no additional coreference clustering is necessary
- global constraints (e.g. transitivity) are easily integrated
- underspecification of antecedent candidates can often be compensated by other members of the emerging coreference sets

Our theory on how to restrict the accessibility of antecedent candidates has proven to be (empirically) successful, as it outperformed other systems. However, we are aware of the fact that we need to explore in a more principled and empirically grounded way, what the parameters of such an evolving discourse model are. We strive for a theory whose decisions, in the best case, relate to the restrictions of human cognitive capacity.

Finally, our implementation of a binding theory is incomplete. Since binding theory provides hard restrictions, it is a crucial component of any theory on antecedent accessibility.

Web demos of the salience based system for English and German are available[9].

Acknowledgements. Our project is funded by the Swiss National Science Foundation (grant 105211-118108). We are grateful to OntoGene[10] for their help and advice regarding the BioNLP shared task.

References

Daniel Büring. 2005. *Binding Theory*. Cambridge Textbooks in Linguistics. Cambridge University Press, Cambridge.

Jie Cai and Michael Strube. 2010. Evaluation metrics for end-to-end coreference resolution systems. In *Proceedings of the 11th Annual Meeting of the Special Interest Group on Discourse and Dialogue*, SIGDIAL '10, pages 28–36, Stroudsburg, PA, USA. Association for Computational Linguistics.

Aron Culotta, Michael Wick, and Andrew McCallum. 2007. First-order probabilistic models for coreference resolution. In *HLT '07: The Conference of the North American Chapter of ACL; Proceedings of the Main Conference*, pages 81–88, Rochester, New York, April. Association for Computational Linguistics.

[9] http://kitt.cl.uzh.ch/kitt/coref/

[10] http://www.ontogene.org/

Walter Daelemans, Jakub Zavrel, Ko van der Sloot, and Antal van den Bosch. 2007. Timbl: Tilburg memory-based learner. Technical report, Induction of Linguistic Knowledge, Tilburg University and CNTS Research Group, University of Antwerp.

Hal Daume III and Daniel Marcu. 2005. A large-scale exploration of effective global features for a joint entity detection and tracking model. In *HLT '05: Proceedings of the conference on Human Language Technology and Empirical Methods in Natural Language Processing*, pages 97–104, Morristown, NJ, USA. Association for Computational Linguistics.

Pascal Denis and Jason Baldridge. 2009. Global joint models for coreference resolution and named entity classification. In *Procesamiento del Lenguaje Natural 42*, pages 87–96, Barcelona: SEPLN.

Christiane Fellbaum. 1998. *WordNet: An Electronic Lexical Database (Language, Speech, and Communication)*. The MIT Press, May.

Jenny Rose Finkel and Christopher D. Manning. 2008. Enforcing transitivity in coreference resolution. In *HLT '08: Proceedings of the 46th Annual Meeting of the ACL on Human Language Technologies*, pages 45–48, Morristown, NJ, USA. Association for Computational Linguistics.

Niye Ge, John Hale, and Eugene Charniak. 1998. A statistical approach to anaphora resolution. In *Proceedings of the Sixth Workshop on Very Large Corpora*, pages 161–171, Montreal, Canada.

Birgit Hamp and Helmut Feldweg. 1997. GermaNet – a lexical-semantic net for German. In *Proceedings of ACL workshop Automatic Information Extraction and Building of Lexical Semantic Resources for NLP Applications*, pages 9–15, Somerset, NJ, USA. Association for Computational Linguistics.

Manfred Klenner. 2007. Enforcing consistency on coreference sets. In *Proceedings of the International Conference on Recent Advances in Natural Language Processing*, pages 323–328, Borovets, Bulgaria.

Shalom Lappin and Herbert J Leass. 1994. An algorithm for pronominal anaphora resolution. *Computational Linguistics*, 20:535–561.

Xiaoqiang Luo, Abe Ittycheriah, Hongyan Jing, Nanda Kambhatla, and Salim Roukos. 2004. A mention-synchronous coreference resolution algorithm based on the bell tree. In *Proceedings of the 42nd Annual Meeting of ACL*, ACL '04, Stroudsburg, PA, USA. Association for Computational Linguistics.

Xiaoqiang Luo. 2005. On coreference resolution performance metrics. In *HLT '05: Proceedings of the conference on Human Language Technology and Empirical Methods in Natural Language Processing*, pages 25–32, Morristown, NJ, USA. Association for Computational Linguistics.

Karin Naumann. 2006. *Manual for the Annotation of Indocument Referential Relations*. SFS (Seminar für Sprachwissenschaft), http://www.sfs.uni-tuebingen.de/tuebadz.shtml.

Vincent Ng. 2010. Supervised noun phrase coreference research: the first fifteen years. In *Proceedings of the 48th Annual Meeting of ACL*, ACL '10, pages 1396–1411, Stroudsburg, PA, USA. Association for Computational Linguistics.

Karthik Raghunathan, Heeyoung Lee, Sudarshan Rangarajan, Nathanael Chambers, Mihai Surdeanu, Dan Jurafsky, and Christopher Manning. 2010. A multi-pass sieve for coreference resolution. In *Proceedings of the 2010 Conference on Empirical Methods in Natural Language Processing*, EMNLP '10, pages 492–501, Stroudsburg, PA, USA. Association for Computational Linguistics.

Altaf Rahman and Vincent Ng. 2009. Supervised models for coreference resolution. In *Proceedings of the 2009 Conference on Empirical Methods in Natural Language Processing: Volume 2 - Volume 2*, EMNLP '09, pages 968–977, Stroudsburg, PA, USA. Association for Computational Linguistics.

Marta Recasens, Lluís Màrquez, Emili Sapena, M. Antònia Martí, Mariona Taulé, Véronique Hoste, Massimo Poesio, and Yannick Versley. 2010. Semeval-2010 task 1: Coreference resolution in multiple languages. In *Proceedings of the 5th International Workshop on Semantic Evaluation*, SemEval '10, pages 1–8, Stroudsburg, PA, USA. Association for Computational Linguistics.

Gerold Schneider. 2008. *Hybrid Long-Distance Functional Dependency Parsing*. Doctoral Thesis, Institute of Computational Linguistics, Univ. of Zurich.

Rico Sennrich, Gerold Schneider, Martin Volk, and Martin Warin. 2009. A New Hybrid Dependency Parser for German. In *Proc. of the German Society for Computational Linguistics and Language Technology 2009 (GSCL 2009)*, pages 115–124, Potsdam, Germany.

Wee M. Soon, Hwee T. Ng, and Daniel. 2001. A machine learning approach to coreference resolution of noun phrases. *Computational Linguistics*, 27(4):521–544, December.

Holger Wunsch, Sandra Kübler, and Rachael Cantrell. 2009. Instance sampling methods for pronoun resolution. In *Proceedings of Proceedings of the International Conference on Recent Advances in Natural Language Processing*, Borovets, Bulgaria.

Xiaofeng Yang, Jian Su, Guodong Zhou, and Chew Lim Tan. 2004. An np-cluster based approach to coreference resolution. In *Proceedings of the 20th International Conference on Computational Linguistics*, COLING '04, Stroudsburg, PA, USA. Association for Computational Linguistics.

Cross-Domain Dutch Coreference Resolution

Orphée De Clercq, Véronique Hoste
LT3, Language and Translation Technology Team
University College Ghent
Groot-Brittannielaan 45
B - 9000 Gent, Belgium
orphee.declercq@hogent.be
veronique.hoste@hogent.be

Iris Hendrickx
Centre of Linguistics
University of Lisbon
Av. Prof. Gama Pinto, 2
1649-003 Lisbon, Portugal
iris@clul.ul.pt

Abstract

This article explores the portability of a coreference resolver across a variety of eight text genres. Besides newspaper text, we also include administrative texts, autocues, texts used for external communication, instructive texts, wikipedia texts, medical texts and unedited new media texts. Three sets of experiments were conducted. First, we investigated each text genre individually, and studied the effect of larger training set sizes and including genre-specific training material. Then, we explored the predictive power of each genre for the other genres conducting cross-domain experiments. In a final step, we investigated whether excluding genres with less predictive power increases overall performance. For all experiments we use an existing Dutch mention-pair resolver and report on our experimental results using four metrics: MUC, B-cubed, CEAF and BLANC. We show that resolving out-of-domain genres works best when enough training data is included. This effect is further intensified by including a small amount of genre-specific text. As far as the cross-domain performance is concerned we see that especially genres of a very specific nature tend to have less generalization power.

1 Introduction

Coreference resolution is the task of automatically recognizing which words or expressions refer to the same discourse entity in a particular text or dialogue.[1] In the last decade considerable efforts have been put in annotating corpora with coreferential relations. Not only a widespread language such as English (e.g. *ACE-2* (Doddington et al., 2004), *ARRAU* (Poesio and Artstein, 2008), *OntoNotes 3.0* (Weischedel et al., 2009)), but also Czech (*PDT 2.0* (Kučová and Hajičová, 2004)), Catalan (*AnCora-Ca* (Recasens and Martí, 2010)) and Italian (*I-CAB* (Magnini et al., 2006))[2] can now rely on substantial resources for coreference research.

One of the challenges in many current NLP tasks is to test their portability across different domains and languages. This portability to other languages was the main objective of the SemEval 2010 Task on Coreference Resolution in Multiple Languages (Recasens et al., 2010). The issue of domain portability was the focus of the ACL 2010 Workshop on Domain Adaptation for NLP (Daumé III et al., 2010).

In this paper we investigate the performance of an existing mention-pair coreference resolver for Dutch (Hoste, 2005; Hendrickx et al., 2008b) across various text genres. More specifically we want to know whether training on out-of-domain data can be done without performance loss. The above-mentioned corpora designed for coreference resolution consist almost exclusively of text from the same genre, i.e. newspaper texts, and as a consequence resulting coreference resolvers are mostly trained on this particular genre. Moreover, when other genres are included, the acquired data are rather scarce: 25K of dialogues in *ARRAU* (Poesio and Artstein, 2008), 23K manuals in *AnATar* (Hammami et al., 2009) or 50K of annotated blogs in *LiveMemories* (Rodríguez et al., 2010). Another related study is the work of Longo and Todirascu (2010). They analyzed a French corpus (50K) consisting of 5 different text genres to develop genre-specific features; in their study

[1] In this article we only discuss nominal coreference, i.e. which coreferential relations exist between noun phrases (common and proper nouns, pronouns).

[2] For a more complete overview we refer to (Recasens, 2010) and (Poesio et al., forthcoming)

they use genre-specific features such as average length of the coreferential chain and average distance separating several mentions of the same referent. An exception to this observation of small datasets is the new OntoNotes 4.0 corpus that is used for the CoNLL 2011 Shared Task on unrestricted coreference resolution, as the corpus contains approximately 1 million words from 5 different text genres.[3] We do see a growing interest in one specific different text genre, namely biomedical text in many NLP tasks, including coreference resolution (e.g Yang et al. (2004), Gasperin and Briscoe (2008), Ngan Nguyen and Tsujii (2008)).

The data for the experiments come from three Dutch corpus projects in which coreference was annotated: COREA (Hendrickx et al., 2008a), DuOMAn (Hendrickx and Hoste, 2009) and SoNaR (Schuurman et al., 2010)[4]. Combining these three resources allows us to work with diverse data spread over different text genres. Another advantage is that all data was annotated following the same approach: first all NPs were pre-tagged based on syntactic dependency structures (Bouma and Kloostermans, 2007) and secondly the COREA guidelines (Bouma et al., 2007) were reused in each project. Though the emphasis in this study is on edited text, we also include unedited text, viz. blogs and news comments (Hendrickx and Hoste, 2009). With this cross-domain portability study, we aim to see which genres perform better or worse and whether it is possible to determine a priori which training data to add to our resolver so as to obtain better results. The results are presented using four of the more frequently used evaluation metrics for coreference research, namely MUC (Vilain et al., 1995), B-cubed (Bagga and Baldwin, 1998), CEAF (Luo and Zitouni, 2005) and BLANC (Recasens and Hovy, 2011).

We show that adding more data to training proves mostly beneficial, especially when genre-specific information is included. Moreover, training a resolver on each genre separately allows us to classify each genre as having good or bad generalization power when applied to other genres. This led us to conduct experiments in which we train on all genres while progressively leaving out the worst-performing cross-domain genres as an attempt to boost overall performance. Although the results are sometimes better, performance does not rise nor drop dramatically. We show that inclusion of some genre-specific training material is necessary, especially when less generalizable genres are to be labeled. However, most effect is perceived by adding more data to training.

The remainder of this paper is organized as follows. In Section 2, we present the datasets and experimental setup of our system and briefly discuss the different evaluation metrics. In Section 3 the results are presented and analyzed, and we report on our experience with the different evaluation metrics. Section 4 concludes this paper by formulating some conclusions and prospects for future work.

2 Datasets and Experimental Setup

In the present study, we aim to investigate the cross-genre portability of an existing mention-pair coreference resolver for Dutch. In order to do so, our system's performance was compared on eight datasets: administrative texts (ADM), autocues (AUTO), texts used for external communication (EXT), instructive texts (INST), journalistic texts (JOUR), medical texts (MED), wikipedia (WIKI), and unedited text (DUO). All data were manually annotated using the COREA guidelines (Bouma et al., 2007). These guidelines allow for the annotation of four relations and special cases are flagged. The four annotated relations are identity (NPs referring to the same discourse entity), bound (expressing properties of general categories), bridge (as in part-whole, superset-subset relations) and predicative. The following special cases were flagged: negations and expressions of modality, time-dependency and identity of sense (as in the so-called paycheck pronouns (Karttunen, 1976)). As annotation environment, the MMAX2 annotation software [5] was used.

To rule out data size as a possible explanation for performance shifts, datasets of equal size (about 30K) were randomly selected. The focus of the current experiments was on resolving identity and predicative relations. Table 1 gives some statistics about each dataset, such as the average sentence length and the number of coreferring NPs.

For all experiments we used an existing coreference resolver for Dutch, developed by Hoste (2005) and Hendrickx et al. (2008b). The system

[3]Website from CoNLL 2011: http://conll.bbn.com

[4]SoNaR is currently still under development.

[5]http://mmax2.net

follows a machine learning approach[6] based on the seminal work of Soon et al. (2001) and represents a mention-pair model. First, a classifier is trained to decide whether a pair of NPs is coreferential or not, after which coreference chains are built for the pairs of NPs that were classified as coreferential.

	#docs	#tokens	avg. senl	#coref NP
ADM	21	30,215	18.1	2,403
AUTO	15	30,058	14.6	2,411
EXT	29	29,940	15.9	2,381
INST	18	29,994	17.5	3,024
MED	213	30,001	14.4	1,995
JOUR	52	30,002	18.2	2,472
WIKI	15	30,340	18.9	3,480
DUO	56	29,740	19.7	3,063

Table 1: Size and number of coreferring NPs per dataset

All datasets were preprocessed in the same way. Tokenisation, lemmatisation, Part-of-Speech tagging and grammatical relations were based on the manually verified output of the Alpino parser (Bouma et al., 2001), i.e. gold standard dependency structures. For the DuOMAn data, however, no gold standard dependency trees were available. Named entity recognition was performed using MBT (Daelemans et al., 2003), trained on the 2002 CoNNL shared task Dutch dataset (Tjong Kim Sang, 2002) and an additional gazetteer lookup. As features we employ string matching, distance between sentences and NPs, grammatical role and named entity overlap, synonym/hypernym lookup using Cornetto (a Dutch database combining Dutch Wordnet (Vossen, 1998) and the Referentie Bestand Nederlands (Martin and Ploeger, 1999)) and local context. All instances were built between NP pairs going 20 sentences back in context. NPs that are not part of a coreferential chain (*singletons*) are included as negative examples. For more information we refer to Hoste (2005) and Hendrickx et al. (2008a).

Since the focus of this study is on genre, we decided not to train on different NP types (pronouns, common nouns and proper names) individually.[7] For all experiments we used Timbl version 6.3 (Daelemans et al., 2010) with default parameter settings.

Our experimental results are evaluated using the four scoring metrics as implemented in the scoring script from the coreference resolution task from the SemEval-2010 competition (Recasens et al., 2010):

- The MUC scoring software (Vilain et al., 1995) counts the number of links between the coreferential elements in the text, and looks how many links are shared or not between the gold standard coreferential chains and the system predictions. As MUC concentrates on links, elements that are not part of a coreferential chain, entities that are only mentioned once (*singletons*), are not taken into account in this scoring method.

- The B-cubed measure (Bagga and Baldwin, 1998) does not consider mere links between elements, but takes into account the coreferential clusters of elements referring to the same entity. B-cubed computes for every individual element in the text the precision and recall by counting how many elements are in the true coreferential cluster and how many in the predicted coreferential cluster.

- The CEAF measure (Luo and Zitouni, 2005) focuses on a one-to-one mapping of elements in the true and predicted coreferential clusters. Both B-cubed and CEAF measures are sensitive to the presence of many singletons, the larger the percentage of singletons, the higher these scores become (Recasens and Hovy, 2011).

- Recently, the BLANC measure (Recasens and Hovy, 2011) was developed to overcome problems with the other scoring methods. This measure is a variant of the Rand Index (Rand, 1971) adapted for coreference resolution and it averages over a score for correctly detecting singletons, and a score for detecting the correct cluster for coreferential elements.

An important remark to make here is that our system does not take into account chains of only one element. As a consequence, contrary to the SemEval-2010 competition, when we compute

[6] For an extensive overview of the different machine learning approaches for coreference resolution, we refer to the surveys of Ng (2010) and Poesio et al. (forthcoming)

[7] Hoste (2005) built a separate learning module for each of these NP types based on the motivation that the impact of different information sources varies per NP type.

	TRAIN	TEST
1.	one genre	that genre
	all genres but one	left out genre
	all genres	one genre
2.	one genre	other genres
3.	all LOO outliers	one genre

Table 2: Three sets of experiments

our scoring metrics, a singleton that is erroneously classified as part of a coreference chain is counted as an error. When it is correctly classified as a singleton, however, this is not represented in the scores.

In order to test cross-genre portability, we ran three sets of experiments (Table 2):

1. In the first set of experiments, we wanted to investigate whether adding more data is beneficial for the classifier. We trained the classifier on each genre individually and compared performance with different training set sizes. Three experiments were conducted: we first trained on each individual genre and tested on the relevant genre using ten-fold cross validation (each fold 27K vs. 3K). In a second experiment, the classifier was trained on all genres except one and tested on the one that was left out (210K vs. 30K). In a third experiment, we used all data, including genre-specific training material for training the classifier, in a ten-fold cross validation set-up (each fold 237K vs. 3K).

2. In a second set of experiments, we focused on the actual cross-domain portability. In order to test this, we each time trained on one genre and tested the performance of the classifier for each of the other genres.

3. Based on the results obtained in the second batch of experiments, we investigated whether some particular genres actually decrease performance when training on all data. In other words, does excluding outlier genres from training data increase performance? This was done by each time leaving out the worst-performing cross-domain genres and performing ten-fold cross validation.

3 Results

The results of the first round of experiments are presented in Figure 1. The dots marked as *individual* present the experiments in which each classifier was trained and tested on the same material. The scores for *All-individual* present experiments in which the classifiers are trained on a large and diverse training set of all different genres except the genre that is held out as a test set. The last experiments in the graph *All+individual* show the result when training on all genres including the held-out genre. Though the B-cubed and CEAF scores are lower than MUC, they present the same tendency: adding more and diverse training material improves performance, especially when genre-specific information is also included.[8] BLANC, however, seems to contradict the other metrics. Though the scores are higher, they reveal that larger training data proves only beneficial for three genres: INST, JOUR and MED. BLANC thus suggests that training only on in-domain material of some genre is the best approach.

This brings us to the cross-genre experiments, where we each time train on one genre and test on all the other genres individually until all genres have been once used as training data.[9] In order to represent the results, we ranked the classifier performance on each genre, ranging from the genre-classifier which on average performs worst when being applied to the other genres to the one performing best. We performed this ranking for each of the four evaluation metrics. The final ranking is visualized in Table 3. Although there are some differences between the metrics -we again observe that BLANC tends to differ more from the others - they all seem to agree that MED (medical text), DUO (unedited text) and INST (instructive text) constitute poor cross-genre training material. JOUR has been selected by MUC, B3 and CEAF as the best material for training on other genres. As we mentioned in Section 1 that most of the currently available datasets annotated with coreferential information consist of newspaper text, this result shows that this might indeed be a good choice.

The four metrics confirmed that three genres had less generalization power, viz. MED, DUO and INST. In the third experiment, we aim to op-

[8]Because of space constraints we only incorporated two graphs in this paper.

[9]Train on ADM = test on AUTO; train on ADM test on DUO;....

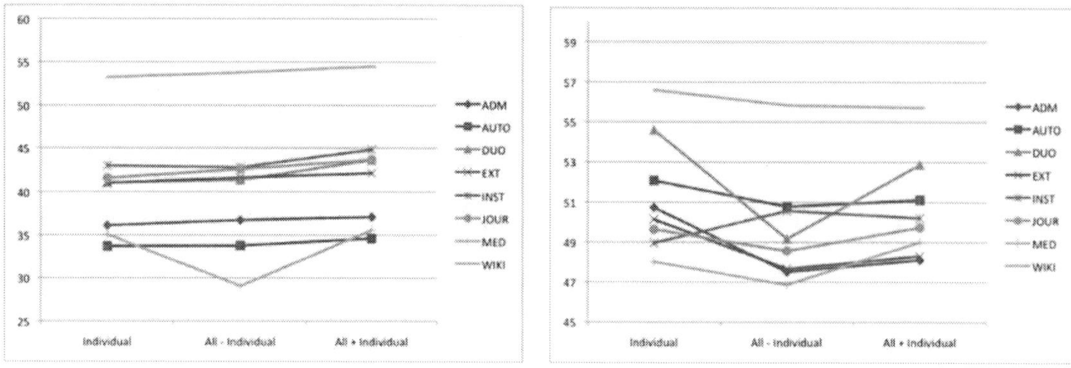

(a) MUC F-measure

(b) BLANC F-measure

Figure 1: Performance comparison for each genre when training only on the genre, all the other genres, or both, respectively

MUC	B3	CEAF	BLANC
MED	MED	MED	MED
DUO	DUO	DUO	DUO
INST	INST	INST	INST
EXT	EXT	EXT	JOUR
WIKI	AUTO	AUTO	ADM
AUTO	ADM	ADM	AUTO
ADM	WIKI	WIKI	EXT
JOUR	JOUR	JOUR	WIKI

Table 3: Comparison of the worst (top) to best-performing (bottom) cross-domain genres per metric.

timize our selection of training data to get the best possible general performance. We hypothesize that leaving out those genres with less predictive power for other genres from the training material will increase overall performance. In this set of experiments we train on all data, including genre-specific information, and test on one genre while progressively leaving out those three genres. The results of this *reversed learning curve* for all metrics can be found in Table 4. Whenever a score is printed in bold, it is the best score obtained for a particular genre.

It is difficult to compare the different metrics with each other. We observe that only the BLANC metric confirms our expectation that the results are almost always better when poor training material is excluded from training. The results as measured with the other 3 metrics, however, show that leaving out data is only beneficial for half of the datasets. Overall, these results do not strongly confirm our hypothesis. An important observation to make is that, for all metrics, the performance gains which are obtained by leaving out data are modest, the effect of removing data is very small. Based on these observations we conclude that to get good generalization performance it is more important to have a large training set than to put time and effort in the composition of this training set.

3.1 Error Analysis

Three genres, viz. MED, DUO and INST, did not score high in the cross-domain experiments and were the first genres to be left out in the final experiments. An error analysis on this data imposed itself. Looking at the data itself we see that MED includes data of a scientific nature consisting of various entries in a medical encyclopedia. DUO contains mostly user-generated text as it consists of texts from blogs and newspaper articles together with a large set of reader comments. This type of data is rather different from the other genres as it is unedited, subjective, informal and more similar to spoken language than the other genres. INST contains various patient information leaflets and manuals in which exactly the same sentences are often repeated with only one word – mostly the name of the product – different. The above observations already hint at the low generalizability of these three genres.

Compared to the other genres, who on average contain 25% of coreferential NPs, we note that MED and INST contain a high number of coreferential NPs (respectively 33% and 37%) and DUO a rather low amount (viz. 18%). Looking at the data statistics given in Table 1, we observe that MED slightly differs from the others: it consists

Train \ Test	ADM	AUTO	DUO	EXT	INST	JOUR	MED	WIKI
MUC								
ALL	37.10	34.61	**43.61**	42.09	**44.81**	43.63	**35.57**	**54.48**
1MinMED	37.26	34.41	43.56	42.01	44.61	44.03		54.07
2MinDUO	**37.39**	**34.85**		**42.29**	44.51	**44.56**	35.44	54.35
3MinINST	37.06	34.00	31.02	41.81		44.46	34.72	54.21
B-cubed								
ALL	27.83	**29.77**	31.45	**30.64**	**31.66**	31.23	**26.08**	**30.84**
1MinMED	27.74	29.64	**31.68**	30.18	**31.66**	31.34		30.46
2MinDUO	**28.02**	29.46		30.11	31.26	**31.81**	25.99	30.58
3MinINST	27.87	29.54	31.02	30.01		31.61	25.18	30.64
CEAF								
ALL	29.48	**30.61**	29.79	**31.36**	28.42	31.42	**29.49**	26.31
1MinMED	29.11	30.33	29.96	30.26	**28.47**	30.86		**26.40**
2MinDUO	**29.73**	29.51		30.09	28.12	**31.62**	29.33	25.99
3MinINST	29.58	30.48	**22.97**	29.16		30.93	28.20	25.14
BLANC								
ALL	48.10	51.11	52.87	48.29	50.21	49.74	**49.01**	55.73
1MinMED	48.49	51.37	**54.70**	48.51	50.72	49.55		**56.66**
2MinDUO	48.73	51.49		48.73	**51.01**	**50.37**	48.15	56.11
3MinINST	**49.71**	**51.59**	54.16	**50.88**		49.61	48.49	56.17

Table 4: Results of the third set of experiments for all metrics and in comparison with training on all data.

of 213 smaller documents and the average sentence length is shorter, viz. 14.4 words. Moreover, looking at the subdivision of NPs we see that MED contains a large number of common nouns (89%) and only few pronouns (5%) and proper nouns (6%). In the other five datasets, this division ranges between 70-75% common nouns and 10-15% pronouns and proper nouns. When using MED as training data this results in a higher number of introduced errors between common nouns. Especially when no string matching features are found between two common nouns the resolver has a lot of difficulty into correctly classifying them. Of all genres we see that with MED pronouns and proper nouns are harder to recognize, which can be explained by their low coverage in the training data. Having a closer look at the DUO dataset, we see that the division between common, proper and pronouns is 64% - 14% - 22% – which is a high number of pronouns. Counterintuitively, this does not mean that resolving pronouns goes better when training on DUO. On the contrary,we see that although the resolution of pronouns rises slightly, more errors are introduced. Dutch pronouns also turned out to be difficult to resolve according to Hoste (2005) because of the inability to distinguish between anaphoric and pleonastic pronouns. The NP subdivision in INST is comparable to the five other genres, with a small preference for proper nouns. The high amount of reoccurring sentences in the data is also reflected in the features, the INST dataset scored best when performing in-domain experiments because of the many exact matches. Furthermore, as many technical NPs are not covered by WordNet (and these semantic features are crucial for most genres), important links between two NPs are missed.

In sum, these three genres have very specific features that seem to make them less predictive for other genres.

4 Conclusion

In this paper we explored the portability of an existing coreference resolver for Dutch when applied to eight different text genres: administrative texts, autocues, texts used for external communication, instructive texts, journalistic texts, medical texts, wikipedia and unedited new media texts. By comparing the performance on three sets of experiments, we found that larger training set size improves performance, especially when genre-specific training material (10%) is included. We saw that excluding poor cross-genre training material does not always results in better scores neither can a drop in performance be perceived. This might imply that training on more data with higher predictive power is more important than training on various text genres. This is something we definitely wish to look into in closer detail in future work. Moreover, we would like to find out how much genre-specific training data is exactly needed to optimize performance. We discovered that especially genres containing very specific (e.g. scientific or unedited) data and having a different subdivision between pronouns, common and proper nous are less equipped for cross-genre experiments and thus have less generalization power.

We also observe that the different evaluation metrics for coreference research in use today, (MUC, B-cubed, CEAF and BLANC) tend to contradict each other and as a consequence hamper interpretation. This is a well-known problem within the community for which no solution has been found yet. In order to allow for a better comparison with the SemEval-2010 competition we intend to have a closer look at the effect of also scoring *singletons*.

Acknowledgments

The work presented in this paper was made possible by the STEVIN programme of the Dutch Language Union within the framework of the SoNaR project under grant number STE07014 and the Portuguese Science Foundation, FCT (Fundação para a Ciência e a Tecnologia). We would like to thank the anonymous reviewers for their helpful comments and valuable suggestions.

References

Amit Bagga and Breck Baldwin. 1998. Algorithms for scoring coreference chains. In *Proceedings of the First International Conference on Language Resources and Evaluation Workshop on Linguistic Coreference*, pages 563–566.

Gosse Bouma and Geert Kloostermans. 2007. Mining Syntactically Annotated Corpora using XQuery. In *Proceedings of the Linguistic Annotation Workshop (held in conjunction with ACL 2007)*, pages 17–24, Prague, Czech Republic.

Gosse Bouma, Gertjan van Noord, and Robert Malouf. 2001. Alpino: Wide coverage computational analysis of dutch. In *Computational Linguistics in the Netherlands 2000: selected papers from the twentieth CLIN meeting*.

Gosse Bouma, Walter Daelemans, Iris Hendrickx, Véronique Hoste, and Anne-Marie Mineur. 2007. The COREA-project, manual for the annotation of coreference in Dutch texts. Technical report, University Groningen.

Walter Daelemans, Jakub Zavrel, Antal van den Bosch, and Ko van der Sloot. 2003. MBT: Memory Based Tagger, version 2.0, Reference Guide. Technical Report ILK Research Group Technical Report Series no. 03-13, Tilburg University.

Walter Daelemans, Jakub Zavrel, Ko Van der Sloot, and Antal van den Bosch. 2010. TiMBL: Tilburg Memory Based Learner, version 6.3, Reference Guide. Technical Report ILK Research Group Technical Report Series no. 10-01, Tilburg University.

Hal Daumé III, Tejaswini Deoskar, David McClosky, Barbara Plank, and Jörg Tiedemann, editors. 2010. *Proceedings of the 2010 Workshop on Domain Adaptation for Natural Language Processing*. Association for Computational Linguistics, Uppsala, Sweden, July.

George Doddington, Alexis Mitchell, Mark Przybocki, Lance Ramshaw, Stephanie Strassel, and Ralph Weischedel. 2004. The Automatic Content Extraction (ACE) Program Tasks, Data, and Evaluation. In *Proceedings of LREC 2004*, pages 837–840, Lisbon, Portugal.

Caroline Gasperin and Ted Briscoe. 2008. Statistical anaphora resolution in biomedical texts. In *Proceedings of the 22nd International Conference on Computational Linguistics (Coling 2008)*, pages 257–264, Manchester, UK, August. Coling 2008 Organizing Committee.

Souha Hammami, Lamia Belguith, and Abdelmajid Ben Hamadou. 2009. Arabic anaphora resolution: Corpora annotation with coreferential links. *The International Arab Journal of Information Technology*, 6(5):481–489.

Iris Hendrickx and Véronique Hoste. 2009. Coreference Resolution on Blogs and Commented News. In *Anaphora Processing and Applications, Lecture Notes in Artificial Intelligence*, volume 5847, pages 43–53, Heidelberg.

Iris Hendrickx, Gosse Bouma, Frederik Coppens, Walter Daelemans, Véronique Hoste, Geert Kloosterman, Anne-Marie. Mineur, Joeri Van Der Vloet, and Jean-Luc Verschelde. 2008a. A coreference corpus and resolution system for Dutch. In *Proceedings of LREC 2008*, pages 144–149, Marrakech, Morocco.

Iris Hendrickx, Véronique Hoste, and Walter Daelemans. 2008b. Semantic and Syntactic features for Anaphora Resolution for Dutch. In *Proceedings of the 9th International Conference on Intelligent Text Processing and Computational Linguistics, Lecture Notes in Computer Science*, volume 4919, pages 351–361, Haifa, Israel.

Véronique Hoste. 2005. *Optimization Issues in Machine Learning of Coreference Resolution*. Ph.D. thesis, Antwerp University.

Lauri Karttunen. 1976. Discourse referents. *Syntax and Semantics*, 7.

Lucie Kučová and Eva Hajičová. 2004. Coreferential relations in the Prague Dependency Treebank. In *Proceedings of DAARC 2004*, pages 97–102, Azores, Portugal.

Laurence Longo and Amalia Todirascu. 2010. Genre-based reference chains identification for french. *Investigationes Linguisticae*, 21:57–75.

Xiaoqiang Luo and Imed Zitouni. 2005. Multi-lingual coreference resolution with syntactic features. In *Proceedings of Human Language Technology Conference and Conference on Empirical Methods in Natural Language Processing*, pages 660–667.

Bernardo Magnini, Emanuele Pianta, Christian Girardi, Matteo Negri, Lorenza Romano, Manuela Speranza, Valentina Bartalesi-Lenzi, and Rachele Sprugnoli. 2006. I-CAB: the Italian Content Annotation Bank. In *Proceedings of LREC 2006*, pages 963–968, Genoa, Italy.

Willy Martin and Jeannette Ploeger. 1999. Tweetalige woordenboeken voor het Nederlands: het beleid van de Commissie Lexicografische Vertaalvoorzieningen. *Neerlandica Extra Muros*, 37:22–32.

Vincent Ng. 2010. Supervised Noun Phrase Coreference Research: The First Fifteen Years. In *Proceedings of the 48th Annual Meeting of the Association for Computational Linguistics*, pages 1396–1411.

Jin-Dong Kim Ngan Nguyen and Junichi Tsujii. 2008. Challenges in pronoun resolution system for biomedical text. In *Proceedings of the Sixth International Language Resources and Evaluation (LREC'08)*, Marrakech, Morocco, may. European Language Resources Association (ELRA).

Massimo Poesio and Ron Artstein. 2008. Anaphoric annotation in the ARRAU corpus. In *Proceedings of LREC 2008*, pages 1170–1174, Marrakech, Morocco.

Massimo Poesio, Simone Paolo Ponzetto, and Yannick Versley. forthcoming. Computational models of anaphora resolution: A survey. *Linguistic Issues in Language Technology*.

William M. Rand. 1971. Objective criteria for the evaluation of clustering methods. *Journal of the American Statistical Association*, 66(336):846–850.

Marta Recasens and Eduard Hovy. 2011. Blanc: Implementing the rand index for coreference evaluation. *Natural Language Engineering*,.

Marta Recasens and M. Antònia Martí. 2010. AnCora-CO: Coreferentially annotated corpora for Spanish and Catalan. *Language Resources and Evaluation*, 44(4):315–345.

Marta Recasens, Lluíz Márquez, Emili Sapena, M. Antònia Martí, Mariona Tauleé, Véronique Hoste, Massimo Poesio, and Yannick Versley. 2010. SemEval-2010 Task 1: Coreference resolution in multiple languages. In *Proceedings of the 5th International Workshop on Semantic Evaluations (SemEval-2010)*, pages 1–8, Uppsala, Sweden.

Marta Recasens. 2010. *Coreference: Theory, Annotation, Resolution and Evaluation*. Ph.D. thesis, Department of Linguistics, University of Barcelona, Barcelona, Spain, September.

Kepa Joseba Rodríguez, Franceska Delogu, Yannick Versley, Egon Stemle, and Massimo Poesio. 2010. Anaphoric annotation of Wikipedia and blogs in the Live Memories Corpus. In *Proceedings of LREC 2010*, pages 157–163, Valletta, Malta.

Ineke Schuurman, Véronique Hoste, and Paola Monachesi. 2010. Interacting Semantic Layers of Annotation in SoNaR, a Reference Corpus of Contemporary Written Dutch. In *Proceedings of LREC 2010*, pages 2471–2477, Valletta, Malta.

Wee Meng Soon, Hwee Tou Ng, and Daniel Chung Yong Lim. 2001. A Machine Learning Approach to Coreference Resolution of Noun Phrases. *Computational Linguistics*, 27(4):521–544.

Erik F. Tjong Kim Sang. 2002. Introduction to the CoNLL-2002 Shared Task: Language-Independent Named Entity Recognition. In *Proceedings of the 6th Conference on Natural Language Learning*, pages 155–158, Taipei, Taiwan.

Marc Vilain, John Burger, John Aberdeen, Dennis Connolly, and Lynette Hirschman. 1995. A Model-Theoretic Coreference Scoring Scheme. In *Proceedings of the Sixth Message Understanding Conference (MUC-6)*, pages 45–52.

Piek Vossen, editor. 1998. *EuroWordNet: a multilingual database with lexical semantic networks*. Kluwer Academic Publishers, Norwell, MA, USA.

Ralph Weischedel, Sameer Pradhan, Lance Ramshaw, Martha Palmer, Nianwen Xue, Mitchell Marcus, Ann Taylor, Craig Greenberg, Eduard Hovy, Robert Belvin, and Ann Houston. 2009. *OntoNotes Release 3.0. LDC2009T24*. Linguistic Data Consortium.

Xiaofeng Yang, Jian Su, GuoDong Zhou, and Chew Lim Tan. 2004. An np-cluster based approach to coreference resolution. In *Proceedings of Coling 2004*, pages 226–232, Geneva, Switzerland, Aug 23–Aug 27.

Finding the Best Approach for Multi-lingual Text Summarisation: A Comparative Analysis

Elena Lloret
University of Alicante
Apdo. de Correos 99
E-03080, Alicante, Spain
elloret@dlsi.ua.es

Manuel Palomar
University of Alicante
Apdo. de Correos 99
E-03080, Alicante, Spain
mpalomar@dlsi.ua.es

Abstract

This paper addresses the problem of multi-lingual text summarisation. The goal is to analyse three approaches for generating summaries in four languages (English, Spanish, German and French), in order to determine the best one to adopt when tackling this issue. The proposed approaches rely on: i) language-independent techniques; ii) language-specific resources; and iii) machine translation resources applied to a mono-lingual summariser. The evaluation carried out employing the JRC corpus – a corpus specifically created for multi-lingual summarisation – shows that the approach which uses language-specific resources is the most appropriate in our comparison framework, performing better than state-of-the-art multi-lingual summarisers. Moreover, the readability assessment conducted over the resulting summaries for this approach proves that they are also very competitive with respect to their quality.

1 Introduction

In the current society, information plays a crucial role that brings competitive advantages to users, when it is managed correctly. However, due to the vast amount of available information, users cannot cope with it, and therefore research into new methods and approaches based on Natural Language Processing (NLP) is crucial, thus resulting in considerable benefits for the society. Specifically, one of these NLP research areas is Text Summarisation (TS) which is essential to condense information keeping, at the same time, the most relevant facts or pieces of information. However, to produce a summary automatically is very challenging. Issues such as redundancy, temporal dimension, coreference or sentence ordering, to name a few, have to be taken into consideration especially when summarising a set of documents (multi-document summarisation), thus making this field even more difficult (Goldstein et al., 2000). Such difficulty also increases when the information is stated in several languages and we want to be capable of producing a summary in those languages, thus not restricting the summariser to a single language (multi-lingual summarisation). The generation of multi-lingual summaries improves considerably the capabilities of TS systems, allowing users to be able to understand the essence of documents in other languages by only reading their corresponding summaries.

Therefore, the aim of this paper is to carry out a comparative analysis of several approaches for generating extractive[1] multi-lingual summaries in four languages (English, French, German and Spanish). These approaches comprise the use of: i) language-independent techniques; ii) language-specific resources; and iii) machine translation resources applied to a mono-lingual summariser. In this way, we can study the advantages and limitations of each approach, as well as to determine which is the most appropriate to adopt for this type of summaries. Although the language-specific resources are limited and perform differently for each language, the results indicate that this approach is the best to adopt, since for each language, more specific information could be obtained, benefiting the final summaries.

The remaining of the paper is organised as follows. Section 2 introduces previous work on multi-lingual TS. Section 3 describes the proposed approaches for generating multi-lingual summaries in detail. Further on, the corpus used, the experiments carried out, the results obtained together with an in-depth discussion is provided

[1]Extractive approaches are those ones which only detect important sentences in documents and extract them, without performing any kind of language generation or generalisation.

in Section 4. Finally, the conclusions of the paper together with the future work are outlined in Section 5.

2 Related Work

Generating multi-lingual TS is a challenging task, due to the fact that we have to deal with multiple languages, each of which has its peculiarities. Attempts to produce multi-lingual summaries started with SUMMARIST (Hovy and Lin, 1999), a system which extracted sentences from documents in a variety of languages, by using English, Japanese, Spanish, Indonesian, and Arabic preprocessing modules and lexicons. Another example of multi-lingual TS system is MEAD (Radev et al., 2004), able to produce summaries in English and Chinese, relying on features, such as sentence position, sentence length, or similarity with the first sentence.

More recently, research in multi-lingual TS has been focused on the analysis of language-independent methods. For instance, in (Litvak et al., 2010b) a comparative analysis of 16 methods for language-independent extractive summarisation was performed in order to find the most efficient language-independent sentence scoring method in terms of summarisation accuracy and computational complexity across two different languages (English and Hebrew). Such methods relied on vector-, structure- and graph-based features (e.g. frequency, position, length, title-based features, pagerank, etc.), concluding that vector and graph-based approaches were among the top ranked methods for bilingual applications. From this analysis, MUSE – MUltilingual Sentence Extractor (Litvak et al., 2010a) was developed, where other language-independent features were added and a genetic algorithm was employed to find the optimal weighted linear combination of all the sentence scoring methods proposed. In (Patel et al., 2007) a multi-lingual extractive language-independent TS approach was also suggested. The proposed algorithm was based on structural and statistical factors, such as location or identification of common and proper nouns. However, it also used stemming and stop word lists, which were dependent on the language. This TS approach was evaluated for English, Hindi, Gujarati and Urdu documents, obtaining encouraging results and showing that the proposed method performed equally well regardless of the language. NewsGist (Kabadjov et al., 2010) is a multi-lingual summariser that achieves better performance than state-of-the-art approaches. It relies on Singular Value Decomposition, which is also a language-independent method, so it can be applied to a wide range of languages, although at the moment, it has been only tested for English, French and German.

Furthermore, Wikipedia[2] is a multi-lingual resource, which has been used for many natural language applications. It contains more than 18 million articles in more than 270 languages, which have been written collaboratively by volunteers around the world. This valuable resource has also been used for developing multi-lingual TS approaches. For instance, (Filatova, 2009) took advantage of Wikipedia information stated across different languages with the purpose of creating summaries. The approach was based on the Pyramid method (Nenkova et al., 2007) in order to account for relevant information. The underlying idea was that sentences were placed on different levels of the pyramid, depending on the number of languages containing such sentence. Thus, the top levels were populated by the sentences that appeared in the most languages and the bottom level contained sentences appearing in the least number of languages. The summary was then generated by taking a specific number of sentences starting with the top level, until the desired length was reached. Moreover, although the multi-lingual approach proposed in (Yuncong and Fung, 2010) aimed at generating complete articles instead of summaries, it is very interesting and it can be perfectly applied to TS. Basically, this approach took an existing entry of Wikipedia as content guideline. Then, keywords were extracted from it, and translated into the target language. The translation was used to query the Web in the target language, so candidate fragments of information were obtained. Further on, these fragments were ranked and synthesised into a complete article.

Different to the aforementioned approaches, in this paper we carried out a comparison between three approaches: i) a language-independent approach; ii) a language-specific approach; and iii) machine translation resources applied to a monolingual TS approach. Our final aim is to analyse them in order to find which is the most suitable for performing multi-lingual TS.

[2] http://www.wikipedia.org/

3 Multi-lingual Text Summarisation

The objective of this section is to explain the three proposed approaches for generating multi-lingual summaries in four languages (English, French, German and Spanish). We developed an extractive TS approach for each case. In particular, we analysed: i) language-independent techniques (Subsection 3.1); ii) language-specific resources (Subsection 3.2); and iii) machine translation resources applied to a mono-lingual summariser (Subsection 3.3). Next, we describe each approach in detail.

3.1 Language-independent Approach

As a language-independent approach for tackling multi-lingual TS, we computed the relevance of sentences by using the term frequency technique. Term frequency was first proposed in (Luhn, 1958), and, despite being a simple technique, it has been widely used in TS due to the good results it achieves (Gotti et al., 2007), (Orăsan, 2009), (Montiel et al., 2009).

The importance of a term in a document will be given by its frequency. At this point, it is worth mentioning that stop words, such as "the", "a", "you", etc. are not taken into account; otherwise the relevance of sentences could be wrongly calculated. In order to identify them, we need a specific list of stop words, depending on the language used. The language-specific processing in this approach is minimal, so it can be considered language-independent, since given a new language it would be very easy to obtain automatic summaries through this approach.

For determining the relevance of sentences, a matrix is built. In this matrix M, the rows represent the terms of the document without considering the stop words, whereas the columns represent the sentences. Each cell $M[i,j]$ contains the frequency of each term i in the document, provided that such term is included in the sentence; otherwise the cell contains a 0. Then, the importance of sentence S_j is computed by means of Formula 1:

$$Sc_{S_j} = \frac{\sum_{i=1}^{n} M[i,j]}{|Terms|} \quad (1)$$

where

Sc_{S_j} = Score of sentence *j*

$M[i,j]$ = value of the cell *[i,j]*

$|Terms|$ = total number of terms in the document.

Once the score for each sentence is calculated, sentences will be ranked in descending order, and the top ones up to a desired length will be chosen to become part of the summary.

Apart from its simplicity, the advantage of this techniques is that it can be used in any language. However, its main limitation is that the relevance of the sentences is only determined through lexical surface analysis, and therefore, semantics aspects are not taken into account.

3.2 Language-specific Approach

Our second proposed approach is very similar to the first one, but instead of term frequency, it employs language-specific resources for each of the target languages. For determining the relevance of sentences, this approach analyses the use of Named Entity Recognisers (NER) and the identification of concepts, by means of their synsets in WordNet (Fellbaum, 1998) or EuroWordNet (Ellman, 2003). On the one hand, named entities can indicate important content, since they refer to specific people, organisations, places, etc. that may be related to the topic of the document. On the other hand, the identification of concepts involves semantic analysis, and therefore, we can identify synonyms or other types of semantic relationships.

These types of resources (NERs and resources like Wordnet) have been commonly employed for generating specific types of summaries (Hassel, 2003), (Bellare et al., 2004), (Chaves, 2001). Moreover, in (Filatova and Hatzivassiloglou, 2004) it was proven that approaches that took into consideration named entities as well as frequent words were appropriate for TS. In light of this, we decided to develop a similar approach, but relying on named entities and concepts.

In particular, we focus on four languages (English, French, German and Spanish). The named entities are identified using different NERs, depending on the language. In this way, we use LingPipe[3] for English, the Illinois Named Entity Tagger[4] (Ratinov and Roth, 2009) for French, the NER for German[5] proposed in (Faruqui and Padó, 2010), and Freeling[6] for Spanish. For detecting concepts, we rely on WordNet for English and EuroWordNet for the remaining languages. Thanks

[3]http://alias-i.com/lingpipe/

[4]http://cogcomp.cs.illinois.edu/page/software_view/4

[5]http://www.nlpado.de/ sebastian/ner_german.html

[6]http://nlp.lsi.upc.edu/freeling/

to these types of resources, this approach uses semantic knowledge, instead of only lexical, as in the case of the term frequency in the language-independent approach.

For computing the relevance of the sentences, a matrix (M) is also built, where the rows represent the entities or concepts of the document and the columns, the sentences. Each cell $M[i,j]$ contains the frequency of appearance of either each entity or concept. As in the previous approach, stop words are not taken into consideration, and in those cases where neither the entity nor the concept is included in the sentence, a 0 is assigned to the cell. Once the matrix has been filled in, Formula 2 is then used to compute the relevance of sentences:

$$Sc_{S_j} = \frac{\sum_{i=1}^{n} M[i,j]}{|NE + Concepts|} \quad (2)$$

where

Sc_{S_j} = Score of sentence *j*
$M[i,j]$ = value of the cell *[i,j]*
$|NE + Concepts|$ = total number of named entities and concepts in the document.

The highest scored sentences, up to a specific length, will be extracted to build the final summary.

The advantages of this approach with respect to the previous one (i.e. the language-independent) is that semantic analysis is applied by using resources such as WordNet or EuroWordNet. This allows us to group synonyms under the same concept. For instance, the words *harassment* and *molestation* represent the same concepts (since they both belong to the same synset in WordNet), so they are grouped together in this approach, whereas in the previous one, where only the frequency of terms is taken into consideration, they are considered two distinct words. In contrast, the drawback of this approach is that such kind of resources may not be available for all languages, and therefore we might have problems in applying this approach. Moreover, the error these resources introduce (e.g. NERs) may negatively affect the performance of the summariser.

3.3 Machine Translation Resources applied to a Mono-lingual Approach

The idea behind this approach is to use an existing mono-lingual summariser for a specific language and then employ a machine translation system for obtaining the summaries in the different languages. In particular, we employ the TS approach proposed in (Lloret and Palomar, 2009) that generates extractive summaries for English. The reason for employing such summariser is its competitive results achieved compared to the state of the art. Briefly, the main features of this approach are: i) redundant information is detected and removed by means of textual entailment; and ii) the Code Quantity Principle (Givón, 1990) is used for accounting relevant information from a cognitive perspective. Therefore, important sentences are identified by computing the number of words included in noun-phrases, taking also into consideration the relative frequency each word has in the document. Once the summaries have been generated, Google Translate[7] is used to translate the summaries into the different target languages (i.e., French, German and Spanish), since it is a free online language translation service that can translate text in more than 50 languages.

The advantage of this approach is that we do not have to develop a particular approach for each language, because we can rely on existing mono-lingual summarisers. Although machine translation has been made great progress in the recent years, and they can translate text into a wide range of languages, the disadvantage associated to using such tools concerns their performance, since wrong translations can negatively affect the quality of the resulting summary.

4 Experimental Framework

The goal of this section is to setup an experimental framework, thus allowing us to analyse the aforementioned approaches in a specific context. Therefore, the corpus employed and the languages used are described in Subsection 4.1. Then, the evaluation methodology proposed and the results obtained together with a discussion is provided in Subsection 4.2.

4.1 Corpus

We used the JRC multi-lingual summary evaluation data[8] for carrying out the experiments, in order to determine which approach should be more appropriate for the task of multi-lingual summarisation. The corpus consists of 20 docu-

[7] http://translate.google.com/
[8] http://langtech.jrc.ec.europa.eu/JRC_Resources.html

	English	French	German	Spanish
No. of words	16,398	18,329	16,837	18,547
Avg. words/document	819.9	916.45	841.45	928.7
Max. words/document	973	1,157	1,025	1,144
Min. words/document	617	698	645	708
No. of NE	511	254	345	326
Avg. NE/document	25.6	12.7	17.25	16.3
Max. NE/document	44	22	37	32
Min. NE/document	3	6	1	1
No. of concepts	3,405	2,376	2,115	3,580
Avg. concepts/document	170.25	118.8	105.75	179
Max. concepts/document	1,353	159	136	231
Min. concepts/document	222	90	78	138

Table 1: Statistical properties of the JRC corpus.

ments grouped into four topics (genetics, Israel-and-Palestine-conflict, malaria and science-and-society). Each document is available in seven languages (Arabic, Czech, English, French, German, Russian and Spanish), and the corpus also contains the manual annotation of important sentences, so it is possible to have four model summaries for each of the documents. Four our purposes, four languages were selected (English, French, German and Spanish), thus dealing with 80 documents.

The type of documents contained in the JRC corpus pertained to the news domain. Table 1 shows some properties of the corpus.

As it can be seen from the table, all the documents have a similar length, the shortest ones having more than 600 words, whereas the longest ones around 1,000 words. Regarding the statistics about the words, it is worth noting that the documents in Romance languages (Spanish and French) have similar characteristics. Analogously, the same happens for the Germanic languages (English and German). However, the highest differences between languages can be found in the number of NE and concepts detected. Whereas for English, the average number of NE is 25, for the remaining languages is at most 17. This depends on the NER employed. The language-specific resources used for detecting concepts (WordNet and EuroWordNet) also influence the number of concepts identified. In this way, Spanish and English are the languages with more concepts.

4.2 Results and Discussion

The JRC corpus was used to generate extractive summaries in four languages (English, French, German, and Spanish), following our three proposed approaches. We generated 20 summaries for each approach and language, thus evaluating 240 different summaries in the end. Two types of evaluation were conducted. On the one hand, the content of the summaries was evaluated in an automatic manner (Subsubsection 4.2.1), whereas on the other hand, their readability was manually assessed (Subsubsection 4.2.2). In addition, a comparison with current multi-lingual TS systems was also carried out (Subsubsection 4.2.3).

4.2.1 Content Evaluation

The automatic summaries were compared to the model ones, using ROUGE (Lin, 2004), a widespread tool for evaluating TS. In this way, the content of the summaries was assessed, since this tool allows to compute recall, precision and F-measure with respect to different metrics, all of them based on how much vocabulary overlap there is between an automatic and model summary. Table 2 shows the F-measure value for ROUGE-1 (R-1), ROUGE-2 (R-2), and ROUGE-SU4 (R-SU4) for each of the proposed multi-lingual TS approaches. R-1 computes the number of common unigram between the automatic and model summary; R-2 computes the number of bi-grams, whereas R-SU4 accounts for the number of bi-grams with a maximum distance of four words in-between.

Moreover, a t-test was performed in order to account for the significance of the results at a 95% level of confidence. Results statistically significant are marked with a star. As it can be seen from the table, the results for the language-independent (LI) and language-specific (LS) approaches are statistically significant compared to the mono-lingual approach combined with machine translation (TS+MT) in all the cases, except for English. Furthermore, from the results obtained, it is worth noting that the LS approach

Language	Approach	R-1	R-2	R-SU4
English	LI	0.53097	0.31777	0.34873
	LS	**0.56530**	**0.37568**	**0.39828**
	TS	0.52823	0.33011	0.35832
French	LI	**0.55758***	0.33777*	0.36116*
	LS	0.55638*	**0.35119***	**0.37316***
	TS+MT	0.50054	0.20505	0.24204
German	LI	0.47886*	0.29219*	0.30646*
	LS	**0.52614***	**0.36849***	**0.38002***
	TS+MT	0.41716	0.15985	0.18180
Spanish	LI	0.57920*	0.36234*	0.39296*
	LS	**0.62351***	**0.42975***	**0.45653***
	TS+MT	0.52886	0.24362	0.28623

Table 2: F-measure results for the content evaluation using ROUGE (LI=language-independent; LS=language-specific; TS= mono-lingual; TS+MT=mono-lingual and machine translation).

obtains better results than the LI approach, in all ROUGE metrics, except R-1 for French, where LI and LS obtain very similar results. In addition, the differences between them are statistically significant for German and Spanish. As it can also be seen, the LS obtains the best results for English and Spanish. This may happens because these languages have a lot of specific resources for dealing with them. In contrast, the performance for French and German linguistic resources may not be as accurate as for the other languages, thus affecting the results. Moreover, it is also worth noting that the performance of the LI approach for German is quite low with respect to the other languages. This is due to the fact that the way of writing in German differs from the others in that it is more agglutinative (e.g. arbeitstag[9]); consequently, the frequency for some of the words in the documents will be computed separately (in the previous example *tag* and *arbeitstag* will have different frequencies). This occurs because in the LI approach we do not rely on any specific resources, such as tokenisers or stemmers; we only use the corresponding stop word list for each language.

4.2.2 Readability Evaluation

From Table 2 we can conclude that the LS approach is the most appropriate to tackle multi-lingual TS. However, we are interested in carrying out a readability assessment, so that the summaries generated by our best approach (LS) can be also assessed with respect to their quality. For conducting this type of assessment, we followed the DUC guidelines[10], and we asked four people (two natives of Spanish and German and two with very advanced knowledge of English and French) to manually evaluate each summary, assigning values from 1 to 5 (1=very poor...5=very good) with respect to five quality criteria: grammaticality, redundancy, clarity, focus and coherence. Results are shown in Table 3.

	English	French	German	Spanish
Grammaticality	3.4	4.3	4.6	3.1
Redundancy	3.8	5.0	4.3	4.8
Clarity	3.6	3.9	4.6	3.8
Focus	4.4	3.9	4.6	4.6
Coherence	4.0	3.5	4.0	3.5

Table 3: Readability Assessment of the language-specific (LS) multi-lingual TS approach.

In general terms, the results obtained in the readability assessment are very good. This means that using the language-specific approach, the resulting summaries are also good with respect to their quality. Concerning this issue, German summaries obtains the best results, all of them above 4 out of 5. The summaries in the remaining languages perform also very good in the coherence and redundancy criteria. It is worth noting that we generated single-document summaries (i.e., the summaries were produced taking only a document as input), so the chances of redundant information decrease. However, in this criteria we also measured the repetition of named entities, so in this sense, despite relying on named entities and concepts, there was not much repeated information in the summaries.

4.2.3 Comparison with Current Multi-lingual Summarisers

With the purpose of widening the analysis and verifying our results, we compared our LS approach to several current multi-lingual TS systems, that also produce extractive summaries as a result. In particular, we selected:

- **Open Text Summarizer**[11] (OTS). This is a multi-lingual summariser able to generate summaries in more than 25 languages, such as English, German, Spanish, Russian or Hebrew. In this approach, keywords are identified by means of word occurrence, and sen-

[9] day at work

[10] http://duc.nist.gov/duc2007/quality-questions.txt

[11] http://libots.sourceforge.net/

tences are given a score based on the the keywords they contain. Some language-specific resources, such as stemmers and stop word lists are employed. It has been shown that this system obtains better performance than other multi-lingual TS systems (Yatsko and Vishnyakov, 2007).

- **MS Word 2007 Summarizer**[12] (MS Word). This summariser is integrated into Microsoft Word 2007 and it also generates summaries in several languages. Since it is a commercial system, the implementation details are not revealed.
- **Essential Summarizer**[13] (Essential). This TS system is a commercial version of the one presented in (Lehmam, 2010). It relies on linguistic techniques to perform semantic analysis of written text, taking into account discursive elements of the text. It is able to produce summaries in twenty languages.

For conducting such comparison, summaries were generated using the aforementioned TS systems in the four languages we dealt with. Then, they were evaluated using ROUGE. Table 4 shows the F-measure results for the ROUGE-1 metric. As before, we performed a t-test in order to analyse the significance of the results for a 95% confidence level (significant results are marked with a star). In most of the cases, our LS approach performs better than the other multi-lingual TS systems, except the OTS which performs slightly better for French and German. Our approach (LS) and OTS performed statistically better than the Essential summariser for German, increasing the results by 20% compared to it. Moreover, for Spanish, LS improves the results of MS Word and Essential summarisers by 9% and 16%, respectively, and this improvement is also statistically significant.

	English	French	German	Spanish
LS	**0.56530**	0.55638	0.52614*	**0.62351***
OTS	0.55732	**0.57745**	**0.53451***	0.60591*
MS Word	0.53591	0.54046	0.48427	0.57396
Essential	0.52622	0.51819	0.43727	0.53978

Table 4: Comparison with current multi-lingual TS systems (F-measure results for ROUGE-1).

[12]http://www.microsoft.com/education/autosummarize.aspx

[13]https://essential-mining.com/es/index.jsp?ui.lang=en

5 Conclusion and Future Work

This paper presented a comparative analysis of three widespread multi-lingual summarisation approaches in order to determine which one would be more suitable to adopt when tackling this task. In particular, we studied: i) a language-independent approach using the term frequency technique; ii) a language-specific approach, relying on specific linguistic resources for each of the target language (named entities recognisers and semantic resources); and finally, iii) a monolingual text summariser for English, whose output was then inputted to a machine translation system in order to generate summaries in the remaining languages. The experiments carried out in English, French, German and Spanish showed that by employing language-specific resources, the resulting summaries performed better than most of the state-of-the-art multi-lingual summarisers.

In the future, we plan to extend our analysis to other languages as well as to investigate other ways of generating multi-lingual summaries, for instance, employing Wikipedia, as in (Filatova, 2009). This would be the starting point to address cross-lingual summarisation, task that we would like to tackle in the long-term.

Acknowledgments

This research is funded by the Spanish Government thorugh the FPI grant (BES-2007-16268) and the projects TIN2006-15265-C06-01 and TIN2009-13391-C04-01; and by the Valencian Government (projects PROMETEO/2009/119 and ACOMP/2011/001). The authors would like to thank also Raúl Bernabeu, Hakan Ceylan, Sabine Klausner, and Violeta Seretan for their help in the manual evaluation of the summaries..

References

Kedar Bellare, Anish Das Sarma, Atish Das Sarma, Navneet Loiwal, Vaibhav Mehta, Ganesh Ramakrishnan, and Pushpak Bhattacharyya. 2004. Generic text summarization using wordnet. In *Proceedings of the 4th International Conference on Language Resources and Evaluation*.

Rui Pedro Chaves. 2001. Wordnet and automated text summarization. In *Proceedings of the 6th Natural Language Processing Pacific Rim Symposium*, pages 109–116.

Jeremy Ellman. 2003. Eurowordnet: A multilingual

database with lexical semantic networks. *Natural Language Engineering*, 9:427–430.

Manaal Faruqui and Sebastian Padó. 2010. Training and evaluating a german named entity recognizer with semantic generalization. In *Proceedings of KONVENS 2010*, Saarbrücken, Germany.

Christiane Fellbaum. 1998. *WordNet: An Electronical Lexical Database*. The MIT Press, Cambridge, MA.

Elena Filatova and Vasileios Hatzivassiloglou. 2004. Event-Based Extractive Summarization. In *Text Summarization Branches Out: Proceedings of the ACL-04 Workshop*, pages 104–111.

Elena Filatova. 2009. Multilingual wikipedia, summarization, and information trustworthiness. In *Proceedings of the IGIR Workshop on Information Access in a Multilingual World*.

Talmy Givón, 1990. *Syntax: A functional-typological introduction, II*. John Benjamins.

Jade Goldstein, Vibhu Mittal, Jaime Carbonell, and Mark Kantrowitz. 2000. Multi-document Summarization by Sentence Extraction. In *NAACL-ANLP Workshop on Automatic Summarization*, pages 40–48.

Fabrizio Gotti, Guy Lapalme, Luka Nerima, and Eric Wehrli. 2007. Gofaisum: A symbolic summarizer for duc. In *Proceedings of the Document Understanding Workshop*.

Martin Hassel. 2003. Exploitation of named entities in automatic text summarization for swedish. In *Proceedings of the 14th Mnordic Conference on Computational Linguistics*.

Eduard Hovy and Chin-Yew Lin. 1999. Automated text summarization in summarist. In *Inderjeet Mani and Mark Maybury, editors*, Advances in Automatic Text Summarization, pages 81–94. MIT Press.

Mijail Kabadjov, Martin Atkinson, Josef Steinberger, Ralf Steinberger, and Erik Van Der Goot. 2010. NewsGist: a multilingual statistical news summarizer. In *Proceedings of the European conference on Machine learning and knowledge discovery in databases: Part III*, pages 591–594.

Abderrafih Lehmam. 2010. Essential summarizer: innovative automatic text summarization software in twenty languages. In *Adaptivity, Personalization and Fusion of Heterogeneous Information*, pages 216–217.

Chin-Yew Lin. 2004. ROUGE: a Package for Automatic Evaluation of Summaries. In *Proceedings of Association of Computational Linguistics Text Summarization Workshop*, pages 74–81.

Marina Litvak, Mark Last, and Menahem Friedman. 2010a. A new approach to improving multilingual summarization using a genetic algorithm. In *Proceedings of the 48th Annual Meeting of the Association for Computational Linguistics*, pages 927–936.

Marina Litvak, Mark Last, Slava Kisilevich, Daniel Keim, Hagay Lipman, and Assaf Ben Gur. 2010b. Towards multi-lingual summarization: A comparative analysis of sentence extraction methods on english and hebrew corpora. In *Proceedings of the 4th Workshop on Cross Lingual Information Access*, pages 61–69.

Elena Lloret and Manuel Palomar. 2009. A gradual combination of features for building automatic summarisation systems. In *Proceedings of the 12th International Conference on Text, Speech and Dialogue*, pages 16–23.

Hans Peter Luhn. 1958. The automatic creation of literature abstracts. In *Inderjeet Mani and Mark Maybury, editors*, Advances in Automatic Text Summarization, pages 15–22. MIT Press.

Romyna Montiel, René García, Yulia Ledeneva, and Rafael Cruz Reyes. 2009. Comparación de tres modelos de texto para la generación automática de resúmenes. *Sociedad Española para el Procesamiento del Lenguaje Natural*, 43:303–311.

Ani Nenkova, Rebecca Passonneau, and Kathleen McKeown. 2007. The pyramid method: Incorporating human content selection variation in summarization evaluation. *ACM Transactions on Speech and Language Processing*, 4(2):4.

Constantin Orăsan. 2009. Comparative Evaluation of Term-Weighting Methods for Automatic Summarization. *Journal of Quantitative Linguistics*, 16(1):67–95.

Alkesh Patel, Tanveer Siddiqui, and U. S. Tiwary. 2007. A language independent approach to multilingual text summarization. In *Large Scale Semantic Access to Content (Text, Image, Video, and Sound)*, RIAO '07, pages 123–132.

Dragomir Radev, Tim Allison, Sasha Blair-Goldensohn, John Blitzer, Arda Celebi, Elliott Drabek, Wai Lam, Danyu Liu, Jahna Otterbacher, Hong Qi, Horacio Saggion, Simone Teufel, Michael Topper, Adam Winkel, and Zhu Zhang. 2004. MEAD - A Platform for Multidocument Multilingual Text Summarization. In *Proceedings of the 4th International Conference on Language Resources and Evaluation*.

Lev Ratinov and Dan Roth. 2009. Design challenges and misconceptions in named entity recognition. In *Proceedings of the 13th Conference on Computational Natural Language Learning*, pages 147–155.

Viatcheslav Yatsko and Timur Vishnyakov. 2007. A method for evaluating modern systems of automatic text summarization. *Automatic Documentation and Mathematical Linguistics*, 41:93–103.

Chen Yuncong and Pascale Fung. 2010. Unsupervised synthesis of multilingual wikipedia articles. In *Proceedings of the 23rd International Conference on Computational Linguistics*, pages 197–205.

Automatically Creating General-Purpose Opinion Summaries from Text

Veselin Stoyanov
Johns Hopkins University
ves@cs.jhu.edu

Claire Cardie
Cornell University
cardie@cs.cornell.edu

Abstract

We present and evaluate the first method known to us that can create rich non-extract-based opinion summaries from general text (e.g. newspaper articles). We first describe two possible representations for opinion summaries and then present our system OASIS, which identifies, and optionally aggregates, fine-grained opinions from the same source on the same topic. We propose new evaluation measures for both types of opinion summary and employ the metrics in an evaluation of OASIS on a standard opinion corpus. Our results are encouraging — OASIS substantially outperforms a competitive baseline when creating document-level *aggregate summaries* that compute the average polarity value across the multiple opinions identified for each source about each topic. We further show that as state-of-the-art performance on fine-grained opinion extraction improves, we can expect to see opinion summaries of very high quality — with F-scores of 54-78% using our OSEM evaluation measure.

1 Introduction

To date, most of the research in opinion analysis (see Related Work section) has focused on the problem of extracting opinions — both at the document level (*coarse-grained opinion information*) and at the level of sentences, clauses, or individual expressions (*fine-grained opinion information*).

In contrast, our work concerns the consolidation of fine-grained information about opinions to create non-extract-based *opinion summaries*, a rich, concise and useful representation of the opinions expressed in a document. In particular, the opinion summaries produced by our system combine opinions from the same source and/or about the same topic and aggregate multiple opinions from the same source on the same topic in a meaningful way. A simple opinion summary is shown in Figure 1. In the sample text, there are seven opinions expressed — two negative and one positive opinion from the American public on the war in Iraq, two negative opinions of Bush on withdrawal from Iraq, and so on. These are aggregated in the graph-based summary. We expect that this type of opinion summary, based on fine-grained opinion information, will be important for information analysis applications in any domain where the analysis of opinions and other subjective language is critical. Our notion of summary is fundamentally different from the extract-based textual summaries used often in Natural Language Processing. We use the term *non-extract-based summary* to make that distinction explicit, but also use *opinion summary* to refer to the summaries that we propose.

In this paper, we present and evaluate OASIS (for Opinion Aggregation and SummarIzation System), the first system known to us that can produce rich non-extract-based opinion summaries from general text.[1] The system relies on automatically extracted fine-grained opinion information and constructs fully automatic opinion summaries in a form that can be easily presented to humans or queried by other NLP applications. In addition, we discuss for the first time different forms of opinion summaries and provide novel methods for quantitative evaluation of opinion summaries.

Unlike most extract-based summarization tasks, we are able to automatically generate gold standard summaries for evaluation. As a result, our

[1] Several systems for summarizing the opinions expressed in product reviews exist (e.g. Hu and Liu (2004), Popescu and Etzioni (2005)). Due to the limited domain, summarizing opinions in product reviews constitutes a substantially different text-understanding problem; it has proven to be easier than the task addressed here and is handled using a very different set of techniques.

> [$_{\text{Source}}$ American public] opinion has [$_{-}$ *turned increasingly against*] [$_{\text{Topic}}$ the Iraq war]. The fourth anniversary of the Iraq war this week was marked by anti-[$_{\text{Topic}}$ war] [$_{-}$ *protests*] during the weekend. There were [$_{\text{Source}}$ some people] out to [$_{+}$ *support*] [$_{\text{Topic}}$ the war] as well, fewer in number but no less vocal.
>
> ...
>
> [$_{\text{Source}}$ Bush] has repeatedly [$_{-}$ *opposed*] [$_{\text{Topic}}$ setting timelines for withdrawing U.S. troops from Iraq]. [$_{\text{Source}}$ He] reiterated [$_{\text{Source}}$ the administration]'s stance that [$_{-}$ *premature*] [$_{\text{Topic}}$ troop withdrawal from Iraq] would leave security to Iraqi forces that [$_{-}$ *cannot yet cope*] with it on their own and allow [$_{\text{Topic}}$ groups like al Qaeda] to establish a base from which to [$_{-}$ *attack*] the US.

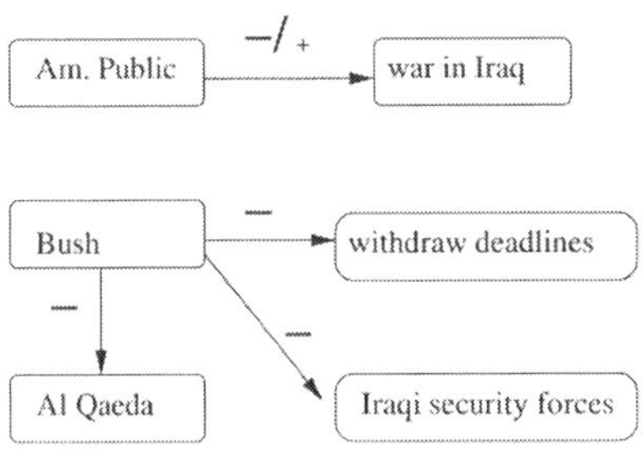

Figure 1: Example text containing opinions (above) and a summary of the opinions (below). In the text, sources and targets of opinions are bracketed; opinion expressions are shown in italics and bracketed with associated polarity, either positive (+) or negative (-). In the summary, entities involved in opinions are shown as nodes and aggregated opinions are shown as directed edges.

evaluation measures require no human intervention.

Our results are encouraging — OASIS substantially outperforms a competitive baseline when creating document-level *aggregate summaries* (like the one in Figure 1). We further show that as state-of-the-art performance on fine-grained opinion extraction improves, we can expect to see opinion summaries of very high quality (F-scores of 54-77% using our OSEM evaluation measure).

2 Opinion Summary Formats

In this section we discuss our notion of opinion summary as motivated by the needs of different applications and uses. In general, we presume the existence of automatically extracted fine-grained opinions, each of which has the following four attributes:

1. Trigger – the word or phrase that signals the expression of opinion in the text.
2. Source – the entity to which the opinion is to be attributed. More precisely, the span of text (usually a noun phrase or pronoun) that specifies the entity to which the opinion is to be attributed.
3. Topic – the topic of the opinion – either an entity (e.g. "Sue dislikes **John**") or a general topic (e.g. "I don't think that **lending money to friends** is a good idea").
4. Polarity – the sentiment (favorability) expressed in the opinion – either positive, negative, or neutral (a non-judgmental opinion that does not express a favorable or unfavorable attitude).

We expect that applications will use summaries of fine-grained opinion information in two distinct ways, giving rise to two distinct summary formats. The two formats differ in the way multiple opinions from the same source about the same topic are combined.

Aggregate opinion summary In an *aggregate opinion* summary, multiple opinions from a source on a topic are merged into a single aggregate opinion that represents the accumulated opinions of the source on that topic considering the document as a whole. Figure 1 depicts an aggregate opinion summary for the accompanying text.

Aggregate opinion summaries allow applications or users to access opinions in a standardized form. They will be needed by applications such as multi-perspective question answering (QA) (Stoyanov et al., 2005; Balahur et al., 2009), for example, which might need to answer questions such as "What is X's opinion toward Y?"

Opinion set summary In an *opinion set* summary, multiple opinions from a source on a topic are collected into a single set (without analyzing them for the overall trend). An opinion set summary of the example in Figure 1 would include, for example, three directed links from *American public* toward *war in Iraq* — one for each of the three expressions of opinion.

Opinion set summaries support fined-grained information extraction of opinions as well as user-directed exploration of the opinions in a document.

3 Related Work

Our works falls in the area of fine-grained subjectivity analysis concerned with analyzing opinions at, or below, the sentence level. Recent work, for example, indicates that systems can be trained to recognize opinions and their polarity, strength, and sources to a reasonable degree of accuracy (e.g. Dave et al. (2003), Riloff and Wiebe (2003), Bethard et al. (2004), Wilson et al. (2004), Yu and Hatzivassiloglou (2003), Choi et al. (2005), Kim and Hovy (2005), Wiebe and Riloff (2005)). Our work builds on research on fine-grained opinion extraction by extracting additional information that allows the creation of concise opinion summaries. In contrast to the opinion extracts produced by Pang and Lee (2004), our summaries are not text extracts, but rather explicitly identify and characterize the relations between opinions and their sources.

Several methods for computing opinions from product reviews exist (e.g. Hu and Liu (2004), Popescu and Etzioni (2005)). Due to properties of the limited domain and genre, however, the problem and approaches have been considerably simplified. In the product domain, summaries have are computed by extracting tuples [product attribute, opinion trigger, polarity] (with the product attribute extraction typically performed as a straightforward dictionary lookup) and computing summary statistics for each attribute.

The only other opinion summarization system in the general domain that we are aware of was perfromed as part of the 2008 text understanding conference (TAC) (Dang, 2008) Opinion Summarization task. The opinion summariztion task provides systems with a target such as "Trader Joe's" and 1 or 2 questions with answers of type SQUISHY LIST. A SQUISHY LIST contains complex concepts, which can overlap, may be expressed in different ways and where boundaries of the concepts are not well defined. In response, systems are expected to produce one fluent summary per target that summarizes the answers to all the questions for the target. Summaries are scored for their content using the Pyramid F-score (Nenkova et al., 2007) borrowed from the field of summarization. Additionally, summaries are manually scored along five dimensions: grammaticality, non-redundancy, structure/coherence, overall readability and overall responsiveness (content + readability).

Our work differs from the 2008 TAC Opinion tasks in several ways: We are always grouping together opinions that belong to the same **source**, while TAC 2008 tasks do not require that sources of opinions are identified. We are interested in grouping together opinions that are on the same **topic**, while the topics for the 2008 TAC Opinion tasks are pre-specified and involve a single named entity. TAC tasks do not always require **polarity** or aggregating polarities of individual opinions. We aim for an **abstract, graph-based representation** of opinions, while the TAC Opinion Summary task aims for extractive summaries.

4 Opinion Summarization System

In this section we describe the architecture of our system, OASIS.

Fine-grained Opinion Extraction OASIS starts with the output of Choi et al.'s (2006) extractor, which recognizes opinion sources and triggers. These predictions can be described as a tuple [opinion trigger, source] with each component representing a span of text in the original document. We enhance these fine-grained opinion predictions by using the opinion polarity classifier from Choi and Cardie (2009), which adds polarity predictions as one of three possible values: *positive*, *negative* or *neutral*. This value is added to the opinion tuple to obtain [opinion trigger, source, polarity] triples.

Source Coreference Resolution Given the fine-grained opinions, our system uses *source coreference resolution* to decide which opinions should be attributed to the same source. For this task, we rely on the partially supervised learning approach of Stoyanov and Cardie (2006). Following this step, OASIS produces opinion triples grouped according to their sources.

Topic Extraction/Coreference Resolution Next, our system labels fine-grained opinions with their topic and decide which opinions are on the same topic. Here, we use the *topic coreference resolution* approach proposed in Stoyanov and Cardie (2008). As a result of this step, OASIS produces opinion four-tuples [opinion trigger, source, polarity, topic name] that are grouped both

Component	Measure	Score
Fine-grained op. extractor	F1	59.7
Polarity classifier	Acc.	65.3
Source coreference resolver	B^3	83.2
Topic coreference resolver	B^3	54.7

Table 1: Performance of components of the opinion summarization system (Acc. refers to Accuracy).

according to their source and their topic. This four-tuple constitutes an opinion set summary.

Aggregating Multiple Opinions Finally, to create an aggregate opinion summary like that of Figure 1, OASIS needs to combine the multiple (possibly conflicting) opinions from a source on the same topic that appear in the opinion set summary. This is done in a straightforward way: the polarity of the aggregate opinion is computed as the average of the polarity of all the opinions from the source on the topic.

Performance of the different subcomponents of our system as it applies to our data (see Section 6) are shown in Table 1. F1 refers to the harmonic average of precision and recall, while the B^3 evaluation metric for coreference resolution (Bagga and Baldwin, 1998) is described in Section 5.[2]

5 Evaluation Metrics

Scientific approach to opinion summarization requires evaluation metrics to quantitatively compare summaries produced by different systems. We propose two new evaluation metrics for opinion summaries inspired by metrics used for coreference resolution and information extraction.

5.1 Doubly-linked B^3 score

Opinion set summaries are similar to the output of coreference resolution – both target grouping a set of items together. Thus, our first evaluation metric is based on a popular coreference resolution measure, the B^3 score (Bagga and Baldwin, 1998). B^3 evaluates the quality of a an automatically generated clustering of items (the system response) as compared to a gold-standard clustering of the same items (the key). It is computed as the recall for each item i: $Recall_i = |R_i \cap S_i|/|S_i|$, where R_i and S_i are the clusters that contains i in the response and the key, respectively. The recall for a document is the average over all items. Precision is computed by switching the roles of the key and the response and the reported score is the harmonic average of precision and recall (the F score).

Opinion summaries differ from coreference resolution in an important way: opinion sets are doubly linked – two opinions are in the same set when they have the same source **and** the same topic. We address this difference by introducing a modified version of the B^3 algorithm – the Doubly Linked B^3 (DLB^3) score . DLB^3 computes the recall for each item (opinion) i as an average of the recall with respect to the source ($recall_i^{src}$) and the recall with respect to the topic ($recall_i^{topic}$). More precisely:

$$\begin{aligned} DLB^3\ recall_i &= (recall_i^{src} + recall_i^{topic})/2 \\ recall_i^{src} &= |R_i^{src} \cap S_i^{src}|/|S_i^{src}| \end{aligned}$$

5.2 Opinion Summary Evaluation Metric

We propose a novel Opinion Summary Evaluation Metric (OSEM) that combines ideas from the ACE score (ACE, 2006) (used for information extraction) and Luo's (2005) CEAF score (used for coreference resolution). OSEM can be used for both opinion set and aggregate summaries.

The OSEM metric compares two opinion summaries – the key, K, and the response, R, containing a number of "summary opinions", each of which is comprised of one or more fine-grained opinions. Each summary opinion is characterized by three attributes (the source name, the polarity and the topic name) and by the set of fine-grained opinions that were joined to form the summary opinion. OSEM evaluates how well the key's summary opinions are extracted in the response by establishing a mapping $f : K \rightarrow R$ between the summary opinions in the key and the response. A value is associated with each mapping defined as: $value_f(K, R) = \sum_{A \in K} match(A, f(A))$, where $match(A, B)$ is a measure of how well opinions A and B match (discussed below). Similarly to the ACE and CEAF score, OSEM relies on the globally optimal matching $f^* = argmax_f(value_f(K, R))$ between the key and the response. OSEM takes CEAF's approach to compute precision

[2] Our scores for fine-grained opinion extraction differ from published results (Choi et al., 2006) because we do not allow the system to extract speech events that do not signal expressions of opinions (i.e. the word "said" when used in objective context: "John said his car is blue.").

Fine-grained opinions	System	DLB^3	OSEM				
			$\alpha = 0$	$\alpha = .25$	$\alpha = .5$	$\alpha = .75$	$\alpha = 1$
Automatic	Baseline	29.20	50.78	37.32	27.90	21.12	25.47
	OASIS	31.24	49.75	41.71	35.82	31.52	41.50
Manual	Baseline	51.12	78.67	60.72	47.04	36.60	28.59
	OASIS	59.82	78.69	69.04	61.47	55.59	54.80
	OASIS + manual src coref	79.85	82.65	79.39	76.68	74.61	74.95
	OASIS + manual tpc coref	80.80	82.40	78.14	74.53	71.56	71.03

Table 2: Scores for the summary system with varying levels of automatic information.

as $value_{f^*}(K, R)/value(R, R)$ and recall as $value_{f^*}(K, R)/value(K, K)$ and report OSEM score as the harmonic average (F-score) of precision and recall. The optimal matching is computed efficiently using the Kuhn-Munkres algorithm.

Finally, $match(A, B)$, the score for a match between summary opinions A and B is computed as a combination of how well the attributes of the summary opinion are matched and how well the individual opinion mentions (i.e. the fine-grained opinions in the text that form the aggregate opinion) are extracted. More precisely we define,

$$match(A, B) = \\ attrMatch(A, B)^{\alpha} * mentOlp(A, B)^{(1-\alpha)},$$

where $attrMatch(A, B) \in [0, 1]$ is computed as an average of how well each of the three attributes (source name, topic name and polarity) of the two summary opinions match. $mentOlp(A, B) = (2 * |A \cap B|)/(|A| + |B|)$ is a measure of how well fine-grained opinions that make up the summary opinion are extracted. Lastly, $\alpha \in [0, 1]$ is a parameter that controls how much weight is given to identifying correctly the attributes of summary opinions vs. extracting all fine-grained opinions.

The α parameter allows us to tailor the OSEM score toward either type of opinion summary. For example, $OSEM_0$ (we will use $OSEM_0$ to refer to the OSEM score with $\alpha = 0$) reflects only how well the response groups together fine-grained opinions from the same source and on the same topic and makes no reference to the attributes of summary opinions. Thus, this value of α is suitable to evaluating opinion set summaries. On the other hand, $OSEM_1$ ($\alpha = 1$) puts all weight on how well the attributes of each summary opinion are extracted, which is suitable for evaluating aggregate opinion summaries. However, $OSEM_1$ does not require summary opinions to be connected to any fine-grained opinions in the text. This can lead to inconsistent summaries getting undeserved credit. For instance, in the example of Figure 1 a system could incorrectly infer that there is a neutral opinion from Bush toward the American public. $OSEM_1$ will give partial credit to such a summary opinion when compared to the negative opinion from Bush toward Al Qaeda, for example. At any other value ($\alpha < 1$) the $mentOlp$ for such an opinion will be 0 giving no partial credit for opinions that are not grounded to a fine-grained opinion in the text. The influence of the α parameter is studied empirically in the next section.

6 Experimental Evaluation

For evaluation we use the MPQA (Wiebe et al., 2005) and $MPQA^{Topic}$ (Stoyanov and Cardie, 2008) corpora.[3] The MPQA corpus consists of 535 documents from the world press, manually annotated with phrase-level opinion information following the annotation scheme of Wiebe et al. (2005). The corpus provides annotations for opinion expressions, their polarities, and sources as well as source coreference. The $MPQA^{Topic}$ corpus consists of 150 documents from the MPQA corpus, which are also manually annotated with opinion topic information, including topic spans, topic labels, and topic coreference.

Our gold-standard summaries are created automatically for each document in the $MPQA^{Topic}$ corpus by relying on the manually annotated fine-grained opinion and source- and topic-coreference information. For our experiments, all components of OASIS are trained on the 407 documents in the MPQA corpus that are not part of the $MPQA^{Topic}$ corpus, with the exception of topic coreference, which uses 5-fold cross-validation on the $MPQA^{Topic}$ corpus.

[3] The MPQA corpus is available at http://nrrc.mitre.org/NRRC/publications.htm.

Taipei, Sept. 26 (CNA) – It is unlikely that the Vatican will establish diplomatic ties with mainland China any time soon, judging from their differences on religious issues, Ministry of Foreign Affairs (MOFA) spokeswoman [$_{\text{Source}}$ Chang Siao-yue] [$_{\text{neu}}$ *said*] Wednesday.
[$_{\text{Source}}$ Chang]'s [$_{\text{neu}}$ *remark*] came in response to a foreign wire [$_{\text{neu}}$ *report*] that mainland China and the Vatican are preparing to bridge their differences and may even pave the way for full diplomatic relations.
[$_{\text{Source}}$ Beijing authorities] are [$_{\text{neu}}$ *expected*] to take advantage of a large religious meeting slated for October 14 in Beijing to develop the possibility of setting up formal relations with the Vatican, [$_{\text{neu}}$ *according*] to the report.
...
[$_{\text{Source}}$ The MOFA spokeswoman] [$_{+}$ *affirmed*] that from the angle of Eastern and Western cultural exchanges, the sponsoring of similar conferences will be instrumental to [$_{\text{Source}}$ mainland Chinese people]'s [$_{+}$ *better understanding*] of Catholicism and its contributions to Chinese society.
As for the development of diplomatic relations between mainland China and the Vatican, [$_{\text{Source}}$ Chang] [$_{-}$ *noted*] that differences between the Beijing leadership and the Holy See on religious issues dates from long ago, so it is impossible for the Vatican to broach this issue with Beijing for the time being.
[$_{\text{Source}}$ Chang] also [$_{+}$ *reaffirmed*] the solid and cordial diplomatic links between the Republic of China and the Vatican.

KEY SUMMARY:

♯ source	opinion	topic
k1. **Chang Siao-yue**	**neutral**	**diplomatic links**
	said remark noted reaffirmed	
k2. **foreign wire**	**neutral**	**diplomatic links**
	report according to	
k3. **Chinese people**	**positive**	**Catholicism**
	better understanding	
k4. **Chang**	**positive**	**conferences**
	affirmed	
k5. **author**	**neutral**	**Beijing authorities**
	are expected	

RESPONSE SUMMARY:

♯ **source**	opinion	topic
r1. **Chang Siao-yue**	**positive**	**pave bridge vatican**
	said remark noted reaffirmed	
r2. **MOFA spokeswoman**	**positive**	**sponsor conference Catholicism**
	affirmed	
r3. **Chinese people**	**neutral**	**sponsor conference Catholicism**
	better understanding	
r4. **Beijing authorities**	**neutral**	**Beijing authorities**
	are expected	

Figure 2: An opinion summary produced by OASIS. The example shows the original article with gold-standard fine-grained opinion annotations above, the key opinion summary in the middle and the summary produced by OASIS below.

6.1 Example

We begin our evaluation section by introducing an example of an output summary produced by OASIS. The top part of Figure 2 contains the text of a document from the MPQA^{Topic} corpus, showing the fine-grained opinion annotations as they are marked in the MPQA corpus. The middle part of Figure 2 shows the gold-standard summary produced from the manual annotations. The summary is shown as a table with each box corresponding to an overall opinion. Each opinion box shows the source name on the left (each opinion is labeled with a unique string, e.g. $k1$ for the first opinion in the key) and the topic name on the right (string equivalence for the source and topic name indicate the same source/topic for the purpose of the example). The middle column of the opinion box shows the opinion characterized by the computed overall opinion shown in the first row and all opinion mentions that were combined to produce the overall opinion shown in subsequent rows (for the purpose of presentation mentions are shown as strings, but in reality they are represented as spans in the original text by the summaries). Finally, the summary produced by OASIS is shown in the bottom part of Figure 2 following the same format.

OASIS performed relatively well on the example summary of Figure 2. This is partially due to the fact that most of the opinion mentions were identified correctly. Additionally, source coreference and topic coreference appear to be mostly accurate, but there are several mistakes in labeling the topic clusters as compared to the gold standard.

Next, we use the example of Figure 2 to illustrate the computation of the OSEM score. The first step of computing the score is to calculate the scores for how well each response opinion matches each key opinion. The four-by-five matrix of scores for matching response opinions to key opinions is shown in Table 3. Scores in the table are computed for value of the α parameter set to .5. As discussed in the previous section, all values of $\alpha < 1$ require that key and response opinions have at least one mention in common to receive a non-zero score. This is illustrated in Table 3, where only four of the 20 match scores are greater than 0.

Based on the scores in Table 3, the optimal match between key and response opinions is $r1 \rightarrow k1$, $r2 \rightarrow k4$, $r3 \rightarrow k3$, and $r4 \rightarrow k5$. The value of this score is 2.91, which translates in OSEM$_{.5}$

α	0.00	0.01	0.10	0.20	0.30	0.40	0.50	0.60	0.70	0.80	0.90	0.99	1.00
OSEM prec	51.5	50.9	47.8	44.6	41.8	39.3	37.1	35.2	33.5	32.0	30.7	29.6	42.8
OSEM recall	48.1	47.6	44.7	41.7	39.0	36.7	34.6	32.8	31.2	29.7	28.5	27.5	40.3
OSEM F1	49.8	49.2	46.2	43.1	40.4	38.0	35.8	33.9	32.3	30.8	29.5	28.5	41.5

Table 4: OSEM precision, recall and F-score as a function of α.

	k1	k2	k3	k4	k5
r1	.58	0	0	0	0
r2	0	0	0	.81	0
r3	0	0	.71	0	0
r4	0	0	0	0	.81

	k1	k2	k3	k4	k5
r1	.33	0	.33	.67	0
r2	0	0	.33	.50	0
r3	.33	.33	.50	.16	.33
r4	.33	.33	0	0	.67

Table 3: OSEM score for each response opinion as matched to key opinions in the example summary of Figure 2 with parameter $\alpha = .5$ (above) and $\alpha = 1.0$ (below).

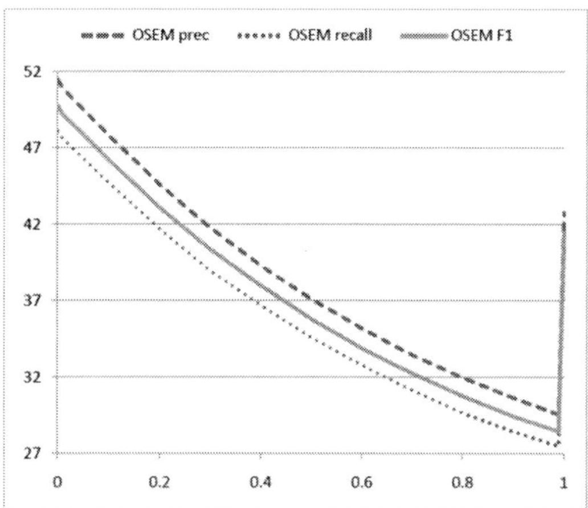

Figure 3: OSEM precision, recall and F-score (x-axis) vs. α (y-axis).

precision of .73 and recall of .58 for an overall $\text{OSEM}_{.5}$ F-score of .65.

Finally, to illustrate the different implications for the score when the α parameter is set to 1, we show the match scores for OSEM_1 in Table 3. Note that there are far fewer 0 scores in Table 3 as compared to Table 3. In the case of this particular summary, the optimal matching between key and response opinions is the same for as the setting of $\alpha = .5$, but this is not always the case. The OSEM_1 precision, recall and F-score for this summary are .50, .60 and .55, respectively.

6.2 Baseline

We compare the performance of our system to a baseline that creates one summary opinion for each fine-grained opinion. In other words, each source and topic mention is considered unique and each opinion is in its own cluster.

6.3 Results

Results are shown in Table 2. We compute $\text{DL}B^3$ score and OSEM score for 5 values of α chosen uniformly over the $[0, 1]$ interval. The top two rows of Table 2 contain results for using fully automatically extracted information.

Compared to the baseline, OASIS shows little improvement when considering opinion set summaries ($\text{DL}B^3$ improves from 29.20 to 31.20, while OSEM_0 worsens from 50.78 to 49.75). However, as α grows and more emphasis is put on correctly identifying attributes of summary opinions, OASIS substantially outperforms the baseline (OSEM_1 improves from 25.47 to 41.50).

Next, we try to tease apart the influence of different subsystems. The bottom four rows of Table 2 contain system runs using gold-standard information about fine-grained opinions (i.e. the [opinion trigger, source, polarity] triple). Results indicate that the quality of fine-grained opinion extractions has significant effect on overall system performance – scores for both the baseline and OASIS improve substantially. Additionally, OASIS appears to improve more compared to the baseline when using manual fine-grained opinion information. The last two rows of Table 2 show the performance of OASIS when using manual information for source and topic coreference, respectively. Results indicate that the rest of the errors of OASIS can be attributed roughly equally to the source and topic coreference modules.

Lastly, the OSEM score is higher at the two extreme values for α (0 and 1) as compared to values in the middle (such as .5). To study this anomaly, we compute OSEM scores for 13 values of α. Results, shown in Table 4, and visualized in Figure 3, indicate that the OSEM score decreases as more weight is put on identifying attributes of summary opinions (i.e. α increases) with a discontinuity at $\alpha = 1$. We attribute this discontinuity to the fact that $OSEM_1$ does not require opinions to be grounded in text as discussed in Section 5.2. Note, however, that the $\alpha = 1$ setting is akin to the standard evaluation scenario for many information extraction tasks.

7 Conclusions

We present and evaluate OASIS, the first general-purpose non-extract-based opinion summarization system known to us. We discuss possible forms of opinion summaries motivated by application needs, describe the architecture of our system and introduce new evaluation measures for objectively judging the goodness of complete opinion summaries. Results are promising – OASIS outperforms a competitive baseline by a large margin when we put more emphasis on computing an aggregate summary.

References

ACE. 2006. Ace 2005 evaluation, November.

A. Bagga and B. Baldwin. 1998. Entity-based cross-document coreferencing using the vector space model. In *In Proceedings of COLING/ACL*.

A. Balahur, E. Boldrini, A. Montoyo, and P. Martínez-Barco. 2009. Opinion and generic question answering systems: a performance analysis. In *Proceedings of the ACL-IJCNLP*.

S. Bethard, H. Yu, A. Thornton, V. Hativassiloglou, and D. Jurafsky. 2004. Automatic extraction of opinion propositions and their holders. In *2004 AAAI Spring Symposium on Exploring Attitude and Affect in Text*.

Y. Choi and C. Cardie. 2009. Adapting a polarity lexicon using integer linear programming for domain-specific sentiment classification. In *Proceedings of EMNLP*.

Y. Choi, C. Cardie, E. Riloff, and S. Patwardhan. 2005. Identifying sources of opinions with conditional random fields and extraction patterns. In *Proceedings of EMNLP*.

Y. Choi, E. Breck, and C. Cardie. 2006. Joint extraction of entities and relations for opinion recognition. In *Proceedings of EMNLP*.

H.T. Dang. 2008. Overview of the TAC 2008 Opinion Question Answering and Summarization Tasks. In *Text Analysis Conference (TAC-2008)*, Gaithersburg, Maryland (USA), November.

K. Dave, S. Lawrence, and D. Pennock. 2003. Mining the peanut gallery: Opinion extraction and semantic classification of product reviews. In *Proceedings of IWWWC*.

M. Hu and B. Liu. 2004. Mining opinion features in customer reviews. In *AAAI*, pages 755–760.

S. Kim and E. Hovy. 2005. Identifying opinion holders for question answering in opinion texts. In *Proceedings of AAAI Workshop on Question Answering in Restricted Domains*.

X. Luo. 2005. On coreference resolution performance metrics. In *Proceedings of EMNLP*.

A. Nenkova, R. Passonneau, and K. McKeown. 2007. The pyramid method: Incorporating human content selection variation in summarization evaluation. *ACM Transactions on Speech and Language Processing*, 4(2).

B. Pang and L. Lee. 2004. A sentimental education: Sentiment analysis using subjectivity summarization based on minimum cuts. In *Proceedings of ACL*.

A.-M. Popescu and O. Etzioni. 2005. Extracting product features and opinions from reviews. In *HLT/EMNLP*.

E. Riloff and J. Wiebe. 2003. Learning extraction patterns for subjective expressions. In *Proceesings of EMNLP*.

V. Stoyanov and C. Cardie. 2006. Partially supervised coreference resolution for opinion summarization through structured rule learning. In *Proceedings of EMNLP*.

V. Stoyanov and C. Cardie. 2008. Topic identification for fine-grained opinion analysis. In *Proceedings of COLING*.

V. Stoyanov, C. Cardie, and J. Wiebe. 2005. Multi-Perspective question answering using the OpQA corpus. In *Proceedings of EMNLP*.

J. Wiebe and E. Riloff. 2005. Creating subjective and objective sentence classifiers from unannotated texts. In *Proceedings of CICLing*.

J. Wiebe, T. Wilson, and C. Cardie. 2005. Annotating expressions of opinions and emotions in language. *Language Resources and Evaluation*, 1(2).

T. Wilson, J. Wiebe, and R. Hwa. 2004. Just how mad are you? Finding strong and weak opinion clauses. In *Proceedings of AAAI*.

H. Yu and V. Hatzivassiloglou. 2003. Towards answering opinion questions: Separating facts from opinions and identifying the polarity of opinion sentences. In *Proceedings of EMNLP*.

Exploring the Usefulness of Cross-lingual Information Fusion for Refining Real-time News Event Extraction: A Preliminary Study

Jakub Piskorski
Institute of Computer Science
Polish Academy of Sciences
Warsaw, Poland
Jakub.Piskorski
@ipipan.waw.pl

Jenya Belayeva, Martin Atkinson
Joint Research Centre
of the European Commission
Ispra, Italy
{Jenya.Belayeva,Martin.Atkinson}
@jrc.ec.europa.eu

Abstract

Nowadays, many influential facts are reported multiple times by different sources and in different languages. This paper presents the results of an experiment on deploying cross-lingual information fusion techniques for refining the results of a large-scale multilingual news event extraction system. An evaluation on a test corpus consisting of 618 event descriptions which refer to 523 real-world events revealed that the description of circa 10% of the events extracted by the mono-lingual systems could be refined. In particular, an overall gain of 6,4% and 4,8% in recall and precision against the best mono-lingual system could be obtained respectively.

1 Introduction

The goal of event extraction is to automatically identify events in free texts and to derive structured and detailed information about them. In the past, a vast bulk of the research focused on the development of mono-lingual event extraction systems that operate on single documents without taking any advantage of global evidence, i.e., without reusing the knowledge acquired in the process of extracting information from other topically-related documents. The advantages of going beyond the classical single-document extraction and exploiting information redundancy to validate facts have recently been explored by various research groups (Downey et al., 2005; Finkel et al., 2005; Ji and Grishman, 2008; Lee et al., 2010; Liao and Grishman, 2010; Mann, 2007; Patwardhan et al., 2007; Poibeau et al., 2008; Yangarber and Jokipii, 2005; Yangarber, 2006). Since nowadays many influential facts are not only reported multiple times by different sources, but also in different languages, the importance of the ability to aggregate and fuse information across documents in several languages is becoming paramount (Ji, 2010). Several experiments on cross-lingual information extraction have been reported (Chen et al., 2009; Sudo et al., 2004; Lee et al., 2010), however, they mainly focused on cross-lingual bootstrapping of ML-based event extraction systems.

This paper presents the results of an experiment aiming at exploring the usefulness of cross-lingual information fusion for refining the results of a real-time multilingual news event extraction engine that is deployed in a large-scale online news monitoring platform. To be more precise, we explored: (a) what fraction of event descriptions extracted could potentially be merged and refined through cross-lingual information fusion; and, (b) whether gain in precision/recall could be obtained. In principle, there are two ways of approaching cross-lingual information fusion in the context of multilingual news event extraction: (1) translate all news articles into one common language for which a high-performance event extraction system exists (e.g., English), and run that system on the translated news (including cross-article fusion), or (2) run mono-lingual event extraction on the native language news articles, then translate (normalize) automatically extracted event descriptions into one common language, and subsequently, perform information fusion. In this paper we explore the latter approach.

The remaining part of this paper is organized as follows. First, the real-time event extraction engine is presented in Section 2. Next, the creation and statistics of the test corpus are described in

Section 3. Subsequently, Sections 4 and 5 present the cross-lingual fusion technique and the results of the experiments. We end with some conclusions in Section 6.

2 Real-time Event Extraction Engine

First, news articles are gathered by Europe Media Monitor (EMM) (Atkinson et al., 2009), a large-scale media monitoring platform[1], which currently retrieves a vast bulk of news articles per day from over 2500 news sources in all major languages. The news articles harvested in a last 4-hour time window are grouped into clusters according to content similarity, using hierarchical agglomerative clustering in a manner as described in (Piskorski et al., 2011).[2] Then news article clusters are categorised using filters, which consist of boolean combinations of multilingual keywords and some metadata.

Next, each cluster is processed by NEXUS, the core event extraction engine, which initially performs shallow linguistic analysis, including, i.a., fine-grained tokenization, sentence splitting, domain-specific dictionary look-up (e.g., for the detection of numerical expressions, quantifiers, person titles, and for the labeling of key terms indicating unnamed person groups), and morphological analysis. In particular, for morphological analysis an extended version of the full-form MULTEXT[3] lexica are used.

Subsequently, a cascade of finite-state extraction grammars[4] is applied on each article in the cluster. The low-level grammars are primarily used for the detection of small-scale structures (e.g., person groups, which might potentially constitute a slot filler). The higher-level grammars consist of simple linear 1/2-slot extraction patterns, similar to those in (Riloff, 1996), e.g., `PER-GROUP <VICTIM> "was killed"` assigns a group of persons followed by a phrase `"was killed"` the role of a victim. These patterns are applied only on the top sentences and the title of each article. The main rationale behind this is that news articles are written in the inverted-pyramid style.[5] Secondly, analysing the entire text might involve handling complex language phenomena (e.g., anaphora resolution), which is hard and requires knowledge intensive processing. In particular, in the context of developing an event extraction system capable of processing news in several languages tackling more complex language phenomena would involve a substantial effort to provide the necessary language-specific resources. Finally, if some crucial information can not be captured from one article in the cluster (due to the simplistic approach mentioned before), it might be extracted from other articles in the same cluster. Let us consider as an example the following sentence.

> *'The United Nations says* ***Somali gunmen*** *who hijacked a U.N.-chartered vessel carrying food aid for tsunami victims* ***have released the ship*** *after holding it for more than two months.'*

The proper extraction of *Somali gunmen* as the actor of a `RELEASE` event would require some syntactical parsing to identify the relative clause that describes the *Somali gunmen*, otherwise the application of a linear extraction pattern might result in assigning the *tsunami victims* the actor role of the `RELEASE` event (incorrect). However, the title and the initial sentence of most of news articles on crisis-related events exhibit relatively simple syntactical structure, e.g., it would be more likely (based on empirical observations) that the same information as in our example is conveyed through a sentence like this:

> ***'Somali gunmen have released the ship*** *after holding it for more than two months.'*

Consequently, the application of the pattern `PER-GROUP <ACTOR> "have released"` would yield a correct extraction of *Somali gunmen* as the actor of the `RELEASE` event.

Since the information about events is scattered over different articles, the last step consists of cross-article cluster-level information fusion in order to produce full-fledged event descriptions, i.e., information extracted locally from each single article in the same cluster is aggregated and validated. This involves: (a) disambiguation on entity roles (as a result of application of extraction patterns the same entity might be assigned different

---

[1] http://press.jrc.it

[2] The article feature vectors are simple word count vectors and no lemmatization is performed.

[3] http://nl.ijs.si/ME/

[4] A grammar consists of pattern-action rules, where the left-hand side of a rule is a regular expression over non-recursive typed feature structures (the recognition pattern), whereas the right-hand side constitutes a list of feature structures, which will be returned in case the recognition pattern is matched. See (Piskorski, 2007) for more details.

[5] The most important parts of the story are placed in the beginning of the article and the least important facts are left toward the end.

roles), (b) computing an estimate of the total number of victims, and (c) event type classification, all accomplished through heuristics.[6]

It is important to note that NEXUS detects only the main event for each news article cluster ('one sense per discourse') (Gale et al., 1992), and 6 language-specific instances of the system have been developed to cover news in English, Italian, Spanish, French, Portuguese, and Russian. In particular, for each language extraction grammars and specialized lexica were acquired using weakly supervised ML techniques and validated by human experts. Noteworthy, certain part of the extraction grammars are shared among languages (Zavarella et al., 2008).

There are several differences in language-specific versions of NEXUS. Currently, Italian, French, Spanish and Portuguese versions fully rely on morphological analysis (MULTEXT), whereas Russian and English system instances do not, i.e., morphological features are not referred to in the extraction patterns. In addition, the Italian, Spanish and Portuguese systems deploy more (abstract) linguistic rules that constitute a partial parser of domain specific phrases. The overall number of extraction patterns used in the Italian, Spanish and Portuguese system varies from 100 to circa 400, whereas the English, French and Russian system deploy thousands of extraction patterns, mainly relying on surface-level text features. Another important difference is that the event type classification for English is done using a blend of category definitions and a statistical classifier, whereas the other 5 language-specific instances rely only on well-defined event category definitions. There are over 30 event category definitions, which can consist of a simple list of related keywords or a combination of lists of words. Most category definitions are defined using Boolean operators with optional proximity operator and wild cards. Alternatively, cumulative positive or negative weights and a threshold can be specified.

The briefly sketched cluster-centric approach to news event extraction, the process of acquisition of language specific resources for NEXUS, and other particularities of NEXUS are given in (Tanev et al., 2008; Tanev et al., 2009; Piskorski et al., 2011). Some other effort aiming at constructing multilingual event extraction based on light-weight linguistic approach is presented in (Lejeune et al., 2010).

[6]For instance, if the same entity has two roles assigned in the same news cluster, preference is given to the role assigned by the most reliable group of patterns, e.g., 2-slot extraction patterns are considered more reliable than 1-slot extraction patterns. In case of event type classification and victim counting heuristics similar in spirit to those described in (Piskorski et al., 2011) were used.

3 Corpus and Event Statistics

For exploring the potential of cross-lingual information fusion a corpus consisting of crisis-related event descriptions automatically extracted by NEXUS on 22 randomly selected (non-continuous) days in 2010 from news in 6 languages has been prepared. In particular, we focused on violent events and natural and man-made disasters. The set of slots we considered includes the following ones: `TYPE`, `LOCATION`, `PERPETRATOR`, `DEAD`, `DEAD-COUNT`, `INJURED`, `INJURED-COUNT`, `KIDNAPPED`, `KIDNAPPED-COUNT`, `ARRESTED`, `WEAPONS`.

The corpus consists of 618 event descriptions. Table 1 gives the statistics on the extracted event descriptions and news sources used. The 618 event descriptions extracted refer to 523 real-world events.

Language	#Event descriptions	#Slots filled in total	#Slots filled on average	#News sources
English	268	963	3.59	783
Spanish	129	454	3.52	174
French	77	273	3.55	224
Italian	50	172	3.44	68
Russian	52	158	3.04	178
Portuguese	42	137	3.26	55
All	618	2157	3.49	1482

Table 1: The statistics of the extracted events.

Out of the 523 events 51 were reported in more then one language. This accounts for circa 9,8% of all extracted events that could be potentially refined through cross-lingual information fusion. The 51 events reported in more than one language include: 33 violence events, 7 natural disasters, 9 man-made disasters and 2 other crisis-related events. Noteworthy, 350 events out of the 523 were detected in non-English news. In the latter group of 'non English' events only 7 were reported in more than two languages, which accounts for 2% of all events in this group. Hence, extraction from English news is crucial in the process of cross-lingual information fusion. The histogram in Figure 1 shows the number of languages in which news report on events in our corpus.

For the 51 events reported in more than one language we manually created the gold-standard

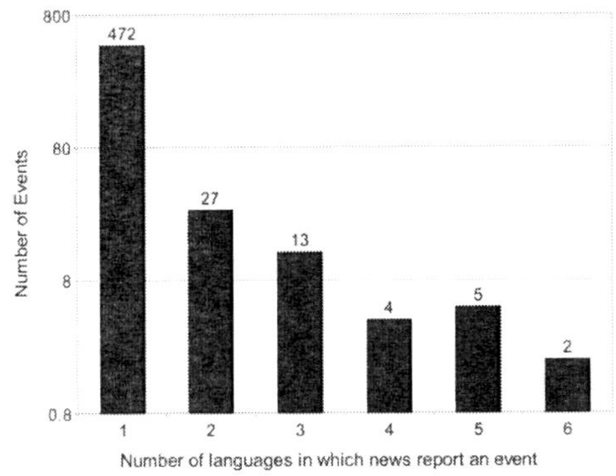

Figure 1: The histogram showing the number of languages in which news report on events.

stand-off annotations based on any information which could be found in news articles in all 6 languages. Furthermore, for the purpose of evaluating mono-lingual systems, we also created for each of the 51 events and a given language (i.e., for each mono-lingual news article cluster) a stand-off annotation based on information which could be found in that particular language only. In total, there were 4252 news articles that refer to the 51 events. In particular, the average number of news articles per cluster which correspond to an event in the set of the 51 events is: 29 (all languages), 55 (English), 16 (Spanish), 21 (Italian), 29 (French), 21 (Portuguese), and 8 (Russian). The annotation task (including the classification of the events) was jointly carried out by two annotators.

For the preparation of the test corpus and annotation, in particular, for linking (manually) of event descriptions across languages, the Event Moderation Tool (EMT) described in (Atkinson et al., 2011) has been used. EMT provides GUI-based tools that can: retrieve automatically extracted event descriptions gathered over time according to a number of different criteria (e.g., event type, date of occurrence, language, source and location), edit, validate, group, translate, and export them into other knowledge repositories.

The test corpus comes from Internet news articles that EMM scrapes and analyses on the fly. The scraped information is governed by copyrights and therefore cannot be reproduced by any means or form without infringement. Hence, as of now, the only corpus that we can provide to the research community are the links to the original articles accompanied with some additional information, i.e., the corresponding event ID that we generated (for 51 events reported in at least two languages) as well as the language of the underlying news article. The resource file URL is available at: http://emm-labs.jrc.it/CLEventResources.csv.[7]

4 Cross-lingual Fusion

The information fusion process is divided into two steps. First, event descriptions extracted by mono-lingual systems are normalized, i.e., all non-numerical slot fillers are translated (converted) into English, whereas geographical names are mapped to their canonical forms using the multi-lingual *GeoNames*[8] gazetteer. In the second step, for each event the corresponding normalized event descriptions are merged into one via the application of simple fusion methods. The computation of the value of each slot in the 'fused' event description is based on the following general assumption: *'If a candidate slot value (returned by at least one of the mono-lingual systems) occurs frequently (more than once) as a filler of a given slot in a collection of event descriptions referring to a certain real-world event, and if this value was 'on average' extracted with high system confidence*[9]*, and if it refers to a more specific concept than the other values in the candidate slot filler set, that increases the likelihood that this slot value is correct'.*

Table 2 shows an example of system response (in as simplified form), i.e., event descriptions extracted by mono-lingual systems, and the result of cross-lingual fusion for an event related to U.S. drone strike that killed eight militants of German nationality in Islamabad.

We now present the fusion method more formally. First, let E denote an event. We denote the set of automatically extracted event descriptions that refer to E as $E_D = \{e_1, \ldots, e_k\}$, where e_i is a set of slot-value pairs. The value of slot x in the event description e is denoted as $e(x)$. We extend this notion to a set of values for slot x in an event description collection $E_D(x) = \{v | \exists e \in E_D \wedge e(x) = v\}$. Next, let $E_D^{x=v} = \{e | e \in E_D \wedge e(x) = v\}$ be the set of event descriptions with certain value v for the slot

[7] It is important to note that some online media do not archive their news. As a consequence of this, a fraction of the links provided in the URL might become inactive relatively soon.

[8] http://www.geonames.org/

[9] 'on average' meaning that the average system confidence was high

LANG	Event Type	Location	Dead (count)	Injured (count)
IT	Air Attack	Islamabad	Germans (3)	- (-)
EN	Armed Conflict	Islamabad	German militants (5)	- (-)
ES	Armed Conflict	Islamabad	German militants (8)	German militants (3)
RU	-	Pakistan	people (8)	- (-)
FR	-	Pakistan	insurgers (8)	- (-)
Fusion	Air Attack	Islamabad	German militants (8)	none (0)

Table 2: Cross-lingual fusion example. The underlined values were selected as slot fillers in the fusion process.

x. Furthermore, we denote systems' confidence of extracting v as the value of $e(x)$ as $conf_e(x, v)$[10]. Let e^* denote the event description resulting from merging the event descriptions in E_D using fusion method M, which is defined as follows:

$$e^*(x) = \underset{v \in E_D(x)}{\text{argmax}}\ Score_M(x, v)$$

where $Score_M(x, v)$ denotes a scoring function specific to method M. For filling non-numerical slots we used the following scoring function:

$$\begin{aligned} Score_M(x, v) &= \sum_{e \in E_D^{x=v}} conf_e(x, v) \cdot \frac{1}{|E_D^{x=v}|} \\ &+ \alpha \cdot |E_D^{x=v}| \\ &+ \beta \cdot |\{v' \in E_D(x)| \wedge v' \supset v\}| \end{aligned}$$

where $\alpha \geq 0$ is a factor determining the importance of the number of occurrences of v as a slot filler for x, and $\beta \geq 0$ is a factor which specifies the degree of boosting slot values, which happen to represent concepts that stand either in 'is-subsumed-by' or 'is-part-of' relation (denoted as '$\supset$') with other concepts in the same slot value set.[11] The rationale of using the latter factor is that, intuitively, a 'more-specific' value co-occurring with a related 'more-generic' concept is more likely to be the correct slot filler among those two. For instance, in $E_D(LOCATION) = \{Spain, Andalucia, Algeciras\}$, *Algeciras* would be boosted by $\beta \cdot 2$ since *Algeciras* is a part of *Andalucia* and *Spain*. Hence, *Algeciras* gets a higher chance of being selected as the location of the event. α and β were set differently for different slot types.

As for numerical slots, the fusion was done in a slightly different way. First of all, the definition of $Score_M(x, v)$ was simplified since the last part (β) does not apply to numbers, and secondly, in case of candidate values, which are significantly distant one from another we selected a maximum (provided that confidence of extracting it is higher than a pre-specified constant), based on a simple assumption that the event is most likely evolving and numbers change continuously, the highest being the more up-to-date one. It is not necessarily the case that the last news article on a certain event reports the most up-to-date figures since there is certain latency between reporting on a given event in different countries. Therefore, we chose the 'maximum' heuristic.

5 Experiments

We have applied the cross-lingual fusion technique presented in Section 4 on the corpus described in Section 3 and we measured extraction precision, recall and F-measure for each language-specific system instance and for the extraction based on cross-lingual information fusion. It is important to note that we assigned basically three scores (for non-numerical slots) for filling each slot: 0 (incorrect), 1 (correct), and 0.5 (partially correct), where 'partially correct' is assigned in cases where the slot fill represents a more generic concept than the one in the gold-standard, or in case of locations, if the slot fill refers to an administrative unit, which encompasses the specific place of an event, e.g., if the event happened in *Islamabad*, we assign the slot fill *Pakistan* the score 'partially correct'.

	Event Type			Location		
	P	R	F	P	R	F
English	86.6	80.7	83.5	82.6	80.7	81.6
Spanish	80.4	61.7	69.8	85.5	85.5	85.5
French	83.3	70.0	76.1	68.8	66.0	67.4
Italian	67.8	63.3	65.5	86.7	86.7	86.7
Russian	81.3	28.3	42.0	61.4	58.7	60.0
Portuguese	73.7	59.2	65.7	**87.5**	55.6	66.7
FUSION	**91.3**	**84.3**	**87.6**	87.3	**87.3**	**87.3**

Table 3: Precision, recall and F-measure figures for the extraction of event type and location.

The overall precision and recall figures is shown in Figure 2. Compared to the performance of the best mono-lingual system a gain of 6,4% and

[10]The confidence is based on a combination of factors, e.g., the reliability of the pattern(s) used to extract a particular value (the likelihood that pattern extract the slot value correctly), the number of articles in which some patterns were triggered (frequency), the overall confidence of the language-specific instance of the event extraction system, etc.

[11]A small in-house ontology was used for this purpose.

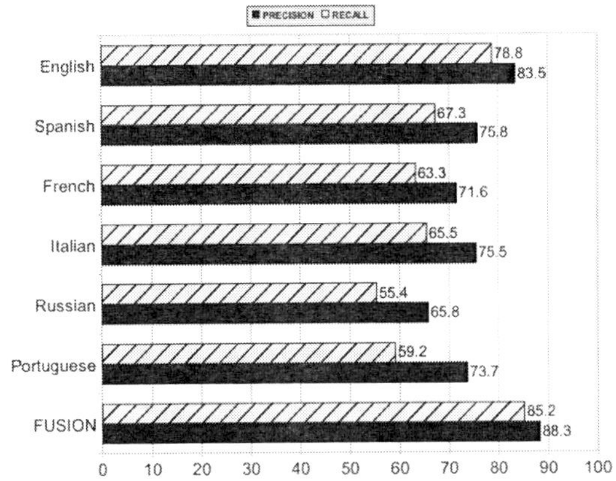

Figure 2: The overall precision (black solid bars) and recall figures for monolingual event extraction vs. event extraction refined by cross-lingual information fusion.

	Non-numerical slots			Numerical slots		
	P	R	F	P	R	F
English	**92.2**	80.8	86.1	73.9	70.8	72.3
Spanish	84.6	69.1	76.1	62.9	51.5	56.6
French	91.6	71.7	80.4	54.1	46.4	50.0
Italian	85.0	51.5	64.1	53.8	41.1	46.6
Russian	91.6	55.0	68.7	75.0	53.5	62.5
Portuguese	83.3	63.1	71.8	50.0	40.0	44.4
FUSION	91.5	**83.5**	**87.3**	**82.6**	**79.6**	**81.1**

Table 4: Precision, recall and F-measure figures for the extraction of numerical and non-numerical slots.

4,8% respectively in the overall recall and precision could be obtained through cross-lingual fusion. Table 3 gives the precision, recall and F-measure for the extraction of the event type and location, whereas Table 4 gives the corresponding figures for the extraction of other non-numerical and numerical slots. As can be observed, a gain of 4-5% and 8% in precision and recall could be obtained for the extraction of event type and numerical slots respectively. The precision for extracting locations and non-numerical slots for the best-scoring mono-lingual system is better than the result of cross-lingual fusion. However, the recall for the same slot types is 0.6% and 2.7% respectively higher in case of cross-lingual fusion.

A small error analysis of cross-lingual fusion was carried out. In case of fusing event type information, it turned out that for 5 out of 51 events in our corpus none of the mono-lingual systems was able to assign any type information. Consequently, the cross-lingual fusion did not result in any improvement in case of those events, i.e., no type information was assigned. In case of 2 other events, all of the mono-lingual systems returned incorrect event type information, which resulted in incorrect cross-lingual fusion. Furthermore, in case of 2 events, the cross-lingual fusion resulted in selection of an event type (extracted by at least one of the mono-lingual systems), which is related to the event type in the gold standard (partially correct extraction), but the latter was not detected by any mono-lingual system. Finally, for 1 event, the cross-lingual fusion resulted in selection of an incorrect event type, although the correct event type was detected by at least one of the mono-lingual systems. The analysis of fusing location information revealed that: (a) in case of 3 events a wrong location was selected, although at least one of the mono-lingual system returned the correct answer, (b) for 4 events the returned location was partially correct, and (c) for 2 events none of the mono-lingual systems provided a correct answer, and, consequently, the error was propagated in the fusion process.

6 Conclusions and Future Work

We presented the results of preliminary explorations on using cross-lingual information fusion to improve the recall/precision of a large-scale multilingual event extraction system. Circa 10% of event descriptions extracted by the mono-lingual systems could be refined, and a gain of 6,4% and 4,8% in the overall recall and precision could be obtained respectively. Since we limited the time window for grouping event descriptions referring to a given event to 1 day only the aforementioned figure of 10% constitutes an approximation of a lower bound for the fraction of crisis-related event descriptions, which can be potentially refined through cross-lingual information fusion. An effort is envisaged to create (multilingual) temporal event chains (Ji et al., 2009), which go beyond 1-day time window, for further explorations on the potential of cross-lingual information fusion for refining event extraction results.

Although the reported improvement in precision and recall appears to be promising, to better assess the actual impact of exploiting multilinguality for refining event descriptions an evaluation of the improvement achieved by merging information from different sources in the same language is planned too. In order to get a better insight into the real contribution of exploiting news in each language a direct one-to-one comparison between the English system (the one with the highest impact) and each of the mono-lingual systems will be carried out too.

Furthermore, we intend to explore the usefulness of deploying cross-lingual information fusion in the context of extracting other types of events. For instance, in (Atkinson et al., 2011) we elaborate on the specifics of reporting on border security-related events (e.g., illegal migration attempts, cross-border crimes, etc.) in online news, which revealed that suchlike events are intuitively less likely to benefit from cross-lingual information fusion.

Future work will also focus on exploring more elaborated fusion techniques (Ji and Grishman, 2008) and comparison with the approach based on translating news articles into one common language and running event extraction and information fusion on the translated articles. Although several authors reported that such an approach is error-prone due to inaccuracy of the state-of-the-art machine translation techniques, it has not been evaluated in the context of a cluster-centric and linguistically-lightweight approach to event extraction as described in this paper.

Our event extraction engine processes only the title and top sentences of each news article. However, processing additional 'relevant' sentences, which could be selected through deployment of some time-efficient sentence ranking measures (Litvak et al., 2010), might lead to a better coverage and is considered to be explored in the future. The inclusion of additional sentences in the event extraction process might also help to estimate the fraction of information which is being missed by the current event extraction engine.

With the emergence of social media, one can observe an ever growing trend of reporting on the same event in many different languages. For instance, the GLOBAL VOICES[12] is a community of bloggers and translators around the globe, who link and translate articles/posts on certain events and issues that are not usually present in international mainstream media. Therefore, we plan to carry out experiments on deploying cross-lingual information fusion techniques to refine event extraction from suchlike information sources.

Although the experiments reported in this paper are preliminary, we strongly believe that the presented work and discussion constitutes useful source of information for researchers and practitioners working on advancing event extraction technology.

[12]http://globalvoicesonline.org

Acknowledgments

We are greatly indebted to all our colleagues in the OPTIMA action at the Joint Research Centre, who are working on *EMM*. In particular, we would like to thank Hristo Tanev and Vanni Zavarella, who are working on the core of NEXUS and language-specific versions of the system, and without whom the presented work would not have been possible.

References

Martin Atkinson and Erik van der Goot. 2009. Near Real-Time Information Mining in Multilingual News. In *Proceedings of the* 18th *World Wide Web Conference 2009.*

Martin Atkinson, Jakub Piskorski, Erik Van der Goot and Roman Yangarber. 2011. Multilingual Real-Time Event Extraction for Border Security Intelligence Gathering. Book chapter in: *Counterterrorism and Open Source Intelligence Series.* Lecture Notes in Social Networks, Vol. 2.

Zheng Chen and Heng Ji. 2009. Can one Language Bootstrap the Other: A Case Study on Event Extraction. In *Proceedings of the NAACL HLT 2009 Workshop on Semi-Supervised Learning for Natural Language Processing.*

Doug Downey, Oren Etzioni and Stephen Soderland. 2005. A Probabilistic Model of Redundancy in Information Extraction. In *Proceedings of IJCAI 2005.*

Jenny Finakel, Trond Grenager and Christopher Manning. 2005. Incorporating Non-local Information into Information Extraction Systems by Gibbs Sampling. In *Proceedings of ACL 2005.*

Gael Lejeune, Antoine Doucet, Roman Yangarber and Nadine Lucas 2010. Filtering News for Epidemic Surveillance: Towards Processing More Languages with Fewer Resources. In *Proceedings of* 4th *Workshop on Cross Lingual Information Access at COLING 2010.*

William Gale, Kenneth Church and David Yarowsky 1992. One Sense per Discourse. In *Proceedings of the workshop on Speech and Natural Language.*, pages 233–237.

Silja Huttunen, Roman Yangarber and Ralph Grishman. 2002. Complexity of Event Structure in IE Scenarios. In *Proceedings of COLING 2002.*

Heng Ji and Ralph Grishman. 2008. Refining Event Extraction through Cross-Document Inference. In *Proceedings of ACL 2008*, pages 254–262.

Heng Ji, Ralph Grishman, Zheng Chen and Prashant Gupta. 2009. Cross-document Event Extraction and Tracking: Task, Evaluation, Techniques and Challenges. In *Proceedings of RANLP 2009*, pages 166–172.

Heng Ji. 2010. Challenges from Information Extraction to Information Fusion. In *Proceedings of ACL 2008*, pages 507–515.

Adam Lee, Marissa Passantino, Heng Ji, Guojun Qi and Thomas Huang. 2010. Enhancing Multi-lingual Information Extraction via Cross-Media Inference and Fusion. In *Proceedings of COLING 2010: Posters*, pages 630–638.

Shasha Liao and Ralph Grishman. 2010. Using Document Level Cross-Event Inference to Improve Event Extraction. In *Proceedings of ACL 2010*, pages 789–797.

Marina Litvak, Mark last and Menahem Friedman. 2010. A new Approach to Improving Multilingual Summarization using a Genetic Algorithm. In *Proceedings of ACL 2010*, pages 927–936.

Gideon Mann. 2007. Multi-document Relationship Fusion via Constraints on Probabilistic Databases. In *Proceedings of HLT/NAACL 2007*.

Martina Naughton, Nicholas Kushmerick and Joseph Carthy. 2006. Event Extraction from Heterogeneous News Sources. In *Proceedings of the AAAI 2006 workshop on Event Extraction and Synthesis*.

Siddharth Patwardhan and Ellen Riloff. 2007. Effective Information Extraction with Semantic Affinity Patterns and Relevant Regions. In *Proceedings of EMNLP-CONLL 2007*.

Jakub Piskorski. 2007. ExPRESS Extraction Pattern Recognition Engine and Specification Suite. In *Proceedings of the* 6th *International Workshop Finite-State Methods and Natural language Processing (FSMNLP 2007)*.

Jakub Piskorski, Hristo Tanev, Martin Atkinson, Erik van der Goot and Vanni Zavarella. 2011. Online News Event Extraction for Global Crisis Surveillance. In *Transactions on Computational Collective Intelligence*, Volume 5, Lecture Notes in Computer Science 6910, pages 182–212, Springer-Verlag Berlin Heidelberg.

Thierry Poibeau, Horacio Saggion and Roman Yangarber. 2008. *Proceedings of the Workshop on Multi-source Multilingual Information Extraction and Summarization (MMIES 2008)*.

Ellen Riloff. 1996. Automatically Generating Extraction Patterns from Untagged Text. In *Proceedings of the* 13th *National Conference on Artificial Intelligence (AAAI-96)*, pages 1044–1049.

Kiyoshi Sudo, Satoshi Sekine and Ralph Grishman. 2004. Cross-lingual Information Extraction System Evaluation. In *Proceedings of COLING 2004*.

Hristo Tanev, Jakub Piskorski and Martin Atkinson. 2008. Real-Time News Event Extraction for Global Crisis Monitoring. In *Proceedings of NLDB 2008*. LNCS, Vol. 5039, pages 207–218, Springer.

Hristo Tanev, Vanni Zavarella, Jens Linge, Mijail Kabadjov, Jakub Piskorski, Martin Atkinson and Ralf Steinberger. 2009. Exploiting Machine Learning Techniques to Build an Event Extraction System for Portuguese and Spanish. *Linguamatica Journal*, Vol.2, pages 55–66.

Earl Wagner, Jiahui Liu, Larry Birnbaum, Kenneth Forbus and James Baker 2006. Using Explicit Semantic Models to Track Situations Across News Articles. In *Proceedings of the AAAI 2006 workshop on Event Extraction and Synthesis*.

Roman Yangarber and Lauri Jokipii. 2005. Redundancy-based Correction of Automatically Extracted Facts. In *Proceedings of HLT/EMNLP 2005*.

Roman Yangarber. 2006. Verification of Facts across Document Boundaries. In *Proceedings of International Workshop on Intelligent Information Access, Helsinki*.

Roman Yangarber, Clive Best, Peter von Etter, Flavio Fuart, David Horby and Ralf Steinberger. 2007. Combining Information about Epidemic Threats from Multiple Sources. In *Proceedings of International Workshop on Multi-source, Multilingual Information Extraction and Summarization at RANLP-2007*.

Zavarella Vanni, Hristo Tanev and Jakub Piskorski. 2008. Event Extraction for Italian Using a Cascade of Finite-State Grammars. In *Proceedings of the* 8th *International Workshop on Finite-State Methods and Natural language Processing (FSMNLP'2008)*.

Temporal Relation Extraction Using Expectation Maximization

Seyed Abolghasem Mirroshandel
Sharif University or Technology, Iran
mirroshandel@ce.sharif.edu

Gholamreza Ghassem-Sani
Sharif University or Technology, Iran
sani@sharif.edu

Abstract

The ability to accurately determine temporal relations between events is an important task for several natural language processing applications such as Question Answering, Summarization, and Information Extraction. Since current supervised methods require large corpora, which for many languages do not exist, we have focused our attention on approaches with less supervision as much as possible. This paper presents a fully generative model for temporal relation extraction based on the expectation maximization (EM) algorithm. Our experiments show that the performance of the proposed algorithm, regarding its little supervision, is considerable in temporal relation learning.

1 Introduction

Lately, the increasing attention to the practical NLP applications such as question answering, information extraction, and summarization have resulted in a growing demand of temporal information processing (Tatu and Srikanth, 2008). In question answering, one may expect the system to answer questions such as *"when an event occurred"*, or *"what is the chronological order of some desired events"*. In text summarization, especially in the multi-document type, knowing the order of events is a useful source of correctly merging related information.

Unlike problems such as part-of-speech tagging, morphological analysis, parsing, and named entity recognition which have been recently addressed with satisfactory results by combining statistical and symbolic methods (Mani et al., 2006), temporal relation extraction that requires deeper semantic analysis are yet to be worked on. One of recent efforts has disclosed that this task is a complicated task, even for human annotators (Mani et al., 2006).

Based on the type of corpora that different temporal relation learning methods use, these methods are divided into three major categories: supervised, semi-supervised, and unsupervised. Supervised methods normally rely on the correct temporal relations of training sentences of a manually tagged corpus. Semi-supervised methods often rely on a partially tagged corpus and need less supervision. Finally, unsupervised methods rely only on raw sentences without any temporal relation annotation. It is obvious that producing the necessary training data (corpora) of supervised and to a less extent semi-supervised methods is a time consuming, hard, and expensive work. Besides, it is very difficult to adapt such methods for new tasks, languages, and/or domains. Consequently, it is in fact the corpus availability that directs the research in this area. For mentioned reasons, we have focused on unsupervised and weakly supervised temporal relation learning.

This paper presents a novel usage of expectation maximization (EM) algorithm for temporal relation learning. The algorithm also employs Allen's interval algebra (Allen, 1984). Our experiments show that the performance of the proposed algorithm is acceptable with respect to little usage of tagged corpora which is used.

The remainder of the paper is organized as follows: section 2 is about previous works on temporal relation extraction. Section 3 explains our proposed method. Section 4 briefly presents the characteristic of the corpora that we have used. Section 5 demonstrates the evaluation of the proposed algorithm. Finally, section 6 includes our conclusions and some possible future works.

2 Temporal Relation Extraction

For a given ordered pair of components (x_1, x_2), where x_1 and x_2 are times and/or events, a temporal information processing system identifies the type of relation that temporally links x_1 to x_2. The relation type can for instance be one of the 14 types proposed in TimeML (Pustejovsky et al., 2003). For example, in *"If all the debt is converted (e_7) to common, Automatic Data will issue (e_8) about 3.6 million shares; last Monday (t_{24}), the company had (e_{25}) nearly 73 million shares outstanding."*, taken from document *wsj_0541* of TimeBank (Pustejovsky et al., 2003), there are two temporal relations between pairs *(e_7, e_8)* and *(t_{24}, e_{25})*. The task of temporal relation extraction is to automatically tag these pairs respectively with the *BEFORE* and *INCLUDES* relations.

2.1 Related Work

There are numerous ongoing researches focused on temporal relation extraction. Existing methods of temporal relation learning, which are mainly fully supervised, can be divided into three categories: 1) Pattern based; 2) Rule based, and 3) Anchor based. These categories are respectively discussed in the next three sub-sections.

Pattern Based Methods

Pattern based methods extract some generic lexico-syntactic patterns for events co-occurrence. Extracting such patterns can be done manually or automatically.

Perhaps the simplest pattern based method is the one that was developed using a knowledge resource called VerbOcean (Chklovski and Pantel, 2005). VerbOcean has a small number of manually selected generic patterns. The style of patterns is in the form of <Verb-X> and then <Verb-Y>. Similar to other manual methods, a major drawback of this method is its tendency to have a high recall but a low precision. Several heuristics have been proposed to resolve the low precision problem (Chklovski and Pantel, 2005; Torisawa, 2006).

On the other hand, automatic methods try to learn a classifier from an annotated corpus, and attempt to improve classification accuracy by feature engineering. MaxEnt classifier is an example of this group (Mani et al., 2006). The state of the art of supervised methods in this group is very similar to the MaxEnt classifier (Chambers et al., 2007). This classifier tries to learn event attributes and event-event features in two consecutive stages. It also uses WordNet to find words' synsets.

Some of researches on pattern based temporal relation classification only work on corpora with specific characteristics, rather than general corpora such as TimeBank (Bethard and Martin, 2008; Bethard et al, 2007a; Lapata and Lascarides 2006; Bethard et al, 2007b; Bethard, 2007). There are also algorithms that work on only limited types of relations (Lapata and Lascarides 2006; Bethard, 2007; Bethard and Martin, 2007; Chambers and Jurafsky, 2008).

In another work, a weakly-supervised algorithm was proposed to classify temporal relation between events (Mirroshandel and Ghassem-Sani, 2010). In that work, it was shown that by applying a bootstrapping technique to some unlabeled documents that were related to the test documents and without any additional annotated data, temporal relations can be classified with satisfactory results.

Rule Based Methods

The common idea behind rule based methods is to design a number of rules for classifying temporal relations. In most existing works, these rules, which are manually defined, are based on Allen's interval algebra (Allen, 1984). One usage of these rules is enlarging the training set (Mani et al., 2006). Reasoning about the certainty of predicted temporal relations is the other utilization of these rules.

Anchor Based Methods

Anchor based methods use information of argument fillers (called anchors) of every event expression as a valuable clue for recognizing temporal relations. These methods rely on the distributional hypothesis (Harris, 1968), and by looking at a set of event expressions whose argument fillers have a similar distribution, try to recognize synonymous event expressions. Algorithms such as DIRT (Lin and Pantel, 2001), TE/ASE (Szpektor et al., 2004), and that of Pekar's system (Pekar, 2006) are examples of anchor based methods.

3 Using EM for Temporal Relation Learning

Due to appropriate results of the expectation maximization (EM) algorithm in some unsupervised tasks of natural language processing such as unsupervised grammar induction (Klein, 2005), unsupervised anaphora resolution (Cherry and Bergsma, 2005; Charniak and Elsner, 2009), and unsupervised coreference resolution (Ng, 2008), we decided to apply EM to temporal relation extraction. Currently, there is no reported work in temporal relation extraction based on EM. Here, we explain how EM can be successfully applied to the task of temporal relation extraction and show that the results are notable in this task. Before that, we first introduce definitions and notations that will be later used in subsequent sections.

3.1 Definitions

In temporal relation learning, system must be able to determine temporal relation r between two events e_1 and e_2. Here, we assume that events are annotated and the learner must find out the relation type r. In general, the relation type can be one of the 14 types proposed in TimeML (Pustejovsky et al., 2003) plus relation *NONE* (which indicates there is no temporal relation between respected pair of events). In this paper, *context* means the sentence (or sentences) containing pairs of examined events.

3.2 The Model

The proposed algorithm operates at the corpus level, inducing valid temporal clustering for all event pairs of a given corpus. More specifically, our algorithm, over a *corpus*, works in two steps: first, according to some temporal clustering distribution *P(TC)*, a temporal clustering *TC* is applied to the event pairs of the *corpus*, and then given that temporal clustering, the *corpus* is generated by using equation (1):

$$P(corpus, TC) = P(TC)P(corpus|TC) \quad (1)$$

To easily incorporate linguistic constraints defined on event pairs, *corpus* is represented by its event pairs, *EventPairs(corpus)*. Now we can assume event pairs are independent and generated by using the following equation:

$$P(corpus|TC) = \prod_{e_i e_j \in EventPairs(corpus)} P(e_i e_j \mid TC_{ij}) \quad (2)$$

where $e_i e_j$ are event pairs, and TC_{ij} are the specified temporal relation type of $e_i e_j$. The marginal probability of *corpus* is computed as follows:

$$P(corpus) = \sum_{All\ possile\ temporal\ clustering\ TC} P(TC)P(corpus|TC) \quad (3)$$

For inducing temporal relations, algorithm runs the EM algorithm on this model. We used a uniform distribution over *P(TC)*.

If we expand the equations, each $e_i e_j$ can be represented by its features, which can potentially be used for determining temporal relation type between events e_i and e_j. Therefore, *P(corpus | TC)* is rewritten using equation (4). Where $e_i e_j^l$ is the value of the lth feature of $e_i e_j$. These features, which are similar to those mentioned in (Chambers and Jurafsky, 2008), are shown in table 1.

$$\prod_{e_i e_j \in EventPairs(corpus)} P(e_i e_j^{1}, e_i e_j^{2}, \ldots, e_i e_j^{k} \mid TC_{ij}) \quad (4)$$

Feature	Description
$Word_1$ & $Word_2$	The text of first and second events
$Lemma_1$ & $Lemma_2$	The lemmatized first and second events heads
$Synset_1$ & $Synset_2$	The WordNet synset for first and second events heads
POS_1 & POS_2	The POS of the first and second events
Event Government $Verb_1$ & $Verb_2$	The verbs that govern the first and second events
Event Government $Verb_1$ & $Verb_2$ POS	The verbs' POS that govern the first and second events
Auxiliary	Any auxiliary adverbs and verbs that modifies the governing verbs
$Class_1$ & $Class_2$	The Class of the first and second events
$Tense_1$ & $Tense_2$	The tense of the first and second events
$Aspect_1$ & $Aspect_2$	The aspect of the first and second events
$Modality_1$ & $Modality_2$	The modality of the first and second events
$Polarity_1$ & $Polarity_2$	The polarity of the first and second events
Tense Match	If two events have the same tense
Aspect Match	If two events have the same aspect
Class Match	If two events have the same class
Tense Pair	Pair of two events' tense
Aspect Pair	Pair of two events' aspect
Class Pair	Pair of two events' class
POS pair	Pair of two events' POS
$Preposition_1$	If first event is in a prepositional phrase or not
$Preposition_2$	If second event is in a prepositional phrase or not
Text order	If the first event occurs first in the document or not
Dominates	If the first event syntactically dominates second event or not
Entity Match	If an entity as an argument is shared between two events

Table 1: The features of events which are used in our algorithm for temporal relation learning

To reduce data sparseness and improve probability estimation, conditional independence assumption is made on these features' value generation. We only assume that *tense* and *aspect* are not independent (i.e., $tense_i$ and $aspect_i$ are dependent), because *tense* and *aspect* define temporal location and event structure, and considering these features together is a powerful source of information in any temporal relation extraction system. By conditional independence assumption, the value of $P(corpus \mid TC)$ can be rewritten as

$$\prod_{e_i e_j \in EventPairs(corpus)} \prod_{All\ features\ l} P\left(e_i e_j^{\,l} \mid TC_{ij}\right) \qquad (5)$$

3.3 The Induction Algorithm

To induce a temporal clustering *TC* on a *corpus*, EM was applied to our proposed model. In the EM algorithm, *corpus* (its event pairs) and temporal clustering *TC* are respectively the observed and unobserved (the hidden) random variables. The EM algorithm includes the following two steps to iteratively estimate the parameters of the model, θ:

E-step: Fix current θ and obtain the conditional temporal clustering likelihoods $P(TC \mid corpus, \theta)$. As a result, for each event pair candidate, a temporal relation type will be selected based on current θ.

Due to inability to consider other relations in pairwise relation learning, some contradictions will be introduced in this step. For example, figure 1 shows an inconsistency in the relations between following events:

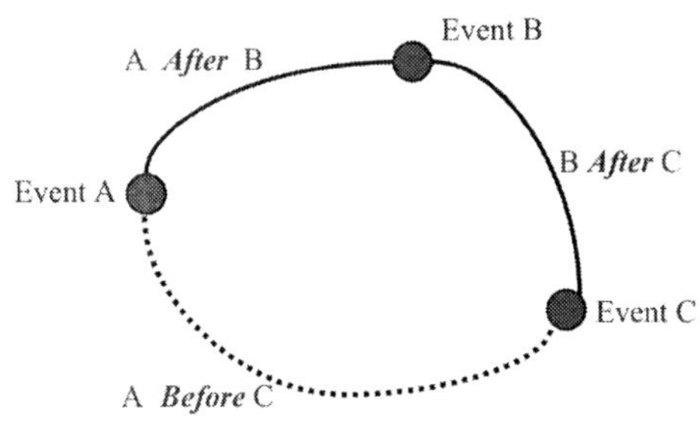

Figure 1: A contradiction in temporal relations between three events A, B, and C.

There are several ways for eliminating such inconsistencies (Mani et al., 2007; Tatu and Srikanth, 2008; Chambers and Jurafsky; 2008). In this paper, we propose a best-first greedy search strategy for temporal reasoning and removing inconsistencies among predicted relations.

First the contradictions in the connected graphs of the text will be discovered with applying a set of rules (e.g., $Before(x, y) \wedge Before(y, z) \rightarrow Before(x, z)$), which are based on Allen's interval algebra (1984). Then the inconsistent relations of each connected graph will be sorted in a list named *SL* based on computed confidence score ($P(TC \mid corpus, \theta)$). In *SL*, the first and the last elements are the most and the least confident relations, respectively.

Now, the algorithm starts from the first relation of *SL*, and pops off this relation and adds it to another list named *FL*. In adding a new relation (r_{new}) to *FL*, the algorithm verifies the consistency between relations of *FL*. If r_{new} is a relation between events e_i and e_j, which introduces an inconsistency into the graph, it will be replaced by the next confident relation between e_i and e_j. These replacements are repeated until *FL* relations will be consistent. When there are no more contradictions in *FL*, algorithm will try to move the next element of *SL* to *FL*. These operations are iterated until there will be no more relations in *SL*. Then the resultant consistent relations in *FL* can be used in the next stages of EM.

M-step: Find θ^{new} that maximizes the equation $\sum_{TC} P(TC \mid corpus, \theta^{old}) \log P(corpus, TC \mid \theta^{new})$ with fixed θ^{old}. In order to predict θ^{new}, different optimization algorithms such as conjugate gradient can be used. However, these methods are slow and costly. In addition, it is difficult to smooth these methods in a desired manner. Therefore, we used smoothed relative frequency estimates.

Now, the EM algorithm can either begin at the E-Step or the M-step, which we start the induction algorithm at the M-step. It is clear that $P(TC \mid corpus, \theta^{old})$ is not available in the first iteration of EM. Instead, an initial distribution over temporal clustering, $P(TC \mid Corpus)$, can be used. Now, there is an important question: how should we initialize $P(TC \mid Corpus)$?

Initialization is an important task in EM, because EM only guarantees to find a local maximum of the likelihood. The quality of such a local maximum is highly dependent on the initial start point. We tested three different ways of initialization: first, we used a uniform distribution over all temporal clustering. Second, we used a small part of a labeled corpus for setting $P(TC \mid Corpus)$. Third, we used some rules for initial estimation of temporal relation types and then used those types for the initial estimation to compute *P(TC | Corpus)*. The detailed accounts of the second and the third methods are discussed in subsection 5.1.

Like many statistical NLP tasks in which smoothing is required to alleviate the problem of data sparseness, smoothing is vital here, too. In particular, in the first few iterations, much more smoothing is required than in later iterations. In our experiments, we used an additive smoothing technique.

4 Corpus Description

In our experiments, we used two standard corpora which had been utilized in evaluation of most previous works: TimeBank (v. 1.2) and Opinion Corpus (Mani et al., 2006). TimeBank includes 183 newswire documents and 64077 words, and Opinion Corpus comprises 73 documents with 38709 words. These two datasets have been annotated based on TimeML (Pustejovsky et al., 2003). There are 14 temporal relations (Event-Event and Event-Time relations) in the TLink class of TimeML. Relation *NONE*, which indicates there is no temporal relation between respected event pairs, must also be considered. For the sake of alleviating the data sparseness problem, we used a converted version of these temporal relations, which contains only four following temporal relations:

BEFORE , AFTER , OVERLAP , NONE

As it was shown in (Bethard et al, 2007a), it is easy to convert 14 TimeML relations into just *BEFORE*, *AFTER*, and *OVERLAP* relations. Here, we merged *BEFORE* and *IBEFORE* relations into only *BEFORE* relations. Similarly *AFTER* and *IAFTER* relations were also merged into *AFTER* relations. All the remaining 10 relation types were collapsed in *OVERLAP* relations.

In our experiments, like several previous works, we merged Opinion and TimeBank to generate a single corpus, which is called OTC. Table 2 shows the converted TLink class distribution over TimeBank and OTC corpora for intra-sentential and general (intra- and inter-sentential) event pairs which are situated in the same document.

Relation Type	TimeBank Corpus		OTC Corpus	
	Intra-Sentential	General	Intra-Sentential	General
BEFORE	593	706	<u>1944</u>	2369
AFTER	549	692	810	1073
OVERLAP	<u>1225</u>	<u>2083</u>	1623	<u>2792</u>
NONE	11309	353401	16768	543918
Total	**13676**	**356882**	**21145**	**550152**

Table 2: The converted TLink class distribution in TimeBank and OTC for intra-sentential and general event pairs.

5 Evaluation

5.1 Experimental Setup

We applied our algorithm to both TimeBank and OTC corpora, using the five-fold cross validation method. The results were evaluated by measuring accuracy. One important point that we should mention is the parameter initialization of EM.

As it was mentioned in section 3.3, we used three different initializations: first, a uniform distribution over all temporal clustering was used; therefore, all temporal clustering in the first step had equal probability. Second, we used a small part of labeled corpora (10% of each relation type) for setting *P(TC | Corpus)*. Relations were selected randomly. Third, we used some rules for initial estimation of temporal relation types and used this initial estimation for computing *P(TC | Corpus)*. The rules were the combination of *GTag* rules (Mani et al., 2006), *VerbOcean* (Chklovski and Pantel, 2005), and some rules derived from certain signal words (e.g., *"on"*, *"during"*, *"when"*, and *"if"*) of the text.

5.2 Results and Discussions

As it is shown in table 2 (in General columns), *NONE* relations dwarf all other relations. As a result, temporal relation learning, because of heavy bias of learner to *NONE* relations, will be very hard (even useless). Regarding this problem, we set up two different types of experiments:

1) Algorithms were applied only for intra-sentential event pairs, considering all relation types (including *NONE*). The results of these experiments are shown in table 3.

2) The *NONE* relations were removed, and algorithms were applied to both intra-sentential and general (intra- and inter-sentential) event pairs. Table 4 shows the results of experiments without considering *NONE* relations.

One important issue in the results of table 3 is that in our experiments, all four mentioned relation types (*BEFORE*, *AFTER*, *OVERLAP*, and *NONE*) have been considered, but in reporting the results, we have reported the aggregated accuracy of only *BEFORE*, *AFTER*, and *OVERLAP* relations, and excluded the accuracy results of *NONE* relations. That is because by considering *NONE*, one could design a simple system which tags all relations to *NONE*, and would get a very high accuracy. But, in that case the comparison would be inappropriate.

In our evaluations, both table 3 and 4, the baselines have been the majority classes for event pair relations ignoring *NONE* relations of the evaluated corpora (i.e., *BEFORE* and *OVERLAP* relations as it is depicted in table 2). The Mani's method is in fact a supervised method which exclusively uses gold-standard features (Mani et al., 2007). The Chambers' method is similar to Mani's, except that it uses some external resources such as WordNet (Chambers et al., 2007). The Mani and Chambers results are different from (or even lower than) their reported results, because of two differences: first, we considered only three temporal relation types while in their experiments, there were six relation types. Second, the results of table 3 are reported by considering *NONE* relations, but in their original works, there was not any *NONE* relation.

Method Type	TimeBank	OTC Corpus
Baseline	<u>51.75</u>	44.41
Mani	31.77	47.24
Chambers	36.03	<u>48.86</u>
EM_1	23.76 (22.10)	32.48 (32.21)
EM_2	28.65 (26.31)	38.68 (36.45)
EM_3	<u>29.81</u> (<u>27.13</u>)	<u>39.92</u> (<u>39.28</u>)

Table 3: The results of proposed method for intra-sentential event pairs on all mentioned relation types including *NONE* relations

Method Type	TimeBank Corpus		OTC Corpus	
	Intra-Sentential	General	Intra-Sentential	General
Baseline	51.75	59.83	44.41	44.79
Mani	54.80	61.55	60.86	60.58
Chambers	<u>62.31</u>	<u>66.79</u>	<u>63.57</u>	<u>62.94</u>
EM_1	41.67 (39.02)	42.09 (40.92)	43.86 (43.75)	42.94 (43.02)
EM_2	46.11 (45.28)	49.54 (<u>48.31</u>)	49.34 (<u>48.35</u>)	<u>50.52</u> (<u>49.34</u>)
EM_3	<u>48.03</u> (<u>46.53</u>)	<u>50.88</u> (47.86)	<u>50.27</u> (48.23)	49.98 (48.78)

Table 4: The results of different methods for intra-sentential and general event pairs by ignoring *NONE* relations.

EM_1, EM_2, and EM_3 are the results of our proposed method with three different initializations. The initializations of EM_1, EM_2, and EM_3 were random, with little supervision (10%), and by using a number of rules, respectively. For EM_1, one question is how this method can determine the label of different classes. In our experiments, EM_1, depending on the type of experiment, only determines three or four different classes ($Class_1$, $Class_2$, $Class_3$, and/or $Class_4$). To label these unlabeled classes, using annotated data, we assigned the labels in such a way that resulted in maximum similarity between predicted and annotated temporal relation types for each event pair.

In tables 3 and 4, the numbers inside parentheses show the results of our proposed algorithm without applying temporal reasoning.

As it is shown in tables 3, all mentioned methods generally demonstrate a weak performance. That is due to the problem's nature. As distribution of different columns of table 2 shows, the number of *NONE* relations, even in the intra-sentential case, is about 7 to 10 times greater than other relations. Therefore, it is very hard for a learning algorithm to precisely determine the relation types. On the other hand, results of table 4, which ignores *NONE* relations, are satisfactory. Comparing proposed method with the baseline, shows that in the cases that supervised methods can beat the baseline method, our weakly supervised method can also work better than the baseline or close to it.

It should be noted that the Chambers' method, which is the most successful method of tables 3 and 4, is in fact the state of the art supervised method, while our proposed method is, based on the initialization approaches, unsupervised or weakly supervised. Among different settings of the proposed method, EM_3 achieved the best results except for the general case of OTC in table 4, where EM_2 achieved better results.

The results show that EM_1 is not very efficient in either first or second type of experiments. It seems that randomized initialization in this hard problem, may cause some divergence in the probability distribution. On the other hand, both EM_2 and EM_3 showed satisfactory results in these problems. Therefore, initialization is a critical factor in our EM method, and some little source of supervision seems crucial for achieving better results.

Comparison of the results of proposed EM algorithm with and without utilization of temporal reasoning shows that using temporal reasoning can be effective on the accuracy of the algorithm. By using temporal reasoning, some inconsistencies are removed in step E of the algorithm and the predicted relations will be more reliable. Then in step M, the update of parameters will be performed more accurately and thus the accuracy of the algorithm iteratively will increase.

Another important point in the comparison of accuracy results is the existence of *NONE* relations. As it is shown in tables 3 and 4, the accuracies in table 3 is much lower than that of in table 4. These differences are all due to the existence of *NONE* relations, which makes problem hard. Figure 2 demonstrates the effects of *NONE* relations on the accuracy of our proposed algorithm. All the experiments have been performed using OTC. We repeated our experiments for different percentage of *NONE* relations. As it is shown, *NONE* relations have had a great impact on the accuracy of the system.

The larger gap between the accuracy of ignoring and consideration of *NONE* relations on TimeBank (in contrast that of OTC) implies that *NONE* relations would have an even greater impact on the accuracy of the algorithm if applied to TimeBank.

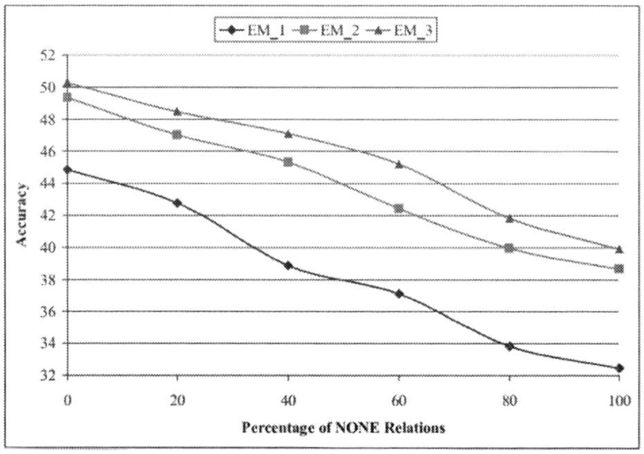

Figure 2: The effect of NONE relations on the accuracy

Figure 2 shows the impact of *NONE* relations on the accuracy (or recall) of the algorithm. Our experiments showed that this impact is even more substantial on the precision of the proposed algorithm. That is because although the algorithm can determine *BEFORE*, *AFTER*, and *OVERLAP* relations with an acceptable rate, but a lot of *NONE* relations will also be recognized. As a result, the precision will substantially decrease. Due to lack of space, we have not reported the precision of the algorithm.

6 Conclusion

In this paper, we have addressed the problem of learning temporal relations between event pairs, which is an interesting topic in natural language processing. Building a suitable corpus is a hard, expensive, and time consuming task. Therefore, we focused on unsupervised and weakly supervised types of learning. We proposed a novel generative model that uses the EM algorithm with some interval algebra reasoning for temporal relation learning. We compared our work with some of successful supervised methods. Our experiments showed that the result of the proposed algorithm, considering its little supervision, is satisfactory.

We think but have not yet verified that using other source of information like narrative information, global relationship between events and times, time expressions, and/or some other useful features of related documents might even further improve the accuracy of the new algorithm.

References

James Allen. 1984. *Towards a General Theory of Action and Time*. Artificial Intelligence, 23, 2, 123-154.

Steven Bethard, James H. Martin, and Sara Klingenstein. 2007a. *Finding Temporal Structure in Text: Machine Learning of Syntactic Temporal Relations*. Journal of Semantic Computing, 1, 4.

Steven Bethard, James H. Martin, and Sara Klingenstein. 2007b. *Timelines from Text: Identification of Syntactic Temporal Relations*. Proceeding of ICSC, 11-18.

Steven Bethard and James H. Martin. 2007. *CU-TMP: Temporal Relation Classification Using Syntactic and Semantic Features*. Proceeding of SemEval-2007, 129-132.

Steven Bethard. 2007. *Finding Event, Temporal and Causal Structure in Text: A Machine Learning Approach*. PhD thesis, University of Colorado at Boulder.

Steven Bethard and James H. Martin. 2008. *Learning Semantic Links from a Corpus of Parallel Temporal and Causal Relations*. Proceeding of ACL-2008, 177-180.

Nathanael Chambers, Shan Wang, and Dan Jurafsky. 2007. *Classifying Temporal Relations between Events*. Proceeding of ACL-2007, 173-176.

Nathanael Chambers and Dan Jurafsky. 2008. *Jointly Combining Implicit Constraints Improves Temporal Ordering*. Proceeding of EMNLP-2008, 698-706.

Eugene Charniak and Micha Elsner. 2009. *EM Works for Pronoun Anaphora Resolution*. Proceedings of EACL-2009, 148-154.

Colin Cherry and Shane Bergsma. 2005. *An Expectation Maximization Approach to Pronoun Resolution*. Proceeding of CoNLL 2005. 88-95.

Timothy Chklovski and Patrick Pantel. 2005. *Global Path-based Refinement of Noisy Graphs Applied to Verb Semantics*. Proceeding of IJCNLP-05, 792-803.

Zellig Harris. 1968. *Mathematical Structure of Language*. John Wiley Sons, New York, 1968.

Dan Klein. 2005. *The Unsupervised Learning of Natural Language Structure*. Ph.D. Thesis, Department of Computer Science, Stanford University.

Mirella Lapata and Alex Lascarides. 2006. *Learning Sentence-Internal Temporal Relations*. Journal of Artificial Intelligence Research, 27, 85-117.

Dekang Lin and Patrick Pantel. 2001. *Dirt-Discovery of Inference Rules From Text*. Proceeding of ACM SIGKDD-2001, 323-328.

Inderjeet Mani, Marc Verhagen, Ben Wellner, Chong M. Lee, and James Pustejovsky. 2006. *Machine Learning of Temporal Relations*. Proceedings of ACL-2006, 753-760.

Inderjeet Mani, Ben Wellner, Marc Verhagen, and James Pustejovsky. 2007. *Three Approaches to Learning Tlinks in TimeML. Technical Report CS-07-268*. Brandeis University, Waltham, USA.

Seyed Abolghasem Mirroshandel, Gholamreza Ghassem-Sani, and Mahdy Khayyamian. 2009. *Using Tree Kernels for Classifying Temporal Relations between Events*. Proceedings of PACLIC-2009, 355-364.

Seyed Abolghasem Mirroshandel and Gholamreza Ghassem-Sani. 2010. *Temporal Relations Learning with a Bootstrapped Cross-document Classifier*. Proceedings of ECAI-2010, 829-834.

Vincent Ng, 2008. *Unsupervised Models for Coreference Resolution*. Proceedings of EMNLP-2008, 640-649.

Victor Pekar. 2006. *Acquisition of Verb Entailment from Text*. Proceeding of NAACL/HLT-2006, 49-56.

James Pustejovsky, Patrick Hanks, Roser Saurí, Andrew See, Robert Gaizauskas, Andrea Setzer, Dragomir Radev, Beth Sundheim, David Day, Lisa Ferro and Marcia Lazo. 2003. *The TimeBank Corpus*. Corpus Linguistics, 647-656.

Idan Szpektor, Hristo Tanev, Ido Dagan, and Bonaventura Coppola. 2004. *Scaling Web-based Acquisition of Entailment Relations*. Proceeding of EMNLP-2004, 41-48.

Marta Tatu and Munirathnam Srikanth. 2008. *Experiments with Reasoning for Temporal Relations between Events*. Proceeding of Coling-2008, 857-864.

Kentaro Torisawa. 2006. *Acquiring Inference Rules with Temporal Constraints by Using Japanese Coordinated Sentences and Noun-Verb Co-Occurrences*. Proceedings of NAACL-2006, 57-64.

Puscasu G. Wvali. 2007. *Temporal Relation Identification by Syntactico-Semantic Analysis*. Proceeding of SemEval-2007, 484–487.

Improving Chunk-based Semantic Role Labeling with Lexical Features

Wilker Aziz, Miguel Rios and **Lucia Specia**
Research Group in Computational Linguistics
University of Wolverhampton
Stafford Street, Wolverhampton, WV1 1SB, UK
{w.aziz, m.rios, l.specia}@wlv.ac.uk

Abstract

We present an approach for Semantic Role Labeling (SRL) using Conditional Random Fields in a joint identification/classification step. The approach is based on shallow syntactic information (chunks) and a number of lexicalized features such as selectional preferences and automatically inferred similar words, extracted using lexical databases and distributional similarity metrics. We use semantic annotations from the Proposition Bank for training and evaluate the system using CoNLL-2005 test sets. The additional lexical information led to improvements of 15% (in-domain evaluation) and 12% (out-of-domain evaluation) on overall semantic role classification in terms of F-measure. The gains come mostly from a better recall, which suggests that the addition of richer lexical information can improve the coverage of existing SRL models even when very little syntactic knowledge is available.

1 Introduction

Identifying the relations that words or groups of words have with verbs in a sentence constitutes an important step for many applications in Natural Language Processing (NLP). This is addressed by the field of Semantic Role Labeling (SRL). SRL has been shown to contribute to many NLP applications, such as Information Extraction, Question Answering and Machine Translation.

Most of the SRL approaches operate via two consecutive steps: i) the identification of the arguments of a target predicate and ii) the classification of those arguments (Gildea and Jurafsky, 2002; Pradhan et al., 2004). Alternatively, graph models can rely on the sequential nature of the shallow semantic parsing and perform both SRL steps simultaneously (Roth and tau Yih, 2005; Cohn and Blunsom, 2005).

Features for SRL are usually extracted from chunks or constituent parse trees. While parse trees allow a set of very informative path-based, structural features, chunks can provide more reliable annotations. Hacioglu et al. (2004) propose the use of base phrases as data representation using Support Vector Machines in order to perform a single argument classification step. Roth and tau Yih (2005) use the same sort of representation with Conditional Random Fields (CRF) as learning algorithm, motivated by the sequential nature of the task. Cohn and Blunsom (2005) use CRF to perform SRL in a single identification/classification step based on features from constituent trees.

Pradhan et al. (2008) point out the lack of semantic features as the bottleneck in argument role classification, a task closely-related to that of word sense disambiguation. Shallow lexical features such as word forms and word lemmas are very sparse. Although named-entity categories have been proposed to alleviate this sparsity problem, they only apply to a fraction of the arguments' words.

In this paper we propose the addition of other forms of lexical knowledge in order to address this problem. The proposed SRL system tags data in a joint identification/classification step using CRF as the learning algorithm. The data is represented with syntactic base phrases such as in (Hacioglu et al., 2004). Besides the shallow syntactic features, we add to the CRF model two new sources of lexicalized knowledge as an attempt to overcome data sparsity and the lack of richer syntactic information: i) selectional preferences and ii) automatically inferred similar words. Although our selection preferences are extracted from WordNet in this particular implementation, they could be extracted from other sources of structured information such as DBpedia[1].

The paper is structured as follows: in Section 2 we give an overview of the related work; in Section 3 we describe the proposed system; in Section 4 we present the results of our experiments. Finally, in Section 5 we present our conclusions and some directions for future work.

2 Related Work

In most previous work, improvements in SRL come from new features used either in the argument identification or in the argument classification step. It is common to train different binary classifiers to perform each of the two steps separately (Gildea and Jurafsky, 2002; Pradhan et al., 2004). In the first step chunks are identified as potential arguments of a given predicate. Xue and Palmer (2004) apply syntax-driven heuristics in order to prune unlikely candidates. In the second step, the selected arguments are individually labeled with semantic roles. Pradhan et al. (2004) use features such as the role of the preceding argument in order to create a dependency between the classification of different arguments.

Hacioglu et al. (2004) propose a single identification/classification step using SVM by labeling chunks within a window centered in the predicated from left to right. The authors propose to label base phrases instead of constituents in a full parse tree. They also change the data representation of the roles to IOB2 notation which is more adequate to shallow parsing. In the proposed representation, the features of base phrases include those that can be extracted from their head words as well as some chunk oriented features (e.g the distance of the chunk to the predicate).

Cohn and Blunsom (2005) approach induces an undirected random field over a parse tree, which allows the joint identification and classification of all predicate arguments. In that direction, but relying on shallow parsing, Roth and tau Yih (2005) use CRF and Integer Linear Programming to group base phrases into labeled predicate arguments.

According to Pradhan et al. (2008) the identification step relies mostly on syntactic information, whereas the classification needs more semantic knowledge. Semantic knowledge is usually represented by lexicalized features such as wordforms, lemmas and named entities. Wordforms and lemmas make very sparse features; while more general features such as named-entities generalize just a fraction of all the nouns that verbs might take as arguments.

To improve argument classification, Zapirain et al. (2010) propose to merge selectional preferences into a state-of-the-art SRL system. They define selectional preference as a similarity score between the predicate, the argument role and the constituent head word. The similarity is computed using different strategies: i) Resnik's similarity measure (Resnik, 1997) based on WordNet (Miller et al., 1990), and ii) different corpus-based distributional similarity metrics, considering both first and second order similarities. They report consistent gains on argument classification by combining models based on different similarity metrics.

In this work we propose to add lexical information in a different fashion. Instead of measuring the similarity between the argument head word and the predicate we: i) understand selectional preferences as categories, such as the usual named-entities, however covering any sort of noun; ii) provide additional evidence of lexical similarity by expanding the head of any base phrase to its 10-most similar concepts retrieved from a distributional thesaurus.

3 Method

According to Hacioglu et al. (2004) SRL systems can be classified as: word-by-word (W-by-W) classifiers, constituent-by-constituent (C-by-C) classifiers and phrase-by-phrase (P-by-P) classifiers. For example, the approach used in (Cohn and Blunsom, 2005) is a C-by-C classifier.

We used the P-by-P approach, in which words are collapsed into base phrases and features of their head words are used. In order to do so, data was lemmatized and part-of-speech tagged using TreeTagger,[2] and shallow parsed (without prepositional attachment) using the OpenNLP toolkit.[3] The chunks were labeled using semantic roles in the IOB2 notation, their tokens were collapsed into base phrases and punctuation was discarded. In order to identify the head of a chunk we used a simple right-most heuristic constrained by the token's POS tag.

Richer lexicalized features were extracted for

[1]http://dbpedia.org/About

[2]http://www.ims.uni-stuttgart.de/projekte/corplex/TreeTagger/

[3]http://incubator.apache.org/opennlp/

head word of the base phrase: i) named-entities, ii) selectional preferences, and iii) similar words. Once the features were extracted, a CRF model was trained using CRF++[4].

3.1 Selectional Preferences

We treated selectional preferences (SP) as categories that can be assigned to any noun. In order to extract those selectional preferences we follow two steps.

First, we tag nouns with word senses using WordNet::SenseRelate::AllWords[5]. Instead of tagging the original input sentences, we remove punctuation and keep only the head of each chunk. As named-entities are not part of WordNet's lexicon, we replace them by their categories in order to aid the WSD step. In addition, simple rules are applied to group pronouns under the same NE categories in a normalization step.

Second, we extract from WordNet the hypernym tree related to the sense of each head noun. A word is assigned a selectional preference if its is subsumed by one of the concepts listed in Figure 1. It is worth noticing that a noun may be assigned multiple selectional preferences.

act 2	animal	artifact
attribute 1	body part	cognition
communication 1	event 3	feeling
food 1,2	group	location
motive 1	natural object	physical object
living thing	person 1,2	phenomenon
plant 2	possession	process 6
quantity	relation 1	relation 2,3,6
shape 1,2	state 2	state 6
substance 1	time	vehicle 1
tool 1	device 1	garment 1
solid	liquid	physical entity
abstraction	thing	

Figure 1: Selectional preferences represented by groups of concepts in WordNet. A concept is represented by a word and its sense information

Motivated by VerbNet's (Kipper et al.,) selectional restrictions, we manually selected the 38 categories listed in Figure 1 and mapped them into the WordNet lexicon. We chose general hypernyms in order to avoid fine-grained sense distinctions, so that the method would be less sensitive to sense-tagging errors.

Figure 2 exemplifies the process of assigning selectional preferences to the noun head words of a sentence. We start with the collapsed chunks and their head words; normalization is performed and then selectional preferences such as *abstraction*, *group*, *physical entity*, *living thing*, *person* are assigned as previously described.

3.2 Most Similar Words

Aiming at producing an SRL system with features that can be easily extracted for different languages and also to provide additional lexical information, we expanded chunks' heads with similar words. For every head word on its base form, regardless its part-of-speech, we selected the 10-most similar words from Lin's distributional thesaurus (Lin, 1998). Lin's thesaurus is an automatically constructed resource that maps words to similar concepts in terms of a distributional lexical similarity metric. The last column in Figure 2 exemplifies similar words retrieved for some chunks.

3.3 Features

We use the CRF learning algorithm, which consists in a framework for building probabilistic models to label sequential data (Lafferty et al., 2001). We extracted the following features:

Head of the Base Phrase: the base phrase's head word was identified using a right-most heuristic constrained by the POS tag of the candidates. The head was taken as the right-most word within the chunk whose POS tag was consistent with the chunk type (e.g. the right-most noun in a noun phrase, the right-most verb in a verb phrase, etc.). For every base phrase, the word form, lemma and POS tag of the head were selected as features. Additionally, named entities were automatically tagged using the OpenNLP and Stanford NER[6] systems with one of the following categories: *person*, *organization*, *location*, *date*, *money* and *percentage*. Besides the actual head, the normalized head was also used: named-entities are replaced by their categories and pronouns are replaced by their most likely SP (e.g. personal pronouns are replaced by *person* if singular or *group* if plural).

Chunk or Base Phrase: the tokens and POS tags within every base phrase were collapsed into a surface and a POS span, respectively. The chunk type, its length and its distance to the target predicate were also selected as features. For the special case of a verb phrase we added as features its main

[4]http://crfpp.sourceforge.net/

[5]http://www.d.umn.edu/ tpederse/senserelate.html

[6]http://nlp.stanford.edu/ner/index.shtml

Chunk	Head	NE	Normalization	WSD	*sp*	*10sim*
Everyone	everyone	O	group	1	abstraction, group	groups, company, organization...
will_tell	tell	O	tell	-	-	ask, remind, telling...
you	you	O	person	1	physical_entity, living_thing, person	persons, man, individuals...
that	that	O	that	-	-	which, it, what...
this_time	time	O	time	7	time, abstraction, cognition	times, period, day...
is	is	O	be	1	-	been, being, was...
different	different	O	different	1	-	various, differing, distinct...
from	from	O	from	ND	-	in, at, of...
1987	1987	DATE	time	7	time, abstraction, cognition	times, period, day...
he	he	O	person	1	physical_entity, living_thing, person	persons, man, individuals...
says	says	O	says	-	-	believe, argue, contend...

Figure 2: Example of feature extraction for the target verb *tell*

verb, its auxiliary or modal verb, its preceding and following prepositions and a flag to indicate passive voice. The voice was identified using a simple heuristic consisted in checking the occurrence of the verbs *to be* or *to get* followed by a past participle form.

Selectional Preferences: as described in 3.1, henceforth referred to as **sp**.

10-most Similar Words: as described in 3.2, henceforth referred to as **10sim**

3.4 Templates

The CRF++ toolkit allows the definition of templates over the basic feature space, that is, rules that combine multiple features. Templates are expanded token-by-token, that is, for every CRF token the original feature set is used to create additional features. Templates can be based on features only, referred to as *unigram templates*, or on the combination of features and predicted labels, referred to as *bigram templates*.

Unigram templates: we created bigrams and trigrams of individual features. Figure 3 shows an example of how the normalized heads were expanded into trigrams, the three right-most columns were generated by template expansion. For every token we combined different features in pairs (e.g. chunk/lemma, chunk/POS, chunk/NE). Finally, for all the resulting features, including the original ones, we also selected their values in a window of 6 tokens centered in the current token.

Bigram templates: we select the two previously assigned semantic role labels as features of the current chunk.

4 Results

We experimented with different configurations of features in order to understand the impact of their contribution. The baseline model (B) contains all features apart from the selectional preferences and the 10-most similar words, the main contributions of this paper. We added the selectional preferences (B+sp) and the most similar words (B+10sim) separately, and built a final model containing all the features (B+10sim+sp), as described in Section 3.

Training was performed using the whole Proposition Bank (Palmer et al., 2005) (except Section 23, which is part of the test set). The Proposition Bank adds a layer of predicate-argument information, or semantic role labels, to the syntactic annotation of the Penn Treebank. The test set used was CoNLL-2005 (Carreras and Màrquez, 2005), which has predicate-argument information for approximately 2.5K sentences from the Wall Street Journal (WSJ) (in-domain evaluation) and 450 sentences from Brown corpus (out-of-domain evaluation).

Table 1 presents the overall results for the SRL taskon the in-domain test set (WSJ), and Table 2 presents the same analysis on the out-of-domain test set (Brown). They also show CoNLL 2005's baseline (Carreras and Màrquez, 2005) and a similar chunk-based SRL (Mitsumori et al., 2005). The figures refer to the weighted average of the performance in correctly classifying target predicates (V), their core arguments (A0 to A5) and their modifiers.

Tables 1 and 2 show that the proposed lexicalized features yielded an important gain in

Chunk	Head (H)	Normalized head (NH)	Previous H	Next H	Previous NH/Current NH/Next NH
Everyone	Everyone	group	-	tell	-/group/tell
will_tell	tell	tell	Everyone	you	group/tell/person
you	you	person	tell	that	tell/person/that
that	that	that	you	time	person/that/time
this_time	time	time	that	is	that/time/be
is	is	be	time	different	time/be/different
different	different	different	is	from	be/different/from
from	from	from	different	1987	different/from/date
1987	1987	date	from	he	from/date/person
he	he	person	1987	says	date/person/say
says	says	say	he	-	person/say/-

Figure 3: CRF template expansion

terms of recall as compared to our baseline (B). In isolation, these features result in similar improvements of approximately 4% in terms of F-measure, whereas together they complement each other yielding about 12% improvement on the out-of-domain dataset. However, disappointingly our system performs worse than that by Mitsumori et al. even though both systems use similar features. In fact, in the out-of-domain task, our system is also outperformed by official baseline.

System	Precision	Recall	F-measure
B	60.04	38.58	46.97
B+10sim	60.15	43.61	50.57
B+sp	61.79	48.11	54.10
B+10sim+sp	65.76	57.35	61.27
CoNLL-baseline	51.13	29.16	37.14
mitsumori	74.15	28.25	71.08

Table 1: In-domain semantic SRL performance

System	Precision	Recall	F-measure
B	38.33	24.34	29.77
B+10sim	44.22	27.27	33.73
B+sp	42.17	27.69	33.43
B+10sim+sp	48.57	37.00	42.00
CoNLL-baseline	62.66	33.07	43.30
mitsumori	63.24	54.20	58.37

Table 2: Out-of-domain SRL performance

One of the reasons for the low performance of our approach may be that we have not yet performed feature nor template engineering. Hacioglu et al. (2004) report an improvement from 61.02% to 69.49% on their average F-measure based on some feature engineering. Our models could also benefit from having additional forms of syntactic information as features (e.g. flat paths between argument candidates and the target predicate). However at this stage of our research we are more concerned about measuring the benefit from adding new lexicalized features over chunk-based SRL approaches with standard features.

Zapirain et al. (2010) evaluate a fairly simple baseline trained using only word lemmas as features as well as their strategies for selectional preferences in isolation. They report an improvement on F-measure of 20% (in-domain) and 30% (out-of-domain) over that baseline. They also report improvements on accuracy of 1% (in-domain) and 2% (out-of-domain) over a robust state-of-the-art SRL system[7]. However, their approach was trained using some gold-standard information, as opposed to a more realistic scenario such as ours, where automatic tools are used to produce all the information needed.

Role	Precision	Recall	F-measure
A0	64.12	38.90	48.42
A1	58.59	44.30	50.45
A2	58.32	50.47	54.11
A3	63.21	40.36	49.26
A4	71.74	65.35	68.39
A5	75.00	75.00	75.00
AM-ADV	27.83	7.21	11.45
AM-CAU	25.00	1.32	2.50
AM-DIR	48.89	28.21	35.77
AM-DIS	47.22	11.49	18.48
AM-EXT	87.50	51.85	65.12
AM-LOC	54.84	18.73	27.93
AM-MNR	43.43	15.19	22.51
AM-MOD	95.06	61.60	74.76
AM-NEG	96.55	60.87	74.67
AM-PNC	42.42	12.28	19.05
AM-PRD	100.00	20.00	33.33
AM-REC	0.00	0.00	0.00
AM-TMP	55.53	25.15	34.62
V	98.05	81.31	88.90
Overall	60.04	38.58	46.97

Table 3: B: In-domain semantic role classification

Table 3 shows the performance of our baseline model in detail. Table 4 shows the relative difference in performance for argument classification between the model improved with the 10-most similar words and the baseline. We can see a considerable gain in recall, particularly for A0 and

[7] www.surdeanu.name/mihai/swirl

A1, which are generally very important arguments in a sentence.

Role	Precision	Recall	F-measure
A0	+0.28	+6.58	+4.19
A1	+0.96	+8.17	+5.33
A2	-0.08	+0.84	+0.45
A3	+0.97	-0.17	+0.37
A4	+5.07	+6.27	+5.74
A5	-8.33	-8.33	-8.33
AM-ADV	-6.09	-2.23	-3.34
AM-CAU	-25	-1.32	-2.50
AM-DIR	+4.05	+1.79	+2.53
AM-DIS	+21.75	+6.69	+10.30
AM-EXT	0.00	+6.48	+4.88
AM-LOC	-0.47	+2.73	+2.84
AM-MNR	-2.25	+2.94	+2.67
AM-MOD	+2.64	-6.04	-3.93
AM-NEG	+3.45	+2.46	+2.88
AM-PNC	+17.58	-0.28	+0.95
AM-PRD	0.00	+5.00	+6.67
AM-REC	0.00	0.00	0.00
AM-TMP	+2.15	+5.64	+5.53
V	-0.26	+10.35	+5.73
Overall	+0.11	+5.03	+3.6

Table 4: B+10sim: In-domain SRL performance per label - relative difference from B

Table 5 shows the relative difference in performance between the model improved with selectional preferences and the baseline. Overall, selectional preferences led to better improvement than the 10-most similar words. This can be explained by the fact that selectional preferences, as defined here, are more linguistically motivated than the 10-most similar words. Moreover, similar words were extracted regardless of the context of the related head words, whereas the selectional preferences were extracted after word sense disambiguation.

Table 6 shows the difference in performance between the baseline and the final model enhanced with all the additional lexical semantic information available.

Overall, the best results were achieved with the combination of both sources of additional lexical information, as they seem to complement each other. Selectional preferences contribute by clustering nouns under linguistically motivated categories. The 10-most similar words bring additional lexical evidence for every head word regardless of its POS tag. We can also see that the most significant improvements are in terms of recall, what was expected, since our classifiers leverage on the additional generalization and expansion of the head words, minimising data sparsity.

Role	Precision	Recall	F-measure
A0	+4.32	+16.04	+12.55
A1	+2.66	+11.99	+8.22
A2	-0.74	+0.66	+0.05
A3	-6.96	-2.41	-3.94
A4	-4.37	-1.98	-3.08
A5	0.00	0.00	0.00
AM-ADV	-5.07	-0.90	-1.57
AM-CAU	+2.27	+2.63	+4.40
AM-DIR	-2.08	0.00	-0.57
AM-DIS	+13.2	+8.10	+11.11
AM-EXT	-9.72	0.00	-2.90
AM-LOC	-3.94	+4.69	+4.15
AM-MNR	-4.91	+1.42	+0.70
AM-MOD	+1.04	-2.40	-1.49
AM-NEG	+3.45	-2.17	-0.70
AM-PNC	-4.92	+0.88	+0.43
AM-PRD	0.00	0.00	0.00
AM-REC	0.00	0.00	0.00
AM-TMP	-3.84	+4.01	+2.66
V	-0.79	+11.73	+6.20
Overall	+1.75	+9.53	+7.13

Table 5: B+sp: In-domain SRL performance per label - relative difference from B

5 Conclusions and Future Work

We presented an SRL system based on CRF which performs the argument identification and classification jointly in one step. We used the phrase-by-phrase approach relying on shallow parsing. The focus of the research was on adding lexical information to the model, while using very simple syntactic features. We added lexicalized features extracted from two resources of very different natures: WordNet and Dekang Lin's distributional similarity thesaurus. The two features led to some improvements when used in isolation, and their combination resulted in the best performance, showing that they complement each other well, as a consequence of the fact that they bring information about words with different POS tags. Our results show that SRL systems can benefit from both linguistically motivated selectional preferences and automatically built thesauri. The additional lexical knowledge helps the machine learning process by providing better generalization over argument head words, which yields some gain in precision and specially noticeable gains in recall.

The approach can be improved in different ways. The use of CRF templates opens a large range of possibilities for feature engineering, which we plan to investigate in the future.

Our selectional preferences were motivated by VerbNet's selectional restrictions, which were then mapped into WordNet's lexicon. Alterna-

Role	Precision	Recall	F-measure
A0	+8.91	+27.22	+20.98
A1	+5.67	+15.36	+11.43
A2	-1.45	-2.54	-2.09
A3	-7.97	-5.42	-6.46
A4	-5.76	-1.98	-3.74
A5	+25.00	0.00	+10.71
AM-ADV	+9.72	+14.86	+16.35
AM-CAU	+13.46	+31.57	+32.96
AM-DIR	+5.16	-2.57	-0.99
AM-DIS	+30.56	+54.73	+53.05
AM-EXT	-0.83	-3.70	-3.22
AM-LOC	+0.81	+16.53	+15.24
AM-MNR	+3.02	+19.44	+17.17
AM-MOD	+2.90	+34.40	+22.21
AM-NEG	-5.06	+32.61	+17.80
AM-PNC	-3.08	+8.77	+8.38
AM-PRD	0.00	0.00	0.00
AM-REC	0.00	0.00	0.00
AM-TMP	+11.64	+32.26	+27.29
V	+0.34	+17.18	+9.54
Overall	+5.72	+18.77	+14.30

Table 6: B+10sim+sp: In-domain SRL performance per label - relative difference from B

tively, one could automatically infer a large set of selectional preference candidates and select the most informative ones via corpus analysis (i.e. using co-occurrence of nouns, their hypernyms and target predicates). Selectional preferences could also be extracted from Wikipedia, or related projects such as the DBpedia, in which concepts are often tagged with structured categories.

Additional shallow syntactic features could also be added to the model, such as flat syntactic paths, clause boundaries and prepositional attachment.

References

Xavier Carreras and Lluís Màrquez. 2005. Introduction to the conll-2005 shared task: semantic role labeling. In *Proceedings of the Ninth Conference on Computational Natural Language Learning*, CONLL '05, pages 152–164.

Trevor Cohn and Philip Blunsom. 2005. Semantic role labelling with tree conditional random fields. In *Proceedings of the Ninth Conference on Computational Natural Language Learning*, CONLL '05, pages 169–172.

Daniel Gildea and Daniel Jurafsky. 2002. Automatic labeling of semantic roles. *Computational Linguistics*, pages 245–288, September.

Kadri Hacioglu, Sameer Pradhan, Wayne Ward, James H. Martin, and Daniel Jurafsky. 2004. Semantic role labeling by tagging syntactic chunks. In *Eighth Conference on Natural Language Learning*, CONLL '04.

Karin Kipper, Anna Korhonen, Neville Ryant, and Martha Palmer. *Language Resources and Evaluation*, pages 21–40, March.

John D. Lafferty, Andrew McCallum, and Fernando C. N. Pereira. 2001. Conditional random fields: Probabilistic models for segmenting and labeling sequence data. In *Proceedings of the Eighteenth International Conference on Machine Learning*, ICML '01, pages 282–289.

Dekang Lin. 1998. Automatic retrieval and clustering of similar words. In *Proceedings of the 36th Annual Meeting of the Association for Computational Linguistics and 17th International Conference on Computational Linguistics*, ACL '98, pages 768–774.

George A. Miller, Richard Beckwith, Christiane Fellbaum, Derek Gross, and Katherine J. Miller. 1990. Wordnet: an on-line lexical database. *Int. J. Lexicograph*, pages 235–244.

Tomohiro Mitsumori, Masaki Murata, Yasushi Fukuda, Kouichi Doi, and Hirohumi Doi. 2005. Semantic role labeling using support vector machines. In *Proceedings of the Ninth Conference on Computational Natural Language Learning*, CONLL '05, pages 197–200.

Martha Palmer, Daniel Gildea, and Paul Kingsbury. 2005. The proposition bank: An annotated corpus of semantic roles. *Computational Linguistics*, pages 71–106, March.

Sameer Pradhan, Wayne Ward, Kadri Hacioglu, and James H. Martin. 2004. Shallow semantic parsing using support vector machines. In *Human Language Technology conference / North American chapter of the Association for Computational Linguistics*, HLT-NAACL '04, May.

Sameer S. Pradhan, Wayne Ward, and James H. Martin. 2008. Towards robust semantic role labeling. *Computational Linguistics*, pages 289–310, June.

Philip Resnik. 1997. Selectional preference and sense disambiguation. In *ACL SIGLEX Workshop on Tagging Text with Lexical Semantics: Why, What, and How?*, April.

Dan Roth and Wen tau Yih. 2005. Integer linear programming inference for conditional random fields. In *Proceedings of the 22nd international conference on Machine learning*, ICML '05, pages 736–743.

Nianwen Xue and Martha Palmer. 2004. Calibrating features for semantic role labeling. In *2004 Conference on Empirical Methods in Natural Language Processing*, EMNLP '04, pages 88–94.

Benat Zapirain, Eneko Agirre, Lluís Màrquez, and Mihai Surdeanu. 2010. Improving semantic role classification with selectional preferences. In *Human Language Technologies: The 2010 Annual Conference of the North American Chapter of the Association for Computational Linguistics*, HLT '10, pages 373–376.

Improving WSD using ISR-WN with Relevant Semantic Trees and SemCor Senses Frequency

Yoan Gutiérrez
Department of Informatics
University of Matanzas, Cuba.
{yoan.gutierrez}@umcc.cu

Sonia Vázquez and Andrés Montoyo
Department of Software and Computing Systems
University of Alicante, Spain.
{svazquez, montoyo}@dlsi.ua.es

Abstract

In this paper we concentrate on the resolution of the semantic ambiguity that arises when a given word has several meanings. This specific task is commonly referred to as Word Sense Disambiguation (WSD). We propose a method that obtains the appropriate senses from a multidimensional analysis (using Relevant Semantic Trees). Our method uses different resources WordNet, WordNet Domains, WordNet-Affects and SUMO, combined with senses frequency obtained from SemCor. Our hypothesis is that in WSD it is important to obtain the most frequent senses depending on the type of analyzed context to achieve better results. Finally, in order to evaluate and compare our results, it is presented a comprehensive study and experimental work using the Senseval-2 and Semeval-2 data set, demonstrating that our system obtains better results than other unsupervised systems.

1 Introduction

The main goal of knowledge technologies is to provide meaning to the huge quantity of information that our multilingual societies generate day to day. A wide range of advanced techniques are required to progressively automate the knowledge lifecycle. For that, after performing an analysis to large data collections it is necessary to develop different approaches to automatically represent and manage a high-level of meaningful concepts (Montoyo *et al.*, 2005). Moreover, to be able to create efficient systems of Natural Language Processing (NLP) it is necessary to turn the information extracted from words in plain text into a Concept Level or meaningful word senses. This representation allows to group words with similar meanings according to the context where they appear.

In order to determine the right meanings of words in different contexts WSD systems have been developed. Furthermore, it has been proved that applications such as Machine Translation, Information Extraction, Question Answering, Information Retrieval, Text Classification, and Text Summarization require knowledge about word meanings to obtain better results. So, WSD is considered an essential task for all these applications (Ide and Véronis, 1998). For this reason many research groups are working on WSD, using a wide range of approaches.

Due to the need of evaluating different approaches to show the improvements of NLP tasks it was created the Senseval[1] competition. The first Senseval was in 1998 at Herstmonceux Castle, Succex (England) and after that every three years a new competition takes place. In Senseval, different NLP tasks are defined in order to evaluate systems using the same repositories and corpus. At present, the results obtained in WSD have been going poorer, because the requirements of each corpus are getting more complex. For example, in Senseval-2 (Cotton *et al.*, 2001) the best system obtained a 69% of accuracy in WSD, three years later in Senseval-3 (Snyder and Palmer, 2004) the best results were around 65.2% of accuracy, next in Semeval-1 (Pradhan *et al.*, 2007) a 59.1% of accuracy was obtained and in Semeval-2 (Agirre *et al.*, 2010) was 55.5%.

Due to the fact that the results are still very low in accuracy we want to go deeply in the resolution of semantic ambiguity. Firstly, we have studied the behavior of the baseline Most Frequent Sense (MFS) in each competition. This baseline has been placed among the top places of the rank; for example, in Senseval-2 a system applying this baseline could have been located on the 2nd place with a 64.58% of accuracy (Preiss, 2006). In Senseval-3 Denys Yuret of Koc University computed a 60.9% and for the same competition Bart Decadt of University of Antwerp provided a baseline of 62.4%, these results could have been located on 7th and 5th positions respectively (Snyder and Palmer,

[1] http://www.senseval.org

2004). In Semeval-1 the baseline was positioned on 9th place of fourteen systems and for the Semeval-2 competition the MFS baseline was located on 6th place. As we can see, this probabilistic procedure can obtain effective results on WSD task, but notice that it does not take into account context information.

Taking into account these facts our hypothesis is that for WSD it is important to obtain the most frequent senses combined with contextual information.

After these considerations, a new question arises: How will we be able to develop a procedure that uses the sense frequencies combined with a technique that takes into account the context information and improves the MFS results?

With the aim to answer this question and to demonstrate our hypothesis we present the following contributions:

- A method that combines MFS with a multidimensional analysis of the context. It uses several semantic resources combined with Relevant Semantic Trees.
- An analysis of how the MFS influences on the Relevant Semantic Trees method.
- An analysis of the behavior of Relevant Semantic Trees and Most Frequent Senses in each one of the semantic dimensions.
- A voting process between MFS and the results of different semantic dimensions.
- An exhaustive evaluation of the proposal.
- A comparison between our results and the systems in the Senseval-2 and Semeval-2 competitions.

In Section 2 we show some related works. Our approach is described in Section 3. The evaluations and analysis are provided in Section 4. Finally, we conclude in Section 5 adding further works.

2 Motivation and related work

Many efforts have been focused on the idea of building semantic networks to help NLP systems such as: MultiWordNet[2] (MWN), Multilingual Central Repository[3] (MCR), Integration of Semantic Resources based on WordNet (ISR-WN) (Gutiérrez *et al.*, 2010b) among others. Each resource has different semantic characteristics and their usage allows to analyze the tasks of NLP from different dimensions. Among all of these resources, ISR-WN has the highest quantity of semantic dimensions aligned, so it is a suitable resource to run our proposal. Next, we present a brief description of ISR-WN.

2.1 Integration of Semantic Resources based on WordNet (ISR-WN)

Integration of Semantic Resources based on WordNet (ISR-WN) (Gutiérrez *et al.*, 2010b) is a new resource that allows the integration of several semantic resources mapped to WN. In ISR-WN, WordNet is used as a core to link several resources such as: SUMO (Niles, 2001), WordNet Domains (WND) (Magnini and Cavaglia, 2000) and WordNet Affect (WNA) (Strapparava and Valitutti, 2004). As (Gutiérrez *et al.*, 2010a) describe, the integrator resource provides a software capable to navigate inside the semantic network.

In order to apply the multidimensionality that this resource provides, we have analyzed related NLP approaches that take into account semantic dimensionality. Addressed to context analysis we have studied (Magnini *et al.*, 2008), (Vázquez *et al.*, 2004) and (Buscaldi *et al.*, 2005). In these works WSD is performed using the WND resource (domain dimension). (Zouaq *et al.*, 2009), (Villarejo *et al.*, 2005) among others, conducted a semantic analysis using SUMO ontology (category dimension), and the Relevant Semantic Trees (RST) (Gutiérrez *et al.*, 2010a) apply several dimensions at once.

Next, we present the RST method which is able to work with different resources based on WordNet.

2.2 Relevant Semantic Trees (RST)

The RST method is able to find the correct senses of each word using Relevant Semantic Trees from different resources. This approach can be used with many resources mapped to WN as we have mentioned above.

In order to measure the association between concepts according to a multidimensional perspective in each sentence, RST uses an Association Ratio (*AR*) modification based on the proposal presented by Vázquez et al. (2004).

3 WSD Method

We propose an unsupervised knowledge-based method that uses the original RST technique including senses frequency of SemCor[4] corpus

[2] http://multiwordnet.fbk.eu/

3 http://www.lsi.upc.es/~nlp/meaning/meaning.html

[4] http://www.cse.unt.edu/~rada/downloads.html#semcor

and using a voting process to find the right senses. The voting process involves MFS (Most Frequent Sense), RST over WND, WNA, WN taxonomy and SUMO. Adding this new information we are able to improve the previous results obtained by the original RST and we also improve the MFS results in Semeval-2 competition. Specifically, we provide a sort of supervised aid (i.e. MFS) to the RST method of Gutiérrez *et al.*(2010a). Our proposal consists of two phases:

- Phase 1. Obtaining the Relevant Semantic Trees.
- Phase 2. Selecting the correct senses:
  - Step 1. Obtaining the RST from candidate senses.
  - Step 2. Obtaining accumulated values of relevance for each resource and frequency sense.
  - Step 3. Voting process to obtain the final senses.

Next, we present how these phases have been developed.

3.1 Obtaining the Relevant Semantic Trees

In this section, we describe how we have used a fragment of the original RST method with the aim to obtain Relevant Semantic Trees from the sentences. Equation 1 is used to measure and obtain the values of Relevant Concepts:

$$AR(C,s) = \sum_{i=1}^{n} AR(C,s_i); \qquad (1)$$

Where

$$AR(C,w) = P(C,w) * \log_2 \frac{P(C,\ w)}{P(C)}; \qquad (2)$$

Where C is a concept; s is a sentence or a set of words (w); s_i is the *i-th* word (w) of the sentence s; *P(C, w)* is joint probability distribution; and *P(C)* is marginal probability.

The first stage is to Pre-process the sentence to obtain all lemmas. For instance, in the sentence "*But it is unfair to dump on teachers as distinct from the educational establishment.*" the lemmas are: [*unfair, dump, teacher, distinct, educational, establishment*]

Vector			
AR	Domain	*AR*	Domain
0.90	Pedagogy	0.36	Commerce
0.90	Administration	0.36	Quality
0.36	Buildings	0.36	Psychoanalysis
0.36	Politics	0.36	Economy
0.36	Environment		

Table 1. Initial Vector of Domain

Next, each lemma is searched through ISR-WN resource and it is correlated with concepts of WND (the dimension used in this example). Table 1 shows the results after applying Equation 1 over the sentence.

After obtaining the Initial Concept Vector of Domains we apply the Equation 3 in order to build the Relevant Semantic Tree related to the sentence.

$$AR(PC,s) = AR(ChC,s) - ND(IC,PC) \qquad ;(3)$$

Where:

$$ND(IC,PC) = \frac{MP(IC,PC)}{TD} \qquad ;(4)$$

Where *AR(PC, s)* represents the *AR* value of *PC* related to the sentence *s*; $AR(ChC,s)$ is the *AR* value calculated with Equation 1 in case of Child Concept *(ChC)* was included in the Initial Vector, otherwise is calculated with the Equation 3; *ND* is a Normalized Distance; *IC* is the Initial Concept from we have to add the ancestors; *PC* is Parent Concept; *TD* is Depth of the hierarchic tree of the resource to use; and *MP* is Minimal Path.

Applying the Equation 3, the algorithm to decide which parent concept will be added to the vector is shown here:

if (AR(PC, s) > 0){
if (PC had not been added to vector)
PC is added to the vector with AR(PC, s) value;
else PC value = PC value + AR(PC, s) value; }

This bottom-up process is applied for each Concept of the Initial Vector to add each Relevant Parent to the vector. After reproducing the process to each Concept of the Initial Vector, the Relevant Semantic Tree is built. As a result, the Table 2 is obtained. This vector represents the Domain tree associated to the sentence such as Figure 1 shows. As we can see, the Relevant Semantic Tree of domains in Figure 1 has associated a color intensity related to the *AR* value of each domain. The more intense the color is the more related *AR* is.

Vector			
AR	Domain	*AR*	Domain
1.63	Social_Science	0.36	Buildings
0.90	Administration	0.36	Commerce
0.90	Pedagogy	0.36	Environment
0.80	RootDomain	0.11	Factotum
0.36	Psychoanalysis	0.11	Psychology
0.36	Economy	0.11	Architecture
0.36	Quality	0.11	Pure_Science
0.36	Politics		

Table 2. Final Domain Vector based on WND

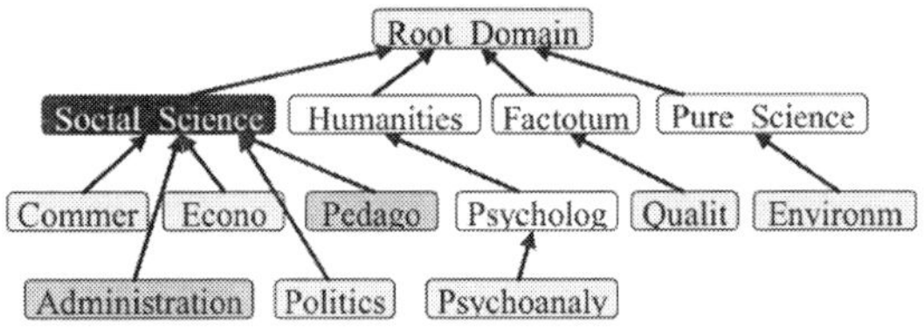

Figure 1. Relevant Semantic Tree from WND

Once the Relevant Semantic Tree is obtained, in case of the Domain dimension the Factotum category is eliminated from the tree. Due to the fact that Factotum is a generic Domain associated to words that appear in general contexts it does not provide useful information (Magnini and Cavaglia, 2000). Moreover, after conducting several experiments we have confirmed that it introduced errors.

3.2 Selecting the correct senses

To select the correct senses, three steps are applied:

Step 1. Obtaining the RST from candidate senses

In this step we associate to each possible sense of each lemma a RST based on each semantic dimension. At this stage the aim of RST is to measure the relation between each Concept and each sense. To do this we use the Equation 2 where we have substituted the variable *w* (word) with the variable sw_i, (sense) where sw_i indicates the *i-th* sense of word *w*. As a result, we convert each RST in a vector. Next, we continue with the complete process adding the parent concepts.

Step 2. Obtaining accumulated values of relevance for each resource and frequency sense

To measure the similarity between the RST of the sentences and senses, we have applied a fragment of the original method from (Gutiérrez *et al.*, 2010a) introducing sense frequency ($Freq_s$) as a new modification. Our goal is to obtain a new value to measure the Most Frequent Sense (MFS) in a given context. The *AR* value is accumulated when a matching exists between the vector elements of the sense and the vector elements of the sentence. The process is shown in the Equation 5.

$$AC(s, ARV) = \frac{\sum_k ARV[Vs_k]}{\sum_{i=1} ARV_i} + Freq_s \quad ; \quad (5)$$

Where *AC* is the *AR* value accumulated for the analyzed elements; *ARV* is the vector of relevant concepts of the sentence with the format: *ARV*[concept1 | *AR* value,...*]*; *Vs* is the vector of relevant concepts of the sense with the format *Vs*[concepts]; Vs_k is the *k-th* concept of the vector *Vs*; *ARV* [Vs_k] represents the value of *AR* assigned to the concept Vs_k for the value *ARV; $Freq_s$* represents the normalized value of frequency sense obtained from *cntlist* file from WN 1.6; and $\sum_{i=1} VRA_i$ is the term that normalizes the result.

AC is calculated for each RST (or Relevant Vector) of each semantic dimension. In this approach we have obtained four *AC* values (for WN taxonomy, WND, WNA and SUMO).

Notice that once we have obtained *AC* values for each sense in each dimension, if the senses calculated do not match with the grammatical category that Freeling (Atserias *et al.*, 2006) suggests, we discriminate these senses adding a zero value to *AC;* in other case we add a one value. Adding these values we can maintain all the candidates in the solution despite the grammatical category is wrong.

Finally, the proposed sense will have the highest *AC* value among all senses in each lemma.

Step 3. Voting process to obtain the final senses

As we have explained above, each semantic dimension provides a possible sense. It is important to remark that the sense frequency is also included as a semantic dimension. So, in order to decide the right sense among the different semantic dimensions sense proposals we use a voting process. To apply this idea we define the next equation:

$$Ps = max_i(max_k(V[VAC]_k)_i); \quad (6)$$

Where *VAC* corresponds to a vector composed by *AC* values of each sense for one lemma; *V [VAC]* is a vector of the *VAC*; *k* corresponds to each resource; $V\,[VAC]_k$: corresponds to *k-th VAC* for resource *k*; $\max_k(V\,[VAC]_k)$: determines the sense with maximum *AC* value of each *VAC*; *i*: is *i-th* sense; $\max_i$: determines the sense that was selected more times by $\max_k$ among all resources; and *Ps*: indicates proposed sense.

The *VAC* format is as follows: VAC [*AC* value sense#1, *AC* value sense#2, *AC* value sense#n]. And the *V [VAC]* format is: *V* [*VAC*-Domains, *VAC*-Emotions, *VAC*-WordNet Taxonomies, *VAC*-SUMO, *VAC*-Frequency *Senses*]

In *VAC* we also define a vector built with the frequency values of SemCor corpus for each lemma. Then we conduct a voting process with five *AC* values. If in an exceptional situation we obtain a tie or disjoin senses, the proposed sense will be the most frequent. We have chosen this option because of empirical studies have demonstrated that MFS works better than others (Molina *et al.*, 2002).

4 Evaluations and Analysis

In this section our purpose is to confirm the hypothesis presented in Section 1. We have evaluated this method with two different test corpus, Senseval-2 on "English All words" task and Semeval-2 on "English All words on Specific Domain" task. Moreover, we have compared our results with the participating systems of the aforementioned competitions. The goal of these experiments is to demonstrate how the sense frequencies combined with RST can improve the original RST results.

4.1 Evaluation with Senseval-2 corpus

First, we analyzed how the addition of the sense frequencies to accumulated value (*AC*) of each sense improved the results of the previous work published on (Gutiérrez *et al.*, 2010a). To do this we used as test corpus the file d00.txt and we conducted some experiments:

- Exp 1: Adding to *AC* value a 0% of $Freq_s$.
- Exp 2: Adding to *AC* value a 50% of $Freq_s$.
- Exp 3: Adding to *AC* value a 100% of $Freq_s$.

In the original method the authors calculated an accumulated value for each resource and summed up all the values to obtain the total accumulated value to combine all resources. In this new approach we also add the $Freq_s$ to the total accumulated value. Table 3 shows how each experiment obtains better results when Sense Frequencies ($Freq_s$) parameter is increased. Notice that we do not keep increasing this weight (i.e. 150%, 200%, etc) because the proposal would become converted only in selection process of MFS.

In order to determine whether the $Freq_s$ enhances the Most Frequent Senses (MFS) baseline, we conducted new experiments.

Next, we show how we have used the original method adding to *AC* the 100% of $Freq_s$ but only using one dimension at the same time:

- Exp4: Using MFS using $Freq_s$
- Exp5: Using WND resource
- Exp6: Using SUMO resource
- Exp7: Using WNA resource
- Exp8: Using WN Taxonomy resource

After doing these experiments we were able to determine which dimension worked better. As we can see on Table 3, these five experiments obtained promising results.

Another experiment was to combine these five experiments in a voting process to obtain even better results. This idea has led us to make our main proposal.

- Exp9: Applying a voting process among Exp4, Exp5, Exp6, Exp7 and Exp8 results

Table 3 shows all the results obtained from d00.txt file of Senseval-2. The result of MFS is underlined and the approach that exceeded it is in bold. We can see that the voting process (Exp9) obtained the best results.

Exp	Precision	Recall	Exp	Precision	Recall
Exp1	0,408	0,407	Exp6	0,561	0,560
Exp2	0,490	0,490	Exp7	0,555	0,554
Exp3	0,535	0,534	**Exp8**	**0,572**	**0,572**
Exp4	0,565	0,564	**Exp9**	**0,575**	**0,575**
Exp5	**0,572**	**0,572**			

Table 3. Results over d00.txt from Senseval-2

Following, we present the results after analyzing the entire corpus of the Senseval-2 competition. For that, we applied two experiments to the entire corpus.

- Exp10: Applying WSD with MFS of $Freq_s$
- Exp11: Applying a voting process using the five dimensions

We show in Table 4 a comparison among the results of the best performances of our voting process, MFS using $Freq_s$ and MFS obtained by (Preiss, 2006). The baseline used by Preiss was based on *cntlist* file from WN 1.7 version and our Exp10 was based on *cntlist* from WN 1.6. Notice, that are different although both are based on frequency information.

English All words - Fine-grained Scoring							
Rank	Precision	Recall		Rank	Precision	Recall	
1	0.690	0.690	S	**Exp11**	**0,610**	**0,609**	U
MFS	0.669	0.646	-	Exp10	0,601	0,599	-
2	0.636	0.636	S	4	0.575	0.569	U
3	0.618	0.618	S	..	..	..	

Table 4. Senseval-2 ranking

As we can see, our approach improves the Exp10 results. These results were obtained by our system, but the baseline MFS results obtained by Preiss were better than ours. This means that we could enhance the MFS that we use. So, we need to integrate in our approach a better MFS resource to obtain better results. Table 4 shows that our proposal would have the best results of all unsupervised methods.

4.2 Evaluation with Semeval-2 corpus

Our approach was also evaluated using corpus from Semeval-2 competition. The voting process obtained 52.7% and 51.5% of precision and recall respectively, improving the MFS baseline with 1% of accuracy. The original method from (Gutiérrez *et al.*, 2010a) was improved on 19.3% of accuracy such as Table 5 shows.

Rank	Precision	Recall	Rank	Precision	Recall
1	0.570	0.555	...	....	...
2	0.554	0.540	...	...	...
3	0.534	0.528	26	0.370	0.345
4	0.522	0.516	27	0.328	0.322
Our	**0,527**	**0,515**	28	0.321	0.315
5	0.513	0.513	29	0.312	0.303
MFS	0.505	0.505	Random	0.23	0.23

Table 5. Semeval-2 ranking

The underlined results pertain to original method from (Gutiérrez *et al.*, 2010a) and the bold results pertain to our approach. As a result, we can see that we can improve the MFS proposal from Semeval-2 competition.

In this competition only were evaluated nouns and verbs. The behavior of our approach for each category was: nouns 54.4% of precision and 53.7% of recall, and verbs 49.4% of precision and 45.4% of recall. Each category is effective in comparison with the best results obtained on this competition.

In order to determine if the annotation of grammatical categories influences on the results, we discovered that the Freeling tool introduced a noise of 2.62% when detecting nouns and for verbs 8.20%. These analyses indicate that the results would be better using another more accurate tool.

4.3 Comparison with newer works

In this section we present a comparison with some relevant WSD methods. We can mention those approaches using page-rank such as (Sinha and Mihalcea, 2007), and (Agirre and Soroa, 2009). These proposals were tested using "English All Words" task corpus from Senseval-2. In both proposals, Page-Rank method has been used to determine the centrality of structural lexical network using the semantic relations of WordNet. Then, to disambiguate each word the most weighted sense was chosen. These approaches obtained 58.6% and 56.37% of recall respectively. Other significant work is the ACL 2004 paper by (Mc.Carthy *et al.*, 2004) where the most frequent senses were obtained from a variety of resources (Reuters Corpus and SemCor Corpus), some of which provide domain information. This proposal obtained a 64% of precision in all-nouns task; this is just 3% higher than our results. However, we achieved better results than Mihalcea and Agirre exceeding them around 5%. This improvement could seem very poor but talking about WSD is a great step forward.

5 Conclusions and further works

In this paper we have presented the hypothesis that for word-sense disambiguation it is important to obtain the Most Frequent Senses depending on the kind of analyzed context. In order to demonstrate this hypothesis, we have studied how several semantic dimensions combined with sense frequencies could improve the obtained results of many approaches that only conducted the WSD analysis with one dimension. We have proposed an adaptation of an unsupervised knowledge-based method that combines the original Relevant Semantic Trees method with senses frequency in a voting process. As a result, we have been able to determine which percentage of sense frequency is needed to help the Relevant Semantic Trees method. Therefore, we have demonstrated that the WSD results are better when more percentage of sense frequency is added.

Moreover, we have conducted different experiments in order to know which semantic dimensions achieve better results. These experiments demonstrated that the Domain dimension (WND) and WordNet dimension (WN Taxonomy) worked better than MFS (Frequency dimension). Also, a voting process has been applied among all dimensions obtaining in Senseval-2 an of 60.9% and achieving the best results of all unsupervised systems. Furthermore, related to Semeval-2 our approach has improved the baseline MFS and the original RST method.

As further work we propose to use other resources on the voting process in order to add more dimensions and also, use a better frequency resource. Apart from that, we also have considered to use another grammatical categorizer, in order to reduce the noise introduced by misclassifying words.

Acknowledgements

This paper has been supported partially by Ministerio de Ciencia e Innovación - Spanish Government (grant no. TIN2009-13391-C04-01), and Conselleria d'Educación - Generalitat

Valenciana (grant no. PROMETEO/2009/119, ACOMP/2010/288 and ACOMP/2011/001).

References

Antonio Molina, Ferran Pla, Encarna Segarra and Lidia Moreno. 2002. Word Sense Disambiguation using Statistical Models and WordNet. *Proceedings of 3rd International Conference on Language Resources and Evaluation*: Las Palmas de Gran Canaria.

Andrés Montoyo, Armando Suárez, German Rigau and Manuel Palomar. 2005. Combining Knowledge- and Corpus-based Word-Sense-Disambiguation Methods. *Journal of Artificial Intelligence*, 23:299-330.

Amal Zouaq, Michel Gagnon and Benoit Ozell. 2009. A SUMO-based Semantic Analysis for Knowledge Extraction. *Proceedings of the 4th Language & Technology Conference*: Poznań, Poland.

Bernardo Magnini and Gabriela Cavaglia. 2000. Integrating Subject Field Codes into WordNet. *Proceedings of Third International Conference on Language Resources and Evaluation (LREC-2000)*: 1413--1418.

Bernardo Magnini, Carlo Strapparava, Giovanni Pezzulo and Alfio Gliozzo. 2008. Using Domain Information for Word Sense Disambiguation. *Proceedings of the First International Conference on Emerging Trends in Engineering and Technology (icetet 2008)*: 1187-1191. Nagpur, India.

Benjamin Snyder and Martha Palmer. 2004. The English All Word Task. *SENSEVAL-3: Third International Workshop on the evaluation of System of the Semantic Analysis of Text*: Barcelona, Spain.

Christiane Fellbaum. 1998. WordNet. An Electronic Lexical Database. *The MIT Press*: University of Cambridge.

Carlo Strapparava and Alessandro Valitutti. 2004. WordNet-Affect: an affective extension of WordNet. *Proceedings of the 4th International Conference on Language Resources and Evaluation (LREC 2004)*: 1083-1086. Lisbon.

Davide Buscaldi, Paolo Rosso and Francesco Masulli. 2005. Integrating Conceptual Density with WordNet Domains and CALD Glosses for Noun Sense Disambiguation. *Proceedings of España for Natural Language Processing (ESTAL-2005)*: 267-276. Alicante, Spain.

Diana Mc.Carthy, Rob Koeling, Julie Weeds and John Carroll. 2004. Finding Predominant Word Senses in Untagged Text. *Proceedings of the 42nd Meeting of the Association for Computational Linguistics (ACL'04)*: 279--286.

Eneko Agirre, Oier López De Lacalle, Christiane Fellbaum, Shu-Kai Hsieh, Maurizio Tesconi, Monica Monachini, Piek Vossen and Roxanne Segers. 2010. SemEval-2010 task 17: All-words word sense disambiguation on a specific domain. *Proceedings of the 5th International Workshop on Semantic Evaluation*: 75-80. Los Angeles, California.

Eneko Agirre and Aitor Soroa. 2009. Personalizing PageRank for Word Sense Disambiguation. *Proceedings of the 12th conference of the European chapter of the Association for Computational Linguistics (EACL-2009)*: Athens, Greece.

Ian Niles. 2001. Mapping WordNet to the SUMO Ontology. *Teknowledge Corporation.*

Jordi Atserias, Bernardino Casas, Elisabet Comelles, Meritxell González, Lluis Padró and Muntsa Padró. 2006. FreeLing 1.3: Syntactic and semantic services in an opensource NLP library. *Proceedings of LREC'06*: Genoa, Italy.

Judita Preiss. 2006. A detailed comparison of WSD systems:an analysis of the system answers for the Senseval-2 English all words task. *Natural Language Engineering,* 12(3):209–228.

Luis Villarejo, Lluís Márquez and German Rigau. 2005. Exploring the construction of semantic class classiers for WSD. *Sociedad Española para el Procesamiento del Lenguaje Natural,* 35: 195-202.

Nancy Ide and Jean Véronis. 1998. Introduction to the Special Issue on Word Sense Disambiguation: The State of the Art. *Computational Linguistics,* 24(1):1-40.

Ravi Sinha and Rada Mihalcea. 2007. Unsupervised Graph-based Word Sense Disambiguation Using Measures of Word Semantic Similarity. *Proceedings of the IEEE International Conference on Semantic Computing (ICSC 2007)*: Irvine, CA.

Sameer S. Pradhan, Edward Loper, Dmitriy Dligach and Martha Stone Palmer. 2007. SemEval-2007 Task-17: English Lexical Sample SRL and All Words. *Proceedings of the 4th International Workshop on Semantic Evaluations (SemEval-2007)*: 87-92. Prague.

Scott Cotton, Phil Edmonds, Adam Kilgarriff and Martha Palmer. 2001. English All word. *SENSEVAL-2: Second International Workshop on Evaluating Word Sense Disambiguation Systems*: Toulouse, France.

Sonia Vázquez, Andrés Montoyo and German Rigau. 2004. Using Relevant Domains Resource for Word Sense Disambiguation. *IC-AI'04. Proceedings of the International Conference on Artificial Intelligence*: Ed: CSREA Press. Las Vegas, E.E.U.U.

Yoan Gutiérrez, Antonio Fernández, Andrés Montoyo and Sonia Vázquez. 2010a. UMCC-DLSI: Integrative resource for disambiguation task. *Proceedings of the 5th International Workshop on Semantic Evaluation*: 427-432. Uppsala, Sweden.

Yoan Gutiérrez, Antonio Fernández, Andrés Montoyo and Sonia Vázquez. 2010b. Integration of semantic resources based on WordNet. *XXVI Congreso de la Sociedad Española para el Procesamiento del Lenguaje Natural,* 45: 161-168. Universidad Politécnica de Valencia, Valencia.

Investigating Advanced Techniques for Document Content Similarity Applied to External Plagiarism Analysis

Daniel Micol and **Rafael Muñoz**
Dept. of Software and Computing Systems
University of Alicante
San Vicente del Raspeig, Alicante, Spain
{dmicol,rafael}@dlsi.ua.es

Óscar Ferrández
Dept. of Biomedical Informatics
University of Utah
Salt Lake City, Utah, USA
oscar.ferrandez@utah.edu

Abstract

We present an approach to perform external plagiarism analysis by applying several similarity detection techniques, such as lexical measures and a textual entailment recognition system developed by our research group. Some of the least expensive features of this system are applied to all corpus documents to detect those that are likely to be plagiarized. After this is done, the whole system is applied over this subset of documents to extract the exact n-grams that have been plagiarized, given that we now have less data to process and therefore can use a more complex and costly function. Apart from the application of strictly lexical measures, we also experiment with a textual entailment recognition system to detect plagiarisms with a high level of obfuscation. In addition, we experiment with the application of a spell corrector and a machine translation system to handle misspellings and plagiarisms translated into different languages, respectively.

1 Introduction

We believe there are two main user scenarios where external plagiarism detection tools are applied, sharing both of them the fact that they have a large source documents corpus. The difference, however, is that the first scenario is based on a large number of suspicious documents being processed at the same time, so the detection approach needs to be highly efficient and scalable. An example of this scenario would be the *1st and 2nd International Competitions on Plagiarism Detection* (Potthast et al., 2009; Potthast et al., 2010), where the corpora contain multiple source and suspicious documents. For this first use case we have developed a system to detect external document plagiarism that is highly efficient and scalable. It contains a first phase where a small subset of source documents are selected as possible candidates to be the origin of the plagiarism for a given suspicious document. Given that this phase processes the whole corpora, it uses a simple and lightweight function to select the subset of candidate source documents. After this is done, a more complex function is applied over this subset to extract which documents contain the plagiarism, and the exact position within these documents. This two-step approach is common among research systems, as described in (Potthast et al., 2009).

The second use case assumes that we only have to process one suspicious document at a time. Therefore, we can apply more complex techniques that are less efficient but highly accurate, as there is less data to process. An example of this use case could be an online system to detect if a scientific manuscript that an author wants to submit to a journal or conference is a plagiarism of a previously published paper. For this second use case we have experimented with more complex and accurate techniques, such as the usage of textual entailment recognition methods developed by our research group. In addition, we have also applied a spell corrector and a machine translation system to handle documents with misspellings and written in different languages.

2 State of the art

Most of the research approaches on external plagiarism analysis contain a simple and efficient heuristic retrieval to reduce the number of source documents to compare against, and a more complex and costly detailed analysis that attempts to extract the exact position of the plagiarized fragment, if any (Potthast et al., 2009). The system that we have developed is in line with this architecture.

With regards to the heuristic retrieval, (Basile et al., 2008; Grozea et al., 2009) decided to apply a document similarity function that would be used as heuristic to determine if a given suspicious and source documents are similar enough to hold a plagiarism relation. (Kasprzak et al., 2009) create an inverted index of the corpus document's contents in order to be able to retrieve efficiently a set of documents that contain a set of n-grams. (Grozea et al., 2009; Stamatatos, 2009) implement a character-level n-gram comparison and apply a cosine similarity function based on term frequency weights. With this approach they extract the 51 most similar source documents to the suspicious one being analyzed. (Basile et al., 2009; Kasprzak et al., 2009) decided to implement a word-level n-gram comparison. Low granularity word n-grams, with a size of 1, have been explored by (Muhr et al., 2009), applying cosine similarity using frequency weights to extract the two most similar partitions for every sentence in a document, using the source document's sentences as centroid.

For the detailed analysis, (Basile et al., 2009) perform a greedy match merging if the distance of the matches is not too high. A more strict approach has been presented by (Muhr et al., 2009), requiring exact sentence matches, and afterwards applying a match merging approach by greedily joining consecutive sentences. In this method, gaps are allowed if the respective sentences are similar to the corresponding sentences in the other document. (Grozea et al., 2009) perform a computation of the distances of adjacent matches, joining them based on a Monte Carlo optimization. Afterwards, they propose a refinement of the obtained section pairs. (Kasprzak et al., 2009) extract matches of word n-grams of length 5, and apply a Match Merging Heuristic to get larger matches. Then they extract the maximum size that shares at least 20 matches, including the first and the last n-gram of the matching sections, and for which 2 adjacent matches are at most 49 not-matching n-grams apart.

3 Methods

We will first present a baseline system that is efficient and scalable, and designed to work for the first use case mentioned above. For this purpose, we will use corpora of thousands of suspicious and source documents, where every suspicious can contain none, one or more plagiarisms of any source documents. After this, we present certain optimizations built on top of our baseline system that will make it more accurate, although slower, and therefore will be applicable in the second use case.

3.1 Baseline system

Our baseline system (Micol et al., 2010), developed for our participation in the *2nd International Competition on Plagiarism Detection* (Potthast et al., 2010), has two phases: document selection, using a heuristic retrieval, and passage matching, performing a more detailed analysis.

The first step is to select a subset of candidate source documents that will later on be compared against a given suspicious document. This should reduce by a large factor the number of document comparisons to perform. To generate this set we will have to loop through all source documents, and given that this set is large, this operation needs to be relatively simple and inexpensive. Our approach to solve this problem is to weight the words in every document and then compare the weights of those terms that appear in both the suspicious and the source documents being compared. Their similarity score will be the sum of the mentioned common term weights.

Once we have a small subset of source documents to compare against for every suspicious one, we can perform a more accurate and costly comparison between pairs of documents. We try to find the largest common substring between suspicious and source documents, requiring a minimum length which will be the n-gram size. Once the n-grams of the source document being compared against have been extracted, we will iterate through the contents of the suspicious document, extract n-grams starting at every given offset, look them up in the list of n-grams of the aforementioned source document, and seek directly to the positions where the given n-gram appears, avoiding unnecessary comparisons. From these offsets we will try to find the largest common substring to both documents.

3.2 DLSITE: a textual entailment recognition system

The baseline system that we have detailed before is suitable for low levels of plagiarism obfuscation, given that it is based on lexical comparisons. If the person who performs the appropriation uses equivalent terms instead of the original ones, or swaps the word order considerably, our system will not perform well and won't recognize these plagiarisms. To be able to detect these sorts of appropriations, we add semantic and syntactic techniques, as well as more advanced lexical measures.

Concretely, we decided to apply DLSITE (Ferrández et al., 2007a), a textual entailment recognition system developed by our research group that analyzes pairs of sentences, being one the text and the other the hypothesis, trying to determine if the hypothesis' meaning can be inferred from the text's. Therefore, with the use of this system, we could detect plagiarisms that are written in different manners, but still share their meaning. DLSITE contains the following modules:

Lexical analysis The lexical module of DLSITE (Ferrández et al., 2007b) computes the extraction of several lexical feature values for a given text-hypothesis pair. These measures are mainly based on word co-occurrences in both the hypothesis and the text, as well as the context where they appear.

Syntactic analysis The syntactic module of DLSITE (Micol et al., 2007) compares the meaning of the text and the hypothesis by generating their corresponding syntactic dependency trees, and then analyzing the similarities of these two structures. It is composed of a pipeline of four submodules, which are syntactic dependency tree construction, filtering, embedded subtree search and graph node matching.

Semantic analysis The semantic module of DLSITE analyzes a text-hypothesis pair from a meaning's perspective, using resources such as WordNet, VerbOcean and FrameNet. Similar research projects have already developed procedures using standard WordNet-based similarities (Corley and Mihalcea, 2005; Hickl and Bensley, 2007). However, in our case we also consider string-based similarities for the final similarity score. This allows us to positively consider entities that, while not appearing in WordNet, are very relevant, instead of penalizing their similarity score. We exploit WordNet relations in order to find semantic paths that connect two concepts through the WordNet taxonomy.

Since verbs have a strong contribution to the sentence's final meaning, we want to measure how the hypothesis' verbs are related to the text's. To achieve this, we exploit the VerbNet lexicon (Kipper et al., 2006), and the VerbOcean and WordNet relationships, trying to find correlations between the main verbs expressed in the hypothesis with those in the text. The underlying intuition about the VerbNet correspondence is that the verbs wrapped in the same VerbNet class or in one of their subclasses have a strong semantic relation since they share the same thematic roles and restrictions, as well as syntactic and semantic frames. Additionally, VerbOcean's relations are good indicators of semantic correspondence between verbs.

Another relevant issue to recognize entailment relations is to analyze the presence and absence of named entities. (Rodrigo et al., 2008) successfully built their system mainly using the knowledge supplied by the recognition of named entities. Other works, such as (Iftene and Moruz, 2009) and our participation in the *Text Analysis Conference 2008* (Balahur et al., 2008), have also proven that knowledge about named entities positively helps in modeling entailments. In our case, rather than constructing the system based on named entity inferences, we study the addition of this knowledge in our textual entailment recognition system.

Therefore, similarly as we did for verbs, we explored ways to find out entity counterparts between the text and the hypothesis. The first step is to recognize named entities, and for this purpose we use our in-house named entity recognizer, called NERUA (Kozareva et al., 2007). Afterwards, we use two surface techniques to discover NE relations: partial entity matching and acronym correspondences between the NEs detected in the hypothesis and the ones in the text.

3.3 Corpus pre-processing

We have identified some scenarios where it would be beneficial to perform additional corpus pre-processing. These are described as follows.

Handling misspellings Given that our method is heavily based on term frequencies, a misspelling in the processed documents could introduce a high level of noise, since they will have a lower document frequency, and therefore a higher idf. Also, if a misspelling appears in a suspicious and a source document, these will be heavily linked by this term, and their similarity score may not be fair when comparing it with other documents. Therefore, it would be beneficial to apply a spell corrector over the documents in our corpora, such as the one described in (Gao et al., 2010). To minimize the impact of false positives from the speller system, we would perform a two-pass algorithm. In the first pass we would not apply the spell corrector, and would try to retrieve all the plagiarisms that our system recognizes. In the second pass we would apply the spell corrector and attempt to extract additional appropriations. By doing this we ensure that we don't loose plagiarisms if the spell corrector system introduces some noise into the data.

Document translation When plagiarizing a document, an author can choose to translate it into a different language. This is the case, for instance, for some of the plagiarized documents of the PAN corpora, which have been translated into Spanish or German (Potthast et al., 2009). These appropriations won't be detected by our system unless we translate them into English, as this is the language in which the source documents are written. As a pre-processing step, we propose to apply a language detector over the set of suspicious documents, and if this tool detects that they are not in English, we execute an automatic translator to transform the corresponding document into English. The detection step is performed using the API of a machine translation application. Given that this is a remote live production system and some of the documents in our corpus can be large, sending the whole text doesn't seem to be the best approach. For the user case where we have a large amount of suspicious documents to process, we send a fragment composed of the first few hundreds of words from a document in order to get a fast and scalable response. This is not completely accurate, as some times documents contain fragments written in different languages. If we only process one suspicious document, we perform a more complex and accurate process. To do this we first split the document content into sentences based on punctuation symbols. Then, we submit three random sentences from the text to the translation application. If all of them return the same language detected, this will be the one of the document. If this is not the case we take another set of three sentences. Similar to what we previously mentioned, we perform a two-pass algorithm in order to reduce the impact of false positives introduced by the translation software.

4 Experimentation and results

As mentioned before, the corpora that we have used to measure and evaluate our system have been provided by the *1st International Competition on Plagiarism Detection*. These are composed thousands of source and suspicious documents, some of the latter containing automatically generated plagiarisms with different levels of obfuscation. In addition, some source documents are written in Spanish or German, but the corresponding plagiarized document has been translated into English.

4.1 Baseline system

To experiment with our system we used the external plagiarism corpora from the *1st International Competition on Plagiarism Detection*. The first aspect we experimented with was trying to determine the optimal number of documents to be selected, given that a larger amount would lead to higher accuracy, but would affect performance negatively. The opposite applies to smaller selected document sets.

Table 1 shows the results from this experiment using different set sizes, where column *Captured* represents the number of plagiarisms that are contained within the set of source documents, and *Missed* those that are not included in this set.

Size	Recall	Captured	Missed
1	0.3260	23,970	49,552
5	0.6875	50,547	22,975
10	0.7781	57,206	16,316
20	0.8282	60,893	12,629
30	0.8479	62,340	11,182
40	0.8595	63,189	10,333
50	0.8698	63,947	9,575
60	0.8760	64,403	9,119
70	0.8820	64,843	8,679
80	0.8869	65,205	8,317
90	0.8905	65,473	8,049
100	0.8941	65,734	7,788

Table 1: Metrics using different selected document set sizes.

Given the values from Table 1, we decided to use a number of documents of 10, since we believe it is the best trade-off between amount of texts and recall. After this step, we executed the passage detection, which produced an overall score of 0.3902. As we can see in these results, the strongest aspect of our baseline system is its precision, where it ranks the third among all participants. On the other hand, recall and granularity were not as good, but still within the top half. The reason why recall is lower is in part due to the fact that we chose 10 source documents per suspicious text to evaluate, giving a maximum coverage value of 77.81%. Apart from this, and since our method is purely lexical, we miss plagiarisms that are not written in similar ways. Finally, documents that are translated will also lower our recall. On the other hand, granularity would have been lower if we had been more aggressive at merging matches, although then precision might have suffered.

4.2 Applying a textual entailment recognition system

Due to the expensive computational cost of executing a textual entailment recognition system, we used the corpora provided for the *Recognizing Textual Entailment* challenges. To simulate that the text-hypothesis pairs in these corpora are documents, we combine the texts into a single document and the hypothesis into another one, and then perform a plagiarism detection using both documents. Table 2 shows the results using our baseline system and the textual entailment recognition method previously described. As we can see in this table, our baseline system doesn't recognize the cases where there is an entailment, given that the pairs are written in a very different way. Applying our textual entailment recognition method provides significant gains.

Corpora	System	Accuracy
RTE-2	Baseline System	0.5000
	Textual Entailment	0.6125
RTE-3	Baseline System	0.5125
	Textual Entailment	0.6800
RTE-4	Baseline System	0.5000
	Textual Entailment	0.6250
RTE-5	Baseline System	0.5000
	Textual Entailment	0.6350

Table 2: Results of our baseline and textual entailment systems using the RTE test corpora.

4.3 Handling misspellings

Given the nature of the corpora provided for the *1st International Competition on Plagiarism Detection*, we cannot apply them to test a speller system given that the plagiarisms are automatically generated and therefore they do not contain misspellings (Potthast et al., 2009). Instead, we evaluate the addition of this module based on the results that spellers achieve in real-world applications.

Typically, web spellers have an accuracy of around 90% assuming an 85% of correctly spelled queries and 15% of misspellings, as described in (Gao et al., 2010). This means that there is clearly a gain of applying these systems as, even though they introduce some noise, in general terms they produce significant benefits. In addition, they are deterministic systems, and given that we apply them to both the source and suspicious document, an incorrect behavior for a given word in a source document would also be applied to the same word in the suspicious, and vice versa. In our system we want to match terms that appear in the same manner, and therefore a false positive or negative produced by the speller system won't hurt the accuracy of our plagiarism detection software.

Assuming a highly misspelled document, the application of a speller could produce a net gain of about 5%, which is a very important increase. In addition, speller systems typically return a normalize score value depending on the confidence of a given candidate. Based on this they either produce a suggestion, when there is lower confidence, or an auto-correction, when there is higher. We could tune our system to use a more or less aggressive speller depending on the user's needs as well as the nature of the input corpora.

4.4 Document translation

The corpora provided for the *1st International Competition on Plagiarism Detection* contains source documents in languages other than English, although the suspicious ones have been translated. Concretely, there are 13,559 source documents in English, and 870 in other languages. Given that the suspicious texts will be in English, our system won't find the plagiarisms associated to those 870 due to language mismatches. To overcome this issue we applied the translator previously described, using different configurations. The parameter we changed was the number of words from the document to submit to the translator, using the first 200, 500 and 1,000 words.

The following table shows the results from applying the language detector over the source documents corpus.

System	Accuracy	Correct	Incorrect	TP	TN	FP	FN
Baseline (no detection)	0.9397	13,559	870	0	13,559	0	870
Detection ($\|words\| = 200$)	0.9936	14,337	92	816	13,521	38	54
Detection ($\|words\| = 500$)	0.9967	14,381	48	843	13,538	21	27
Detection ($\|words\| = 1,000$)	0.9974	14,392	37	847	13,545	14	23

Table 3: Results from applying the language detector over the source documents corpus.

We define positives as the documents that have been translated, and negatives those that have been not. In this table we can see that there is a 5.77% increase in accuracy if we apply a language detector using the first 1,000 words of a document. However, given that we use a two-pass algorithm, the number of FPs would be 0, which means that the final accuracy after applying a language detection software would be 0.9984, which is a 5.87% higher than the baseline. This means that, assuming a perfect translator and plagiarism detector, our system's score could increase in almost six points, which is a big improvement. The final gain will depend on the user's document translation software choice.

5 Conclusions and future work

In this paper we have presented a baseline system for external plagiarism analysis mainly based on lexical similarities, and a set of more advanced techniques that could be beneficial to external plagiarism analysis. While the baseline system is very efficient and produces reasonable results, the application of the aforementioned advanced techniques can have a very significant impact, depending on the corpus' nature. However, these latter methods decrease our overall system's performance considerably, so they are not applicable to large corpora.

We have also explained two scenarios where we believe that plagiarism detection tools are applied. In the first of them, where we would have a large suspicious documents corpus, the application of advanced techniques would not be feasible given their low efficiency. Therefore, in this case we would have to use our baseline system which is mainly based on lexical measures. On the other hand, in the second user scenario, where we only have one suspicious document to analyze, the application of the aforementioned advanced techniques is suitable given the smaller amount of data to process. In this case we will be able to achieve higher accuracy rates and support a larger number of obfuscation cases. Therefore, there is a trade-off between accuracy and response time, which will be in large determined by the size of the corpus to process.

As future work we would like to apply a word alignment algorithm to detect plagiarisms, such as the one described in (Och, 2002). This would be a more flexible and accurate approach, rather than forcing the words to appear in the same position in both documents being analyzed, although its computational cost would also be considerably higher. This should allow our system to recognize higher levels of obfuscation than our current approach. In addition, it would be very beneficial for multilingual plagiarism analysis. This kind of task presents the challenge that words might not appear in the same order, not even after a machine translation tool has been applied. Hence, applying the aforementioned word alignment algorithm would allow us to handle better multilingual plagiarism.

Acknowledgements

This research has been partially funded by the Spanish Ministry of Science and Innovation (grant TIN2009-13391-C04-01) and the Conselleria d'Educació of the Spanish Generalitat Valenciana (grants PROMETEO/2009/119 and ACOMP/2010/286). Furthermore, we would like to thank Dario Bigongiari and Michael Schueppert for their help and support.

References

Alexandra Balahur, Elena Lloret, Óscar Ferrández, Andrés Montoyo, Manuel Palomar, and Rafael Muñoz. 2008. The DLSIUAES Team's Participation in the TAC 2008 Tracks. In *Notebook Papers of the Text Analysis Conference, TAC 2008 Workshop*, Gaithersburg, Maryland, USA, November.

Chiara Basile, Dario Benedetto, Emanuele Caglioti, and Mirko Degli Esposti. 2008. An example of mathematical authorship attribution. *Journal of Mathematical Physics*, 49:125211–125230.

Chiara Basile, Dario Benedetto, Emanuele Caglioti, Giampaolo Cristadoro, and Mirko Degli Esposti. 2009. A Plagiarism Detection Procedure in Three Steps: Selection, Matches and "Squares". In *Proceedings of the SEPLN'09 Workshop on Uncovering Plagiarism, Authorship and Social Software Misuse*, pages 19–23, San Sebastián (Donostia), Spain, September.

Courtney Corley and Rada Mihalcea. 2005. Measuring the Semantic Similarity of Texts. In *Proceedings of the ACL Workshop on Empirical Modeling of Semantic Equivalence and Entailment*, pages 13–18, Ann Arbor, Michigan, USA, June.

Óscar Ferrández, Daniel Micol, Rafael Muñoz, and Manuel Palomar. 2007a. A Perspective-Based Approach for Solving Textual Entailment Recognition. In *Proceedings of the ACL-PASCAL Workshop on Textual Entailment and Paraphrasing*, pages 66–71, Prague, Czech Republic, June.

Óscar Ferrández, Daniel Micol, Rafael Muñoz, and Manuel Palomar. 2007b. DLSITE-1: Lexical Analysis for Solving Textual Entailment Recognition. In *Natural Language Processing and Information Systems*, volume 4592, pages 284–294.

Jianfeng Gao, Xiaolong Li, Daniel Micol, Chris Quirck, and Xu Sun. 2010. A Large Scale Ranker-Based System for Search Query Spelling Correction. In *Proceedings of the 23rd International Conference on Computational Linguistics*, pages 358–366, Beijing, China, August.

Cristian Grozea, Christian Gehl, and Marius Popescu. 2009. ENCOPLOT: Pairwise Sequence Matching in Linear Time Applied to Plagiarism Detection. In *Proceedings of the SEPLN'09 Workshop on Uncovering Plagiarism, Authorship and Social Software Misuse*, pages 10–18, San Sebastián (Donostia), Spain, September.

Andrew Hickl and Jeremy Bensley. 2007. A Discourse Commitment-Based Framework for Recognizing Textual Entailment. In *Proceedings of the ACL-PASCAL Workshop on Textual Entailment and Paraphrasing*, pages 171–176, Prague, Czech Republic, June.

Adrian Iftene and Mihai-Alex Moruz. 2009. UAIC Participation at RTE5. In *Notebook Papers of the Text Analysis Conference, TAC 2009 Workshop*, Gaithersburg, Maryland, USA, November.

Jan Kasprzak, Michal Brandejs, and Miroslav Křipač. 2009. Finding Plagiarism by Evaluating Document Similarities. In *Proceedings of the SEPLN'09 Workshop on Uncovering Plagiarism, Authorship and Social Software Misuse*, pages 24–28, San Sebastián (Donostia), Spain, September.

Karin Kipper, Anna Korhonen, Neville Ryant, and Martha Palmer. 2006. Extending Verbnet with Novel Verb Classes. In *Proceedings of the Fifth International Conference on Language Resources and Evaluation (LREC 2006)*, Genova, Italy, June.

Z. Kozareva, Ó. Ferrández, A. Montoyo, and R. Muñoz. 2007. Combining data-driven systems for improving Named Entity Recognition. *Data and Knowledge Engineering*, 61(3):449–466.

Daniel Micol, Óscar Ferrández, and Rafael Muñoz. 2007. DLSITE-2: Semantic Similarity Based on Syntactic Dependency Trees Applied to Textual Entailment. In *Proceedings of the TextGraphs-2 Workshop*, pages 73–80, Rochester, New York, USA, April.

Daniel Micol, Óscar Ferrández, Fernando Llopis, and Rafael Muñoz. 2010. A Lexical Similarity Approach for Efficient and Scalable External Plagiarism Detection. In *Proceedings of the SEPLN'10 Workshop on Uncovering Plagiarism, Authorship and Social Software Misuse*, Padua, Italy, September.

Markus Muhr, Mario Zechner, Roman Kern, and Michael Granitzer. 2009. External and Intrinsic Plagiarism Detection Using Vector Space Models. In *Proceedings of the SEPLN'09 Workshop on Uncovering Plagiarism, Authorship and Social Software Misuse*, pages 47–55, San Sebastián (Donostia), Spain, September.

Franz Josef Och. 2002. *Statistical machine translation: from single-word models to alignment templates*. Ph.D. thesis, RWTH Aachen.

Martin Potthast, Benno Stein, Andreas Eiselt, Alberto Barrón Cedeño, and Paolo Rosso. 2009. Overview of the 1st international competition on plagiarism detection. In *Proceedings of the SEPLN'09 Workshop on Uncovering Plagiarism, Authorship and Social Software Misuse*, pages 1–9, San Sebastián (Donostia), Spain, September.

Martin Potthast, Benno Stein, Andreas Eiselt, Alberto Barrón Cedeño, and Paolo Rosso. 2010. Overview of the 2nd international competition on plagiarism detection. In *Proceedings of the SEPLN'10 Workshop on Uncovering Plagiarism, Authorship and Social Software Misuse*, Padua, Italy, September.

Álvaro Rodrigo, Anselmo Peñas, and Felisa Verdejo. 2008. Towards an Entity-based recognition of Textual Entailment. In *Notebook Papers of the Text Analysis Conference, TAC 2008 Workshop*, Gaithersburg, Maryland, USA, November.

Efstathios Stamatatos. 2009. Intrinsic Plagiarism Detection Using Character n-gram Profiles. In *Proceedings of the SEPLN'09 Workshop on Uncovering Plagiarism, Authorship and Social Software Misuse*, pages 36–37, San Sebastián (Donostia), Spain, September.

Using Cognates in a French - Romanian Lexical Alignment System: A Comparative Study

Mirabela Navlea
Linguistique, Langues, Parole (LiLPa)
Université de Strasbourg
22, rue René Descartes
BP, 80010, 67084 Strasbourg cedex
navlea@unistra.fr

Amalia Todiraşcu
Linguistique, Langues, Parole (LiLPa)
Université de Strasbourg
22, rue René Descartes
BP, 80010, 67084 Strasbourg cedex
todiras@unistra.fr

Abstract

This paper describes a hybrid French - Romanian cognate identification module. This module is used by a lexical alignment system. Our cognate identification method uses lemmatized, tagged and sentence-aligned parallel corpora. This method combines statistical techniques, linguistic information (lemmas, POS tags) and orthographic adjustments. We evaluate our cognate identification module and we compare it to other methods using pure statistical techniques. Thus, we study the impact of the used linguistic information and the orthographic adjustments on the results of the cognate identification module and on cognate alignment. Our method obtains the best results in comparison with the other implemented statistical methods.

1 Introduction

We present a new French - Romanian cognate identification module, integrated into a lexical alignment system using French - Romanian parallel law corpora.

We define cognates as translation equivalents having an identical form or sharing orthographic or phonetic similarities (common etymology, borrowings). Cognates are very frequent between close languages such as French and Romanian, two Latin languages with a rich morphology. So, they represent important lexical cues in a French - Romanian lexical alignment system.

Few linguistic resources and tools for Romanian (dictionaries, parallel corpora, MT systems) are currently available. Some lexically aligned corpora or lexical alignment tools (Tufiş *et al.*, 2005) are available for Romanian - English or Romanian - German (Vertan and Gavrilă, 2010). Most of the cognate identification modules used by these systems are purely statistical. As far as we know, no cognate identification method is available for French and Romanian.

Cognate identification is a difficult task due to the high orthographic similarities between bilingual pairs of words having different meanings. Inkpen *et al.* (2005) develop classifiers for French and English cognates based on several dictionaries and manually built lists of cognates. Inkpen *et al.* (2005) distinguish between:

- cognates (*liste* (FR) - *list* (EN));
- false friends (*blesser* ('to injure') (FR) - *bless* (EN));
- partial cognates (*facteur* (FR) - *factor* or *mailman* (EN));
- genetic cognates (*chef* (FR) - *head* (EN));
- unrelated pairs of words (*glace* (FR) - *ice* (EN) and *glace* (FR) - *chair* (EN)).

Our cognate detection method identifies cognates, partial and genetic cognates. This method is used especially to improve a French - Romanian lexical alignment system. So, we aim to obtain a high precision of our cognate identification method. Thus, we eliminate false friends and unrelated pairs of words combining statistical techniques and linguistic information (lemmas, POS tags). We use a lemmatized, tagged and sentence-aligned parallel corpus. Unlike Inkpen *et al.* (2005), we do not use other external resources (dictionaries, lists of cognates).

To detect cognates from parallel corpora, several approaches exploit the orthographic similarity between two words of a bilingual pair. An efficient method is the 4-gram method (Simard *et al.*, 1992). This method considers two words as cognates if their length is greater than or equal to 4 and at least their first 4 characters are common. Other methods exploit Dice's coefficient (Adam-

son and Boreham, 1974) or a variant of this coefficient (Brew and McKelvie, 1996). This measure computes the ratio between the number of common character bigrams of the two words and the total number of two word bigrams. Also, some methods use the Longest Common Subsequence Ratio (LCSR) (Melamed, 1999; Kraif, 1999). LCSR is computed as the ratio between the length of the longest common substring of ordered (and not necessarily contiguous) characters and the length of the longest word. Thus, two words are considered as cognates if LCSR value is greater than or equal to a given threshold. Similarly, other methods compute the distance between two words, which represents the minimum number of substitutions, insertions and deletions used to transform one word into another (Wagner and Fischer, 1974). These methods use exclusevly statistical techniques and they are language independent.
On the other hand, other methods use the phonetic distance between two words belonging to a bilingual pair (Oakes, 2000). Kondrak (2009) identifies three characteristics of cognates: recurrent sound correspondences, phonetic similarity and semantic affinity.
Thus, our method exploits orthographic and phonetic similarities between French - Romanian cognates. We combine n-grams methods with linguistic information (lemmas, POS tags) and several input data disambiguation strategies (computing cognates' frequencies, iterative extraction of the most reliable cognates and their deletion from the input data). Our method needs no external resources (bilingual dictionaries), so it could easily be extended to other Romance languages. We aim to obtain a high accuracy of our method to be integrated in a lexical alignment system. We evaluate our method and we compare it with pure statistical methods to study the influence of used linguistic information on the final results and on cognate alignment.
In the next section, we present the parallel corpora used for our experiments. In section 3, we present the lexical alignment method. We also describe our cognate identification module in section 4. We present the evaluation of our method and a comparison with other methods in section 5. Our conclusions and further work figure in section 6.

2 The Parallel Corpus

In our experiments, we use a legal parallel corpus (*DGT-TM*[1]) based on the *Acquis Communautaire* corpus. This multilingual corpus is available in 22 official languages of EU member states. It is composed of laws adopted by EU member states since 1950. *DGT-TM* contains 9,953,360 tokens in French and 9,142,291 tokens in Romanian.
We use a test corpus of 1,000 1:1 aligned complete sentences (starting with a capital letter and finishing with a punctuation sign). The length of each sentence has at most 80 words. This test corpus contains 33,036 tokens in French and 28,645 in Romanian.
We use the *TTL*[2] tagger available for Romanian (Ion, 2007) and for French (Todiraşcu *et al.*, 2011) (as Web service[3]). Thus, the parallel corpus is tokenized, lemmatized, tagged and annotated at chunk level.
The tagger uses the set of morpho-syntactic descriptors (MSD) proposed by the Multext Project[4] for French (Ide and Véronis, 1994) and for Romanian (Tufiş and Barbu, 1997). In the Figure 1, we present an example of TTL's output: *lemma* attribute represents the lemmas of lexical units, *ana* attribute provides morpho-syntactic information and *chunk* attribute marks nominal and prepositional phrases.

```
<seg lang="FR"><s id="ttlfr.3">
<w lemma="voir" ana="Vmps-s">vu</w>
<w lemma="le" ana="Da-fs"
chunk="Np#1">la</w>
<w lemma="proposition" ana="Ncfs"
chunk="Np#1">proposition</w>
<w lemma="de" ana="Spd"
chunk="Pp#1">de</w>
<w lemma="le" ana="Da-fs"
chunk="Pp#1,Np#2">la</w>
<w lemma="commission" ana="Ncfs"
chunk="Pp#1,Np#2">Commission
</w>
<c>;</c>
</s></seg>
```

Figure 1 TTL's output for French (in XCES format)

[1] http://langtech.jrc.it/DGT-TM.html
[2] Tokenizing, Tagging and Lemmatizing free running texts
[3] https://weblicht.sfs.uni-tuebingen.de/
[4] http://aune.lpl.univ-aix.FR/projects/multext/

3 Lexical Alignment Method

The cognate identification module is integrated in a French - Romanian lexical alignment system (see Figure 2).

In our lexical alignment method, we first use GIZA++ (Och and Ney, 2003) implementing IBM models (Brown *et al.*, 1993). These models build word-based alignments from aligned sentences. Indeed, each source word has zero, one or more translation equivalents in the target language. As these models do not provide many-to-many alignments, we also use some heuristics (Koehn *et al.*, 2003; Tufiş *et al.*, 2005) to detect phrase-based alignments such as chunks: nominal, adjectival, verbal, adverbial or prepositional phrases.

In our experiments, we use the lemmatized, tagged and annotated parallel corpus described in section 2. Thus, we use lemmas and morpho-syntactic properties to improve the lexical alignment. Lemmas are followed by the two first characters of morpho-syntactic tag. This operation morphologically disambiguates the lemmas (Tufiş *et al.*, 2005). For example, the same French lemma *change* (*=exchange, modify*) can be a common noun or a verb: *change_Nc* vs. *change_Vm*. This disambiguation procedure improves the GIZA++ system's performance.

We realize bidirectional alignments (FR - RO and RO - FR) with GIZA++, and we intersect them (Koehn *et al.*, 2003) to select common alignments.

To improve the word alignment results, we add an external list of cognates to the list of the translation equivalents extracted by GIZA++. This list of cognates is built from parallel corpora by our own method (described in the next section).

Also, to complete word alignments, we use a French - Romanian dictionary of verbo-nominal collocations (Todiraşcu *et al.*, 2008). They represent multiword expressions, composed of words related by lexico-syntactic relations (Todiraşcu *et al.*, 2008). The dictionary contains the most frequent verbo-nominal collocations extracted from legal corpora.

To augment the recall of the lexical alignment method, we apply a set of linguistically-motivated heuristic rules (Tufiş *et al.*, 2005):

a) we define some POS affinity classes (a noun might be translated by a noun, a verb or an adjective);
b) we align content-words such as nouns, adjectives, verbs, and adverbs, according to the POS affinity classes;
c) we align chunks containing translation equivalents aligned in a previous step;
d) we align elements belonging to chunks by linguistic heuristics. We develop a language dependent module applying 27 morpho-syntactic contextual heuristic rules (Navlea and Todiraşcu, 2010). These rules are defined according to morpho-syntactic differences between French and Romanian.

The architecture of the lexical alignment system is presented in the Figure 2.

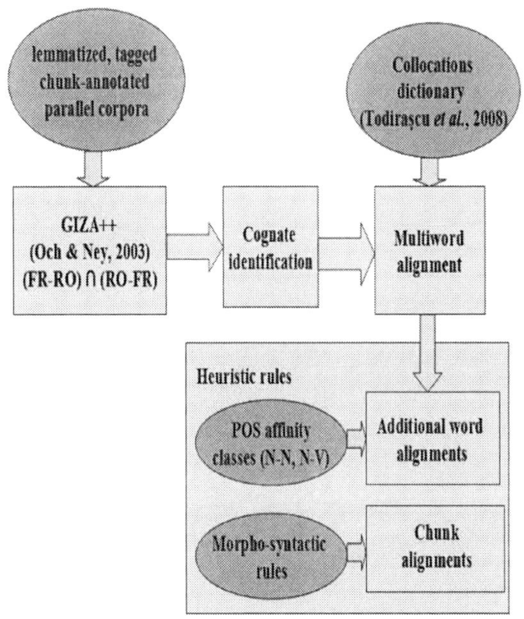

Figure 2 Lexical alignment system architecture

4 Cognate Identification Module

In our hybrid cognate identification method, we use the legal parallel corpus described in section 2. This corpus is tokenized, lemmatized, tagged, and sentence-aligned.

Thus, we consider as cognates bilingual word pairs respecting the linguistic conditions below:

1) their lemmas are translation equivalents in two parallel sentences;
2) they have identical lemmas or have orthographic or phonetic similarities between lemmas;
3) they are content-words (nouns, verbs, adverbs, etc.) having the same POS tag or belonging to the same POS affinity class. We filter out short words such as prepositions and conjunctions to limit noisy output. We also detect short cognates such as *il* 'he' vs. *el* (personal pronoun), *cas* 'case' vs. *caz* (nouns). We

avoid ambiguous pairs such as *lui* 'him' (personal pronoun) (FR) vs. *lui* 's' (possessive determiner) (RO), *ce* 'this' (demonstrative determiner) (FR) vs. *ce* 'that' (relative pronoun) (RO).

To detect orthographic and phonetic similarities between cognates, we look at the beginning of the words and we ignore their endings.

We classify the French - Romanian cognates detected in the studied parallel corpus (at the orthographic or phonetic level), in several categories:

1) cross-lingual invariants (numbers, certain acronyms and abbreviations, punctuation signs);
2) identical cognates (*document* 'document' vs. *document*);
3) similar cognates:
    a) 4-grams (Simard *et al.*, 1992); The first 4 characters of lemmas are identical. The length of these lemmas is greater than or equal to 4 (***auto**rité* vs. ***auto**ritate* 'authority').
    b) 3-grams; The first 3 characters of lemmas are identical and the length of the lemmas is greater than or equal to 3 (***acte*** vs. ***act*** 'paper').
    c) 8-bigrams; Lemmas have a common sequence of characters among the first 8 bigrams. At least one character of each bigram is common to both words. This condition allows the jump of a non identical character (***souscrire*** vs. ***subscrie*** 'submit'). This method applies only to long lemmas (length greater than 7).
    d) 4-bigrams; Lemmas have a common sequence of characters among the 4 first bigrams. This method applies for long lemmas (length greater than 7) (***homolo**gué* vs. ***omolog**at* 'homologated') but also for short lemmas (length less than or equal to 7) (***groupe*** vs. ***grup*** 'group').

We iteratively extract cognates by identified categories. In addition, we use a set of orthographic adjustments and some input data disambiguation strategies. We compute frequency for ambiguous candidates (the same source lemma occurs with several target candidates) and we keep the most frequent candidate. At each iteration, we delete reliable considered cognates from the input data. We start by applying a set of empirically established orthographic adjustments between French - Romanian lemmas, such as: diacritic removal, phonetic mappings detection, etc. (see Table 1).

Levels of orthographic adjustments	**French**	**Romanian**	**Examples FR - RO**
diacritics	x	x	d**é**p**ô**t - d**e**p**o**zit
double contiguous letters	x	x	ra**pp**ort - ra**p**ort
consonant groups	ph	f [f]	**ph**ase - **f**ază
	th	t [t]	mé**th**ode - me**t**odă
	dh	d [d]	a**dh**érent - a**d**erent
	cch	c [k]	ba**cch**ante - ba**c**antă
	ck	c [k]	sto**ck**age - sto**c**are
	cq	c [k]	gre**cq**ue - gre**c**
	ch	ş [ʃ]	fi**ch**e - fi**ş**ă
	ch	c [k]	**ch**apitre - **c**apitol
q	q (final)	c [k]	cin**q** - cin**c**i
	qu(+i) (medial)	c [k]	é**q**uilibre - e**c**hilibru
	qu(+e) (medial)	c [k]	mar**q**uer - mar**c**a
	qu(+a)	c(+a) [k]	**q**ualité - **c**alitate
	que (final)	c [k]	prati**q**ue - practi**c**ă
intervocalic s	v + s + v	v + z + v	pré**s**ent - pre**z**ent
w	w	v	**w**agon - **v**agon
y	y	i	**y**aourt - **i**aurt

Table 1 French - Romanian cognate orthographic adjustments

While French uses an etymological writing and Romanian generally has a phonetic writing, we identify phonetic correspondences between lemmas. Then, we make some orthographic adjustments from French to Romanian. For example, cognates *stockage* 'stock' (FR) vs. *stocare* (RO) become *stocage* (FR) vs. *stocare* (RO). In this example, the French consonant group *ck* [k] become *c* [k] (as in Romanian). We also make adjustments in the ambiguous cases, by replacing with both variants (*ch* ([ʃ] or [k])): ***fiche*** vs. *fişă* 'sheet'; ***chapitre*** vs. *capitol* 'chapter'.

We aim to improve the precision of our method. Thus, we iteratively extract cognates by identified categories from the surest ones to less sure candidates (see Table 2).

To decrease the noise of the cognate identification method, we apply two supplementary strategies. We filter out ambiguous cognate candidates (*autorité - autoritate|autorizare*), by computing their frequencies in the corpus. In this case, we keep the most frequent candidate pair. This strategy is very effective to augment the precision of the results, but it might decrease the recall in certain cases. Indeed, there are cases where French - Romanian cognates have one form in French, but two various forms in Romanian (*spécification* 'specification' vs. *specificare* or *specificaţie*). We recover these pairs by using regular expressions based on specific lemma endings (*ion* (fr) vs. *re|ţie* (ro)).

Then, we delete the reliable cognate pairs (high precision) from the input data at the end of the extraction step. This step helps us to disambiguate the input data. For example, the identical cognates *transport* vs. *transport* 'transportation', obtained in a previous extraction step and deleted from the input data, eliminate the occurrence of candidate *transport* vs. *tranzit* as 4-grams cognate, in a next extraction step.

We apply the same method for cognates having POS affinity (N-V; N-ADJ). We keep only 4-grams cognates, due to the significant decrease of the precision for the other categories 3 (b, c, d).

Extraction steps by category of cognates	Content-words / Same POS	Frequency	Deletion from the input data	Precision (%)
1 : cross lingual invariants			x	100
2 : identical cognates	x		x	100
3 : 4-grams (lemmas' length >= 4) ;	x	x	x	99.05
4 : 3-grams (lemmas' length >=3) ;	x	x	x	93.13
5 : 8-bigrams (long lemmas, lemmas' length >7)	x		x	95.24
6 : 4-bigrams (long lemmas, lemmas' length > 7)	x			75
7 : 4-bigrams (short lemmas, lemmas' length =< 7)	x	x		65.63

Table 2 Precision of cognate extraction steps

5 Evaluation and Methods' Comparison

We evaluated our cognate identification module against a list of cognates initially built from the test corpus, containing 2,034 pairs of cognates.

In addition, we also compared the results of our method with the results provided by pure statistical methods (see Table 3). These methods are the following:

a) thresholding the Longest Common Subsequence Ratio (LCSR) for two words of a bilingual pair; This measure computes the ratio between the longest common subsequence of characters of two words and the length of the longest word. We empirically establish the threshold of 0.68.

$$LCSR\,(w1,w2) = \frac{length\,(common\_substring\,(w1,w2))}{\max(\,length\,(w1), length\,(w2))}$$

b) thresholding DICE's coefficient ; We empirically establish the threshold of 0.62.

$$DICE\,(w1,w2) = \frac{2 * number\_common\_bigrams}{total\_number\_bigrams\,(w1,w2)}$$

c) 4-grams ; Two words are considered as cognates if they have at least 4 characters and their first 4 characters are identical.

We implemented these methods using orthographically adjusted parallel corpus (see Table 1). Moreover, we evaluate 4-grams method on the initial parallel corpus and on the orthographically adjusted parallel corpus to study the impact of orthographic adjustments step on the quality of the results.
These methods generally apply for words having at least 4 letters in order to decrease the noise of the results. Cognates are searched in aligned parallel sentences. Word characters are almost parallel (***rembourser*** vs. ***rambursare*** 'refund').

Methods	P (%)	R (%)	F (%)
LCSR	44.13	58.95	50.47
DICE	56.47	60.91	58.61
4-grams	91.55	72.42	80.87
Our method	**94.78**	**89.18**	**91.89**

Table 3 Evaluation and methods' comparison; P=Precision; R=Recall; F=F-measure

Our method extracted 1,814 correct cognates from 1,914 provided candidates. The method obtains the best scores (precision=94.78% ; recall=89.18% ; f-measure=91.89%), in comparison with the other implemented methods. The 4-grams method obtains a high precision (90.85%), but a low recall (47.84%). Orthographic adjustments step improves significantly the recall of 4-grams method with 24.58% (see Table 4). This result is due to the specific properties of the law parallel corpus. Indeed, many Romanian terms were borrowed from French and these terms present high orthographic similarities.

Methods	P (%)	R (%)	F (%)
4-grams - Adjustments	90.85	**47.84**	62.68
4-grams + Adjustments	91.55	**72.42**	80.87

Table 4 Evaluation of the 4-grams method before and after orthographic adjustments step

However, our method extracts some ambiguous candidates such as *numéro 'number'* - *nume 'name'*, *compléter* 'complete' - *compune* 'compose'. Some of these errors were avoided by keeping the most frequent candidate in the studied corpus. So, the remaining errors mainly concern hapax candidates.
Also, some cognates were not extracted: *heure - oră* 'hour', *semaine - săptămână* 'week', *lieu - loc* 'place'. These errors concern cognates sharing very few orthographic similarities.

The lowest scores are obtained by the LCSR method (f-measure=50.47%), followed by the DICE's coefficient (f-measure=58.61%). These general methods provide a high noise due to the important orthographic similarities between the words having different meanings. Their results might be improved by combining statistical techniques with linguistic information such as POS affinity or by combining several association scores.

As we mentioned, the output of the cognate identification module is exploited by a French - Romanian lexical alignment system (based on GIZA++) described in section 3. We compared the set of cognates provided by GIZA++ with our results to study their impact on cognate alignment. GIZA++ extracted 1,532 cognates representing a recall of 75.32% (see Table 5). Our cognate identification module significantly improved the recall with 13.86%.

Systems	Number of extracted cognates	Number of total cognates	Recall (%)
GIZA++	1,532	2,034	75.32
Our method	1,814		89.18

Table 5 Improvement of our method's recall

6 Conclusions and Further Work

We present a French - Romanian cognate identification module required by a lexical alignment system. Our method combines statistical techniques and linguistic filters to extract cognates from lemmatized, tagged and sentence-aligned parallel corpus. The use of the linguistic information and the orthographic adjustments significantly improves the results compared with pure statistical methods. However, these results are dependent of the studied languages, of the corpus domain and of the data volume. We need more experiments using other corpora from other domains to be able to generalize. Our system should be improved to detect false friends by using external resources.

Cognate identification module will be integrated in a French - Romanian lexical alignment system. This system is part of a larger project aiming to develop a factored phrase-based statistical machine translation system for French and Romanian.

References

George W. Adamson and Jillian Boreham. 1974. The use of an association measure based on character structure to identify semantically related pairs of words and document titles, *Information Storage and Retrieval*, 10(7-8):253-260.

Chris Brew and David McKelvie. 1996. Word-pair ex-traction for lexicography, in *Proceedings of International Conference on New Methods in Natural Language Processing*, Bilkent, Turkey, 45-55.

Peter F. Brown, Vincent J. Della Pietra, Stephen A. Della Pietra, and Robert L. Mercer. 1993. The mathematics of statistical machine translation: Parameter estimation, *Computational Linguistics*, 19(2):263-312.

Nancy Ide and Jean Véronis. 1994. Multext (multilingual tools and corpora), in *Proceedings of the 15th International Conference on Computational Linguistics, CoLing 1994*, Kyoto, pp. 90-96.

Diana Inkpen, Oana Frunză, and Grzegorz Kondrak. 2005. Automatic Identification of Cognates and False Friends in French and English, RANLP-2005, Bulgaria, Sept. 2005, p. 251-257.

Radu Ion. 2007. *Metode de dezambiguizare semantică automată. Aplicaţii pentru limbile engleză şi română, Ph.D. Thesis*, Romanian Academy, Bucharest, May 2007, 148 pp.

Philipp Koehn, Franz J. Och, and Daniel Marcu. 2003. Statistical Phrase-Based Translation, in *Proceedings of Human Language Technology Conference of the North American Chapter of the Association of Computational Linguistics, HLT-NAACL 2003*, Edmonton, May-June 2003, pp. 48-54.

Grzegorz Kondrak. 2009. Identification of Cognates and Recurrent Sound Correspondences in Word Lists, in *Traitement Automatique des Langues (TAL)*, 50(2) :201-235.

Olivier Kraif. 1999. Identification des cognats et alignement bi-textuel : une étude empirique, dans *Actes de la 6ème conférence annuelle sur le Traitement Automatique des Langues Naturelles, TALN 99*, Cargèse, 12-17 juillet 1999, 205-214.

Dan I. Melamed. 1999. Bitext Maps and Alignment via Pattern Recognition, in *Computational Linguistics*, 25(1):107-130.

Mirabela Navlea and Amalia Todiraşcu. 2010. Linguistic Resources for Factored Phrase-Based Statistical Machine Translation Systems, in *Proceedings of the Workshop on Exploitation of Multilingual Resources and Tools for Central and (South) Eastern European Languages, 7th International Conference on Language Resources and Evaluation*, Malta, Valletta, May 2010, pp. 41-48.

Michael P. Oakes. 2000. Computer Estimation of Vocabulary in Protolanguage from Word Lists in Four Daughter Languages, in *Journal of Quantitative Linguistics*, 7(3):233-243.

Franz J. Och and Hermann Ney. 2003. A Systematic Comparison of Various Statistical Alignment Models, in *Computational Linguistics*, 29(1):19-51.

Michel Simard, George Foster, and Pierre Isabelle. 1992. Using cognates to align sentences, in *Proceedings of the Fourth International Conference on Theoretical and Methodological Issues in Machine Translation*, Montréal, pp. 67-81.

Amalia Todiraşcu, Ulrich Heid, Dan Ştefănescu, Dan Tufiş, Christopher Gledhill, Marion Weller, and François Rousselot. 2008. Vers un dictionnaire de collocations multilingue, in *Cahiers de Linguistique*, 33(1) :161-186, Louvain, août 2008.

Amalia Todiraşcu, Radu Ion, Mirabela Navlea, and Laurence Longo. 2011. French text preprocessing with TTL, in *Proceedings of the Romanian Academy, Series A,* Volume 12, Number 2/2011, pp. 151-158, Bucharest, Romania, June 2011, Romanian Academy Publishing House. ISSN 1454-9069.

Dan Tufiş and Ana Maria Barbu. 1997. A Reversible and Reusable Morpho-Lexical Description of Romanian, in Dan Tufiş and Poul Andersen (eds.), *Recent Advances in Romanian Language Technology*, pp. 83-93, Editura Academiei Române, Bucureşti, 1997. ISBN 973-27-0626-0.

Dan Tufiş, Radu Ion, Alexandru Ceauşu, and Dan Ştefănescu. 2005. Combined Aligners, in *Proceedings of the Workshop on Building and Using Parallel Texts: Data-Driven Machine Translation and Beyond*, pp. 107-110, Ann Arbor, USA, Association for Computational Linguistics. ISBN 978-973-703-208-9.

Cristina Vertan and Monica Gavrilă. 2010. Multilingual applications for rich morphology language pairs, a case study on German Romanian, in Dan Tufiş and Corina Forăscu (eds.): *Multilinguality and Interoperability in Language Processing with Emphasis on Romanian*, Romanian Academy Publishing House, Bucharest, pp. 448-460, ISBN 978-973-27-1972-5.

Robert A. Wagner and Michael J. Fischer. 1974. The String-to-String Correction Problem, *Journal of the ACM*, 21(1):168-173.

*** Formatting Issue - Best Available Paper/Graphic ***

Highly Multilingual Coreference Resolution Exploiting a Mature Entity Repository

Josef Steinberger, Jenya Belyaeva, Jonathan Crawley, Leonida Della-Rocca, Mohamed Ebrahim, Maud Ehrmann, Mijail Kabadjov, Ralf Steinberger and **Erik van der Goot**
EC Joint Research Centre
21027, Ispra (VA), Italy
name.surname@jrc.ec.europa.eu

Abstract

In this paper we present an approach to large-scale coreference resolution for an ample set of human languages, with a particular emphasis on time performance and precision. One of the distinctive features of our approach is the use of a mature multilingual named entity repository (persons and organizations) gradually compiled over the past few years. Our experiments show promising results – an overall precision of 94% tested on seven different languages. We also present an extrinsic evaluation on seven languages in the context of summarization where we gauge the contribution of the coreference resolver towards the end summarization performance.

1 Introduction

Recent work on coreference resolution has been largely dominated by machine learning approaches and predominantly for the English language (Ng and Cardie, 2002; Ponzetto and Strube, 2006; Luo, 2007). This is in great part due to the availability of annotated corpora such as MUC-6/7 (Hirschman, 1998), ACE-2/3/4/5 (NIST, 2004), GNOME (Poesio et al., 2004) and large-scale crowdsourcing efforts like Phrase Detectives.[1]

One of the big advantages of machine learning approaches is that they are reasonably easy to reproduce given that the set of input features are documented well, since there are many good open-source platforms for machine learning (e.g., WEKA[2]) and machine-learning-based coreference (e.g., BART[3] (Versley et al., 2008)).

However, intrinsic evaluations can pose problems. As pointed out by (Stoyanov et al., 2009) there is too much variation in reported results across data sets to be able to draw robust conclusions on the state-of-the-art in the area for which they proposed a method for reporting results on a data set that makes it easier to predict performance on other data sets (by breaking down results into names, types of pronouns, nominals etc.). Also, intrinsic evaluations can be highly sensitive to preprocessing (Mitkov, 2002).

There is agreement in the community on the level of resolution difficulty on major types of coreferential expressions. For instance, proper names are considered to be the easiest to resolve, followed by pronouns, in turn followed by common nouns. One of the main reasons why common noun coreference is challenging is because they often share little or no surface linguistic features with their antecedents and require world or encyclopedic knowledge for their resolution (see (Kabadjov, 2007) for a study for English). For instance, Ponzetto and Strube (2006) proposed to use WordNet and Wikipedia to address the problem of bringing in world and/or encyclopedic knowledge into their system for coreference resolution in English reporting improvements for common noun resolution.

In this work we address two important remaining gaps in coreference resolution. Firstly, we are interested in highly multilingual coreference. Secondly, we address the problem of common noun coreference by exploiting a large lexical resource, the named entity database, compiled over the past few years by automatically extracting names from hundreds of thousands of online news articles in twenty languages (and subsequently cleaning the most frequent names by a human moderator). The coreference resolver we present is designed to work as part of the Europe Media Monitor (EMM) system[4] for online news analysis and aggregation.

[1] http://www.phrasedetectives.org.
[2] http://www.cs.waikato.ac.nz/ml/weka/.
[3] http://www.bart-coref.org/.
[4] http://emm.newsbrief.eu/overview.html

In order to evaluate the effectiveness of our approach we carry out two separate evaluations: one intrinsic and one extrinsic in the context of summarization.

The rest of the paper is organized as follows: in the next section (2) we describe our named entity database which is the backbone of our approach; in 3, we present our approach to coreference followed by a discussion of experimental results in 4. Then, in 5 we briefly survey related work on coreference resolution and finally conclude and give pointers to future work.

2 The Multilingual Named Entity Database

The historical repository of EMM's person and organization titles is a by-product of the Named Entity Recognition (NER) process, which has been applied daily to tens of thousands of multilingual news articles per day since 2004. Titles are parts of the name recognition patterns, and each time a name is found, EMM keeps track of the titles found next to the name. The result is a large multilingual repository of titles and other attributes about names. In this section, we thus try to give an overview of the NER process and hence information about the title repository.

EMM's NER is performed by applying language-independent recognition patterns to text. The hand-written language-independent recognition patterns use slots to make reference to various language-specific lists of words, phrases and regular expressions. By doing this, the system is modular and a new language can simply be plugged in by adding the language-specific parameter file, containing the relevant word lists for each slot. Pouliquen and R. Steinberger (2009) describe the types of slots and list a number of patterns. A typical and simple pattern is the one that requires that uppercase words adjacent to any title are likely to be person or organization names (e.g., *President* `Upper Upper`). As the strings indicating that neighboring uppercase words in a name are not necessarily titles, we refer to them more generally as Trigger Words. The trigger word list of elements thus contains conventional titles (e.g., *Dr.*, *Mr.*, *President*), professions and occupations (e.g., *spokeswoman*, *artist*, *playboy*, *tennis player*), roles inside teams (*secretary*, *defense player*, *short-stop*), adjectives referring to countries, regions, locations, ethnic groups or religions (e.g., *Iraqi*, *Latin-American*, *Parisian*, *Berber*, *Catholic*), and a variety of other strings that may indicate that the adjacent uppercase words are a person (e.g., *XX-year-old*, *has declared*, *deceased*). These lists are mostly produced using empirical methods or machine learning, but they are always manually verified. The rules are partially cascaded and allow for large combinations of trigger words, e.g., to recognize the uppercase words in the following apposition construction as a name: `Upper Upper`, *former 56-year-old Afghan Foreign Minister*.

As the patterns exist and are applied to twenty languages, the list of trigger words contains words in all these languages. Some of these trigger words are not suitable so we remove them from the lists. Age expressions such as *XX-year-old* or verbal phrases such as *has declared* were thus manually removed.

Patterns to recognize organizations have different shapes and the trigger words are usually part of the organization name (e.g., *Bank* and *Club* in *Chartered Bank* or *Motor Sport Club*). These typical organization name parts are also used for the co-reference resolution task.

3 Coreference Algorithm

3.1 System Architecture

The coreference resolution module is built for inclusion in a larger pipeline architecture, where an input text document undergoes several processing phases during which the source is augmented with layers of meta data such as named entities. The data interchange format between processing phases is RSS, a light-weight type of XML typically used by on-line news providers.

3.2 Lookup of Known Named Entities

Known entities are entities that have been found in at least five different news clusters in the past in the EMM system. For all known entities morphological or other spelling variants are automatically generated according to hand-written rules. For example, for *Angela Merkel*, the genitive version *Merkels* will be pre-generated and recognized, and Arabic names using the infix *al* will be pre-generated with and without *al*, as well as with and without linking hyphens (*Moussab al-Zarqawi*, *Moussab al Zarqawi*, *Moussab Zarqawi*). For the actual lookup, a finite state tool that allows patterns and partial case sensitivity is used, employing entity information that has been gathered over a number of years from the EMM production system to recognize known entities within the text (currently, there are over 1.2 million distinct entities in the named entity repository). The RSS is then marked up with additional meta information about the entities found (see (Crawley and Wagner, 2010) for more details).

3.3 Entity Guessing

As we are interested in grounding name references to real-life entities and we thus need to disambiguate between people having the same surname (or first name), we only look for entities consisting of at least two name parts.

The entity guessing comprises two parts, the first is a parallel lexical tokenization of the text, using classifying tokenizers, gazetteers, pattern matchers and simple tokenizers as well as any previously defined entities from further up the processing chain. The second part is a sequence of finite state grammars that pick and choose appropriate tokens for a given rule from the parallel token streams passing the output on to the next grammar in the sequence building ever more complex constructs and disambiguating on the way.

3.4 Merging of NE Variants

The entity normalization takes place once the entities have been discovered and is used as a means of merging entities with newly found aliases, such as when an existing entity is written in a script we have not seen it in before or has been slightly misspelt. This is done by transliterating the name from any unicode range into the Latin unicode range using a statistical matrix for ngram substitutions. Some normalization may be performed and vowels are removed to create a consonant signature which is then used to perform a lookup for the most likely candidates with the list of known entities. This is to reduce the number of values for eventual comparison using a string similarity metric. The closest match is then selected and, if within a fine-grained tolerance, the value is assigned as a new alias. Otherwise it is assumed a new entity and assigned a new id.

3.5 Coreference Resolver

When an RSS file reaches the coreference resolution module, it already contains the list of known and guessed entities. The resolution is run only over the known entities. The resolver module does the following for each article:

1. Loads all known and guessed entities
2. For each known entity it searches the resources for its possible references (titles from the entity-title table, name parts directly from the entity mention).
3. The reference-entity map is created; it associates each possible reference (step 2) to a known entity.[5]
4. The matcher component finds all possible mentions of any entity (i.e., name parts[6], titles) in the text.[7]
5. The resolver links mentions (step 4) to entities using the reference-entity map, given that the following conditions are met:
   (a) The entity has been already introduced.[8]
   (b) The entity reference is not a constituent of a known or guessed entity mention (or their title).
6. The resolved mentions are merged in order to create a non-overlapping sequence of entity mentions with the following rules:
   (a) If the mention is part of a longer mention leave only the longer one (e.g., 'former US president' would outweigh 'president').
   (b) If the mentions are next to each other and they are assigned to the same entity they are concatenated.
   (c) If the mentions are next to each other and they are assigned to a different entity a name part will outweigh a title (probably an incorrect title).
   (d) Otherwise consider only the latter mention.

4 Evaluation

We carry out a precision-focused intrinsic evaluation over EMM data and an extrinsic evaluation in the context of summarization where we measure the contribution of coreference towards summarization performance. We describe each in turn below.

4.1 Intrinsic Evaluation: EMM Data

In order to evaluate our coreference system we compiled a corpus of news articles in seven different languages: English, German, Italian, Spanish, French, Russian and Arabic, thus, covering a

[5] Ambiguous references are ignored (e.g., title 'president' is not considered as a coreference candidate in the case of an article in which two entities carry the title 'president').

[6] We are also aware of names with infixes like 'de la Vega'.

[7] Because of efficiency reasons it uses lists of all possible name parts and titles, not only those found in the article – the resources are loaded during the matcher's initialization.

[8] The candidate mention appears after the first mention of the entity identified by the name recognition module.

Table 1: Corpus statistics.

Language	News articles	Words	Words per art.
English	149	56891	382
German	45	18213	405
Italian	117	14082	120
Spanish	94	18772	200
French	96	35046	365
Russian	149	24435	164
Arabic	67	24400	364
Overall	717	191839	268

diverse set of language family branches as are Germanic, Romance, Slavic and Semitic.[9]

Statistics about the corpus are shown in table 1. Overall, we gathered 717 news articles containing almost 200k words.

4.1.1 Corpus and Quick Annotation

We ran each news article through the EMM pipeline. After that we asked native speakers of the seven languages to go over the news articles and mark whether each highlighted mention points to the correct entity or not, whereby measuring precision.[10] A highlighted mention could be one of three things: a known named entity recognized by the named entity disambiguation system, a mention of an entity guessed by the named entity guesser, or a mention recognized and attached to a coreference chain by the coreference resolver. The human subjects marked each entity mention via a simple HTML interface.

4.1.2 Results and Discussion

We present separate performance results for named entity disambiguation (table 2) and for coreference resolution (table 3). In both cases we report precision.

Overall, the named entity disambiguation precision was high; 95% of the 2631 named entities recognized by the system were correct (see table 2). The recognition precision of person names in Arabic was the lowest, 81.7%. We discuss the possible reasons for that in our detailed error analysis below. The type of entities entailed by the category 'Others' is mostly mentions to organizations, but also some other prominent named entities such

[9]In principle, since the coreference method we propose builds on the named entity repository (2), it can be straightforwardly applied to all the languages covered by the repository (currently 20).

[10]As pointed out earlier, we are interested in precision and not in recall, since the large volume of news articles passing through the EMM pipeline makes up for potential loss in recall.

Table 2: Quality of named entity recognition in the analyzed languages. Values correspond to: Precision (Correct/Recognized).

Language	Persons	Others	All
English	97.0% (419/432)	89.5% (256/286)	94.0% (675/718)
German	97.5% (230/236)	100.0% (46/46)	97.9% (276/282)
Italian	92.1% (151/164)	100.0% (76/76)	94.6% (227/240)
Spanish	95.7% (180/188)	96.0% (72/75)	95.8% (252/263)
French	98.4% (432/439)	97.2% (278/286)	97.9% (710/725)
Russian	97.7% (130/133)	100.0% (35/35)	98.2% (165/168)
Arabic	81.7% (125/153)	100.0% (82/82)	88.1% (207/235)
Overall	95.5% (1667/1745)	95.4% (845/886)	95.5% (2512/2631)

Table 3: Quality of coreference resolution. Values correspond to: Precision (Correct/Recognized).

Language	Person name parts	Person titles	Organiz. head nouns	All
English	99.2% 237/239	72.7% 40/55	94.4% 34/36	94.2% 311/330
German	99.0% 104/105	86.7% 13/15	100.0% 1/1	97.5% 118/121
Italian	94.1% 16/17	75.0% 9/12	100.0% 1/1	86.8% 26/30
Spanish	100.0% 41/41	72.7% 16/22	100.0% 4/4	91.0% 61/67
French	98.1% 51/52	61.2% 52/85	13.3% 2/15	69.1% 105/152
Russian	100.0% 45/45	100.0% 7/7	– 0/0	100.0% 52/52
Arabic	92.9% 92/99	100.0% 2/2	40.0% 2/5	90.6% 96/106
Overall	98.0% 586/598	70.2% 139/198	71.0% 44/62	89.6% 769/858

as events (e.g., Woodstock Festival).

We present the coreference performance in three distinct categories: *person name parts*, *person titles* and *organization head nouns* (see table 3).

Not surprisingly, the overall coreference resolution of proper names yields high precision (98%), since resolution difficulty increases as folows: proper names pronouns common noun phrases, in particular definite descriptions. Perhaps more notably, these results provide evidence that this is also the case across languages, with Arabic being lowest with 92.9%.

What is more significant, however, is the performance on *person titles*, which entail mostly refer-

Table 4: Types of errors.

Type of error	Person name parts	Person titles	Organiz. head nouns	All
Indefinite NP		18	13	32
Res. sparseness		11	3	14
Different POS		18	1	20
Error propag.	9			9
Other	3	12	1	16
Overall	12	59	18	89

ences by means of definite descriptions not sharing a head noun with the antecedent, where the system surpasses the 70% threshold (with the exception of French with 61.2%). It is worth pointing out that these are largely regarded as among the most challenging to resolve, mainly because their resolution requires real-world knowledge.

It should be noted also that our system is an end-to-end system, whose input is free text akin to (Mitkov, 2002; Kabadjov, 2007).

In what follows we discuss several representative examples.

Arabic. In the following example the system recognizes بَابَا (*Pope*) as the correct reference to the preceding recognized person بنديكتوس السَادس عشر (*Benedikt XVI*), because our resources capture that *Pope* is one of the titles of *Benedikt XVI* (بنديكتوس السَادس عشر, 'Benedikt XVI' بَابَا, 'Pope'):

(1) يعتزم بَابَا الفَاتيكَان **بنديكتوس السَادس عشر** القيَام بزيَاره الَى كنيس يهودي في العَاصمة الَايطالية رومَا في ثَاني زيَارة من نوعهَا في تَاريخ الكنيسة الكَاثولكية. وتَاتي زيَارة **البَابَا** في وقت .... الحرب العَالمية الثَانية.

English. And here is a similar example in English:

(2) Bruce, who has until 31 December to respond to the FA's request, had asked [Andre Mariner] to look at Turner's red card again... "I hope [the referee] looks at it again. I doubt it, though."

Russian. And finally an example in Russian (, 'Mahmoud Ahmadinejad' , 'leader'):

(3)

4.1.3 Detailed Error Analysis

In this section we discuss the most prominent types of errors and give illustrative examples for Arabic and French.[11] We adopt a precision-focused error analysis.

Precision-focused analysis of errors. We have grouped system errors into five major categories (see table 4): *indefinite noun phrases* (the system wrongly links an indefinite noun phrase to an antecedent), *resource sparseness* (errors due to incomplete database of names and/or titles), *different part-of-speech* (the system assumes a wrong part-of-speech, e.g., *official* as adjective or noun), *error propagation* (errors at the named entity lookup stage propagate on to the coreference resolution) and a general category *Other* for all the remaining errors. To illustrate these error types, we give a few representative examples next.

Arabic. While working on Arabic articles we were faced with some difficulties related to issues of ambiguity, propagation of errors from the NER module and a relative lack of resources compared to other languages. Ambiguity of Arabic person and organization names is mainly due to the relatively high polysemy of Arabic words, the widespread omission of diacritic vowels in written text and the lack of capitalization in the Arabic writing system. For example, some of the very common person names in Arabic like رمضَان *Ramdan* , شعبَان *Shaban* and رجب *Ragab* also stand for month names, so if we have an Entity called محمد رمضَان *Mohamed Ramdan* and at a later distance in text the word رمضَان *Ramdan*, it is difficult to decide if this is a reference to the previous entity or if it is the name of a month. Moreover, the lack of diacritic vowels increases the number for possible readings for a given word, if we have for example the name سَيد عمر *Sayad Amr* and the name part عمر *Amr* in a non vocalized text, the word عمر *Amr* could have four different meanings,

[11] We left out examples for other languages due to space contraints.

whereas if we had the word in the vocalized form عُمَر *Umar*, the only possible meaning would be that of a proper name. A different kind of ambiguity results from the fact that in most Arabic countries there is no real distinction between first and last names. So, the reference to a person's full name could be done by any of the parts of the name, that is, usually in news articles references to "Saddam Hussein" would use the first part of his name, whereas references to "Muhammad Husni Mubarak" would use the third part of the name.

French. There were several errors due to incorrect recognition of named entity boundaries (i.e., error propagation). For instance, in the following example (example 4), the reference to *Ligue 2* has been wrongly recognized as *Ligue* and subsequently identified as coreferential with *Ligue 1*:

(4) Neuf des dix matches de cette 20e journée de [Ligue 1] sont programmés ce soir à 21h, avec notamment un intéressant Lille-PSG. En bas de tableau, le match de la peur oppose Grenoble, quasiment assuré de descendre en *[Ligue]* 2, à Saint-Etienne, 18e et premier relégable.

4.2 Extrinsic Evaluation via Summarization: Project-Syndicate Data

Kabadjov (2007) argued that Summarization is a suitable task for evaluating extrinsically coreference resolution systems. Here, we take on their proposal and in this section we discuss experiments with an LSA-based summarizer integrated with the coreference resolver described above on a publicly available corpus[12] for evaluating multi-document multilingual[13] summarization systems (Turchi et al., 2010).[14]

Our approach for integrating a coreference resolver into an LSA-based summarization system draws on the method put forward by (Steinberger et al., 2007). The intuition behind this choice is that in addition to capturing pure lexical co-occurrence the extended system is also capable of capturing entity co-occurrence which takes the summarization process to a more semantically-aware level.

4.2.1 Experimental Results

The experimental results are presented in table 5. Each summary score is computed by first calculating the intersection of sentences selected by the summarizer with those selected by at least two annotators divided by the number of sentences in the system summary.[15]

The first thing we observe is that overall (see bottom part of table 5) for target summaries of size three sentences or smaller incorporating cross-document coreference works better than the baseline LSA case and both perform better than two baseline summarizers: one selecting the first sentence of each document in the cluster (labeled 'Lead' in table 5) and another one selecting random sentences (labeled 'Random'). One possible reason for that is that by adopting a more semantically-aware representation the summarization machinery is able to produce succinct summaries of better quality than the LSA-only method, but as soon as the summarization compression rate is relaxed the benefit of including entities becomes less visible (and even in some cases yields worse results).

The variation in summarization performance across languages can be in part explained by the inconsistent performance of the coreference resolver due to lack of or noisy resources for the languages. For instance, for languages like English and German we have good coreference resolution performance which also translates into decent summarization performance, whereas for Czech the performance is notably lower.

5 Related work

Representatives of machine learning work on coreference are (Ng and Cardie, 2002; Luo, 2007) for supervised learning and (Haghighi and Klein, 2007) for unsupervised.

In more recent work, (Stoyanov et al., 2009) provides a comprehensive discussion of the state of the art coupled with extensive experiments on the standard corpora for English: MUC-6, MUC-7, ACE-2, ACE-3, ACE-4 and ACE-5. Recasens and Hovy (2010) explore the impact on coreference resolution performance by varying several prominent contextual factors; they measure performance across corpora, languages, annotation schemes and preprocessing. However, their set of languages consisted of English and Spanish only.

The most closely related experiment to ours is that of the SemEval-2010 task 1 (Recasens et al., 2010), which covered coreference evaluation on six languages.

[12]This is different from the dataset used for the intrinsic evaluation.

[13]Seven languages: English, French, German, Spanish, Russian, Arabic and Czech.

[14]Data publicly available for download at: `http://langtech.jrc.ec.europa.eu/JRC_Resources.html`.

[15]For a discussion on how this evaluation metric compares with ROUGE see (Turchi et al., 2010).

Table 5: Summarization Results.

Summarizers	Summary Size (number of sentences)					
	1	3	5	10	15	20
	English					
LSA+Coref	1.0	.67	.6	.6	.5	.43
LSA	0	.67	.6	.6	.47	.45
	French					
LSA+Coref	.5	.67	.6	.55	.47	.43
LSA	0	.5	.6	.45	.47	.4
	German					
LSA+Coref	1.0	.83	.7	.55	.47	.35
LSA	.5	.5	.7	.55	.43	.38
	Spanish					
LSA+Coref	1.0	.83	.7	.45	.37	.4
LSA	.5	.67	.5	.5	.37	.43
	Russian					
LSA+Coref	1.0	.67	.6	.65	.53	.6
LSA	1.0	.67	.6	.5	.57	.6
	Arabic					
LSA+Coref	0	.5	.7	.55	.47	.5
LSA	.5	.67	.5	.6	.53	.53
	Czech					
LSA+Coref	0	.67	.6	.5	.43	.48
LSA	.5	.67	.7	.7	.53	.48
	Overall					
LSA+Coref	.64	.69	.64	.55	.46	.45
LSA	.43	.62	.6	.56	.48	.46
Lead	-	-	.3	.25	.26	.25
Random	.22	.22	.22	.22	.22	.22

6 Conclusion

In this paper we presented an approach to large-scale coreference resolution for a broad spectrum of human languages with precision and efficiency in mind. The backbone of our algorithm is a mature multilingual named entity database semi-automatically compiled over the past few years.

We reported an overall precision of 94% tested on seven different languages and presented a detailed error analysis with illustrative examples from our corpus.

We performed an extrinsic evaluation on seven languages in the context of the task of summarization. We concluded that producing short informative summaries (from one to three sentences) is better achieved by bringing in cross-document coreference than without it.

In future work, we intend to carry out a comprehensive extrinsic evaluations in the context of end-goal tasks like Sentiment Analysis and Quotation extraction. We also plan to perform an additional intrinsic evaluation on the SemEval'10 corpus.

References

J.B. Crawley and G. Wagner. 2010. Desktop text mining for law enforcement. In *Proceedings of IEEE ISI*, pages 138–140.

A. Haghighi and D. Klein. 2007. Unsupervised coreference resolution in a nonparametric bayesian model. In *Proceedings of ACL*, pages 848–855.

L. Hirschman. 1998. MUC-7 coreference task definition, version 3.0. In *Proceedings of MUC*. NIST.

M. Kabadjov. 2007. *A Comprehensive Evaluation of Anaphora Resolution and Discourse-new Recognition*. Ph.D. thesis, Department of Computer Science, University of Essex, December.

X. Luo. 2007. Coreference or not: A twin model for coreference resolution. In *Proceedings of NAACL*.

R. Mitkov. 2002. *Anaphora Resolution*. Longman.

V. Ng and C. Cardie. 2002. Improving machine learning approaches to coreference resolution. In *Proceedings of ACL*.

NIST. 2004. The ace evaluation plan.

M. Poesio, R. Stevenson, B. Di Eugenio, and J. M. Hitzeman. 2004. Centering: A parametric theory and its instantiations. *Computational Linguistics*, 30(3):309–363.

S.P. Ponzetto and M. Strube. 2006. Exploiting semantic role labeling, WordNet and Wikipedia for coreference resolution. In *Proceedings of HLT-NAACL*, pages 192–199.

B. Pouliquen and R. Steinberger. 2009. Automatic construction of multilingual name dictionaries. In *Learning Machine Translation*. MIT Press, NIPS series.

M. Recasens and E. Hovy. 2010. Coreference resolution across corpora: Languages, Coding schemes, and Preprocessing Information. In *Proceedings of ACL*, pages 1423–1432.

M. Recasens, L. Marquez, E. Sapena, M.A. Martí, M. Taulé, V. Hoste, M. Poesio, and Y. Versley. 2010. SemEval-2010 Task 1: Coreference Resolution in Multiple Languages. In *Proceedings of ACL*, pages 1–8.

J. Steinberger, M. Poesio, M. Kabadjov, and K. Ježek. 2007. Two uses of anaphora resolution in summarization. *Information Processing and Management*, 43(6):1663–1680.

V. Stoyanov, N. Gilbert, C. Cardie, and E. Riloff. 2009. Conundrums in noun phrase coreference resolution: Making sense of the state-of-the-art. In *Proceedings of ACL-IJCNLP*.

M. Turchi, J. Steinberger, M. Kabadjov, and R. Steinberger. 2010. Using parallel corpora for multilingual (multi-document) summarisation evaluation. In *Proceedings of CLEF*, pages 52–63.

Y. Versley, S.P. Ponzetto, M. Poesio, V. Eidelman, A. Jern, J. Smith, X. Yang, and A. Moschitti. 2008. BART: A modular toolkit for coreference resolution. In *Proceedings of LREC*.

Singletons and Coreference Resolution Evaluation

Sandra Kübler
Indiana University
skuebler@indiana.edu

Desislava Zhekova
University of Bremen
zhekova@uni-bremen.de

Abstract

This paper presents an empirical study on the influence of singletons on the evaluation of coreference resolution systems. We present results on two English data sets used in the SEMEVAL 2010 shared task 1 and the CONLL 2011 shared task using the scorers of both shared tasks. We show that singletons, both in the gold standard and in the system output, have an immense impact on the overall evaluation – in an experiment where the coreference resolution results remain unchanged over the different settings.

1 Introduction

In the last decade, the task of Coreference Resolution has become an important enterprise in Natural Language Processing. At the same time, the need for proper benchmarking increased over time. In the last year, two major shared tasks were concerned with coreference resolution: the SEMEVAL 2010 task 1 "Coreference Resolution in Multiple Languages" (Recasens et al., 2010) and the CONLL shared task 2011 "Modeling Unrestricted Coreference in OntoNotes" (Pradhan et al., 2011). Both shared tasks introduced a new element into the definition of coreference resolution: The detection of mentions. Previous to these shared tasks, the availability of gold standard mentions was often assumed, and research concentrated on the resolution of coreference relationships between mentions. (e.g. (Luo et al., 2004; Denis and Baldridge, 2007)).

However, in many approaches to coreference resolution, the problem is even more restricted, and the coreference resolution component expects only such mentions that are coreferent in the present context, i.e. no singletons are present in the data. "Singleton" is a cover term for mentions that are never coreferent, such as in `in general` or `on the contrary`, and mentions that are potentially coreferent but occur only once in a document. If the extraction of mentions is part of the task definition, then filtering singletons is generally necessary since methods for mention identification often overgenerate and produce all noun phrases (NPs), including all singletons. *Twinless mentions* (Stoyanov et al., 2009) are mentions that have been identified by a coreference resolution system but are not included in the gold data, or vice versa. Twinless mentions can lead to considerable changes in overall system performance, and Stoyanov et al. (2009) report that at that time B^3 was not prepared to handle them. For the CONLL shared task, the metrics were updated to obtain "better alignment for B^3 and CEAF so that the gold standard set and the system output have the same number of mentions" (p.c. S. Pradhan). In this paper, we investigate how the presence of singletons in either gold standard or in the system output influences the results. We compare the English data sets of the SEMEVAL and the CONLL shared task and the two versions of the scorer used there.

A simple solution was chosen by Rahman and Ng (2011), who remove twinless mentions that the coreference resolution system identifies as singletons with the motivation that the system should be rewarded for identifying the mentions as a whole, and can still be punished for their incorrectly resolved coreference. Yet, this approach is only applicable when the gold standard answers are available for evaluation. It can be used to address shortcomings of the evaluation metrics and to gain a more

	CEAF			MUC			B^3			BLANC		
	R	P	F_1	R	P	F_1	R	P	F_1	R	P	F_1
SINGLETONS	71.2	71.2	71.2	0.0	0.0	0.0	71.2	100	83.2	50.0	49.2	49.6
ALL-IN-ONE	10.5	10.5	10.5	100	29.2	45.2	100	3.5	6.7	50.0	0.8	1.6

Table 1: Baseline scores for the English data set in the SEMEVAL task 1.

	IM			MUC			B^3			$CEAF_E$			BLANC		
	R	P	F_1	R	P	F_1	R	P	F_1	R	P	F_1	R	P	F_1
SEMEVAL scorer															
ABC, DE	100	100	100	66.7	66.7	66.7	73.3	73.3	73.3	80.0	80.0	80.0	58.3	58.3	58.3
ABC, DE, Y	100	83.3	90.9	66.7	66.7	66.7	73.3	61.1	66.7	80.0	53.3	64.0	51.8	52.3	49.8
ABC, DE, X	83.3	100	90.9	66.7	66.7	66.7	61.1	73.3	66.6	53.3	80.0	64.0	58.3	58.3	58.3
CONLL scorer															
ABC, DE	100	100	100	66.7	66.7	66.7	73.3	73.3	73.3	80.0	80.0	80.0	58.3	58.3	58.3
ABC, DE, Y	100	83.3	90.9	66.7	66.7	66.7	73.3	73.3	73.3	80.0	80.0	80.0	58.3	58.3	58.3
ABC, DE, X	100	100	100	66.7	66.7	66.7	77.8	77.8	77.8	86.7	86.7	86.7	65.9	65.9	65.9

Table 2: Coreference scores on an artificial example.

objective overview of the system coreference performance. But it is not possible in a real world system.

The remainder of the paper is structured as follows: Section 2 discusses coreference evaluation metrics and their behavior in the presence of singletons. Section 3 describes the English data sets from the shared tasks, which we use for our investigation, and section 4 gives a short description of the coreference resolution system that we use. In section 5, we investigate the influence of singletons in the gold standard and system sets for both data sets, and in section 6, we investigate how the presence and treatment of pronoun singletons influences scoring results on the CONLL data set.

2 Coreference Evaluation

Apart from the open research question how to distinguish singletons from coreferent mentions, there is the question how the standard evaluation metrics, MUC (Vilain et al., 1995), B^3(Bagga and Baldwin, 1998), CEAF (Luo, 2005), and BLANC (Recasens and Hovy, 2011), react to the presence of singletons in the data. Recasens et al. (2010) present two baselines, one in which every mention in the data set is considered a singleton, and one in which all mentions are grouped into one chain. The singleton baseline reaches high scores for the metrics CEAF and B^3, with an overall performance of above 70% for English. The MUC metric, on the other hand, is not at all sensitive to the existence of singleton mentions. Yet, for the second baseline, in which all mentions were linked to one single entity, the MUC metric reported the highest results. Table 1 shows the results for both baselines.

Let us consider a small artificial example, in which the gold standard contains two coreference chains, `A-B-C` and `D-E` and the system erroneously attached `A` to the chain `D-E`. Then, we introduce one singleton in the gold standard, `X` and one in the system output `Y`. Since, the metrics in the CONLL shared task were modified to handle singletons (cf. section 1) we use both versions of the scorer, the SEMEVAL scorer and the CONLL scorer. The results are presented in table 2. This example shows that with the SEMEVAL scorer, all metrics but MUC, are sensitive to singletons in the system output and in the gold standard data. However, the presence of a singleton (Y) in the system output leads to a decrease in the results while an additional singleton (X) in the gold standard increases results although the system output is unchanged. With the CONLL scorer, all metrics are insensitive to singletons in the system output. An additional singleton in the gold standard still increases scores for B^3, $CEAF_E$ (mention-based CEAF), and BLANC. Overall, this scorer leads to higher system results.

However, the above example is a small, artificial example. It remains unclear how the results change in real world situations in which a large number of coreference chains provide the grounds for many types of errors. For this reason, we empirically investigate the influence of singletons on the English

```
1 0 By IN (TOP(S(PP* - - - Speaker#1 * (ARGM-TMP* (ARGM-TMP*   -     -
1 1 1940 CD (NP*)) - - - Speaker#1 (DATE) *) *)              (29)  (1)
1 2 , , * - - - Speaker#1 * * *                              -     -
1 3 China NNP (NP(NP(NP* - - - Speaker#1 (GPE) (ARG0* (ARG0*  (31   (2)|(3|(4|(5
1 4 's POS *) - - - Speaker#1 * * *                           31)  5)
1 5 War NNP *) - - - Speaker#1 (EVENT) * *                   -     (6)|4)
1 6 of IN (PP* - - - Speaker#1 * * *                         -     -
1 7 Resistance NNP (NP(NP*) - - - Speaker#1 (ORG) * *        -     (7)|(8|(9)
1 8 against IN (PP* - - - Speaker#1 * * *                    -     -
1 9 Japan NNP (NP*))))) - - - Speaker#1 (GPE) *) *)          (72)  (10)|(11)|8)|3)
1 10 had VBD (VP* have 03 - Speaker#1 * (V*) *               -     (12)
1 11 entered VBN (VP* enter 01 1 Speaker#1 * * (V*)          -     (13)
1 12 a DT (NP* - - - Speaker#1 * * (ARG1*                    -     (14
1 13 stalemate NN *))) - - - Speaker#1 * * *)                -     14)
1 14 . . *)) - - - Speaker#1 * * *                           -     -
```

Table 3: An example sentence from the CoNLL shared task data set.

data sets of the SemEval and the CoNLL shared task. We investigate different strategies of handling singletons, and their influence on results of a robust coreference resolution system, UBIU.

3 The Shared Task English Data Sets

Both shared tasks for coreference resolution in the last year, the SemEval 2010 task 1 (Recasens et al., 2010) and the CoNLL shared task 2011 (Pradhan et al., 2011), included an English data set, based on OntoNotes (Hovy et al., 2006). However, both data sets differ in the texts selected for their assembly as well as in the annotations on the gold standard. We discuss these differences below.

3.1 The SemEval English Data Set

The SemEval task 1 (Recasens et al., 2010) aimed at the evaluation and comparison of coreference resolution systems in a multilingual environment targeting six languages (Catalan, Dutch, English, German, Italian, Spanish). The main focus of the task was on system portability across different languages and the importance of various linguistic annotations for the system performance for all languages.

All data sets contained linguistic annotation at the morphological, syntactic, and semantic levels, including both gold standard and automatic annotations. The task description defined that only NP constituents and possessive pronouns were considered mentions; nominal predicates, appositives, expletive NPs, attributive NPs, and NPs within idioms were not considered mentions. The task description also specified that singletons were included in the data annotations since they represent coreference chains containing a single mention.

3.2 The CoNLL 2011 Shared Task Data Set

The CoNLL 2011 shared task (Pradhan et al., 2011) was defined as modeling unrestricted coreference. This shared task focused on English as its only language, and it also used the OntoNotes corpus as its basis. The task definition specifies that names, nominal mentions, and pronouns are considered mentions. Additionally, verbs that are coreferent with a noun phrase are marked as mentions. Singletons are not considered mentions. The annotation in the data set included POS tags, syntactic information, semantic role labeling, and WordNet information and corpus-based number and gender information.

Table 3 shows an example sentence from the CoNLL shared task data set with automatic annotations. Here, mention (72), `Japan` is coreferent with the mention `the enemy's` in the following sentence. Since in contrast to the SemEval data set, singletons are not annotated as mentions, noun phrases such as `China's War of Resistance` are not annotated as mentions. The last column in the example is not from the data set but is generated by UBIU (see below).

4 UBIU

UBIU (Zhekova and Kübler, 2010) was developed as a multilingual coreference resolution system. For such a task, a robust approach is necessary to make the system applicable for a variety of languages. Pronoun resolution results for German show that a mention pair model gives higher results than more complex architectures (Wunsch, 2009), thus we use a mention-pair approach, in combination with TiMBL (Daelemans et al., 2007), a memory-based learner that labels the feature vectors from the test set based on the k nearest neighbors in the training data. Based on a non-exhaustive parameter optimization on the development set, we use the *IB1* algorithm, weighted overlap as similarity metric, and gain ratio for weighting. The number of nearest neighbors is $k = 3$. The classifier is preceded by a mention extractor, which identifies possible mentions, and a feature extractor to gather the information required for classification in the form of vector features.

The mention extractor uses POS, syntactic, and lemma information that was provided in the CoNLL data set. An example of its output for the example sentence is given in the last column of table 3. Syntactic information is used to assign a mention to each of the noun phrases existing according to that annotation. Additionally, possessive pronouns and proper nouns, which are selected based on POS information are assigned a separate mention. Since verbs can be coreferent, additional mentions are included for each verb with a predicate lemma.

The feature extractor creates a feature vector for each possible pair of a mention and all its possible antecedents in a context of 3 sentences. Since mentions are represented by their syntactic head, the module uses a heuristic to select the rightmost noun in a noun phrase. However, since postmodifying prepositional phrases may be present in the mention, the noun may not be followed by a preposition.

Initially, UBIU used a wide set of features (Zhekova and Kübler, 2010), which constitutes a subset of the features by Rahman and Ng (2009). Our experiments in the CoNLL 2011 shared task (Zhekova and Kübler, 2011) showed that adding additional information, such as WordNet or number/gender information, does not improve performance for our system when applied on the CoNLL data set. For this reason, we use the basic feature set shown in table 4.

Another important step is to separate singleton mentions from coreferent ones since only the latter are annotated in OntoNotes. Our mention extractor overgenerates in that it extracts all possible mentions, and only after classification, the system can decide which mentions are singletons.

#	Feature Description
1	m_j - the antecedent
2	m_k - the mention to be resolved
3	Y if m_j is a pronoun; else N
4	number - S(ingular) or P(lural)
5	Y if m_k is a pronoun; else N
6	C if the m. are the same string; else I
7	C if one m. is a substring of the other; else I
8	C if both m. are pronominal and the same string; else I
9	C if the m. are non-pronominal and the same string; else I
10	C if m. are pronominal and either the same pronoun or differ only w.r.t. case; NA if at least one is not pronominal; else I
11	C if the m. agree in number; I if they disagree; NA if the number for one or both mentions cannot be determined
12	C if both m. are pronouns; I if neither are pronouns; else NA
13	C if both m. are Prop. N.; I if neither are Prop. N; else NA
14	sentence distance between the mentions

Table 4: The pool of features used in the base feature set.

5 Singletons in the SemEval and CoNLL Data Sets

In this section, we investigate the influence of singletons on the evaluation of UBIU. Since the system's coreference resolution performs below the state of the art systems, we assume that a wide range of errors will be present in the system output. We compare the system performance based on the data sets from the shared tasks, and we evaluate the system output with the two versions of the scorer from the shared tasks. For both data sets, we train UBIU on the training data. For the SemEval data, we test on the test set, for the CoNLL set, we use the development set since the gold standard annotation for the test set is not available yet. Overall, we have four different settings for the experiment w.r.t. singletons:

1. G+S/S+S: Singletons are included in the gold standard (i.e. training and test data) and in the system output.
2. G+S/S-S: Singletons are included in the gold standard but are removed in the system output.
3. G-S/S+S: Singletons are removed from the gold standard but not from the system output.
4. G-S/S-S: Singletons are removed from the gold standard and from the system output.

The coreference resolution information in the system data remains the same over all settings, the only changes made to the data sets concern the singletons. Since the CoNLL data set does not include singletons, we can only evaluate the last two settings for this data set. The results of these evaluations are

	IM			MUC			B^3			$CEAF_E$			BLANC		
	R	P	F_1	R	P	F_1	R	P	F_1	R	P	F_1	R	P	F_1
							SEMEVAL data – SEMEVAL scorer								
G+S/S+S	88.12	81.54	84.70	19.82	62.80	30.13	64.10	79.01	70.78	79.96	57.46	66.87	50.79	78.51	50.03
G+S/S-S	14.32	92.86	24.81	19.82	63.75	30.24	7.06	74.01	12.89	3.99	44.13	7.32	60.35	74.01	62.54
G-S/S+S	71.23	10.00	17.54	24.86	6.13	9.83	42.87	11.49	18.13	53.91	2.89	5.49	50.03	51.83	17.36
G-S/S-S	56.93	12.52	20.53	24.86	6.14	9.85	28.52	8.93	13.60	39.22	6.34	10.92	50.12	52.51	20.46
							SEMEVAL data – CONLL scorer								
G+S/S+S	87.72	81.18	84.32	19.77	62.64	30.05	73.92	96.24	83.62	91.02	71.51	80.10	53.48	78.78	55.90
G+S/S-S	14.04	91.10	24.34	19.77	63.59	30.16	73.91	96.41	83.68	91.09	71.45	80.09	53.48	79.50	55.91
G-S/S+S	45.38	6.37	11.17	12.61	3.11	4.99	86.92	43.79	58.24	20.53	39.42	27.00	50.36	50.19	50.22
G-S/S-S	37.90	8.33	13.66	12.61	3.11	5.00	86.25	42.22	56.69	20.55	42.20	27.64	51.11	50.57	50.72
							CONLL data – SEMEVAL scorer								
G-S/S+S	96.55	18.55	31.12	31.25	25.12	27.85	38.07	17.06	23.57	61.98	3.66	6.91	50.01	51.63	22.85
G-S/S-S	65.16	40.16	49.69	33.87	27.29	30.23	26.94	31.86	29.20	46.04	17.09	24.93	50.84	65.01	38.33
							CONLL data – CONLL scorer								
G-S/S+S	95.11	18.27	30.66	30.59	24.58	27.26	68.11	64.25	66.12	34.16	36.88	35.47	53.44	59.15	54.80
G-S/S-S	62.71	38.66	47.83	30.59	24.65	27.30	67.06	62.65	64.78	34.19	40.16	36.94	54.10	60.29	55.67

Table 5: System results with and without singletons on the SEMEVAL and CONLL data.

shown in table 5. Overall, there are considerable differences in the results, ranging in F-score from 4.99 in the SEMEVAL data set with the G-S/S+S setting and the MUC metric of the CONLL scorer to 83.68 in the same data set with the G+S/S-S setting and the B^3 metric of the CONLL scorer. This is disconcerting given that there is no difference in system quality, but simply in the representation of singletons. The differences between settings within a single metric are similarly extreme: B^3's F-score, for example, ranges from 70.78 to 12.89, on the same data set using the same scorer, the only difference is the presence of singletons in the system output.

A comparison of the scores for mention identification (IM) shows that the scorer version has a considerable influence on the results on the SEMEVAL data set: In the G-S/S+S setting, recall decreases from 71.23% to 45.38%. In the CONLL data set, this effect is also present, but to a lesser degree: The F-score decreases from 31.12 to 30.66 in the same setting. Any setting with a difference in the presence of singletons between gold standard and system output results in extreme differences in precision and recall. When singletons are present in the system output but not in the gold standard, recall is boosted; precision profits from the presence of singletons in the gold standard. The fact that UBIU obtains higher IM scores on the CONLL data set may be due to the strategy for mention detection, which was developed explicitly for the CONLL data set.

Contrary to our expectation that MUC will remain constant across the 4 settings, there is a significant decrease in F-score on the SEMEVAL data set between the settings in which the gold standard contains singletons and the one where it does not. The F-scores drop from approximately 30 to 9. Additionally, while there is no significant difference between the settings in which there are no singletons in the gold standard for the SEMEVAL set, the CONLL set shows a deterioration of approximately 3 percent points from G-S/S+S to G-S/S-S for the SEMEVAL scorer. The B^3 results of the SEMEVAL scorer closely model mention quality. Additionally, the results of the CONLL scorer are significantly higher than those by the SEMEVAL scorer. In the G-S/S-S setting, for example, the F-score ranges from 13.60 to 56.69 on the SEMEVAL data and from 29.20 to 64.78 on the CONLL data. $CEAF_E$ and BLANC show similar trends.

A comparison of UBIU on the two data sets shows that based on the majority of the metrics, the CONLL shared task was the easier of the two. All of the results for the CONLL set are higher than for the SEMEVAL set, with the only exception of MUC for the G-S/S-S setting. This is surprising given that the CONLL task also included verbal coreference, which should be a challenge for a system whose features were developed for nominal coreference. However, the CONLL training set was also more extensive with 2374 documents, in comparison to 322 documents in the SEMEVAL training set.

	IM			MUC			B^3			$CEAF_E$			BLANC		
	R	P	F_1	R	P	F_1	R	P	F_1	R	P	F_1	R	P	F_1
							SEMEVAL scorer								
AllS	96.55	18.55	31.12	31.25	25.12	27.85	38.07	17.06	23.57	61.98	3.66	6.91	50.01	51.63	22.85
NoS	58.86	38.42	46.50	33.87	27.29	30.23	25.13	29.62	27.19	40.56	17.26	24.22	50.86	63.97	37.61
PronS	65.16	40.16	49.69	33.87	27.29	30.23	26.94	31.86	29.20	46.04	17.09	24.93	50.84	65.01	38.33
AttP	70.52	28.69	40.78	28.70	12.35	17.27	26.94	16.03	20.10	40.54	14.29	21.13	50.51	57.15	32.64
							CONLL scorer								
AllS	95.11	18.27	30.66	30.59	24.58	27.26	68.11	64.25	66.12	34.16	36.88	35.47	53.44	59.15	54.80
NoS	56.44	36.84	44.59	30.59	24.65	27.30	67.06	62.65	64.78	34.19	40.16	36.94	54.10	60.29	55.67
PronS	62.71	38.66	47.83	30.59	24.65	27.30	67.06	62.65	64.78	34.19	40.16	36.94	54.10	60.29	55.67
AttP	67.76	27.56	39.18	25.68	11.05	15.45	75.97	42.30	54.34	21.44	42.02	28.39	52.56	52.19	52.36

Table 6: System results with varying treatment of pronouns.

6 Pronominal Singletons in the System Output

Here, we have a closer look at pronoun singletons in the system output. We include all types of anaphoric pronouns in our investigation, i.e. personal, reflexive, demonstrative, and possessive pronouns. Relative and indefinite pronouns are not annotated as mentions in the data and thus excluded from our study. Since most of the pronouns are inherently anaphoric, we know that, apart from expletive pronouns, they must be part of a coreference chain. We examine the effect of singleton pronouns on the scorers' results.

We use the CONLL data set for this study since it does not contain singletons. This means, the expectation for the system is that it does not include singletons in the answers. On the system side, we investigate the following four settings:

1. AllS: In this setting, singletons are not filtered out, i.e. all mentions for pronouns, NPs, names, verbs, etc. remain in the final system.
2. NoS: This setting filters out all singletons, i.e. all mentions that were marked by the mention extractor but for which the coreference resolution module did not find any coreferring mentions, are deleted from the system answers.
3. PronS: This is similar to the NoS setting, but here all the pronominal singletons remain in the answers. I.e. the filter deletes all NP mentions, but does not delete any pronoun mentions.
4. AttP: In the final setting, singleton pronouns are attached to an antecedent. I.e. the system enforces coreference for all pronouns. If the coreference resolution module does not find an antecedent for the pronoun, a heuristic enforces coreference to the closest preceding mention. As in the NoPron setting, all singletons that do not consist of a pronoun are deleted.

The results of the system performance given the above settings are shown in table 6. Similar to the findings in section 5, there is a difference between the scores achieved by the SEMEVAL scorer and the CONLL scorer. The CONLL MUC scores are somewhat lower while the CONLL B^3, $CEAF_E$, and BLANC scores are higher by a wide margin to maximally 2.8 times the original F-score.

The mention quality (IM) shows the expected results: For the AllS setting, the system reaches a very high recall of 96.55/95.11%, but at the same time a very low precision, which also results in the lowest F-score. Since all the singletons are included in the system answer, a high number of mentions are found, but many of the identified mentions are twinless singletons. When we exclude all singletons in the NoS setting, recall reaches its lowest value, but precision profits so that the F-score is higher overall than the AllS score. Forcing the pronouns into a coreference relation has a positive influence on recall, which increases to 70.52/67.76%, but a negative influence on precision, which decreases to 28.78/27.56%. These results show that adding the pronouns and their coreferent mentions has a positive influence on recall but the missing separation of expletive pronouns from anaphoric ones has a detrimental effect on precision.

MUC, which should not be sensitive to singletons in the system answers, shows the same scores for the settings with no singletons (NoS) and with only pronominal singletons. Given the CoNLL scorer, all metrics show the same scores for the NoS and PronS settings, thus they are insensitive towards the presence of non-pronominal singleton. However, for the setting with all singletons, all scores based on the SEMEVAL scorer are considerably lower than for the settings without singletons or with only pronominal singletons. The reason for this difference is unclear at this point and needs to be investigated further.

7 Conclusion and Future Work

In this paper, we investigated the influence of singletons in the gold standard as well as in the system output on coreference resolution evaluation. We have shown that all metrics are affected by the presence of singletons in the gold standard. Especially in a setting in which both the gold standard and the system output contain singletons, the evaluation scores of both versions of the scorer are artificially boosted. However, the presence of singletons in the system output also has an effect on evaluation, but to a considerably lesser degree. This means that a system may not always be rewarded for having a reliable filter for singletons. Including singletons in the training data is a necessary step towards more realistic settings. However, including singletons in the gold standard for evaluation artificially boosts results.

Acknowledgment

This work is based on research supported by the US Office of Naval Research (ONR) Grant #N00014-10-1-0140. We also gratefully acknowledge the support of the Deutsche Forschungsgemeinschaft (DFG) through the Collaborative Research Center SFB/TR 8 Spatial Cognition (Project I5-DiaSpace).

References

Amit Bagga and Breck Baldwin. 1998. Algorithms for scoring coreference chains. In *Proceedings of the LREC Workshop on Linguistic Coreference*, Granada, Spain.

Walter Daelemans, Jakub Zavrel, Ko van der Sloot, and Antal van den Bosch. 2007. TiMBL: Tilburg memory based learner – version 6.1 – reference guide. Technical Report ILK 07-07, ILK-CL, Tilburg University.

Pascal Denis and Jason Baldridge. 2007. Joint determination of anaphoricity and coreference resolution using integer programming. In *Proceedings of HLT-NAACL 2007*, Rochester, NY.

Eduard Hovy, Mitchell Marcus, Martha Palmer, Lance Ramshaw, and Ralph Weischedel. 2006. Ontonotes: The 90% solution. In *Proceedings of HLT-NAACL*, New York, NY.

Xiaoqiang Luo, Abe Ittycheriah, Hongyan Jing, Nanda Kambhatla, and Salim Roukos. 2004. A mention-synchronous coreference resolution algorithm based on the bell tree. In *Proceedings of ACL*, Barcelona, Spain.

Xiaoqiang Luo. 2005. On coreference resolution performance metrics. In *Proceedings of HLT-EMNLP*, Vancouver, Canada.

Sameer Pradhan, Lance Ramshaw, Mitchell Marcus, Martha Palmer, Ralph Weischedel, and Nianwen Xue. 2011. CoNLL-2011 shared task: Modeling unrestricted coreference in OntoNotes. In *Proceedings of CoNLL 2011*, Portland, OR.

Altaf Rahman and Vincent Ng. 2009. Supervised models for coreference resolution. In *Proceedings of EMNLP*, Singapore.

Altaf Rahman and Vincent Ng. 2011. Narrowing the modeling gap: A cluster-ranking approach to coreference resolution. *JAIR*, 40:469–521.

Marta Recasens and Eduard Hovy. 2011. BLANC: Implementing the Rand Index for coreference evaluation. *Natural Language Engineering*.

Marta Recasens, Lluìs Màrquez, Emili Sapena, M. Antònia Martí, Mariona Taulé, Véronique Hoste, Massimo Poesio, and Yannick Versley. 2010. SemEval-2010 task 1: Coreference resolution in multiple languages. In *Proceedings of SemEval*, Uppsala, Sweden.

Veselin Stoyanov, Nathan Gilbert, Claire Cardie, and Ellen Riloff. 2009. Conundrums in noun phrase coreference resolution: Making sense of the state-of-the-art. In *Proceedings of ACL-AFNLP*, Singapore.

Marc Vilain, John Burger, John Aberdeen, Dennis Connolly, and Lynette Hirschman. 1995. A model-theoretic coreference scoring scheme. In *Proceedings of MUC-6*, Columbia, MD.

Holger Wunsch. 2009. *Rule-Based and Memory-Based Pronoun Resolution for German: A Comparison and Assessment of Data Sources*. Ph.D. thesis, Universität Tübingen.

Desislava Zhekova and Sandra Kübler. 2010. UBIU: A language-independent system for coreference resolution. In *Proceedings of SemEval*, Uppsala, Sweden.

Desislava Zhekova and Sandra Kübler. 2011. UBIU: A Robust System for Resolving Unrestricted Coreference. In *Proceedings of CoNLL: Shared Task*, Portland, OR.

Modelling Entity Instantiations

Andrew McKinlay
School of Computing
University of Leeds, UK
scs4ajm@comp.leeds.ac.uk

Katja Markert
School of Computing
University of Leeds, UK
markert@comp.leeds.ac.uk

Abstract

We introduce the problem of detecting *Entity Instantiations*, a type of entity relation in which a set of entities is introduced, and either a member or subset of this set is mentioned afterwards. We perform the first, reliable, corpus study of Entity Instantiations, concentrating on intersentential annotation. We then develop the first automatic instantiation detector, which incorporates lexical, contextual and world knowledge and shows significant improvements over a strong baseline.

1 Introduction

In this paper we annotate and classify *Entity Instantiations*. An Entity Instantiation is a non-coreferent entity relationship, where a *set* of entities is mentioned, and then a *member* or *subset*[1] of this set is introduced. Example 1 shows a pair of sentences with the set in bold and set member in italics.[2] Examples 2 and 3 show a pair of sentences with a set in bold and subset in italics.

(1) a. **Some European funds** recently have skyrocketed.
  b. *Spain Fund* has surged to a startling 120% premium.

(2) a. **Bids totalling $515 million** were submitted.
  b. *Accepted offers* ranged from 8.38% to 8.395%

(3) a. In the aftermath of the downturn **many manufacturers** have struggled.
  b. *Those relying on foreign imports* have had the most difficulty.

The detection of Entity Instantiations is not tackled in ACE (ACE, 2000–2005) or MUC (MUC, 1987–1998), the two most popular schemes of semantic relation annotation. It is, however, important as it can supplement knowledge about the member or subset. In Example 4 below, the Entity Instantiation between *'several EU countries'* and *'the UK'* gives us the knowledge that not only are interest rates dropping in the UK, but inflation is rising as well. Entity Instantiations can also aid the interpretation of sentiment — in Example 5, the author's thoughts about the pay of Wayne Rooney can be inferred from the negative sentiment of the first sentence. In some instances, the member or subset is even uninterpretable without the set. In Example 3, *'Those relying on foreign imports'* requires *'many manufacturers'* to interpret the missing head noun. The problem of detecting these types of Entity Instantiation overlaps with bridging anaphora.

(4) a. Inflation has increased sharply in **several EU countries**.
  b. In *the UK*, this has accompanied a drop in interest rates.

(5) a. **Footballers** are vastly overpaid.
  b. Manchester United pay *Wayne Rooney* £200,000 per week.

The interpretation of Entity Instantiations can often be difficult. Entity Instantiations occur in a variety of forms. Participating noun phrases (NPs) include pronouns and proper nouns, can

[1] When we refer to a subset, we mean a *proper* subset. We consider two equal sets to be coreferent, and not participating in an Entity Instantiation.

[2] Examples 1, 2, 3, 8 and 9 are adapted from the Penn Treebank Wall Street Journal Corpus (Marcus et al., 1993).

have missing head nouns (see Example 3) and fulfil various grammatical roles in a sentence. The two participants in an Entity Instantiation can have word overlap (see Example 1) or synonymous head nouns (see Example 2), but are often not related in such a simple manner. For instance, in Example 5, one needs to know that Wayne Rooney is a footballer to identify the Entity Instantiation. Additionally, correct interpretation of an Entity Instantiation often needs contextual knowledge. In Examples 6 and 7, the contextual information about the attitudes of the workers is necessary to establish whether an Entity Instantiation exists.

(6) a. **Some workers** are opposed to strike action.

b. *John Smith* fears that a strike could damage the industry's public perception.

(7) a. **Some workers** are opposed to strike action.

b. *David Jones*, however, is willing to put his job on the line for the cause. *(Not an instantiation.)*

In this paper we present an annotated corpus of Entity Instantiations, containing 648 annotated instantiations over 25 texts. We then use this corpus to train and test an automatic Entity Instantiation identifier, which gains significant improvements over a unigram baseline.

2 Related Work

Our work is related to Relation Extraction (RE), which is the discovery of semantic relations between pairs of entities. Much of the work in this field is connected to the Message Understanding Conferences (MUC, 1987–1998) and the NIST Automatic Content Extraction (ACE, 2000–2005) programs, both of which provide annotated corpora of semantic relations. The ACE-2004 scheme includes 7 broad relation types, divided into a total of 23 subtypes, such as *ART.User-Owner* to indicate the ownership of an object by a person, and *ORG-AFF.Employment* to represent the employment of a person by an organisation.

Entity Instantiations are not considered in the MUC and ACE annotation schemes, which consider relationships between different *types* of entity, such as those between persons and locations, rather than our groups and instances of entities of the same type. However, the algorithms used to classify these semantic relationship might still be applicable to our problem.

A variety of automatic RE algorithms have been developed, falling largely into two groups; those that learn from tree-kernels and those that use traditional, flat features. In one approach of the first type, (Zhou et al., 2007) use tree kernels to capture the structured information held in the parse trees of entities. They implement an algorithm which dynamically decides how much context to include as part of the tree, and in conjunction with some flat features it achieves an F-score of 75.8% on the 7 broad relation types in the ACE-2004 dataset.

Two recent flat-featured approaches successfully exploit background knowledge to improve RE. (Chan and Roth, 2010) implement features which use Wikipedia queries to search for *parent-child* relationships between entities. They attain an F-score of 68.2% at the coarse-grained level and 54.4% at the fine-grained level on a set of directed, sentence-internal relations from the ACE-2004 dataset. (Sun et al., 2011) generate large-scale word clusters from the TDT5 corpus and incorporate information regarding which cluster the mention head word belongs to. This method results in an F-score of 71.5%.

Our work is also related to the problem of bridging anaphora. A bridging anaphor is an anaphor that is not coreferent to its antecedent, but connected by another relationship, such as meronymy. Prior work in theoretical linguistics and corpus linguistics (Asher and Lascarides, 1998; Fraurud, 1990; Poesio and Vieira, 1998) has offered significant insight into bridging. A number of bridging publications also refer to set membership or subset relationships specifically (Clark, 1975; Prince, 1981; Gardent et al., 2003). Further work has concentrated on the development of algorithms for the resolution of bridging anaphora. (Markert et al., 1996; Vieira and Poesio, 2000) create end-to-end systems for bridging resolution, while both (Markert et al., 2003) and (Poesio et al., 2004) tackle solely part-of bridging references.

Our work differs from bridging in that often Entity Instantiations are not anaphoric (see Examples 1, 4, 5 and 6). There is, however, some overlap. For instance, in Example 3 the subset *'Those relying on foreign imports'* requires knowledge of the set *'manufacturers'* to be understood.

Our work is also related to (Recasens et al., 2010), in which the authors develop a typology of near-identity coreference relationships, including largely overlapping sets. Set membership relations, however, are not tackled.

3 Corpus Study

To create a gold standard corpus creation we annotate full texts from the Penn Treebank (PTB) Wall Street Journal corpus (Marcus et al., 1993) for the presence of two types of Entity Instantiation:

Set Member A set of entities is introduced, and a *single member* of that set is mentioned.

Subset A set of entities is introduced, and a smaller *subset* of these is mentioned.

We limit our annotation to instantiations that occur *between* adjacent sentences. We do not annotate intrasententially, as we suspect that many intrasentential instantiations may be easily discoverable by syntactic analysis (for example, the instantiations in *'Some football managers, such as Sir Alex Ferguson'* and *'Among these workers, John Smith'*)..

Our annotation tool automatically identifies plural and singular noun phrases (NPs) that are candidates for participating in Entity Instantiations, separately displaying plural-plural NP pairs for subset annotation and plural-singular NP pairs for set member annotation. We automatically remove NPs that are appositions or predicates, and therefore not mentions. Our tool also includes the option to manually mark noun phrases as *"Not a mention"*. We use this to exclude instances of non-referential *it*, noun phrases that are idiomatic — such as *pie in the sky* — and generic pronouns.

The annotator then indicates whether each pair of NPs forms an Entity Instantiation. We annotate each pair of sentences twice; once with potential sets in first sentence and potential set members and subsets in the second sentence, and once with potential sets in the second sentence and potential set members and subsets in the first sentence.

3.1 Agreement Study

To ascertain the reliability and replicability of our annotations, we undertook a short agreement study. Five texts containing a total of 6,177 NP pairs were independently annotated by the two authors of this study, and their agreement was measured in the following three variations:

1. Does this pair of candidate noun phrases participate in a set membership/subset relationship or not?

Method	# of items tested	Kappa	Agreement
1	6177 pairs of NPs	0.6504	97.31%
2	2994 NPs	0.6403	95.23%
3	607 sentence pairs	0.7317	91.09%

Table 1: Agreement Statistics

2. Does this candidate set member/subset participate in a set membership/subset relationship with any potential set or not?

3. Is there an Entity Instantiation between these two sentences?

The results of the agreement study, including percentage agreement and chance corrected agreement (Kappa, (Cohen, 1960)), are presented in Table 1. Our agreement about which candidates were *"Not a mention"* was $\kappa = 0.7146$. These agreement statistics show reasonable agreement on the task, and that our annotation scheme is reliable and replicable.

There were several re-occurring types of disagreements. It was often difficult for annotators to establish whether a pair of sets were subsets, coreferent or overlapping. In Example 8, one can interpret *'men'* to mean either the men belonging to Baker or the general set of men, and this interpretation directly affects whether *'them'* is considered a subset.

Another problematic issue was systematic polysemy. In Example 9, *'Most cosmetic purchases'* might comprise a set of transactions or a set of products. The result of this interpretation then affects whether one considers *'lipstick'* to be a set member.

We also found that disagreements often propagated. A single decision about the relationship between two entities early on in a text can result in a large number of follow-on disagreements.

(8) a. Baker had lots of **men**.
    b. But she didn't trust *them* and didn't reward trust.

(9) a. **Most cosmetic purchases** are unplanned.
    b. *Lipstick* is often bought on a whim.

3.2 Further Annotation

After the successful agreement study, a further 20 texts were annotated by the first author of this study in order to complete the corpus. The frequency of Entity Instantiations over the final 25

Entity Instantiation	# NP pairs	%
Set Member	468	1.616
Subset	180	0.621
No inst. plural-singular	18758	64.76
No inst. plural-plural	9560	33.00
Total	28966	100

Table 2: Frequency of Entity Instantiations in 25 texts

texts is shown in Table 2. We found that a mean of 26 instantiations occurred per text, and that set membership instantiations occur considerably more frequently than subset instantiations.

4 Automatic Instantiation Detection

We use a supervised machine learning approach to detect which NP pairs comprise Entity Instantiations. Below we detail our feature set, experimental set-up and results.

4.1 Features

Our features fall into five broad categories; *surface*, *salience*, *syntactic*, *contextual* and *knowledge*. These categories contain both features that pertain to a single NP, and those that represent cross-NP relationships.

Surface features. Our surface features consist of unigrams, part-of-speech tags, lemmas, and dependency-parse[3] derived heads of each NP. We calculate Levenshtein's distance between the strings representing the unigrams, lemmas, head word and head lemma of each NP, hoping to capture pairs like *'funds'* and *'fund'* (see Example 1). We also calculate the distance in characters and words between NP pairs, and include these along with versions normalised by the total length of the two sentences containing the NPs. Additionally we include a boolean feature which represents the order of the NPs — True for candidate set NP in the first sentence and candidate set member/subset NP in the second sentence and False for the reverse order.

Salience features. As an indicator of the salience of each NP we include: its grammatical role, derived from dependency parse data; whether it is the first mention of that entity in the sentence or document; the number of mentions of the entity prior to this in the document; and the overall number of mentions of the entity in the document. We approximate the number of entity mentions by judging noun phrases with identical heads to be coreferent, as in (Barzilay and Lapata, 2008).

[3]Our dependency parses are generated from the gold standard PTB tree.

Syntactic features. We include five syntactic features, representing syntactic parallelism and pre- and post-modification. The modification type includes values that represent apposition, conjunction, pre modification and bare nouns. Our intuition is that set members and subsets are often more heavily modified than the sets that they are part of, as in *footballers → footballers playing in the Premiership*, *European countries → European nations that use the Euro*.

Contextual features. We include several contextual features, hypothesising that NPs that occur in similar contexts may be more likely to be Entity Instantiations. We retrieve the Levin class (Levin, 1993) of each NP's head verb, as well as the verb itself, noting examples such as Example 1 which has two similar verbs, *'surge'* and *'skyrocket'*. We also calculate whether each NP is in a quotation, and include an approximation of the discourse relations present in the two sentences by identifying likely discourse connectives and mapping them to their most frequent explicit relation in the Penn Discourse Treebank (PDTB) (Prasad et al., 2008). In cases such as Example 7, the presence of the discourse connective *'however'* appears useful in establishing that no instantiation is present. Note that we do *not* use any PDTB annotations to discover the presence of implicit or explicit discourse relations in the two sentences.

Knowledge-based features. Our knowledge-based features are organised into four categories:

WordNet. We use WordNet to establish whether the head words of NPs that are *not* named entities are synonyms or hyponyms, in an effort to identify pairs such as *'offers'* and *'bids'* in Example 2.

Freebase. We use Freebase (Bollacker et al., 2008), a freely-available repository of structured knowledge, to attempt to establish the relatedness of NPs. Each entity in Freebase is associated with a list of topics, which loosely represent hyponyms of the entity. For example, the topics listed for *'Wayne Rooney'* include *['Person', 'Football player', 'Athlete', '2010 World Cup Athlete']*. For each NP representing a potential set member or subset, we search Freebase using their Search API, choosing those matching entities that have a relevance score over 35. We then retrieve a list of topics for each entity and compare these topics to our potential set NP. If one of the topics is equal to, synonymous with, or has a Levenshtein distance of 1 from our potential set, the feature is True. Otherwise the feature is False.

Google PMI. We also use Google for discovering potential set membership and subset relations. We calculate Point-wise Mutual Information from hit counts for our potential Entity Instantiations, based on the notion that the pattern "X and other Y", where X is a potential set member or subset and Y is a potential set, indicates hyponymy (Hearst, 1992; Markert and Nissim, 2005). We use the following formula to calculate the value of our feature:

$$\text{G-PMI}(X, Y) = \frac{hits(\text{“}X\text{ and other }Y\text{”})}{hits(\text{“}X\text{”}) \times hits(\text{“and other }Y\text{”})}$$

Animacy. We attempt to establish whether the animacy of the two NPs match, reasoning that pairs of NPs that do not have the same animacy are highly unlikely to participate in an Entity Instantiation.

We use a list of animate pronouns, lists of animate and inanimate words distributed as part of the Stanford Deterministic Coreference Resolution System (Ji and Lin, 2009; Lee et al., 2011), and named entity information generated by the Stanford Named Entity Recognizer (Finkel et al., 2005) to ascertain the animacy of each NP. Our feature has three possible values; Match if the two NPs have the same animacy, No Match if they do not, and Not Present if we cannot calculate the animacy of one of the NPs. Not Present occurs in only 6% of pairs.

4.2 Experimental Set-up and Results

We divide our data set into two; plural-plural NP pairs that are labelled either *subset* or *no-instantiation* and plural-singular NP pairs that are labelled either *set member* or *no-instantiation*. We use the machine learner ICSIBoost (Favre et al., 2007). ICSIBoost is an open source implementation of Boostexter (Schapire and Singer, 2000), an algorithm which combines simple 'rules-of-thumb' — in this case, decision stumps — to produce a classifier. We apply 10-fold cross-validation for testing and training in all our experiments, keeping pairs from the same text in the same fold, to avoid rewarding the learning of very specific rules about the unigrams present which will not generalise well.

Due to the nature of the annotation study, there are many more pairs of candidates between which no Entity Instantiation has been annotated than those that have. Only 2.32% of the 28,966 pairs of candidates in the corpus have a set member or subset annotation. We therefore experiment with two different datasets.

Firstly, we used random sub-sampling to produce a balanced data set in which only 50% of the annotated pairs were non-relations, and used this for both training and testing. Results on the sub-sampled data are shown in Table 3.

Secondly, we experimented with the original, highly skewed data. Training on the original data resulted in a classifier that almost never predicted an instantiation, so we experimented with some simple techniques to improve precision and recall. These comprised randomly subsampling the negative examples so that they made up 50% or 75% of the training data, and oversampling the positive examples in the training data by a factor of 10, 20 or 40. The results of these experiments are shown in Table 4.

For comparison, results for a baseline whose sole features are the unigrams of the two NPs are also included. The Precision, Recall and F-Measure scores shown are for the positive examples in each set.

4.3 Discussion

On a balanced data set, our best features show highly significant improvements over the unigram baseline[4]. We performed a feature ablation study, removing each group of features from our model in turn, the results of which are present in Table 3. Our knowledge-based features are particularly good for identifying instantiations. Upon further investigation, we discovered that our Google PMI feature is the most effective of this feature group, with large PMI values often being indicative of instantiations.

Our salience features aid classification significantly for set members but not subsets. This indicates that set members are often first mentions of an entity that are mediated from a set, but subsets function less often in this way. In general, sub-

[4] $p < 10^{-8}$ and 10^{-4} for set members and subsets respectively with McNemar's χ^2 test (McNemar, 1947).

	Set Members				Subsets			
Feature set	**Accuracy**	**P**	**R**	**F**	**Accuracy**	**P**	**R**	**F**
Majority	50.0%	—	—	—	50.0%	—	—	—
Unigrams	58.8%	0.692	0.316	0.434	52.9%	0.565	0.255	0.352
All	68.9%♣	0.782	0.525	0.628	65.2%	0.724	0.489	0.584
All - Surface	66.6%	0.717	0.550	0.622	62.00%	0.651	0.516	0.576
All - Salience	65.5%♠	0.739	0.479	0.582	65.4%♣	0.730	0.489	0.586
All - Syntax	68.0%	0.770	0.512	0.615	65.2%	0.732	0.479	0.579
All - Contextual	67.7%	0.792	0.479	0.597	63.0%	0.674	0.505	0.578
All - World Knowledge	64.4%◇	0.766	0.413	0.537	60.6%♠	0.675	0.410	0.510

Table 3: Results on balanced data set

♣ Algorithm with highest accuracy
♠ Significantly *worse* than ♣, significance $p < 0.005$, McNemar's χ^2 test.
◇ Significantly *worse* than ♣, significance $p < 0.001$, McNemar's χ^2 test.

	Set Members				Subsets			
Method	**Accuracy**	**P**	**R**	**F**	**Accuracy**	**P**	**R**	**F**
Original Set	97.39%	0.2979	0.0289	0.0527	97.90%	0.1852	0.0266	0.0465
Undersampling 50/50	83.31%	0.0782	0.5227	0.1361	76.47%	0.0453	0.5585	0.0839
Undersampling 75/25	94.60%	0.1275	0.1963	0.1546	93.28%	0.0838	0.2500	0.1255
Oversampling x10	96.89%	0.2500	0.1178	0.1601	97.47%	0.1685	0.0798	0.1083
Oversampling x20	96.38%	0.2129	0.1632	0.1848	97.21%	0.1557	0.1011	0.1226
Oversampling x40	95.24%	0.1690	0.2272	0.1938	96.51%	0.1346	0.1489	0.1414

Table 4: Results on unbalanced data set

sets appear harder to detect than set membership relations, but the smaller size of the subset data set likely contributes to this.

Learning from the original, highly skewed data is much more difficult, and our highest F-scores are 0.1938 and 0.1414 for set members and subsets, respectively (see Table 4). Learning from data with this sort of distribution is difficult, regardless of the domain. In future we intend to use techniques such as SMOTE (Chawla et al., 2002) and One-Sided Selection (Kubat and Matwin, 1997) to address this heavy skew.

5 Conclusion and Future Work

We propose a novel Information Extraction task: the detection of Entity Instantiations. This task is potentially important for a variety of NLP problems, such as question answering and sentiment analysis. We have presented the first corpus study of Entity Instantiations, achieving good levels of annotator agreement. Our supervised machine learning classifier achieves an F-score of 0.628 for set member relations and 0.586 for subset relations on a balanced set, making good use of a variety of features, including world-knowledge and salience criteria.

In the future, we intend to expand our annotation to include intrasentential and further distant Entity Instantiations, as well as our current instantiations between adjacent sentences. Future machine learning approaches to consider are tree-kernel based approaches such as (Zhou et al., 2007). To tackle the high skew in our data, we will use techniques such as those detailed in (Kubat and Matwin, 1997) and (Chawla et al., 2002), and also look to methods such as active learning to acquire more positive instantiation examples.

Acknowledgements

Andrew McKinlay is funded by an EPSRC Doctoral Training Grant. This research draws on data provided by the University Research Program for Google Search, a service provided by Google to promote a greater understanding of the web.

References

ACE. 2000-2005. Automatic Content Extraction. `http://www.ldc.upenn.edu/Projects/ACE/`.

N. Asher and A. Lascarides. 1998. Bridging. *Journal of Semantics*, 15(1):83–113.

R. Barzilay and M. Lapata. 2008. Modeling local coherence: An entity-based approach. *Computational Linguistics*, 34(1):1–34.

K. Bollacker, C. Evans, P. Paritosh, T. Sturge, and J. Taylor. 2008. Freebase: a collaboratively created graph database for structuring human knowledge. In *Proceedings of the 2008 ACM SIGMOD International Conference on Management of Data*, pages 1247–1250.

Y.S. Chan and D. Roth. 2010. Exploiting background knowledge for relation extraction. In *Proceedings of COLING 2010*, pages 152–160.

N.V. Chawla, K.W. Bowyer, L.O. Hall, and W.P. Kegelmeyer. 2002. Smote: synthetic minority over-sampling technique. *Journal of Artificial Intelligence Research*, 16(1):321–357.

H.H. Clark. 1975. Bridging. In *Proceedings of the 1975 Workshop on Theoretical Issues in Natural Language Processing*, pages 169–174.

J. Cohen. 1960. A coefficient of agreement for nominal scales. *Educational and psychological measurement*, 20(1):37–46.

B. Favre, D. Hakkani-Tür, and S. Cuendet. 2007. ICSIboost. `http://code.google.come/p/icsiboost`.

J.R. Finkel, T. Grenager, and C. Manning. 2005. Incorporating non-local information into information extraction systems by Gibbs sampling. In *Proceedings of ACL 2005*, pages 363–370.

K. Fraurud. 1990. Definiteness and the processing of noun phrases in natural discourse. *Journal of Semantics*, 7(4):395.

C. Gardent, H. Manuelian, and E. Kow. 2003. Which bridges for bridging definite descriptions. In *Proceedings of the EACL 2003 Workshop on Linguistically Interpreted Corpora*, pages 69–76.

M.A. Hearst. 1992. Automatic acquisition of hyponyms from large text corpora. In *Proceedings of COLING 1992*, pages 539–545.

H. Ji and D. Lin. 2009. Gender and animacy knowledge discovery from web-scale n-grams for unsupervised person mention detection. In *Proceedings of PACLIC 2009*.

M. Kubat and S. Matwin. 1997. Addressing the curse of imbalanced training sets: one-sided selection. In *Proceedings of ICML 1997*, pages 179–186.

H. Lee, Y. Peirsman, A. Chang, N. Chambers, M. Surdeanu, and D. Jurafsky. 2011. Stanfords multi-pass sieve coreference resolution system at the conll-2011 shared task. In *Proceedings of the CoNLL-2011 Shared Task*, pages 28–34.

B. Levin. 1993. *English verb classes and alternations: A preliminary investigation.* University of Chicago press.

M.P. Marcus, M.A. Marcinkiewicz, and B. Santorini. 1993. Building a large annotated corpus of English: The Penn Treebank. *Computational Linguistics*, 19(2):313–330.

K. Markert and M. Nissim. 2005. Comparing knowledge sources for nominal anaphora resolution. *Computational Linguistics*, 31(3):367–402.

K. Markert, M. Strube, and U. Hahn. 1996. Inferential realization constraints on functional anaphora in the centering model. In *Proceedings of CogSci 1996*, pages 609–614.

K. Markert, N. Modjeska, and M. Nissim. 2003. Using the web for nominal anaphora resolution. In *Proceedings of EACL 2003 Workshop on the Computational Treatment of Anaphora*, pages 39–46.

Q. McNemar. 1947. Note on the sampling error of the difference between correlated proportions or percentages. *Psychometrika*, 12(2):153–157.

MUC. 1987-1998. The NIST MUC website: `http://www.itl.nist.gov/iaui/894.02/related_projects/muc/`.

M. Poesio and R. Vieira. 1998. A corpus-based investigation of definite description use. *Computational Linguistics*, 24:183–216, June.

M. Poesio, R. Mehta, A. Maroudas, and J. Hitzeman. 2004. Learning to resolve bridging references. In *Proceedings of ACL 2004*, page 143.

R. Prasad, N. Dinesh, A. Lee, E. Miltsakaki, L. Robaldo, A. Joshi, and B. Webber. 2008. The Penn Discourse TreeBank 2.0. In *Proceedings of LREC 2008*, pages 2961–2968.

E.F. Prince. 1981. Toward a Taxonomy of Given-New Information. *Radical Pragmatics*, 3:223–255.

M. Recasens, E. Hovy, and M.A. Martı. 2010. A typology of near-identity relations for coreference (NIDENT). In *Proceedings of LREC 2010*, pages 149–156.

R.E. Schapire and Y. Singer. 2000. BoosTexter: A boosting-based system for text categorization. *Machine learning*, 39(2):135–168.

A. Sun, R. Grishman, and S. Sekine. 2011. Semi-supervised relation extraction with large-scale word clustering. In *Proceedings of ACL-HLT 2011*, pages 521–529.

R. Vieira and M. Poesio. 2000. An empirically based system for processing definite descriptions. *Computational Linguistics*, 26(4):539–593.

G.D. Zhou, M. Zhang, D.H. Ji, and Q.M. Zhu. 2007. Tree Kernel-Based Relation Extraction with Context-Sensitive Structured Parse Tree Information. In *Proceedings of EMNLP-CoNLL 2007*, pages 728–736.

A New Scheme for Annotating Semantic Relations between Named Entities in Corpora

Mani EZZAT[(1)(2)]
[(1)]INaLCO-CRIM
49bis av. Belle Gabrielle
75012 Paris
[(2)] ARISEM
1-5 rue Carnot
91883 Massy
mani.ezzat@gmail.com

Thierry POIBEAU[(3)]
[(3)] LaTTiCe-CNRS and ENS
1, rue Maurice Arnoux
92120 Montrouge, France
thierry.poibeau@ens.fr

Abstract

Although several studies have developed models and type hierarchies for named entity annotation, no such resource is available for semantic relation annotation, despite its utility for various applications (e.g. question answering, information extraction). In this paper, we show that there are two issues in semantic relation description, one concerning knowledge engineering (what to annotate?) and the other concerning language engineering (how to deal with modality and modifiers?). We propose a new annotation scheme, making it possible to have both a precise and tractable annotation. A practical experiment shows that annotators using our scheme were able to quickly annotate a large number of sentences with very high inter-annotator agreement.

1 Introduction

A large number of natural language applications (e.g. information extraction, question answering, automatic summarization) require a precise analysis of the linguistic content of the text. Since the Message Understanding Conferences in the 1990s, there is a general agreement on the different steps required to perform this analysis: *i)* relevant elements (mostly named entities) are first recognized and tagged, then *ii)* relations between these elements are extracted. This generic schema does not preclude the existence of other steps in the analysis (*e.g.* anaphora resolution, discourse structure recognition), but the recognition of basic elements and relations between them is nevertheless a shared basis among a large number of systems (Jurafsky and Martin, 2009).

This of course explains why there has been an increasing amount of research both on named entity recognition and on relation analysis in the last 20 years (MUC6, 1995; Appelt and Martin, 1999). However, the maturity of these two tasks differs to a large extent. As for named entity recognition, a large number of tools, data and gold standard are available for very different languages. The success rate is often above .9 or even .95 F-measure for major categories (person's names, location's names) in newspapers (Collins and Singer, 1999). Entity types are to a certain extent normalized and formalized in large hierarchies (see for example the hierarchy proposed by Sekine which is now a de facto standard (Sekine et al., 2002)).

In comparison, it is interesting to observe that only a few annotated corpora and no real gold standard exist for semantic relations[1]. A first explanation is that relation analysis largely depends on the task and on the kind of corpora being analyzed. However, we do not think that this is enough to explain the current situation: for example question-answering systems are supposed to address any kinds of questions and thus require a generic approach for relation analysis.

It is of course difficult to normalize the set of all possible relations. The clusters of verbs described in Wordnet (synsets, clusters of near-synonym verbs) (Fellbaum, 1998) or Framenet (clusters of verbs sharing the same argument structure) (Fillmore et al., 2003) are a good basis and our goal is not to propose a new classification of verbs and/or events. Nevertheless, annotation schemes proposed so far do not go beyond simple events themselves. From this perspective, they are inadequate in that they do not provide enough room between a yes or no option (the relation can be identified or not), whereas texts constantly report relations along with modalities, negations, etc.

This is the reason why, in this paper, we propose a tractable annotation scheme allowing one to annotate relations more accurately, with a level of generality that makes our scheme both tractable and extensible. We do not focus on event them-

[1]One of our reviewers suggested previous studies (like (Carlson et al., 2002; Poesio and Artstein, 2008), among several others). However, none of these propose a general scheme for semantic relation annotation. They generally deal with a specific theory (e.g. Rhetorical Structure Theory (Carlson et al., 2002)) or a specific phenomenon (e.g. anaphora resolution (Poesio and Artstein, 2008)). Recent frameworks like ACE take profits of all these studies but a large number of problems remains unsolved, see (ACE, 2008a).

selves, but we propose to annotate contextual information for a more thorough analysis of relations expressed in texts. Contextual information includes negations, modalities and reported speech, which are surprisingly poorly represented in most schemes.

We first show why semantic relation annotation is difficult. We then present previous schemes that have been proposed in different frameworks, esp. the Message Understanding Conferences (MUC) (Grishman and Sundheim, 1996) and the Automatic Content Extraction (ACE) conferences, as well as their limitations. We then propose our own scheme and present two experiments showing that annotators using our scheme were able to quickly annotate a large number of sentences with a very high accuracy.

2 Why is Relation Annotation a Difficult Task?

We consider different issues related to semantic relation analysis for event detection. Note that we do not focus on the analysis of lexical relations themselves (e.g. synonymy, meronymy, hyponymy, etc.) since there has been a huge body of research on this topic so far (Cruse, 1986). We consider that lexical semantics is outside the scope of this study, even if this kind of knowledge plays a prominent role in relation analysis (and therefore, in various tasks like information extraction or question answering).

In our view, there are two main issues in relation annotation. The first one is a knowledge engineering problem, the second one a linguistic representation problem.

2.1 A Knowledge Engineering Problem

In most annotation schemes, one has to take a binary decision, *i.e.* whether to annotate or not the relation. There are of course some clear cases. For example, if one is interested in companies acquiring other companies, the following sentences should obviously be considered as positive examples:

- *Google has bought Irish company Green Parrot Pictures in an attempt to improve the quality of video uploaded to YouTube.*
- *Google Buys Mobile Ad Company for $750M*
- *Google buys YouTube for $1.65 billion*

However, most cases are not that clear. Since relations refer to semantic concepts and since those concepts can be difficult to grasp, some examples cannot be tagged accurately without a proper representation of the domain. Some examples are impossible to classify, since the text does not provide enough information to decide if the event (*the purchase*) has been completed or not:

- *Under the Note Purchase Agreement: (a) Dolphin Fund II acquired convertible notes of the Issuer in the aggregate principal amount of $988,900, which convertible notes were convertible, as of January 15, 2003 into 3,826,270 shares of Common Stock*

In this example, the text is complex, refers to domain specific concepts and does not even give the key to the annotator: it is not explicitly said if the result of the transaction means a transfer of the control of the company or not.

All these refer to knowledge engineering problems: most of the time, a good command of domain knowledge is necessary to be able to annotate accurately the different examples in the text. As seen above, this knowledge is not enough when some information is missing or when the text is underspecified.

2.2 A linguistic engineering problem

The linguistic side of the problem is of course not completely disconnected from the knowledge engineering point of view. Let's consider the following examples:

- *Rumors Swirling Around A Google Acquisition of Groupon...*
- *Is Google Buying Groupon For Several Billion Dollars?*

One can see that the first sentence does not refer to a pure fact since the main information is introduced by the phrase "Rumors Swirling Around". In the second example, it is the fact that information appears with a question mark that makes it uncertain.

More generally, relation annotation is inseparable from the analysis of hedge expressions. According to J. Watts (Watts, 2003), hedge expressions are "linguistic expressions which weaken the illocutionary force of a statement: by means of attitudinal predicates (*I think, I don't think, I mean*) or by means of adverbs such as *actually*, etc.". Modal auxiliaries (*may, would...*) should also be include in this list.

- *Google May Acquire Groupon for $6 Billion*
- *If Google would acquire Salesforce.com, it wouldn't be about CRM only.*

In the previous examples, modal auxiliaries make it clear that these sentences are not about facts but possibilities.

For some kinds of events, one can easily find speculations (*e.g.* rumors in the financial domain). Speculations can also use the negative form:

- *Google will NOT acquire Twitter in 2011.*

- *Why Google Will Not Acquire Twitter*

All these examples show that texts are not just about facts but include a lot of other phenomena (modals, negation, etc.) that make annotation a difficult task.

This is of course not new, and a lot of studies have tried to address some of these complex linguistic questions (*e.g.* analyzing the scope of modalities or negations). However, these questions are not directly addressed by most existing annotation schemes, especially the most popular ones.

3 Existing Schemes for Semantic Relation Annotation

Semantic relation analysis is a traditional task for the language understanding community. Despite the lack of generic resources (as seen in the introduction), a large number of works involve relation annotation. As a consequence, relation annotation has been identified as a separable and re-usable task from the Message Understanding Conferences on.

3.1 Early Work in Relation Annotation

Text understanding has been explored since the beginning of natural language processing, and involves since the beginning the recognition of semantic relations between textual entities.

During the 1970s, a number of applications tried to establish a link between texts and databases. This kind of analysis typically requires to be able to connect together different pieces of information. Ad hoc relations were defined and recognized in texts in order to fill databases and subsequently be able to access these databases with natural language queries (see for example the LUNAR system developed by Woods to access databases on materials collected on the moon (Woods, 1973)).

Semantic networks (e.g. conceptual graphs (Sowa and Way, 1986)) provided a framework to standardize the representation of this kind of information, but did not normalize the annotation itself.

3.2 The Message Understanding Conferences (MUC)

The Message Understanding Conferences refer to a series of evaluation campaigns organized by DARPA from 1987 to 1998 (MUC6, 1995; MUC7, 1998). The goal was for DARPA and other funding institutions to be able to track the progress of different strategies for information extraction (*i.e.* the extraction of structured knowledge from unstructured texts). We will not detail here the evolution of MUC during these 12 years, since good overviews are available elsewhere (Grishman and Sundheim, 1996).

What is interesting from our perspective is the fact that for MUC-6, in 1995, named entity recognition was recognized as an independent task. Three other tasks ("co-reference annotation", "template element" and "scenario template") were proposed for evaluation, and these were mainly based on the identification of relevant relations between named entities, and between named entities and their attributes.

Here, the evaluation was clearly task-oriented: a limited number of texts from the targeted domain were carefully selected for evaluation. Modifiers, negations and other hedge expressions were only marginally represented and not really integrated in the annotation framework. Most systems did not take these elements into account, with no major penalty. Of course, this kind of strategy can lead to major errors, which can be a serious problem when the system is used in the real world.

3.3 Automatic Content Extraction (ACE)

Automatic Content Extraction refers to a series of evaluation campaigns held between 2000 and 2008 and organized by the Linguistic Data Consortium (LDC). Contrary to what was done in the framework of MUC, the evaluation is not task-oriented but technology-oriented, in that it is supposed to provide general guidelines that are not limited to a given domain (Doddington et al., 2004; ACE, 2008b).

ACE considers for example issues related to modality (ACE, 2008b). A fact can be tagged as ASSERTED or as OTHER (all other cases). As we have seen in the previous section, there are far more than two cases to consider in order to be able to accurately tag texts. Moreover, the guidelines provide rather unclear rules like "If we think of the situations described by sentences as pertaining to possible descriptions of the world (or as 'possible worlds') then we can think of ASSERTED Relations as pertaining to situations in 'the real world', and we can think of OTHER Relations as pertaining to situations in 'some other world defined by counterfactual constraints elsewhere in the context'" (ACE, 2008a).

The authors give the following example: "*We are afraid Al-Qaeda terrorists will be in Baghdad*". Since "The presence of Al-Qaeda terrorists in Baghdad is a situation being described as holding in the counterfactual world defined by 'our' fears", the example should be consider as being ASSERTED. They also give an example that should not be considered as being ASSERTED: "*If the inspectors can get plane tickets today, then they will be in Baghdad on* Tuesday". This sentence is not ASSERTED because "the inspectors (they) are in Baghdad only in the worlds where they get plane tickets today" (ACE, 2008a).

So a fact is asserted when it is "interpreted relative to the 'Real' world" and not asserted (OTHER) when the fact "is taken to hold in a particular counterfactual world". Finally, "negatively defined relations (e.g. "*John is not in the house*") [should] not be annotated" following the ACE proposal.

In our view, there are several problems with this scheme:

1. there are more than two values to be considered. The distinction between ASSERTED and OTHER is not enough to get a fine grained description of relations in texts (for example, this annotation does not say if the event is completed or ongoing, if it is sure, probable or just possible) . Moreover, it seems important to annotate the source of the assertion when possible;

2. there is no reason to exclude negative events. Moreover, from an applicative point of view, this knowledge is often of paramount importance for the domain (*e.g.* knowing/speculating that Google will not buy Twitter in 2011 may have a major impact on investment people);

3. the notion of real world *vs* counterfactual world is not really operational for the task. It does not provide enough evidence for the annotator to make her decision.

Most recent frameworks do not seem to answer these issues, even for the "event detection" task; they often contain domain specific annotation (Aitken, 2002; Mcdonald et al., 2004; Jayram et al., 2006; Shen et al., 2007; Kim et al., 2008) or focus on a certain type of information (Morante and Daelemans, 2009). So we need to build on the ACE scheme in order to overcome some of its shortcomings.

4 A New Relation Annotation Scheme

Semantic relations correspond to a core event with most of time additional information related to the event. These additional pieces of information are most of the time encoded through negations, modalities and higher level clauses (for reported speech for example). Our contribution addresses these elements.

4.1 Basic Event Encoding

We consider that a semantic relation is part of the linguistic expression of an event. This relation is most of the time expressed by a predicate, either a verb (*Google buys YouTube*) or a noun (*the purchase of Youtube by Google...*). The predicate governs some arguments (*Google, Youtube*) that can be tagged more or less precisely (*arg1, arg2; agent, patient; buyer, target;* etc.). Linguistic descriptions of verb hierarchies provide an accurate basis for this kind of analysis (see Wordnet (Fellbaum, 1998) or Framenet (Fillmore et al., 2003), as detailed above). These hierarchies must be adapted with respect to the domain but they are anyway as far as it can be re-usable.

Existing frameworks like MUC or ACE provided precise guidelines for this kind of information. We build on these guidelines for our experiments.

4.2 Enunciative Modalities

The description of basic events must be completed in order to take into account the different issues we have described above (knowledge engineering as well as linguistic engineering issues). We consider three basic attributes directly associated with relations in order to express the degree of completeness of the event: COMPLETED, ONGOING, POSSIBLE.

- if the process is done and over, it is COMPLETED;
- if the process has begun is not yet accomplished, it is ONGOING;
- if the process has not begun, it is POSSIBLE.

Moreover, the event can be NEGATED (e.g. see *Google will NOT acquire Twitter in 2011*).

The event can also be reported directly or by different sources, which means we have to annotate the relation as being DIRECT (*Google Buys Mobile Ad Company for $750M*) or INDIRECT and, for the latter, we also have to annotate the SOURCE when possible (see for example "*Rumors Swirling Around A Google Acquisition of Groupon*" where the PROCESS is reported, therefore INDIRECT and the "*rumors*" are the source). Table 1 gives some examples along with their annotation.

More detailed annotation schemes are possible, especially to deal with different kinds of modalities (epistemic, deontic, etc.). We do not think it is appropriate to have a so fine grained description as these categories will be inappropriate for most language understanding applications. Note that this more fine grained categorization is not incompatible with our scheme. It just requires that some of the categories are refined.

5 Experiments

We present here a method to quickly extract potential relevant sentences from corpora using collocations. These sentences are then manually annotated in order to check the operability of our scheme.

Sentence	Annotation
Rumors Swirling Around A Google Acquisition of Groupon	POSSIBLE, INDIRECT, SOURCE='rumors'
Google will NOT acquire Twitter in 2011	POSSIBLE, DIRECT, NEGATED
Google Buys Mobile Ad Company for $750M	COMPLETED, DIRECT
Is Google Buying Groupon For Several Billion Dollars?	POSSIBLE, DIRECT
Google announced on Friday that it has entered into an agreement to acquire Widevine	ONGOING, INDIRECT, SOURCE='Google'

Table 1: English examples with annotations.

5.1 Extracting Potentially Relevant Sentences from Corpora

The extraction of relevant sentences from corpora is a long and labour intensive task. Most of the time, one must read a large number of texts in order to find only a few relevant sentences. This is both inefficient and time-consuming.

In order to reduce the time spent on this step, we have developed a series of tools allowing one to retrieve relevant documents and then identify potentially relevant sentences. Our approach is simple and easy to reproduce: the idea is to use collocations as a basis for filtering sentences from corpora. The approach can be compared to previous experiments described for example by Riloff with the AutoSlog system (Riloff, 1993). Information extraction patterns involve arguments that can be used to find relevant predicates and, in turn, relevant predicates can be used to find relevant arguments. The same strategy can be used to identify relevant sentences.

We reproduced this idea by first fixing named entity types. Sentences containing these types are then retrieved if named entities appear within a certain distance (in most experiments we used a sliding window with a distance inferior to 10 between the two named entities) (Freitag, 1998). This technique makes it possible to retrieve a certain number of sentences (the method can be parametrized to adjust the number of retrieved sentences). User studies (made with a representative sample of potential end-users who are not trained linguists) have proven that experts can describe the kind of relations they are looking for and the kind of entities these relations involve. They are practically able to use the tools we have developed and are able to perform their analysis a lot quicker with this approach.

For example, in the case of companies buying other companies, only sentences that contain at least two company names are extracted. This of course eliminates relevant sentences containing less than two company names (esp. sentences containing anaphora) but, after manual inspection, we assume we get a representative set of sentences anyway, since anaphora do not fundamentally change the deep semantic structure. So, even if anaphora are not taken into consideration here, they can be analyzed and integrated in subsequent steps without any problem.

For the company buyout task, the system provided more than 1000 potentially relevant sentences in a few minutes (extracted from a 2.9 million word corpus). It then took less than one hour for an expert to manually check these sentences and discard non relevant ones. More than 50% of the extracted sentences were relevant but this represents less than 5% of the corpus (and always less than 10% of the corpus, even with other domains and relations). This proves that the approach is both efficient and accurate.

5.2 Corpus annotation

Our experiment is based on the previous set of sentences extracted from different sources, mainly from financial newswires and newspapers (see table 2 for some examples). A reduced experiment has been done on English texts (see examples in table 1 and in section 2) but a larger experiment has been done on French, using texts from the same domain. This ensures that our annotation scheme is largely language independent.

This corpus is automatically analyzed using a state-of-the art named entity tagger[2]. Sentences containing two company names are extracted. As a result, one hundred sentences are extracted and these sentences are annotated according to the above scheme by two human annotators.

5.3 Inter-annotator agreement

Interannotator agreement is relatively straightforward to calculate, although there are dependencies between tags (e.g. SOURCE is relevant only in case of INDIRECT speech). For each sentence, we compare the set of tags added by annotator A and by annotator B. If the tags do not fully correspond,

[2]Tha ARISEM named entity recognizer.

Twitter dément la rumeur de rachat par Apple	NEGATED, INDIRECT, SOURCE='rumeur'
Areva a racheté pour 1,62 milliard d'euros la part de Siemens dans la co-entreprise Areva NP, ouvrant la voie à un rapprochement entre Siemens et le russe Rosatom, selon le journal allemand Die Welt, qui cite les porte-parole des deux groupes, s'exprimant dans un document qui sera publié lundi.	COMPLETED, INDIRECT, SOURCE='les porte-parole des deux groupes'
Selon Apple4us, un des plus gros blogs chinois au sujet d'Apple, la firme de Cupertino aurait racheté EditGrid, un service de tableurs en ligne basé à Hong Kong, pour une somme comprise entre 10 et 30 millions de dollars.	COMPLETED, INDIRECT, SOURCE='Apple4us'
Amazon aurait racheté la jeune pousse américaine Touchco basée à New York pour développer son offre de lecteurs de livres numériques Kindle.	POSSIBLE, DIRECT
Le possible rachat du Parisien-Aujourd'hui en France par le groupe Dassault inquiète.	POSSIBLE, DIRECT
La société Acom27 dirigée par Monsieur et Madame Garnot n'a absolument pas été rachetée par les éts Cochet.	NEGATED, DIRECT

Table 2: French examples used for evaluation.

we consider that there is a disagreement. Dependencies between tags are not taken into account. This is not a problem as it penalizes the evaluation, rather that the other way round (i.e. results are lower than they would be if we were taking into account these dependencies).

We then computed Cohen's kappa (Cohen, 1960) and obtained 0.94, which means a near perfect agreement, according to the usual interpretation of Cohen's kappa results (Fleiss, 1981). This proves that our method is both efficient and accurate.

Some sentences are hard to classify between DIRECT and INDIRECT, especially when the event is negated, for example when a company denies rumors (*Twitter dément la rumeur de rachat par Apple — Twitter denies the rumor of a buyout by Apple*). In this case, the experts agreed on NEGATED and INDIRECT. The cases of disagreement are rare and affect quite specific sentences (with negation or with a complex structure); they can all be solved after discussion between domain experts.

However, this scheme does not cover all possible cases and should be extended for specific needs. Since it is open (and built upon existing schemes) it can easily be extended to cover new cases and new applications.

6 Conclusion

In this paper, we have presented an annotation scheme that is more precise that what has been proposed for the MUC and the ACE conferences. Our scheme allows one to quickly annotate relations in texts without sacrificing accuracy.

We have proven this result through an experiment on texts from the financial domain, both in English and in French. Additionally, we have shown that it is possible to quickly retrieve relevant examples just by accessing the corpus with key collocations.

The perspectives are twofold. First, we need to annotate a larger number of texts from different domains to ensure the utility of our scheme. Second, we need to explore different specializations of this scheme, as different needs will probably be expressed in the future to get a more precise annotation, concerning modalities for example.

References

ACE. 2008a. *ACE (Automatic Content Extraction) English Annotation Guidelines for Relations.* Linguistic Data Consortium, Univ. Pennsylvania.

ACE. 2008b. Automatic Content Extraction 2008 Evaluation Plan (ACE08) — Assessment of Detection and Recognition of Entities and Relations Within and Across Documents. In *Proceedings of the Automatic Content Extraction conference*, Gaithersburg.

J. Aitken. 2002. Learning information extraction rules : An inductive logic programming approach. In *15th European Conference on Artificial Intelligence*, Lyon.

Douglas Appelt and David Martin. 1999. Named Entity Extraction from Speech: Approach and Results Using the TextPro System. In *Proceedings of the DARPA Broadcast News Workshop*, pages 51–54, Herndon.

Lynn Carlson, Daniel Marcu, and Mary Ellen Okurowski. 2002. Building a discourse-tagged corpus in the framework of rhetorical structure theory. In Jan van Kuppevelt and Ronnie Smith, editors, *Current Directions in Discourse and Dialogue*. Kluwer Academic Publishers.

Jacob Cohen. 1960. A coefficient of agreement for nominal scales. *Educational and Psychological Measurement*, 20(1):37–46.

M. Collins and Y. Singer. 1999. Unsupervised models for named entity classification. In *Proceedings of Conf. on Empirical Methods in Natural Language Processing*, Univ. of Maryland.

D.A. Cruse. 1986. *Lexical semantics*. Cambridge University Press, Cambridge.

G. Doddington, A. Mitchell, M. Przybocki, L. Ramshaw, S. Strassel, and R Weischedel. 2004. Automatic Content Extraction (ACE) Program. In *Proceedings of 4th International Conference on Language Resources and Evaluation (LREC)*, pages 837–840, Lisbon.

Chritiane Fellbaum, editor. 1998. *WordNet: An Electronic Lexical Database*. MIT Press, Cambridge, MA.

Charles J. Fillmore, Christopher Johnson, and Miriam Petruck. 2003. Background to Framenet. *International Journal of Lexicography*, 16.3: 235–250.

Joseph L. Fleiss. 1981. *Statistical methods for rates and proportions*. John Wiley, New York.

Dayne Freitag. 1998. Multistrategy learning for information extraction. In *Proceedings of International Conference on Machine Learning (ICML)*, Madison.

Ralph Grishman and Beth Sundheim. 1996. Message understanding conference 6 – A brief history. In *Proceedings of the International Conference on Computational Linguistics (COLING)*, pages 466–471, Copenhagen.

T.S. Jayram, R. Krishnamurthy, S. Raghavan, S. Vaithyanathan, and H. Zhu. 2006. Avatar information extraction system. *IEEE Data Engineering Bulletin*.

Daniel Jurafsky and James H. Martin. 2009. *Speech and Language Processing: An Introduction to Natural Language Processing, Speech Recognition, and Computational Linguistics*. Prentice-Hall.

Jin-Dong Kim, Tomoko Ohta, and Jun'ichi Tsujii. 2008. Corpus annotation for mining biomedical events from literature. *BMC Bioinformatics*, 10(9).

Daniel M. Mcdonald, Hsinchun Chen, Hua Su, and Byron B. Marshall. 2004. Extracting gene pathway relations using a hybrid grammar: the arizona relation parser. *Bioinformatics*, 20:3370–3378.

Roser Morante and Walter Daelemans. 2009. Learning the scope of hedge cues in biomedical texts. *Proceedings of the Workshop on BioNLP BioNLP 09*, page 28.

MUC6. 1995. Proceedings of the 6th Message Understanding Conference.

MUC7. 1998. Proceedings of the 7th Message Understanding Conference.

Massimo Poesio and Ron Artstein. 2008. Anaphoric Annotation in the ARRAU Corpus. In *Proceedings of the International Conference on Language Resources and Evaluation (LREC)*, Lisbon.

Ellen Riloff. 1993. Automatically Constructing a Dictionary for Information Extraction Tasks. In *Proceedings of AAAI 1993 (Association for the Advancement of Artificial Intelligence)*, Washington.

Satoshi Sekine, Kiyoshi Sudo, and Chikashi Nobata. 2002. Extended Named Entity Hierarchy. In *Proceedings of the Third International Conference on Language Resources and Evaluation (LREC)*, pages 1818–1824, Las Palmas.

Warren Shen, AnHai Doan, Jeffrey F. Naughton, and Raghu Ramakrishnan. 2007. Declarative information extraction using datalog with embedded extraction predicates. In *Proceedings of the 33rd international conference on Very large data bases*, VLDB '07, pages 1033–1044. VLDB Endowment.

John F. Sowa and Eileen C. Way. 1986. Implementing a semantic interpreter using conceptual graphs. *IBM Journal of Research and Development*, 30(1):57–69.

Richard J. Watts. 2003. *Politeness*. Cambridge university Press, Cambridge.

W. A. Woods. 1973. Progress in natural language understanding: an application to lunar geology. In *Proceedings of the June 4-8, 1973, national computer conference and exposition*, AFIPS '73, pages 441–450, New York, NY, USA. ACM.

Prototypical Opinion Holders: What We can Learn from *Experts* and *Analysts*

Michael Wiegand and **Dietrich Klakow**
Spoken Language Systems
Saarland University
D-66123 Saarbrücken, Germany
{Michael.Wiegand|Dietrich.Klakow}@lsv.uni-saarland.de

Abstract

In order to automatically extract opinion holders, we propose to harness the contexts of prototypical opinion holders, i.e. common nouns, such as *experts* or *analysts*, that describe particular groups of people whose profession or occupation is to form and express opinions towards specific items. We assess their effectiveness in supervised learning where these contexts are regarded as labeled training data and in rule-based classification which uses predicates that frequently co-occur with mentions of the prototypical opinion holders. Finally, we also examine in how far knowledge gained from these contexts can compensate the lack of large amounts of labeled training data in supervised learning by considering various amounts of actually labeled training sets.

1 Introduction

Building an opinion holder (OH) extraction system on the basis of supervised classifiers requires large amounts of labeled training data which are expensive to obtain. Therefore, alternative methods requiring less human effort are required. Such methods would be particularly valuable for languages other than English as for most other languages sentiment resources are fairly sparse.

In this paper, we propose to leverage contextual information from prototypical opinion holders (protoOHs), such as *experts* or *analysts*. We define prototypical opinion holders as common nouns denoting particular groups of people whose profession or occupation is to form and express opinions towards specific items. Mentions of these nouns are disproportionately often OHs:

1. ***Experts*** agree it generally is a good idea to follow the manufacturers' age recommendations.
2. Shares of Lotus Development Corp. dropped sharply after ***analysts*** expressed concern about their business.

Since protoOHs are common nouns they should occur sufficiently often in a large text corpus in order to gain knowledge for OH extraction. We examine different ways of harnessing mentions of protoOHs for OH extraction. We compare their usage as labeled training data for supervised learning with a rule-based classifier that relies on a lexicon of predictive predicates that have been extracted from the contexts of protoOHs. Moreover, we investigate in how far the knowledge gained from these contexts can compensate the lack of large amounts of actually labeled training data in supervised classification by considering various amounts of labeled training sets.

2 Related Work

There has been much research on supervised learning for OH extraction. Choi et al. (2005) explore OH extraction using CRFs with several manually defined linguistic features and automatically learnt surface patterns. The linguistic features focus on named-entity information and syntactic relations to opinion words. Kim and Hovy (2006) and Bethard et al. (2004) examine the usefulness of semantic roles provided by FrameNet[1] for both OH and opinion target extraction. More recently, Wiegand and Klakow (2010) explored convolution kernels for OH extraction and found that tree kernels outperform all other kernel types. In (Johansson and Moschitti, 2010), a re-ranking approach modeling complex relations between multiple opinions in a sentence is presented.
Rule-based OH extraction heavily relies on lexical cues. Bloom et al. (2007), for example, use a list of manually compiled communication verbs.

[1] framenet.icsi.berkeley.edu

3 Data

As a large unlabeled (training) corpus, we chose the North American News Text Corpus. As a labeled (test) corpus, we use the MPQA corpus.[2] We use the definition of OHs as described in (Wiegand and Klakow, 2010). The instance space are all noun phrases (NP) in that corpus.

4 Method

In this paper, we propose to leverage contextual information from prototypical opinion holders (protoOHs) by which we mean common nouns denoting particular groups of people whose profession or occupation it is to form and express opinions towards specific items. The set of protoOHs that we use are listed in Table 1. It has been created ad-hoc. We neither claim completeness nor have made any attempts to tune it to our data.

Though mentions of protoOHs are likely to present OHs, not every mention is an OH:

3. Canada offered to make some civilian *experts* available.

We try to solve this problem by exclusively looking at contexts in which the protoOH is an *agent* of some predicate. Bethard et al. (2004) state that 90% of the OHs are realized as agents on their dataset. This heuristic would exclude Sentence 3 as *some civilian experts* should be considered the *patient* of *make available* rather than its agent.

We use grammatical dependencies from a syntactic parser rather than the output of a semantic parser for the detection of agents as in our initial experiments with semantic parsers the detection of agents of predicate adjectives and nouns was deemed less reliable. The grammatical dependency relations that we consider implying an agent are illustrated in the left half of Table 2.

We consider two different methods for extracting an OH from the contexts of protoOHs: supervised learning and rule-based classification.

4.1 Supervised Learning

The simplest way of using the contexts of agentive protoOHs is by using supervised learning. This means that on our unlabeled training corpus we consider each NP with the head being an agentive protoOH as a positive data instance and all the remaining NPs occurring in those sentences as negative instances. With this definition we train a supervised classifier based on *convolution kernels* (Collins and Duffy, 2001) as this method has been shown to be quite effective for OH extraction (Wiegand and Klakow, 2010). Convolution kernels derive features automatically from complex discrete structures, such as syntactic parse trees or part-of-speech sequences, that are directly provided to the learner. Thus a classifier can be built without the taking the burden of implementing an explicit feature extraction. We chose the best performing set of tree kernels (Collins and Duffy, 2001; Moschitti, 2006) from that work. It comprises two tree kernels based on constituency parse trees and a tree kernel based on semantic role trees. Apart from a set of sequence kernels (Taylor and Christianini, 2004), this method also largely outperforms a traditional vector kernel using a set of features that were found predictive in previous work. We exclude sequence and vector kernels in this work not only for reasons of simplicity but also since their addition to tree kernels only results in a marginal improvement. Moreover, the features in the vector kernel heavily rely on task-specific resources, e.g. a sentiment lexicon, which are deliberately avoided in our low-resource classifier as our method should be applicable to any language (and for many languages sentiment resources are either sparse or do not exist at all).

In addition to Wiegand and Klakow (2010), we have to discard the content of candidate NPs (e.g. the candidate opinion holder NP $[NP_{Cand}[NNS$ *advocates*$]]$ is reduced to $[NP_{Cand}]$), the reason for this being that in our automatically generated training set, OHs will always be protoOHs. Retaining them in the training data would cause the learner to develop a detrimental bias towards these nouns (our resulting classifier should detect any OH and not only protoOHs).

4.2 Rule-based Classifier

Instead of training a supervised classifier, we can also construct a rule-based classifier on the basis of the agentive protoOHs. The classifier is built on the insight that the most predictive cues for OH extraction are predicates (Wiegand and Klakow,

[2]www.cs.pitt.edu/mpqa/databaserelease

advocate, agitator, analyst, censor, consultant, critic, defender, demonstrator, examiner, expert, inspector, marketer, observer, opponent, optimist, pessimist, proponent, referee, respondent, reviewer, supporter, surveyor

Table 1: ProtoOHs considered in the experiments.

Learning/Extraction Phase		Rule-Based Classification	
Pattern	Example	Pattern	Example
protoOH <NSUBJ> verb	*Experts* criticized$_{PRED_V}$ the proposal.	NP <NSUBJ> extracted verb	*Clinton* criticized$_{PRED_V}$ Chavez.
protoOH <NSUBJ> adj	*Experts* are critical$_{PRED_A}$ of the proposal.	NP <NSUBJ> extracted adj	*Clinton* is critical$_{PRED_A}$ of Chavez.
protoOH <by-OBJ> verb	The proposal was criticized$_{PRED_V}$ by *experts*.	NP <by-OBJ> extracted verb	Chavez was criticized$_{PRED_V}$ by *Clinton*.
protoOH <by-OBJ> noun	They faced criticism$_{PRED_N}$ by *experts*.	NP <by-OBJ> extracted noun	Chavez ignored the criticism$_{PRED_N}$ by *Clinton*.
protoOH <POSS> noun	The *experts'* criticism$_{PRED_N}$ ...	NP <POSS> extracted noun	Chavez ignored *Clinton*'s criticism$_{PRED_N}$.

Table 2: Agentive patterns for finding predictive predicates (left half) and for classification (right half).

2010). We, therefore, mine the contexts of agentive protoOHs (left half of Table 2) for discriminant predicates (i.e. verbs, nouns, and adjectives). That is, we rank every predicate according to its correlation, i.e. we use *Pointwise Mutual Information*, of having agentive protoOHs as an argument. The highly ranked predicates are used as predictive cues. The resulting rule-based classifier always classifies an NP as an OH if its head is an agent of a highly ranked discriminative predicate (as illustrated in the right half of Table 2).

The supervised kernel-based classifier from §4.1 learns from a rich set of features. In a previous study on reverse engineering making implicit features within convolution kernels visible (Pighin and Moschitti, 2009), it has been shown that the learnt features are usually fairly small subtrees. There are plenty of structures which just contain one or two leaf nodes, i.e. sparse lexical information, coupled with some further structural nodes from the parse tree. These structures are fairly similar to low-level features, such as bag of words or bag of ngrams, in the sense that they are weak predictors and that there are plenty of them. For such types of features, it has been shown in both subjectivity detection (Lambov et al., 2009) and polarity classification (Andreevskaia and Bergler, 2008) that they generalize poorly across different domains. On the other hand, very few high-level features describing the presence of certain semantic classes or opinion words perform consistently well across different domains. These features can either be incorporated within a supervised learner (Lambov et al., 2009) or a lexicon-based rule-based classifier (Andreevskaia and Bergler, 2008). We assume that our rule-based classifier based on discriminant predicates (they can also be considered as some kind of semantic class) used in combination with very common grammatical relations will have a similar impact as those high-level features used in the related tasks mentioned above. Domain-independence is also an important issue in our setting, since our training and test data originate from two different corpora (which can be considered two different domains).

4.2.1 Self-training

A shortcoming of the rule-based classifier is that it incorporates no (or hardly any) domain knowledge. In other related sentiment classification tasks, i.e. subjectivity detection and polarity classification, it has been shown that by applying self-training, i.e. learning a model with a supervised classifier trained on low-level features (usually bag of words) using the domain-specific instances labeled by a rule-based classifier, more in-domain knowledge can be captured. Thus, one can outperform the rule-based classifier (Wiebe and Riloff, 2005; Tan et al., 2008).

Assuming that the same can be achieved in OH extraction, we train a classifier with convolution kernels (=low level features) on the output of the rule-based classifier run on our target corpus. The set of labeled data instances is derived from the sentences of the MPQA corpus in which the rule-based classifier predicts at least one OH, i.e. the instances the classifier labels as OHs are used as positive instances while the remaining NPs are labeled as negative. Unlike §4.1 we do not discard the content of the candidate NPs. In these labeled training data, OHs are not restricted to protoOHs. We, therefore, assume that among the domain-specific features the supervised classifier may learn could be useful prior weights towards some of these domain-specific NPs as to whether they might be an OH or not.

4.2.2 Generalization with Clustering and Knowledge Basis

We also examine in how far the coverage of the discriminant predicates can be increased with the usage of clustering. Turian et al. (2010) have shown that in semi-supervised learning for named-entity recognition, i.e. a task which bears some resemblance to the present task, features referring to the clusters corresponding to groups of specific words with similar properties (induced in an unsupervised manner) help to improve performance.

In the context of our rule-based classifier, we augment the set of discriminant predicates by all words which are also contained in the cluster associated with these discriminant predicates. Hopefully, due to the strong similarity among the words within the same cluster, the additional words will have a similar predictiveness as the discriminant predicates. Unlike our extraction phase for OH extraction in which only the correlation between predicates and protoOHs are considered (Table 2), we may find additional predicates as the clustering is induced from completely unrestricted text.

The extension of discriminant predicates can also be done by taking into account manually built general-purpose lexical resources, such as WordNet.[3] One simply adds the entire set of synonyms of each of the predicates.

4.3 Incorporation into Supervised Classifiers with Actually Labeled Data

We also want to investigate the effectiveness of the knowledge from our rule-based classifier that has been learned on the unlabeled corpus (§4.2) in supervised learning using actually labeled training data from our target corpus, i.e. the MPQA corpus. In particular, we will examine in how far this knowledge (when used as a feature in supervised learning) can compensate the lack of a sufficiently large labeled training set. For that experiment the labeled corpus, i.e. MPQA corpus, will be split into a training set and a test set.

Again, we use the supervised learner based on tree kernels (§4.1). We also augment the tree kernels themselves with additional information by following Wiegand and Klakow (2010) who add for each word that belongs to a predictive semantic class another node that directly dominates the pertaining leaf node and assign it a label denoting that class. While Wiegand and Klakow (2010) made use of manually built lexicons, we use our predictive predicates extracted from contexts of protoOHs. For instance, if *doubt* is such a predicate, we would replace the subtree $[VBP\ doubt]$ by $[VBP\ [PRED_{OH}\ doubt]]$. Moreover, we devise a simple vector kernel incorporating the prediction of the rule-based classifier. All kernels are combined by plain summation.

5 Experiments

The documents were parsed using the Stanford Parser.[4] Semantic roles were obtained by using the parser by Zhang et al. (2008).

5.1 Supervised Learning

All experiments using convolution kernels were done with the *SVM-Light-TK* toolkit.[5] We test two versions of the supervised classifier. The first considers any mention of a protoOH as an OH, while the second is restricted to only those mentions of a protoOH which are an agent of some predicate. We also experimented with different amounts of (pseudo-)labeled training data from our unlabeled corpus varying from 12500 to 150000 instances. We found that from 25000 instances onwards the classifier does not notably improve when further training data are added. The results of the classifier (using 150000 data instances) are listed in Table 3. The restriction of protoOHs to agents increases performance as expected (see §4).

5.2 The Different Rule-based Classifiers

In order to build a rule-based classifier, we first need to determine how many of the ranked predicates are to be used. This process is done separately for verbs, nouns, and adjectives. For verbs, F-Score reaches its maximum at approximately 250 which is the value we chose in our subsequent experiments. In a similar fashion, we determined 100 for both nouns and adjectives.

Table 4 lists the most highly ranked verbs that are extracted.[6] As an indication of the intrinsic

[3] wordnet.princeton.edu

[4] nlp.stanford.edu/software/lex-parser.shtml

[5] disi.unitn.it/moschitti

[6] The ranked predicates are available at: www.lsv.uni-saarland.de/ranlp/data.tgz

Classifier	Prec	Rec	F1	Prec	Rec	F1
Supervised	*all contexts*			*agentive contexts*		
	27.62	15.36	19.75	41.45	28.75	33.95
Rule-based	*without heuristics*			*with heuristics*		
AL	**40.18**	33.32	36.43	46.04	30.94	37.00
SL	35.21	34.90	35.05	**49.64**	31.66	38.66
AL+SL	35.00	55.36	42.89	45.16	50.65	47.75
V250	39.75	51.24	44.77	46.25	46.94	46.60
V250+A100	39.88	53.43	45.67	46.56	48.89	47.70
V250+N100	39.18	54.08	45.44	45.40	49.62	47.42
V250+A100 +N100	39.31	**55.93**	**46.17**	45.71	**51.57**	**48.47**

Table 3: Performance of the different classifiers.

say†	see†	wonder*	recommend$^{\dagger *}$
expect*	question	complain$^{\dagger *}$	view$^{\dagger *}$
believe$^{\dagger *}$	contend*	consider*	concede*
predict*	speculate*	accuse*	attribute
agree*	point	praise$^{\dagger *}$	acknowledge*
argue*	fear$^{\dagger *}$	describe†	testify
call	worry*	claim$^{\dagger *}$	hope*
estimate	charge	tell	disagree*
warn†	forecast	change	conclude
note†	find†	cite†	look*
think$^{\dagger *}$	doubt*	anticipate	write
suggest$^{\dagger *}$	caution†	try*	criticize*

Table 4: List of verbs most highly correlating with protoOHs; †: included in AL; *: included in SL.

quality of the extracted words, we mark the words which can also be found in task-specific resources, i.e. communication verbs from the Appraisal Lexicon (AL) (Bloom et al., 2007) and opinion words from the Subjectivity Lexicon (SL) (Wilson et al., 2005). Both resources have been found predictive for OH extraction (Bloom et al., 2007; Wiegand and Klakow, 2010).

Table 3 (lower part) shows the performance of the rule-based classifiers based on protoOHs using different parts of speech. As hard baselines, the table also shows other rule-based classifiers using the same dependency relations as our rule-based classifier (see Table 2) but employing different predicates. As lexical resources for these predicates, we again use AL and SL. The table also compares two different versions of the rule-based classifier being the classifier as presented in §4.2 (left half of Table 3) and a classifier additionally incorporating the two **heuristics** (right half):

- If the candidate NP follows *according to*, then it is labeled as an OH.
- The candidate NP can only be an OH if it represents a person or a group of persons.

These are commonly accepted heuristics which have already been used in previous work as features (Choi et al., 2005; Wiegand and Klakow, 2010). The latter rule requires the output of a named-entity recognizer[7] for checking proper nouns and WordNet for common nouns.

As far as the classifier built with the help of protoOHs is concerned, adding highly ranked adjectives and nouns consistently improves the performance (mostly recall) when added to the set of highly ranked verbs. The heuristics further improve the rule-based classifier which is achieved by notably increasing precision.

None of the baselines is as robust as the best rule-based classifier using protoOHs (i.e. V250+A100+N100). Considering our discussion in §4.2, it comes as no surprise that the best (pseudo-)supervised classifier does not perform as well as our best rule-based classifier (induced by protoOHs). The fact that, in addition to that, our proposed method also largely outperforms the rule-based classifier relying on both AL and SL when no heuristics are used and is still slightly better when they are incorporated supports the effectiveness of our method.

5.2.1 Performance of Subsets of ProtoOHs

In the previous section, we evaluated predicates often co-occurring with the entire set of protoOHs (Table 1). Therefore, we should also check how individual protoOHs or special subsets perform in order to find out whether the simple approach of considering the entire set is the optimal setting. For these experiments we use the configuration: V250+N100+A100 without heuristics.

We found that the performance of individual protoOHs varies and that the performance cannot be fully ascribed to the frequency of a protoOH with agentive contexts. For example, though *proponent* and *demonstrator* occur similarly often with those contexts, we obtain an F-Score of 44.75 when we use the predicates from the context of the former while we only obtain an F-Score of 32.70 when we consider the predicates of the latter.

We also checked whether it would be more effective to use only a subset of protoOHs and compared the performance produced by the five best protoOHs, the five most frequent protoOHs, and

[7]We use the Stanford tagger: `nlp.stanford.edu/software/CRF-NER.shtml`

	without heuristics			*with heuristics*		
Type	Prec	Rec	F1	Prec	Rec	F1
Baseline	**39.31**	55.93	46.17	**45.71**	51.57	48.47
+Clus	35.87	63.23	45.78	44.17	58.01	50.15
+WN	37.52	59.46	46.01	44.35	54.42	48.87
+SelfTr	39.14	62.71	**48.20**	44.38	59.61	50.88

Table 5: Performance of extended rule-based classifiers.

the entire set of protoOHs. The performance of the different subsets is very similar (i.e. 46.44, 46.28, and 46.17), so we may conclude that the configuration that we proposed, namely to consider all protoOHs, is more or less the optimal configuration for this method.

5.2.2 Self-training and Generalization

Table 5 shows the performance of our method when extended by either self-training (SelfTr) or generalization. For generalization by clustering (Clus), we chose Brown clustering (Brown et al., 1992) which is the best performing algorithm in (Turian et al., 2010). The clusters are induced on our unlabeled corpus (see §3). We induced 1000 clusters (optimal size). For the knowledge-based generalization (WN), we used synonyms from WordNet 3. For both Clus and WN, we display the results extending only the most highly ranked V100+N50+A50 since it provided notably better results than extending all predicates, i.e. V250+N100+A100 (our baseline). The table shows that only self-training consistently improves the results. The impact of generalization is less advantageous since by increasing recall precision drops more dramatically. Only Clus in conjunction with the heuristics manages to preserve sufficient precision.

5.3 Incorporating Knowledge from ProtoOHs into Supervised Learning

As a maximum amount of labeled training data we chose 60000 instances (i.e. NPs) which is even a bit more than used in (Wiegand and Klakow, 2010). In addition, we also test 1%, 5%, 10%, 25% and 50% of the training set. From the remaining data instances, we use 25000 instances as test data. In order to deliver generalizing results, we randomly sample the training and test partitions five times and report the averaged results.

We compare four different classifiers, a plain classifier using only the convolution kernel configuration from previous experiments (TKPlain), the augmented convolution kernels (TKAug) where additional nodes are added indicating the presence of an OH predicate (§4.3), the augmented convolution kernels with the vector kernel encoding the prediction of the best rule-based classifier (induced by protoOHs) without heuristics (TKAug+VK) and the classifier incorporating those heuristics (TKAug+VK[heur]). Instead of just using one feature encoding the overall prediction we use several binary features representing the occurrence of the individual groups of predicates (i.e. verbs, nouns, or adjectives) and prediction types (direct predicate or predicate from cluster extension). We also include the prediction of the self-trained classifier. The performance of these different classifiers is listed in Table 6. Recall from §4.1 that we want to examine cases in which no task-specific resources and no or few labeled training data are available. This is why the different classifiers presented should primarily be compared to our own baseline (TKPlain) and not the numbers presented in previous work as they always use the maximal size of labeled training data and additionally task-specific resources (e.g. sentiment lexicons).

The results show that using the information extracted from the unlabeled data can be usefully combined with the labeled training data. Tree augmentation causes both precision and recall to rise. This observation is consistent with (Wiegand and Klakow, 2010) where, however, AL and SL are considered for augmentation. When the vector kernel with the prediction of the rule-based classifier is also included, precision drops slightly but recall is notably boosted resulting in an even more increased F-Score. The results also show that for the setting that we have in focus, i.e. using only few labeled training data, our proposed method is particularly useful. For example, when TKPlain is as good as the best classifier exclusively built from unlabeled data (50.88% in Table 5), i.e. at 10%, there is a very notable increase in F-Score when the additional knowledge is added, i.e. the F-Score of TKAug+VK[heur] is increased by approx. 4% points. The degree of improvement towards TKPlain decreases the more labeled training data are used. However, when 100% of the labeled data are used, all of the other classifiers using additional information still outperform TKPlain.[8]

[8]The improvement is statistically significant using pair-

	TKPlain *(Baseline)*			TKAug			TKAug + VK			TKAug + VK[heur]		
Training Size	**Prec**	**Rec**	**F1**	**Prec**	**Rec**	**F1**	**Prec**	**Rec**	**F1**	**Prec**	**Rec**	**F1**
600 (1%)	52.14	31.49	38.63	**54.18**	34.44	41.52	49.60	**46.74**	47.38	51.47	46.63	**48.20**
3000 (5%)	51.69	43.80	47.39	**53.17**	45.92	49.27	50.68	54.48	52.50	51.40	**56.84**	**53.97**
6000 (10%)	53.31	50.39	51.78	**54.22**	51.91	52.99	51.13	58.33	54.46	52.14	**59.55**	**55.57**
15000 (25%)	54.75	57.96	56.31	**55.52**	59.08	57.24	52.96	63.76	57.86	53.02	**64.46**	**58.18**
30000 (50%)	55.14	62.69	58.66	**55.82**	64.06	59.65	53.40	66.89	59.38	53.02	**67.75**	**59.91**
60000 (100%)	55.94	66.80	60.88	**56.68**	68.56	**62.05**	54.60	70.30	61.46	54.92	**71.30**	62.04

Table 6: Performance of supervised classifiers incorporating the prediction of the rule-based classifier.

6 Conclusion

We proposed to harness contextual information from prototypical opinion holders for opinion holder extraction. We showed that mentions of such nouns when they are agents of a predicate are a useful source for automatically building a rule-based classifier. The resulting classifier performs at least as well as classifiers depending on task-specific lexical resources and can also be extended by self-training. We also demonstrated that this knowledge can be incorporated into supervised classifiers and thus improve performance, in particular, if only few labeled training data are used.

Acknowledgements

This work was funded by the German Federal Ministry of Education and Research (Software-Cluster) under grant no. "01IC10S01" and the Cluster of Excellence for Multimodal Computing and Interaction. The authors thank Alessandro Moschitti, Josef Ruppenhofer, Ines Rehbein and Yi Zhang for their technical support and interesting discussions.

References

A. Andreevskaia and S. Bergler. 2008. When Specialists and Generalists Work Together: Overcoming Domain Dependence in Sentiment Tagging. In *ACL/HLT*.

S. Bethard, H. Yu, A. Thornton, V. Hatzivassiloglou, and D. Jurafsky. 2004. Extracting Opinion Propositions and Opinion Holders using Syntactic and Lexical Cues. In *Computing Attitude and Affect in Text: Theory and Applications*.

K. Bloom, S. Stein, and S. Argamon. 2007. Appraisal Extraction for News Opinion Analysis at NTCIR-6. In *NTCIR-6*.

P. Brown, P. deSouza, R. Mercer, V. Della Pietra, and J. Lai. 1992. Class-based n-gram models of natural language. *Computational Linguistics*, 18.

wise t-test, where $p < 0.05$.

Y. Choi, C. Cardie, E. Riloff, and S. Patwardhan. 2005. Identifying Sources of Opinions with Conditional Random Fields and Extraction Patterns. In *HLT/EMNLP*.

M. Collins and N. Duffy. 2001. Convolution Kernels for Natural Language. In *NIPS*.

R. Johansson and A. Moschitti. 2010. Reranking Models in Fine-grained Opinion Analysis. In *COLING*.

S. Kim and E. Hovy. 2006. Extracting Opinions, Opinion Holders, and Topics Expressed in Online News Media Text. In *ACL Workshop on Sentiment and Subjectivity in Text*.

D. Lambov, G. Dias, and V. Noncheva. 2009. Sentiment Classification across Domains. In *EPIA*.

A. Moschitti. 2006. Making Tree Kernels Practical for Natural Language Learning. In *EACL*.

D. Pighin and A. Moschitti. 2009. Reverse Engineering of Tree Kernel Feature Spaces. In *EMNLP*.

S. Tan, Y. Wang, and X. Cheng. 2008. Combining Learn-based and Lexicon-based Techniques for Sentiment Detection without using Labeled Examples. In *SIGIR*.

J. Taylor and N. Christianini. 2004. *Kernel Methods for Pattern Analysis*. Cambridge University Press.

J. Turian, L. Ratinov, and Y. Bengio. 2010. Word Representations: A Simple and General Method for Semi-supervlsed Learning. In *ACL*.

J. Wiebe and E. Riloff. 2005. Creating Subjective and Objective Sentence Classifiers from Unannotated Texts. In *CICLing*.

M. Wiegand and D. Klakow. 2010. Convolution Kernels for Opinion Holder Extraction. In *HLT/NAACL*.

T. Wilson, J. Wiebe, and P. Hoffmann. 2005. Recognizing Contextual Polarity in Phrase-level Sentiment Analysis. In *HLT/EMNLP*.

Y. Zhang, R. Wang, and H. Uszkoreit. 2008. Hybrid Learning of Dependency Structures from Heterogeneous Linguistic Resources. In *CoNLL*.

Multiword Expressions and Named Entities in the Wiki50 Corpus

Veronika Vincze[1], **István Nagy T.**[2] and **Gábor Berend**[2]
[1]Hungarian Academy of Sciences, Research Group on Artificial Intelligence
vinczev@inf.u-szeged.hu
[2]Department of Informatics, University of Szeged
{nistvan,berendg}@inf.u-szeged.hu

Abstract

Multiword expressions (MWEs) and named entities (NEs) exhibit unique and idiosyncratic features, thus, they often pose a problem to NLP systems. In order to facilitate their identification we developed the first corpus of Wikipedia articles in which several types of multiword expressions and named entities are manually annotated at the same time. The corpus can be used for training or testing MWE-detectors or NER systems, which we illustrate with experiments and it also makes it possible to investigate the co-occurrences of different types of MWEs and NEs within the same domain.

1 Introduction

In natural language processing (NLP), a challenging task is the proper treatment of multiword expressions (MWEs). Multiword expressions are lexical items that can be decomposed into single words and display lexical, syntactic, semantic, pragmatic and/or statistical idiosyncrasy (Sag et al., 2002; Kim, 2008; Calzolari et al., 2002) thus, they often pose a problem to NLP systems.

Named Entity Recognition (NER) is another widely researched topic in NLP. There are several methods developed for many languages and domains, which are tested on manually annotated databases, e.g. the MUC-6 and MUC-7 and the CoNLL-2002/2003 challenges aimed at identifying NEs in newswire texts (Grishman and Sundheim, 1995; Chinchor, 1998; Tjong Kim Sang, 2002; Tjong Kim Sang and De Meulder, 2003). Multiword named entities can be composed of any words or even characters and their meaning cannot be traced back to their parts. For instance, *Ford Focus* refers to a car and has nothing to do with the original meaning of *ford* or *focus*, thus, it is justifiable to treat the whole expression as one unit.

In this paper, we present our corpus called Wiki50 which contains 50 Wikipedia articles annotated for multiword expressions and named entities. To the best of our knowledge, this is the first corpus in which MWEs and NEs are annotated at the same time. We describe the categories occurring in the database, provide some statistical data on their frequency and finally, we demonstrate how noun compounds and named entities can be automatically detected by applying some dictionary-based and machine learning methods.

2 Related corpora and databases

Several corpora and databases of MWEs have been constructed for a number of languages. For instance, Nicholson and Baldwin (2008) describe a corpus and a database of English compound nouns (BNC dataset in Table 1). As for multiword verbs, corpora and databases for English (Cook et al., 2008), German (Krenn, 2008), Estonian (Muischnek and Kaalep, 2010) and Hungarian (Vincze and Csirik, 2010) have been recently developed. The Prague Dependency Treebank is also annotated for multiword expressions (Bejcek and Stranák, 2010).

As for named entities, several corpora have been constructed, for instance, within the framework of the ACE project (Doddington et al., 2004) and for international challenges such as the CoNLL-2002/2003 datasets (Tjong Kim Sang, 2002; Tjong Kim Sang and De Meulder, 2003) or the MUC datasets (Grishman and Sundheim, 1995; Chinchor, 1998) – just to name a few.

As can be seen, although there are a number of corpora and databases annotated for MWEs, they typically focus on only one specific type of MWE. That is, there are hardly any corpora that contain manual annotation for several types of English MWEs at the same time. On the other hand, to the best of our knowledge, there exist no corpora where various types of MWEs are annotated together with NEs. Named entities often consist of more than one word, i.e. they can be seen as a specific type of multiword expressions / noun compounds (Jackendoff, 1997). Although both noun compounds and multiword named entities consist of more than one word, they form one semantic unit and thus, they should be treated as one unit in NLP systems. Taking the example of POS-tagging, the linguistic behavior of compound nouns and multiword NEs is the same as that of single-word nouns, thus, they are preferably tagged as nouns (or proper nouns) even if the phrase itself does not contain any noun (e.g. *has-been* or *Die Hard*). Once identified as such, they can be treated similarly to single words in syntactic parsing for example. Our corpus makes it possible – for the first time – to compare (co-)occurrences of different types of MWEs and NEs and to evaluate the performance of MWE-detectors and NER systems within the same domain.

3 The Wiki50 corpus

When constructing our corpus, we selected 50 random articles from the English Wikipedia. The only selectional criterion applied was that each article should consist of at least 1000 words and they should not contain lists, tables or other structured texts (i.e. only articles with running texts were included). In this section, we present the types of multiword expressions and named entities annotated in our corpus.

3.1 Multiword expressions

A **compound** is a lexical unit that consists of two or more elements that exist on their own. Orthographically, a compound may include spaces (*high school*) or hyphen (*well-known*) or none of them (*headmaster*). We annotated only nominal and adjectival compounds in the database since they are productive and cannot be identified with lists. Our main goal being to develop a corpus for evaluating MWE detectors, we annotated only compounds with spaces since hyphenated compounds (e.g. *self-esteem*) can be easily recognized and are not included in our definition of multiword expressions (i.e. 'words with spaces').

Verb-particle constructions (VPCs, also called phrasal verbs or phrasal-prepositional verbs) are combined of a verb and a particle/preposition (see e.g. Kim (2008)). They can be adjacent (as in *put off*) or separated by an intervening object (***turn** the light **off***). They can be compositional, i.e. it can be computed from the meaning of the preposition and the verb (*lie down*) or non-compositional (*do in* meaning "kill"). VPCs are also marked in the database and their respective parts (i.e. verb and particle) are also annotated in order to facilitate the automatic detection of constructions where the two parts are not adjacent (e.g. ***spit** it **out***).

An **idiom** is a MWE whose meaning cannot (or can only partially) be determined on the basis of its components (Sag et al., 2002; Nunberg et al., 1994). Although most idioms behave normally as syntax and morphology are concerned, i.e. they can undergo some morphological change (e.g. *He spills/spilt the beans*), their semantics is totally unpredictable. **Proverbs** express some important facts thought to be true by most people, e.g. *The early bird catches the worm.* Idioms and proverbs are both annotated in our corpus.

Light verb constructions (LVCs) consist of a nominal and a verbal component where the noun is usually taken in one of its literal senses but the verb usually loses its original sense to some extent e.g. *to give a lecture*, *to come into bloom*, *the problem lies (in)*. The nominal and the verbal component of such constructions are also marked within the light verb construction (hierarchical annotation) for they can be separated from each other within context (e.g. in passive sentences).

There are **other types of MWEs** that do not fit into the above categories (some of them are listed in Jackendoff (1997)) such as *status quo*, *c'est la vie* and *ad hoc*. Although they are composed of perfectly meaningful parts in the original language, in English, these words do no exist on their own hence it is impossible to derive their meaning from their parts and the expression must be stored as a whole. They are also labeled as MWEs in the database. So are multiword verbs that cannot be classified as VPCs or LVCs (e.g. *to voice act* or *drink and drive*).

3.2 Named entities

In our database, the four basic types of named entities are marked: persons (PER), organizations (ORG), locations (LOC) and miscellaneous (MISC). We applied tag-for-meaning annotation in the corpus, that is, occurrences of e.g. country names could refer to an organization and a loca-

Corpus	Sentence	Token
CoNLL-2003	14,987	203,621
Wikipedia	4,350	114,570
BNC dataset	1000	21,631

Table 1: Size of various NE and MWE annotated corpora in terms of sentence and token number

tion as well depending on the context, thus, they were classified as belonging to different categories in such cases.

3.3 Segmentation of data

Sentence boundaries were also manually annotated in the database: sentences ending with an abbreviated form (e.g. *He lives in L.A.*), where the full stop belongs to the named entity and marks the sentence boundary at the same time, are distinctively marked.

The corpus exists in two versions: in the distilled version, segmentation errors (e.g. missing spaces) were corrected manually, and irrelevant parts of the documents (e.g. references or footnotes) were filtered. The other version – being more noisy – can be used in web-mining applications since no such modifications were carried out on the texts collected from the web. Both versions of the corpora are available under the Creative Commons license at `http://rgai.inf.u-szeged.hu/mwe`.

3.4 Statistics on corpus data

In the following, some statistical data on the distilled version of the corpus are provided. The corpus consists of 4350 sentences and 114,570 tokens, which size makes it comparable to other existing corpora (see Table 1). Table 2 summarizes the number of occurrences of the annotated categories and the number of unique phrases (i.e. no multiple occurrences are counted here) as well as the average and variance of the number of the various annotations per token.

4 The process of annotation and error analysis

Two linguists carried out the annotation of the corpus. 15 articles out of the 50 were annotated by both of them and differences were later resolved. The agreement rates between the two annotators are represented in Table 3.

As the data show, NEs in general are easier to identify for humans than MWEs. Among MWEs, note that for many categories it was mostly recall that was responsible for the decrease in F-measure. This can be related to the complexity of the annotation task: in 4350 sentences 12,832 elements were marked (i.e. 2.95 elements per sentence), not including the hierarchical categories, which probably led to the fact that annotators were prone to overlook certain expressions in running text. It was especially true for VPCs and MWEs classified as 'other' – VPCs typically consist of short elements, which may make it hard to recognize them in running text. The high precision value of the VPC class suggests that this category is relatively easy to classify (if recognized in text). This is somewhat different for NEs: here the capitalization may be an important feature in detecting NEs while reading, which causes that NEs were almost always annotated (i.e. recall values are higher) hence their agreement rates are higher.

Category	Occurrence	Unique	Avg. frequency
Noun Comp.	2929	2405	0.0263±2.1E-4
Adj. Comp.	78	60	0.0008±1.1E-6
VPC	446	342	0.0038±8.9E-6
LVC	368	338	0.0030±4.9E-6
Idiom	19	18	0.0002±1.2E-7
Other	21	17	0.0002±8.1E-8
MWE sum	3861	3180	0.0342±2.0E-4
PER	4093	1533	0.0352±5.8E-4
ORG	1498	893	0.0133±2.0E-4
LOC	1558	705	0.0150±2.5E-4
MISC	1827	952	0.0166±2.3E-4
NE sum	8976	4083	0.0801±7.5E-4

Table 2: Identified occurrences of categories in the corpus and their relative per-token frequencies

It seems that frequent MWE categories reach higher agreement rates than rare ones (cf. Table 2). In the latter case with only a few tens of examples, one single erroneous annotation or lack of annotation weighed much more than in cases when several hundreds (or even thousands) of examples could be found. As opposed to MWEs there were no underrepresented NE categories, which yields that the overall agreement rate calculated for NEs is higher than that of MWEs.

The κ-measure of the whole annotation (i.e. including NEs and MWEs) is 0.6938, which can be considered as a fairly good agreement rate.

4.1 Errors in MWE annotation

MWE annotation errors can be classified into two groups. The lack of annotation by one of the annotators may be related to conceptual differ-

Category	Precision	Recall	F-score	Jaccard	κ-measure
Noun Comp.	0.7135	0.7089	0.7112	0.5518	0.6414
Adj. Comp.	0.5625	0.4286	0.4865	0.3214	0.4841
VPC	0.8831	0.5620	0.6869	0.5231	0.6792
LVC	0.7454	0.6721	0.7069	0.5467	0.6980
Idiom	0.5556	0.5556	0.5556	0.3846	0.5545
Other	1.0	0.1429	0.25	0.1429	0.2497
MWE sum	0.7320	0.6816	0.7059	0.5329	0.5797
PER	0.9794	0.9802	0.9798	0.9605	0.9708
ORG	0.8322	0.7515	0.7898	0.6526	0.7716
LOC	0.9042	0.9103	0.9073	0.8303	0.8953
MISC	0.8921	0.8986	0.8953	0.8105	0.8781
NE sum	0.9635	0.9544	0.9589	0.8603	0.6789

Table 3: Agreement rates between annotators

ences (e.g. hyphenated noun compounds were not to be marked, however, one annotator occasionally marked phrases like *brother-in-law* as noun compounds) and lack of attention: the annotator simply did not recognize one instance of an element annotated elsewhere in the text. A typical example for the latter case is VPCs, which are usually short and therefore it is hard to catch them in running text for the human annotator. Concerning the second group of errors, here the same expression was marked with two different labels. Interestingly, a common source of error was that certain elements were annotated as noun compounds by one of the annotators and as named entities by the other annotator such as Latinate or botanical names (*Torrey Pine*), buildings (*City Hall*), names of positions or committees (*Board of Trustees*) etc. These issues might be eliminated with more detailed annotation guidelines, however, all of these mismatches were later disambiguated, yielding the gold standard annotation of the corpus.

4.2 Errors in NE annotation

In NE annotation, most of the cases where only one of the annotators marked the phrase were related to fictional objects. Many articles described a video game or a fantasy world in which a lot of special objects (e.g. *Trap Cards*) were annotated as miscellaneous by one of the annotators while the other did not mark them. On the other hand, different labels were also assigned to the same phrases. Besides NE-MWE differences, certain NEs were annotated as different NE-subtypes, which is partly connected to metonymic annotation. For instance, names of countries or states could be annotated as locations and organizations according to context but sometimes the two annotators did not agree on whether it should be marked as a location or an organization. Another example was person-like fictional characters (e.g. *Zombie Werewolf*): one annotator labeled them as a person while the other as miscellaneous. Again, these cases are hard to determine without deeper knowledge of the story and more refined guidelines are necessary for their annotation.

4.3 Nested expressions

A special type of annotation differences concerned nested expressions. A multiword expression may contain another multiword expression (***carbon monoxide*** *leak*), a named entity may include another named entity (***New York*** *City*) or a MWE may include a NE (***FBI*** *special agent*) and may be part of an NE (*Tallulah* ***High School***). Although it was assumed that in each case the longest unit is marked, sometimes this principle was not observed by one of the annotators, which resulted in annotation errors. This issue may be resolved with hierarchical annotation where elements within the longest unit are also annotated, which we plan to carry out in the future.

5 Experiments

In this section, we describe our dictionary-based and machine learning based approaches to identify noun compounds and named entities in the corpus.

5.1 Dictionary based approaches

We used several Wikipedia-based approaches to automatically identify noun compounds, which

Threshold	Match	Merge	POS rules	Combined
100	0.2915	0.3093	0.2742	0.2901
50	0.3391	0.3599	0.3289	0.3479
20	0.4133	0.4332	0.4104	0.4295
10	0.4560	0.4751	0.4597	0.4801
5	0.4715	0.4883	0.4872	0.5051
2	0.4749	0.4976	0.5158	0.5420
1	0.4528	0.4751	0.5334	0.5609

Table 4: Effect of various heuristics using dictionary based methods

were evaluated on the above described corpus. Our methods were motivated by the encyclopedic nature of Wikipedia: as opposed to dictionaries, it mostly contains nominal concepts. Thus, we assumed that by using internal links of Wikipedia[1], a list of possible noun compounds can be gathered. This list consists of the anchor texts of all internal links with their frequencies (how many times this text span occurred as a link) comprising 2-4 lowercase tokens. The list was later filtered for special (non-English) characters and words not typical of noun compounds (such as auxiliaries or quantifiers).

In the first approach we marked a phrase as a noun compound if it occurred in the list and its frequency exceeded the current threshold (Match). In the second case, we assumed that if *a b* is a possible noun compound and *b c* too, they can be merged, so *a b c* is also a noun compound. In this case, *a b c* was only accepted as a noun compound if *a b* and *b c* occurred in the list and the frequency of the whole phrase exceeded the current threshold (Merge). As for the the third approach, several part-of-speech based patterns such as `JJ (NN|NNS)` were created. A potential noun compound in the text was accepted if it appeared in the list, its POS code sequence matched one of the patterns and its frequency exceeded the current threshold (POS rules). POS codes were determined using Stanford POS Tagger (Toutanova and Manning, 2000). Finally, we combined these approaches: we accepted a potential noun compound if it appeared in the list, its POS code sequence matched our patterns, furthermore, merges were allowed too (Combined). Results in terms of F-measure are shown in Table 4, from which it can be seen that best results were obtained when all the above mentioned extensions were combined and no frequency threshold was considered.

[1]Articles included in our corpus were not considered when collecting links.

leave-one-out	R	P	F
MWE	58.07	69.86	63.42
MWE + NE	65.65	72.44	68.68
NE	85.58	86.02	85.81
NE + MWE	87.07	87.28	87.18

Table 5: Results of leave-one-out approaches in terms of precision (P), recall (R) and F-measure (F). MWE: our CRF extended with automatically collected MWE dictionary, MWE+NE: our CRF with MWE features extended with NEs as feature, NE: our CRF trained with basic feature set, NE+MWE: our CRF model extended with MWEs as feature.

5.2 Machine Learning approaches

In addition to the above-described approach, we defined another method for automatically identifying noun compounds. The Conditional Random Fields (CRF) classifier was used (MALLET implementations (McCallum, 2002)) with the feature set used in Szarvas et al. (2006). To identify noun compound MWEs we used Wiki50 to train CRF classification models (they were evaluated in a leave-one-document-out scheme). Results are shown in the *MWE* row of Table 5.

In order to use Wiki50 only for testing purposes, we automatically generated a train database for the CRF trainer. The train set consists of 5,000 randomly selected Wikipedia pages and we ignored those containing lists, tables or other structured texts. Since this document set has not been manually annotated, dictionary based noun compound labeling was considered as the gold standard. As a result, we had a less accurate but much bigger training database. The CRF model was trained on the automatically generated train database with the above presented feature set. Results can be seen in the *CRF* row of Table 6. However, the database included many sentences without any labeled noun compounds hence negative examples were overrepresented. Therefore, we thought it necessary to filter the sentences: only those with at least one noun compound label were retained in the database (*CRF+SF*). With this filtering methodology the CRF could build a better model. The above-described feature set was completed with the information that a token is a named entity or not. The *MWE+NE* row of Table 5 shows that this feature proved very effective in the leave-one-document-out scheme, so we used it in the auto-

Approach	R	P	F
DictCombined	52.47	59.45	55.75
CRF	44.38	58.42	50.44
CRF+SF	53.39	56.66	54.98
CRF+NE	45.81	58.37	51.33
CRF+NE+SF	53.12	55.89	54.47
CRF+OwnNE+SF	53.29	57.60	55.36
CRF+OwnNELeft+SF	53.44	57.60	55.44
CRF+MWELeft+SF	53.53	58.74	56.02

Table 6: Results of different methods for noun compounds in terms of precision (P), recall (R) and F-measure (F). DictCombined: combination of dictionary based methods, CRF: our CRF model trained on automatically generated database, SF: sentences without any MWE label filtered, NE: NEs marked by Stanford NER used as feature, OwnNE: NEs marked by our CRF model (trained on Wikipedia) used as feature, OwnNELeft: the NE labeling selected as feature and the standard noun compound notation removed, MWELeft: the NE feature deleted and the standard noun compound notation selected.

matically generated train database too. As shown in the *CRF+NE* row of Table 6, the CRF model which was trained on the automatic training set could achieve better results with this feature than the original *CRF*.

First, the Stanford NER model was used for identifying NEs. However, we assumed that a model trained on Wikipedia could identify NEs more effectively in Wikipedia (i.e. in the same domain). Therefore, we merged the four NE classes marked in Wiki50 into one NE class to train the CRF with the above described common features set. Results are shown in the *NE* row of Table 5.

The *CRF+OwnNE+SF* row in Table 6 represents results achieved when the NEs identified by using the entire Wiki50 as the training dataset functioned as a feature. Although the *CRF+NE+SF* (when NEs were identified by the Stanford model) did not achieve better results than the *CRF+SF*, our Wikipedia based CRF model to identify NEs in the automatically generated training dataset (*CRF+OwnNE SF*) yielded better F-score than *CRF+SF*, which means that NEs are useful in the identification of noun compounds.

Sometimes it was not unequivocal to decide whether a multiword unit is a noun compound or a NE. However, we assumed that a term can occur either as a NE or a noun compound. Therefore, if the dictionary method marked a particular word as noun compound and the NE model also marked it as NE, we had to decide which mark to delete. The *CRF+OwnNELeft+SF* row in Table 6 shows results we achieved if the NE labeling was selected as feature and the standard noun compound notation was removed, whereas the row *CRF+MWELeft+SF* refers to the scenario when the NE feature was deleted, and the standard noun compound notation remained.

5.3 Named Entity Recognition with MWEs

We investigated the usability of noun compounds in named entity recognition. So we used Wiki50 to train CRF classification models with the basic feature set, which was extended with the feature noun compound MWE for NE recognition and they were evaluated in a leave-one-document-out scheme. Results of these approaches are shown in the *NE+MWE* row of Table 5. Comparing these results to those of the *NE* method (when the CRF was trained without the noun compound feature), noun compounds are also beneficial in NE identification.

6 Discussion

For identifying noun compounds we examined dictionary based and machine learning based methods too. The approaches we applied heavily rely on Wikipedia. The dictionary based approach made use of the automatically collected list from Wikipedia. The machine learning method exploited automatically generated training data. These were less accurate but much bigger than the available manually annotated training sets.

Our results demonstrate that previously known noun compounds are beneficial in NER and identified NEs enhance MWE detection. This may be related to the fact that multiword NEs and noun compounds are similar from a linguistic point of view as discussed above – moreover, in some cases, it is not easy to determine even for humans whether a given sequence of words is a NE or a MWE (capitalized names of positions such as *Prime Minister* or taxonomic names, e.g. *Torrey Pine*). In the test databases, no unit was annotated as NE and MWE at the same time, thus, it was necessary to disambiguate cases which could be labeled by both the MWE and the NE systems. By fixing the label of such cases, disambiguity is eliminated, that is, the training data are less noisy, which leads to better overall results.

7 Conclusions

In this paper, Wiki50, the first corpus in which multiword expressions and named entities are annotated at the same time was presented. Corpus data make it possible to investigate the co-occurrences of different types of MWEs and NEs within the same domain. The corpus consists of 50 Wikipedia articles (4350 sentences) and is freely available for research purposes. We also conducted various experiments on the identification of noun compounds and named entities in the corpus by dictionary-based and machine learning methods as well. We hope that our corpus will enhance the training and testing of MWE-detectors and NER systems.

Acknowledgments

This work was supported by the Project "TÁMOP-4.2.1/B-09/1/KONV-2010-0005 – Creating the Center of Excellence at the University of Szeged", supported by the European Union and co-financed by the European Regional Development Fund and by the project MASZEKER financed by the National Innovation Office of the Hungarian government.

References

Eduard Bejcek and Pavel Straňák. 2010. Annotation of multiword expressions in the Prague Dependency Treebank. *Language Resources and Evaluation*, 44(1-2):7–21.

Nicoletta Calzolari, Charles Fillmore, Ralph Grishman, Nancy Ide, Alessandro Lenci, Catherine MacLeod, and Antonio Zampolli. 2002. Towards best practice for multiword expressions in computational lexicons. In *Proceedings of LREC-2002*, pages 1934–1940, Las Palmas.

Nancy A. Chinchor. 1998. Overview of MUC-7/MET-2. In *Proceedings of MUC-7*.

Paul Cook, Afsaneh Fazly, and Suzanne Stevenson. 2008. The VNC-Tokens Dataset. In *Proceedings of the LREC Workshop Towards a Shared Task for Multiword Expressions (MWE 2008)*, pages 19–22, Marrakech, Morocco, June.

George Doddington, Alexis Mitchell, Mark Przybocki, Lance Ramshaw, Stephanie Strassel, and Ralph Weischedel. 2004. The Automatic Content Extraction (ACE) Program – Tasks, Data and Evaluation. In *Proceedings of LREC 2004*, pages 837–840.

Ralph Grishman and Beth Sundheim. 1995. Design of the MUC-6 evaluation. In *Proceedings of MUC-6*, pages 1–12, Stroudsburg, PA, USA. ACL.

Ray Jackendoff. 1997. *The Architecture of the Language Faculty*. MIT Press, Cambridge, MA.

Su Nam Kim. 2008. *Statistical Modeling of Multiword Expressions*. Ph.D. thesis, University of Melbourne, Melbourne.

Brigitte Krenn. 2008. Description of Evaluation Resource – German PP-verb data. In *Proceedings of the LREC Workshop Towards a Shared Task for Multiword Expressions (MWE 2008)*, pages 7–10, Marrakech, Morocco, June.

Andrew Kachites McCallum. 2002. Mallet: A machine learning for language toolkit. http://mallet.cs.umass.edu.

Kadri Muischnek and Heiki Jaan Kaalep. 2010. The variability of multi-word verbal expressions in Estonian. *Language Resources and Evaluation*, 44(1-2):115–135.

Jeremy Nicholson and Timothy Baldwin. 2008. Interpreting Compound Nominalisations. In *LREC 2008 Workshop: Towards a Shared Task for Multiword Expressions (MWE 2008)*, pages 43–45, Marrakech, Morocco.

Geoffrey Nunberg, Ivan A. Sag, and Thomas Wasow. 1994. Idioms. *Language*, 70:491–538.

Ivan A. Sag, Timothy Baldwin, Francis Bond, Ann Copestake, and Dan Flickinger. 2002. Multiword Expressions: A Pain in the Neck for NLP. In *Proceedings of CICLing-2002*, pages 1–15, Mexico City, Mexico.

György Szarvas, Richárd Farkas, and András Kocsor. 2006. A Multilingual Named Entity Recognition System Using Boosting and C4.5 Decision Tree Learning Algorithms. In *Discovery Science*, pages 267–278.

Erik F. Tjong Kim Sang and Fien De Meulder. 2003. Introduction to the CoNLL-2003 Shared Task: Language-Independent Named Entity Recognition. In *Proceedings of CoNLL-2003*, pages 142–147. Edmonton, Canada.

Erik F. Tjong Kim Sang. 2002. Introduction to the CoNLL-2002 Shared Task: Language-Independent Named Entity Recognition. In *Proceedings of CoNLL-2002*, pages 155–158. Taipei, Taiwan.

Kristina Toutanova and Christopher D. Manning. 2000. Enriching the knowledge sources used in a maximum entropy part-of-speech tagger. In *Proceedings of EMNLP 2000*, pages 63–70, Stroudsburg, PA, USA. ACL.

Veronika Vincze and János Csirik. 2010. Hungarian corpus of light verb constructions. In *Proceedings of Coling 2010*, pages 1110–1118, Beijing, China. Coling 2010 Organizing Committee.

Towards the Automatic Merging of Lexical Resources: Automatic Mapping

Muntsa Padró
IULA
Universitat Pompeu Fabra
Barcelona, Spain
muntsa.padro@upf.edu

Núria Bel
IULA
Universitat Pompeu Fabra
Barcelona, Spain
nuria.bel@upf.edu

Silvia Necsulescu
IULA
Universitat Pompeu Fabra
Barcelona, Spain
silvia.necsulescu@upf.edu

Abstract

Lexical Resources are a critical component for Natural Language Processing applications. However, the high cost of comparing and merging different resources has been a bottleneck to have richer resources with a broad range of potential uses for a significant number of languages. With the objective of reducing cost by eliminating human intervention, we present a new method for automating the merging of resources, with special emphasis in what we call the mapping step. This mapping step, which converts the resources into a common format that allows latter the merging, is usually performed with huge manual effort and thus makes the whole process very costly. Thus, we propose a method to perform this mapping fully automatically. To test our method, we have addressed the merging of two verb subcategorization frame lexica for Spanish, The results achieved, that almost replicate human work, demonstrate the feasibility of the approach.

1 Introduction

The production, updating, tuning and maintenance of Language Resources for Natural Language Processing is currently being considered as one of the most promising areas of advances for the full deployment of Language Technologies. The reason is that these resources that describe, in one way or another, the characteristics of a particular language are necessary for Language Technologies to work.

Although the re-use of existing resources such as WordNet (Fellbaum, 1998) in different applications has been a well known and successful case, it is not very frequent. The different technology or application requirements, or even the ignorance about the existence of other resources, has provoked the proliferation of different, unrelated resources that, if merged, could constitute a richer repository of information augmenting the number of potential uses. This is especially important for under-resourced languages, which normally suffer from the lack of broad coverage resources. The research reported in this paper was done in the context of the creation of a gold-standard for subcategorization frames of Spanish verbs to be used in lexical acquisition (Korhonen, 2002). We wanted to merge two hand-written, large scale Spanish lexica to obtain a new one that is richer and validated. Because subcategorization frames contain highly structured information, it was considered a good scenario for testing new lexical resource merging methods.

Several attempts at resource merging have been addressed and reported in the literature. Teufel (1995) and Chan & Wu (1999) were concerned with the merging of several source lexica for PoS tagging. The merging of more complex lexica has been addressed by Crouch and King (2005) who produced a Unified Lexicon with lexical entries for verbs based on their syntactic subcategorization in combination with their meaning, as described by WordNet, Cyc (Lenat, 1995) and VerbNet (Kipper et al., 2000).

In this context, a proposal such as the Lexical Markup Framework, LMF (Francopoulo et al. 2008) is an attempt to standardize the format of computational lexica as a way to avoid the complexities of merging lexica with different structures. But there is no particular facility to easy the mapping from non-standard into standard.

Molinero et al (2009) build a morphological and syntactic lexicon for Spanish (*Leffe*) by merging four different lexica. They convert these sources into the *Alexina* format which is compatible with LMF in order to merge them. Nevertheless, both the mapping to this common format and the merging of the resources is done using manually developed rules that need a deep knowledge of the lexica to be merged.

The research presented here is closely related to Necsulescu et al (2011), that presents a method to automatically merge lexica using graph unification mechanism. To do so, the lexica need to be represented as feature structures. Again, the conversion of the lexica into the common format (in this case a graph structure) is performed developing a set of manual rules.

Despite the undeniable achievements of the research just mentioned, most of it reports the need for a significant amount of human intervention to extract information of existing resources and to represent it in a way that can be compared with another lexicon, or towards proposed standards, such as the mentioned LMF. Thus, there is still room for improvement in reducing human intervention. This constituted the main challenge of the research reported in this paper: finding a method that can perform blind, but semantic preserving operations to allow for automatically merging two lexical resources, in this particular case two subcategorization frame (SCF) lexica for Spanish, as we did in Necsulescu et al. (2011).

In next section we introduce the proposed method for automatic mapping and merging of information. Section 3 presents the obtained results, and in section 4 we state the conclusions and the future work.

2 Merging Lexica

Basically, merging of lexica has two well defined steps (Crouch and King, 2005). In the first, because information about the same phenomenon can be expressed differently, the existing resources have to be mapped into a common format, which makes merging possible in a second step. While automation of the second step has already proved to be possible, human intervention is still critically needed for the first. In addition to the cost of manual work, note that the exercise is completely adhoc for the particular resources to be merged. The cost is what explains the lack of interest in merging existing resources, even though it is critically needed, especially for under-resourced languages. Any cost reduction will have a high impact in the actual re-use of resources.

Thus, our objective was to reduce human intervention in the first step by devising a blind, semantic preserving mapping algorithm that covers the extraction of the information and the conversion into a format that allows, later, the merging.

In our experiments, we wanted to merge two subcategorization lexica developed for rule-based grammars: the Spanish working lexicon of the Incyta Machine Translation system (Alonso, 2005) and the Spanish working lexicon of the Spanish Resource Grammar, SRG, (Marimon, 2010) developed for the LKB framework (Copestake, 2002). Note that different senses under the same lemma are not distinguished in these lexica, and thus, are not addressed in the research reported here[1]. SRG and Incyta lexica encode the same phenomena related to verbal complements, their role and categorical characteristics expressed as restrictions. SCFs in the SRG lexicon are formulated in terms of feature-attribute value pairs, so they have a graph structure. In the Incyta lexicon, SCFs are represented as a list of parenthesis with less structured internal information[2]. In both cases, a lemma can have more than one SCF, and it is indeed the most frequent case as we will see later. For more details about these two lexica, see Necsulescu et al. (2011).

In order to approach current proposals for standard formats (Francopoulo et al. 2008; Ide & Bunt, 2010) that recommend graph-based and attribute-value formalisms, we choose to map Incyta information towards SRG format which was closer to the standard recommendations. The devised method was to find semantically equivalent pieces of information and to substitute the parenthetical list by the attribute-value equivalent matrix.

[1] These characteristics made it not advisable to use LMF where lemma and sense are the mandatory information for a lexical entry.

[2] Decorated lists, parenthetical or otherwise marked, have been a quite common way of representing SCF information, i.e. COMLEX, VERBNET among others.

2.1 Semantic Preserving Mapping

Our experiment to avoid manual intervention when converting the two lexica into a common format with a blind, semantic preserving method departs from the idea of Chan and Wu (1999) to compare information contained in the same entries of different lexica, looking for significant equivalences. However they were working only with part-of-speech tags, while we handle complex, structured information. Note that we need to automatically learn correspondences for both, labels (such as the label of a noun phrase) and structures (e.g. the representation of a prepositional phrase that is fulfilled by a clause phrase in indicative mode).

The basic requirement for the automatic mapping is to have a number of verbs encoded in both lexica to be compared. Then it is possible to assess that a piece of the code in lexicon A corresponds to a piece of code in lexicon B since a significant number of other verbs hold the same correspondence. Thus, when a correspondence is found, the relevant piece in A will be substituted by the piece in B, performing the conversion into the target format.

Since we wanted our method to not be informed by human knowledge of the lexica, in order to make it applicable to more than one lexicon, the first point to solve was how to compare SCF code with no available previous information about their internal semantics. The code in Incyta lexicon is as in example (1).

(1) (($SUBJ N1 N0 (FCP 0 INT) (MD-0 IND) (MD-INT SUB)) ($DOBJ N1))

Therefore, the information that had to be discovered was the following:

- Incyta lexicon marks each SCF as a list of parenthesis, where the first level of parenthesis indicates the list of complements.
- Each component of the list begins with an identifier followed, without necessarily any formal marker, by additional information about properties of the component in the form of tags. For example, in (1) above, direct object ($DOBJ) is fulfilled by a noun phrase (N1).
- Incyta marks disjunction as a simple sequence of tags. In (1), subject ($SUBJ) may be fulfilled by N1 (noun phrase) or N0 (clause phrase). Furthermore, properties of one of the elements in the disjunction are specified in one or more parenthesis following the tag, as it is the case of N0 in (1). The 3 parenthesis after N0 are in fact properties of its realization: it is a sentential complement (FCP) whose verb should appear in indicative (MD-0 IND) unless it is an interrogative clause (MD-INT SUB).

We devised an algorithm that could discover this internal structure in Incyta SCFs. Our algorithm first splits every SCF in all possible ways according to formal characteristics (complete parenthetical components for Incyta and complete attribute-value matrices for SRG) and looks for the most frequently repeated pieces along the whole lexicon, so it is assessed that a particular piece is a meaningful unit. Note that we wanted to discover minimal units in order to handle different information encoding granularity. If we would have mapped entire SCFs or large pieces of them, the system could substitute information in A with information in B, possibly missing a difference.

Note that when performing the mapping for small pieces we ensure that we save as much the information as possible in the original lexicon, but this also causes the mapping result to not be a complete SCF. Since the ultimate goal is merging the two lexica, it is in the merging step that the partial elements will obtain the missing parts.

To sum up, our algorithm does the following with the Incyta SCF code:

1. Split SCF into each parentheses that conforms the list (this is to find $SUBJ and $DOBJ in 1).
2. For each of these pieces, it considers the first element as its key, and recursively splits the following elements.
3. It detects the relationship among the different elements found inside the parentheses by assessing which of them always occur together. For (1), it will detect that FCP appears only when there is a N0, and that MD-0 appears only when we have seen (FCP 0). In this way, we will obtain the constituents of the parentheses grouped according to their dependency.

Once extracted the different parts of each Incyta SCF and joined the elements that are correlated, our algorithm does the mapping:

1. For each element extracted from the Incyta SCF, it creates a list of verbs that contain it. This list is represented as a binary vector whose element *i* is 1 if the verb in position *i* is in the list.

2. It splits the SRG graphs following the feature-value attributes and builds a binary vector with the verbs that contain each element.
3. For each Incyta SCF minimal unit, it assesses the similarity with each SRG unit comparing the two binary vectors using the Jaccard distance measure, especially suited for binary vectors and as in (Chan and Wu, 1999).
4. It chooses as the corresponding elements those that maximize similarity.

Once the corresponding elements have been extracted, a new feature structure is constructed substituting Incyta units with those from SRG and the actual merging with the SRG lexicon is done. Since the SCFs have a graph structure, we used a unification mechanism (NLTK, Bird 2006) to merge both lexica, lemma by lemma, as in Necsulescu et al. (2011). Thus, we obtained, totally automatically, a new lexicon that contains SCF information from both lexica.

3 Evaluation and Results

To evaluate the results of our automatic mapping algorithm, we used the resulting lexicon of Necsulescu et al (2011) work as our gold-standard. To create this lexicon, Necsulescu et al (2011) developed a manually built set of extraction rules that converted Incyta list-based SCF's into SRG-like feature structures. Once both dictionaries were reliably converted into the same format, they were merged by using unification, thus obtaining a richer lexicon that we have used as the gold-standard for the automatic mapping exercise.

In order to evaluate the quality of the automatic mapping step, we compared the lexicon resulting from the merging of the SRG and the automatically mapped Incyta lexicon with the gold-standard. This comparison was first carried out by looking for identical SCFs in the entries of every particular verb. However, the results of the automatic mapping are in some cases parts of SCFs, because of the piece splitting process. As said, merging adds the lacking information in numerous cases, but the Incyta SCFs that do not unify with any SRG SCF remain incomplete. Also, there are cases in which the manually converted frame has more information than the automatic one, but the SCFs resulting from the automating mapping subsumes the one in the gold-standard, so they may be considered correct, although incomplete. Thus, in a second measure, we also count these pieces that are compatible with SCFs in the gold-standard as a positive result.

The evaluation is done using traditional precision, recall and F1 measures for each verb and then we compute the mean of these measures over all the verbs. The results, shown in table 1, are near 88% of F1 even in the strict case of identical SCFs. If we compare SCFs that unify, the results are even more satisfactory.

	P	R	F1
A-identical	87,35%	88,02%	87,69%
B-compatible	92,35%	93,08%	92,72%

Table 1: Average results of the mapping exercise

In Figure 1 we can see the performance in terms of number of SCFs under a lemma that are the same in the gold-standard and in the merged lexicon. We also plot the ratio of verbs that have a particular number of SCFs or less. The verbs that have one or two SCFs (about 50% of the verbs) obtain high values, as it may be expected. Nevertheless, 95% of verbs (those with 11 or less SCFs per lemma) obtain at least F1=80% when counting strictly equal SCFs and F1 over 90% when counting unifying SCFs. Note that these figures are the lower threshold, since verbs with less SCFs have better results, as it can be seen in Figure 1. To summarize, we consider that the obtained precision and recall of all verbs, even those with more than two SCFs, are very satisfactory.

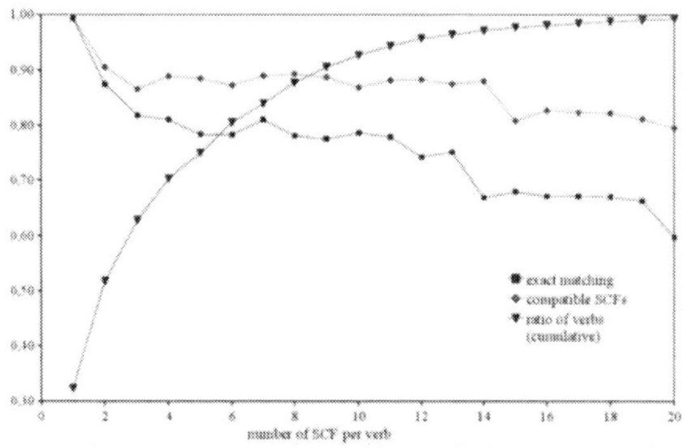

Figure 1: Average F1 and cumulative number of verbs with respect to the number of SCFs

As for the error analysis, the results revealed that some SCFs in the gold-standard are not in the automatically built lexicon. One case is SCFs with adverbial complements. Our algorithm maps adverbials onto PPs and the resulting SCF misses part of the original information. Nevertheless, our algorithm correctly adds information when there are gaps in one of the dictionaries. It is able to learn correspondences such as "INT" (Incyta for interrogative clause) to "q" in SRG and to add this information when it is missed in a particular entry of the SRG lexicon but available in the Incyta entry.

4 Conclusions and Future Work

We have proposed a method to reduce human intervention in the merging of lexical resources. In order to unify different lexica, the resources need to be mapped into a comparable format. To reduce the cost of extracting and comparing the contents, we proposed a method to make the mapping automatically. We consider the results obtained very satisfactory. Our method rids the manual information extraction phase, which is the big bottleneck for the re-use and merging of language resources.

The strongest point of our method is that it can be applied without the need of knowing the structure nor the semantics of the lexica to be compared. This allows us to think our method can be extended to other types of Lexical Resources. The only requirement is that all resources to be merged contain some common data. Although further work is needed for assessing how much common data guarantees the same results, the current work is indicative of the feasibility of our approach.

It is important to note that the results presented here are obtained without using what Crouch and King (2005) call patch files. Automatic merging produces consistent errors that can be objects of further refinement. Thus, it is possible to devise specific patches that correct or add information in particular cases where either wrong or incomplete information is produced. It is future work to study the use of patch files to improve our method.

Acknowledgments

This project has been funded by the PANACEA project (EU-7FP-ITC-248064) and the CLARA project (EU-7FP-ITN-238405).

References

Juan Alberto Alonso, András Bocsák. 2005. Machine Translation for Catalan-Spanish. The Real Case for Productive MT; In Proceedings of the tenth Conference on European Association of Machine Translation (EAMT 2005), Budapest, Hungary.

Steven Bird. 2006. NLTK: the natural language toolkit. In Proceedings of the COLING/ACL on Interactive presentation sessions. Association for Computational Linguistics, Morristown, NJ, USA.

Ignacio Bosque and Violeta Demonte, Eds. (1999): Gramática descriptiva de la lengua española, R.A.E. - Espasa Calpe, Madrid.

Daniel K. Chan and Dekai Wu. 1999. Automatically Merging Lexicons that have Incompatible Part-of-Speech Categories. Joint SIGDAT Conference on Empirical Methods in Natural Language Processing and Very Large Corpora (EMNLP/VLC-99). Maryland.

Ann Copestake. 2002. Implementing Typed Feature Structure Grammars. CSLI Publications, CSLI lecture notes, number 110, Chicago.

Dick Crouch and Tracy H. King. 2005. Unifying lexical resources. Proceedings of Interdisciplinary Workshop on the Identification and Representation of Verb Features and Verb Classes. Saarbruecken; Germany.

Christiane Fellbaum. 1998. WordNet: An Electronic Lexical Database. MIT Press.

Gil Francopoulo, Núria Bel, Monte George, Nicoletta Calzolari, Mandy Pet, and Claudia Soria. 2008. Multilingual resources for NLP in the lexical markup framework (LMF). Journal of Language Resources and Evaluation, 43 (1).

John Hughes, Clive Souter, and E. Atwell. 1995. Automatic Extraction of Tagset Mappings from Parallel-Annotated Corpora. Computation and Language.

Nancy Ide and Harry Bunt. 2010. Anatomy of Annotation Schemes: Mapping to GrAF. Proceedings of the Fourth Linguistic Annotation Workshop, ACL 2010

Daniel Jurafsky and James H. Martin. 2009. Speech and Language Processing: An Introduction to Natural Language Processing, Speech Recognition, and Computational Linguistics. 2nd edition. Prentice-Hall.

Karin Kipper, Hoa Trang Dang, and Martha Palmer. 2000. Class-based construction of a verb lexicon. In Proceedings of AAAI/IAAI.

Anna Korhonen. 2002. Subcategorization Acquisition. PhD thesis published as Technical Report UCAM-CL-TR-530. Computer Laboratory, University of Cambridge

Doug Lenat. 1995. Cyc: a large-scale investment in knowledge infrastructure. In CACM 38, n.11.

Christopher D. Manning and Hinrich Schütze. 1999. Foundations of Statistical Natural Language Processing. MIT Press, Cambridge, MA, USA.

Montserrat Marimon. 2010. The Spanish Resource Grammar. Proceedings of the Seventh Conference on International Language Resources and Evaluation (LREC'10). Paris, France: European Language Resources Association (ELRA).

Miguel A. Molinero, Benoît Sagot and Nicolas Lionel. 2009. Building a morphological and syntactic lexicon by merging various linguistic resources. In Proceeding of 17th Nordic Conference on Computational Linguistics (NODALIDA-09), Odense, Danemar.

Monica Monachini, Nicoletta Calzolari, Khalid Choukri, Jochen Friedrich,Giulio Maltese, Michele Mammini, Jan Odijk & Marisa Ulivieri. 2006. Unified Lexicon and Unified Morphosyntactic Specifications for Written and Spoken Italian. In Calzolari et al. (eds.), LREC2006: 5th International Conference on Language Resources and Evaluation: Proceedings, pp. 1852-1857, Genoa, Italy.C.J.

Silvia Necsulescu, Núria Bel, Muntsa Padró, Montserrat Marimon and Eva Revilla: Towards the Automatic Merging of Language Resources. In Proceedings of WoLeR 2011. Ljubljana, Slovenia.

Pollard and I.A. Sag. 1994. Head-driven PhraseStructure Grammar. The University of Chicago Press, Chicago.

Simone Teufel. 1995. A Support Tool for Tagset Mapping. In EACL-Sigdat 95.

Unsupervised Learning for Persian WordNet Construction

Mortaza Montazery
NLP Lab, School of ECE, College of Engineering, University of Tehran, Tehran, Iran
Mortaza.gh@gmail.com

Heshaam Faili
NLP Lab, School of ECE, College of Engineering, University of Tehran, Tehran, Iran
hfaili@ut.ac.ir

Abstract

In this paper we introduce an unsupervised learning approach for WordNet construction. The whole construction method is an Expectation Maximization (EM) approach which uses Princeton WordNet 3.0 (PWN) and a corpus as the data source for unsupervised learning. The proposed method can be used to construct WordNet in any language. Links between PWN synsets and target language words are extracted using a bilingual dictionary. For each of these links a parameter is defined that shows probability of selecting PWN synset for target language word in corpus. Model parameters are adjusted in an iterative fashion. In our experiments on Persian language, by selecting 10% of highly probable links trained by the EM method, a Persian WordNet was obtained that covered 7,109 out of 11,076 distinct words and 9,427 distinct PWN synsets with a precision of more than 86%.

1 Introduction

One of the most important challenges with respect to Natural Language Processing is the existence of ambiguity in different levels of natural language. Word sense ambiguity is one of these ambiguities. One solution for dealing with these problems is to generate knowledge repositories where human knowledge about natural language can be encoded. WordNet is a rich repository of knowledge about words that has been constructed to deal with word sense ambiguity problem.

The first WordNet was constructed for English language in Princeton University under direction of George A. Miller (Fellbaum, 1998). English words in four categories noun, verb, adjective and adverb have been grouped into sets of cognitive synonyms that are called synset. By proving of usefulness of Princeton WordNet (PWN), construction of WordNet for other languages has been considered. Two great efforts in constructing WordNet for other languages are EuroWordNet (Vossen, 1999) and BalkaNet (Tufiș, Cristea, & Stamou, 2004). The former deals with European's languages such as English, Dutch, German, French, Spanish, Italian, Czech and Estonian. The second one deals with languages from Balkan zone such as Romanian, Bulgarian, Turkish, Slovenian, Greek and Serbian.

Manual construction of WordNet is a time consuming task and requires linguistic knowledge. The estimation of the average time for building a lexical entry depends on the polysemy of the words in the synsets, on the available lexical resources and definitely on the WordNet building tools. Thus automated approaches for WordNet construction or enrichment have been proposed to facilitate faster, cheaper and easier development. In this way several automatic methods have been proposed for constructing WordNet for Asian languages such as Japanese, Arabic, Thai and Persian that use PWN and other existing lexical resources.

In (Shamsfard M. , 2008) a semi-automated method has been proposed for developing a Persian lexical ontology called FarsNet. About 1,500 verbs and 1,500 nouns have been gathered manually to make WorldNet's core. Then two heuristics and a Word Sense Disambiguation (WSD) method have been used to find the most likely related Persian synsets. According to the first heuristic, a Persian word has only one synset if it is translated to a single English word that has only one sense in PWN. In this case no ambiguity exists for the Persian word whose one of synsets will be equivalent to that of English word. In other cases, second heuristic is used: if two translations of a Persian word have only one common synset then this common synset is linked to the

Persian word. The existence of a single common synset implies the existence of a single common sense between the two words and therefore their Persian translations shall be connected to this synset (Shamsfard M. , 2008). For words whose English translations have more than one synset and the second heuristic could not find the appropriate synset, a WSD method has been used to select the correct synset. For each candidate synset, a score is calculated using the measure of semantic similarity and synset gloss words. Manual evaluation of the proposed automatic method in this research shows 70% correctness and covers about 6,500 entries on PWN.

In (Montazery & Faili, 2010), an automatic method for Persian WordNet construction based on PWN has been introduced. The proposed approach uses two monolingual corpora for English and Persian and a bilingual dictionary in order to make a mapping between PWN synsets and Persian words. In this paper, Persian words have been linked to PWN synsets in two different ways. Some links were selected directly by using some heuristics that recognize these links as unambiguous. Another type of links is ambiguous, in which a scoring method is used for selecting the appropriate synset. In order to select an appropriate PWN synset for ambiguous links, a score for each candidate synset of a given Persian word is calculated and a synset with maximum score is selected as a link to the Persian word. The manual evaluation on selected links on 500 randomly selected Persian words shows about 76.4% quality respect to precision measure. By augmenting the Persian WordNet with the unambiguous words, the total accuracy of automatically extracted Persian WordNet becomes 82.6%.

The automated approaches for WordNet construction vary according to the resources that are available for a particular language (Fišer, 2008). In (Fišer, 2008) multilingual parallel corpora have been used for the construction of Slovene WordNet. Their experiments were conducted on two different corpora. The first corpus contains five languages (English, Czech, Romanian, Bulgarian and Slovene), 100,000 words per language and it has already been sentence-aligned and tagged. The second corpus is the biggest parallel corpus of its size in 21 languages (about 10 million words per language) and it is paragraph-aligned but is not tagged, lemmatized, sentence or word-aligned. Both corpora have been sentence and word-aligned. Word-alignments have been used to create bilingual lexicons. For noise reduction purpose in the lexicon, only 1:1 links between words of the same part of speech have been taken into account and all alignments occurring only once have been discarded. Multilingual lexicon and already existing WordNet for each language have been used in order to construct Slovene WordNet. For English, PWN has been used while for Czech, Romanian and Bulgarian WordNets from the BalkaNet project have been used. For each lexicon entry synset ids from each WordNet are extracted and, if there is an overlap of synset ids across all languages, then it is assumed that the words in question all describe the concept marked with this id. Finally, the concept is extended to the Slovene part of the multilingual lexicon entry and the synset id common to all the languages is assigned to it (Fišer, 2008). Fišer (2008) also has extended her proposed method to include multi-word expression in generated Slovene WordNet.

There have been some other efforts to create a WordNet for Persian language (Shamsfard, et al., 2010; Mansoory & Bijankhan, 2008; Rouhizadeh, Shamsfard, & Yarmohammadi, 2008; Famian, 2007); but there exists no Persian WordNet yet that covers all Persian words in dictionary and is comparable with PWN.

In this paper, a fully automated language-independent unsupervised ML-based method for constructing a large-scale WordNet for any language is proposed. The method just needs some available resources such as PWN, machine readable dictionaries and monolingual corpus to train ontology for a target language. The approach implements an Expectation/Maximization (EM) algorithm which iteratively estimates the probability of selecting a candidate synset for a given target language word. Although the whole method is language-independent and it just works with the mentioned resources, we tested it on Persian language to retrieve a large-scale Persian WordNet.

The rest of the paper is organized as follows. Section 2 presents our method for constructing Persian WordNet automatically. Experimental results and evaluations of the proposed method are explained in section 3. Finally conclusion and future works are presented in section 4.

2 Persian WordNet Construction Method

The process is started by making an initial WordNet that consists of words in Persian language and the links between them and PWN synsets. Each Persian word may have several English translations and each English translation may also have several PWN synsets. Candidate synsets of a given Persian word are the union of all PWN synsets of its English translations. We think that each candidate synset of a given Persian word may be one of its probable senses. Our proposed method tries to estimate this probability. If a candidate synset represents a correct sense of Persian word, we expect the occurrence of this sense in a Persian corpus which contains that word.

For each Persian word w and each PWN synset t, $\theta_{w,t}$ is considered as probability of selecting PWN synset t for Persian word w. That is:

$$\forall w,t: \theta_{w,t} \in [0,1] \quad (1)$$

$$\forall w: \sum_{t} \theta_{w,t} = 1 \quad (2)$$

In order to estimate these parameters we can divide the number of times that a Persian word w occurs with PWN synset t in a Persian tagged corpus to the number of times that a Persian word w appears in that Persian tagged corpus. However, this simple method needs a Persian sense tagged corpus. Because, there is no such corpus, we use an EM method to estimate the probability of selecting a PWN synset for each Persian word of corpus. The idea is as follows: first we make a Persian WordNet with an initial value for the mentioned parameters, then for each word occurred in a Persian corpus the probability of selecting its senses is estimated using current value of parameters and words in context. Probabilities calculated in this step are used to update the parameters of the model.

The EM algorithm is a general method of finding the maximum-likelihood estimate of the parameters of an underlying distribution from a given data set when the data is incomplete or has missing values (Bilmes, 1998). Consider a sequence of Persian word w_1^n with length n and its corresponding sense tag sequence t_1^n. Assuming the independence between each pair of (w_i, t_i) we have:

$$\begin{aligned} P(w_1^n, t_1^n|\Theta) &= \prod_i P(w_i, t_i|\Theta) \\ &= \prod_{(w,t)\in(w_1^n,t_1^n)} P(w,t|\theta)^{n(w,t)} \\ &= \prod_{(w,t)\in(w_1^n,t_1^n)} \theta_{w,t}{}^{n(w,t)} \end{aligned} \quad (3)$$

Where Θ is the set of all parameters $\theta_{w,t}$ and $n(w,t)$ represents the number of times that word w appears with sense tag t in word-sense tag sequence (w_1^n, t_1^n). Log-likelihood function $L(\Theta)$ is defined as below:

$$\begin{aligned} L(\Theta) &= \log P(w_1^n, t_1^n|\Theta) \\ &= \sum_{(w,t)\in(w_1^n,t_1^n)} n(w,t) * \log \theta_{w,t} \end{aligned} \quad (4)$$

Because there is no such sense tagged corpus, we assume these tags to be hidden variables and the surface words to be observations. The EM algorithm first finds the expected value of the log-likelihood function with respect to the unknown data T_1^n given the observed data w_1^n and the current parameter values. This expected value is shown with $Q(\Theta, \Theta^{j-1})$ and is calculated as follows:

$$\begin{aligned} Q(\Theta, \Theta^{j-1}) &= E\left(L(\Theta)\middle|w_1^n, \Theta^{j-1}\right) \\ &= \sum_{T_1^n} L(\Theta) * P(T_1^n|\, w_1^n, \Theta^{j-1}) \end{aligned} \quad (5)$$

Where Θ^{j-1}stands for the current parameters value that we use to evaluate the expectation and Θ is the new parameters value that we optimize to increase Q. The second step (the M-step) of the EM algorithm is used to maximize the expectation value which was computed in the first step. That is, we find:

$$\Theta^j = argmax_{\Theta}\left(Q(\Theta, \Theta^{j-1})\right) \quad (6)$$

In order to maximize $Q(\Theta, \Theta^{j-1})$ subject to constraint has shown in formula (2), we introduce the Lagrange multiplier λ and to find the expression for $\theta_{w,t}$, we should to solve the following equation:

$$\frac{\partial}{\partial \theta_{w,t}}\left[Q(\Theta, \Theta^{j-1}) - \lambda(\sum_{t'} \theta_{w,t'} - 1)\right] = 0 \quad (7)$$

Whit solving differential equation (7), we obtain the new value of parameters as follows:

$$\theta_{w,t}^j = \frac{\sum_{T_1^n \, s.t.\; t\in T_1^n}\left(n(w,t) * P(T_1^n|w_1^n, \Theta^{j-1})\right)}{\sum_{t'}\sum_{T_1^n \, s.t.\; t'\in T_1^n}\left(n(w,t') * P(T_1^n|w_1^n, \Theta^{j-1})\right)} \quad (8)$$

However, in order to calculate new estimation of parameters, according to the formula (8) we must iterate over all possible sense tagged sequences T_1^n for Persian word sequence w_1^n. But the number of such sense tagged sequences is exponential with respect to the length of sequence. In this step we assume that the probability of assigning a sense tag t for word w_i is dependent only on w_i and other surrounding words in the sequence and is independent from the sense tags of other neighboring words. By this assumption, we simplify formula (8) as follows:

$$\theta_{w,t}^{j} = \frac{\sum^{n}_{\substack{j=1 \\ w_j=w, t_j=t}} P\left(t_j = t \middle| w_1^n, \theta^{j-1}\right)}{n(w)} \quad (9)$$

The formula (9) implies that the probability of assigning sense tag t to word w is equal to average of conditional probability $P\left(t \middle| w_1^n, \Theta^{j-1}\right)$ $P\left(t \middle| w_1^n, \theta^{j-1}\right)$ over different occurrences of w in w_1^n. For applying the formula, a method to estimate the mentioned conditional probability is required. This method can be regarded as a WSD method which will be described in section 2.2.

2.1 Model Initialization

As in iterations of EM methods is guaranteed to increase the log likelihood function of observed data but there is no guarantee that the method converge to a maximum likelihood estimator (Bilmes, 1998). Depending on starting values, the EM method may converge to a local maximum of the observed data likelihood function. So, in our experiments initial value of $\theta_{w,t}$ has been initiated as follows.

FarsNet is the first published WordNet for Persian language that organized about 18,000 Persian words in about 10,000 synsets. Table 1 shows some statistics about FarsNet. For about 6,500 synsets in FarsNet equivalent synset in PWN have been identified. We have used these synsets for initializing model parameters.

	#Words	#Synsets
Noun	9,351	5,180
Adjective	3,935	2,526
Verb	4,380	2,305
Total	17,046	10,011

Table 1: Statistics of FarsNet

Suppose Persian word w has n candidate synsets such that m candidate synsets between them are equivalent with m synsets of w in FarsNet. With these assumptions $\theta_{w,t}$ is initiated as follows.

$$\theta_{w,t} = \begin{cases} \dfrac{1 + n\alpha}{n + nm\alpha}, & if\ t\ is\ between\ m\ synset \\ \dfrac{1}{n + nm\alpha}, & otherwise \end{cases}$$

In our experiments we used value 0.05 for parameter α.

2.2 Word Sense Disambiguation

WSD is the task of selecting the correct sense for a word in a given context. WSD methods can be classified into two types: supervised and unsupervised methods (Agirre & Edmonds, 2007). The former uses statistical information gathered from training on a corpus that has already been semantically disambiguated. Unlike supervised methods that require sense-tagged corpus, unsupervised methods just use a raw corpus and don't need any annotated data. Based on the types of used resources, unsupervised methods are classified into the following methods: raw corpus-based, dictionary-based and knowledge-based (Agirre & Edmonds, 2007).

In order to identify the sense of each word of corpus according to the initial Persian WordNet, knowledge based methods have been used. In (Agirre & Edmonds, 2007), three categories of knowledge based methods which use WordNet as their source of knowledge have been described: WordNet gloss based, conceptual density based and relative based. A gloss is a definition of synset in WordNet; WordNet gloss based approach is similar to dictionary based approach. However because our initial Persian WordNet does not have Persian gloss, this approach can not been applied to generate Persian sense-tagged corpus. Conceptual distance among the senses of a word in a context is used in conceptual density based approaches. In these approaches sense with shortest conceptual distance from words of context is selected. A conceptual distance is usually defined as the number of links between two concepts in a hierarchical lexical database such as WordNet or a thesaurus. In WordNet several relations between synsets and words are defined such as synonym, hypernym and hyponym. Relative based approaches use these relations to extract the relatives of each polysemous word from WordNet for WSD.

In our experiments a relative based WSD method similar to the one presented in (Seo, Chung, Rim, Myaeng, & Kim, 2004) has been used. In (Seo, Chung, Rim, Myaeng, & Kim, 2004) for a word in a context, a set of related words are extracted from WordNet and then the highest probable relative that can be substituted with the word in the context is chosen. In order to calculate the probability of selecting a relative, co-occurrence frequency has been used. Now consider Persian word w that occurred in the word sequence w_1^n and its sense correspond to PWN synset t. In our Persian WordNet there are other words that have the same PWN synset t in their candidate synsets. These words are synonyms of Persian word w with some probability that were estimated using parameter Θ. We consider a window around w and calculate the correlation of words linked to PWN synset t with words appeared in the window as a score of this sense in this context. That is:

$$Score(w,t) = \frac{\sum_{w'} \sum_{w''} \theta_{w',t} * PMI(w', w'')}{n} \quad (10)$$

In this formula, w' represents words that have t as their candidate synset and n is the number of such words and w'' represents the words appeared in a window around w. This score is based on the idea that synonym words occurred in similar context and then maximum score is obtained for a sense whose linked words have highest association with the words of the context. In our experiments point-wise mutual information has been used in order to measure association between two words. Point-wise mutual information between two words w and w' is defined as follows:

$$PMI(w,w') = \log_2\left(\frac{P(w,w')}{P(w) * P(w')}\right) \quad (11)$$

According to formula (10), we can define the probability of selecting sense tag t_i for word w_i in context w_1^n as follows:

$$P\left(t_i \middle| w_1^n, \Theta^{j-1}\right) = \frac{Score(w,t)}{\sum_{t'} Score(w,t')} \quad (12)$$

The proposed EM method is repeated until the changes of probability of selecting a candidate synset for a Persian word becomes negligible.

3 Experiments and Evaluation

In order to generate initial Persian WordNet as mentioned in section 2, Aryanpour [1] Persian/English dictionary has been used to find equivalent English translations of each Persian word. Also, PWN version 3.0 was used to extract candidate synsets of Persian words.

In order to implement the E-step of proposed method we should select a Persian corpus and calculate the probability of selecting each candidate synset of Persian words using formula (10). To get better WSD result, we used an available POS-tagged Persian corpus instead of raw-corpus. Using this corpus has the benefit that formula (10) is calculated only for senses of word that have the same POS tag to those identified in the corpus and also candidate synsets of Persian words can be pruned according to their POS and appeared POS of Persian word. For this purpose Bijankhan POS-tagged corpus (BijanKhan, 2004) has been considered and all unique words that fall into three categories noun, adverb and adjective have been selected to generate initial Persian WordNet. Now consider Persian word w with POS tag p in Persian corpus. We want to calculate the probability of selecting each sense of w regarding its context. To do this, all senses of w in generated Persian WordNet that have POS p are extracted and their probabilities are calculated using formula (10). Probabilities of selecting other senses of w with different POS tags are considered to be zero in this context. Whereas words in corpus appear in inflected form, extraction of candidate synsets from our Persian WordNet may not perform properly. Thus in order to deal with this problem, before beginning our iterative method we performed a shallow stemming process for Persian on corpus. This process converts nouns to its singular form.

In order to calculate PMI between each pair of Persian words, Hamshahri text corpus has been used. Hamshahri is one of the online Persian newspapers in Iran that has been published for more than 20 years and its archive has been presented to the public. In (AleAhmad, Amiri, Darrudi, Rahgozar, & Oroumchian, 2009) this archive has been used and a standard text corpus with 318,000 documents has been constructed. In order to count the number of co-occurrences of two words w and w', a window with the size of 20 words has been considered.

In our experiments, we used 1,000 documents as training data set. All unique words in corpus fall into just three categories noun, adjective and adverb and there exist entry for each of them in bilingual dictionary were selected to generate the initial Persian WordNet. In table 2 the number of PWN synsets covered by initial Persian WordNet using words in 1,000 documents has been shown.

POS	1,000 documents
Noun	22,988
Adjective	6,121
Adverb	480
Total	29,589

Table 2: Number of PWN synsets covered in initial Persian WordNet with respect to number of documents

[1] http://www.aryanpour.com/

Table 3 shows the number of words in initial Persian WordNet and number of their related candidate synsets. This table also shows average number of occurrence of words in documents.

	1,000 documents
# Words	11,076
# candidate synsets	111,919
Average number of occurrence	110.6

Table 3: Number of words and candidate synsets and average number of occurrence with respect to number of documents

The learning process will be iterated until the maximum changes in probabilities become less than a predefined threshold. In our experiments, we set the threshold to be 0.001. After the termination of EM algorithm, a WordNet in target language and the probabilities of selecting each candidate synsets to each word are acquired. Based on the threshold value has been set before, the model is converged to its final state after 73 iterations.

In order to evaluate the accuracy of trained WordNet, we generate a test set manually that contains 1365 randomly selected links between Persian words and PWN synsets. These links are manually divided into two categories: correct and incorrect. The number of links in each category with respect to the different POS tags has been shown in table 4. The average number of initial candidate synsets of words in this test set is about 66. It means that the words in this test set have high polysemy.

POS	Correct	Incorrect	Total
Noun	452	386	838
Adjective	300	87	387
Adverb	67	73	140

Table 4: Number of correct and incorrect links in test set

In figure 1, the curve indicating the relation between the precision and recall is shown. If we select the highest 10% of probable links as final Persian WordNet, the precision about 86.7% is achieved. In this case, the Persian WordNet contains 7,109 distinct words from 11,076 words appeared in corpus and covers 9,427 distinct PWN synsets. By selecting more links, less precision is retrieved. In the case of accepting all trained links after removing links with probability zero, the lowest precision, about 66%, is achieved.

In table 5, the mean average precision (MAP) over different recall rates with respect to different POS tags is shown. The highest precision is acquired for adjective which is 89.7% while the lowest precision is for noun, which is about 61%.

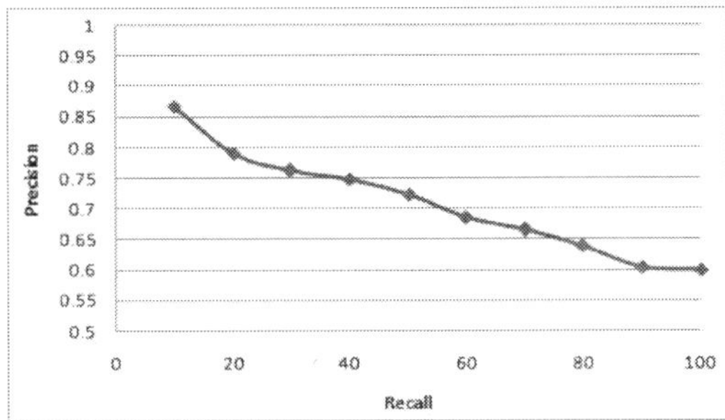

Figure 1: Recall Precision curve

	MAP
Noun	0.612
Adjective	0.897
Adverb	0.656

Table 5: Mean average precision with respect to different POS tags

4 Conclusion

In this paper we have presented a language-independent unsupervised EM method for automatically linking PWN synsets to Persian words using pre-existing lexical resources such as Persian text corpus, PWN and bilingual dictionary.

In the first step (E-step) of EM method, for each Persian word in corpus the probability of selecting each of its candidate synsets is calculated then these probabilities are used in the second step (M-step) to update probability of selecting candidate synsets of each Persian word. The final Persian WordNet is obtained by removing links those probabilities are less than a threshold or by selecting the top probable links as correct links. However the result of this method is dependent to the corpus that is used in E-step. In fact, the probability of selecting correct candidate synsets of a given Persian word that haven't appeared in corpus will be zero and these synsets will be ignored.

We guess that better results can be obtained by using more effective methods to initialize the parameter values rather than using FarsNet which may initialize some senses with higher values even if they have not even been observed in the corpus.

References

Agirre, E., & Edmonds, P. (2007). *Word Sense Disambiguation Algorithms and Applications.* Springer.

AleAhmad, A., Amiri, H., Darrudi, E., Rahgozar, M., & Oroumchian, F. (2009). Hamshahri: A standard Persian text collection. *Journal of Knowledge-Based Systems , 22* , 382-387.

BijanKhan, M. (2004). The Role of the Corpus in Writing a Grammar: An Introduction to a Software. *Iranian Journal of Linguistics, vol. 19, no. 2* .

Bilmes, J. (1998). A gentle tutorial of the EM algorithm and its application to parameter estimation for Gaussian mixture and hidden Markov models. *ICSI*, (pp. 1-13). U.C. Berkeley.

Famian, A. A. (2007). Towards Building a WordNet for Persian Adjectives. *In Proceedings of the 3rd Global wordnet conference*, (pp. 307-309).

Fellbaum, C. (1998). *Wordnet: An Electronic Lexical Database.* Bradford Books.

Fišer, D. (2008). Using Multilingual Resources for Building SloWNet Faster. *The Fourth Global WordNet Conference*, (pp. 185-193). Szeged, Hungary.

Mansoory, N., & Bijankhan, M. (2008). The Possible Effects of Persian Light Verb Constructions on Persian WordNet. *The Fourth Global WordNet Conference*, (pp. 297-303). Szeged, Hungary.

Montazery, M., & Faili, H. (2010). Automatic Persian WordNet Construction. *the 23rd International conference on computational linguistics* (pp. 846-850). Beijing, China: Coling 2010 Organizing Committee.

Rouhizadeh, M., Shamsfard, M., & Yarmohammadi, M. A. (2008). Building a WordNet for Persian Verbs. *The Fourth Global WordNet Conference*, (pp. 406-412). Hungary.

Seo, H.-C., Chung, H., Rim, H.-C., Myaeng, S. H., & Kim, S.-H. (2004). Unsupervised word sense disambiguation using WordNet relatives. *ELSEVIER* , 253-273.

Shamsfard, M. (2008). Developing FarsNet: A Lexical Ontology for Persian. *The Fourth Global WordNet Conference*, (pp. 413-418). Szeged, Hungary.

Shamsfard, M. (2008). Towards Semi Automatic Construction of a Lexical Ontology for Persian. *In Proceedings of the Sixth International Language Resources and Evaluation (LREC'08).* Marrakech, Morocco.

Shamsfard, M., Hesabi, A., Fadaei, H., Mansoory, N., Famian, A., Bagherbeigi, S., et al. (2010). Semi Automatic Development of FarsNet; The Persian WordNet. *5th Global WordNet Conference (GWA2010).* Mumbai, India.

Tufis,, D., Cristea, D., & Stamou, S. (2004). BalkaNet: Aims, methods, results and perspectives. a general overview. *Romanian Journal of Information Science and Technology* .

Vossen, P. (1999). *EuroWordNet General Document.* Version 3 Final University of Amsterdam EuroWordNet LE2-4003, LE4-8328.

Domain Independent Authorship Attribution without Domain Adaptation

Rohith K Menon
Department of Computer Science
Stony Brook University
rkmenon@cs.stonybrook.edu

Yejin Choi
Department of Computer Science
Stony Brook University
ychoi@cs.stonybrook.edu

Abstract

Automatic authorship attribution, by its nature, is much more advantageous if it is domain (i.e., topic and/or genre) independent. That is, many real world problems that require authorship attribution may not have in-domain training data readily available. However, most previous work based on machine learning techniques focused only on in-domain text for authorship attribution. In this paper, we present comprehensive evaluation of various stylometric techniques for cross-domain authorship attribution. From the experiments based on the Project Gutenberg book archive, we discover that extremely simple techniques based on stopwords are surprisingly robust against domain change, essentially ridding the need for domain adaptation when supplied with a large amount of data.

1 Introduction

Many real world problems that require authorship attribution, such as forensics (e.g., Luyckx and Daelemans (2008)) or authorship dispute for old literature (e.g., Mosteller and Wallace (1984)) may not have in-domain training data readily available. However, most previous work to date has focused on authorship attribution only for in-domain text (e.g., Stamatatos et al. (1999), Luyckx and Daelemans (2008), Raghavan et al. (2010)). On limited occasions researchers include heterogeneous (cross-domain) dataset in their experiments, but they only report the performance on heterogeneous dataset is much lower than that of homogeneous dataset, rather than directly tacking the problem of cross-domain or domain independent authorship attribution (e.g., Peng et al. (2003)).

The lack of research for cross-domain scenarios is perhaps only reasonable, given that it is understood in the community that the prediction power of machine learning techniques does not transfer well over different domains (e.g., Blitzer et al. (2008)). However, the seminal work of Blitzer et al. (2006) has shown that it is possible to mitigate the problem by examining distributional difference of features across different domains, and derive features that are robust against domain switch. Therefore, one could expect that applying domain adaptation techniques to authorship attribution can also help with cross-domain authorship attribution.

Before hasting into domain adaptation for authorship attribution, we take a slightly different push to the problem: we first examine whether there exist domain-independent features that rarely change across different domains. If this is the case, and if such features are sufficiently informative, then domain adaptation might not be required at all to achieve high performance in domain-independent authorship attribution. Therefore, we conduct a comprehensive empirical evaluation using various stylistic features that are likely to be common across different topics and genre.

From the experiments based on the Project Gutenberg book archive, we indeed discover stylistic features that are common across different domains. Against our expectations, some of such features, stop-words in particular, are extremely informative, essentially ridding of the need for domain adaptation, if supplied with a large amount of data. Due to its simplicity, techniques based on stop-words scale particularly well over a large amount of data, in comparison to more computationally heavy techniques that require parsing (e.g., Raghavan et al. (2010)).

2 Domain Independent Cues for Author Identification

The study of authorship attribution requires careful preparation of dataset, in order not to draw overly optimistic conclusions. For instance, if the dataset consists of text where each author writes about a distinctive and exclusive topic, the task of author attribution reduces to topic categorization, a much easier task in general (e.g., (Mikros and Argiri, 2007)). Such statistical models that rely on topics will not generalize well over text in previously unseen topics or genre. Random collection of data is not the solution to this concern, as many authors are biased toward certain topics and genre. In order to avoid such pitfall of inadvertently benefiting from topic bias, we propose two different ways of data preparation: First approach is to ensure that multiple number of authors are included per topic and genre, so that it is hard to predict the author purely based on topical words. Second approach is to ensure that multiple domains (i.e., topics and/or genre) are included per author, and that test dataset includes domains that are previously unseen in the training data.

Next we discuss stylistic features that are likely to be common across different domains. In this study, we compare the following set of features: (1) n-gram sequences as a baseline, (2) part of speech sequences that capture shallow syntactic patterns, (3) modified $tf - idf$ for n-gram that captures repeated phrases, (4) mood words that capture author's unique emotional traits, and (5) stop word frequencies that capture author's writing habit with common words. Each of these features is elaborated below.

2.1 N-gram Sequences as a Topic Dependent Baseline

We conjecture that N-gram sequences are not robust against domain changes, as N-grams are powerful features for topic categorization (e.g., (Türkoğlu et al., 2007)). We therefore set N-gram based features as baseline to quantify how much domain change affects the performance. Normalized frequency of the most frequent 100 stemmed (Porter, 1997) 3-grams[1] are encoded as features.

2.2 3-gram Part-of-Speech Sequences to Capture Favorite Sentence Structure

To capture the syntactic patterns unique to authors, we use 3-gram sequence of part-of-speech (POS) tags. To be robust across domain change, we use only the most frequent 100 3-grams of part-of-speech tags as features. To encode a feature from each such 3-gram POS sequence, we use the frequency of each POS sequence normalized by the number of POS grams in the document. We expect these shallow syntactic patterns will help characterize the favorite sentence structure used by the authors. We make use of Stanford parser (Klein and Manning, 2003) to tag the part-of-speech tags for the given document.

2.3 Modified $tf - idf$ for 3-gram Sequences

$Tf - idf$ provides a score to a term indicating how informative each term is, by multiplying the frequency of the term within the document (term frequency) by the rarity of the term across corpus (inverse document frequency). $tf - idf$ is known to be highly effective for text categorization. In this work, we experiment with modified $tf - idf$ in order to accommodate the nature of author attribution more directly. We propose two such variants:

tf-iAf* – *Term-Frequency Inverse-Author-Frequency

In this variant, we take inverse-*author*-frequency instead of inverse-*document*-frequency, as the terms that occur across many authors are not as informative as the terms unique to a given author. For training data, we compute $tf\text{-}iAf$ based on known authors of each document, however in test data, we do not have access to the authors of each document. Therefore, we set $tf\text{-}iAf$ of the test data as tf of the test data weighted by iAf of the training data. We generate these features for top 500 3-gram sequences ordered by $tf\text{-}iAf$ scores from each author. We compute different $tf\text{-}iAf$ values for different authors. The exact formula we use for a given author i is given below:

$$Tfiaf_i = \sum_{j=1}^{K_i} \frac{f_{ij}}{N_{ij}} * iaf_i{}^2$$

where f_{ij} is the frequency of a 3-gram for $author_i$ in document D_{ij}, D_{ij} is the jth document by $author_i$, N_{ij} is the total number of 3-grams in document D_{ij}, and K_i is the number of documents written by $author_i$. We take the second power of inverse-author-frequency, as the number of authors is much smaller than the number of documents in a corpus.

[1] For all ngram based features, 3-gram (N=3) was chosen because increasing N increased sparseness and decreasing N failed to capture common phrases.

***tf-iAf-tpf* – Term-Frequency Inverse-Author-Frequency Topic-Frequency**

In this variant, we augment the previous approach with *topic*-frequency, which is the number of different topics a given term appears for a given author. We generate these features for top 500 3-gram sequences ordered by $tf\text{-}iAf\text{-}tpf$ scores from each author. Again, we compute different $tf\text{-}iAf\text{-}tpf$ values for different authors. The exact formula for a given author i is given below:

$$TfiafTpf_i = Tfiaf_i * tpf_i^2$$

where we take the second power to the topic frequency, as the number of distinctive topics is small in general.

2.4 Mood Words to Capture Emotional Traits

We conjecture that mood words[2] will reveal unique emotional traits of each author. In particular, either the use of certain types of mood words, or the lack of it, will reveal common mood or tone in documents that is orthogonal to the topics or genre. To encode features based on mood words, we include the normalized frequency of each mood word in a given document in the feature vector. Normalization is done by dividing frequency by total number of words in the document. We consider in total a list of 859 mood words.

2.5 Stop-words to Capture Writing Habit

Many researchers reported that the usage patterns of stop-words are a very strong indication of writing style (Arun et al. (2009), Garca and Martn (2007)). Based on 659 stop words obtained, we encode features as the frequency of each stop-word normalized by total number of words in the document [3]. These normalized frequencies indicate two important characteristics of stop-word usage by authors:

(1) Relative usage of function words by authors.
(2) Fraction of function words in document.

3 Dataset with Varying Degree of Domain Change

In order to investigate the topic influence on authorship attribution, we need a dataset that consists of articles written by prolific authors who wrote on a variety of topics. Furthermore, it would be ideal if the dataset already includes topic categorization, so that we do not need to manually categorize each article into different topics and genre.

Fortunately, there is such a dataset available online: we use the project Gutenberg book archive (`http://www.gutenberg.org`) that contains an extensive collection of books. In order to remove topic bias in authors, we rely on the catalog of project Gutenberg. Categories of project Gutenberg correspond to the mixture of topics and genre.

There are two types of categories defined in project Gutenberg: the first is LCSH (Library of Congress Subject Headings)[4] and the second is LCC (Library of Congress Classification).[5] Examples of LCSH and LCC categories are shown in Table 1 and Table 2 respectively. As can be seen in Table 1, the categories of LCSH are more fine-grained, and some of the categories are overlapping eg: *"history"* and *"history and criticism"*. In contrast, the categories of LCC are more coarse-grained so that they are more distinctive from each other.

In the next section, we present following four experiments in the order of increasing difficulty. We use the term topics, genre, and domains interchangeably in what follows, as LCC & LCSH categories are mixed as well.

(1) **Balanced topic:** Topics in the test data are guaranteed to appear in the training data.
(2) **Semi-disjoint topic using LCSH:** Topics in the test data differ from topics in the training according to LCSH.
(3) **Semi-disjoint topic using LCC:** Topics in the test data differ from topics in the training according to LCC.
(4) **Perfectly-disjoint topic using LCC:** Topics in the test data differ from topics in the training according to LCC, and documents with unknown categories are discarded to create perfectly disjoint training and test data, while in (2) and (3) documents with unknown categories are added to maintain large dataset.

[2]The list of mood words is obtained from `http://moods85.wordpress.com/mood-list/`

[3]The list of stopwords is obtained from `http://www.ranks.nl/resources/stopwords.html`

[4]`http://www.loc.gov/aba/cataloging/subject/weeklylists/`

[5]`http://www.loc.gov/catdir/cpso/lcco/`

American drama, Eugenics, American poetry, Fairy tales, Architecture, Family, Art, Farm life, Authors, Fiction, Ballads, Fishing, Balloons, France, Children, Harbors, Civil War, History, Conduct of life, History and criticism, Correspondence, History – Revolution, Country life, Cycling, Description and travel, ...

Table 1: Examples of LCSH Categories.

Music And Books On Music, Philosophy, Psychology, Fine Arts, Religion, Auxiliary Sciences Of History, Language And Literature, World History (Non Americas), Science, History Of The Americas, Medicine, Geography, Anthropology, Agriculture, Recreation, Social Sciences, Technology, Political Science, ...

Table 2: Examples of LCC Categories.

4 Experimental Results

We present four experiments in the order of increasing difficulty. In all experiments, we use the SVM classifier with sequential minimal optimization (SMO) implementation available in the Weka package (Hall et al., 2009). We used polynomial kernel with regularization parameter C = 1.

4.1 Balanced Topic

Configuration We identify a set of 14 authors who had written at least 25 books and also had written books in at least 6 categories. This amounts to 844 books in total for all authors. Table 3 tabulates the author statistics.

In our first experiment, we randomly split the 844 books into 744 training data and 100 testing data with 14 authors. This setting is simpler than true topic disjoint scenario where there is no intersection between topics in training and testing sets. Nevertheless, this setting is not an easy one, as we only consider authors who have written for more than 6 topics, which makes it harder to benefit from topic bias in authors. Note that a random guess will give an accuracy of $\frac{1}{14}$ only.

Result Table 4 tabulates the accuracy, precision, recall and f-score obtained for various features described in Section 2. Note that f-scores (including precision and recall) are first computed for each author, then we take the macro average over different authors. We perform 8-way cross validation for this setup. The first row — N-GRAM — is the baseline. It is interesting that n-gram-based features suffer in this experimental setting already, even though we do not deliberately change the topics across training and test data. All other features

Author	Total	LCC	LCSH
Andrew Lang	63	(36, 8)	(16, 12)
Charles Kingsley	45	(10, 6)	(2, 2)
Charlotte Mary	59	(27, 5)	(11, 9)
G K Chesterton	37	(22, 7)	(7, 6)
H G Wells	43	(38, 7)	(12, 10)
Jacob Abbott	48	(33, 9)	(15, 14)
John Morley	27	(8, 5)	(6, 6)
John Ruskin	38	(16, 8)	(8, 7)
R M Ballantyne	97	(85, 9)	(5, 5)
Robert Louis	80	(28, 2)	(19, 6)
Thomas Carlyle	35	(6, 5)	(1, 1)
Thomas Henry	41	(12, 4)	(4, 3)
William Dean	95	(38, 6)	(25, 19)
William Henry	113	(24, 4)	(2, 2)

Table 3: Author statistics. Numbers in parentheses (x, y) under LCC and LCSH columns indicate the number of books categorized (x) and the number of unique categories the author has written in (y).

Features	Acc	Prec	Rec	F1
NGram	61.22	64.75	59.51	58.02
Tflaf	90.82	94.69	91.54	92.10
TflafTpf	84.69	86.02	85.61	84.96
POSGram	91.84	93.19	91.22	91.51
MoodWord	95.92	94.99	96.28	95.22
StopWord	**97.96**	**99.21**	**97.92**	**98.45**
All	93.88	95.30	94.68	94.41

Table 4: Balanced Topic (Experiment-1)

demonstrate strong performance, mostly achieving F-score and accuracy well above 90%, with the exception of TflafTpf.

Stop-word based features achieve the highest performance with 98.45% in F-score and 97.96% in accuracy. This echoes previously reported studies (e.g., Arun et al. (2009)) that indicate that stop words can reveal author's unique writing styles and habits. We are nonetheless surprised to see the performance of stopword based features is higher than that of more sophisticated approaches such as Tflaf or TflafTpf.

It is unexpected to see that tfiaf-tpf performs worse than tfiaf or POS-grams. We conjecture the cause can be attributed to the fact that we calculate tfiaf-tpf only from the set of books which are categorized by LCC. We calculate tfiaf-tpf only from LCC categorized books because only these categories at the root level are truly disjoint. Because we select tfiaf-tpf ngrams only from the subset of the books in training, it is possible that we could have missed some ngrams which would otherwise have high tfiaf-tpf scores.

High performance for mood words, reaching 95.22% in F-score and 95.92% in accuracy confirms our hypothesis that it can reveal author's unique emotional traits that are orthogonal to particular topics.

Note on the Baseline Because the baseline scores are very low, we also experimented with other variants with baselines not included in the table for brevity. First, we tested with increased number of n-grams. That is, instead of using top 100 3-grams per document, we experiment with top 500 3-grams per document. This did not change the performance much however. We also tried to incorporate all 3-grams, but we could not fit such features based on all 3-grams into memory, as our dataset consists of many books in their entirety. We conclude the discussion on the first experiment by highlighting two important observations:

- First, POS 3-gram features are also based on top 100 POS 3-grams per document, and *these unlexicalized features perform extremely well with 91.51% f-score and 91.84% accuracy, using the identical number of features as the baseline.*
- Second, all features presented here are highly *efficient* and *scalable*.

4.2 Semi-Disjoint Topic using LCSH

Configuration In the second experiment, we use categories from LCSH. As shown in Table 1, these categories were not completely disjoint. As a result, we split training and test data with manual inspection on the LCSH categories to ensure training and test data are as disjoint as possible. In this experiment, we focus on 6 authors out of 14 authors considered in the previous dataset in order to make it easier to split training and test data based on disjoint topics. In particular, we place books in fiction, essays and history categories in the training set, and the rest in the test set. This results in 202 books for training and 72 books for testing.

Despite our effort, this split is not perfect: first, it might still allow topics with very subtle differences to show up in both training and test data. Second, the training set includes books that are not categorized by LCSH categories. As a result, these books with unknown categories might accidentally contain books whose topics overlap with the topics included in the test data. Nevertheless, author attribution becomes a much harder task than before, because a significant portion of training and test data consists of disjoint topics.

Features	Acc	Prec	Rec	F1
NGram	52.78	57.69	53.61	52.66
TfIaf	87.50	89.73	86.15	84.53
TfIafTpf	81.94	82.29	80.22	79.47
POSGram	86.11	88.89	84.81	85.57
MoodWord	87.50	88.28	84.90	85.77
StopWord	**98.61**	**98.81**	**98.72**	**98.72**
All	93.06	94.23	92.44	92.47

Table 5: Semi-Disjoint Topics using LCSH (Experiment-2)

Result Table 5 tabulates the results. As expected, the overall performance drops for almost all approaches. The only exceptional case is stop word based features, the top performer in the previous experiment. It is astonishing that the performance of stop word based features in fact does not drop at all, achieving 98.72% in f-score and 98.61% in accuracy. As before, the mixture of all features actually decrease the performance. Overall the performance of most approaches look strong however, as most achieve scores well above 80% in f-score and accuracy. Baseline performs very poorly again, as n-grams are more sensitive to topic changes than other features.

4.3 Semi-Disjoint Topic using LCC

Configuration For the third experiment, we use categories from LCC instead of LCSH. As described earlier, top categories of LCC are more disjoint than those of LCSH. We choose 5 authors who have written in "Language and literature" in addition to other categories. We then create a training set with books in categories that are not "Language and Literature". We also include books with unknown categories into the training dataset to maintain a reasonably large dataset. The test set consists of books in a single topic "Language and Literature". This split results in 146 books for training, and 112 books for testing.

Result Table 6 tabulates the result. Again, the f-score (including precision and recall) are first computed per-author, then we take the macro aver-

Features	Acc	Prec	Rec	F1
NGram	70.54	70.95	64.88	65.84
TfIaf	93.75	95.66	89.76	91.37
TfIafTpf	88.39	91.89	82.18	83.40
POSGram	93.75	94.80	89.23	90.14
MoodWord	**100.00**	**100.00**	**100.00**	**100.00**
StopWord	**100.00**	**100.00**	**100.00**	**100.00**
All	98.21	98.67	96.67	97.51

Table 6: Semi-Disjoint Topics using LCC (Experiment-3)

Features	Acc	Prec	Rec	F1
NGram	56.76	55.33	55.50	53.07
TfIaf	86.49	89.00	89.39	87.35
TfIafTpf	94.59	95.00	96.36	95.33
POSGram	64.86	69.57	71.17	69.33
MoodWord	81.08	83.83	83.12	81.84
StopWord	**97.30**	**97.50**	97.14	97.13
All	**97.30**	**97.50**	**98.18**	**97.71**

Table 7: Perfectly-Disjoint Topics using LCC (Experiment-4)

age over all authors. Surprisingly, the performance of all approaches increased. We conjecture the reason to be overlap of unknown categories with categories in the test dataset.

Stop word and mood based features achieve 100% prediction accuracy in this setting. However, we should like to point out that this extremely high performance of simple features are attainable only when supplied with sufficiently large amount of data. See Section 4.5 for discussions related to the performance change with reduced data size.

4.4 Perfectly-Disjoint Topic using LCC

Configuration Finally, we experiment on a set of data which were truly topic independent, and we try to learn the author cues from one topic and use it to predict the authors of books written in different topics. In this experiment, the training set consists of books in a single topic "Language and Literature", which used to be the test dataset in the previous experiment. For test, we take the training dataset from the previous experiment and remove those books with unknown categories to enforce fully disjoint topics between training and testing. This split results in 112 documents in the training data and 37 documents in the test data.

Result Table 7 tabulates the result. Note that this experiment is indeed the harder that the previous experiment, as the performance of the most approaches dropped significantly. Here we find that the performance of tfiaf-tpf is very strong achieving 95.33% in f-score and 94.59% in accuracy. Note that in all of previous experiments, tfiaf-tpf performed considerably worse than tfiaf. This is because this experiment is the only experiment that discards all books with unknown categories, which makes it possible for tfiaf-tpf to exploit the topic information more accurately. In fact, the performance of tfiaf-tpf is now almost as good as that of stop word based features, our all time top performer that achieves 97.13% in f-score and 97.30% in accuracy in this experiment. Mood words and pos-grams, previously high performing approaches do not appear to be very robust with drastic domain changes.

4.5 Perfectly-Disjoint Topic using LCC with Reduced Data

In this section, we briefly report how the performance of all approaches changes when we reduce the size of the data. For brevity, we report this only with respect to the last experiment. Table 8 show the results, when we reduce the size of data down to 10% and 50% respectively, by taking the first x% of each book in the training and test data. In comparison to Table 7, overall performance drops with reduced data. From these results, we conclude that (1) when faced with data reduction, the relative performance of stop word based features stands out even more, and that (2) high performance of simple features are attainable when supplied with sufficiently large amount of data.

5 Related Work

Stamatatos (2009) provides an excellent survey of the field. One of the prominent approaches in authorship attribution is the use of style markers (Stamatatos et al., 1999). Our approaches make use of such style markers implicitly and more systematically.

The work of Peng et al. (2003) by using character level n-grams achieve state-of-the-art performance (90%) on homogeneous (in-domain) but drops significantly (74%) on heterogeneous (cross-domain) data in accuracy. In contrast, we present approaches that perform extremely well even on heterogeneous data.

Features	Acc_{10}	$F1_{10}$	Acc_{50}	$F1_{50}$
NGram	37.84	39.40	48.65	46.78
TfIaf	32.43	30.57	72.97	75.43
TfIafTpf	32.43	33.11	62.16	62.87
POSGram	24.32	31.16	62.16	64.23
MoodWord	40.54	36.77	70.27	67.10
StopWord	**64.86**	**65.38**	**91.89**	**92.12**
All	37.84	39.24	75.68	77.01

Table 8: Perfectly-Disjoint Topics using LCC (Reduced to 10% and 50% of the original data)

Another interesting technique that is explored for authorship attribution is the use of PCFG in the work of Raghavan et al. (2010). They show that PCFG models are effective in authorship attribution, although their experiments were conducted only on homogeneous datasets. The approaches studied in this paper are much simpler and highly scalable, while extremely effective.

6 Conclusion

We have presented a set of features for authorship attribution in a domain independent setting. We have demonstrated that the features we calculate are effective in predicting authorship while being robust against topic changes. We show the robustness of our features against topic changes by evaluating the features under increasing topic disjoint property of training and test documents. These experiments substantiate our claim that the features we propose capture the stylistic traits of authors that persist across multiple domains. The simplicity of our features also makes it scalable and hence can be applied to large scale data.

References

R. Arun, V. Suresh, and C.E.V. Madhavan. 2009. Stopword graphs and authorship attribution in text corpora. In *Semantic Computing, 2009. ICSC '09. IEEE International Conference on*, pages 192 –196.

John Blitzer, Ryan McDonald, and Fernando Pereira. 2006. Domain adaptation with structural correspondence learning. In *Conference on Empirical Methods in Natural Language Processing*, Sydney, Australia.

John Blitzer, Koby Crammer, Alex Kulesza, Fernando Pereira, and Jenn Wortman. 2008. Learning bounds for domain adaptation. In *Advances in Neural Information Processing Systems 21*, Cambridge, MA. MIT Press.

Antonio Miranda Garca and Javier Calle Martn. 2007. Function words in authorship attribution studies. *Literary and Linguistic Computing*, 22(1):49–66.

Mark Hall, Eibe Frank, Geoffrey Holmes, Bernhard Pfahringer, Peter Reutemann, and Ian H. Witten. 2009. The weka data mining software: an update. *SIGKDD Explor. Newsl.*, 11:10–18, November.

Dan Klein and Christopher D. Manning. 2003. A parsing: fast exact viterbi parse selection. In *Proceedings of the 2003 Conference of the North American Chapter of the Association for Computational Linguistics on Human Language Technology - Volume 1*, NAACL '03, pages 40–47, Stroudsburg, PA, USA. Association for Computational Linguistics.

Kim Luyckx and Walter Daelemans. 2008. Authorship attribution and verification with many authors and limited data. In *Proceedings of the 22nd International Conference on Computational Linguistics (Coling 2008)*, pages 513–520, Manchester, UK, August. Coling 2008 Organizing Committee.

George Mikros and Eleni K. Argiri. 2007. Investigating topic influence in authorship attribution. In *PAN*.

Frederick Mosteller and David L. Wallace. 1984. *Applied Bayesian and Classical Inference: The Case of the Federalist Papers*. Springer-Verlag.

Fuchun Peng, Dale Schuurmans, Shaojun Wang, and Vlado Keselj. 2003. Language independent authorship attribution using character level language models. In *Proceedings of the tenth conference on European chapter of the Association for Computational Linguistics - Volume 1*, EACL '03, pages 267–274, Stroudsburg, PA, USA.

M. F. Porter, 1997. *An algorithm for suffix stripping*, pages 313–316. Morgan Kaufmann Publishers Inc., San Francisco, CA, USA.

Sindhu Raghavan, Adriana Kovashka, and Raymond Mooney. 2010. Authorship attribution using probabilistic context-free grammars. In *Proceedings of the ACL 2010 Conference Short Papers*, ACLShort '10, pages 38–42, Stroudsburg, PA, USA.

E. Stamatatos, N. Fakotakis, and G. Kokkinakis. 1999. Automatic authorship attribution. In *Proceedings of the ninth conference on European chapter of the Association for Computational Linguistics*, EACL '99, pages 158–164, Stroudsburg, PA, USA.

Efstathios Stamatatos. 2009. A survey of modern authorship attribution methods. *J. Am. Soc. Inf. Sci. Technol.*, 60:538–556, March.

Filiz Türkoğlu, Banu Diri, and M. Fatih Amasyali. 2007. Author attribution of turkish texts by feature mining. In *Proceedings of the intelligent computing 3rd international conference on Advanced intelligent computing theories and applications*, ICIC'07, pages 1086–1093, Berlin, Heidelberg. Springer-Verlag.

Cultural Configuration of Wikipedia: Measuring Autoreferentiality in Different Languages

Marc Miquel Ribé
Universitat Politècnica de Catalunya
mmiquel@lsi.upc.edu

Horacio Rodríguez
Universitat Politècnica de Catalunya
horacio@lsi.upc.edu

Abstract

Among the motivations to write in Wikipedia given by the current literature there is often coincidence, but none of the studies presents the hypothesis of contributing for the visibility of the own national or language related content. Similar to topical coverage studies, we outline a method which allows collecting the articles of this content, to later analyse them in several dimensions. To prove its universality, the tests are repeated for up to twenty language editions of Wikipedia. Finally, through the best indicators from each dimension we obtain an index which represents the degree of *autoreferentiality* of the encyclopedia. Last, we point out the impact of this fact and the risk of not considering its existence in the design of applications based on user generated content.

1 Introduction

"Wikipedia is a free web-based, collaborative, multilingual encyclopedia project supported by the non-profit Wikimedia Foundation", this is the way Wikipedia (WP) is defined in the starting article of the English language edition. What it does not say is that it is the seventh most visited webpage in the Internet and sixteen million articles prove its participation success. It requires a very complex governance system and one of its requisites and rule for achieving the goal of gathering all the human knowledge is maintaining the neutral point of view (NPOV) in its articles.

The repository implements the *wiki technology*, which applies to the ease in creating or modifying text collaboratively as well as the property of linking words to other articles. Due to this differentiated characteristic which enhances the navigation through the content and also for being the focus of attention, WP becomes a highly studied object whose nature is social and technical – textual, relational and quantitative (Ortega et al., 2007) – and is often analyzed by means of disciplines like Data Mining, Information Retrieval or Natural Language Processing.

Although WP maintains its goal and main rules in the almost three hundred language editions in which it is available, the English one is by far the biggest in number of articles. Every WP community decides on which articles are a priority to create, organizes in what is called wikiprojects and ultimately writes the text. Both users and creators of a language edition share a common cultural background and specificities in the writing style. However, when studies approach the community in terms of motivation they coincide they do it for fun, for appeal of the ideology or some sort of altruism (Nov, 2007). However, some informal surveys in Catalan WP association 'Amical Viquipèdia' showed how the national topics were a focus of interest for writing and conflict. Could it not be then that some editors get involved due to some sort of cultural motivation related to their own national or linguistic sphere too?

Yet in WP ideology there is no reason for this to occur, this content exists in any language edition. *Autoreferentiality* concept we propose stands out to describe the interest of a culture on itself, which in WP translates to the interest of editors for their own local content in a WP language edition. Our study makes two contributions: first, we show empirically how by an algorithm using the relations among categories and articles it is possible to retrieve a kind of content which is local to a language; second, how by the use of all kinds of WP features we can understand the importance of this content. We present this theoretical and practical work which will be extended to 20 languages in order to see if its results can be generalized and to give a stronger validity than studies limited to the English language edition.

2 Related Work

There has been research on WP regarding many different aspects, but just a few on cultural questions. Pfeil et al. (2006) in their study proved how different behaviors in editing can be related to the culture. Other study from Hecht and Gergle (2010) focused on the differences in concepts common to several languages using Explicit Semantic Analysis by Gabrilovich et al. (2007).

In the context of topical coverage, studies like Kittur et al. (2009) quantify the content and classify the WP articles into general topics. The study showed a big amount of content related to the social sciences sphere and thus more culturally sensitive. However, the closest work on cultural content related problematic has been presented by Hecht (2009), who introduced the concept *self-focus bias* as *"occurring when contributors to a knowledge repository encode information that is important and correct to them and a large proportion of contributors to the same repository, but not important and correct to contributors of similar repositories"*. While he remarked this lack of consensus in theory, his implementation took the geographically located articles shared among languages to see its prominence by the number of incoming links each article had. As such, Hecht's study could make us understand how for each language edition the geographically located articles in their speaking territories were more important to their editors than other geographically labeled articles. However, it is left to be answered the problematic for many other kinds of content which can be included in the definition. Also, it did not compare strictly the existence of a particular content in different language editions since it assumed only those articles which were in available in different languages and then were universal.

In the following pages we want to introduce a different approach to the self-focus or autoreferentiality question. We explain how we relate it closely to the WP object characteristics and how from them we can understand the importance attributed to some information.

3 Approach

We introduce two stages in which we identify and measure autoreferentiality. First, by collecting all the articles which are likely to be included in a local content representative set, then obtaining their features and giving value in relation to the whole language edition articles. For this, we used a tool called wikAPIdia, which counts with multilingual compatibility and is Java and MySQL based. Differently than many systems using WP as knowledge source and limit themselves to the last articles, we used complementary material as history edits for our purpose.

3.1 Measuring Autoreferentiality

Autoreferentiality shows the degree by which a higher interest on local content is manifested in a language edition. An article is the indivisible unit of analysis within its features. We assume that a higher value in some features represents a higher interest, which in different set of articles can be compared by their average values. The features can be considered as interest indicators and grouped in different dimensions which illustrate the WP object. We will divide the analysis in seven dimensions: Semantic, Isolation, Effort, Prominence, Endogamy, Edition and Temporal. The first refers to the selection of articles, *Semantic* (1), takes into account their semantic value and will be extended on the next section.

Following, the other dimensions are about article qualities or the activity by which they are created. *Isolation* (2) explains if an article exists in other language editions and it is checked on the use of Interwiki links[1]. Hence, if there is external interest for a particular concept (which we assume lower for local content), it will be related to the number of this kind of links. *Effort* (3) is quantitative as it is measured by two indicators made out of the amount of bytes and outlinks – links which appear on the text and point to other articles. *Prominence* (4) complements measuring the number of inlinks, IL, the number of category memberships of an article, CM, and the PageRank (PR) value an article has. *Endogamy* (5) wants to know how prominent is the local content within itself, first by measuring the number of inlinks directed to the set which come from the same set, EIL, and second by measuring the number of category memberships of selected articles which already belong to the local content selection, ECM. *Edition* (6) is similar to second but represents a higher interest in number of edits, ED, number of editors and what we call a diversity coefficient. This calculated indicator is the number of editors, EDT, which are necessary to fulfill a high percentage of edits (for instance, we chose 80%) in relation to all the editors which contributed at least once to an article. The higher the coefficient the more diversified is the

[1] Interwiki links are those from one wiki to another.

editing. We assume it lower since there are highly motivated users by editing local content.

Lastly, *Temporal* (7) dimension is defined by the rate of article as indicator. First, comparing the relative values obtained by the rate of articles created in the selected set of articles, RR, and those created in all language edition, IRR. The hypothesis is that the local content will show higher relative rate. Second, looking at the subtraction of these relative values according to the periods and observing if the local content starts to grow or decay earlier than the general trend.

All in all, our end goal is merging the values of the optimal indicators in one single index which helps in comparing WP language editions (I). Therefore we will obtain the indicator from the feature using the next formula which subtracts the average of a feature (f) on the set by the average of all language edition and relates to this last one. The *Isolation* dimension interwiki links and the Edition dimension diversity coefficient will assume the opposite subtraction. It is expected that both average of features will be lower for the selected set of articles than for all language edition articles. The two endogamy indicators will calculate their value by considering the percentage of inlinks/category memberships to the set coming from the set (endo-inlinks and endo-category memberships), then subtracting 50 (minimum for endogamy) and relating it to 50 again as a range of significant data.

$$(1)\quad Ind.Value(l,f) = \frac{\underset{\forall articles \in Selection}{avg(f_i)} - \underset{\forall articles \in L.edition}{avg(f_i)}}{\underset{\forall articles \in L.edition}{avg(f_i)}}$$

Once we have an indicator value for all the language editions we can create an average value of them. This will explain how representative an indicator is and will work as a fair weighting in the index creation.

$$(2)\quad Ind.Weighting(f) = \underset{\forall l \in languages}{avg}(Ind.Value(f,l))$$

Then a partial index value is the multiplication of an indicator for a language, the general weighting and the percentage of the local content to all the articles from a language edition. The final index value will be the sum of all the partial values.

$$(3)\quad PartialIdx.Value(l) = \sum_{f=1}^{m}(Ind.Value(l,f)\cdot Ind.Weighting(f)\cdot setpercentage(l))$$

3.2 Selection of Articles

The selection of the twenty languages from all five continents represent a variety in both sociological use, spread in their respective territories and community activity in WP, in number of articles and users' involvement[2]. Hence we consider these factors independent enough from results.

Local content will be heterogeneous in any language. It can include writers and geographic places, music and historical objects. We understand it is relative to the language, to the people who are native writers of the language and to the territory where it is spoken, its legacy and activities. Nastase and Strube (2008) studied the titles of articles and categories and found how relevant they were for propagating semantic relations.

Our method of gathering the local content uses first a retrieval of articles and categories which include certain keywords in their titles, to later crawl the category memberships iteratively. If an article can be reached through two different paths it just appears once. From level zero (the one which includes the keywords) to level three, the content is tightly related to the keywords. Although usually there is seven to ten levels, after the third there appear some interferences with articles which can hardly be considered.

For instance, in a language like Catalan we might use the words which refer to the Catalan speaking territories, their demonym and language names (if the same language has more than one). These would be "catalunya", "català", but also "valencia" or "mallorquí" and would retrieve titles in articles and categories like "escriptors de catalunya" or "dret català", referring to writers and law. Then, any article which hangs from these two categories may specialize in some concepts or aspects and develop the topic.

4 Results

In this study, first we determine whether the scope of the local content in a WP language edition. If the selection process using keywords collected a great amount of articles this may infer later in a great autoreferentiality. In Table 1 we see the number of articles in January 2011 for each language edition and the selected percent-

[2] English has not been considered due its size and difficulties in processing in all dimensions.

age. There is no relation between the size of the language and the scope of local content. Small language editions like Icelandic or Swahili do not have higher percentage than big ones like Italian or Dutch, although these last have more articles in local content. Their values oscillate between 14,08% and 52,06% (mean 24,89%).

Languages	Nº Art. Lang. Edition	Selected. %
Arabic	134253	23,41
Catalan	301304	14,08
Chinese	334175	25,57
Czech	184251	25,65
Danish	141767	31,00
Dutch	650733	14,82
Finnish	261678	21,29
Guarani	1371	38,37
Hebrew	114496	27,73
Hungarian	182467	23,53
Indonesian	149509	12,19
Icelandic	42023	24,83
Italian	777906	14,83
Japanese	737085	52,06
Korean	155256	26,35
Norwegian	290629	19,63
Romanian	155763	31,01
Swahili	21193	23,88
Swedish	382801	28,01
Turkish	155242	19,56

Table 1. Extension of local content

In Table 2, we can see the average of the selected articles is up to three times smaller than that of the whole language edition articles. In the last column, the indicator value is made from the difference between both averages (formula 1), related to the one from all language articles. It is not important the selected set of articles has a low average if the average of all the language edition articles is low too. *Isolation*, measured by the number of interwiki links, wants to prove a smaller external interest. Less interwiki links means the article is no replicated to many other languages. In Table 3, we see in the last row that the standard deviation applied to the average of the set is much higher than on the average of all language editions for interwiki links. This means that there are few articles which have a greater number of interwiki links than the average and these may be those which have interest in other language editions. These could be around emblematic locations, institutions or famous celebrities. The resulting weighting is a high value like 74,4 which proves a good for showing the difference between local content and other kinds.

Languages	Avg. Sel.Set	Avg. Lang.	Diff.	Ind.Val.
Arabic	3,1	7,7	4,6	59,8
Catalan	1,4	6,4	5,0	78,6
Chinese	1,4	5,8	4,4	75,7
Czech	1,7	8,3	6,6	79,1
Danish	2,5	9,0	6,5	71,8
Dutch	1,2	5,5	4,3	78,4
Finnish	1,0	8,0	7,0	87,4
Guarani	10,7	16,9	6,2	36,7
Hebrew	3,0	10,1	7,1	70,2
Hungarian	2,8	8,0	5,2	65,4
Indonesian	0,9	7,1	6,2	87,0
Icelandic	1,3	8,8	7,4	84,7
Italian	2,5	4,9	2,4	49,5
Japanese	0,7	3,7	3,0	80,0
Korean	1,2	8,1	6,9	85,4
Norwegian	1,0	6,3	5,3	84,2
Romanian	1,4	7,9	6,5	82,6
Swahili	2,9	14,6	4,4	80,2
Swedish	1,2	6,4	5,2	81,7
Turkish	2,2	7,5	5,3	70,7

Table 2. Results for Isolation indicator

The procedure is repeated for other dimensions like *Effort*, represented by bytes, B, and Outlinks, OL. Both of them resulted in positive indicator weightings, although they are not fully confirmed as positive indicator for all cases. Our assumption was that a higher interest in local content would be reflected in longer articles and more linked towards other articles, which is just partially confirmed. *Prominence*, shows how only category membership's indicator is positive in all cases. It is proved that articles from the selected set are better socially annotated for all tested language, which results in a good weighting indicator of value 42,73. Other indicators from the dimension like number of inlinks and PageRank are irregular and like those from dimension *Effort* it cannot be concluded the local content represents a relational interest to define the whole encyclopedia. Again, the standard deviation shows us there is more variation in the selected set than in all language edition articles.

Dimensions	Isolat.	Effort		Prominence			Endogamy		Edition			Temporal	
Languages	IW	B	OL	IL	CM	PR	EIL	ECM	ED	EDT	DC	RR	IRR
Arabic	59,8	11,3	22,3	21,3	19,6	-22,10	21,20	31,70	-33,10	5,50	11,00	-24,62	-32,31
Catalan	78,6	-18,5	-15	-43,7	52,3	-26,30	35,30	63,10	16,90	1,30	9,00	-18,64	-10,17
Chinese	75,7	-5,8	33,7	5,7	54,2	20,60	40,90	60,30	27,10	19,20	3,70	-9,23	63,08
Czech	79,1	-8,7	-4,1	-33,9	27,5	-10,70	51,90	29,40	-25,00	7,00	5,40	-12,31	-33,85
Danish	71,8	-9,5	11,2	-23,1	36,5	-19,00	47,90	90,10	-8,90	-9,40	0,50	-15,38	-50,77
Dutch	78,4	24,9	36,3	2,4	43,6	85,50	43,00	55,30	-55,80	-35,40	29,00	-20,00	-72,31
Finnish	87,4	-3,6	5,4	-23,1	13	4,50	53,00	37,80	-42,40	-14,90	8,90	-12,31	-49,23
Guarani	36,7	15,5	69,3	34,3	14,3	6,50	51,80	90,80	-37,90	-28,50	-11,10	-41,54	-64,62
Hebrew	70,2	8,8	26	-18	43,9	-21,10	54,10	61,80	-43,10	-25,10	-4,70	-24,62	-40,00
Hungarian	65,4	-4,8	12	-32,6	43,3	31,70	40,00	40,00	-56,60	-2,10	42,00	-16,92	60,00
Indonesian	87	26,2	52,7	52,5	103,6	56,30	11,00	53,80	22,50	65,90	-9,90	-21,54	-15,38
Icelandic	84,7	35,4	10,9	-22,8	61,3	-6,80	50,00	82,40	161,20	275,70	-19,00	-18,46	-38,46
Italian	49,5	55	69,7	23,3	72,5	2,10	25,70	57,80	90,80	64,20	5,80	-15,25	13,56
Japanese	80	-1,7	16,6	-9,5	20,4	69,70	70,50	41,20	-59,40	-45,80	14,10	16,92	-58,46
Korean	85,4	2,1	43,6	-5,7	50,4	-22,80	64,60	34,00	-25,50	23,10	0,00	-15,38	-29,23
Norwegian	84,2	-8,5	6,7	-33,2	47,1	29,30	24,20	11,60	-20,70	24,40	8,20	-20,00	-46,15
Romanian	82,6	-3,1	0,3	-26,5	33,7	-39,90	64,50	40,70	-19,60	-30,80	18,40	-30,77	-67,69
Swahili	80,2	-24,9	9,8	-17,2	20,4	-64,70	76,10	39,00	110,70	289,90	45,80	-23,08	-41,54
Swedish	81,7	-3,9	1,3	-22,1	26,7	108,30	56,40	8,70	-28,90	-15,00	11,90	-10,77	-40,00
Turkish	70,7	-1,4	16	-12,9	70,2	-44,4	23,7	40,1	42,6	37,3	2,40	-27,69	-12,31
Weighting	74,46	4,24	21,24	-9,24	42,73	6,84	45,29	48,48	0,74	30,33	8,57	-18,08	-28,29
S.D.(Ind.Val.)	14,05	17,68	20,79	22,29	23,37	39,73	22,59	26,53	52,48	80,77	14,49	30,15	45,8
S.D.(AvgSet)	1,28	0,35	0,46	0,42	0,29	29,58	0,53	0,24	0,72	0,51	0,14		
S.D(AvgLEdit)	0,41	0,27	0,42	0,42	0,3	24,52			0,32	0,31	0,07		

[3]

Table 3. All indicators values

Those levels which are closer to the zero (containing the keywords in the title) accumulate more effort and are more prominent because they are more general and often inlinked by the specialized ones in the following levels.

In *Endogamy*, both indicators are fulfilled showing how the selected content represents a semantic unity around the keywords. The special procedure for this case implied that endogamy means at least half of the inlinks coming from the same set and then percentage surpassing 50 related to the 50 as a range. With the high value of the indicator tested in inlinks, the local content proved to be defined having a common set of terms which were the core of the selected set. With category memberships it showed how these articles are often classified in several categories which are different but semantically close. For instance, an eminent personality is categorized by his profession but also the city where was born and political positions.

Edition indicators ED or EDT are not positive for all cases. Equally to others, there is almost twice variation in the selected articles than in all articles, which means local content can raise interest in the community but not all the degrees of specialization of the topic receive the same. When the standard deviation is calculated for the indicator values on all languages they give a very high variation which means the communities' responses to this content are very different. The other indicator, diversity coefficient, does not give positive for all cases but it is more stable in its values. It also reflects a tendency of few editors writing the biggest amount of the articles even more emphasized.

From last dimension, *Temporal*, we can conclude the assumption that the article creation in local content would show more interest in time is false. Although the rates show how local content is mostly created while there is a good period of creation for the whole language edition, the relative amount created is not higher for the local content than for the whole language edition. In short, local content is mostly characterized by having few interwiki links and being highly cat-

[3] IW: interwiki links, B: bytes, OL: outlinks, IL:inlinks, CM:category memberships, PR: PageRank, EIL: endogamy inlinks, ECM: endogamy category memberships, ED: edits, EDT: editors, DC: diversity coefficient, RR: relative rate, IRR: increment relative rate. S.D: standard deviation.

egorized. These are the two indicators which can express better the difference of the selected set to all the articles from the language edition. These two represent first an interest not corresponded to other language editions and then a higher will of having it well classified. Endogamy indicators also proved how this content is around the same topic despite it is heterogeneous and can be classified in many other categories like those used by Kittur et al. (2009). When looking at the standard deviation of all the indicator weightings we see how the most stable is diversity coefficient followed by Interwiki links.

With all the indicators already measured and evaluated, the last step is creating the index. Yet, we have another constraint besides having a positive value in the weighting, which is not being correlated among them and therefore avoid redundancy. We checked all the indicators for three different size language editions (Italian, Czech and Romanian) and saw four different correlations: bytes with outlinks, inlinks with endo-inlinks, category memberships with category memberships from set and number of edits with number of editors. Then we select first those which are most independent and from the couples those with higher weighting value. These are interwiki links (*Isolation*), bytes (*Effort*), category memberships (*Prominence*), inlinks from set (*Endogamy*), number of editors and diversity coefficient (*Edition*). In Table 4 we can see the ranking of the overall index.

Languages	Index Value	Position
Icelandic	48,71	1
Japanese	47,41	2
Swahili	46,58	3
Korean	34,43	4
Romanian	30,21	5
Danish	28,01	6
Swedish	26,98	7
Hebrew	25,82	8
Czech	24,60	9
Guarani	23,80	10
Hungarian	21,36	11
Turkish	21,17	12
Norwegian	20,27	13
Finnish	19,60	14
Indonesian	17,59	15
Italian	16,94	16
Arabic	16,33	17
Chinese	16,26	18
Dutch	14,21	19
Catalan	13,35	20

Table 4. Overall results Autoreferentiaity index

5 Discussion

Usually, motivation was approached by classic social sciences methodologies which discuss about where it resides, in the individual by itself or in it while is acting. Further than that, an analysis on the content cannot provide a clear answer on motivation but it can explain what are the cultural preferences and in which degree. While most of the research assumes the results obtained from English language as valid for all language editions, this study remarks how differences exist, they are important to those who create the product, and furthermore they finally shapes the encyclopedia in several dimensions. In the initial selection of articles which represent the local content we found that the extension it covered from the encyclopedia had nothing to do with the sociological characteristics from the community of speakers neither the one involved in WP. But regardless the size of the WP language edition, a non-negligible percentage covered almost a quarter of the total articles.

That said, any of the dimensions we proposed cover different aspects of WP's articles information. What is interesting is that while they vary in number of bytes, they vary less in number of editors and there is a subgroup much more active. This is the confirmation editors change their habits of editing depending on the content they are about to write.

All in all, those indicators which proved more consistent for all languages and their selected articles are the interwiki links and the category memberships, followed by the two from the endogamy inlinks and category memberships. It is paradigmatic that the first, which represented the lack of interest in other languages and was very intrinsic to the definition of autoreferentiality, was also the one with higher value and less variation among the language editions. The second one, showed how in the social annotation process of creating content in articles and structuring it in categories, editors prefer local content to be more precise to all the sorts of content in which can belong. This is important for the future semantic web in which the information must be tagged. And the third, related to endogamy, show how this content shares a sense of unity. No matter how heterogeneous are the articles in discourse or general topic that when they are sorted in categories, on the descendent way from those which include the keywords, they will include some pieces of text (and therefore links) which will tend to refer to themselves. Also, one of the correlations we noticed was that the more endogamy in terms of inlinks, the less interwiki links it had. In other words, the less permeated is a culture by other topics and then diverse, the less connections from abroad.

6 Conclusions and future lines

In this study, first we determined with a simple technique method the scope of the local content in WP language editions, which is in average a 24%. Choosing key words which are very tight to each language like the territories where they are spoken proved right to obtain local content, although a good choice of key words like the territory names and gentilics from the language edition was key to avoid losing content. Most of content comes from the main territory name. While this selection could have been influenced by the noisy category structure, studying after the category memberships as a feature of the content and discovering local content has more categories memberships reinforced the method.

Our results according to our methodology for creating an index showed that autoreferentiality value can increase due to several dimensions. Languages like Japanese and Icelandic gave a high and similar final value but the first relied more on the isolation of their content and their endogamy and the second had a much higher number of editors interested in contributing to local content articles. Since there is no direct relation between features, the extension of the local content and autoreferentiality, every community and its composition must be studied as a different case. For instance, any insight on the general trends the features can show like the length of articles or the very active subgroups of users could be related to a qualitative study which would explain much better motivation works and the social interactions.

To conclude, we want to remark how important understanding autoreferentiality can be when designing applications which retrieve information from WP or another user generated repository. The confirmation of an interest from users in a content in which they identify and develop might not necessarily be considered a bias. While the encyclopedia goal remains in the vague 'collecting all the human knowledge', local content exists part of this collection and because the editors spontaneously created it. Any software which applies to retrieve information from WP or any dataset might be designed aware of giving a better context. Once our best conclusion is the uniqueness of some content in any language, our future work will be on understanding how cultural configuration can be explained by particular topics.

Acknowledgments

This work has been partially funded by KNOW2 (TIN2009-14715-C04-04)

Eduard Aibar, Amical Viquipèdia, Joan Campàs, Marcos Faúndez. Diana Petri, Pere Tuset, Fina Ribé, Jordi Miquel, Joan Ribé, Peius Cotonat.

References

Gabrilovich, E. and Markovitch, S. (2007). *Computing Semantic Relatedness using Wikipedia-based Explicit Semantic Analysis*. 20th Joint Conference for A.I. (IJCAI '07), *1606-16*

Halavais, Alexander and Kaclkaff, Derek. 2008. *An analysis of topical coverage of Wikipedia. Journal of Computer-Mediated Communication.* 13(2)

Hecht, Brent and Gergle, Darren. 2009. *Measuring self-focus bias in community-maintained knowledge repositories.* In C38;T'09: Proc. of the 4th international conf. on Communities and technologies, 11-20, New York, NY, USA, 2009.

Hecht, Brent and Gergle, Darren. 2010. *The Tower of Babel meets web 2.0: user-generated content and its applications in a multilingual context,* 291-300. ACM.

Kittur, Aniket and chi, Ed H. and Suh, Bongwon. 2009. *What's in Wikipedia?: mapping topics and conflict using socially annotated category structure.* CHI'09: Proceedings of the 27th international conference on Human factors in computing systems. pages 1509-1512. ACM. Boston, MA, USA.

Ortega, Felipe and Gonzalez Barahona, Jesus M.. 2007. *Quantitative analysis of the Wikipedia community of users.* WikiSym '07: Proceedings of the 2007 International symposium on Wikis. Pages 75-86. ACM. Montreal, Québec, Canada.

Nastase, Vivi and Strube, Michael. 2008. *Decoding Wikipedia categories for knowledge acquisition.* AAAI'08: Proceedings of the 23rd national conference on Artificial intelligence. Pages 1219-1224. AAI Press. Chicago, Illinois.

Nov, Oded. *What motivates Wikipedians?* 2007. Communic. ACM. 60-64. New York, NY, USA.

Pfeil, Ulrike and Zaphiris, Panayiotis and Ang, Chee S. 2006. *Cultural Differences in Collaborative Authoring of Wikipedia.* Journal of Computer-Mediated Communication. 12(1).

Yang, Heng-Li and Lai, Cheng-Yu. 2010. *Motivations of Wikipedia content contributors.* Computer Human Behaviour. 26(6).

Combining Relational and Attributional Similarity for Semantic Relation Classification

Preslav Nakov
Department of Computer Science
National University of Singapore
13 Computing Drive
Singapore 117417
nakov@comp.nus.edu.sg

Zornitsa Kozareva
University of Southern California
Information Sciences Institute
4676 Admiralty Way
Marina del Rey, CA 90292-6695, USA
kozareva@isi.edu

Abstract

We combine relational and attributional similarity for the task of identifying instances of semantic relations, such as PRODUCT-PRODUCER and ORIGIN-ENTITY, between nominals in text. We use no pre-existing lexical resources, thus simulating a realistic real-world situation, where the coverage of any such resource is limited. Instead, we mine the Web to automatically extract patterns (verbs, prepositions and coordinating conjunctions) expressing the relationship between the relation arguments, as well as hypernyms and co-hyponyms of the arguments, which we use in instance-based classifiers. The evaluation on the dataset of SemEval-1 Task 4 shows an improvement over the state-of-the-art for the case where using manually annotated WordNet senses is not allowed.

1 Introduction

Recently, the natural language processing (NLP) community has shown renewed interest in the problem of deep language understanding, which was inspired by the notable progress in this important research direction in the last few years. Today, lexical semantics tasks such as word sense disambiguation, semantic role labeling, and textual entailment are already well-established and are gradually finding their way in real NLP applications, while a number of new semantic tasks are emerging. One such example is the task of extracting semantic relations between nominals from text, which has attracted a lot of research attention following the creation of two benchmark datasets as part of SemEval-1 Task 4 (Girju et al., 2007) and SemEval-2 Task 8 (Hendrickx et al., 2010).

The ability to recognize semantic relations in text could potentially help many NLP applications. For example, a question answering system facing the question *What causes tumors to shrink?* would need to identify the CAUSE-EFFECT relation between *shrinkage* and *radiation* in order to be able to extract the answer from the following sentence: *The period of tumor shrinkage after radiation therapy is often long and varied.* One can also imagine a relational search engine that can serve queries such as "*find all X such that X causes wrinkles*", asking for all entities that are in a particular relation with a given entity (Cafarella et al., 2006). Finally, modeling semantic relations has been shown to help statistical machine translation (Nakov, 2008a).

The task of identifying semantic relations in text is complicated by their heterogeneous nature. Thus, it is often addressed using non-parametric instance-based classifiers like the k nearest neighbors (kNN), which effectively reduce it to *measuring the relational similarity* between a testing and each of the training examples. The latter is studied in detail by Turney (2006), who distinguishes between *attributional similarity* or correspondence between attributes, and *relational similarity* or correspondence between relations. Attributional similarity is interested in the similarity between two *words* (or nominals, noun phrases), A and B. In contrast, relational similarity focuses on the relationship between two *pairs* of words (or nominals, noun phrases), i.e., it asks how similar the relations A:B and C:D are. Measuring relational similarity directly is hard, and thus it is rarely done directly. Instead, relational similarity is typically modeled as a function of two instances of attributional similarity: (1) between A and C, and (2) between B and D.

Going back to semantic relations, there is a similar split between two general lines of research. The first one learns the relation directly, e.g., using suitable patterns that can connect the arguments (Hearst, 1992; Turney and Littman, 2005; Nakov and Hearst, 2006; Kim and Baldwin, 2006; Pantel and Pennacchiotti, 2006; Davidov and Rappoport, 2008; Nakov, 2008b; Nakov and Hearst, 2008; Katrenko et al., 2010). This is useful for context-dependent relations like CAUSE-EFFECT, which are dynamic and often episodic in nature, e.g., *My Friday's exam causes me anxiety.* The second line focuses on the arguments, e.g., by generalizing them over a lexical hierarchy (Rosario et al., 2002; Girju et al., 2005; Kim and Baldwin, 2007; Ó Séaghdha, 2009). This works well for relations like PART-WHOLE, which are more permanent and context-independent, e.g., *door-car*.

An important advantage of argument modeling approaches is that they can benefit from many preexisting lexical resources. For example, systems using WordNet (Fellbaum, 1998) had sizable performance gains for SemEval-1 Task 4. However, this advantage was mainly due to manually annotated WordNet senses for the relation arguments being provided for this task. There was a restricted track where using them was not allowed: this track was dominated by relation modeling approaches.

Relation and argument modeling have their strengths and weaknesses, but there have been little attempts to combine them, which is our main objective. We use no lexical resources, thus simulating a realistic real-world situation, where the coverage of any such resource is limited. Instead, we mine the Web to extract linguistic patterns expressing the relation (verbs, prepositions, and coordinating conjunctions), as well as hypernyms and co-hyponyms of its arguments. We combine (a) relational and (b) attributional similarity between (i) the first and (ii) the second argument,[1] using weights that are tuned separately for each individual relation.

While semantic relations can hold between different parts of speech, e.g., between a verb and a noun, we focus on relations between nominals.[2]

[1]We will call the first relation argument a *modifier* and the second one a *head*, e.g., for PART-WHOLE, the modifier will be the PART and the head will be the WHOLE.

[2]A nominal is a noun or a base noun phrase (NP), excluding named entities. A base NP is a noun and its premodifiers, e.g., nouns, adjectives, determiners. For example, *coffee* and *guy* are nouns, *coffee boy* is a base NP, but *the coffee guy from our office* is a complex NP and thus not a nominal.

The most relevant related publication is that of Ó Séaghdha and Copestake (2009), who combine attributional and relational features using kernels. However, they are interested in a special kind of relations: between the nouns in a noun-noun compounds like *steel knife*. Moreover, they use the British National Corpus instead of the Web, which is known to cause data sparseness issues (Lapata and Keller, 2004), they do not focus on linguistically motivated relational features such as verbs and prepositions explicitly, they use co-hyponyms but not hypernyms to generalize the relation arguments, and they give equal weights to the similarities between heads and between modifiers.

The remainder of the paper is organized as follows: Section 2 introduces our Web mining methods for argument and relation modeling, Section 3 presents our experimental setup, Section 4 discusses the results, and Section 5 concludes and points to some directions for future work.

2 Method

2.1 Overview

As we said above, we combine argument modeling and relation modeling for the task of extracting semantic relations between nominals from text.

Given the heterogeneous nature of semantic relations, we use a non-parametric instance-based classifier: kNN. This effectively reduces the task to measuring the relational similarity between a given testing example and each of the training examples: we first need to find the training example that is most similar to the target testing example; then we assume they should have the same label.

For argument modeling, we generalize the arguments of each training/testing example using a set of possible hypernyms and co-hyponyms. For example, given *the guy who makes coffee*, which is an instance of the PRODUCT-PRODUCER relation, we generate a list of potential hypernyms such as *drink* and *beverage* for *coffee*, and *person* and *human* for *guy*. We further generate co-hyponyms for the arguments, e.g., *tea* and *milk* for *coffee*, and *girl* and *boy* for *guy*. These hypernyms and co-hyponyms are extracted from the Web and there is a frequency of extraction associated with each of them, which we use to build a hypernym/co-hyponym frequency vector for each argument and for each example. We then use these *argument vectors* to measure *attributional similarity* between training and testing examples.

For relation modeling, we mine the Web to find verbs, prepositions and coordinating conjunctions that can express the typical relationship between the arguments of the target example, e.g., we generate verbs like *make* and *brew*, prepositions like *with*, and coordinating conjunctions like *and* for the arguments *guy* and *coffee* of *the guy who makes coffee*. Again, the paraphrasing verbs and prepositions and the coordinating conjunctions are extracted from the Web, and there is a frequency of extraction associated with each of them, which we incorporate into a *relational vector* and use to measure *relational similarity* between training and testing examples.

2.2 Argument Modeling

We model the arguments using a distribution over Web-derived hypernyms and co-hyponyms.

Multiple knowledge harvesting procedures have been proposed in the literature for the automatic acquisition of hyponyms (Hearst, 1992; Paşca, 2007; Kozareva et al., 2008) and hypernyms (Ritter et al., 2009; Hovy et al., 2009).

While we could have used any of them for our experiments, we chose the method of Kozareva et al. (2008), which (i) can extract hypernyms and hyponyms simultaneously, (ii) has been shown to achieve higher accuracy than the methods described in (Paşca, 2007; Ritter et al., 2009), and also (iii) is easy to implement. It uses a doubly-anchored pattern (DAP) of the following general form:

"*sem-class* such as $term_1$ and $term_2$"

where *sem-class* stands for a semantic class, and $term_1$ and $term_2$ are members of this class.

In our experiments, we use the following two-placeholder form of DAP, which takes only one noun as a parameter and simultaneously extracts pairs of its hypernyms and co-hyponyms:

"* such as *noun* and *"

We execute the pattern against *Google*, trying both a plural and a singular form of *noun*, and we collect the returned snippets. Then, we extract the terms from the * positions, and we build a frequency vector of hypernyms and co-hyponyms. Table 1 shows an example for *coffee guy*.

2.3 Relation Modeling

We model the relation itself as a distribution over Web-derived verbs, prepositions, and coordinating conjunctions that can connect the target nouns.

Frequency	Hyp./co-hyp. for arg. 1/2
311	cohyp_arg1:tea
175	hyper_arg1:beverage
102	hyper_arg1:drink
80	hyper_arg1:item
59	hyper_arg1:product
51	cohyp_arg1:chocolate
32	cohyp_arg1:cocoa
27	cohyp_arg1:soda
24	hyper_arg1:crop
22	hyper_arg1:food
21	cohyp_arg1:sugar
19	cohyp_arg1:fruit
19	hyper_arg1:stimulant
...	...
119	hyper_arg2:people
21	hyper_arg2:friend
...	...

Table 1: **Vector of hypernyms and co-hyponyms for the two arguments of *coffee guy*.**

Following Nakov and Hearst (2008), we use generalized patterns of the form:

"`noun1 THAT? * noun2`"
"`noun2 THAT? * noun1`"

where `noun1` and `noun2` are inflected variants of the head nouns in the relation arguments, `THAT?` stands for *that*, *which*, *who* or the empty string, and `*` stands for up to eight instances[3] of the search engine's star operator.

We instantiate these generalized patterns and we submit them to *Google* as exact phrase queries. We then collect the snippets for all returned results (up to 1,000). We split the extracted snippets into sentences, and we filter out all incomplete ones and those that do not contain the target nouns. We POS tag the sentences using the *Stanford POS tagger* (Toutanova et al., 2003) and we make sure that the word sequence following the second mentioned target noun is non-empty and contains at least one non-noun, i.e., that the snippet includes the entire noun phrase of the second noun in the pattern instantiation. This is because we want the second noun in the pattern instantiation to be the head of an NP: if the NP in incomplete, the second noun could be a modifier in that partial NP.

[3]Using multiple instances of the star operator increases the number of possible instantiations of the generalized pattern and allows extracting additional snippets.

Frequency	Paraphrase
58	V:have
54	V:make
34	V:get
32	V:sell
31	V:serve
30	V:sip
17	V:buy
16	V:want
16	V:pour
13	RV:be made by
12	V:bring
11	P:with
9	RP:from
4	C:and
...	...

Table 2: **Vector of paraphrases for *coffee guy*.**

We then run the *OpenNLP tools*[4] to shallow parse the sentences and to extract the verbs, prepositions and coordinating conjunctions connecting the two nouns. Finally, we lemmatize all extracted verbs.

As a result, we end up with quadruples, each of which includes the following: (i) a pattern, i.e., a lemmatized verb, a preposition, or a coordinating conjunction, (ii) a pattern type, i.e., V for verb, P for preposition, or C for coordinating conjunction, (iii) direction, i.e., relative order of the arguments in the pattern (R marks reverse), and (iv) frequency of extraction.

We concatenate the first three components of these quadruples to form typed directed patterns. We then build frequency vectors for them using the frequency of extraction to represent the semantics of the relation itself. Table 2 shows the resulting relational vector for *coffee guy*.

3 Experiments and Evaluation

In this section, we describe the dataset, the classifier, the similarity measures, and the way we combine relational and attributional similarity.

3.1 Dataset

We use with the dataset from SemEval-1 Task 4 on *Classification of Semantic Relations between Nominals* (Girju et al., 2009), which is the most popular dataset for our problem; using it allows for a direct comparison to state-of-the-art systems that were evaluated on it.

[4]OpenNLP: `http://opennlp.sourceforge.net`

Each example in the dataset consists of a sentence annotated with two target nominals, e_1 and e_2, which are to be judged on whether they are in a given target relation or not. In addition, manually annotated WordNet 3.0 senses for these nominals are provided. The Web query the task organizers used to mine the sentence from the Web is also made available.

Here is a fully annotated training example (note that, for the test examples, the `"true"`/`"false"` labels are hidden from the system):

```
"The production assistant is
basically the <e1>guy</e1> who
makes <e2>coffee</e2> and goes to
the post office."
WordNet(e1) = "guy%1:18:00::",
WordNet(e2) = "coffee%1:13:00::",
Origin-Entity(e2, e1) = "true",
Query = "the * makes * coffee"
```

In our experiments, we ignored the WordNet senses and the Web query since having them is unrealistic for a real-world application.

Table 3 shows the seven semantic relations defined by the task along with the positive/negative instance distribution and one example instance for each relation. In SemEval-1 Task 4, each relation is considered in isolation, i.e., there are seven separate classification tasks, and there are separate training and testing datasets for each of them. For each relation, the examples are annotated with true/false labels, depending on whether they are instances of the relation. Each of the seven datasets consists of 140 training and 71-93 testing examples per relation, approximately 50% of which are positive.

3.2 Classifier and Similarity Measures

Due to the small size of the individual training datasets and because of the heterogeneity of the examples, we found it hard to train a good model such as SVM or logistic regression. Therefore, we opted for a non-parametric classifier: kNN, and more precisely, 1-nearest-neighbor. Because of its sensitivity to the similarity function, we experimented with three weighting schemes: (1) frequency, (2) TF.IDF, and (3) TF.IDF with add-one smoothing for the IDF part. Each of these schemes was combined with the following *cosine* and *Dice* similarity functions:

Relation	Training Data positive	size	Test Data positive	size	Example
CAUSE-EFFECT	52.14%	140	51.25%	80	hormone (CAUSE) – growth (EFFECT)
INSTRUMENT-AGENCY	50.71%	140	48.71%	78	laser (INSTRUMENT) – printer (AGENCY)
PRODUCT-PRODUCER	60.71%	140	66.67%	93	honey (PRODUCT) – bee (PRODUCER)
ORIGIN-ENTITY	38.57%	140	44.44%	81	alcohol (ENTITY) – grain (ORIGIN)
THEME-TOOL	41.43%	140	40.84%	71	copyright (THEME) – law (TOOL)
PART-WHOLE	46.43%	140	36.11%	72	leg (PART) – table (WHOLE)
CONTENT-CONTAINER	46.43%	140	51.35%	74	pear (CONTENT) – basket (CONTAINER)

Table 3: **SemEval-1 Task 4:** The seven semantic relations defined by the task along with the distribution of positive/negative instances and one example for each relation.

$$cosine(A,B) = \frac{\sum_{i=1}^{n} a_i b_i}{\sqrt{\sum_{i=1}^{n} a_i^2}\sqrt{\sum_{i=1}^{n} b_i^2}} \quad (1)$$

$$Dice(A,B) = \frac{2 \times \sum_{i=1}^{n} \min(a_i, b_i)}{\sum_{i=1}^{n} a_i + \sum_{i=1}^{n} b_i} \quad (2)$$

We further experimented with the information-theoretic similarity measure of Lin (1998).

3.3 Experimental Setup

For each example in the SemEval-1 Task 4 dataset, we removed all modifiers from the target entities e_1 and e_2, retaining their head nouns only; below we will still refer to them as e_1 and e_2 though. We then mined the Web to extract features, as described in Section 2 above:

(1) **relational features:** verbs, prepositions, and coordinating conjunctions connecting e_1 and e_2 (see Table 2);

(2) **attributional features:** hypernyms and co-hyponyms of e_1 and e_2 (see Table 1).

We used the type (1) features as a baseline, and we studied the impact of combining them with type (2) features using the following five linear weights: w_{mod} for the modifier, w_{head} for the head, w_{rel} for the relation, w_{hyp} for the hypernyms, and w_{coh} for the co-hyponyms.

We tuned the values of these parameters using leave-one-out cross-validation on the development set, trying all values in [0.0; 1.0] with a step of 0.1, subject to the following two constraints:

$$w_{mod} + w_{head} + w_{rel} = 1$$
$$w_{hyp} + w_{coh} = 1$$

These tuned weights were then used to calculate the final similarity score s as follows:

$$s = w_{mod} s_m + w_{head} s_h + w_{rel} s_r$$
$$s_m = w_{hyp} s_{hyp}(m_1, m_2) + w_{coh} s_{coh}(m_1, m_2)$$
$$s_h = w_{hyp} s_{hyp}(h_1, h_2) + w_{coh} s_{coh}(h_1, h_2)$$

where $s_{hyp}(m_1, m_2)$ is the similarity between the hypernyms of the modifiers, $s_{coh}(m_1, m_2)$ is the similarity between the co-hyponyms of the modifiers, $s_{hyp}(h_1, h_2)$ is the similarity between the hypernyms of the heads, $s_{coh}(h_1, h_2)$ is the similarity between the co-hyponyms of the heads, and s_r is the relational similarity.

We also did two restricted experiments: (a) with hypernyms only, i.e., setting $w_{hyp} = 1$, and (b) with co-hyponyms only, i.e., setting $w_{coh} = 1$.

4 Results and Discussion

Following the experimental setup for SemEval-1 Task 4, we trained and evaluated a separate system for each of the seven relations.

The macro-averaged accuracy over all relations is shown in Table 4. Several interesting observations can be made about it. First, we can see consistent improvements over the corresponding baseline for all three combined systems, for all similarity measures and for all weighting schemes, ranging from 0.5% to 19.5% absolute. Second, in 15 of the 21 experimental conditions involving attributional patterns, the improvements over the corresponding baselines are statistically significant as measured by the χ^2 test. Third, we improve by 1.4% absolute even over our strong baseline, *Dice w/ TF.IDF, smoothed*, which achieves 68.1% accuracy. Note that this baseline is better than the best accuracy of 66.0% achieved at SemEval-1 Task 4 for systems of *type A*, which do not use the Web query or the WordNet senses (Girju et al., 2007).

Similarity measures	Baseline	+(Hyp.&Co-hyp.)		+Hypernyms		+Co-hyponyms	
	Accuracy	Accuracy	Δ	Accuracy	Δ	Accuracy	Δ
cosine w/ frequency	62.2	*67.8	+5.5	*68.3	+6.1	***68.4**	**+6.2**
cosine w/ TF.IDF	59.4	*69.3	+9.9	*68.6	+9.2	***70.3**	**+10.9**
cosine w/ TF.IDF, smoothed	63.9	***70.1**	**+6.2**	*67.8	+3.9	*69.3	+5.4
Dice w/ frequency	62.5	***68.9**	**+6.4**	*68.1	+5.6	*67.0	+4.5
Dice w/ TF.IDF	51.8	***71.3**	**+19.5**	*67.4	+15.6	*66.8	+15.0
Dice w/ TF.IDF, smoothed	68.1	**69.5**	**+1.4**	68.7	+0.6	69.3	+1.2
Lin's measure	66.2	68.0	+1.8	**68.2**	**+2.0**	66.7	+0.5

Table 4: **Overall macro-averaged results for all seven relations.** The baseline system uses relational patterns only, while the following systems combine relational and attributional features using linear interpolation. Shown are the accuracy and the absolute difference (in %) compared to the baseline. The highest results in each row appear in bold. Statistically significant improvements over the baseline are marked with a star.

Fourth, our best overall accuracy of 71.3% represents a statistically significant improvement not only over our corresponding baseline of 51.8% but also over the best result of 66.0% achieved at SemEval-1 Task 4 for systems of *type A*. It is also higher (but no statistically significant difference) than the state-of-the-art result of Davidov and Rappoport (2008), who achieved 70.1%.

The evaluation results for each of the seven individual relations are shown in Table 5. We can see that not all relations benefit equally well from using attributional patterns in addition to relational ones. The most sizable improvements are for THEME-TOOL, which shows statistically significant improvements for all evaluation measures, ranging from +7.1% to +23.9% absolute. Very large consistent improvements can be also observed for PRODUCT-PRODUCER and ORIGIN-ENTITY. The results are somewhat mixed for relations like CAUSE-EFFECT, CONTENT-CONTAINER, INSTRUMENT-AGENCY and PART-WHOLE; still, the improvements are more sizable than the decreases.

We can further see that relations like THEME-TOOL and ORIGIN-ENTITY are best characterized by the properties of their arguments, which makes them a good fit for attributional methods. In contrast, relations like INSTRUMENT-AGENCY and PRODUCT-PRODUCER, are better expressed by patterns: verbs, prepositions and coordinations.

The weights in Table 5 suggest that, overall, the co-hyponyms are more important than the hypernyms, and the relations are typically determined primarily by the modifier and the relational similarity. There is also a lot of variety for the individual relations. For example, for THEME-TOOL, it is the head that matters most.

Note that for two of the relations, we achieve results that are better than the best results achieved at SemEval-1 Task 4, even by systems that used WordNet and the original search engine query. In particular, for ORIGIN-ENTITY, we achieve up to 77.8% accuracy, which is statistically significantly better than the 72.8% at SemEval-1 Task 4. We also improve for THEME-TOOL, but our 74.7% is only marginally better than 74.6%.

5 Conclusion and Future Work

We have studied the combination of relational and attributional similarity for the task of semantic relation classification in text. Using the dataset for SemEval-1 Task 4, we have shown statistically significant improvements over a strong baseline that uses relational similarity only, and even a small improvement over the state-of-the-art. We have further studied the extent of the improvement across seven individual relations.

In future work, we plan to do a similar study for the dataset for SemEval-2 Task 8, where, given its size and the specifics of the relation definitions, which are much more context-dependent, we will need to model the local context, in addition to relational and attributional similarity measures.

Acknowledgments

This research is partially supported (for the first author) by the *SmartBook project*, funded by the Bulgarian National Science Fund under Grant D002-111/15.12.2008.

We would like to thank the anonymous reviewers for their detailed and constructive comments, which have helped us improve the paper.

	Baseline	Accuracy	Δ	w_{mod}	w_{head}	w_{rel}	w_{hyp}	w_{coh}
CAUSE-EFFECT								
cosine w/ frequency	66.3	65.0	-1.3	1.0	0.0	0.0	0.1	0.9
cosine w/ TF.IDF	62.5	*70.0	+7.5	0.5	0.0	0.5	0.4	0.6
cosine w/ TF.IDF, smoothed	67.5	68.8	+1.3	0.6	0.0	0.4	0.4	0.6
Dice w/ frequency	63.7	65.0	+1.3	0.6	0.1	0.3	0.1	0.9
Dice w/ TF.IDF	68.8	68.8	0.0	0.9	0.0	0.1	0.1	0.9
Dice w/ TF.IDF, smoothed	71.3	70.0	-1.3	0.6	0.0	0.4	0.3	0.7
Lin's measure	68.8	66.3	-2.6	0.0	0.0	1.0	0.0	1.0
INSTRUMENT-AGENCY								
cosine w/ frequency	67.9	71.8	+3.9	0.0	0.4	0.6	0.5	0.5
cosine w/ TF.IDF	62.8	*70.5	+7.7	0.0	0.1	0.9	1.0	0.0
cosine w/ TF.IDF, smoothed	73.1	70.5	-2.6	0.1	0.1	0.8	0.0	1.0
Dice w/ frequency	67.9	66.7	-1.2	0.2	0.1	0.7	0.6	0.4
Dice w/ TF.IDF	56.4	*69.2	+12.8	0.0	0.4	0.6	1.0	0.0
Dice w/ TF.IDF, smoothed	61.5	65.4	+3.9	0.1	0.2	0.7	0.1	0.9
Lin's measure	61.5	55.1	-6.4	0.1	0.0	0.9	0.0	1.0
PRODUCT-PRODUCER								
cosine w/ frequency	58.1	*65.6	+7.5	0.2	0.7	0.1	0.5	0.5
cosine w/ TF.IDF	57.0	*72.0	+15.0	0.3	0.0	0.7	0.4	0.6
cosine w/ TF.IDF, smoothed	60.2	*71.0	+10.8	0.1	0.2	0.7	0.1	0.9
Dice w/ frequency	62.4	*66.7	+4.3	0.7	0.1	0.2	0.0	1.0
Dice w/ TF.IDF	58.1	*73.1	+15.0	0.5	0.1	0.4	0.3	0.7
Dice w/ TF.IDF, smoothed	68.8	72.0	+3.2	0.2	0.1	0.7	0.8	0.2
Lin's measure	74.2	74.2	0.0	0.2	0.2	0.6	0.2	0.8
ORIGIN-ENTITY								
cosine w/ frequency	56.8	*72.8	+16.0	0.5	0.5	0.0	0.3	0.7
cosine w/ TF.IDF	55.6	*70.4	+14.8	0.3	0.2	0.5	0.2	0.8
cosine w/ TF.IDF, smoothed	66.7	*71.6	+4.9	0.2	0.0	0.8	0.0	1.0
Dice w/ frequency	58.0	*74.1	+16.1	0.5	0.5	0.0	0.1	0.9
Dice w/ TF.IDF	50.6	*77.8	+27.2	0.5	0.5	0.0	0.1	0.9
Dice w/ TF.IDF, smoothed	69.1	71.6	+2.5	0.3	0.2	0.5	0.1	0.9
Lin's measure	60.5	*69.1	+8.6	0.5	0.4	0.1	0.2	0.8
THEME-TOOL								
cosine w/ frequency	54.9	*69.0	+14.1	0.1	0.9	0.0	0.2	0.8
cosine w/ TF.IDF	47.9	*69.0	+21.1	0.0	1.0	0.0	0.3	0.7
cosine w/ TF.IDF, smoothed	56.3	*74.7	+18.4	0.1	0.9	0.0	0.4	0.6
Dice w/ frequency	57.7	*64.8	+7.1	0.2	0.8	0.0	0.3	0.7
Dice w/ TF.IDF	42.3	*66.2	+23.9	0.0	0.8	0.2	0.4	0.6
Dice w/ TF.IDF, smoothed	62.0	*71.8	+9.8	0.0	1.0	0.0	0.3	0.7
Lin's measure	54.9	*67.6	+12.7	0.1	0.9	0.0	0.1	0.9
PART-WHOLE								
cosine w/ frequency	72.2	63.9	-8.3	0.8	0.0	0.2	0.8	0.2
cosine w/ TF.IDF	70.8	68.1	-2.7	0.6	0.0	0.4	0.9	0.1
cosine w/ TF.IDF, smoothed	62.5	*68.1	+5.6	0.5	0.0	0.5	0.3	0.7
Dice w/ frequency	70.8	*80.6	+9.8	0.5	0.0	0.5	0.3	0.7
Dice w/ TF.IDF	40.3	*80.6	+40.3	0.7	0.0	0.3	0.7	0.3
Dice w/ TF.IDF, smoothed	75.0	75.0	0.0	0.0	0.0	1.0	0.0	1.0
Lin's measure	69.4	72.2	+2.8	0.2	0.0	0.8	0.9	0.1
CONTENT-CONTAINER								
cosine w/ frequency	59.5	*66.2	+6.7	0.8	0.1	0.1	0.5	0.5
cosine w/ TF.IDF	59.5	*64.9	+5.4	0.0	0.0	1.0	0.0	1.0
cosine w/ TF.IDF, smoothed	60.8	*66.2	+5.4	0.0	0.1	0.9	0.0	1.0
Dice w/ frequency	56.8	*64.9	+8.1	0.3	0.0	0.7	0.4	0.6
Dice w/ TF.IDF	45.9	*63.5	+17.6	0.5	0.2	0.3	0.7	0.3
Dice w/ TF.IDF, smoothed	68.9	60.8	-8.1	0.6	0.0	0.4	1.0	0.0
Lin's measure	74.3	71.6	-2.7	0.5	0.1	0.4	0.7	0.3

Table 5: **Results for the individual relations.** The baseline uses relational patterns only; the rest combine relational and attributional patterns for hypernyms & co-hyponyms. Shown are the accuracy and the absolute difference (in %) compared to the baseline. Statistically significant improvements are marked with a star.

References

Michael Cafarella, Michele Banko, and Oren Etzioni. 2006. Relational Web search. Technical Report 2006-04-02, University of Washington, Department of Computer Science and Engineering.

Dmitry Davidov and Ari Rappoport. 2008. Classification of semantic relationships between nominals using pattern clusters. In *Proceedings of ACL*, pages 227–235.

Christiane Fellbaum, editor. 1998. *WordNet: An Electronic Lexical Database*. MIT Press.

Roxana Girju, Dan Moldovan, Marta Tatu, and Daniel Antohe. 2005. On the semantics of noun compounds. *Comput. Speech Lang.*, 4(19):479–496.

Roxana Girju, Preslav Nakov, Vivi Nastase, Stan Szpakowicz, Peter Turney, and Deniz Yuret. 2007. Semeval-2007 task 04: Classification of semantic relations between nominals. In *Proceedings of SemEval*, pages 13–18.

Roxana Girju, Preslav Nakov, Vivi Nastase, Stan Szpakowicz, Peter Turney, and Deniz Yuret. 2009. Classification of semantic relations between nominals. *Lang. Resour. Eval.*, 43(2):105–121.

Marti Hearst. 1992. Automatic acquisition of hyponyms from large text corpora. In *Proceedings of COLING*, pages 539–545.

Iris Hendrickx, Su Nam Kim, Zornitsa Kozareva, Preslav Nakov, Diarmuid Ó Séaghdha, Sebastian Padó, Marco Pennacchiotti, Lorenza Romano, and Stan Szpakowicz. 2010. Semeval-2010 task 8: Multi-way classification of semantic relations between pairs of nominals. In *Proceedings of SemEval*, pages 33–38.

Eduard Hovy, Zornitsa Kozareva, and Ellen Riloff. 2009. Toward completeness in concept extraction and classification. In *Proceedings of EMNLP*, pages 948–957.

Sophia Katrenko, Pieter W. Adriaans, and Maarten van Someren. 2010. Using local alignments for relation recognition. *J. Artif. Intell. Res.*, 38:1–48.

Su Nam Kim and Timothy Baldwin. 2006. Interpreting semantic relations in noun compounds via verb semantics. In *Proceedings of COLING/ACL*, pages 491–498.

Su Nam Kim and Timothy Baldwin. 2007. Interpreting noun compounds via bootstrapping and sense collocation. In *Proceedings of PACLING*, pages 129–136.

Zornitsa Kozareva, Ellen Riloff, and Eduard Hovy. 2008. Semantic class learning from the web with hyponym pattern linkage graphs. In *Proceedings of ACL*, pages 1048–1056.

Mirella Lapata and Frank Keller. 2004. The Web as a baseline: Evaluating the performance of unsupervised Web-based models for a range of NLP tasks. In *Proceedings of HLT-NAACL*, pages 121–128.

Dekang Lin. 1998. An information-theoretic definition of similarity. In *Proceedings of ICML*, pages 296–304.

Preslav Nakov and Marti Hearst. 2006. Using verbs to characterize noun-noun relations. In *Proceedings of AIMSA*, pages 233–244.

Preslav Nakov and Marti Hearst. 2008. Solving relational similarity problems using the web as a corpus. In *Proceedings of ACL*, pages 452–460.

Preslav Nakov. 2008a. Improved statistical machine translation using monolingual paraphrases. In *Proceedings of ECAI*, pages 338–342.

Preslav Nakov. 2008b. Noun compound interpretation using paraphrasing verbs: Feasibility study. In *Proceedings of AIMSA*, pages 103–117.

Diarmuid Ó Séaghdha and Ann Copestake. 2009. Using lexical and relational similarity to classify semantic relations. In *Proceedings of EACL*, pages 621–629.

Diarmuid Ó Séaghdha. 2009. Semantic classification with WordNet kernels. In *Proceedings of HLT-NAACL*, pages 237–240.

Marius Paşca. 2007. Organizing and searching the world wide web of facts – step two: harnessing the wisdom of the crowds. In *Proceedings of WWW*, pages 101–110.

Patrick Pantel and Marco Pennacchiotti. 2006. Espresso: leveraging generic patterns for automatically harvesting semantic relations. In *Proceedings of ACL*, pages 113–120.

Alan Ritter, Stephen Soderland, and Oren Etzioni. 2009. What is this, anyway: Automatic hypernym discovery. In *Proceedings of AAAI Spring Symposium*, pages 88–93.

Barbara Rosario, Marti Hearst, and Charles Fillmore. 2002. The descent of hierarchy, and selection in relational semantics. In *Proceedings of ACL*, pages 247–254.

Kristina Toutanova, Dan Klein, Christopher Manning, and Yoram Singer. 2003. Feature-rich part-of-speech tagging with a cyclic dependency network. In *Proceedings of HLT-NAACL*, pages 252–259.

Peter Turney and Michael Littman. 2005. Corpus-based learning of analogies and semantic relations. *Machine Learning*, 60(1-3):251–278.

Peter Turney. 2006. Similarity of semantic relations. *Comput. Linguist.*, 32(3):379–416.

In Search of Missing Arguments: A Linguistic Approach

Josef Ruppenhofer
Dept. of Information Science
and Language Technology
Hildesheim University
ruppenho@uni-hildesheim.de

Philip Gorinski and Caroline Sporleder
Computational Linguistics
Saarland University
{philipg,csporled}@coli.uni-saarland.de

Abstract

Semantic argument structures are often incomplete in that core arguments are not locally instantiated. However, many of these implicit arguments can be linked to referents in the wider context. In this paper we explore a number of linguistically motivated strategies for identifying and resolving such null instantiations (NIs). We show that a more sophisticated model for identifying definite NIs can lead to noticeable performance gains over the state-of-the-art for NI resolution.

1 Introduction

Semantic Role Labeling (SRL) is traditionally concerned with identifying the overtly realized arguments of a predicate. However, in a natural discourse only a relatively small proportion of the theoretically possible semantic arguments tend to be locally instantiated in the same clause or sentence that contains the target predicate. The other arguments are so-called *null instantiations* (NIs). Even core arguments of a predicate, i.e., those that express participants which are necessarily present in the situation which the predicate evokes (see Section 2 for a more detailed explanation of core vs. peripheral arguments), are frequently not instantiated in the local context. While null instantiated arguments are not locally realized, they can often be inferred from the context.

Consider examples (1) and (2) below (taken from Arthur Conan Doyle's "The Adventure of Wisteria Lodge" and part of the SemEval-10 Task-10 corpus (Ruppenhofer et al., 2010)). We use A and B in the examples to indicate speakers.[1] In a frame-semantic analysis of (1) *interesting* evokes the `Mental_stimulus_stimulus_focus` (`Mssf`) frame. This frame has two core semantic arguments, EXPERIENCER and STIMULUS, as well as eight peripheral arguments, such as TIME, MANNER, DEGREE. Of the two core arguments, neither is actually realized in the same sentence. Only the peripheral argument DEGREE (DEG) is instantiated and realized by *most*. To fully understand the sentence, it is necessary to infer the fillers of the EXPERIENCER and STIMULUS roles, i.e., the reader needs to make an assumption about what is interesting and to whom. For humans this inference is easy to make as the EXPERIENCER (EXP) and STIMULUS (STIM) roles are actually filled by *he* and *a white cock* in the previous sentence. (Note that the two utterances in (1) are spoken by the same person.) Similarly, in (2) *right* evokes the `Correctness` (`Corr`) frame, which has four core arguments, only one of which is filled locally, namely SOURCE (SRC), which is realized by *You* (and co-referent with *Mr. Holmes*). However, another argument, INFORMATION (INF), is filled by the preceding sentence (spoken by a different speaker, namely Holmes), which provides details of the fact about which Holmes was right.

(1) A. ["A white cock,"]$_{Stim}$ said [he]$_{Exp}$. "[Most]$_{Deg}$ **interesting**$_{Mssf}$!"

(2) A. ["Your powers seem superior to your opportunities."]$_{Inf}$
B. "[You]$_{Src}$'re **right**$_{Corr}$, Mr. Holmes."

While humans have no problem inferring uninstantiated roles that can be filled from the linguistic context, this is beyond the capacity of state-of-the-art semantic role labeling systems, which tacitly ignore all roles that are not instantiated locally. SRL systems thus disregard much argument-level information that is potentially necessary for solving text understanding tasks such as question answering or information extraction. That the problem of locally unrealized roles is not restricted

[1] We provide this information for clarity, it is not explicitly marked in the corpus.

to the genre of narrative texts as in the examples above is evidenced by a study by Gerber and Chai (2010) who annotated implicit roles for a set of high frequency nouns in NomBank, which provides predicate argument structure annotation for nominals in the Wall Street Journal portion of the Penn Treebank. They found that implicit arguments add another 65% to the coverage of overtly instantiated roles in NomBank. Hence, the problem also arises in the news domain, at least with nominal arguments, which tend to realize fewer roles overtly due to a more restrictive syntax.

Intuitively, it is not surprising that even core arguments often remain locally unexpressed since a coherent discourse is not a collection of sentences expressing random states-of-affairs but typically is concerned with a limited set of situations which tend to be interconnected. Hence, it is unlikely that an evocation of a situation in a given sentence immediately provides exhaustive information about all possible participants. It is much more likely that this information is spread out over several sentences. Traditional, sentence- or clause-based SRL is therefore clearly a simplification, albeit one that is useful as a first approximation.

In this paper, we propose a number of strategies for identifying implicit arguments and inferring their antecedents from the context. Our aim is not so much to provide a perfect system that gives the best possible performance; rather our work is of an exploratory nature. We investigate different linguistically motivated strategies for dealing with null instantiated arguments and thereby hope to shed more light on the nature of such arguments as well as evaluating potential avenues for future research on automatically inferring referents for such arguments.

This paper is structured as follows. In the next section we provide an overview of how FrameNet models semantic argument structures and null instantiations. Section 3 discusses previous approaches to null instantiation resolution. In Section 4 we describe the data we used in our experiments. The following two sections (5 and 6) describe our model and the experiments. Finally, we conclude in 7.

2 Arguments and Null Instantiations in FrameNet

A predicate argument structure in FrameNet consists of a *frame* evoked by a target predicate. Each frame defines a number of potentially possibly arguments or *frame elements* (FEs). For some FEs, FrameNet explicitly specifies a *semantic type*. For instance, the EXPERIENCER of the `Mental_stimulus_stimulus_focus` frame (see ex. 1) is defined to be of type 'sentient'. We make use of this information in the experiments. The set of FEs is split into core arguments, peripheral arguments, and extra-thematic arguments. *Core arguments* are seen as essential components of a frame; they distinguish the frame from other frames and represent participants which are necessarily present the situation evoked by the frame, though they may not be overtly realized in a given context. *Peripheral arguments* are optional and generalize across frames, in that they can be found in all semantically appropriate frames. Typical examples are TIME or MANNER. Finally, *extra-thematic arguments* are those that situate the event described by the target predicate against another state-of-affairs. For example, *twice* can express the extra-thematic argument ITERATION. Since only core arguments are essential to a frame, only they are analyzed as null instantiated if missing. Peripheral and extra-thematic arguments are, by definition, optional anyway.

Matters are complicated by the fact that not all core arguments of all frames can be realized simultaneously. Some frames have core arguments that are mutually exclusive. For example, in the `Similarity` (`Sim`) frame the entities being compared for similarity can either be expressed by different FEs as in (3) or collectively as in (4). The frame therefore provides three FEs ENTITY_1 (ENT1), ENTITY_2 (ENT2), and ENTITIES (ENTS), where the first two FEs are mutually exclusive with the third. These two sets are said to form an *exclusion set*. At the same time, ENTITY_1 and ENTITY_2 are said to be in a *Requires* relation, which means that occurrence of one of these two core FEs requires that the other core FE occur as well.

(3) $[\text{How}]_{\textit{Dimension}}$ is $[\text{it}]_{\textit{Ent1}}$ **similar**$_{\textit{Sim}}$ [to my solution]$_{\textit{Ent2}}$?

(4) $[\text{They}]_{\textit{Ents}}$ are $[\text{very}]_{\textit{Degree}}$ **similar**$_{\textit{Sim}}$.

CoreSets define another type of relation that is important in the context of null instantiations. The idea behind CoreSets is that FEs can be interdependent, i.e., express similar semantic content, which makes it unlikely that all of them will be overtly realized in a given context. An example are the SOURCE (SRC), PATH (PTH), and GOAL (GOAL) FEs of the `Motion` (`Mtn`) frame. They can be expressed together as in (5) (Ruppenhofer et al., 2006) but it is more likely that only one or two of them will be expressed (6). FEs that are interdependent in such way are grouped together in CoreSets. As long as one FE from a CoreSet is expressed, none of the others is annotated as omitted. If none is expressed, the contextually most relevant one is annotated as null-instantiated.

(5) [Fred]$_{Theme}$ **went**$_{Mtn}$ [from Berkeley]$_{Src}$ [across North America and the Atlantic Ocean]$_{Pth}$ [to Paris]$_{Goal}$.

(6) [Fred]$_{Theme}$ **went**$_{Mtn}$ [to Paris]$_{Goal}$.

The annotation of null instantiations in SemEval-10 Task-10 follows the practice adopted by FrameNet, which is rooted in the work of Fillmore (1986). Omissions of core arguments of predicates are categorized along two dimensions, the licensor and the interpretation they receive. An NI can either be licensed by a particular lexical item or a particular grammatical construction. For example, in (7) the omission of the AUTHORITIES making the arrest is licensed by the passive construction. Such an omission can apply to any predicate with an appropriate semantics that allows it to combine with the passive construction. On the other hand, the omission in (8) is lexically specific: the verb *arrive* allows the GOAL to be unspecified but the verb *reach*, also a member of the `Arriving` frame, does not (9).

(7) [A drunk burglar]$_{Sspct}$ was **arrested**$_{Arrest}$ after accidentally handing his ID to his victim.

(8) [We]$_{Thm}$ **arrived**$_{Arrive}$ [at 8pm]$_{Tm}$.

(9) *[We]$_{Thm}$ **reached**$_{Arrive}$ [at 8pm]$_{Tm}$

The above two examples also illustrate the second major dimension of variation. Whereas, in (7) the protagonist making the arrest is only existentially bound within the discourse (an instance of indefinite null instantiation, INI), the GOAL location in (8) is an entity that must be accessible to speaker and hearer from the discourse or its context (definite null instantiation, DNI). Finally, note that the licensing construction or lexical item fully and reliably determines the interpretation. Whereas missing by-phrases have always an indefinite interpretation, whenever *arrive* omits the GOAL lexically, the GOAL has to be interpreted as definite.

As INIs do not need to be accessible within a context, the task of resolving NIs is restricted to DNIs. The complete task can then be modeled as a pipeline consisting of three sub-tasks: (i) identifying potential NIs by taking into account information about core arguments and relations between them, (ii) automatically distinguishing between DNIs and INIs by identifying NI licensing constructions or lexical items, and (iii) resolving NIs classified as DNIs to a suitable referent.

3 Related Work

The most closely related piece of work is the system building performed in the context of the SemEval-10 Task-10 (Ruppenhofer et al., 2010). The two participating systems which addressed the NI resolution task took very different approaches. Tonelli and Delmonte (2010) developed a knowledge-based system called VENSES++ that builds on an existing text understanding system (Delmonte, 2008). VENSES++ employs deep syntactic parsing and uses hand-crafted lexicons to generate logical forms. It then makes use of a rule-based anaphora resolution procedure before employing two different strategies for identifying and resolving NIs. For verbal predicates, argument pattern templates generated from FrameNet data are used to identify missing predicates and classify lexically licensed NIs as DNI or INI. The only type of constructionally licensed NIs that can be detected by the system are those of agents in passive constructions. NIs are resolved by reasoning about the semantic similarity between an NI and a potential filler using WordNet. For nominal predicates, the system employs a common sense reasoning module that builds upon ConceptNet (Liu and Singh, 2004). The system is conservative and has a relatively high precision, e.g., 64.2% for the DNI v. INI distinction, but a low recall, identifying less than 20% of the NIs correctly.

The second system (Chen et al., 2010) is statistical and extends an existing semantic role labeler (Das et al., 2010). The system first classifies NIs as DNI or INI and then tries to find fillers for the former. Resolving DNIs is modeled in the same way as labeling overt arguments, however the search space is extended to pronouns, NPs, and nouns outside the sentence.[2] When evaluating a potential filler, the syntactic features which

[2]This disregards other role fillers such as whole sentences as in example (2) above.

are used in argument labeling of overt arguments are replaced by two semantic features: The system checks first whether a potential filler in the context fills the null-instantiated role overtly in one of the FrameNet sentences, i.e. whether there is a precedent for a given filler-role combination among the overt arguments of the frame in FrameNet. If not, the system calculates the distributional similarity between filler and role. The surface distance between a potential filler and an NI is also taken into account. While Chen et al.'s system has a higher recall than VENSES++, its performance is still relatively low, e.g., the accuracy for the DNI v. INI classification is 55%. The authors argue that data sparseness is the biggest problem.

Also very closely related is Gerber and Chai (2010), which presents a study of implicit arguments for a group of frequent nominal predicates. Gerber and Chai (2010) model the task as a classical supervised task and implement a number of syntactic, semantic, and discourse features such as the the sentence distance between an NI and its potential filler, their mutual information, and the discourse relation holding between the spans containing the target predicate and the potential filler.

While both Gerber and Chai (2010) and the SemEval-10 Task-10 deal with finding fillers for uninstantiated arguments, there are important differences between the two data sets, which make the results not directly comparable. Gerber and Chai's corpus consists of newswire texts (Wall Street Journal), which is annotated with NomBank/PropBank roles. The data cover 10 nominal predicates from the commerce domain, with—on average—120 annotated instances per predicate. The Task-10 corpus consists of narrative texts annotated under the FrameNet paradigm. Crucially, this corpus provides annotations for running texts not for individual occurrences of selected target predicates. It thus treats many different general-language predicates of all parts of speech. While the overall size of the corpus in terms of sentences is comparable to Gerber and Chai's corpus, the SemEval corpus contains many more target predicates and fewer instances for each.[3] These properties make it much harder to obtain good results on the SemEval corpus, which is supported by the fact that the NI resolution results obtained by the Task-10 participants are significantly below those reported by Gerber and Chai (2010).

While the SemEval-10 Task-10 is harder than the problem tackled by Gerber and Chai (2010), we also believe it is more realistic. Given the complexity of annotating semantic argument structures in general and null instantiations in particular, it seems infeasible to annotate large amounts of text with the required information. Hence, automated systems will always have to make do with scarce resources. We investigate different strategies of incorporating linguistic background knowledge to overcome this data sparseness problem, e.g., by explicitly modeling the DNI v. INI distinction, which is ignored by Gerber and Chai (2010). We also think that the task is best modeled as a semi-supervised task which combines the training data with FrameNet data not annotated for NIs.

Another line of research that is related to the goals of our effort is the work on zero pronoun resolution in pro-drop languages such as Japanese or Spanish. Iida et al. (2007) discuss the relevance of the semantic role labeling and zero-anaphora resolution tasks to each other and study how methods used in one task can help in the other. Still, their work is different from our task in two respects. First, it has a different coverage. Of the kinds of omissions that we consider to be null instantiations, Iida et al. (2007) target only the subset of constructionally licensed omissions. In addition, they seem to treat cases of co-instantiation or argument sharing—for instance subjects shared across conjoined VPs—as involving argument omission, which is not how similar cases would be treated in our FrameNet-style annotations. Second, in their system implementation Iida et al. (2007) use only syntactic patterns but no semantic information about the semantic class ($\approx$ frame) of the predicate missing an argument or about the interrelations between the predicate missing an argument and the predicate(s) where coreferent mentions of the missing argument appear. Palomar et al. (2001) similarly use syntactic rather than semantic information in their work on Spanish, which only allows constructionally licensed subject omissions.

4 Data

In our experiments we used the corpus distributed for the SemEval-10 Task-10 on "Linking Events and Their Participants in Discourse" (Ruppenhofer et al., 2010). The data set consists of two

[3]E.g., Ruppenhofer et al. (2010) report that there are 1,703 frame instances covering 425 distinct frame types, which gives an average of 3.8 instances per frame.

texts from Arthur Conan Doyle, "The Adventure of Wisteria Lodge"(1908) and "The Hound of the Baskervilles" (1901/02). From the first text, the second part entitled "The Tiger of San Pedro" (henceforth "Tiger") was annotated and served as training data in the task; from the second text (henceforth "Hound") chapters 13 and 14 were annotated and served as test data. The annotation consists of frame-semantic argument structure, coreference chains, and information about null instantiation, i.e., the NI type (DNI vs. INI) and the filler, if available in the text. Table 1 provides basic statistics about the data set.

In a qualitative analysis, we also considered a randomly chosen subset of 50 frame instances from the training data with at least one uninstantiated FE-set (see Section 6).

5 Modeling

We approach our three sub-decisions separately. The first sub-task, determining which, if any, frame elements are missing relies on information from the FrameNet release. Of particular importance is information about the three types of relationships between the core Frame elements: CoreSet, Excludes, and Requires. Given that we start with gold standard annotation of the overtly instantiated elements, we reason about the FE relations in the frame at issue to determine which FEs are to be considered as missing. For instance, consider the instance of the `Similarity` frame evoked by *different* in (10).

(10) Falkner can be related to the "New South" literature but [his approach]$_{Ent1}$ was **different**$_{Sim}$.

As discussed in Section 2, there are two FE-relation instances defined for the `Similarity` frame: a Requires relation between ENTITY_1 and ENTITY_2 and an Excludes relation between ENTITIES and ENTITY_1 and ENTITY_2. Given that ENTITY_1 is instantiated, we conclude due to the Excludes relation that ENTITIES does not have to be treated as NI; given the Requires relation, we conclude that ENTITY_2 does.

Our second sub-decision is to decide whether a frame element that we have found to be null-instantiated has an anaphoric (DNI) or an existential (INI) interpretation. Our approach for making this decision is the following. First, we check whether the omission we are looking at is licensed by a specific grammatical construction which specifies the interpretation type of the argument it suppresses. For instance, we would treat the missing by-phrase agent of a passive as omitted with existential interpretation. Besides passive, we only consider imperatives at this point, although there are additional but less frequently occurring valence-suppressing constructions.

In our specific case of (10), there is no relevant construction that we can blame the omission on and we thus consider the omission to be lexically licensed. Since that is so, we next look at the FrameNet annotations for the specific frame evoking element. Either we only look at the annotations of the particular lexical unit that occurs in our text, or we consider statistics aggregated across all lexical units in a frame. In either case, for the frame element under consideration we choose that type of interpretation type that is more common in the annotated data. For *different* we find that uninstantiated cases of ENTITY_2 are always labeled DNI and so in processing (10) we would choose DNI as well. Heuristics are needed when there either are no relevant annotations or when the frequencies of DNI and INI are tied.[4] The simplest heuristic is to simply choose one interpretation type as a default, which is what we do.

The final decision we have to make concerns uninstantiated FEs for which we have settled on the anaphoric interpretation type. For these, we have to locate, if possible, a coreferring antecedent mention. Any coreferring mention will do since we evaluate against coreference chains.[5] In theory, we could use customized strategies for antecedent finding depending, for instance, on whether the null instantiation is licensed by a construction or by a lexical item, or depending on the identity of the null-instantiated frame element. However, at the moment we treat the problem of antecedent finding in the same way for all null-instantiated frame elements.

One approach we pursue for identifying a suitable mention/chain relies on the semantic types that FrameNet specifies for frame elements. Specifically, we look up in FrameNet the semantic type(s) of the FE that is unexpressed. With that in-

[4] One might additionally choose to employ heuristics when the number of annotated instances is very small, or when the frequencies of DNI and INI are very close, though not tied. We have not used such heuristics here.

[5] Note that we have chains of length 1, since we for instance need to be able to reify whole sentences as referents that can be the antecedents for unexpressed MESSAGE, CONTENT or similar FEs of predicates such as *know* or *confess*.

data set	sentences	tokens	frame instances	frame types	overt frame elements	DNIs (resolved)	INIs
train	438	7,941	1,370	317	2,526	303 (245)	277
test	525	9,131	1,703	452	3,141	349 (259)	361

Table 1: Statistics for the SemEval-10 Task-10 corpus

formation in hand, we consider all the coreference chains that are active in some window of context, where being active means that one of the member mentions of the chain occurs in one of the context sentences. We try to find chains that share at least one semantic type with the FE in question. This is possible because for each chain, we have percolated the semantic types associated with any of their member mentions to the chain.[6] If multiple chains remain that are compatible with the FE in question, we select between them by some criterion. In particular, we prefer to link the FE to that chain that has the mention closest to the FE in question in terms of intervening leaf nodes.[7] If we find no chain at all within the window that has semantic types compatible with our FE, we guess that the FE has no antecedent.[8] Note also that in our current set-up we have defined the semantic type match to be a strict one. For instance, if our FE has the semantic type *Entity* and an active chain is of the type *Sentient*, we will not get a match even though the type *Sentient* is a descendant of *Entity* in the hierarchy in which semantic types are arranged.

6 Experiments

To gain a better understanding of our results for the full NI resolution task, we performed a qualitative analysis on a subset of 50 frames from the training set, in which one or more Frame elements were uninstantiated. We focus here on the first two sub-decisions that have to be made in the automatic analysis of null instantiations: which specific FEs should be treated as null-instantiated and which interpretation type the relevant FEs have.

The distribution of frames in this set was as follows: 33 frames occurring only once, 4 instances of `Arriving`, 3 instances of `Self-motion` and 2 of `Departing`. In 3 of the 6 instances of `Calendric_unit` and in all 3 instances of `Self-motion`, our NI analysis system made errors. These are two challenging frames to handle which happen to be frequent in our data.

We also see that in our data, we have many nouns as frame evoking elements (FEEs). 28 of 50 FEEs are nouns, 15 verbs, and 7 adjectives. This distribution also contributes to an overall lower performance of our system because the error rate is highest for nouns, middling for adjectives, and lowest for verbs.[9] In our first system setting, where we use frame-level NI statistics and where we use INI as the default interpretation type when FrameNet either has no relevant data or shows equal probability for DNI and INI, the error rate on nouns is 53.6%, on adjectives 28.6%, and on verbs 13.3%.

In the first setting with INI as default, the system made no error on 31 of the 50 frames (62%). The 50 frame instances analyzed contain 62 FE-Sets that are not instantiated. (Recall that a single predicate may omit more than one argument at the same time.) Of these 62 sets, 38 are classified correctly as INI or DNI (61.3%) and the remaining 24 incorrectly. The predominant error type is the system positing INI where the gold value is DNI (16 of 24). The remaining errors are the other way around.

Given that for our data set, the baseline of guessing the DNI majority class is 52.2%, our system configuration has noticeably better precision at 62%. Importantly, we also have 100% recall for uninstantiated FE-sets unlike the systems in the SemEval task.

In our second NI analysis setting, we again use

[6]In the official FrameNet database, not every frame element is assigned a semantic type. We modified our copy of FrameNet so that every FE does have a semantic type by simply looking up in WordNet the path from the name of a frame element to the synsets that FrameNet uses to define semantic types.

[7]Other criteria are easily conceivable. We might, for instance, use a tree-based distance measure, or link the FE to the chain that has the most mentions within the window of context.

[8]Alternatively, we could have widened the window of context in the hope of hitting upon a suitable chain.

[9]The same differences among the parts-of-speech can also be seen, for instance, in the performance on labeling of explicit FEs where the treatment of verbal predicators is more successful.

	Accuracy
Maj. Baseline	52.2%
PerFrame	61.3%
PerLU	66.0%

Table 2: Distinguishing DNIs and INIs

INI as the default value but we use lexical unit-specific NI-statistics rather than aggregate statistics over all lexical units in the frame. Doing so improves the result a bit: we classify 41 of 62 FE-sets (66%) correctly, for a 4.7% improvement over the previous setting. Table 2 provides a summary of the results.

Finally, we look at the sources of error for our first setting. As noted above, there were 19 frame instances where at least one FE-set was classified incorrectly. The main reasons for these errors were:

- With 5 frames instances, the error results because the aggregate frame-level statistics are distorted. This is due to two reasons: there are few annotated instances, or a "deviant" lexical unit is overrepresented.

- In another 5 frame instances, the use of INI as a default is inappropriate. These are cases where either no lexical unit in the frame is annotated at all, or where the frame was created and annotated before the practice of annotating missing arguments was adopted.

- In 4 frame instances, a misclassification occurs because the instance of the frame in our test data occurs in a special linguistic context that overrides the majority interpretation type that can be observed in the FrameNet data. For instance, the context in our data may be generic, while the majority of cases in FrameNet annotations are episodic.

- 4 frame instances belong to the linguistically difficult frames where the gold standard analysis itself may not be fully worked out. A good example of this is Calendric unit.

While our manually inspected data set is small, it seems we must conclude from this qualitative analysis that even a reasonable, linguistically motivated use of the available FrameNet data won't yield the correct result for NI-classification in all cases. One difficulty arises from FrameNet's annotation practice, which does not select instances randomly. Hence, the statistics about indefinite v. definite interpretations for a given FE that can be gleaned from FrameNet are not necessarily accurate. At this point, we do not know the exact number of frames where, for instance, a skew in the annotated LUs or the annotated instances of a particular LU would lead to incorrect classifications. But even if FrameNet had annotated a large number of randomly chosen instances for all LUs, our current system would not achieve perfect performance because it lacks a way of detecting constructions and contexts (such as generic or habitual sentences) that can override the majority interpretation type. Complementing our system with an additional analysis step which attempts to identify different event types thus seems beneficial. The work by Reiter and Frank (2010) and Mathew and Katz (2009) on generic NPs and sentences could be a starting point.

Since there are only very few resolved NIs in the 50 frame data set we used to evaluate the first two sub-tasks, we evaluated the NI resolution task (i.e., the third sub-task) on the whole SemEval-2010 Task-10 test set. We employed the best performing SemEval system, SEMAFOR (Chen et al., 2010), as a baseline. Even though our NI resolution strategy is still fairly basic, taking only the semantic type of potential fillers into account, our system reduces the resolution errors for the complete pipeline by 14% compared to SEMAFOR. This may be due to the fact that our DNI v. INI classification is better. As the DNI v. INI distinction was not evaluated for the shared task, we cannot directly compare our results on this sub-task against SEMAFOR. However, Chen et al. (2010) provide a confusion matrix for argument classification (Table 3 in their paper), which suggests that only 3% of DNIs are correctly identified. The majority of unidentified DNIs are misclassified as INIs (52%).

SEMAFOR is, however, a bit better at identifying the correct boundaries for correctly found antecedents (100% NI linking overlap v. 89% for our system). The reason for this may be that we consider more varied antecedents. In particular, we also consider full sentence antecedents. Example (11) illustrates the problem of identifying the correct boundaries for full sentence antecedents. The gold annotation identifies both (a) and (b) as the antecedent of the CONTENT FE of the `Experiencer_focus` frame evoked by *pleasure* in (c), while our system resolved the NI only to (b).

(11) a. "I must congratulate you, Inspector, on handling so distinctive and instructive a case.
b. Your powers, if I may say so without offence, seem superior to your opportunities."
c. Inspector Baynes's small eyes twinkled with **pleasure**$_{Exp\_foc}$.

7 Conclusion

We presented a novel approach to recognizing and resolving null instantiations. We split the task in three sub-task: identification of NIs, distinguishing definite and indefinite NIs, and resolving NIs to a suitable referent in the text. We paid particular attention to the first two sub-tasks. The first task was addressed by making use of background knowledge about interdependencies between frame elements. For the second task, we employed a hybrid system which combined rules for identifying syntactic constructions with statistics about DNI v. INI distributions for different lexical units or frames. For the resolution task we made use of FrameNet's semantic type information for frame elements which we enriched with semantic information from WordNet.

We showed that our system has a noticeably better performance on the whole pipeline than the best system participating in the SemEval-10 NI resolution task. This is probably due to the fact that we employ a more sophisticated system for identifying DNIs.

However, an error analysis revealed that there are also areas where our system could be improved. Obtaining reliable statistics for lexically licensed NIs from FrameNet proves difficult because FrameNet data were not randomly selected. It may be possible to overcome this shortcoming by trying to glean information about NIs from unannotated data, e.g., by using semantic similarity to cluster syntactic arguments. A preprocessing component which identifies different event types (generics, habituals etc.) might also help to identify DNIs in a more reliable fashion. Furthermore, our strategy for finding antecedents is still fairly basic. Adding additional features, e.g., along the lines of Gerber and Chai (2010) will probably lead to better performance.

Acknowledgments

This research has been funded by the German Research Foundation DFG (MMCI Cluster of Excellence and grant PI 154/9-3).

References

D. Chen, N. Schneider, D. Das, N. A. Smith. 2010. SEMAFOR: Frame Argument Resolution with Log-Linear Models. In *Proc. of SemEval-2010*, 264–267.

D. Das, N. Schneider, D. Chen, N. A. Smith. 2010. Probabilistic Frame-semantic Parsing. In *Proc. of NAACL-HLT-10*, 948–956.

R. Delmonte. 2008. *Computational Linguistic Text Processing Lexicon, Grammar, Parsing and Anaphora Resolution*. Nova Science, New York.

C. Fillmore. 1986. Pragmatically Controlled Zero Anaphora. In *Proceedings of the Twelfth Annual Meeting of the Berkeley Liguistics Society*, 95–107.

M. Gerber, J. Y. Chai. 2010. Beyond NomBank: A Study of Implicit Arguments for Nominal Predicates. In *Proc. of ACL-2010*, 1583–1592.

R. Iida, K. Inui, Y. Matsumoto. 2007. Zero-anaphora Resolution by Learning Rich Syntactic Pattern Features. *ACM Transactions on Asian Language Information Processing (TALIP)*, 6:1:1–1:22.

H. Liu, P. Singh. 2004. ConceptNet: A Practical Commonsense Reasoning Toolkit. *BT Technology Journal*, 22(4):211–226.

T. Mathew, G. Katz. 2009. Supervised categorization of habitual and episodic sentences. In *Sixth Midwest Computational Linguistics Colloquium*, Bloomington, Indiana.

M. Palomar, L. Moreno, J. Peral, R. Muñoz, A. Ferrández, P. Martínez-Barco, M. Saiz-Noeda. 2001. An Algorithm for Anaphora Resolution in Spanish Texts. *Computational Linguistics*, 27:545–567.

N. Reiter, A. Frank. 2010. Identifying Generic Noun Phrases. In *Proc. of ACL-10*, 40–49.

J. Ruppenhofer, M. Ellsworth, M. R. L. Petruck, C. R. Johnson, J. Scheffczyk. 2006. FrameNet II: Extended Theory and Practice. available at `http://framenet.icsi.berkeley.edu/index.php?option=com_wrapper&Itemid=126`.

J. Ruppenhofer, C. Sporleder, R. Morante, C. Baker, M. Palmer. 2010. SemEval-2010 Task 10: Linking Events and Their Participants in Discourse. In *Proc. of SemEval-2010*, 45–50.

S. Tonelli, R. Delmonte. 2010. VENSES++: Adapting a Deep Semantic Processing System to the Identification of Null Instantiations . In *Proc. of SemEval-2010*, 296–299.

Enlarging Monolingual Dictionaries for Machine Translation with Active Learning and Non-Expert Users

Miquel Esplà-Gomis, Víctor M. Sánchez-Cartagena, Juan Antonio Pérez-Ortiz
Transducens Research Group
Departament de Llenguatges i Sistemes Informàtics
Universitat d'Alacant, Spain
{mespla,vmsanchez,japerez}@dlsi.ua.es

Abstract

This paper explores a new approach to help non-expert users with no background in linguistics to add new words to a monolingual dictionary in a rule-based machine translation system. Our method aims at choosing the correct paradigm which explains not only the particular surface form introduced by the user, but also the rest of inflected forms of the word. A large monolingual corpus is used to extract an initial set of potential paradigms, which are then interactively refined by the user through active machine learning. We show the results of experiments performed on a Spanish monolingual dictionary.

1 Introduction

Rule-based machine translation (MT) systems heavily depend on explicit linguistic data such as morphological dictionaries, bilingual dictionaries, grammars, and structural transfer rules (Hutchins and Somers, 1992). Although some automatic acquisition is possible, collecting these data usually requires in the end the intervention of domain experts (mainly, linguists) who master all the encoding and format details of the particular MT system. We should, however, open the door to a broader group of non-expert users who could collaboratively enrich MT systems through the web.

In this paper we present a novel method for enlarging the monolingual dictionaries in rule-based MT systems by non-expert users. An automatic process is first run to collect as much linguistic information as possible about the new word to be added to the dictionary and, after that, the resulting set of potential hypothesis is filtered by eliciting additional knowledge from non-experts with no linguistic background through *active learning* (Olsson, 2009; Settles, 2010), that is, by interactively querying the user in order to efficiently reduce the search space. As these users do not possess the technical skills which are usually required to fill in the dictionaries, this elicitation is performed via a series of simple and easy yes/no questions which only require *speaker-level* understanding of the language. Our method does not only incorporate to the dictionary the particular surface form introduced by the user (for example, *wants*), but it also discovers a suitable paradigm for the new word so that all the word forms of the corresponding lexeme and their morphological information (such as *wanted, verb, past* or *wanting, verb, gerund*) are also inserted.

This work focuses on monolingual dictionaries. These dictionaries have basically two types of data: *paradigms*, that group regularities in inflection, and *word entries*. The paradigm assigned to many common English verbs, for instance, indicates that by adding the ending *-ing*, the gerund is obtained. Paradigms make easier the management of dictionaries in two ways:

1. by reducing the quantity of information that needs to be stored, thereby creating more compact data structures, and

2. by simplifying revision and validation by describing the regularities in the dictionary; for example, describing the inflection of a verb by giving its stem and inflection model ("it is conjugated as") is safer than writing all the possible conjugated forms one by one.

Once the most frequent paradigms in a dictionary are defined, entering a new inflected word is generally limited to writing the stem and choosing an inflection paradigm. We show a semi-automatic method for the assignment of new words to the existing paradigms in a monolingual dictionary, which interrogates the user when it cannot automatically find enough evidence for unambiguously determining the correct paradigm. Note that as paradigms in MT usually contain morphological information (gender, noun, tense, etc.) on every inflected word form, our method also avoids the user from identifying all these linguistic data.

In our experiments we will use the free/open-source rule-based MT system Apertium (Forcada et al., 2011). Apertium[1] is being currently used to build MT systems for a variety of language pairs. Every word is assigned to a paradigm in Apertium's monolingual dictionaries, and specific paradigms are defined for words with irregular forms. In addition, all the lexical information is included in the paradigms; as a result, there exist paradigms which only contain lexical information and do not add any suffix to the corresponding stem; the paradigm for the proper nouns is a good example of this.

Once a word and its corresponding translation have been added to the monolingual dictionaries of the source and target languages, respectively, of a MT system, the next step is to link both of them by adding the corresponding entry in the bilingual dictionary. How to adapt this task to non-experts is out of the scope of this paper and will be tackled in future works.

Social Translation. In spite of the vast amount of contents and collaboratively-created knowledge uploaded to the web during the last years, linguistic barriers still pose a significant obstacle to universal collaboration as they lead to the creation of "islands" of content, only meaningful to speakers of a particular language. Until *fully-automatic high-quality* MT becomes a reality, massive online collaboration in translation may well be the only force capable of tearing down these barriers (Garcia, 2009) and produce large-scale availability of multilingual information. Actually, this collaborative translation movement is happening nowadays, although still timidly, in applications such as Cucumis.org, OneHourTranslation.com or the Google Translator Toolkit[2].

The resulting scenario, which may be called *social translation*, will need efficient computer translation tools, such as reliable MT systems, friendly postediting interfaces, or shared translation memories. Remarkably, collaboration around MT should not only concern the postediting of raw machine translations, but also the creation and management of the linguistic resources needed by the MT systems; if properly done, this can lead to a significant improvement in the translation engines. Since as many hands as possible are necessary for the task, speakers that, in principle, do not have the level of technical know-how required to improve MT systems or manage linguistic resources must be involved, and, consequently, software that can make those tasks easier and elicit the knowledge of both experts and non-experts must be developed (Font-Llitjós, 2007; Sánchez-Cartagena and Pérez-Ortiz, 2010). This large-scale collaboration implies a change of paradigm in the way linguistic resources are managed and a series of conditions should hold in order to fully accomplish the goals of this social translation scenario (Pérez-Ortiz, 2010).

Knowledge Elicitation and Active Learning. Two of the more prominent works related to the elicitation of knowledge for building or improving MT systems are those by Font-Llitjós (2007) and McShane et al. (2002). The former proposes a strategy for improving both transfer rules and dictionaries by analysing the postediting process performed by a non-expert through a special interface. McShane et al. (2002) design a complex framework to elicit linguistic knowledge from informants who are not trained linguists and use this information to build MT systems into English; their system provides users with a lot of information about different linguistic phenomena to ease the elicitation task. Ambati et al. (2010) show how to apply an active learning (Olsson, 2009) strategy to the configuration of a statistical machine translation.

Automatic Extraction of Resources. Many approaches have been proposed to deal with the automatic acquisition of linguistic resources for MT, mainly, transfer rules and bilingual dictionaries, even for the specific case of the Apertium platform (Caseli et al., 2006; Sánchez-Martínez and Forcada, 2009). The automatic identification of morphological rules (a problem for which paradigm identification is a potential resolution strategy) has also been subject of many recent studies (Monson, 2009; Creutz and Lagus, 2007; Goldsmith, 2010; Walther and Nicolas, 2011).

Novelty. Our work introduces some novel elements compared to previous approaches:

1. Unlike the Avenue formalism used in the work by Font-Llitjós (2007), our MT system is a *pure* transfer-based one in the sense that a single translation is generated and no language model is used to score a set of possible candidate translations. Therefore, we are interested in the unique right answer and assume that an incorrect paradigm cannot be assigned to a new word.

[1] `http://www.apertium.org`

[2] `http://translate.google.com/toolkit`

2. Bartusková and Sedlácek (2002) also present a tool for semi-automatic assignment of words to declination patterns; their system is based on a decision tree with a question in every node. Their proposal, however, focuses on nouns and is aimed at experts because of the technical nature of the questions.

3. Our approach is addressed to non-experts, including those who probably cannot define even vaguely what, for instance, an adverb is, but who can intuitively identify whether a particular word is correct under the rules for forming words in their language; therefore, the answer to as few as possible simple questions is our main source of information in addition to what an automated extraction method may deliver in a first step. Font-Llitjós (2007) already anticipated the advisability of incorporating an active learning mechanism in her transfer rule refinement system, asking the user to validate different translations deduced from the initial hypothesis. However, this active learning approach has not yet been undertaken. Unlike the work by McShane et al. (2002), we want to relieve users of acquiring linguistic skills.

4. Our work focuses on identifying the paradigm which could be assigned to a word, a task more restrictive than decompounding a word into a set of morphemes. In the work by Monson (2009) some errors are tolerated in the final output of the system.

5. Our mid-term intention is to develop a system in line with the social translation principles which may be used to collaboratively build MT systems from scratch. This will also include the semi-automatic learning of the paradigms or the transfer rules which better serve the translation task, and which do not need necessarily correspond to the linguistically motivated ones.[3]

Outline of the Paper. The rest of the paper is organised as follows. Section 2 introduces our method for semi-automatic assignment of words to paradigms. A brief outline of the format used by the dictionaries of the Apertium MT system is given in section 3. Section 4 presents our experimental set-up and Section 5 discusses the results attained. The experiments performed pose some limitations in our approach or in the way in which data is currently represented in Apertium's dictionaries, which are discussed in section 6, together with some ideas on how to cope with them in future work. Finally, the paper ends with some conclusions.

[3]For example, a single inferred paradigm could group inflections for verbs like *wait* (ϵ, *-s*, *-ed*, *-ing*) and nouns like *waiter* (ϵ, *-s*), whereas an expert would probably write two different paradigms in this case.

2 Methodology

In this work we focus on languages which generate inflections by adding suffixes to the stems of words, as happens, for example, with Romance languages; our approach, however, could be easily adapted to inflectional languages based on different ways of adding morphemes. Let $P = \{p_i\}$ be the set of paradigms in a monolingual dictionary. Each paradigm p_i defines a set of suffixes $F_i = \{f_{ij}\}$ which are appended to stems to build new inflected word forms, along with some additional morphological information. The dictionary also includes a list of stems, each labelled with the index of a particular paradigm; the *stem* is the part of a word that is common to all its inflected variants. Given a *stem/paradigm pair* composed of a stem t and a paradigm p_i, the *expansion* $I(t, p_i)$ is the set of possible word forms resulting from appending all the suffixes in p_i to t. For instance, an English dictionary may contain a paradigm p_i with suffixes $F_i = \{\epsilon$,*-s*, *-ed*, *-ing*$\}$ (ϵ denotes the empty string), and the stem *want* assigned to p_i; the expansion $I(\text{want}, p_i)$ consists of the set of word forms *want*, *wants*, *wanted* and *wanting*. We also define a *candidate stem* t as an element of $\text{Pr}(w)$, the set of possible prefixes of a particular word form w.

Given a new word form w to be added to a monolingual dictionary, our objective is to find both the candidate stem $t \in \text{Pr}(w)$ and the paradigm p_i which expand to the largest possible set of morphologically correct inflections. To that end, our method performs three tasks: obtaining the set of all compatible stem/paradigm candidates which generate, among others, the word form w when expanded; giving a *confidence score* to each of the stem/paradigm candidates so that the next step is as short as possible; and, finally, asking the user about some of the inflections derived from each of the stem/paradigm candidates obtained in the first step. Next we describe the methods used for each of these three tasks.

It is worth noting that in this work we assume that all the paradigms for the words in the dictionary are already included in it. The situation in which for a given word no suitable paradigm is available in the dictionary will be tackled in the future, possibly by following the ideas in related works (Monson, 2009).

2.1 Paradigm Detection

The first step for adding a word form w to the dictionary is to detect the set of *compatible* paradigms. To do so, we use a *generalised suffix tree* (GST) (McCreight, 1976) containing all the possible suffixes included in the paradigms in P. Each of these suffixes is labelled with the index of the corresponding paradigms. The GST data structure allows to retrieve the paradigms compatible with w by efficiently searching for all the possible suffixes of w; when a suffix is found, the prefix and the paradigm are considered as a candidate stem/paradigm pair. In this way, a list L of candidate stem/paradigm pairs is built; we will denote each of these candidates with c_n.

The following example illustrates this stage of our method. Consider a simple dictionary with only three paradigms:

p_1: f_{11}=ϵ, f_{12}=*-s*
p_2: f_{21}=*-y*, f_{22}=*-ies*
p_3: f_{31}=*-y*, f_{32}=*-ies*, f_{33}=*-ied*, f_{34}=*-ying*

Assume that a user wants to add the new word w=*policies* to the dictionary. The candidate stem/paradigm pairs which will be obtained after this stage are:

c_1=*policies*/p_1, c_2=*policie*/p_1, c_3=*polic*/p_2, c_4=*polic*/p_3

2.2 Paradigm Scoring

Once L is obtained, a *confidence score* is computed for each stem/paradigm candidate $c_n \in L$ using a large monolingual corpus C. One possible way to compute the score is

$$\text{Score}(c_n) = \frac{\sum_{\forall w' \in I(c_n)} \text{Appear}_C(w')}{\sqrt{|I(c_n)|}},$$

where $\text{Appear}_C(w')$ is a function that returns 1 when the inflected form w' appears in the corpus C and 0 otherwise, and I is the expansion function as defined before. The square root term is used to avoid very low scores for large paradigms which include lot of suffixes.

One potential problem with the previous formula is that all the inflections in $I(c_n)$ are taken into account, including those that, although morphologically correct, are not very usual in the language and, consequently, in the corpus. To overcome this, $\text{Score}(c_n)$ is redefined as

$$\text{Score}(c_n) = \frac{\sum_{\forall w' \in I'_C(c_n)} \text{Appear}_C(w')}{\sqrt{|I'_C(c_n)|}},$$

where $I'_C(c_n)$ is the difference set

$$I'_C(c_n) = I(c_n) \setminus \text{Unusual}_C(c_n).$$

The function $\text{Unusual}_C(c_n)$ uses the words in the dictionary already assigned to p_i as a reference to obtain which of the inflections generated by p_i are not usual in the corpus C. Let $T(p_i)$ be a function retrieving the set of stems in the dictionary assigned to the paradigm p_i. For each of the suffixes f_{ij} in F_i our system computes

$$\text{Ratio}(f_{ij}, p_i) = \frac{\sum_{\forall t \in T(p_i)} \text{Appear}_C(tf_{ij})}{|T(p_i)|},$$

and builds the set $\text{Unusual}_C(c_n)$ by concatenating the stem t to all the suffixes f_{ij} with $\text{Ratio}(f_{ij}, p_i)$ under a given threshold Θ.

Following our example, the following inflections for the different candidates will be obtained:

$I(c_1)$={*policies*, *policiess*}
$I(c_2)$={*policie*, *policies*}
$I(c_3)$={*policy*, *policies*}
$I(c_4)$={*policy*, *policies*, *policied*, *policying*}

Using a large monolingual English corpus C, word forms *policies* and *policy* will be easily found; the other inflections (*policie*, *policiess*, *policied* and *policying*) will not be found. To simplify the example, assume that $\text{Unusual}_C(c_n) = \emptyset$ for all the candidates; the resulting scores will be: $\text{Score}(c_1)$=0.71, $\text{Score}(c_2)$=0.71, $\text{Score}(c_3)$=1.41, $\text{Score}(c_4)$=1.

2.3 Active Learning Through User Interaction

Finally, the best candidate is chosen from L by querying the user about a reduced set of the inflections for some of the candidate paradigms $c_n \in L$. To do so, our system firstly sorts L in descending order by $\text{Score}(c_n)$. Then, users are asked to confirm whether some of the inflections in each expansion are morphologically correct (more precisely, whether they *exist* in the language); the only possible answer for these questions is *yes* or *no*. In this way, when an inflected word form w' is presented to the user

- if it is accepted, all $c_n \in L$ for which $w' \notin I(c_n)$ are removed from L;

- if it is rejected, all $c_n \in L$ for which $w' \in I(c_n)$ are removed from L.

Note that c_1, the best stem/paradigm pair according to Score, may change after updating L. Questions are asked to the user until only one single candidate remains in L. In order to ask as few questions as possible, the word forms shown to the user are carefully selected. Let $G(w', L)$ be a function giving the number of $c_n \in L$ for which $w' \in I(c_n)$. We use the value of $G(w', L)$ in two different phases: *confirmation* and *discarding*.

Confirmation. In this stage our system tries to find a suitable candidate c_n, that is, one for which all the inflections in $I(c_n)$ are morphologically correct. In principle, we may consider that the inflections generated by the best candidate c_1 in the current L (the one with the highest score) are correct. Because of this, the user is asked about the inflection $w' \in I(c_n)$ with the lowest value for $G(w', L)$, so that, in case it is accepted, a significant part of the paradigms in L are removed from the list. This process is repeated until

- only one single candidate remains in L, which is used as the final output of the system; or

- all $w' \in I(c_1)$ are generated by all the candidates remaining in L, meaning that c_1 is a suitable candidate, although there still could be more suitable ones in L.

If the second situation holds, the system moves on to the *discarding* stage.

Discarding. In this stage, the system has accepted c_1 as a possible solution, but it needs to check whether any of the remaining candidates in L is more suitable. Therefore, the new strategy is to ask the user about those inflections $w' \notin I(c_1)$ with the highest possible value for $G(w', L)$. This process is repeated until

- only c_1 remains in L, and it will be used as the final output of the system; or

- an inflection $w' \notin I(c_1)$ is accepted, meaning that some of the other candidates is better than c_n.

If the second situation holds, the system removes c_1 from L and goes back to the *confirmation* stage.

For both *confirmation* and *discarding* stages, if there are many inflections with the same value for $G(w', L)$, the system chooses the one with higher $\text{Ratio}(f_{ij}, p_i)$, that is, the most usual in C.

It is important to remark that this method cannot distinguish between candidates which generate the same set $I(c_n)$. In the experiments, they have considered as a single candidate.

In our example, the ordered list of candidates will be $L = (c_3, c_4, c_1, c_2)$. Choosing the inflection in $I(c_3)$ with the smaller value for $G(w', L)$ the inflection *policy*, which is only generated by two candidates, wins. Hopefully, the user will accept it and this will make that c_1 and c_2 be removed from L. At this point, $I(c_3) \subset I(c_4)$, c_3 is suitable and, consequently, the system will try to discard c_4. Querying the user about any of the inflections in $I(c_4)$ which is not present in $I(c_3)$ (*policied* and *policying*) and getting user rejection will make the system to remove c_4 from L, confirming c_3 as the most suitable candidate.

3 Monolingual Dictionaries in Apertium

A small example follows to show how a simple entry is encoded in the English Apertium's monolingual dictionary. A paradigm named *par123* to be used in English nouns with singular ending in *-um* which change it to *-a* to form the plural form will be defined in XML as follows:

```
<pardef n="par1">
  <e><p>
    <l>um</l>
    <r>um<s n="n"/><s n="sg"/></r>
  </p></e>
  <e><p>
    <l>a</l>
    <r>um<s n="n"/><s n="pl"/></r>
  </p></e>
</pardef>
```

Now, the words *bacterium/bacteria* and *datum/data* will be defined as follows:

```
<e lm="bacterium">
  <i>bacteri</i>
  <par n="par123"/>
</e>
<e lm="datum">
  <i>dat</i>
  <par n="par123"/>
</e>
```

The part inside the *i* element contains the stem of the lexeme, which is common to all inflected forms, and the element *par* refers to the assigned paradigm. In this case, *bacterium* will be analysed into `bacterium<n><sg>` and *bacteria* into `bacterium<n><pl>`.

It is also possible to create entries in the dictionaries consisting of two or more words if these words are considered to build a single *translation unit*. Dictionaries may also contain *nested paradigms* used in other paradigms (for instance, paradigms for enclitic pronoun combinations are included in all Spanish verb paradigms).

It is clear that it may be hard for non-experts to incorporate new entries to the dictionaries unless methods, like the one proposed in this paper, exist to conveniently elicit their language knowledge.

4 Experiments

The aim of the experiments is to asses, in a realistic scenario, whether our semi-automatic methodology is valid to find out, for a given word, its most suitable paradigm. Therefore, a group of people has been told to add a set of words to a monolingual dictionary using our methodology. For this task, we chose the Apertium Spanish monolingual dictionary from the language pair Spanish–Catalan. First, the dictionary was filtered to remove

- word entries belonging to a closed part-of-speech category: when building a monolingual dictionary from scratch, words from closed categories are usually included first, since they are very frequent in source texts;

- word entries assigned to a paradigm which only contains an empty suffix: these paradigms usually define proper nouns, which may be identified using other methods;

- multi-word units, which are out of the scope of this paper;

- prefix inflection entries: as our methodology is designed to deal with suffix inflection, the only entry found in the dictionary with prefix inflection was discarded;

- redundant paradigms, which generate the same inflections with the same lexical information and are, therefore, equivalent.

A test set was created with words extracted from the filtered dictionary. Firstly, a stem assigned to each of the paradigms p_i with $1 < |T(p_i)| < 10$ was added. To build a more realistic test set, we chose one more stem from those paradigms p_i with $10 \leq |T(p_i)|$ in order to have more words assigned to very common paradigms. Then, we obtained, for each pair stem/paradigm, all the possible word forms and included the most common ones into the test set using the $\mathrm{Ratio}(f_{ij}, p_i)$ value. In this way, we obtained 226 words: 106 extracted from the first group of paradigms and 120 from the second one. Obviously, the stems from which we obtained the words included in the test set were removed from the dictionary.

Then, the test set was split into 10 subsets, and each subset was assigned to a different human evaluator. Each evaluator in an heterogeneous group of non-experts was then asked to introduce each of the words in their test set using our system. Experiments were run using the filtered dictionary and a word list obtained from the Spanish Wikipedia dump[4] as the monolingual corpus C.

The different evaluation metrics obtained from the human evaluation process are:

- *success rate*: number of words from the test set that have been tagged with the paradigm assigned to them in the original Apertium dictionary. This is the most straightforward metric to evaluate our methodology;

- *average precision and recall*: precision (P) and recall (R) were computed as

$$P(c, c') = |I(c) \cap I(c')| \cdot |I(c)|^{-1},$$

$$R(c, c') = |I(c) \cap I(c')| \cdot |I(c')|^{-1},$$

  where c is the stem/paradigm pair chosen by our system and c' is the pair originally in the dictionary. Confidence intervals were estimated with 99% statistical confidence with a *t-test*;

- *average number of questions*: average number of questions made by our system for each word in the test set;

- *average number of initial paradigms*: the average number of compatible paradigms initially found as possible solutions in the first stage of our method.

The value of the threshold Θ used to compute the set $\mathrm{Unusual}_C(c_n)$ defined in Section 2 was 0.1.

Finally, an alternative approach without user interaction was designed as a baseline so that the impact of active learning could be better evaluated. The baseline consists of directly choosing the first element in the list L as the most suitable candidate. The average position of the right candidate in L has also been computed.

[4]http://dumps.wikimedia.org/eswiki/20110114/eswiki-20110114-pages-articles.xml.bz2

5 Results and Discussion

We evaluated our approach and computed the results following the metrics depicted in Section 4. The average number of initial candidates detected by our approach was 56.4; this metric was specially high for verbs, whereas it was much lower for nouns and adjectives. The average number of questions asked to the users by the active learning approach for the test set was 5.2, which is reasonably small considering that the 56.4 initial paradigms on average and that the average position of the right candidate in L was 9.1. Figure 1 shows an histogram representing the position of the right candidate in the initial list L for each word in the test set. We also observed that, in average, users needed around 30 seconds in average to find the paradigm of each word in the test set.

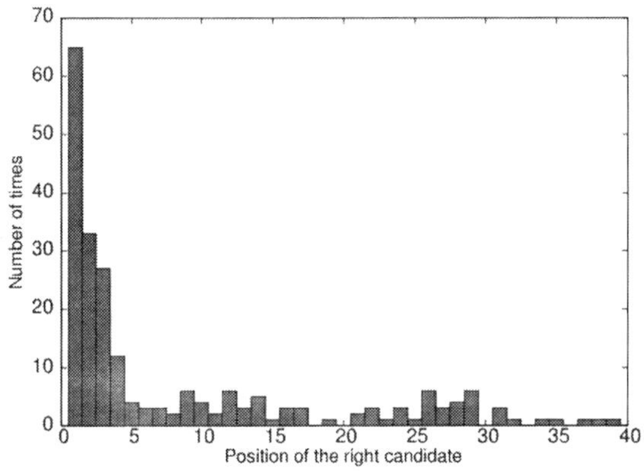

Figure 1: Histogram representing the distribution of the position of the right candidate in the initial list of candidates L for each word in the test set.

We obtained a success rate of 72.9% for the active learning approach with a precision of $P = 87\% \pm 5$ and a recall of $R = 87\% \pm 5$. These results stress the fact that those words which were assigned to incorrect paradigms, were assigned to paradigms generating similar inflections. These results are clearly better than those obtained by the baseline approach, with a success rate of 28.9%, a precision of $P = 70.3\% \pm 6$ and a recall of $R = 62.77\% \pm 7$.

Taking a closer look at the results, we observed some relevant causes for the errors. On the one hand, we detected human errors for words which should have been accepted but were rejected or vice-versa. These mistakes, caused by a lack of knowledge of the users (for example, about accentuation rules), should be taken into account in the future; they could be solved, for instance, by using *reinforcement questions* or combining the answers of different users for the same or similar words. Moreover it could be possible to give a kind of *confidence score* to the paradigms in the dictionary based on how frequently words are incorrectly assigned to them.

We also observed that most of the words which were not assigned to the expected paradigm were verbs. Spanish morphological rules allow multiple concatenations of enclitic pronouns at the end of verbs. In many occasions, users rejected forms of verbs with too many enclitic pronouns or for which some concrete enclitics had no semantic sense. This happens because, in order to reduce the number of possible paradigms, Apertium's dictionaries can assign some words to existing paradigms which are a superset of the correct one; since the included semantically incorrect word forms will never occur in a text to translate, this, in principle, may be safely done.

6 Limitations and Work Ahead

In this paper we have described a system for interactively enlarging dictionaries and selecting the most suitable paradigm for new words. Our preliminary experiments have brought to light several limitations of our method which will be tackled in the future.

Detection of lexical information. One of the most important limitations of our approach is that, as already commented in Section 2, candidate paradigms generating the same $I(c_n)$ set cannot be distinguished. This situation usually holds when the expansions of two different stem/paradigm pairs are equal but the lexical information in each paradigm is different. For example, in Spanish two different paradigms may contain the same suffixes F=$\{\epsilon$, -$s\}$ although one of them generates substantives and the other one generates adjectives.

We have started to explore a method to semi-automatically obtain this lexical information. A statistical part-of-speech tagger may be used to obtain initial hypothesis about the lexical properties of a word w; this information could then be refined by querying users with complete sentences in which w plays different lexical roles.

Lack of suitable paradigms. Our approach assumes that all the paradigms for a particular language are already included in the dictionary, but it could be interesting to have a method to also add new paradigms. The work by Monson (2009) could be a good start for the new method.

Other improvements. We plan to improve our approach by using simple statistical letter models of bigrams or trigrams to discard candidates generating morphologically unlikely word forms, or by using additional information in the scoring stage, such as word context, number of occurrences, etc.

7 Conclusions

We have shown an active learning method for adding new entries to monolingual dictionaries. Our system allows non-expert users with no linguistic background to contribute to the improvement of RBMT systems. The Java source code for the tool described in this paper is published[5] under an open-source license.

Acknowledgements

This work has been partially funded by Spanish Ministerio de Ciencia e Innovacin through project TIN2009-14009-C02-01 and by Generalitat Valenciana through grant ACIF/2010/174 from VALi+d programme.

References

Vamshi Ambati, Stephan Vogel, and Jaime Carbonell. 2010. Active learning and crowd-sourcing for machine translation. In *Proceedings of the Seventh conference on International Language Resources and Evaluation, LREC 2010.*

Dita Bartusková and Radek Sedlácek. 2002. Tools for semi-automatic assignment of czech nouns to declination patterns. In *Proceedings of the 5th International Conference on Text, Speech and Dialogue*, pages 159–164, London, UK. Springer-Verlag.

Helena Caseli, Maria Nunes, and Mikel Forcada. 2006. Automatic induction of bilingual resources from aligned parallel corpora: application to shallow-transfer machine translation. *Machine Translation*, 20:227–245.

Mathias Creutz and Krista Lagus. 2007. Unsupervised models for morpheme segmentation and morphology learning. *ACM Trans. Speech Lang. Process*, 4.

Ariadna Font-Llitjós. 2007. *Automatic improvement of machine translation systems*. Ph.D. thesis, Carnegie Mellon University.

Mikel L. Forcada, Mireia Ginestí-Rosell, Jacob Nordfalk, Jim O'Regan, Sergio Ortiz-Rojas, Juan Antonio Pérez-Ortiz, Felipe Sánchez-Martnez, Gema Ramírez-Sánchez, and Francis M. Tyers. 2011. Apertium: a free/open-source platform for rule-based machine translation. *Machine Translation*. doi: 10.1007/s10590-011-9090-0.

Ignacio Garcia. 2009. Beyond translation memory: Computers and the professional. *The Journal of Specialised Translation*, 12:199–214.

John A. Goldsmith, 2010. *The Handbook of Computational Linguistics and Natural Language Processing*, chapter Segmentation and morphology. Wiley-Blackwell.

W. J. Hutchins and H. L. Somers. 1992. *An introduction to machine translation*. Academic Press, London.

Edward M. McCreight. 1976. A space-economical suffix tree construction algorithm. *Journal of the Association for Computing Machinery*, 23:262–272, April.

Marjorie McShane, Sergei Nirenburg, James Cowie, and Ron Zacharski. 2002. Embedding knowledge elicitation and MT systems within a single architecture. *Machine Translation*, 17:271–305.

Christian Monson. 2009. *ParaMor: From Paradigm Structure to Natural Language Morphology Induction*. Ph.D. thesis, Carnegie Mellon University.

Fredrik Olsson. 2009. A literature survey of active machine learning in the context of natural language processing. Technical report, School of Electronics and Computer Science, University of Southampton.

Juan Antonio Pérez-Ortiz. 2010. Social Translation: How Massive Online Collaboration Could Take Machine Translation to the Next Level. In *Second European Language Resources and Technologies Forum: Language Resources of the Future, FlarenetNet Forum 2010*, pages 64–65, Barcelona, Spain.

Víctor M. Sánchez-Cartagena and Juan Antonio Pérez-Ortiz. 2010. Tradubi: open-source social translation for the Apertium machine translation platform. In *Open Source Tools for Machine Translation, MT Marathon 2010*, pages 47–56.

Felipe Sánchez-Martínez and Mikel L. Forcada. 2009. Inferring shallow-transfer machine translation rules from small parallel corpora. *Journal of Artificial Intelligence Research*, 34:605–635.

Burr Settles. 2010. Active learning literature survey. Technical report, Computer Sciences Technical Report 1648, University of WisconsinMadison.

Géraldine Walther and Lionel Nicolas. 2011. Enriching morphological lexica through unsupervised derivational rule acquisition. In *Proceedings of the International Workshop on Lexical Resources*.

[5] `https://apertium.svn.sourceforge.net/svnroot/apertium/branches/apertium-dixtools-paradigmlearning`

Morphological Analysis of Biomedical Terminology with Analogy-Based Alignment

Vincent Claveau
IRISA-CNRS
Vincent.Claveau@irisa.fr

Ewa Kijak
IRISA-Univ. Rennes 1
Ewa.Kijak@irisa.fr

Abstract

In the biomedical domain, many terms are neoclassical compounds (composed of several Greek or Latin roots). The study of their morphology is important for numerous applications since it makes it possible to structure, translate, retrieve them efficiently...

In this paper, we propose an original yet fruitful approach to carry out this morphological analysis by relying on Japanese, more precisely on terms written in kanjis, as a pivot language. In order to do so, we have developed a specially crafted alignment algorithm relying on analogy learning. Aligning terms with their kanji-based counterparts provides at the same time a decomposition of the term into morphs, and a kanji label for each morph.

Evaluated on a dataset of French terms, our approach yields a precision greater than 70% and shows its relevance compared with existing techniques. We also illustrate the interest of this approach through two direct applications of the produced alignments: translating unknown terms and discovering relationships between morphs for terminological structuring.

1 Introduction

In many domains, accessing the information in documents or collections of documents is guided by the use of well-defined terms, which form a terminology of the domain. This is particularly true in the biomedical domain where there is a long tradition of terminologies development for structuring the knowledge as well as accessing it. An example is the MeSH (Medical Subject Headings) www.nlm.nih.gov/mesh terminology which is used to index the very popular PubMED database (www.pubmed.gov). Knowing how to handle these terms, understanding them, translating them or building semantic relationships between them are thus essential operations for applications like enrichment of bilingual lexicons, or more generally machine translation, information retrieval...

In this framework, the work presented here is interested in the morphology of simple terms from the biomedical domain as a basis for the terminological analysis. More precisely, we present a technique aiming at breaking up a term into its morphological components, namely morphs, and associating in the same time semantic knowledge to these morphs. Note that in this paper, we distinguish morphs, elementary linguistic signs (segments), from morphemes, equivalence classes with identical signified and close significants (Mel'čuk, 2006). We therefore tackle the same issue already raised in some studies (Deléger et al., 2008; Markó et al., 2005, for example), but we try here to suppress the costly human operations required by these studies.

The original idea at the heart of our approach is to use the multilingualism of existing terminological databases. We exploit Japanese as a pivot language, or more precisely terms written in kanjis, to help decomposing the terms of other languages into morphs and associate them with the corresponding kanjis, in a fully automatic way. Thus, kanjis play the role of a semantic representation for morphs. The main advantage of kanjis in this respect is that Japanese terms can be seen as a concatenation of elementary words which are easier to find in general language dictionaries. For example, the term photochimiotherapy can be translated in Japanese by 光化学療法; splitting and aligning these two terms gives: photo ↔ 光 ('light'), chimio ↔ 化学 ('chemistry'), thérapie ↔ 療法 ('therapy'). Our approach chiefly relies on the hypothesis that the composition of terms in kanjis is the same than those of English or French simple terms. This hypothesis can be seen as peremptory, but the results presented below in this paper show that it is a reasonable hypothesis. Finally, our approach provides, at the same time 1) an effective way to split terms into morphs, 2) the semantic meaning of each morph as they are actually used.

This morphological analysis thus relies on an essential step which consists in aligning English or French terms with Japanese ones taken from a multilingual terminology. To do so, we propose a new alignment technique, particularly suited to this kind of data, which mixes *Forward-Backward* algorithm and analogy-based machine learning. After a presentation of related work in Section 2, either in terms of applications or methods, we describe this alignment technique in Section 3. Results of the morphological analysis are detailed in Section 4. In Section 5, we illustrate the interest of such analysis through two applications. The first one shows that our technique can be used to translate and analyse never-seen-before terms. The second application illustrates how the morphs and their obtained semantic labels can be used from a terminological point of view.

2 Related work

Many studies have used morphology for terminological analysis. This is more particularly the case in the biomedical domain where terminologies are central to many applications and where terms are constructed by operations like neo-classical composition (e.g. *chemotherapy*, built from the Greek pseudo-word *chemo*, and *therapy*), which are very regular, and very productive. Unfortunately, no comprehensive database of morphs with semantic information is available, and splitting a term into morphs is still an issue. One can distinguish two views of the use of morphology as a tool for term (or word) analysis. In the lexematic view, relations between terms rely on the word form, but without the need to split them into morphs (Grabar and Zweigenbaum, 2002; Claveau and L'Homme, 2005, for example). Beside this implicit use of morphology, the morphemic view chiefly relies on splitting the term into morphs as a first step. Many studies have been made in this framework. They either rely on partially manual approaches, as the already mentioned ones (Deléger et al., 2008; Markó et al., 2005) in which morphs and combination rules are provided by an expert, or on more automatic approaches. The latter usually try to find recurrent letter patterns as morph-candidate. But such techniques cannot associate a semantic meaning with these morphs. To our knowledge, no existing work makes the most of a pivot language to perform an automatic morphological analysis, as we propose in this study.

From a more technical point of view, the use of a bilingual terminology also evokes studies in transliteration, particularly Katakana or Arabic (Tsuji et al., 2002; Knight and Graehl, 1998, for example), or in translation. In this framework, let us cite the work of Morin and Daille (2010). They propose to map complex terms written in kanjis with French ones, by using morphological rules. Yet, here again, these rules are to be given by an expert, and this study only concerns a special case of derivation. Moreover such an approach cannot handle neo-classical compounds. In other studies, translation methods for biomedical terms which considers terms as simple sequences of letters have been proposed (Claveau, 2009, inter alia). Even if the goal is different here, such approaches share some similarities with the one presented here. Indeed, they all require aligning the words at the letter level. In most cases, this is performed with 1-1 alignment algorithm, that is, algorithm only capable to align one character, which can be empty, of the source language word with one another character of the target language word. Yet, in recent work about phonetization (Jiampojamarn et al., 2007), authors have shown that *many-to-many* alignment could yield interesting results.

3 Analogy for alignment

Our alignment technique is mainly based on an *Expectation-Maximization* (EM) algorithm that we briefly present in the next sub-section (Jiampojamarn et al., 2007, for more details and examples of its use). The second sub-section explains the modification made to this standard algorithm so that it can naturally and automatically handle morphological variation, which is a phenomenon inherent to our morph splitting problem.

3.1 EM Alignment

The alignment algorithm at the heart of our approach is standard: it is a *Baum-Welch* algorithm, extended to map symbol sub-sequences and not only 1-1 alignments. In our case, it takes as input French terms with their kanji translations, taken from a multilingual terminology for instance. The maximum length of the sub-sequences of letters and kanjis considered for alignment are parametrized by $maxX$ and $maxY$.

For each term pair (x^T, y^V) to be aligned (T and V being the lengths of the terms in letters or kanjis), the EM algorithm (see Algorithm 1) proceeds as follows. It first computes the partial counts of every possible mapping between sub-sequences of kanjis and letters (*Expectation* step). These counts are stored in table γ, and are then used to estimate the alignment probabilities in table δ (*Maximization* step).

The *Expectation* step relies on a *forward-backward* approach (Algorithm 2): it computes the *forward* probabilities α and *backward* probabilities β. For each position t, v in the terms, $\alpha_{t,v}$ is the sum of the probabilities of all the possible alignments of (x_1^t, y_1^v), that is, from the beginning of the terms to the current position, according to the current alignment probabilities in δ (cf. Algorithm 4). $\beta_{t,v}$ is computed in a similar way by considering (x_t^T, y_v^V). These probabilities are then used to re-estimate the counts in γ. In this version of the EM algorithm, the *Maximization* (Algorithm 3) simply consists in computing the δ alignment probabilities by normalizing the counts in γ.

Algorithm 1 *EM Algorithm*

Input: list of pairs (x^T, y^V), $maxX$, $maxY$
while changes in δ **do**
 initialization of γ to 0
 for all pair (x^T, y^V) **do**
  γ = Expectation(x^T, y^V, $maxX$, $maxY$, γ)
 δ = Maximization(γ)
return δ

Algorithm 2 *Expectation*

Input: (x^T, y^V), $maxX$, $maxY$, γ
$\alpha :=$ Forward-many2many(x^T, y^V, $maxX$, $maxY$)
$\beta :=$ Backward-many2many(x^T, y^V, $maxX$, $maxY$)
if $\alpha_{T,V} > 0$ **then**
 for $t = 1...T$ **do**
  for $v = 1...V$ **do**
   for $i = 1...maxX$ s.t. $t - i \geq 0$ **do**
    for $j = 1...maxY$ s.t. $v - j \geq 0$ **do**
     $\gamma(x_{t-i+1}^t, y_{v-j+1}^v) \mathrel{+}= \frac{\alpha_{t-i,v-j}\delta(x_{t-i+1}^t, y_{v-j+1}^v)\beta_{t,v}}{\alpha_{T,V}}$
return γ

Algorithm 3 *Maximization*

Input: γ
for all sub-sequence a s.t. $\gamma(a, \cdot) > 0$ **do**
 for all sub-sequence b s.t. $\gamma(a, b) > 0$ **do**
  $\delta(a, b) = \frac{\gamma(a,b)}{\sum_x \gamma(a,x)}$
return δ

Algorithm 4 *Forward-many2many*

Input: (x^T, y^V), $maxX$, $maxY$
$\alpha_{0,0} := 1$
for $t = 0...T$ **do**
 for $v = 0...V$ **do**
  if $(t > 0 \vee v > 0)$ **then**
   $\alpha_{t,v} = 0$
  if $(v > 0 \wedge t > 0)$ **then**
   for $i = 1...maxX$ s.t. $t - i \geq 0$ **do**
    for $j = 1...maxY$ s.t. $v - j \geq 0$ **do**
     $\alpha_{t,v} \mathrel{+}= \delta(x_{t-i+1}^t, y_{v-j+1}^v)\alpha_{t-i,v-j}$
return α

The EM process is repeated until the probabilities δ are stable. When the convergence is reached, the alignment simply consists in finding the mapping that maximizes $\alpha(T, V)$. In addition to this resulting alignment, we also store the final alignment probabilities δ, which are used to split unseen terms (cf. Section 5.1).

This technique is not very different from the one used in statistical translation. Yet, some particularities are worth noting: this approach allows us to handle *fertility*, that is the capacity to align from or to empty substrings (for lack of space, it does not appear in the above simplified version); conversely, *distortion*, that is reordering of morphs, cannot be handled easily without major changes in this algorithm.

3.2 Automatic morphological normalisation

The maximization step simply compute the translation probabilities of a kanji sequence into a letter sequence. For example, for the kanji 菌 ('*bacteria*'), there may exist one entry in δ associating it with bactérie, one with bactério (as in bactério/lyse) and another one with bactéri (in myco/bactéri/ose), each with a certain probability. This dispersion of probabilities, which is of course harmful for the algorithm, is caused by morphemic variation: bactério, bactérie, and bactéri are 3 morphs of the same morpheme, and we would like their probabilities to reinforce each other. The adaptation we propose aims at making the maximization phase able to automatically group the different morphs belonging to a same morpheme. To achieve this goal, we use a simple but well suited technique relying on formal analogical calculus.

3.2.1 Analogy

An analogy is a relation between 4 elements that we note: $a : b :: c : d$ which can be read *a is for b what c is for d* (Lepage, 2000, for more details about analogies). Analogies have been used in many NLP studies, especially for translation of sentences (Lepage, 2000) or terms (Langlais and Patry, 2007; Langlais et al., 2008). Analogies are also a key component in the previously mentioned work on terminology structuring (Claveau and L'Homme, 2005). We rely on this latter work to formalize our normalization problem. In our framework, one possible analogy may be: dermato : dermo :: hémato : hémo. Knowing that dermato and dermo belong to a same morpheme, one can infer that this is the case for hémato and hémo. Such an analogy, build on the graphemic representation of words, is said a formal analogy. After Stroppa and Yvon (2005), formal analogies can be defined in terms of factorizations. Let a be a string (a term in our case) over an alphabet Σ, a factorization of a, noted f_a, is a sequence of n factors $f_a = (f_a^1, ..., f_a^n)$, such that $a = f_a^1 \oplus f_a^2 \oplus ... \oplus f_a^n$, where $\oplus$ denotes the concatenation operator. A formal analogy can be defined by as:

Definition 1 $\forall(a, b, c, d) \in \Sigma, [a : b :: c : d]$ *iff there exist factorizations* $(f_a, f_b, f_c, f_d) \in (\Sigma^{*n})^4$ *of* (a, b, c, d) *such that,* $\forall i \in [1, n], (f_b^i, f_c^i) \in \{(f_a^i, f_d^i), (f_d^i, f_a^i)\}$ *. The smallest n for which this definition holds is called the degree of the analogy.*

As for most European languages, French morphology is mostly concerned with prefixation and suffixation. Thus, we are looking for formal analogies of degree at most 3 (ie, 3 factors: prefix $\oplus$ base $\oplus$ suffix). In our approach, such analogies are searched by trying to build a rule rewriting the prefixes and the suffixes to move from dermato to dermo and to check that this rule also applies to hémato-hémo. The base is considered as the longest common sub-string (lcss) between the 2 words. In the previous example, the rewriting rule r would be:
$r = \text{lcss}(\text{morph}_1, \text{morph}_2) \ominus \text{ato} \oplus \text{o}$.
This rule makes it possible to rewrite dermato into dermo and hémato into hémo; thus, hémato,hémo is in analogy with dermato,dermo.

3.2.2 Using analogy for normalization

The main problem is that we do not have examples of morphs that are known a priori to be related (like dermato and dermo in the previous example). Thus, we use a simple bootstrapping technique: if two morphs are stored in γ as possible translations of the same kanji sequence, and if these two morphs share a sub-string longer than a certain threshold, then we assume that they both belong to the same morpheme. From these bootstrap pairs, we build the prefixation and suffixation rewriting rules allowing us to detect analogies, and thus to group pairs of morphs (which can be very short, unlike the bootstrapping pairs). The more a rule is found, the more certain it will be. Therefore, we keep all the analogical rules generated at each iteration along with their number of occurrence, and we only apply the most frequently found ones. The whole process is thus completely automatic.

This new *Maximization* step is summarized in Algorithm 5. It ensures that all the morphs supposed to belong to the same morpheme have equal and reinforced alignment probabilities.

Algorithm 5 *Maximization* with analogical normalization

Input: γ
for all sub-sequence a s.t. $\gamma(a, \cdot) > 0$ **do**
  for all m_1, m_2 s.t. $\gamma(a, m_1) > 0 \wedge \gamma(a, m_2) > 0 \wedge$ lcss(m_1, m_2) > threshold **do**
    build the prefixation and suffixation rule r for m_1, m_2
    increment the score of r
  for all sub-sequence b s.t. $\gamma(a, b) > 0$ **do**
    build the set $\mathcal{M}$ of all morphs associated to b with the help of the n most frequent analogical rules from the previous iteration

$$\delta(a, b) = \frac{\sum_{c \in \mathcal{M}} \gamma(a, c)}{\sum_x \gamma(a, x)}$$

return δ

4 Experiments

4.1 Evaluation Data

The data used for our experiments are extracted from the UMLS MetaThesaurus (Tuttle et al., 1990), which group several terminologies for several languages. In the MetaThesaurus, each term is associated with a concept identifier (CUI) which facilitates the Japanese/French pairs extraction. We only consider Japanese terms composed of kanjis, and only simple (one-word) French terms. About 8,000 pairs are formed this way. An ending mark (';') is added to each term.

We randomly selected 1,600 pairs among these 8,000 pairs in order to evaluate the performance of our alignment technique. These 1,600 pairs have been aligned manually to serve as gold standard.

4.2 Alignment results

We evaluate our approach in terms of precision: an alignment is considered as correct only if all the components of the pair are correctly aligned (thus, it is equivalent to the sentence error rate in standard machine translation).

For each pair, the EM algorithm indicates the probability of the proposed alignment. Therefore, it is possible to only consider alignments having a probability greater than a given threshold. By varying this threshold, we can compute a precision according to the number of terms aligned. Figure 1 presents the results obtained on the 1,600 test pairs. We indicate the curves produced by the EM algorithm with and without our morphemic normalization. For comparison purpose, we also report the results of GIZA++ (Och and Ney, 2003), a reference tool in machine translation. The different IBM models and sets of parameters available in GIZA++ were tested; the results reported are the best ones (obtained with IBM model 4).

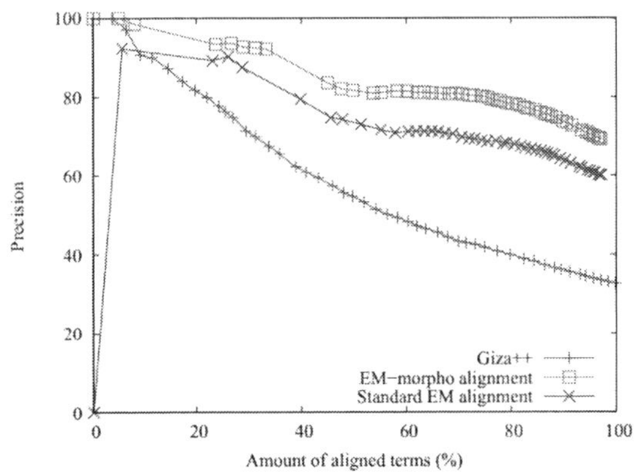

Figure 1: Precision of alignment according to the number of test pairs aligned

As expected, the interest of the morphemic normalization appears clearly in this figure; it yields a 70% precision in the worst case (that is, when all the terms are kept for alignment). Indeed, the normalization brings a 10% improvement whatever the number of aligned pairs.

A manual examination of the results shows that most of the errors are caused by the falsification of our hypothesis: some French-Japanese pairs cannot be decomposed in a similar way. For example, the French term anxiolytiques (anxiolytics) is translated by a sequence of kanjis meaning literally 'drugs for depression'. Among these errors, some pairs imply terms that are not neoclassical compounds in French, Japanese or both (eg. méninges (meninges) is translated by 脳膜 'brain membrane'). Other errors are caused by a lack of training data: some morphs or sequences only appear once, or only combined with another morph, which mislead the segmentation.

5 Using the morph/kanji alignments

In this section, we present two ways of exploiting the results produced by our morphological analysis technique. The first one aims at translating unseen terms and the second one aims at structuring terminologies by finding related terms or morphs.

5.1 Translating and analysing unknown terms

The alignment technique that we propose can be used as a first step to translate an unknown term (i.e a term absent from the training data of our alignment algorithm). Translating terms has already been tackled in several studies, mostly to reduce the *out-of-vocabulary* errors in machine translation tasks. Most of these studies look for translations in textual resources: parallel or comparable corpora (Chiao and Zweigenbaum, 2002; Fung and Yee, 1998), Web (Lu et al., 2005). Others have considered this problem without external resources; in this case, the approach rely on the similarities between the terms in the two languages (cognates) (Schulz et al., 2004, for example), or on the similarities of rewriting operations to go from one term to its equivalent in the other language (Langlais and Patry, 2007; Claveau, 2009). Our work falls into this category.

In the experiment reported here, we translate French terms into Japanese. In practice, we use the probabilities from δ to generate the most probable translation. The approach is straightforward: the morph translation probabilities in δ are used in a Viterbi-like algorithm; thus, we do not use a language model in addition to the translation model.

It is important to note that this translation process also produce the alignment of the source term into its translation. As a result, it also segments the initial term and label them with the corresponding kanjis. Therefore, it corresponds to the morpho-semantic analysis of the unknown term.

For the need of this experiment, 128 terms and their kanji translations have been selected at random to form the test set (of course, they have been removed from the alignment training set). These French terms are translated as explained above with the help of the *delta* table, and the generated translations are compared with the expected ones.

Reference	UMLS	Web
Correctly translated (and segmented)	58	82
Incorrectly translated (or segmented)	34	10
Not translated	36	36

Table 1: Unknown terms translation results

The results of this small experiment are presented in Table 1. 58 of 128 terms, that is 45%, have been correctly translated and segmented. There are two types of errors: either a wrong translation has been proposed (it concerns 34 terms), or no translation was found (36 terms). When examining these untranslated terms, we find without any surprise that they are either words which are not neo-classical compounds, or compounds having one or several components that do not appear in the training data of the alignment algorithm. The precision on the terms for which a translation is proposed is thus 63%; this result is very promising given the simplicity of our implementation of the translation. It is also worth noting that, among the errors, most of the proposed translations are correct paraphrase, absent from the UMLS but attested on the Web in bio-medical Japanese websites; with this wider reference, the precision on translated terms reaches 89 %.

5.2 Morph analysis

Once all the terms are aligned, one can study the recurrent correspondences between French morphs and kanjis. These correspondences can be shed into light through different techniques: Galois lattices (kanjis would be the intention and morph the extension), in a distributional analysis manner, or by analysing the kanji-morph graph with small-world, connected components... In this paper we propose to use such a graph representation: the vertices represent kanjis and morphemes (i.e a set of morphs grouped during the analogical step of the alignment), and the edges are weighted according to the number of times that a particular morpheme is aligned with a kanji sequence among the 8,000 training pairs from the UMLS. Figure 2 shows a small excerpt of the resulting graph. The size of the edge lines is proportional to the associated weight.

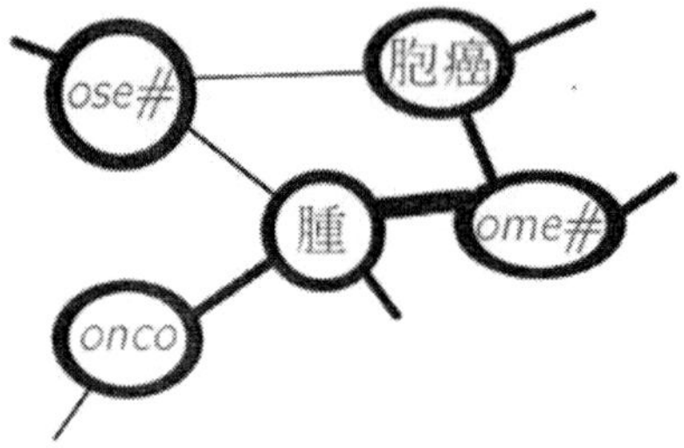

Figure 2: Morpheme-kanji graph

This representation allows us to easily explore the different kinds of neighbourhood of a morpheme: each vertex receives an amount of energy which is propagated to the connected vertices proportionally to the edge's weight. Figures 3 and 4 respectively present the kanjis (manually translated in English in this figure) and the morphemes reached, in the form of tag clouds, for the French morpheme ome (oma in English, a suffix for cancer-related terms). The size and color represent the energy that reach the neighbouring kanji (respectively the morpheme) vertices. The reached vertices are expected to be conceptually related and to exhibit translation relations or synonymy, as one can see in these examples. Thus, Figure 3 represents a sort of semantic profile of the morpheme ome, in which the kanjis are used as semantic tags, while Figure 4 proposes synonyms and quasi-synonyms morphemes of the suffix ome. It is interesting to see that other related suffixes are found, but also prefixes like onco.

The alignment and the segmentation produced by our algorithm also make it possible to study

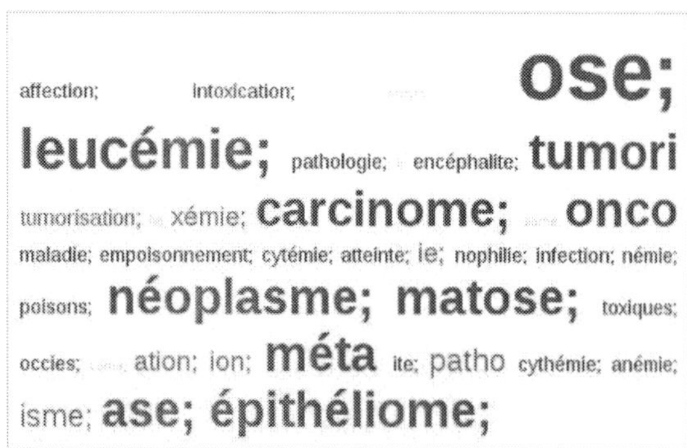

Figure 4: Morpheme cloud for morpheme ome

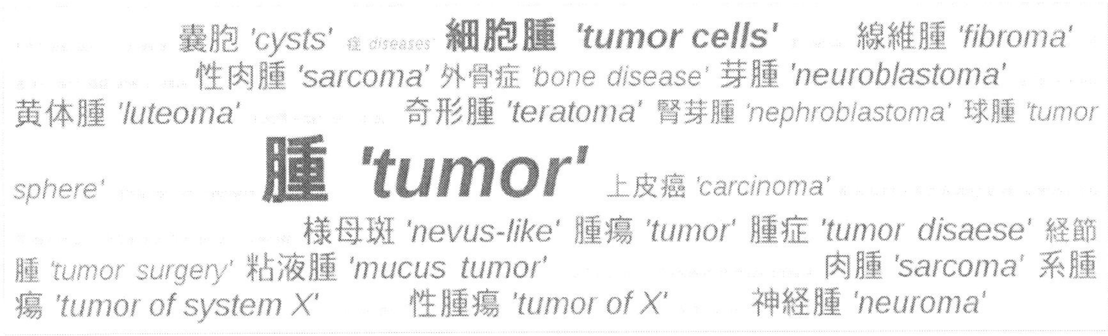

Figure 3: Kanji cloud for ome

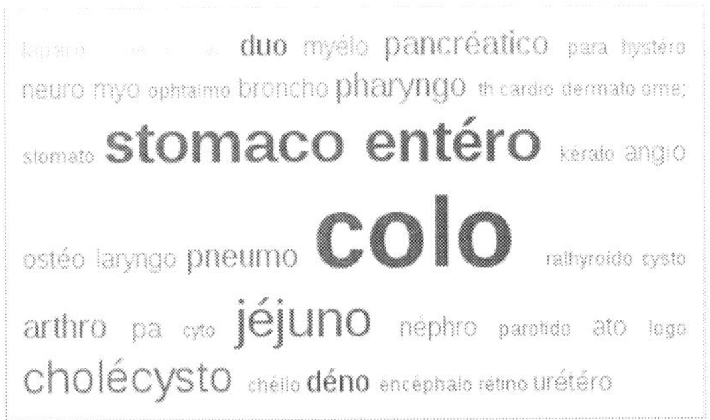

Figure 5: Morpheme cloud for gastro second-order affinities

the co-occurrences of morphemes in French terms. One can study first-order affinities (which morphemes are frequently associated with other morphemes) and, more interesting, second order affinities (morphemes sharing the same co-occurring morphemes). The second-order affinity allows us to group morpheme according to their paradigm. For instance, the tag cloud in Figure 5 illustrates the morphemes associated with gastro (morpheme for stomach) according to this second order affinity. Most of the morphemes identify organs, and the closest ones are for biologically close organs.

This information of different nature (other benefits from these alignments can be derived) makes it possible to identify relationships between terms, or build synonyms, or explore the termbase using these morphological elements. Yet, to our knowledge, such specialized morpho-semantic resources do not exist. It makes a direct evaluation of these three different uses of the alignment results impossible.

6 Conclusion

The original idea of making the most of another language like Japanese in order to help the morphologically decomposition and analysis of compounds offers many new opportunities to automatically handle biomedical terms. The new alignment approach based on analogy that we propose takes the particularities of the data into account in order to yield high quality results. Since this whole process is entirely automatic, it makes it possible to overcome the limits of terminological systems, like the one of Deléger et al. (2008), which heavily rely on manually populating a morphological database.

Many perspectives are foreseen for this work. First, from a technical point of view, we plan to consider more complex segmentation than the linear one we implemented. Indeed, the syntactic properties of the kanjis (some of them expect an agent or object), could help to better structure the different morphemes. One could also exploit the semantic relations between kanjis that can be easily found in general Japanese dictionaries.

Concerning the analysis aspects illustrated in the last section, many possibilities are also under consideration. As the links between morphs that we produce are not typed, the use of heuristics (such as string inclusion used by Grabar and Zweigenbaum (2002)) or techniques from distributional analysis could provide useful additional information to better characterize the relationships. Yet, the problem of evaluating this type of work arises, especially the ground truth construction, since such resources do not exist.

Finally, an adaptation of these principles for complex terms is under study. The main difficulty in this case is to manage the reordering of the words composing these terms, and thus manage the distortion in the alignment algorithm.

References

Yun-Chuang Chiao and Pierre Zweigenbaum. 2002. Looking for French-English translations in comparable medical corpora. Journal of the American Medical Informatics Association, 8(suppl).

Vincent Claveau and Marie-Claude L'Homme. 2005. Structuring terminology by analogy-based machine learning. In Proc. of the 7th International Conference on Terminology and Knowledge Engineering, TKE'05, Copenhaguen, Denmark.

Vincent Claveau. 2009. Translation of biomedical terms by inferring rewriting rules. In Violaine Prince and Mathieu Roche, editors, Information Retrieval in Biomedicine: Natural Language Processing for Knowledge Integration. IGI - Global.

Louise Deléger, Fiammetta Namer, and Pierre Zweigenbaum. 2008. Morphosemantic parsing of medical compound words: Transferring a french analyzer to english. International Journal of Medical Informatics, 78(Supplement 1):48–55.

Pascale Fung and Lo Yuen Yee. 1998. An IR approach for translating new words from non-parallel, comparable texts. In Proc. of 36th Annual Meeting of the Association for Computational Linguistics ACL, Montréal, Canada.

Natalia Grabar and Pierre Zweigenbaum. 2002. Lexically-based terminology structuring: Some inherent limits. In Proc. of International Workshop on Computational Terminology, COMPUTERM, Taipei, Taiwan.

Sittichai Jiampojamarn, Grzegorz Kondrak, , and Tarek Sherif. 2007. Applying many-to-many alignments and hidden markov models to letter-to-phoneme conversion. In Proc. of the conference of the North American Chapter of the Association for Computational Linguistics, Rochester, New York, USA.

Kevin Knight and Jonathan Graehl. 1998. Machine transliteration. Computational Linguistics, 24(4):599–612.

Philippe Langlais and Alexandre Patry. 2007. Translating unknown words by analogical learning. In Proc. of Joint Conference on Empirical Methods in Natural Language Processing and Computational Natural Language Learning (EMNLP-CoNLL), pages 877–886, Prague, Czech Republic, June.

Philippe Langlais, François Yvon, and Pierre Zweigenbaum. 2008. Translating medical words by analogy. In Proc. of the workshop on Intelligent Data Analysis in bioMedicine and Pharmacology (IDAMAP) 2008, Washington, DC.

Yves Lepage. 2000. Languages of analogical strings. In Proc. of the 18th conference on Computational linguistics, COLING'00, Universität des Saarlandes, Saarbrücken, Germany.

Wen-Hsiang Lu, Shih-Jui Lin, Yi-Che Chan, and Kuan-Hsi Chen. 2005. Semi-automatic construction of the Chinese-English MeSH using web-based term translation method. In Proc. of AMIA annual symposium.

Kornél Markó, Stefan Schulz, and Udo Han. 2005. Morphosaurus - design and evaluation of an interlingua-based, cross-language document retrieval engine for the medical domain. Methods of Information in Medicine, 44(4).

Igor Mel'čuk. 2006. Aspects of the Theory of Morphology. Trends in Linguistics. Studies and Monographs. Mouton de Gruyter, Berlin, March.

Emmanuel Morin and Béatrice Daille. 2010. Compositionality and lexical alignment of multi-word terms. Language Resources and Evaluation (LRE), 44.

Franz Josef Och and Hermann Ney. 2003. A systematic comparison of various statistical alignment models. Computational Linguistics, 29(1):19–51.

Stefan Schulz, Kornel Markó, Eduardo Sbrissia, Percy Nohama, and Udo Hahn. 2004. Cognate Mapping - A Heuristic Strategy for the Semi-Supervised Acquisition of a Spanish Lexicon from a Portuguese Seed Lexicon. In Proc. of the 20th International Conference on Computational Linguistics, COLING'04, Geneva, Switzerland.

Nicolas Stroppa and François Yvon. 2005. An analogical learner for morphological analysis. In Proceeedings of the 9th CoNLL, pages 120–127, Ann Arbor, MI, USA.

Keita Tsuji, Béatrice Daille, and Kyo Kageura. 2002. Extracting French-Japanese word pairs from bilingual corpora based on transliteration rules. In Proc. of the 3rd International Conference on Language Resources and Evaluation, LREC'02, Las Palmas de Gran Canaria, Spain.

Mark Tuttle, David Sherertz, Nels Olson, Mark Erlbaum, David Sperzel, Lloyd Fuller, and Stuart Neslon. 1990. Using meta-1 – the 1st version of the UMLS metathesaurus. In Proc. of the 14th annual Symposium on Computer Applications in Medical Care (SCAMC), pages 131–135, Washington, USA.

Adaptability of Lexical Acquisition for Large-scale Grammars

Kostadin Cholakov†, Gertjan van Noord†, Valia Kordoni‡, Yi Zhang‡

† University of Groningen, The Netherlands
‡ Saarland University and DFKI GmbH, Germany
{k.cholakov,g.j.m.van.noord}@rug.nl
{kordoni,yzhang}@coli.uni-saarland.de

Abstract

In this paper, we demonstrate the portability of the lexical acquisition (LA) method proposed in Cholakov and van Noord (2010a). Here, LA refers to the acquisition of linguistic descriptions for words which are not listed in the lexicon of a given computational grammar, i.e., words which are unknown to this grammar. The method we discuss was originally developed for the Dutch Alpino system, and the paper shows that the method also applies to the GG (Crysmann, 2003), a computational HPSG grammar of German. The LA method obtains very similar results for German (84% F-measure on learning unknown words). Extending the GG with the lexical entries proposed by the LA method causes an important improvement in parsing accuracy for a test set of sentences containing unknown words. Furthermore, in a smaller experiment, we show that the linguistic knowledge the LA method provides can also be used for sentence generation.

1 Introduction

Computational grammars of natural language lie at the heart of various wide-coverage symbolic parsing systems. At present, such systems have been integrated into real-world NLP applications, such as IE, QA, grammar checking, MT and intelligent IR. This integration, though, has reminded us of some of the problems which the aforementioned grammars encounter when applied to naturally occurring text, in particular lack of lexical coverage. Since such grammars usually rely on hand-crafted lexicons containing elaborate linguistic descriptions, words not listed in the lexicon, i.e. words unknown to the grammar, pose a major issue in the employment of the grammars for real-life applications. In this context, *lexical acquisition* refers to the acquisition of correct lexical descriptions for unknown words.

Various LA techniques for computational grammars have been proposed in the past. Cussens and Pulman (2000) used a symbolic approach employing *inductive logic programming*, while Erbach (1990), Barg and Walther (1998) and Fouvry (2003) followed a unification-based approach. Other approaches have treated LA as a classification task where the unknown word is mapped to a finite set of labels. Baldwin (2005) has extracted features from various linguistic resources (POS taggers, chunkers, etc.) and used a set of binary classifiers to learn lexical entries for a large-scale grammar of English (ERG; (Copestake and Flickinger, 2000)). Zhang and Kordoni (2006) and Cholakov et al. (2008), on the other hand, have trained a maximum entropy (ME) classifier with features extracted from the grammar in order to acquire new lexical entries for the ERG and the GG (Crysmann, 2003), respectively. Extending this line of research, Cholakov and van Noord (2010a) have proposed a technique for learning unknown words for the Dutch Alpino grammar (van Noord, 2006) which takes into account the morphology of the unknown word and various contexts which it occurs in. In each case, however, LA is performed within a single parsing system, in a single framework, and mostly for a single language. It is unclear to what extent the various techniques can be used for a different language or parsing architecture.

The main motivation for the current work is

to explore the challenging task of employing one such LA technique, the one proposed in Cholakov and van Noord (2010a) – henceforth C&vN– for another system and another language. The C&vN technique is an obvious candidate for such a generalisation challenge, since Cholakov and van Noord (2010a) claim explicitly that the method should apply to other systems and languages provided some conditions are met. The conditions listed in Cholakov and van Noord (2010a) are: a finite set of labels which unknown words are mapped onto, a syntactic parser, and a morphological component which generates the paradigm(s) of a given unknown word. As a further motivation for our choice we note that the method of C&vN can be extended to deal with wrong and incomplete lexical descriptions of words which are already in the lexicon (Cholakov and van Noord, 2010b). However, this extension is beyond the scope of the current paper.

The choice of German and the GG (Crysmann, 2003) as the target for our case study lies in the fact that German is a language with somewhat richer morphology than Dutch, which affects the design of the grammar and makes LA more challenging. A further challenge is posed by the fact that the GG, unlike Alpino, does not have a full form lexicon. Instead, lexical entries define only the stem of the word and all other forms are derived by applying various morphological rules defined in the grammar. In the case of the GG, the LA method has the additional task of mapping unknown words to their stems and, at the same time, the descriptions it acquires should be detailed enough to allow for the proper application of the morphological rules.

Naturally, one could employ other techniques for LA with the GG but our purpose is to show that we can avoid implementing system specific solutions by adapting an existing LA method.

The remainder of the paper is organised as follows. Section 2 describes the adoption of the discussed LA method to the GG. Section 3 presents the experiments conducted with the grammar and evaluates the performance of the LA algorithm. Section 4 investigates how the LA method affects parsing accuracy on sentences containing unknown words and explores the possibility of using newly acquired lexical entries in a small sentence realisation task. Section 5 concludes the paper.

2 Lexical Acquisition for German

In this section, we explain the main steps in the method presented in C&vN and we focus on issues which arise from porting it to the GG.

2.1 The Parsing Setup

The GG is a stochastic attribute-value grammar based on typed feature structures. The GG types are strictly defined within a type hierarchy. The grammar contains constructional and lexical rules, as well as a lexicon where words are assigned lexical types. Currently, it consists of 5K types, 115 rules and the lexicon contains approximately 55K entries. There are 411 distinct lexical types which words can be mapped onto.

We employ the PET system (Callmeier, 2000) to parse with the GG. PET is a system for efficient processing of unification-based grammars. It is an industrial strength implementation of a typed-feature structure formalism (Carpenter, 1992). The system comprises a sophisticated preprocessor, a bottom-up chart parser and a grammar compiler.

2.2 Constructing a Set of Labels for Learning

In C&vN the unknown words are mapped onto a finite set of labels, namely the linguistic descriptions contained in the Alpino lexicon. In the case of the GG, the unknown words have to be mapped onto lexical type(s) from the GG lexicon. We consider only open-class lexical types: nouns, adjectives, verbs and adverbs. In the case of Alpino, C&vN do not consider adverbs because adjectives which are used adverbially are listed as adjectives in the lexicon. The remaining adverbs are a closed class. In the GG, such adjectives are listed as adverbs and therefore the adverbs are also a target for lexical acquisition.

A further difference with Alpino is that the definitions of the lexical types in the GG are not explicit enough for the purposes of LA. Consider the lexical entry for *Abfahrten* (departures):

```
abfahrt-n := count-noun-le &
 [ MORPH.LIST.FIRST.STEM < "Abfahrt" >,
   SYNSEM.LKEYS [ --SUBJOPT -,
                  KEYAGR c-n-f,
                  KEYREL "_abfahrt_n_rel",
                  KEYSORT temp_move_poly,
                  MCLASS nclass-9 ] ].
```

The lexical type 'count-noun-le' shows that the word is a countable noun[1]. The KEYAGR feature

[1] *le* stands for lexeme.

indicates case, number and gender. In the example above, case and number are left underspecified while the gender is set to feminine. The value of SUBJOPT shows that this noun is always used with an article and MCLASS indicates its morphological paradigm. The KEYREL and KEYSORT features define the semantics of the word.

When performing LA with the GG, we need to learn not only the lexical type but also the information encoded in the various type features. For this purpose, we include the values of features which we consider relevant for LA into the type definitions. In the case of *Abfahrten* we include the value of the gender from the KEYAGR feature turning the lexical type into *count-noun-le_f*. Only features designating morphosyntactic agreement are considered. For all noun types and predicative adjectives this is the KEYAGR feature. For verb types allowing for prepositional complements, we consider the COMPAGR and the OCOMPAGR features which indicate the case of the the (oblique) complement. By creating such *expanded* lexical types, we give the LA method access to the information contained in the selected features.

The remaining features do not contribute to LA and they are also likely to cause data sparseness. When adding words to the lexicon, some of those features can safely be left underspecified while others (e.g., KEYREL) can be assigned default values. Experiments have shown that such mildly less constrained lexical entries do not affect the parsing accuracy since the ambiguity they create usually dissolves in the context of the unknown word.

2.3 Paradigm Generation and Its Importance

C&vN use the paradigm of the unknown word as an important source of morphological features for the classification process. However, as stated above, unlike Alpino, the GG does not have a full form lexicon. We see in the lexical entry of *Abfahrten* that the STEM feature defines only the stem of the word. All other morphological forms are derived by applying various morphological rules defined in the GG to the word stem. For this reason, we employ the paradigm not only as a source of features for the classifier but also as a way to map the unknown word to its stem.

The stem for nouns is the singular nominative noun form, for adjectives it is the base noninflected form and for verbs it is the root form. Adverbs in German have a single form which is used as the value of the STEM feature in adverb entries. Some nouns (e.g., *Baukosten* (building costs)) do not have all forms typical for German nouns. In such cases, the word itself is set as the value of the STEM feature.

Due to the GG design, it is not straightforward to use the morphological rules of the grammar for paradigm generation. Following a technique developed for generating the paradigms of Dutch words (Cholakov and van Noord, 2009), we created a German finite state morphology. The morphology does not have access to any linguistic information and thus, it generates all possible paradigms allowed by the word orthography. Then, the number of search hits Yahoo returns for each form in a given paradigm is combined with some simple heuristics to disambiguate the output of the morphology and to determine the correct paradigm(s). For words predicted to be nouns, we also apply heuristics to guess the gender.

One could argue that there is a simpler approach for mapping the various forms of the unknown word to its stem. For instance, the TreeTagger POS tagger (Schmid, 1994) could provide both POS and stem information with high accuracy. However, the generation of the paradigms allows us to extract contexts in which other forms of a given unknown word occur and thus, we have access to much more and linguistically diverse data. For example, C&vN show the benefits of having access to other forms of a word predicted to be a verb for learning subcategorization frames.

2.4 Classifier and Features

We employ the maximum entropy based classifier[2] and the features used for unknown word prediction as described in C&vN. The probability of a lexical type t, given an unknown word and its context c is:

$$(1) \qquad p(t|c) = \frac{exp(\sum_i \Theta_i f_i(t,c))}{\sum_{t' \in T} exp(\sum_i \Theta_i f_i(t',c))}$$

where $f_i(t,c)$ may encode arbitrary characteristics of the context and $< \Theta_1, \Theta_2, ... >$ can be evaluated by maximising the pseudo-likelihood on a training corpus (Malouf, 2002).

Table 1 shows the features for *Abfahrten*. Row **(i)** contains 4 separate features derived from the prefix of the word and 4 other suffix features are

[2]TADM; `http://tadm.sourceforge.net/`

given in row **(ii)**. The two features in rows **(iii)** and **(iv)** indicate whether the word starts with a separable particle and if it contains a hyphen, respectively. Since it is the stem of the unknown word we add to the lexicon, we also experimented with prefix and suffix features extracted from the stem. We assumed that those could allow for a better generalization of morphological properties but they proved to be less informative for the classifier.

Further, the paradigm generation method outputs a single paradigm for *Abfahrten* indicating that this word is a singular feminine noun. This information is explicitly used as a feature in the classifier which is shown in row **(v)** of Table 1.

Features
i) A, Ab, Abf, Abfa
ii) n, en, ten, rten
iii) particle_yes #in this case *Ab*
iv) hyphen_no
v) noun_feminine
vi) count-noun-le_f, mass-noun-le_f
vii) noun⟨f⟩

Table 1: Features for *Abfahrten*

Rows **(vi)** and **(vii)** show syntactic features obtained from what C&VN refer to as 'parsing with universal types'. Each unknown word is assigned the target types belonging to the POS of the paradigm(s) generated for this word. For example, *Abfahrten* is assigned all noun types from the set of types we want to learn. Sentences containing the unknown word and other of its forms are parsed with PET in best-only mode. For each sentence only the best parse selected by the disambiguation model of the parser is preserved. Then, the lexical type that has been assigned to the form of *Abfahrten* occurring in this parse is stored.

We employ the most frequently used type(s) (based on an empirical threshold) as features in the classifier (row **vi**). Further, as illustrated in row **(vii)**, each feature value we have attached to the type definition of the considered types (the part after the underscore) is also taken as a separate feature.

3 Experiments with Development Data

3.1 Experiment Setup

In our experiments with the GG, an open-class lexical type is considered if it has at least 10 lexical entries in the lexicon mapped onto it and it is assigned to at least 15 distinct words occurring in large corpora parsed with PET and the GG. The parsed corpus we use consists of roughly 2.5M sentences randomly selected from the German part of the Wacky project (Kilgarriff and Grefenstette, 2003). The Wacky project aims at the creation of large corpora for different languages, including German, from various web sources, such as online newspapers and magazines, legal texts, internet fora, etc.

Following these criteria, we have selected 39 open-class types out of the 411 lexical types defined in the GG. As described in Section 2.2, we re-defined the type definitions of the 39 types which resulted in the creation of 68 *expanded* types. This number is smaller than the 611 types used in the experiments with Alpino because the GG does not have a full form lexicon. Table 2 gives more details about the type distribution.

	Original types	Expanded types
Total	39	68
-nouns	5	15
-verbs	28	45
-adjectives	4	6
-adverbs	2	2

Table 2: Distribution of the target lexical types

In order to train and test the classifier, 2400 less frequent words are temporarily removed from the lexicon of the GG. Of these, 2000 are used for training, and 400 words are used for testing. We assume that less frequent words are typically unknown and, in order to simulate their behaviour, all 2400 words we removed from the lexicon have between 40 and 100 occurrences in the parsed corpus. Experiments with a minimum lower than 40 occurrences have shown that this is a reasonable threshold to filter out typos, tokenization errors, etc. The distribution of the parts-of-speech for the 2400 words is listed in Table 3 (some words have more than a single part-of-speech).

3.2 Evaluation of the Paradigm Generation Component

Since paradigms play such a crucial role in the experiments with the GG, we first evaluate the performance of the paradigm generation component.

Table 3 shows the overall results and the results for each POS. *Accuracy* indicates how many of the generated paradigms are correct. In the

	overall	nouns	adj	verbs
total	2954	1196	651	694
accuracy(%)	96.45	91.09	100	99.54

Table 3: Paradigm generation results

paradigms generated for verbs there were three mistakes. However, the generated verb stems were all correct. Similarly, the stems for all nouns were correct, including the stems of 98 nouns which contained a mistake in their paradigm. In 91 cases the singular genitive form was incorrect, in another 12 cases the predicted gender was wrong. The mapping of the words to their correct stems is correct in all cases.

3.3 Evaluation of the Classifier

Let us now investigate the performance of the classifier. We allow prediction of multiple types per word but we discard the types accounting together for less than 5% of probability mass. Additionally, there are three baseline methods:

- *Naive*– each unknown word is assigned the most frequent expanded type in the lexicon: *count-noun-le_f*
- *Naive POS*– the word is given the most frequent expanded type for the POS of each paradigm generated for it
- *GG*– the unknown word is assigned the most frequently used type in the parsing stage (e.g., for *Abfahrten*, this is *count-noun-le_f* from row vi) in Table 1)

The overall results are given in Table 4 together with the result C&vN reported for Alpino. Table 5 breaks down the results for each POS. Precision indicates how many types found by the method are correct and recall indicates how many of the lexical types of a given word are actually found. The presented results are the average precision and recall for the 400 test words. The original lexical types which the words had before they were removed from the GG lexicon are used as a gold standard for comparison.

The LA model improves upon the baselines, and performs very similar to the results reported for Dutch. The German model achieves somewhat better recall which is balanced by lower precision. Figure 1 shows that the F-measure reaches 70%

Model	Prec(%)	Rec(%)	F-meas(%)
Naive	21.75	21.07	21.41
Naive POS	58.96	47.65	52.7
GG	67	48.96	56.58
LA with the GG	82.04	86.5	84.21
LA with Alpino	89.08	80.52	84.58

Table 4: Overall experiment results

POS	Prec(%)	Rec(%)	F-meas(%)
Nouns	91	93.85	92.4
Adj	88.89	93.07	90.93
Verbs	65.02	69.64	67.25
Adverbs	75.32	76.32	75.82

Table 5: Detailed results for the LA model

already at 100 training words. It goes up to 80% when 300 words are used for training the curve flattens out at 1600 training words. The results indicate that the method of C&vN can be successfully applied outside the environment which it was primarily developed for.

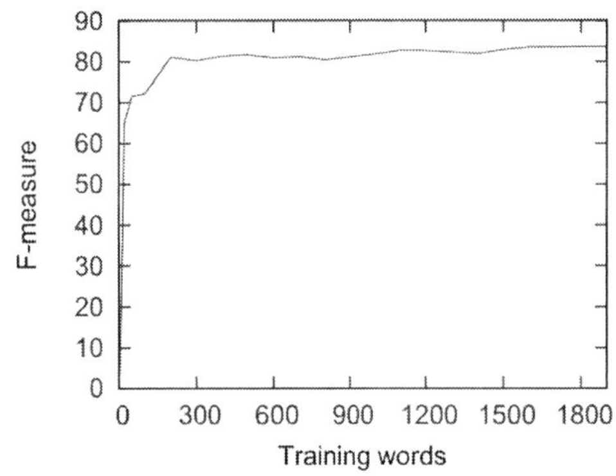

Figure 1: Learning curve

Predicting lexical entries for verbs is the hardest task for the LA model. The classifier has a strong bias towards assigning transitive and intransitive verb types. It either fails to predict infrequent frames or it wrongly predicts a transitive type for intransitive verbs and vice versa. Another difficulty for the model is the distinction which the GG makes between ergative and non-ergative verbs.

The main issue with adverbs is that many of them can be used as adjectives as well. As a consequence, the classifier has a strong bias towards predicting an adverb type for words for which an adjective type has also been predicted. Further, it also has a bias towards assigning one of the two adverb types, namely, *intersect-adv-le*. Finally, no pattern in the errors for nouns and adjectives can be identified.

4 Tests with Real Unknown Words

4.1 LA and Parsing Accuracy

Once we have a trained model, we want to investigate how LA affects parsing accuracy.

We conducted an experiment with a test set of 450 sentences which all contain unknown words. The sentences are randomly selected from a German newspaper corpus containing 614K sentences. The articles in the corpus deal with various domains. For this experiment, we parse the 450 sentences with PET, under two conditions. In the first case, the standard lexicon of the GG is used, whereas in the second case, we add to the GG lexical entries acquired offline by the LA method. The standard GG model includes a guesser which assigns generic types to the unknown words. Some of the morphosyntactic features in these types are left underspecified and the semantic features receive default values. The experiment therefore compares the difference in parsing accuracy of the built-in guesser with the LA model.

From the 450 sentences, we selected the 113 sentences which PET/GG was able to parse with the standard lexicon as well as with the extended lexicon (for this reason, the accuracy figures below are relatively high). For 100 out of the 113 sentences a correct parse is produced (among the set of parses) by at least one of the methods. In the standard setup, a correct parse can be produced for 89 sentences. For the setup with LA, this number increases to 99 sentences. The correct parses for the 100 sentences were used as our gold standard, to be able to report the accuracy numbers below, for the best parse. These 100 sentences have an average sentence length of 17.72 words, and contain 106 distinct unknown words. Accuracy is measured in terms of labelled brackets. The results are listed in Table 6.

Model	Accuracy	msec/sentence
GG-standard	92.80	9824
GG + LA	94.51	9911

Table 6: Results with real unknown words

Adding the lexical entries proposed by the LA model leads to an increase in parsing accuracy. This result is consistent with the one reported for C&VN for Dutch.

The increase in parsing accuracy has to do mainly with the fact that the built-in guesser assigns noun types to the vast majority of the unknown words. Many of the features in those entries are left underspecified which creates a lot of ambiguity and which makes it harder for the parser disambiguation model to select the correct analysis. As mentioned in Section 2.2, the LA model also leaves some of the features underspecified or assigns default values to them. Still, the information it provides is much more linguistically accurate which helps for ambiguity resolution and the production of the correct parse.

4.2 LA for Sentence Realisation

As a further evaluation, extending the evaluation methodology of C&VN, we also investigate if the acquired lexical entries affect sentence realisation.

The GG adopts Minimal Recursion Semantics (MRS, Copestake et al. (2005)) as semantic representation. This, together with the fine-grained linguistic information in the GG lexical types, allows for finding the textual realisations for a given input semantic representation. Sentence realisation with the GG is performed within the LKB grammar engineering platform which provides an efficient generation engine. This engine is essentially a chart-based generator (Kay, 1996) with various optimisations for MRS and packed parse forest (Carroll and Oepen, 2005).

As there are less ordering constraints in the semantic representation (comparing to the word sequence in parsing inputs), the computation is intrinsically more expensive. While in parsing the ambiguity in the less constrained lexical entries acquired with LA dissolves quickly in its context, there is a potential risk of overgeneration in sentence realisation.

We conduct an indicative experiment with 14 unknown words from the test set used in Section 4.1. These words have been assigned verb types by the classifier. The focus of the experiment is on verbs because of the large number of possible subcategorization frames, which is a major source for overgeneration and can severely damage the quality of the sentence realisations.

We have extracted a test set of 64 sentences from the Wacky web corpus we used in Section 3.1, each of which contains one of the 14 selected words. We parse those sentences with the GG using the verb lexical entries acquired for the 14 unknown words with LA. Some of the sentences are edited to make sure that there are no other unknown words in them. The best MRS is recorded, and sent back to the generation engine. The generated realisations are recorded and compared with the original input sentence. The average sentence length of the selected 64 sentences is 7.66 tokens.

We construct manually another sentence set where the 14 unknown words are replaced by verbs from the GG lexicon. Each replacement verb belongs to the same lexical type and has the same type features as the lexical entry acquired for the unknown word it replaces. This comparison set indicates what the performance of the GG would be with fully constrained, but otherwise similar lexical entries.

There were 3.28 realisations per sentence for the test set versus 3.16 for the comparison one. As for accuracy, a realisation is considered correct if it is an exact match of the original sentence (excluding punctuation). Despite the higher number for realisations per sentence for the test set, the quality of the realisations is the same for both sets– for 60 sentences a correct realisation is produced. Thus, the entries acquired with LA can be employed for both parsing and realisation.

5 Conclusion

We addressed the challenging issue of generalising LA techniques for computational grammars by applying the method of C&VN, originally developed for the Dutch Alpino grammar, to the GG, an HPSG grammar for German. This resulted in improved parsing accuracy. The modifications we made to adopt the method to the linguistic properties of German and the design of the GG did not change its fundamental principles and the basic steps of the algorithm it implements.

Moreover, we have also shown that the lexicon acquired with this method may also be used for generation, something that to our knowledge has not been tried so far in similar linguistic processing architectures. The successful adaptation of the discussed LA method for the GG also suggests that such architectures share common design principles which makes it possible for common solutions to be developed.

References

Tim Baldwin. 2005. Bootstrapping deep lexical resources: Resources for courses. In *Proceedings of the ACL-SIGLEX 2005 Workshop on Deep Lexical Acquisition*, Ann Arbor, USA.

Petra Barg and Markus Walther. 1998. Processing unknown words in HPSG. In *Proceedings of the 36th Conference of the ACL*, Montreal, Quebec, Canada.

Ulrich Callmeier. 2000. PET– a platform for experimentation with efficient HPSG processing techniques. In *Journal of Natural Language Engineering*, volume 6, pages 99–107. Cambridge University Press.

Bob Carpenter. 1992. *The Logic of Typed Feature Structures*. Cambridge University Press.

John Carroll and Stephan Oepen. 2005. High efficiency realization for a wide-coverage unification grammar. In *Proceedings of the 2nd International Joint Conference on Natural Language Processing (IJCNLP 2005)*, pages 165–176, Jeju Island, Korea.

Kostadin Cholakov and Gertjan van Noord. 2009. Combining finite state and corpus-based techniques for unknown word prediction. In *Proceedings of the 7th Recent Advances in Natural Language Processing (RANLP) conference*, Borovets, Bulgaria.

Kostadin Cholakov and Gertjan van Noord. 2010a. Acquisition of unknown word paradigms for large-scale grammars. In *Proceedings of the 23rd International Conference on Computational Linguistics (COLING-2010)*, Beijing, China.

Kostadin Cholakov and Gertjan van Noord. 2010b. Using unknown word techniques to learn known words. In *Proceedings of the Conference on Empirical Methods in Natural Language Processing (EMNLP 2010)*, Cambridge, MA.

Kostadin Cholakov, Valia Kordoni, and Yi Zhang. 2008. Towards domain-independent deep linguistic processing: Ensuring portability and re-usability of lexicalised grammars. In *Proceedings of COLING 2008 Workshop on Grammar Engineering Across Frameworks (GEAF08)*, Manchester, UK.

Ann Copestake and Dan Flickinger. 2000. An open-source grammar development environment and broad-coverage English grammar using HPSG. In *Proceedings of the 2nd International Conference on Language Resource and Evaluation (LREC 2000)*, Athens, Greece.

Ann Copestake, Dan Flickinger, Carl J. Pollard, and Ivan A. Sag. 2005. Minimal recursion semantics: an introduction. *Research on Language and Computation*, 3(4):281–332.

Berthold Crysmann. 2003. On the efficient implementation of German verb placement in HPSG. In *Proceedings of RANLP 2003*, Borovets, Bulgaria.

James Cussens and Stephen Pulman. 2000. Incorporating linguistic constraints into inductive logic programming. In *Proceedings of the Fourth Conference on Computational Natural Language Learning*.

Gregor Erbach. 1990. Syntactic processing of unknown words. IWBS report 131. Technical report, IBM, Stuttgart.

Frederik Fouvry. 2003. Lexicon acquisition with a large-coverage unification-based grammar. In *Companion to the 10th Conference of EACL*, pages 87–90, Budapest, Hungary.

Martin Kay. 1996. Chart generation. In *Proceedings of the 34th Annual Meeting of the Association for Computational Linguistics*, pages 200–204, Santa Cruz, California, USA, June. Association for Computational Linguistics.

Adam Kilgarriff and G Grefenstette. 2003. Introduction to the special issue on the web as a corpus. In *Computational Linguistics*, volume 29, pages 333–347.

Robert Malouf. 2002. A comparison of algorithms for maximum entropy parameter estimation. In *Proceedings of the 6th conference on Natural Language Learning (CoNLL-2002)*, pages 49–55, Taipei, Taiwan.

Helmut Schmid. 1994. Probabilistic part-of-speech tagging using decision trees. In *Proceedings of the International Conference on New Methods in Language Processing*, Manchester, UK.

Gertjan van Noord. 2006. At last parsing is now operational. In *Proceedings of TALN*, Leuven, Belgium.

Yi Zhang and Valia Kordoni. 2006. Automated deep lexical acquisition for robust open text processing. In *Proceedings of the Fifth International Conference on Language Resourses and Evaluation (LREC 2006)*, Genoa, Italy.

Integration of Data from a Syntactic Lexicon into Generative and Discriminative Probabilistic Parsers

Anthony Sigogne
Université Paris-Est, LIGM
sigogne@univ-mlv.fr

Matthieu Constant
Université Paris-Est, LIGM
mconstan@univ-mlv.fr

Éric Laporte
Université Paris-Est, LIGM
laporte@univ-mlv.fr

Abstract

This article evaluates the integration of data extracted from a syntactic lexicon, namely the Lexicon-Grammar, into several probabilistic parsers for French. We show that by modifying the Part-of-Speech tags of verbs and verbal nouns of a treebank, we obtain accurate performances with a parser based on Probabilistic Context-Free Grammars (Petrov et al., 2006) and a discriminative parser based on a reranking algorithm (Charniak and Johnson, 2005).

1 Introduction

Syntactic lexicons are rich language resources that may contain useful data for parsers like subcategorisation frames, as they provide, for each lexical entry, information about its syntactic behaviors. Most of the time, these lexicons only deal with verbs. Few, like the Lexicon-Grammar (Gross, 1994), deal with other categories like nouns, adjectives or adverbs. Many works on symbolic parsing studied the use of a syntactic lexicon, in particular linguistic formalisms like Lexical-Functional Grammars [LFG] (Kaplan and Maxwell, 1994; Riezler et al., 2002; Sagot, 2006) or Tree Adjoining Grammars [TAG] (Joshi, 1987; Sagot and Tolone, 2009; de La Clergerie, 2010). For probabilistic parsing, we can cite LFG (Cahill, 2004; O'Donovan et al., 2005; Schluter and Genabith, 2008), Head-Driven Phrase Structure Grammar [HPSG] (Carroll and Fang, 2004) and Probabilistic Context-Free Grammars [PCFG] (Briscoe and Carroll, 1997; Deoskar, 2008). The latter has incorporated valence features to PCFGs and lexicons and observes slight improvements on performances. However, lexical resources that contain valence features were obtained automatically from a corpus. Furthermore, valence features are mainly used on verbs. In this paper, we will show how we can exploit information contained in the Lexicon-Grammar in order to improve probabilistic parsers. We will in particular focus on verbs and verbal nouns[1].

In section 2, we describe the probabilistic parsers used in our experiments. Section 3 briefly introduces the Lexicon-Grammar. We detail information contained in this lexicon that can be used for parsing. Then, in section 4, we present methods to integrate this information into parsers and, in section 5, we describe our experiments and discuss the obtained results.

2 Statistical parsers

In our experiments, we used two types of parsers: a generative parser that generates the *n-best* parses (n most probable parses) for a sentence according to a PCFG; a reranker that reranks the *n-best* parses generated from the PCFG parser according to a discriminative probabilistic model.

2.1 Non-lexicalized PCFG parser

The PCFG parser, used into our experiments, is the Berkeley Parser (called BKY thereafter) (Petrov et al., 2006)[2]. This parser is based on a non-lexicalized PCFG model. The main problem of non-lexicalized context-free grammars is that pre-terminal symbols encode too general information which weakly discriminates syntactic ambiguities. BKY tries to handle the problem by generating a grammar containing complex pre-terminals. It follows the principle of latent annotations introduced by (Matsuzaki et al., 2005). It consists in creating iteratively several grammars, which have a tagset increasingly complex. For each iteration, a symbol of the grammar is splitted in several symbols

[1] Verbal nouns are nouns playing the role of a predicate in the sentence.

[2] The Berkeley parser is freely available at http://code.google.com/p/berkeleyparser/downloads/list

according to the different syntactic behaviors of the symbol that occur in a treebank. Parameters of the latent grammar are estimated with an algorithm based on Expectation-Maximisation (EM). Within the framework of French, (Seddah et al., 2009) have shown that BKY produces *state-of-the-art* performances. They have also shown that several parsers, based on the lexicalized paradigm (phrasal nodes are annotated with their headword), achieved lower scores than BKY.

2.2 Reranking parser

We have also experimented the integration of a reranker as a post-process of BKY output. For a given sentence s, a reranker selects the best parse y among the set of candidates $Y(s)$ according to a scoring function V_θ :

$$y^\star = argmax_{y \in Y(s)} V_\theta(y) \quad (1)$$

The set of candidates $Y(s)$ is the *n-best* parses output of the baseline parser (BKY in our case), $Y(s) = \{y_1, y_2, ..., y_n\}$. The *n-best* parses correspond to the n most probable parses according to the probability model of the parser. The scoring function V_θ is defined by the dot product of a weight vector θ and a feature vector f :

$$V_\theta(y) = \theta.f(y) = \sum_{j=1}^{m} \theta_j.f_j(y) \quad (2)$$

where the feature vector $f(y)$ is a vector of m functions $f = (f_1, f_2, ..., f_m)$, and each feature function f_j maps a parse y to a real number $f_j(y)$. The first feature $f_1(y)$ is the probability of the parse given by the n-best parser (cf. (Charniak and Johnson, 2005)). All remaining features are integer values, and each of them is the number of times that the feature occurs in parse y. Features belong to feature schemas which are abstract schemas from which specific features are instantiated. Feature schemas that we used during our experiments are specified in the table 1. For example, a feature $f_{10}(y)$, which is an instance of the feature schema *Rule*, counts the number of times that a nominal phrase in y is the head of a rule which has a determinant and a noun as children. The weight vector θ can be estimated by a machine learning algorithm from a treebank corpus which contains the gold parse for each sentence. In our case, we will use the Maximum Entropy estimator, as in (Charniak and Johnson, 2005).

Feature schemas	
Rule	Edges
Word	WordEdges
Heavy	Heads
HeadTree	WProj
Bigrams$^\triangle$	NgramTree
Trigrams$^\triangle$	

Table 1: Features used in this work. Those with a $^\triangle$ are from (Collins, 2000), and others are from (Charniak and Johnson, 2005)

3 Lexicon-Grammar

The Lexicon-Grammar [LG] is the richest source of syntactic and lexical information for French[3] that focuses not only on verbs but also on verbal nouns, adjectives, adverbs and frozen (or fixed) sentences. Its development started in the 70's by Maurice Gross and his team (Gross, 1994). It is a syntactic lexicon represented in the form of tables. Each table encodes lexical items of a particular category sharing several syntactic properties (e.g. subcategorization information). A lexical item is a lemmatized form that can be present in one or more tables depending on its meaning and its syntactic properties. Each table row corresponds to a lexical item and a column corresponds to a property (e.g. syntactic constructions, argument distribution, and so on). A cell encodes whether a lexical item accepts a given property. Figure 1 shows a sample of verb table *12*. In this table, we can see that the verb *chérir* (*to cherish*) accepts a human subject (pointed out by a + in the property *N0 =: Nhum*) but this verb cannot be intransitive (pointed out by a − in the property *N0 V*). Recently, these tables have been made consistent and explicit (Tolone, 2011) in order to be

N0 =: Nhum	N0 =: le fait Qu P	N0 =: V1-inf W	<ENT>Ppv	Ppv =: Neg	<ENT>V	Neg	N0 V	N1 =: Qu Pind	Qu P = V0-inf W	N1 =: Qu P = Aux V0-inf W	N1 = Ppv	[passif par]	[passif de]
+	-	-	<E>	-	chérir	-	-	-	-	-	+	+	+
+	-	-	<E>	-	comprendre	-	+	-	-	-	+	+	+
+	-	-	<E>	-	critiquer	-	+	-	-	-	+	+	+
+	-	-	<E>	-	débiner	-	-	-	-	-	+	+	+

Figure 1: Sample of verb table *12*

[3] We can also cite lexicons like LVF (Dubois and Dubois-Charlier, 1997), Dicovalence (Eynde and Piet, 2003) and Lefff (Sagot, 2010).

exploitable for NLP. They also have been transformed in a XML-structured format (Constant and Tolone, 2008)[4]. Each lexical entry is associated with its table identifier, its possible arguments and its syntactic constructions.
For the verbs, we manually constructed a hierarchy of the tables on several levels[5]. Each level contains classes which group LG tables which may not share all their defining properties but have a relatively similar syntactic behavior. Figure 2 shows a sample of the hierarchy. The tables *4, 6* and *12* are grouped into a class called *QTD2* (transitive sentence with two arguments and sentential complements). Then, this class is grouped with other classes at the superior level of the hierarchy to form a class called *TD2* (transitive sentence with two arguments). The characteristics of

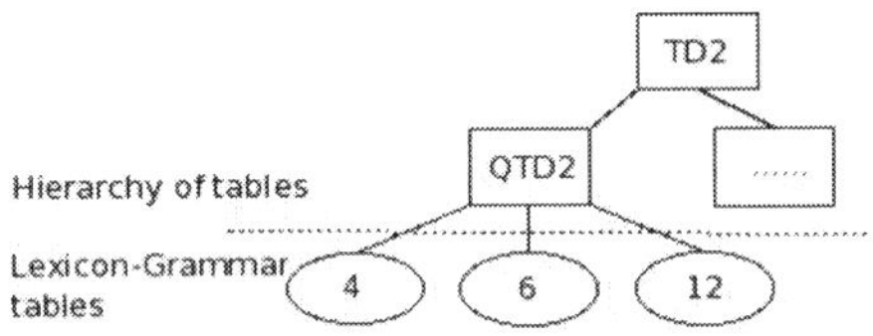

Figure 2: Sample of the hierarchy of verb tables

each level are given in the table 2[6] (level 0 represents the set of tables of the LG). We can state that there are 5,923 distinct verbal forms for 13,862 resulting entries in tables of verbs. The column *#classes* specifies the number of distinct classes. The columns *AVG_1* and *AVG_2* respectively indicate the average number of entries per class and the average number of classes per distinct verbal form.

Level	#classes	AVG_1	AVG_2
0	67	207	2.15
1	13	1,066	1.82
2	10	1,386	1.75
3	4	3,465	1.44

Table 2: Characteristics of the hierarchy of verb tables

The hierarchy of tables have the advantage of reducing the number of classes associated with each verb of the tables. We will see that this ambiguity reduction is crucial in our experiments.

4 Exploitation of the Lexicon-Grammar data

Many experiments about parsing, within the framework of French (Crabbé and Candito, 2008; Seddah et al., 2009), have shown that refining the tagset of the training corpus improves performances of the parser. We will follow their works by integrating information from the Lexicon-Grammar to part-of-speech tags. In this article, we will only focus on tables of verbs and verbal nouns.

Table identifiers of the lexical entries are important hints about their syntactic behaviors. For example, the table *31R* indicates that all verbs belonging to this table are intransitive. The first experiment, called **AnnotTable**, consists in augmenting the part-of-speech tag with the table identifier(s) associated with the noun or the verb. For example, the verb *chérir* (*to cherish*) belongs to the table *12*. Therefore, the induced tag is *#tag_12*, where *#tag* is the POS tag associated with the verb. For an ambiguous verb like *sanctionner* (*to punish*), belonging to two tables *6* and *12*, the induced tag is *#tag_6_12*.

Then, in the case of verbs, we have done variants of the previous experiment by taking the hierarchy of verb tables into account. This hierarchy provides a tagset with a size which varies according to the level in the hierarchy. Identifiers added to tags depend on the verb and the specific level in the hierarchy. For example, the verb *sanctionner*, belonging to tables *6* and *12*, has a tag *#tag_QTD2* at level 1. In the case of ambiguous verbs, for a given level in the hierarchy, suffixes contain all classes the verb belongs to. This experiment will be called **AnnotVerbs** thereafter. In the case of verbal nouns, as such a hierarchy of tables does not exist, we experimented two other methods. The first one, called **AnnotIN**, consists in adding a suffix *IN* to the tag of a noun if this noun occurs in the syntactic lexicon, and therefore if it is a verbal noun. The second method, called **AnnotNouns**, consists in creating a hierarchy of noun tables from the table of classes of verbal nouns. This hierarchy is made accordingly to the maximum

[4]These resources are freely available at http://infolingu.univ-mlv.fr>Language_Resources> Lexicon_Grammar>Download

[5]The hierarchy of verb tables is available at : http://igm.univ-mlv.fr/~sigogne/arbre-tables.xlsx

[6]We can also state that 3,121 verb forms (3,195 entries) are unambiguous. This means that all their entries occur in a single table.

number of arguments that a noun of a table can have according to defining properties specified for this table. As a consequence, the hierarchy has a single level. For example, nouns of the table *N_aa* can have at most 2 arguments contrary to those of table *N_an04* which can have only one. The characteristics of each level are specified in table 3[7] (level 0 represents the set of tables of the Lexicon-Grammar). We can state that there are 8,531 distinct nominal forms for 12,351 resulting entries in tables of nouns.

Level	#classes	AVG_1	AVG_2
0	76	162	1.43
1	3	3,413	1.2

Table 3: Characteristics of the hierarchy of noun tables

5 Experimental setup

For our experiments, we used the richest treebank for French, the French Treebank, (later called FTB) (Abeillé et al., 2003), containing 20,860 sentences and 540,648 words from the newspaper *Le Monde* (version of 2004). As this corpus is small, we used a *cross-validation* procedure for the evaluation. This method consists in splitting the corpus into *p* equal parts, then we compute training on *p-1* parts and evaluations on the remaining part. We can iterate this process *p* times. This allows us to calculate an average score for a sample as large as the initial corpus. In our case, we set the parameter *p* to 10. We also used the part-of-speech tagset defined in (Crabbé and Candito, 2008) containing 28 different tags describing some complementary morphological and syntactic features (e.g. verb mood, clitics, ...)[8]. Compound words have been merged in order to obtain a single token.

In the following experiments, we will test the impact of modifying the tagset of the training corpus, namely the addition of information from the Lexicon-Grammar described in the section 4. Results on evaluation parts are reported using the standard protocol called PARSEVAL (Black et al., 1991) for sentences smaller than 40 words. The score f-measure (F1) takes into account the bracketing and categories of nodes (including punctuation nodes). For each experiment, we have reported the *Baseline* results (i.e. the results of BKY trained on the original treebank without annotations from the Lexicon-Grammar). We have also indicated the percentage of distinct annotated verbs and verbal nouns in the entire corpus for each annotation method[9].

5.1 Annotation of verb tags

We first conducted experiments on verbs described in section 4, namely *AnnotTable* and *AnnotVerbs*. The experimental results are shown in the table 4. In the case of the method *AnnotVerbs*, we varied two parameters, *Lvl* (for Level) indicating the level of the hierarchy used and *Amb.* (for Ambiguity) indicating that a tag of a verb is changed only if this verb belongs to a number of classes less than or equal to the number specified by this parameter.

Method	Lvl/Amb.	F1/Tagging	Absolute gains (F1)
Baseline	-/-	85.05/97.43	
AnnotTable	-/1	84.49/97.29	
AnnotVerbs	1/1	85.06/97.46	
AnnotVerbs	2/1	85.35/97.41	
AnnotVerbs	3/1	**85.39/97.49**	
AnnotVerbs	2/2	84.60/97.35	
AnnotVerbs	3/2	85.20/97.48	

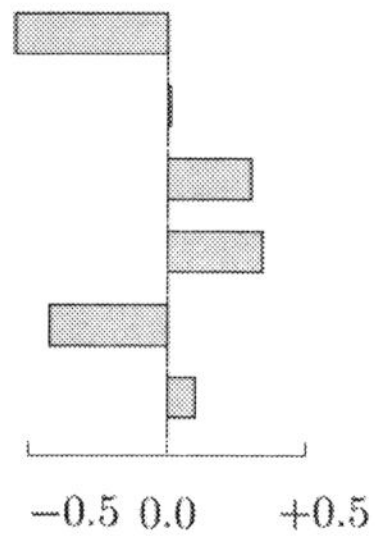

Table 4: Results from cross-validation evaluation according to verb annotation methods

Method	Size of tagset	% annotated verbs
Baseline	28	-
AnnotTable	228	18,6%
AnnotVerbs 1/1	89	21,5%
AnnotVerbs 2/1	76	22,5%
AnnotVerbs 3/1	47	33,9%
AnnotVerbs 2/2	246	44,7%
AnnotVerbs 3/2	75	55,7%

Table 5: Size of tagset and percentage of annotated verbs according to verb annotation methods

For non-ambiguous verbs, we observe that the experiment *AnnotTable* highly deteriorates performances. This comes most probably from the

[7]The number of non-ambiguous nouns is 6126 for 6175 entries.

[8]There are 6 distinct tags for verbs and 2 distinct tags for nouns.

[9]The corpus contains 3058 distinct verbal forms and 17003 distinct nominal forms.

grammar which is too fragmented because of the significant size of the part-of-speech tagset (as shown in table 5). However, the effect is reversed as soon as we use levels of the hierarchy of tables (levels 2 and 3 only). The use of the table hierarchy causes the increase of the number of verbs annotated as non-ambiguous and the decrease of the size of the tagset. Considering ambiguous verbs do not improve performances (results are shown only for levels 2 and 3 with maximal ambiguity of 2) because of the large size of the tagset (as for experiment *AnnotTable*).

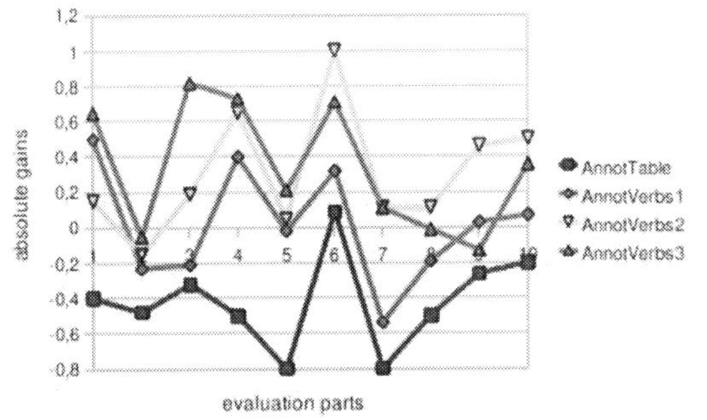

Figure 3: Absolute gains (F1) of verb annotation methods on evaluation parts (baseline is the horizontal line at 0 on y axis)

We can see on Figure 3 absolute gains according to verb annotation methods on evaluation parts. We have displayed curves for methods *AnnotTable* and *AnnotVerbs*X, where X is the level in the hierarchy (without ambiguity). Higher we are in the hierarchy of tables, the more we obtain better performances. Levels 2 and 3 are globally above the baseline for most of their evaluation parts. Therefore, this would mean that table identifiers of verbs and the hierarchy are a real help for parsing and do not produce a random effect. On table 6, we

Phrase label	Meaning	Error reduction
Ssub	subordinate clause	5,3% (52)
Sint	internal clause	3,6% (47)
PP	prepositional phrase	3,1% (272)
Srel	relative clause	2,2% (17)
NP	nominal phrase	2,1% (347)
VPinf	infinitive phrase	2,1% (34)

Table 6: Top most error reductions according to phrase label

can see the top most error reductions according to phrase label, for the best verb annotation method (*AnnotVerbs* with level 3 of the hierarchy). For each phrase, the column called *Error reduction* indicates the average error reduction rate associated with the corresponding average number of error corrected (inside brackets). The NP and PP phrases are those that have the highest number of errors corrected (the low reduction rate can be explained by the fact that these two phrases have the highest number of errors). Furthermore, they are linked to each other because, generally, a PP has a NP kernel. Therefore, if a NP is corrected, the corresponding PP is also corrected (if it is the only error).

5.2 Annotation of noun tags

For verbal nouns, we successively conducted several experiments *AnnotTable*, *AnnotNouns* and *AnnotIN*, described in section 4. Results are given in table 7. As for verbs, we have reported the results for the experiment *AnnotNouns* with respect to the parameter *Ambiguity* (the maximum number of classes being associated with a noun is 3).

Method	Amb.	F1/Tagging	Absolute gains (F1)
Baseline	-	85.05/97.43	
AnnotTable	1	85.10/97.42	
AnnotNouns	1	85.13/97.48	
AnnotNouns	2	85.16/97.47	
AnnotNouns	3	85.05/97.41	
AnnotIN	-	**85.20/97.54**	
			−0.5 0.0 +0.5

Table 7: Results from cross-validation evaluation according to noun annotation methods

Method	Size of tagset	% annotated nouns
Baseline	28	-
AnnotTable	98	8,6%
AnnotNouns 1	33	11,2%
AnnotNouns 2	38	16,5%
AnnotNouns 3	39	16,9%
AnnotIN	30	16,9%

Table 8: Size of tagset and percentage of annotated verbal nouns according to noun annotation methods

The various noun annotation methods slightly increase performances of the parser. Unlike verbs, the method *AnnotTable* does not degrade performances because there are much less nouns in the corpus belonging to the syntactic lexicon (less than 9% as shown in table 8), hence the limited impact of the new tagset. The use of a simple hierarchy of the noun tables, through experiment *AnnotNouns*, achieves positive gains but, here, insignificant. Moreover, we obtain a slight improvement by annotating some ambiguous nouns. Surprisingly, the method which gives the best result, despite its simplicity, is *AnnotIN*. We can see in

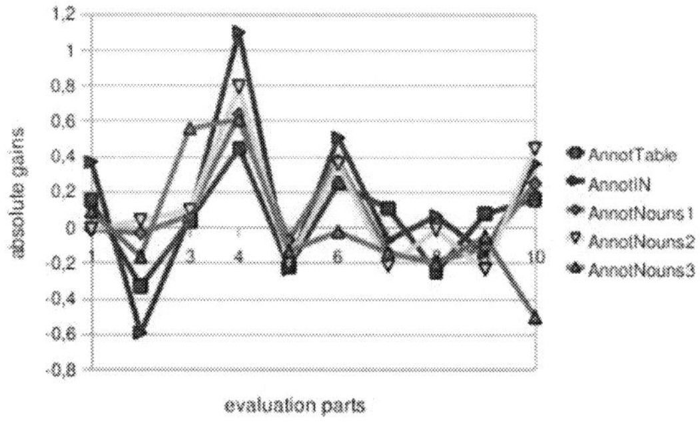

Figure 4: Absolute gains (F1) of noun annotation methods on evaluation parts (baseline is the horizontal line at 0 on y axis)

Figure 4 absolute gains according to noun annotation methods on all evaluation parts. Unlike verbs, absolute gains are closer to the baseline. The best method *AnnotIN* is able to improve significantly 4 of 10 evaluation parts (+0,4 to +0,8).

5.3 Combination of annotations

In a final experiment with BKY, we combined the best methods of verb and verbal noun annotations, that are *AnnotIN* for verbal nouns and *AnnotVerbs* for verbs (level 3 without ambiguity). Results are shown in table 9.

Method	F1
Baseline	85.05
Combination	**85.32**

Table 9: Results from cross-validation evaluation according to combination of annotations

Combination of annotations does not increase the gains obtained with the method *AnnotVerbs* and we even observe a slight decrease.

5.4 Impact on a reranker

We also experimented the integration of a discriminative reranker (cf. section 2). We practically set to 10 the number of parses generated by BKY for each sentence (therefore, the 10 most probable parses). The following experiment consists in evaluating the impact of the modification of the tagset on a reranker. We called *Reranker(Baseline)* the experiment using the reranker with BKY trained on the original corpus (without annotations from the Lexicon-Grammar). *Reranker(AnnotVerbs)* is the experiment based on BKY that is trained on the corpus annotated by the best verb annotation method, *AnnotVerbs* (level 3 of hierarchy without ambiguity). Results are shown in table 10. The column named *Oracle F1/Tagging* indicates oracle scores for f-measure and tagging accuracy. An oracle score is the best global score that we could obtain whether we choose, for each input sentence, the best parse from the n-best parses. With this score, we can estimate the performance limit of a parser and the global quality of parses generated.

Method	F1/Tagging	Oracle F1/Tagging
BKY(Baseline)	85.05/97.43	-
BKY(AnnotVerbs)	85.39/97.49	-
Reranker(Baseline)	86.51/97.42	91,72/98.03
Reranker(AnnotVerbs)	**86.71/97.49**	**91.99/98.08**

Table 10: Results from cross-validation evaluation for reranking process.

First, we can see that *Reranker(Baseline)* improves performances with an absolute gain of +1,46 as compared with the baseline. These results are comparable to scores obtained for English (Charniak and Johnson, 2005). Then, we observe that the experiment *Reranker(AnnotVerbs)* increases the f-measure by +0,2 compared with *Reranker(Baseline)* (and to a lesser extent, the tagging accuracy by +0,07). The power of the discriminative model of the reranker implies that the gap of performances between the two experiments based on the reranker is less than the one obtained from experiments only based on BKY (+0,2 against +0,34). In addition, the oracle f-measure is improved (+0,27), which means that analyses generated by BKY are slightly better. We can see on Figure 5 absolute gains given by the reranker on all evaluation parts according to the two methods described above. Globally, the method *Reranker(AnnotVerbs)* has a curve slightly above the one of *Reranker(Baseline)*. Note that the first one outperforms the latter on 8 of 10 evaluation parts. All these observations confirm that the syntactic lexicon through the experiment *AnnotVerbs* is able to improve performances on both

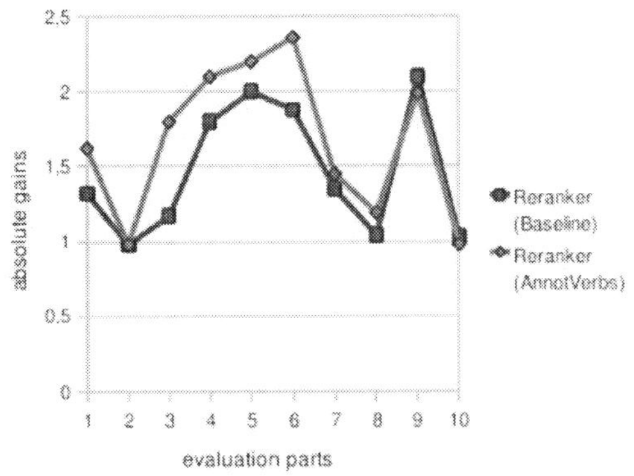

Figure 5: Absolute gains (F1) given by the reranker on evaluation parts (BKY(baseline) is the horizontal line at 0 on y axis)

a generative parser based on a PCFG grammar (BKY), and a discriminative parser (reranker).

6 Conclusions

The work described in this paper shows that by adding some information from a syntactic lexicon like the Lexicon-Grammar, we are able to improve performances of several probabilistic parsers. These performances are mainly obtained thanks to a hierarchy of verb tables that can limit ambiguity in terms of number of classes associated with a verb. This has the effect of increasing the coverage of verbs annotated according to the level of granularity used. However, once we include some ambiguity, performances drop. Results obtained on verbal nouns with a simple hierarchy of tables are insignificant but suggest a degree of progress with a more complex hierarchy as the one available for verbs.

In the near future, we plan to reproduce these experiments by taking into account of word clustering methods introduced by (Koo et al., 2008; Candito and Crabbé, 2009; Candito and Seddah, 2010). Thanks to a semi-supervized algorithm, these methods can reduce the size of the lexicon of the grammar by grouping words according to their behaviors in a treebank. These methods could be complementary to annotation methods described in this paper. Moreover, we plan to exploit the LFG formalism in order to use a syntactic lexicon more easily than for PCFGs, as many works have reported performance improvements for these models (Cahill, 2004; Deoskar, 2008).

References

A. Abeillé, L. Clément, and F. Toussenel. 2003. Building a treebank for French. In Anne Abeillé, editor, *Treebanks*, Kluwer, Dordrecht.

E. Black, S.Abney, D. Flickinger, C. Gdaniec, R. Grishman, P. Harrison, D. Hindle, R. Ingria, F. Jelinek, J. Klavans, M. Liberman, M. Marcus, S. Roukos, B. Santorini, and T. Strzalkowski. 1991. A procedure for quantitatively comparing the syntactic coverage of english grammars. In *Proceedings of the DARPA Speech and Naturale Language Workshop*, pages 306–311.

T. Briscoe and J. Carroll. 1997. Automatic extraction of subcategorization from corpora. In *Fifth Conference on Applied Natural Language Processing*, pages 356–363, Washington DC, USA.

A. Cahill. 2004. *Parsing with Automatically Acquired, Wide-Coverage, Robust, Probabilistic LFG Approximations*. Ph.D. thesis, Dublin City University, Dublin 9.

Marie Candito and B. Crabbé. 2009. Improving generative statistical parsing with semi-supervised word clustering. In *Proceedings of the 11th International Conference on Parsing Technology (IWPT'09)*, pages 138–141.

Marie Candito and D. Seddah. 2010. Parsing word clusters. In *Proceedings of the first NAACL HLT Workshop on Morphologically-Rich Languages (SPRML2010)*, pages 76–84, Los Angeles, California.

J. Carroll and A. C. Fang. 2004. The automatic acquisition of verb subcategorisations and their impact on the performance of an HPSG parser. In *Proceedings of the 1st International Conference onNatural Language Processing*, Sanya City, China.

E. Charniak and M. Johnson. 2005. Coarse-to-fine n-best parsing and MaxEnt discriminative reranking. In *Proceedings of the 43th Annual Meeting of the Association for Computational Linguistics (ACL05)*.

M. Collins. 2000. Discriminative reranking for natural language parsing. In *Proceedings of the 17th ICML*, pages 175–182.

M. Constant and E. Tolone. 2008. A generic tool to generate a lexicon for NLP from Lexicon-Grammar tables. In *Actes du 27ème Colloque Lexique et Grammaire*, L'Aquila, Italie.

B. Crabbé and Marie Candito. 2008. Expériences d'analyse syntaxique statistique du français. In *Actes de la 15ème Conférence sur le Traitement Automatique des Langues Naturelles (TALN'08)*, pages 45–54, Avignon, France.

E. de La Clergerie. 2010. Building factorized TAGs with meta-grammars. In *Proceedings of the 10th International Conference on Tree Adjoining Grammars and Related Formalisms*, pages 111–118.

T. Deoskar. 2008. Re-estimation of lexical parameters for treebank PCFGs. In *Proceedings of the 22nd International Conference on Computational Linguistics (Coling 2008)*, pages 193–200, Manchester, Great Britain.

J. Dubois and F. Dubois-Charlier. 1997. *Les verbes français*. Larousse-Bordas.

K. Eynde and M. Piet. 2003. La valence: l'approche pronominale et son application au lexique verbal. *Journal of French Language studies*, pages 63–104.

M. Gross. 1994. Constructing Lexicon-grammars. In Atkins and Zampolli, editors, *Computational Approaches to the Lexicon*, pages 213–263.

A. K. Joshi. 1987. An introduction to tree adjoining grammars. In Alexis Manaster-Ramer, editor, *Mathematics of Language*, pages 87–115, Amsterdam/Philadelphia. John Benjamins Publishing Co.

R. Kaplan and J. Maxwell. 1994. *Grammar writer's workbench, version 2.0*. Rapport technique, Xerox Corporation.

T. Koo, X. Carreras, and M. Collins. 2008. Simple semi-supervised dependency parsing. In *Proceedings of ACL-08*.

T. Matsuzaki, Y. Miyao, and J. Tsujii. 2005. Probabilistic cfg with latent annotations. In *Proceedings of ACL-05*, pages 75–82, Ann Arbor, USA.

R. O'Donovan, A. Cahill, A. Way, M. Burke, and J. van Genabith. 2005. Large-scale induction and evaluation of lexical resources from the Penn-II and Penn-III treebanks. In *Proceedings of the First International Joint Conference on Natural Language Processing (IJCNLP'04)*.

S. Petrov, L. Barrett, R. Thibaux, and D. Klein. 2006. Learning accurate, compact, and interpretable tree annotation. In *Proceedings of the 21st International Conference on Computational Linguistics and 44th Annual Meeting of the Association for Computational Linguistics*, Sydney, Australia.

S. Riezler, T. King, R. Kaplan, R. Crouch, J. Maxwell, and M. Johnson. 2002. Parsing the Wall Street Journal using a lexical-functional grammar and discriminative estimation techniques. In *Proceedings of the Annual Meeting of the ACL*, University of Pennsylvania.

B. Sagot and E. Tolone. 2009. Intégrer les tables du Lexique-Grammaire à un analyseur syntaxique robuste à grande échelle. In *Actes de la 15ème Conférence sur le Traitement Automatique des Langues Naturelles (TALN'09)*, Senlis, France.

B. Sagot. 2006. *Analyse automatique du français: lexiques, formalismes, analyseurs*. Ph.D. thesis, Université Paris VII.

B. Sagot. 2010. The lefff, a freely available, accurate and large-coverage lexicon for french. In *Proceedings of LREC 2010*, La Valette, Malte.

N. Schluter and J. Van Genabith. 2008. Treebank-based Acquisition of LFG Parsing Resources for French. In *Proceedings of LREC08*, Marrakech, Morocco.

D. Seddah, Marie Candito, and B. Crabbé. 2009. Adaptation de parsers statistiques lexicalisés pour le français : Une évaluation complète sur corpus arborés. In *Actes de la 15ème Conférence sur le Traitement Automatique des Langues Naturelles (TALN'09)*, Senlis, France.

E. Tolone. 2011. *Analyse syntaxique à l'aide des tables du Lexique-Grammaire du français*. Ph.D. thesis, Université Paris-Est Marne-la-Vallée.

Pattern Learning for Event Extraction using Monolingual Statistical Machine Translation

Marco Turchi, Vanni Zavarella, Hristo Tanev
European Commission - Joint Research Centre (JRC), IPSC - GlobeSec
Via Fermi 2749, 21020 Ispra (VA) - Italy
marco.turchi@jrc.ec.europa.eu,
{vanni.zavarella, hristo.tanev}@ext.jrc.ec.europa.eu

Abstract

Event extraction systems typically take advantage of language and domain-specific knowledge bases, including patterns that are used to identify specific facts in text; techniques to acquire these patterns can be considered one of the most challenging issues. In this work, we propose a language-independent and weakly-supervised algorithm to automatically discover linear patterns from texts. Our approach is based on a phrase-based statistical machine translation system trained on monolingual data. A bootstrapping version of the algorithm is proposed. Our method was tested on patterns with different domain-specific semantic roles in three languages: English, Spanish and Russian. Performance shows the feasibility of our approach and its capability of working with texts in various languages.

1 Introduction

Multilingual event extraction task consists of retrieving information about particular facts from text documents in different languages and producing event-description templates, which typically contain slots about event participants, location, time and means.

In this work we use an event extraction system which aims at identifying violent events, man made and natural disasters and humanitarian crises, in title and first sentence of news reports. An event is represented as a template, whose main slots correspond to *event-specific semantic roles*, such as: *event-type*, *killed-victims*, *injured-victims*, *perpetrators*, and others. Slot fillers are typically extracted by matching linear patterns in text. For example, *killed <PERSON-GROUP>* represents a sample pattern for the semantic role *DEAD-VICTIM*. It will match text snippets like *killed five people*, where *five people* fills the pattern slot *<PERSON-GROUP>*[1]. In this paper, we are concerned with surface-level, one-slot patterns which accept as slot fillers person names/descriptions such as *two Italian women*.

Building a lexicon of linear patterns is a crucial step in the development and customization of an event extraction system, particularly in news texts which are characterized by an open domain and a large vocabulary. Different approaches have been proposed but most of them require a large manual effort and linguistic expertise. Moreover, due to lexical and syntactic variability and to Zipf's law-based word distribution in language, acquired patterns can only partially cover the range of linguistic constructions. These are serious obstacles faced by every effort to adapt an event extraction system across domains or languages.

In order to address these problems, we put forward a novel language-independent and weakly-supervised algorithm to automatically learn linear event extraction patterns from an unannotated corpus of texts. The method allows knowledge-poor pattern acquisition without any data annotation. It is based on the noisy-channel model developed for Phrase-Based Statistical Machine Translation (PBSMT).

For a particular event-specific semantic role (e.g. *DEAD-VICTIM*) a pattern is proposed as seed. The most frequent person group fillers are selected both automatically from a document collection running an event extraction grammar (Tanev et al., 2009) or manually. Then, a monolingual PBSMT system, separately trained on pairs of comparable sentences from the same language, is used to translate the associations: filler-seed. The new patterns are extracted from the top translations using the mean reciprocal rank (Voorhees,

[1]Notice that *"X pattern"* and *"pattern X"* are two different patterns, with *X* occupying a different position wrt the pattern.

2000). This process is bootstrapped passing iteratively the new patterns and the fillers to the algorithm.

Such an approach depends on availability of a corpus of monolingual sentence pairs conveying approximately the same information. The solution we explore is to use pairs composed by the title and the first sentence of a news article. The main idea is that they report about the same content expressed in different ways. A PBSMT system trained on this data produces, as output of the translation process, lexical or morphological variations of the initial seed.

Our algorithm was tested on three languages, namely English, Spanish and Russian, belonging to three different language groups. Manual and application-based evaluations show the adaptability of our approach across languages and domains.

2 Related Work

Systems for automatic event detection and extraction typically use some form of language and domain-specific patterns. Many event extraction systems use syntactic patterns, (Riloff, 1993), or combinations of patterns and statistical classifiers, (Grishman et al., 2005). In the multilingual context, where syntactic parsers are not always available, automatically learned linear patterns are an important resource for event detection and can reach a reasonable level of performance, as shown in (Tanev et al., 2009).

The first pattern learning systems, such as CRYSTAL, (Soderland et al., 1995), and AutoSlog (Riloff, 1993), use manually-annotated corpora. (Riloff, 1996) proposes a weakly supervised method which is an improved version of AutoSlog. This method requires as input a set of text documents, which are manually classified as relevant or irrelevant to a topic. Although this is less demanding than annotating the document content, it is still a time-consuming task. Weakly supervised methods, reported so far, require much less human input than annotating a corpus, but they strongly depend on linguistic knowledge, preventing them from easy adaptation between domains and languages.

Relevant to our work, the multilingual weakly supervised approaches, (Tanev and Wennerberg, 2008) and (Tanev et al., 2009), are based on annotation propagation in semantically consistent document clusters. They share some features with our approach: they use bootstrapping; they only weakly depend on the language; they are domain independent. The disadvantage of these approaches is that clustering is computationally expensive, which prevents this method from scaling to very large corpora.

Another research area, significant to our work is the unsupervised discovery of paraphrases. (Barzilay and Lee, 2003) proposes an approach, which is based on aligned comparable corpora. Unfortunately, such corpora are not easy to be acquired, especially in the multilingual context. In order to go around this obstacle, some approaches use distributional similarity for paraphrase acquisition: For example TEASE, (Szpektor et al., 2004), learns syntactic patterns which paraphrase a seed pattern, but it uses a full syntactic parser, thus making not applicable in a multilingual context. A language independent algorithm to paraphrase English sentences using a Statistical Machine Translation (SMT) system is proposed by (Quirk et al., 2004), where training data are extracted from Web pages and parallel sentences identified using edit distance.

Compared to the aforementioned approaches, our algorithm is more adaptable across languages, since it does not use any language-specific processing. Moreover, our training corpora are easy-to-acquire and more focused on the type of text analysed by the event extraction system, which allowed us to significantly extend training data sets compared to other algorithms based on monolingual machine translation.

3 Monolingual Phrase Based Statistical Machine Translation

Phrase Based Model (Koehn et al., 2003) is an extension of the noisy channel model, introduced by (Brown et al., 1994), using phrases rather than words. The best translation $\hat{e}$ of a source sentence f is obtained by maximizing the probability $p(e|f)$ computed by the product of three components: ϕ, the probability of translating a source phrase f into a target phrase e, d, the distance-based reordering model that drives the system to penalize significant reordering of words during translation and, p_{LM}, the language model probability which assigns a higher probability to fluent/grammatical sentences. Different weight can be associated to each component. For more details see (Koehn et al., 2003). Probabilities are estimated counting the frequency of the phrases in the parallel corpus.

In classical PBSMT, a system is trained using parallel data: each sentence in a source language is associated with correctly translated sentence in a target language. In our approach, we use monolingual comparable data: source and target sentences are respectively the first sentence of the body and the title of a news article in a selected language, for example:

First Sentence: *Twenty-five people were killed in the latest round of Afghan violence this week.*

Title: *25 civilians dead as Taliban intensifies attacks in Afghanistan.*

The main idea is that the two sentences convey the same information in different style, e.g. *Twenty-five people were killed* and *25 civilians dead*. This is grounded on a well-established news writing practice, the so called "inverted pyramid" method, which suggests to re-state the core factual content of a news story at the opening of the article body, (Bell, 1991).

Consequently, a translation in our monolingual PBSMT consists of finding the most probable sentence in the "title" style that contains the same information of the input sentence in the "content" style. In this work, the PBSMT technique allows the extraction of patterns that are indistinctly constituted by either a sequence of words (phrase) or a single word.

4 Pattern Learning Algorithm

The proposed method for pattern acquisition consists of two parts. The first one is the core algorithm with an initial pattern (seed) and a set of fillers, produces a set of reliable new linear patterns. To increase the number of patterns, the core algorithm is then embedded in a bootstrapping schema where it is repeatedly called. In the next Sections, these methods are described in detail.

Core Approach The basic algorithm takes advantage of a monolingual PBSMT system to find lexical and morphological variants of a seed and it is made of three phases: *association*, *translation* and *recombination*. In the first phase, see Fig. 1.a, a set of associations is created pairing the seed, *X killed*, with a set of person/person group fillers, *soldiers*, ... *policemen*, which can be either provided manually or extracted by a person recognition grammar. Each single association is passed to a monolingual translation system, see Fig. 1.b, that produces the top fifty best translations of the association ranked according to $p(e|f)$.

Each seed could be translated by itself, independently from the fillers. However, some initial experiments showed that the filler text snippets help the algorithm to contextualize the translation, e.g. *shot X* with the filler *civilians* or *pictures*. Without any person group context, the extracted variants may end up covering different meanings. Furthermore, filler position crucially defines who or what is doing or undergoing an action in transitive verb group patterns (e.g. *A soldier shot* or *shot a soldier*) so that translating them alone can generate patterns with event roles in inverted position.

In terms of machine translation, the usage of the person group requires the translation of the full association, person group plus seed, rather than using the translation model as a look-up table for the seed only. This means that the SMT may also produce a variation of the person group adding extra noise to the output. To reduce the impact of the presence of the person group, each association is passed to the SMT system with an option that forces PBSMT not to modify the filler in the output, but to use it to contextualize the translation, e.g. *soldiers* and *policemen* are present in their original form in Fig. 1.b.

For a single seed, sets of translations are generated according to the number of associations, and the same new pattern can be ranked in a different position inside different sets, e.g. *are killed* as shown in Fig. 1.b. The last step consists of extracting all the new patterns from the sets of translations and re-ranking them in a reliability order, see Fig. 1.c. To make the new patterns comparable across sets, in each translation the person group is substituted by a X. The recombination of the patterns in a unique list can be done merging and reranking all of them using a mathematical operator based on $p(e|f)$, e.g. average, but $p(e|f)$ is a local property of each set of translations because includes the contribution of the filler.

The main idea that we propose consists of using a global metric that takes advantage of the local rank inside of each set. For this purpose we use the Mean Reciprocal Rank (MRR), (Voorhees, 2000), a metrics used in information retrieval to evaluate any process that produces a list of possible responses to a query. The mean reciprocal rank for a sample of queries Q is reported in Eq. 1 where

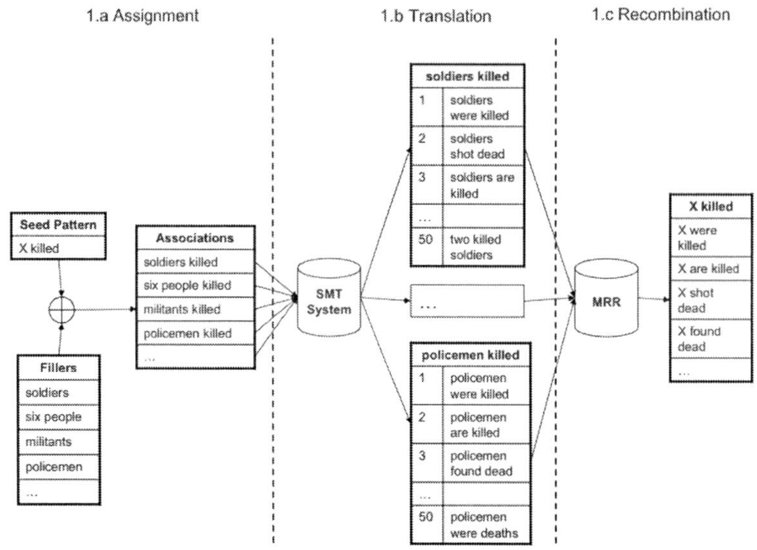

Figure 1: Extraction of new patterns using the seed "*X killed*".

$rank$ is the rank of the first correct answer.

$$MRR = \frac{1}{|Q|}\sum_{i=1}^{Q}\frac{1}{rank_i} \quad (1) \qquad MRR(np) = \frac{1}{|A|}\sum_{i=1}^{A}\frac{1}{rank_i(np)} \quad (2)$$

We adapt the MRR in the following way: the number of queries is the number of associations, and the answers to a query are the fifty translations of a certain association. The MRR of a new pattern, np, is shown in Eq. 2, where A is the number of associations for a seed and $rank_i(np)$ is the position of np in the set of translations of the association i.

High rank of a new pattern in a set of translations guarantees its correctness while MRR based on the ranked translations guarantees that those new patterns that are on top positions in various sets received a high rank in the final list. Top patterns are selected from the final list by picking up those that have MRR value bigger than 10% of the MRR value of the best pattern.

Bootstrapping. The core algorithm is embedded in a bootstrapping framework. Starting from the original seed, called "root seed", each new pattern produced by the core algorithm can be considered an input seed for another instance of the core algorithm. This procedure can be iterated over all the new patterns.

This approach increases the number of retrieved patterns, but can create unwanted noise. At each bootstrapping step, the produced patterns can be semantically divergent from the "root seed" because a seed can be semantically ambiguous or polysemous and one of the fillers can be too generic to pick up a unique sense. We tackle this problem by introducing a stop criterion in the bootstrapping framework, whose goal is to select only those new patterns that are semantically similar to the "root seed". The selected patterns are only propagated to the next iteration and the seed that produced them is added to the final results.

The concept of semantic similarity between a surface pattern and the seed is modelled by simply using set intersection.We assume that the new patterns produced by the expansion of the "root seed" are the most semantically similar to it. This is confirmed by the value of the macro-precision of the produced patterns in English which is equal to 82%. According to this, we consider the expansion of the "root seed" as a gold standard, GS, for the bootstrapping approach.

At a certain bootstrapping step t, a new pattern, np^t, is passed to the core algorithm, CA, producing a set of new patterns, $S(np^t)$. np^t is semantically correlated to the "root seed" if and only if the intersection between GS and $S(np^t)$ is not empty. It means that $S(np^t)$ should have at least one new pattern in common with the gold standard for being semantically correlated to the "root seed". If the condition is true, np^t is added to the final results and the new patterns, that are not in common with the gold standard, are propagated to next bootstrapping iterations. Otherwise the bootstrapping is stopped, np_t is not considered a reliable pattern and not included in the final results. The stop criterion forces each new pattern at iteration t to be validated using information produced at iteration $t+1$ before being added to final results.

The stop criterion is not highly restrictive, it reduces the number of computations and guarantees a semantic similarity between the "root seed" and new patterns. The final output of the bootstrapping process is the union without duplicates of all the new patterns that are evaluated as correct by the stop criterion.

5 Experimental Setup

In this work, we use Moses, (Koehn et al., 2007), a complete phrase-based translation toolkit for research purposes.

Training data are extracted from a title and first sentence of news articles gathered during a one year time span from 01/07/2008 to 01/07/2009. We perform experiments in three languages: English, Russian and Spanish. For each language, we respectively use ~2,87M, ~2,19M and ~1,48M sentence pairs. Nine event predicates are chosen, which are important for analysis of political, crisis and violence-related news (for example *DEAD-VICTIM*). For each of them a highly frequent and unambiguous linguistic realization is selected as a single-slot seed pattern, for each of the three languages: *X sentenced* (1), *criticized X* (2), *X visited* (3), *X were killed* (4), *X met with* (5), *X were evacuated* (6), *X were wounded* (7), *supported X* (8) and *X launched an attack* (9) [2]. In each language, seed patterns are integrated with person/person group recognition rules, as proposed in (Tanev et al., 2009), and run on a news corpus to extract a set of person/person group fillers: the 20 most frequent are then paired with the seed pattern and fed to the PBSMT system[3].

6 Evaluation and Results

We evaluate by running only four iterations of bootstrapping, where the fourth is used to validate the new patterns extracted at iteration 3. An average of about 55, 74 and 39 new patterns over all the predicates are acquired for English, Russian and Spanish, respectively. There were rates of 3.6%, 0.3% and 4.8% ungrammatical patterns. For a seed that was not in the test set, *X was kidnapped*, we experimented running more iterations of bootstrapping, finding that at each iteration the number of correct patterns grew about 1.5 times on average, at the cost of a small decrease of precision (about 20%). The number of new patterns is relatively small, because we wanted to test the generative power of the algorithm when fed with a minimal input of only one seed pattern.

We performed a direct evaluation of the output pattern Accuracy and then we evaluated indirectly the Precision and Recall via running an extraction system. Ungrammatical patterns are considered inapplicable and discarded from accuracy evaluation while we keep them for evaluating extraction performance.

Pattern Accuracy. Pattern Accuracy evaluation was performed by asking a language expert to rate each pattern as either "correct" (semantically sound and non-ambiguous), "correct-in-context" (partially ambiguous but semantically sound in some linguistic context) or "incorrect". A "lenient" Accuracy score was computed as the ratio of both the "correct" and "correct-in-context" patterns over the total, while "strict" accuracy only includes "correct" patterns.

Id	English		Russian		Spanish	
	Strict	Lenient	Strict	Lenient	Strict	Lenient
1	0.42	0.66	0.68	0.70	0.32	0.36
2	0.43	0.61	0.00	0.00	0.19	0.29
3	0.51	0.78	0.23	0.33	0.29	0.40
4	**0.64**	0.81	0.52	0.64	**0.83**	**1.00**
5	0.57	0.80	**0.76**	**0.87**	0.77	0.77
6	0.59	**0.83**	0.50	0.64	0.26	0.30
7	0.35	0.47	0.30	0.34	0.57	0.57
8	0.31	0.37	0.62	0.85	0.31	0.38
9	0.61	0.69	0.48	0.60	0.00	0.00
	0.49	**0.67**	**0.46**	**0.55**	**0.39**	**0.45**

Table 1: Manual evaluation of pattern accuracy. Highest values are highlighted.

Average Kappa score between two annotators over the 9 pattern sets for English was 0.58, which is in the higher range "moderate agreement" class according to (Fleiss, 1981). However, the Kendall tau-b rank correlation coefficient, (Lapata, 2006), turns out to be a more suitable evaluation metrics as it better accounts for the natural ordering of the rank classes. We measured a 0.79 score ($p < 10^{-3}$), consequently we assumed the anno-

[2] In the next Sections, we refer to each pattern using the number close to it.

[3] Notice that fillers could have been manually produced as well, so that the overall algorithm is not really dependent on the person recognition grammar.

tation task is grounded and performed it with one single annotator for Spanish and Russian.

Pattern Accuracy scores for each predicate are shown in Table 1 together with macro-averages. Among correct patterns in all the seeds, morphological variants can be observed (including mood, tense, number) as well as lexical shifts and a few verb form alternations (e.g. active-passive). A common source of noise is the assignment of the filler position to a wrong verb argument (e.g. *X were killed* → *X kills*; *supported X* → *X favour*). This is due to the reordering model in the PBSMT system that considers the incorrect position of the filler as probable as the correct one, so forcing the translation system to output the wrong pattern.

Overall, pattern Accuracy figures closely correlates with the size of the training corpora for the PBSMT systems in the three languages.

Extraction systems based on the same schema (initial seed plus bootstrapping approach in a unsupervised manner) have accuracy on new patterns from 40% to 50% (e.g. the Web-based system by (Szpektor et al., 2004)), consequently we consider the performance of our method for pattern learning really encouraging.

Event Extraction Precision and Recall. In order to measure Recall and Precision of the new pattern sets, we compared performance of a baseline extraction system (**BL**), containing person entity grammar and the single seed extraction pattern, against a target system (**TG**), that adds the set of the discovered patterns to the seed, and then against a clean target system (**CT**), that adds only those discovered patterns that are human-evaluated as "correct" and "correct-in-context".

Recall was measured in the following way: for each event predicate, a set of 20 news article sentences reporting about that event type were manually collected then the person/person group entity expressions were replaced in text with a constant expression detectable by the person recognition grammar, so as to make the results unaffected by the performance of the grammar itself. Then the number of successful detections of that filler was checked.

As for the Precision, the baseline and target systems were both run on a corpus of titles and first sentences of news articles collected during 10 days, resulting in about 5.79M, 3.29M and 700k words for English, Russian and Spanish respectively. From all the system outputs, a set of 20 were randomly collected, discarding duplicates, and the correctness of extracted fillers were manually evaluated. Answers were rated as correct when at least one of the fillers extracted was at least partially overlapping with the full person entity expression actually in text [4].

Table 2 shows Precision and Recall scores of the discovered patterns in an extraction task[5]. The Recall of the TG system is raising constantly from the baseline values across all the predicates and for each language. Recall can be improved raising the number of correct patterns added to the system. This, as mentioned in Section 6, can be done by increasing the number of bootstrapping steps. Precision of the TG system is also constantly dropping. However, this decrease can be significantly limited via human pattern selection, as can be seen from the performance of the CT. system Overall, the automatic approach proposed here, coupled with a lightweight human post-processing step, generates a good quality pattern lexicon for information extraction.

For the TG system, performance seems to be largely variable across predicate types, and this partially correlates with the pattern accuracy figures too. However, performances seem to be independent from domain variation, with the best results spreading over the violent, political or judicial event domains. This suggests that domain adaptation of an event extraction system can be easily achieved in our method by providing a suitable amount of training data in the corresponding subject domain, so as to reduce the ambiguity of the language.

7 Conclusions

We proposed a language-independent and weakly-supervised bootstrapping algorithm to learn linear patterns from text, based on a phrase-based statistical machine translation system trained on monolingual data.

Among the different methods that have been proposed for extracting linear patterns from text, our approach is completely language independent, and it relies on freely available data such as news articles. Training data for the SMT system do not require any heavy pre-processing and such sen-

[4]E.g. *soldiers* is taken as a correct system answer for the *injured-victim* role in a sentence like "*3 German soldiers were wounded*"

[5]F-measure scores could not be computed on such Precision and Recall figures coming from different test sets

Id	English						Russian						Spanish					
	P			R			P			R			P			R		
	BL	**TG**	**CT**	**BL**	**TG**	**CT**	**BL**	**TG**	**CT**	**BL**	**TG**	**CT**	**BL**	**TG**	**CT**	**BL**	**TG**	**CT**
1	0.90	0.40	**0.85**	0.10	0.30	0.30	1.00	0.40	0.80	0.10	0.50	0.30	na	0.00	0.25	0.00	0.36	**0.35**
2	1.00	0.50	0.40	0.25	0.45	0.45	0.00	0.50	na	0.00	0.00	0.00	na	0.00	0.25	0.05	0.20	0.05
3	0.90	0.30	0.60	0.10	0.40	0.40	0.95	0.30	0.85	0.10	**0.70**	**0.65**	1.00	0.60	0.70	0.20	0.30	0.35
4	1.00	0.60	0.65	0.00	0.30	0.30	1.00	**0.60**	0.90	0.25	0.80	0.80	1.00	**1.00**	**1.00**	0.10	0.15	0.15
5	0.95	**0.60**	0.50	0.00	0.40	0.30	1.00	**0.60**	**0.95**	0.10	0.45	0.40	1.00	**1.00**	**1.00**	0.00	**0.50**	0.05
6	0.93	0.25	0.55	0.05	0.30	0.30	0.95	0.25	0.80	0.00	0.45	0.45	1.00	0.10	**1.00**	0.00	0.05	0.05
7	0.90	0.05	0.45	0.00	**0.70**	0.65	1.00	0.05	0.80	0.00	0.30	0.05	1.00	0.30	**1.00**	0.05	0.05	0.05
8	0.50	0.15	0.30	0.00	0.80	**0.80**	0.64	0.15	0.45	0.10	0.55	0.55	na	0.35	0.30	0.00	0.15	0.25
9	1.00	0.25	0.35	0.00	0.35	0.35	1.00	0.25	0.70	0.00	0.50	0.35	na	na	na	0.00	0.00	0.00
	0.90	**0.34**	**0.52**	**0.06**	**0.43**	**0.38**	**0.84**	**0.34**	**0.78**	**0.07**	**0.47**	**0.39**	**1.00**	**0.42**	**0.69**	**0.04**	**0.20**	**0.14**

Table 2: Pattern performance in an extraction task. "na" values for Precision mean that there were no extracted fillers for that test set. For each language, the biggest improvement (or smallest decrease) over the pattern types compared to the baseline is underlined.

tence pair collections can be easily built for any language and target domain from the news.

The new extracted patterns, in the "title" style, contain exactly the kind of variation in linguistic constructions that the event extraction system has to deal with during the detection process on title and first sentence of a news article. Performance analysis confirms this assumption and shows the feasibility of the approach both across languages and domains.

From an evaluation of the output patterns we noticed a degradation of the Accuracy after the first iteration of the algorithm. It is our intention to investigate the role of the bootstrapping criterion and model the similarity condition with some robust measure of distributional similarity between pattern sets.

Acknowledgments

Special thanks go to Francesca Torti from University of Parma for her essential statistical support.

References

Barzilay R., and Lee L. (2003) Learning to Paraphrase: An Unsupervised Approach Using Multiple-Sequence Alignment. *Proceedings of HLT-NAACL*, 16–23. Edmonton, Canada.

Bell A. (1991) *The Language of News Media*. Blackwell Publishers, Oxford.

Brown P.F., Della Pietra S., Della Pietra V.J., and Mercer R.L. (1994) The Mathematic of Statistical Machine Translation: Parameter Estimation. *Computational Linguistics*, 19(2) 263–311.

Fleiss J.L. (1981) *Statistical methods for rates and proportions*. John Wiley, New York, USA.

Grishman R., Westbrook D., and Meyers A. (2005) NYU's English ACE 2005 system description. *Proceedings of the ACE, Evaluation Workshop*.

Koehn P., Och F.J., and Marcu D. (2003) Statistical phrase-based translation. *Proceedings of NAACL*, 48–54, Morristown, USA.

Koehn P., Hoang H., Birch A., Callison-Burch C., et al. (2007) Moses: Open source toolkit for statistical machine translation. *Proceedings of ACL*, 45(2).

Lapata, M. (2006) Automatic evaluation of information ordering: Kendall's tau. *Computational Linguistics*, 32(4) 471–484.

Quirk C., Brockett C., and Dolan W. (2004) Monolingual machine translation for paraphrase generation. *Proceedings of EMNLP*, 149. Barcelona, Spain.

Riloff E. (1993) Automatically Constructing a Dictionary for Information Extraction Tasks. *Proceedings of the Eleventh National Conference on Artificial Intelligence*, 811–816. Seattle, USA.

Riloff E. (1996) Automatically Generating Extraction Patterns from Untagged Text. *Proceedings of AAAI*, 1044–1049. Portland, USA.

Soderland S., Fisher D., Aseltine J., and Lehnert W. (1995) CRYSTAL: Inducing a conceptual dictionary. *Proceedings of IJCAI*, 1314–1319. Canada.

Szpektor I., Tanev H., Dagan I., and Coppola B. (2004) Scaling Web-based Acquisition of Entailment Relations. *Proceedings of EMNLP*, 41–48. Spain.

Tanev H., and Wennerberg P. (2008) Learning to Populate an Ontology of Politically Motivated Violent Events. *Mining Massive Data Sets for Security*, IOS Press, 311–322.

Tanev H., Zavarella V., Linge J., Kabadjov M., et al. (2009) Exploiting Machine Learning Techniques to Build an Event Extraction System for Portuguese and Spanish. *Linguamatica*, 2(1) 55–66.

Voorhees E.M. (2000) The TREC-8 question answering track report. *NIST Special Publication*, 77–82.

META-DARE: Monitoring the Minimally Supervised ML of Relation Extraction Rules

Hong Li **Feiyu Xu** **Hans Uszkoreit**

German Research Center for Artificial Intelligence (DFKI), LT-Lab
Alt-Moabit 91c, 10559 Berlin, Germany
{lihong,feiyu,uszkoreit}@dfki.de
http://www.dfki.de/lt/

Abstract

This paper demonstrates a web-based online system, called META-DARE[1]. META-DARE is built to assist researchers to obtain insights into seed-based minimally supervised machine learning for relation extraction. META-DARE allows researchers and students to conduct experiments with an existing machine learning system called DARE (Xu et al., 2007). Users can run their own learning experiments by constructing initial seed examples and can monitor the learning process in a very detailed way, namely, via interacting with each node in the learning graph and viewing its content. Furthermore, users can study the learned relation extraction rules and their applications. META-DARE is also an analysis tool which gives an overview of the whole learning process: the number of iterations, the input and output behaviors of each iteration, and the general performance of the extracted instances and their distributions. Moreover, META-DARE provides a very convenient user interface for visualization of the learning graph, the learned rules and the system performance profile.

1 Introduction

Seed-based minimally supervised machine learning within a bootstrapping framework has been widely applied to various information extraction tasks (e.g., (Hearst, 1992; Riloff, 1996; Brin, 1998; Agichtein and Gravano, 2000; Sudo et al., 2003; Greenwood and Stevenson, 2006; Blohm and Cimiano, 2007)). The power of this approach is that it needs only a small set of examples of either patterns or relation instances and can learn and discover many useful extraction rules and relation instances from unannotated texts. Within this framework, Xu et al. (2007) develop a learning approach, called DARE, which learns relation extraction rules for dealing with relations of various complexity by utilizing some relation examples as semantic seed in the initialization and has achieved very promising results for the extraction of complex relations. In the recent years, more and more researchers are interested in understanding the underlying process behind this approach and attempt to identify relevant learning parameters to improve the system performance.

Xu (2007) investigates the role of the seed selection in connection with the data properties in a careful way with our DARE system. Xu (2007) and Li et al. (2011) describe the applications of DARE system in different domains for different relation extraction tyes, for example, the Nobel-Prize-Winning event, management succession relations defined in MUC-6, marriage relationship, etc. Uszkoreit et al. (2009) describe a further empirical analysis of the seed construction and its influence on the learning performance and show that size, arity and distinctiveness of the seed examples play various important roles for the learning performance. Thus, the system demonstrated here, called META-DARE, serves as a monitoring and analysis system for conducting various experiments with seed-based minimally supervised machine learning. META-DARE is also aimed to assist researchers to understand the DARE algorithm and its rule representation and the interaction between rule learning and relation instance extraction. It allows users to construct different seed sets with respect to size, arity and specificity to start experiments on the example domains. Moreover, it provides a detailed survey of all learning iterations including the learned rules and extracted instances and their respective properties. Finally, it delivers a qualitative analysis of the learning per-

[1] http://dare.dfki.de/

formance.

As a web service, it offers a very user-friendly visualization of the learning graph and allows users to interact with the learning graph and study the interaction between learning rules and extracted relation instances. Each rule and extracted instance is presented in a feature structure format. Furthermore, the wrong instances extracted by DARE are visually extra marked so that users can investigate them and learn lessons from them. As a side effect, META-DARE is a very useful and effective tool for teaching information extraction.

The paper is organized as follows: Section 2 outlines the overall architecture, while Section 3 explains the experiment corpus. Section 4 describes the DARE system and the learning algorithm. In Section 5, we introduce the seed selector. Section 6 reports the visualization functions of META-DARE. Section 7 gives a conclusion and discusses future ideas.

2 META-DARE: Overall Architecture

Figure 1 depicts the overall architecture of the META-DARE system.

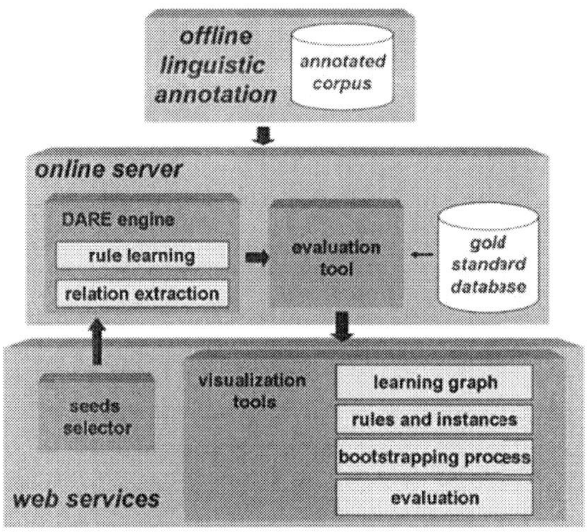

Figure 1: META-DARE: Overall architecture

META-DARE contains three major parts:

- **Online server**: This module is responsible for learning, extracting and evaluation. Its core component is the *DARE engine* for *rule learning* and *relation extraction*. The *evaluation tool* is responsible for validation of the extracted instances against our gold standard databases.
- **Offline linguistic annotation**: This component automatically annotates the corpus texts with named entity information and dependency tree structures using standard NLP tools. All annotations are stored in XML format.
- **Web services**: This part is responsible for user interaction and visualization of learning, extraction and evaluation results. The component *Seeds Selector* allows users to choose their own initial seed set for their experiments. The *visualization tools* present the learning graph and allow users to view learned rules, extracted instances and their interactions. Furthermore, evaluation results of the extracted instances are presented in tabular form.

3 Experiment Corpus

In META-DARE, we use the standard Nobel-Prize corpus described in (Xu et al., 2007), which contains mentionings of the Nobel Prize award events. The target relation for our experiment domain is a quaternary tuple about a person obtaining Nobel Prize in a certain year and in a certain area, described as follows:

$$\langle Person, Prize, Area, Year \rangle .$$

There are 3312 domain related documents (18MB) from online newspapers such as NYT, BBC and CNN. To facilitate our learning, the corpus is preprocessed with several NLP tools (see component "offline linguistic annotation"). We utilize the named entity recognize tool **SProUT** to annotate seven types of named entities: *Person, Location, Organization, Prize, Year, PrizeArea* (Drozdzynski et al., 2004). Furthermore, we apply the dependency parser **MiniPar** for obtaining grammatical functions (Lin, 1998). Users can access the annotations via the system web page where the named entities are highlighted and the dependency structures are presented in a tree format.

4 DARE: Bootstrapping Relation Extraction with Semantic Seed

The core engine in META-DARE is DARE (**D**omain **A**daptive **R**elation **E**xtraction), a minimally supervised machine learning framework for extracting relations of various complexity (Xu et

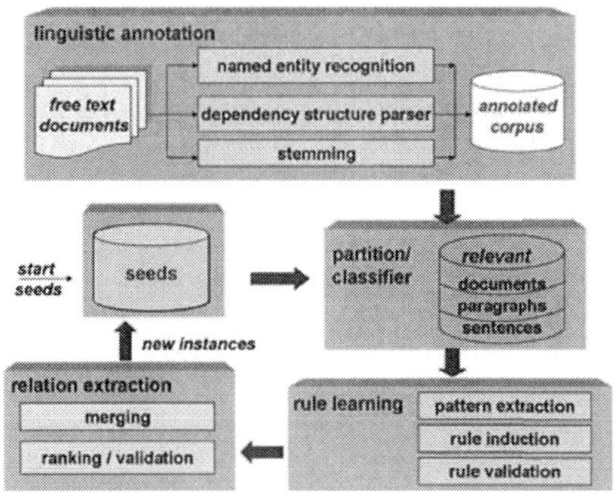

Figure 2: DARE system architecture

al., 2007). Figure 2 illustrates the DARE system architecture.

DARE learns rules from un-annotated free texts, taking some relation instances as examples in the initialization. The learned extraction rules are then applied to the texts for detection of more relation and event instances. The newly discovered relation instances become new seeds for learning more rules. The learning and extraction processes interact with each other and are integrated in a bootstrapping framework. The whole algorithm works as follows:

1. **Input**:
   - A set of un-annotated natural language texts, preprocessed by named entity recognition and dependency parser
   - A trusted set of relation instances, initially chosen ad hoc by the users, as *seeds*.
2. **Partition/Classifier**: Apply seeds to the documents and divide them into relevant and irrelevant documents. A document is relevant if its text fragments contain a minimal number of the relation arguments of a seed and the distance among individual arguments does not exceed the defined width of the textual window.
3. **Rule learning**:
   - **Pattern extraction**: Extract linguistic patterns which contain seed relation arguments as their linguistic arguments and compose the patterns to relation extraction rules.
   - **Rule induction**: Induce relation extraction rules from the set of patterns using compression and generalization methods.
   - **Rule validation**: Rank and validate the rules based on their domain relevance and the trustworthiness of their origin.
4. **Relation extraction**: Apply induced rules to the corpus, in order to extract more relation instances. The extracted instances will be merged and validated.
   - **Merging**: Merge the compatible instances.
   - **Ranking and validation**: Rank and validate the new relation instances.
5. **Stop** if no new rules and relation instances can be found, else repeat step 2 to step 4 with the new seeds resulted from the current step 4.

DARE learns rules basically from the dependency tree structures and proposes a novel compositional rule representation model which supports bottom-up rule composition. A rule for a *n*-ary relation can be composed of rules for its projections, namely, rules that extract a subset of the *n* arguments. Furthermore, it defines explicitly the semantic roles of linguistic arguments for the target relation.

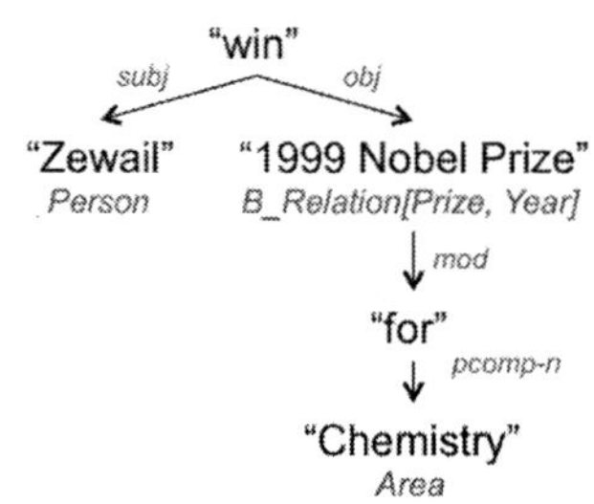

Figure 3: dependency tree example

Let us look at the following example in our experiment domain. Given the following example (1) as our seed which describes a person *Ahmed Zewail* won the *Nobel* Prize in the area of *Chemistry* in the year of *1999*, all four arguments occur in the following sentence (2) in our experiment corpus. The dependency tree structure of sentence (2) is showed in Figure 3.

(1) ⟨*Ahmed Zewail, Nobel, Chemistry, 1999*⟩

(2) *Ahmed Zewail* won the *1999 Nobel* Prize for *Chemistry*.

The rule extracted from example (2) is illustrated in Figure 4, headed by the verb "win". This rule extracts all four arguments for the target relation, where the two arguments *Prize* and *Year* are extracted by its binary projection rule specified as the value of the feature *HEAD* belonging to the grammar function *OBJ* (object). The binary rule detects the *Prize* and *Year* arguments in a complex NP such as "the 1999 Nobel Prize".

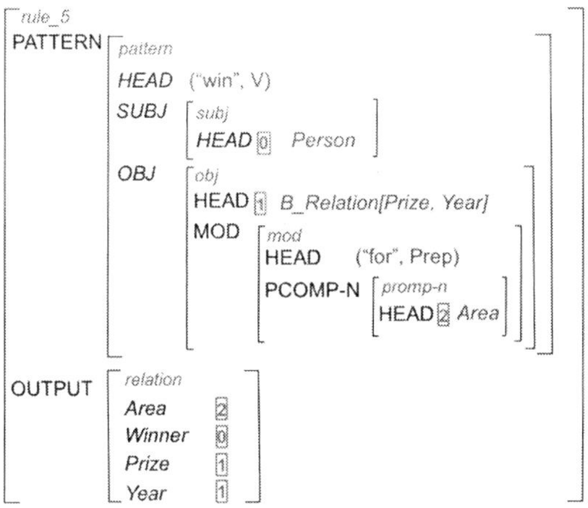

Figure 4: Learned relation extraction rule example

5 Seeds Selector for Seed Construction

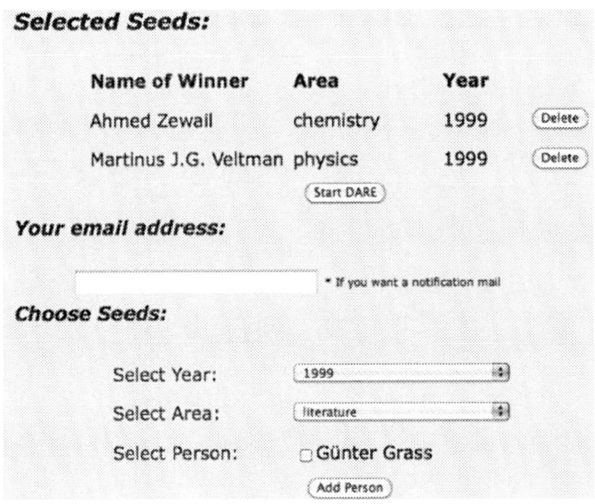

Figure 5: Seed selector

META-DARE offers users a web interface for seed construction[2]. Figure 5 illustrates a seed construction example. Users can choose their seed examples according to the following parameters:

[2] http://dare.dfki.de/start_demo.jsp

- **Size**: users can select as many winning events as available.
- **Year**: users can choose winners belonging to a certain year.
- **Area**: users can add their preferred area.
- **Person name**: users are allowed to select their preferred person name.

Given a valid email address from the user, the system is able to dispatch a notification automatically when the experiment ends.

6 Visualization for Monitoring

META-DARE allows users to access and monitor the following elements of the bootstrapping process:

- Learning graph: Users have access to the whole learning graph and can also zoom in the graph and interact with each node and view its content.
- Learned rule: Each learned rule is presented as a feature structure and is linked to its seeds and sentences from which it is extracted.
- Evaluation results: The distribution of the extracted instances and their precision is presented in tabular form.

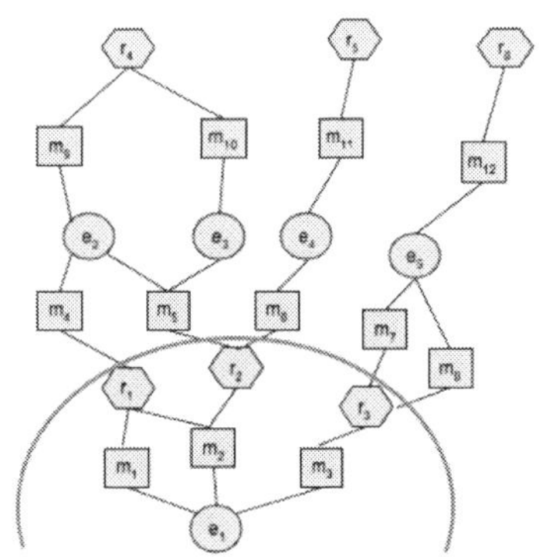

Figure 6: Learning graph starting from semantic seed. e_i: *relation instances*; r_i: *extraction rules*; m_j: *textual snippets*

6.1 Learning Graph

A learning graph in DARE is a graph whose vertices are relation instances, extraction rules and text units as depicted in Figure 6. The learning process starts with instances (e.g., e_1) as seeds and finds textual snippets (e.g., m_1, m_2, m_3) which

	4	3-arity			2	
	arity	(W. P. A.)	(W. P. Y.)	sum	arity	sum
correct	142	61	20	81	74	297
sum	155	88	21	109	107	371
precision	91.61%	69.32%	95.24%	74.31%	69.16%	80.05%

Table 1: Distribution of extracted instances and their precision

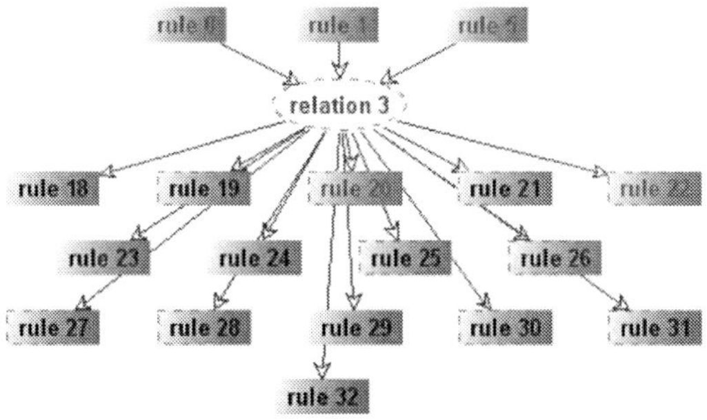

Figure 7: Interaction of rule application and rule learning

match the seeds and then extract pattern rules (e.g, r_1, r_2, r_3). Figure 6 represents the extraction and learning process as a growing graph (Uszkoreit et al., 2009).

The learning graph visualized in META-DARE mainly focuses on the interaction between the learned rules and their seed instances[3]. Figure 7 shows that all three learned rules $rule$ 0, $rule$ 1 and $rule$ 5 detect the same relation instance $relation$ 3 as follows:

(3) ⟨*Robert Mundell, Nobel, Economics, 1999*⟩

which further helps to learn many new rules including $rule$ 18 and $rule$ 19 etc. The nodes not framed by dashed lines, such as $rule$ 23 and $rule$ 24 are rules that cannot discover any new relation instances. The foreground colors of the nodes indicate the evaluation information (see Section 6.2).

If users click one of these rules, they can view the rule presentation as depicted in Figure 4.

The sentences mentioning extraction rules or instances are also presented on the web page. The following example shows two sentences from which $relation$ 3 is extracted.

(4)
1. *Canadian economist Robert Mundell won the Nobel in economics for introducing foreign trade, capital movements, and currency swings into Keynesian economics in the early 1960s. (nyt, 1999-10-13)*
2. *The Canadian-born professor Robert Mundell has won the 1999 Nobel Prize for Economics. (bbc, 1999-10-14)*

[3]`http://dare.dfki.de/graph.jsp?f_id=example`

6.2 Visualization of Evaluation Results

With the help of the gold standard database about the Nobel prize winners, we are able to automatically evaluate the extracted instances. In our evaluation, we take following aspects into account:

- overall performance of the relation extraction: precision and recall
- detailed analysis of the extracted instances: distribution of relation instances with various arities and their precision.
- highlighting of the wrong instances and indications of error sources

Table 1 lists the extraction results and their evaluations after one experiment run with only one example as seed. This seed is mentioned in example (1). We classify the extracted relation instances into different groups depending on their argument combinations. The overall precision of this experiment is 80.05% with 297 correct instances. The precision of instances with all four arguments given is pretty high, namely, 91.61%. They cover almost half of extracted instances. Among the instances with three arguments, there are two argument combinations where *W* stands for winners, *P* for prize names, *Y* for years and *A* for areas. The combination *(W.P.Y)* has achieved a very good precision but contains only few instances. In our experiment, we consider only instances at least containing a person name as instance candidates. This experiment confirms our observation that instances which cover more arguments of the target relation have in general better precision values.

In Table 2 and Table 3, we summarize four different experiments depending on different seed configurations. Table 2 lists the configuration of

id	instance number		prize area	year
1	1		chemistry	1999
2	1		chemistry	1998
3	2		peace	1998
4	12	3	medicine	1998
		2	chemistry	
		2	peace	
		1	literature	
		3	physics	
		1	economics	

Table 2: Different seed constructions

id	bootstrapping steps	extracted instances		learned rules
		sum	4-arity	
1	7	372	156	1151
2	10	374	156	1146
3	6	373	159	1147
4	5	374	163	1117

Table 3: Performance comparison of different seed constructions mentioned in Table 2

seed construction in the four experiments. The first two experiments apply only one seed example and both seed examples are in the same area *Chemistry*, but in a different year. The seed in the third experiment contains two examples in the area *Peace*, while the fourth contains all twelve winners in the year *1998*. If we compare the number of the learned rules and the learned instances in Table 3, all four experiments do not differ too much from each other. However, with more examples in the fourth run, the system needs only five iterations. As reported in (Uszkoreit et al., 2009), the Nobel corpus owns a data property close to a small world. With one single example, the system can achieve very good performance. Therefore, all four experiments share similar performance in our evaluations.

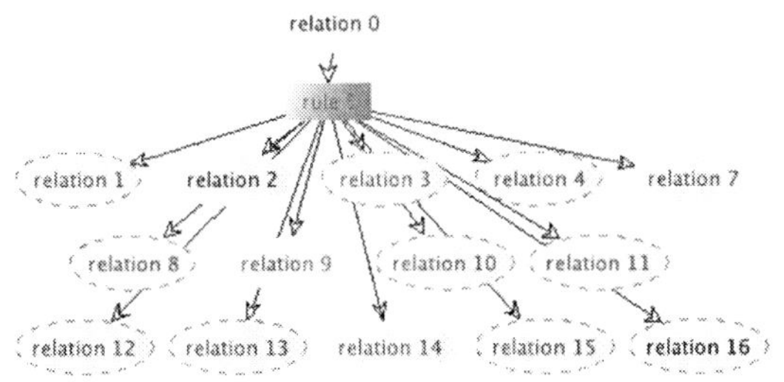

Figure 8: Highlighting of the wrong instances and indications of error sources

As illustrated in Figure 7 and 8, META-DARE also highlights the dangerous or bad rules and wrong relation instance. As described in Xu et al. (2010), the acquired rules are divided into four groups according to the extraction results:

- useless, if the rule does not extract any instances.
- good, if the rule extracts only correct instances.
- dangerous, if the rule extract both correct and wrong instances.
- bad, if the rule extract only bad instances.

In the learning graph, the rules from different group are colored in the following way:

- useless rules: not framed by dashed lines
- good rules: black foreground
- dangerous or bad rules: red foreground

In a similar way, the extracted instances are colored as follows:

- correct instance: blue foreground
- wrong instance: red foreground
- not evaluable: black foreground, such as instance about other prize-winning events but not noble-prize-winning
- useless seed: not framed by dashed lines. With these instances no rules are learned.

For example, in Figure 7 $rule$ 23 and $rule$ 24 are the useless rules, while $rule$ 20 and $rule$ 22 have extracted the wrong instances. $Rule$ 0, $rule$ 1 and $rule$ 5 are the dangerous rules. In Figure 8 $Relation$ 9 is a wrong instance but it does not contribute more errors. $rule$ 5 is a dangerous rule. The users can study the rule and the corresponding sentences from which this rule is learned.

7 Conclusion and Future Work

We demonstrate the META-DARE system which implements the minimally supervised machine learning approach DARE for learning rules and extracting relation instances. META-DARE provides a user-friendly web interface to allow researchers to conduct their own experiments and to obtain insights in the bootstrapping process such as the learning graphs, the learned rules and the iteration behaviors. Furthermore, the evaluation results and the highlighting of the errors are very useful to investigate the learning algorithms and to develop improvement solutions.

META-DARE is an initial approach to an online monitoring system of seed-based minimally supervised machine learning approaches. We plan to integrate more domains and target relations as described in (Xu, 2007; Li et al., 2011). Since DARE is domain adaptive, the META-DARE can be easily customized if users might provide additional corpora and definitions of new relations for a new domain. It might be also useful if META-DARE can display the ranking information computed by the confidence estimation component (Xu et al., 2010) for the instances and the rules. Furthermore, in addition to seed construction, we would like to allow more interactions with the DARE system in the near future, such as adding or selecting negative examples for learning negative rules (Uszkoreit et al., 2009), evaluating the instances or rules during the bootstrapping or correcting the linguistic annotation of NLP tools. An even ambitious plan is to integrate other similar rule learning systems and compare their performance with each other.

Acknowledgements

This research was conducted in the context of the DFG Cluster of Excellence on Multimodal Computing and Interaction (M2CI), projects Theseus Alexandria and Alexandria for Media (funded by the German Federal Ministry of Economy and Technology, contract 01MQ07016), and project TAKE (funded by the German Federal Ministry of Education and Research, contract 01IW08003).

References

Eugene Agichtein and Luis Gravano. 2000. Snowball: Extracting relations from large plain-text collections. In *Proceedings of the 5th ACM International Conference on Digital Libraries (DL'00)*, San Antonio, TX, June.

S. Blohm and P. Cimiano. 2007. Using the Web to Reduce Data Sparseness in Pattern-based Information Extraction. *Proceedings of the 11th European Conference on Principles and Practice of Knowledge Discovery in Databases (PKDD)*, September.

Sergey Brin. 1998. Extracting patterns and relations from the world wide web. In *WebDB Workshop at 6th International Conference on Extending Database Technology, EDBT'98*.

Witold Drozdzynski, Hans-Ulrich Krieger, Jakub Piskorski, Ulrich SchŁfer, and Feiyu Xu. 2004. Shallow processing with unification and typed feature structures — foundations and applications. *Knstliche Intelligenz*, (1):17–23.

Mark A. Greenwood and Mark Stevenson. 2006. Improving semi-supervised acquisition of relation extraction patterns. In *Proceedings of the Workshop on Information Extraction Beyond The Document*, pages 29–35, Sydney, Australia, July. Association for Computational Linguistics.

M.A. Hearst. 1992. Automatic Acquisition of Hyponyms om Large Text Corpora. *Proceedings of the Fourteenth International Conference on Computational Linguistics*.

Hong Li, Feiyu Xu, and Hans Uszkoreit. 2011. Minimally supervised rule learning for the extraction of biographic information from various social domains. In *Proceedings of RANLP 2011*.

D. Lin. 1998. Dependency-based evaluation of MINIPAR. *Workshop on the Evaluation of Parsing Systems*, pages 317–330.

Ellen Riloff. 1996. Automatically generating extraction patterns from untagged text. In *Proceedings of Thirteenth National Conference on Artificial Intelligence (AAAI-96)*, pages 1044–1049. The AAAI Press/MIT Press.

K. Sudo, S. Sekine, and R. Grishman. 2003. An improved extraction pattern representation model for automatic IE pattern acquisition. *Proceedings of ACL 2003*, pages 224–231.

Hans Uszkoreit, Feiyu Xu, and Hong Li. 2009. Analysis and improvement of minimally supervised machine learning for relation extraction. In *14th International Conference on Applications of Natural Language to Information Systems*. Springer.

Feiyu Xu, Hans Uszkoreit, and Hong Li. 2007. A seed-driven bottom-up machine learning framework for extracting relations of various complexity. In *Proceedings of ACL 2007, 45th Annual Meeting of the Association for Computational Linguistics*, Prague, Czech Republic, 6.

Feiyu Xu, Hans Uszkoreit, Sebastian Krause, and Hong Li. 2010. Boosting relation extraction with limited closed-world knowledge. In *Proceedings of the 23rd International Conference on Computational Linguistics*. Association for Computational Linguistics, o.A.

Feiyu Xu. 2007. *Bootstrapping Relation Extraction from Semantic Seeds*. Phd-thesis, Saarland University.

Mining Transliterations from Wikipedia using Dynamic Bayesian Networks

Peter Nabende
Alfa-Informatica, University of Groningen
p.nabende@rug.nl

Abstract

Transliteration mining is aimed at building high quality multi-lingual named entity (NE) lexicons for improving performance in various Natural Language Processing (NLP) tasks including Machine Translation (MT) and Cross Language Information Retrieval (CLIR). In this paper, we apply two Dynamic Bayesian network (DBN)-based edit distance (ED) approaches in mining transliteration pairs from Wikipedia. Transliteration identification results on standard corpora for seven language pairs suggest that the DBN-based edit distance approaches are suitable for modeling transliteration similarity. An evaluation on mining transliteration pairs from English-Hindi and English-Tamil Wikipedia topic pairs shows that they improve transliteration mining quality over state-of-the-art approaches.

1 Introduction

Transliteration mining is aimed at addressing the problem of *unknown* words in NLP applications of which named entities (NEs) constitute the highest percentage. Currently, there is growing interest in using automated methods to harness large amounts of correct multi-lingual named entities (NEs) from various ever accumulating Web-based data resources such as newspaper websites and online encyclopedia (most notably Wikipedia) with the aim of improving word coverage and the effectiveness of NLP systems such as MT and CLIR.

In this paper, we present the application of two DBN-based edit distance approaches in mining transliterations from Wikipedia. Our motivation to apply the DBN-based approaches for modeling transliteration is founded on our observation of their successful application in NLP tasks (such as cognate identification (2005) and pronunciation classification (2005)) which have requirements similar to transliteration mining. While transliteration mining currently demands new approaches to complement or improve performance over existing methods, there was not yet any investigation about the use of the DBN-based edit distance approaches for mining transliteration pairs from 'noisy' data. The first approach is based on the classic HMM framework but models two observation sequences (hence the name Pair HMM) instead of one observation sequence. The second approach is based on the representation and implementation of a *memoryless stochastic transducer* (initially proposed by Ristad and Yianilos (1998) as a DBN model for learning string edit distance. We propose to evaluate the use of the two approaches in mining transliterations with respect to two subtasks. In the first subtask, we follow the same evaluation setup as that for a recent shared task on transliteration mining (Kumaran et al., 2010b) while using the same standard corpora. This first subtask ensures a comparison of the DBN model results against those for state-of-the-art systems that participated in the shared task since the DBN models are applied to the same standard transliteration corpora. In the second subtask, we investigate the possibility of applying proposed DBN models in mining transliterations from Wikipedia's article content in addition to the Wikipedia paired topics.

2 Wikipedia

Wikipedia is a free Web-based multi-lingual encyclopedia with an ever increasing number of articles in over 270 languages. In some articles for each language Wikipedia, access is provided to pages about the same topic in other language Wikipedias. Figure 1 shows two Wikipedia articles about the same topic, one in English titled as "Arab spring" while the other is in Arabic and is accessed using the Arabic Wikipedia interlanguage link (WIL) which exists on the English page as shown.

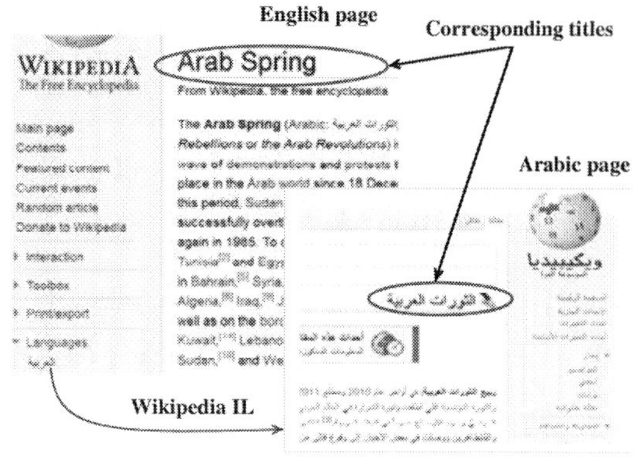

Figure 1: Two Wikipedia articles about the same topic but written using different writing systems.

Many studies have recently found it inexpensive to automatically construct multi-lingual lexicons by using only Wikipedia inter-language links. In the first subtask, we use Wikipedia topic pairs that have been identified from inter-language links to constitute the collection of raw data to which the DBN models are applied and evaluated for mining transliteration pairs. In the second subtask, we propose to extend the application of the DBN models beyond mining from only linked text to also mining from the unlinked text in comparable articles. We postulate that the possibility to apply DBN models in mining from noisy unlinked comparable Wikipedia text would imply an extended use in mining transliterations from a variety of other similar sources where we expect to get many named entities such as from many emerging bilingual newspaper websites. In the following section, we introduce the concepts underlying the framework of DBNs and the models we have proposed to evaluate in mining transliteration pairs.

3 Dynamic Bayesian networks

The possibility to have random variables relate to time in a Bayesian network enables DBNs to represent probability distributions over a sequence of random variables comprising of observations that are related to an underlying sequence of hidden states. A DBN model is formally defined as a pair $\langle \mathcal{B}_0, \mathcal{B}_{\rightarrow} \rangle$ where $\mathcal{B}_0$ is a Bayesian network over an initial distribution over states, and $\mathcal{B}_{\rightarrow}$ is a two slice Temporal Bayes Net (2-TBN) (Murphy, 2002). It is the 2-TBN that is *unrolled* a number of times to fit a given observation sequence while providing the semantic definitions of the DBN over the whole observation sequence. The structure of a DBN is a directed acyclic graph (DAG) where each node represents a domain variable of interest, and each directed arc represents the dependency between the two nodes it connects. The DBN framework already generalizes various methods including some of the common and successful methods in NLP such as HMMs. HMMs, being the simplest DBNs, provide a natural starting point for our investigation of the use of DBNs in mining transliteration pairs. The classic HMMs in particular have already been applied in detecting transliteration pairs from bilingual text. However, because of space restrictions, we defer the introduction of HMMs in general and proceed to introduce the edit distance-based Pair HMMs for modeling transliteration similarity.

3.1 Pair HMMs

The Pair HMM approach is based on modifications to a pairwise alignment finite state automaton (Durbin et al., 1998). In this paper, we build upon the Pair HMM structure proposed by Mackay and Kondrak (2005) to compute word similarity. Figure 2 is a finite state representation of a Pair HMM similar to the one proposed by Mackay and Kondrak (2005). The Pair HMM in Figure 2 models word similarity as an edit operation cost for measuring the similarity between two words. The edit operations are encoded in the edit operation states

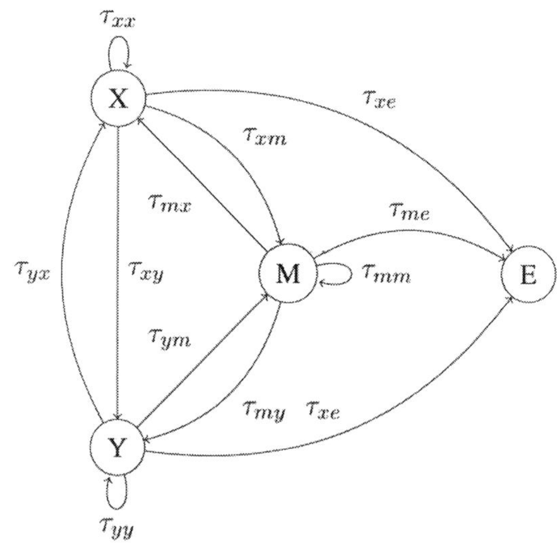

Figure 2: A finite state representation of a Pair HMM for modeling edit operations using three emission states: M (match), X (delete), and Y (insert). The τ's illustrate transition parameters.

which are denoted in Figure 2 by three nodes as follows: M (for emitting an aligned pair of symbols), X (for deleting a symbol from one word), and Y (for inserting a symbol) in the other word. The E node denotes the non-emitting end state. With respect to related work, we do not include a start state and instead assume that the edit operation process starts in any of the edit states where the three starting parameters are defined to be the same as the transition parameters from the M state to one of the edit states including M. We base our application of the Pair HMMs on a number of requirements that were proposed by Nabende et al. (2010) in adapting Mackay and Kondrak's word similarity Pair HMM for computing transliteration similarity. Specifically, we ensure the use of distinct emission parameters in the deletion (X) and insertion (Y) states because of different writing systems. Nabende (2010c) also investigated the effect of transition parameter changes on identifying English-Russian transliteration pairs and the result was that transition parameters are important for computing transliteration similarity. With respect to this paper, we also conducted an investigation on changes in transition parameters for seven language pairs and the conclusion was the same, that transition paramters are important for computing transliteration similarity. Therefore, the Pair HMMs we apply in transliteration mining are based on the finite state representation in Figure 2 but with different settings for transition parameters. In one setting we used only three transition parameters where the transition parameter takes the same value for outward transitions from a given edit state. In the second setting, we used five transition parameters where we assume some symmetries in the source and target language. We used similar parameters for transitions to and from the deletion and insertion states as in Mackay and Kondrak (2005). That is, we used the same parameter for staying in the X or Y state, another same parameter for moving from either X or Y to the end state, and the same parameter from the substitution state to the X or Y state. In the third setting, we used nine distinct parameters for transitions between the Pair HMM states. Apart from evaluating the effect of transition parameters, we also evaluated the use of different Pair HMM scoring algorithms including the following: the forward and Viterbi algorithms, and their combination with a random Pair HMM to compute log-odds ratios which we use as transliteration similarity estimates. The results for our preliminary investigation showed a stable and better transliteration identification performance for the three different Pair HMMs when we compute the transliteration similarity estimates as log-odds ratios of the Pair HMM forward score and the random model score compared to the other scoring algorithms.

3.2 Transduction-based DBN models

The second edit distance-based DBN approach that we propose for mining transliterations from Wikipedia finds its origins as an alternative DBN representation of a *memoryless stochastic transducer* using the general probabilistic graphical modeling (PGM) framework. The DBN template-based representation simplifies the investigation of a variety of edit operation-specific dependencies for computing word similarity and has led to successful applications in pronunciation classification (Filali and Bilmes, 2005) and cognate identification (Kondrak and Sherif, 2006). In this approach, random variables are defined to correspond to the objects that contribute to the computation of edit distance for a pair of words. The main objects of interest include: an edit operation variable (denoted by Z_i); source and target character variables; variables that capture the position of the characters in the source and target words; and consistency variables that check the yield of the edit operation variable against the actual pair of characters at a given position. The dependencies between the random variables follow naturally. For example, the following include some of the dependencies that were defined by Filali and Bilmes (2005) to model the memoryless stochastic transducer. Dependencies between string position variables (sp_i and tp_i) and character variables (s_i and respectively t_i) (where the idea is that knowledge about a position in a string leads to knowledge about the character at that position. For consistency checking, consistency variables are defined to depend on the character variables and the edit operation variable. Filali and Bilmes (2005) use an ASR-based graphical modeling approach where a *frame* is used to represent a set of random variables and their attributes at a given time. In the ASR-based graphical modeling approach, the term *prologue frame(s)* is used to refer to the initial Bayesian network $\mathcal{B}_0$ and the term *chunk frame* is used to refer to the Bayesian network that is *un-*

rolled a number of times to fit a given observation sequence as defined for a 2-TBN. Using the ASR-based notation, the initial, chunk and epilogue networks that model the memoryless stochastic transducer are as shown in Figure 3. The DBN template defined by the three networks in Figure 3 is also referred to as *memoryless and context-independent* (MCI) since it models the memoryless stochastic transducer which is also context-independent in the sence that the edit operation variable has no local dependencies on the source and target characters, but has a global context dependency that allows it to generate the source and target strings.

In Figure 3, the sp_i and tp_i nodes refer to variables used to track the current position in the source and target strings respectively. The sp_i and tp_i combined with z_{i-1} capture the transition semantics in the network. The s_i and t_i variables represent the current character in the source and target strings respectively. The sc_i and tc_i nodes enforce consistency constraints by having a fixed observed value 1 where the only configuration of their parents is such that the source component of the edit operation variable z_i is s_i or an empty symbol and the target component of z_i is t_i or an empty symbol ϵ, and that z_i does not generate (ϵ, ϵ). e_i denotes the 'end' variable which is a 'switching' parent of z_i and it is used to indicate when we are past the end of both the source and target strings; that is, when $sp_i > m$ and $tp_i > n$ where *m* and *n* are the lengths of the source and target strings respectively. The *se* and *te* nodes represent variables that ensure that we are past the end of the source and target strings respectively. Most of the edges in Figure 3 represent deterministic relationships between variables, more specifically, edges that are associated with position variables, consistency variables, character variables and end variables. For these, we use deterministic conditional probability tables. The emission probabilities that are used to generate the source and target strings are encoded in the edit operation variable z_i by way of dense conditional probability tables.

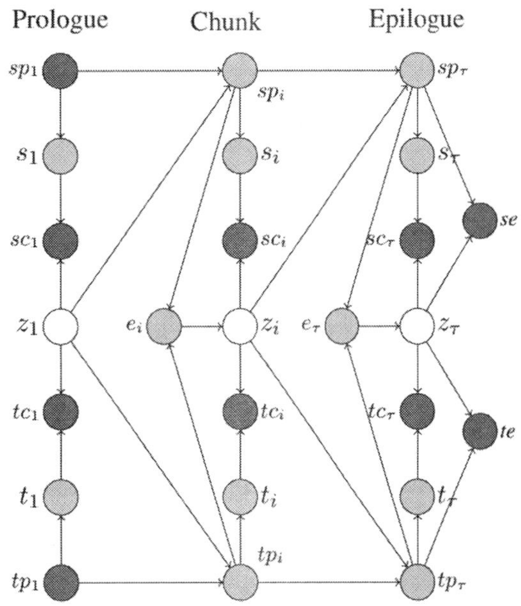

Figure 3: Graphical representation for the MCI DBN template. Following the common convention for representing graphical models, dark nodes represent observed variables which can be either deterministic or stochastic, gray nodes represent deterministic hidden variables, and unshaded nodes represent hidden variables. Adapted from Filali and Bilmes (2005).

In Nabende (2010a), three DBN model generalizations based on the MCI DBN model were adapted to compute transliteration similarity and identify transliterations between English and Russian NEs. In the preliminary experiments in this paper, we evaluate the three DBN model generalizations that were adapted in Nabende (2010a) on the same seven language pairs that we used to evaluate several Pair HMMs as described in section 3.1 above. The three DBN model generalizations represent different dependencies on the edit operation random variables including: edit operation *memory* dependencies that capture memory from previous edit states of a DBN model; *contextual* dependencies of the edit operation variable on either source and / or target string elements; and dependencies that account for the *length* of the edit steps needed to represent an observation sequence.

3.3 Preliminary transliteration identification experiments

We conducted a preliminary transliteration identification (TI) experiment to help choose DBN models for use in mining transliteration pairs from Wikipedia. Several Pair HMMs and transduction-based DBN models introduced in the previous section were evaluated on standard transliteration corpora (Li et al., 2009; Li et al., 2010) for seven language pairs including: English-Bangla (e-b), English-Chinese (e-c), English-Hindi (e-h),

Models	e-b	e-c	e-h	e-k	e-r	e-t	eth
	Top-1 accuracy						
Phm	93	68	**89**	**86**	89	83	62
Mci	87	30	75	72	98	65	35
Mem	89	49	72	57	89	72	49
Cs1	96	70	86	84	98	83	74
Cs2	96	80	86	85	97	85	79
Ct1	95	68	84	84	98	84	76
Ct2	96	**82**	86	86	98	**86**	**85**
Ls1	96	71	83	77	98	84	73
Ls2	95	70	85	81	98	80	70

Table 1: DBN model transliteration identification results involving seven language pairs. The row with Phm represents the best Pair HMM result per language pair. The remaining results are for the transduction-based models with Mci referring to the MCI DBN template in Figure 3. cs1 and ct1 refer to context-dependent DBN models where Z_i depends on the current source (cs1) or target (ct1) character. In Cs2 and ct2, Z_i depends on the current and previous characters.

English-Kannadda (e-k), English-Russian (e-r), English-Tamil (e-t), and English-Thai (eth). Table 1 shows the TI Top-1 accuracy results (out of 100%) for the transduction-based DBN models against the best Pair HMMs (represented by Phm) involving the seven language pairs. As Table 1 shows, the context-dependent DBN models generally achieve a better performance compared to other DBN models. Table 1 also shows that Pair HMMs outperform the transduction-based DBN models in identifying transliterations between English and Hindi, and between English and Kannada. Based on the TI Top-1 accuracy results in Table 1, we chose to evaluate the Pair HMMs and context-dependent DBN models in mining transliterations from Wikipedia.

4 Transliteration mining experiments

4.1 Experiments using NEWS 2010 shared task Wikipedia data

We applied the best Pair HMMs and context-dependent DBN models from the preliminary TI experiments above to transliteration data provided for the NEWS 2010 shared task (Kumaran et al., 2010a) on mining single word transliteration pairs for three language pairs: English-Hindi, English-Russian, and English-Tamil. Two sets of data were provided per language pair including: 1000 hand picked pairs of single NEs as seed data for training transliteration mining systems; and many noisy Wikipedia topic pairs obtained using Wikipedia inter-language links (WILs) as raw data. Our data pre-processing on the noisy Wikipedia topic pairs involved using simple regular expressions to filter out most of the irrelevant entities including: characters from other writing systems; temporal and numeric expressions; and punctuation symbols. To reduce on data sparseness, we converted all characters in the English and Russian datasets to lowercase. After pre-processsing, the remaining number of Wikipedia topic pairs per language pair were as follows: 14620 (86.2%) for English-Hindi, 296053 (85.6%) for English-Russian, and 13249 (95.4%) for English-Tamil.

Evaluation setup and results

We used the seed datasets to train each Pair HMM and context-dependent DBN models. We trained each Pair HMM using the Baum-Welch expectation maximization algorithm and each context-dependent DBN model using a generalized expectation maximization algorithm. We then applied the trained models to compute transliteration similarity between candidate NEs from each Wikipedia topic pair. After the application of each model, we checked the similarity estimates assigned by the model to candidate transliteration pairs which enabled us to specify different threshold scores ranging from a low threshold for which the system suggests many candidate pairs as transliteration pairs to a high threshold where the system suggests very few candidate pairs as transliteration pairs. The transliteration mining results from each model are evaluated using three related metrics: Precision (P), Recall (R), and F-score.

$$\mathrm{P} = \frac{\mathrm{TP}}{\mathrm{TP}+\mathrm{FP}}, \quad \mathrm{R} = \frac{\mathrm{TP}}{\mathrm{TP}+\mathrm{FN}}$$

$$\mathrm{F} = \frac{2 \times \mathrm{P} \times \mathrm{R}}{\mathrm{P}+\mathrm{R}}$$

where TP, FP, and FN refer to true positives, false positives, and false negatives respectively.

In order to compare the DBN model results against those reported for the NEWS 2010 shared task on transliteration mining, we checked a subset of the transliteration mining result per language pair to set a subjective threshold score that we thought would result in an optimal dis-

Model	P	R	F
PHMM3_FLO	0.930	0.976	0.952
PHMM3_IterT_FLO	0.959	0.949	**0.954**
PHMM9_FL0	0.934	0.975	0.954
PHMM9_IterT_FLO	0.936	0.976	**0.955**
CONs2	0.911	0.891	0.901
NEWS 2010 best result	0.954	0.895	0.924

Table 2: DBN model results against NEWS 2010 shared task results for English-Hindi. P refers to Precision, R to recall, and F to F-score.

crimination between true transliteration and non-transliteration pairs. Table 2 shows the results for the DBN models against the best shared task result on the English-Hindi dataset. In Table 2, the Pair HMMs have in an F-score value that is better than that for the best shared task result while the CONs2 model also posts a promising result.

Table 3 shows the results for Pair HMMs and a context-dependent DBN model against the best shared task result on the English-Tamil dataset. The Pair HMMs again achieve a better F-score value compared to the best shared task result. However, the CONs2 model has a relatively poor performance than it did for English-Hindi above.

For the English-Russian dataset, we applied a context-dependent DBN model (Cont1) that models the dependency of the edit operation variable Z_i on the current target character. Table 4 shows the results of Cont1 against the best shared task result and against those of a Pair HMM with nine distinct transition parameters that was also evaluated during the shared task (Nabende, 2010b). For the English-Russian dataset, none of the DBN models achieved an F-score better than that of the shared task result. Table 4 shows that the context-dependent DBN models results in a better F-score over the Pair HMM using only the forward algorithm to compute transliteration similarity.

Model	P	R	F
PHMM3_FLO	0.913	0.966	0.936
PHMM5_FLO	0.923	0.955	0.939
CONs2	0.790	0.852	0.820
NEWS2010 best result	0.923	0.906	0.914

Table 3: DBN model results against NEWS 2010 shared task results for English-Tamil.

Model	P	R	F
Cont1	0.835	0.815	0.825
PHMM9_F_NEWS2010	0.780	0.834	0.806
NEWS2010 best result	0.880	0.869	0.875

Table 4: DBN model results against NEWS 2010 shared task results for English-Tamil.

4.2 Experiments using Wikipedia's article content

For this set of experiments, we used Wikipedia inter-language links to automatically acquire seed data by restricting our search to only person names following the structured nature of information in Wikipedia infoboxes. For test data, we identified some ten of the most visited pages during the month of August 2009 to serve as our source for mining transliterations. The data pre-processing steps here are similar to those described in the previous section. Our evaluation set comprised of 4811 English NEs and 9334 Russian NEs after pre-processing. From the candidate NEs, we hand-picked 264 transliteration pairs to form the gold set.

We applied three Pair HMMs (PHMM3, PHMM5, and PHMM9) and a context-dependent DBN model to mine transliterations from English-Russian Wikipedia article text in a manner similar to how we applied them in mining transliterations from Wikipedia topic pairs. We trained the DBN models on the automatically acquired seed data and then applied the trained models to compute transliteration similarity between candidate NEs. All the Pair HMMs use the log-odds ratio involving the forward algorithm to compute transliteration similarity. We evaluate the models at different cut-offs of the number of the top-ranked suggestions of transliteration pairs for each model. Table 5 shows theresults for the top ranked 200 suggestions per model. Table 5 shows that the

Model	P	R	F
PHMM3_FLO	0.530	0.402	0.457
PHMM5_FLO	0.755	0.572	0.651
PHMM9_FLO	0.630	0.477	0.543
CONs1	0.760	0. 576	0.655

Table 5: Transliteration mining results for a cut-off of 200 top-ranked suggestions of English-Russian candidate pairs as true transliteration pairs.

context-dependent DBN model achieves a slightly better F-score than the Pair HMMs for the first 200 suggestions of transliteration pairs using the models. However, we found out that an increase in recall resulted in a faster drop of precision for the context-dependent DBN model compared to the drop for the Pair HMMs.

5 Conclusions and future work

In this paper, we evaluated several DBN models in mining transliterations from Wikipedia. Pair HMMs achieved fair improvements in transliteration mining quality over state-of-the-art methods for mining transliterations from English-Hindi and English-Tamil Wikipedia topic pairs. The results also showed the possibility of applying the DBN approaches in mining transliteration pairs from comparable Wikipedia article content with context-dependent models performing better than the Pair HMMs on an English-Russian dataset.

As future work, we would like to evaluate more transduction-based DBN models in mining transliteration pairs from comparable Wikipedia content for other language pairs and on larger datasets than the ones used in this paper.

Acknowledgments

Research in this paper was funded through a second NPT Uganda project from 2007–2011.

References

Richard Durbin, Sean R. Eddy, Anders Krogh, and Graeme Mitchison. 1998. *Biological Sequence Analysis: Probabilistic Models of Proteins and Nucleic Acids.* Cambridge University Press, Cambridge, UK.

Karim Filali and Jeff Bilmes. 2005. A Dynamic Bayesian Framework to model context and memory in edit distance learning: An application to pronunciation classification. *Proceedings of the Association for Computational Linguistics (ACL)*, Ann-Arbor, Michigan.

Grzegorz Kondrak and Tarek Sherif. 2006. Evaluation of several phonetic similarity algorithms on the task of cognate identification. *Proceedings of the COLING-ACL Workshop on Linguistic distances*, pp. 43–50, Sydney, Australia.

A Kumaran, Mitesh M. Khapra, and Haizhou Li. 2010. Whitepaper of NEWS 2010 Shared Task on Transliteration Mining, *Proceedings of the 2010 Named Entities Workshop*, pp. 29–38, Uppsala, Sweden.

A Kumaran, Mitesh M. Khapra, and Haizhou Li. 2010. Report of NEWS 2010 Transliteration Mining shared task. *Proceedings of the 2010 Named Entities Workshop*, pp. 21–28, Uppsala, Sweden.

Haizhou Li, A Kumaran, Vladmir Pervouchine, and Min Zhang. 2009. Report of NEWS 2009 Machine transliteration shared task. *ACL/IJCNLP 2009 Named Entities Workshop (NEWS 2009)*, Suntec, Singapore.

Haizhou Li, A Kumaran, Min Zhang, and Vladmir Pervouchine. 2010. Whitepaper of NEWS 2010 transliteration generation shared task. *Proceedings of the 2010 Named Entities Workshop*, pp. 12–20, Uppsala, Sweden.

Wesley Mackay and Grzegorz Kondrak. 2010. Computing Word and identifying cognates with Pair Hidden Markov models. *Proceedings of the ninth Conference on Computational Natural Language Learning (CONLL 2005)*, pp. 40–47 Ann Arbor, Michigan.

Kevin P. Marphy. 2002. *Dynamic Bayesian Networks: Representation, Inference and Learning*. PhD Thesis, UC Berkeley, Computer Science Division.

Peter Nabende, Jörg Tiedeman, and John Nerbonne. 2010. Pair Hidden Markov model for named entity matching. *Innovations and advances in computer sciences and engineering*, pp. 497–502, Springer Heidelberg.

Peter Nabende. 2010. Applying a Dynamic Bayesian network framework to transliteration identification. Proceedings of the seventh International language resources and evaluation conference (LREC 2010), pp.244–251, Valletta, Malta.

Peter Nabende. 2010. Mining transliterations from Wikipedia using Pair HMMs. *Proceedings of the 2010 Named Entities Workshop, ACL 2010*, pp. 76–80, Uppsala, Sweden.

Peter Nabende. 2010. Comparison of applying Pair HMMs and DBN models in transliteration identification. *Proceedings of the 20th Computational Linguistics in Netherlands meeting*, pp. 107–122, Amsterdam, The Netherlands.

Eric S. Ristad and Peter N. Yianilos. 1998. Learning string edit distance. *Trans. on Pattern Recognition and Machine Intelligence*, 20(5):522–532.

Martijn Wieling, Therese Leinonen, and John Nerbonne. 2007. Inducing sound segment differences using Pair Hidden Markov Models. In J. Nerbonne, M. Ellison, and G. Kondrak (eds.), *Computing and Historical Phonology: 9th Meeting of ACL Special Interest Group for Computational Morphology and Phonology Workshop*, pp. 48–56, Prague, Czech Republic.

Detecting Opinions Using Deep Syntactic Analysis

Caroline Brun
Xerox Research Centre Europe
Meylan, France
Caroline.Brun@xrce.xerox.com

Abstract

In this paper, we present an opinion detection system built on top of a robust syntactic parser. The goal of this system is to extract opinions associated with products but also with characteristics of these products, i.e. to perform feature-based opinion extraction. To carry out this task, and following a target corpus study, the robust syntactic parser is enriched by associating polarities to pertinent lexical elements and by developing generic rules to extract relations of opinions together with their polarity, i.e. positive or negative. These relations are used to feed an opinion representation model. A first evaluation shows very encouraging results, but numerous perspectives and developments remain to be investigated.

1 Introduction

Opinion mining (or sentiment analysis) arouses great interest in recent years both in academia and industry. With the emergence of discussion groups, forums, blogs, web sites compiling consumer reviews on various subjects, there is a huge mass of documents containing information expressing opinions. This constitutes a very important data source for monitoring various applications (business intelligence, product and service benchmarking, technology watch). Consequently, numerous research works at the crossroads of NLP and data mining, are focusing on the problem of opinion detection and mining. In this paper, we present an opinion detection system developed in the framework of the European Project Scoop[1]. This system uses a robust parser specifically adapted for opinion detection, and we focus here on recent developments made for English. Our goal is to extract opinions related to the main concepts commented in the reviews (e.g. products, movies, books...), but also on the features associated to these products (such as certain characteristics of the products, their price, associated services, etc...).

After a brief review of related work, we describe a corpus analysis conducted on a first target corpus consisting of reviews about printers, copiers and scanners. The following section describes in details the building of the opinion detection system, which makes an intensive use of syntactic information. Finally, we present a preliminary evaluation of the performances of this system and conclude on our perspectives.

2 State of the Art

Besides works about lexical resources acquisition for opinion mining, discussed in section 4.3.2, two main types of works can be distinguished: those aiming at classifying texts according to an overall polarity (positive, negative and sometimes neutral), generally based on supervised approaches (such as (Pang et al. 2002), or (Charton and Acuna-Agost 2007)), and those aiming at extracting precise information about positive or negative aspects of a given product or topic. The latter consider that the main concept (e.g. a product) is related to several features (e.g. quality, print speed and resolution for a printer), that can be evaluated separately. Our system belongs to this category. In this case, the goal is to identify related features and opinions expressed about these features. Three sub-tasks are considered: feature extraction, discovery of opinions about these features, and eventually production of a summary of the information associated with a given feature. In order to extract features, methods are generally based on frequency criteria coupled with linguistically-based heuristic, see for example (Yi et al. 2003) or (Popescu and Etzioni 2005). In order to extract opinions about features, a wide range of methods have been proposed: (Hu and Liu 2004) extract the linguistic segments containing a concept and count the polarity of the polar vocabulary present in the same segment. (Vernier et al. 2009) propose a symbolic method to detect and categorize opinions locally expressed in a set of multi-domain

[1] http://www.scoopproject.eu/overview.html

blogs. Some systems use syntactic dependencies to link source and target of the opinion as in (Kim and Hovy 2006) or (Bloom et al. 2007). Our system belongs to this family, as we believe that syntactic processing of complex phenomena (negation, comparison and anaphora) is a necessary step to perform feature-based opinion mining. A specificity of our system is a two level architecture: it relies on a first level, general and valid across all domain and corpora, and on a second level, adapted for each sub-domain of application.

3 Corpus Study

In order to build our opinion detection system, we used a corpus of reviews available on the website "Epinion"[2]. This is a general site compiling millions of user reviews about products, movies, books, etc. As our first target application deals with consumer reviews about printers, we extracted a corpus of about 3,500 printer reviews from this site. These reviews are semi-structured and contain the following information: The product name; the overall score (from 0 to 5 stars); the review title; the creation date; the sections "Pros", "Cons" and "Bottom Line" and the content of the review in free text, with the assessment: "Recommended": "yes" or "no".

This study revealed two important points:

(a) Complex linguistic phenomena are involved in the expression of opinions, and need to be taken into account to build an efficient extraction system:

Syntactic or lexical negation, which inverses the polarity of opinions, as in the following examples:

- *I **can't** use it **without** problems.*
- *There is **no way** I can recommend this printer*

Modality, which affects the strength of the opinion:

- *Considering the high cost of the printer, the quality **should be** outstanding.*

Comparison, which express an opinion comparatively:

- *I would be **happier** with a **better** price.*
- *Performance is **better than** many competing laser printers.*

Anaphora, impacting the detection of the topic of an opinion: In the following example, taken from a review about the "*Xerox DocuPrint P8ex Laser Printer*", the author refers to many other products (underlined text) that are not the main topic of the review (bold text):

***Xerox DocuPrint P8ex Laser Printer**: When my previous printer (HP LaserJet 5: it was really good at the time) did not last as long as I would like it to have lasted.... I had one functional HP remaining (this one also a good, reliable product but ancient and so slow), one NEC and then I bought **this Xerox**.*

(b) Regarding the subjective vocabulary, i.e. the vocabulary expressing whether an opinion is positive or negative, it is necessary to take into account the following problems:

Ambiguities, because the same word in a given domain can express opinions of different polarity, for example, the adjective "fast" in the domain of printers:

- *It uses ink twice as **fast**.* [Negative]
- *It is a **fast**, high quality printer.* [Positive]

Domain-dependent polarity, because the polarity of a given word can vary across domains:

- *It walks like a **lemon** and quacks like a **lemon*** [Negative]: In product reviews, "lemon" is negative, while this word is generally neutral.
- *(i)Pros: Completely **unpredictable**, Nicholas Cage is awesome.* [Positive]. (ii) *The only problem is that the HP software that runs it appears to be very flaky and **unpredictable**.* [Negative]. In the domain of movie reviews, "unpredictable" is used positively, whereas it is negative in the domain of printers.

Following this study, we designed system with a two level-architecture: the first level contains generic vocabulary, of constant polarity across domains, as well as generic extraction rules, while the second level contains domain-dependent polar vocabulary and specific extraction rules. This system, which benefits of the incremental architecture of the parser we use, is described in detail in the next section.

4 Our System

4.1 Model of an Opinion

Our goal is to develop a system for extracting opinions on product reviews. We not only aim at classifying reviews as positive or negative (document-level opinion mining), but also at extracting finer-grained opinions expressed about specific features related to a main concept (e.g. speed, print quality etc. in the case of a printer). It seems indeed very interesting to detect precise-

[2] http://www.epinions.com/

ly what users like or dislike about a given product, because an overall opinion on a review, either positive or negative, does not necessarily reflect the fact that the user likes or does not like the product as a whole. To achieve this goal, we adopt the formal representation of an opinion given proposed by (Liu, B. 2010): an opinion is a five place predicate of the form $(o_j, f_{jk}, so_{ijkl}, h_i, t_l)$, where:

- o_j is the target object of the opinion (the main concept)
- f_{jk} is a feature associated to the object o_j
- so_{ijkl} is the value (positive or negative) of the opinion expressed by the opinion holder h_i about the feature f_{jk}
- h_i is the opinion holder
- t_l is the time when the opinion is expressed.

Our opinion extraction system is designed on top of a robust syntactic parser (XIP, see below). We use this parser to extract, from syntactic relations already extracted by a general dependency grammar, semantic relations in order to instantiate the five place predicates compliant with this model.

4.2 XIP in Brief

We use the Xerox Incremental Parser, XIP, (Ait-Mokthar et al., 2002) as a fundamental component of our system, in order to extract deep syntactic dependencies, which are an intermediary step to the extraction of semantic relations of opinion. The parser also includes a module for named entity. For this project, since the first application focuses on reviews about printers, a preliminary adaptation was to integrate the recognition of printer names into the NER module.

4.3 Design of the System

As said before, we aim at extracting from customer reviews, semantic relations to instantiate five place predicates modeling an opinion. In the context of our application, we can simplify the extraction of the required information, considering that the moment in time when the opinion is expressed is the date of creation of the document and that the opinion holder is the review's author. Moreover, if not mentioned explicitly in the sentence, by default, the object of an opinion is the main topic of the review, i.e., in our case, the product reviewed. For reasons of implementation, we also model the polarity of an opinion as a feature (whose value is "positive" or "negative") associated with the sentiment semantic relation. Finally, an argument of the sentiment relation is the predicate carrying the opinion. This information can be useful for a subsequent phase of normalization. So we want to extract semantic relations of the form:

SENTIMENT[POLARITY](MAIN-CONCEPT, FEATURE, PREDICATE), for example:

(1)"*This printer is slow*":

➔ SENTIMENT[NEG](printer, _ , slow)

(2)"*The laser print quality is great*"

➔ SENTIMENT[POS](Default, print quality, great)

In the first example, the predicate carrying the opinion is "slow", the object is "printer", the opinion relates to this object entirely and the sentiment is negative. In the second example, the predicate carrying the opinion is "great", the associated feature is "print quality", and as it is not explicitly mentioned, the object of the opinion is the main topic of the review (*Default*).

In order to extract such semantic relationships, we have first extracted the associated features from our corpus, then implemented a polar lexicon, and finally design hand-crafted sentiment extraction rules, according to the two-level architecture mentioned before. These different development steps are now described in detail.

4.4 Associated Feature Extraction

The main concepts of our first application are the topic discussed in customer reviews about printers: the vocabulary denoting these concepts is: *printer*, *copier*, *scanner*, *machine*, and *product*.

To extract the associated features related to these concepts, we use a method partly similar to what is proposed in (Popescu and Etzioni 2005): They seek meronymy relationships (part-whole) to identify related features. We use our parser to extract, from our corpus, the most frequent nouns modifying a main concept, i.e. matching the two following syntactic relations:

•MODIFIER-PRE(MAIN-CONCEPT,CANDIDATE-FEATURE), which matches for example "*printer quality*", where "*quality*" would be extracted as a feature candidate.

•MODIFIEUR_PREP[OF](CANDIDATE-FEATURE, MAIN-CONCEPT), which matches for example "*the speed of the machine*" for which "*speed*" would be extracted as a candidate feature.

We calculate the frequencies for each candidate feature, and get a list of 736 feature candidates. To filter the noise, we apply the following heuristic: we consider that a candidate is actually a related feature if it is in attributive syntactic rela-

tion at least once with the adjectives "good" or "bad" in the corpus. These syntactic relations are again extracted automatically using the parser.
At the end, we get a list of 76 related features, the most frequent being: *quality, speed, photo, color, software, cartridge, price, resolution...* A manual verification reveals that these words are indeed related features: they refer either to hardware parts of the products (*cartridge, drum*), functional characteristics (*resolution, speed*) or related concepts (*price, support, warranty*).

4.5 Building the Lexicon

The vocabulary encoding the polarity (positive or negative) associated with subjective words contains adjectives ("beautiful" (positive), "ugly" (negative)), nouns ("talent" (positive), "nuisance" (negative)), verbs ("love" (positive), "hate" (negative)) adverbs, ("admirably" (positive), "annoyingly" (negative)). Many studies address this problem. For example, (Agarwal and Bhattacharyaa 2006) are classifying adjectives according to their polarity by using a small set of "seed" adjectives, of known polarity, and calculate their degree of association with other adjectives in a large corpus, the underlying idea being that close adjectives tend to co-occur. (Vegnaduzzo 2004) also classifies adjectives according to their polarities using seed adjectives and a method based on the distributional similarity of the syntactic context. (Esule and Sebastiani 2006) develop SentiWordnet: they carry out a quantitative analysis of definitions ("glosses") associated with Wordnet synsets using different statistical classifiers to provide three measures for each synset: positivity, negativity and objectivity. This work is particularly challenging and interesting; however, we could not use it in our application, because the ambiguity of each Wordnet lexical entry is preserved. Moreover, this is a very general resource that would not fulfill completely our application needs: for example, the adjective "fast", mainly considered as objective by SentiWordnet, it is either positive ("fast printer") or negative ("fast ink consumption") in printer's domain. As we do not have at our disposal a manually opinion-annotated corpus, we once again used the syntactic dependencies provided by the parser. We automatically extract a set of syntactic relations, on the entire corpus of reviews to select the vocabulary which is potentially subjective. These relationships are filtered according to the presence of a main concept, or an associated feature, or the personal pronoun "I" in a syntactic relationship.

We extract the following relations:

•ATTRIBUTE(CONCEPT|FEATURE,CANDIDATE) to extract nouns and adjectives in attributive position with a main concept or an associated feature, as in "*the **size** of the printer is **huge***";

•ATTRIBUTE(PRON_PERS(I), CANDIDATE), to extract nouns and adjectives in attributive position with the personal pronoun "I" as in "***I** am extremely **unhappy*** ";

•MODIFIER(CONCEPT|FEATURE, CANDIDATE) to extract adjectives modifying a main concept or an associated feature, as in "*It prints **great photos***";

•SUBJECT-VERB_OBJECT(PRON_PERS(I), CANDIDATE, CONCEPT|FEATURE), to extract verbs whose subject is "I" and direct object is a main concept or an associated feature, as in "***I appreciate** the **speed** of the printer*";

•SUBJECT-VERB-OBJECT(CONCEPT|FEATURE, CANDIDATE, PRON_PERS(I)), to extract verbs whose subject is a main concept or a related feature, and object is the personal pronoun "I" as in "***I** am **disappointed** with this **product***";

•SUBJECT-VERB(CONCEPT|FEATURE, CANDIDATE), to extract verbs whose subject is a main concept or a related feature, as in "*this **printer stinks**!*".

The results of the extraction are then filtered according to the syntactic category of the candidate and its number of occurrences in the corpus. Then these candidates are analyzed manually to attach to them the appropriate polarity (positive or negative) and to include them in the general or in the domain-dependant vocabulary. We then use WordNet to find synonyms and antonyms of the selected words. Finally, we obtain 130 verbs in the general lexicon and 42 in the specialized lexicon, 465 adjectives in the general lexicon and 230 in the specialized lexicon, and 145 nouns in the general lexicon and 42 in the specialized lexicon. We thus constructed a "generic" lexicon of polarity, valid for any application and a specialized lexicon, related to the domain of printers.
Moreover, as we work with a robust parser adapted to extract semantic relations of sentiment, the mere mention of polarities in the lexicon is not completely adequate for the development of sentiment extraction rules. It is also necessary to encode information within the predicates in order to be able to detect the scope of the opinions. Typically, we associate semantic features to verbs, indicating if the scope of the opinion is the subject (1), or the direct object of verbs, (2), or on a prepositional complement, (3):
(1) "*These **printers** never cease to **amaze** me.*"

(2) "*I* ***appreciate*** *the* ***swiftness*** *of this machine.*"
(3) "*We have had several* ***problems*** *with a* ***LaserJet.***"

We needed also to add semantic features to domain specific vocabulary occurring in some specific opinion expressions. Indeed, in the domain of printers, examples of type (4) or (5) are frequents:

(4) "*This machine was very* ***easy*** *to* ***setup***".
(5) "*It is so* ***easy*** *to* ***operate.***"

Here, it is the combination [easy + to + verb expressing a functional characteristic of the printer] that denotes a positive opinion. We therefore assigned semantic features for verbs of this type in the specialized lexicon.

At the end of this step, we have an attested list of polar words, enriched with syntactico-semantic information. In order to extend the coverage of the lexicon for adjectives, which are intensively used to express opinions, we combined the methods proposed by (Hatzivassiloglou and McKeown 97) and (Monceau et al 2009). They both use information about syntactic conjunction of adjectives to statistically predict their polarity, the underlying idea being that conjunctions give information about the orientation of adjectives: we use our attested list of polar adjectives enriched with 300 hand-coded objective adjectives to train a standard SVM classifier (SVM-multiclass, (Joachim 1999)). In order to do this, we extract from the British National Corpus[3], with the robust parser, all conjunction relations involving attested polar and objective adjectives, for all types of conjuncts ("and", "or", "neither nor" and "but"). For each adjective (negative, positive or objective), we count the number of times it is coordinated with a negative, positive, or objective adjective, for the four type of conjuncts. These numbers of occurrences are used as the values of 12[4] features to train the 3 classes SVM. We used about 350 attested polar adjectives, and 200 objective adjectives for training, and keep about 100 polar adjectives and 100 objective adjectives for validation. We use the resulting model to classify all unknown adjectives appearing in a coordination relation with an attested adjective within the BNC. We end up with 9692 new adjectives, among which 1777 are classified as negative, 1329 as positive and 6586 as objective. From these results, we manually validated 1302 negative adjectives and 995 positive adjectives, and integrate them into the general polar lexicon.

4.6 Rule Development

Once encoded the polar vocabulary, we developed a set of hand-crafted rules, on top of the output of the deep syntactic parser, to extract semantic relationships denoting opinions. The rules are also divided into two subsets: generic rules and domain-specific rules.

The generic rules are testing, for a semantico-syntactic pattern detected by the parser, the presence of polar vocabulary within the arguments of syntactic relationships. For example:

If(SUBJ-N(#1[polarity,!polarity:!,topic-subj],
#2[main-concept]))
➔ SENTIMENT[polarity](#2,_#1)

Indicates that if the parser has detected that the subject (#2) of a verb (#1) expressing an opinion (feature *polarity*, either positive or negative) is a main concept (feature *main-concept*) then a relationship of sentiment is created using percolation (!polarity:!). This rule associates a positive or negative value to the output relation according to the orientation of the verb. It matches:

- "*These* ***printers#2*** *never cease to* ***amaze#1*** *me*"
- "*I was quite* ***disappointed#1*** *with this* ***machine#2***"

Similar rules are also developed if the scope of the opinion is an associated feature. Moreover, when neither a main concept nor an associated feature is mentioned in the sentence, relations with default values are extracted:

Very nice! → SENTMENT[POS](default,_,nice)
Do not buy! → SENTIMENT[NEG](default,_,buy).

In the current system, about 60 generic rules are developed to cover the majority of structures identified from the corpus study.

We have also focused on the treatment of negation, since this phenomenon reverses the polarity of opinions. This treatment follows two axes. First, we developed rules to deal with the very frequent cases of negation in telegraphic style ("*Not quite as fast as HP says*"), to deal with the interaction between quantification and negation ("*I never had so many problems*") or double negation ("*I cannot say I do not appreciate this printer*"). Then, we developed rules reversing the polarity according to the scope of the negation, built on top of the sentiment relations extracted in the previous processing step. These rules allow to affect the proper polarity to examples like "*I really do not like this feature*"; "*This is not a good photo printer*".

[3] About 100539584 words.
[4] 4 coordination types * 3 classes of adjectives.

In addition, a layer of domain specific rules has been developed, to handle expressions such as:

- *It is **easy** to **set up**.* [Positive]
- *It **uses** a lot of **ink**.* [Negative]

which are specific to the domain: generally "easy" can not be considered as a positive word ("It is easy to lose money" has a negative connotation). However, the association [easy + to + verb indicating a functional characteristic of the printer] expresses a positive opinion. Similarly, a verb of consumption ("consume", "use", "eat" ...) with a consumable item of the printer ("ink", "paper", "cartridge",...) as direct object denotes a negative opinion. About twenty such domain-dependent rules, based on the semantic features encoded in the domain-dependent lexicon, have been developed.

Finally, a few rules take into account the structure of the reviews of the site "Epinion", using some structural clues ("*Cons*", "*Pro*", "*Recommended*"...) to calculate the opinions. For example, "*Cons: none*" indicate a very positive opinion.

The set of sentiment-related rules is now fairly stable. We must continue our development efforts to address the problems of modality, comparisons, and integrate a coreference module to the system.

4.7 Evaluation

As we do not have a corpus of annotated printer reviews, in terms of positive or negative opinion relations, we used the structure of the "Epinion" reviews, in order to assess the performance of our system in a "coarse" way: since the user explicitly states whether he recommends or not the printer, we consider the corpus as annotated for classification. We then use the relations of opinions extracted by our system to train a SVM binary classifier (SVMLight, Joachims 1999) in order to classify the reviews as positive (i.e. recommended) or negative (i.e. not recommended). The experimental setup consists in 313 reviews extracted randomly from the initial corpus to train the SVM classifier, 293 reviews extracted randomly for validation and 2735 reviews extracted randomly for testing. The SVM features are the relations of opinion on a given target and their values are the frequencies of these relations, e.g. OPINION-POSITIVE-on-SPEED:2, OPINION-NEGATIVE-on-PRICE:1 , etc. We calculated the baseline using simple keyword-based SVM classification, without syntactic analysis. We therefore evaluate the system ability to classify documents according to an overall opinion.

Table 1 shows the results obtained on the test corpus (2735 test reviews).

	Favorable reviews	Unfavorable reviews	Total reviews
Number	2066	669	2735
Classified as "positive"	1996	128	2124
Classified as "negative"	70	541	611
Accuracy	97%	81%	93%
Baseline Accuracy	87%	51%	79%

Table 1: Coarse evaluation on the printer corpus

These results are very encouraging since they are in line with state of the art results, obtained for similar classification tasks, cf. (Pang et al. 2002) or (Paroubek et al. 2007).

To validate the quality of our general grammar, and to assess its portability, we conducted a similar second evaluation, in the domain of movie reviews. For this experiment we only use the general opinion extraction grammar and no specialized grammar. The experimental conditions are otherwise exactly the same as before. The results are given in Table II. Results are also very satisfactory. The slight difference is probably due to the lack of specialized grammar rules.

	Favorable Reviews	Unfavorable reviews	Total
Number	1343	420	1763
Classified as positive	1281	122	1403
Classified as negative	62	298	360
Accuracy	95%	71%	89%
Baseline Accuracy	83%	46%	74%

Table 2: Coarse evaluation on the movie corpus

In both cases, the system shows the same trend, it has more difficulty to properly classify unfavorable reviews. There are several explanations for this: first, as the polar vocabulary is partly extracted from the reviews themselves, and as the proportion of unfavorable reviews is small, there might be a coverage problem for the negative vocabulary. Moreover, it seems that the authors use a different discourse whether they recommend o not a product or a film: a brief analysis of the errors on unfavorable reviews shows that authors tend to use comparison with other products or movies they have preferred. For now, our system deals only partially with comparison and does not yet integrate a coreference module, many positive opinions about other products or films are incorrectly credited to the account of the main topic of the review.

In conclusion, we are aware that this is a preliminary evaluation, since our final goal is fine-grained opinion extraction. We plan to make another evaluation, using a reference corpus manually annotated with sentiment relations.

5 Conclusion

In this paper, we present a system extracting opinions on online product reviews. This system uses deep syntactic relations provided by a robust dependency parser in order to extract sentiment relationships. These relationships are intended to instantiate a formal model of representation of the opinions. We have developed semi-automatically a dedicated lexicon associating polarities and semantic features to words. We have then developed a set of generic and domain-dependant hand-crafted rules for extracting relations of opinions. The evaluation of the performances of the system on coarse-grained classification of reviews is very encouraging. We will pursue the developments in order to take account complex linguistic phenomena not yet well not covered, namely comparative constructions, modality and coreference. The coreference module pre-exists but requires modifications for its integration within our system. We then plan to conduct a fine-grained evaluation.

References

A. Agarwal, P. Bhattacharya. 2006. Augmenting Wordnet with Polarity Information on Adjectives. *3rd International Wordnet Conference*, Jeju Island, Korea, South Jeju (Seogwipo)

Salah Ait-Mokthar, Jean-Pierre Chanod. 2002, Robustness beyond Shallowness: Incremental Dependency Parsing. *Special Issue of NLE Journal*.

E. Charton, R. Acuna-Agosy. 2007. Quel modèle pour détecter une opinion? Trois propositions pour généraliser l'extraction d'une idée dans un corpus, *Deft'07*, Grenoble.

X. Ding, B. Liu, P.Yu. 2008. A Holistic Lexicon-Based Approach to Opinion Mining. *Proceedings of the international conference on Web search and web data mining*, WSDM '08, ACM.

E. Dubreil, M. Vernier, L. Monceaux, B. Daille. 2008. Annotating Opinion – Evaluation of Blogs, Workshop on LREC 2008 Conference, Sentiment Analysis: Metaphor, Ontology and Terminology (EMOT-08), Marrakech, Morocco.

A. Esuli, F. Sebastiani. 2006. SENTIWORDNET: A Publicly Available Lexical Resource for Opinion Mining. In 5th Conference on Language Resources and Evaluation (LREC'06), pp. 417-422.

C. Hagège, C. Roux. 2002. Entre syntaxe et sémantique: normalisation de la sortie de l'analyse syntaxique en vue de l'amélioration de l'extraction d'information à partir de textes. *TALN 2003*, Batz-sur-Mer, France, 11-14 Juin.

M. Hu, B. Liu. 2004. Mining and summarizing customer reviews. ACM SIGKDD International Conference on Knowledge Discovery & Data Mining (KDD-2004), Seattle, Washington, USA.

T. Joachims. 1999: Making large-Scale SVM Learning Practical. Advances in Kernel Methods - Support Vector Learning, B. Schölkopf and C. Burges and A. Smola (ed.), MIT Press.

V. Hatzivassiloglou, K. McKeown. 1997. Predicting the semantic orientation of adjectives. In Proceedings of the Joint ACL/EACL Conference, pp. 174–181.

B. Liu. 2010. Sentiment Analysis and Subjectivity, Chapter of Handbook of Natural Language Processing, 2nd edition.

L. Monceaux, B. Daille, E. Dubreil 2009. Catégorisation des évaluations dans un corpus de blogs multi-domaine. Revue des nouvelles technologies de l'information (RNTI).

B. Pang, L. Lee, S. Vaithyanathan. 2002. Thumbs up? Sentiment classification using machine learning techniques. In Proceedings of the Conference on Empirical Methods in Natural Language Processing (EMNLP), pages 79–86.

P. Paroubek Berthelin J.B., El Ayari S., Grouin C., Heitz T., Hurault-Plantet M., Jardino M., Khalis Z., Lastes M. 2007. Résultats de l'édition 2007 du DÉfi Fouille de Textes, *Deft'07*, Grenoble.

A. Popescu, O. Etzioni. 2005. Extracting product features and opinions from reviews. Actes de Conference on Empirical Methods in Natural Language Processing (EMNLP).

S. Vegnaduzzo. 2004. Acquisition of subjective adjectives with limited resources. Actes de AAAI spring symposium on exploring attitude and affect in text: Theories and Applications, Stanford, US.

J. Yi, T. Nasukawa, A. Valerio, H. Zhang. 2003. Sentiment Analyzer: Extracting Sentiments about a Given Topic Using natural Language Processing Techniques. ICDM'03: 3rd IEEE International Conference on Data Mining, pp. 427.

Hong Yu, Vassileos Hazivassiloglou. 2003. Towards Answering Opinion Questions: Separating Facts from Opinions and Identifying the Polarity of Opinions, EMNLP 2003, Sapporo, Japan.

Using Visual Information to Predict Lexical Preference

Shane Bergsma
Dept. of Computer Science and HLTCOE
Johns Hopkins University
sbergsma@jhu.edu

Randy Goebel
Dept. of Computing Science
University of Alberta
goebel@cs.ualberta.ca

Abstract

Most NLP systems make predictions based solely on linguistic (textual or spoken) input. We show how to use *visual* information to make better *linguistic* predictions. We focus on selectional preference; specifically, determining the plausible noun arguments for particular verb predicates. For each argument noun, we extract visual features from corresponding images on the web. For each verb predicate, we train a classifier to select the visual features that are indicative of its preferred arguments. We show that for certain verbs, using visual information can significantly improve performance over a baseline. For the successful cases, visual information is useful even in the presence of co-occurrence information derived from web-scale text. We assess a variety of training configurations, which vary over classes of visual features, methods of image acquisition, and numbers of images.

1 Introduction

Selectional preferences quantify the plausibility of predicate-argument pairs. We focus on predicting the plausibility of a noun argument (e.g. *pasta*) occurring as the direct object of a verb predicate (e.g. *eat*). Such knowledge is useful since many NLP tasks require determining the actual argument from the alternatives that arise because of syntactic, semantic or anaphoric ambiguity. Previous uses of selectional preferences include prepositional-phrase attachment (Hindle and Rooth, 1993), word-sense disambiguation (Resnik, 1997), pronoun resolution (Dagan and Itai, 1990), and semantic role labeling (Erk, 2007).

The compatibility of a predicate and an argument can be quantified by counting how often they occur together in a large text corpus (Hindle and Rooth, 1993), but many plausible pairs are absent even from web-scale text (Bergsma et al., 2008). We therefore seek to *generalize* from observed pairs in order to make inferences for unseen combinations. Some approaches back off to counts over argument classes (Resnik, 1996; Rooth et al., 1999; Clark and Weir, 2002; Ó Séaghdha, 2010; Ritter et al., 2010), Others interpolate over similar words (Dagan et al., 1999; Erk, 2007). Text-based approaches work best for arguments that are *frequent* in text, but, paradoxically, frequent arguments are the arguments for which generalization is least needed. This provides motivation to look beyond text in order to make better predictions for infrequent or out-of-vocabulary arguments.

We propose using *visual* features to identify a verb's preferred arguments. Visual information may play a role in the human acquisition of word meaning (Feng and Lapata, 2010b). For computers, there is a massive amount of visual data to exploit. Billions of images are added to websites like Facebook and Flickr every month. The challenge of associating words and images is reduced because many users label their images as they post them online, providing an explicit link between a word and its visual depiction. Bergsma and Van Durme (2011) used these explicit word-image connections in order to find words in different languages having the same meaning (translations); pairs of words are proposed as translations if their visual depictions are visually similar.

In this paper, we use online images to help predict a predicate's selectional preferences. For each verb-noun pair, (v, n), we retrieve labeled images of n from the web, and apply computer vision techniques to extract visual features from the images. We then use the DSP model of Bergsma et al. (2008) to combine the visual features collected for n into a single plausibility score for (v, n). In the original DSP model, each verb has a corre-

Figure 1: Which out-of-vocabulary nouns are plausible direct objects for the verb *eat*? Each row corresponds to a noun: 1. *migas*, 2. *zeolite*, 3. *carillon*, 4. *ficus*, 5. *mamey* and 6. *manioc*.

sponding classifier that scores noun arguments on the basis of various *textual* features. We use this discriminative framework to incorporate the visual information as new, *visual* features.

Our experiments evaluate the ability of these classifiers to correctly predict the selectional preferences of a small set of verbs. We evaluate two cases: 1) the case where the nouns are all assumed to be out-of-vocabulary, and the classifiers must make predictions without any corpus-based co-occurrence information, and 2) the case where we assume access to noun-verb co-occurrence information derived from web-scale N-gram data.

We show that visual features are useful for some verbs, but not for others. For verbs taking abstract arguments without definitive visual features, the classifier can often learn to disregard the visual data. On the other hand, for verbs taking *physical* arguments (such as food, animals, or people), the classifier can make accurate predictions using the nouns' visual properties. In these cases, visual information remains useful even after incorporating the web-scale statistics.

2 Visual Selectional Preference

Consider determining whether the nouns *carillon*, *migas* and *mamey* are plausible arguments for the verb *eat*. Existing systems are unlikely to have such words in their training data, let alone information about their edibility. However, after inspecting a few images returned by a Google search for these words (Figure 1), a human might reasonably predict which words are edible. Humans make this determination by observing both intrinsic visual properties (pits, skins, rounded shapes and fruity colors) and extrinsic visual context (circular plates, bowls, and other food-related tools) (Oliva and Torralba, 2007).

We propose using similar information to predict the plausibility of arbitrary verb-noun pairs. That is, we aim to learn the distinguishing visual features of all nouns that are plausible arguments for a given verb. This differs from work that has aimed to recognize, annotate and retrieve objects defined by a single phrase, such as *tree* or *wrist watch* (Feng and Lapata, 2010a). These approaches learn from labeled images during training in order to assign words to unlabeled images during testing. In contrast, we analyze labeled images (during training and testing) in order to determine their visual compatibility with a given predicate. Our approach does not need labeled training images for a *specific* noun in order to assess that noun during testing; e.g. we can make a reasonable prediction for the plausibility of *eat mamey* even if we've never encountered *mamey* before.

We now specify how we automatically 1) download a set of images for each noun, 2) extract visual features from each image, and 3) combine the visual features from multiple images into plausibility scores. Scripts, code and data are available at: `www.clsp.jhu.edu/~sbergsma/ImageSP/`.

2.1 Mining noun images from the web

To obtain a set of images for a particular noun argument, we submit the noun as a query to either the Flickr photo-sharing website (`www.flickr.com`), or Google's image search (`www.google.com/imghp`). In both cases, we download the thumbnails on the results page directly rather than downloading the source images. Flickr returns images by matching the query against user-provided tags and accompanying text. Google retrieves images based on the image caption, file-name, and surrounding text (Feng and Lapata, 2010a). Images obtained from Google are known to be competitive with "hand prepared datasets" for training object recognizers (Fergus et al., 2005).

2.2 Extracting visual features from images

A range of features have been developed in the vision community, typically with the aim of improving content-based image retrieval (Deselaers et al., 2008). We follow previous work in using features in a *bag-of-words* representation that ignores the spacial relationship between image components.

Color Histogram Our first set of features are extracted from the color histogram of the image. We partition the color space by dividing the R, G, and B values of the pixel colors into equal-sized bins. For a given image, we count the number of pixels that occur within each RGB bin. Each color bin and its count is used as a feature dimension and its value, respectively. We describe how we choose the number of bins in Section 3.

SIFT Keypoints Additional features are derived from the image's SIFT (scale-invariant feature transform) keypoints (Lowe, 2004). SIFT keypoints are detected at visually-distinct image locations. Each keypoint has a corresponding *descriptor vector* that identifies a location's unique visual properties. SIFT keypoints are conceptually similar to local features identified by so-called *corner detectors*. Corner detectors find image locations that have "large gradients in all directions at a predetermined scale" (Lowe, 2004). Unlike typical corner detectors, SIFT keypoints are invariant to scaling and rotation. They are also robust to illumination, noise and distortion. We identify SIFT keypoints using David Lowe's software: `www.cs.ubc.ca/~lowe/keypoints/`. SIFT keypoints are taken from images converted to grayscale.

Since each keypoint is itself a vector, we quantize the keypoints by mapping them to a set of K discrete visual words. This set of words forms the visual vocabulary of our bag-of-words representation. The set of words is obtained by clustering a random selection of keypoints into K cluster centroids using the K-means algorithm. The final feature representation for an image consists of a feature dimension for each visual word; each feature value is the number of keypoints in the image that have that word as their nearest centroid.

We generate different clusterings (and thus different vocabularies) separately for each verb predicate. For each verb, we randomly sample 500,000 keypoints from the set of downloaded images for that verb's potential argument nouns, and run the clustering over these keypoints. Section 3 describes how we choose the number of clusters, K.

2.3 Combining features with the DSP model

We use DSP (Bergsma et al., 2008) to generate a plausibility score for a verb-noun pair, (v, n). Let Φ be a function that generates features for nouns, $\Phi : n \rightarrow (\phi_1 ... \phi_k)$. We explain below how, for each n, we aggregate visual features across multiple images to create features in $\Phi(n)$. DSP determines whether n is a plausible argument of v by scoring $\Phi(n)$ using a verb-specific set of learned weights, $\boldsymbol{w}_v = (w_1 ... w_k)$. The weights are trained for each v in order to distinguish the verb's positive nouns from its negatives in training data (the generation of training data is also explained below). The weights can be learned using any binary classification algorithm; we use logistic regression. At test time, we generate a final compatibility score (prediction) via the logistic function:

$$\text{Score}(v, n) = \frac{exp(\boldsymbol{w}_v \cdot \Phi(n))}{1 + exp(\boldsymbol{w}_v \cdot \Phi(n))} \quad (1)$$

Our discriminative model differs from a recent generative model over words and visual features by Feng and Lapata (2010b). In that work, including visual features resulted in better topic clusters, which indirectly improved (topic-derived) word-word associations. In our work, visual features are directly exploited by a discriminative model, allowing us to use arbitrary and potentially interdependent visual attributes in our representation.

Generating Examples We follow Bergsma et al. (2008)'s approach by first calculating the pointwise mutual information (PMI) between predicate verbs and (direct object) argument nouns in a large parsed corpus. For each verb predicate, v, we create positive examples, (v, n), by pairing v with *all* nouns, n, such that v and n have a positive PMI, i.e. $\text{PMI}(v, n) > 0$. For each of these positives pairs (e.g. *eat pasta*), we generate two *pseudo*-negative examples, (v, n'), by randomly pairing v with some nouns n' that either did not occur with v (and hence PMI is undefined) or have $\text{PMI}(v, n') \leq 0$ (e.g., *eat distribution, eat wheelchair*). As in Bergsma et al. (2008), pseudo-negatives n' are chosen to have similar corpus frequency to the original positive noun, n.

We use this approach to generate both training examples for learning the DSP classifier and also separate test examples for evaluating the model's predictions. We train and evaluate a classifier for each v separately from all other verbs. For each v, we take 85% of examples for training, 7.5% for development, and 7.5% for final testing.

Generating Features The DSP model allows us to use any information that might indicate a noun's compatibility with a verb; we simply encode this information as features in the noun's feature representation, $\Phi(n)$. Bergsma et al. used DSP's flexibility to include novel string-based features of the noun argument (e.g., the verb *become* prefers lower-case direct objects; *accuse* prefers capitalized ones). We augment $\Phi(n)$ with visual features.

Since we download multiple images for each noun, n, we have multiple color histograms and multiple bags of SIFT keypoints. To generate a single feature representation, $\Phi(n)$, we first sum the color and SIFT-keypoint feature vectors, respectively, across all the images in n's image set. We then normalize each sum vector to unit length, and include all of the resulting normalized features as additional features in $\Phi(n)$.

In summary, we can produce a score for a (v, n) pair at test time as follows: 1) select the appropriate weights, $\boldsymbol{w}_v$, for verb v, 2) generate the composite (normalized) feature vector, $\Phi(n)$, for noun n, and 3) score the features with the weights using the formula for $\text{Score}(v, n)$ (Equation (1) above). In practice, this score is exactly what is returned by our logistic regression software package. We can use this score directly, or, for hard classifications, predict positive if the returned probability is greater than 0.5 and otherwise predict negative.

3 Experimental Set-up

Task and Data The task is to predict whether a particular verb-noun pair, previously unseen during training of the DSP classifier, is a positive or a negative example, as defined in Section 2.3 above. We evaluate using *Accuracy*: the proportion of examples correctly classified on test data. We calculate significance using *McNemar's test*.

Since the negatives are pseudo-negatives, this kind of evaluation is also known as a pseudo-disambiguation evaluation. While the set-up of pseudo-disambiguation evaluations has varied in NLP (Chambers and Jurafsky, 2010), we use an identical set-up to Bergsma et al. (2008): we generate positive and negative examples for DSP from a parsed and processed copy of the AQUAINT corpus, and use the same PMI-threshold (i.e. 0) and positive-to-negative ratio (i.e. 1:2).

We evaluate on nouns in the direct object position of seven verbs: *eat*, *inform*, *hit*, *kill*, *park*, *hunt* and *shoot down*. The total number of training examples for these verbs varies from roughly 500 to 10,000 instances, while the number of test instances varies from roughly 50 to 1000 instances.

We chose these seven verbs as test cases because we speculated they might benefit from visual information to different degrees (e.g. we expected indicative food-features for *eat*, but perhaps less helpful human-features for *inform*, etc.). Ideally one would like to automatically categorize all the verbs for which visual features might be helpful, but it is natural to first demonstrate the benefits of visual information in certain cases in order to motivate further study. Importantly, note that while we hand-selected a set of verb predicates, our evaluation data is based on real observed arguments of these predicates, and in particular not on nouns for which we would *a priori* expect visual information to be predictive. Our evaluation is thus focused, but realistic.

Classifier In all cases, we use an L2-regularized logistic regression model for DSP's base classifier, and train it via LIBLINEAR (Fan et al., 2008). We optimize the regularization parameter on the development data.

Visual Features For each noun,[1] we take the first six images returned from both Google and Flickr, and extract the corresponding visual features as described above. While we later discovered that the more images we have, the better the results (Figure 2), we initially decided to use only six images mainly for computational reasons; downloading and processing images is space and time-intensive.

Rather than selecting fixed values for the size of the color bins and the number of SIFT centroids, we take advantage of our model's flexibility to use features over different granularities: we use separate features with both 64 and 512 color bins, and with both 100 and 1000 SIFT centroids. The flexibility to include visual information at different levels of granularity is one of the chief advantages of the discriminative model.

Test Configurations We are primarily interested in whether visual information can lead to

[1]For a given verb in our corpus, DSP actually provides plausibility scores for both nouns and multi-word noun phrases; we refer to both of these as 'nouns' for convenience.

System	*eat*	*inform*	*hit*	*kill*	*park*	*hunt*	*shoot down*	Average
Baseline	68.3	68.0	68.7	67.7	69.9	67.6	70.0	68.6
+ Visual Features via Flickr	75.8	68.0	**68.8**	67.2	69.9	69.6	70.0	69.9
+ Visual Features via Google	***79.5***	**68.2**	68.7	***68.5***	69.9	***76.5***	**72.0**	**71.9**

Table 1: Using visual features from Google significantly improves accuracy (%) over the baseline system on *eat* ($p<0.001$), *kill* ($p<0.1$) and *hunt* ($p<0.1$).

better predictions on out-of-vocabulary (OOV) nouns, but obtaining a sufficiently-large test set of labeled OOV instances is difficult. We therefore first provide results on *simulated* OOV arguments (Section 4.1), where we assume no corpus-based knowledge is available to the DSP classifier. That is, we initially exclude corpus-based features from our models. We compare visual models to ones that only use features for the noun string (such features are always available). Our string features are binary features that indicate the 'shape' of the noun via the regular expression maps: [A-Z]+ → A, and [a-z]+ → a. E.g., *Al Unser Jr.* will have the one feature '*Aa Aa Aa.*'.

In the second part of our results (Section 4.2), we test whether visual information can help even in the presence of high-quality corpus-based features. We use Keller and Lapata (2003)'s approach to obtain web-scale co-occurrence frequencies for the verb-noun pair. That is, we retrieve counts for the pattern "V Det N" from a web-scale Google N-gram corpus (Lin et al., 2010). Here, V is any inflection of the verb, Det is *the*, *a*, *an*, or the empty string, and N is the noun. We include the log-count of this pattern as a feature, and also include separate features for the log-counts of the noun and verb themselves. By multiplying these features by appropriate weights, a classifier can generate a (web-based) PMI score.

4 Results

4.1 Results on OOV nouns

We now compare the use of visual features to string-based features alone (Baseline), simulating out-of-vocabulary arguments by assuming no corpus-based knowledge is available for the noun features. For these verbs, we actually found the Baseline with only string features to be no better than picking the majority-class.

Visual features significantly improve performance for 3 of the verbs (Table 1). Visual features do not improve (but also do not impair) accuracy on the verbs that have mostly abstract or general arguments. For example, one can "*hit turbulence*," "*hit record*," or "*hit the slopes*," but there are no visual features that can help select these nouns. Macro-averaged accuracy across all verbs increases from a baseline of 68.6% to 71.9% using Google-derived visual features.

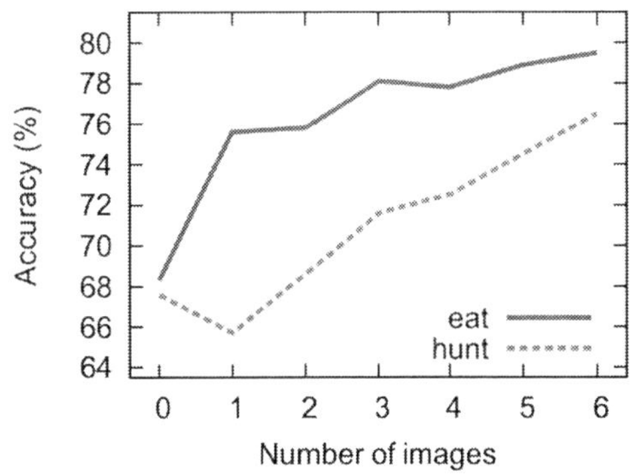

Figure 2: The more images, the more accurate: Performance on the verbs *eat* and *hunt* as features are extracted from a varying number of images.

The features obtained from Google images perform better than features from Flickr (Table 1). Inspecting the retrieved image sets, we observe that compared to Flickr, Google tends to retrieve more consistent, more canonical images for a particular noun. For example, Google's top results for the query "buffalo" are exclusively images of buffalo animals. On Flickr, "buffalo" returns images of the city of Buffalo, buffalo hides, and pictures of buffalo animals alongside people, cars, birds, etc. For our purposes, the consistency of the Google images is better; it makes learning and predicting easier for the visual classifier.

We provide further analysis using Google images only. Figure 2 shows that, as we use more images, accuracy on the verbs *eat* and *hunt* improves and is not yet leveling off. With computation only linear in the number of images, adding even more images is one possible way to improve accuracy.

Table 2 shows the contribution of the two visual feature types for classifying arguments involving

Features	Accuracy
All Features	79.5
-Color Histogram	78.4
-SIFT Keypoint	78.1
-Color & -SIFT	68.3

Table 2: Accuracy on *eat* as different feature classes are removed.

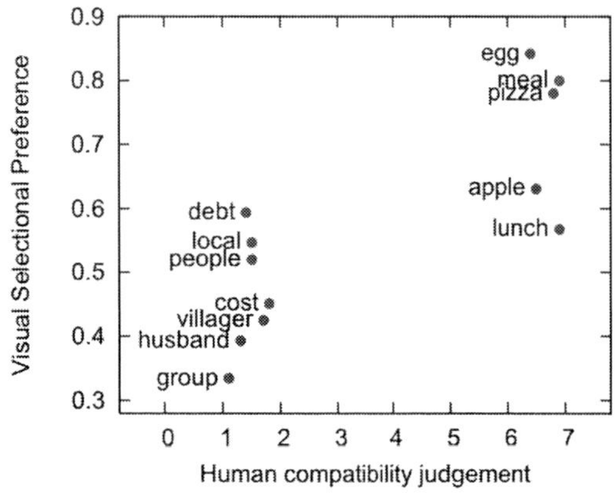

Figure 3: Visual selectional preference correlates well with human judgments: arguments of the verb *eat* are plotted using visual and average human compatibility scores.

the verb *eat*. Either visual feature type helps a lot on its own; together they further improve accuracy.

We also tried replacing our logistic classifier with kernelized SVMs, which have previously proved useful for object recognition (Chapelle et al., 1999). While kernel-SVMs can implicitly consider all combinations of features (resulting in the encoding of richer visual information), we found the resulting gains over linear classifiers to be minimal. The kernelized SVMs also took much longer to train and apply. The further development of effective while still efficient visual features remains an important direction for future work.

Figure 3 compares the scores of the visual system (computed via Equation (1)) to human plausibility judgments (described by Padó et al. (2006)).[2] The human scores are the average judgments for the question, "how common is it to *eat* X?" where X is a given noun. Participants responded with scores from 1 (very uncommon) to 7 (very common). These average judgments have a high correlation with our predicted scores; the

[2]Available online at `http://www.nlpado.de/~ulrike/data/pado_plausibility.tgz`

System	*eat*	*kill*	*hunt*
Baseline	68.3	67.7	67.6
+ Visual Features alone	79.5	68.5	76.5
+ Web Co-occ alone	85.1	74.0	76.5
+ Web Co-occ & Visual	**85.7**	**74.3**	**78.4**

Table 3: Visual features improve accuracy (%) even when web co-occurrence information is used.

Pearson correlation coefficient is 0.803. The visual system does a good job on the nouns *egg*, *meal*, *pizza* and *apple*, but ranks *debt* above (the somewhat abstract) *lunch*. Looking at the Google images for *lunch*, we note that clearer pictures of food occur beyond the top 6 images, and hence using more images would likely improve scoring.

Finally, we note that for *eat*, we found the visual system's accuracy was consistent across nouns of different frequencies. This contrasts with systems using text-based features; these perform much better on more frequent nouns (Bergsma et al., 2008).

4.2 Results with web-scale statistics

We have shown that visual information can result in significantly improved performance in cases where no corpus-based information is available. Do these gains hold up when high-quality corpus-based information is available?

On those verbs where visual information helped in the OOV setting, visual information remains helpful even with features encoding web-scale co-occurrence statistics (Table 3).[3] Note the gains from adding visual features are consistent in all three cases, but not statistically significant, as the proportion of nouns where the visual features can help is now much smaller.

These final results are somewhat sobering. Visual information is not helpful for every verb, and even in the positive cases, it is not very helpful when combined with existing text-based features. However, the exploitation of visual information is still in its infancy in NLP. Using search engines to obtain images for NLP today is perhaps similar to how search engines were also used to obtain web-scale *text* statistics for NLP a decade ago. While we leveraged a relatively small number of visual features from a relatively small number of images,

[3]Not surprisingly, on the verbs where visual features were not effective earlier, visual features remains ineffective here; these features tend to actually impair performance when added to the web-scale co-occurrence features.

future advances in computer vision and large-scale data processing will allow richer visual information to be extracted and applied to NLP problems.

5 Conclusion

We have shown that it is possible to predict verb-noun selectional preference purely on the basis of visual information. For a given noun, web images are downloaded, processed, and then analyzed by classifiers corresponding to different verbs. Each verb classifier is trained to identify the visual properties that distinguish the verb's preferred arguments. Statistically-significant improvements were obtained on three verbs and visual data remains helpful even in the presence of high-quality web-scale co-occurrence information.

These results give us a good basis for moving forward. We know where we should get our images (Google), which features are useful (both color and SIFT) and how many images to use (as many as possible). It remains to be seen which other predicates, which other predicate-argument relationships, and which other NLP problems can benefit from visual information.

References

S. Bergsma and B. Van Durme. 2011. Learning bilingual lexicons using the visual similarity of labeled web images. In *Proc. IJCAI*.

S. Bergsma, D. Lin, and R. Goebel. 2008. Discriminative learning of selectional preference from unlabeled text. In *Proc. EMNLP*, pages 59–68.

N. Chambers and D. Jurafsky. 2010. Improving the use of pseudo-words for evaluating selectional preferences. In *Proc. ACL*, pages 445–453.

O. Chapelle, P. Haffner, and V. Vapnik. 1999. Support vector machines for histogram-based image classification. *IEEE Transactions on Neural Networks*, 10(5):1055–1064.

S. Clark and D. Weir. 2002. Class-based probability estimation using a semantic hierarchy. *Computational Linguistics*, 28(2):187–206.

I. Dagan and A. Itai. 1990. Automatic processing of large corpora for the resolution of anaphora references. In *Proc. COLING*, pages 330–332.

I. Dagan, L. Lee, and F. C. N. Pereira. 1999. Similarity-based models of word cooccurrence probabilities. *Mach. Learn.*, 34(1-3):43–69.

T. Deselaers, D. Keysers, and H. Ney. 2008. Features for image retrieval: an experimental comparison. *Information Retrieval*, 11:77–107.

K. Erk. 2007. A simple, similarity-based model for selectional preference. In *Proc. ACL*, pages 216–223.

R.-E. Fan, K.-W. Chang, C.-J. Hsieh, X.-R. Wang, and C.-J. Lin. 2008. LIBLINEAR: A library for large linear classification. *Journal of Machine Learning Research*, 9:1871–1874.

Y. Feng and M. Lapata. 2010a. Topic models for image annotation and text illustration. In *Proc. HLT-NAACL*, pages 831–839.

Y. Feng and M. Lapata. 2010b. Visual information in semantic representation. In *Proc. HLT-NAACL*, pages 91–99.

R. Fergus, L. Fei-Fei, P. Perona, and A. Zisserman. 2005. Learning object categories from Google's Image Search. In *Proc. ICCV*, pages 1816–1823.

D. Hindle and M. Rooth. 1993. Structural ambiguity and lexical relations. *Computational Linguistics*, 19(1):103–120.

F. Keller and M. Lapata. 2003. Using the web to obtain frequencies for unseen bigrams. *Computational Linguistics*, 29(3):459–484.

D. Lin, K. Church, H. Ji, S. Sekine, D. Yarowsky, S. Bergsma, K. Patil, E. Pitler, R. Lathbury, V. Rao, K. Dalwani, and S. Narsale. 2010. New tools for web-scale N-grams. In *Proc. LREC*, pages 2221–2227.

D. G. Lowe. 2004. Distinctive image features from scale-invariant keypoints. *IJCV*, 60:91–110.

D. Ó Séaghdha. 2010. Latent variable models of selectional preference. In *Proc. ACL*, pages 435–444.

A. Oliva and A. Torralba. 2007. The role of context in object recognition. *Trends in Cognitive Sciences*, 11(12):520–527.

U. Padó, F. Keller, and M. Crocker. 2006. Combining syntax and thematic fit in a probabilistic model of sentence processing. In *Proc. CogSci*, pages 657–662.

P. Resnik. 1996. Selectional constraints: An information-theoretic model and its computational realization. *Cognition*, 61:127–159.

P. Resnik. 1997. Selectional preference and sense disambiguation. In *Proc. ACL SIGLEX Workshop on Tagging Text with Lexical Semantics: Why, What, and How?*

A. Ritter, Mausam, and O. Etzioni. 2010. A latent dirichlet allocation method for selectional preferences. In *Proc. ACL*, pages 424–434.

M. Rooth, S. Riezler, D. Prescher, G. Carroll, and F. Beil. 1999. Inducing a semantically annotated lexicon via EM-based clustering. In *Proc. ACL*, pages 104–111.

Systematic Knowledge Acquisition for Question Analysis

Dat Quoc Nguyen[†,♯] and **Dai Quoc Nguyen**[†,♯] and **Son Bao Pham**[†,‡]
[†] Faculty of Information Technology
University of Engineering and Technology
Vietnam National University, Hanoi
{datnq, dainq, sonpb}@vnu.edu.vn
[‡] Information Technology Institute
Vietnam National University, Hanoi

Abstract

For the task of turning a natural language question into an explicit intermediate representation of the complexity in question answering systems, all published works so far use rule-based approach to the best of our knowledge. We believe it is because of the complexity of the representation and the variety of question types and also there are no publicly available corpus of a decent size. In these rule-based approaches, the process of creating rules is not discussed. It is clear that manually creating the rules in an ad-hoc manner is very expensive and error-prone. In this paper, we focus on the process of creating those rules manually, in a way that consistency between rules is maintained and the effort to create a new rule is independent of the size of the current rule set. Experimental results are promising where our system achieves better performance and requires much less time and cognitive load compared to previous work.

1 Introduction

The goal of question answering systems is to give answers to the user's questions instead of ranked lists of related documents as used by most current search engines (Hirschman and Gaizauskas, 2001). Natural language question analysis component is the first component in any question answering systems. This component creates an intermediate representation of the input question, which is expressed in natural language, to be utilized in the rest of the system.

In this paper, we introduce a language independent approach to systematically build a knowledge base for analyzing natural language questions. Natural language questions will be transformed into intermediate representation elements which include construction type of question, class of question, keywords in question and semantic constraints between them.

Some question answering systems such as Aqualog (Lopez et al., 2007) and Vietnamese question answering system (VnQAS) (Nguyen et al., 2009) manually defined a list of sequence pattern structures to analyze questions. As rules are created in an ad-hoc manner, these systems share a common difficulty in managing interaction between rules and keeping consistency. In our approach, we present an approach utilizing Ripple Down Rules (Compton and Jansen, 1990) (Richards, 2009) knowledge acquisition methodology to acquire rules in a systematic manner which avoids unintended interaction between rules.

In section 2, we provide some related works and describe our overall system architecture in section 3. We present our knowledge acquisition approach for question analysis in section 4. We describe our experiments in section 5. Discussion and conclusion will be presented in section 6.

[♯]Both authors contributed equally to this work.

2 Related works

2.1 Question analysis in question answering systems

Early NLIDB systems used pattern-matching technique to process user's question and generate corresponding answer (Androutsopoulos, 1995). A common technique for parsing input questions in NLIDB approaches is syntax analysis where a natural language question is directly mapped to a database query (such as SQL) through grammar rules. Nguyen and Le (Nguyen and Le, 2008) introduced a NLIDB question answering system in Vietnamese employing semantic grammars. Their system includes two main modules: QTRAN and TGEN. QTRAN (Query Translator) maps a natural language question to an SQL query while TGEN (Text Generator) generates answers based on the query result tables. QTRAN uses limited context-free grammars to analyze user's question into syntax tree via CYK algorithm.

Recently, some question answering systems that used semantic annotations generated high results in natural language question analysis. A well known annotation based framework is GATE (Cunningham et al., 2002) which have been used in many question answering systems especially for the natural language question analysis module such as Aqualog (Lopez et al., 2007), QuestIO (Damljanovic et al., 2008), VnQAS (Nguyen et al., 2009).

Aqualog and VnQAS are ontology-based question answering systems for English and Vietnamese respectively. Both systems take a natural language question and an ontology as its input, and return answers for users based on the semantic analysis of the question and the corresponding elements in the ontology. General architecture of these systems can be described as a waterfall model where a natural language question is mapped to an intermediate representation. The subsequent modules of the system process the intermediate representation to provide queries with respect to the input ontology. These systems perform semantic and syntactic analysis of the input question through the use of processing resources wrapped as GATE plug-ins such as word segmentation, sentence segment and part-of-speech tagging.

2.2 Single Classification Ripple Down Rules

In this section we present the basic idea of Ripple-Down Rules (RDR) (Compton and Jansen, 1990) which inspired our approach. RDR allows one to add rules to a knowledge base incrementally without the need of a knowledge engineer. A new rule is only created when the KB performs unsatisfactorily on a given case. The rule represents an explanation for why the conclusion should be different from the KB's conclusion on the case at hand.

A Single Classification Ripple Down Rules (SCRDR) tree is a binary tree with two distinct types of edges. These edges are typically called *except* and *if-not* edges. Associated with each node in a tree is a *rule*. A rule has the form: *if* α *then* β where α is called the *condition* and β the *conclusion*.

Cases in SCRDR are evaluated by passing a case (a sentence to be classified in our case for example) to the root of the tree. At any node in the tree, if the condition of a node N's rule is satisfied by the case, the case is passed on to the exception child of N using the *except* link if it exists. Otherwise, the case is passed on to the N's *if-not* child. The conclusion given by this process is the conclusion from the last node in the RDR tree which *fired* (satisfied by the case). To ensure that a conclusion is always given, the root node typically contains a trivial condition which is always satisfied. This node is called the *default* node.

A new node is added to an SCRDR tree when the evaluation process returns the wrong conclusion. The new node is attached to the last node in the evaluation path of the given case with the *except* link if the last node is the *fired* rule. Otherwise, it is attached with the *if-not* link.

RDR based approaches have been used to tackle NLP tasks such as POS tagging (Nguyen et al., 2011), text classification and information extraction (Pham and Hoffmann, 2006).

3 Our Question Answering System Architecture

The architecture of our question answering system is shown in Figure 1. It includes two components: the Natural language question analysis engine and the Answer retrieval.

The question analysis component consists of three modules: preprocessing, syntactic analysis and semantic analysis. It takes the user question as an input and returns a query-tuple representing the question in a compact form. The role of this intermediate representation is to provide structured information of the input question for later processing such as retrieving answers. Our contribution focuses on the semantic analysis module by proposing a rule language and a systematic processing to create rules in a way that interaction between rules are controlled and consistency are maintained.

Similar to VnQAS (Nguyen et al., 2009), the answer retrieval component includes two main modules: Ontology Mapping and Answer Extraction. It takes an intermediate representation produced by the question analysis component and an Ontology as its input to generate semantic answers.

To set the context for the discussion on the systematic knowledge acquisition process in the semantic analysis module, we will describe our question analysis component in details.

We wrapped existing linguistic processing modules for Vietnamese such as Word Segmentation, Part-of-speech tagger (Pham et al., 2009) as GATE plug-ins. Results of the modules are annotations capturing information such as sentences, words, nouns and verbs. Each annotation has a set of feature-value pairs. For example, a word has a feature *category* storing its part-of-speech tag. This information can then be reused for further processing in subsequent modules. New modules are specifically designed to handle Vietnamese questions using patterns over existing linguistic annotations. This is achieved using GATE JAPE (Java Annotation Pattern Engine) transducers, a set of JAPE grammars. A JAPE grammar allows one to specify regular expression pattern based on semantic annotations.

3.1 Preprocessing module

The preprocessing module generates *TokenVn* annotations representing a Vietnamese word with features such as part-of-speech. Vietnamese is a monosyllabic language; hence, a word may contain more than one token.

However, the Vietnamese word segmentation module is not trained for question domain. There are question phrases, which are indicative of the question categories such as *"phải không"*, tagged as multiple *TokenVn* annotations. In this module we identify those phrases and mark them as single annotations with corresponding feature *"question-word"* and its semantic categories such as $HowWhy_{cause\ |\ method}$, $YesNo_{true\ or\ false}$, $What_{something}$, $When_{time\ |\ date}$, $Where_{location}$, $Many_{number}$, Who_{person}. In fact, this information will be used in creating rules in the semantic analysis module at a later stage.

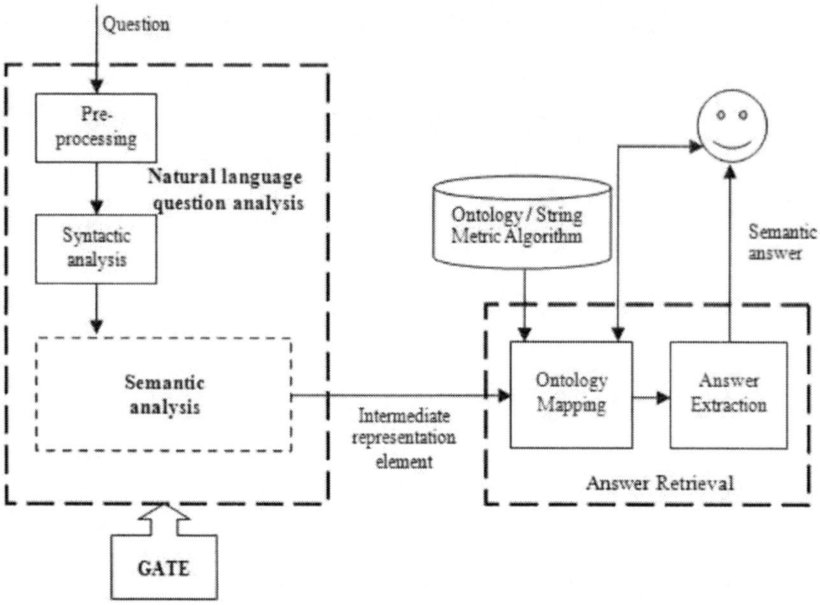

Figure 1: Architecture of our question answering system.

In addition, we marked phrases that refer to comparing-phrases (such as *"lớn hơn$_{greater\ than}$"* *"nhỏ hơn hoặc bằng$_{less\ than\ or\ equal\ to}$"* ...) or special-words (for example: abbreviation of some words on special-domain) by single *TokenVn* annotations.

3.2 Syntactic analysis

This module is responsible for identifying noun phrases and the relations between noun phrases. The different modules communicate through the annotations, for example, this module uses the *TokenVn* annotations, which is the result of the preprocessing module.

Concepts and entities are normally expressed in noun phrases. Therefore, it is important that we can reliably detect noun phrases in order to generate the *query-tuple*. We use *JAPE* grammars to specify patterns over annotations. When a noun phrase is matched, an annotation *NounPhrase* is created to mark up the noun phrase. In addition, its *type* feature is used to identify the concept and entity that is contained in the noun phrase using the following heuristic:

If the noun phrase contains a single noun (not including numeral nouns) and does not contain a proper noun, it contains a *concept*. If the noun phrase contains a proper noun or contains at least three single nouns, it contains an *entity*. Otherwise, concepts and entities are determined using a manual dictionary. In this step, a manual dictionary is built for describing concepts and their corresponding synonyms in the Ontology.

In addition, question-phrases are detected by using noun phrases and question-words identified by the preprocessing module. *QUTerm* or *QU-E-L-MC* annotations are generated to cover question-phrases with corresponding *category* feature which gives information about question categories.

The next step is to identify *relations* between noun phrases or noun phrases and question-phrases. When a phrase is matched by one of the relation patterns, an annotation *Relation* is created to markup the relation.

For example, with the following question:

"liệt kê tất cả các sinh viên có quê quán ở Hà Nội?"

"list all students whose hometown is Hanoi?"

The phrase *"có quê quán ở$_{have\ hometown\ of}$"* is the relation phrase linking the question-phrase *"liệt kê tất cả các sinh viên$_{list\ all\ students}$"* and the noun-phrase *"Hà Nội$_{Hanoi}$"*.

3.3 Semantic analysis module

The semantic analysis module identifies the query-tuples to generate the intermediate representation of the input question using the annotations generated by the previous modules. We will present a systematic knowledge acquisition approach by building a SCRDR KB of rules in the next section.

4 Ripple Down Rules for Question Analysis

Unlike existing approaches for question analysis for English (Lopez et al., 2007) and Vietnamese (Nguyen et al., 2009) where manual rules are created in an ad-hoc manner, we will describe a language independent approach to analyze natural language questions by applying Ripple Down Rules methodology to acquire rules incrementally. Rules are structured in an exception-structure and new rules are only added to correct errors of existing rules.

A SCRDR knowledge base is built to identify the question structure and to produce the query-tuples as the intermediate representation. Figure 2 shows the GUI of our natural language question analyzer. We will first describe the intermediate representation used in our approach, and then propose a rule language for extracting this intermediate representation for a given input question.

4.1 Intermediate Representation of an input question

Aqualog (Lopez et al., 2007) performs semantic and syntactic analysis of the input English question through the use of processing resources provided by GATE (Cunningham et al., 2002). When a question is asked, the task of the question analysis component is to transfer the natural language question to a Query-Triple with the following format (generic term, relation, second term). Through the use of JAPE grammars in GATE, AquaLog identifies terms and their relationship. Following VnQAS (Nguyen et al., 2009), the intermediate representation used in our approach is more complex aiming to cover a wider variety of question types. It consists of a *question-structure* and one or more *query-tuple* in the following format:

(question-structure, question-class, $Term_1$*, Relation,* $Term_2$*,* $Term_3$*)*

where $Term_1$ represents a concept (object class), $Term_2$ and $Term_3$, if exist, represent entities (objects), *Relation* (property) is a semantic constraint between terms in the question. This representation is meant to capture the semantic of the question.

Simple questions only have one *query-tuple* and its *question-structure* is the query-tuple's question-structure. More complex questions such as composite questions have several sub-questions, each sub-question is represented by a separate *query-tuple*, and the *question-structure* captures this composition attribute. Composite questions such as:

"danh sách tất cả các sinh viên của khoa công nghệ thông tin mà có quê quán ở Hà Nội?"

"list all students in the Faculty of Information Technology whose hometown is Hanoi?"

has question structure of type *And* with two query-tuples where ? represents a missing element: *(UnknRel , List , sinh viên*$_{student}$ *, ? , khoa công nghệ thông tin*$_{Faculty\ of\ Information\ Technology}$ *, ?)* and *(Normal , List , sinh viên*$_{student}$ *, có quê quán* $_{has\ hometown}$ *, Hà Nội*$_{Hanoi}$ *, ?).*

This representation is chosen so that it can represent a richer set of question types. Therefore, some terms or relation in the tuple can be missing. Existing noun phrase annotations and relation annotations are potential candidates for terms and relations respectively. Following VnQAS (Nguyen et al., 2009), we define the following question structures: *Normal, UnknTerm, UnknRel, Definition, Compare, ThreeTerm, Clause, Combine, And, Or, Affirm, Affirm_3Term, Affirm_MoreTuples* and question categories: *HowWhy, YesNo, What, When, Where, Who, Many, ManyClass, List* and *Entity*.

4.2 Rule language

A rule is composed of a condition part and a conclusion part. A condition is a regular expression pattern over annotations using JAPE grammar in GATE (Cunningham et al., 2002). It can also post new annotations over matched phrases of the pattern's sub-components. The following example of a pattern shows the posting an annotation over the matched phrase:

```
( ( {TokenVn.string == "liệt kê_list"} |
    {TokenVn.string == "chỉ ra_show"} )
  {NounPhrase.type == Concept} ) : QU_LIST
```

This pattern would catch phrases starting with a TokenVn annotation covering either the word "liệt kê$_{list}$" or the word "chỉ ra$_{show}$", followed by a NounPhrase which must have feature type equal to Concept. When applying this pattern on a text fragment, QU_LIST annotations would be posted over phrases matching this pattern. As annotations have feature value pairs, we can impose constraints on annotations in the pattern by requiring that a feature of an annotation must have a particular value.

The rule's conclusion contains the question structure and the tuples corresponding to the intermediate representation where each element in the tuple is specified by a newly posted annotations from matching the rule's condition in the following order:

(question-structure, question-class, $Term_1$*, Relation,* $Term_2$*,* $Term_3$*)*

All newly posted annotations have the same prefix RDR and the rule index so that a rule can refer to annotations of its parent rules. Examples of rules and how rules are created and stored in exception structure will be explained in details in the next section.

Given a new input question, a rule's condition is considered satisfied if the whole input question is matched by the condition pattern. The conclusion of the fired rule outputs the intermediate representation of the input question.

To create rules for capturing structures of questions, we use patterns over annotations such as TokenVn, NounPhrase, Relation, annotations capturing question-phrases like QUTerm, QU-E-L-MC (Entity, List, ManyClass)... and their features.

4.3 Knowledge Acquisition Process

The following examples show how the knowledge base building process works. When we encountered the question:

"trường đại học Công Nghệ có bao nhiêu sinh viên?" ("how many students are there in the College of Technology?")

[NounPhrase trường đại học Công Nghệ$_{the\ College\ of\ Technology}$ NounPhrase][Has có$_{has}$ Has] [QU-E-L-MC bao nhiêu sinh viên$_{how\ many\ students}$ QU-E-L-MC]

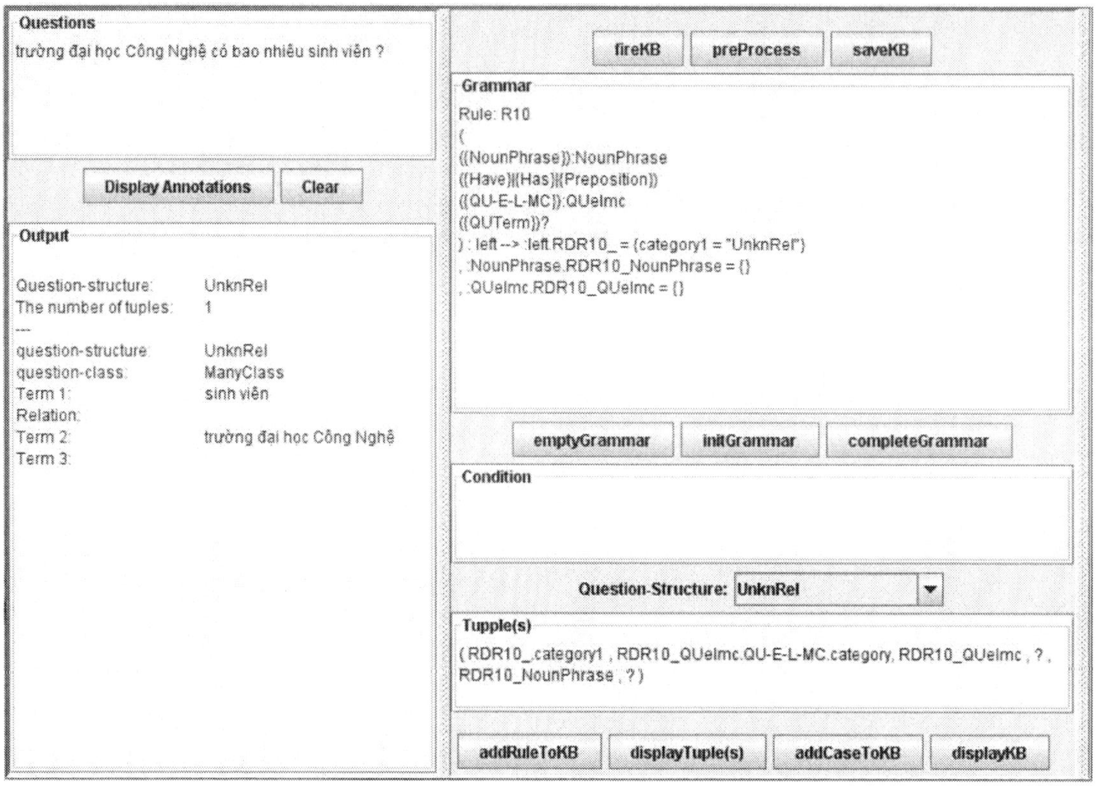

Figure 2: Question Analysis module to create the intermediate representation of question *"trường đại học Công Nghệ có bao nhiêu sinh viên?"("how many students are there in the College of Technology?")*.

Supposed we start with an empty knowledge base, the fired rule is default rule that gives empty conclusion. This can be corrected by adding the following rule to the knowledge base:

Rule: R10

(
({NounPhrase}):NounPhrase
({Have}|{Has}|{Preposition})
({QU-E-L-MC}):QUelmc
({QUTerm})?
) : left --→ :left.RDR10_ = {category1 = "UnknRel"}
, :NounPhrase.RDR10_NounPhrase = { }
, :QUelmc.RDR10_QUelmc = { }

Conclusion: question-structure of *UnknRel* and tuple *(RDR10_.category1 , RDR10_QUelmc.QU-E-L-MC.category, RDR10_QUelmc , ? , RDR10_NounPhrase , ?)*.

If the condition of rule **R10** matches the whole input question, a new annotation RDR10_ will be created covering the whole input question and new annotations RDR10_NounPhrase and RDR10_QUelmc will be created to cover sub-phrases of the input question.

If rule **R10** is fired, the matched input question is deemed to have a query-tuple with question-structure taking the value of *category1* feature of RDR10_ annotation, question-class taking the value of *category* feature of QU-E-L-MC annotation co-covering the same span as RDR10_QUelmc annotation, $Term_1$ is the string covered by RDR10_QUelmc, $Term_2$ is the string covered by RDR10_NounPhrase while $Term_3$ and *Relation* are unknown.

When we encounter the question:

"trường đại học Công Nghệ có bao nhiêu sinh viên là Nguyễn Quốc Đạt?" ("How many students named Nguyen Quoc Dat are there in the College of Technology?")

[RDR10_ *trường đại học Công Nghệ có bao nhiêu sinh viên* RDR10_] [Are là$_{Are}$ Are] [NounPhrase Nguyễn Quốc Đạt$_{Nguyen\ Quoc\ Dat}$ NounPhrase]

Rule **R10** is the fired rule but gives the wrong conclusion of question-structure of *UnknRel* and tuple *(UnknRel , ManyClass , sinh viên$_{student}$, ? , trường đại học Công Nghệ$_{the\ College\ of\ Technology}$, ?)*. The following exception rule was added to knowledge base to correct that:

Rule: R38

(
{RDR10_} ({Are}|{Is})
({NounPhrase}):NounPhrase
):left --→ :left.RDR38_ = {category1 = "ThreeTerm"}
, :NounPhrase.RDR38_NounPhrase = { }

Conclusion: question-structure of *ThreeTerm* and tuple *(RDR38_.category1 , RDR10_QUelmc.QU-E-L-MC.category , RDR10_QUelmc , ? , RDR10_NounPhrase , RDR38_NounPhrase)*.

Using rule **R38**, the output of the input question is question-structure of *ThreeTerm* and tuple *(ThreeTerm , ManyClass , sinh viên$_{student}$, ? , trường đại học Công Nghệ$_{the\ College\ of\ Technology}$, Nguyễn Quốc Đạt$_{Nguyen\ Quoc\ Dat}$)*

With the question *"quê quán của những sinh viên nào là Hà Nội?"* (*"which students have hometown of Hanoi?"*)

[RDR10_ [RDR10_NounPhrase *quê quán$_{hometown}$* RDR10_NounPhrase] [Preposition *của$_{of}$* Preposition] [RDR10_QUelmc *những sinh viên nào$_{which\ students}$* RDR10_QUelmc] RDR10_][Are *là$_{are}$* Are] [RDR38_NounPhrase *Hà Nội$_{Hanoi}$* RDR38_NounPhrase]

it will be satisfied by rule **R38**. But rule **R38** gives the wrong conclusion of question-structure of *ThreeTerm* and tuple *(ThreeTerm , Entity , sinh viên$_{student}$, ? , quê quán$_{hometown}$, Hà Nội$_{Hanoi}$)* because *quê quán$_{hometown}$* is a relation for linking *sinh viên$_{student}$* and *Hà Nội$_{Hanoi}$*. We can add a following exception rule **R76** to correct the conclusion by using constrains via rule condition:

Rule: R76

({RDR38_}):left

--→ :left.RDR76_ = {category1 = "Normal"}

Condition: RDR10_NounPhrase.hasAnno == NounPhrase.type == Concept

Conclusion: question-structure of *Normal* and tuple *(RDR76_.category1 , RDR10_QUelmc.QU-E-L-MC.category , RDR10_QUelmc , RDR10_NounPhrase , RDR38_NounPhrase , ?)*

The condition of rule **R76** matches a RDR10_NounPhrase annotation that has a NounPhrase annotation covering their substring with *Concept* as its *type* feature. The extra annotation constrain *hasAnno* requires that the text covered by the annotation must contain the specified annotation. With the rule **R76**, we have the correct output containing the question-structure of *Normal* and tuple *(Normal , Entity , sinh viên$_{student}$, quê quán$_{hometown}$, Hà Nội$_{Hanoi}$, ?)*.

5 Experiments

We experiment our system for both Vietnamese and English using the same intermediate representation.

5.1 Question Analysis for Vietnamese

For this experiment, we build a knowledge base of 92 rules from a corpus containing 400 questions and evaluate its quality on an unseen corpus of 102 questions in the same domain of college (university). The corpus of 400 questions were generated based on a seed corpus of 115 questions. Table 1 shows the number of exception rules in each layer where every rule in layer n is an exception rule of a rule in layer $n-1$. The only rule that is not an exception rule, is the default rule in layer 0. This indicates that the exception structure is indeed present and even extends to level 4.

Layer	Number of rules
1	26
2	41
3	20
4	4

Table 1: Number of exception rules in layers in our SCRDR KB.

In our experiment, we implemented the question analysis component of VnQAS (Nguyen et al., 2009) on the same corpus as in building our knowledge base. Table 2 gives the number of correctly analyzed questions of our system and system of (Nguyen et al., 2009) respectively where our system performs slightly better.

Type	Number of questions	Percent
Our system	88	86.3%
Question analysis component of (Nguyen et al., 2009)	83	81.4%

Table 2: Number of correctly analyzed questions.

Our method took one expert about 13 hours to build a KB based on the training corpus. However, most of the time was spent in looking at questions to determine if they belong to the structure of interest and which phrases in the sentence need to be extracted for the intermediate representation. The actual time required to create 92 rules by one expert is only about 5 hours in total. In contrast, implementing question analysis component of VnQAS (Nguyen et al., 2009) took about 75 hours for creating rules in an ad-hoc manner. Anecdotal account indicates that the cognitive load in creating rules in our approach is much less compared to that in VnQAS (Nguyen et al., 2009) as in our case, we do not have to consider other rules when crafting a new rule.

Table 3 presents the source of error for the 14 questions that our system incorrectly extract. It clearly shows that most errors come from unexpected structures. This could be easily rectified by adding more exception rules to the current knowledge base, especially when we have a bigger training set that contain a larger variety of question structure types.

Reason	Number of questions
Unknown structures of questions	12
Word segmentation was not trained for question-domain	2

Table 3: Error results.

5.2 Question Analysis for English

For the experiment in English, we take 170 English question examples of AquaLog's corpus. Using our ap-

http://technologies.kmi.open.ac.uk/aqualog/examples.html

proach, we built a knowledge base of 59 rules including the default one. It took 7 hours to build the knowledge base, which includes 3 hours of actual time to create all rules. The table 4 shows the numbers of rules in English knowledge base layers.

Layer	Number of rules
1	9
2	13
3	20
4	11
5	5

Table 4: Number of exception rules in layers in our English SCRDR KB.

As the intermediate representation of our system is different to Aqualog and there is no common test set available, it is impossible to directly compare our approach with Aqualog on the English domain. However, this experiment is indicative of the ability in using our system to quickly build a new knowledge base for a new domain and a new language.

6 Conclusion

We believe our approach is important especially for under-resourced languages where annotated data is not available. Our approach could be combined nicely with the process of annotating corpus where on top of assigning a label or a representation to a question, the experts just have to add one more rule to justify their decision using our system. Incrementally, an annotated corpus and a rule-based system can be obtained simultaneously.

The structured data used in the evaluation falls into the category of querying database or ontology but the problem of question analysis we tackle go beyond that, as it is a process that happens before the querying process. It can be applied to question answering in open domain against text corpora as long as the technique requires an analysis to turn the input question to an explicit representation of some sort.

In this paper, we introduced a language independent approach for systematically acquiring rules for converting a natural language question into an intermediate representation in a question answering system. Experimental results of our system on a wide range of questions are promising with accuracy of 86.3% for the Vietnamese corpus. Notably, the time it takes to get the system up to this performance is much less compared to previous works.

In the future, we will extend our system to employ a *near match* mechanism to improve the generalization capability of existing rules in the knowledge base and to assist the rule creation process.

Acknowledgements

This work is partially supported by the Research Grant from Vietnam National University, Hanoi No. QG.10.23.

The authors would like to acknowledge Vietnam National Foundation for Science and Technology Development (NAFOSTED) for their financial support to present the work at the conference.

References

L. Androutsopoulos. 1995. Natural language interfaces to databases - an introduction. *Nat. Lang. Eng.*, 1:29–81.

P. Compton and R. Jansen. 1990. A philosophical basis for knowledge acquisition. *Knowl. Acquis.*, 2(3):241–257.

Hammish Cunningham, Diana Maynard, Kalina Bontcheva, and Valentin Tablan. 2002. GATE: A Framework and Graphical Development Environment for Robust NLP Tools and Applications. In *Proc. of ACL*, pages 168–175.

Danica Damljanovic, Valentin Tablan, and Kalina Bontcheva. 2008. A text-based query interface to owl ontologies. In *Proc. of LREC*, pages 205–212.

L. Hirschman and R. Gaizauskas. 2001. Natural language question answering: the view from here. *Nat. Lang. Eng.*, 7(4):275–300.

Vanessa Lopez, Victoria Uren, Enrico Motta, and Michele Pasin. 2007. Aqualog: An ontology-driven question answering system for organizational semantic intranets. *Web Semant.*, 5(2):72–105.

Anh Kim Nguyen and Huong Thanh Le. 2008. Natural language interface construction using semantic grammars. In *Proc. of PRICAI*, pages 728–739.

Dai Quoc Nguyen, Dat Quoc Nguyen, and Son Bao Pham. 2009. A vietnamese question answering system. In *Proc. of KSE*, pages 26–32.

Dat Quoc Nguyen, Dai Quoc Nguyen, Son Bao Pham, and Dang Duc Pham. 2011. Ripple down rules for part-of-speech tagging. In *Proc. of CICLing*, pages 190–201.

Son Bao Pham and Achim Hoffmann. 2006. Efficient knowledge acquisition for extracting temporal relations. In *Proc. ECAI*, pages 521–525.

Dang Duc Pham, Giang Binh Tran, and Son Bao Pham. 2009. A hybrid approach to vietnamese word segmentation using part of speech tags. In *Proc. of KSE*, pages 154–161.

Debbie Richards. 2009. Two decades of ripple down rules research. *Knowl. Eng. Rev.*, 24(2):159–184.

A Semi-Automatic, Iterative Method for Creating a Domain-Specific Treebank

Corina Dima **Erhard Hinrichs**
Department of Linguistics
University of Tübingen
corina.dima, erhard.hinrichs@uni-tuebingen.de

Abstract

In this paper we present the development process of NLP-QT, a question treebank that will be used for data-driven parsing in the context of a domain-specific QA system for querying NLP resource metadata. We motivate the need to build NLP-QT as a resource in its own right, by comparing the Penn Treebank-style annotation scheme used for QuestionBank (Judge et al., 2006) with the modified NP annotation for the Penn Treebank introduced by Vadas and Curran (2007). We argue that this modified annotation scheme provides a better interface representation for semantic interpretation and show how it can be incorporated into the NLP-QT resource, without significant loss in parser performance.

The parsing experiments reported in the paper confirm the feasibility of an iterative, semi-automatic construction of the NLP-QT resource similar to the approach taken for QuestionBank. At the same time, we propose to improve the iterative refinement technique used for QuestionBank by adopting Hwa (2001)'s heuristics for selecting additional material to be hand-corrected and added to the data set at each iteration.

1 Introduction

Question-Answering (QA) systems have a long history in the field of natural language processing. In the 1970s and 1980s QA systems focused on natural language interfaces to domain-specific data bases or expert systems. Such systems typically used hand-crafted, rule-based front ends for parsing and semantic interpretation. With the increased availability of large-scale textual resources, QA systems more recently have focused on domain-independent broad-coverage information retrieval applications that typically employ more shallow processing techniques for question analysis and answer matching.

The intended application for the research reported in the present paper is more in the tradition of the earlier, domain-specific QA systems in that it aims to provide a natural language front-end to large repositories of metadata about language tools and resources that are made available by the CLARIN[1] project. However, instead of relying on a parser with hand-crafted grammar rules, it employs a robust data-driven parser that requires annotated training data in the form of a treebank.

Since the natural language front end for the intended QA system is English, the simplest solution would be to use a statistical parser such as the Berkeley (Petrov and Klein, 2007) or Stanford (Klein and Manning, 2003) parser with an existing language model obtained from the Penn Treebank (Marcus et al., 1993). However, it is well known that parser performance drops when analyzing text from domains other than that represented in the training data (Sekine, 1997; Gildea, 2001). In particular, Judge et al. (2006) have shown that language models obtained from the Penn Treebank perform far worse on questions than on their original test data. The Bikel (2004) parser they employ has an F-Score of 82.97 when tested on Section 23 of the Penn-II Treebank and an F-Score of 78.77 when tested on the 4000 questions in QuestionBank. Judge et al. (2006) attribute this loss of per-

[1] CLARIN project - http://www.clarin.eu

formance to two factors: (i) in the genre of newspaper texts, which the Penn Treebank is based on, questions are not a high frequency syntactic construction, and (ii) if wh-type constructions occur at all in the Penn Treebank, they predominantly involve relative clause constructions or indirect questions, but not unembedded questions. Therefore, a parser trained on Penn Treebank data, routinely misanalyses unembedded questions as these other two construction types. In fact, it was this poor parser performance that led Judge et al. to create QuestionBank, a special-purpose treebank based on SemEval data sets for Question Answering (QA).The data include the SemEval QA data from 1999-2001, part of the 2003 set (2000 questions), and another 2000 questions provided by the Cognitive Computation Group at the University of Illinois, which were also test data for developing QA systems. Training a statistical parser on QuestionBank data, possibly in combination with Penn Treebank data, therefore seems to be an attractive alternative. In fact, this is precisely how Judge et al. train their parser. However, for reasons explained in more detail in sections 2 and 3, we will adopt annotation guidelines for questions that differ from the Penn Treebank-style annotation used in QuestionBank. Rather, we will follow a more hierarchical annotation style for NPs that has been proposed by Vadas and Curran (2007) and that provides an easier interface for semantic interpretation. Section 3 will introduce the Vadas and Curran (2007) annotation style and will motivate why it is appropriate for the QA system envisaged here. Section 4 will present a set of parsing experiments for the Berkeley parser trained on different combinations of treebank data discussed in sections 2 and 3. The final section summarizes the main results of this paper and discusses directions for future research.

2 Data Collection for Querying NLP Resource Metadata

One of the main reasons to create a new data set of questions and not use some already existing set has to do with the specific subject domain of the QA system to be developed. All the questions should concern particular pieces of information associated with language resources or with different application domains of natural language processing. In order to obtain a realistic data set of this sort, we harvested the questions from mailing lists like LinguistList[2] and Corpora List[3], as well as from the Stack Overflow[4] questions tagged with "nlp".

The mailing lists have a history of 20 years and have a lot of extra content other than user queries. Therefore, all the posts had to be browsed through in order to manually extract only the relevant questions from the whole post. For example, information about the person asking the question was deleted from the original posts, since such information is not relevant for a QA system. Spelling and grammar errors were then removed from the extracted questions. A number of 2500 questions were harvested until the moment of writing, but the goal is to gather a 10.000 questions corpus that should provide enough training and testing data when converted into a treebank.

The data below provide some typical examples that have been collected from the three sources:

(1) Where can I find a corpus of German newspapers from the 17th century until the 1950s?

(2) What good introductory books on the subject of natural language processing, parsing and tagging are there?

(3) Where can I find the Orleans corpus of spoken French (created by Michel Blanc and Patricia Biggs)?

(4) Where can I find a parallel corpus of translations in English, French, German and Italian, ideally containing news stories?

(5) Where can I find a free or available English tagger other than Brill's tagger?

Apart from the more restricted subject domain, the NLP Resource Metadata Questions significantly differ from the SemEval data used in QuestionBank in at least two other respects:

- The average length of the SemEval questions in QuestionBank is 47.58 characters and 9.45 words, whereas the NLP Questions average 81.17 characters and 12.88 words.

- Moreover, the distribution of questions types is quite different in the two cases. The SemEval data set used for QuestionBank is intended to query encyclopedic knowledge from sources such as Wikipedia. This means that the questions essentially include all possible question words such as *who*, *what*, *which*, *where*, *when*, *why*, *how*, etc. When

[2]LinguistList - http://linguistlist.org/

[3]Corpora List - http://www.hit.uib.no/corpora/

[4]Stack Overflow - http://stackoverflow.com/

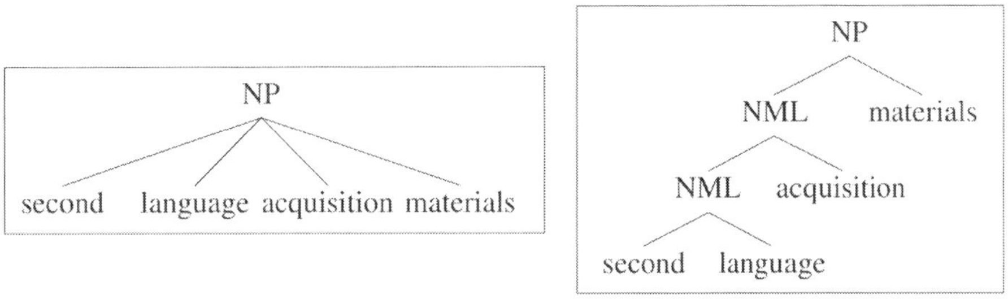

Figure 1: Comparing annotations for the compound noun *second language acquisition materials*: Penn-style annotation on the left, Vadas and Curran (2007) style annotation on the right

Question Word	% in QB	% in NLP-QT
Are there	0	5.45
At what	0.075	0
For what	0.025	0
How	3.75	0.5
How *	8.2	0
In what	0.825	0
In which	0.15	0
Is there	0	16.81
On what	0.075	0
On which	0.075	0
What	57.35	0.98
When	5	0.05
Where	6.075	75.07
Which	1.925	0.09
Who	11.375	0.1
Why	1.2	0
Other	3.822	0.93

Table 1: Distribution of question types in the two datasources; *How ** stands for questions like *how many, how much, how far, how long* etc.

querying NLP resource metadata, the emphasis is to a large extent on *where* and *is there* questions; the percentage for each type of question in the two datasources is showed in Table 1.

3 Comparing the Annotation of Base NPs

There is yet another property of both QuestionBank and the Penn Treebank that limits its usefulness for the QA application considered here. This concerns the flat-structure annotation style for noun phrases adopted in both resources. For example, in the question *Where can I find a German corpus containing second language acquisition materials?* the compound noun *second language acquisition materials* would be annotated in these resources as a single flat NP, as shown in the left column of Figure 1. Such a flat annotation does not provide sufficient information about the scope of each member of the compound. It is precisely this type of shortcoming that led Vadas and Curran (2007) to revise the Penn Treebank annotation style for NPs along the following lines:

- If the intended scope of a base NP leads to a strictly right-branching structure, then the Penn Treebank annotation remains unchanged.
- If the intended scope is partially or completely left-branching, then an extra node is introduced into the tree for each left-branching structure. The label of this node is either NML or JJP, depending on the lexical head of the local tree (noun or adjective, respectively).

The resulting annotation for the compound noun *second language acquisition materials* is shown in the right column of Figure 1.

From the point of view of semantic interpretation, the more contoured Vadas and Curran (2007) annotation style is to be preferred since it reflects the type of answer that is required, namely *materials for second language acquisition*, but not for example *acquisition materials for second language*, or *the second (batch) of language acquisition materials*.

It is precisely for this reason that we adopt the annotation style of Vadas and Curran (2007) for the NLP Resource Metadata Questions Treebank (henceforth abbreviated as NLP-QT).

4 Experimental Results

This section summarizes the set of experiments that we have conducted with the Vadas and Curran (2007) annotation style for NPs and in particular with the NLP-QT data set. We discuss two types of experiments:

- comparing the performance of the parser using different annotation styles for base NPs,
- experiments for optimizing the language model of a statistical parser in order to assist with the semi-automatic creation of the treebank.

All the experiments were performed with the Berkeley parser. The results are summarized in Table 2 and Table 3.

4.1 Parsing Results for Different Annotation Styles

Using Bikel (2004)'s parser, Vadas and Curran (2007) report that the parsing results slightly decrease when the parser is trained on the Penn Treebank with the modified annotation style for NPs. As Table 2 shows, we obtain a similar result when testing on section 23 of the Penn Treebank, using the Berkeley parser trained on sections 02-21 of the same treebank: there is minor drop in F-score from 90.43 to 89.96. We also confirm Gildea's finding that testing a parser on test sets from a different domain than the training sets results in a significant loss of performance: when using the same models that we used for the Penn Treebank experiments, the average F-score for test data from the Question Bank in a 10-fold cross-validation experiment is 79.944 for the model trained on the original Penn Treebank and 77.607 for the model trained on the modified Penn Treebank.

The above experiments were designed as a baseline for comparing the performance of the parser trained only on Penn Treebank data. But since our primary interest is in parsing questions as accurately as possible, we conducted a second set of experiments, summarized in the lower half of Table 2. Here additional training data from the Question Bank was added to both the original and the modified Penn Treebank training data. The decrease in performance caused by adding the QuestionBank training data together with the modified NP annotation on section 23 is comparable to the one caused by adding the modified NP annotation alone (a decrease from 90.263 to 90.04, whereas for the original Penn Treebank data the F-score decreased from 90.43 to 89.96), but this slight decrease is more than offset by the increase in semantic information obtained from the Vadas and Curran (2007) annotation for complex base NPs. Even more noteworthy is the big jump in F-score from 77.607 to 92.658 when adding the QuestionBank data to the training data.

4.2 Semi-automatic Creation of NLP-QT

The creation of a treebank is a time-consuming and expensive task if all the annotation has to be performed manually. It is therefore useful to investigate whether at least parts of the annotation can be performed automatically or by a combination of automatic analysis and manual post editing. To this end, we performed a set of parsing experiments, again using the Berkeley parser, where the test data are taken both from the QuestionBank and a seed set of 500 manually annotated questions from the NLP-QT. The results are shown in Table 3.

As in the experiments shown in the previous subsection, the performance with a model trained purely on Penn Treebank data (with NPs annotated in the Vadas and Curran (2007) style) serves as a baseline (the model is called *np-wsj* in the table). This model is then enriched by first adding annotated data from Question Bank and then by adding the manually annotated questions from the NLP-QT. We refer to these models as *np-wsjqb* and *np-wsjqblq_500*, respectively. The results are very encouraging on several dimensions:

1. overall parsing performance on the test data for both the *np-wsjqb* and the *np-wsjqblq_500* models is very good
2. adding questions from the NLP-QT yields a desired increase in performance
3. almost two-thirds of all questions from the test data yield a completely correct parse.

These three findings together make a semi-automatic construction of the NLP-QT entirely feasible. In fact, we are currently constructing the NLP-QT treebank in this semi-automatic fashion, using the same iterative approach to treebank construction adopted for the QuestionBank data by Judge et al. This approach involves iterations of manual post correction of automatically generated

Models	Section 23 of Penn Treebank			QuestionBank test section		
	Prec.	Recall	F-score	Prec.	Recall	F-score
Orig. PTB	90.480	90.390	90.430	79.285	80.617	79.944
PTB w/ NPs	90.000	89.920	89.960	77.546	77.670	77.607
Orig. PTB + QB	90.317	90.211	90.263	93.618	92.801	93.207
PTB w/ NPs + QB	90.095	89.985	90.040	92.592	92.725	92.658

Table 2: Comparison of parser performance when trained on different data sources with different annotation styles

Models	Questions test set			
	Prec.	Recall	F-score	Exact match
np-wsj	78.525	78.780	78.651	30.231
np-wsjqb	91.256	91.499	91.375	63.111
np-wsjqblq_500	92.128	92.186	92.157	64.801

Table 3: Parser performance increases when adding hand-corrected question data to the training set

	% of total	Avg. char. length	Avg. word length	Avg. const. no
Correct	48.59	61.55	11.41	20.94
Incorrect	51.41	100.96	17.85	31.96

Table 4: Average length and constituent count for the correctly/incorrectly parsed questions

parses, adding this post-corrected data set to the previously used training material and then retraining the parser with the enlarged data set.

One question that was not addressed in the approach by Judge et al. concerns the selection of the additional trees that will be manually corrected and then added to the training and test material in the next iteration. As Hwa (2001) has pointed out, this selection process can be critical in minimizing the amount of data that needs to be hand-corrected during grammar induction. She suggests several simple heuristics for ranking the candidate trees, two of which will be considered here. One heuristic is based on the often observed fact that, on average, longer sentences are harder to parse correctly than shorter ones. A second, related and somewhat more fine-grained variant of the first heuristic is based on the number of constituents obtained by the automatic parse of a sentence. Since the automatic parse is often at least partially incorrect, the constituent count of the parser will typically be just an estimate of the actual constituent count and related complexity of the sentence. Hwa suggests that when trees are added, the selected trees should match the average constituent count and length profile of the trees that were incorrectly parsed in the previous iteration.

We adopt Hwa's approach in the construction of the NLP-QT treebank. In order to use it effectively, it is necessary to inspect the results of the parser and in particular create an automatic profile of the completely correct versus partially incorrect parses. This type of error analysis is the subject of the next section.

4.3 Error Analysis

Table 4 summarizes the profiling of the 500 questions from the NLP-QT used in the 10-fold validation experiment. On average, 48.59 % of all sentences received an entirely correct parse. The average length in characters and in words as well as the average number of constituents of the correctly parsed sentences differ significantly from the questions where the parse is only partially correct.

These results provide a sound basis for applying Hwa's selection method: in the next iteration of optimizing the statistical model for the parser, sampling should focus on questions that match as closely as possible the character, word, and constituent count of the partially incorrect parse trees.

In order to get an impression of the kinds of mistakes that are made by the Berkeley parser, we are presenting two partially incorrect parse trees for the sentences in 6 and 7.

(6) Is there any freely available text corpus for Croatian, no smaller than 20k words?

(7) Where can I find information on chunking French and German texts?

The trees obtained by the Berkeley parser for these two sentences are shown in Figures 2 and 3, respectively. They exhibit the following typical attachment mistakes and misgroupings of conjuncts in a coordination structure:

The parse tree generated by the Berkeley parser for sentence 6 (Figure 2) contains several errors: two attachment errors (the PP *for Croatian* is not attached as a post-head modifier to the nominal head *text corpus*, but rather attached high as a sister of the preceding NP. Likewise, the modifier starting with *no smaller ...* is treated as an ADJP rather than an NP and is attached as well as a sister of the preceding NP and PP rather than to the complex NP *any ... for Croatian* in the gold parse. Moreover, the JJP *freely available* is incorrectly labelled as an ADJP.

The parse tree for sentence 7 (Figure 3) fails on the correct grouping and labelling of the coordinate structure *French and German texts*. The tagger treats the lexical token *chunking* as a noun (NN), rather than a gerund (VBG), and the lexical token *French* as a plural noun (NNS) rather than as an adjective (JJ). The parser then combines these two items into an NP, which is then coordinated with the NP *German texts*.

By hand correcting parse trees similar to the ones just discussed and by including them in the data set for retraining the parsing model in the next iteration, the performance of the parser on the types of constructions in question will improve and thereby minimize the amount of manual post editing as much as possible.

5 Conclusion and Future Work

In this paper we have presented the development process of the NLP-QT resource that will be used for data-driven parsing in the context of a domain-specific QA system for querying NLP resource metadata. We have motivated the need to build NLP-QT as a resource in its own right by comparing the Penn Treebank-style annotation scheme used for QuestionBank with the modified NP annotation for the Penn Treebank introduced by Vadas and Curran (2007). We have argued that this modified annotation scheme provides a better interface representation for semantic interpretation and have shown how it can be incorporated into the NLP-QT resource, without significant loss in parser performance.

The parsing experiments reported in the paper confirm the feasibility of an iterative, semi-automatic construction of the NLP-QT resource similar to the approach taken for QuestionBank. At the same time, we propose to improve the iterative refinement technique used for QuestionBank by adopting Hwa's heuristics for selecting additional material to be hand-corrected and added to the data set at each iteration.

Another important aspect in the creation of a treebank how to ensure a consistent and correct annotation of the linguistic material. Automatic error detection techniques that can be used to test the accuracy of the annotation have already been described in works like Květoň and Oliva (2002), for the part of speech annotation level, and Dickinson and Meurers (2005), for the syntactic annotation level. In future work on the NLP-QT, we plan to employ such methods in order to identify and to correct inconsistencies in the annotation.

References

Dan Bikel. 2004. *A distributional analysis of a lexicalized statistical parsing model.* Proceedings of the 2004 Conference on Empirical Methods in Natural Language Processing (EMNLP 2004).

Markus Dickinson and W. Detmar Meurers. 2005. *Prune Diseased Branches to Get Healthy Trees! How to Find Erroneous Local Trees in a Treebank and Why It Matters.* Proceedings of the 4th Workshop on Treebanks and Linguistic Theories (TLT 2005).

Daniel Gildea. 2001. *Corpus Variation and Parser Performance.* Proceedings of the 2001 Conference on Empirical Methods in Natural Language Processing (EMNLP 2001), 167–202.

Rebecca Hwa. 2001. *On Minimizing Training Corpus for Parser Acquisition.* Proceedings of the 2001 workshop on Computational Natural Language Learning - Volume 7.

John Judge, Aoife Cahill, and Josef van Genabith. 2006. *QuestionBank: Creating a Corpus of Parse-Annotated Questions.* Proceedings of the 21st International Conference on Computational Linguistics and the 44th annual meeting of the Association for Computational Linguistics (Coling-ACL 2006).

Pavel Květoň and Karel Oliva. 2002. *Achieving an Almost Correct PoS-Tagged Corpus.* Proceedings of the 5th International Conference Text, speech and dialogue (TSD 2002).

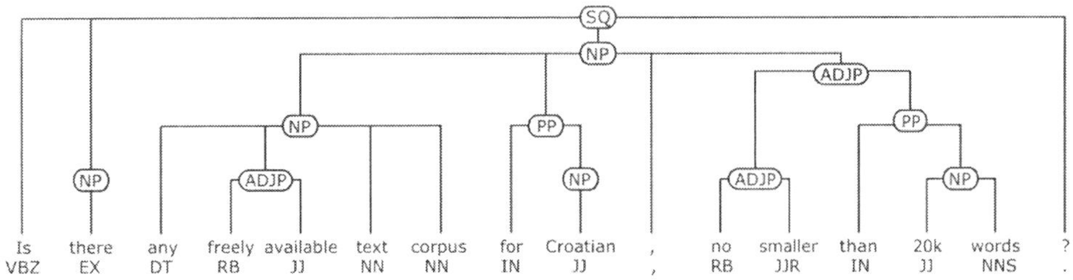

(a) Incorrect parse

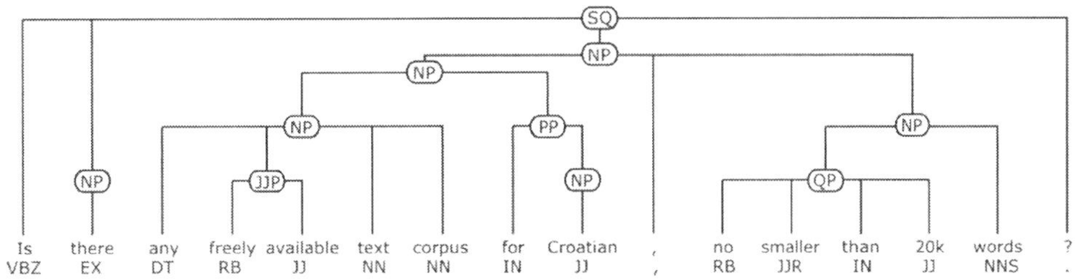

(b) Correct parse

Figure 2: Incorrect (top) and correct (bottom) parse for example 6

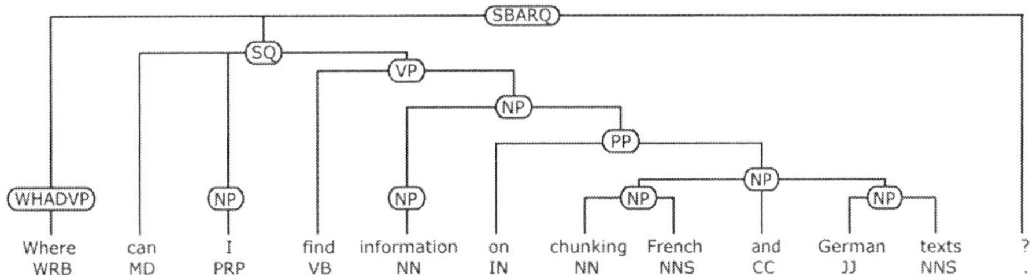

(a) Incorrect parse

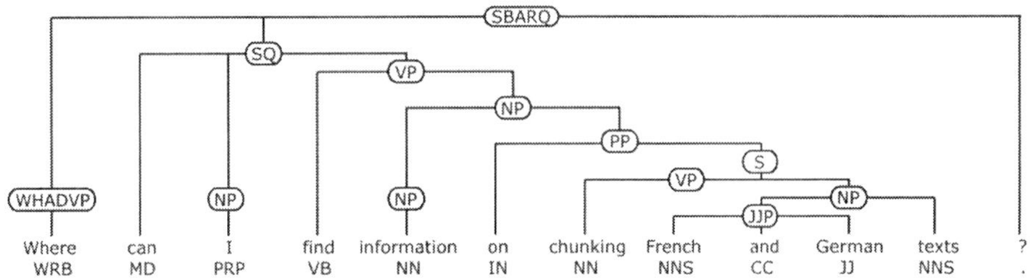

(b) Correct parse

Figure 3: Incorrect (top) and correct (bottom) parse for example 7

Dan Klein and Christopher D. Manning. 2003. *Accurate Unlexicalized Parsing.* Proceedings of the 41st Annual Meeting on Association for Computational Linguistics - Volume 1 (ACL 2003), 423–430.

Mitchell P. Marcus, Beatrice Santorini, and Mary Ann Marcinkiewicz. 1993. *Building a Large Annotated Corpus of English: The Penn Treebank.* Computational Linguistics 19, 313–330.

Slav Petrov and Dan Klein. 2007. *Improved Inference for Unlexicalized Parsing.* Proceedings of NAACL HLT 2007.

Satoshi Sekine. 1997. *The Domain Dependence of Parsing.* Proceedings of the Fifth Conference on Applied Natural Language Processing, 96–102.

David Vadas and James R. Curran. 2007. *Adding Noun Phrase Structure to the Penn Treebank.* Proceedings of the 45th Annual Meeting of the Association for Computational Linguistics (ACL-07), 240–247.

Determining Immediate Constituents of Compounds in GermaNet

Verena Henrich
University of Tübingen
verena.henrich@uni-tuebingen.de

Erhard Hinrichs
University of Tübingen
erhard.hinrichs@uni-tuebingen.de

Abstract

In order to be able to systematically link compounds in GermaNet to their constituent parts, compound splitting needs to be applied recursively and has to identify the immediate constituents at each level of analysis. Existing tools for compound splitting for German only offer an analysis of all component parts of a compound at once without any grouping of subconstituents. Thus, existing tools for splitting compounds were adapted to overcome this issue. Algorithms combining three heterogeneous kinds of compound splitters are developed to achieve better results. The best overall result with an accuracy of 92.42% is achieved by a hybrid combined compound splitter that takes into account all knowledge provided by the individual compound splitters, and in addition some domain knowledge about German derivation morphology and compounding.

1 Introduction

The present paper presents a compound splitter for German that is tailored to the needs of systematically enriching the set of lexical relations of *GermaNet* (Kunze and Lemnitzer, 2002; Henrich and Hinrichs, 2010), the German version of the Princeton WordNet for English (Fellbaum, 1998). Compounding is a highly productive word formation process resulting in complex words with two or more constituent parts. Baroni et al. (2002) report that almost half (47%) of the word types in the APA German news corpus are compounds.

For GermaNet, the numbers are comparable: The morphological analyzer *SMOR* (Schmid et al., 2004) for German classifies 46.89% of all lexical units contained in release 6.0 of GermaNet as compounds. Among those, nominal compounds make up 95% and are thus by far the largest class of compounds. It is for this reason that we concentrate exclusively on the treatment of nominal compounds in the present study.

Given the prevalence of compounds in GermaNet and its current coverage of 84586 lexical units, a systematic treatment of compounds is badly needed in order to enhance the usability of GermaNet for a wide variety of NLP applications, including machine translation, natural language generation, information extraction, etc. The size of GermaNet and the high frequency of compounds clearly prohibit a purely manual solution and mandate an automatic treatment. The treatment of compounds for GermaNet needs to be systematic along at least three dimensions: (i) it should cover all combinations of word classes present in GermaNet which can enter into noun compounding, (ii) it should apply to all lexical units already entered into GermaNet, and (iii) it should be extendable to all compounds which are candidates for inclusion in GermaNet in future data releases.

2 Nominal Compounds in German

Peter Eisenberg (Eisenberg, 2006) defines four major subclasses for compounds, where the rightmost head constituent is a noun.

1. Noun + Noun: *Apfelbaum* 'apple tree'.
2. Adjective + Noun: *Weißbrot* 'white bread'.
3. Verb + Noun: *Esstisch* 'eating table'.
4. Preposition + Noun: *Oberarm* 'upper arm'.

In addition to these four major classes, there is a small class of bound morphemes (i.e., morphemes that cannot appear as an independent word), such as *Him-*[1], that can also serve as the initial constituent of a nominal compound:

[1] In the German linguistics literature such bound morphemes are referred to as *unikale Elemente*.

5. Bound Morpheme + Noun: *Himbeere* 'raspberry'.

What makes compound splitting for German a challenging task is the fact that compounding is not always simple string concatenation, but often involves the presence of intervening linking elements or the elision of word-final characters in the non-head constituent of a compound[2]. Word-final *e*, for example, is absent in compounds such as *Hüftschwung* 'hip swing', whose non-head constituent is *Hüfte* 'hip'. While such elision cases are relatively rare, the presence of linking morphemes in nominal compounds is a much more frequent phenomenon. Eisenberg (2006) distinguishes between the following linking elements: *n* (*Blumenvase*: *Blume* + *n* + *Vase*; 'flower vase'), *s* (*Zweifelsfall*: *Zweifel* + *s* + *Fall*; 'case of doubt'), *ns* (*Glaubensfrage*: *Glaube* + *ns* + *Frage*; 'question of believe'), *e* (*Pferdewagen: Pferd* + *e* + *Wagen*; 'horse carriage'), *er* (*Kindergarten*: *Kind* + *er* + *Garten*), *en* (*Heldenmut*: *Held* + *en* + *Mut*; 'hero's courage'), *es* (*Siegeswille*: *Sieg* + *es* + *Wille*; 'will to win'), and *ens* (*Schmerzensschrei*: *Schmerz* + *ens* + *Schrei;* 'scream of pain').

3 Modeling Compounds in GermaNet

GermaNet is a lexical semantic network that is modeled after the Princeton WordNet for English. It partitions the lexical space into a set of semantic concepts (modeled by *synsets*) that are interlinked by semantic relations. A synset is a set of words (called *lexical units*) where all the words are taken to have the same meaning. There are two types of semantic relations in GermaNet. *Conceptual relations* hold between two synsets, including hypernymy, part-whole relations, entailment, or causation. *Lexical relations* hold between two individual lexical units.

To the best of our knowledge, a systematic treatment of compounds is largely absent from monolingual wordnets presently available. The only programmatic approach for how to treat compounds is documented in the final report of the *EuroWordNet* project (Vossen, 2002) from which the following illustrative example is taken:

```
guitar player
  HAS_HYPERONYM player
  CO_AGENT_INSTRUMENT guitar
```

[2] Langer (1998) presents a frequency table for German linking morphemes and elisions, according to which approximately half of the compounds he investigated contain some kind of linking morpheme or elision.

In this EuroWordNet proposal, compounds such as *guitar player* are linked via conceptual relations to their component parts. The compound as a whole is related via the hypernymy relation to its head constituent (*player*) and via the bidirectional CO_ROLE relation to its modifier constituent (*guitar*). This CO_ROLE relation is then further specified by the particular thematic role realized by the modifier constituent. In short, the EuroWordNet treatment focuses on the semantics of compounds.

The current proposal of how to treat compounds in GermaNet is to some extent more modest in that it focuses on the morphosyntactic structure of compounds and leaves a semantic treatment to future work. A strong requirement for a compounding analysis for GermaNet is that it has to reflect the recursive nature of compounding in the case of compounds that have more than two constituent parts such as *Kraftfahrzeugsteuer* 'motor vehicle tax'. The immediate constituents of this compound are *Kraftfahrzeug* and *steuer*, with the first constituent then splitting further into *Kraft* and *fahrzeug*, etc. (see Figure 1). In order to be able to systematically link compounds in GermaNet to their constituent parts, compound splitting needs to be applied recursively and has to identify only the immediate constituents at each level of analysis.

Figure 1. Compounds in GermaNet.

4 Related Work on Compound Splitting

For German, there are a number of morphological tools available that include compound splitting, such as GERTWOL (Haapalainen and Majorin, 1994), SMOR (Schmid et al., 2004), ASV Toolbox (Witschel and Biemann, 2005), BananaSplit[3], and Morfessor (Creutz and Lagus, 2005). After an initial evaluation of all publicly available tools, SMOR and ASV Toolbox are used as baseline tools for the present project.

[3] See http://niels.drni.de/s9y/pages/bananasplit.html

SMOR is a morphological analyzer for German inflection and productive word formation including composition, which has been developed at the University of Stuttgart. It provides analyses consisting of sequences of morphemes enriched with morphological information, however without grouping them into immediate constituents. Furthermore, although SMOR disambiguates its results to a certain extend, for many compounds there are still several distinct sequences of morphemes provided.

ASV Toolbox has been developed at the University of Leipzig. It comprises several tools for linguistic classification and clustering, amongst them compound splitting, which is included in the tool described as *ASV Toolbox Baseforms*[4]. The result of the compound analysis identifies all constituent parts of the compound without internal bracketing. It reduces inflected word forms of constituents to their base forms.

5 Compound Splitting Algorithms

Three individual compound splitters are used in the present project: a compound splitter incorporating GermaNet (GN-CS) developed by the authors of this paper, a modified version of SMOR (SMOR-CS), and a modified version of the ASV Toolbox compound splitter (ASV-CS).

5.1 Compound Splitter Incorporating GermaNet (GN-CS)

This compound splitter is especially tailored for determining compounds in GermaNet and their immediate constituents. It uses pattern matching for gathering all potential modifiers and heads of a compound, considering intervening linking morphemes and the elision of word-final characters (as described in section 2). In case the pattern matching yields more than one potential modifier-head composition, the correct constituents are verified incorporating the semantic resource GermaNet and its graph structure. For example, compositions having both constituents in GermaNet are preferred over compositions where only one constituent is an existing entry in GermaNet. Further, more probability is assigned to compositions of simple string concatenation than to compositions showing a linking morpheme or the elision of word-final characters.

The availability of semantic relations, such as part-whole relations, direct or indirect hypernymy, or synonymy, is employed as well. Thus, a modifier or head that is semantically related to the compound determines the correct splitting of compounds into its immediate constituents with high probability. The following example illustrates this. For the compound *Flughafengelände* 'airport area', all relevant parts of the two candidate parses *Flug* + *Hafengelände* and *Flughafen* + *Gelände* are existing entries in GermaNet, i.e., existing words. Further, both potential analyses show neither linking morphemes nor the elision of word-final characters. In this case, the usage of GermaNet's semantic relations determines, that *Flughafen* is a holonym of the compound *Flughafengelände*, and thus clearly and correctly determines the modifier, resulting in the correct parse *Flughafen* + *Gelände*.

If there are two different modifier-head combinations having both their heads as hypernyms of the compound, GN-CS disambiguates the correct splitting by taking into account the hypernym's distances[5]. The splitting belonging to the head with the larger hypernym distance is preferred.[6] For example, *Nachttischlampe* 'bedside lamp' has both hypernyms *Tischlampe* 'table lamp' (hypernym distance is 1, i.e., direct hypernym) and *Lampe* 'lamp' (hypernym distance is 2, i.e., indirect hypernym). Thus, *Nachttischlampe* is correctly split into *Nachttisch* + *Lampe*.

5.2 Modified SMOR Compound Splitter (SMOR-CS)

To achieve better results in the specific task of determining compounds in GermaNet and their immediate constituents, SMOR's output has been adapted. Some steps, such as the denominalization of the head constituents or the splitting of all affixes, need to be reverted. Other results, such as the splitting into more than two constituents or the indication of more than one splitting possibility, require further processing. For example, SMOR splits *Änderungsanforderung* 'change request' into *ändern* + *ung* + *an* + *fordern* + *ung*. After reverting the denominalization and the separation of prefixes and suffixes, SMOR-CS returns: *Änderung* + *Anforderung*.

For those compounds with several distinct results, it is not trivial to disambiguate the correct splitting. Furthermore, the splitting of compounds having more than two constituents, such

[4] See http://wortschatz.uni-leipzig.de/~cbiemann/software/toolbox/Baseforms%20Tool.htm

[5] Here, *hypernym distance* describes the path length between the compound and a direct or indirect hypernym, i.e., a direct hypernym has a hypernym distance of one.

[6] Preference of longer hypernym distance may seem counterintuitive, but surprisingly turns out to be the correct heuristic.

as *Brennstofflagerungsbehälter* ('fuel storage container'), which is split into *brennen* + *Stoff* + *lagern* + *Behälter* cannot be used in this form for determining immediate constituents, since the constituents are not grouped.

5.3 Modified ASV Toolbox Compound Splitter (ASV-CS)

The output of the ASV Toolbox compound splitter is further processed in order to better fit the needs of the present project. To enhance the reliability of the determined constituents, the enhanced compound splitter ASV-CS searches for entries in GermaNet. If a result consists of more than two constituents, the different bracketing alternatives need to be verified. This is done by incorporating GermaNet's graph structure in the same way as for GN-CS (see section 5.1).

6 Combination of Compound Splitters

It has been shown for various NLP tasks, such as part-of-speech tagging (van Halteren et al., 2001) or word sense disambiguation (Florian and Yarowsky, 2002), that multiple classifier systems outperform single decision systems. Further, the performance of such methods is usually better the more diverse the individual systems are (Polikar, 2006). Thus, having three classifiers[7] (compound splitters) available that produce diverse results, the application of a combined method seems reasonable. As the compound splitters in the present project each return exactly one decision, the range of applicable combination algorithms is restricted. In the following subsection, the application of *majority voting* and *weighted majority voting* is described. Further, a combined algorithm, which is developed by the authors of this paper, is presented.

6.1 Majority Voting (MV) and Weighted Majority Voting (WMV)

In majority voting, equal weight is given to all compound splitters when voting for a result (i.e., a splitting of a compound into its immediate constituents). The votes from all compound splitters are summed up and the result with the highest number of votes is selected. In case a compound splitter does not return an analysis, it is disregarded, while the other two compound splitters vote for the final result.[8] In weighted majority voting, individual compound splitters are assigned different weights in such a way that the combination of weights minimizes errors.[9]

6.2 Combined Hybrid Compound Splitter (CH-CS)

In order to further increase performance, we created a hybrid combined compound splitter that takes into account all knowledge provided by the individual compound splitters, but that also takes into account some domain knowledge about German derivation morphology and compounding. One of the frequent mistakes made is to treat words like *Gutherzigkeit*[10] 'kindheartedness' or *Teilhaberschaft*[11] 'partnership' as compounds, while in reality these are complex nouns formed by derivation morphology. The hybrid model therefore incorporates knowledge about derivation morphology and filters out such erroneously marked compounds. As will be shown in the evaluation section, the hybrid model outperforms all individual compound splitters as well as the other combined compound splitters in all tasks described in section 7.

7 Evaluation

The automatic predictions of compounds and their immediate constituents are manually verified. The order of the manual verification is in the order of the IDs of the lexical units, which is actually randomly concerning the nouns themselves. For the purpose of evaluation, 68743[12] nouns were chosen, of which 42191 (61.37%) are compounds and 26552 (38.63%) are not. The evaluation is fourfold: (i) section 7.1 evaluates how many compounds are correctly identified, (ii) section 7.2 evaluates how many predicted compounds are split at the correct position, (iii) how many compounds are correctly predicted

[7] The task of compound splitting is, in a strict sense, not a classification task, because there is no predefined result set, such as a tagset for part-of-speech tagging. The results of the compound splitters are rather variable and, from a technical point of view, describe arbitrary content (although describing the splitting of a compound into its immediate constituents).

[8] In case of a tie, giving priority to SMOR-CS turned out to be the best strategy.

[9] Experimenting with several weighting combinations resulted in giving weight 2.0 to SMOR-CS, 0.9 to GN-CS, and 0.8 to ASV-CS. This adjustment helps in cases where both GN-CS and ASV-CS agree on an erroneous analysis.

[10] SMOR-CS treats *Gutherzigkeit* erroneously as a compound, although it is derived from the adjective *gutherzig* with the derivation suffix *-keit*.

[11] *Teilhaberschaft* is derived from the noun *Teilhaber* with the derivation suffix *-schaft*.

[12] Altogether, there are 93407 nouns in GermaNet. Note that all foreign words and named entities are disregarded in this evaluation.

regarding the word forms of their immediate constituents is evaluated in section 7.3, and, finally, (iv) there is an error analysis in section 7.4.

7.1 Identification of Compounds

The first part of the evaluation concerns the prediction whether a noun in GermaNet is a compound or not. Table 1 lists all *true positives* (TP; correctly identified compounds), *false positives* (FP; erroneously identified as a compound), *true negatives* (TN; correctly identified as no compound), and *false negatives* (FN; erroneously not identified as a compound). The numbers are separately calculated for the individual algorithms and for the combined algorithms.

Algorithm	*TP*	*FP*	*TN*	*FN*
GN-CS	38489	1559	24993	3702
SMOR-CS	33765	544	26008	8426
ASV-CS	36356	555	25997	5835
MV & WMV	39675	1806	24746	2516
CH-CS	41894	1974	24578	297

Table 1: Identification of Compounds

The reason for MV and WMV performing alike in this task of identifying compounds is that in case a compound splitter does not return an analysis, it is disregarded. This means that, if at least one compound splitter returns a result, both MV and WMV decide that this noun is a compound regardless of any weighting.

There are remarkable improvements especially in the numbers of true positives and false negatives of the combined algorithms compared to the individual ones. The reason for these remarkable differences is obvious: the individual splitting algorithms are very heterogeneous, which leads to an improved overall coverage. Table 2 shows the calculated percentages for accuracy, precision, and recall of the task of identifying compounds.

Algorithm	*Accuracy*	*Precision*	*Recall*
GN-CS	92.34%	96.11%	91.23%
SMOR-CS	86.95%	98.41%	80.03%
ASV-CS	90.70%	98.50%	86.17%
MV & WMV	93.71%	95.65%	94.04%
CH-CS	96.70%	95.50%	99.30%

Table 2: Accuracy, Precision, and Recall of Identifying Compounds

Highest accuracy and best recall are achieved by CH-CS, whereas ASV-CS and SMOR-CS yield highest precision. The values in this section (Tables 1 and 2) are gathered with the aim of identifying if a noun in GermaNet is a compound or not. The correctness of the splitting into two constituents is considered in the following sections.

7.2 Predicting Immediate Splitting Position

This part of the evaluation regards the splitting position. It is evaluated for all 42191 compounds whether the predicted position at which the algorithms split the compounds into two constituents is correct. An obvious error is, e.g., the splitting of *Tiefkühltruhe* 'deep-freezer' into *tief* + *Kühltruhe* instead of *tiefkühlen* + *Truhe*. An example of an erroneous splitting that is not as obvious is the splitting of *Muskelshirt* 'muscle shirt' into *Muskel* + *Hirt* instead of *Muskel* + *Shirt*. In contrast, the predicted position of the splitting *Bundfaltenhose* 'pleated pants' into *Bundfalten* + *Hose* (instead of *Bundfalte* + *Hose*) is correct, although this example reveals a wrong inflection of the modifier. The evaluation results are presented in Table 3; where the accuracy specifies the number of correctly predicted splitting positions divided by the total number of compounds.

Algorithm	*Correct position*	*Erroneous position*	*Accuracy*
GN-CS	37779	4411	89.54%
SMOR-CS	32863	9326	77.89%
ASV-CS	35407	6783	83.92%
MV	38548	3636	91.38%
WMV	38688	3496	91.71%
CH-CS	40010	2181	94.83%

Table 3: Predicting Immediate Splitting Position

For the task of predicting the immediate splitting position again all combined algorithms outperform the individual compound splitters.

7.3 Prediction of Immediate Constituents

This section evaluates the correctness of the entire prediction of two immediate constituents, including word class and inflection. The predicted constituents for all 42191 compounds are analyzed and the results listed in Table 4. The evaluation takes into account, that for some compounds, there is more than one composition correct. For *Nachtspeicherheizung* 'night storage heater', e.g., two internal groupings are semantically correct: *Nacht* + *Speicherheizung* and *Nachtspeicher* + *Heizung*. In other compounds, two word classes are possible for the modifier. For example, *Spielecke* 'kid's corner' might be composed of *Spiel* + *Ecke* or *spielen* + *Ecke*.

Algorithm	*Correct constituents*	*Erroneous constituents*	*Accuracy*
GN-CS	32738	9449	77.60%
SMOR-CS	31757	10432	75.27%
ASV-CS	31621	10568	74.95%
MV	33349	8832	79.06%
WMV	33176	9005	78.65%
CH-CS	38994	3197	92.42%

Table 4: Prediction of Immediate Constituents

Table 4 reveals that all combined compound splitters outperform the individual compound splitters in the main task of the present project, i.e., in determining immediate constituents of compounds in GermaNet. The best overall result with an accuracy of 92.42% is achieved by the hybrid combined compound splitter CH-CS.

7.4 Error Analysis

To distinguish different cases that cause erroneous predictions of the immediate constituents, the following error types were identified. The occurrences of these error types – presented in Table 5 – are gathered for the combined algorithm CH-CS only as this error classification is done in a manual verification step.

- *Position*: The proposed splitting position is wrong, e.g., *Eislaufbahn* 'ice rink' is split into *Eis* + *Laufbahn* instead of *Eislauf* + *Bahn*.
- *Not parsed*: Some compounds are recognized but not parsed. For example, a compound such as *Kreuzschlitzschraubenzieher* ,Philips screwdriver', consisting of four parts, is recognized as a compound, but not grouped into its immediate constituents.
- *Wrong lemma*: For some predictions, the lemmatization of the modifier is erroneous. For example, the immediate lemmatized constituents of *Hühnerleiter* 'chicken ladder' are *Huhn* and *Leiter*, but CH-CS splits the compound into *Hühner* + *Leiter* without lemmatizing the modifier.
- *Word class*: The modifier has been assigned a wrong word class. Two different subcases are distinguished:
  1. The proposed word does not exist. For example, *Mischanlage* 'mixing plant' is erroneously split into *Misch* + *Anlage*, but the modifier needs to be the verb *mischen*, because a noun like *Misch* does not exist.
  2. The proposed word (class) has a wrong reading, e.g., the splitting of *Allesschneider* 'slicing maschine' into *All* + *Schneider* instead of *alles* + *Schneider* reveals a wrong reading of the modifier.
- *False negatives*: Those compounds that are erroneously not identified as a compound.

Error type	*CH-CS*
Position	384 (12.01%)
Not parsed	1490 (46.60%)
Wrong lemma	207 (6.47%)
Word class 1	325 (10.17%)
Word class 2	311 (9.73%)
False negatives	297 (9.29%)
Other	183 (5.72%)
Total errors	3197

Table 5: Occurrences of Different Error Types

Two (obvious) causes of errors are identified in Table 6: bound morphemes and missing entries in GermaNet. Bound morphemes such as *Him-* in *Himbeere* 'raspberry' (cf. section 2 above) are a common source of error because the algorithm cannot reliably identify such words. Second, if either the modifier or the head is not in GermaNet, the algorithm may propose a wrong splitting. For example, the correct splitting of *Feincordhose* 'narrow wale corduroy pants' is *Feincord* + *Hose*, but as *Feincord* is not in GermaNet, the algorithm erroneously proposes *fein* + *Cordhose* as those two constituents are entries in GermaNet.

Error type	*Total*	*Bound morpheme*	*No entry in GermaNet*
Position	384	18 (4.7%)	280 (72.9%)
Not parsed	1490	98 (6.6%)	1061 (71.2%)
Wrong lemma	207	7 (3.4%)	150 (72.5%)
Word class 1	325	112 (34.5%)	226 (69.5%)
Word class 2	311	14 (4.5%)	87 (28.0%)
FN	297	15 (5.2%)	153 (51.5%)
Other	183	2 (1.1%)	23 (12.6%)
Total errors	3197	266 (8.3%)	1980 (61.9%)

Table 6: Causes of Errors

A third error type is identified for false positives – actually for 35.3% of all false positives (696 of 1974): Words like *Bausparen* 'building society savings' or *Zusammenprall* 'collision' are frequently treated as compounds, while these are nouns derived from compound verbs.

8 Conclusion and Future Work

Existing tools for splitting compounds were adapted to overcome issues with determining immediate constituents of compounds. Combinatory algorithms using three heterogeneous kinds of compound splitters are developed to achieve better results. As the combined compound splitting algorithms all outperform the individual compound splitters, the overall combined result should improve further, including even more individual compound splitters. The best overall result with an accuracy of 92.42% is achieved by a hybrid combined compound splitter that takes into account all knowledge provided by the individual compound splitters, and in addition some domain knowledge about German derivation morphology and compounding.

There are two obvious problems with the used individual compound splitters. First, lemmatized forms are never generated by GN-CS. Extending GN-CS with a lemmatizer to determine base forms can enhance this drawback. Second, the immediate constituents of compounds consisting of more than two or three constituents are not determined by SMOR-CS and ASV-CS, respectively. This issue can be improved through bracketing those compounds by ASV-CS and SMOR-CS.

In future work, we plan to automatically predict compound-internal relations between the now determined immediate constituents by using GermaNet's relations. This would also mean that the immediate compound constituents would have to be automatically disambiguated. Further, an automatic extension of GermaNet with compounds by using statistical information of existing compounds in GermaNet is envisioned.

Acknowledgments

The research reported in this paper was jointly funded by the SFB 833 grant of the DFG and by the CLARIN-D grant of the BMBF.

We would like to thank our research assistant Sarah Schulz for her help with the evaluation reported in Section 7. Special thanks go to our GermaNet colleague Reinhild Barkey for extensive discussions on the syntax and semantics of compounds and on their modeling in GermaNet.

References

Marco Baroni, Johannes Matiasek, and Harald Trost. 2002. Predicting the Components of German Nominal Compounds. *Frank van Harmelen (eds.), Proceedings of the 15th European Conference on Artificial Intelligence (ECAI)*, Amsterdam: IOS Press, 470-474.

Mathias Creutz and Krista Lagus. 2005. Unsupervised Morpheme Segmentation and Morphology Induction from Text Corpora Using Morfessor 1.0. *Publications in Computer and Information Science*, Report A81. Helsinki University of Technology Helsinki, Finland.

Peter Eisenberg. 2006. *Das Wort – Grundriss der deutschen Grammatik*. 3rd edition, Verlag J. B. Melzer, Stuttgart/Weimar, Germany.

Christiane Fellbaum (eds.). 1998. *WordNet – An Electronic Lexical Database*. The MIT Press.

Radu Florian and David Yarowsky. 2002. Modeling consensus: classifier combination for word sense disambiguation. In *Proceedings of the ACL-02 conference on Empirical methods in natural language processing (EMNLP '02)*, Vol. 10. Association for Computational Linguistics, Stroudsburg, PA, USA, 25-32.

Mariikka Haapalainen and Ari Majorin. 1994. *GERTWOL: Ein System zur automatischen Wortformerkennung Deutscher Wörter*. Technical report, Lingsoft Inc. https://files.ifi.uzh.ch/cl/volk/LexMorphVorl/Lexikon04.Gertwol.html

Verena Henrich and Erhard Hinrichs. 2010. GernEdiT – The GermaNet Editing Tool. In *Proceedings of the Seventh Conference on International Language Resources and Evaluation (LREC 2010)*, main conference. Valletta, Malta.

Claudia Kunze and Lothar Lemnitzer. 2002. GermaNet – representation, visualization, application. In *Proceedings of LREC 2002*, main conference, Vol V. pp. 1485-1491.

Stefan Langer. 1998. Zur Morphologie und Semantik von Nominalkomposita. *Tagungsband der 4. Konferenz zur Verarbeitung natürlicher Sprache*, KONVENS, pp. 83–97.

Robi Polikar. 2006. Ensemble based systems in decision making. In *IEEE Circuits and Systems Magazine*, 16(3):21–45.

Helmut Schmid, Arne Fitschen, and Ulrich Heid. 2004. SMOR: A German Computational Morphology Covering Derivation, Composition, and Inflection. In *Proceedings of the IVth International Conference on Language Resources and Evaluation (LREC 2004)*, p. 1263-1266, Lisbon, Portugal.

Hans van Halteren, Walter Daelemans and Jakub Zavrel. 2001. Improving accuracy in word class tagging through the combination of machine learning systems. In *Compuational Linguistics*, 27, 2, 199-229.

Piek Vossen. 2002. EuroWordNet General Document. EuroWordNet Project LE2-4003 & LE4-8328 report, Version 3, Final, University of Amsterdam.

Hans F. Witschel and Chris Biemann. 2005. Rigorous dimensionality reduction through linguistically motivated feature selection for text categorisation. In *Proceedings of NODALIDA 2005*, Joensuu, Finland.

Segmentation and Clustering of Textual Sequences: a Typological Approach

Christelle Cocco, Raphaël Pittier, François Bavaud and Aris Xanthos
University of Lausanne, Switzerland
{Christelle.Cocco,Raphael.Pittier,
Francois.Bavaud,Aris.Xanthos}@unil.ch

Abstract

The long term goal of this research is to develop a program able to produce an automatic segmentation and categorization of textual sequences into discourse types. In this preliminary contribution, we present the construction of an algorithm which takes a segmented text as input and attempts to produce a categorization of sequences, such as narrative, argumentative, descriptive and so on. Also, this work aims at investigating a possible convergence between the typological approach developed in particular in the field of text and discourse analysis in French by Adam (2008) and Bronckart (1997) and unsupervised statistical learning.

1 Introduction

An increasing amount of research has been conducted concerning text genre detection using POS (part-of-speech) tags since the work of Biber (1988). For instance, Malrieu and Rastier (2001) describe how to classify texts according to genres (comedy, tragedy, drama...) or discourses (literary, legal, political...) using POS-tags.

POS-tags can be determined in an unsupervised way (see *e.g.* Schmid (1994)) and their distribution happens to differ according to types of texts, such as narrative, explicative and so on. Hence, developing automatic discourse type detection, which is of interest to the linguistic community, seems practicable.

Thus, the purpose of the present study is to cluster clauses of a text into discourse types, *i.e.* to develop a tool for type detection with a limited quantity of annotated texts. We limit ourselves to the use of simple bag-of-words models on which fuzzy and K-means clustering are applied.

Specifically, the aim is twofold: firstly, the construction of a program which takes a segmented text as input and produces a categorization of sequences of clauses by clustering, based principally on POS-tags; secondly, the comparison of this clustering with the typology proposed by a human expert, corresponding to discourse types. Thus, this preliminary work aims at investigating a possible convergence between unsupervised statistical learning on the one hand, and the typological approach developed in particular in the field of French linguistics by Adam (2008) and in language psychology by Bronckart (1997) on the other hand.

As a first step, sample texts were manually annotated, that is segmented (section 2.1) and classified (section 2.2). Then, the clauses resulting from the previous segmentation were clustered on the basis of their POS distribution (sections 2.3 and 2.4). It appeared that the latter vary across the typological classes proposed by the expert (section 3.1) which were compared to those resulting from fuzzy and K-means clustering processes (sections 3.2 and 4). Future developments are proposed in section 5.

2 Method

2.1 Segmentation

The first step of this research was to create a corpus of annotated texts. For that purpose, a human expert has been working on 19th century French short stories by Maupassant. Only one genre is examined, because distributions of POS-tags vary with genre as mentioned in the introduction. For the same reason, only one author is considered (see *e.g.* Koppel and Schler (2003)) in this preliminary work. Annotation was carried out by means of XML tags, which is becoming a standard practice in this field (see *e.g.* Daoust et al. (2010)).

It transpired that segmentation into sentences

Texts	♯ sentences	♯ clauses	♯ tokens		♯ types		% discourse types according to the human expert					
			with punct.	without punct.	wordforms	tags	nar	dial	descr	expl	arg	inj
"Un Fou?"	150	316	2'635	2'185	764	28	33.54	14.56	10.44	14.56	18.67	8.23
"L'Orient"	88	189	1'750	1'488	654	27	28.04	25.93	20.11	19.05	4.23	2.65
"Un Fou"	266	400	3'140	2'574	837	29	44.75	1.75	13.25	11.75	17.00	11.50
Total	504	905	7'525	6'247	2'255	30	37.35	11.27	13.70	14.25	14.92	8.51

Table 1: Statistics of the three annotated texts by Maupassant. Number of sentences as considered by TreeTagger (Schmid, 1994). Number of clauses as segmented by the human expert. Number of tokens including punctuation and compounds as tagged by TreeTagger. Number of simple tokens without punctuation and figures, considering compounds as separated tokens. Number of wordform types. Number of POS-tag types. Percentage of clauses for each discourse type (nar=narrative, dial=dialogal, descr=descriptive, expl=explicative, arg=argumentative, inj=injunctive).

was not sufficiently fine-grained for the envisioned analysis, so the expert was instructed to segment the texts at the clause level.

2.2 Classification by a human expert

To be able to compare the results of the automatic clustering with a classification according to the typological approach developed in particular by Adam (2008; 2005) and Bronckart (1997), the expert was then asked to classify the clauses into six types. In fact, Adam proposes a classification of textual sequences into five types: narrative, argumentative, descriptive, explicative and dialoged sequences. However, we decided to add an injunctive type, following Bronckart. The expert decision to classify clauses was based partly upon formal criteria, such as punctuation, typical words, tense of verbs and semantics; and partly upon his linguistic and literary knowledge. Table 1 shows descriptive statistics about annotated texts.

An important issue inherent in this task is that the typological structure of the text is hierarchical rather than linear. This means that a sequence of a given type may contain sequences of other types. The number of inclusions is not limited. For the purpose of annotation, the use of XML tags appears to be appropriate, since it allows us to describe trees. However, taking into account the full hierarchical structure represents an additional difficulty for the automatic clustering procedure; in this first approach, the problem is treated as linear, *i.e.* only the leaves of the tree structure are considered (for the clauses). For instance, in the extract given in table 2, the first three clauses are regarded as narrative; the forth as injunctive; the fifth as argumentative; and the others as explicative.

```
<div type="narratif">
<e>Je le trouvai tantôt couché sur un divan,
 en plein rêve d'opium.</e>
<e>Il me tendit la main sans remuer le corps,</e>
<e>et me dit :</e><cr/>
  <div type="dialogal">
    <div type="injonctif">
    <e>Reste là, parle,</e>
    </div>
    <div type="argumentatif">
    <e>je te répondrai de temps en temps,</e>
      <div type="explicatif">
      <e>mais je ne bougerai point,</e>
      <e>car tu sais qu'une fois la drogue avalée</e>
      <e>il faut demeurer sur le dos.</e><cr/>
      </div>
    </div>
  </div>
</div>
```

Table 2: Annotated extract of "L'Orient" by Maupassant. <e> refers to clause.

pared with the limited database of annotated clauses created by the expert. As a consequence, only POS-tags (*e.g.* noun, adjective, verb present, demonstrative pronoun, and so on) are used to cluster clauses.

In more detail, this program involves several steps. Firstly, the text is divided into n clauses (based on the manual annotation). Secondly, POS-tags are attributed to all the words of each clause with TreeTagger (Schmid, 1994), yielding a distribution over POS-tags. Thus a contingency table between clauses and POS-tags is obtained.

As a next step, clauses are categorized with the thermodynamic clustering procedure, a variant of fuzzy K-means, which amounts to minimizing a free energy term, made up of an energy (the within-cluster dispersion) and an entropy (the clause-cluster mutual information). In a nutshell, fuzzy clustering aims at assigning each clause to the various clusters in a probabilistic fashion. At each iteration step, the membership z_i^g of sentence

2.3 Automatic fuzzy clustering

The general principle is to perform a maximally unsupervised classification (clustering) to be com-

i in group g is defined by the following equation (Rose et al., 1990; Bavaud, 2009):

$$z_{ig} = \frac{\rho_g \exp(-\beta D_i^g)}{\sum_{h=1}^{m} \rho_h \exp(-\beta D_i^h)} \tag{1}$$

where $\rho_g = \sum_{i=1}^{n} f_i z_{ig}$ is the relative weight of group g and f_i is the relative weight of clause i, D_i^g is the chi-squared dissimilarity between clause i and the centroid of group g, and β is the inverse temperature parameter controlling the number of groups (a larger β implies more groups). At the outset, centroids are chosen randomly (uniformly distributed memberships).

In addition, the user must choose the initial number m of groups, the number $N_{\max}$ of maximum iterations and the relative temperature t_{rel} defining the inverse temperature $\beta := 1/(t_{\text{rel}} \times \Delta)$, where $\Delta := \frac{1}{2}\sum_{ij} f_i f_j D_{ij}$ is total inertia and D_{ij} is the chi-squared dissimilarity between clauses i and j.

Moreover, groups whose profiles are close enough are aggregated, thus reducing the initial number of groups m to the final number of groups M (Bavaud, 2009). In that case, memberships of sentences of similar groups are added in the following way: $z_{i[g \cup h]} = z_{ig} + z_{ih}$. Two groups are considered close if $\theta_{gh}/\sqrt{\theta_{gg}\theta_{hh}} \geq 1 - 10^{-5}$ where $\theta_{gh} = \sum_{i=1}^{n} f_i z_{ig} z_{ih}$ measures the overlap between groups g and h (Bavaud, 2010).

Also, a factorial correspondence analysis (FCA) is performed to produce a low dimensional representation of the chi-squared dissimilarities D_{ij} between clauses (and between POS-tags).

At the end of the process, each clause is attributed to the most probable group and the results are plotted in 2D (figures 3 and 4).

Moreover, observing the dependency of the effective number of groups as well as evaluation measures (figures 1 and 2) provides a guidance for determining suitable values of the temperature.

2.4 K-means clustering

We also compared the above fuzzy algorithm to the well-known K-means method (see *e.g.* Manning and Schütze (1999)). As for the former, chi-squared dissimilarities are calculated in the algorithm. Two versions are investigated, a weighted and a non-weighted (*i.e.* uniform weights for each clause) approaches.

In K-means, the number m of groups (and not the relative temperature) must be chosen *a priori*. We have concentrated on $m = 6$ (the number of groups in the expert classification) as well as on values of m corresponding to performance peaks in the fuzzy version (see figures 1 and 2).

2.5 Evaluation criteria

Regarding the evaluation, the aim is to compare automatic clustering and expert classification. In addition to χ^2 statistic which measures the dependence between the two classifications, a certain number of similarity indices between partitions exist, among which the Jaccard index, noted J, seems to be a good indicator (Denœud and Guénoche, 2006; Youness and Saporta, 2004):

$$J = \frac{\sum_i \sum_j n_{ij}^2 - n}{\sum_i n_{i\bullet}^2 + \sum_j n_{\bullet j}^2 - \sum_i \sum_j n_{ij}^2 - n} \tag{2}$$

where n_{ij} is the number of clauses belonging to the unsupervised cluster i and the manual class j.

Another interesting measure is the corrected Rand index (Denœud and Guénoche, 2006):

$$RC = \frac{r - \text{Exp}(r)}{\text{Max}(r) - \text{Exp}(r)} \tag{3}$$

with $r = \frac{\sum_{i,j} n_{ij}(n_{ij}-1)}{2}$,
$\text{Exp}(r) = \frac{\sum_i n_{i\bullet}(n_{i\bullet}-1)\sum_j n_{\bullet j}(n_{\bullet j}-1)}{2n(n-1)}$,
$\text{Max}(r) = \frac{\sum_i n_{i\bullet}(n_{i\bullet}-1)+\sum_j n_{\bullet j}(n_{\bullet j}-1)}{4}$.

3 Results

3.1 Relevance of the method

To ensure that the choice of using POS-tags is relevant in this context, the dependence between the classification of clauses made by the human expert and the POS-tags they contain must be established. Table 3 reports the corresponding independence ratios ($R_{w,c}$ in Li et al. (2008)) for the three annotated texts by Maupassant. An independence ratio greater than 1 shows a mutual attraction, whereas if it is less than 1, it shows a mutual repulsion. Furthermore, stars in this table indicate the most significant chi2 term-category dependance for each POS-tag with 2 degrees of freedom in relation to $\chi^2_{1-0.001}[2] = 10.83$ (Yang and Pedersen, 1997; Li et al., 2008). It appears that a number of POS-tags are relevant for the types investigated, such as adjectives for the descriptive type ($q = 1.62$ and chi2 $= 27.88$), simple past tense for the narrative type ($q = 2.60$ and chi2 $= 110.55$) or future tense for the dialogal type ($q = 4.63$ and chi2 $= 62.10$). Satisfactorily enough, the value of the chi-square on the contingency table between POS-tags and discourse types (chi2 $= 752.6$ with df $= 145$) is large, denoting a highly significant link between classes and POS-tags ($p < 10^{-15}$). Moreover, research into genre detection using POS-tags reports interesting results (Karlgren and Cutting, 1994; Kessler et al., 1997; Malrieu and Rastier, 2001), which are, to some extent, relevant for type detection.

	nar	dial	descr	expl	arg	inj
ABR	**2.92**	0.00	0.00	0.00	0.00	0.00
ADJ	0.78	1.07	**1.62***	1.10	0.85	0.75
ADV	0.96	1.02	0.71	1.17	1.04	**1.39**
DET:ART	0.91	0.97	1.15	0.83	**1.22**	0.93
DET:POS	**1.27**	0.76	0.95	0.80	0.93	0.77
INT	**1.34**	**1.34**	0.00	1.05	0.95	0.94
KON	0.93	1.03	0.75	1.19	**1.25**	0.84
NAM	1.00	1.15	1.11	1.03	0.33	**2.15**
NOM	0.92	0.89	**1.20**	0.87	1.15	1.03
NUM	**1.51**	0.52	1.05	0.93	0.74	0.00
PRO	**2.92**	0.00	0.00	0.00	0.00	0.00
PRO:DEM	0.69	0.97	0.95	**1.52**	1.42	0.58
PRO:IND	0.68	1.34	1.08	**1.45**	1.33	0.00
PRO:PER	**1.30***	1.03	0.58	1.05	0.86	0.67
PRO:REL	0.70	1.14	1.25	**1.28**	1.01	1.07
PRP	0.96	0.99	**1.18**	0.98	1.04	0.77
PRP:det	0.59*	1.45	1.31	0.65	1.19	**1.78**
PUN	0.95	0.99	1.15	0.80	1.00	**1.34**
PUN:cit	0.00	4.11*	0.80	0.00	0.23	**4.91**
SENT	**1.16**	0.96	0.79	1.08	0.83	1.05
VER:cond	1.29	0.97	0.00	0.87	**1.83**	0.00
VER:futu	0.53	**4.63***	0.39	0.44	0.17	1.37
VER:impf	1.44	0.38	**2.06***	0.34	0.50	0.12
VER:infi	1.07	0.78	0.89	**1.50**	0.91	0.53
VER:pper	**1.26**	0.91	0.98	0.90	0.80	0.57
VER:ppre	**1.42**	1.09	1.05	0.78	0.31	0.81
VER:pres	0.81	0.98	0.71	1.34	1.07	**1.79***
VER:simp	**2.60***	0.10	0.32	0.00	0.28	0.00
VER:subi	0.53	0.00	0.59	**5.26***	0.00	0.00
VER:subp	0.32	**3.58**	0.00	1.61	0.64	1.67

Table 3: Independence ratio for the three texts by Maupassant (q): numbers indicate the ratio of the observed counts to their expected values under independence. The strongest mutual attraction for each POS-tag is in bold characters. Stars in cells point out the most significant chi-squared per POS-tag ($\alpha = 0.001$).[2]

3.2 Results with automatic fuzzy clustering

Figures 1 to 6 present the results for the method described above. The number of groups after aggregation and the corrected Rand index as a function of the relative temperature are shown for the text "Un Fou?" in figure 1. These curves are obtained with an initial number of groups $m = 316$ corresponding to the number of clauses $n = 316$ and a number of maximum iterations of $N_{max} = 400$. The entire process is executed around 20 times for each relative temperature (with randomly chosen initial memberships) and so, values in graphics represent the mean of these 20 simulations. With the same parameters, figure 2 shows the evolution of the Jaccard index with the rela-

[2]A complete explanation about the signification of POS-tags in the table is available on `http://www.ims.uni-stuttgart.de/~schmid/french-tagset.html`

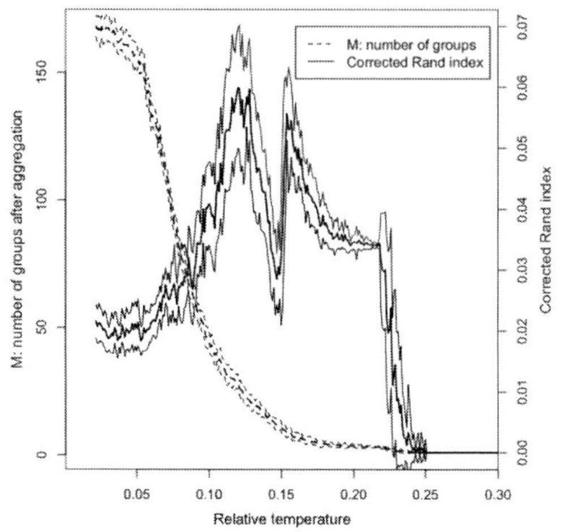

Figure 1: "Un Fou?" by Maupassant: number of groups and corrected Rand index as a function of the relative temperature. For each curve, the thick line represents the mean and the two thin lines represent the standard deviation.

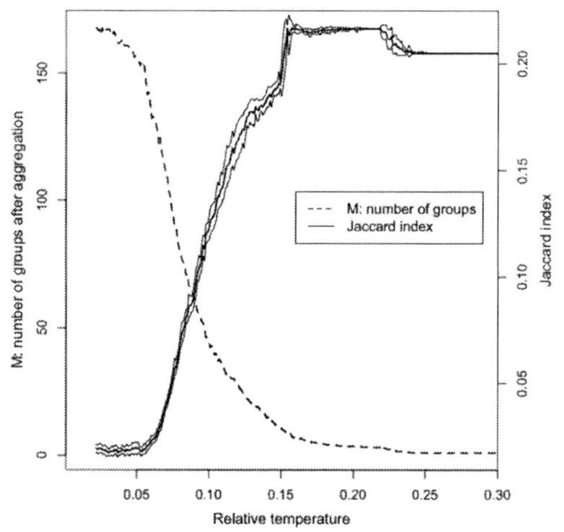

Figure 2: "Un Fou?" by Maupassant: Jaccard index according to the relative temperature. The curve of number of groups is given for reminder.

tive temperature. In figure 1, the two remarkable peaks for the corrected Rand index correspond to around 26 and 8.5 groups after aggregation. Figure 2 shows that Jaccard index increases when the number of groups decreases until there is only one group. However, the maximum of Jaccard index appears around 8 groups as does the second maximum of the corrected Rand index. It is obvious that the two indexes give different results. On the one hand, the Jaccard index takes a non-zero value in presence of single group, an artefact due to the absence of correction for self-similarity in (2). On the other hand, the corrected Rand index can take negative values, which means that results are worse than chance.

Similar studies were made for "L'Orient" and "Un Fou". For the former, the corrected Rand index decreases when the relative temperature increases, with two small local maxima for around 96 and 30 goups. For the latter, corrected Rand index is always negative, except with small relative temperatures which correspond to 180 groups. And for the both texts, Jaccard index increases while the number of groups decrease monotically until it becomes maximal for one group.

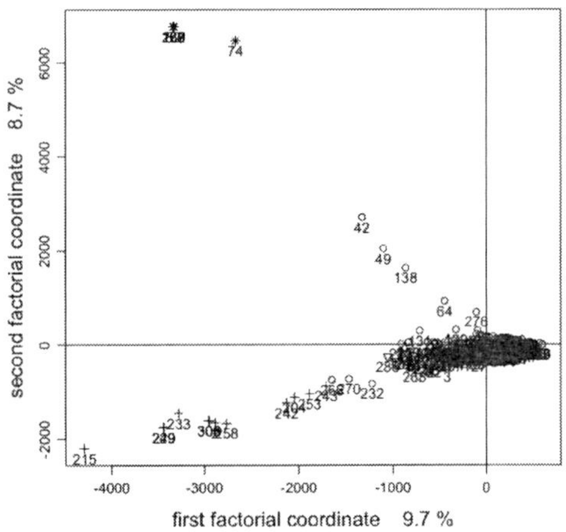

Figure 3: Clustering of clauses of "Un Fou?" by Maupassant (each symbol belongs to one of the eight clusters and numbers correspond with the position of clauses in the text).

Finally, an example for "Un Fou?" is given in figures 3 to 6 with the following parameters: $m = 316$, $N_{\max} = 400$ and $t_{rel} = 0.157$ designed to produce $M = 8$ groups after aggregation, because the two evaluation indexes have interesting value

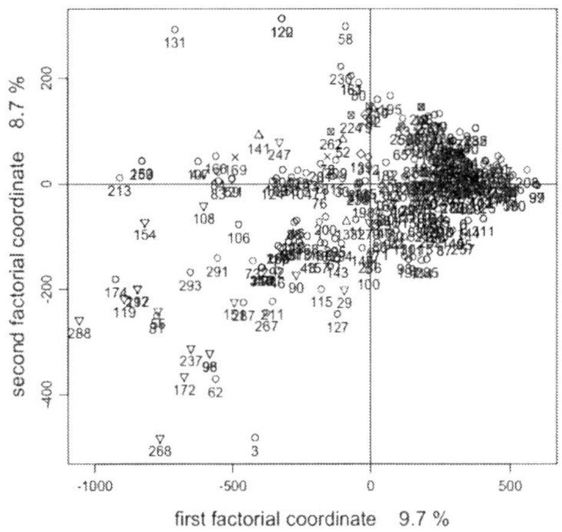

Figure 4: Zoom of figure 3.

for this number of group. In figure 3, all clauses ($n = 316$) are represented in a 2D plot. Figure 5 represents dissimilarities between POS-tags in the same space as figure 3. For all these figures, dissimilarities are not well represented, since the expressed inertia is only 18.4%.

4 Preliminary evaluation

		Classes identified by the expert						Total
		arg	descr	dial	expl	inj	nar	
Clusters	1	48	30	33	34	15	101	261
	2	4	0	2	1	0	0	7
	3	0	0	1	1	0	0	2
	4	0	0	2	0	0	0	2
	5	0	2	2	0	8	0	12
	6	2	0	1	0	3	0	6
	7	5	0	5	4	0	3	17
	8	0	1	0	6	0	2	9
Total		59	33	46	46	26	106	316

Table 4: Cross-counts between unsupervised and manual classification.

Table 4 shows cross-counts between automatic clusters and classes assigned by the human expert corresponding to the analysis of figures 3 to 6. The chi square reveals a strong relation between automatic clustering and expert classification (chi2 $=$ 137.28 with df $= 35$ and $p < 10^{-13}$). For this table, other evaluation criteria are less satisfactory ($RC = 0.06$ and $J = 0.22$).

In addition to the results obtained above with the fuzzy clustering, K-means (respectively fuzzy clustering) was performed on the three texts for 6 groups (respectively with a relative temperature yielding around 6 groups) and on "Un Fou?" and "L'Orient" for a number of groups (respectively relative temperature) corresponding to the best

	Method	♯S	m	M		$N_{\max}$	N_{eff}		chi2		df		J		RC	
				mean	sd		mean	sd	mean	sd	mean	sd	mean	sd	mean	sd
"Un Fou?"	NW K-means	300	6	-	-	200	14.26	4.49	155.96	28.34	25	-	.18	.01	.06	.02
	W K-means	300	6	-	-	200	16.18	5.60	152.46	28.21	25	-	.15	.01	.07	.02
	fuzzy t_{rel}=0.165	40	316	6.1	1.71	400	182	49.1	104.26	14.70	25.5	8.53	.21	.00	.04	.01
	NW K-means	89	26	-	-	200	12.62	3.16	338.04	19.58	125	-	.07	.01	.05	.01
	W K-means	225	26	-	-	200	11.68	2.78	335.66	16.56	125	-	.07	.00	.05	.01
	fuzzy t_{rel}=0.125	40	316	23.8	2.66	400	195.1	73.2	265.29	20.42	113.9	12.83	.17	.01	.06	.01
"L'Orient"	NW K-means	300	6	-	-	200	12.66	3.76	63.09	8.94	25	-	.15	.01	.02	.01
	W K-means	300	6	-	-	200	12.42	3.81	69.95	13.75	25	-	.14	.01	.04	.02
	fuzzy t_{rel}=0.18	40	189	6.48	0.82	400	161.2	61.5	48.24	5.83	27.38	4.08	.20	.00	-.01	.00
	NW K-means	144	30	-	-	200	9.22	2.25	225.97	19.95	145	-	.06	.01	.03	.01
	W K-means	207	30	-	-	200	8.76	1.79	229.74	19.69	145	-	.06	.00	.04	.01
	fuzzy t_{rel}=0.117	40	189	30.8	3.04	400	290.8	63.2	220.92	29.93	149	15.20	.13	.01	.01	.01
"Un Fou"	NW K-means	300	6	-	-	200	17.00	6.22	63.20	16.45	25	-	.16	.01	-.04	.01
	W K-means	300	6	-	-	200	17.80	6.43	70.61	19.33	25	-	.15	.01	.00	.01
	fuzzy t_{rel}=0.188	40	400	6.08	1.07	400	89.1	27.5	142.89	11.72	25.38	5.36	.24	.01	-.04	.02

Table 5: Comparison of results between K-means (non-weigthed (NW) and weighted (W)) and fuzzy clustering algorithms. ♯S denotes the number of random starts on which the mean and the standard deviation (sd) are computed for evaluation criteria and other values. N_{eff} refers to the effective number of iterations needed to stabilize the group centroid positions.

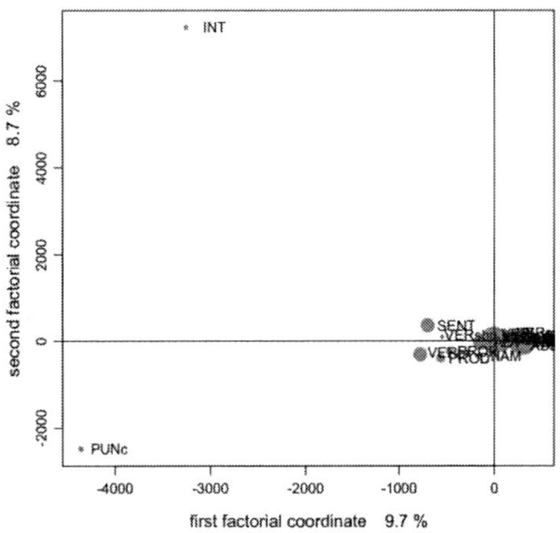

Figure 5: Representation of POS-tags of "Un Fou?" by Maupassant.

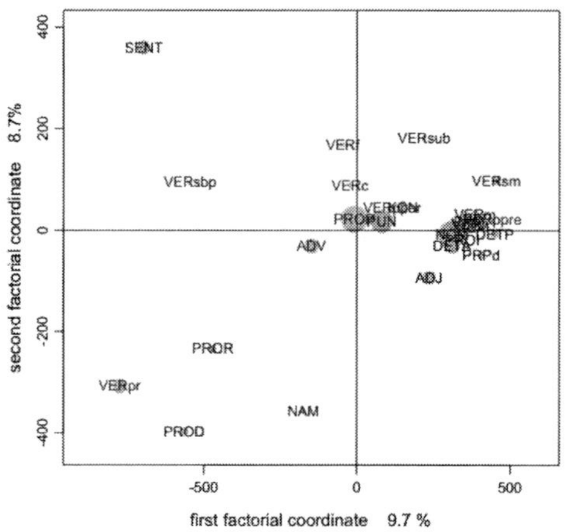

Figure 6: Zoom of figure 5.

performances. Evaluation criteria for the three texts and all methods are summarized in table 5. It is obvious that the three evaluation criteria do not imply the same conclusions. For instance, chi2 values indicates that for "Un Fou?" and 6 groups, the non-weighted K-means induces the most promising classification. Regarding the Jaccard index, the fuzzy clustering seems to involve better results. As for the corrected Rand, it shows that weighted K-means improves the clustering. However, a certain number of regularities transpire. For "Un Fou?"and 26 groups, the weighted K-means never implies the best results according to the three criteria, while for "L'Orient" and "Un Fou", the non-weighted K-means never induces the best classification. Finally, the corrected Rand index is low, or even negative, for "Un Fou". Perhaps it is due to the fact that this text is partly different, even if it is a short story as the both other texts. Indeed, this text is made of a journal part.

To conclude, all these preliminary results must be considered with caution, in regard to the small size of the sample, annotated by a unique expert.

5 Work in progress

Despite encouraging first results, demonstrating the dependence between the clusters obtained based on POS-tags and the linguistic types assessed by the human expert, the limitations are obvious, and further improvements have to be explored. First of all, it will be interesting to apply a bi- or trigram model to replace individual POS-tags. Besides this, using only POS-tags might reveal itself no sufficient, and calling for considering the inclusion of typical words which discriminate, in a certain proportion, the different discourse types. And, in the same line, feature selection between POS-tags could improve results (see *e.g.* Yang and Pedersen(1997); Li et al. (2008)). It is also crucial to consider and exploit the hierarchical structure of discourse types. One way to do this could be to take into account the dominance of one type over others in a part of the hierarchical structure. Moreover, the use of other measures of clause dissimilarities, alternative to the chi-squared distances, may improve clustering results. Furthermore, combining fuzzy clustering and K-means as in the "simulated annealing" approach of Rose et al. (1990) should be explored. Finally, the possibility of automatically segmenting the text into clauses should be considered.

References

Jean-Michel Adam. 2005. *La linguistique textuelle: Introduction à l'analyse textuelle des discours*. Armand Colin, Paris.

Jean-Michel Adam. 2008. *Les textes: types et prototypes, 2nd edition*. Armand Colin, Paris.

François Bavaud. 2009. Aggregation invariance in general clustering approaches. *Advances in Data Analysis and Classification*, 3(3):205–225.

François Bavaud. 2010. Euclidean Distances, Soft and Spectral Clustering on Weighted Graphs. *ECML PKDD 2010: European Conference on Machine Learning and Principles and Practice of Knowledge Discovery in Databases*, J.L. Balcázar et al. (Eds.), 6321:103–118.

Douglas Biber. 1988. *Variation across Speech and Writing*. Cambridge University Press, Cambridge, UK.

Jean-Paul Bronckart. 1997. *Activité langagière, textes et discours: pour un interactionisme socio-discursif*. Delachaux et Niestlé, Lausanne; Paris.

François Daoust, Yves Marcoux and Jean-Marie Viprey. 2010. L'annotation structurelle. *JADT 2010: 10th International Conference on Statistical Analysis of Textual Data*.

Lucile Denœud and Alain Guénoche. 2006. Comparison of Distances Indices Between Partitions. *Data Science and Classification*, 21–28.

Jussi Karlgren and Douglass Cutting. 1994. Recognizing text genres with simple metrics using discriminant analysis. *Proceedings of the 15th conference on Computational linguistics*, 2. Kyoto, Japan.

Brett Kessler, Geoffrey Nunberg and Hinrich Schütze. 1997. Automatic detection of text genre. *Proceedings of the 35th Annual Meeting of the Association for Computational Linguistics*, 32–38. Madrid, Spain.

Moshe Koppel and Jonathan Schler. 2003. Exploiting Stylistic Idiosyncrasies for Authorship Attribution. *Proceedings of IJCAI'03 Workshop on Computational Approaches to Style Analysis and Synthesis*, 69–72.

Yanjun Li, Congnan Luo and Soon M. Chung. 2008. Text Clustering with Feature Selection by Using Statistical Data. *IEEE Transactions on Knowledge and Data Engineering*, 20(5):641–652.

Denise Malrieu and François Rastier. 2001. Genres et variations morphosyntaxiques. *Traitement Automatique des langues*, 42(2):548–577.

Christopher D. Manning and Hinrich Schütze. 1999. *Foundations of Statistical Natural Language Processing*. The MIT Press, Cambridge, MA.

Guy de Maupassant. 1883. L'Orient. *Le Gaulois*, September 13. `http://un2sg4.unige.ch/athena/selva/maupassant/textes/orient.html`. Thierry Selva. accessed 2011, March 5.

Guy de Maupassant. 1884. Un Fou?. *Le Figaro*, September 1. `http://un2sg4.unige.ch/athena/maupassant/maup_fou.html`. Thierry Selva. Accessed 2011, February 7.

Guy de Maupassant. 1885. Un Fou. *Le Gaulois*, September 2. `http://un2sg4.unige.ch/athena/selva/maupassant/textes/unfou.html`. Thierry Selva. Accessed 2011, April 26.

Kenneth Rose, Eitan Gurewitz and Geoffrey C. Fox. 1990. Statistical mechanics and phase transitions in clustering. *Physical Review Letters*, 65(8):945–948.

Helmut Schmid. 1994. Probabilistic part-of-speech tagging using decision trees. *Proceedings of the International Conference on New Methods in Language Processing*, 44–49.

Yiming Yang and Jan O. Pedersen. 1997. A Comparative Study on Feature Selection in Text Categorization. *Proceedings of the Fourteenth International Conference on Machine Learning*, 412–420.

Genane Youness and Gilbert Saporta. 2004. Une méthodologie pour la comparaison de partitions. *Revue de statistique appliquée*, 52(1):97–120.

A Contextual Classification Strategy for Polarity Analysis of Direct Quotations from Financial News

Brett Drury
LIAAD-INESC
Portugal
brett.drury@gmail.com

Gaël Dias
HULTIG, Portugal
DLU/GREYC, France
ddg@di.ubi.pt

Luís Torgo
Fac. Sciences
LIAAD-INESC, Portugal
ltorgo@inescporto.pt

Abstract

Quotations from financial leaders can have significant influence upon the immediate prospects of economic actors. Indiscreet or candid comments from senior business leaders have had detrimental effects upon their organizations. Established polarity classification techniques perform poorly when classifying quotations because they display a number of complex linguistic features and lack of training data. The proposed strategy segments the quotations by inferred "opinion maker" role and then applies individual polarity classification strategies to each group of the segmented quotations. This strategy demonstrates a clear advantage over applying classical classification techniques to the whole corpus of quotations. While modelling contextual information with Random Forests based on a vector of unigrams plus the "opinion maker role" reaches a maximum F-measure of 52.85%, understanding the "bias" of the quotation maker previously based on its lexical usage allows 86.23% F-measure for "unbiased" quotations and 71.10% F-measure for "biased" quotations with the Naive Bayes classifier.

1 Introduction

Quotations from business leaders or government ministers can have profound effects upon the immediate and future prospects of economic actors. This phenomenon was demonstrated in a 1991 speech by Gerald Ratner at the Institute of Directors. He described his company's products as "*crap*" (Ratner, 2007) and that a pair of earrings sold by his company were "*cheaper than a prawn sandwich but probably wouldn't last as long*" (Ratner, 2007). His company (Ratners) lost 500 million pounds in value and had to change its name to Signet to distance itself from his speech. There are other, less colourful, examples of quotations impacting the financial prospects of an economic actor. Mervyn King, the governor of the Bank of England, declared in 2008 that "*now seems likely that Britain is entering a recession*"[1]. The day after, the British Pound promptly lost value on the foreign exchange markets.

Quotations are arguably an important source of information for researchers trying to determine the financial prospects of an economic actor. However, analysing quotations in terms of conveyed opinion is a non-trivial task because (1) quotations may contain metaphors, euphemisms, slang, obscenities, invented words or negations and (2) their polarity mainly depends on the context of the quotation and in particular, the opinion maker.

Most of the strategies proposed so far for polarity classification or opinion mining have been focusing on positively or negatively labelling word/phrases (Hatzivassiloglou and McKeown, 1997; Strapparava and Mihalcea, 2008), sentences (Hatzivassiloglou and Wiebe, 2000; Turney, 2002) or texts (Pang et al., 2002; Chesley et al., 2006) independent of their context.

Recently, the context of opinion has been addressed and research literature has revealed two different approaches. The first approach was proposed by (Al Masum Shaikh et al., 2007). The underlying idea is to either group the affective information into sets of emotions or to associate the affective information with the opinion of its readers. The contextual information is the reader in contrast to the writer. For example, the following neutral statement in terms of the writer "*Real Madrid won the Spanish Football Cup against FC Barcelona*" can be interpreted as a negative emotion for a Barcelona fan and as a positive one for

[1] http://news.bbc.co.uk/2/hi/business/7682723.stm, consulted in 2011 (Gloomy forecasts for UK economy).

a Real Madrid fan. These studies show a user-centric approach based on personalization. Second, some works have been emerging, which focus on polarity detection of texts based on contextual information such as the author, the reader or the text. In particular, (Balahur and Steinberger, 2009) identified the main tasks for news opinion mining: (1) the definition of the target, (2) the separation of the good and bad news content from the good and bad sentiment expressed on the target and (3) the analysis of clearly marked opinion that is expressed explicitly, not needing interpretation or the use of world knowledge. In particular, they show that it is important to distinguish three different possible views on newspaper articles: author, reader and text. These have to be addressed differently at the time of analysing sentiment, especially the case of author intention and reader interpretation, where specific profiles must be defined if the proper sentiment is to be extracted. Moreover, (Balahur et al., 2010) presented a work on mining opinions about entities in English language news, in which they tested the relative suitability of various sentiment dictionaries and attempted to separate positive or negative opinions from good or bad news. In their experiments, they tested whether or not subject domain-defining vocabulary should be ignored and results showed that in the context of news opinion mining, subject oriented classification produces better performance than classical strategies.

This paper is concerned with a "market view" of the sentiment in quotations made by an economic actor. A "market view" is expressed either in the rise or fall of a financial instrument or significant increase in trading volume. Classical sentiment classification may assist, but the motivation of the quote maker may inhibit the effectiveness of these techniques as shown in (Balahur and Steinberger, 2009). For example, business leaders lie and when they lie they use opinionated language (Larcker and Zakolyukina, 2010). This characteristic of direct speech will inhibit classical techniques to identify "actionable" information to use in a trading strategy. The research problem is to identify "actionable" information in quotations from financial news.

The proposed approach is predicated upon the following assumptions: (1) certain economic actors are compelled to speak in a highly rhetorical manner which conveys no actionable information, (2) rhetorical language contains overtly positive lexicon and (3) certain economic actors are compelled to speak in an objective manner. The final assumption is that an implied role i.e. biased (rhetorical features) or unbiased (non-rhetorical features) can be assigned through job role or specific lexicon extraction.

The proposed approach seeks to group opinion makers by their implied role and apply separate classification strategies to their quotations. This strategy demonstrates a clear advantage over applying classical classification techniques to the whole corpus of quotations. While modelling contextual information with Random Forests based on a vector of unigrams plus the "opinion maker role" reaches a maximum F-measure of 52.85%, understanding the "bias" of the quotation maker previously based on its lexical usage allows 86.23% F-measure for "unbiased" quotes and 71.10% F-measure for "biased" quotes with Naive Bayes.

2 One-Step Learning Strategy

This section will cover the initial experiments and lay some foundations for the justification of the work contained in this paper. The sub-sections will cover the data acquisition process, the learner selection and the influence of the "opinion maker role" of the writer as a feature.

2.1 Data Acquisition

A large number of news stories (>300,000) were collected from freely available sources on the Internet. The news stories were gathered from Really Simple Syndication (RSS) feeds during the period from October 2008 until June 2010. News story meta-data was added by the Open Calais web service[2]. Open Calais identifies quotations, the quotation maker and on occasion job titles and organization affiliations. This process yielded 180,956 quotations, a subset of which were hand-labelled as positive, negative and neutral. The annotation process was conducted by a single annotator. Some examples are given in sentences (1), (2) and (3).

(1) *Mr Cowgill said the relative strength was a result of the differences between male and female consumers.* (neutral)

(2) *BBT is trading up on the news as they would likely be able to assume the deposits at an*

[2]http://www.opencalais.com/, consulted in 2011.

attractive price. (positive)

(3) *About 60 per cent of summer crops could be hurt badly by insufficient rainfall subsequently dragging down agricultural performance which has already been modest in recent quarters.* (negative)

2.2 Baseline Experiments

The assumption of this work is that the role of the quotation maker influences the polarity and the influence over the financial market. The baseline experiments are designed to demonstrate that the addition of the "opinion maker role" as a feature provides a demonstrable gain in F-measure for a classifier. We conducted three different experiments with different feature sets: (1) unigrams, (2) unigrams plus the job role (JR) and (3) unigrams plus the "opinion maker role" (OMR). In particular, the job role was extracted from the Open Calais metadata and the annotator added the "opinion maker role". The annotator selected the "opinion maker role" on the following definitions: (1) *biased* if the opinion maker has a clear affiliation to a company (CEO, CIO etc.) and (2) *unbiased* if the opinion maker is independent of an economic actor and should be free from bias (analysts, economists etc.). The experiments were conducted with the first ranked learner (Random Forests) and a mid ranked classifier (Naive Bayes) based on the classifier ranking assigned by the landmarking tools (Pfahringer et al., 2000) implemented in Rapidminer (Mierswa et al., 2006) to ensure that any gain would not be learner specific. The estimated F-measures were calculated with a 10-fold cross validation technique and are presented in Table 1.

Classifier	Features	F-Measure
Rand For.	Unigrams	46.91% $\pm$4.07
Rand For.	Unigrams + JR	46.37% $\pm$3.06
Rand For.	Unigrams + OMR	52.85% $\pm$3.40
N. Bayes	Unigrams	49.01% $\pm$4.75
N. Bayes	Unigrams + JR	49.66% $\pm$5.10
N. Bayes	Unigrams + OMR	50.54% $\pm$4.39

Table 1: Experiments Estimated F-Measures.

The experiments demonstrate a small gain by a using the inferred role of the opinion maker, but the gains are within the margin of error. There are, however, gains for both learners and therefore provide some evidence for the "inferred role" assisting the learner. As a consequence, we propose in the next section the analysis of the language of "biased" and "unbiased" quotation makers in order to see if the "inferred role" can automatically be identified based on a specific language usage and then propose a two-step learning process to improve the accuracy of our learning process.

3 Quote Maker Language Analysis

This section describes the lexical analysis of two job roles: CEOs and Analysts. These two job roles conform to the annotation rules when labelling the baseline experimental data with "opinion maker roles". CEOs are assumed to be part of the "biased" class because they have a direct affiliation with a company whereas analysts are normally independent and therefore are part of the "unbiased" class. If the initial assumption is correct, then the CEOs' quotes would be likely to have rhetorical features whereas the analysts' ones would not.

3.1 The CEOs Lexicon

The expected lexicon of CEOs should contain overtly positive language, which is designed to manipulate the public opinion. The initial lexicon analysis was aimed at extracting adjectives, as adjectives are known to be the conveyors of the opinionated language (Wiebe et al., 2004). For that purpose, we used the Pointwise Mutual Information (PMI) to calculate the affinity of an adjective to a quotation by a person with the job role of CEO. The PMI is defined in Equation 1 where "adj" represents an adjective and "cl" is the job role of CEO.

$$PMI(adj, cl) = \log_2 \frac{Pr(adj, cl)}{Pr(adj)Pr(cl)}. \quad (1)$$

All the adjectives, which scored above zero were assumed to be a member of the CEO's lexicon. As such, 1,401 adjectives were extracted and ranked in order of their PMI score. The majority of the adjectives are positive and there are few negative adjectives. In particular, the first negative adjective is ranked 87. Conversely, the negative language was not exaggerated, however the positive language was domain specific as for example, "win-win", "mission-critical" and exaggerated, as for example, "superb", "immense". In particular, negative adjectives tended to have the lowest PMI scores. A further analysis was made of frequent and infrequent unigrams and bigrams. The analysis was limited to the top and bottom 100 terms.

The most frequent terms were positive whereas the infrequent terms were either atypical words or negative words. In summary, the lexicon of the CEO is overwhelmingly positive, which is, nevertheless contradictory as the quotes were harvested between 2008 and 2010, which was a time of a severe economic crisis.

3.2 Analysts Lexicon

Compared to the CEOs' language, the Analysts' language should be more measured because the analysts' job function is to provide objective advice. The lexicon analysis was the same as for the CEOs i.e. analysis of specific adjectives using the PMI and analysis of frequent and infrequent terms i.e. unigrams and bigrams. The adjective analysis revealed a smaller lexicon, 415 adjectives compared with the 1,401 in the CEO lexicon. The next difference is the higher ranking of negative words. The highest ranking of a negative word is for the adjective "*speculative*", which had the rank of 2. Comparatively, the highest ranked negative word in the CEO lexicon had a rank of 87. The analysis of frequent and infrequent terms revealed a lack of opinionated language. This is contrary to the CEOs' language who seems to use positively opinionated language.

In summary, there is clear evidence that there are significant differences in the lexicons of CEOs and Analysts. The lexicon difference in conjunction with the baseline experiments provides justification for the two-step strategy as it will be possible to identify the role of the quotation maker by his language. The next section will describe a methodology to identify "biased" from "unbiased" quotation makers based on their language.

4 Market View of Quotations

The identification of quotations, which contain "actionable information" is a non-trivial task. Manual selection of data is a labourious task and can be impractical because of the volume of information. For example, our data set contained 180,956 quotations. A specific aim of this paper was to identify "real-world" effects of quotations. Consequently, the first attempt to label quotes was to align quotes with market movements as in (Lavrenko et al., 2000). A baseline experiment was conducted where the ticker symbol of the affiliation of the quote maker was retrieved from Yahoo! Finance and the opening and closing price was recorded. The category of the quote would then be inferred based upon the following conditions: (1) a negative category would be inferred if the share price fell by more than 1%, (2) a positive category would be inferred if the share price rose by more than 1% and (3) a neutral category would be inferred if the share price rose or fell by less or equal than 1%. The evaluation of the automatic labelling was based on a 10-fold cross validation process with the unigrams of the quotations as the only features compared to the manual labelling initially performed. The results are presented in the Table 2.

Learner	Categories	F-Measure
Rand For.	Neut & No-Neut	39.58% ±0.0
Rand For.	Neut, Pos & Neg	22.50% ±0.0
N. Bayes	Neut & No-Neut	67.42% ±4.28
N. Bayes	Neut, Pos & Neg	54.12% ±3.70

Table 2: Automatic Labelling F-Measure

The results are clear. Automatic alignment with the market has its flaws. Quotations may appear with a market movement by chance and consequently the inferred label may be false. In fact, this result reproduces other experiments with automatic alignment (Drury et al., 2011). To avoid this kind of problems and achieve acceptable results, auto-alignment of texts with markets requires a form of constraint (Drury et al., 2011). In this paper, we propose a label propagation algorithm for quotations made by an identifiable CEO to improve the automatic labelling of quotations based on the market movement.

4.1 Labelling and Learning CEOs Quotes

The first assumption is that the majority of quotations made by CEOs are likely to be "bluster" and therefore may contain rhetorical language (which is not informative), whereas a small subset would contain useful information. The imbalance between the two categories would ensure that some quotations would "move the market" simply because they would be unexpected. There is some evidence in the research literature to suggest that the element of surprise can move markets (Bomfim and N., 2000). However, surprise is usually infrequent. To confirm our assumption, a human expert aligned a selection of CEO quotations with the movements in the market. The rules for the manual market alignment were the ones explained above with one difference that the human annotator would make the final decision if the quotation was responsible for the market movement or not. The human annotator found that for every "useful" quotation, there were 100 "bluster" quotations. In fact, it was not possible for the human annotator to align all the CEO quotations in a reasonable period of time. Therefore, once the human annotator had selected a sufficient number of quotations, a further automated process was required. A form of semi-supervised learning was chosen where labels of known data are propagated to unlabelled data via clustering algorithms. The RapidMiner Top Down Clustering operator was chosen as the number of clusters was selected by the operator. The process goes as follows. The seed set of manually annotated quotations is clustered with unlabelled data in groups of 1,000 documents. Clusters with more than 75% of labelled data from a single category have their labels propagated to the quotes in the cluster without labels. This process continues until no further labels are propagated.

This clustering process was executed in three steps: (1) for the initial CEO data (positive), (2) for the quotations attributed to a person with an identifiable job role which was not a CEO (negative) and (3) for quotes attributed to a person with no identifiable job role (neutral). At the end of the process, there were 1,242 quotations which were determined to contain "useful" information. These quotations were split into positive and negative categories with manual alignment with the market. This process was then evaluated based on a 10-fold cross validation with the unigrams of the quotations as the only features showing that regularities can be found as presented in Table 3.

Learner	Categories	F-Measure
Rand For.	Neut & No-Neut	88.28% ± 2.29
Rand For.	Neut, Pos & Neg	67.10% ± 2.82
N. Bayes	Neut & No-Neut	82.75% ± 3.31
N. Bayes	Neut, Pos & Neg	70.71% ± 3.31

Table 3: Automatic CEO Labelling F-Measure

4.2 Labelling and Learning Analysts Quotes

The role of the analyst has an arguably different role to that of a CEO. Analysts are not required to "bluster" or mislead, and often they tend to reach a consensus (Tamura and Hiromichi, 2003). An analyst consensus ensures that there is a "lack of surprise" and consequently, a quotation from an analyst is unlikely to move the market. In these conditions, auto-alignment with the market is unlikely to be a profitable strategy. The proposed strategy was to manually extract adjectives from the Analyst lexicon and expand them with WordNet (Miller, 1990) based on existing semantic relationships. The polarity of the adjectives was then inferred by calculating the PMI score for the adjective and its category (i.e. positive or negative) as in (Turney, 2002). As a consequence, in order to collect as strong as possible quotations, a high precision rule classifier selected quotations with three or more adjectives from one category. The classification task was only into positive and negative categories because analysts are assumed not to "bluster" and that the economics of the news publishing business will ensure that quotations will be sufficiently interesting to the general reader before it is published (McManus, 1988). In this case, as there exist many quotations from real-world texts, label propagation was not necessary. Results are shown in Table 4 performed over a 10-fold cross-validation strategy with the unigrams of the quotations as the only features and show how regularities can be found this way.

Learner	Categories	F-Measure
Rand For.	Pos & Neg	83.24% ± 2.85
N. Bayes	Pos & Neg	86.23% ± 2.27

Table 4: Automatic Analyst Labelling F-Measure

5 Two-Step Learning Strategy

The initial assumption was that understanding the job role of the opinion maker is likely to lead to improved classification performance upon the contribution of the quotation over the market. On one hand, the quotations with a high level of rhetorical features are assumed to carry no useful information with respect to the financial market. In particular, the quote makers who use rhetorical language are assumed to have the inferred role of "biased" and the groups of individuals who do not use rhetorical language are assumed to be "unbiased". This was verified in section 3. On the other hand, we know that "biased" people are likely to have loyalties to companies or organizations, whereas "unbiased" people are usually independent because they are employed by companies who provide impartial advice to client. As a consequence, our two-step strategy aims at first learning the "inferred role" of the opinion maker and second applying a unigram classification model to extract positive and negative quotations within the context of the market.

As we showed in section 4, if we are capable of clearly identifying the "inferred role" of the opinion maker, it is likely that we obtain improved performance over classification of quotations as positive, negative or neutral within the context of the financial market. In fact, as shown in section 3, as "biased" and "unbiased" opinion makers use different languages and different linguistic features, learning job roles should be possible. For that purpose, we automatically built a suitable data set through the same clustering process as was used for identifying data for CEOs i.e. the label propagation algorithm. In particular, the data was split into two categories, "bluster", (i.e. the meaningless category from the CEO data) and "non-bluster", (i.e. the remaining data from both the analysts and CEO data sets). As a consequence, the clusters, which contained 75% of a single category had their labels propagated and the job titles from the propagated and labelled data were recorded. To better understand the kind of job roles associated to both classes "bluster" and "non-bluster", we calculated a PMI score for each job title and its affinity to each category. A sample of job titles and their categories are presented in Table 5 and evidence how job role can easily be discovered.

Bluster	Non-Bluster
Chairman, CTO, Co-head, Company President	Chief Economist, Credit Analyst, Chief economic adviser

Table 5: Automatic Identification of Job Roles

The initial assumption is based on the fact that separate strategies take advantage of the individual linguistic characteristics of the hypothesized "inferred roles" in the corpus of the quotation makers. The hypothesized "inferred roles" are in fact "biased" (i.e. quotes made by people with known loyalties to companies/organizations) and "unbiased" (i.e. quotes made by other people without links to companies/organizations). In fact, the market view technique identifies meaningful quotes from the "biased", but fails to identify quotations from the "unbiased" group because the later group often fails to move the market with their pronouncements. A rule approach works well with the "unbiased" group, but performs worst with the "biased" group because the quotations in the training set are overly positive due to the inclusion of quotes from the "bluster" group. As a consequence, it is compulsory to first identify the "inferred role" of the quotation maker so that the genre specific learner is correctly applied to the given quotation. In fact, the "inferred roles" are based upon job title. The job titles, which have a predominance of rhetorical language and therefore cluster together are for our purposes "biased". The roles, which have a lack of rhetorical language also cluster together and are assumed to be "unbiased". So, by applying this two-step strategy, we obtain improved results over the baseline presented in Table 1. In particular, we performed a 10-fold cross validation with the unigrams of the quotations from each category individually as the only features. The results are presented in the Table 6.

Group	Learner	F-Measure
Unbiased	Rand For.	83.24% $\pm$(2.85)
Unbiased	N. Bayes	86.23 % $\pm$(2.27)
Biased	Rand For.	64.03% $\pm$(2.58)
Biased	N. Bayes	71.10% $\pm$(6.45)

Table 6: Comparison of Inferred Roles

Clustering is a computational expensive process, consequently when classifying a large groups of quotations it is not possible to use this process to separate the quotes into their respective latent groups. The group separation is done by job title as discovered previously. It was therefore possible to accurately separate the potential quotes by keywords into their latent groups. While modelling contextual information with Random Forests based on a vector of unigrams plus the "inferred role" reaches a maximum F-measure of 52.85%, understanding the "bias" of the quotation maker previously based on his job role allows 86.23% F-measure for "unbiased" authors and 71.10% F-measure for "biased" authors with the Naive Bayes classifier.

6 Conclusions

This paper has provided some evidence that grouping quote makers by their latent roles can assist in polarity classification tasks. The paper demonstrates that quote makers latent role predetermines their language in direct quotations and consequently quotations by members of these latent roles are susceptible to different forms of analysis. In this paper, we provided evidence of the existence of two latent groups, but we are not arguing that there are only two latent groups in a quotation corpus. It is possible that smaller groups exist with subtle language characteristics, which may be exploited with separate strategies. As a summary, we can conclude that understanding the writer motivation of any quotation, and in the broad area of opinion mining, is a key factor for the success of automatic classification.

References

M. Al Masum Shaikh, H. Prendinger, and M. Ishizuka. 2007. Emotion sensitive news agent: An approach towards user centric emotion sensing from the news. In *Proceedings of the IEEE/WIC/ACM International Conference on Web Intelligence (WIC 2007)*, pages 614–620.

A. Balahur and R. Steinberger. 2009. Rethinking sentiment analysis in the news: from theory to practice and back. In *Proceedings of the 1st Workshop on Opinion Mining and Sentiment Analysis*. University of Sevilla.

A. Balahur, R. Steinberger, M. Kabadjov, V. Zavarella, E. van der Goot, M. Halkia, B. Pouliquen, and J. Belyaeva. 2010. Sentiment analysis in the news. In *Proceedings of the 7th Conference on International Language Resources and Evaluation*.

Bomfim and Antulio N. 2000. Pre-announcement effects, news, and volatility: Monetary policy and the stock market. Technical report, Board of Governors of the Federal Reserve System.

P. Chesley, B. Vincent, L. Xu, and R. Srihari. 2006. Using verbs and adjectives to automatically classify blog sentiment. In *Proceedings of the AAAI Symposium on Computational Approaches to Analyzing Weblogs (AAAI/CAAW 2006)*, pages 27–29.

B. Drury, L. Torgo, and J.J Almedia. 2011. Classifying news stories to estimate the direction of a stock market index. In *Proceedings of the 3rd Workshop on Intelligent Systems and Applciations*. `http://goo.gl/J7yv5`.

V. Hatzivassiloglou and K.R. McKeown. 1997. Predicting the semantic orientation of adjectives. In *Proceedings of the 8th Conference on European Chapter of the Association for Computational Linguistics (EACL 1997)*, pages 174–181.

V. Hatzivassiloglou and J. Wiebe. 2000. Effects of adjective orientation and gradability on sentence subjectivity. In *Proceedings of the 18th International Conference on Computational Linguistics (COLING 2000)*, pages 299–305.

D.F. Larcker and A. Zakolyukina. 2010. Detecting deceptive discussions in conference calls.

V. Lavrenko, M. Schmill, D. Lawrie, P. Ogilvie, D. Jensen, and J. Allan. 2000. Language models for financial news recommendation. In *Proceedings of the 9th International Conference on Information and Knowledge Management (CIKM 2000)*, pages 389–396.

J. McManus. 1988. An economic theory of news selection. In *Annual Meeting for Education in Journalism and Mass Communication*.

I. Mierswa, M. Wurst, R. Klinkenberg, M. Scholz, and T. Euler. 2006. Yale: Rapid prototyping for complex data mining tasks. In *Proceedings of the 12th ACM SIGKDD International Conference on Knowledge Discovery and Data Mining (KDD 2006)*, pages 935–940.

G. A. Miller. 1990. Wordnet: an on-line lexical database. *International Journal of Lexicography*, 3(4).

B. Pang, L. Lee, and S. Vaithyanathan. 2002. Thumbs up?: Sentiment classification using machine learning techniques. In *Proceedings of the Conference on Empirical Methods in Natural Language Processing (EMNLP 2002)*, pages 79–86.

B. Pfahringer, H. Bensusan, and C. Giraud-Carrier. 2000. Meta-learning by landmarking various learning algorithms. In *Proceedings of the 17th International Conference on Machine Learning, (ICML 2000)*, pages 743–750.

Gerald Ratner. 2007. *The Rise and Fall... and Rise Again*. Wiley, J.

C. Strapparava and R. Mihalcea. 2008. Learning to identify emotions in text. In *Proceedings of the 2008 ACM Symposium on Applied Computing (SAC 2008)*, pages 1556–1560.

Tamura and Hiromichi. 2003. Individual-analyst characteristics and forecast error. *Financial Analysts Journal*.

P.D. Turney. 2002. Thumbs up or thumbs down?: Semantic orientation applied to unsupervised classification of reviews. In *Proceedings of the 40th Annual Meeting on Association for Computational Linguistics (ACL 2002)*, pages 417–424.

J. Wiebe, T. Wilson, R. Bruce, M. Bell, and M. Martin. 2004. Learning subjective language. *Computational Linguistics*, 30(3):277–308.

On the Contribution of MWE-based Features to a Readability Formula for French as a Foreign Language

Thomas François
Aspirant F.N.R.S.
Centre for Natural Language Processing
Institut Langage et Communication
UCLouvain
thomas.francois@uclouvain.be

Patrick Watrin
Centre for Natural Language Processing
Institut Langage et Communication
UCLouvain
patrick.watrin@uclouvain.be

Abstract

This study aims to assess the usefulness of multi-word expressions (MWEs) as features for a readability formula that predicts the difficulty of texts for French as a foreign language. Using a MWE extractor combining a statistical approach with a linguistic filter, we define 11 predictors. These take into account the density and the probability of MWEs, but also their internal structure. Our experiments show that the predictive power of these 11 variables is low and that a simple approach based on the average probability of n-grams is more effective.

1 Introduction

With the success of the communicative and action-oriented approach in the teaching of a second or foreign language (L2), teachers are encouraged to work on authentic texts in order to bring their students in contact with real linguistic data. The web is a valuable source for such documents, but the search for a document tailored to the level of the students may sometimes be tedious. In this context, readability studies may help. They aim to develop tools capable of assessing the difficulty of texts for a given population through textual features only (such as the number of letters per word, the number of words per sentence, etc.).

However, while many studies have examined the readability of English L1 (Chall and Dale, 1995), there are far fewer studies on readability in an L2, especially in French as a foreign language (FFL). In most cases, formulas for native speakers have been applied to L2 texts. However, the validity of such an approach is far from established, because it relies on three suspect assumptions : (1) the understanding of readers in the L2 is comparable to that of native speakers, (2) the textual features considered in L1 formulas are relevant to L2 reading, and (3) the weighting of these variables may be the same in a formula for L1 and L2.

If some work by Greenfield (2004) supports this vision, other authors disagree and consider that the peculiarities of the reading process in the L2, described by Koda (2005) among others, must be taken into account by designers of readability formulas. Of these dimensions, the interferences between the L1 and L2 of the learners are certainly among the most studied topics (Uitdenbogerd, 2005; Laroche, 1979). Moreover, François (2009) has shown that considering verb modes and tenses leads to the significant improvement of a L2 formula.

However, there is another textual aspect that is likely to be a good predictor of lexical difficulty for L2 readers: collocations and idioms. A good knowledge of these items is indeed associated with a fluent and appropriate use of the language (Pawley and Syder, 1983). We can therefore expect that L2 readers, especially beginners, encounter difficulties in processing these lexical chains and that texts which contain a large number of collocations and idioms are likely to be more difficult. Nevertheless, this assumption has not yet been addressed by a comprehensive study, be it for English as a second or foreign language (EFL), or for FFL. That is why we have dedicated this paper to this issue, which we explore through the specific case of FFL.

In section 2, we summarize a set of research findings about collocations and their processing, especially when reading a text in L2. Section 3 is a description of both the corpus and the lexical extractor we used to analyze the relationship between some characteristics of MWEs and the difficulty of the text for readers of FFL. The results of these experiments are reported and discussed in Section 4 before we conclude with some perspectives for future research.

2 MWEs and Text Difficulty

In this paper, we refer to MWEs as a set of linguistic objects the meaning and structure of which can be more or less frozen (collocations, compound words, idioms, etc.). From a statistical point of view, this class of objects commonly refers to "strings of words that are more frequently associated than it would be only by chance (Dias et al., 2000, 213).

These lexical entities have been shown to be processed by native speakers faster on average than free combinations (Underwood et al., 2004), both in reading and in oral production. This result may be interpreted as to mean that MWEs are fully or partially stored in long-term memory (Pawley and Syder, 1983) and can be recovered as such, thereby relieving short-term memory whose capacity is limited. Therefore, the processing of MWEs should be faster in reading and oral production, at least for natives, who are familiar with most of these.

For L2 learners, it has been demonstrated that their collocational knowledge lags far behind their general vocabulary knowledge (Bahns and Eldaw, 1993). Surprisingly, some studies on the L2 reading of MWEs reported a facilitating effect similar to the one of native speakers for advanced L2 learners (Underwood et al., 2004). It should be noted that such studies focus on reading time, which is related to the recognition of collocations, but do not evaluate their impact on comprehension. Underwood et al. (2004) reported that some of their subjects, for which a faster processing of collocations was observed, did not know the meaning of nearly a third of them. Therefore, we assume that at beginner or intermediate level, this facilitating effect is likely to be counterbalanced by the fact that the MWEs encountered are (1) mostly unknown to readers and (2) even more difficult to elucidate using the context as their meaning can be non-compositional.

A common method to estimate to what extent a MWE is known in a given population is to use its objective frequency. However, the hypothesis that MWEs that are less frequent in the language may be more difficult to read has hardly been explored in readability. Weir and Anagnostou (2008) suggested using the mean of the absolute frequency of all MWEs in a text as an indication of its difficulty. However, they did not report any experiments related to this hypothesis. In a previous article, Ozasa et al. (2007) had presented an EFL readability formula for Japanese learners that includes, among other variables, an index of textbook-based idiom difficulty. However, this variable was not significant in its multiple linear regression model, since the p-value of the t-test for coefficient significance was $0,61$ (Ozasa et al., 2007, 4).

In view of these results, it is not clear whether MWE-based features may be effective predictors of text readability in L2. However, we believe that the studies mentioned above have approached the issue only superficially. In this paper, we investigate further how MWEs can be used within an L2 readability formula through the specific case of FFL.

3 Methodology

To conduct our experiments, it was necessary to (1) collect a corpus that was already annotated in terms of difficulty, and (2) develop an extractor of nominal MWEs.

3.1 The Corpus

The corpus used to develop a readability formula should be labelled for reading-difficulty level, a task that implies agreement on the difficulty scale. In the context of foreign language teaching in Europe, an obvious choice is the *Common European Framework of Reference for Languages* (CEFR) (Council of Europe, 2001). The CEFR normally has six levels – A1 (Breakthrough); A2 (Waystage); B1 (Threshold); B2 (Vantage); C1 (Effective Operational Proficiency) and C2 (Mastery). However, to better reflect the evolution of learners, which is faster in the early stages of learning, we split the first three levels into two, thereby obtaining a total of nine levels.

Another positive aspect of using the CEFR is that, since its introduction, FFL textbooks have undergone a kind of standardization. It is thus feasible to gather a large number of documents that have already been labelled in terms of the CEFR scale by experts. We postulated that the level of a text is equivalent to the level of the textbook it comes from. Following this assumption, we first gathered a corpus of 1,895 texts (about 500K words) selected from FFL textbooks, using the same criteria as François (2009). We then randomly selected 50 texts per level (thus retaining 450 texts) to establish a test corpus in which the *a priori* probability of each class is similar. To do otherwise would have resulted in a biased model.

3.2 The Extractor

Regarding the extraction process of MWEs, we use a three-step state-of-the-art procedure which draws on the work of Daile (1995) and Smadja (1993) in that it combines a linguistic filter with association measures (AM). Concretely, the texts are first POS tagged to clear most lexical ambiguities[1]. We then identify all nominal MWE candidates in the tagged text with the help of a library of transducers [2] (or syntactic patterns). Finally, the list of candidates is submitted to the statistical validation module which assigns an AM to each of them. After some experiments, we retained the *fair log-likelihood ratio* (Silva and Lopes, 1999) as our AM, since it allows to process units that are longer than bigrams.

As with all measures of association, the proper functioning of this AM requires a consistent frequency mass, which was not available from the texts in our corpus. To overcome this problem, we used a frequency reference, which is a database of n-grams with their frequencies, as suggested by Watrin and François (2011). The reference allows an efficient on-the-fly computation of AMs, even in reduced contexts, provided that the frequencies stored in the database have been counted on a large corpus. For this study, we used two differents corpora as references:

- The 5-grams of Google (Michel et al., 2011), which represents the largest corpus currently available for French. Only contemporary n-grams were kept, i.e. those that relate to texts published between 2000 and 2008. We therefore obtained 1.117.140.444 5-grams. However, it must be stressed that the tokenization carried out in this resource remains very basic. It considers the following chains as 5-grams: " , l ' arbre est " or " un pique - nique . ".
- A set of newspaper articles published in 2009 in the Belgian daily *Le Soir* for a total of 5.000.000 5-grams. In this case, we were able to define our own tokenization and to consider such items as " pique-nique " or " l' " as one word.

To optimize the size of the references as well as their access time, we used a PATRICIA tree (Morrison, 1968) to store the n-grams. This data structure allows the compression of n-grams sharing a common prefix and that of nodes with only one child node, which results in queries carried out in constant time. We were then able to extract all the MWE candidates terms from the texts of our test corpus.

We then faced one last problem: what criterion should we use to decide whether a candidate term is actually a collocation ? The *log-likelihood ratio* being distributed according to a chi-square law with one degree of freedom, one possible approach is to select the MWEs for which the AM obtained is higher than 3.84 (which corresponds to $\alpha = 0.05$). However, as the size of the reference corpus increases, this solution becomes meaningless since high frequencies of occurrences generate high scores for the chi-square. Therefore, more and more phenomena appear significant (Kilgarriff, 2005).

The common solution to this issue is to empirically set a higher threshold. It has an obvious flaw: the threshold is only valid for a given corpus or one of comparable size. Once more, the use of a reference circumvents this difficulty: since the size is constant, an optimal threshold can be fixed once and for all. In our study, the selected threshold values were function of the precision of the extractor (see 4.1).

4 Results and Discussion

4.1 The Predictive Efficiency of the MWEs

From the extractor described above, it was possible to define 11 variables that aimed at taking into account various facets of MWEs. These were:

- The proportion of nominal MWEs to the number of words in the text (**NCPW**).
- The mean size (in number of words) of nominal MWEs in the text (**MSize**).
- 4 variables representing the proportion of the

[1] Tagging is done with the *TreeTagger* (Schmid, 1994).

[2] To apply our transducers to the tagged text, we use *Unitex* (Paumier, 2003). The output of the process is a file containing only the recognized sequences.

following grammatical structures : *N N* ; *N PREP (DET) N* ; *A N*, and *N A*.

- The mean probability of all nominal MWEs in the text, the probabilities used coming from our two references (**MeanP**). We also computed the 75th percentile of the same probabilities distribution **P75**.

- 3 variables that are the mean probabilities of nominal MWEs of size 2 (**MP2Coll**), size 3 (**MP3Coll**), and size 4 (**MP4Coll**). Longer units were not considered, since they were too scarce.

- For the sake of comparison, we also computed two conventional variables: the number of letters per word (**NLW**) and the number of words per sentence (**NWS**.

Furthermore, we manipulated the threshold θ used for the selection of MWEs. In this way, we were able to estimate how the strength of association between the components of MWEs impacts on the predictive power of the above variables. Four thresholds were selected for each of the two references: a zero threshold where all nominal structures were considered, a second and a fourth one respectively corresponding to a 30% and 50% precision for our extractor, and an intermediate value as the third threshold. Table 1 shows the Pearson correlation coefficients (r) between the 11 aforementioned variables and the level of difficulty of the texts in our test corpus [3]

These results provide valuable lessons. First, when one roughly analyses the strength of associations, it can be noticed that several variables are significantly correlated with the difficulty of the texts, in particular **NPCW** and the NA structure. It is a interesting outcome, since neither the simple **NPCW** variable, nor structural information had been previously considered in the readability literature. Furthermore, **MeanP** mostly appeared as not being significantly correlated with difficulty, a result that is congruent with that of Ozasa *et al.* (2007).

A second significant observation is that increasing θ, and thus strengthening the level of cohesion among MWEs, tends to weaken the association between most of our variables and difficulty. Faced with these results, one might conclude that MWEs are not as good predictors as the simple complex nominal structures ($\theta = 0$). However, it seems more accurate to limit this deficiency to MWEs that are detected automatically using statistical techniques. Among the best candidates of our corpus, we find MWEs such as "effet de serre (greenhouse effect) or "développement durable (sustainable development), which are relevant in the context of L2 reading, but we also found "mardi soir (late Tuesday) or "million d'euros (millions of euros), which are less relevant.

Third, as relying on correlations to conclude that a variable is a good predictor for readability does not suffice, we investigated this issue for our two best variables: **NPCW** and the NA structure. In a predictive model such as a readability formula, the informative contribution of each variable depends on the other factors in the formula. If two variables are highly correlated, they are likely to provide redundant information. In our case, although the significance level of **NPCW** and the NA structure are high, their raw correlation remains well below that of the two classic variables : **NLW** ($r = 0.58$) and **NWS** ($r = 0.578$). It is therefore not obvious that the two selected MWEs variables will be good predictors.

To clarify this issue, we compared a baseline readability formula using only **NLW** and **NWS** as predictors with the same formula which also comprised the **NPCW** and the NA structure [4]. It turns out that the contribution of the two MWE predictors is non significant ($\chi^2 = 2.98$; $p - value = 0.08$) [5], hence demonstrating that MWE-based variables do not provide really new information compared to traditional variables.

Faced with this inadequacy of variables based on automatically detected MWEs to the context of readability, we asked ourselves a second question. Would a simpler model, namely an n-gram model, be more efficient although it considers only sequences of tokens without any linguistic motivation ?

[3] In order to compute this metric, the difficulty levels A1 to C2 were converted into a discrete scale ranging from 1 to 9.

[4] The statistical model used for this comparison is based on an ordinal logistic regression, described in more detail in François (2009)

[5] The statistical technique used to compare the two models equates each of them to an explicative hypothesis of the data and calculates their log-likelihood ratio which is multiplied by the constant -2 in order to be distributed according to a chi-square law.

	Le Soir				Google			
Thresholds θ	0	15	25	43	0	139	4000	9931
NCPW	0.30^3	0.14^2	0.13^2	0.14^2	0.17^3	0.10^1	0.15^2	0.15^2
MSize	-0.02	0.03	-0.03	-0.02	-0.12^1	-0.19^3	-0.14^2	-0.18^3
NN	-0.24^3	-0.14^2	-0.01	0.03	-0.22^3	-0.13^2	0.004	0.007
NPN	0.05	0.13^2	0.09	0.11^1	0.04	0.06	0.15^2	0.17^3
AN	-0.05	-0.03	0.02	0.08	-0.07	0.03	0.08	0.09^1
NA	0.36^3	0.30^3	0.27^3	0.22^3	0.37^3	0.32^3	0.25^3	0.28^3
P75	-0.16^2	-0.10^1	-0.11^1	-0.15^2	-0.0001	0.02	-0.01	0.03
MeanP	-0.03	-0.03	-0.04	-0.05	0.15^2	0.16^2	0.14^1	0.09
MeanP2	-0.12^1	-0.18^3	-0.19^3	-0.20^3	-0.0007	-0.03	-0.06	-0.0005
MeanP3	-0.12^1	-0.12^1	-0.05	0.05	-0.02	0.03	0.02	0.02
MeanP4	-0.09	-0.07	-0.02	-0.08	-0.10^1	-0.05	0.01	0.02

Table 1: Pearson correlation between independent variables and text difficulty. Significance levels are noted as follows: $^1p < 0.05$; $^2p < 0.01$; $^3p < 0.0001$

4.2 N-gram Models

In contrast to MWEs, the use of n-gram models in readability is not new. They were first applied to the field by Si and Callan (2001) as a set of unigram models specific to every level of difficulty. Pitler and Nenkova (2008) later showed that even a single unigram model is an efficient predictor for readability. Meanwhile, higher order models have been developed by Schwarm and Ostendorf (2005) or Kate *et al.* (2010). The former authors selected the perplexity of a trigram model as one of their predictors, while the latter preferred to directly use the normalized probability outputted by the n-gram model (see Equation 1).

In this study, we defined the 7 following variables to assess the efficiency of n-gram models in the context of readability:

- The normalized log-probability of every text (**normTLProb**), which is in keeping with Kate *et al.* (2010) and is expressed as follows:

$$\text{normTLProb} = \frac{1}{m} \sum_{i=1}^{m} \log P(w_i|h) \qquad (1)$$

  where $P(w_i|h)$ is the probability of word i conditioned on the historic h limited to the $n-1$ previous words, and m stands for the number of words in the text to analyze.

- The mean (**MeanProb**) and the median (**MedianProb**) of the conditional probabilities distribution for a given text.

- Furthermore, as probabilities of MWEs were not expressed in a conditional form, but rather as a sequence's probability, we also take into consideration the probabilities of n-grams in our references. We used the arithmetic mean (**meanNGProb**), the median (**medianNGProb**), and the geometrical mean (**gmeanNGProb**) of those probabilities for a given text.

- Once more, for the sake of comparison, we developed a unigram model, based on *Lexique3* probabilites (New et al., 2007) **UnigM**.

We computed all these variables for each order of model from 2 to 5 using the frequencies stored in our two references: *Le Soir* and Google. Unfortunately, only the bigram model proved to be relevant to our approach. The discriminative capability of higher-order models suffers too much from the smoothing, since the number of unknown n-grams increases proportionally to the model order. As the probability of unknown events is always the same, the resulting variables are not discriminative enough once the order exceeds the bigram. Therefore, we only considered this level for our experimentations. The correlations of the 6 bigram-based variables with difficulty are shown in Table 2.

Again, our analyses provide some food for thought. A first observation is the complete inefficiency of variables based on a conventional bigram (r is 0.003 and -0.06 for **normTLProb**). This outcome seems highly surprising in comparison with previously reported results for English. Schwarm and Ostendorf (2005), for instance, reported successfully using n-gram models, even though they do not describe individual correlations for this variable and their good overall performance is obtained using many predictors. Such a low association is even more surprising as the

	normTLProb	MeanProb	MedianProb	meanNGProb	medianNGProb	gmeanNGProb
Google	$0,003$	$0,33^3$	$-0,04$	$0,38^3$	$-0,001$	$-0,03$
Le Soir	-0.06	$0,18^3$	$-0,01$	$0,25^3$	$-0,09$	$-0,0007$

Table 2: Correlation between the bigram-based variables and difficulty. Significance levels are noted as follows: $^1p < 0.05$; $^2p < 0.01$; $^3p < 0.0001$

unigram model **UnigM** conversely shows a strong correlation ($r = -0.57$).

However, **MeanProb**, which is also based on conditional probabilities, appears significant ($r =$ 0.33 and 0.18), as does **meanNGProb** ($r = 0.38$ and 0.25). **gmeanNGProb**, where probabilities of sequences are multiplied as in the classic n-gram model, is also uncorrelated with difficulty. Therefore, this lack of association might come from the fact that we multiply probabilities instead of adding them up.

Considering our two significant variables, **meanNGProb** and **MeanProb**, one may wonder if they provide valuable information to assess the difficulty of texts. It should be noted that both features are extremely intercorrelated ($r = 0.975$) as one might expect. Therefore, it makes no sense to add them both to our baseline formula. We therefore compared this baseline with the enhanced version including only **medianNGProb** and, this time, this led to a significant improvement ($R = 0,67$; $\chi^2 = 11,66$; $p - value = 0,0006$). In relation to our research, it is particularly interesting to note that **medianNGProb** is more informative than a finer variable (**MeanP**) which requires a complex procedure to detect MWEs.

With respect to the models based on bigrams, one last surprising observation is the direction of the correlation. In our data, more complex texts are, on average, composed of more frequent units. This result is completely opposed to that of the classic unigram model: **UnigM** shows a strong negative correlation ($r = -0.57$) which is consistent with the assumption that more frequent words are easier. For this assumption to be applicable to higher order models, it would require that a similar pattern be found: less frequent word sequences should be more complex to read. Unexpectedly, this is not what we obtained. Although this result questions the validity of such an assumption, there may be other explanations. One is that the language used in beginner texts might be less likely, since it often use an "unnatural" style.

5 Conclusion

In this study, we investigated what would be the contribution of variables based on automatically extracted MWEs for a FFL readability formula. These were found to be negligible, both in absolute terms and compared with a simpler approach based on n-grams models. This replicates and extends the results of Ozasa et al. (2007) on English. Our experiment emphasizes how taking into account linguistic notions through an automatic approach may not always lead to satisfactory results in the context of L2 readability. Indeed, the NLP processing we used seems to generate too many approximations (coverage issue of the references, extraction errors, etc.) that reduce the effectiveness of our variables.

Regarding the n-grams, we found two interesting predictors for a readability formula: **meanNGProb**, and **MeanProb**. Besides, some of our results appeared surprising: (1) the conventional n-gram models proved ineffective on our data ($r = -0,06$), yet they are widely used in the field; (2) the negative association between objective frequency and difficulty, observed for unigram models, was not replicated for longer sequences. These two issues need to be further investigated to determine whether they are due to peculiarities of our data or not.

Finally, we wonder whether these results would be replicated (1) if verbal MWEs were taken into account instead of nominal ones ; (2) if the detection of MWEs were done manually (although it would be a huge work), and (3) if only idioms, semantically more opaque, were considered. This last perspective, intellectually attractive, must be tempered since it is likely that this kind of MWEs is too rare in texts to be analyzed with a statistical approach.

References

J. Bahns and M. Eldaw. 1993. Should We Teach EFL Students Collocations? *System*, 21(1):101–14.

J.S. Chall and E. Dale. 1995. *Readability Revisited:*

The New Dale-Chall Readability Formula. Brookline Books, Cambridge.

Council of Europe and Education Committee and Council for Cultural Co-operation. 2001. *Common European Framework of Reference for Languages: Learning, Teaching, Assessment*. Press Syndicate of the University of Cambridge.

Béatrice Daille. 1995. Combined approach for terminology extraction: lexical statistics and linguistic filtering. Technical report, Lancaster University.

G. Dias, S. Guilloré, and J.G.P. Lopes. 2000. Extraction automatique dassociations textuelles à partir de corpora non traités. In *Proceedings of 5th International Conference on the Statistical Analysis of Textual Data*, pages 213–221.

T. François. 2009. Combining a statistical language model with logistic regression to predict the lexical and syntactic difficulty of texts for FFL. In *Proceedings of the 12th Conference of the EACL : Student Research Workshop*, pages 19–27.

J. Greenfield. 2004. Readability formulas for EFL. *Japan Association for Language Teaching*, 26(1):5–24.

R. Kate, X. Luo, S. Patwardhan, M. Franz, R. Florian, R. Mooney, S. Roukos, and C. Welty. 2010. Learning to predict readability using diverse linguistic features. In *Proceedings of the 23rd International Conference on Computational Linguistics (Coling 2010)*, pages 546–554.

A. Kilgarriff. 2005. Language is never ever ever random. *Corpus linguistics and linguistic theory*, 1(2):263–276.

K. Koda. 2005. *Insights into second language reading: A cross-linguistic approach*. Cambridge University Press, Cambridge.

J.M. Laroche. 1979. Readability measurement for foreign-language materials. *System*, 7(2):131–135.

J.B. Michel, Y.K. Shen, A.P. Aiden, A. Veres, M.K. Gray, The Google Books Team, J.P. Pickett, D. Hoiberg, D. Clancy, P. Norvig, J. Orwant, S. Pinker, M.A. Nowak, and E.L. Aiden. 2011. Quantitative analysis of culture using millions of digitized books. *Science*, 331(6014):176–182.

D.R. Morrison. 1968. PATRICIA - practical algorithm to retrieve information coded in alphanumeric. *Journal of the ACM*, 15(4):514–534.

B. New, M. Brysbaert, J. Veronis, and C. Pallier. 2007. The use of film subtitles to estimate word frequencies. *Applied Psycholinguistics*, 28(04):661–677.

T. Ozasa, G. Weir, and M. Fukui. 2007. Measuring readability for Japanese learners of English. In *Proceedings of the 12th Conference of Pan-Pacific Association of Applied Linguistics*.

Sébastien Paumier. 2003. *De la reconnaissance de formes linguistiques à l'analyse syntaxique*. Ph.D. thesis, Université de Marne-la-Vallée.

A. Pawley and F.H. Syder. 1983. Two puzzles for linguistic theory: nativelike selection and nativelike fluency. In J. Richards and R. Schmitt, editors, *Language and Communication*, pages 191–225. Longman, London.

E. Pitler and A. Nenkova. 2008. Revisiting readability: A unified framework for predicting text quality. In *Proceedings of the Conference on Empirical Methods in Natural Language Processing*, pages 186–195.

H. Schmid. 1994. Probabilistic part-of-speech tagging using decision trees. In *Proceedings of International Conference on New Methods in Language Processing*, volume 12. Manchester, UK.

S.E. Schwarm and M. Ostendorf. 2005. Reading level assessment using support vector machines and statistical language models. *Proceedings of the 43rd Annual Meeting on Association for Computational Linguistics*, pages 523–530.

L. Si and J. Callan. 2001. A statistical model for scientific readability. In *Proceedings of the Tenth International Conference on Information and Knowledge Management*, pages 574–576. ACM New York, NY, USA.

J.F. Silva and G.P. Lopes. 1999. A local maxima method and a fair dispersion normalization for extracting multi-word units from corpora. In *Sixth Meeting on Mathematics of Language*.

F. Smadja. 1993. Retrieving collocations from text: Xtract. *Computational linguistics*, 19(1):143–177.

S. Uitdenbogerd. 2005. Readability of French as a foreign language and its uses. In *Proceedings of the Australian Document Computing Symposium*, pages 19–25.

G. Underwood, N. Schmitt, and A. Galpin. 2004. The eyes have it: An eye-movement study into the processing of formulaic sequences. In N. Schmitt, editor, *Formulaic sequences: acquisition processing and use*, pages 155–172. John Benjamins, Amsterdam.

P. Watrin and T. François. 2011. N-gram frequency database reference to handle MWE extraction in NLP applications. In *Proceedings of the 2011 Workshop on MultiWord Expressions: from Parsing and Generation to the Real World (ACL Workshop)*, pages 83–91.

G.R.S. Weir and N.K. Anagnostou. 2008. Collocation frequency as a readability factor. In *Proceedings of the 13th Conference of the Pan Pacific Association of Applied Linguistics*.

Exploiting Hidden Morphophonemic Constraints for Finding the Underlying Forms of 'weak' Arabic Verbs

Allan Ramsay
School of Computer Science
University of Manchester
Manchester M13 9PL, UK
Allan.Ramsay@manchester.ac.uk

Hanady Mansour
Department of Arabic,
College of Arts and Sciences
Qatar University, State of Qatar
hanadyma@qu.edu.qa

Abstract

We present a treatment of Arabic morphology which allows us to deal with 'weak' verbs by paying attention to the underlying phonological process. This provides us with a very clean way of thinking about such verbs, and also makes maintenance of the lexicon very straightforward.

1 Introduction

It is well known that Arabic morphology is complex: the language uses a combination of concatenative and discontinuous processes, and the effects of these are obscured by the fact that many phonologically significant items (short vowels, geminations) are not written in modern Arabic.

We present a treatment of Arabic morphology which covers the standard cases, but which has two significant advantages. (i) We delay making decisions about the underlying form until we have the information that is necessary for getting the decision right. Unlike most attempts at diacriticisation, we do not enumerate all the possible forms and then try to choose between them. Instead we leave decisions on specific diacritics until we are in a position to get them right–*e.g.* we delay choosing between declarative and interrogative present tense prefixes for a verb until we know whether it is being used in a statement or a question. This enables us to weave morphological and syntactic processing together very efficiently, as described below. (ii) We can take account of the phonological processes that produce the varying forms of 'weak' verbs without having to declare these verbs as belonging to a special class. Weak verbs are in fact regular verbs whose spelling reflects a small set of phonological contractions. Our analysis allows us to obtain 'underlying forms' for the surface forms of weak verbs which show how they are related to their roots.

2 Basic Mechanisms

The basic problems of Arabic morphology are well known. A single word may have numerous forms, marking various syntactic features, where a form may have a combination of prefixes and affixes and the vowels at the heart of the word may vary. Thus كَتَبَ (**kataba**) ... are all forms of a single verb, with a variety of prefixes and suffixes marking such things as tense, agreement and mode, and with each form involving different vowels between the consonants كْ؟تْ؟بْ (**k?t?b**). The situation is made worse by the fact that the short vowels, and a number of other significant items, are not generally written. This means that the full forms كَتَبَ (**kataba**), كُتِبَ (**kutiba**), ... are all written as كتب (*ktb*). To make things even worse, Arabic generally forms families of words around a single root. These are sometimes marked by derivational prefixes, but in many cases there is no visible prefix of this kind, so that the written form كتب (*ktb*) also corresponds to a plural noun (كُتُبٌ (**kutub**)) and to two forms of two different verbs, كَتَبَ (**kataba**) and كُتِبَ (**kutiba**) (active and passive of '*to write*') كَتَّبَ (**kattaba**) and كُتِّبَ (**kuttiba**) (active and passive of '*to make write*'). Thus we have three sets of interlinked problems: different forms of the same word may be written quite differently, different forms of the same word may be written the same but have different underlying sets of vowels, and different words may be written the same (and may or may not have different underlying sets of vowels).

We follow fairly standard practice by describing a word in terms of a template and a set of fillers (*e.g.* (McCarthy and Prince, 1990)); we use a categorial description of the way roots and affixes combine (Bauer, 1983); in order to improve the efficiency of the process of lexical lookup, we store the lexicon as a lexical trie; and then we add a set of spelling rules to account for the variations in surface forms that are observed under various conditions.

2.1 Characters

We represent the graphemes that make up a word as bundles of information that we will refer to as 'characters'. A character has a number of properties. It has (usually) a written form; it has an 'underlying' form, which might be a diacritic mark (and hence unwritten in normal text) and which can be used to derive the phonetic transcription; it can be classified as being a consonant or a vowel, and in the latter case it can be either long or short; and it has various other features, which we will introduce as they become relevant. Thus the semi-vowel و (w) is represented as in Fig. 1 (note that this item marked as being both a consonant and a vowel, since it has the properties of both).

```
character(char( و (w)),
        underlying("w"),
        vc(+vowel, +consonant, +long))
```

Figure 1: The character و (w)

To save space we will sometimes simply write a character like the one in Fig. 1 as #و (w), but whenever you see something of this form you should try to remember that it is just a shorthand for a complex object of the kind shown in Fig. 1.

2.2 Templatic Specification of Lexical Items

In order to know what forms a word may take, you need to know three things: what are the consonants in the root, what are the vowels that fill the gaps between those consonants under different conditions, and are the consonants geminated?

We therefore represent a root by providing a template, as in Fig. 2.

```
history(diacritics(choices(actvPres(["o","u"]),
                           actvPast(["a","a"]),
                           psvPast(["u","i"]),
                           psvPres(["o","a"]))),
                   actualVowels(A)))
        consonants(targetConsonants(B),
                   actualConsonants(B)))
```

Figure 2: Template for one sense of ك؟ت؟ب (k?t?b)

This template specifies the vowels that are to be used for filling the gaps in the root for different tense/voice combinations. The slot for the 'actual vowels' will be bound to one of the options, once the tense and voice are actually known. The template further specified that the underlying consonants are the same as the ones that appear in the written form–we will see examples where this is not so below.

2.3 Categorial Treatment of Inflectional Morphology

In addition to describing how the vowels and consonants of the root change in the underlying form depending on the tense and mood (for verbs) and the number and gender (for nouns), we have to specify the patterns of affixes that a given root takes. We do this using a categorial description of the affixes that a given item requires in order to complete itself. We make two assumptions: (i) we assume that an open-class word will typically be obtained from an underlying root via a derivational suffix. Thus we assume that استك؟ت؟ب (*āstk?t?b*), مك؟ت؟ب (*mk?t?b*), اك؟ت؟ب (*āk?t?b*) and so on are all obtained by adding a derivational prefix to the root ك؟ت؟ب (*k?t?b*). For consistency we further assume that forms with no visible derivational affix are nonetheless obtained from the root by adding an empty prefix. (ii) We assume that each individual affix specifies what further affixes are required, using the extended categorial rules in Fig. 3 to process words strictly from right to left, as proposed by (Ades and Steedman, 1982) for handling syntactic relations. Allowing each affix to specify what else is required allows roots to require variable numbers of affixes, *e.g.* the derivational affix است (*āst*) which obtains a verb from ك؟ت؟ب (*k?t?b*) starts a different chain of affixes from the prefix م (*m*) which obtains a noun from this root. This provides a more flexible approach to describing the structure of a word than using a context-free grammar, as suggested by (Kiraz, 2001).

$$G / H \Longrightarrow G / I,\ I / H$$
$$G \backslash H \Longrightarrow G / I,\ I \backslash H$$

Figure 3: Combinatory categorial rules

Consider the written form يستكتب (*ystktb*). This has two possible readings, as an active transitive verb or as the passive form of that verb. In both cases it is made out of a number of pieces, as shown in Fig. 4.

يَ+اِيسْتَ+كُتِبْ+٠+؟ (**ya+īsta+kotib+0+?**),

يُ+اُوسْتُ+كُتَبْ+٠+؟ (**yu+ūstu+kotab+0+?**)

Figure 4: Possible structure for يستكتب (*ystktb*)

Fig. 4 shows that يستكتب (*ystktb*) is actually made out of five pieces–the root ك؟ت؟ب (*k?t?b*), the derivational prefix ايست (*īst*), a tense circumfix consisting of the prefix ي؟ (*y?*) and an empty suffix, and an agreement marker whose form cannot be decided out of context. The slot fillers in the root and the tense prefix vary depending on whether the verb is active or passive, with the phonological consequence that the prefix would be pronounced '*yaasta*' in the active and '*yuustu*' in the passive. The underlying form of the agreement marker cannot in fact be determined until the mood of the verb is known–it will be ُ (**u**) if the verb is used in a statement or a question, َ (**a**) if it is being used in a context where a subjunctive is required, and ْ () if a jussive is intended.

2.4 The Lexicon as a Trie

We store the lexicon as a trie. This is a well-known technique for managing dictionaries, since it facilitates lexical lookup. The only slightly odd thing about the trie we use is that it contains arcs with unknown items, to mark the fact that roots have holes in them which can be filled in a variety of ways. In particular, a single hole may be filled by either an (unwritten) short vowel or a (written) long vowel, depending on fine-grained syntactic factors. This makes the normal processing of traversing the trie more complex, but is unavoidable: how we deal with this is discussed in Section 2.5.

2.5 Spelling Rules

In most languages, phonological processes and other quirks of the writing system mean that there are a range of 'boundary effects' where elements of a word are joined together. The prefix *im-* on the English words '*impossible*' and '*imperfect*', for example, is a variant on the negation prefix *in-* that appears on '*incorrect*' and '*indecisive*' which arises because it is easier to get from saying '*m*' to '*p*' (because they both involve closing your lips) than to get from '*n*' to '*p*'.

Phenomena of this kind are generally dealt with by specifying 'spelling rules', often in the form of finite-state automata of some kind. We will write such rules using the format */L/*$\boxed{P}$*/R/*$\Longrightarrow Q$, meaning that if P occurs in a context where it is preceded by L and followed by R then it should be replaced by Q, as suggested by (Chomsky and Halle, 1968). We will use *c0, c1, ...* to denote arbitrary consonants, *v0, v1, ...* to denote vowels and *x0, x1, ...* to denote arbitrary consonants, and we will add specific features by including them in square brackets [...]. If the context is unimportant then we will write /???/. It is important to note that we are using these rules in the reverse of the standard direction: morphophonemic rules are usually used to describe what the surface form would be given a particular set of constituents. We are using these rules to recover the underlying form from the surface forms. This should be borne in mind when reading the rules below.

There are numerous such cases in Arabic: we will illustrate the form of our rules by considering the feminine agreement marker, which is pronounced differently depending on whether it is the last element of the word to which it is attached.

We assume that the canonical form of this item is the one that appears at the end of a word, which is pronounced '*ha*', and is written as ة (*t*). We then have a spelling rule that says that if you see a ت (*t*) in the middle of a word, it might actually be this item, having undergone a change in the way it is written to reflect the fact that it is easier to say '*ta*' than '*ha*' in the middle of a word. The rule in Fig. 5 says that if the written form of a word contains a consonant $\#c0$, where this consonant is not a slot filler (*−query*), and this is followed by an ordinary ت (*t*) and another character $\#x0$, then maybe the underlying item was the feminine marker ة (*t*), which has been replaced by ت (*t*) to reflect the change in pronunciation of this item when it appears in the middle of a word (note that this character carries the marker $+taa$ to indicate that it is not just the normal character #ت (*t*)). Thus application of this rule to the word دارستان (*dārstā-n*) produces the underlying form دَارِسْةَانْ (**dāristān**)[1]

/c0:[*−query*]*/*$\boxed{\text{\#ت (t)}}$*/x0/* $\Longrightarrow$ #ة (**t**):[+*taa*]

Figure 5: Rule for tamarbuta replacement

Application of spelling rules is interwoven with the search through the lexical trie. You cannot search the trie effectively without being aware of the potential application of these rules, but it is unrealistic either to apply the rules to lexical entries before constructing the tree (since this would lead to an explosion in the size of the trie) or to apply them blindly to the surface string (because this would again lead to the construction of an exponentially large number of forms, many of which have no correspondents in the lexicon). Our strategy is to apply rules as they become relevant during traversal of the trie. That way we do not apply rules to strings that have no counterparts in the trie, but we do apply them as soon as their effect would lead to exploration of a branch. The left-hand con-

[1]This might look a little odd, since it has the word final version of the feminine marker appearing in the middle of the word, but that's the whole point of this rule: the item in question *is* the feminine marker, but because it is in a word-internal position it has undergone a phonological change.

text of the antecedent of a rule is thus the route that has been followed so far through the trie, the right-hand context is the currently unconsumed portion of the input string, and the consequent of the rule is the branch of the trie that is to be explored.

We also use rules of this kind to insert the 'fillers' into the templatic descriptions of roots. As noted above, we include the gaps between the consonants in a root as arcs in the trie. These gaps can in general be filled either by short (unwritten) vowels or by long (written) ones. In any particular form of a given root, the way that they are to be filled is determined, but since you do not know which form you have until you have looked the word up, and possibly not until you have examined its syntactic role, you have to allow for all possible ways of traversing these arcs. To do this we make use of the two rules in Fig. 6.

/c1:[−query]/[c2:[−query, −taa]] /???/
⟹?: [+vowel, −long, +query, +inserted]

/c1:[−query]/[v1:[+long, −query]:B] /???/
⟹?:[+long, +inserted, −multiple]:C
if[underlying]@B↔ [underlying]@C

Figure 6: Rules for slot-fillers

The first of these rules says that if you've just traversed a consonant *c1*, and the next character is another consonant *c2*, where neither *c1* nor *c2* is itself a query or the tarmabuta, then you might try inserting an unspecified short vowel, i.e. an item whose surface form is *?*, so that it can be used to traverse an arc for a slot filler. The second rule in Fig. 6 says that if you have just traversed a consonant *c1*, and the next character is a long vowel *B*, then you can try replacing the long vowel by a *?* which is marked as being long, and which shares the same *underlying* character as the original long vowel.

Between them these rules allow us to account for the slot-and-filler structure of Arabic nouns and verbs, since we simply introduce *?*s at appropriate points, marking them as corresponding to short or long vowels appropriately, and in the case of long vowels remember what the actual underlying form of the long vowel was.

There are a number of other spelling rules, which can be used to account for a range of phenomena from fairly trivial things (such as the fact that the hamza can be omitted on word-initial characters) to more interesting cases such as the deletion of the second occurrence of a repeated consonant after a sukun (*e.g.* obtaining the underlying form جَدَدْ (**ğadod**) from the written form جد (*ğd*)).

2.6 Delayed Decisions about Underlying Forms

In general, just looking at a word will not tell you what the short vowels in its underlying form are. Consider, for instance, the word يدرس (*ydrs*). This has a number of interpretations, as the active and passive forms of verbs meaning 'study' and 'teach', but even if we consider just one of these, say the active form of the version meaning 'study', we see that there are a number of possibilities. In particular, it could occur in a context requiring an indicative form, *e.g.* as the main verb of a declarative sentence, or in one requiring a subjunctive form (*e.g.* after certain complementisers and modifiers), or one requiring a jussive form. The final agreement marker takes different forms in the different kinds of context, as shown in Fig. 7.

(1) a. يدرس الولد الدرس. (*ydrs ālwld āldrs.*)
b. لن يدرس الولد الدرس. (*nl ydrs ālwld āldrs.*)

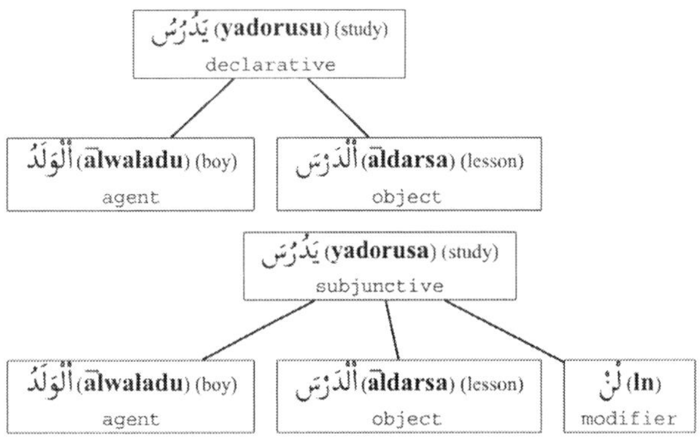

Figure 7: indicative/subjunctive forms of يدرس (*ydrs*)

Generating both these versions as soon as you saw the written form would be a major problem for any system that was going to attempt to parse the input text, since it would double the number of analyses that needed to be explored.

There are plenty of similar instances. Even in Fig. 7, for instance, the nouns الولد (*ālwld*) and الدرس (*āldrs*) have different case markers (الْوَلَدُ (**ā-lwalad-u**) and الدَّرْسَ (**āldars-a**)), because الولد (*ālwld*) is the subject and الدرس (*āldrs*) is the object. But these case markers cannot be determined until the syntactic role of these items is known (and, indeed, not until the context in which the verb itself

	past actv	past psv	present actv	present psv
1st pers sing	وَقَفْتُ (waqaftu)	وُقِفْتُ (wuqiftu)	أَقِفُ (ʔa'qifu)	أُوْقَفُ (ʔawqafu)
1st pers not sing	وَقَفْنَا (waqafnā)	وُقِفْنَا (wuqifnā)	نَقِفُ (naqifu)	نُوْقَفُ (nwqafu)
2nd pers sing masc	وَقَفْتَ (waqafta)	وُقِفْتَ (wuqifta)	تَقِفُ (taqifu)	تُوْقَفُ (twqafu)
2nd pers sing fem	وَقَفْتِ (waqafti)	وُقِفْتِ (wuqifti)	تَقِفِيْنَ (taqifyna)	تُوْقَفِيْنَ (twqafyna)
2nd pers dual	وَقَفْتُمَا (waqaftumā)	وُقِفْتُمَا (wuqiftumā)	تَقِفَانِ (taqifāni)	تُوْقَفَانِ (twqafāni)
2nd pers plural masc	وَقَفْتُمْ (waqaftum)	وُقِفْتُمْ (wuqiftum)	تَقِفُوْنَ (taqifwna)	تُوْقَفُوْنَ (twqafwna)
2nd pers plural fem	وَقَفْتُنَّ (waqaftuna)	وُقِفْتُنَّ (wuqiftuna)	تَقِفْنَ (taqifna)	تُوْقَفْنَ (twqafna)
3rd pers sing masc	وَقَفَ (waqafa)	وُقِفَ (wuqifa)	يَقِفُ (yaqifu)	يُوْقَفُ (ywqafu)
3rd pers sing fem	وَقَفَتْ (waqafat)	وُقِفَتْ (wuqifat)	تَقِفُ (taqifu)	تُوْقَفُ (twqafu)
3rd pers dual masc	وَقَفَا (waqafā)	وُقِفَا (wuqifā)	يَقِفَانِ (yaqifāni)	يُوْقَفَانِ (ywqafāni)
3rd pers dual fem	وَقَفَتَا (waqafatā)	وُقِفَتَا (wuqifatā)	تَقِفَانِ (taqifāni)	تُوْقَفَانِ (twqafāni)
3rd pers plural masc	وَقَفُوَا (waqafwā)	وُقِفُوَا (wuqifwā)	يَقِفُوْنَ (yaqifwna)	يُوْقَفُوْنَ (ywqafwna)
3rd pers plural fem	وَقَفْنَ (waqafna)	وُقِفْنَ (wuqifna)	يَقِفْنَ (yaqifna)	يُوْقَفْنَ (ywqafna)

Figure 8: Full conjugation for وقف (*wqf*) (attested by (Khwask, 1992; El-Dahdah, 1991))

appears is known, because in some contexts subjects are marked as being accusative). Again, generating all the possibilities at the point when you look the word up will multiply the options that a parser would have to explore: if we had generated the nominative, accusative and genetive forms of the two nouns, and the indicative, subjunctive and jussive forms of the verb, when we looked up the words in (1)(a) then we would have had to look at potentially 27 times as many possibilities.

To cope with this, we use 'just-in-time constraints' (similar to Hewitt (1971)'s 'if-added demons', or to 'watched literals' in theorem proving (Moskewicz et al., 2001)) to leave an unspecified item in the underlying form, to be filled in when the required information becomes available. Thus the forms that are produced when we first look up the words يدرس (*ydrs*), الولد (*ālwld*) and الدرس (*āldrs*) are يَدْرُسُ؟ (**yadrus?**), الْوَلَدُ؟ (**ālwalad?**) and الْدَرْسُ؟ (**āldars?**), where the ?s indicate that there is some element of the word which is not yet known, because the contextual information that would fix it is not yet available.

3 Weak Verbs

So far so good. We can produce fine-grained diacriticisations using a combination of slot-and-filler templates, a lexical trie and a set of spelling rules, and we can delay decisions about the underlying form until relevant syntactic information turns up. We now turn to the question of 'weak' verbs.

These are verbs whose root contains a semivowel (usually و (*w*), ي (*y*) or ا (*ā*)), which sometimes appears in the written form and sometimes goes missing or changes its form. These words do not appear to fit the normal slot-and-filler pattern, since the set of consonants in the written form appears to vary, so it does not look as though you can set a single template and fill in the slots. A typical example is the verb وقف (*wqf*), whose conjugation is given in Fig. 8.

The awkward thing about Fig. 8 is that most of the table looks as though it corresponds to a verb whose root is وقف (*wqf*), but in the column for the active present tense the initial و (*w*) is missing.

Why is it missing here and nowhere else? Crucially, why is it missing in the column for the present active but not the column for the present passive?

The only differences between the active and passive are that the *underlying* forms of the prefixes are different–the active prefix is يَ (**ya-**), the passive one is يُ (**yu-**)–and that the diacritics that fill in the slots may be different.

It is hard to see what the diacritics for the active present of وقف (*wqf*) would be. Because the initial consonant has disappeared there is no obvious trace of a vowel following the position where it would have been, but it seems reasonable to assume that it is a ـَ (**a**), since the cases where we can see the diacritics seem fairly regular, and a ـَ (**a**) for the first diacritic in the active present is common for regular verbs. It therefore looks as though the initial وْ (**w**) disappears if it is preceded by a ـَ (**a**) in the underlying form. There is, of course, no trace of this in the written form, and there is indeed no trace of it in the phonetic form, but the underlying process is that the awkwardness of pronouncing أَوَ (**awa**) has led to the deletion of the وَ (**wa**)

We therefore introduce a spelling rule which says that if you have just traversed a consonant and an (unwritten) ـَ (**a**), and the next item is a consonant, you should consider the possibility that a وْ (**w**) has been deleted from the surface form. This

	past actv	past psv	present actv	present psv
1st pers sing	شَكَوْتُ (šakawtu)	شُكِيتُ (šukiytu)	أَشْكُو (ʼaʼškuw)	أُشْكَى (ʼaʼškaā)
1st pers not sing	شَكَوْنَا (šakawnā)	شُكِينَا (šukiynā)	نَشْكُو (naškuw)	نُشْكَى (nuškaā)
2nd pers sing masc	شَكَوْتَ (šakawta)	شُكِيتَ (šukiyta)	تَشْكُو (taškuw)	تُشْكَى (tuškaā)
2nd pers sing fem	شَكَوْتِ (šakawti)	شُكِيتِ (šukiyti)	تَشْكِينَ (taškiyna)	تُشْكَيْنَ (tuškayna)
2nd pers dual	شَكَوْتُمَا (šakawtumā)	شُكِيتُمَا (šukiytumā)	تَشْكُوانِ (taškuwāni)	تُشْكَيَانِ (tuškayāni)
2nd pers plural masc	شَكَوْتُمْ (šakawtum)	شُكِيتُمْ (šukiytum)	تَشْكُونَ (taškuwna)	تُشْكَيْنَ (tuškayna)
2nd pers plural fem	شَكَوْتُنَّ (šakawtuna)	شُكِيتُنَّ (šukiytuna)	تَشْكُونَ (taškuwna)	تُشْكَيْنَ (tuškayna)
3rd pers sing masc	شَكَا (šakā)	شُكِيَ (šukiya)	يَشْكُو (yaškuw)	يُشْكَى (yuškaā)
3rd pers sing fem	شَكَتْ (šakat)	شُكِيَتْ (šukiyat)	تَشْكُو (taškuw)	تُشْكَى (tuškaā)
3rd pers dual masc	شَكَوَا (šakawā)	شُكِيَا (šukiyā)	يَشْكُوانِ (yaškuwāni)	يُشْكَيَانِ (yuškayāni)
3rd pers dual fem	شَكَتَا (šakatā)	شُكِيَتَا (šukiyatā)	تَشْكُوانِ (taškuwāni)	تُشْكَيَانِ (tuškayāni)
3rd pers plural masc	شَكَوَا (šakawā)	شُكُوا (šukuwā)	يَشْكُونَ (yaškuwna)	يُشْكَوْنَ (yuškawna)
3rd pers plural fem	شَكَوْنَ (šakawna)	شُكِينَ (šukiyna)	يَشْكُونَ (yaškuwna)	يُشْكَيْنَ (yuškayna)

Figure 9: Conjugation for شكو (*škw*) (attested by (Khwask, 1992; El-Dahdah, 1991))

rule only applies if the وْ (w) is also followed by an unwritten ـَ (a), so we will insert this as well. Note that the item being rewritten here is in fact the empty string: this rule just inserts وْ (w), ـَ (a) between *c0*, ـَ (a) and *c1*.

/*c0*, #ـَ (a)/[∅]/*c1*/ $\Longrightarrow$ #وْ (w), #ـَ (a)

Figure 10: Spelling rule for missing وْ (w)

Fig. 10 says that if you have just traversed arcs corresponding to a consonant *c0* and a gap which was filled by an unwritten vowel whose underlying form was ـَ (a), and the next character to be scanned is another consonant *c1*, then you could try inserting a وْ (w) and a following gap-filler which also has underlying form ـَ (a).

This rule allows us to spot that the surface form تقف (*tqf*) corresponds to an underlying diacriticisation تَوَقُفَ (**tawaqufa**), but not to the passive form تُوُقِفَ (**tuwuqifa**) because in the latter case the underlying vowel in the prefix was ـُ (u), which does not trigger the rule.

Now consider the conjugation of شكو (*škw*), as shown in Fig. 9. Much of this can be accounted for by assuming that the diacritics for the four tense/mood combinations for this verb are *actvPast=["a", "a"], psvPast=["u", "i"], actvPres=["o", "u"], psvPres=["o", "a"]*. The past active column is accounted for by the rule in Fig. 10: the third singular masculine and feminine and third dual feminine forms have suffixes which begin with ـَ (a) added to them, so Fig. 10 deletes the final أَوْ (aw) from the root to produce شكا (*škā*), شَكَتْ (**škt**) and شَكَوَا (**škwā**) as the surface forms. The other cases are slightly more complex. Most of the present active column leaves the end of the root unchanged as أُو (**uw**), most of the passive past column is produced by a rule of the form /???/[∅]/#ـِ (i)#يْ (y)/ $\Longrightarrow$ #ـُ (u)#وْ (w) and most of the passive present is produced by /#ـَ (a)/[#يْ (ā)]/v0[-long]/$\Longrightarrow$ #وْ (w) and /#ـَ (a),# يْ (y)/[∅]/???/$\Longrightarrow$#وْ (w).

In each of these columns, however, there are cases that do not fit the main pattern. Why, for instance, is the 2nd person singular feminine active present tense تَشْكِينَ (**taškiyna**) when every other entry in this column has شْكُو (**škuw**) as its root? Inspection of the components of this item show that it is made up of تَ+شْكُو+اِينَ (**tu+škuw+iyna**). But in that case the rule /???/[∅]/#ـِ (i)#يْ (y)/ $\Longrightarrow$ #ـُ (u)# وْ (w) that we introduced to cover the past passive forms applies here also, producing the observed form. Similarly, the presence of يُشْكَوْنَ (**yuškawna**) as the 3rd person plural masculine passive present appears odd in the passive present column, where most of the time شْكَوْ (**škaw**) has been turned to شْكَي (**šky**); but again consideration of the components of يُشْكَوْنَ (**yuškawna**) as يُ+شْكَوْ+وْنَ (**yu+škaw+wna**) shows that the relevant rule here is /#وْ (w)/[∅]/???/ $\Longrightarrow$ #وْ (w) (i.e. the وْ (w) at the end of the stem is deleted in the surface form) rather than /#ـَ (a),#يْ (y)/[∅]/???/$\Longrightarrow$#وْ (w).

Thus the vast majority of the cases in Fig. 9 arise very straightforwardly by applying spelling rules which reflect simple phonological processes. If you look only at the surface forms, these rules are hard to spot, but looking at the full underlying forms they become much more apparent. The case of the 3rd person masculine plural passive past, however, requires a little more attention. The basic building blocks here are شُكِوْ+وَا (**šukiw+wā**).

Applying produces شُكِيْ+وَا (šukiy+wā). But then the sequence اِيْ+وْ (iy+w) is itself awkward, so a subsequent rule /???/#ِ (i), #يْ (y)/#وْ (w)/ ⟹ #ُ (u) comes into play, leading finally to شُكُوا (šukuwā).

We thus have the rules in Fig. 11:

/*c0*, #َ (a)/∅/*c1*/⟹#وْ (w), #َ (a)
/???/∅/#ِ (i)#يْ (y) / ⟹ #ُ (u)#وْ (w)
/#َ (a)/#ىْ (ā)/v0[-long]/⟹ #وْ (w)
/#َ (a)#يْ (y)/∅/???/⟹#وْ (w)
/#وْ (w)/∅/???/ ⟹ #وْ (w)
/???/#ِ (i), #يْ (y)/#وْ (w)/ ⟹ #ُ (u)

Figure 11: Spelling rules for وْ (w)

These rules are phonologically plausible, in that they all reflect changes in pronunciation that arise from awkward combinations of phonemes. Applying them allows us to reconstruct the underlying forms from the surface forms, without having to put complex descriptions in the lexicon. We can simply say that شكو (*škw*) is a regular verb, with the slot fillers given above, rather than having to list all the forms of the stem and assigning very precise sets of affixes to them, as in for instance the Buckwalter analyser (Buckwalter, 2004).

Lexicons that require multiple specifications for a single item are hard to maintain, since you have to know a great deal about the meanings of the tags that say what affixes will attach to a given item (see (Algihaad and Abdelfatah, 2009) for a similar approach). It is much easier to simply say that شكو (*škw*) is a regular verb that takes *actvPast=["a", "a"], psvPast=["u", "i"], actvPres=["o", "u"], psvPres=["o", "a"]* as its diacritics, and to let the spelling rules look after the surface appearance. Indeed, the Buckwalter analyser misses out a number of the forms in Fig. 9, notably several of the passive forms (and some cases which have both active and passive readings, e.g. يشكون (*yškwn*)). The output of this analyser also relies on the sense tagging (given as the English gloss) to link the different forms of a single word. The morphological analysis of شكت (*škt*), for instance, is given as شَكْ+اَتْ (šk+at). The only way to ascertain that this is a form of the same word as the others in Fig. 9 is by noting that they have same English gloss–there is nothing in the structure that makes the link clear.

4 Conclusions

We have shown how using phonologically motivated spelling rules allows us to treat Arabic weak-initial and weak-final verbs in exactly the same way as other verbs, specifying a template and a set of slot fillers for the various tense/mood combinations (the same approach also works for weak-middle verbs, but there was no space to discuss these here). This has two major advantages: it provides a very clear separation between the cause of the apparent irregularity of these verbs and their actual adherence to the usual slot-and-filler pattern of Arabic verbs; and by providing this separation, it makes it easy to maintain the lexicon. Comparison with a small number of examples shows that this approach provides correct analyses for several cases which the Buckwalter analyser misses.

References

Ades, A E and M J Steedman. 1982. On the order of words. *Linguistics and Philosophy*, 4:517–558.

Algihaad, A and A Abdelfatah. 2009. Morphological analyizer for arabic verbs. In *3rd IEEE International Conference on Arabic Language Processing (CITAL'09)*, Rabat, Morocco. IEEE.

Bauer, L. 1983. *English Word Formation*. CUP, Cambridge.

Buckwalter, T. 2004. Buckwalter Arabic morphological analyzer version 2.0. Linguistic Data Consortium.

Chomsky, N and M Halle. 1968. *The sound pattern of English*. MIT Press, Cambridge, Mass.

El-Dahdah, A. 1991. *Dictionary of Arabic verb conjugation*. Liprairie du Liban.

Hewitt, C. 1971. Planner: a language for proving theorems in robots. In *2nd International Joint Conference on Artificial Intelligence*.

Khwask, Z. 1992. *Lessons in Syntax and Morphology*. Dar Almarefah Alghamayah, Alexandria, Egypt.

Kiraz, G. 2001. *Computational Nonlinear Morphology: with emphasis on Semitic languages*. Cambridge University Press, Cambridge.

McCarthy, J and A Prince. 1990. Prosodic morphology and templatic morphology. In Eid, M and J McCarthy, editors, *Perspectives on Arabic linguistics II: papers from the second annual symposium on Arabic linguistics*, pages 1–54, Amsterdam. Benjamins.

Moskewicz, M, C Madigan, Y Zhao, L Zhang, and S Malik. 2001. Chaff: Engineering an efficient SAT solver. In *39th Design Automation Conference*, Las Vegas.

A Confidence Model for Syntactically-Motivated Entailment Proofs

Asher Stern
Dept. of Computer Science
Bar-Ilan University
Ramat Gan, Israel
astern7@gmail.com

Ido Dagan
Dept. of Computer Science
Bar-Ilan University
Ramat Gan, Israel
dagan@cs.biu.ac.il

Abstract

This paper presents a novel method for recognizing textual entailment which derives the hypothesis from the text through a sequence of parse tree transformations. Unlike related approaches based on tree-edit-distance, we employ transformations which better capture linguistic structures of entailment. This is achieved by (a) extending an earlier deterministic knowledge-based algorithm with syntactically-motivated on-the-fly transformations, and (b) by introducing an algorithm that uniformly learns costs for all types of transformations. Our evaluations and analysis support the validity of this approach.

1 Introduction

Recognizing Textual Entailment (RTE) is the task of determining whether a given textual statement (a hypothesis), **H**, can be inferred by a given text passage, **T** (Dagan et al., 2005). In recent years, the task has attracted considerable interest, with research evolving around the six RTE challenges, organized by PASCAL[1] and later under the NIST Text Analysis Conference (TAC)[2]. While some of the proposed RTE systems employed quite shallow and ad-hoc techniques, a few principled approaches for modeling entailment inference began emerging as well.

This paper focuses on an appealing approach attempted in several previous works, which, like most RTE systems, utilizes parse-based representations of the text and hypothesis. Within this approach the parse-tree of **H** is explicitly generated from that of **T** by applying a sequence of tree transformation operations. In analogy to logic, that sequence can be referred to as a *proof*, by which the target proposition, represented as a parse tree, is generated from the given text propositions using appropriate proof steps.

In one line of these works (Wang and Manning, 2010; Heilman and Smith, 2010; Mehdad and Magnini, 2009) the tree-transformation operations followed mostly traditional *tree edit distance* operations, such as node insertion, deletion and substitution, and learned their costs according to the given RTE training data. As described in more detail in Section 2, these transformations do not necessarily capture the syntactic structure of entailment-preserving transformations.

On the other hand, a rich inventory of knowledge-based operations was employed by Bar-Haim et al. (2007a). Their operations enable transforming complete sub-trees which do capture the syntactic structure of entailment inferences. Nevertheless, their work did not include a learning component for estimating proof costs and their tree-transformations were based only on available knowledge resources, without providing on-the-fly operations that could compensate for some inevitably missing knowledge.

In this work we aim to combine the complementing advantages of the above mentioned works while filling in some missing gaps. We utilize knowledge-based sub-tree transformations, following (Bar-Haim et al., 2007a), but augment them with a set of *on the fly* transformations that correspond to syntactically-motivated entailment inferences, whose reliability can be learned using syntactic features. We further apply a cost model for entailment proofs and introduce an iterative learning scheme that estimates reliability weights based on the "best" (lowest-cost) proofs for the training pairs.

Evaluations show that our current implementation, including an initial set of knowledge resources and linguistic analysis, achieves compa-

[1] http://pascallin.ecs.soton.ac.uk/Challenges/RTE/
[2] http://www.nist.gov/tac/

rable results to other proof-based systems. We conclude the paper by pointing at the generality and flexibility of our framework and suggest several research directions which can be naturally integrated into it.

2 Background

As pointed above, a promising approach in RTE research is applying a sequence of operations (a proof) on the given text, **T**, to reveal whether and how it entails the hypothesis, **H**. The advantage of this approach is that it allows composition of knowledge, where in many cases information from one knowledge resource becomes relevant only after a previous operation was performed.

Methods that follow this approach should deal with three main aspects. First, they have to decide how to represent **T** and **H**. Second, they have to define the set of proof operations. Third, they have to define a method to estimate the likelihood that a generated sequence of operations indeed preserves entailment.

Raina et al. (2005) used a logical representation, and accordingly defined the set of operations by a commonly used theorem proving method (resolution refutation). However, since state-of-the-art methods that transform a text into logical representation are less robust than syntactic parsers, the logical representation is rarely used.

Syntactic parse trees provide a common representation in text understanding systems in general, and for RTE in particular. The corresponding proof operations are thus tree-transformations that subsequently change the parse tree of **T** until **H**'s parse tree is obtained.

Mostly, the selected tree-transformations followed standard ("insert", "delete", "substitute") or custom tree edit distance operations (Mehdad and Magnini, 2009; Wang and Manning, 2010; Heilman and Smith, 2010) However, those sets of operations are often not linguistically-motivated and thus do not necessarily reflect the nature of the RTE problem. In addition, utilizing knowledge resources (both linguistic knowledge and world knowledge) is limited in such systems. Consider, for example, transformation of a parse-tree from a passive form to an active form. Such transformation can be done by a sequence of mostly deletion and insertion operations, however, such sequence misses to capture the syntactic structure of the transformation. Similarly, resources that in-

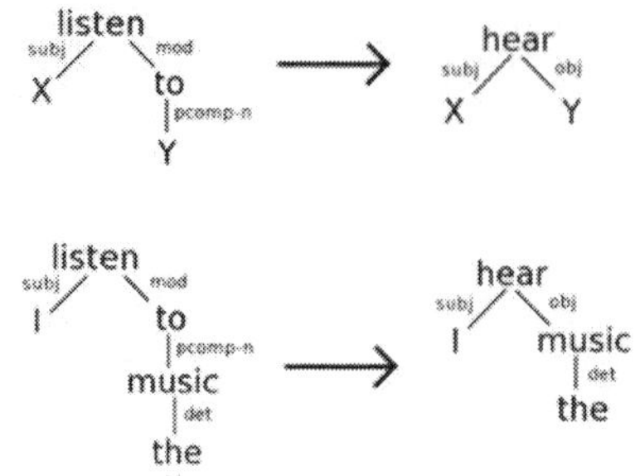

Figure 1: The figure demonstrates the rule *X listen to Y* → *X hear Y*, along with its application to the sentence "I listen to the music."

dicate semantic similarity of two sub-trees, e.g. DIRT (Lin and Pantel, 2001), would be utilized naturally by substitution of a complete sub-tree by another, which cannot be performed by the above tree-edit-distance operations.

In contrast, a set of linguistically-motivated operations was proposed independently by Harmeling (2009) and by Bar-Haim et al. (2007a). While the set of operations defined by Harmeling (2009) was limited and included mostly ad-hoc heuristics, the operations defined by Bar-Haim et al. (2007a) were designed to capture a broad range of linguistic and world knowledge. Their primary operations are applications of *Entailment Rules*, which substitute complete sub-trees and generate new parse-trees, based on knowledge resources (see Figure 1 and Table 1).

However, unlike other methods that followed the proof-style approach, the method of Bar-Haim et al. (2007a) does not estimate the likelihood that a generated proof is valid. Another problem is that in most cases, there is no sequence of operations that completely generates **H**. Rather, starting from **T**, the operations generate new trees that become more similar, but not identical to **H**[3] (Bar-Haim, 2010).

To summarize, two main challenges are involved in transformational proof-style inferences over syntactic parse trees. The first is defining a method to estimate the likelihood that a given proof preserves entailment. The second is to define operations that are linguistically-motivated and reflect the RTE problem space. So far, all proof-style systems addressed either the first or the

[3]On the RTE datasets, a hybrid framework was introduced by Bar-Haim et al. (2007b), which uses an approximate match mechanism for final classifications.

Rule Type	Description	Examples
Lexical Rules	Substitution of a single node, capturing lexical entailment. Both *lhs* and *rhs* are single nodes.	novel → book walk → go
Lexical Syntactic Rules	Tree transformations that change the tree's lexical items as well as the tree's structure.	"X file lawsuit against Y" → "X accuse Y" "X listen to Y" → "X hear Y"
Generic Syntactic Rules	Tree structure transformations. Capture linguistic phenomena (e.g. passive-active).	X *V(active)* Y → Y is *V(passive)* by X

Table 1: Types of Entailment Rules. Note that for simplicity the examples are presented as strings, though the actual definition and implementation are based on sub-trees, as in Figure 1

second challenge, but not both. As described next, in this work we propose a principled integrated solution to those two challenges.

3 A Cost-based Proof Model

In our framework we adopt the linguistically-motivated entailment operations proposed by Bar-Haim et al. (2007a), and extend them with syntactically-motivated on-the-fly operations to enable generation of complete proofs (Sec. 3.1). The extended framework is then integrated with a learning method similar to the one proposed for logic representations by (Raina et al., 2005) as follows. We propose a cost model, which assigns a cost for each entailment proof (Sec. 3.2), and introduce a search algorithm that finds the "best proof" with respect to the cost model (Sec. 3.3). Finally we describe a method to iteratively learn the parameters of the cost model (Sec. 3.4).

3.1 Inference Formalism

The model presented here assumes a single-sentence hypothesis, similar to the RTE challenges, though it can be easily adjusted to multi-sentence hypotheses as well.

Given a (**T**,**H**) pair, the system first constructs the dependency parse trees[4] of **T** and **H**. Each node in those trees contains information about one lexical item (i.e. a word or a multi-word expression), which includes its lemma and its part-of-speech, and optionally other information, such as Named Entity type[5]. Each edge is labelled with a dependency relation (e.g. *subject*, *object*).

Let $\mathcal{T}$ be a set of dependency parse trees that were constructed for **T**'s sentences, and let h be the dependency parse tree constructed for **H**. The system iteratively extends $\mathcal{T}$ with additional trees, by applying *tree generation operations*, until there exists a tree $t \in \mathcal{T}$, such that h is embedded in t.

[4]We used the Minipar parser (Lin, 1998b)

[5]We used Stanford NE recognizer (Finkel et al., 2005)

We will use the following notations: Let $\mathcal{T}$ be a set of trees, o be a tree generation operation, and t be a tree. $\mathcal{T} \vdash_o t$ denotes that t can be generated from $\mathcal{T}$ using the operation o. We will use the $\vdash$ notation also for the resulting extended set of trees, that is:

$$\mathcal{T} \vdash_o \mathcal{T} \cup \{t\}$$

Let $O = (o_1, o_2 \dots o_m)$ be a sequence of operations. The notation $\mathcal{T} \models_O \mathcal{T}'$ means that $\mathcal{T}'$ can be generated from $\mathcal{T}$ by applying iteratively the operations in O. Finally, a sequence of operations is called a *proof*, P, if $\mathcal{T} \models_P \mathcal{T}'$ such that h is embedded in one of the trees in $\mathcal{T}'$.

Although a more accurate definition of a proof would require that h would be identical to one of the trees in $\mathcal{T}'$, rather than being embedded in one of them, our relaxed definition is a common heuristic simplifying the proof construction process.

3.1.1 Entailment rules

The primary operations in Bar-Haim et al. (2007a) are applications of *Entailment Rules*. An entailment rule is composed of two sub-trees, named *left hand side* (*lhs*) and *right hand side* (*rhs*), intended to capture an entailment relation between its two sides (See Table 1). For example, a simple lexical rule is "music → art", where both sub-trees consist of single nodes.

Let r = *(lhs, rhs)* be a rule and t be a parse-tree, such that *lhs* is embedded in t. An *application* of r on t is a generation of a new tree, t', which is identical to t, but with the instance of *lhs* in t being replaced by *rhs*. If the underlying meaning of t entails the meaning of t', then we would consider the application of r as *valid*. It should be noted that in (Bar-Haim et al., 2007a) all rule-applications, based on the set of rules given to the system, were considered valid for any arbitrary (**T**,**H**) pair, an assumption which we relax in our cost-based model.

A rule's *lhs* and *rhs* may contain *variables*, i.e.

nodes in which the lemma is not specified. When such a rule is applied, the system first instantiates the variables with actual lemmas, according to the original tree, and then replaces the *lhs* by the instantiated *rhs* (As exemplified in Figure 1). As described in Section 2 and Table 1, such entailment rules are able to capture a broad range of linguistic and world knowledge. It should be noted that in our current implementation generic-syntactic rules were not integrated yet. Incorporating and extending the set of generic-syntactic rules is currently under work.

3.1.2 Co-reference Operations

Co-reference Substitution is a tree manipulation that is performed according to co-reference information, given by an external co-reference resolver[6]. Given two mentions m_1 and m_2 of the same entity, not necessarily in the same parse-tree, we define the operation of replacing the sub-tree rooted by m_1 by the sub-tree rooted by m_2 as *Co-reference Substitution.*

3.1.3 On The Fly operations

As described in Section 2, the original scheme of Bar-Haim et al. (2007a) recognized a **(T,H)** pair as entailing if and only if **H** could be generated by a sequence of co-reference substitutions and applications of rules from the given set of knowledge resources. Inevitably that scheme suffers very limited recall[7].

Utilizing our learning scheme as described below, we are able to overcome that difficulty, by adding an additional set of *on the fly* tree-transformations. Though those operations are not justified by a pre-given knowledge base, an estimation of their correctness likelihood can be learned, based on syntactic features. For example, moving a complete sub-tree is defined as an atomic operation, in contrast to the regular tree-edit-distance operations, in which such transformation requires a sequence of "insert" and "delete" operations.

An initial set of on-the-fly operations which is implemented in our system is specified in Table 2. The validity of applying such operations is estimated by the cost-model, described next, using the features listed in Table 3. Those operations represent simple transformations required to handle differences between two dependency-parse-trees, and are applied when parts of the hypothesis tree are missing in a given tree in $\mathcal{T}$.

Operation-Name	Operation-Description
Insert Node	Insert a new node in an arbitrary position in a parse tree.
Move sub tree	Disconnect a sub tree rooted by n from its parent $p(n)$ and connect it as a child of another node in the tree, $p'(n)$.
Change Relation	Change the relation (the edge label) between a node n and its parent $p(n)$.
Flip Part-Of-Speech	Change a node's part-of-speech.
Cut Multi-Word	Remove some of the words from a multi-word expression, as identified by the parser
Single-Word to Multi-Word	Replace a word by a multi word expression containing it, e.g. "Bond" → "James Bond".

Table 2: *on-the-fly* operations in our system.

This set of operations can be extended in the future by using additional linguistic resources, e.g. by identifying the semantic role of the inserted and moved nodes, or by adding on-the-fly substitutions, scored by distributional similarity.

3.2 Cost Model

Given a proof P, we want to estimate its correctness likelihood. Under the assumption that some or all of the operations in P might be incorrect - for example due to inaccuracies of the knowledge bases, wrong co-reference resolution or incorrect on-the-fly operations - we define a *cost model* to quantify the proof's likelihood to be correct. Following the cost model applied by Raina et al. (2005) to logic proofs, we use an additive linear model in which each operation is characterized by a set of features and the operation's total cost is a weighted linear combination of those features. Formally, let $o \in P$, let $F^{(o)} = (F_1^{(o)}, F_2^{(o)}, \ldots F_D^{(o)})^T$ be a feature vector characterizing o, and let w be a corresponding *weight vector*. The total cost of o (denoted by $C_w(o)$) is defined as:

$$C_w(o) \triangleq \sum_{i=1}^{D} w_i \cdot F_i^{(o)} = w^T \cdot F^{(o)} \qquad (1)$$

The cost of a sequence of operations (and in particular of a proof) is naturally defined as the sum of costs of all operations. Thus, given a proof

[6]We used BART co-reference resolver (Versley et al., 2008)

[7]As mentioned earlier, to increase recall in practical RTE datasets, a hybrid framework was introduced by Bar-Haim et al. (2007b), which uses an approximate match mechanism for final classifications.

$P = (o_1, o_2, \ldots o_m)$, its total cost, denoted by $C_w(P)$, is:

$$C_w(P) \triangleq \sum_{j=1}^{m} C_w(o_j) \quad (2)$$

Let $F^{(P)} = \sum_{j=1}^{m} F^{(o_j)}$. Combining (1) and (2), we get:

$$C_w(P) \triangleq \sum_{i=1}^{D} w_i \cdot F_i^{(P)} = w^T \cdot F^{(P)} \quad (3)$$

The last equation provides a way to represent a complete proof by a single feature-vector, which is simply the sum of all operations' vectors. We will use this feature representation in the learning and classification phases.

For each (**T**,**H**) pair there might be many proofs. However, for positive pairs, we assume there exists a "correct" proof, i.e. a proof that is composed of only valid operations (though many other incorrect proofs exist as well), while for negative pairs non of the proofs is correct. An optimal weight vector, w^*, would assign low costs to correct proofs while incorrect proofs will be assigned high costs. Therefore, distinguishing between positive pairs and negative pairs should be done by examining their lowest-cost proofs.

In the next sub-sections we describe how to search for lowest-cost proofs ("best proofs") and how to learn the optimal weight vector.

3.2.1 Modelling Operations by Features

As a convention, all features are assigned zero-or-negative values, interpreted as penalty. For each value v_i assigned to a feature F_i, $v_i = 0$ means that no penalty is implied by that feature, while $|v_i| \gg 0$ implies a high penalty by that feature. Following that convention, all weights should be assigned zero-or-positive values, since adding an operation cannot improve the confidence of a proof. This implies that an operation's total cost $C_w(o)$, and a proof's total cost $C_w(P)$ are zero-or-negative. The higher the absolute cost value, the lower the likelihood of the proof's correctness.

Features were defined for each knowledge resource, for co-reference substitution and for on-the-fly operations, as summarized in Table 3. For knowledge resources, features were defined as follows. Many knowledge resources provide numerical scores, indicating rules' reliability, which we use for the corresponding feature value. The knowledge resources that provide such scores and were used in the current system are DIRT (Lin and Pantel, 2001), Wikipedia rules (Shnarch et al., 2009), Lin similarity (Lin, 1998a), and Directional-Similarity[8] (Kotlerman et al., 2010). For knowledge resources that do not provide a numerical information about rule reliability, the corresponding feature-value is set to (-1). In the current system, WordNet[9] (Fellbaum, 1998; Miller, 1995), an in-house Geographical data-base, and VerbOcean[10] (Chklovski and Pantel, 2004) were included.

Some on-the-fly operations incorporate numerical information that reflects how likely it is that the meaning of the text is changed by applying them. As an example, for the insert-node operation we use the "Maximum Likelihood Estimation" (MLE) of the occurrence probability of the inserted word in a large news corpus[11]. The underlying assumption here is that it is more likely that inserting frequent words would still preserve entailment than inserting rare words.

3.3 Searching for the best proof

Searching for the best proof is done iteratively. Starting from $\mathcal{T}$ as the original text's trees, and a given weight vector, the system adds all the trees that can be generated by applying any generation-operation on $\mathcal{T}$. Since that scheme makes $\mathcal{T}$ grow exponentially, we use a simple beam search pruning approach as follows.

A constant beam size K is predetermined. In each iteration $\mathcal{T}$ is pruned such that its number of trees will be no more than K. Since every tree in $\mathcal{T}$ was generated by a sequence of operations, we define the cost of a tree as the cost of the sequence that was used to generate that tree. We use that cost, in addition to estimations about the difference between a given tree to the hypothesis tree, in order to decide which tree should be pruned out, such that after each iteration $|\mathcal{T}| \leq K$. Finally, the lowest cost generated tree which embeds h is returned.

[8]A rule-base of lexical entailment rules automatically extracted by means of directional distributional similarity.

[9]We used the following WordNet relations: *hypernymy*, *holonymy*, *verb-entailment* and *synonymy*

[10]Only the relation "stronger" was used.

[11]We used Reuters Corpus, Volume 1+2 (RCV1-2). Available at http://trec.nist.gov/data/reuters/reuters.html

#	Feature	Value
1	Wikipedia	$\log(m)$, where m is the estimated accuracy of the method used to learn the given Wikipedia rule, as described in (Shnarch et al., 2009). $0 \leq m \leq 1$.
2	Lin Similarity	$\log(sim)$, where sim is the similarity score given for that rule according to (Lin, 1998a). $0 \leq sim \leq 1$.
3	Directional-Similarity	$\log(sim)$, where sim is the similarity score given for that rule according to (Kotlerman et al., 2010). $0 \leq sim \leq 1$.
4	DIRT	$\log(sim)$, where sim is the similarity score given for that rule according to (Lin and Pantel, 2001). Note that $0 \leq sim \leq 1$.
5	WordNet	-1
6	VerbOcean	-1
7	Geographical Database	-1
8 9 10 11	Insert Verb Insert non-verb content word Insert non-content word insert Named Entity	$\log(f)$, where f is the MLE of the occurrence probability for the inserted lemma in the Reuters news corpus.
12, 13, 14, 15	Insert verb / content word / non-content word / Named Entity - that exist in other parts of the text	$\log(f)$, where f is the MLE of the occurrence probability for the inserted lemma in the Reuters news corpus.
16	Change relation of a node to its parent, from "subject" to "object" or vice versa	-1
17 18	Move Sub Tree rooted by n from $p(n)$ to $p'(n)$, s.t. the path from n to $p'(n)$ contains a verb All other "move Sub Tree" operations	$-l$, where l is the length of the path between n and $p'(n)$ in the original tree.
19	Single-word to Multi-word	$\log(\min_{f \in \mathcal{F}}(f))$ where $\mathcal{F}$ is the set of MLE of the occurrence probabilities corresponding to the added words. The probabilities were calculated using the Reuters News corpus.
20	Cut Multi-word	-1
21	Flip part-of-speech	-1
22	Co-reference	-1

Table 3: Features and their values for each (knowledge and on-the-fly) operation. Note that all values are negative.

3.4 Iterative Weight Estimation

We would like to classify a proof P, represented by a feature vector F, as "correct" if its cost is low.

Formally, let (w, b) be a weight vector and a threshold. P is classified as correct if and only if

$$w \cdot F + b \geq 0 \quad (4)$$

and as incorrect otherwise. The goal of parameter estimation is thus finding optimal (w^*, b^*).

If our training set was a set of binary-labelled vectors (F_i, l_i), $i \in \{1 \dots n\}$, we could apply directly a linear training algorithm to find (w^*, b^*). However, our training set is a set of labelled text pairs, for which the proofs that determine the corresponding feature vectors should be constructed by the system. Yet, as explained at the end of Section 3.2, only the lowest-cost proofs should be considered to distinguish between positive and negative pairs, while finding those proofs through the search algorithm of Section 3.3 requires knowing the optimal weight vector.

We therefore use an iterative learning scheme to overcome this circularity problem, as follows (see Algorithm 1). We start with an initial weight vector and threshold, (w_0, b_0), set manually by a reasonable guess. Using the algorithm in Section 3.3 we find a lowest-cost proof for each pair, resulting in n labelled feature vectors, $(F_1, l_1) \dots (F_n, l_n)$, where l_i is the binary entailment annotation. Next, we use a standard linear learning algorithm to learn new parameters, (w_1, b_1). We iteratively improve the weights vectors and the proofs until con-

Algorithm 1 Parameters Estimation

```
Require: Training set: (T_1,H_1,l_1) ... (T_n,H_n,l_n)
(w_0, b_0) ← a reasonable guess of weights vector and threshold
i ← 0
repeat
    Find P_1 ... P_n by the method described in 3.3, using (w_i, b_i)
    Construct the corresponding feature vectors F^(P_1) ... F^(P_n).
    use (F^(P_1), l_1) ... (F^(P_n), l_n) as a training set to a linear classifier, resulting new parameters (w_{i+1}, b_{i+1}).
    i ← i + 1
until convergence
```

System	RTE-1	RTE-2	RTE-3	RTE-5
Learning and abductive reasoning (Raina et al., 2005)	57.0 %			
Probabilistic Calculus of Tree Transformations (Harmeling, 2009)		56.39 %	57.88 %	
Probabilistic Tree Edit model (Wang and Manning, 2010)		63.0 %	61.10 %	
Deterministic Entailment Proofs (Bar-Haim et al., 2007b)			61.12 %	63.80 %
Our System Accuracy (Recall % / Precision %)	57.13% (81.0/54.8)	61.63% (76.2/59.0)	67.13% (87.2/63.3)	63.50% (75.7/60.9)
Median of all submissions in challenge	55.20 %	58.13 %	61.75 %	61.00 %
Best System in challenge	58.6 %	75.3 %	80.0 %	73.5 %

Table 4: Accuracy of proof-based systems on RTE datasets, followed by median results and best results of all systems participated in those challenges.

vergence. Since there is no theoretical bound on the convergence rate, we limit the number of iterations by a predefined constant. In practice, however, only few iterations are required for convergence.

4 Evaluation

We ran experiments on the first, second, third and fifth RTE datasets[12] (Dagan et al., 2005; Bar-Haim et al., 2006; Giampiccolo et al., 2007; Bentivogli et al., 2009) and compared our system to other proof-style systems. Each dataset consists of 600 to 800 (**T**,**H**) pairs, half of them are positive, and the other half are negative. For the underlying linear classifier, required by Algorithm 1, we used linear-SVM[13]. The value of K, described in Section 3.3, was set to 135, according to tuning done on the training set. The results for our system, presented in Table 4, show comparable performance to other systems on most datasets, with notably higher performance in RTE-3.

Operation	avg. in positives	avg. in negatives	ratio
Insert Named Entity	-0.006	-0.016	2.67
Insert content word	-0.038	-0.094	2.44
DIRT	-0.013	-0.023	1.73
"subject" $\leftrightarrow$ "object"	-0.025	-0.040	1.60
Flip part-of-speech	-0.098	-0.101	1.03
Lin similarity	-0.084	-0.072	0.86
WordNet	-0.064	-0.052	0.81

Table 5: The average value of certain features in positive pairs and negative pairs, taken from an experiment on the RTE-2 test set.

As indicated by the results, our system indeed assigns, on average, higher costs to negative pairs than to positive ones. Further insight into this behavior is obtained by Table 5. The table presents a sample of features' average values. The upper rows of the table present features whose average absolute value in negative pairs is significantly higher than in positive pairs, while the features in the lower rows have similar average values in positive and negative pairs.

The former features indicate that there are some operations that tend to be part of the "best" proof for negative pairs more frequently than for positive pairs. A reasonable explanation for this phenomenon is that the system learned that some operations are less reliable than other operations, and tried to avoid them whenever possible. However, these operations could not be avoided in negative pairs, resulting in higher feature values.

5 Conclusions and Future Work

Two main concepts underlie this paper. The first is automatic estimation of the quality of proofs required to recognize textual-entailment. The second concept is a complete framework of linguistically-motivated proof operations for recognising textual-entailment. The main contribution of this paper is showing how those two concepts can be integrated, to leverage the advantages of both.

The linguistically-motivated framework presented here is based on the framework proposed by (Bar-Haim et al., 2007a), with a significant extension of on-the-fly operations required for making it robust and complete. Many additional linguistically-motivated entailment operations can be naturally integrated into this framework. For example, lexical, syntactic and semantic attributes like verb-tense and polarity (negation) can be easily handled, much like part-of-speech and named-entity (Bar-Haim et al., 2007a). Another example is temporal inference (e.g. "this afternoon $\rightarrow$ today") which can be integrated easily by proper substitutions based on an appropriate knowledge

[12]The RTE-4 dataset had no training dataset

[13]We used SVM-Light, available at http://svmlight.joachims.org/

resource (similar to the one proposed by Wang and Zhang (2008)). Yet another example is addressing more types of co-reference based operations (Mirkin et al., 2010). Finally, as noted earlier, the current set of on-the-fly operations may be extended, which will likely improve the system's performance.

Acknowledgements

This work was partially supported by the Israel Science Foundation grant 1112/08 and by the PASCAL-2 Network of Excellence of the European Community FP7-ICT-2007-1-216886.

References

Roy Bar-Haim, Ido Dagan, Bill Dolan, Lisa Ferro, Danilo Giampiccolo, Bernardo Magnini, and Idan Szpektor. 2006. The second pascal recognising textual entailment challenge. In *Proceedings of the Second PASCAL Challenges Workshop on Recognising Textual Entailment.*

Roy Bar-Haim, Ido Dagan, Iddo Greental, and Eyal Shnarch. 2007a. Semantic inference at the lexical-syntactic level. In *Proceedings of AAAI.*

Roy Bar-Haim, Ido Dagan, Iddo Greental, Idan Szpektor, and Moshe Friedman. 2007b. Semantic inference at the lexical-syntactic level for textual entailment recognition. In *Proceedings of ACL-PASCAL Workshop on Textual Entailment and Paraphrasing.*

Roy Bar-Haim. 2010. *Semantic Inference at the Lexical-Syntactic Level.* Ph.D. thesis, Bar-Ilan Univeristy.

Luisa Bentivogli, Bernardo Magnini, Ido Dagan, H.T. Dang, and D. Giampiccolo. 2009. The fifth pascal recognizing textual entailment challenge. In *proceeding of TAC.*

Timothy Chklovski and Patrick Pantel. 2004. Verbocean: Mining the web for fine-grained semantic verb relations. In *Proceedings of EMNLP.*

Ido Dagan, Oren Glickman, and Bernardo Magnini. 2005. The PASCAL recognising textual entailment challenge. In Joaquin Quiñonero Candela, Ido Dagan, Bernardo Magnini, and Florence d'Alché Buc, editors, *MLCW*, volume 3944 of *Lecture Notes in Computer Science*, pages 177–190. Springer.

Christiane Fellbaum, editor. 1998. *WordNet An Electronic Lexical Database.* The MIT Press, Cambridge, MA ; London, May.

Jenny Rose Finkel, Trond Grenager, and Christopher D. Manning. 2005. Incorporating non-local information into information extraction systems by Gibbs Sampling. In *Proceedings of ACL.*

Danilo Giampiccolo, Bernardo Magnini, Ido Dagan, and Bill Dolan. 2007. The third pascal recognizing textual entailment challenge. In *RTE '07 Proceedings of the ACL-PASCAL Workshop on Textual Entailment and Paraphrasing.*

Stefan Harmeling. 2009. Inferring textual entailment with a probabilistically sound calculus. *Natural Language Engineering*, 15(4):459–477.

Michael Heilman and Noah A. Smith. 2010. Tree edit models for recognizing textual entailments, paraphrases and answers to questions. In *HLT-NAACL.*

Lili Kotlerman, Ido Dagan, Idan Szpektor, and Maayan Zhitomirsky-geffet. 2010. Directional distributional similarity for lexical inference. *Natural Language Engineering*, 16:359–389.

Dekang Lin and Patrick Pantel. 2001. DIRT - discovery of inference rules from text. In *Proceedings of ACM SIGKDD Conference on Knowledge Discovery and Data Mining.*

Dekang Lin. 1998a. Automatic retrieval and clustering of similar words. In *Proceedings of COLING-ACL.*

Dekang Lin. 1998b. Dependency-based evaluation of minipar. In *Proceedings of the Workshop on Evaluation of Parsing Systems at LREC 1998*, Granada, Spain.

Yashar Mehdad and Bernardo Magnini. 2009. Optimizing textual entailment recognition using particle swarm optimization. In *Proceedings of the 2009 Workshop on Applied Textual Inference.*

George A. Miller. 1995. Wordnet: A lexical database for english. *Commun. ACM*, 38(11):39–41.

Shachar Mirkin, Ido Dagan, and Sebastian Pado. 2010. Assessing the role of discourse references in entailment inference. In *Proceedings of ACL.*

Rajat Raina, Andrew Y. Ng, and Christopher D. Manning. 2005. Robust textual inference via learning and abductive reasoning. In *Proceedings of AAAI.*

Eyal Shnarch, Libby Barak, and Ido Dagan. 2009. Extracting lexical reference rules from Wikipedia. In *ACL-IJCNLP.*

Yannick Versley, Simone Paolo Ponzetto, Massimo Poesio, Vladimir Eidelman, Alan Jern, Jason Smith, Xiaofeng Yang, and Ro Moschitti. 2008. BART: A modular toolkit for coreference resolution. In *Proceedings of ACL, Demo Session.*

Mengqiu Wang and Christopher D. Manning. 2010. Probabilistic tree-edit models with structured latent variables for textual entailment and question answering. In *Proceedings of COLING.*

Rui Wang and Yajing Zhang. 2008. Recognizing textual entailment with temporal expressions in natural language texts. In *Proceedings of the IWSCA.*

Learning Script Participants from Unlabeled Data

Michaela Regneri * **Alexander Koller** † **Josef Ruppenhofer** ‡ **Manfred Pinkal** *

* Department of Computational Linguistics, Saarland University
{regneri,pinkal}@coli.uni-saarland.de
† Department of Linguistics, University of Potsdam
koller@ling.uni-potsdam.de
‡ Department of Information Science and Language Technology, University of Hildesheim
Josef.Ruppenhofer@uni-hildesheim.de

Abstract

We introduce a system that learns the participants of arbitrary given scripts. This system processes data from web experiments, in which each participant can be realized with different expressions. It computes participants by encoding semantic similarity and global structural information into an Integer Linear Program. An evaluation against a gold standard shows that we significantly outperform two informed baselines.

1 Introduction

Scripts (Schank and Abelson, 1977) represent commonsense knowledge about the events that stereotypically constitute a certain activity. For instance, the "restaurant" script might specify that the patron enters, the waiter shows the patron to their seat, eventually the patron eats a plate of food, and so forth. There has always been agreement that script knowledge can be highly useful for a variety of applications in artificial intelligence and computational linguistics, including commonsense reasoning for text understanding (Cullingford, 1977; Mueller, 2004), information extraction (Rau et al., 1989) and automated storytelling (Swanson and Gordon, 2008). But there is hardly an area where the discrepancy between the felt importance of a type of knowledge and the inability to provide any substantial amount of this knowledge for serious applications is greater.

Recently, several groups have tackled the problem using unsupervised methods for learning script-like knowledge from text corpora or data obtained through web experiments (Chambers and Jurafsky, 2008; Chambers and Jurafsky, 2009; Regneri et al., 2010). For the first time, they open up a perspective to wide-coverage resources of script knowledge. However, each of these approaches handles only specific aspects of script information: Chambers and Jurafsky (2009) learn *narrative schemas* and their participants; they group verbs into schemas by virtue of shared participants assuming that this is an indicator for being part of the same stereotypical activity, without knowing the actual scenarios. The system of Regneri et al. (2010) learns the temporal order of events occurring in specific stereotypical scenarios, but does not determine participants.

In this paper, we present a system that automatically learns sets of participants associated with specific scenarios. We take the approach of Regneri et al. as our starting point. In this earlier work, several experimental subjects described what happens in a given scenario in a web experiment; the system then learns what event descriptions from different subjects refer to the same event, and how they are temporally ordered, using Multiple Sequence Alignment (Durbin et al., 1998). The specific problem we consider is to group the different noun phrases occurring throughout a script into equivalence classes, resulting in one class for each participant. Our solution combines diverse sources of information, including semantic similarity and structural information from the sequence alignment, in an Integer Linear Program (Wolsey, 1998, *ILP*). The desired equivalence classes then correspond to an optimal solution of the ILP. We not only show that our system significantly outperforms a high-precision baseline, but also that it substantially exploits global structural information. The process is almost entirely unsupervised: We rely on annotated data only for training a handful of similarity thresholds and for evaluation. We expect our approach to scale up and help obtain a broad-coverage knowledge base of scripts with participants through web experiments.

Plan of the paper. The paper starts by reviewing related work. We will then define the exact script learning problem we tackle here. Next, we show how participants can be learned, and then present

	ESD 1	ESD 2	ESD3
1	put food on plate	put food in bowl	put food on dish
2	open microwave	open door	open oven
3	put plate in	put food inside	place dish in oven
4	close microwave	close door	close
5	∅	enter time	select desired length
6	press start	push button	∅
7		...	

Figure 1: Alignment for the MICROWAVE scenario.

the evaluation before we finally conclude.

2 Related Work

Many papers on scripts and their application perspectives have been published in the seventies (Schank and Abelson, 1977; Barr and Feigenbaum, 1981). Script knowledge was manually modeled, and never exceeded a handful of domains and implementations operating on them.

Scenario frames in FrameNet (Baker et al., 1998) are another approach to modeling scripts and their participants. They describe how a stereotypical activity is made up of smaller events (frames), which share roles (frame elements) specifying people and objects involved in the events.

The supervised approach of Mani et al. (2006) learns temporal event relations from TimeBank (Pustejovsky et al., 2006).

All of these approaches rely on elaborate manual annotation efforts, and so it is unclear how they would scale to wide-coverage resources.

Chambers and Jurafsky (2008; 2009) exploit coreference chains and co-occurrence frequency of verbs in text corpora to extract *narrative schemas* describing sequences of events and their participants.[1] Because this approach is fully unsupervised, its coverage is in principle unlimited. Each schema provides a family of verbs and arguments related by the same narrative context. Roughly speaking, event sequences are induced by grouping verbs in the same schema if they tend to share the same arguments. Within the schemas, events are represented as verbs, while the relations between the verbs remain underspecified: Two verbs of a schema might describe the same, different or contradictory events. The aim here is not to collect data describing predetermined activities, but rather to establish verb groups that share an (unknown) underlying scenario.

Regneri et al. (2010) (henceforth, RKP) propose an alternative approach with complementary strengths and weaknesses. The starting point are specific scenarios, and human users answer questions like “what happens in a restaurant?”. From the data collected in this way, a mining algorithm learns both which phrases describe the same subevent and how these sub-events are ordered temporally. This guided way of learning script data produces representations associated with known scenarios, and also opens up the possibility of learning about activities that are too stereotypical to be elaborated much in text corpora (and which thus can’t be induced from there). However, the approach is limited by its reliance on scenarios that have to be determined beforehand. Tying in with this previous work, we compute participants using Integer Linear Programming to globally combine information from diverse sources. ILP has been applied to a variety of different problems in NLP (Althaus et al., 2004; Barzilay and Lapata, 2006; Berant et al., 2010), including coreference resolution (Denis and Baldridge, 2007; Finkel and Manning, 2008).

3 Scripts and Participants

We formalize the problem of computing participants of a script as one of computing equivalence classes of mentions occurring in script-related event descriptions. In this respect our task is similar to coreference resolution.

Our algorithm takes the raw data and processed outputs of RKP as its starting point. The RKP data consist of a collection of *event sequence descriptions (ESDs)*, each of which is written by one annotator to describe how a scenario plays out. RKP compute an *alignment table* out of the ESDs (Fig. 1) using Multiple Sequence Alignment (Durbin et al., 1998, *MSA*). The columns of this alignment table represent the original ESDs, possibly interspersed with some gaps (“∅”). The non-gaps in each row are *aligned*, and thus presumably describe the same event in the scenario (cf. *open microwave*, *open door*, and *open oven* in Fig. 1). The MSA algorithm assumes a *cost function* for substitutions (= aligning two non-gaps) and *gap costs* for aligning gaps with non-gaps to compute the lowest-cost alignment of the ESDs.

In our work, we compute script-specific participants using the alignment tables. For example, we want to find out that *plate*, *bowl* and *dish* fill the same role in the microwave script. We call a mention of a participant (typically a noun phrase) in

[1]See http://cs.stanford.edu/people/nc/schemas

some event description a *participant description*. Our system is intended to group participant descriptions into equivalence classes, which we call *participant description sets* (PDS).

4 Computing Participants

Learning participants from aligned ESDs is done in two steps: First, we identify candidate participant descriptions in event descriptions. Then, we partition the participant descriptions for each scenario into sets. The sets correspond to script-specific participants, their members are possible verbalizations of the respective participants.

4.1 Identifying participant descriptions

We consider participant descriptions to be the noun phrases in our data set, and thus reduce the task of their identification to the task of syntactic parsing. Parsing event descriptions is a challenge because the data is written in telegraphic style (cf. Fig. 1). The subject (typically the protagonist) is frequently left implicit, and nouns lack determiners, as in *start microwave*. In our experiments, we use the Stanford parser (Klein and Manning, 2003). Under the standard model, parsing accuracy for phrase structure trees is only 59% on our data (evaluated on 100 hand-annotated example sentences). The scores for dependency links between predicates and direct objects indicate how many noun phrase heads are correctly identified. Here the standard parser reaches 81% precision. The most frequent and most serious error is misclassification of the phrase-initial verb (like *start*) as a noun, which often leads to subsequent errors in the rest of the phrase.

Our available dataset of event descriptions is much too small to serve as a training corpus of its own. To achieve sufficient parsing accuracy, we combine and modify existing resources to build the parser model: we re-train the parser on a corpus consisting of the Penn Treebank (Marcus et al., 1993) and modified versions of the ATIS and Brown corpora (Dahl et al., 1994; Francis and Kucera, 1979). Modification consists in deleting all subjects in the sentences and deleting the determiners. To maintain accuracy on whole sentences, the original version of the modified corpora is added to the training set as well. The adaptation raises the accuracy for whole phrase structure trees to 72%, and the direct object link precision to 90%.

Out of those parses, we can now extract all noun phrases for further processing. The last step for participant identification consists in adding the "implicit protagonist" whenever the subject position in the parse tree is empty.

4.2 Participant Description Sets

The next task consists in the actual learning of script participants, more specifically: We will propose a method that groups participant descriptions occurring in the ESDs for a given scenario into participant description sets (PDSs) that comprise different mentions of one participant.

We assume that two token-identical participant descriptions always have the same word sense and represent the same participant, not only in one ESD, but across all event descriptions within a scenario. This extends the common "one sense per discourse" heuristic (Gale et al., 1992) with a "one participant per sense" assumption on top of that. The resulting loss of precision is only minimal, and we can take participant description types (PTs) rather than tokens to be basic entities, which drastically reduces the size of the basic entity set.

We also exploit structural information given in the alignment tables: If two PTs occur in aligned event descriptions, we take this as a piece of evidence that they belong to the same participant. In the example of Fig. 1, this supports identification of "time" and "desired length".

We complement this structural indicator by semantic similarity information: In the example of Fig. 1, the identification of "bowl" and "dish" is supported by WordNet hyponymy. We use semantic similarity information in different ways:

- WordNet synonymy of PTs, as well as synonymy and direct hyponymy of the head of multiword PTs (like *full can* and *full container*) guarantee participant identity
- A WordNet based semantic similarity score is used as a soft indicator of participant identity

We combine all these information sources by modeling the equivalence-class problem as an Integer Linear Program (Wolsey, 1998, *ILP*). An ILP computes an assignment of integer values to a set of variables, maximizing a given *objective function*. Additional linear equations and inequalities can constrain the possible value assignments.

The problem we want to solve is to determine for each pair pt_i and pt_j in the set of PTs

$\{\mathrm{pt}_1, \ldots, \mathrm{pt}_n\}$ whether they belong to the same equivalence class. We model this in our ILP by introducing variables x_{ij} which can take the values 0 or 1; if x_{ij} takes the value 1 in a solution of the ILP, this means that the tokens of pt_i and the tokens of pt_j belong to the same PDS.

Objective function

We use the objective function to encode semantic similarity and structural information from the alignment. We require the ILP solver to maximize the value of the following linear term:

$$\sum_{i,j=1,i\neq j}^{n} (\mathrm{struc}(pt_i, pt_j) \cdot \mathrm{sim}(pt_i, pt_j) - \theta) \cdot x_{ij} \tag{1}$$

$\mathrm{sim}(i, j)$ stands for the semantic similarity of pt_i and pt_j and is computed as follows:

$$\mathrm{sim}(pt_i, pt_j) = \begin{cases} lin(pt_i, pt_j) + \eta & \text{if } pt_i \text{ and } pt_j \\ & \text{are hyponyms} \\ lin(pt_i, pt_j) & \text{otherwise} \end{cases} \tag{2}$$

For computing similarity, we use Lin's (WordNet-based) similarity measure (Lin, 1998; Fellbaum, 1998), which performs better than several distributional measures which we have tried. Direct hyponymy is a particularly strong indicator; therefore we add the empirically determined constant η to sim in this case.

θ is a cutoff which is also optimized empirically. Every pair with a similarity lower than θ adds a negative score to the objective function when its variable is set to 1. In the final solution, pairs with a similarity score smaller than θ are thus avoided whenever possible.

$\mathrm{struc}(i, j)$ encodes structural information about pt_i and pt_j, i.e. how tokens of pt_i and pt_j are related in the alignment table. Eq. 3 defines this:

$$\mathrm{struc}(pt_i, pt_j) = \begin{cases} \lambda_+ & \text{if } pt_i \text{ and } pt_j \text{ from} \\ & \text{same row} \\ \lambda_- & \text{if } pt_i \text{ and } pt_j \text{ from} \\ & \text{same column and unrelated} \\ 1 & otherwise \end{cases} \tag{3}$$

If pt_i and pt_j are aligned at least once (i.e., their enclosing event descriptions are paraphrase candidates), $\mathrm{struc}(i, j)$ takes a constant value λ_+ greater than 1, thus boosting the similarity of pt_i and pt_j. If the tokens of pt_i and pt_j occur in the same *column* (i.e., they are alternately used by the same subject in an ESD) and the two types have no direct WordNet link, $\mathrm{struc}(pt_i, pt_j)$ takes a constant value smaller than 1 (λ_-) and lowers the similarity score. Both values are empirically optimized.

Hard Constraints

We add a constraint $x_{ij} = 1$ for a pair i, j if one of the following conditions holds:

- pt_i and pt_j share a synset in WordNet
- pt_i and pt_j have the same head (like *laundry machine* and *machine*)
- pt_i and pt_j are both multiword expressions, their modifiers are identical and their heads are either synonyms or hyponyms

Furthermore, if pt_i is the implicit protagonist, we add the constraint $x_{ij} = 1$ if pt_j is a first or second person pronoun, and $x_{ij} = 0$ otherwise.

Finally, we ensure that the ILP groups the participant types into equivalence classes by enforcing symmetry and transitivity. Symmetry is trivially encoded by the following constraint over all i and j:

$$x_{ij} = x_{ji} \tag{4}$$

Transitivity can be guaranteed by adding the following constraints for each i, j, k:

$$x_{ij} + x_{jk} - x_{ik} \leq 1 \tag{5}$$

This is a standard formulation of transitivity, used e.g. by Finkel and Manning (2008).

5 Evaluation

We evaluate our system against a gold standard of 10 scenarios. On average, one scenario consists of 180 event descriptions, containing 54 participant description types realized in 233 tokens. The scenarios are EAT AT A FAST FOOD RESTAURANT, RETURN FOOD (IN A RESTAURANT), PAY WITH CREDIT CARD, TAKE A SHOWER, FEED A PET DOG, MAKE COFFEE, HEAT SOMETHING IN A MICROWAVE, MAIL A LETTER, BUY SOMETHING FROM A VENDING MACHINE, and DO LAUNDRY. The VENDING MACHINE and LAUNDRY scenarios were used for parameter optimization. The parameter values we determined were $\theta = 5.3, \eta = 0.8, \lambda_+ = 3.4$ and $\lambda_- = 0.4$. We solve the ILP using LPSolve (Berkelaar et al., 2004).

SCENARIO	PRECISION				RECALL				F-SCORE			
	full	sem	align	base	full	sem	align	base	full	sem	align	base
LAUNDRY*	0.85	0.76	0.53	0.93	0.75	0.83	0.89	0.57	**0.80**	0.79	0.67	0.70
VENDING M.*	0.80	0.74	0.57	0.84	0.78	0.83	0.97	0.62	**0.79**	0.78	0.72	0.72
FAST FOOD	0.82	0.65	0.55	0.87	0.82	0.85	0.84	0.70	**0.82**	0.74	0.66	0.78
RETURN FOOD	0.80	0.78	0.53	0.88	0.44	0.52	0.63	0.34	0.57	***0.62***	0.57	0.49
COFFEE	0.85	0.77	0.53	0.92	0.80	0.81	0.98	0.68	**0.82**	0.79	0.68	0.78
FEED DOG	0.81	0.67	0.53	0.90	0.88	0.92	0.94	0.57	**0.84**	0.78	0.68	0.70
MICROWAVE	0.89	0.78	0.55	0.93	0.84	0.84	0.89	0.70	**0.86**	0.81	0.68	0.80
CREDIT CARD	0.90	0.82	0.60	0.94	0.54	0.54	0.64	0.40	**0.67**	0.65	0.62	0.56
MAIL LETTER	0.92	0.78	0.54	0.96	0.88	0.88	0.93	0.74	**0.90**	0.83	0.68	0.84
SHOWER	0.87	0.79	0.57	0.94	0.83	0.83	0.86	0.66	**0.85**	0.81	0.69	0.77
AVERAGE*	0.85	0.75	0.55	0.91	0.75	0.79	0.86	0.60	• **0.79**	• 0.76	0.66	0.71
AVERAGE	0.86	0.76	0.55	0.92	0.75	0.77	0.84	0.60	• **0.79**	0.75	0.66	0.71

Figure 2: Results for the full system, the system without structural constraints (sem), the system with structural information only (align) and the naive baseline. Participant descriptions with the right head are considered correct. Starred scenarios have been used for parameter optimization, *average** includes those scenarios, the unmarked average doesn't. A black dot (•) means that the difference to the next lower baseline is significant with $p < 0.05$. The difference between full and base is significant at $p < 0.001$.

5.1 Gold Standard

We preprocessed the 10 evaluation scenarios by aligning them with the RKP algorithm. Two annotators then labeled the 10 aligned scenarios, recording which noun-phrases referred to the same participant. Specifically, the labelers were shown, in order, the sets of aligned event descriptions. For instance, for the microwave script, they would first encounter all available alternative descriptions for putting food on some dish. From each aligned description, the annotators extracted the participant-referring NPs, which were then grouped into blocks of coreferent mentions. After all sets of component-event descriptions had been processed, the annotators also manually sorted the previously extracted blocks into coreferent sets. Implicit participants, typically missing subjects, were annotated, too. For the evaluation, we include missing subjects but do not consider other implicit participants. Each annotator labeled 5 of the scenarios independently, and reviewed the other annotator's work. Difficult cases, mostly related to metonymies, were solved in consultation.

5.2 Baseline and Scoring Method

The system sorts participant descriptions into their equivalence classes, thus we evaluate whether the equivalence statements are correct and whether the classes it found are complete. Speaking in terms of participant description sets, we evaluate the purity of each set (whether all items in a set belong there) and the set completeness (whether another set should have been merged into the current one).

5.2.1 Baselines

We compare our system with three baselines: As a naïve baseline (*base*), we group participant descriptions together only if they are string-equal. This is equivalent to just employing the type-abstraction step we took in the full system and ignoring other information sources.

Additionally, we show the influence of the structural information with a more informed baseline (*sem*): we replicate our full system but just use the semantic similarity including all hard constraints, without any structural information from the alignment tables. This is equivalent to setting $\mathrm{struc}(i, j)$ in equation 1 always to 1.

In order to show that semantic similarity and the alignment indeed provide contrastive knowledge, we test a third baseline that contains the structural information only (*align*). Here we group all noun phrases i and j together if $\mathrm{struc}(i, j) > 1$ and the pair (i, j) meets all hard constraints.

All parameters for the baselines were optimized separately using the same scenarios as for the full system.

5.2.2 Scoring Method

Because the equivalence classes we compute are similar to coreference sets, we apply the b^3 evaluation metric for coreference resolution (Bagga and Baldwin, 1998). b^3 defines precision and recall as follows: for every token t in the annotation, take the coreference set C_t it is assigned to. Find the

np-matching	PRECISION				RECALL				F-SCORE			
	full	sem	align	base	full	sem	align	base	full	sem	align	base
Gold Tokens	0.92	0.81	0.54	0.97	0.86	0.88	0.96	0.71	0.89	0.84	0.70	0.81
Matching Head	0.86	0.76	0.55	0.92	0.75	0.77	0.84	0.60	0.79	0.75	0.66	0.71
Strict Matching	0.82	0.74	0.52	0.91	0.70	0.71	0.77	0.59	0.74	0.71	0.62	0.71

Figure 3: Averaged evaluation results for three scoring methods: *Gold Tokens* uses gold standard segmentation. *Matching head* uses parsing for PD extraction and phrases with the right head are considered correct. *Strict* requires the whole phrase to match.

set C_{t+gold} that contains t in the gold standard, and assign $precision_t$ and $recall_t$:

$$precision_t = \frac{|C_t \cap C_{t+gold}|}{|C_t|} \quad (6)$$

$$recall_t = \frac{|C_t \cap C_{t+gold}|}{|C_{t+gold}|} \quad (7)$$

Overall precision and recall is averaged over all tokens in the annotation. Overall F_1 score is then computed as follows:

$$F_1 = \frac{2 * precision * recall}{precision + recall} \quad (8)$$

Unlike in coreference resolution, we have the problem that we compare gold-standard annotations against tokens extracted from automatic parses. However, the b^3-metric is only applicable if the gold standard and the test data contain the same set of tokens. Thus we apply b^3_{sys}, a variant of b^3 introduced by Cai and Strube (2010). b^3_{sys} extends the gold standard and the test set such that both contain the same set of tokens. Roughly speaking, every token that appears in the gold standard but not in the test set is copied to the latter and treated as singleton set, and vice versa. See Cai and Strube for details.

With the inaccurate parser, noun phrases are often parsed incompletely, missing modifiers or relative clauses. We therefore consider a participant description as equivalent with a gold standard phrase if they have the same head. This relaxed scoring metric evaluates the system realistically by punishing parsing errors only moderately.

5.3 Results

5.3.1 Scores

Figure 2 shows the results for our system and three baselines. *full* marks the complete system, *sem* is the baseline without structural information, *align* uses exclusively structural information and *base* is the naïve string matching baseline. The starred scenarios were used for parameter optimization and excluded from the final average score. (The AVERAGE* row includes those scenarios.) In terms of the average F-Score, we outperform the baselines significantly ($p < 0.05$, paired two-sample t-test on the f-scores for the different scenarios) in all three cases. The system difference to the naïve baseline even reaches a significance level of $p < 0.001$. While the naïve baseline always gets the best precision results, the *align*-baseline performs best for recall. The latter is due to the numerous alignment errors, which sometimes lead to a simple partition in subjects and objects. Our system finds the best tradeoff between precision and recall, gaining 15% recall on average compared to the naïve baseline and just losing about 6% precision. *sem* and the naïve baseline differ only moderately. This shows that semantic similarity information alone is not sufficient for distinguishing the different participant descriptions, and that the exploitation of structural information is crucial. However, the structural information by itself is worthless: high precision loss makes *align* even worse than the naïve baseline.

Fig. 3 compares the same-head scoring metric described in the previous section *(Matching Head)* against two other approaches of dealing with wrongly recognized NP tokens: *Strict Matching* only accepts two NP tokens as equivalent if they are identical; *Gold Tokens* means that our PDS identification algorithm runs directly on the gold standard tokens. This shows that parsing accuracy has a considerable effect on the overall performance of the system. However, our system robustly outperforms the baselines regardless of the matching approach.

5.3.2 Example Output

Fig. 4 illustrates our system's behavior showing its output for the MICROWAVE scenario. Each rectangle on the left represents one PDS, which we rep-

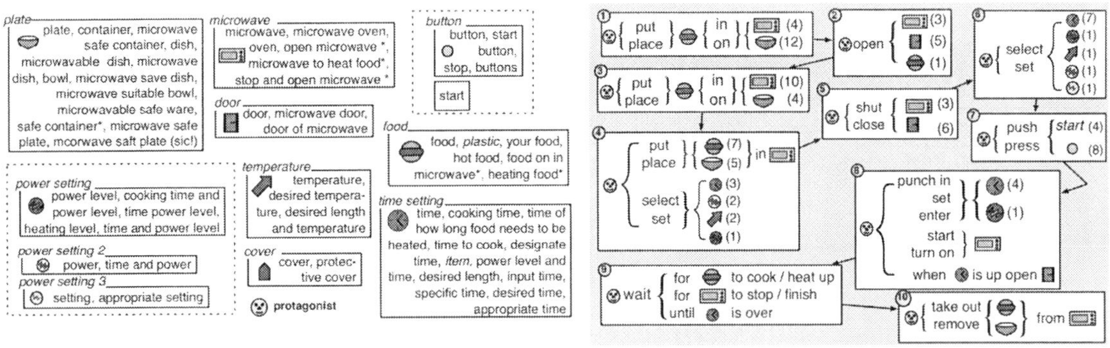

Figure 4: The participants we extracted for the MICROWAVE scenario, and a participant-annotated excerpt from the original graph. Descriptions in *italics* indicate sorting mistakes, asterisks (*) mark parsing mistakes. Dotted boxes frame PDSs that actually belong together but were not combined by the algorithm.

resent by an icon in the graph to the right.[2] The participant types in the sets are ordered by frequency, starting with the most frequent one. The labels of the sets are script role labels and were introduced for readability. Note that the structural alignment information allows us to correctly classify *plate* and *container*, and *stop* and *button*, as equivalent, although they are not particularly similar in WordNet. However, especially for rare terms, our algorithm seems too strict: it did not combine the three *power setting* PDSs. Also, we cannot tell start from stop buttons, which is mainly due to the fact that most people did not distinguish them at all but just called them *button(s)* (some microwaves just have one button). The separate grouping of *start* is also related to parsing errors: *start* was mostly parsed as a verb, even when used as object of *push*.

The right part of Fig. 4 shows a version of the RKP temporal script graph for this scenario, with all NP tokens replaced by icons for their PDSs. Ten of its nodes are shown with their temporal ordering, marked by the edges and additionally with encircled numbers. Alternative PDSs are marked with their absolute frequencies. As the subject is always left out in the example data, we assume an implicit protagonist in all cases. The figure demonstrates that we can distinguish the participants, even though the event alignment has errors.

6 Conclusion

We have presented a system that identifies script participants from unlabeled data by grouping equivalent noun phrases together. Our system combines semantic similarity and global structural information about event alignments in an ILP. We have shown that the system outperforms baselines that are restricted to each of these information sources alone; that is, both structural and similarity information are essential.

We believe that we can improve our system in a number of ways, e.g. by training a better parser or switching to a more sophisticated semantic similarity measure. One particularly interesting direction for future work is exploiting participant information to improve the alignments; this would allow us to merge the "put food in microwave" nodes in the graph of Fig. 4, which look identical once noun phrases have been abstracted into participants. We could achieve this by jointly modeling the event alignment problem and the participant identification problem in the same ILP.

While our approach to learning participants is unsupervised once some parameters have been optimized on a small amount of labeled data, we can only obtain a large-scale knowledge base of scripts if we can collect large amounts of scenario descriptions. Thus the next step must demonstrate that this can be done, without requiring the manual selection of scenarios to ask people about. A promising approach is collecting data through online games; this has been shown to be successful in other domains (e.g. by von Ahn and Dabbish (2008)), and we are optimistic that we can apply this here as well.

Acknowledgments

We're indebted to Ines Rehbein who carryied out the parser experiments. We thank the anonymous reviewers and particularly Nate Chambers for their

[2]We omit some PDSs in the presentation for lack of space.

helpful comments. – This work was funded by the Cluster of Excellence "Multimodal Computing and Interaction" in the German Excellence Initiative, and the SALSA project of the German Research Foundation DFG.

References

Ernst Althaus, Nikiforos Karamanis, and Alexander Koller. 2004. Computing locally coherent discourses. In *Proc. of ACL-04*.

Amit Bagga and Breck Baldwin. 1998. Algorithms for scoring coreference chains. In *Proc. of LREC-98*.

Collin F. Baker, Charles J. Fillmore, and John B. Lowe. 1998. The berkeley framenet project. In *Proc. of COLING-98*.

Avron Barr and Edward Feigenbaum. 1981. *The Handbook of Artificial Intelligence, Volume 1*. William Kaufman Inc., Los Altos, CA.

Regina Barzilay and Mirella Lapata. 2006. Aggregation via set partitioning for natural language generation. In *Proc. of HLT-NAACL 2006*.

Jonathan Berant, Ido Dagan, and Jacob Goldberger. 2010. Global learning of focused entailment graphs. In *Proc. of ACL-10*.

Michel Berkelaar, Kjell Eikland, and Peter Notebaert. 2004. lp_solve, a Mixed Integer Linear Programming (MILP) solver Version 5.0. Website.

Jie Cai and Michael Strube. 2010. Evaluation metrics for end-to-end coreference resolution systems. In *Proc. of SIGDIAL 2010*.

Nathanael Chambers and Dan Jurafsky. 2008. Unsupervised learning of narrative event chains. In *Proc. of ACL-08: HLT*.

Nathanael Chambers and Dan Jurafsky. 2009. Unsupervised learning of narrative schemas and their participants. In *Proc. of ACL-IJCNLP 2009*.

Richard Edward Cullingford. 1977. *Script application: computer understanding of newspaper stories*. Ph.D. thesis, Yale University, New Haven, CT, USA.

Deborah A. Dahl, Madeleine Bates, Michael Brown, William Fisher, Kate Hunicke-Smith, David Pallett, Christine Pao, Alexander Rudnicky, and Elizabeth Shriberg. 1994. Expanding the scope of the ATIS task: the ATIS-3 corpus. In *Proceedings of the HLT-94*, HLT '94.

Pascal Denis and Jason Baldridge. 2007. Joint determination of anaphoricity and coreference resolution using integer programming. In *Proc. of HLT-NAACL 2007*.

Richard Durbin, Sean Eddy, Anders Krogh, and Graeme Mitchison. 1998. *Biological Sequence Analysis*. Cambridge University Press.

Christiane Fellbaum. 1998. *WordNet: An Electronical Lexical Database*. The MIT Press, Cambridge, MA.

Jenny Rose Finkel and Christopher D. Manning. 2008. Enforcing transitivity in coreference resolution. In *Proc. of ACL-08: HLT*.

W. N. Francis and H. Kucera, 1979. *Manual of Information to Accompany a Standard Corpus of Present-Day Edited American English, for use with Digital Computers*. Department of Linguistic, Brown University.

William A. Gale, Kenneth W. Church, and David Yarowsky. 1992. One sense per discourse. In *Proceedings of the workshop on Speech and Natural Language*.

Dan Klein and Christopher D. Manning. 2003. Accurate unlexicalized parsing. In *Proc. of ACL-03*.

Dekang Lin. 1998. An information-theoretic definition of similarity. In *Proc. of ICML-98*.

Inderjeet Mani, Marc Verhagen, Ben Wellner, Chong Min Lee, and James Pustejovsky. 2006. Machine learning of temporal relations. In *Proc. of COLING/ACL-2006*.

Mitchell P. Marcus, Mary Ann Marcinkiewicz, and Beatrice Santorini. 1993. Building a large annotated corpus of english: the penn treebank. *Comput. Linguist.*, 19.

Erik T. Mueller. 2004. Understanding script-based stories using commonsense reasoning. *Cognitive Systems Research*.

James Pustejovsky, Marc Verhagen, Roser Sauri, Jessica Littman, Robert Gaizauskas, Graham Katz, Inderjeet Mani, Robert Knippen, and Andrea Setzer. 2006. TimeBank 1.2. Linguistic Data Consortium.

Lisa F. Rau, Paul S. Jacobs, and Uri Zernik. 1989. Information extraction and text summarization using linguistic knowledge acquisition. *Information Processing and Management*.

Michaela Regneri, Alexander Koller, and Manfred Pinkal. 2010. Learning script knowledge with web experiments. In *Proc. of ACL-10*.

Roger C. Schank and Robert P. Abelson. 1977. *Scripts, Plans, Goals and Understanding*. Lawrence Erlbaum, Hillsdale, NJ.

Reid Swanson and Andrew S. Gordon. 2008. Say anything: A massively collaborative open domain story writing companion. In *Proc. of ICIDS 2008*.

Luis von Ahn and Laura Dabbish. 2008. Designing games with a purpose. *Commun. ACM*, 51(8).

Laurence Wolsey. 1998. *Integer programming*. Wiley-Interscience.

Towards Minimal Recursion Semantics over Bulgarian Dependency Parsing

Kiril Simov
LMD, IICT-BAS
kivs@bultreebank.org

Petya Osenova
LMD, IICT-BAS
petya@bultreebank.org

Abstract

The paper discusses the transferring rules of the output from a dependency parser for Bulgarian into RMRS analyses. This task is required by the machine translation compatibility between Bulgarian and English resources. Since the Bulgarian HPSG grammar is still being developed, a repairing mechanism has been envisaged by parsing the Bulgarian data with the Malt Dependency Parser, and then retrieving RMRS analyses by exploring the linguistic knowledge within BulTreeBank-DP.

1 Introduction

Recently a number of machine translation efforts have focused on grammatical formalisms in performing source language analysis, transfer rule application and target language generation. It is worth mentioning several works, such as (Bond, 2005) exploiting DELPH-IN infrastructure for developing of HPSG grammars, (Riezler and Maxwell III, 2006) using LFG grammar, (Oepen et al, 2007) working on a hybrid architecture consisting of an LFG grammar, an HPSG grammar, partial parsing, and (Bojar and Hajic, 2008) using the Functional Generative Description framework to language analysis on analytical and tectogrammatical level. All the approaches rely on the advances in the development of deep grammar natural language parsing. The approaches share similar architecture and techniques to overcome the drawbacks of the deep processing in comparison to statistical shallow methods.

Within the above mentioned context, we are constructing a Bulgarian-to-English translation system, based on HPSG. The transfer rules are implemented on the level of MRS (Minimal Recursion Semantic) structures (Copestake et al, 2005). The HPSG deep grammar for Bulgarian still has a limited coverage. Thus, for many input sentences it will fail to produce MRS analyses. In such cases, we rely on a dependency parser (Malt parser trained on the BulTreeBank data) to produce a dependency parse for the sentence. Then, we construct an RMRS (Robust Minimal Recursion Semantic) analysis over the dependency parse. Thus our input processing architecture consists of two grammars – HPSG grammar which produces MRS structures, and Dependency grammar which produces RMRS structures. The resulting semantic analysis is the input for the transfer module of the machine translation system. The paper focuses on the dependency tagset and the rules for the construction of RMRS analyses over the dependency parses. It is structured as follows: First, the context of our work is presented. Then our dependency tagset is discussed. In the following section the HPSG-based Bulgarian grammar BURGER is briefly outlined. Finally, the basic rules for the construction of the RMRS analyses from dependency parses are described.

2 Background

Our approach is inspired by the work on MRS and RMRS (see (Copestake, 2003; 2007)) and the previous work on transfer of dependency analyses into RMRS structures described in (Spreyer and Frank, 2005) and (Jakob et al, 2010).

MRS is introduced as an underspecified semantic formalism (Copestake et al, 2005). It is used to support semantic analyses in HPSG English grammar – ERG (Copestake and Flickinger, 2000), but also in other grammar formalisms like LFG. The main idea is the formalism to rule out spurious analyses resulting from the representation of logical operators and the scope of quantifiers. Here we will present only basic definitions from (Copestake et al, 2005). For more details the cited publication should be consulted. An MRS structure is a tuple <*GT*, *R*, *C*>, where *GT* is the top handle, R is a bag of EPs (elementary predicates) and *C* is a bag of handle constraints, such that there is no handle *h* that outscopes *GT*. Each elementary predication contains exactly four components: (1) a handle which is the label of the EP; (2) a relation; (3) a list of zero or more ordinary variable arguments of the relation; and (4) a list of zero or more handles corresponding to scopal arguments of the relation (i.e., holes). Here is an example of an MRS structure for the sentence "*Every dog chases some white cat.*"

<h0, {h1: every(x,h2,h3), h2: dog(x), h4: chase(x, y), h5: some(y,h6,h7), h6: white(y), h6: cat(y)}, {}>

The top handle is *h0*. The two quantifiers are represented as relations *every(x, y, z)* and *some(x, y, z)* where *x* is the bound variable, *y* and *z* are handles determining the restriction and the body of the quantifier. The conjunction of two or more relations is represented by sharing the same handle (*h6* above). The outscope relation is defined as a transitive closure of the immediate outscope relation between two elementary predications – EP immediately outscopes EP' iff one of the scopal arguments of EP is the label of EP'. In this example the set of handle constraints is empty, which means that the representation is underspecified with respect to the scope of both quantifiers. Here we finish with the brief introduction of the MRS formalism. The rest of the definitions will be introduced when necessary in the text.

RMRS is introduced as a modification of MRS which to capture the semantics resulting from the shallow analysis. Here the following assumptions are taken into account – the shallow processor does not have access to a lexicon. Thus it does not have access to arity of the relations in EPs. Therefore, the representation has to be underspecified with respect to the number of arguments of the relations. Additionally, the forming of the relation names follows such conventions that provide possibilities to construct a correct semantic representation only on the base of information provided by a POS tagger, for example. The arguments are introduced separately by argument relations between the label of a relation and the argument. The names of the argument relations follow some standardized convention like RSTR, BODY, ARG1, ARG2, etc. These argument relations are grouped in a separate set in a given RMRS structure. Both representations MRS and RMRS could be transferred to each other under certain conditions. In the paper we follow the representation of RMRS used in (Jakob et al, 2010), which defines an RMRS structure as a quadruple < *hook*, *EP-bag*, *argument set*, *handle constraints* >, where a hook consists of three elements *l:a:i*, *l* is a label, *a* is an anchor and *i* is an index. Each elementary predication is additionally marked with an anchor – *l:a:r(i)*, where *l* is a label, *a* is an anchor and *r(i)* is a relation with one argument of appropriate kind – referential index or event index. The argument set contains argument statements of the following kind *a:ARG(x)*, where *a* is anchor which determines for which relation the argument is defined, *ARG* is the name of the argument, and *x* is an index or a hole variable or handle (*h*) for scopal predicates. The handle constraints are of the form *h =q l*, where h is a handle, l is a label and *=q* is the relation expressing the constraint similarly to MRS. *=q* sometimes is written as *qeq*.

RMRS was used in analyses of two dependency treebanks – TIGER treebank of German and Prague Dependency Treebank of Czech. The work on Prague Dependency Treebank presented in (Jakob et al, 2010) first assigns elementary predications to each node in the tectogrammatical tree. Then the elementary predications for the nodes are combined on the basis of the dependency annotation in the trees. Similar approach is taken by us, except that the analyses from which we start are not trees on tectogrammatical level. Thus, our trees contain nodes for each token in the sentences.

3 Bulgarian Dependency Parsing

Many parsers have been trained on data from BulTreeBank. Especially successful was the MaltParser of Joakim Nivre (Nivre et al., 2006). It works with 87.6 % accuracy. The following text describes the dependency relations produced by the parser.

Here is a table with the dependency tagset related to the Dependency part of the BulTreeBank. This part has been used for training of the dependency parser:

adjunct 12009	Adjunct (optional verbal argument)
clitic 2263	Short forms of the possessive pronouns
comp	Complement (arguments of non-verbal

18043	heads, non-finite verbal heads, copula, auxiliaries)
conj 6342	Conjunction in coordination
conjarg 7005	Argument (second, third, ...) of coordination
indobj 4232	Indirect Object (indirect argument of a non-auxiliary verbal head)
marked 2650	Marked (clauses, introduced by a subordinator)
mod 42706	Modifier (dependants which modify nouns, adjectives, adverbs; also the negative and interrogative particles)
obj 7248	Object (direct argument of a non-auxiliary verbal head)
subj 14064	Subject
pragadjunct 1612	Pragmatic adjunct
punct 28134	Punctuation
xadjunct 1826	Clausal adjunct
xcomp 4651	Clausal complement
xmod 2219	Clausal modifier
xprepcomp 168	Clausal complement of preposition
xsubj 504	Clausal subject

In addition to the dependency tags we have also morphosyntactic tags attached to each word (Simov et. al, 2004). For each lexical node the lemma is assigned. The number under the name of each relation indicates how many times the relation appears in the dependency version of BulTreeBank. We have also statistics for the triples <DependentWordForm, Relation, HeadWordForm>. It is used for defining the rules for constructing RMRS structures over the dependency parses produced by the Malt parser.

The dependency relations here reflect the original HPSG analyses in BulTreeBank and are conformant to the dependency relations schema of the CoNLL shared task (2006). Thus, some of them are more specific (such as, *obj*, *indobj*, *clitic*, *subj*, etc.), while others are more general (such as, *comp* and *mod*). Since the reflexive accusative and dative clitics are always marked as *comp*, a dictionary check is needed to determine whether these clitics are part of the lexeme, or they mark a voice alternation. Also, when there is an auxiliary verb, it becomes the root of the sentence, and since the main verb as well as the personal clitic are both marked with the same relation (comp), a check with the morphosyntactic information is needed. Here is an example for the sentence 'The peoples afterwards have revenged them mercilessly':

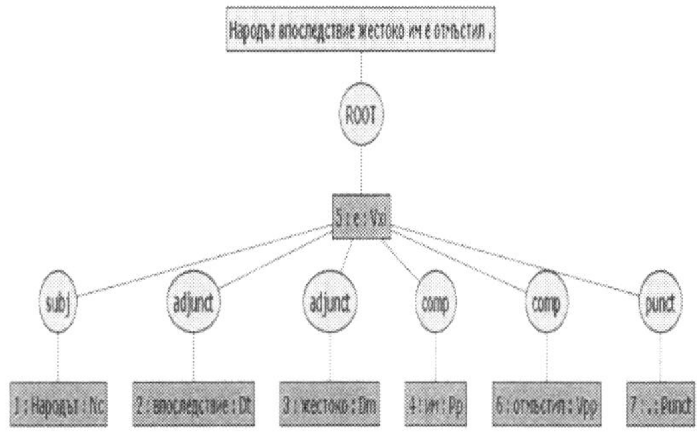

The missing information in comparison with the HPSG-based version is the constituent structure, the coreferential relations and ellipses. As it can be seen from the above description, some of the relations in the dependency tagset are very general (the *comp* relation, for example). More specific information could be inferred on the basis of the morphosyntactic information of the two lexical nodes and the dependency relation between them. This allows us to write rules for constructing RMRS for different configurations in the dependency trees (see section 5). In the above example, the participle (node 6) determines the relation of the main verb and the dative clitic (node 4) determines the plurality and the third person of the indirect object. More on the specificities of this schema in comparison with another dependency schema for Bulgarian is discussed in (Kancheva 2010).

4 The BURGER Grammar and the MRS Analysis

BURGER is the realization of the Matrix Grammar (Bender et. al 2002) to Bulgarian language. It is implemented in LKB - Linguistic Knowledge Builder (Bender et. al 2010). Its first version is made available at the DELPH-IN Consortium site, and it is described in (Osenova 2010).

The work on the grammar included several tasks: a lexicon building for Bulgarian within the required format; adapting of the type hierarchy to the Bulgarian grammar model; addition of language specific principles for Bulgarian; preparing of a test-suite with sentences, which to illustrate the main linguistic phenomena in Bulgarian and to demonstrate the capacity of the grammar (including also negative examples on the basis of the Bulgarian BulTreeBank Corpus).

Here is an example of the lexical entry for the verb *чета* 'read':

cheta := v_np_i1_le &
[**STEM** < "чета" >,
SYNSEM.LKEYS.KEYREL.PRED
"чета_v_rel"].

As it can be seen, the lexical entry uses the Latin transliteration of the Bulgarian word. The Cyrillic sequence is presented in the feature **STEM**. The mnemonic name **v_np_i_le** means that this word is a verb, which takes an NP as its complement, and it is in an imperfective aspect. The ending **le** has only technical functions.

In general, the Grammar Matrix provides a semantic approach to the description of a language. For example, the verbs, the adjectives, the adverbs and the prepositions are viewed as introducing events. Bulgarian, however, lacks a grammar, which describes all the phenomena at the semantic-syntactic interface. The existing research is mainly focused on the morphology and syntax only. Concerning Bulgarian, its rich morphology seems to conflict with the requirements behind the semantic approach. Thus, the adjectives, participles, numerals happen to have *morphologically* definite forms, while the definiteness marker is not a *semantic* property of these categories. For that reason, the most important thing in the grammar was to keep Syntactic and Semantic features separate. This distinction concerns, for example, definiteness and tense properties. All the parses are also augmented with the corresponding MRS.

BURGER covers all the syntactic phenomena, presented in the international testset of the Grammar Matrix plus the language specific features, such as clitics behavior, da-construction, prodropness, lexical aspect etc (193 sentences).

Here is an example of an MRS for the sentence *не лай* 'do not bark', where the negative particle *не* 'no' is treated as a verb:

```
[LTOP: h1
 INDEX: e2 [E.ASPECT: imperfective E.MOOD: imperative SF: comm]
 RELS:<
     [ "negation_rel"
         LBL: h1
         ARG0: e2
         ARG1: h3
     [ "лая_v_rel"
         LBL: h4
         ARG0: e2
         ARG1: x5 [x PNG.NUMBER singular PNG.PERSON 2nd SF comm]
 HCONS <h3 qeq h4>]
```

Here the main verb 'bark' is represented as an event (the value of ARG0), which takes an unexpressed subject (the value of ARG1) being of underspecified gender, singular, second person. The negative particle is encoded as a verb, which introduces a negation relation. In this relation, ARG0 structure-shares with the ARG0 of the event 'bark', and ARG1 is the scope over the event 'bark'.

5 RMRS for Bulgarian Dependency Parses

In this section we present a set of rules for transfer of dependency parses into RMRS presentations. The information input for the RMRS structures is based on the following linguistic annotation – the lemma (*Lemma*) for the given wordform; the morphosyntactic tag (*MSTag*) of the wordform, and the dependent relations in the dependency tree. In cases of quantifiers we have access to the lexicon used in BURGER. Here we present the rules for some of the most important combinations. The approach of (Jakob et al, 2010) is adopted. Also, we take into account the MRS structures produced by BURGER in order to be able to compare them to RMRS structures produced over the dependency trees. Thus, the algorithm for producing of RMRS from a dependency parse is implemented via two types of rules:

1. *<Lemma, MSTag> → EP-RMRS*

The rules of this type produce an RMRS including an elementary predicate.

2. *<DRMRS, Rel, HRMRS> → HRMRS'*

The rules of this type unite the RMRS constructed for a dependent node (*DRMRS*) into the current RMRS for a head node (*HRMRS*). The union (*HRMRS'*) is determined by the relation (*Rel*) between the two nodes. In the rest of the section we present examples of these rules.

First, we start with assigning EPs for each lemma in the dependency tree. These EPs are similar to node EPs of (Jakob et al, 2010). Each EP for a given lemma consists of a predicate generated on the basis of the lemma string. When the lemma is a quantifier and thus it is a part of the BURGER lexicon, we copy the related information about its relation and arguments – RESTRICTION (RSTR) and BODY. Additionally, the morphosyntactic features of the wordform are presented. On the basis of the part-of-speech tag the type of ARG0 is determined – referential index or event index. After this initial step the basic RMRS structure for each lemma in the sentence is compiled. Below we discuss the exploitation of the rest of the information in the dependency tree – the types of links to the other lemmas as well as the further contribution of the morphosyntactic features. Here is an example for the verb 'чета' (to read):

< l1:a1:e1,
{ l1:a1:чета_v_rel(e1) },
{ a1:ARG1(x1) },
{} >

In this example we also include information for the unexpressed subject (ARG1) which is always incorporated in the verb form. In case the subject is expressed, it will be connected to the same referential index. For some types of nodes the EP RMRS will include information only for arguments of the predicate of the head node.

The short forms of pronouns (clitics) do not introduce a semantic relation. The semantic relation is introduced only by their full counter-parts. It is rather straightforward transfer, since the short forms are annotated as clitics, while the full forms are assigned grammatical roles – object or indirect object. Thus, the full forms in verbal domain are automatically transferred as ARG2 and ARG3 of the corresponding verb. In this transfer we always connect the object to argument ARG2 slot and indirect object to ARG3 slot. For example, the sentence *чета му я* (Read-I him-dative her-accusative, 'I read it to him') will have the following representation:

< l1:a1:e1,
{ l1:a1:чета_v_rel(e1) },
{ a1:ARG1(x1), a1:ARG2(x2),
a1:ARG3(x3) },
{} >

The EP RMRS for the accusative clitic introduces only the information for ARG2 and appropriate grammatical features for the variable x2 (third person, singular, feminine). Similarly EP RMRS for the dative clitic provides ARG3 and its grammatical features (third person, singular, masculine). When this information is incorporated into the head RMRS, the anchors for the ARG2 and ARG3 are changed with respect to the anchor of the head.

The subject is mapped to ARG1. It is worth noting that the Subject argument is partially determined during the previous step in building EPs, because Bulgarian is a pro-drop language, and the main subject properties are considered part of the verb form. Here is an example for the sentence *момче му я чете* (Boy him-dative her-accusative read, 'A boy reads it to him):

< l2:a4:e1,
{ l1:a1:момче_n_rel(x1),
l2:a4:чета_v_rel(e1) },
{ a4:ARG1(x1), a4:ARG2(x2),
a4:ARG3(x3) },
{} >

Another example with an explicit direct object for the sentence *момче му чете книга* (Boy him-dative reads book, 'A boy reads a book to him'):

< l2:a3:e1,
{ l1:a1:момче_n_rel(x1),
l2:a3:чета_v_rel(e1),
l3:a4:книга_n_rel(x2) },
{ a3:ARG1(x1), a3:ARG2(x2),
a3:ARG3(x3) },
{} >

A problematic case is the passive construction in which the arguments are represented as alternating dependency relations. In this case the lemma is consulted for the semantic presentation, and the indirect object relation is assigned as a PP-relation, which introduces the Subject.

The modifying words (*mod*) – adjectives, adverbs or nouns introduce a modifier relation. When the modifier is definite, then the information is treated only on the syntactic level. Thus, the head is considered semantically definite, and the information is divided between the two levels of analysis.

The complements of the copula need the information from the morphosyntactic tag, since the adjective, adverb and PPs raise their INDEX to the semantically vacuous copula. In contrast to them, the nouns introduce a referential INDEX, which, however, is not raised to the copula.

When an auxiliary verb is recognized, which takes a participle as a complement, and then depending on the participle, the transfer is realized accordingly. For example, if the participle is aorist, then it is in active voice. If it is passive, then the semantics follows the strategy from above.

The transfer of the impersonal verbs into RMRS also relies on the morphosyntactic tags. They introduce a restriction on its subject to be pro-nominal, 3rd person, singular, neuter. The relation *xcomp* is transformed into a constraint, which ensures that the ARG1 of the modal qeqs the label of the verb in the da-construction (analytical substitute form for the Old Bulgarian infinitive).

Here is a simplified representation of the sentence *Трябва да му кажа.* (Must to him-dat tell-I, 'I have to tell him'):

```
< l1:a1:e1,
  { l1:a1:трябва_v_rel(e1),
    l2:a4:кажа_v_rel(e2) },
  { a1:ARG2(e2),
    a4:ARG1(x1),
    a4:ARG3(x2) },
  {} >
```

The *xmod* relation connects a clause to a nominal head. When the clause is introduced by a relative pronoun, its RMRS is incorporated in the RMRS of the head and the index introduced by the relative pronoun is made the same as the index of the head. In cases when the clause is not introduced by a relative clause the event index of the clause is nominalised and the new referencial index is made the same as the index of the head.

The *xsubj* relation is incorporated in the head RMRS depending on the kind of the dependent clause. If it is a relative clause then the index of the relative pronoun is made equal to the index introduced by the unexpressed subject of the head. In the other cases the event represented by the clause is nominalized and the new referential index is made equal to the index of the unexpressed subject of the head.

The *marked* relation is always connected to a subordinate conjunction. The subordinate conjunction introduces a two argument relation, where both arguments are events. In this case the RMRS of the dependent clause is added to the RMRS assigned to the conjunction. Additionally, the index of the second argument is made equal to the index of the dependent clause.

The *xprepcomp* relation is treated as an ordinary *prepcomp* relation, but the index of ARG1 is an event.

The canonical coordination is handled relatively straightforwardly. The *conj* label introduces a coordination relation, and *conjarg* is mapped to the right index R-INDEX. Then, the left index L-INDEX is taken by the above level, which contains the grammatical role of the whole coordination phrase.

The *pragadjunct* introduces different types of modifiers on pragmatic level like vocatives, parenthetical expressions, etc. For the moment, we incorporate the RMRS of the dependent element in the RMRS of the head without additional constraints, but these cases require more work in future.

The relation *punct* is ignored.

The incorporation of the dependent RMRS into the head RMRS is done recursively from the leaves of the tree up. After the construction of the RMRS of the tree root, we need to add the missing quantifiers for the unbound referential indexes. For each such index the algorithm determines the handle with a widest scope and uses it as a RSTR argument.

Here is a pseudo code of the main algorithm RMRS which selects the root of the input tree and calls the recursive function which calculates the RMRS for the sentence:

```
algorithm rmrs
  Input: DTree (dependency tree in CoNLL format)
    Output: < hook, EP-bag, argument set, handle
      constraints > (RSMS structure for the sentence)
  RootNode ← root(DTree)
  setEnumerators()
  RMRS ← nodeRMRS(DTree, RootNode)
  return addQuantifiers(RMRS)
end_algorithm
```

The function root(*DTree*) selects the root of the tree. The function nodeRMRS(*DTree*, *Node*) constructs recursively RMRS structure for the subtree starting at node *Node*. The subtree is part of the whole tree for the sentence – *DTree*. The function setEnumerators() sets the initial numbers for labels, referential and event variables. For anchors we use the token numbers that are already in the CoNLL format of the dependency tree. The function addQuantifiers(*RMRS*) introduces the missing quintifiers in the final RMRS. Here is the pseudo code for the function:

```
function nodeRMRS(DTree, CurrentNode)
  NodeEP ← nodeEP(DTree, CurrentNode)
  for DNode in depNodes(DTree, CurrentNode)
    DNodeRMRS ← nodeRMRS(DTree, DNode)
    DRel ← nodeRel(DTree, DNode)
    NodeEP ← union(NodeEP, DNodeRMRS, DRel)
  end_for
  return NodeEP
end_function
```

This function first calls the function for constructing RMRS for the elementary predication for the current node in the dependency tree – nodeEP(*DTree*, *CurrentNode*). This function implements the first kind of rules mentioned above. It has access to the lemma and the grammatical information for the current node. The predicate name is constructed on the basis of the lemma and the part of speech (for example, чета_v_rel), the argument type is determined on the basis the grammatical information – event or referential index. Additional information can be added for other arguments of the verbs as it was described above. In case of access to a lexicon, the function will be tuned to the information within the lexicon. This will be relevant for the case of the valency lexicon.

The function depNodes(*DTree*, *CurrentNode*) returns a set of nodes in the tree which are dependent of the current node. For each of them the function nodeRMRS(*DTree*, *Node*) is called. The result of this recursive call is incorporated within the current RMRS on the basis of the dependency relations. This is done by the function union(*NodeEP*, *DNodeRMRS*, *DRel*). This function is defined by the second kind of rules described above. Note that all the relevant information is available in the already constructed RMRS structures for the head node as well as the dependent nodes and the type of the relations.

The rules of the first kind are 118. They correspond to a reduced morphosyntactic tagset of (Simov et al. 2004). The rules of the second kind are 53. The construction of these rules follows the statistics, presented in section 3. We first implemented rules for most frequent combinations. As much as we can not be sure that the treebank contains examples of all possible combinations we implement 'catch all' which just construct the union of the sets within the two RMRSes.

6 Evaluation

We do not have a gold standard corpus of dependency trees with manually constructed RMRS. Thus, we cannot determine a real evaluation of the performance of the proposed algorithm. However, we have a dataset covered by BURGER grammar for which the correct analyses, including MRS, are selected. Therefore, we decided to evaluate the algorithm with respect to this dataset.

First, we annotated the sentences in the dataset as dependency trees. Then, we ran the parser over the sentences and manually corrected the result. Next, we applied the algorithm over the resulting trees and produced the RMRS for each dependency tree. In the same time, we transferred the MRS, constructed by BURGER into RMRS representations.

Comparing the two RMRS structures for the same sentence is done by comparing the information related to each index in the RMRS. Intuitively, the expectation was that the RMRS constructed on the base of the dependency analysis would contain less information than the one produced by BURGER. Intuitively, less information here means that the indexes participate in reduced number of relations; the relations have smaller number of arguments; and also smaller number of handle constraints. Needless to say, the relations, arguments and constraints have to be identical when present in both structures.

The actual comparison was performed by constructing of a mapping from indexes, labels, anchors and handles in one of the RMRS into the indexes, labels and handles in the other one. The mapping has to respect the type of the indexes.

Let RMRS-D be the structure produced from the dependency tree and let RMRS-B be the structure produced by BURGER. If there exists a mapping from RMRS-D into RMRS-B such that:

- for each index **i**, each anchor **a**, each label **l** and each relation **r** such that l:a:r(i) is in RMRS-D then for the corresponding label l', anchor a' and index i' it is true that l':a':r(i') is in RMRS-B;
- for each anchor **a**, each index **i** and argument **ARG** such that a:ARG(i) is in RMRS-D then for the corresponding anchor a' and index i' it is true that a':ARG(i') is in RMRS-B;
- for each handle **h** and each label **l** such that **h =q l** is in RMRS-D then for the corresponding handle h' and label l' it is true that h' =q l' is in RMRS-B; and
- if l':a':i' is the hook of RMRS-B and for at least one of its elements there is a mapping from a corresponding element in RMRS-D, then there are mappings for all elements and original triple l:a:i is the hook of RMRS-D.

then we say that RMRS-D is substructure of RMRS-B. The last condition is very strong and is subject to further refinement. But in our work with this example dataset it has not caused any troubles. In all other cases we say that both structures are incompatible.

On the basis of the dataset covered by BURGER (193 sentences) we achieved 77% of compatibility of RMRSes.

The main sources of incompatibility are: relation names and principles of BURGER. In the case of the relation names, it could happen that in BURGER there are more relation names that share a lemma string. For example, трябва_v_1_rel and трябва_v_2_rel is represented in dependency RMRS as трябва_v_rel. In BURGER there are some cases when the subordinate conjunction is incorporated in the clause RMRS, but in the dependency we do not have such a rule. In the first case the wrong match is acceptable in our opinion as much as we do not have access to a lexicon for most of the lemmas in the sentences. For the second case we have to modify the rules in the algorithm.

7 Conclusion

In this paper we presented an algorithm for transferring of information from dependency parses into RMRS. This information will be used in a Bulgarian-English machine translation system when the HPSG grammar fails to produce an analysis. We hope that the algorithm will produce the right number and types of indexes with appropriate relations between them which to allow the addition of missing information on the basis of statistics over a parallel treebank.

The algorithm needs augmentation with a rich lexicon and a more elaborate treatment of some constructions for the production of appropriate RMRS. These resources are under development.

We have to say that an evaluation with more examples is necessary, because the 193 do not demonstrate all the dependency relations in the dependency tagsets. Another task which is under development is the creation of a gold corpus of manually annotated RMRS structures.

8 Acknowledgments

This work has been supported by the European project EuroMatrixPlus (IST-231720).

References

Bender, Flickinger and Oepen. 2002: E. Bender, D. Flickinger and S. Oepen. *The Grammar Matrix: An Open-Source Starter-Kit for the Rapid Development of Cross-Linguistically Consistent Broad-Coverage Precision Grammars.* Carroll, John, Nelleke Oostdijk, and Richard Sutcliffe, eds. Proced-ings of the Workshop on Grammar Engineering and Evaluation at the 19th International Confer-ence on Computational Linguistics. Taipei, Taiwan. pp. 8-14.

E. Bender, Scott Drellishak, Antske Fokkens, Laurie Poulson and Safiyyah Saleem. 2010. *Grammar Customization.* In Research on Language and Computation, volume 8, issue 1. Springer.

Francis Bond, Stephan Oepen, Melanie Siegel, Ann Copestake and Dan Flickinger. 2005. *Open Source Machine Translation with DELPH-IN.* In: Proceedings of the Open-Source Machine Translation Workshop at the 10th Machine Translation Summit. pp 15-22.

Bojar, Ondrej and Hajic, Jan. 2008. Phrase-based and deep syntactic English-to-Czech statistical machine translation. In: StatMT '08: Proceedings of the Third Workshop on Statistical Machine Translation. pp. 143--146.

Ann Copestake, Dan Flickinger, Carl Pollard, and Ivan A. Sag. 2005. Minimal Recursion Semantics: An Introduction. Research on Language and Computation, 3(4). pp 281–332.

Ann Copestake and Dan Flickinger. 2000. Open source grammar development environment and broad-coverage English grammar using HPSG. In Proceedings of the 2nd International Conference on Language Resources and Evaluation. pp 591–598.

Ann Copestake. 2003. Robust Minimal Recursion Semantics (working paper). http://www.cl.cam.ac.uk/~aac10/papers

Ann Copestake. 2007. *Applying Robust Semantics.* In Proceedings of the 10th Conference of the Pacific Assocation for Computational Linguistics (PACLING), pages 1–12, Melbourne, Australia.

Max Jakob, Lopatková, M., Kordoni, V. 2010. *Mapping between Dependency Structures and Compositional Semantic Representations.* In: Proceedings of the Seventh conference on International Language Resources and Evaluation (LREC'10), ELRA.

Stanislava Kancheva. 2010. *Representation of the Grammatical Roles for Bulgarian in the Dependency Grammar.* (unpublished Master Thesis). In Bulgarian.

Joakim Nivre, Johan Hall, Jens Nilsson. 2006. *MaltParser: A data-driven parser-generator for dependency parsing.* In Proc. of LREC-2006. pp 2216-2219.

Stephan Oepen, Erik Velldal, Jan Tore Loenning, Paul Meurer, Victoria Ros'en and Dan Flickinger. 2007. *Towards Hybrid Quality-Oriented Machine Translation - On Linguistics and Probabilities in MT.* In: Proc. of the 11th Conference on Theoretical and Methodological Issues in MT.

Petya Osenova. 2010: *The Bulgarian Resource Grammar.* VDM.

Riezler, Stefan and Maxwell III, John T. 2006. *Grammatical machine translation.* In: HLT-NAACL. pp 248-255.

Kiril Simov, Petya Osenova and Milena Slavcheva. 2004. *BTB-TR03: BulTreeBank Morphosyntactic Tagset.* BulTreeBank Technical Report № 03.

Kathrin Spreyer and Anette Frank. 2005. *Projecting RMRS from TIGER Dependencies.* In Stefan Müller, editor, Proceedings of the 12th HPSG Conference, pages 354–363, Lisbon, Portugal.

Discourse Structures to Reduce Discourse Incoherence in Blog Summarization

Shamima Mithun
Concordia University
Computer Science & Software Eng.
Montreal, Canada
s_mithun@encs.concordia.ca

Leila Kosseim
Concordia University
Computer Science & Software Eng.
Montreal, Canada
kosseim@cse.concordia.ca

Abstract

Discourse incoherence is an important and typical problem with multi-document extractive summaries. To address this issue, we have developed a schema-based summarization approach for query-based blog summaries that utilizes discourse structures. In our schema design, we tried to model discourse structures which are typically used by humans in their summary writing in response to a particular question type. In our approach, a sentence instantiates a specific slot of the schema based on its discourse structures. To validate our approach, we have built a system named BlogSum and have evaluated its performance through 4 human participants using a likert scale of 1 to 5. The evaluation results show that our approach has significantly improved summary coherence compared to the summaries with no discourse structuring without compromising on content evaluation.

1 Introduction

Research on text summarization dates back since the 1950s and with the growth of the Internet it has become a popular research topic in last decade. Text summarization reduces text search time by providing the most relevant information from the documents which enables users to comprehend more quickly the main ideas of a set of documents. Over time, different summarization techniques have been developed and evaluated. Although significant improvement continues to be made, the summaries generated automatically are by no means of the same quality as their human created counter parts. The area in which automatic summaries differ most from human generated summaries is text coherence (Otterbacher et al., 2002; Conroy and Dang, 2008; Genest et al., 2009).

Coherence problems can be the result of different phenomena: discourse incoherence, redundancy, temporal incoherence, grammatical mistakes or many other linguistic problems. In a manual analysis of 15 summaries, (Otterbacher et al., 2002) showed that coherence problems are caused mostly by discourse incoherence (34%) where the main concern is the lack of relations between sentences as well as in the overall summary.

Recently, (Genest et al., 2009) demonstrated that the performance of automatic summarizers in term of linguistic quality is significantly weaker compared to that of a baseline consisting of sentences extracted from the source documents by 5 human extractors and added to the summary without any modification. This result indicates that there is still much space to improve coherence of summaries even for pure extractive summaries.

1.1 Discourse Incoherence

Computational theories on discourse coherence were introduced by (Hobbs, 1985; Mann, 1988). According to (Mann, 1988), a discourse is coherent if the hearer knows the communicative role of each of its portion; that is, if the hearer knows how the speaker intends each clause to relate to each other. As a result, a summary will exhibit discourse incoherence if the reader cannot identify the communicative intentions of the writer from the clauses or if the clauses do not seem to be interrelated.

Consider the following summary (ID:T1001.8[1]) which contains discourse incoherence problems (shown in Figure 1). The summary for the question is incoherent. Even though all the sentences are relevant to the query, improper sentence ordering degrades the coherence of this summary. In ad-

[1]The summary is taken from the TAC 2008 opinion summarization track.

dition, sentence 3 contains a pronoun *(it)* without having an antecedent. One possible better ordering for this summary would be 4-3-1-2 or 4-3-2-1.

Figure 1: A Sample Summary

Topic: *Carmax*
Question: *What motivated positive opinions of Carmax from car buyers?*
Summary:
(1) It's like going to disney world for car buyers.
(2) have to say that Carmax rocks.
(3) We bought it at Carmax, and I continue to have nothing bad to say about that company.
(4) After our last big car milestone, we've had an odyssey with cars.

A summary with poor coherence confuses the readers and degrades the quality and readability of the summary. The proper sentence order significantly improves the readability of summaries. (Lapata, 2003) experimentally showed that the time to read a summary strongly correlates with the arrangement of sentences.

1.2 State of the Art

Currently, most of the automatic summarization systems for news articles use an extractive approach. In general, this approach works in two steps: in the first step, the most salient sentences are extracted from the source documents and in the second step, these sentences are ordered to create a summary. Since in the first step, sentences may be selected from multiple documents or without consideration to their interdependency with other sentences this may cause text incoherence. Moreover, in multi-document summarization, documents may be written by different writers who have different perspectives and writing styles thus exasperating coherence problems. To improve coherence, the second step tries to reorder the selected sentences appropriately.

As part of the sentence ordering, two major types of approaches are used to address coherence: making use of chronological information (McKeown et al., 2002), and learning the natural order of sentences from large corpora (Barzilay and Lee, 2004; Lapata, 2003). However, in the first case, if the source documents are not event-based, the quality of the summaries will be degraded because temporal cues are missing. In the later case, probabilistic models of text structures are trained on a large corpus. If the genre of the corpus and the source documents mismatch then they will perform poorly.

Summarization for opinionated text is a recent endeavor. Query-based blog summarization approaches have been first developed in the TAC 2008 opinion summarization track. Most of these summarization approaches (e.g. (Murray et al., 2008)) use sentence scores for summary generation. Some of these approaches (e.g. (Kumar and Chatterjee, 2008)) use the sentence order of the original documents to specify the sentence order of the summary. Recent work (e.g. (Paul et al., 2010)) on blog summarization also mostly use sentence scores for summary generation. However, these approaches hardly can be effective in coherence improvement. To the best of our knowledge, text schemata and discourse relations, found effective in news summarization and question answering (Blair-Goldensohn and McKeown, 2006; Sauper and Barzilay, 2009), were never used in blog summarization.

In our research, we try to reduce discourse incoherence of extractive summaries; and in particular in query-based blog summaries. In this work, we propose a domain independent query-based blog summarization approach to address discourse incoherence using discourse structures in the framework of schemata. To verify our approach we have developed a system called BlogSum and evaluated its performance using the Text Analysis Conference (TAC 2008) opinion summarization track data[2].

2 Discourse Structures to Reduce Discourse Incoherence

In our research, we are interested in query-based blog summarization. Nowadays, because of the rapid growth of the Social Web, a large amount of informal opinionated texts are available on any topic. Query-based opinion summarizers present what people think or feel on a given topic in a condensed manner to analyze others' opinions regarding a specific question (e.g. *Why do people like Starbucks better than Dunkin Donuts?*). This research interest motivated us to develop an effective query-based multi-document opinion summarization approach for blogs and we utilize discourse structures in the framework of schema to improve discourse coherence.

[2]http://www.nist.gov/tac/

2.1 Previous Work on Schemas

(McKeown, 1985) introduced a schema-based approach for text planning based on the observation that certain standard patterns of discourse organization (schema) are more effective to achieve a particular discourse goal. (McKeown, 1985) demonstrated the usability of this schema-based approach for a domain-dependent question answering application. In this application, she designed various schemata that incorporate discourse structures which are typically used in human writing for a specific question type (e.g. *identification*). In most recent summarization work, (Sauper and Barzilay, 2009) also tried to utilize discourse structures learned from domain relevant articles to design schemata (or templates) for structured domains (e.g. Wikipedia pages).

We also believe that for any domain, for a particular type of query, certain types of sentences if organized in a certain order can meet the communicative goal more effectively and create a more coherent text. For example, to take (McKeown, 1985)'s example, to define an entity or event (e.g. *what is a ship?*) it is natural to first include the identification of the item as a member of a generic class, then to describe the object's constituency or attributes followed by a specific example and so on. On the other hand, a comparison of two objects should use another combination to be effective and coherent.

2.2 Our Schema-based Approach

In our schema-based approach, the basic units of a schema are *rhetorical predicates* which characterize the structural purposes of a text and delineate the discourse relations between propositions.

2.2.1 Our Set of Rhetorical Predicates

Six main types of rhetorical predicates which have been found most useful for our blog summarization application were considered:

1. Attributive: Provides details about an entity or event. It can be used to illustrate a particular feature about a concept - e.g. *Mary has a pink coat.*
2. Comparison: Gives a comparison and contrast among different situations - e.g. *Perhaps that's why for my European taste Starbucks makes great espresso while Dunkin's stinks.*
3. Contingency: Provides cause, condition, reason, evidence for a situation, result or claim - e.g. *The meat is good because they slice it right in front of you.*
4. Illustration: Is used to provide additional information or detail about a situation - e.g. *Allied Capital is a closed-end management investment company that will operate as a business development concern.*
5. Attribution: Provides instances of reported speech both direct and indirect which may express feelings, thoughts, or hopes - e.g. *I said actually I think Zillow is great.*
6. Topic-opinion: Can be used to express an opinion; an agent can express internal feeling or belief towards an object or an event - e.g. *The thing that I love about their sandwiches is the bread.*

Rhetorical relations characterized by *comparison*, *illustration*, and *contingency* predicates are also considered by other research groups (e.g. (Carlson, 2001)). We consider three additional classes of predicates *attributive*, *attribution*, and *topic-opinion*. The *attributive* predicate and the *attribution* predicate are also listed in Grimes' predicates (McKeown, 1985) and (Carlson, 2001)'s relations list, respectively. We introduced *Topic-opinion* predicates to represent opinions which are not expressed by reported speech.

2.2.2 Schemata Design

In our schema-based approach, sentences need to be classified and organized based on what rhetorical predicates they contain. We designed and associated appropriate schemata (e.g. *compare and contrast*) to generate a summary that answers specific types of questions (e.g. *comparison, suggestion*) by defining constraints on the types of predicates (e.g. *comparison, attribution*) and the order in which they should appear in the output summary for a particular question type. In our approach, schemata help to ensure the global coherence of the summary.

Figure 2 shows a sample schema that can be used to answer a *comparison* question. According to this schema, a sentence to be included in the beginning of the summary needs to be classified as either a *Comparison* predicate or a *Contingency* predicate followed by *Topic-opinion* or *Attribution* predicates then by *Illustration* predicates. More formally, one or more *Comparison* or *Contingency* predicates followed by zero or many

Topic-opinion or *Attribution* predicates followed by zero or many *Illustration* predicates can be used[3].

Figure 2: A Sample Schema

Predicates & Constraints
Predicate: {*Comparison/Contingency*} +
Constraint: Compared objects, Sentence focus
Predicate: {*Topic-opinion/Attribution*} *
Constraint: Sentence polarity
Predicate: *Illustration**

From Figure 2, we can see that constraints are also defined on predicates based on their semantic content. In the example, the *Comparison* and *Contingency* predicates must contain all objects or events which are being compared and the topic[4] of the sentence needs to be the focus of the sentence; and *Topic-opinion* and *Attribution* predicates must have the same polarity as the question. In order to answer a different type of questions, a different schema would be more appropriate. In this approach, schemata will help to improve coherence by specifying a higher level text organization by constraining the order of the predicates.

3 BlogSum

In order to test our approach, we have built a system called BlogSum. Given an initial question on a particular topic and a set of related blogs, BlogSum performs sentence selection then content organization.

3.1 Content Organization

The content organization requires as input a ranked list of sentences from the document set. In our test, we have developed our own sentence extractor based on question similarity, topic similarity, and subjectivity scores. However, any other sentence ranker could have been used. The role of content organization is to select a few sentences from the candidate sentences and order them so as to produce a coherent and query relevant summary. For content organization, BlogSum performs the following tasks: A) Question Categorization, B) Schema Selection, C) Predicate Identification, and D) Sentence Selection and Ordering.

[3]Following (McKeown, 1985)'s notations, the symbol / indicates an alternative, * indicates that the item may appear 0 to n times, + indicates that the item may appear 1 to n times.

[4]Text specified in the Target in the TAC 2008 task data.

3.1.1 Question Categorization

Our content organization approach first categorizes questions to determine which schema will better convey the expected communicative goal of the answer for a particular question type and should be used for text planning.

By analyzing the TAC 2008 opinion summarization track questions manually, we have identified 3 categories of questions based on their communicative goals, namely: *comparison*, *suggestion*, and *reason*.

1. *Comparison* questions ask about the differences between objects - e.g. *Why do people like Starbucks better than Dunkin Donuts?*
2. *Suggestion* questions ask for suggestions to solve some problems - e.g. *What do Canadian political parties want to happen regarding NAFTA?*
3. *Reason* questions ask for reasons for some claim - e.g. *Why do people like Mythbusters?*

To automatically identify a unseen question into one of these 3 categories, we have designed lexical patterns by analyzing the same set of questions which we used to identify question categories.

3.1.2 Schema Selection

Based on the observation that for a particular question type, sentences need to be organized in a specific order to be coherent, we have designed three schemata, one for each question type, 1) *comparison*, 2) *suggestion*, and 3) *reason*. To design these schemata, we have analyzed 50 summaries generated by participating systems at the TAC 2008 opinion summarization track. From our analysis, we have derived which question types should contain which type of predicates. Each schema is designed based on giving priority to its associated question type and subjective sentences as we are generating summaries for opinionated texts. For each type of schema, we have also defined constraints on the predicates based on their semantic content to improve the question relevance. As part of the schema selection, BlogSum selects the associated schema for a specific question category to select and order sentences for the final summary.

It must be noted that schemata can be designed in different ways. However, our current content organization approach allows the generation of different summaries for particular question types by providing flexible sentence selection and reordering strategies.

3.1.3 Predicate Identification

In our approach, candidate sentences need to be classified into a predefined set of rhetorical predicates to fill the various slots of the matched schema - we called this process predicate identification.

In (Mithun and Kosseim, 2011), we have introduced a domain independent approach to identify which rhetorical predicates are conveyed by a sentence. As specified in (Mithun and Kosseim, 2011), predicates can describe a single proposition or the relation between propositions. To identify the predicates between propositions - e.g. *evidence*, we have used the SPADE discourse parser (Soricut and Marcu, 2003). On the other hand, in order to identify predicates within a single proposition - e.g. *attributive*, we have used three other taggers: comparison (Jindal and Liu, 2006), topic-opinion (Fei et al., 2008), and our attributive tagger (Mithun and Kosseim, 2011). By combining these approaches, a sentence is tagged with all possible predicates that it may contain and ready to be used in a schema.

3.1.4 Sentence Selection and Ordering

In BlogSum, sentence selection and ordering is accomplished in the following manner:

First, candidate sentences fill particular slots in the selected schema based on which rhetorical predicate they convey and whether they fulfil the semantic constraints. This process is performed for each candidate sentence based on their extraction score until the maximum summary length is reached. Since the use of schemata alone is not sufficient to achieve a total order; for example there may be several sentences that can fill a particular slot of a selected schema, we have used post-schemata heuristics to improve this partial order and coherence. These heuristics include: topical similarity, explicit discourse markers, and context. At the end of the sentence ordering process, to create a total order, we finally use the rank of the sentences in the original list of candidates. Let us now describe the post-schemata heuristics.

1. **Topical Similarity**: In the schema for a particular predicate type (e.g. *contingency*), we tried to use topical similarity in order to group sentences that describe the same topic together. To find topically similar sentences we used the cosine similarity using *tf.idf*.

2. **Explicit Discourse Markers**: To further improve discourse coherence, we add conjunctive markers based on the sentences' topical similarity and polarity value. For example, if two sentences are topically similar, our approach will place them next to each other and make a single sentence out of them using a conjunctive marker (e.g. *and*) even though these sentences may not adjacent in the candidate list. If BlogSum finds another sentence on this topic, it will position that sentence together using another conjunctive marker.

3. **Context:** To improve discourse coherence further, if a potential sentence starts with a pronoun without having a potential antecedent, we include its previous sentence from the source document as a context from the original document.

3.1.5 An Example to Describe Content Organization

To illustrate the content organization process, let us take the following example:

Question: *What motivated positive opinions of Carmax from car buyers?*

Figure 3: Partial Candidate List

(1) With Carmax you will generally always pay more than from going to a good used car dealer.
(2) We bought it at Carmax, and I continue to have nothing bad to say about that company.
(3) Carmax did split the bill which made me happy.
(4) Not sure if you have a Carmax near you, but I've had 2 good buying experiences from them.
(5) have to say that Carmax rocks.
(6) At Carmax, the price is the price and when you want a car you go get one.
(7) Sometimes I wonder why all businesses can't be like Carmax.
(8) Arthur Smith, 36, has been living in a van outside the CarMax lot, 24 hours a day, for more than a month.

The above question has been classified as a *Reason* type question based on the question pattern matching. A subset of the candidate sentences generated by BlogSum for this question is shown in Figure 3. For this question, the *Reason* schema is used to order the sentences. The *Reason* schema and the final order of the sentences are shown in Figure 4. In Figure 4, the constraints "sentence polarity", "compared objects", and "sentence focus" indicate that the sentence needs to have the same polarity as the question, the sentence needs to contain all objects which are being compared, and the topic of the sentence needs to be the focus of the sentence, respectively.

Figure 4: Summary Generated using the Reason Schema

Schema	Sentences
Predicate: $\{$*Topic-opinion/ Attribution*$\}^+$ Constraint: sentence polarity.	(2-1) After our last big car milestone, we've had an odyssey with cars. (2, 4) We bought it at Carmax, and I continue to have nothing bad to say about that company; not sure if you have a Carmax near you, but I've had 2 good experiences from them. (3) Moreover, Carmax did split the bill which made me happy. (5) have to say that Carmax rocks.
Predicate: $\{$*Contingency/ Comparison*$\}^*$ Constraint: compared objects, sentence focus.	(7) Sometimes I wonder why all businesses can't be like Carmax.
Predicate: *Attributive** Constraint: sentence focus.	(6) At Carmax, the price is the price and when you want a car you go get one.

In this sample, we can see that the schema did not include sentences 1 and 8 in the final summary even though the summary is within the length limit. This is because these sentences did not fit within the *Reason* schema. Though sentence 1 was classified as containing a *comparison* predicate, it did not fulfil the semantic constraint (shown in Figure 4) that the topic of the sentence (Carmax) be the focus of the sentence[5]. On the other hand, sentence 8 was not included, because it did not contain any of the rhetorical predicate which can fill the slots of this schema.

We can see that since for the sentence 2, the antecedent of the pronoun *it* is missing, our context heuristic added the preceding sentence 2-1 of sentence 2 from the source document. Our approach placed sentences 2 and 4 next to each other because of their topical similarity and also merged them using the conjunctive marker ';'. We can also see that the system added the discourse marker "Moreover" in sentence 3. In the summary, sentences 6 and 7 are also reordered compared to the candidate list based on the rhetorical predicate category they contained.

4 Evaluation

In order to test our approach, we have evaluated BlogSum-generated summaries for coherence and overall readability.

4.1 Corpus and Experimental Design

In this evaluation, we have used the TAC 2008 opinion summarization track data. The data set consists of 50 questions on 28 topics; on each topic one or two questions are asked and 10 to 50 relevant documents are given. For each question, one summary was generated by OList and one by BlogSum and the maximum summary length was restricted to 250 words. To evaluate coherence, we did not use the ROUGE metric because from a manual analysis (Blair-Goldensohn and McKeown, 2006) found that the ordering of content within the summaries is an aspect which is not evaluated by ROUGE. Instead, 4 participants manually rated 50 summaries from OList and 50 summaries from BlogSum for coherence with respect to the question for which the summary is generated using a blind evaluation. These summaries were rated on a likert scale of 1 to 5 where 1 refers to "very poor" and 5 refers to "very good". As a baseline, we used the original ranked list of candidate sentences (OList), and we compared it to the final summaries which are generated by BlogSum after applying the discourse structuring.

4.2 Results

In the evaluation, to calculate the score of BlogSum and OList for a particular question, we calculated the average scores of all annotators' ratings to that question. Table 1 shows the performance comparison between BlogSum and OList.

[5]To identify this, we test if the subject or object of the sentence is the topic.

We can see that 52% of the time BlogSum summaries were rated better than OList summaries; 30% of the time both performed equally; and 18% of the time BlogSum was weaker than OList. This means that 52% of the time, our approach has improved the coherence compared to that of the original candidate list (OList).

Table 1: Summary of the Comparison

Comparison	%
BlogSum Score > OList Score	52%
BlogSum Score = OList Score	30%
BlogSum Score < OList Score	18%

Table 2 shows the performance of BlogSum versus OList on each likert scale; where Δ shows the performance difference. From Table 2, we can see that BlogSum outperformed OList in the scale of "very good" and "good" by 16% and 8%, respectively; and improved the performance in "barely acceptable" and "poor" categories by 12% and 14%, respectively.

Table 2: Performance of BlogSum vs. OList

Category	OList	BlogSum	Δ
Very Good	8%	24%	16%
Good	22%	30%	8%
Barely Acceptable	36%	24%	-12%
Poor	22%	8%	-14%
Very Poor	12%	14%	2%

We have also evaluated if the difference in performance between BlogSum and OList was statistically significant using the t-test. The t-test results show that in a two-tailed test, BlogSum performed significantly better than OList with a p-value of 0.0223.

In this experiment, we also calculated the inter-annotator agreement using Cohen's kappa coefficient to verify the annotation subjectivity. We have found that the average pair-wise inter-annotator agreement is substantial with the kappa-value of 0.76.

4.3 Error Analysis

From the evaluation results of Table 2, we can see that about 54% of the time the coherence of BlogSum is categorized as "very good" or "good"; about 24% of the time "barely acceptable"; but still, about 22% of the time the summaries were considered "poor" or "very poor". From an error analysis, we have found that many of the summaries are ranked in the lower categories because of their question irrelevance, an incorrect polarity identification or a predicate tagging error. Although the annotators were asked to evaluate coherence only, they found it difficult to abstract all other factors and assign a high score to a coherent text that did not answer the question properly.

The evaluation results of Table 1 show that 52% of the time our approach has improved the coherence over the original candidate list (OList). However, in 18% of the time (9 summaries), our approach was weaker than OList. We have analyzed these 9 summaries and found that in 4 cases, some sentences were tagged with the wrong polarity; as a result when the post-schemata heuristics were applied (e.g. conjunctive marker) they made the summaries weaker. In 3 cases, sentences were tagged with the wrong predicates thus they were included in the final summaries yet they should not have and in 2 other cases, BlogSum excluded sentences which were actually potential sentences again because of a wrong polarity identification and predicate tagging.

In order to determine if the improvement in coherence was done at the expense of content, we evaluated this aspect by using the TAC 2008 opinion summarization track data and the ROUGE metric using answer nuggets (provided by TAC), which had been created to evaluate participants' summaries at TAC, as gold standard summaries. In this evaluation, we compared original candidate list (OList) to BlogSum-generated final summaries. The ROUGE scores are also calculated for all 36 submissions in the TAC 2008 opinion summarization track. In this experiment, BlogSum achieved a better F-Measure for ROUGE-2 and ROUGE-SU4 compared to OList. Results show that BlogSum gained 18% and 16% in F-Measure over OList using ROUGE-2 and ROUGE-SU4, respectively. Compared to the other systems, BlogSum ranked third and its F-Measure score difference from the best system is very small. Both BlogSum and OList performed better than the average systems.

5 Conclusion and Future Work

In this work, we have used discourse structures with the help of schema to improve discourse coherence of query-based blog summaries. In our schema based approach, we exploited discourse structures in schema design and in instantiating the schema to fill a slot. We have developed a query-based blog summarization system called BlogSum to validate our approach. The performance of BlogSum was evaluated manually using the TAC 2008 question answering track data by 4 human participants in a likert scale of 1 to 5. The results indicate that about 54% of the summaries are rated as "very good" or "good" as opposed to 30% for the summaries with no discourse structuring. The evaluation results also show that our approach has significantly improved summary coherence compared to that of the original candidate list without compromising on content.

An error analysis following the human evaluation has shown that an important source of error in low ranking summaries is question irrelevance. As a result, we plan to test our content organization strategies with a better initial candidate list. In the future, we also plan to evaluate the individual contribution of the post-schemata heuristics to the overall coherence of the summaries.

Acknowledgement

The authors would like to thank the anonymous referees for their comments on a previous version of the paper.

This work was financially supported by NSERC.

References

Barzilay, R., Lee, L.: Catching the Drift: Probabilistic Content Models, with Applications to Generation and Summarization. *In Proceedings of HLT-NAACL*, 113–120 (2004), Boston, USA.

Blair-Goldensohn, S., McKeown, K.R.: Integrating Rhetorical-Semantic Relation Models for Query-Focused Summarization. *In Proceedings of the Document Understanding Conference (DUC) Workshop at NAACL-HLT*, (2006), New York, USA.

Carlson, L., Marcu, D.: Discourse Tagging Reference Manual. University of Southern California Information Sciences Institute, ISI-TR-545, 2001.

Conroy, J. M., Dang, H. J.: Mind the Gap: Dangers of Divorcing Evaluations of Summary Content from Linguistic Quality. *In Proceedings of the 22nd International Conference on Computational Linguistics (Coling)*, 145–152 (2008), Manchester, UK.

Fei, Z., Huang, X., Wu, L.: Mining the Relation between Sentiment Expression and Target Using Dependency of Words. *PACLIC20: Coling 2008: Proceedings of the 20th Pacific Asia Conference on Language, Information and Computation*, 257–264 (2008), Wuhan, China.

Genest, P., Lapalme, G., Yousfi-Monod, M: HEXTAC: the Creation of a Manual Extractive Run. *In Proceedings Text Analysis Conference*, (2010), Gaithersburg, USA.

Hobbs, J. R.: On the Coherence and Structure of Discourse. Center for the Study of Language and Information, Stanford University, Report No. CSLI-85-37, 1985.

Jaidka, K., Khoo, C. S. G., Na, J.: Imitating Human Literature Review Writing: An Approach to Multi-document Summarization. *In Proceedings of the 12th International Conference on Asia-Pacific Digital Libraries*, 116–119 (2010), Gold Coast, Australia.

Jindal, N., Liu, B.: Identifying Comparative Sentences in Text Documents. *In Proceedings of ACM SIGIR*, 244–251 (2006), Seattle, USA.

Kumar, S., Chatterjee, D.: IIIT Kharagpur at TAC 2008: Statistical Model for Opinion Summarization. *In Proceedings Text Analysis Conference*, (2008), Gaithersburg, USA.

Lapata, M.: Probabilistic Text Structuring: Experiments with Sentence Ordering. *In Proceedings of the Annual Meeting of ACL*, 545–552 (2003), Sapporo, Japan.

Mann, W., Thompson S.: Rhetorical Structure Theory : Toward a Functional Theory of Text Organisation. *J. Text*, 3(8):234-281, 1988.

Marcu, D.: From Discourse Structures to Text Summaries. *Proceedings of the ACL'97/EACL'97 Workshop on Intelligent Scalable Text Summarization*, 82–88 (1997), Madrid, Spain.

McKeown, K.R.: Discourse Strategies for Generating Natural-Language Text. *J. Artificial Intelligence*, 27(1):1–41, 1985.

McKeown, K., Klavans, J., Hatzivassiloglou, V., Barzilay, R., Eskin, E.: Towards Multidocument Summarization by Reformulation: Progress and prospects. *AAAI/IAAI*, 27–36 (2002), Edmonton, Canada.

Mithun, S., Kosseim, L.: Comparing Approaches to Tag Discourse Relations. *In Proceedings (1) of CICLing*, 328–339 (2011), Tokyo, Japan.

Murray, G., Joty, S., Carenini, G., Ng, R.: The University of British Columbia at TAC 2008. *In Proceedings Text Analysis Conference*, (2008), Gaithersburg, USA.

Otterbacher, J. C., Radev, D. R., Luo, A.: Revisions that Improve Cohesion in Multi-document Summaries: A Preliminary Study. *In Proceedings of the Workshop on Automatic Summarization (including DUC 2002)*, 27–36 (2002), Philadelphia, USA.

Paul, M. J., Zhai. C., Girju, R.: Summarizing contrastive viewpoints in opinionated text. *In Proceedings of the 2010 Conference on Empirical Methods in Natural Language Processing*, 65–75 (2010).

Sauper, C., Barzilay, R.: Automatically Generating Wikipedia Articles: A Structure-Aware Approach. *In Proceedings of the Joint Conference of ACL and AFNLP*, 208–216 (2009), Suntec, Singapore.

Soricut, R., Marcu, D.: Sentence Level Discourse Parsing using Syntactic and Lexical Information. *In Proceedings of NAACL'03*, 149–156 (2003), Edmonton, Canada.

Parallel Suffix Arrays for Linguistic Pattern Search

Johannes Goller
Macmillan, Digital Science
Chiyoda Bldg., 2-37 Ichigayatamachi
Shinjuku-ku, Tokyo
jogojapan@gmail.com

Abstract

The paper presents the results of an analysis of the merits and problems of using suffix arrays as an index data structure for annotated natural-language corpora. It shows how multiple suffix arrays can be combined to represent layers of annotation, and how this enables matches for complex linguistic patterns to be identified in the corpus quickly and, for a large subclass of patterns, with greater theoretical efficiency than alternative approaches. The results reported include construction times and retrieval times for an annotated corpus of 1.9 billion characters in length, and a range of example patterns of varying complexity.

1 Introduction

Empirical linguistic studies require access to large corpora of text, and they benefit greatly when the text is stored in a form that enables the efficient retrieval of specific elements, such as sentences that match a pattern defined by a linguist. The size and contents of the corpus, the type and structure of its annotations, and the form of patterns involved vary greatly; the present paper deals with the requirements of only a subset of linguistic studies, which are characterized as follows:

- The corpus is large (hundreds of millions of words), but not extremely large (hundreds of millions of documents);
- Annotations exist in any number of layers, for example a layer of part-of-speech (POS) annotations and a layer of semantic role labels, but the annotations on each individual layer are non-overlapping and non-ambiguous;
- A pattern is essentially a regular expression, made up of literals (to be matched against the text), annotations (each with a specification of the layer it is expected to be found in) and wildcard elements ("gaps");
- The retrieval results are expected to be delivered within seconds or minutes (that is, not necessarily as fast as web search), and to be comprehensive (that is, to contain all matches, not only the top-N defined by some relevancy ranking);
- New patterns are generated constantly, perhaps by many different users or automated programs in parallel, while the text is largely static.

Corpus search engines that respond to a similar, albeit not identical, set of requirements include the Corpus Workbench[1], WebCorp Linguist's Search Engine[2] and Manatee/Bonito (Rychlý, 2007). The implementation of all of these systems relies on the principle of inverted files, which is the main alternative to the suffix arrays presented here[3]. Both approaches are described and briefly compared in section 2, a direct comparison is also available in (Puglisi et al., 2006). Sections 3 and 4 introduce the concept of parallel suffix arrays and describe how it enables annotations and complex pattern search, including patterns equivalent to finite state machines. Section 5 describes results obtained using an actual implementation of parallel suffix arrays.

2 The Two Main Approaches to Indexing

2.1 Inverted Files

The concept of inverted files requires the text to be *tokenized*, that is, to be segmented into tokens

[1] http://cwb.sourceforge.net/
[2] http://www.webcorp.org.uk/
[3] Suffix arrays are frequently used for n-gram analyses (e.g. Yamamoto and Church (1998)), but without the ability to process complex search patterns.

(usually roughly equivalent to words). The index consists of a searchable dictionary of the tokens (e.g. a hash table or sorted list), and a link connecting each token with its inverted list, i.e. the list of positions where the token is found (where the position of a token is defined as the token offset, i.e. the number of tokens to its left).

The match result for a search pattern that consists of a single token t is then readily retrieved by determining the dictionary entry corresponding to t (which if hashing is used typically takes $O(|t|)$ time, where $|t|$ is the length of t in characters) and returning the entire inverted list I_t. The length of the list corresponds to the number of occurrences of t, $\mathrm{occ}(t)$. If the pattern is a sequence of tokens $P := t_1, \dots, t_r$, the retrieval strategy is to determine all inverted lists in $O(|t_1|) + \dots + |t_r|)$ time, to then identify the inverted list of the least frequent token, i.e. I_{t_μ} such that $\mu = \mathrm{argmin}_i \, \mathrm{occ}(t_i)$, and to finally check for each of the positions $p \in I_{t_\mu}$ whether it lies in a match for the entire pattern P. That requires, for each p a look-up in the remaining $r-1$ inverted lists, specifically, for each $1 \leq k < \mu$, a look-up to check whether $p - k \in I_{t_{\mu-k}}$, and for each $1 \leq k < (r - \mu)$ to check whether $p + k \in I_{t_{\mu+k}}$. Since inverted lists are usually stored as sorted lists of integers, a look-up in I_{t_i} requires $O(\log\, \mathrm{occ}(t_i))$ time, hence the total time taken to identify all matches for P is

$$O(\sum_k |t_i| + \mathrm{occ}(t_\mu) \sum_{k \neq \mu} \log\, \mathrm{occ}(t_k)) \qquad (1)$$

Storing annotations in the index is straightforward: Modify the inverted lists so as to store positions as character offsets (rather than token offsets), and the length of t in characters along with each occurrence of t. Annotations can then be indexed in the same way as ordinary tokens, with character offset and length, and the procedure above can be modified so as to take into account the length of each t_i when computing the positions of adjacent tokens. This enables patterns using a mix of text and annotations, i.e. with some of the t_i referring to text, others to annotation. The time bound of (1) is unchanged.

2.2 Suffix Arrays

A *suffix array* is any representation of the lexicographically sorted list of all suffixes of a text, where *suffix* is defined as any substring beginning

	1	2	3	4	5	6	7	8	9
T=	a	b	x	a	b	d	a	e	$
SA=	9	4	1	7	5	2	6	8	3
bwt=	e	x	$	d	a	a	b	a	b
lcp=	0	0	2	1	0	1	0	0	0

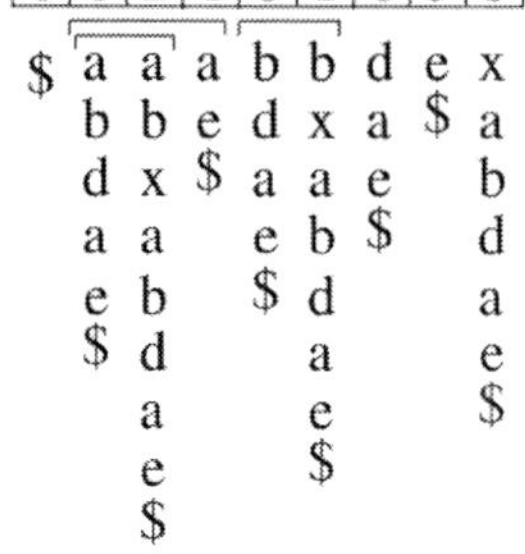

Figure 1: Suffix array SA for the string T =abxabdae$, along with auxiliary data structures *bwt*, *lcp* and "brackets" indicating the match ranges for substrings ab, a and b.

somewhere in the text and ending at the end of the text, i.e. there are n suffixes in a text of length n. Rather than storing copies of all the substrings, the suffix array is usually represented as a list of n integers, each indicating the starting position of a suffix. An example of this is shown in Fig. 1: The suffix array itself consists only of the integer list SA; the lower part of Fig. 1 shows the strings corresponding to each position, written vertically. Suffix arrays have an important property related to substring searches: Given a text T, its suffix array SA and a search pattern P, the set of starting positions of matches for P in T forms a continuous range in SA, as each match is the initial part of a suffix of T. Because of the lexicographical sorting, these suffixes must be adjacent to each other in the suffix array. For example, the set of matches for substring ab in Fig. 1 is the range [2; 3] of SA (corresponding to positions 4 and 1 of T). This shall be called the **range property** of suffix arrays.

Recent improvements in search algorithms for suffix arrays, cf. Navarro and Mäkinen (2007), make it possible to identify the match range for P in $O(|P|)$ time[4], and since no tokenization is required, recombining matches for individual tokens as in the case of inverted files is unnecessary. However, it is impossible to store annotation-related information in the suffix array. The follow-

[4]Strictly speaking, the time is bound by $O(|P|(1 + \log|\Sigma|/\log\log n))$, where $|\Sigma|$ is the size of the alphabet. However that is asymptotically equivalent to $O(|P|)$ when the alphabet is as much smaller than the text as it is the case for large-scale natural-language corpus search. See Navarro and Mäkinen (2007, 42) for details.

ing two sections describe a new concept, *parallel suffix arrays*, and how it enables annotations and more powerful search patterns.

3 Parallel Suffix Arrays

The first step is to allow annotations to enter the index. In the following it is assumed that a text $T \in \Sigma^*$ of length n is given, and one layer of q annotations

$$A = ((a_1, p_1, \ell_1), (a_2, p_2, \ell_2), \dots, (a_q, p_q, \ell_q))$$

such that each annotation (a_i, p_i, ℓ_i) consists of a label $a_i \in \Sigma^*$, a starting position $p_i < n$ and a length ℓ_i. p_i indicates where in T the substring annotated with a_i starts, ℓ_i indicates the number of T-characters it covers. For example, given

$$T = \text{is but a dream within a dream}$$

and POS-annotations V, Conj etc., the annotation layer might look like this:

$$A = ((\text{V}, 1, 2), (\text{Conj}, 4, 3), (\text{Det}, 8, 1), (\text{N}, 10, 5), (\text{Prep}, 16, 6), (\text{Det}, 23, 1), (\text{N}, 25, 5)) .$$

There are two ways to bring these annotations into the suffix-array-based index for T:

Method 1: Single-integer annotations. Three steps need to be performed: (1) Each distinct annotation label is mapped to a unique integer (e.g. using a hash table), that is, a new annotation alphabet Λ is created, in which each annotation is represented as one integer. (2) An extra integer is introduced in Λ, below represented by $\emptyset$, which is used as a dummy annotation for all areas of T that are not covered by any element of A (in the example above, this applies to the space characters between words). (3) A is replaced by a string $A' \in \Lambda^*$ containing the new annotation symbols in the order of the T-positions they refer to, and a bitvector $B^{T \leftrightarrow A}$ of length n indicating the starting positions of annotations relative to T. The example above now becomes:

$$A' = 1\emptyset 2\emptyset 3\emptyset 4\emptyset 5\emptyset 3\emptyset 4$$
$$B^{T \leftrightarrow A} = 10110011110000110000011110000 ,$$

where V has been mapped to 1, Conj to 2, and so forth. The next step is to construct a suffix array $\text{SA}_{A'}$ from the Λ-string A', along with auxiliary data structures required for fast searches, cf. Navarro and Mäkinen (2007). That enables fast searches for sequences consisting solely of annotations. It will later be shown how the bitvector is used to accomplish searches for mixed patterns, that is, patterns that contain both, T-sequences and A-sequences.

Method 2: Complex annotations. In some situations annotations are themselves complex and one would like to be able to search inside them, rather than mapping them to atomic integers. This is accomplished by appending a new character $\sharp \notin \Sigma$ to every label a_i as a separation mark, and then concatenating all labels to a new string A':

$$A' = \text{V}\sharp\text{Conj}\sharp\text{Det}\sharp\text{N}\sharp\text{Prep}\sharp\text{Det}\sharp\text{N}\sharp$$

In addition, two bitvectors $B^{T \leftrightarrow A}$ and $B^{A \leftrightarrow A}$ are defined, the former in the same way as in method 1, while the latter is of length $|A'|$ and has a 1 wherever a new annotation starts in A':

$$B^{A \leftrightarrow A} = 101000010001010000100010$$

Again, a suffix array $SA_{A'}$ for A' enables searching for substrings of annotations as well as sequences of annotations. The $\sharp$-symbols prevent undesired matches across annotation-boundaries.

How the bitvectors are used for mixed T/A' patterns. Both the bitvector of the first, and the bitvectors of the second method need to undergo an indexing process, during which a *rank* index and a *select* index are generated for each bitvector, defined as follows: Let B be a bitvector of length b and $i, j < b$, then

$$\texttt{rank}_B(i) := \text{the total number of 1s in } B[1..i]$$
$$\texttt{select}_B(j) := i \text{ s.t. there are } j \text{ 1s in } B[1..i] .$$

Using techniques described by Jacobson (1989), it is possible to construct, in $O(b)$ time, data structures that implement these functions, such that a lookup can be performed in $O(1)$ time and no more than $b + o(b)$ bits of space are consumed in total (including the bitvector itself). In the case of single-integer annotations (method 1), $\texttt{rank}_{B^{T \leftrightarrow A}}$ and $\texttt{select}_{B^{T \leftrightarrow A}}$ are constructed; in the case of complex annotations, these and $\texttt{rank}_{B^{A \leftrightarrow A}}$ and $\texttt{select}_{B^{A \leftrightarrow A}}$ are constructed. In addition, in both cases the inverse suffix arrays for T and A' must be computed and stored in memory: Given a suffix array SA, its inverse is defined as

$$\text{invSA}[j] := i \text{ such that } \text{SA}[i] = j ,$$

and invSA can be generated from SA in linear time. To see how these data structures work together, consider a mixed pattern $\sigma\lambda$, where $\sigma \in \Sigma^*$ is a substring match against T and λ is a substring match against the annotations. We first assume that method 1 was used, hence that $\lambda \in \Lambda^*$ is a sequence of annotations mapped to integers. The next step is to search the suffix arrays and determine the match ranges (l_σ, r_σ) for σ in SA_T and (l_λ, r_λ) for λ in $\mathrm{SA}_{A'}$. Clearly, the number of occurrences of σ in T is $\mathrm{occ}(\sigma) = r_\sigma - l_\sigma$, the number of matches for λ is $\mathrm{occ}(\lambda) = r_\lambda - l_\lambda$. We must now check, for each σ-match, whether it is followed by a λ-match. Let $l_\sigma \leq x < r_\sigma$ one of the σ-matches. It begins at position $p = \mathrm{SA}_T[x]$ of T and it is $|\sigma|$ characters in length. Hence it is followed by a λ-match if and only if an A-annotation starts at $p + |\sigma|$ and that annotation corresponds to a λ-match in A', which is the case iff the corresponding position in A' is a suffix in the match range (l_λ, r_λ). We therefore verify, for the candidate offset $q := p + |\sigma|$:

A-element exists:	$B^{T\leftrightarrow A}[q] = 1$	(2)
Location in A':	$q' := \mathtt{rank}_{B^{T\leftrightarrow A}}(q)$	(3)
Is q' a λ-match:	$l_\lambda \leq \mathrm{invSA}_A[q'] < r_\lambda$	(4)

If SA and invSA are available for random access, all of the above can be tested in $O(1)$ time, hence it takes $O(\mathrm{occ}(\sigma))$ time to compute the set of $\sigma\lambda$-matches from the two individual match ranges. Moreover, the procedure works in the reverse direction, too, starting from the λ-matches and determining those among them that are preceded by a σ-match (using `select` instead of `rank`; the time consumption becomes $O(\mathrm{occ}(\lambda))$). Hence it is possible to choose the matching direction according to whichever part of the pattern has fewer matches, i.e. let $\mathrm{occ}_\mu := \min(\mathrm{occ}(\sigma), \mathrm{occ}(\lambda))$, then the match combination can be computed in $O(\mathrm{occ}_\mu)$ time.

Without giving a detailed proof, we note that this result can be extended to general sequential patterns $t_1 \cdots t_r$, $t_i \in \Sigma^*, \Lambda^*$: The match combination time depends only on the least frequent (i.e. most specific) element t_μ, that is, including the time taken to determine the match range for each t_i, the total asymptotic time is

$$O\Big(\sum_k |t_k| + \mathrm{occ}(t_\mu)\Big), \qquad (5)$$

which is obviously better than with inverted files, where the match combination time depends on the frequency of all elements, as shown in (1). This shall be called the **least-frequency property** of parallel suffix arrays[5]. It should also be noted that for subsequences $t_e \cdots t_f$ such that all elements refer to the same layer, i.e. $\forall t_i \in \Sigma^*$ or $\forall t_i \in \Lambda^*$, no match combination is required at all, since the suffix arrays do not rely on tokenization, hence $t' := t_e \cdots t_f$ can be searched for as a single element in $O(|t'|)$ time.

Moreover, it is possible to define gaps of fixed length (measured in terms of number of T-characters, or alternatively, as number of A-annotations) between the individual elements, e.g. a pattern like $\sigma \overset{A:3}{\bowtie} \lambda$, indicating a distance of 3 arbitrarily A-annotated elements between σ and λ, can be evaluated in the same asymptotic time (because the length ℓ of the three wildcard elements following σ can be computed for each match candidate using `rank` and `select`, and then added to the candidate position, $q := p + |\sigma| + \ell$ used in (2) and (3) before the match range check for λ).

The property also holds when complex annotations and method 2 are used, at least when searching for prefixes of annotations, rather than arbitrary substrings of them. The distance calculations must then be made using the rank/select indexes for $B^{T\leftrightarrow A}$ to map positions between T and A, and those for $B^{A\leftrightarrow A}$ to compute the string length of annotations in A'. If arbitrary substring matching in annotations is required, the match process is delayed by a factor related to the length of λ, as every position inside the annotation must be checked for being a possible match continuation.

4 Complex Patterns

4.1 General patterns

Multiple annotation layers

It is straightforward to add further layers of annotation, e.g. semantic or morphological information, constituent classes etc. Each layer $A_1, A_2, \ldots$ is represented by an annotation string A'_i, a bitvector $B^{T\leftrightarrow A_i}$, and $B^{A_i\leftrightarrow A_i}$ if it is complex. Direct mappings between layers A_i, A_j are unnecessary, as they can be emulated using $B^{T\leftrightarrow A_i}$ and $B^{T\leftrightarrow A_j}$. Hence, total space consumption of the index grows in an additive manner as layers are added.

[5]The name *parallel suffix arrays* refers to the view of SA_T and $\mathrm{SA}_{A'}$ as parallel layers, both related to the same underlying text.

Branching patterns

An important step towards more powerful search patterns is the ability to process branching patterns, that is, patterns that specify multiple alternatives. This shall be denoted using a new operator $\oplus$, such that a pattern $\oplus(e_1, e_2, \ldots, e_m)$ is defined as matching all substrings of T that match any of the subexpressions e_i. If all e_i are distinct Σ-strings, the individual match sets for each e_i are disjoint, and the final result corresponds to the union set of the match ranges for the e_i.

But if some of the e_i refer to annotations or are themselves complex, i.e. sequential patterns or $\oplus$-expressions, the individual match sets might not be disjoint, causing the end result to contain duplicate matches, which makes it difficult to read and might cause frequency counts to be wrong. Hence, **duplicate elements must be detected** and removed from the individual match sets. This can be done either by creating a searchable result set representation, such as a hash table or tree, and inserting the matches one by one, rejecting matches that were inserted before; or, it can be done by creating a simpler, non-searchable result list and checking for each match for any e_i whether it is also a match for one of the other e_j, $j < i$. Both these methods are available when inverted files are used instead of suffix arrays, too, but if the second method is used, suffix arrays often have an advantage because the member check for the e_j, if it is a Σ- or Λ-string, involves only an $O(1)$ range check, whereas it would be logarithmic in an inverted file.

Sequences of complex elements

In section 3, the least-frequency property was established for sequential patterns, consisting of atomic elements and fixed-length-gaps, i.e. expressions like

$$e_1 \overset{Q_1:x_1}{\bowtie} e_2 \overset{Q_2:x_2}{\bowtie} \cdots \overset{Q_{m-1}:x_{m-1}}{\bowtie} e_m\,,$$

where $e_i \in \Sigma^*, \Lambda^*$; $Q_i \in \{\Sigma, \Lambda\}$; x_i integers. For even more powerful search patterns, it is important that the above can also be processed if the e_i are themselves complex, i.e. sequences or branching elements. This is indeed possible; the pattern then becomes a graph, and determining the least-frequent element, at which the matching should start, becomes a non-trivial problem. The number of matches of a sequence or branching subelement cannot be calculated accurately before the entire matching process has finished, but an upper bound can be determined: For a sequence, it is the frequency of its least-frequent subelement, for a branching element it is the sum of the frequencies of its branches. Based on this, it is possible to recursively determine the estimated best atomic subelement of the graph for the match combination process to begin. Once it has begun, the least-frequency property takes full effect during the processing of sequential substructures, and the range property accelerates the duplicate-checks where branching substructures are involved, as described above. Both is not true of inverted files, hence the theoretical performance of parallel suffix arrays is, generally, superior even for the most complex patterns.

Iteration

Another useful operator in powerful linguistic search patterns is the iteration operator, which is denoted by $\circledast(e)$ for any atomic or complex expression e. It corresponds to a sequence

$$e \overset{T:0}{\bowtie} e \overset{T:0}{\bowtie} \cdots \overset{T:0}{\bowtie} e$$

of undetermined length. Since all its elements are identical, the least-frequency property is preserved, even if the matching simply starts on the left end, or alternatively on the right end, and continues as long as new matches are found. Therefore, iteration elements can itself become part of complex patterns, and the three operations $\overset{Q:x}{\bowtie}$, $\oplus$ and $\circledast$ establish a pattern syntax with the power of regular expressions, over an annotated text with any number of annotation layers, and including fixed-length gaps (wildcards).

4.2 Gap-filling

In order to analyse linguistic patterns in specific contexts, it is desirable that not only substrings matching the entire pattern are identified, but that selected parts of the patterns, especially matches for gaps or annotation elements, can be extracted and separately returned as frequency lists. For example, if one wants to investigate the syntactic environment of "discussion", i.e. usages like "discussion on", "discussion with" etc., one might use a pattern like

$$\texttt{discussion} \overset{T:0}{\bowtie} \underbrace{\texttt{<Prep><Det>}}_{(*)} \overset{T:0}{\bowtie} \texttt{<N>}$$

and then obtain a frequency list of the content that matched the part marked by $(*)$. Parallel suffix arrays are particularly well-suited for this purpose: Firstly, it is easy to keep track of the beginning and ending offsets of the desired subexpressions during the matching processing; secondly, frequency lists are easy to generate: Given starting positions p_1, p_2 of two matches for $(*)$, a comparison of invSA$[p_1]$ and invSA$[p_2]$ in $O(1)$ time suffices to determine their lexicographic order. Once the matches are in lexicographic order, identifying duplicates and counting the frequencies of distinct strings is easy.

4.3 Look-betweens and negation

Another feature related to gaps is the ability to define some of their content partially. The three types of patterns below are examples of this:

$$\text{(a) } e_1 \overset{Q:x:y}{\bowtie} e_2 \quad \text{(b) } e_1 \overset{Q:x:y}{\bowtie} [?e_3] e_2 \quad \text{(c) } e_1 \overset{Q:x:y}{\bowtie} [!e_3] e_2$$

(a) represents a gap of length $x \leq \ell \leq y$ elements on the annotation level Q; (b) requires that somewhere inside the gap there must be a match for e_3 (positive look-between); (c) means there must be no match for e_3 in the gap (negative look-between). Without going into further detail, it should be noted that these types of patterns can be incorporated into the matching process using match combination techniques similar to those described in section 3. There is, however, a specific disadvantage of suffix arrays when processing variable-length gaps $e_1 \overset{Q:x:y}{\bowtie} e_2$: Assuming that $\text{occ}(e_1) \leq \text{occ}(e_2)$, let (p, ℓ) be the position and length of a match for e_1. Let (q_i, p_i, ℓ_i) be a Q-annotation located at $p_i = p + \ell$, and

$$(q_{i+1}, p_{i+1}, \ell_{i+1}), \ldots, (q_{i+y}, p_{i+y}, \ell_{i+y})$$

the following y Q-annotations. Then we need to check whether a match for e_2 is found at any of the positions $p_{i+x}, \ldots, p_{i+y}$, which requires $\delta := y - x + 1$ look-ups in invSA$_Q$. Hence, the gap length variability δ becomes a factor in the time complexity of the match combination process. That is not the case when inverted files are used: It then suffices to check for matches at p_{i+x} and p_{i+y} stored in the inverted list for e_2. Since the inverted list is sorted, all other relevant matches must be located between these too and can be retrieved in one step.

5 Implementation and Results

5.1 Index construction and operation

The system has been implemented as a C++ program that takes as input a file containing the text T with three layers of annotations in XML: A_{POS} (POS-annotations); A_{lem} (baseforms of words, indexed using method 1 (see section 3); A_{cPOS} (POS along with morphological information; indexed using method 2).

The index construction is performed by first establishing the parallel layers and bitvectors and then creating SA$_Q$, invSA$_Q$ and, as an auxiliary data structure used to enable faster suffix array search, the wavelet tree $\texttt{WVT}_Q$ (Grossi et al., 2003) for each layer $Q \in \{T, A_{\text{POS}}, A_{\text{lem}}, A_{\text{cPOS}}\}$. For the construction of SA$_Q$, a multi-threaded version of the DC-algorithm (Kärkkäinen et al., 2006) is used, invSA$_Q$ is computed in a trivial way in one pass over SA$_Q$, and the wavelet tree $\texttt{WVT}_Q$ is constructed using a simple multi-threaded method (for details see Goller (2011)). The only highly time-consuming steps are the constructions of SA$_Q$ and $\texttt{WVT}_Q$. Their running times are given in Table 1.

For efficient pattern search, it is necessary to keep all data structures in main memory at all times. Compression methods for SA, invSA and WVT are available, cf. Navarro and Mäkinen (2007), but unfortunately, using them causes the time complexity of pattern search to be increased by a factor of $\Omega(\log n)$, eliminating the advantage it has over inverted files. As a result, using parallel suffix arrays requires a large amount of RAM. The implementation used to obtain the results described above was found to require $\approx (0.06 \cdot N)/1024$ MB for a corpus of N characters with the three annotation layers described above. Hence, on a 32-bit desktop computer with about 3 GB of memory available, a corpus of ≈ 52 million characters (≈ 7 million words) can be processed efficiently. Therefore, although optimizing the implementation's use of RAM is certainly possible, it is quite clear that possibilities to use the described approach in linguistic practice depend on whether servers with sufficiently large RAM are available, and affordable.

5.2 Pattern Search

Table 2 presents response times for various kinds of patterns and illustrates, as expected, that the performance varies greatly depending on the complexity of the pattern; more specifically, it de-

	Threads Used	Hard drive	Available RAM	SA_T	WVT_T	SA_{POS}	WVT_{POS}	SA_{lem}	WVT_{lem}	SA_{cPOS}	WVT_{cPOS}
A	10	NFS	128 GB	3:17	3:48	1:30	1:13	1:27	11:46	3:03	2:03
B	20	Direct	512 GB	2:00	3:06	0:50	1:05	0:49	8:05	2:00	1:57
C	45	Direct	512 GB	2:00	2:37	0:51	0:54	0:55	6:16	1:49	1:43

Table 1: Construction times on three different system configurations. The text is 1.97 billion characters (375 million words) in length and contains approx. 27,000 distinct baseforms of words. Test A was performed on a server with AMD-Opteron CPUs 8356 (total 16 threads) and the hard drive mounted through NFS, tests B and C were conducted on a server with Intel Xeon X7560 processors (total 64 threads) and the hard drive installed locally. Time durations are given in the format h:mm.

	Pattern	#results	Search time (ms)	Extraction time (ms)
P1	millions	5,857	106	200
P2	thousands of	7,526	74	399
P3	#thousand# of	7,696	168	343
P4	discussion⟨IN⟩⟨NN⟩	1,296	213	80
P5	discussion$pr$$n$	1,894	372	118
P6	discussion[$pr$$n$]	1,894	530	111
P7	#preparation# $\overset{A_{POS}:0:2}{\bowtie} \langle IN \rangle \overset{T:0}{\bowtie} \oplus (\langle NN \rangle, \langle NNS \rangle)$	752	191	28
P8	$\langle JJ \rangle \langle NN \rangle \langle NN \rangle \overset{A_{POS}:0:2}{\bowtie} \langle IN \rangle \overset{T:0}{\bowtie} \oplus (\langle NN \rangle, \langle NNS \rangle)$	13,229	4,065	621
P9	$\langle NN \rangle \langle NN \rangle \overset{A_{POS}:0:2}{\bowtie} \langle IN \rangle \overset{T:0}{\bowtie} \oplus (\langle NN \rangle, \langle NNS \rangle)$	129,723	36,711	5,178

Table 2: Pattern processing times using hardware configuration A (see Table 1). Search time (identifying the set of match positions) and extraction time (extracting matches, but not including result printing). #..#-elements refer to A_{lem}, ⟨..⟩ to A_{POS}, $..$ to A_{cPOS}. Elements enclosed in [..] are marked for separate extraction and frequency counting (gap-filling). Times are in milliseconds.

pends on the "most specific atomic element" of the pattern. An element is atomic, if it refers to one layer (text or annotation) exclusively and contains no gaps. For example, the POS sequence $\langle$JJ$\rangle\langle$NN$\rangle\langle$NN$\rangle$ in P8, which would consist of three tokens in a standard inverted-file configuration, is atomic, as all three sub-elements refer to the same layer A_{POS} and can therefore be matched against $\text{SA}_{A_{\text{POS}}}$ in a single step. In accordance with the least-frequency property, the overall response time for the entire pattern depends on the number of occurrences of the most specific atomic element, which in this case is $\langle$JJ$\rangle\langle$NN$\rangle\langle$NN$\rangle$, rather than such high-frequency individual tokens as $\langle$JJ$\rangle$ or $\langle$NN$\rangle$. If the most specific atom is modified to be less specific, as in P9, the search time is increased by a factor of ≈ 9.

5.3 Discussion and Conclusion

The approach presented appears to be effective, especially for complex patterns that contain at least one relatively specific element. It provides efficient solutions for special tasks like context-specific pattern matching and frequency-list generation (described as gap-filling above), and it does not require any kind of tokenization, neither on the level of the main text, nor on the level of annotations and is hence suitable for corpora that involve annotations on the morpheme level, or across token boundaries, as well as for languages or writing systems that are hard to tokenize. Its biggest disadvantage is its high memory consumption, which however is likely to be less important in the future, as ever larger RAM hardware becomes available at increasingly low cost.

Although this has not been discussed in detail in previous sections, it is important to point out that the approach is *not* suitable in situations that call for frequent updates to the text or the annotations. The index structures described above, especially rank and select indexes for bit vectors as well as the suffix arrays themselves cannot be updated efficiently. Although data structures for suffix arrays that can be searched as well as dynamically updated are known, cf. (Russo et al., 2008; González and Navarro, 2008), using them would cause delays in the order of $O(\log n)$ (where n is the length of the text) in lookups of `select`, `rank` and SA, hence rendering the system considerably less efficient the corresponding version of an inverted file based system.

There are plans to release an open-source version of the implementation used for the tests described above as a corpus exploration tool for linguists before the end of the year.

References

Johannes Goller. 2011. *Exploring text corpora using index structures. PhD thesis.* To appear, Centrum für Informations- und Sprachverarbeitung, Ludwig-Maximilians-Universität München.

Rodrigo González and Gonzalo Navarro. 2008. Improved dynamic rank-select entropy-bound structures. In *LNCS 4957/2008, LATIN 2008: Theoretical Informatics*, pages 374–386, Berlin / Heidelberg. Springer.

Roberto Grossi, Ankur Gupta, and Jeffrey Scott Vitter. 2003. High-order entropy-compressed text indexes. In *SODA '03: Proceedings of the 14th annual ACM-SIAM symposium on discrete algorithms*, pages 841–850, Philadelphia, PA, USA. Society for Industrial and Applied Mathematics.

Guy Jacobson. 1989. Space-efficient static trees and graphs. In *Proc. of the 30th IEEE Symposium on Foundations of Computer Science (FOCS)*, pages 549–554.

Juha Kärkkäinen, Peter Sanders, and Stefan Burkhardt. 2006. Linear work suffix array construction. *J. ACM*, 53(6):918–936.

Gonzalo Navarro and Veli Mäkinen. 2007. Compressed full-text indexes. *ACM Comput. Surv.*, 39(1):2.

Simon Puglisi, W. Smyth, and Andrew Turpin. 2006. Inverted files versus suffix arrays for locating patterns in primary memory. In Fabio Crestani, Paolo Ferragina, and Mark Sanderson, editors, *String Processing and Information Retrieval*, volume 4209 of *Lecture Notes in Computer Science*, pages 122–133. Springer Berlin / Heidelberg.

Luís M. Russo, Gonzalo Navarro, and Arlindo L. Oliveira. 2008. Dynamic fully-compressed suffix trees. In *CPM '08: Proceedings of the 19th annual symposium on Combinatorial Pattern Matching*, pages 191–203, Berlin, Heidelberg. Springer-Verlag.

P. Rychlý. 2007. Manatee/bonito – a modular corpus manager. In P. Sojka and A. Horák, editors, *First Workshop on Recent Advances in Slavonic Natural Language Processing 2007*, Faculty of Informatics, Masaryk University, Botanická 68a, 60200 Brno, Czech Republic.

Mikio Yamamoto and Kenneth W. Church. 1998. Using suffix arrays to compute term frequency and document frequency for all substrings in a corpus. *Computational Linguistics*, 27:28–37.

A Mechanism to Restrict the Scope of Clause-Bounded Quantifiers in 'Continuation' Semantics

Anca Dinu
Faculty of Foreign Languages and Literatures, University of Bucharest
anca_d_dinu@yahoo.com

Abstract

This paper presents a formal mechanism to properly constrain the scope of negation and of certain quantificational determiners to their minimal clause in continuation semantics framework introduced in Barker and Shan (2008) and which was subsequently extended from sentential level to discourse level in Dinu (2011). In these works, type shifting is employed to account for side effects such as pronominal anaphora binding or quantifier scope. However, allowing arbitrary type shifting will result in overgenerating interpretations impossible in natural language. To filter out some of these impossible interpretations, once the negation or the quantifiers reach their maximal scope limits (that is their minimal clause), one should force their scope closing by applying a standard type shifter *Lower*. But the actual mechanism that forces the scope closing was left underspecified in previous work on continuation semantics. We propose here such a mechanism, designed to ensure that no lexical entries having the scope bounded to their minimal clause (such as *not, no, every, each, any*, etc) will ever take scope outside.

1 Introduction

The starting point of this paper is the continuation semantics introduced in Barker and Shan (2008) and extended from sentential level to discourse level in Dinu (2011). In this framework, type shifting is used to account for side effects such as pronominal anaphora binding or quantifier scope. However, allowing arbitrary type shifting will result in overgenerating interpretations impossible in natural language. To filter out these impossible interpretations, we first need to understand the scope behavior of each scope-taking lexical entry: its maximal scope limits and the scope precedence preferences w.r.t. other lexical entries. Second, we should force the scope closing of the quantifiers by applying a standard type shifter *Lower* (which is equivalent to identity function application), once their scope limits were reached. But the actual mechanism that ensures the scope closing was left underspecified in previous work on continuation semantics.

In what follows, we propose such a mechanism, designed to ensure that no lexical entry having the scope bounded to its minimal clause (such as *not, no, every, each, any*, etc) will ever take scope outside, thus getting right discourse truth conditions.

The programming language concept of continuations was successfully used by Barker and Shan in a series of articles (Barker 2002, Barker 2004, Shan 2005, Shan and Barker 2006, Barker and Shan 2008) to analyze intra-sentential linguistic phenomena (focus fronting, donkey anaphora, presupposition, crossover, superiority, etc). Moreover, (de Groote, 2006) proposed an elegant discourse semantics based on continuations. Continuations are a standard tool in computer science, used to control side effects of computation. They are a notoriously hard to understand notion. Actually, understanding what a continuation is per se is not so hard. What is more difficult is to understand how a grammar based on continuations (a 'continuized' grammar) works. The basic idea of continuizing a grammar is to provide subexpressions with direct access to their own continuations (future context), so subexpressions are modified to take a continuation as an argument. A continuized grammar is said to be written in *continuation passing style*. Continuation passing style is in fact a restricted (typed) form of λ-calculus.

Historically, the first continuation operators were undelimited (e.g., call/cc or J). An undelimited continuation of an expression represents "the entire (default) future for the computation" of that expression. Felleisen (1988) introduced delimited continuations (sometimes called 'composable' continuations) such as control ('C') and prompt ('%'). Delimited continuations represent the future of the computation of the expression up to a certain boundary. Interestingly, the natural-language phenomena discussed here make use only of delimited continuations.

For instance, if we take the local context to be restricted to the sentence, when computing the meaning of the sentence *John saw Mary*., the default future of the value denoted by the subject is that it is destined to have the property of seeing Mary predicated of it. In symbols, the continuation of the subject denotation j is the function $\lambda x.saw\,\boldsymbol{m}\,x$. Similarly, the default future of the object denotation $\boldsymbol{m}$ is the property of being seen by John, the function $\lambda y.\boldsymbol{saw}\,y\,j$; the continuation of the transitive verb denotation *saw* is the function $\lambda R.R\,m\,j$; and the continuation of the verb phrase *saw Mary* is the function $\lambda P.P\,j$. This simple example illustrates two important aspects of continuations:

(1) every meaningful subexpression has a continuation;

(2) the continuation of an expression is always relative to some larger expression containing it.

Thus, when *John* occurs in the sentence *John left yesterday*., its continuation is the property $\lambda x.\boldsymbol{yesterday}\,\boldsymbol{left}\,x$; when it occurs in *Mary thought John left*., its continuation is the property $\lambda x.\boldsymbol{thought}\,(\boldsymbol{left}\,x)\,m$ and when it occurs in the sentence *Mary or John left*., its continuation is $\lambda x.(\boldsymbol{left}\,\boldsymbol{m}) \vee (\boldsymbol{left}\,x)$ and so on.

It is worth mentioning that some results of traditional semantic theories are particular cases of results in continuation semantics:

- The generalized quantifier type from Montague grammar (Montague, 1970) <<<e,t>,t>,t> is exactly the type of quantificational determiners in continuation-based semantics;
- The <<t,t>,t> type of sentences in dynamic semantics is exactly the type of sentences in continuation-based semantics. In fact, dynamic interpretation constitutes a partial continuization in which only the category S has been continuized.

This is by no means a coincidence, MG only continuizes the noun phrase meanings and dynamic semantics only continuizes the sentence meanings, rather than continuizing uniformly throughout the grammar as it is done in continuation semantics.

2 Preliminaries

We use Barker and Shan's (2008) tower notation for a given expression, which consists of three levels: the top level specifies the syntactic category of the expression couched in categorial grammar, the middle level is the expression itself and the bottom level is the semantic value:

$$\begin{array}{c} syntactic\ category \\ expression \\ semantic\ value \end{array}$$

The syntactic categories are written $\frac{C|B}{A}$, where *A*, *B* and *C* can be any categories. We read this counter clockwise as "the expression functions as a category *A* in local context, takes scope at an expression of category *B* to form an expression of category *C*."

The semantic value in linear notation $\lambda k.f[k(x)]$ is equivalently written vertically as $\frac{f[\,]}{x}$ omitting the future context (continuation) *k*. Here, *x* can be any expression, and *f[ ]* can be any expression with a gap *[ ]*. Free variables in *x* can be bound by binders in *f [ ]*. This vertical (layered) notational convention is meant to make the combination process of two expressions easier (more visual) then in linear notation. Here there are the two possible modes of combination (Barker and Shan 2008):

$$\left(\begin{array}{cc} \frac{C|D}{A/B} & \frac{D|E}{B} \\ left-exp & right-exp \\ \frac{g[\,]}{f} & \frac{h[\,]}{x} \end{array}\right) = \begin{array}{c} \frac{C|E}{A} \\ left-exp\ right-exp \\ \frac{g[h[\,]]}{f(x)} \end{array}$$

$$\left(\begin{array}{cc} \frac{C|D}{B} & \frac{D|E}{B\backslash A} \\ left-exp & right-exp \\ \frac{g[\,]}{x} & \frac{h[\,]}{f} \end{array}\right) = \begin{array}{c} \frac{C|E}{A} \\ left-exp\ right-exp \\ \frac{g[h[\,]]}{f(x)} \end{array}$$

Below the horizontal lines, combination proceeds simply as in combinatory categorial grammar: in the syntax, *B* combines with *A/B* or *B\A* to form *A*; in the semantics, *x* combines with *f* to form *f(x)*. Above the lines is where the combination machinery for continuations kicks in. The syntax combines the two pairs of categories by a kind of cancellation: the *D* on the left cancels with the *D* on the right. The semantics combines the two expressions with gaps by a kind of composition: we plug *h[ ]* to the right into the gap of *g[ ]* to the left, to form *g[h[ ]]*. The expression with a gap on the left, *g[ ]*, always surrounds the expression with a gap on the right, *h[ ]*, no matter which side supplies the function and which side supplies the argument below the lines. This fact expresses the generalization that the default order of semantic evaluation is left-to-right.

When there is no quantification or anaphora involved, a simple sentence like *John came.* is derived as follows:

$$\begin{pmatrix} DP & DP\backslash S \\ John & came \\ j & came \end{pmatrix} = \begin{matrix} S \\ John\ came \\ came\ j \end{matrix}$$

In the syntactic layer, as usual in categorical grammar, the category under slash (here DP) cancels with the category of the argument expression; the semantics is function application.

Quantificational expressions have extra layers on top of their syntactic category and on top of their semantic value, making essential use of the powerful mechanism of continuations in ways proper names or definite descriptions do not. For instance, below is the derivation of *A man came.*:

$$\begin{pmatrix} \frac{S|S}{DP}/N & N & \frac{S|S}{DP\backslash S} \\ a & man & came \\ \lambda P.\frac{\exists x.P(x)\wedge[\,]}{x} & man & \frac{[\,]}{\mathbf{came}} \end{pmatrix} = \begin{matrix} \frac{S|S}{S} \\ a\ man\ came \\ \frac{\exists x.man(x)\wedge[\,]}{\mathbf{came}\ x} \end{matrix}$$

Comparing the analysis above of *John came* with that of *A man came* reveals that came has been given two distinct values. The first, simpler value is the basic lexical entry, the more complex value being derived through the standard type-shifter Lift, proposed by Partee and Rooth (1983), Jacobson (1999), Steedman (2000), and many others:

$$\begin{matrix} A \\ expression \\ x \end{matrix} \overset{Lift}{\Longrightarrow} \begin{matrix} \frac{B|B}{A} \\ expression \\ \frac{[\,]}{x} \end{matrix}$$

Syntactically, Lift adds a layer with arbitrary (but matching!) syntactic categories. Semantically, it adds a layer with empty brackets. In linear notation we have: $x \overset{Lift}{\Longrightarrow} \lambda k.k(x)$.

To derive the syntactic category and a semantic value with no horizontal line, Barker and Shan (2008) introduce the type-shifter Lower. In general, for any category *A*, any value *x*, and any semantic expression *f[ ]* with a gap, the following type-shifter is available:

$$\begin{matrix} \frac{A|S}{S} \\ expression \\ \frac{f[\,]}{x} \end{matrix} \overset{Lower}{\Longrightarrow} \begin{matrix} A \\ expression \\ f[x] \end{matrix}$$

Syntactically, Lower cancels an *S* above the line to the right with an *S* below the line. Semantically, Lower collapses a two-level meaning into a single level by plugging the value *x* below the line into the gap *[ ]* in the expression *f[ ]* above the line. Lower is equivalent to identity function application.

The third and the last type shifter we need is one that accounts for binding. We adopt the idea (in line with Barker and Shan (2008)) that the mechanism of binding is the same as the mechanism of scope taking. Binding is a term used both in logics and in linguistics with analog (but not identical) meaning. In logics, a variable is said to be bound by an operator (as the universal or existential operators) if the variable is inside the scope of the operator. If a variable is not in the scope of any operator, than the variable is said to be free. In linguistics, a binder may be a constituent such as a proper name (*John*), an indefinite common noun (*a book)*, an event or a situation, etc. Anaphoric expressions such as pronouns (*he, she, it, him, himself*, etc), definite common nouns (*the book, the book that John read*), demonstrative pronouns (like *this, that*), etc. act as variables that take the value of (are bind by) a previous binder.

In order to give a proper account of anaphoric relations in discourse, we need to formulate an explicit semantics for both the binder and the anaphoric expressions to be bound. Any determiner phrase (DP) may act as a binder, as the Bind rule from Barker and Shan (2008) explicitly states:

$$\begin{matrix} \frac{A|B}{DP} \\ expression \\ \frac{f[\,]}{x} \end{matrix} \overset{Bind}{\Longrightarrow} \begin{matrix} \frac{A|DP \rhd B}{DP} \\ expression \\ \frac{f([\,]x)}{x} \end{matrix}$$

At the syntactic level, the Bind rule says that an expression that functions in local context as a DP may offer to bind an anaphoric expression to the right ((Barker and Shan 2008) encode that by the sign ⊳). At the semantic level, the expression transmits (copies) the value of the variable x. In linear notation, the semantic part of the Bind rule looks like this: $\lambda k.f[k(x)] \overset{Bind}{\Longrightarrow} \lambda k.f([k(x)]x)$

As for the elements that may be bound, (Barker and Shan 2008) give the following lexical entry for the singular pronoun *he*:

$$\frac{DP \rhd S|S}{\begin{matrix} DP \\ he \end{matrix}} \qquad \frac{\lambda y.[\,]}{y}$$

To account for multiple anaphoric expressions (and their binders) or for inverse scope of multiple quantifiers, each binder can occupy a different scope-taking level in the compositional tower. With access to multiple levels, it is easy to handle multiple binders. Analyzing pronouns as two-level rules is the same thing as claiming that pronouns take scope (see Dowty (2007), who also advocates treating pronouns as scope-takers). Then, a pronoun or another anaphoric expression chooses its binder by choosing where to take scope. So, distinct scope-taking levels correspond to different binders, layers playing the role of indices: a binder and the pronoun it binds must take effect at the same layer in the compositional tower. A superior level takes scope at inferior levels and left expressions take scope at right expressions, to account for left-to-right natural language order of processing.

Dinu (2011) extends the formalism from sentence level to discourse level, giving the sentence connectors such as the dot the following semantics:

$$\begin{matrix} S\backslash(S/S) \\ . \\ \lambda p\lambda q.p\wedge q \end{matrix}$$

that is, the dot is a function that takes two sentence denotations and returns a sentence denotation (the conjunction of original sentence denotation).

For two affirmative sentences with no anaphoric relations and no quantifiers, such as *John came. Mary left.*, the derivation trivially proceeds as follows:

$$\begin{matrix} S \\ John\ came \\ \mathbf{came}\ j \end{matrix} \quad \begin{matrix} S\backslash(S/S) \\ . \\ \lambda p\lambda q.p\wedge q \end{matrix} \quad \begin{matrix} S \\ Mary\ left \\ \mathbf{left}\ m \end{matrix} = \begin{matrix} S \\ John\ came.Mary\ left \\ \mathbf{came}\ j \wedge \mathbf{left}\ m \end{matrix}$$

As one sees above, there is no need in this simple case to resort to type shifting at all. Nevertheless, type shifting and the powerful mechanism of continuations are employed when dealing with linguistic side effects such quantifier scope or binding. For instance, to derive the denotation of *A man came. He whistled.*, type lifting, type lowering and Bound rule become necessary:

$$\frac{S|S}{DP}/N \quad N \qquad \frac{S|S}{DP}$$

$$\begin{matrix} a \\ \lambda P.\dfrac{\exists x.P(x)\wedge[\,]}{x} \end{matrix} \quad \begin{matrix} man \\ \mathbf{man} \end{matrix} = \begin{matrix} a\ man \\ \dfrac{\exists x.\mathbf{man}(x)\wedge[\,]}{x} \end{matrix}$$

$$\overset{Bind}{\Longrightarrow} \frac{S|DP \rhd S}{\begin{matrix} DP \\ a\ man \end{matrix}} \quad \frac{\exists x.\mathbf{man}(x)\wedge([\,]x)}{x}$$

$$\frac{S|DP \rhd S}{\begin{matrix} DP \\ a\ man \end{matrix}} \frac{\exists x.\mathbf{man}(x)\wedge([\,]x)}{x} \quad \frac{DP \rhd S|DP \rhd S}{\begin{matrix} DP\backslash S \\ came \end{matrix}} \frac{[\,]}{\mathbf{came}} =$$

$$\frac{S|DP \rhd S}{\begin{matrix} S \\ a\ man\ came \end{matrix}} \quad \frac{\exists x.\mathbf{man}(x)\wedge([\,]x)}{\mathbf{came}\ x}$$

$$\frac{DP \rhd S|S}{\begin{matrix} DP \\ he \end{matrix}} \frac{\lambda y.[\,]}{y} \quad \frac{S|S}{\begin{matrix} DP\backslash S \\ whistled \end{matrix}} \frac{[\,]}{\mathbf{whistled}} = \frac{DP \rhd S|S}{\begin{matrix} S \\ he\ whistled \end{matrix}} \frac{\lambda y.[\,]}{\mathbf{whistled}\ y}$$

$$\frac{S|DP \rhd S}{\begin{matrix} S \\ a\ man\ came \end{matrix}} \frac{\exists x.\mathbf{man}(x)\wedge([\,]x)}{\mathbf{came}\ x} \quad \frac{DP \rhd S|DP \rhd S}{\begin{matrix} S\backslash(S/S) \\ . \end{matrix}} \frac{[\,]}{\lambda p\lambda q.p\wedge q} \quad \frac{DP \rhd S|S}{\begin{matrix} S \\ he\ whistled \end{matrix}} \frac{\lambda y.[\,]}{\mathbf{whistled}\ y}$$

$$= \frac{S|S}{\begin{matrix} S \\ a\ man\ came.he\ whistled \end{matrix}} \frac{\exists x.\mathbf{man}(x)\wedge(\lambda y.[\,]x)}{\mathbf{came}\ x \wedge \mathbf{whistled}\ y} \overset{Lower}{\Longrightarrow}$$

$$\begin{matrix} S \\ a\ man\ came.he\ whistled \\ \exists x.\mathbf{man}(x)\wedge(\lambda y.[\mathbf{came}\ x \wedge \mathbf{whistled}\ y\,]x) \end{matrix}$$

$$= \begin{matrix} S \\ a\ man\ came.he\ whistled \\ \exists x.\mathbf{man}(x)\wedge(\mathbf{came}\ x \wedge \mathbf{whistled}\ x) \end{matrix}$$

Note that the denotations of *came* and *whistled* were also lifted so as to match the ones of *a* and *he*, both being scope-takers. The last equality sign is due to routine lambda conversion.

3 Restricting the Scope of Clause-Bounded Lexical Entries

A first proposal for the lexical entry for the negation could look like this:

$$\begin{array}{c} \dfrac{S|S}{(DP\backslash S)/(DP\backslash S)} \\ not \\ \dfrac{\neg[\,]}{[\,]} \end{array}$$

meaning that negation functions in local context as a verb modifier and takes scope at a sentence to give a sentence.

Using this denotation for *not*, the piece of discourse *John does not own a car.* is interpreted as (ignoring the auxiliary *does* for simplicity):

$$\begin{array}{cccc} \dfrac{S|S}{DP} & \dfrac{S|S}{(DP\backslash S)/(DP\backslash S)} & \dfrac{S|S}{(DP\backslash S)/DP} & \dfrac{S|S}{DP} \\ John & not & own & a\ car \\ \dfrac{[\,]}{\boldsymbol{j}} & \dfrac{\neg[\,]}{[\,]} & \dfrac{[\,]}{\boldsymbol{own}} & \dfrac{\exists x.\,\boldsymbol{car}(x)\wedge[\,]}{x} \end{array}$$

$$= \begin{array}{c} \dfrac{S|S}{S} \\ John\ not\ own\ a\ car \\ \dfrac{\neg(\exists x.\,\boldsymbol{car}(x)\wedge[\,])}{\boldsymbol{own}\ x\ \boldsymbol{j}} \end{array} \xrightarrow{Lower} \begin{array}{c} S \\ John\ not\ own\ a\ car \\ \neg(\exists x.\,\boldsymbol{car}(x)\wedge \boldsymbol{own}\ x\ \boldsymbol{j}) \end{array}$$

meaning that there is no car that John owns, a fair approximation of the intended meaning.

It is generally accepted that negation cannot take scope outside its minimal clause. But, if we do not restrict the possible scope of negation, continuing the discourse with the sentence **It is red.*, could result in the following derivation:

$$\begin{array}{ccc} \dfrac{S|DP\rhd S}{S} & \dfrac{DP\rhd S|DP\rhd S}{S\backslash(S/S)} & \dfrac{DP\rhd S|S}{S} \\ John\ not\ own\ a\ car & . & It\ is\ red \\ \dfrac{\neg(\exists x.\,\boldsymbol{car}(x)\wedge[\,]x)}{\boldsymbol{own}\ x\ \boldsymbol{j}} & \dfrac{[\,]}{\lambda p\lambda q.\,p\wedge q} & \dfrac{\lambda y.\,[\,]}{\boldsymbol{is\ red}\ y} \end{array}$$

$$= \begin{array}{c} \dfrac{S|S}{S} \\ John\ not\ own\ a\ car.\ It\ is\ red \\ \dfrac{\neg(\exists x.\,\boldsymbol{car}(x)\wedge\lambda y.[\,]x)}{\boldsymbol{own}\ x\ \boldsymbol{j}\wedge\boldsymbol{is\ red}\ y} \end{array} \xrightarrow{Lower}$$

$$\begin{array}{c} S \\ John\ not\ own\ a\ car.\ It\ is\ red \\ \neg(\exists x.\,\boldsymbol{car}(x)\wedge\lambda y.[\,\boldsymbol{own}\ x\ \boldsymbol{j}\wedge \boldsymbol{s\ red}\ y]x) \end{array}$$

$$= \begin{array}{c} S \\ John\ not\ own\ a\ car.\ It\ is\ red \\ \neg(\exists x.\,\boldsymbol{car}(x)\wedge[\,\boldsymbol{own}\ x\ \boldsymbol{j}\wedge \boldsymbol{is\ red}\ x]) \end{array}$$

which would incorrectly assert that there is no car which is owned by John and which is red. Moreover, *it* would wrongly refer back to *a car*. In fact, if we do not restrict the possible scope of negation, any following sentence may be wrongly interpreted inside the scope of negation.

In order to block such interpretations, we could adopt a similar strategy with the one proposed in Barker and Shan (2008): to force the scope closing of *not* immediately after the interpretation of its minimal clause, by applying Lower. This also closes the scope of any other *DP* inside the scope of negation, so it becomes impossible for it to bind subsequent anaphoric expressions. But this strategy leaves the actual mechanis that insures the scope closing unspecified. As Barker and Shan put it, when referring to the scope closing of *every*, "Like most leading accounts of donkey anaphora, we provide no formal mechanism here that bounds the scope-taking of universals".

In what follows, we propose such a mechanism within the continuation semantics framework. The mechanism is designed to ensure that no lexical entries having the scope bounded to their minimal clause (such as *not, no, every, each, any*, etc) will ever take scope outside.

We introduce a new category for clauses: *C*, of the same semantic type as the category *S*, namely *t*. *C* is the minimal discourse unit, whereas *S* is contains at least one such unit.

We constrain by definition the lexical entries with clause-bounded scope to take scope only at clauses. For instance, here there are the lexical entries for *not, no* and *every*:

$$\begin{array}{c} \dfrac{C|C}{(DP\backslash C)/(DP\backslash C)} \\ \text{not} \\ \dfrac{\neg[\,]}{[\,]} \end{array} \qquad \begin{array}{c} \dfrac{C|C}{DP}/N \\ \text{no} \\ \lambda P.\dfrac{\neg\exists x.\,(P(x)\wedge[\,])}{x} \end{array}$$

$$\begin{array}{c} \dfrac{C|C}{\dfrac{C|C}{DP}/N} \\ \text{every} \\ \forall x.[\,] \\ \hline \lambda P.\dfrac{P(x)\rightarrow[\,]}{x} \end{array}$$

After the full interpretation of the minimal clause which they appear in, the category *C* has to be converted to category *S*. Specifically, one can use the following silent lexical entry:

$$\begin{array}{c} S/C \\ \Phi \\ \lambda p.\,p([\,]) \end{array}$$

This step ensures that clauses (of category *C*) can be further processed as pieces of discourse (of category *S*), because all discourse connectors (such as the dot or *if*) are allowed to take only expressions of category *S* as arguments.

We modify the Lower rule such that category *C* may also be lowered similarly to category *S*:

$$\begin{array}{c}\frac{A|C}{C}\\ expression\\ \frac{f[\,]}{x}\end{array} \overset{Lower}{\Longrightarrow} \begin{array}{c}A\\ expression\\ f[x]\end{array}$$

With this clause-restricting mechanism, the derivation of *John does not own a car.* becomes:

$$\begin{array}{c}\frac{C|C}{DP}\\ John\\ \frac{[\,]}{\boldsymbol{j}}\end{array} \begin{array}{c}\frac{C|C}{(DP\backslash C)/(DP\backslash C)}\\ not\\ \frac{\neg[\,]}{[\,]}\end{array} \begin{array}{c}\frac{C|C}{(DP\backslash C)/DP}\\ own\\ \frac{[\,]}{own}\end{array} \begin{array}{c}\frac{C|C}{DP}\\ a\ car\\ \frac{\exists x.\boldsymbol{car}(x)\wedge[\,]}{x}\end{array}$$

$$= \begin{array}{c}\frac{C|C}{C}\\ John\ not\ own\ a\ car\\ \frac{\neg(\exists x.\boldsymbol{car}(x)\wedge[\,])}{\boldsymbol{own}\ x\ \boldsymbol{j}}\end{array} \overset{Lower}{\Longrightarrow} \begin{array}{c}C\\ John\ not\ own\ a\ car\\ \neg(\exists x.\boldsymbol{car}(x)\wedge\ \boldsymbol{own}\ x\ \boldsymbol{j})\end{array}$$

Now that the scope of negation is closed, it is obviously impossible for it to stretch over the following discourse. We only have to change the category *C* into *S* in order to connect it to the discourse:

$$\begin{array}{c}S/C\\ \Phi\\ \lambda p.p([\,])\end{array} \begin{array}{c}C\\ John\ not\ own\ a\ car\\ \neg(\exists x.\boldsymbol{car}(x)\wedge\ \boldsymbol{own}\ x\ \boldsymbol{j})\end{array}$$

$$= \begin{array}{c}S\\ John\ not\ own\ a\ car\\ \lambda p.p([\neg(\exists x.\boldsymbol{car}(x)\wedge\ \boldsymbol{own}\ x\ \boldsymbol{j})])\end{array}$$

$$= \begin{array}{c}S\\ John\ not\ own\ a\ car\\ \neg(\exists x.\boldsymbol{car}(x)\wedge\ \boldsymbol{own}\ x\ \boldsymbol{j})]\end{array}$$

What about the binding capabilities of the expressions in a clause whose scope has been closed? The subject, for instance, should be able to bind subsequent anaphora. It can do so by lifting over the negation and being available to bind from that position:

$$\begin{array}{c}\frac{S|DP\rhd S}{\frac{C|C}{DP}}\\ John\\ \frac{[\,]\boldsymbol{j}}{\frac{[\,]}{\boldsymbol{j}}}\end{array} \begin{array}{c}\frac{DP\rhd S|DP\rhd S}{\frac{C|C}{(DP\backslash C)/(DP\backslash C)}}\\ not\\ \frac{[\,]}{\frac{\neg[\,]}{[\,]}}\end{array} \begin{array}{c}\frac{DP\rhd S|DP\rhd S}{\frac{C|C}{(DP\backslash C)/DP}}\\ own\\ \frac{[\,]}{\frac{[\,]}{\boldsymbol{own}}}\end{array} \begin{array}{c}\frac{DP\rhd S|DP\rhd S}{\frac{C|C}{DP}}\\ a\ car\\ \frac{[\,]}{\frac{\exists x.\boldsymbol{car}(x)\wedge[\,]}{x}}\end{array}$$

$$= \begin{array}{c}\frac{S|DP\rhd S}{\frac{C|C}{C}}\\ John\ not\ own\ a\ car\\ \frac{[\,]\boldsymbol{j}}{\frac{\neg\exists x.\boldsymbol{car}(x)\wedge[\,]}{\boldsymbol{own}\ x}}\end{array} \overset{Lower}{\Longrightarrow} \begin{array}{c}\frac{S|DP\rhd S}{C}\\ John\ not\ own\ a\ car\\ \frac{[\,]\boldsymbol{j}}{\neg\exists x.\boldsymbol{car}(x)\wedge\boldsymbol{own}\ x}\end{array}$$

$$\begin{array}{c}\frac{S|S}{S/C}\\ \Phi\\ \frac{[\,]}{\lambda p.p([\,])}\end{array} \begin{array}{c}\frac{S|DP\rhd S}{C}\\ John\ not\ own\ a\ car\\ \frac{[\,]\boldsymbol{j}}{\neg\exists x.\boldsymbol{car}(x)\wedge\boldsymbol{own}\ x}\end{array} = \begin{array}{c}\frac{S|DP\rhd S}{S}\\ John\ not\ own\ a\ car\\ \frac{[\,]\boldsymbol{j}}{\neg\exists x.\boldsymbol{car}(x)\wedge\boldsymbol{own}\ x}\end{array}$$

$$\begin{array}{c}\frac{S|DP\rhd S}{S}\\ John\ not\ own\ a\ car\\ \frac{[\,]\boldsymbol{j}}{\neg\exists x.\boldsymbol{car}(x)\wedge\boldsymbol{own}\ x}\end{array} \begin{array}{c}\frac{DP\rhd S|DP\rhd S}{S\backslash(S/S)}\\ .\\ \frac{[\,]}{\lambda p\lambda q.p\wedge q}\end{array} \begin{array}{c}\frac{DP\rhd S|S}{S}\\ He\ came\ by\ foot\\ \frac{\lambda y.[\,]}{\boldsymbol{came\ by\ foot}\ y}\end{array}$$

$$= \begin{array}{c}\frac{S|S}{S}\\ John\ not\ own\ a\ car.He\ came\ by\ foot\\ \frac{\lambda y.[\,]\boldsymbol{j}}{\neg\exists x.\boldsymbol{car}(x)\wedge\boldsymbol{own}\ x\wedge\boldsymbol{came\ by\ foot}\ y}\end{array} \overset{Lower}{\Longrightarrow}$$

$$\begin{array}{c}S\\ John\ not\ own\ a\ car.He\ came\ by\ foot\\ \neg\exists x.\boldsymbol{car}(x)\wedge\boldsymbol{own}\ x\wedge\boldsymbol{came\ by\ foot}\ \boldsymbol{j}\end{array}$$

It is conceivable that an indefinite in direct object position may also rise from its minimal negated clause to give the inverse scope interpretation. This interpretation may sometimes be ruled out on pragmatic grounds as being too uninformative (for instance, there is a car that John does not own is not a valid interpretation for *John does not own a car.*) or may be the preferred interpretation (there is a certain colleague Mary does not like is the preferred interpretation *of Mary does not like a colleague.*). Also, there are lexical entries such as negative polarity items (for instance, *any*) or definite descriptions (such as *John, the man, the man who entered)* that, when in direct object position of a negated verb phrase, take wide scope over negation and thus bind subsequent anaphora. For instance, here it is the derivation of *Mary does not like John. He is rude.*:

$$\begin{array}{c}\frac{S|S}{\frac{C|C}{DP}}\\ Mary\\ \frac{[\,]}{\frac{[\,]}{\boldsymbol{m}}}\end{array} \begin{array}{c}\frac{S|S}{\frac{C|C}{(DP\backslash C)/(DP\backslash C)}}\\ not\\ \frac{[\,]}{\frac{\neg[\,]}{[\,]}}\end{array} \begin{array}{c}\frac{S|S}{\frac{C|C}{DP\backslash C}}\\ like\\ \frac{[\,]}{\frac{[\,]}{\boldsymbol{like}}}\end{array} \begin{array}{c}\frac{S|DP\rhd S}{\frac{C|C}{DP}}\\ John\\ \frac{[\,]\boldsymbol{j}}{\frac{[\,]}{\boldsymbol{j}}}\end{array} =$$

$$\begin{array}{c}\dfrac{S|DP \rhd S}{\dfrac{C|C}{C}}\\ \textit{Mary not like John}\\ \dfrac{[\,]j}{\dfrac{\neg[\,]}{\mathbf{like}\ j\ m}}\end{array} \xRightarrow{Lower} \begin{array}{c}\dfrac{S|DP \rhd S}{C}\\ \textit{Mary not like John}\\ \dfrac{[\,]j}{\neg[\,\mathbf{like}\ j\ m]}\end{array}$$

$$\begin{array}{c}\dfrac{S|S}{S/C}\\ \Phi\\ \dfrac{[\,]}{\lambda p.\,p([\,])}\end{array} \quad \begin{array}{c}\dfrac{S|DP \rhd S}{C}\\ \textit{Mary not like John}\\ \dfrac{[\,]j}{\neg[\,\mathbf{like}\ j\ m]}\end{array} = \begin{array}{c}\dfrac{S|DP \rhd S}{S}\\ \textit{Mary not like John}\\ \dfrac{[\,]j}{\neg[\,\mathbf{like}\ j\ m]}\end{array}$$

$$\begin{array}{c}\dfrac{S|DP \rhd S}{S}\\ \textit{Mary not like John}\\ \dfrac{[\,]j}{\neg[\,\mathbf{like}\ j\ m]}\end{array} \quad \begin{array}{c}\dfrac{S|S}{S\backslash(S/S)}\\ .\\ \dfrac{[\,]}{\lambda p \lambda q.\,p \wedge q}\end{array} \quad \begin{array}{c}\dfrac{DP \rhd S|S}{S}\\ \textit{He is rude}\\ \dfrac{\lambda y.[\,]}{\mathbf{is\ rude}\ y}\end{array}$$

$$\begin{array}{c}\dfrac{S|S}{S}\\ = \textit{Mary not like John. He is rude} \xRightarrow{Lower}\\ \dfrac{\lambda y.[\,]j}{\neg[\,\mathbf{like}\ j\ m] \wedge \mathbf{is\ rude}\ y}\end{array}$$

$$\begin{array}{c}S\\ \textit{Mary not like John. He is rude}\\ \lambda y.[\neg[\,\mathbf{like}\ j\ m] \wedge \mathbf{is\ rude}\ y\,]j\end{array}$$

$$\begin{array}{c}S\\ = \textit{Mary not like John. He is rude}\\ \neg[\,\mathbf{like}\ j\ m] \wedge \mathbf{is\ rude}\ j\end{array}$$

The scope behavior of the quantificational determiners *every* and *any* may be accounted for in a similar manner. Consider for instance the following examples:

*John does not know every poem. *It is nice.*

*John does not know any poem. *It is nice.*

The interpretative difference between *every* and *any* is made (in line with Quine and Geach among others) by the scope behavior of the two quantificational determiners. *Any* prefers to take wide scope, whereas *every* rather takes narrow scope:

$$\begin{array}{c}\dfrac{C|C}{\dfrac{C|C}{DP}}\\ \textit{John}\\ \dfrac{[\,]}{\dfrac{[\,]}{\mathbf{j}}}\end{array} \begin{array}{c}\dfrac{C|C}{\dfrac{C|C}{(DP\backslash C)/(DP\backslash C)}}\\ \textit{not}\\ \dfrac{\neg[\,]}{\dfrac{[\,]}{[\,]}}\end{array} \left(\begin{array}{c}\dfrac{C|C}{\dfrac{C|C}{(DP\backslash C)/DP}}\\ \textit{know}\\ \dfrac{[\,]}{\dfrac{[\,]}{\mathbf{know}}}\end{array} \begin{array}{c}\dfrac{C|C}{\dfrac{C|C}{DP/N}}\\ \textit{every}\\ \dfrac{\neg\exists x.[\,]}{\lambda P.\dfrac{P(x) \wedge \neg[\,]}{x}}\end{array} \begin{array}{c}\dfrac{C|C}{N}\\ \textit{poem}\\ \dfrac{[\,]}{\mathbf{poem}}\end{array}\right)$$

$$\begin{array}{c}\dfrac{C|C}{\dfrac{C|C}{C}}\\ = \textit{John not know every poem} \xRightarrow{Lower\ two\ times}\\ \dfrac{\neg[\neg\exists x.[\,]]}{\dfrac{\mathbf{poem}(x) \wedge \neg[\,]}{\mathbf{know}\ x\ \mathbf{j}}}\end{array}$$

$$\begin{array}{c}C\\ \textit{John does not know every poem}\\ \neg[\neg\exists x.[\mathbf{poem}(x) \wedge \neg[\mathbf{know}\ x\ \mathbf{j}\,]\,]]\end{array}$$

$$\begin{array}{c}S/C\\ \Phi\\ \lambda p.\,p([\,])\end{array} \quad \begin{array}{c}C\\ \text{John does not know every poem}\\ \neg[\neg\exists x.[\mathbf{poem}(x) \wedge \neg[\text{know } x\ \mathbf{j}\,]\,]]\end{array} =$$

$$\begin{array}{c}S\\ \textit{John does not know every poem}\\ \neg[\neg\exists x.[\mathbf{poem}(x) \wedge \neg[\mathbf{know}\ x\ \mathbf{j}\,]\,]]\end{array}$$

which means that there is (at least) one poem that John does not know, a fare approximation of the intended meaning. In this context, the interpretation of *It is nice.* crashes, because *it* cannot find a suitable antecedent into the preceding discourse. It would have been useless for *poem* to offer to bind in the first place, because *not* takes scope over it and negation has to close its scope before its minimal clause is interpreted in discourse.

The interpretation of the quantificational determiner *any* in discourse proceeds similarly:

$$\begin{array}{c}\dfrac{C|C}{\dfrac{C|C}{DP}/N}\\ \textit{any}\\ \dfrac{\neg\exists x.[\,]}{\lambda P.\dfrac{P(x) \wedge \neg[\,]}{x}}\end{array} \begin{array}{c}\dfrac{C|C}{N}\\ \textit{poem}\\ \dfrac{[\,]}{\mathbf{poem}}\end{array} = \begin{array}{c}\dfrac{C|C}{\dfrac{C|C}{DP}}\\ \textit{any poem}\\ \dfrac{\neg\exists x.[\,]}{\dfrac{\mathbf{poem}(x) \wedge \neg[\,]}{x}}\end{array}$$

$$\xRightarrow{Lift} \begin{array}{c}\dfrac{C|C}{\dfrac{C|C}{\dfrac{C|C}{DP}}}\\ \textit{any poem}\\ \dfrac{\neg\exists x.[\,]}{\dfrac{\mathbf{poem}(x) \wedge \neg[\,]}{\dfrac{[\,]}{x}}}\end{array}$$

$$\begin{array}{c}\dfrac{C|C}{\dfrac{C|C}{\dfrac{C|C}{DP}}}\\ \textit{John}\\ \dfrac{[\,]}{\dfrac{[\,]}{\dfrac{[\,]}{\mathbf{j}}}}\end{array} \begin{array}{c}\dfrac{C|C}{\dfrac{C|C}{\dfrac{C|C}{(DP\backslash C)/(DP\backslash C)}}}\\ \textit{not}\\ \dfrac{[\,]}{\dfrac{[\,]}{\dfrac{\neg[\,]}{[\,]}}}\end{array} \left(\begin{array}{c}\dfrac{C|C}{\dfrac{C|C}{\dfrac{C|C}{(DP\backslash C)/DP}}}\\ \textit{know}\\ \dfrac{[\,]}{\dfrac{[\,]}{\dfrac{[\,]}{\mathbf{know}}}}\end{array} \begin{array}{c}\dfrac{C|C}{\dfrac{C|C}{\dfrac{C|C}{DP}}}\\ \textit{any poem}\\ \dfrac{\neg\exists x.[\,]}{\dfrac{\mathbf{poem}(x) \wedge \neg[\,]}{\dfrac{[\,]}{x}}}\end{array}\right)$$

$$\begin{array}{c}\dfrac{C|C}{\dfrac{C|C}{\dfrac{C|C}{DP}}}\\ = \textit{John not know any poem} \xRightarrow{Lower\ three\ times}\\ \dfrac{\neg\exists x.[\,]}{\dfrac{\mathbf{poem}(x) \wedge \neg[\,]}{\dfrac{\neg[\,]}{\mathbf{know}\ x\ \mathbf{j}}}}\end{array}$$

$$\begin{array}{c} C \\ \textit{John does not know any poem} \\ \neg\exists x.\,\boldsymbol{poem}(x) \land [\boldsymbol{know}\ x\ j\,] \end{array}$$

which means that there is no poem that John knows, a fare approximation of the intended meaning. It cannot be argued that it is the negation which prevents further referring to *any poem*, because *any* takes wide scope over negation. Obviously, the same mechanism prevents *poem* to bind subsequent anaphora both in the case of *every* and of *any*.

Notice that there is a third intermediate possibility of scope taking, with negation taking scope at the second level of the compositional tower:

$$\begin{array}{c} C|C \\ \hline C|C \\ \hline DP \\ John \\ [\,] \\ \hline [\,] \\ \hline \boldsymbol{j} \end{array} \left(\begin{array}{c} C|C \\ \hline C|C \\ \hline (DP\backslash C)/(DP\backslash C) \\ not \\ [\,] \\ \hline \neg[\,] \\ \hline [\,] \end{array} \left(\begin{array}{c} C|C \\ \hline C|C \\ \hline (DP\backslash C)/DP \\ know \\ [\,] \\ \hline [\,] \\ \hline \boldsymbol{know} \end{array} \left(\begin{array}{c} C|C \\ \hline C|C \\ \hline DP/N \\ any \\ \neg\exists x.[\,] \\ \hline \lambda P.\dfrac{P(x) \land \neg[\,]}{x} \end{array} \begin{array}{c} C|C \\ \hline N \\ poem \\ [\,] \\ \hline \boldsymbol{poem} \end{array} \right)\right)\right)$$

$$\begin{array}{c} \mathrm{C|C} \\ \hline \mathrm{C|C} \\ \hline \mathrm{C} \\ = \text{John not know any poem} \\ \neg\exists \mathrm{x}.[\,] \\ \hline \neg(\mathbf{poem}(\mathrm{x}) \land \neg[\,]) \\ \hline \mathbf{know}\ \mathrm{x\ j} \end{array}$$

$$\xrightarrow{\text{Lower two times}} \begin{array}{c} \mathrm{C} \\ \text{John does not know any poem} \\ \neg\exists \mathrm{x}.\neg[\mathbf{poem}(\mathrm{x}) \land \neg[\mathbf{know}\ \mathrm{x\ j}\,]] \end{array}$$

$$\begin{array}{c} \mathrm{S} \\ = \text{John does not know any poem} \\ \neg\exists \mathrm{x}.\neg\mathbf{poem}(\mathrm{x}) \lor \mathbf{know}\ \mathrm{x\ j} \end{array}$$

This interpretation is impossible in natural language. Thus, it may be said that *any* obligatory takes wide scope over negation not only with its general (first level) scope, but also with its nuclear scope.

4 Conclusions

To conclude, allowing arbitrary type shifting overgenerates interpretations impossible in natural language. In order to filter some of them out, we proposed a mechanism that forbids clause bounded lexical entries to take scope outside their minimal clause. For this natural language fragment, the mechanism and the scope precedence preference of the lexical entries (for instance, *not* > indefinites, *not* > *every*, *not* < *any*) ensures the right discourse truth conditions.

References

Barker, Chris. 2002. Continuations and the nature of quantification. *Natural Language Semantics* 10(3). 211-242.

Barker, Chris. 2004. Continuations in natural language. In Hayo Thielecke, editor, Proceedings of *the fourth ACM SIGPLAN workshop on continuations*, pages 55-64, 2004.

Barker, C and Shan Chung-chieh. 2008. Donkey anaphora is in-scope binding. In *Semantics and Pragmatics* Volume 1, pages 1-46.

Dowty, David. 2007. Compositionality as an empirical problem. In Chris Barker & Pauline Jacobson (eds.), *Direct compositionality*. Oxford University Press.

Dinu, Anca. 2011. Versatility of 'continuations' in discourse semantics. Fundamenta Informaticae (to appear).

de Groote, Philippe. 2006. Towards a montagovian account of dynamics. In *Semantics and Linguistic Theory* XVI.

Jacobson, Pauline. 1999. Towards a variable-free semantics. *Linguistics and Philosophy* 22(2). 117-185.

M. Felleisen. 1988. The theory and practice of first-class prompts. In J. Ferrante and P. Mager, editors, Proceedings of the *Fifteenth Annual ACM Symposium on Principles of Programming Languages*, pages 180-190, San Diego, California, Jan. 1988. ACM Press.

Montague, Richard. 1970. The Proper Treatment of Quantification in English. In R. Thomason (ed). *Formal Philosophy: Selected Papers of Richard Montague*,247-270. New Haven:Yale.

Partee, Barbara H. & Mats Rooth. 1983. Generalized conjunction and type ambiguity. In Rainer Buerle, Christoph Schwarze & Arnim von Stechow. (eds.), *Meaning, use, and interpretation of language*, 361-383.Walter de Gruyter and Co.

Shan, Chung-chieh and Chris Barker. 2006. Explaining crossover and superiority as left-to-right evaluation. *Linguistics and Philosophy* 29.1:91-134.

Shan, Chung-chieh. 2005. *Linguistic side effects*. Ph.D. thesis, Harvard University.

Steedman, Mark. 2000. *The syntactic process*. MIT Press.

A Support Tool for Deriving Domain Taxonomies from Wikipedia

Lili Kotlerman[*], **Zemer Avital**[§], **Ido Dagan**[*], **Amnon Lotan**[♯], **Ofer Weintraub**[§]
[*]Bar-Ilan University, [§]Orca Interactive Ltd., [♯]Tel Aviv University
*lili.dav@gmail.com, zemer.avital@orcainteractive.com, dagan@cs.biu.ac.il,
amnonlot@post.tau.ac.il, ofer.weintraub@orcainteractive.com*

Abstract

Organizing data into category hierarchies (taxonomies) is useful for content discovery, search, exploration and analysis. In industrial settings targeted taxonomies for specific domains are mostly created manually, typically by domain experts, which is time consuming and requires a high level of expertise. This paper presents an algorithm and an implemented interactive system for automatically generating target-domain taxonomies based on the Wikipedia Category Hierarchy. The system also enables human post-editing, facilitated by intelligent assistance.

1 Introduction

Hierarchies of category names (taxonomies) are very useful for effective information access (Käki (2005), Stoica et al. (2007)). When geared for a specific domain or data collection, such hierarchies can highly benefit the tasks of content discovery, search, exploration and analysis. Our project, carried out by the Natural Language Processing group at Bar-Ilan University and Orca Interactive Ltd., aimed at semi-automatic generation of a taxonomy for the domain of general video content in order to enhance search and improve recommendations in a personalized video recommendation system.

This paper delivers two main contributions: (1) a novel algorithm for automatic generation of target-domain taxonomies and (2) an interactive taxonomy editing tool, which helps human editor to post-edit and improve automatically generated taxonomies by providing her with intelligent assistance.

Automatic taxonomy generation approaches can be roughly divided into two classes: corpus-based and knowledge-based. We suggest a knowledge-based algorithm, deriving focused target-domain taxonomies from the Wikipedia Category Hierarchy (WCH). WCH covers a very wide range of topics and is assumed to embed smaller taxonomies suitable for specific domains. The algorithm is thus aimed at extracting such taxonomies from WCH.

Since automatic techniques for taxonomy creation are not accurate enough, in real-life applications some human post-editing is usually employed. Our taxonomy editing tool was designed to facilitate this process. It provides the editor with intelligent assistance, based on statistical similarity in a domain corpus along with WCH. Our initial experiments in the video domain show considerable reduction of time needed for taxonomy generation, as well as improvement of the taxonomy quality, compared to a manually created taxonomy.

In Section 2 we describe some prior art and essential background. Section 3 describes our suggested taxonomy generation algorithm, while Section 4 describes the taxonomy editing tool.

2 Background

2.1 Taxonomy Generation

Two major approaches to automatic domain taxonomy generation can be identified in the literature. The first is the corpus-based approach, in which hierarchical clustering methods are applied either directly to keyword terms extracted from a target-domain corpus for generating a keyword hierarchy, or to the documents in the corpus with further extraction of category names as keywords frequent in each cluster[1]. These methods consider distributional corpus statistics and reflect the actual trends in the data, yet the resulting hierarchies are rather noisy and category names are not easily understandable.

[1]See a summary at (Krishnapuram and Kummamuru, 2003)

The second, knowledge-based approach relies on manually constructed lexical hierarchies, such as WordNet (Fellbaum, 1998). For example, the Castanet algorithm (Stoica et al., 2007) utilizes *is-a* relations within WordNet to organize keywords into a hierarchy. Such hierarchies are more accurate than those obtained by clustering. Some related studies that compare clustering with knowledge-based category systems show that participants prefer categories (Pratt et al., 1999). The disadvantage of such hierarchies is their limited coverage.

In our work we follow the knowledge-based approach. We suggest utilizing the most comprehensive category hierarchy available, namely Wikipedia Category Hierarchy, in order to obtain relatively accurate taxonomies and avoid the disadvantage of limited coverage. In addition, we combine distributional information to better reflect the actual trends in the data, similarly to corpus-based methods.

2.2 Wikipedia Categories

The majority of Wikipedia articles, each usually describing a single topic, have been manually assigned to one or multiple categories. These categories are arranged in a hierarchy, which we refer to as Wikipedia Category Hierarchy (WCH). WCH is widely used for research, including generation of large-scale taxonomies and ontologies (de Melo and Weikum (2010), Ponzetto and Navigli (2009), Ponzetto and Strube (2007), Suchanek et al. (2007)). Yet, to the best of our knowledge, WCH was never previously used to address our task of creating focused target-domain taxonomies.

The main advantages of WCH are that it is multilingual, covers almost all conceivable topics and is constantly evolving, thus never going out of date. WCH has a single root node. Deeper-level categories have many subcategories and parent categories, while Wikipedia articles are placed at the leaves of the hierarchy. Thus, the hierarchy approximates a directed acyclic graph (DAG). In our work to obtain a strict DAG we performed a preprocessing step that removed the few cycles existing in WCH. Figure 1 presents an excerpt of WCH for ancestors of the *surfing* node.

2.3 Distributional Similarity

To derive target-domain taxonomies from WCH, our algorithm utilizes distributional similarity

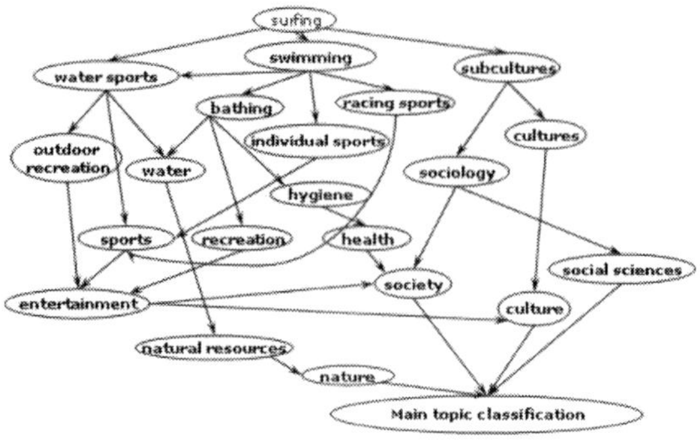

Figure 1: Paths from the *surfing* node to the root of WCH. The edges are directed from subcategories towards parent categories.

scores between category names. The distributional similarity approach assumes that terms that appear with similar context words have similar meanings.

We suggest that if similarity scores are calculated based on a corpus representing a target domain, then terms distributionally similar to a given category name c indicate the typical context or sense of c in the given domain. For example, in the recipes domain *cookie* will be similar to *biscuit*, while in texts about the Web *cookie* will be most similar to *file*.

In our work we used a directional distributional similarity measure (Kotlerman et al., 2010), which learns directional similarities between specific terms and more general ones, e.g. *koala→animal*, *wedding→marriage*. This type of similarity better corresponds to our task of building category hierarchies, in which the relations between category nodes are directional - from specific to more general ones.

3 Generating an Initial Domain Taxonomy

As explained in Section 2.2, WCH covers a very broad range of conceivable subjects and fields of interest and thus embeds various target-domain taxonomies. Accordingly, we define a target-domain taxonomy as a subtree of WCH and determine our goal as deriving such a subtree from WCH. Our preliminary analysis within the video domain showed that indeed almost all the desirable domain categories were found in WCH.

We address our goal in three stages:

1. Detect *target categories* - a subset of WCH categories relevant for the target domain.
2. Form an initial subtree by picking out for each

target category a single path to the root of WCH amongst all possible paths.

3. Prune the resulting hierarchy to retain only the most relevant categories and obtain a taxonomy of the desired size.

3.1 Detecting Target Categories

To define a relevant subset of WCH nodes we suggest using a set of keywords, including multi-word ones, representing the important concepts of the domain. Such keywords can be extracted from a corpus representing a target domain, which is a common practice for automatic taxonomy generation, or obtained from a target-domain collaborative tagging system. For our target video domain we used keywords obtained from the IMDb[2] collaborative tagging system, where users assign keywords to movie descriptions.

The keyword set is intersected with the set of WCH category names in order to obtain the list of target categories. Keywords not found in WCH are discarded. In our experiments most of the discarded keywords indeed were not valuable as category names e.g. *based on novel*, *young boy*. Others had a synonymous keyword found in WCH, e.g. *automobile accident* and *car accident*.

We note that it is worth using an exhaustive list of target categories, larger than the desired taxonomy size. Though not all of the target categories will be retained during pruning, each one will contribute when deciding on the importance of its parent category.

For each of the resulting target categories its *domain frequency* is specified, which can stand either for the number of corresponding keyword's occurrences in the target-domain documents or for the number of documents annotated with this keyword in a (manual) tagging system.

3.2 Deriving a Target Taxonomy Subtree

In Figure 2 we present the outline of our suggested algorithm, which given WCH and a set of target categories C as its input generates a target taxonomy tree T. As explained above, to generate the taxonomy tree a single path from each target category to the root of WCH should be chosen. We address this goal iteratively, by processing at each step one *current* target category c (step a) and selecting for it a single parent category p', based the on weighting heuristics we explain below (steps

[2] `http://www.imdb.com/`

Input: W - Wikipedia Category DAG C - list of target categories sorted by depth in W **Output:** T - taxonomy tree

1. Initialize T as an empty tree
2. While C not empty do:
   a. Pop a category c from the head of the list C
   b. P = all parents of c in W
   c. $p' = argmax_{p \in P}(weight(c, p))$
   d. Add edge ($c \rightarrow p'$) to the taxonomy tree T
   e. If p' not in $C \cup T$: add p' to C
3. Prune T to remove marginal categories

Figure 2: Algorithm outline.

b and c). If the selected parent category is not found in the list of target categories then it is added to the list to further proceed with the path construction (step e). We sort the input list of target categories by their depth in WCH, so that daughter categories would be processed before their parents.

Below we describe the method we suggest for selecting the most suitable parent p' for a given target category c. As can be seen from the outline, the highest-scoring parent is selected, while we suggest the weight assigned to each candidate parent p to be the product of two factors:

$$weight(c, p) = w_{self}(p) \cdot w_{daughter-parent}(c, p)$$

- *self weigh* of the parent, which does not depend on the identity of the current target category c, but rather quantifies the importance of the candidate parent to be included in the target-domain taxonomy;
- *daughter-parent weight* that allows considering preferences related to the current target category c when choosing its parent.

For calculating both of these weights we suggest a *backward and forward looking* approach, aiming to look beyond the single local edge and consider a wider perspective of categories' ancestors and descendants when choosing the parent category at each step.

Self weight. When calculating the self-weight of a candidate parent p we consider the following criteria for its importance and relevance for the target-domain taxonomy. The category should:

1. Represent a concept or topic prominent within the target domain (local-relevance).
2. Represent a general, not too narrow topic or concept (local-importance).

3. Have a relevant category of high importance amongst its ancestors (look forward).
4. Have many important and relevant categories amongst its descendants (look backward).

We reflect the first two criteria in a local self weight (lsw) of a category, which we define as follows:

$$lsw(p)=freq_{domain}(p) + \frac{freq_{W}(p)}{depth(p)},$$

where $freq_{domain}(p)$ is the domain frequency (as defined in 3.1) of category p, $freq_{W}(p)$ is the number of Wikipedia articles that belong to the category p or its subcategories in WCH, and $depth(p)$ is the length of the shortest path from p to the root of WCH. This simple heuristic promotes categories frequent in the target-domain corpus, while being general enough to cover many Wikipedia articles and be placed not too far from the hierarchy root.

To address the 3rd and 4th criteria we define the self weight of a candidate parent p as follows:

$$w_{self}(p) = lsw(p) + \frac{\sum_{a\epsilon A} lsw(a)}{|A|} + \frac{\sum_{d\epsilon D} lsw(d)}{|D|}$$

where A is the set of p's ancestors and D is the set of p's descendants in WCH.

Daughter-parent weight. By introducing a daughter-parent weight we expect to improve the selection of the most appropriate path from WCH, which leads from the current category c to the root node. We do that by considering the preferences induced by a target category when choosing its parent. We note that different candidate parents of a target category tend to represent different contexts, and sometimes "senses", for the category. For example, *Albert Einstein* falls among others under the categories *theoretical physicists*, *zionists* and *American vegetarians*.

We suggest that a target category c can assign a score to its candidate parent p by means of directional distributional similarity (see Section 2.3) $sim(c \rightarrow p)$, calculated using a corpus of the target domain. This provides implicit context selection for c in the target domain and ensures that the most relevant parent is preferred. Similarly to self weight calculation, we suggest combining direct (local) scoring by the current target category for a candidate parent with transitive (backward-forward) scoring:

$$w_{daughter-parent}(c,p) = \frac{\sum_{b\epsilon B} \sum_{f\epsilon F} sim(b \rightarrow f)}{|B| \cdot |F|}$$

where F is the "forward" set containing the candidate parent p and its ancestors in WCH and B is the "backward" set containing the current target category c and all of its descendants in the current taxonomy tree T. We use descendants from T and not from WCH because deeper categories in WCH are proceeded before higher ones and thus at each step the current target category c represents not only itself, but also the target categories (if any) that have already selected c to be their parent and whose preferences when selecting their path to the root should also be considered.

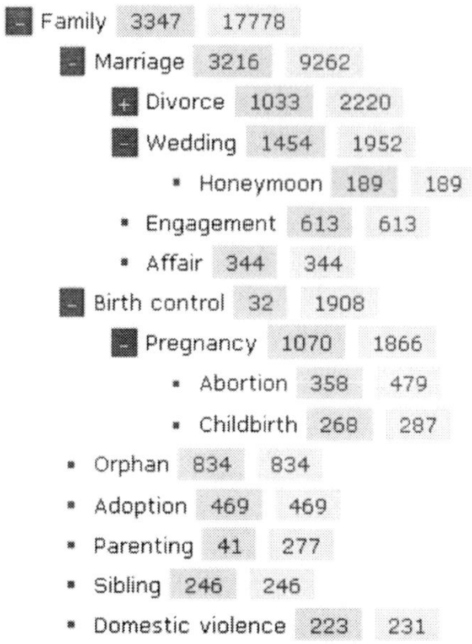

Figure 3: A screen shot of a portion of a target-domain taxonomy automatically generated by our algorithm for the movies domain, based on IMDb keywords.

3.3 Pruning

When a target subtree is extracted from WCH, we apply a pruning procedure in order to retain only the most relevant categories and obtain a taxonomy of a desired size. The size can be specified by the user as a parameter of the algorithm. We employ the following simple pruning procedure:

1. For each category calculate its *sub-tree weight* by summing its own and all its sub-categories' domain frequencies.
2. Prune categories whose sub-tree weight is lower than a threshold. Define the threshold to be depth-dependent, requiring a higher sub-tree frequency for deeper levels of the tree.

Figure 3 shows a sample from a resulting taxonomy tree generated by our algorithm for the movie domain.

4 Taxonomy Editing Tool

Automatically-generated taxonomies are usually not accurate enough and thus human inspection and post-editing is practically a necessity. In this section we describe our taxonomy post-editing tool, which aims to help the editor to correct some of the decisions made by the taxonomy generation algorithm, while making her work efficient in terms of both time and the quality of the resulting taxonomy. We note that the intelligent assistance suggested by our support tool can be applied to improve the output of any taxonomy generation algorithm.

The utility of the tool can be demonstrated thought three typical editing scenarios: (1) pruning the taxonomy from irrelevant categories, (2) enriching important categories with additional subcategories, which were not included in the initial taxonomy and (3) moving categories placed under an inappropriate parent to another place in the taxonomy. Below we provide examples for these scenarios.

The tool allows generating first an initial taxonomy of a desired size and then supports standard browsing and editing operations over it, such as creating, deleting and renaming categories. For each category the tool displays its domain frequency and sub-tree weight (cumulative frequency, Section 3.3) as in Figure 3. These statistics help the editor in deciding whether to delete a category or perhaps to enrich it with additional subcategories if the current subcategories do not suffice. They also attract the editor's attention to problematic parts in the hierarchy. For example, the category *meat* received a high sub-tree weight (614), while counting only 58 occurrences in the target-domain corpus. The editor will see that 500 out of 614 occurrences were contributed by the *rabbit* category, which should rather be a subcategory of *animals* in the video domain.

While it is relatively easy for the editor to notice that a category is placed under a wrong parent, identifying an appropriate parent category is more difficult. Similarly, it is not easy to identify which additional daughters should be added to a given category. The tool's on-demand assistance described below helps the editor in these situations by providing suggestions for alternative parent categories and suitable subcategories.

Figure 4 presents an example of the on-demand assistance offered to the editor after clicking on

Figure 4: Part of the assistance view for the *Children* category.

the *children* category. The category, along with its current path from the root, is displayed at the top, with assistance information below. We see that the *children* category was placed under the *nature→time→human development* category due to the biological "sense" of the word *children*, while in the video domain it would be more suitable to place this category under the *family* category.

The tool uses two sources for suggesting both parent categories and daughter categories - WCH and distributional similarity calculated over the target-domain corpus (Section 2.3). From Figure 4 we see that information from the two sources is complementary and each source has its pros and cons. Distributional similarity is more noisy, but allows the editor to better understand the characteristic contexts of the specified category in the target domain and adds relevant suggestions not found in WCH.

For the example in Figure 4 the editor will see that there were no alternative parent categories in WCH, which explains the system's failure in placing the *chidren* category. She might then move *chidren* under the *family* category, which is the first choice suggested by distributional similarity.

She might then want to check what interesting subcategories are suggested for *children*, which is an important category in the domain (over 1800 occurrences), but had no subcategories in the automatically generated taxonomy. She might decide to add the *orphan* category suggested by WCH, as well as *boys* and *girls* suggested by distributional similarity as subcategories of *children*. We note that the editor can add and move categories in a single click without leaving the assistance window.

4.1 Initial Evaluation of the Tool

We performed initial evaluation by performing the task of generating a small taxonomy of 100 categories for the video domain. Creating a taxonomy manually, given the initial set of keywords and their domain frequencies, took about 20 hours. Post-editing of the automatically generated taxonomy (by another person) by means of the editing tool was accomplished in about 5 hours. The editor requested an initial taxonomy about twice as large as the required one and edited it mostly by removing some of the categories. Dozens of categories were enriched with additional subcategories and some were moved under a different parent category using the tool's assistance (Figure 4). In addition, the taxonomy generated using the tool included interesting categories not present in the manually created one.

The tool documents all the editor's actions in a detailed log file to enable further analysis and evaluations, including quantifying human editing effort.

5 Conclusions and Future Work

In this paper we presented a novel algorithm and an implemented interactive system for automatic generation of target-domain taxonomies. The algorithm combines knowledge-based and corpus-based techniques by deriving a taxonomy from Wikipedia Category Hierarchy, while relying on corpus statistics and distributional similarity. The system includes a taxonomy editing tool, facilitating human post-editing by means of intelligent assistance.

Our initial evaluations showed considerable reduction of time needed to create a taxonomy using the tool comparing to manual taxonomy creation. In the future we plan to conduct elaborate user studies to evaluate the quality of the algorithm and the usefulness of the assistance provided by the tool.

Acknowledgments

This work was supported by the NEGEV project (www.negev-initiative.org). We would like to thank Sonya Liberman for her help with the WCH.

References

G. de Melo and G. Weikum. 2010. Menta: inducing multilingual taxonomies from wikipedia. In *CIKM*.

C. Fellbaum. 1998. *WordNet – An Electronic Lexical Database*. MIT Press.

M. Käki. 2005. Findex: search result categories help users when document ranking fails. In *CHI*.

L. Kotlerman, I. Dagan, I. Szpektor, and M. Zhitomirsky-Geffet. 2010. Directional distributional similarity for lexical inference. *JNLE*, 16.

R. Krishnapuram and K. Kummamuru. 2003. Automatic taxonomy generation: Issues and possibilities. In *IFSA*.

S. P. Ponzetto and R. Navigli. 2009. Large-scale taxonomy mapping for restructuring and integrating wikipedia. In *IJCAI*.

S. P. Ponzetto and M. Strube. 2007. Deriving a large-scale taxonomy from wikipedia. In *AAAI*.

W. Pratt, M. A. Hearst, and L. M. Fagan. 1999. A knowledge-based approach to organizing retrieved documents. In *AAAI/IAAI*.

E. Stoica, M. Hearst, and M. Richardson. 2007. Automating creation of hierarchical faceted metadata structures. In *NAACL/HLT*.

F. M. Suchanek, G. Kasneci, and G. Weikum. 2007. Yago: A large ontology from wikipedia and wordnet.

Barrier Features for Classification of Semantic Relations

Anita Alicante
University "Federico II", Naples, Italy
anita.alicante@unina.it

Anna Corazza
University "Federico II", Naples, Italy
corazza@na.infn.it

Abstract

Approaches based on machine learning, such as Support Vector Machines, are often used to classify semantic relations between entities. In such framework, classification accuracy strongly depends on the set of features which are used to represent the input to the classifier. We are proposing here a new type of features, namely the *barrier features*, which can be used in addition to more usual features, such as n-grams of PoS, word suffixes and prefixes, hypernyms from WordNet etc., and to the parse tree of the whole sentence. Barrier features aim at giving a compact representation of the context of each entity involved in the relation. The effectiveness of the new features is assessed on documents from the TREC data set annotated by Roth and Yih. The obtained results show not only that the performance of the proposed approach are state-of-the-art but also that such improvement is due to the introduction of the barrier features.

1 Introduction

Different approaches have been proposed for the identification of entities and relations in text. In this paper we focus only on the task of classification of semantic relations, that is of assigning to each semantic relation a label taken from a finite set, and therefore we assume that pairs of related entities are given us together with their labels. In general, not all relation labels are compatible with every pair of entity types. Table 3 reports all such constraints in the considered data set. Thus not all relation labels can be compatible with all entity pairs and therefore we decompose the problem in several binary classifications, one for each possible relation label and apply Support Vector Machines (SVMs) to each of these subtasks.

Moreover, by applying SVMs with a combination of different kernel functions we can handle together different kinds of information, both structured and not. In fact, we applied tree kernels (Moschitti, 2006) to the whole sentence parse tree and a linear kernel to a vector of binary features extracted from the words surrounding each of the involved entities. Among the latter, we introduce a novel kind of binary feature, which we call *barrier features* and experimentally prove that they improve classification performance. Although inspired by the barrier rules of the constraint grammar framework proposed in (Karlsson et al., 1995) for PoS tagging, barrier features have been completely redesigned for this task as binary values rather than rules.

The experimental assessment of the approach is performed on the newswire documents annotated by Roth and Yih (Roth and Yih, 2004). The best published results for relation classification on this data set have been obtained by the $M_{O|K}$ system, described in (Giuliano et al., 2007). The following Section 2 is devoted to the discussion of related works. Afterwards, the approach we are proposing is presented in Section 3, with a discussion of the adopted features, and in particular of barrier features. In Section 4 the experimental assessment is described. In the final section some planned development of the presented results are considered.

2 Related work

In the past few years a lot of works have been devoted to relation extraction and classification. Because of space limitation, we are giving a preference here to systems which have been assessed on the Roth and Yih data set. Systems assessed on other data sets include (Beamer et al., 2007; Davidov and Rappoport, 2008) for the Task 4 of SemEval07, (Rink and Harabagiu, 2010) for the Task08 of SemEval10 and (Kambhatla, 2004; Culotta and Sorensen, 2004; Guodong et al., 2005;

GuoDong et al., 2006; Qian et al., 2008) for the Automatic Content Extraction (ACE), which is not freely available.

Systems devoted to relation extraction and classification usually first extract and label entities and afterwards relations. An important exception to this two pass approach is represented by (Roth and Yih, 2007), where entity and relation extraction and labeling are integrated and (Kate and Mooney, 2010) where a new method for joint entity and relation extraction is presented using a "card-pyramid" graph.

Most relation labeling systems are based on some machine learning approach, and build a classifier which associates a label to a representation of the input sentence. In such approaches the representation of the input is crucial, as only the information it contains can be used for labeling. Nearly all such systems consider some form of parsing: the complete parse tree of the input sentence is considered, among the others, by (Miller et al., 2000) and (Kambhatla, 2004), which considers both constituency and dependency parse trees. Another approach based on dependency parse trees is presented in (Reichartz et al., 2009). Systems that instead of the complete parse tree only consider some form of shallow parsing include (Giuliano et al., 2007) and (Zhang et al., 2005).

We compare our performance with the $M_{O|K}$ on the Roth and Yih data set (Giuliano et al., 2007). In addition to presenting a novel approach to relation extraction and labeling, they evaluate the effect of automatic named-entity recognition on its performance. Their approach is based on shallow linguistic features, which are combined with semantic information, such as WordNet hypernym relations of the candidate entities. Kernels are employed to combine two different information sources: the global context where the two entities appear and (independently) the two local contexts of the entities. A specific kernel function is associated to each of the different types of information.

3 The proposed approach

3.1 Problem definition

In this subsection, we briefly introduce a few definitions together with some examples. A sentence of length n is a string of n tokens $S = t_1t_2 \dots t_n$ and can include a number $N \geq 0$ of entities $\{E_1, E_2, \dots, E_N\}$, each corresponding to a sequence of consecutive tokens, that is a substring of S. The entity indexes follow their order in the sentence, and each entity is labeled by an *entity-type* in a finite set E of labels. Although in the corpus we used for assessment entities are also represented by noun phrases, this definition is more general.

A subset of all ordered entity pairs corresponds to relations: $R_{i,j} = (E_i, E_j)$; E_i is called *agent* and E_j *target*, where the entities E_i and E_j can be composed by one or more tokens of the sentence and E_i can either precede or follow E_j. This definition excludes cross-sentence relations. A label taken from a finite set R of possible labels is associated to each relation. We are considering the task of associating the correct label to each relation, that is the *classification* task of *sematic relations*.

For the sake of clarity, let us consider the example sentence s_1 of Table 1. It contains four different relations containing six entities, namely (e_1, e_2) with label "work for", (e_2, e_3) with label "orgbased in", (e_4, e_5) labeled as "work for", and (e_5, e_6) for "orgbased in". Indeed, entities e_2 and e_5 are involved in two different relations.

3.2 The proposed solution

For each possible relation label we build a binary classifier based on SVMs which takes as input both a feature vector and the parse tree of the whole sentence. The former refers to the two input entities and its elements are therefore called *entity features*, while the latter refers to the whole sentence. Entity features include word and PoS unigrams, PoS bigrams and trigrams, word prefixes and suffixes, word length, and a set of word features indicating whether the initial letter is upper case, whether all letters are upper or lower case and whether the token contains a period or number or hyphen. Furthermore, we also included the most likely WordNet[1] (Fellbaum, 1998) sense tag for each token involved in the entity, which always corresponds to the first one in the list of possible senses, together with all the hypernyms.

These two sets of features are combined in the SVM-based classifier by integrating two kernels, namely tree kernels (Moschitti, 2006) and a linear kernel. The former is applied to the parse tree and evaluate the similarity between two trees in terms

[1] `http://wordnet.princeton.edu/`

s_1	Also being considered are $\langle e_1 \rangle$*Judge Ralph K. Winter* $\langle /e_1 \rangle$of the $\langle e_2 \rangle$*2nd U. S. Circuit Court of Appeals*$\langle /e_2 \rangle$ in $\langle e_3 \rangle$*New York City* $\langle /e_3 \rangle$ and $\langle e_4 \rangle$*Judge Kenneth Starr* $\langle /e_4 \rangle$ of the $\langle e_5 \rangle$*U. S. Circuit Court of Appeals*$\langle /e_5 \rangle$ for the $\langle e_6 \rangle$*District of Columbia*$\langle /e_6 \rangle$, said the source, who spoke on condition of anonymity.
s_2	The/DT spy/NN ,/, high-ranking/JJ $\langle e2 \rangle$Korean/JJ CIA/NNP$\langle /e2 \rangle$ official/JJ $\langle e1 \rangle$Sohn/NNP Ho/NNP Young/NNP$\langle /e1 \rangle$,/, wanted/VBD to/TO defect/VB ....

Table 1: *Example sentences taken from the Roth and Yih data set used for assessment.*

of the number of fragments they have in common; the latter has been chosen in the system tuning phase as described in Section 4. The same weight is associated to the two kernels.

3.2.1 Barrier features

In addition to these, we consider a novel kind of features, which we call *barrier features*, to model the context of each token in entities. Their definition is based on the set of PoS tags in a window surrounding the token. The length of the window varies and is based on the PoS's of the corresponding tokens: for each token in the entity (*trigger*), an *endpoint* token is chosen on the basis of the PoS of the trigger. In fact, for each token in the entity the corresponding endpoint is defined as the closest preceding or following token having one of the PoS associated with the PoS of the considered token. Such (trigger PoS, endpoint PoS) pairs are predefined and depend on the considered language: in the experiments we used the ones reported in Table 2.

In the task we are considering here, barrier features aim at describing the syntactic context of tokens in entities, which can only be nouns or adjectives. Therefore, we only considered patterns for this PoS, while completely disregarding other important PoS tags including verbs. On the other hand, endpoints try to bound the interesting context of the considered trigger. The choice of the pairs (trigger PoS, endpoint PoS) has been inspired by the corresponding barrier rules. We think that their favourable impact is connected to their complementarity to simpler features like bigrams and trigrams on one side and the complete parse tree on the other. We plan to explore the possibility of considering other pairs in the future.

In the experiments described in Section 4 barrier features only consider the case where the endpoint token precedes the entity. An entity token can have several endpoints and a new barrier feature corresponding to the set of PoS's between the endpoint and the token is introduced for every possible endpoint. If no endpoint is found before the entity token, the set of all the PoS tags from the beginning of the sentence to this entity are considered. As the barrier features are based on *sets* of tags, order and possible repetitions of tags are not considered.

3.3 Smoothing

A very large number of different barrier features can occur in addition to all other usual features and therefore the choice of the smoothing strategy is crucial. First of all, if the feature we observe in the input to the classifier does not exist in the set of features collected on the training set, then we consider all barrier features having the same (trigger PoS, endpoint PoS) pair and a PoS's set including the considered one. A side effect of this strategy is that more than one barrier feature can be positive (equal to 1) at the same time.

Furthermore, we introduce for every kind of feature a new feature UNKNOWN which intuitively corresponds to the unseen (rare) case. We train this feature by cumulating all cases having less than 3 occurrences. Therefore, there is an UNKNOWN feature for barriers, one for word unigrams, one for PoS unigrams, and so on. Whenever an input would not activate any value for a given type of features, the corresponding UNKNOWN feature is set.

In the sentence s_2 in Table 1 the relation corresponding to the entity pair (e_1, e_2) is labeled as *work for*. As entity e_2 is composed by two tokens ("Korean CIA") the corresponding feature vector results from the OR combination of the features corresponding to each token. If the entity were composed by only one token, the feature vector would only contain 1's in correspondence of the features computed for this token.

Thus, features based on words are extracted from the window "The/DT spy/NN ,/, high-ranking/JJ Korean/JJ CIA/NNP". Barrier features construction is based on a window whose length is not predetermined, but depends on the PoS's of the tokens preceding the one we are considering, in this case "CIA". Since "CIA" PoS is NNP, we apply the first rule reported in Table 2: the endpoint is the closest determiner preceding the token *CIA*, namely *The*. In this case the endpoint does not belong to the entity, but this is not always so. The resulting barrier feature is then given by the set {*JJ, NN, ,*}, and contains, as discussed, only one repetition of *JJ*, corresponding to the tokens *high-ranking/JJ Korean/JJ* , *spy/NN* and *,/,*.

Endpoint	Trigger
DT	NN, NNP
PRP	NNS
JJ	JJR, RBR

Table 2: *Endpoints PoS and Trigger PoS of the barrier features employed in the assessment.*

All features we consider are binary, taking values 0 if the considered pattern does not occur, 1 otherwise. The entity feature vector is constructed by merging a different feature vector for each of the tokens composing the considered entities by a logical OR: the element of the final vector takes value 1 if the corresponding features takes value 1 in at least one of the all involved vectors. More precisely, let $E_i = t_{i,1}, ..., t_{i,k_i}$ and $E_j = t_{j,1}, ..., t_{j,k_j}$ be the two entities we are considering. To obtain the feature vector corresponding to this entity pair, we merge the feature vectors of $t_{i,1}, ..., t_{i,k_i}$ and $t_{j,1}, ..., t_{j,k_j}$ corresponding to both entities. Note that this representation is independent of the order of the two considered entities.

4 Experimental evaluation

The aim of the experimental assessment is twofold: to verify whether the system employing barrier features is competitive with state of the art systems, and to evaluate the role of barrier features in the results. Performance is evaluated by computing Precision (P), Recall (R) and F_1, as usual.

4.1 Data set

For experimental assessment we used the data set used by Roth and Yih (Roth and Yih, 2004), derived from TREC corpus[2], which is freely available. It includes three types of entities, namely PER (person), LOC (location) and ORG (organization) and the five types of binary relations reported in Table 3.

Relation	Example	agent	target
work for	employ-company	PER	ORG
kill	murderer-victim	PER	PER
live in	Clinton-USA	PER	LOC
located in	Rome - Italy	LOC	LOC
orgbased in	Harvad -U.S.	ORG	LOC

Table 3: List of relations with the type of the involved entities and the number of occurrences in the Roth Yih Data set.

The Roth and Yih data set is not divided in training and test set. Therefore assessment is performed by following the 5-fold cross validation protocol, as in (Giuliano et al., 2007; Roth and Yih, 2007; Kate and Mooney, 2010).

4.2 System tuning and kernel choice

The Roth and Yih data set comes along with the correct PoS tagging and therefore we consider gold case PoS's while constructing the features, as in (Giuliano et al., 2007). Then, the syntactic parse tree is automatically associated to each input sentence by using the Stanford Parser (Klein and Manning, 2003a; Klein and Manning, 2003b)[3], by employing the grammar for English distributed together with the parser. For the sake of precision, we mention that we do not give correct PoS's in input to the parser.

The classification was performed by using the SVM package SVMLight-TK[4] (Moschitti, 2006), which is based on SVMLight (Joachims, 1999), but also includes tree kernels, offering the possibility of combining tree-structured features with vectors, which is what we need to combine the input syntactic tree with the entity feature vector. In such approach, a further kernel can be introduced in addition to the tree kernel to apply to the unstructured features. To choose this second kernel, we compared the performance of different combinations including the tree kernel alone and in conjunction with other kernels.

As the data set has not been split in training and test sets, performance has been evaluated by fol-

[2]The annotated data are freely available at `http://l2r.cs.uiuc.edu/~cogcomp/Data/ER/conll04.corp`

[3]The parser can be freely downloaded from `http://nlp.stanford.edu/software/lex-parser.shtml`.

[4]The package is available from `http://dit.unitn.it/~moschitt/Tree-Kernel.htm`.

lowing a 5-fold cross-validation protocol, including 5 iterations with a different split in training and test sets at each step. The choice of the best kernel combination has been again based on a 5-fold cross-validation protocol, applied to the training set defined at each iteration. Significantly, the linear kernel showed the best performance for all split.

4.3 System performance

Assessment considers five classifiers, one for each relation. The data set is divided in subsets corresponding to the different relations. For each relation, training has been performed by considering gold positive examples for the considered relation while negative examples are represented by all the other pairs of entities having labels compatible with the relation. In this way, the number of negative examples is much larger than for positive examples. The SVM implementation we used allows to balance the number of positive and negative examples by a cost factor. We set it to the rate between the number of negative and positive examples. Table 4 reports the comparison between the performance of our system and the results presented in (Giuliano et al., 2007) for the $M_{O|K}$ system. With the only exception of the *located in* relation, our system has an F_1 larger than $M_{O|K}$ both on single relations and on average. Although we are not able to estimate the statistical significance of such comparison because we do not have the output of that system on each sentence, we think that this consistency is quite convincing. Note however that in two cases their precision is better than ours, and in three cases their recall is better. However, the average values are always better for our system. Although we are not reporting the exact results here, we noticed that the WordNet features (hypernyms of each entity tokens) do not give any significant improvement on performance.

4.4 Barrier feature contribution

Last but not least, we tried to understand the contribution of barrier feature to the global system performance. In order to obtain a numerical estimation, we run exactly the same experiment with and without barrier features. Results are reported in Table 4 and show that their contribution to performance is always relevant and on average can be evaluated in an improvement in F_1 of nearly the 15%.

5 Conclusions and future work

In this work we proposed a new kind of features for classifying semantic relations and showed how they are indeed effective in improving classification performance. Experimental assessment on the Roth and Yih data set not only shows that they performance are state of the art, but also that their contribution is relevant.

In the future, we plan to assess the barrier features on new data sets and on different tasks, such as relation extraction and entity classification. As the number of possible barrier features is very large, we plan to invest on the search for an effective smoothing strategy, in order to limit as much as possible the effect of data sparsity.

6 Aknowledgments

We are in debt with Giorgio Satta for indicating us the potentialities of barrier rules.

References

Brandon Beamer, Suma Bhat, Brant Chee, Andrew Fister, Alla Rozovskaya, and Roxana Girju. 2007. UIUC: A Knowledge-rich Approach to Identifying Semantic Relations between Nominals. In *Proc. of SemEval07: the Fourth International Workshop on Semantic Evaluations*, pages 386–389, Prague, Czech Republic, June. Association for Computational Linguistics.

Aron Culotta and Jeffrey Sorensen. 2004. Dependency tree kernels for relation extraction. In *Proc. of ACL04: 42nd Meeting of the Association for Computational Linguistics , Main Volume*, pages 423–429, Barcelona, Spain, July.

Dmitry Davidov and Ari Rappoport. 2008. Classification of Semantic Relationships between Nominals Using Pattern Clusters. In *Proc. of ACL-08: HLT*, pages 227–235, Columbus, Ohio, June. Association for Computational Linguistics.

Christiane Fellbaum, editor. 1998. *WordNet: An Electronic Lexical Database*. MIT Press, Cambridge, MA.

Claudio Giuliano, Alberto Lavelli, and Lorenza Romano. 2007. Relation extraction and the influence of automatic named-entity recognition. *ACM Trans. Speech Lang. Process.*, 5(1):1–26.

Zhou Guodong, Su Jian, Zhang Jie, and Zhang Min. 2005. Exploring various knowledge in relation extraction. In *ACL '05: Proceedings of the 43rd Annual Meeting on Association for Computational Linguistics*, pages 427–434, Morristown, NJ, USA. Association for Computational Linguistics.

	OS No Barrier Features			OS With Barrier Features			$M_{O\|K}$		
Relation	**P**	**R**	**F1**	**P**	**R**	**F1**	**P**	**R**	**F1**
kill	70.30	71.29	70.79	92.39	**75.63**	83.17	82.80	81.00	81.89
live in	73.26	63.65	68.12	74.69	**73.39**	74.33	78.00	65.80	71.38
work for	66.22	63.12	64.63	**76.38**	86.18	80.99	76.80	80.00	78.37
located in	61.53	72.23	71.88	**70.00**	**75.40**	**72.60**	79.60	76.00	77.76
orgabased in	68.13	66.33	67.22	86.58	77.70	81.90	74.30	77.20	75.72
average	69.89	67.32	68.53	80.01	77.66	78.54	78.30	76.00	77.02

Table 4: Comparison of performance of Our System (OS) with and without barrier features and the best performing one $M_{O|K}$ on the Roth and Yih data set.

Zhou GuoDong, Su Jian, and Zhang Min. 2006. Modeling commonality among related classes in relation extraction. In *Proceedings of the 21st International Conference on Computational Linguistics and the 44th annual meeting of the Association for Computational Linguistics*, ACL-44, pages 121–128, Stroudsburg, PA, USA. Association for Computational Linguistics.

Thorsten Joachims. 1999. Making large-scale support vector machine learning practical. In *Advances in kernel methods: support vector learning*, pages 169–184. MIT Press, Cambridge, MA, USA.

Nanda Kambhatla. 2004. Combining lexical, syntactic, and semantic features with maximum entropy models for information extraction. In *Proc. of ACL04: Companion Volume to the Proceedings of 42st Annual Meeting of the Association for Computational Linguistics*, pages 178–181, Barcelona, Spain, July. Association for Computational Linguistics.

Fred Karlsson, Atro Voutilainen, Juha Heikkila, and Arto Anttila, editors. 1995. *Constraint Grammar: A Language-Independent System for Parsing Unrestricted Text.* Mouton de Gruyter.

Rohit J. Kate and Raymond J. Mooney. 2010. Joint entity and relation extraction using card-pyramid parsing. In *Proceedings of the Fourteenth Conference on Computational Natural Language Learning*, CoNLL '10, pages 203–212, Stroudsburg, PA, USA. Association for Computational Linguistics.

Dan Klein and Christopher D. Manning. 2003a. Accurate unlexicalized parsing. In *Proc. of ACL 03 of the 41st Annual Meeting on Association for Computational Linguistics*, pages 423–430, Morristown, NJ, USA. Association for Computational Linguistics.

Dan Klein and Christopher D. Manning. 2003b. Fast exact inference with a factored model for natural language parsing. In *Proc of NIPS03: In Advances in Neural Information Processing Systems*, pages 3–10. MIT Press.

Scott Miller, Heidi Fox, Lance Ramshaw, and Ralph Weischedel. 2000. A novel use of statistical parsing to extract information from text. In *Proc. of ANLP00: In 6th Applied Natural Language Processing Conference*, pages 226–233.

Alessandro Moschitti. 2006. Making tree kernels practical for natural language learning. In *EACL*.

Longhua Qian, Guodong Zhou, Fang Kong, Qiaoming Zhu, and Peide Qian. 2008. Exploiting constituent dependencies for tree kernel-based semantic relation extraction. In *Proceedings of the 22nd International Conference on Computational Linguistics - Volume 1*, COLING '08, pages 697–704, Stroudsburg, PA, USA. Association for Computational Linguistics.

Frank Reichartz, Hannes Korte, and Gerhard Paass. 2009. Dependency tree kernels for relation extraction from natural language text. In Wray Buntine, Marko Grobelnik, Dunja Mladenić, and John Shawe-Taylor, editors, *Machine Learning and Knowledge Discovery in Databases*, volume 5782, chapter 18, pages 270–285. Springer Berlin Heidelberg, Berlin, Heidelberg.

Bryan Rink and Sanda Harabagiu. 2010. Utd: Classifying semantic relations by combining lexical and semantic resources. In *Proceedings of the 5th International Workshop on Semantic Evaluation*, pages 256–259, Uppsala, Sweden, July. Association for Computational Linguistics.

D. Roth and W. Yih. 2004. A Linear Programming Formulation for Global Inference in Natural Language Tasks. In *Proc. of CoNLL-2004*, pages 1–8. Boston, MA, USA.

D. Roth and W. Yih. 2007. Global inference for entity and relation identification via a linear programming formulation. In Lise Getoor and Ben Taskar, editors, *Introduction to Statistical Relational Learning*. MIT Press.

Min Zhang, Jian Su, Danmei Wang, Guodong Zhou, and Chew Lim Tan. 2005. Discovering relations between named entities from a large raw corpus using tree similarity-based clustering. In *Proc. of IJCNLP05: International Joint Conference on Natural Language Processing*, pages 378–389.

A Reflective View on Text Similarity

Daniel Bär, Torsten Zesch, and Iryna Gurevych
Ubiquitous Knowledge Processing Lab
Computer Science Department, Technische Universität Darmstadt
Hochschulstrasse 10, D-64289 Darmstadt, Germany
www.ukp.tu-darmstadt.de

Abstract

While the concept of *similarity* is well grounded in psychology, *text similarity* is less well-defined. Thus, we analyze text similarity with respect to its definition and the datasets used for evaluation. We formalize text similarity based on the geometric model of *conceptual spaces* along three dimensions inherent to texts: *structure*, *style*, and *content*. We empirically ground these dimensions in a set of annotation studies, and categorize applications according to these dimensions. Furthermore, we analyze the characteristics of the existing evaluation datasets, and use those datasets to assess the performance of common text similarity measures.

1 Introduction

Within the natural language processing (NLP) community, similarity between texts (*text similarity*, henceforth) is utilized in a wide range of tasks, e.g. automatic essay grading (Attali and Burstein, 2006) or paraphrase recognition (Tsatsaronis et al., 2010). However, *text similarity* is often used as an umbrella term covering quite different phenomena. Therefore, we formalize text similarity and analyze the datasets used for evaluation.

We argue that the seemingly simple question "How similar are two texts?" cannot be answered independently from asking *what properties make them similar*. Goodman (1972) gives a good example regarding the baggage check at an airport: While a spectator might compare bags by shape, size, or color, the pilot only focuses on a bag's weight, and the passenger compares them by destination and ownership. Similarly, texts also have certain inherent properties (*dimensions*, henceforth) that need to be considered in any attempt to judge their similarity. Consider, for example, two novels by Leo Tolstoy[1]. A reader may readily argue that these novels are completely dissimilar due to different plots, people, or places (i.e. dissimilar *content*). On the other hand, another reader may argue that both texts are indeed highly similar because of their *stylistic* similarities. Hence, text similarity is a loose notion unless we provide a certain frame of reference. Therefore, we introduce a formalization based on *conceptual spaces* (Gärdenfors, 2000). Furthermore, we discuss the datasets used for evaluating text similarity measures. We analyze the properties of each dataset by means of annotation studies and a critical view on the performance of common similarity measures.

2 Formalization

In psychology, *similarity* is well formalized and captured in formal models such as the *set-theoretic model* (Tversky, 1977) or the *geometric model* (Widdows, 2004). In an attempt to overcome the traditionally loose definition of *text similarity*, we rely on a conceptual framework based on *conceptual spaces* (Gärdenfors, 2000). In this model, objects are represented in a number of geometric spaces. For example, potential spaces related to countries are *political affinity* and *geographical proximity*. In order to adapt this model to texts, we need to define explicit spaces (i.e. *dimensions*) suitable for texts. Therefore, we analyzed common NLP tasks with respect to the relevant dimensions of similarity, and then conducted annotation studies to ground them empirically.

Table 1 gives an overview of common NLP tasks and their relevant dimensions: *structure*, *style*, and *content*. *Structure* thereby refers to the internal developments of a given text, e.g. the order of sections. *Style* refers to grammar, usage, mechanics, and lexical complexity (Attali and Burstein, 2006). *Content* addresses all facts and

[1] A famous 19th century Russian writer of realist fiction and philosophical essays

Task	*str*	*sty*	*c*
Authorship Classification		✓	
Automatic Essay Scoring	✓	✓	✓
Information Retrieval	✓	✓	✓
Paraphrase Recognition			✓
Plagiarism Detection		✓	✓
Question Answering			✓
Short Answer Grading	✓	✓	✓
Summarization	✓		✓
Text Categorization			✓
Text Segmentation	✓		✓
Text Simplification	✓		✓
Word Sense Alignment			✓

Table 1: Classification of common NLP tasks with respect to the relevant dimensions of text similarity: *structure (str)*, *style (sty)*, and *content (c)*

their relationships within a text. For example, the task of automatic essay scoring (Attali and Burstein, 2006) typically not only requires the essay to be about a certain topic (*content* dimension), but also an adequate style and a coherent structure are necessary. However, in authorship classification (Holmes, 1998) only *style* is important.

Taking this dimension-centric view on text similarity also opens up new perspectives. For example, standard information retrieval usually considers only the *content* dimension (keyword overlap between query and document). However, a scholar in digital humanities might be interested in texts that are similar to a reference document with respect to style and structure, while texts with similar content are of minor interest. In this paper, we only address dimensions inherent to texts, and do not consider dimensions such as user intentions.

2.1 Empirical Grounding

In order to empirically ground the proposed dimensions of text similarity, we conducted a number of exemplary annotation studies. The results show that annotators indeed distinguish between different dimensions of text similarity.

Content vs. Structure In this study, we used the dataset by Lee et al. (2005) that contains pairwise human similarity judgments for 1,225 text pairs. We selected a subset of 50 pairs with a uniform distribution of judgments across the whole similarity range. We then asked three annotators: "How similar are the given texts?" We then computed the Spearman correlation of each annotator's ratings with the gold standard: $\rho_{A_1} = 0.83$, $\rho_{A_2} = 0.65$, and $\rho_{A_3} = 0.85$. The much lower correlation of the annotator A_2 indicates that a different dimension might have been used to judge similarity.

To further investigate this issue, we asked the annotators about the reasons for their judgments. A_1 and A_3 consistently focused only on the content of the texts and completely disregarded other dimensions. A_2, however, was also taking structural similarities into account, e.g. two texts were rated highly similar because of the way they are organized: First, an introduction to the topic is given, then a quotation is stated, then the text concludes with a certain reaction of the acting subject.

Content vs. Style The annotators in the previous study only identified the dimensions *content* and *structure*. *Style* was not addressed, as the text pairs were all of similar style, and hence that dimension was not perceived as salient. Thus, we selected 10 pairs of short texts from Wikipedia (WP) and Simple Wikipedia[2] (SWP). We used the first paragraphs of WP articles and the full texts of SWP articles to obtain pairs of similar length. Pairs were formed in all combinations (WP-WP, SWP-WP, and SWP-SWP) to ensure that both similarity dimensions were salient for some pairs. For example, an article from SWP and one from WP about the same topic share the same content, but are different in style, while two articles from SWP have a similar style, but different content.

We then asked three annotators to rate each pair according to the *content* and *style* dimensions. The results show that WP-WP and SWP-SWP pairs are perceived as stylistically similar, while WP-SWP pairs are seen similar with respect to their content.

2.2 Discussion

The results demonstrate that humans indeed distinguish the major dimensions of text similarity. Also, they seem intuitively able to find an appropriate dimension of comparison for a given text collection. Smith and Heise (1992) refer to that as *perceived similarity* which "changes with changes in selective attention to specific perceptual properties." Selective attention can be modeled using dimension-specific similarity measures. The scores for all dimensions are computed in parallel, and then summed up for each text pair.[3] Thereby, we automatically obtain the discriminating dimension (see Figure 1). A, B, and C are documents of

[2] Articles written in Simple English use a limited vocabulary and easier grammar than the standard Wikipedia.

[3] The last step requires all measures to be normalized.

Dataset	Text Type / Domain	Length in Terms (⌀)	# Pairs	Rating Scale	# Judges per Pair
30 Sentence Pairs (Li et al., 2006)	Concept Definitions	5–33 (11)	30	0–4	32
50 Short Texts (Lee et al., 2005)	News (Politics)	45–126 (80)	1,225	1–5	8–12
Computer Science Assignments (Mohler and Mihalcea, 2009)	Computer Science	1–173 (18)	630	0–5	2
Microsoft Paraphrase Corpus (Dolan et al., 2004)	News	5–31 (19)	5,801	binary	2–3

Table 2: Statistics for text similarity evaluation datasets

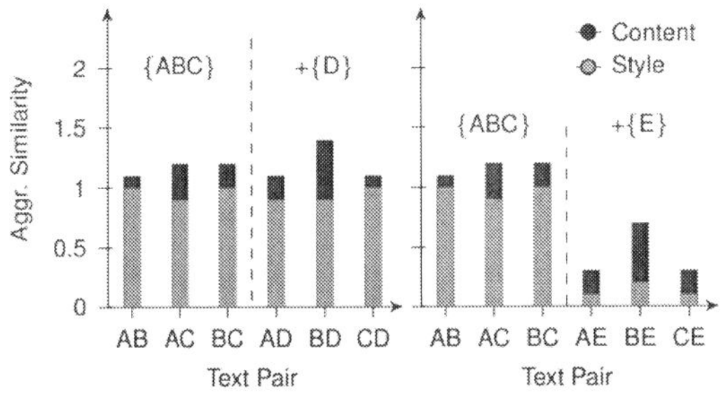

Figure 1: Combination of specialized text similarity measures to determine the salient dimension. Left: Adding document D makes *content* salient. Right: Adding document E makes *style* salient.

the same style but rather different content (as indicated by the comparable height of the stacked bars). Adding another text D of the very same style, but where the content is rather similar to B, changes the situation to what is shown in Figure 1 (left). The pair BD stands out as its aggregated score is significantly higher than that of the others. In contrast, adding document E which is written with a different style, results in the situation as shown in Figure 1 (right). Even though B and E have rather similar content, the content dimension will not become salient because of the dominance of the style dimension. Consequently, the better measures for a certain dimension are available, the better this automatic discrimination will work. Developing such dimension-specific measures, however, requires evaluation datasets which are explicitly annotated according to those dimensions. In the next section, we analyze whether the existing datasets already fulfill this requirement.

3 Evaluation Datasets

Four datasets are commonly used for evaluation (see Table 2). They contain text pairs together with human judgments about their perceived similarity. However, none of those datasets has yet undergone a thorough analysis with respect to the dimensions of text similarity encoded therein.

3.1 30 Sentence Pairs

Li et al. (2006) introduced 65 sentence pairs which are based on the noun pairs by Rubenstein and Goodenough (1965). Each noun was replaced by its definition from Collins Cobuild English Dictionary (Sinclair, 2001). The dataset contains judgments from 32 subjects on *how similar in meaning* one sentence is to another. Li et al. (2006) selected 30 pairs to reduce the bias in the frequency distribution (*30 Sentence Pairs*, henceforth).

We conducted a re-rating study to evaluate whether text similarity judgments are stable across time and subjects. We collected 10 judgments per pair asking: "How close do these sentences come to meaning the same thing?"[4] The Spearman correlation of the aggregated results with the original scores is $\rho = 0.91$. We conclude that text similarity judgments are stable across time and subjects. It also indicates that humans indeed share a common understanding on what makes texts *similar*.

In order to better understand the characteristics of this dataset, we performed another study. For each text pair we asked the annotators: "Why did people agree that these two sentences are (not) close in meaning?" We collected 10 judgments per pair in the same crowdsourcing setting as before.

To our surprise, the annotators only used lexical semantic relations between *terms* to justify the similarity relation between *texts*. For example, the text pairs about `tool/implement` and `cemetery/graveyard` were consistently said to be *synonymous*. We conclude that – in this setting – humans reduce *text* similarity to *term* similarity.

As the text pairs are originally based on term pairs, we computed the Spearman correlation between the text pair scores and the original term pair scores. The very high correlation of $\rho = 0.94$ shows that annotators indeed judged the similarity between *terms* rather than *texts*. We conclude

[4]Same question as in the original study by Li et al. (2006). We used Amazon Mechanical Turk via CrowdFlower.

Measure	r	ρ
Cosine Baseline	.81	.83
Term Pair Heuristic	.83	.84
ESA (Wikipedia)	.61	.77
ESA (Wiktionary)	.77	.82
ESA (WordNet)	.75	.80
Kennedy and Szpakowicz (2008)	.87	-
LSA (Tsatsaronis et al., 2010)	.84	.87
OMIOTIS (Tsatsaronis et al., 2010)	.86	.89
STASIS (Li et al., 2006)	.82	.81
STS (Islam and Inkpen, 2008)	.85	.84

Table 3: Results on the 30 Sentence Pairs dataset

that this dataset encodes the content dimension of similarity, but a rather constrained one.

Evaluation Results Table 3 shows the results of state of the art similarity measures obtained on this dataset. We used a cosine baseline and implemented an additional baseline which disregards the actual texts and only takes the target noun of each sentence into account. We computed their pairwise term similarity using the metric by Lin (1998) on WordNet (Fellbaum, 1998). Our heuristic achieves Pearson $r = 0.83$ and Spearman $\rho = 0.84$. The block of results in the middle shows our implementation of Explicit Semantic Analysis (ESA) (Gabrilovich and Markovitch, 2007) using different knowledge sources (Zesch et al., 2008). The bottom rows show scores previously obtained and reported in the literature. None of the measures significantly[5] outperforms the baselines. Given the limitation of encoding rather *term* than *text* similarity and the fact that the dataset is also very small (30 pairs), it is questionable whether it is a suitable evaluation dataset for *text* similarity.

3.2 50 Short Texts

The dataset by Lee et al. (2005) comprises 50 relatively short texts (45 to 126 words[6]) which contain newswire from the political domain. In analogy to the study in Section 3.1, we performed an annotation study to show whether the encoded judgments are stable across time and subjects. We asked three annotators to rate *"How similar are the given texts?"*. We used the same uniformly distributed subset as in Section 2.1. The resulting Spearman correlation between the aggregated results of the annotators and the original scores is $\rho = 0.88$. This shows that judgments are quite stable across time and subjects.

[5] $\alpha = .05$, Fisher Z-value transformation

[6] Lee et al. (2005) report the shortest document having 51 words probably due to a different tokenization strategy.

Measure	r
Cosine Baseline	.56
ESA (Wikipedia)	.46
ESA (Wiktionary)	.53
ESA (WordNet)	.59
ESA (Gabrilovich and Markovitch, 2007)	**.72**
LSA (Lee et al., 2005)	.60
WikiWalk (Yeh et al., 2009)	**.77**

Table 4: Results on the 50 Short Texts dataset. Statistically significant[7] improvements in bold.

In Section 2.1, two annotators had a content-centric view on similarity while one subject also considered structural similarity important. When combining only the two content-centric annotators, the correlation is $\rho = 0.90$, while it is much lower for the other annotator. Thus, we conclude that this dataset encodes the content dimension of text similarity.

Evaluation Results Table 4 summarizes the results obtained on this dataset. We used a cosine baseline, and our implementation of ESA applied to different knowledge sources. The results at the bottom are scores previously obtained and reported in the literature. All of them significantly outperform the baseline.[7] In contrast to the *30 Sentence Pairs*, this dataset encodes a broader view on the content dimension of similarity. It obviously contains text pairs that are similar (or dissimilar) for reasons beyond partial string overlap. Thus, the dataset might be used to intrinsically evaluate text similarity measures.

However, the distribution of similarity scores in this dataset is heavily skewed towards low scores, with 82% of all term pairs having a text similarity score between 1 and 2 on a 1–5 scale. This limits the kind of conclusions that can be drawn as the number of the pairs in the most interesting class of highly similar pairs is actually very small.

Another observation is that we were not able to reproduce the ESA score on Wikipedia reported by Gabrilovich and Markovitch (2007). We found that the difference probably relates to the cut-off value used to prune the vectors as reported by Yeh et al. (2009). By tuning the cut-off value, we could improve the score to 0.70, which comes very close to the reported score of 0.72. However, as this tun-

[7] $\alpha = .01$, Fisher Z-value transformation

Measure	r
Cosine Baseline	.44
ESA (Mohler and Mihalcea, 2009)	.47
LSA (Mohler and Mihalcea, 2009)	.43
Mohler and Mihalcea (2009)	.45

Table 5: Results on the Computer Science Assignments dataset

ing is done directly on the evaluation dataset, it probably overfits the cut-off value to the dataset.

3.3 Computer Science Assignments

The dataset by Mohler and Mihalcea (2009) was introduced for assessing the quality of short answer grading systems in the context of computer science assignments. The dataset comprises 21 questions, 21 reference answers and 630 student answers. The answers were graded by two teachers – not according to stylistic properties, but to the extent the content of the student answers matched with the content of the reference answers.

Evaluation Results We summarize the results obtained on this dataset in Table 5. The scores are reported without *relevance feedback* (Mohler and Mihalcea, 2009) which distorts results by changing the reference answers. None of the measures significantly[8] outperforms the baseline. This is not overly surprising, as the textual similarity between the reference and the student answer only constitutes part of what makes an answer the correct one. More sophisticated measures that also take lexical semantic relationships between terms into account might even worsen the results, as typically a specific answer is required, not a similar one. We conclude that similarity measures can be used to grade assignments, but it seems questionable whether this dataset is suited to draw any conclusions on the performance of similarity measures outside of this particular task.

3.4 Microsoft Paraphrase Corpus

Dolan et al. (2004) introduced a dataset of 5,801 sentence pairs taken from news sources on the Web. They collected binary judgments from 2–3 subjects whether each pair captures a paraphrase relationship or not (83% interrater agreement). The dataset has been used for evaluating text similarity measures as, by definition, paraphrases need to be similar with respect to their content.

[8] $\alpha = .05$, Fisher Z-value transformation

Measure	F-measure
Cosine Baseline	.81
Majority Baseline	.80
ESA (Wikipedia)	.80
LSA (Mihalcea et al., 2006)	.81
Mihalcea et al. (2006)	.81
OMIOTIS (Tsatsaronis et al., 2010)	.81
PMI-IR (Mihalcea et al., 2006)	.81
Ramage et al. (2009)	.80
STS (Islam and Inkpen, 2008)	.81
Finch et al. (2005)	.83
Qiu et al. (2006)	.82
Wan et al. (2006)	.83
Zhang and Patrick (2005)	.81

Table 6: Results on Microsoft Paraphrase Corpus

Evaluation Results We summarize the results obtained on this dataset in Table 6. As detecting paraphrases is a classification task, we use an additional *majority baseline* which classifies all results according to the predominant class of true paraphrases. The block of results in the middle contains measures that are not specifically tailored towards paraphrase recognition. None of them beats the cosine baseline. The results at the bottom show measures which are specifically tailored towards the detection of a bidirectional entailment relationship. None of them, however, significantly outperforms the cosine baseline. Obviously, recognizing paraphrases is a very hard task that cannot simply be tackled by computing text similarity, as sharing similar content is a necessary, but not a sufficient condition for detecting paraphrases.

3.5 Discussion

We showed that all four datasets encode the *content* dimension of text similarity. The *Computer Science Assignments* dataset and the *Microsoft Paraphrase Corpus* are tailored quite specifically to a certain task. Thereby, factors exceeding the similarity of texts are important. Consequently, none of the similarity measures significantly outperformed the cosine baseline. The evaluation of similarity measures on these datasets is hence questionable outside of the specific application scenario. The *30 Sentence Pairs* dataset was found to rather represent the similarity between *terms* than *texts*. Obviously, it is not suited for evaluating text similarity measures. However, the *50 Short Texts* dataset currently seems to be the best choice. As it is heavily skewed towards low similarity scores, though, the conclusions that can be drawn from the results are limited. Further datasets are necessary to guide the development of measures along other dimensions such as *structure* or *style*.

4 Conclusions

In this paper, we reflected on *text similarity* as a foundational technique for a wide range of tasks. We argued that while *similarity* is well grounded in psychology, *text similarity* is less well-defined. We introduced a formalization based on *conceptual spaces* for modeling text similarity along explicit dimensions inherent to texts. We empirically grounded these dimensions by annotation studies and demonstrated that humans indeed judge similarity along different dimensions. Furthermore, we discussed common evaluation datasets and showed that it is of crucial importance for text similarity measures to address the correct dimensions. Otherwise, these measures fail to outperform even simple baselines.

We propose that future studies aiming at collecting human judgments on text similarity should *explicitly* state which dimension is targeted in order to create reliable annotation data. Further evaluation datasets annotated according to the *structure* and *style* dimensions of text similarity are necessary to guide further research in this field.

Acknowledgments

This work has been supported by the Volkswagen Foundation as part of the Lichtenberg-Professorship Program under grant No. I/82806, and by the Klaus Tschira Foundation under project No. 00.133.2008. We thank György Szarvas for sharing his insights into the ESA similarity measure with us.

References

Yigal Attali and Jill Burstein. 2006. Automated essay scoring with e-rater v.2.0. *Journal of Technology, Learning, and Assessment*, 4(3).

Bill Dolan, Chris Quirk, and Chris Brockett. 2004. Unsupervised Construction of Large Paraphrase Corpora: Exploiting Massively Parallel News Sources. In *Proc. of the 20th International Conference on Computational Linguistics*.

Christiane Fellbaum. 1998. *WordNet: An Electronic Lexical Database*. MIT Press.

Andrew Finch, Young-Sook Hwang, and Eiichiro Sumita. 2005. Using machine translation evaluation techniques to determine sentence-level semantic equivalence. In *Proc. of the 3rd Intl. Workshop on Paraphrasing*, pages 17–24.

Evgeniy Gabrilovich and Shaul Markovitch. 2007. Computing Semantic Relatedness using Wikipedia-based Explicit Semantic Analysis. In *Proc. of the 20th Intl. Joint Conference on Artificial Intelligence*, pages 1606–1611.

Peter Gärdenfors. 2000. *Conceptual Spaces: The Geometry of Thought*. MIT Press.

Nelson Goodman. 1972. Seven strictures on similarity. In *Problems and projects*, pages 437–446. Bobbs-Merrill.

David I. Holmes. 1998. The Evolution of Stylometry in Humanities Scholarship. *Literary and Linguistic Computing*, 13(3):111–117.

Aminul Islam and Diana Inkpen. 2008. Semantic Text Similarity Using Corpus-Based Word Similarity and String Similarity. *ACM Transactions on Knowledge Discovery from Data*, 2(2):1–25.

Alistair Kennedy and Stan Szpakowicz. 2008. Evaluating Roget's Thesauri. In *Proceedings of the 46th Annual Meeting of the Association for Computational Linguistics: Human Language Technologies*, pages 416–424.

Michael D. Lee, Brandon Pincombe, and Matthew Welsh. 2005. An empirical evaluation of models of text document similarity. In *Proceedings of the 27th Annual Conference of the Cognitive Science Society*, pages 1254–1259.

Yuhua Li, David McLean, Zuhair Bandar, James O'Shea, and Keeley Crockett. 2006. Sentence Similarity Based on Semantic Nets and Corpus Statistics. *IEEE Transactions on Knowledge and Data Engineering*, 18(8):1138–1150.

Dekang Lin. 1998. An information-theoretic definition of similarity. In *Proceedings of International Conference on Machine Learning*, pages 296–304.

Rada Mihalcea, Courtney Corley, and Carlo Strapparava. 2006. Corpus-based and Knowledge-based Measures of Text Semantic Similarity. In *Proceedings of the 21st National Conference on Artificial Intelligence*.

Michael Mohler and Rada Mihalcea. 2009. Text-to-text Semantic Similarity for Automatic Short Answer Grading. In *Proc. of the Europ. Chapter of the ACL*, pages 567–575.

Long Qiu, Min-Yen Kan, and Tat-Seng Chua. 2006. Paraphrase Recognition via Dissimilarity Significance Classification. In *Proceedings of the Conference on Empirical Methods in Natural Language Processing*, pages 18–26.

Daniel Ramage, Anna N. Rafferty, and Christopher D. Manning. 2009. Random Walks for Text Semantic Similarity. In *Proceedings of the Workshop on Graph-based Methods for Natural Language Processing*, pages 23–31.

Herbert Rubenstein and John B. Goodenough. 1965. Contextual correlates of synonymy. *Communications of the ACM*, 8(10):627–633.

John Sinclair, editor. 2001. *Collins COBUILD Advanced Learner's English Dictionary*. HarperCollins, 3rd edition.

Linda B. Smith and Diana Heise. 1992. Perceptual similarity and conceptual structure. In B. Burns, editor, *Percepts, Concepts, and Categories*. Elsevier.

George Tsatsaronis, Iraklis Varlamis, and Michalis Vazirgiannis. 2010. Text relatedness based on a word thesaurus. *Journal of Artificial Intell. Research*, 37:1–39.

Amos Tversky. 1977. Features of similarity. In *Psychological Review*, volume 84, pages 327–352.

Stephen Wan, Dras Mark, Robert Dale, and Cécile Paris. 2006. Using dependency-based features to take the "parafarce" out of paraphrase. In *Proc. of the Australasian Language Technology Workshop*, pages 131–138.

Dominic Widdows. 2004. *Geometry and Meaning*. Center for the Study of Language and Information.

Eric Yeh, Daniel Ramage, Christopher D. Manning, Eneko Agirre, and Aitor Soroa. 2009. WikiWalk: Random walks on Wikipedia for Semantic Relatedness. In *Proceedings of the Workshop on Graph-based Methods for Natural Language Processing*, pages 41–49.

Torsten Zesch, Christof Müller, and Iryna Gurevych. 2008. Using Wiktionary for Computing Semantic Relatedness. In *Proc. of the 23rd AAAI Conf. on AI*, pages 861–867.

Yitao Zhang and Jon Patrick. 2005. Paraphrase Identification by Text Canonicalization. In *Proc. of the Australasian Language Technology Workshop*, pages 160–166.

Evaluating the Robustness of EmotiBlog for Sentiment Analysis and Opinion Mining

Ester Boldrini, Javi Fernández, José Manuel Gómez and Patricio Martínez-Barco
GPLSI – University of Alicante
{eboldrini; javifm; jmgomez; patricio}@dlsi.ua.es

Abstract

Preliminary research demonstrated the EmotiBlog annotated corpus relevance as a Machine Learning resource to detect subjective data. In this paper we compare EmotiBlog with the JRC Quotes corpus in order to check the robustness of its annotation. We concentrate on its coarse-grained labels and carry out a deep Machine Learning experimentation also with the inclusion of lexical resources. The results obtained show a similarity with the ones obtained with the JRC Quotes corpus demonstrating the EmotiBlog validity as a resource for the SA task.

1 Introduction and Motivation

Due to the birth of the Web 2.0 and the wide employment of the new textual genres we have an exponential increase of the subjective information. We also have a recent explosion of interest in Sentiment Analysis (SA), a subtask of Natural Language Processing (NLP), in charge of identifying the opinions related to a specific target (Liu, 2006). Subjective data has a great potential; it can be exploited by business organizations or individuals, for ads placements, but also for the Opinion Retrieval/Search, etc (Liu, 2007). Our research is motivated by the lack of resources, methods and tools to effectively process subjective information. Our main purpose is to demonstrate that the *EmotiBlog* corpus can be a robust resource to overcome the challenges SA brings. For these first experiments we take into account its coarse-grained annotation; however in the future we will concentrate on the finer-grained annotation. We train our Machine Learning (ML) system with *EmotiBlog Kyoto*[1] and *EmotiBlog Phones*[2] corpora, but also with the *JRC Quotes*[3] collection. These experiments are possible since the corpora share some common annotated elements (Section 3), thus allowing a larger dataset and comparable results. Then, we train our system with some of the features of *EmotiBlog* and we also integrate 2 lexical resources to reach a wider coverage. We also employ NLP techniques (stemmer, lemmatiser, bag of words, etc.) to improve the results obtained with the supervised ML models. In previous works it has been demonstrated that *EmotiBlog* is a beneficial resource for Opinionated Question Answering (OQA) as stated Balahur et al. (2009c and 2010) or Automatic Opinionated Summarization (Balahur et al. 2009a). Thus, our first objective is to demonstrate that *EmotiBlog* is a useful resource to train ML systems for SA. The combination of training from *EmotiBlog* and *JRC Quotes* is beneficial since it provides more data for the common labelled elements. As a consequence, our second purpose is to demonstrate that a deeper text classification is crucial (Section 2). We believe there is a need for determining the emotion intensity (*high/medium/ low*) and the emotion type apart from other elements presented in Boldrini et al. (2010).

2 Related Work

The first step of SA research consists in building up lexical resources of affect, such as *WordNet Affect* (Strapparava and Valitutti, 2004), *SentiWordNet* (Esuli and Sebastiani, 2006), or *MicroWNOP* (Cerini et. al., 2007). Moreover, (Wiebe 2004) focused the idea of subjectivity around that of private states setting the benchmark for subjectivity analysis. Authors show that the discrimination between objective/subjective discourses is crucial for the SA, as part of Opinion Information Retrieval (TREC Blog tracks[4] and the TAC 2008 competitions[5]), Information

[1] The *EmotiBlog* corpus is composed by blog posts on the Kyoto Protocol, Elections in Zimbabwe and USA election, but for this research we only use the *EmotiBlog* Kyoto (about the Kyoto Protocol)

[2] it is an EmotiBlog extension with reviews of mobiles

[3] http://langtech.jrc.ec.europa.eu/JRC_Resources.html

[4] http://trec.nist.gov/data/blog.html

[5] http://www.nist.gov/tac/

Extraction (Riloff and Wiebe, 2003) and QA (Stoyanov et al., 2005) systems. Related work also includes sentiment classification using unsupervised methods (Turney, 2002), ML techniques (Pang and Lee, 2002), scoring of features (Dave, Lawrence and Pennock, 2003), using PMI, or syntactic relations and other attributes with SVM (Mullen and Collier, 2004). Research in classification at a document level included sentiment classification of reviews (Ng, Dasgupta and Arifin, 2006). Neviarouskaya (2010) classified texts using fine-grained attitude labels basing its work on the compositionality principle and an approach based on the rules elaborated for semantically distinct verb classes and Tokuhisa (2008) proposed a data-oriented method for inferring the emotion of a speaker conversing with a dialogue system from the semantic content of an utterance. Wilson et al 2009 worked on mixed results and for Ghazi et al 2010 the hierarchy was better on two datasets. Our work starts from the conclusions drawn by (Boldrini et al 2010). They showed that the different levels of annotation that *EmotiBlog* contains offers important information on the structure of subjective texts, leading to an improvement of the performance of systems trained on it.

3 Corpora

The corpus we mainly employed in this research is *EmotiBlog*[6] *Kyoto* extended with the collection of mobile phones (*EmotiBlog Phones*): the *EmotiBlog Full*. The first part is a collection of blog posts in English extracted from the web containing opinions about the Kyoto Protocol, while the second part is composed by reviews of mobiles phones extracted from Amazon[7]. *EmotiBlog* annotation model contemplates *document/sentence/ element levels of annotation* (Boldrini et al. 2010), and distinguishes *objective/subjective* discourse Boldrini et al. (2009a). For all of these elements, common attributes are annotated: *polarity*, *degree* and *emotion*. Two experienced annotators labelled this collection and previous work done by Boldrini et al, 2009a) detected a high percentage of inter-annotator agreement, thus proving a reliable tagging. We also used the *JRC* Quotes corpus[8] (1590 English quotations extracted from the news and manually annotated for the sentiment expressed towards entities mentioned inside the quotation) (Balahur et al., 2010c).

4 ML Experiments and Discussion

For demonstrating that *EmotiBlog* is a robust resource for ML, we performed a series of experiments using different approaches, corpus elements and resources.

4.1 EmotiBlog without Semantic Information

First we used *EmotiBlog Kyoto* and *Phones* and a combination of them (*EmotiBlog Full*).

	Classification	Samples	Categories
EmotiBlog Kyoto	Objectivity	557	2
	Polarity	203	2
	Degree	209	3
	Emotion	132	5
	Obj+Pol	550	3
	Obj+Pol+Deg	549	6
EmotiBlog Phones	Objectivity	418	2
	Polarity	245	2
	Degree	236	3
	Emotion	234	4
	Obj+Pol	417	3
	Obj+Pol+Deg	409	7
EmotiBlog Full	Objectivity	974	2
	Polarity	448	2
	Degree	445	3
	Emotion	366	5
	Obj+Pol	967	3
	Obj+Pol+Deg	958	7

Table 1: # of samples and categories by classification

Classifying either objectivity or polarity is simpler than degree or emotion due to the smaller number of categories these last ones contain. For the polarity evaluation we need the objectivity to have been evaluated previously (*subjective/objective* discrimination) to work with the selected subjective sentences. The same situation applies for the *degree*, since we have to determine if it refers to the *positive/negative* polarity. The consequence of this process is that the classification errors of polarity and objectivity are propagated affecting the final degree evaluation. Thus we combined the classifications to check if this approach improves the results for evaluating *polarity* and *degree*. We combined *polarity* with *objectivity* (*Obj+Pol*), with 3 resulting categories: *objective*, *positive* and *negative*. We also combined *degree+objectivity+pola-rity* with the 7 resulting categories.

[6] Available on request from authors

[7] www.amazon.com

[8] http://langtech.jrc.ec.europa.eu/JRC_Resources.html

In this first step we use the classic *bag of words* (**word**) and to reduce the dimensionality we employ *stemming* (**stem**), *lemmatization* (**lemma**) and *dimensionality reduction by term selection* (TSR) methods. For TSR, we compare two approaches, *Information Gain* (**ig**) and *Chi Square* (**x2**), since they reduce the dimensionality substantially with no loss of effectiveness (Yang and Pedersen, 1997). We have applied these techniques with a different number of selected terms for each of them (**ig50**, **ig100**, ... **ig1000**). For weighting these features we evaluate the most common methods: *binary weighting* (**binary**), *tf/idf* (**tfidf**) and *tf/idf normalized* (**tfidfn**) (Salton and Buckley, 1988). We also included as weighting technique the one use by Gómez et al. (2006) in IR tasks to evaluate its reliability in different domains (**jirs**). It is similar to *tf/idf* but it does not take into account term frequencies. We will also use its normalized version (**jirsn**). As supervised learning method we use *Support Vector Machines* (SVM) due to its good performance in text categorization (Sebastiani, 2002) and the promising results obtained in previous studies (Boldrini et al. 2009b). The best results are shown in in Table 2. Due to the high number of experiments (about 1 million) and ML adjustment parameters carried out, for space reasons we present only the best performance obtained. As baseline we employed a classifier that always chooses the most frequent class. Our best results are obtained with *lemmatisation* (high number of features) and *stemming* (with few features). Experiments with TSR obtain higher scores, without any significant difference between *x2* and *ig*. The number of features selected by TSR range s between 100 and 800, depending on the number of classes and samples of the classification (the bigger they are, the more features are needed). In addition, if we do not apply *stemmer* or *lemmatiser*, the number of features must be increased for better results. Using TSR improves the results. The *tf/idf* performs better except for the polarity, where *tf/idf normalised* works better. No significant differences were found between using the normalised version of *tf/idf*, *jirs* or *jirs normalised*. In general any feature weight technique works better than the *binary* one, giving similar results independently from the method selected. We can observe that the results obtained with *Kyoto* and *Phones* corpora separately are better than using both corpora (*Full*) to build the ML model. Moreover, the learned ML models of *Kyoto* and *Phones* corpora are more specialized. They are only appropriate for classifying opinions about their own domain, the Kyoto. As we can deduce from the experiments, objectivity and polarity classifications evaluation is less problematic due to the low number of categories of each one of them. In addition, once we have detected the objectivity, the polarity is easier to determinate although the number of samples for polarity is a 41% smaller and both have the same number of categories. The first task is more complex, because the feature space vectors in the two objectivity categories are closer and we have more ambiguity in objectivity classification than in polarity classification. Terms as '*bad*', '*good*', '*excellent*' or '*awful*' clearly determine the polarity of the sentences but it is more difficult to find this kind of terms for the objectivity. Although the combinations of categories (*Obj+Pol* and *Obj+Pol+Deg*) give lower *f-measure*, this does not mean that these approaches are not adequate. In order to obtain the score for polarity and degree in Table 2, we

	Classification	Baseline	word		lemma		stem	
		f-measure	f-measure	techniques	f-measure	techniques	f-measure	techniques
EmotiBlog Kyoto	Objectivity	0.4783	0.6440	tfidf, chi950	0.6425	tfidfn	**0.6577**	**tfidfn, chi250**
	Polarity	0.5694	0.7116	jirsn, ig400	0.6942	tfidf, ig200	**0.7197**	**tfidf, ig500**
	Degree	0.3413	0.5884	tfidf, ig900	**0.6296**	**tfidf, ig350**	0.6146	tfidfn, ig600
	Emotion	0.1480	0.4437	tfidfn, ig350	**0.4665**	**jirsn, ig650**	0.4520	jirsn, ig650
	Obj+Pol	0.4881	0.5914	jirsn, ig600	0.5899	tfidfn, ig750	**0.6064**	**jirsn, ig250**
	Obj+Pol+Deg	0.4896	0.5612	jirsn	**0.5626**	**jirsn**	0.5433	tfidf, ig700
EmotiBlog Phones	Objectivity	0.4361	0.6200	jirsn, ig900	**0.6405**	**tfidfn, chi500**	0.6368	tfidfn, ig600
	Polarity	0.7224	**0.7746**	**tfidf, ig250**	0.7719	tfidfn	0.7516	tfidfn, ig500
	Degree	0.5153	0.6156	tfidfn	**0.6174**	**jirsn, ig650**	0.6150	tfidf, ig650
	Emotion	0.7337	0.7555	jirsn, ig450	**0.7828**	**jirsn, ig150**	0.7535	tfidf, ig350
	Obj+Pol	0.3057	0.5287	tfidf, ig650	**0.5344**	**tfidfn, ig900**	0.5227	tfidf, ig850
	Obj+Pol+Deg	0.2490	0.4395	tfidf, ig700	0.4424	tfidf	**0.4557**	**tfidf, ig600**
EmotiBlog Full	Objectivity	0.3705	0.5964	jirsn, ig150	0.6080	jirsn, chi100	**0.6229**	**jirsn, ig350**
	Polarity	0.3880	0.6109	tfidfn, ig1000	**0.6196**	**tfidf, chi100**	0.6138	tfidf, chi50
	Degree	0.4310	0.5655	jirsn	0.5526	jirsn	**0.5775**	**jirsn, ig450**
	Emotion	0.3990	0.5675	jirsn, ig850	**0.5712**	**tfidfn, ig800**	0.5644	jirsn, ig800
	Obj+Pol	0.3749	0.5332	tfidf	0.5381	tfidf, ig700	**0.5431**	**tfidf**
	Obj+Pol+Deg	0.3807	0.4794	tfidf, ig700	0.4903	tfidf	**0.4923**	**jirsn**

Table 2: Experiments without semantic information

preselected only the subjective sentences for the polarity and degree evaluation, not possible in the real-world. We would need first to automatically classify the objectivity, then the polarity and the degree. This methodology drags errors in each evaluation. If we calculate the *precision* (P) instead of the *f-measure* of the best experiment for each category separately and obtain their final precision by propagating the error multiplying their precisions, the polarity measure does not seem to be so good. It is important to underline that, for the propagation of the objectivity categories, we only take into account the subjective precision and not the objective one (when we evaluate objectivity and polarity using the *Full* corpus we obtain a precision of **0.71** and **0.72** respectively). Therefore, the propagated precision would be the product of these values (0.51), which is 12% lower than evaluating *Obj+Pol* together (0.58). This is more significant if we evaluate degree separately, which gives us a precision 37% lower.

	Combination	Precision
EB Kyoto	P(Obj) · P(Pol)	0.4352
	P(Obj+Pol)	**0.6113**
	P(Obj) · P(Pol) · P(Deg)	0.2852
	P(Obj+Pol+Deg)	**0.4571**
EB Phones	P(Obj) · P(Pol)	0.5154
	P(Obj+Pol)	**0.5584**
	P(Obj) · P(Pol) · P(Deg)	0.3316
	P(Obj+Pol+Deg)	**0.4046**
EB Full	P(Obj) · P(Pol)	0.5090
	P(Obj+Pol)	**0.5771**
	P(Obj) · P(Pol) · P(Deg)	0.3097
	P(Obj+Pol+Deg)	**0.4912**

Table 3: Precisions by combination of categories

In Table 3 we show the best results with the 3 main corpora. These improvements appear in all evaluations independently from the corpus and techniques used. The combination of categories improves the final results from 8.34% to 68.39%. The more categories are combined the bigger is the improvement because in the case of separate categories, the ML process has no information about the rest of categories when is learning for only one of them. When combining several categories we are adding this valuable information to the ML process and removing an important part of the propagation error.

4.2 EmotiBlog with Semantic Information

In order to check the impact of including the semantic relation as learning feature, we group features by their semantic relations, to increase the coverage and reduce the samples' dimensionality. The challenge here is *Word Sense Disambiguation* (WSD). We suppose that choosing the wrong sense of a term would introduce noise in the evaluation and a lower performance. But if we include all term senses term in the set of features, the TSR could remove the not useful ones (this disambiguation method would be adequate). We used two lexical resources: *WordNet* (WN) and *SentiWordNet* (SWN). The first one since it contains a huge quantity of semantic relations between English terms, and the second since the use of this specific OM resource demonstrated to improve the results of OM systems (Abulaish et al. 2009). It assigns to some of the synsets of WN three sentiment scores: *positivity*, *negativity* and *objectivity*. As the synsets in SWN are only the opinionated ones, we want to test if expanding only with those ones can improve the results. In addition, we want to introduce the sentiment scores into the ML system by adding them as new attributes. For example, if we get a synset *S* with a positivity score of 0.25 and a negativity score of 0.75, we add a feature called *S* (with the score given by the weighting technique) but also two more features: *S-negative* and *S-positive* with their negative and positive scores respectively. These experiments with lexical resources have been carried out with five different configurations using: only SWN synsets (**swn**), only WN synsets (**wn**), both SWN and WN synsets (**swn+wn**), only SWN synsets including sentiment scores (**swn+scores**) and both SWN and WN synsets including also the mentioned sentiment scores (**swn+wn+scores**). In case a term is not found in any of the lexical resources, then its lemma is used. Moreover, to solve the ambiguity, two techniques have been adopted: including all its senses and let the TSR methods perform the disambiguation (mentioned **swn**, **wn**, **swn+wn**, **swn+scores** and **swn+wn+scores**), but also including only the most frequent sense for each term (**swn1**, **wn1**, **swn1+wn1**, **swn1+scores** and **swn1+wn1+scores**).

Except for a few cases, the semantic information from WN and SWN improves the final results (+7.12%). We observed that the experiments using semantic information are always in the top results. Using only WN does not perform as well as with SWN, because it only contains information about subjective features, an important thing when selecting the best features for the classification task. From Table 4 we notice that TSR is present in almost all experiments with semantic information. Thus TSR techniques are adequate approximations for removing noise from the training corpus features. Again, the weighting techniques do not seem to have a big influence in opinion classification, but *tf/idf* and *jirs* perform always better than the *binary* approach. The best results include the lexical resources (always in the top positions). In Table 4 we see that SWN is present in all the best results, and the sentiment scores in 55% of them. Moreover, SWN and its scores appear in almost all best results for *EmotiBlog Full*. This technique seems to be better for not domain-specific corpus. It is important to stress upon the fact that methods, which use *ig* and *x2* improve the majority of the results confirming our hypothesis they are adequate for disambiguation.

	Classification	f-measure	Techniques
EmotiBlog Kyoto	Objectivity	0.6647	swn+wn+scores, tfidf, chi900
	Polarity	0.7602	swn1, tfidfn, chi550
	Degree	0.6609	swn1, jirsn, ig550
	Emotion	0.4997	swn, tfidf, chi450
	Obj+Pol	0.5893	swn, tfidfn
	Obj+Pol+Deg	0.5488	swn1+wn1, tfidf
EmotiBlog Phones	Objectivity	0.6405	swn1+wn1+scores, jirsn, ig1000
	Polarity	0.8093	swn+scores, tfidfn, ig550
	Degree	0.6306	swn1+wn1, tfidfn, ig150
	Emotion	0.8133	swn+wn+scores, jirsn, ig350
	Obj+Pol	0.5447	swn+wn+scores, tfidfn, chi200
	Obj+Pol+Deg	0.4445	swn1, jirsn
EmotiBlog Full	Objectivity	0.6274	swn+wn, jirsn, chi650
	Polarity	0.6374	swn1+scores, jirsn, chi350
	Degree	0.6101	swn1+wn1+scores, tfidf, ig1000
	Emotion	0.5747	swn+wn+scores, jirsn, ig450
	Obj+Pol	0.5493	swn+wn+scores, tfidf, chi950
	Obj+Pol+Deg	0.4980	swn+wn+scores, jirsn

Table 4: Results with semantic information

4.3 Experiments with the JRC Corpus

We have applied the same ML techniques with the *JRC Quotes* corpus. We can observe in first instance that experiments adding lexical resources, either WN or SWN, obtain better score than experiments without it (Table 5). Using only WN performs better than adding SWN (because the number of objective sentences in *JRC Quotes* is greater than the number of subjective ones). That is why the information that SWN provides does not have the same impact with this corpus. The *binary* weighting technique also performs worse than the rest of techniques, which seem to be indifferent for *EmotiBlog*. The precisions combining the classifications objectivity and polarity are also better than calculating the precisions separately and propagating the errors. In general, the *f-measure* is worse than in the ones with *EmotiBlog* despite the fact that the *JRC Quotes* is bigger.

	Classification	f-measure	Techniques
Baseline	Objectivity	0.5363	-
	Polarity	0.3880	-
	Obj+Pol	0.5363	-
Word	Objectivity	0.6022	tfidfn, ig950
	Polarity	0.5163	jirsn
	Obj+Pol	0.5648	tfidfn, ig100
Lemma	Objectivity	0.6049	jirsn
	Polarity	0.5240	tdidfn, ig800
	Obj+Pol	0.5697	jirs
Stem	Objectivity	0.6066	jirsn
	Polarity	0.5236	tfidfn, ig450
	Obj+Pol	0.5672	tfidf
WN	Objectivity	**0.6088**	wn1, jirsn, ig650
	Polarity	**0.5340**	wn1, tfidfn, ig800
	Obj+Pol	**0.5769**	wn1, jirsn, ig700
SWN + WN	Objectivity	0.6054	swn1+wn1, jirsn
	Polarity	0.5258	swn+wn+scores, jirsn
	Obj+Pol	0.5726	swn1+scores, jirsn

Table 5: Experiments with JRC

The cause of this is that its annotation process instructions are: *If the annotator doubts when deciding if a sentence is objective or subjective, then he must leave it blank, and If a sentence has been left blank, then the sentence is supposed to be objective.* These rules cause several subjective sentences to be tagged as objective creating noise to our ML approaches.

	EB Kyoto	EB Phones	EB Full	JRC
Objectivity	**0.6647**	0.6405	0.6274	0.6088
Polarity	0.7602	**0.8093**	0.6374	0.5340
Obj+Pol	**0.5893**	0.5447	0.5493	0.5769

Table 6. Comparison of best results per classification/corpus.

5 Conclusions and Future Works

The corpora we employed are *EmotiBlog* and the *JRC Quotes* collection. We processed all the combinations of TSR, tokenisation and term weighting for a total of 1M experiments, showing only the most significant results. The SA is a challenging task and there is room for improvement. For target detection we will employ learning models based on sequence of words (*n-grams*, *Hidden Markov Models*, etc.) to find the topic of published opinion and making a comparative assessment of different techniques. We will also merge both corpora (*EmotiBlog* and *JRC Quotes*) and other collections to have more data for the ML models. We will take into account the totality of the *EmotiBlog* annotation to improve our ML models with this fine-grained data. We observed that experimenting with the same techniques both of the corpora obtained close or higher results demonstrating that the *EmotiBlog* is a valid resource.

References

Abulaish, M., Jahiruddin, M., Doja, N. and Ahmad, T. 2009. Feature and Opinion Mining for Customer Review Summarization. PReMI 2009, LNCS 5909, pp. 219–224, 2009. Springer-Verlag Berlin Heidelberg.

Balahur A., Lloret E., Boldrini E., Montoyo A., Palomar M., Martínez-Barco P. 2009a. Summarizing Threads in Blogs Using Opinion Polarity. In Proceedings of ETTS workshop. RANLP.

Balahur, A., Boldrini, E., Montoyo, A., Martínez-Barco, P. 2009c. Opinion and Generic Question Answering systems: a performance analysis. In Proceedings of ACL, 2009, Singapore.

Balahur, A., Boldrini, E., Montoyo, A., Martínez-Barco, P. 2010b. Opinion Question Answering: Towards a Unified Approach. In Proceedings of the ECAI conference.

Balahur, A., Boldrini, E., Montoyo, A., Martínez-Barco 2009b. P. Cross-topic Opinion Mining for Realtime Human-Computer Interaction. ICEIS 2009.

Balahur Alexandra, Ralf Steinberger, Mijail Kabadjov, Vanni Zavarella, Erik van der Goot, Matina Halkia, Bruno Pouliquen & Jenya Belyaeva (2010c). Sentiment Analysis in the News. In: Proceedings of the 7th International Conference on Language Resources and Evaluation (LREC'2010), pp. 2216-2220. Valletta, Malta, 19-21 May 2010.

Balahur, A., Boldrini, E., Montoyo, A., Martínez-Barco, P. 2010. A Unified Proposal for Factoid and Opinionated Question Answering. In Proceedings of the COLING conference.

Boldrini, E., Balahur, A., Martínez-Barco, P., Montoyo, A. 2010. EmotiBlog: a finer-grained and more precise learning of subjectivity expression models. In Proceedings of LAW IV, ACL.

Boldrini, E., Balahur, A., Martínez-Barco, P., Montoyo, A. 2009a: EmotiBlog: an Annotation Scheme for Emotion Detection and Analysis in Non-traditional Textual Genres. In Proceedings of DMIN, Las Vegas.

Cerini S., Compagnoni V., Demontis A., Formentelli M., and Gandini G. 2007. Language resources and linguistic theory: Typology, second language acquisition. English linguistics (Forthcoming), chapter Micro-WNOp: A gold standard for the evaluation of automatically compiled lexical resources for opinion mining. Franco Angeli Editore, Milano, IT.

Dave K., Lawrence S., Pennock, D. 2003. "Mining the Peanut Gallery: Opinion Extraction and Semantic Classification of Product Reviews". In Proceedings of WWW-03.

Esuli A., Sebastiani F. 2006. SentiWordNet: A Publicly Available Resource for Opinion Mining. In Proceedings of the 6th International Conference on Language Resources and Evaluation, LREC 2006, Genoa, Italy.

Gómez, J.M.; Buscaldi, Bisbal, E.; D.; Rosso P.; Sanchis E. QUASAR: The Question Answering System of the Universidad Politécnica de Valencia. In Accessing Multilingual Information Repositories. LNCS 2006. 439-448.

Liu 2006. Web Data Mining book. Chapter 11

Liu, B. (2007). Web Data Mining. Exploring Hyperlinks, Contents and Usage Data. Springer, first edition.

Mullen T., Collier N. 2004. Sentiment Analysis Using Support Vector Machines with Diverse Information Sources. In Proceedings of EMNLP.

Neviarouskaya, A., Prendinger, H. and Ishizuka, M. 2010. User study on AffectIM, an avatar-based Instant Messaging system employing rule-based affect sensing from text. Int. Journal of Human-Computer Studies 68(7):432–450.

Ng V., Dasgupta S. and Arifin S. M. 2006. Examining the Role of Linguistics Knowledge Sources in the Automatic Identification and Classification of Reviews. In the proceedings of the ACL, Sydney.

Pang B., Lee L, Vaithyanathan, S. 2002. Thumbs up? Sentiment classification using machine learning techniques. In Proceedings of EMNLP-02, the Conference on Empirical Methods in Natural Language Processing.

Salton, G. and Buckley, C. (1988). "Term Weighting Approaches in Automatic Text Retrieval." In: Information Processing and Management, 24(5).

Strapparava C. Valitutti A. 2004. WordNet-Affect: an affective extension of WordNet. In Proceedings ofthe 4th International Conference on Language Resources and Evaluation, LREC.

Turney P. 2002. Thumbs Up or Thumbs Down? Semantic Orientation Applied to Unsupervised Classification of Reviews. ACL 2002: 417-424.

Wilson, T., Wiebe, J., Hwa, R. 2006. Recognizing strong and weak opinion clauses. Computational Intelligence 22 (2): 73-99

Yang, J. and and Pedersen, O. 1997. A comparative study of feature selection in text categorization. In: ICML '97: Proceedings of the Fourteenth International Conference on Machine Learning. San Francisco, CA, USA: Morgan Kaufmann Publishers Inc., pp. 412–420.

Hybrid System for Plagiarism Detection

Javier R. Bru
University of Alicante
javier.r.bru@gmail.com

Patricio Martínez-Barco
University of Alicante
patricio@dlsi.ua.es

Rafael Muñoz
University of Alicante
rafael@dlsi.ua.es

Abstract

The Internet boom in recent years has increased the interest in the field of plagiarism detection. A lot of documents are published on the Net everyday and anyone can access and plagiarize them. Of course, checking all cases of plagiarism manually is an unfeasible task. Therefore, it is necessary to create new systems that are able to automatically detect cases of plagiarism produced. In this paper, we introduce a new hybrid system for plagiarism detection which combines the advantages of the two main plagiarism detection techniques. This system consists of two analysis phases: the first phase uses an intrinsic detection technique which dismisses much of the text, and the second phase employs an external detection technique to identify the plagiarized text sections. With this combination we achieve a detection system which obtains accurate results and is also faster thanks to the pre-filtering of the text.

1 Introduction

Plagiarism detection is a topic that has always received some interest. Authors have worried about other people stealing their intellectual property, in other words, having their work plagiarized. With the recent increase in the importance of the Internet plagiarism has become a real problem. Anyone anywhere in the world can access any document, plagiarize and publish it as their own. Each author cannot spend all his or her time watching that nobody copies his or her work, so it is very important to create systems that can automatically detect cases of plagiarism.

The research in this field is mainly divided into two branches: external plagiarism detection and intrinsic plagiarism detection. Each one has its own advantages and disadvantages. In this paper we introduce a new plagiarism detection system that combines these two detection techniques, joining their main advantages and avoiding their disadvantages. This system has a first phase that uses an intrinsic detection technique to identify text sections that are most likely to be plagiarism. This phase helps us to filter the text and discard much of it, thus the next phase must analyze less text. The second phase is based on an external detection technique, which employs text comparisons to identify plagiarized sections. This technique, although slow, is very precise for plagiarism detection. Moreover, the problem of slowness is mainly solved thanks to the filtering of text done in the previous phase.

The benefits of this combination of detection techniques are the merge of the speed of intrinsic detection and the precision of external detection. We also avoid their disadvantages. In intrinsic detection we improve precision with the second analysis phase. About external detection, which is a very slow technique, we increase speed thanks to the filtering of text in the first phase.

The remainder of this paper is organized as follows. In Section 2 we detail how the first phase of intrinsic plagiarism detection is implemented. The future implementation of the second phase of external detection is described in Section 3. In Section 4 we show the preliminary results obtained with the system developed so far. In Section 5 conclusions are presented. Finally, future work, especially external detection phase, is included in Section 6.

2 Intrinsic Detection

Intrinsic plagiarism detection technique does not require a reference collection with original documents. This technique only analyzes the suspicious document trying to find changes in the author's writing style. For that purpose, we use stylometry, which is the application of the study of linguistic style. Stylometry is based on the idea that each author has an individual writing style depending on unconscious habits. There are many stylometric features, for instance, count ing the number of punctuation marks, sentence length, or number of stopwords.

Our system employs the Averaged Word Frequency Class (Meyer zu Eissen et al, 2007) as writing style measure. A document's averaged word frequency class quantifies the style complexity and the size of the author's vocabulary. This measure has the advantage that is independent of the length and structure of text. This is suitable for our system because we take sentences as text units and these are of variable length and structure. Another salient property is it works with word frequencies, so this measure can be used with documents written in different languages.

In order to make the intrinsic analysis of the suspicious document we must first calculate the document's averaged word frequency class. To this end, we divide the document into sentences and calculate the averaged word frequency class each of them. The measure of a sentence is the average of the word frequency class of every word of the sentence. Then, there only remains to calculate the average of measures of all sentences.

The next step is to identify the plagiarized sections of the text. We calculate the averaged word frequency class of all the sentences of the document following the process described above. These measures are compared with the document's averaged word frequency class. Those sentences which have a significantly different value from the document's averaged value are considered as plagiarism.

The difference between the value of the sentences and the value of the whole document is determined by a percentage set by the user. We have defined this difference as the Percentage Deviation (PD), which determines the results obtained by the intrinsic analysis. If PD is low, much plagiarism is detected because the difference between the values is low. Many false positives are also detected and little text is discarded. However, if PD is high we detect less plagiarism but the amount of discarded text is higher.

The benefits from this analysis phase are mainly two. First, we achieve to identify the text sections most likely to be plagiarized. Those sections are confirmed in the next analysis phase. Second and more important, we discard much of the text. Only plagiarized sentences are stored, so the next phase must process less text. This is important because external detection is a very slow technique.

3 External Detection

The second analysis phase of our system uses an external plagiarism detection technique. This technique is based in a reference corpus of source documents. The suspicious document is compared with all the source documents to find identical or similar text sections. If the comparison is successful we can confirm a plagiarism in the suspicious document and the source document which has been copied from. In our system only the probably plagiarized sentences identified in the previous phase are compared with the reference corpus. This speeds up the process considerably.

Currently, we are working on this phase and only an initial part is completed about the verbatim plagiarism. This type of plagiarism is known as a copy word for word without any change on the text. To identify verbatim plagiarism we compare the plagiarized sentences obtained in the previous intrinsic phase with every sentence of every document of the reference corpus. The comparison is made word for word. If the number of equal words is greater than 90 % the suspicious sentence is considered plagiarism and the reference sentence is its source. This method has a high accuracy as long as the plagiarized sentence has not been modified from its source.

But the verbatim plagiarism is the less common case. As expected, the plagiarist does not want his or her copy to be detected, for which he uses obfuscation methods in the text. These obfuscation methods try to hide the copies changing the plagiarized text. There are different obfuscation techniques such as: (i) removing, inserting, or replacing the words of the sentence, (ii) changing the words by their synonyms, antonyms, hyponyms, or hypernyms, and (iii) changing the structure of the sentence. In short, any technique that prevents a direct comparison between the plagiarized sentence and the source sentence is an obfuscation technique.

Our next step is to continue working to detect this type of more complex plagiarisms. Among the papers that can inspire us, we emphasize two which are appropriate for us. Firstly, the application PPChecker (Nam Oh Kang et al, 2006) is interesting because it also works on sentence level and is based on plagiarism pattern checking. This application is able to find subtle changes in the words and structure of the sentences. Secondly, an algorithm which works with sentences too (White and Joy, 2004). It measures the similarity between sentences based on the number of words in common and the length of the sentences. If a certain threshold is exceeded, the sentences are considered equal, in other words, one sentence is the plagiarism of the other. This algorithm is able to detect sophisticated obfuscation like paraphrasing, reordering, or merging sentences.

Another possibility considered is not utilizing a reference corpus. The comparisons between the suspicious document and source documents can be made through the Internet. This is the method used by the application SNITCH (Niezgoda and Way, 2006). Thus, the text sections of the suspicious document are searched on the Internet. If one section is found, the section is plagiarism because someone had to copy it. This is an interesting technique because we do not have to build the reference corpus, which is a complex and long task in many cases.

Whatever the used method, the objective of this analysis phase is to confirm the plagiarism detected in the previous phase thanks to the precision of the external detection techniques. In addition, the false positives detected in the intrinsic phase are easily discarded in this phase.

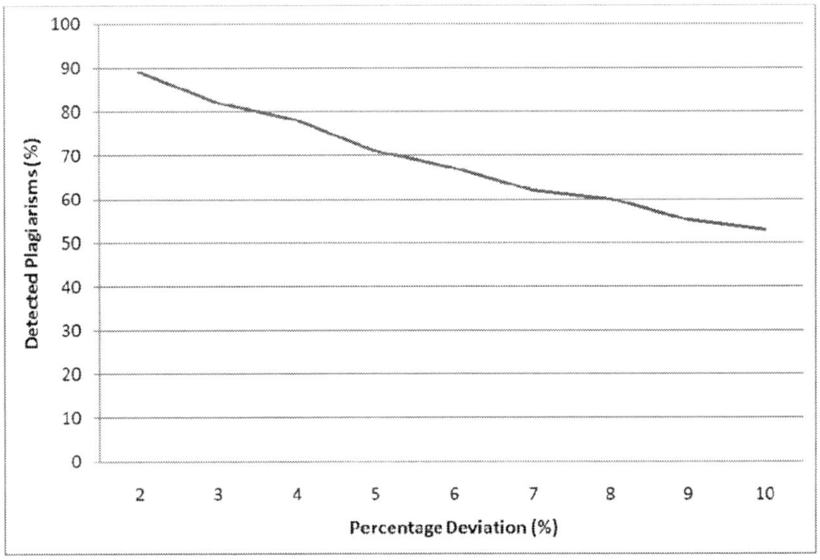

Figure 1: Detected plagiarisms depending on PD parameter value.

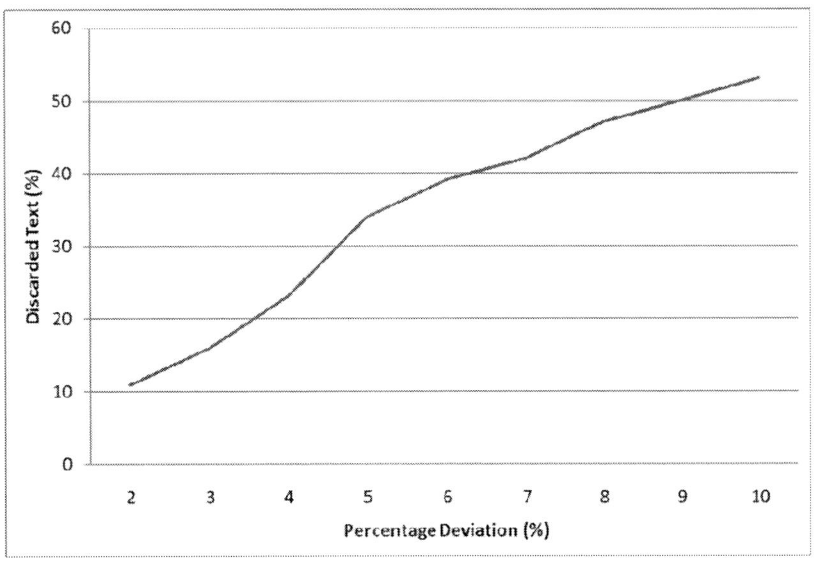

Figure 2: Amount of discarded text depending on PD parameter value.

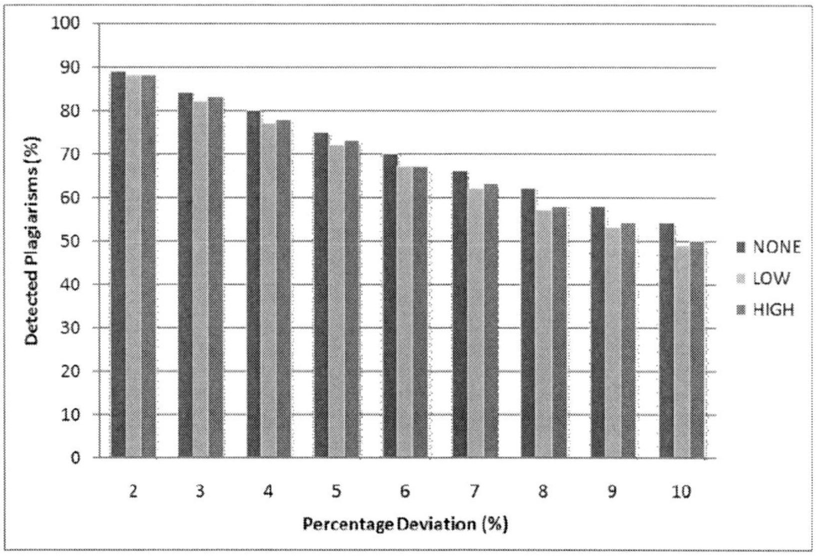

Figure 3: Detected plagiarisms according to PD parameter and corpus complexity.

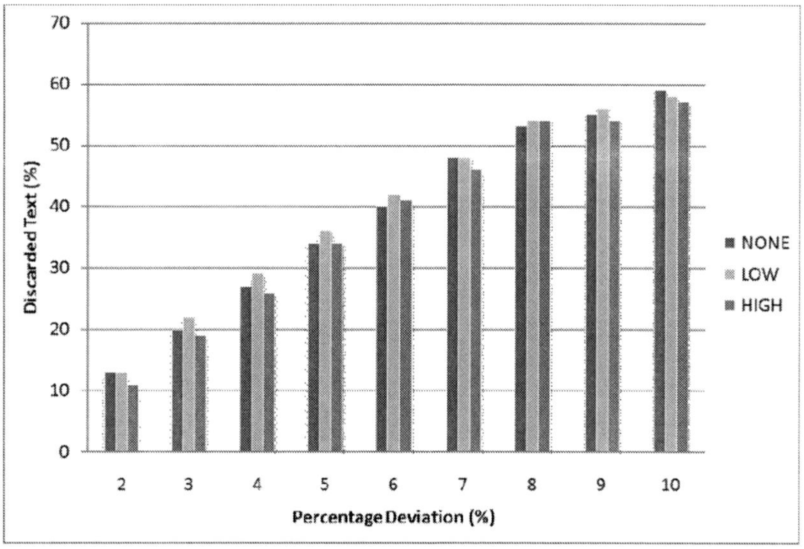

Figure 4: Discarded text according to PD parameter and corpus complexity.

4 Experiments

This section presents the preliminary tests performed with the developed system so far. The tests have been carried out with the PAN-PC-10 corpus (Potthast et al, 2010), which was created for the 4th International Workshop on Uncovering Plagiarism, Authorship, and Social Software Misuse. This is a detailed corpus which contains 64,558 artificial and 4,000 simulated plagiarism cases spread over nearly 6,000 suspicious documents. It also contains over 11,000 source documents to make comparisons. All the documents have an extension between 10 and 1,000 pages. The included plagiarisms are very varied and can be verbatim or obfuscated copies. Several obfuscation strategies have been used: (i) manual obfuscation realized by a human, (ii) random text operations, (iii) semantic word variations, and (iv) word shuffling. Therefore, this is a good corpus to do different tests to achieve exhaustive results.

For the intrinsic detection phase the system tries to find the plagiarism cases in the suspicious documents collection of the corpus without utilizing a reference collection. The Percentage Deviation (PD) parameter seen in Section 2 has been established to a 5% value.

Intrinsic Phase Results		
Sentences plagiarized	4,182,604	
Sentences detected	2,999,834	(71%)
Total text (characters)	3,495,686,760	
Discarded text (characters)	1,208,801,781	(34%)

Table 1: Results of the Intrinsic Detection Phase

As shown in Table 1, the intrinsic phase of the system is able to detect the 71% of the plagiarisms included in the suspicious collection and discards the 34% of all text (more than a third of the text). Therefore, the next phase of external detection only has to compare the 66% of text of all suspicious collection. The time taken to process more than 3GB of the suspicious collection has been 47 minutes, which shows the speed of this intrinsic technique.

As said in Section 2, varying the value of PD parameter we can change the results of the intrinsic detection phase. If PD is decreased, the difference between plagiarized sentence's value and document's averaged value is lower. This makes the plagiarism detection task more restrictive. Detection percentages regarding the PD values are shown in Figure 1. On the other hand, the PD parameter affects the amount of discarded text. Unlike before, more text is discarded when PD value is high. Values of discarded text are represented in Figure 2.

Therefore, the PD value must be low when the primary objective is to detect plagiarism as much as possible. If our priority is to discard much of the text we must assign a high PD value. It would be interesting for large corpuses when the second analysis phase should analyze the least amount of text. It is necessary to find an intermediate value for PD parameter that provides a balance between the number of detected plagiarisms and the amount of discarded text. Through various tests we have determined that the optimum value for PD is 5%.

Moreover, we have also tested how the PD parameter affects the results depending on the corpus complexity. To achieve this test we have divided the PAN corpus according to the level of plagiarism complexity included in each document. For this, we have used the own division made by its authors. The documents of the corpus are classified in three types depending on the obfuscation level: high, low or none. The tests done with these three groups are represented in Figures 3 and 4. It can be seen that percentage of detected plagiarisms is similar for each subcorpus. Only the group without obfuscation obtains slightly higher results. The discarded text is also constant for each group. With this it is shown that PD parameter influences the results but the parameter itself is not influenced by the corpus complexity. Thus, this is positive because we do not have to worry about the configuration of PD parameter in function of complexity of the corpus we work on.

Regarding the external detection phase, we have only tested the completed part so far. Tests have been carried out with verbatim plagiarism and results show that virtually 100% of plagiarism is detected. This is logical because this type of plagiarism is easily identified by direct comparisons of text. Now we are working with more complex types of plagiarism and all different obfuscation strategies.

5 Conclusions

The system which is being implemented shows promising results in the plagiarism detections field. The intrinsic detection phase has given good results in the detection of plagiarisms as well getting to discard a considerable part of the text. This benefits the next external phase and ultimately decreases the system runtime. The intrinsic phase has also been flexible and adjustable depending on our needs: more plagiarism detection or more discarded text. The number of detected plagiarisms and the amount of discarded text can change through Percentage Deviation parameter setting. The tests have proved that the system is able to detect nearly 90% of the plagiarism cases and discard more than half of the text. Because one thing is against the other finding a balance between both terms is recommended.

Moreover, we have tested that the results for a certain PD value are constant regardless of the corpus complexity. We only have to set PD parameter to obtain good results but we do not have to previously check the obfuscation level of the corpus. This simplifies the intrinsic detection task and makes the system independent of the used corpus.

The external detection phase will make the system more precise in the task of plagiarism detection thanks to the high precision of the external detection techniques. The work being done at this phase will allow the system to detect all types of obfuscation strategies and therefore more plagiarism cases will be identified.

In conclusion, our system is able to offer good results in the plagiarism detection. Moreover, the detection is done at high speed, which is very interesting due to the large number of documents to analyze nowadays.

6 Future Work

In the short term our future work is concentrated in completing the second phase of the system. The external detection phase must be able to confirm nearly 100% of the detected plagiarisms in the intrinsic phase and remove as many false positives as possible. In order to do this, the system must identify a large number of obfuscation techniques like changing the word order or the sentence structure. The more techniques are identified, the more plagiarism is detected and more types of documents can be analyzed.

Once the system has been completed, we can improve the different phases of the system. The intrinsic phase can be perfected to detect more plagiarism without harming the amount of discarded text. It would also be interesting to reduce the number of false positives obtained in this phase.

The external detection phase can also be improved to detect more types of plagiarism. For instance, we can add another algorithm to detect translated plagiarisms, in other words, plagiarisms where the source text has been written in one language and the plagiarized text has been translated into another language.

References

Sven Meyer zu Eissen, Benno Stein, and Marion Kulig. 2007. *Plagiarism detection without reference collections*. Advances in Data Analysis, Studies in Classification, Data Analysis, and Knowledge Organization, pp. 359-366.

Nam Oh Kang, Alexander Gelbukh and Sang Yong Han. 2006. *PPChecker: Plagiarism Pattern Checker in Document Copy Detection*. Text, Speech and Dialogue Proceedings, Lecture Notes in Artificial Intelligence, volume 4188, pp. 661-667.

Daniel R. White and Mike S. Joy. 2004. *Sentence-based natural language plagiarism detection*. Journal on Educational Resources in Computing, volume 4, issue 4.

Sebastian Niezgoda and Thomas P. Way. 2006. *SNITCH: a software tool for detecting cut and paste plagiarism*. ACM SIGCSE Bulletin, volume 38, issue 1, pp. 51-55.

Martin Potthast, Benno Stein, Alberto Barrón-Cedeño, Paolo Rosso. 2010. *An Evaluation Framework for Plagiarism Detection*. Proceedings of the 23rd International Conference on Computational Linguistics, COLING 2010, Beijing, China.

Data-Driven Approach Using Semantics for Recognizing and Classifying TimeML Events in Italian

Tommaso Caselli
ILC-CNR, Pisa
tommaso.caselli@ilc.cnr.it

Hector Llorens
DLSI - Universidad de Alicante
hllorens@dlsi.ua.es

Borja Navarro-Colorado
DLSI - Universidad de Alicante
borja@dlsi.ua.es

Estela Saquete
DLSI - Universidad de Alicante
stela@dlsi.ua.es

Abstract

We present a data-driven approach for recognizing and classifying TimeML events in Italian. A high-performance state-of-the-art approach, TIPSem, is adopted and extended with Italian-specific semantic features from a lexical resource. The resulting approach has been evaluated over the official TempEval2 Italian test data. The analysis of the results shows a positive impact of the semantic features both for event recognition and classification. Moreover, the presented data-driven approach has been compared with an existing rule-based prototype over the same data set. The results are directly comparable and show that the machine learning strategy better deals with the complexity of the tasks.

1 Introduction

Recognizing and classifying events is a strategic task in order to improve the performance of many NLP applications such as automatic summarization and question answering (Q.A.). In NLP, different definitions of event can be found regarding the target application. Recently, TimeML (Pustejovsky et al., 2003a) introduced a rich specification language for annotating and classifying events and it has been applied to English documents (the TimeBank corpus (Pustejovsky et al., 2003b)). The SemEval TempEval-1 and TempEval-2 international evaluation excercises (Verhagen et al., 2007; Verhagen et al., 2010), have provided the NLP community with gold standard resources for comparative evaluations of different systems. In addition to this, TempEval-2 made available TimeML annotated data in languages other than English, namely Italian, French, Spanish, Chinese and Korean. Unfortunately, there were only participants for English and Spanish.

This paper focuses on the recognition and classification of TimeML events in Italian by means of a state of the art data driven approach, TIPSem (Llorens et al., 2010), which obtained competitive results in the TempEval tasks for English and Spanish. To the best of our knowledge this is the first data-driven approach which is developed for this language and differs from state-of-the-art approches developed for English for the use of specific lexical semantic features. In particular, the Italian-specific semantic features have been obtained from a semi-automatically built *event lexicon* which has been derived from the SIMPLE/CLIPS lexicon (Ruimy et al., 2003), following the proposal in Caselli (2009). The objectives of this paper are (i) evaluating TIPSemIT over the official TempEval-2 data for Italian and assessing the impact of the semantic resource, and (ii) comparing the performance of data-driven to rule-based approaches in Italian over the same data. Section 2 reports a short background on the TimeML specifications. Section 3 describes the adaptation of TIPSem approach to Italian. Section 4 is devoted to the different evaluation experiments introduced above and, finally, section 5 focuses on conclusions and future work.

2 TimeML specifications for events

In TimeML an event is defined as something that happens or holds true. Natural language (NL) offers a variety of means to realize events, such as verbs (*andare* [to go]), complex VPs (light verb constructions, *fare una doccia* [to have a shower], or idioms), nouns (nominalizations - *volo* [flight], *costruzione* [building] - second order nominals - *assemblea* [meeting] - and type-coercions), predicative constructions (*essere ricco* [to be rich]), prepositional phrases (*a bordo* [on board]) or adjectival phrases (*dormiente* [dormant]). Two innovative aspects introduced by TimeML with respect to event recognition and classification concern (i) the extent of the text span to be annotated and (ii) the classes. As for the text span of the <EVENT> tag, TimeML implements the notion of minimal chunk, i.e. only the head of the constituent(s) realizing an event must be annotated and not the entire phrase(s). This distinction is of utmost importance, since phrases can include more than one event instance. To clarify, consider example 1, where the extent of the event phrase is in bold and the event elements are marked with the <EVENT> tag.

(1) *Marco **deve andare a casa**.* [Marco has to go home]

```
Marco <EVENT id="001"
...>deve</EVENT> <EVENT id="002"
...>andare</EVENT> a casa .
```

Events's classes are established by means of criteria that characterize their nature as irrealis, factual, possible, reported, intensional and so forth, thus departing from theoretical linguistic approaches (Vendler, 1967). In this way, seven classes have been identified, namely:

- REPORTING: the action of a person, an organization declaring something or informing about an event (e.g. say, tell...);
- PERCEPTION: events which involve the physical perception of another event (e.g. see, hear...);
- I_ACTION: events which give rise to an intensional relation with their event argument (e.g. try...);
- I_STATE: events which give rise to an intensional state with their event argument (e.g. love, want...);
- STATE: temporally bound circumstances in which something obtains (e.g. peace, be in love...);
- OCCURRENCE: events which describe thighs that happen in the world (e.g. happen, come...);
- ASPECTUAL : events which describe an aspectual predication of another event (e.g. start, finish...).

Notice that the same event item may belong to different classes according to the linguistic context in which it occurs. To clarify, consider the following examples where the event *pensare* [to think] is classified both as OCCURRENCE and I_STATE:

(2) *Marco pensa.* [Marco thinks.]

```
Marco <EVENT id="001"
class="OCCURRENCE" ...>pensa</EVENT>
```

(3) *Marco pensa di andare a casa.* [Marco thinks to go home]

```
Marco <EVENT id="001"
class="I_STATE" ...>pensa</EVENT> di
<EVENT id="002" class="OCCURRENCE"
...>andare</EVENT> a casa .
```

3 TIPSemIT: Adapting TIPSem to Italian

TIPSem is a state-of-the-art data-driven approach which uses conditional random fields (CRF) (Lafferty et al., 2001) and semantic features.

We address the problem of event detection as a sequence labeling problem, which can be also seen as a classification problem. In this bounding task, we use IOB2 labels to classify all the tokens. Given an input text, each token must be classified as being the beginning of an event, inside an event, or outside an event. The resulting IOB2 alphabet consists of B-*event*, I-*event* and O. Example 4 illustrates the event recognition problem for the sentence in example 3.

(4)

input text	problem	solution
Marco	(B-event | I-event | O)	O
pensa	(B-event | I-event | O)	B-event
di	(B-event | I-event | O)	O
andare	(B-event | I-event | O)	B-event
a	(B-event | I-event | O)	O
casa	(B-event | I-event | O)	O
.	(B-event | I-event | O)	O

The classification problem is similarly defined but restricted to those tokens which are assigned the labels B-*event* or I-*event*; e.g.:

(5)

input text	problem	solution
pensa - B-event	(TimeML Classes)	I_ACTION
andare - B-event	(TimeML Classes)	OCCURRENCE

One of the most challenging part of our work is represented by the extent of the data set. As a matter of fact, the TempEval-2 data set for Italian is not very large, containing 27,152 tokens for training and 4,995 for test[1]. Our proposal maintains TIPSem machine learning environment and the general morphological features, but, in order to reduce the impact of data sparseness, we have integrated the learner with an additional semantic resource, a derived event lexicon from the SIMPLE/CLIPS lexicon (Ruimy et al., 2003; Caselli, 2009).

The tasks of event recognition and classification are tackled in a two-step approach. First, events are recognized and then the recognized events are classified. In recognition the features are obtained at the token level. The *morphological features* used are:

- lemma
- Treebank-like PoS obtained by a statistical tagger (Dell'Orletta, 2009);
- token (word)

In the development of the models we have combined the morphological features in contexts of different window sizes.

The *semantic features* are obtained from the event derived lexicon. This lexicon has been created from a mapping between the TimeML event classes and the SIMPLE/CLIPS entries at the ontological level and it is composed by 8,721 lemmas (1,068 for adjectives, 4,614 for nouns, 3,390 for verbs). The mapping has been realized in a semi-automatic way. The SIMPLE/CLIPS ontology is a multidimensional type system based on both hierarchical and non-hierarchical conceptual relations. The Event top node has seven subtypes (Perception, Aspectual, State, Act, Psychological Event, Change, Cause Change) which can be associated to one or more TimeML classes. Semantic information plays a primary role in the assignment of the TimeML classes. However, the semantic information is not always a necessary and sufficient condition for its classification. Other levels of linguistic information, such as the argument structure, may influence the class assignment. The mapping provides each event denoting expression with one or more default TimeML classes. The assignment of the right class is strictly dependent on the occurrence of each token in the text/discourse. The availability of this knowledge to the system

```
dimorare        STATE
dimostrare      I_ACTION-OCCURRENCE-STATE
dipanare        I_ACTION-OCCURRENCE
dipartirsi      I_ACTION-OCCURRENCE
dipendere       OCCURRENCE
dipingere       I_ACTION-OCCURRENCE
diplomarsi      I_ACTION-OCCURRENCE
diradare        I_ACTION-OCCURRENCE
diramare        I_ACTION-OCCURRENCE
dire    REPORTING-OCCURRENCE
```

Figure 1: Verb entries of the event lexicon.

should be useful for improving event classification. Its use in event recognition has been tested as well. Figure 1 illustrates a short portion of the lexicon for verb entries.

4 Evaluation

Evaluation is divided in two experiments that correspond to the objectives of this paper. The Italian TempEval-2 data contains 4,543 events in the training set and 834 in the test set. In Table 1, we report the distributions of the event tokens in the seven TimeML classes for training and test.

We set as baseline for the evaluation a previous realization of a TimeML event detector and classification system for Italian, the TimeML TULE Converter[2] (Robaldo et al., 2011). The Converter takes as input the syntactic trees of the sentences in a document built by the TULE parser (Lesmo and Lombardo, 2002). The TULE Converter implements two different sets of rules: a group for event recognition which takes into account morphological features (PoS) and dependency relations with a set of "event trigger expressions" and a group for event classification. In particular for classification, the TULE converter exploits the derived event lexicon for having access to the TimeML class(es) associated with each event lemma and then integrates this information with syntactic information.

We have developed three data driven models to capture, incrementally, the influence of the features. The basic model, TIPSemIT_basic uses only the basic morphological features, namely lemma, token and PoS without any context window combination. The other two best performing models differ from the basic one for the combination of morphological features and presence of semantic features. In particular, TIPSemIT_FPC5 has

[1]Available at http://timeml.org/site/timebank/timebank.html

[2]The reported results differ from those published in the referred paper as the TempEval test set was not used for the evaluation. At the time of writing this article a new version of the TULE Converter has been developed only for event detection (Robaldo et al., in press). New experiments and comparisons will be performed when the Converter will be finalized also for event classes.

been obtained by adding a five window size context for lemma, token and fine-grained PoS together with bigrams for lemma and PoS. Finally, TIPSemIT_FPC5Sem adds semantic features to the previous model.

Event Classes	# training set	# test set
OCCURRENCE	2,360	456
STATE	1,089	166
I_ACTION	288	58
I_STATE	502	88
REPORTING	216	47
PERCEPTION	13	1
ASPECTUAL	75	18
Total events	4,543	834

Table 1: Event classes in TempEval-2 data

4.1 Event recognition

Table 2 reports the results for event recognition obtained by the described models.

Models	P	R	F1
TULE Converter	0.84	0.74	0.79
TIPSemIT_basic	0.90	0.77	0.83
TIPSemIT_FPC5	0.89	0.81	0.85
TIPSemIT_FPC5Sem	0.91	0.83	0.87

Table 2: Event recognition - TempEval-2 data

Although we have a very reduced corpus at disposal, TIPSemIT_basic obtains a better result with respect to the baseline in terms of precision (0.90 *vs.* 0.84) while the recall is not satisfactory (only +2%). A relative low number of events is recognized and it is close to that of the baseline system (644/834 *vs.* 624/834). It is interesting to notice that this model is not able to correctly identify 12 verb token realized by past participle forms. This is due to the PoS tagger which considers absolute past participle forms as adjectives when they are not followed by specific complement phrases (e.g. "*PP_da + NP*") making their identification as events more challenging. The TULE TimeML Converter does not suffer from this kind of issues, since the tagging approach adopted is different. In particular, we have observed that all events realized by verbs were correctly annotated.

The similarity of the results with respect to the recall is not surprising. The low recall of the baseline system (TimeML TULE Converter) is due to the fact that the system is not able to identify items, words and constructions which have not been implemented in the rules. Similarly, TIPSemIT_basic suffers from data sparseness. The reduced dimensions of the training set and the features used are not sufficient enough to identify previously "unseen" event instances nor to generalize information about the linguistic contexts of occurrence. The precision obtained by TIPSemIT_basic is higher than that of the TimeML TULE Converter, showing that the data-driven approach has a lower number of false positives with respect the rule-based system (72 *vs.* 117). This difference suggests that better recognition rules are to be developed, taking into account more complex features (both morphosyntactic and semantic, i.e. word-sense disambiguation). As for TIPSemIT_FPC5, the precision is slightly lower than the previous model (0.89), but the model is well balanced (recall=0.81). The increase in recall is +7% with respect to the baseline and +4% with respect to TIPsemIT_basic. The combination of PoS appears as a good strategy for approaching WSD of events realized by PoS other than verbs, especially for nouns as previously demonstrated by (Mohammad and Pedersen, 2004) (+26 nouns; +15 adjectives; +5 prepositional phrases). This model can detect instances of events which are out of range for the TimeML TULE Converter, in particular for nouns. For instance, the noun "*fuga*" [escape/flight] in example 6 is not recognized by the TimeML TULE Converter because the rules are not able to identify the causative construction realized by the presence of the preposition "*per*" [for/due to].

(6) *[...] evacuta per una* ***fuga*** *di gas.* [evacuated due to a flight of gas.]

Finally, TIPSemIT_FPC5Sem shows the highest recall (689/834 = 83%). The use of the event lexicon appears to be useful for the recognition of event nouns (+36 tokens) and adjectives (+13 tokens). One of the main contribution of the event lexicon is the reduction of data sparseness. The dimension of the training corpus is small and in order to obtain generalizations on event readings of lexical items such as nouns and adjectives a relevant number of instances are necessary. The presence of the event lexicon overcomes this limitation.

We carried out a 10-fold cross validation experiment to check if the improvement over the

TIPSemIT basic model is significant. With the results obtained, we performed a one-tailed paired t-test which showed that the mean F1 relative error reduction (21%) is statistically significant with a confidence of 99.5% ($p = 0.005$).

4.2 Event classification

The classification approaches have been evaluated over the events recognized by the best recognition model (i.e. TIPSemIT_FPC5Sem). Table 3 shows the results obtained.

Models	Accuracy
TULE Converter	0.65
TIPSemIT_basic	0.74
TIPSemIT_FP	0.74
TIPSemIT_FPC5	0.74
TIPSemIT_FPC5Sem	0.77

Table 3: Event classification - TempEval-2 data

For event classification, the TULE Converter exploits the derived event lexicon for having access to the default TimeML class and then integrates this information with syntactic information. The Converter's accuracy is lower (-12%) than that obtained by TIPSemIT_C5Sem. The primary source of errors for the Converter is due to parsing errors which prevent the activation of the corresponding rule(s), thus decreasing the number of correctly classified events. The performance improvement of the TIPSemIT_FPC5Sem with respect to the other models is due to the contribution of the event lexicon. In particular, we register an improvement in the classification of less frequent classes in the data such as I_STATE (52% *vs.* 73%), ASPECTUAL (41% *vs.* 65%) and REPORTING (53% *vs.* 68%), with the exception of I_ACTION.

In terms of number of event tokens correctly classified, the access to the event lexicon improves the classification of 42 tokens with respect to TIPSemIT_basic and TIPSemIT_FPC5. It is worth noticing that the context windows differentiating TIPSemIT_FPC5 from TIPSemIT_basic do not contribute at all to an improvement in classification, while this feature has a positive impact on event recognition.

A detailed error analysis of the event classes shows that the access to the default class information is clearly an advantage for reducing the impact of data sparseness. For instance, the verb "RAFFORZARE" [strenghten] occurs twice in the training set, and both occurrences belong to two different classes, namely OCCURRENCE and I_STATE. In the test set, this verb appears twice, once classifed as STATE, as it is realized by a past participle form, and another as I_STATE. Both TIPSemIT_basic and TIPSemIT_FPC5 can correctly classify the STATE instance thanks to the PoS information but fail in the classification of the I_STATE one. On the contrary, TIPSemIT_FPC5Sem correctly classify both cases. The correct classification of the I_STATE instance is due to the event lexicon. A 10-fold experiment has been performed to check if the improvement over TIPSemIT basic for event classification is significant. A one-tailed paired t-test showed that the mean accuracy relative error reduction (7%) is statistically significant with a confidence of 99.5% ($p = 0.005$).

However, the event lexicon is not perfect. In particular, we have observed that the coverage of the lexicon, i.e. the number of entries, must be extended especially for nouns an adjectives.

5 Conclusions and future works

This paper focuses on the adaptation to Italian of a data-driven state of the art approach based on CRF for event recognition and classification, TIPSem. Our proposal, TIPSemIT_FPC5Sem includes an Italian-specific semantic resource and has been evaluated over the available gold-standard Italian data.

The results obtained are satisfactory and show an overall improvement of 0.08% for event recognition and 0.12% in classification accuracy with respect to the baseline, i.e. the TimeML TULE Converter. This suggests that the proposed semantic features are useful for learning both event recognition and classification models.

In event recognition, the semantic features help to improve the recall without introducing too many false positives (689 events *vs.* 624 in the baseline and 644 in TIPSemIT_basic) and with a positive impact for the most difficult cases such as eventive nouns and adjectives. The results obtained from the TIPSemIT_basic and the TIPSemIT_FPC5 models are very interesting. Apparently the combination of context windows as features provides necessary information for improving event recognition even with a relative poor set of training data.

In event classification, more complex features are required. These rely on a combination of semantic and syntactic information. In addition to this, the class variability that each event lemma may give rise to requires a relatively large set of data for training. However, the results of TIPSemIT_FPC5Sem have proved that the issue of data sparseness can be dealt with *ad hoc* lexical resources, such as the derived event lexicon, which can be obtained from existing ones with a small effort.

It is worth noticing that the TIPSemIT models have a better performance with respect to the rule-based system. For instance, TIPSemIT_basic outperforms the TimeML TULE Converter in terms of precision with a reduced number of false positives. In general, the better performance of the data-driven models both in recognition and classification is due to the limitations of a rule-based approach to model complex cases. Implementing handcrafted rules for recognizing and classifying the eventive reading of nouns, adjectives and prepositional phrases is not easy and a machine learning solution appears to better deal with the complexity of the tasks.

As future work, we are planning to run a different set of experiments with more training and test data for Italian in order to assess the value of the data-driven approach, and the contribution of the semantic resource for event processing. Also, different context-window sizes will be compared. Moreover, we propose to experiment the impact of syntactic dependencies as a feature, which may facilitate the recognition and classification of events.

References

T. Caselli. 2009. *Time, events and temporal relations: an empirical model for temporal processing of Italian texts*. Ph.D. thesis, Dept. of Linguistics, University of Pisa.

T. Caselli. 2010. It-timeml: Timeml annotation scheme for italian - version 1.3.1. Technical report, ILC-CNR, Pisa.

F. Dell'Orletta. 2009. Ensemble system for part-of-speech tagging. In *EVALITA 2009 - Proceedings of the 11th Conference of the Italian Association for Artificial Intelligence*.

J. D. Lafferty, A. McCallum, and Fernando C. N. P. 2001. Conditional random fields: Probabilistic models for segmenting and labeling sequence data. In *Proceedings of the 18th ICML*, pages 282–289. Morgan Kaufmann.

L. Lesmo and V. Lombardo. 2002. Transformed subcategorization frames in chunk parsing. In *In Proc. of the 3rd Int. Conf. on Language Resources and Evaluation (LREC 2002)*, pages 512–519, Las Palmas.

H. Llorens, E. Saquete, and B. Navarro-Colorado. 2010. TIPSem (English and Spanish): Evaluating CRFs and Semantic Roles in TempEval-2. In *Proceedings of the 5th International Workshop on Semantic Evaluation*, pages 284–291. ACL.

S. Mohammad and T. Pedersen. 2004. Combining lexical and syntactic features for supervised word sense disambiguation. In *Proceedings of the Conference on Computational Natural Language Learning*, pages 25–32.

J. Pustejovsky, J. Castao, R. Saurì, R. Ingria, R. Gaizauskas, A. Setzer, and G. Katz. 2003a. TimeML: Robust specification of event and temporal expressions in text. In *Fifth International Workshop on Computational Semantics (IWCS-5)*.

J. Pustejovsky, P. Hanks, R. Saurí, A. See, R. Gaizauskas, A. Setzer, D. Radev, B. Sundheim, D. Day, L. Ferro, and M. Lazo. 2003b. The TIMEBANK Corpus. In *Corpus Linguistics*, pages 647–656.

L. Robaldo, T. Caselli, I. Russo, and M. Grella. 2011. From italian text to timeml document via dependency parsing. In Alexander Gelbukh, editor, *Computational Linguistics and Intelligent Text Processing*, volume 6609 of *Lecture Notes in Computer Science*, pages 177–187. Springer Berlin / Heidelberg.

L. Robaldo, T. Caselli, and M. Grella. in press. Rule-based creation of timeml documents from dependency trees. In *Proceedings of the 12th Conference of the Italian Association for Artificial Intelligence*.

N. Ruimy, M. Monachini, E. Gola, N. Calzolari, M.C. Del Fiorentino, M. Ulivieri, and S. Rossi. 2003. A computational semantic lexicon of italian: *SIMPLE. Linguistica Computazionale XVIII-XIX, Pisa*, pages 821–64.

Z. Vendler, 1967. *Linguistics and philosophy*, chapter Verbs and times, pages 97–121. Cornell University Press, Ithaca, NY.

M. Verhagen, R. Gaizauskas, F. Schilder, M. Hepple, G. Katz, and J. Pustejovsky. 2007. Semeval-2007 task 15: Tempeval temporal relation identification. In *Proceedings of the Fourth International Workshop on Semantic Evaluations (SemEval-2007)*, pages 75–80, June.

M. Verhagen, R. Saurí, T. Caselli, and J. Pustejovsky. 2010. Semeval-2010 task 13: Tempeval-2. In *Proceedings of the 5th International Workshop on Semantic Evaluation*, pages 57–62, Uppsala, Sweden. ACL.

Can Alternations Be Learned? A Machine Learning Approach To Romanian Verb Conjugation

Liviu P. Dinu
Faculty of Mathematics and Computer Science
University of Bucharest
ldinu@funinf.cs.unibuc.ro

Emil Ionescu
Faculty of Letters
University of Bucharest
emilionescu@unibuc.ro

Vlad Niculae
Faculty of Mathematics and Computer Science
University of Bucharest
vlad@vene.ro

Octavia-Maria Şulea
Faculty of Foreign Languages and Literatures
University of Bucharest
mary.octavia@gmail.com

Abstract

In this paper we look at the conjugation of the Romanian verb, in particular, at its irregularities, from a machine learning point of view. Our attempt is to predict the presence or absence of any alternation in the stem (apophony), using n-gram representations of the infinitive. We combine formal labelling mechanisms with learning methods in order to build a general conjugational model.

1 Introduction

The problem that we approached in this paper deals with phonological alternations in the stem of the Romanian irregular verbs during their conjugation. What we attempted to investigate, using machine learning techniques, was whether there is reason to believe that a pattern can be identified in the conjugation of the Romanian verb and whether that pattern could be learnt through automatic means such that, given the infinitive form of a verb, its correct conjugation could be produced.

Like other Romance languages, Romanian has traditionally received a Latin-inspired classification of verbs into 4 conjugational classes (or sometimes 5, where the 4th conjugation is divided between verbs with the infinitive ending in i and î, respectively) based on the ending of their infinitival form alone (Costanzo, 2011). However, this infinitive-based classification has often been found inadequate due to the many conjugational patterns that have been found in each class and to its inability to account for the behavior of partially irregular verbs (those whose stem has a smaller number of allomorphs than the completely irregular such as "a fi") during their conjugation. There have been, thus, numerous attempts throughout the history of Romanian Linguistics to give other conjugational classifications.

Lombard (1955) combined the traditional 4 infinitive-based conjugational classes with the information related to the variation in the suffix received by 1st and 4th conjugational class verbs in the indicative first person singular form and came up with 6 classes. Other classifications based on the way Romanian verbs conjugate include (Ciompec et. al., 1985 in Costanzo, 2011), who proposed 10 conjugations, and Felix (1964) who came up with 12 conjugations by looking at the inflection of the verbs and the number of allomorphs of the stem. Moisil (1960) proposed 5 regrouped classes of verbs and introduced the method of letters with variable values, in his computer scientific effort toward a "mechanical grammar". Papastergiou et al. (2007) have developed a classification from a (second) language acquisition point of view, dividing the 1st and 4th traditional classes into 3 and respectively 5 subclasses, each with a different conjugational pattern, and offering rules for alternations in the stem.

Finally, Barbu (2007) offered a highly comprehensive classification of the verb conjugation in Romanian.This classification was based on a corpus of more than 7000 verbs, representing verbs of contemporary Romanian, and distinguished 41 conjugational classes which cover the whole corpus. The corpus has also been used in the present research.

As stated before, our focus has been on capturing rules of variation in the stem for partially irregular verbs like a aştepta (to wait), which becomes eu aştept (I wait) and el aşteaptă (he waits) in the "indicativ prezent" tense. It can be seen that the letter e in the stem changes to ea during conjugation, this rich morphology making the language seem difficult to acquire. Attempts to formalize rules from a computer scientific point of view date back to Moisil in 1960. Such (incomplete) rules can be formulated as context-sensitive grammars, since the alternations are determined by the (phonologic) context in which certain characters (phonemes) appear. This lead us to the idea of analyzing the Romanian verbs from a machine learning point of view: what can one find out by looking at n-gram representation of the infinitives?

In the following, we give a brief description of the context-sensitive grammar rules that we've developed based on a slight modification to Moisil's concept of letters with variable values, a discussion of the implementation of these rules as a parser, and the machine learning techniques applied to the infinitives of a particular class of verbs from a selected corpus.

2 Capturing Verb Alternations in Context-Sensitive Rules

For the moment we limited the discussion to verbs ending in -ta, for which Dinu and Ionescu (2011) gave two rules that, according to our findings, cover 80% of the alternations that appear.

The first rule is for the variable letter t_0 and can be described as:

$$t_0 = \begin{cases} [\text{ţ}]\text{in the context}\#\_[\text{i}]\# \\ [\text{t}]\text{in the context}\#\_[\text{e}] \vee [\text{a}] \vee [\text{ă}] \vee [\text{î}] \vee [\Phi]\# \end{cases}$$

The second rule is for the variable letter u_0 and amounts to:

$$u_0 = \begin{cases} [\text{oa}]\text{in the context}\#\_[\text{ă}] \vee [\text{e}]\# \\ [\text{o}]\text{in the context}\#\_[\text{i}] \vee [\Phi]\# \\ [\text{u}]\text{in the context}\#\_\text{stressed vowel}]\# \end{cases}$$

For example, the verb "a purta" (to wear) has the lemma pu_0rt_0. The third person singular "el poartă" (he wears) is matched by the first context for u_0 and the second context for t_0. The second person singular "tu porţi" (you wear) is matched by the second context for u_0 and by the first context for t_0.

These rules can be formulated as a context sensitive grammar $G = (V_N, V_T, \Sigma, P)$ in the following way:

$$P = \begin{cases} \Sigma \to \$\alpha T_0\#|\$\alpha U_0\beta T_0\# \\ \Sigma \to \$\alpha T_0\text{i}\#|\$\alpha U_0\beta T_0\text{i}\# \\ \Sigma \to \$\alpha T_0\text{ă}\#|\$\alpha U_0\beta T_0\text{ă}\# \\ \Sigma \to \$\alpha T_0\text{ăm}\#|\$\alpha U_0\beta T_0\text{ăm}\# \\ \Sigma \to \$\alpha T_0\text{aţi}\#|\$\alpha U_0\beta T_0\text{aţi}\# \\ T_0\# \to \#\text{t} \\ T_0\text{i}\# \to \#\text{ţi} \\ T_0\text{ă}\# \to \#\text{tă}|\&\text{tă} \\ T_0\text{ăm}\# \to \#\text{tăm}|!\text{tăm} \\ T_0\text{aţi}\# \to \#\text{taţi}|!\text{taţi} \\ x\# \to \#x, \text{for all } x \in V_T \\ x\& \to \&x, \text{for all } x \in V_T \\ x! \to !x, \text{for all } x \in V_T \\ U_0! \to \#\text{u} \\ U_0\# \to \#\text{o} \\ U_0\& \to \#\text{oa} \\ \$\# \to \lambda \end{cases}$$

V_N is the set of non-terminals, V_T is the set of terminals (the alphabet), Σ is the starting non-terminal and P is the set of production rules. For the Romanian language, $V_T = \{$a, ă, â, b, ...$\}$. α and β are arbitrary strings from V_T^*. Note that this is the reunion of the two grammars G_1 and G_2 given in (Dinu and Ionescu, 2011).

The power of this grammar does not lie in its language: some of its derivations are general enough to accept any string over the alphabet ending in the letter t, for example. However, derivations in this grammar represent a generative process that can build present indicative forms of verbs.

The way verbal forms are parsed by this grammar with regard to the arbitrary α and β is very important. Take the verb "a certa" (to scold or to quarrel). At the second person singular form, in the present indicative tense, it becomes "tu cerţi" (you scold) which is accurately modeled by the T_0 alternation. However its third person singular form "el ceartă" (he scolds) exhibits an alternation in the stem vowel "e" that is not captured by these rules. The form "ceartă" is however generated by the grammar, as:

$$\Sigma \to \$\text{cear}T_0\text{ă}\# \to \$\text{cear}\#\text{tă} \to \\ \to \$\#\text{ceartă} \to \text{ceartă}.$$

Therefore, we cannot say that the grammar models this alternation. How can we tell? Note that if we would assume that these derivations completely explain the alternations, it would mean that the verb has two allomorphs for the stem, "cert" and "ceart", yet we have no alternating "e" vowel rule to account for that variation. This leads to the natural restriction that for a verb to be considered fully modeled by the grammar we previously described, α and β need to remain the same during the derivation of all its forms. This is equivalent to saying that the variable letters should be the only alternations in the stem of a partially irregular verb.

Such grammars are hard to control methods that cannot directly solve the problem of conjugating a verb starting from its infinitive form. We used a simplification of this system to assign labels to verbs depending on how they are conjugated and what alternations they present.

3 Labeling Method

The correct derivations in the grammar presented in the previous section can be formulated as regular expressions. Furthermore, we can associate a particular regular expression for each one of the six possible forms of a verb in this tense. For example, the regular expressions for the conjugation pattern of the word "a cânta" (to sing) at the first person singular is ^(.+)t$, while for the second person singular it is ^(.+)ţi$, therefore catching the t-ţ alternation. Note that the dot accepts any letter in the Romanian alphabet. The restriction is that, for each of the six forms, the value of the capturing groups (the characters captured by the bracketed part of the expressions) remains constant. These groups correspond to all parts of the stem that remain unchanged and ensure that, given the infinitive and the regular expressions, one can produce a correct conjugation. When the stem has no alternation, the expression will contain only one such capturing group that represents the whole stem.

We will use the term "rule" to refer to a set of six regular expressions describing the conjugation of a verb. We started incrementally adding rules to cover more of the verbs in the dataset, and arrived at a total of 14 rules. We dropped the rules that only covered one or two verbs, and eliminated these verbs from the dataset. We ended up with seven rules covering 616 of the 628 verbs ending in -ta (98.1%).

An example of one such rule, covering the verb "a tresălta", is:

Person	Regexp	Example
1st singular	^(.+)a(.+)t$	tresalt
2nd singular	^(.+)a(.+)ţi$	tresalţi
3rd singular	^(.+)a(.+)tă$	tresaltă
1st plural	^(.+)ă(.+)tăm$	tresăltăm
2nd plural	^(.+)ă(.+)taţi$	tresăltaţi
3rd plural	^(.+)a(.+)tă$	tresaltă

It can be observed that the forms of the verb are consistently accepted by the regular expressions of the rule, with the two groups in brackets always having the values "tres" and "l". This rule is the 5th in our line of 7 rules. Below are listed all 7 of them:

- the 1st rule accepts verbs like "a ajuta" (to help), which has an alternation in the stem of the sort t→ţ due to palatalization (determined by the 2nd person singular suffix "i")
- the 2nd rule accepts verbs like "a exista" (to exist), which has an alternation in the stem of the type s→ş, due to palatalization as well
- the 3rd rule accepts verbs like "a deştepta" (to awake/arouse), whose stem has an alternation of the type a→ea
- the 4th rule accepts verbs like "a deşerta" (to empty), with a stem alternation of the type e→a
- the 5th rule accepts verbs like "a tresălta" (to start, to take fright), with a stem alternation of the kind ă→a
- the 6th rule accepts verbs like "a desfăta" (to delight), with a stem alternation of the type ă→a in the 3rd person, and ă→e in the 2nd person singular
- the 7th rule accepts verbs like "a decapita" (to decapitate), which conjugates with "ez" suffixes (-ez, -ezi, -ează, -ăm, -aţi, -ează)

These rules were run against the dataset of conjugated Romanian verbs (only those ending in -ta), and a label was assigned to each of the distinct infinitives found, such that the end result consists of a dataset of 616 infinitives, each labeled from 0 to

6 depending on how the verb is inflected during conjugation.

4 Posing the Learning Problem

4.1 Objectives

The problem that we are aiming to solve is to determine how to conjugate a verb, given its infinitive form. The traditional infinitive-based classification taught in school does not take one all the way. Many variations exist within these 4 classes.

The rules from the previous section allow us to separate the verbs ending in -ta into more specific classes, knowing their inflected forms. By assigning the correct label to an infinitive of a verb not inlcuded in our dataset, one obtains all required information in order to produce a correct conjugation. We will now tackle the problem of fitting a model that is able to predict this labelling.

The context sensitive nature of the alternations leads to the idea of n-gram representations. A text feature extractor can be tuned to convert a list of verbs into a data matrix. The features of this data matrix are the substrings of length up to n that occur in the data, and the values can be taken either as occurence counts or simply as binary indicators of occurence. While occurence counts are useful in, for example, information retrieval, we have found that for such character-level applications, frequencies are less relevant than occurence, and it is not useful to give larger weight to n-grams that appear more often.

4.2 Approach

In order to get from a list of strings to a data format suitable for machine learning algorithms, we put together a feature extractor that returns a sparse matrix.

The feature extractor takes two parameters: the maximum n-gram size and whether to binarize the features. It is based on a character n-gram analyzer that takes a Unicode string as input and outputs a list of n-grams that constitute it. For the input "cânta", and for $n = 3$ it would produce the list "c", "â", "n", "t", "a", "câ", "ân", "nt", "ta", "cân", "ânt", "nta". The second component of the feature extractor is the vectorizer. This takes a list of unicode strings as input, runs the analyzer on all of them, then establishes the "vocabulary" of features as the set of distinct n-grams outputted by the analyzer. Afterwards, the vectorizer transforms every string in the dataset into a vector of the same size as the vocabulary. If we want to count features, the i-th element of the vector vector will contain the number of times the i-th n-gram appears in the word. If we want binary features, the vector will contain ones and zeros, indicating whether the n-gram appears or not in the word.

The average word length in the set of infinitives ending in -ta is 7.48. The larger we choose n, the more features the model will have, and therefore the more complex it will be. Considering both of these aspects, we decided on using the value $n = 3$.

The model is built as a pipeline. The list of verbs first passes through the feature extractor and is then fed into the classifier. For classification we evaluated Naive Bayes and linear support vector machines. When using counted features, we used multinomial Naive Bayes, while in the case of binarized features we used Bernoulli Naive Bayes. The support vector classifier uses the one-versus-all approach. Due to the limited size of the dataset, all scores are estimated using leave-one-out cross-validation.

The value of the regularization parameter C for the SVM is decided by a grid search. This consists in defining grid points for fixed parameter values, then fitting and evaluating a model for each grid point using cross-validation.

The system was put together using the scikits.learn machine learning library for the Python programming language (scikits.learn). It provides text feature extraction tools as described above, a linear support vector machine implementation based on the efficient liblinear library, and an automatic grid search framework for tuning the parameters.

4.3 Results

We first looked at how the Naive Bayes score varies as a function of n, the maximum n-gram length. The results can be seen in figure 1. Considering the fact that the number of features grows exponentially with n, the value of $n = 3$ seems to offer an acceptable model compexity trade-off versus classification score.

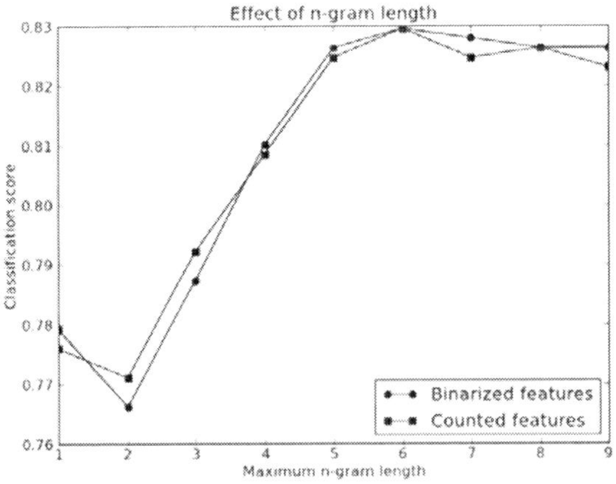

Figure 1: Evolution of Naive Bayes scores as we vary n.

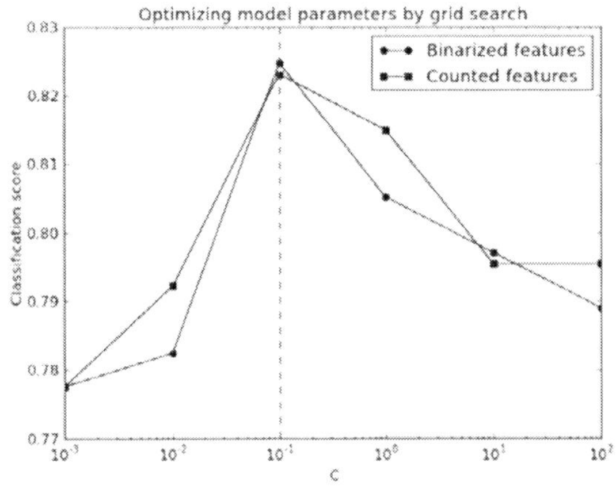

Figure 2: Determining the optimal value for the model parameters

The grid search for optimizing the support vector machine's C, detailed in figure 2 parameter shows that binary features perform better, and the value of C that maximizes the success rate within the grid is found at 10^{-1}, with an accurate classification rate of 82.47%. Precision, recall and F_1 scores for this optimal classifier are presented in table 1. It can be seen that even the poorly represented classes are accounted for. The last class (with label 6), which contains verbs that conjugate without alternations, is the most clearly separated.

class	precision	recall	F_1	support
0	0.65	0.38	0.48	106
1	0.38	0.23	0.29	13
2	1.00	0.60	0.75	5
3	1.00	0.25	0.40	4
4	1.00	0.80	0.89	5
5	1.00	0.25	0.40	4
6	0.85	0.95	0.90	479
avg/total	0.81	0.82	0.80	616

Table 1: Scores estimated by cross validation for the support vector classifier.

The results show that indeed, n-gram based features for classification can give good results for such morphological tasks that are difficult to solve using simple decision rules.

5 Conclusions and Future Works

Our results show that the labelling system based on the verb conjugation model we developed for verbs ending in -ta can be learned with reasonable accuracy. We are currently working on a more extensive system for labelling the infinitives, based on a near exhaustive conjugational model for the Romanian verb.

Our future work will revolve around a more exhaustive classification of the verbs such that, for each class, there is a simple and deterministic way to produce the correct present tense forms, given the infinitive. Following recent works in Romanian linguistics and the study of Romanian as a foreign language such as (Papastergiou et al., 2007), wherein a newer, more comprehensive and in-depth infinitive-based classification of the Romanian verb is given, we aim to extend these results to all verbs, not just the ones ending in -ta, and obtain a usable present tense indicative conjugator for the Romanian language.

6 Acknowledgements

We would like to thank the anonymous reviewers for their insight and constructive criticism which have helped us greatly in polishing this article. We would also like to thank Ana-Maria Barbu for the very useful corpus without which this article wouldn't have existed.

References

Ana-Maria Barbu. *Conjugarea verbelor românești. Dicționar: 7500 de verbe românești grupate pe clase de conjugare*. Bucharest: Coresi, 2007. 4th edition, revised. (In Romanian.) (263 pp.).

Angelo Roth Costanzo. *Romance Conjugational Classes: Learning from the Peripheries*. PhD thesis, Ohio State University, 2011.

Liviu Dinu and Emil Ionescu. A context sensitive approach to the problem of phonetic alternations. submitted, 2011.

Jiři Felix. *Classification des verbes roumains*, volume VII. Philosophica Pragensia, 1964.

Alf Lombard. *Le verbe roumain. Etude morphologique*, volume 1. Lund, C. W. K. Gleerup, 1955.

Grigore C. Moisil. Probleme puse de traducerea automată. conjugarea verbelor în limba română. *Studii si cercetări lingvistice*, XI(1):7–29, 1960.

I. Papastergiou, N. Papastergiou, and L. Mandeki. Verbul românesc - reguli pentru înlesnirea însuşirii indicativului prezent. In *Romanian National Symposium "Directions in Romanian Philological Research", 7th Edition*, May 2007.

scikits.learn. scikits.learn, Apr 2011. URL `http://scikit-learn.sourceforge.net`.

A New Representation Model for the Automatic Recognition and Translation of Arabic Named Entities with NooJ

Héla Fehri
Laboratory MIRACL, University of Sfax
hela.fehri@fss.rnu.tn

Kais Haddar
Laboratory MIRACL, University of Sfax
kais.haddar@fss.rnu.tn

Abdelmajid Ben hamadou
Laboratory MIRACL, University of Sfax
abdelmajid.benhamadou@isimsf.rnu.tn

Abstract

Recognition and translation of named entities (NEs) are two current research topics with regard to the proliferation of electronic documents exchanged through the Internet. The need to assimilate these documents through NLP tools has become necessary and interesting. Moreover, the formal or semi-formal modeling of these NEs may intervene in both processes of recognition and translation. Indeed, the modeling makes more reliable the constitution of linguistic resources, limits the impact of linguistic specificities and facilitates transformations from one representation to another. In this context, we propose an approach of recognition and translation based on a representation model of Arabic NEs and a set of transducers resolving morphological and syntactical phenomena.

1 Introduction

The formal or semi-formal modeling of NEs can be involved in recognition and translation process. It enables to constitute more reliable linguistic resources. Indeed, such a modeling can represent all the constituents of a NE in a standard manner and limit the impact of linguistic specificities. In fact, a formal representation of Arabic NEs can help, firstly, in the identification of dictionaries and grammars required for a given application and, secondly, in the use of advanced linguistic methods of translation (i.e., transfer or pivot method). This abstraction level favors the reuse of certain linguistic resources. The elaboration of a formal and generic representation of an NE is not an easy task because, on the one hand, we have to find a representation that takes into consideration the concept of recursion and length of NE. In fact, a NE can be formed by other NEs. So, its length is not known in advance. On the other hand, the representation to be proposed should also contain a sufficient number of features that can represent any NE independently of the domain and grammatical category.

It is in this context that the present work is situated. In fact, the main objective is to propose an approach of recognition and translation of Arabic NEs based on a representation model, a set of bilingual dictionaries and a set of transducers resolving morphological and syntactical phenomena related to the Arabic NEs and implemented with the linguistic platform NooJ (Silberztein, 2005).

In this paper, we present, firstly, a brief overview of the state-of the art. Next, we describe the hierarchy type of Arabic NEs and the identified problems in recognition and translation processes. Then, we detail our proposed representation model. After that, we give a general idea of our resources construction and their implementation in the linguistic platform NooJ. Finally, the paper concludes with some perspectives.

2 Related work

Research on NEs revolves around two complementary axes: the first involves the typing of NEs while the second concerns the identification and translation of NEs. As for the identification, the tagging and the translation of NEs, they have been implemented for multiple languages based on different approaches: linguistic (Coates-Stephens, 1993), statistic (Borthwick et al., 1998) and hybrid (Mikheev et al., 1998) approaches. In what follows, we focus on the linguistic approach.

Regarding the recognition of NEs, based on the linguistic approach, we cite the work presented in (Friburger, 2002). This work allows the extraction of proper names in French. The proposed method is based on multiple syntactic transformations and some priorities that are implemented with transducers. We can cite also the work described in (Mesfar, 2007). The elaborated method is applied on a biomedical domain. Other Arabic works are dealing with the recognition of elliptical expressions (Hasni et al., 2009) and most important categories in Arabic script (shaalan et al., 2009).

Other works have been dedicated to the translation of different structure (e.g., NE) from one language to another. We can cite the work presented in (Barreiro, 2008) dealing with the translation of simple sentences from English to Portuguese. Additionally, the work of (Wu, 2008) provides a noun translation of French into Chinese.

The literature review shows that the already proposed translation approaches are not well specified (e.g., lack of abstraction and genre). Each one addresses a particular phenomenon without taking into account other phenomena. We should also mention that there are few works that proposed a modeling of NEs for explicitly representing the effects of meaning within the NE and explaining phenomena like synecdoche and the metonymy (Poibeau, 2005). However, these works don't treat the concept of embedded NEs which is very important and can help to implement the recognition and the translation process of NEs. Furthermore, all translations using NooJ platform adopt a semi-direct approach of translation, in which the recognition task is combined with that of translation. Thus, the reuse of such work has become limited, which does not promote multilingualism.

3 Hierarchy of Arabic NEs and identified problems

3.1 Hierarchy of Arabic NEs

The hierarchy of Arabic NEs that we propose is inspired from MUC conferences (Grishman, 1995). This hierarchy does not differ from other typologies of other languages. In fact, categories that make up the proposed hierarchy are common to almost all domains. Indeed, our contribution focuses on the refinement done in different categories in various levels. In order to do this refinement, we must choose a domain. In our work, we chose the sport domain. Therefore, all our examples are related to this domain and especially to the category of place names belonging to the category of proper names but we should mention that our work is also applied to place names regardless of the domain. Figure 1 illustrates the suggested hierarchy.

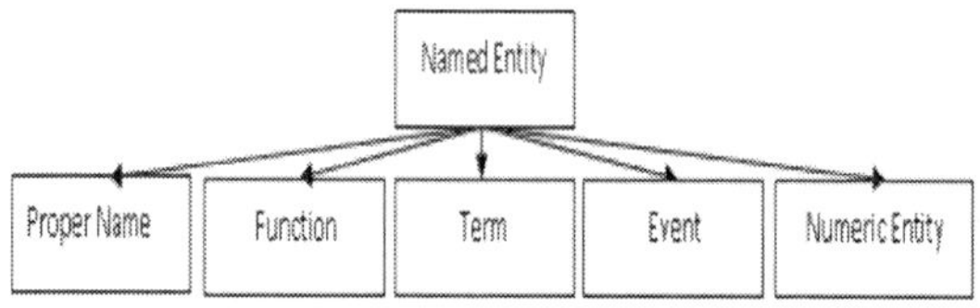

Figure 1: NE Hierarchy of the sport domain

Let's note that the proposed typological model comes as a result of the study of various forms of denomination of sports names (e.g., stadium, swimming pools, teams names) on corpora and lists of official names of the sport domain available on the Internet for Arabic countries

This proposed hierarchy allows the typing of the main constituents of NEs from a set of predefined categories. In fact a NE can be composed of others NEs. It is obvious that if a NE contains several NEs, it can cause different problems such as polysemy as mentioned in (Poibeau, 2005). However, it proves also the concept of embedded NEs. So, a modeling by a set of features may be an appropriate solution to explicitly represent this notion. In fact, it can help the process of recognition and translation of NEs. Later, we detail our proposed model allowing the implementation of the process of recognition and translation of NEs.

3.2 Identified problems in recognition and translation of Arabic NEs

Problems in Arabic NE' recognition: Arabic NE' recognition needs to solve some problems. For example, we can cite:

Proper name problem. In Arabic, there is a big challenge for finding those proper names in the text because they do neither start with capital letter as in many other languages, nor do they have special sign to identify and distinguish between them and other words in the text.

Syntactic problem. Arabic NE grammar is rich and variant. Indeed, the length of NE (number of constituents) is not known in advance.

Problems in Arabic NE' translation: In our work, NE' translation is done from Arabic to

French. The study of this process shows that there exist many problems. For example, we cite:

- Gender feature correspondence. Gender feature value is not always the same for Arabic word and its equivalent in French. For example, the word مســبح *swimming pool* is masculine but its translation to French *piscine* is feminine.
- Ambiguity between capital name and city name. For example, the toponym تــونس *Tunisia* can be translated to *Tunisie* or *Tunis* in French.
- Arabic adjective position is different in French. For example, ملعب عبد العزيز**الأولمبي** *malaab Abdelaziz* ***el oulimpi*** *Abdelaziz* ***Olympic*** *stadium* is translated to *Stade* ***olympique*** *Abdelaziz.*

4 Proposed model for representing Arabic NEs

The model that we propose is used to formalize and to identify Arabic NEs. This model is inspired by formalisms based on structural features like Head-driven Phrase Structure Grammar (Pollard et al., 1994). Its features are inspired from the concepts "Head and Expansion" introduced by (Bourigault, 2002).

The essential characteristics of the feature structure of the proposed model are: an element of the structure can be atomic or complex and an internal structure of an element is defined by its attributes and values.

4.1 Structure and features of the proposed model

Each NE has a type and is composed of two parts: one is essential and the other is extensional. The essential part is also a NE and has itself essential and extensional parts. This proves the recursion for an NE. The type of a NE "Type_EN" is usually indicated by a trigger word. The essential part is represented by the feature "Tête_EN" (head of NE) and the trigger word is represented by the feature "Mot_declencheur". The extensional part represents the final form that composes the NE. It does not admit a type because it is preceded by a lexical item "Element_EN" (e.g., preposition, special character). Then, it can not be considered as a NE but it can contain a NE. Its existence or non-existence doesn't affect the well-formation of the NE. This part is represented by the feature "Fin_EN".

The value of the feature "Tête_EN" can be atomic or structured. If it is structured, then it is composed by the features "Mot_déclencheur", "Tête_EN", "Fin_EN" and "Type_EN". The "Mot_déclencheur" value is simple or composed. Indeed, the trigger word can be formed by a word or a sequence of words. It can also be empty. The "Fin_EN" value can be atomic or structured. If it is structured, then it is composed by the features "Element_EN", "Tête_EN" and "Fin_EN". It can also be empty. The feature "Type_EN" value is always simple or composed but not empty. In fact, it represents one of the categories identified in the NE hierarchy. The "Element_EN" value is always simple. The structure can be equipped with a set of principles allowing the construction and evaluation of NE-representation.

4.2 Principles of the proposed model

Saturation principle: A structure is called saturated if it can be considered as a well-formed NE. That means, it consists of a NE head ("Tête_EN") whose value is not empty. Figure 2 describes an example of a formal representation that satisfies a saturation principle.

El *Riadh* **الرياض**

Tête_EN	الرياض
Fin_EN	ϕ
Type_EN	Ville

Figure 2: Representation of the word الرياض *el Riadh*

Non-saturation principle: A structure is called unsaturated if it isn't a NE and can be completed to become a NE. That means, it is formed only by a NE end (*"Fin_EN"*) or if the value of the feature "Tête_EN" is empty. For example, in the word بالرياض *bi Riadh,* the value of the feature "Tête_EN" is empty because this word doesn't have a type. Thus, this word cannot be considered as a NE. It doesn't satisfy the saturation principle. However, it should be noted that this word can contain a NE. The two mentioned principles allow us to avoid ambiguity between a NE-word (or set of words) and a non NE-word.

4.3 Literal translation representation

Word-to-word translation consists to translate each feature value composing a NE structure representation. This translation is done with bilingual dictionaries without any risk of information loss. For instance, in the NE ملعب الملك عبد العزيز الدولي Malaab el malik Abd el Aziz el doali bil Riadh, the word ملعب *malaab stadium* is translated to *stade*, the word الملك *el malik king* to *roi*, the adjective الدولي *el doali international* to *international and* the preposition ب *bi in* to *de*.

Let's note that the representation of a word-to-word translation is not sufficient to generate a well formed NE in the target language. Therefore, readjustment rules are necessary and should be associated in translation process.

5 NooJ implementation of the set of transducers

The NooJ implementation of our system requires two phases process: recognition of Arabic NEs phase and translation phase in which the transliteration process is integrated.

5.1 Phase of recognition

The proposed representation model helps us to identify the necessary resources for the recognition and translation of NEs. In fact, each structured feature "Tête_EN" containing not empty features, other than the feature "Type_EN", is transformed into a grammar. Whereas, each elementary NE (value of "Tête_EN" feature is atomic) will be transformed into a dictionary.

From the NE representation in the considered model, we have created the following transducer:

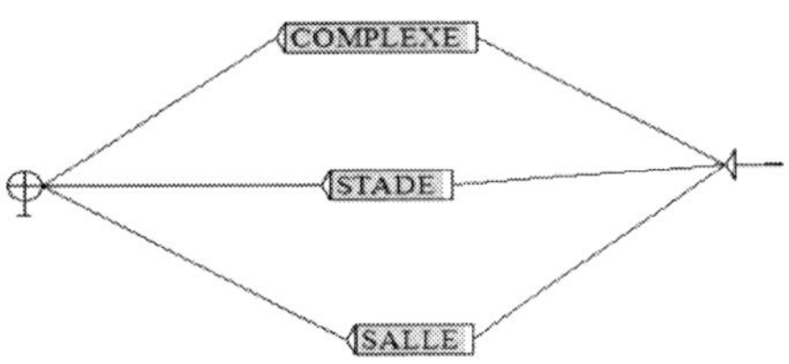

Figure 3. Main transducer of NE' recognition

The transducer of Figure 3 allows recognition of NEs belonging in the sport place name category. Each path of each sub-graph represents a rule extracted in the study corpus.

In the recognition phase, we have solved the problems related to the Arabic language (eg, agglutination) establishing morphological grammars built into the platform NooJ. This phase contains 19 graphs respecting the production rules identified in the study corpus.

5.2 Phase of translation

Word-to-word translation: To implement the process of word-to-word translation in the platform NooJ, we built a syntactic grammar allowing the translation of each word composing a NE with the exception of words not found in dictionaries, or can not be translated (number, special character, etc..). This grammar takes as input the NE list extracted by the transducer of Figure 3 allowing the recognition and it is described by the transducer of Figure 4.

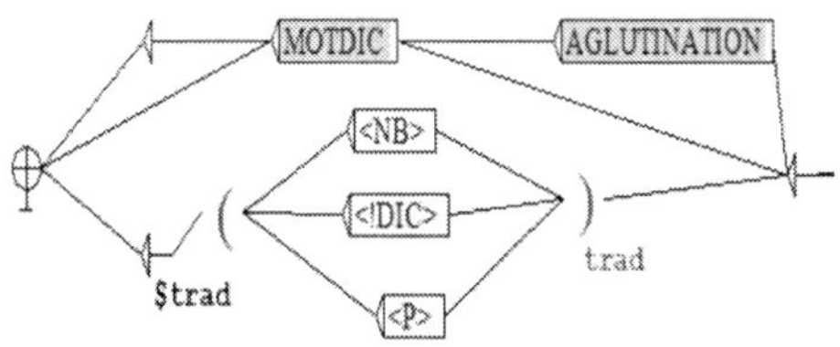

written in PERL, C++, JAVA, etc. In our work, we use C#.

6 Experimentation and evaluation

The experimentation of our resources is done with the linguistic platform NooJ. As mentioned above, this platform uses (syntactic and morphological) grammars already built and dictionaries. To the resources of NooJ, we added these dictionaries: Team Names (5785 entries), Sport Names (337 entries), Capital and country Names (610 entries), Personality Names (300 entries), Trigger words (20 entries) and Functions Names (100 entries).

In addition to the mentioned dictionaries, we use other dictionaries existing in NooJ like dictionary of adjectives, nouns and First Names. To these dictionaries, we add some entries related to the sport domain. We also add French translations of all entries in all mentioned dictionaries. Let's note that the First Name dictionary remains monolingual because its entries can be transliterated. To experiment and evaluate our work, we have applied our resources to two types of corpus: sport and education.

6.1 Experimentation of recognition phase

To evaluate a recognition phase, we have applied our resources to a corpus formed by 4000 texts (94,5 Mo) of sport domain (different of the study corpus). It contains 180000 NEs belonging to different categories of sport domain (e.g., player name, name of sport, sports term). In these NEs, there are 40000 NEs belonging to the category place name. These NEs are manually identified using NooJ queries.

Let's note that NE is detected if it satisfies one of the paths described by the transducer of Figure 3. Indeed, a transducer is characterized by an initial node and one or many end nodes. If multiple paths are verified, we maintain the longest one.

The obtained results give 98% of precision, 90% of recall and 94% of F-measure. This measures show that there are problems that are not yet resolved. Some problems are related to the lack of standards for writing proper names (e.g., el hamza) and the absence of some words in the dictionaries. This causes a silence. Other problems are related to specific concepts in the Arabic language as metaphor.

We have also applied our resources to the education domain. We have collected a corpus composed of 300 texts (14.5 Mo) containing university 3000 institution names. The performance measure of the obtained results gives 98% of precision, 70% of recall and 82% of F-measure. We deduce that silence is increased. This is caused by the incompleteness of specific dictionaries to this domain and lack of some paths in the developed transducers. So our resources are applicable regardless of the domain, provided that we use the same features adopted in dictionaries we have built. It is evident that for reasons specific to the field, we should sometimes add other paths and other sub-graphs, but we do not have to redo everything.

6.2 Experimentation of translation phase

The translation phase is applied to the extracted Arabic NEs during the recognition phase. Note that erroneous results are inherited. Therefore, heuristics filtering are necessary before the translation process. The obtained results of the translation phase are illustrated in Figure 5.

Figure 5: Extract of results of word-to-word translation

As shown in Figure 5, the proper problems of this phase involve multiple translations that can be assigned to a word. For example, the selected lines in Figure 5 represent the NE' translation ملعب مدينة الباسل الرياضية بدرعا *malaab madinat el bacel el riadhiya bi deraa stadium of city Bacel sportive in Deraa*. In this NE, the word مدينة *madina* can be translated to the word "cité" *city* or "ville" *country*. NooJ displays all possibilities. In this case, the adjective can resolve this ambiguity. In fact, the adjective الرياضية *el riadhiya sportive* is generally related to the city and not to the country. Let's note that the word "باسل" *Bacel* remains in the source language because it is a first name, so it will be transliterated later.

Our method provides 97% of well translated NEs while ensuring the specificities of the target language. The obtained result is promising and shows that there are some problems not resolved. These problems are related to the multiple translations assigned to a toponym (e.g., تونس *tounis* can be translated in tunis or tunisie).

The proposed representation model facilitates the implementation and the building of the linguistic resources with the platform NooJ. It facilitates also the transformation from the semi-direct translation to transfer translation. Indeed, we have separated the NE' recognition of their translation. In addition, it helps the promotion to the reuse of the needed grammars. In fact, it is sufficient to change the inputs (i.e., dictionaries, morphological grammars) of the syntactic grammars for the desired results. Thus, for example, if we want to translate Arabic NE to another language other than French, the recognition module can be reused with some modifications if necessary (related to the specificities of the domain).

7 Conclusion and perspectives

In this paper, we have proposed an approach for recognition and translation of Arabic NEs (eventually NE from other language) based on a representation model, a set of bilingual dictionaries and a set of transducers resolving morphological and syntactical phenomena related to the Arabic NEs. Moreover, we have given an idea of the hierarchy types of Arabic NEs and of the identified problems in the recognition and translation processes. Besides, we have described the representation model structure, its features and principles that should be satisfied. We have also given an experimentation and evaluation on the sports and education domains proving that our resources can be reused independently of the domain. The experimentation and the evaluation are done in the linguistic platform NooJ. The obtained results are satisfactory.

As perspectives, we seek to improve the model by introducing other features related to the semantics. Furthermore, we are currently identifying heuristics filtering enabling finer translation.

References

Barreiro, A. 2008. *Port4NooJ: an open source, ontology-driven Portuguese linguistic system with applications in machine translation.* NooJ'08, Budapest.

Borthwick, A., Sterling, J., Agichtein, E. Grishman, R. 1998. *NYU: Description of the MENE Named Entity System as used in MUC-7.* In Proc. of the Seventh Message Understanding Conference (MUC-7).

Bourigault, D. 2002. *UPERY : un outil d'analyse distributionnelle étendue pour la construction d'ontologies à partir de corpus.* TALN.

Coates-Stephens, S. 1993. *The Analysis and Acquisition of Proper Names for the Understanding of Free Text.* In Computers and the Humanities, Kluwer Academic Publishers, Vol. 26(5-6), Hingham, MA, p. 441-456.

Friburger, N. 2002. *Reconnaissance automatique des noms propres.* PhD thesis, university of François Rabelais.

Grishman, R. 1995. *Where's the Syntax? The NYU MUC-6 System.* In Acts of MUC-6, Morgan Kaufmann Publishers, San Francisco.

Hasni, E., Haddar, K., Abdelwahed, A. 2009. *Reconnaissance des expressions elliptiques arabes avec NOOJ.* In proceedings of the 3rd International Conference on Arabic Language Processing (CITALA'09) sponsored by IEEE Morocco Section, 4-5 May 2009, Rabat, Morocco, pp 83-88.

Mesfar, S. 2007. *Named Entity Recognition for Arabic Using Syntactic grammars.* NLDB 2007 Paris, 28-38.

Mikheev, A., Grover, C. et Moens, M. 1998. *Description of the LTG system used for MUC -7.* In Proc. of 7th Message Understanding Conference (MUC-7), http://www.itl.nist.gov/iad/ 894.02/ related_projects/muc/.

Poibeau, T. 2005. *Sur le statut référentiel des entités nommées.* Laboratory of data processing of Paris North – CNRS and University Paris 13.

Pollard, C., Sag., I.A. 1994. *Head-Driven Phrase Structure Grammar.* Published by the press in the University of Chicago, Edition Golgoldmittu, Chicago, LSLI.

Shaalan, K., Raza, H. 2009. NERA: *Named Entity Recognition for Arabic.* Published in Journal of the American Society for Information Science and Technology, Volume 60 Issue 8.

Silberztein, M. 2004. *NooJ : an Object-Oriented Approach.* In INTEX pour la Linguistique et le Traitement Automatique des Langues. C. Muller, J. Royauté M. Silberztein Eds, book of the MSH Ledoux. Presses University of Franche-Comte, pp. 359-369.

Wu, M. 2008. *La traduction automatique français-chinois pour les groupes nominaux avec NooJ.* Budapest.

Training Data in Statistical Machine Translation – The More, the Better? –

Monica Gavrila
University of Hamburg, Germany
gavrila@informatik.uni-hamburg.de

Cristina Vertan
University of Hamburg, Germany
cristina.vertan@uni-hamburg.de

Abstract

Current statistical machine translation (SMT) systems are stated to be dependent on the availability of a very large training data for producing the language and translation models. Unfortunately, large parallel corpora are available for a limited set of language pairs and for an even more limited set of domains.

In this paper we investigate the behavior of an SMT system exposed to training data of different sizes and types. Our experimental results show that even parallel corpora of modest sizes can be used for training purposes without lowering too much the evaluation scores. We consider two language pairs in both translation directions for the experiments: English-Romanian and German-Romanian.

1 Introduction

Statistical machine translation (SMT) is the most frequently used paradigm, especially when a translation system has to be implemented for a new (less researched) language pair. The pure statistical approach has the advantage that no additional bilingual linguistic expertise is required. Once the training data is available, open-source, language independent systems can be reused. However, the quality of the results is strongly influenced by the size and type of the available training data.

State-of-the-art literature tends to share the opinion that the larger the data, the better the results. (Suresh, 2010) shows that a larger corpus size for training increases the quality of a Moses-based SMT system, for the Europarl corpus for English-French. The same conclusion appears also in (Koehn et al., 2003), for German-English. In (Brants et al., 2007) experiments for Arabic-English data with billions of tokens are presented and a dependency between the output quality and the size of the training data is also demonstrated.

Unfortunately, large amount of parallel training data is available only for a restricted number of language pairs and domains. Additionally, the training step on large corpora is time and (computing-) resources consuming. On the other hand, smaller corpora can be more easily achieved and have the advantage of requiring less time for training. They also offer the possibility of manually correcting and creating the data.

Experiments with smaller data for Serbian-English (approx. 2.6K sentences) are presented in (Popovic and Ney, 2006). In the same paper also experimental results for Spanish-English, with different data sizes are reported. The systems trained on smaller data give acceptable results. However, the trend remains the same: larger data provides better results.

For English-Romanian, SMT systems are presented in (Cristea, 2009) and (Ignat, 2009), with BLEU results of 0.5464 and 0.3208, respectively. Although both systems use as training and test data parts of the JRC-Acquis corpus, the architecture described in (Cristea, 2009) involves the use of linguistic resources and the system implemented in (Ignat, 2009) uses pivot languages. As long as comparisons are not made on identical training and test data, it is difficult to estimate if, overall, the inclusion of linguistic tools increases significantly the performance. The SMT results for Romanian-English, German-Romanian and Romanian-German reported in (Ignat, 2009) are 0.3840, 0.2373 and 0.2415, respectively. For Romanian-English the BLEU score obtained in (Cristea, 2009) is 0.4604.

Especially for MT systems embedded in online applications, which face a dynamic domain change and involve several language pairs, it is extremely important to be aware of the small amount of training data which is available. Such a case is the ATLAS content management system, developed within the EU-Project "Applied Language Technology for Content Management Systems"[1]. In this project a machine translation (MT) engine should be available to translate abstracts from various domains across twelve language pairs.

In this paper we present the results of a Moses-based SMT system, trained on different types of small size corpora (2.2K). For comparison reasons we additionally consider a larger corpus (330K). Especially with respect to the availability of parallel corpora and linguistic resources, Romanian can be considered a lesser resourced language[2].

We chose two language pairs (English-Romanian and German-Romanian) in both directions of translations and, in contrast to (Popovic and Ney, 2006), we use for all experiments the same language pairs. The language pair Romanian (ro)-German (ge) is particularly interesting as both languages present morphological and syntactical features which do not occur in English (en) and make the process of translation even more challenging.

In the following sections we present the Moses-based SMT system used and the data employed in our experiments (Section 2), the translation results and their interpretation (Section 3). Conclusions and further work are described in Section 4.

2 Experimental Setting

2.1 The SMT System

Our MT system follows the description of the baseline architecture provided at the Sixth Workshop on SMT[3] and uses Moses[4]. Moses implements the statistical paradigm and allows the user to train automatically translation models (TM) for the involved language pair. It is assumed that the user has the required training data. The target language model (LM) and the word alignment for the parallel corpus are obtained through external applications. We used for our experiments SRILM[5] and GIZA++ [6], respectively.

Two changes have been made to the specifications of the Workshop on SMT: we left out the tuning step and considered the language model (LM) order 3 (instead of 5). Leaving out the tuning step is motivated by previous experiments we made, in which the tuned system did not always provide the best results. A reason for choosing the order three for the LM was provided by the results shown in the presentation of the SMART[7] project (Rousu, 2008), in which it was stated that "3-grams work generally the best".

2.2 Data Description

We want to study the influence of the training data on the translation results. Therefore, we use for our experiments three corpora of different sizes, which have various compilation methods: **JRC-Acquis_L** (a large-size parallel corpus, automatically aligned at sentence level), **JRC-Acquis_S** (a small-size parallel corpus, automatically aligned at sentence level), and **RoGER_S** (a small-size technical manual, manually compiled and aligned at sentence level).

The first corpus (**JRC-Acquis_L**) is part of the JRC-Acquis[8], a freely available parallel corpus in 22 languages, which consists of European Union documents of legal nature. In order to reduce errors we considered only the one-to-one sentence alignments obtained with Vanilla[9]. In fact, the alignment is realized at paragraph level[10], where a *paragraph* can be a simple or complex sentence, or a sub-sentential phrase (such as a noun phrase). More details on JRC-Acquis can be found in (Steinberger et al., 2006).

Filtering the sentence alignments had different influences on the data-size. For English - Romanian, from 391324 links ($< p >$-alignments) in 6557 documents, only 336509 links were retained. Subsequently, the cleaning step[11] of the SMT system reduced the translation model (TM) to 240219 links. This represents approx. 61.38% of the initial corpus. For German - Romanian, from 391972

[1] http://www.atlasproject.eu.

[2] While the interest for translation from or into German or English appeared in an early stage of MT, an increased demand for automatic translation from and into Romanian was noticed after the enlargement of the European Union in 2007.

[3] http://www.statmt.org/wmt11/baseline.html.

[4] http://www.statmt.org/moses/, (Koehn et al., 2007).

[5] http://www.speech.sri.com/projects/srilm/, (Stolcke, 2002).

[6] Details on GIZA++ can be found in (Och and Ney, 2003).

[7] www.smart-project.eu - last accessed on June 27th, 2011.

[8] The JRC Collection of the Acquis Communautaire: http://wt.jrc.it/lt/Acquis/.

[9] See http://nl.ijs.si/telri/Vanilla/.

[10] The tag $< p >$ from the initial HTML files.

[11] The cleaning step is integrated in Moses and supposes the elimination of sentences longer than 40 words.

links in 6558 documents, only 324448 links were considered for the LM. The TM was reduced to 238172 links (i.e 60.76% of the initial corpus).

The corpus is not manually corrected. Therefore, translation, alignment or spelling errors might influence negatively the output quality.

The tests were run on 897 (3 x 299) sentences, which were not used for training. Sentences were randomly removed from different parts of JRC-Acquis to ensure a relevant lexical, syntactic and semantic coverage. These test sets of 299 sentences represent in the following sections the data sets **Test 1**, **Test 2**, and **Test 3**. **Test 1+2+3** is formed from all 897 sentences. The test data has no sentence length restriction. Some statistical information on JRC-Acquis_L are summarized in Table 1, in which an item represents a word, a number or a punctuation sign.

Data	No. of items	Voc.* size	Average sent.* length
en – ro			
Training (SL)	3579856	39784	14.90
LM Romanian	9572058	81616	28.45
Test 1 (SL)	6424	1048	21.48
Test 2 (SL)	7523	735	25.16
Test 3 (SL)	5609	1111	18.76
Test 1+2+3 (SL)	19556	2345	21.80
ro – en			
Training (SL)	3386495	55871	14.10
LM English	9955983	55856	29.59
Test 1 (SL)	5672	1245	18.97
Test 2 (SL)	7194	923	24.06
Test 3 (SL)	5144	1355	17.20
Test 1+2+3 (SL)	18010	2717	20.08
ge – ro			
Training (SL)	3256047	76600	13.67
LM Romanian	9122333	80484	28.12
Test 1 (SL)	5325	1140	17.81
Test 2 (SL)	10286	1439	34.40
Test 3 (SL)	5125	1292	17.23
Test 1+2+3 (SL)	20763	3000	23.15
ro – ge			
Training (SL)	3453586	56219	14.50
LM German	8469146	121969	26.10
Test 1 (SL)	5432	1294	18.17
Test 2 (SL)	11488	1663	38.42
Test 3 (SL)	5317	1388	17.78
Test 1+2+3 (SL)	22237	3336	24.79

Table 1: Corpus statistics for JRC-Acquis_L (* voc = vocabulary, sent=sentence).

The second corpus we used is **JRC-Acquis_S**, a sub-corpus of JRC-Acquis_L, which consists of 2333 sentences. The sentences were extracted from the middle of JRC-Acquis_L. From these, 133 sentences were randomly selected as test data. The remaining 2200 sentences represent the training data. The statistics on this corpus are presented in Table 2.

Data SL	No. of items	Voc.	Average sent. length
en – ro			
Training	75405	3578	34.27
Test	4434	992	33.33
ro – en			
Training	72170	5581	32.80
Test	4325	1260	32.51
ge – ro			
Training	69735	5929	31.69
Test	3947	1178	29.67
ro – ge			
Training	75156	6390	34.16
Test	4366	1320	32.82

Table 2: Statistics for JRC-Acquis_S.

RoGER_S, the third corpus in this paper, is a parallel corpus, consisting of technical texts in four languages[12], which is manually aligned at sentence level. The text is preprocessed by replacing concepts such as numbers or web pages with '*meta-notions*': numbers = NUM, websites = WWW etc. More about the RoGER corpus can be found in (Gavrila and Elita, 2006). RoGER_S has the same number of training and test sentences as JRC-Acquis_S. The main difference to JRC-Acquis_S is the correctness of the translations and sentence alignments. The statistical information about this corpus is presented in Table 3.

Data SL	No. of items	Voc.	Average sent. length
en – ro			
Training	27889	2367	12.68
Test	1613	522	12.13
ro – en			
Training	28946	3349	13.16
Test	1649	659	12.40
ge – ro			
Training	28361	3230	12.89
Test	1657	604	12.46
ro – ge			
Training	28946	3349	13.16
Test	1649	659	12.40

Table 3: Statistics for RoGER_S.

3 Evaluation and Interpretation of Translation Results

3.1 Automatic Evaluation

The obtained translations have been evaluated using two automatic metrics: BLEU and TER. The choice of the metrics is motivated by the available

[12] Romanian, German, English, Russian.

resources and, for comparison reason, by the results reported in the literature. The comparison was done with only one reference translation, as we work in a realistic scenario with dynamic domain change (see section 1.)

Although criticized, **BLEU** (**bil**ingual **e**valuation **u**nderstudy) is the score mostly used for MT evaluation in the last couple of years. It measures the number of n-grams, of different lengths, of the system output that appear in a set of reference translations. More details about BLEU[13] can be found in (Papineni et al., 2002).

TER[14] calculates the minimum number of edits required to get from obtained translations to the reference translations, normalized by the average length of the references. It considers insertions, deletions, substitutions of single words and an edit-operation which moves sequences of words. More information about TER can be found in (Snover et al., 2006).

In Table 4 we present the results we obtained for all three corpora. The boldface numbers represent the highest scores for the specific language combination and evaluation metric.

Score	RoGER_S	JRC-Acquis_S	JRC-Acquis_L (Test 1+2+3)
		en – ro	
BLEU	0.4386	**0.4801**	0.4015
TER	**0.3784**	0.5032	0.5023
		ro – en	
BLEU	0.4765	**0.4904**	0.4255
TER	**0.3465**	0.4509	0.4457
		ge – ro	
BLEU	0.3240	0.2811	**0.3644**
TER	**0.5239**	0.6658	0.6113
		ro – ge	
BLEU	0.3405	0.2926	**0.3726**
TER	**0.5570**	0.6816	0.6112

Table 4: Evaluation results (all three corpora).

The results from Table 4 for Romanian-English are overall similar with state-of-the art evaluation described in Section 1. For Romanian-German our result overtake the system presented in (Ignat, 2009). However, a truly one-to-one comparison is not possible, as we do not work with identical test and training data as the referred systems.

Even for same training data evaluation results may vary across test sets, as presented in Table 5. Here we show how dependent are the SMT results on the test data. As the size and domain-type of the test data (**Test 1** - **Test 3**) is identical, the differences in BLEU and TER score can be explained only through lexical and syntactical variation across test-sets. Some sources for these variations are represented by out-of-vocabulary words (OOV-words) and the number of test sentences already found in training data. An overview of these two aspects in all the three corpora can be seen in Tables 6 and 7. As expected, best results are obtained for the test data set which has less OOV-words and which contains most sentences in the training data: **Test 2**. As it is not the topic of this paper, we will not extend the explanation for these variations or present any possible solutions.

Score	Test 1	Test 2	Test 3	Test 1+2+3
		en – ro		
BLEU	0.3997	**0.4179**	0.3797	0.4015
TER	0.5007	**0.4898**	0.5208	0.5023
		ro – en		
BLEU	0.2545	**0.5628**	0.4271	0.4255
TER	0.5020	**0.3756**	0.4684	0.4457
		ge – ro		
BLEU	0.2955	**0.4244**	0.2884	0.3644
TER	0.6200	**0.5905**	0.6438	0.6113
		ro – ge		
BLEU	0.2953	**0.4411**	0.2939	0.3726
TER	0.6437	**0.5588**	0.6791	0.6112

Table 5: Evaluation results for JRC-Acquis_L

Corpus	No. of OOV-Words (% from voc. size)	Sentences in the corpus
	JRC-Acquis_L	
	en – ro	
Test 1	33 (3.15%)	69 (23.07%)
Test 2	2 (0.27%)	134 (44.81%)
Test 3	96 (8.64%)	85 (28.42%)
Test 1+2+3	131 (5.59%)	288 (21.10%)
	ro – en	
Test 1	51 (4.10%)	69 (23.07%)
Test 2	7 (0.76%)	117 (39.13%)
Test 3	111 (8.19%)	81 (27.09%)
Test 1+2+3	169 (6.22%)	267 (29.76%)
	ge – ro	
Test 1	69 (6.05%)	73 (24.41%)
Test 2	53 (3.68%)	121 (40.46%)
Test 3	187 (14.47%)	83 (27.75%)
Test 1+2+3	309 (10.30%)	277 (30.88%)
	ro – ge	
Test 1	44 (3.40%)	76 (25.41%)
Test 2	97 (5.83%)	109 (36.45%)
Test 3	105 (7.56%)	79 (26.42%)
Test 1+2+3	246 (7.37%)	264 (29.43%)

Table 6: Analysis of the test data sets (JRC-Acquis_L)

[13]We considered the NIST/BLEU implementation *mteval_v12*, as on `http://www.itl.nist.gov/iad/mig/tests/mt/2008/scoring.html`.

[14]TER (translation error rate.) as implemented on `http://www.cs.umd.edu/~snover/tercom/` - last accessed on 12.01.2010.

Corpus	No. of OOV-Words (% from voc. size)	Sentences in the corpus
RoGER_S		
en – ro		
Test	60 (11.49%)	37 (27.81%)
ro – en		
Test	84 (12.75%)	34 (25.56%)
ge – ro		
Test	101 (16.72%)	31 (23.30%)
ro – ge		
Test	84 (12.75%)	34 (25.56%)
JRC-Acquis_S		
en – ro		
Test	72 (7.25%)	38 (28.57%)
ro – en		
Test	129 (10.23%)	33 (24.81%)
ge – ro		
Test	171 (14.51%)	41 (30.82%)
ro – ge		
Test	160 (12.12%)	40 (30.07%)

Table 7: Analysis of the test data sets (RoGER and JRC-Acquis_S)

In the next subsection we will show more detailed the sensitivity of SMT systems to training and test data size and type.

3.2 Interpretation of the Results

In Table 4 we presented the variation of BLEU and TER scores across the three corpora. In (Koehn et al., 2003) a log-linear dependency between the size of the training corpora and the BLEU scores was observed. In contrast, our results cannot confirm this dependency for all language pairs investigated[15]. While for German-Romanian the log-linear dependency seem to be preserved, for English-Romanian the BLEU scores for JRC-Acquis_S are better than the ones for JRC-Acquis_L. Also worth to remark is that the BLEU scores for the other small corpus – ROGER_S –, are in the case of English-Romanian between the other two BLEU scores, and in the case of Romanian-English closer to the BLEU score for JRC-Acquis_S. This leads us to the conclusion that the hypothesis of log-linear dependency has to be tested before one decides to invest a lot of work in collecting large data sets. Giving the fact that in both of our experiments, as well as in (Koehn et al., 2003), the log-linear dependency was noticed in case of language pairs involving German, it could be an indication that the German specific morphological features, in special the dynamic word composition, could be a reason for this behavior. The high number of compounds in German may imply a higher data-sparseness, which can be compensated only through large amounts of training data.

[15]We also do not exclude the difference in the results due also to different evaluation methodology. However, this aspect is not analyzed in this paper

Another interesting observation can be done regarding the TER Scores. The best TER scores were obtained, independent of the chosen language pair, for the ROGER_S corpus. One explanation is the particular syntax of this corpus: technical short sentences, in which the translation usually preserves the SL word order, as far as the syntax in both source and target languages allows. In contrast, in JRC-Acquis one finds often reformulations or shorter sentences. As TER measures the differences between output and reference translation in number of insertions, deletions and replacements, this may be cause of alternation of the TER scores.

Given the fact that the BLEU scores for the ROGER_S corpus are also in line with current state-of-the-art systems, we can conclude that for technical domains a small, manually corrected corpus can be successfully used for obtaining a reasonable translation output.

All the results we have presented reinforce the idea that SMT is fully dependent on the training and test data size and type and on the evaluation procedure. We will further show how dependent the results are to all the steps involved in the translation and evaluation processes by presenting the results in Table 8. We evaluated the results for the JRC-Acquis_S corpus, when no detokenization or recasing in the post-processing has been done. In contrast to the information from Table 4, in this last case, the translation evaluation scores are better. This shows that, next to the training and test data itself, sometimes pre- or post-processing steps affect (negatively) the evaluation scores.

Language Pair	BLEU	TER
en – ro	0.5359	0.3586
ro – en	0.5573	0.3279
ge – ro	0.3051	0.5808
ro – ge	0.3279	0.5796

Table 8: Results for JRC-Acquis_S (no recasing, no detokenization)

4 Conclusions

The results presented and discussed in this paper let us conclude that there is not always an a priori size which can be recommended for developing a standard SMT systems independent of language pair and domain. The experiments we made showed (again) how dependent SMT results are on training and test data and on all processing steps. Especially for on-line applications which embed MT systems, where translation domain changes dynamically and a large number of language pairs is involved, a framework criteria for the training and test data is necessary. Our further work includes more experiments with different data (type and size) and language pairs. Also the associated statistical confidence intervals need to be calculated to have a better view on the evaluation results.

Acknowledgments

Ideas and results presented in this paper are part of Monica Gavrila's PhD research, conducted at the University of Hamburg, and of the ATLAS EU-Project (`www.atlasproject.eu`), supported through the ICT-PSP-Programme of the EU-Commission.

References

Thorsten Brants, Ashok C. Popat, Peng Xu, Franz J. Och, and Jeffrey Dean. 2007. Large language models in machine translation. In *Proceedings of the 2007 Joint Conference on Empirical Methods in Natural Language Processing and Computational Natural Language Learning*, pages 858–867, Prague, Czech Republic.

Dan Cristea. 2009. Romanian language technology and resources go to europe. Presentated at the FP7 Language Technology Informative Days, January, 20-11. To be found at: ftp://ftp.cordis.europe.eu/pub/fp7/ict/docs/language-technologies/cristea_en.pdf - last accessed on 10.04.2009.

Monica Gavrila and Natalia Elita. 2006. Roger - un corpus paralel aliniat. In *In Resurse Lingvistice şi Instrumente pentru Prelucrarea Limbii Române Workshop Proceedings*, pages 63–67, December. Workshop held in November 2006, Publisher: Ed. Univ. Alexandru Ioan Cuza, ISBN: 978-973-703-208-9.

Camelia Ignat. 2009. *Improving Statistical Alignment and Translation Using Highly Multilingual Corpora*. Ph.D. thesis, INSA - LGeco- LICIA, Strasbourg, France, June, 16th. It can be found on: http://sites.google.com/site/cameliaignat/home/phd-thesis - last accessed on 3.08.09.

Philipp Koehn, Franz Josef Och, and Daniel Marcu. 2003. Statistical phrase-based translation. In *NAACL '03: Proceedings of the 2003 Conference of the North American Chapter of the Association for Computational Linguistics on Human Language Technology*, pages 48–54, Morristown, NJ, USA. Association for Computational Linguistics.

Philipp Koehn, Hieu Hoang, Alexandra Birch, Chris Callison-Burch, Marcello Federico, Nicola Bertoldi, Brooke Cowan, Wade Shen, Christine Moran, Richard Zens, Chris Dyer, Ondrej Bojar, Alexandra Constantin, and Evan Herbst. 2007. Moses: Open source toolkit for statistical machine translation. In *Annual Meeting of the Association for Computational Linguistics (ACL), demonstration session*, pages 177–180, Prague, Czech Republic, June.

Franz Josef Och and Hermann Ney. 2003. A systematic comparison of various statistical alignment models. *Computational Linguistics*, 29(1):19–51.

Kishore Papineni, Salim Roukos, Todd Ward, and Wei-Jing Zhu. 2002. Bleu: a method for automatic evaluation of machine translation. In *Proceedings of the 40th Annual Meeting on Association for Computational Linguistics, Session: Machine translation and evaluation*, pages 311 – 318, Philadelphia, Pennsylvania. Publisher: Association for Computational Linguistics Morristown, NJ, USA.

Maja Popovic and Hermann Ney. 2006. Statistical machine translation with a small amount of bilingual training data. In *LREC-2006: Fifth International Conference on Language Resources and Evaluation. 5th SALTMIL Workshop on Minority Languages: Strategies for developing machine translation for minority languages*, pages 25–29, Genoa, Italy, May.

Juho Rousu. 2008. Workpackage 3 advanced language models. Online, January. SMART Project.

Matthew Snover, Bonnie Dorr, Richard Schwartz, Linnea Micciulla, and John Makhoul. 2006. A study of translation edit rate with targeted human annotation. In *Proceedings of Association for Machine Translation in the Americas*, pages 223–231, August.

Ralf Steinberger, Bruno Pouliquen, Anna Widiger, Camelia Ignat, Tomaz Erjavec, Dan Tufis, and Daniel Varga. 2006. The jrc-acquis: A multilingual aligned parallel corpus with 20+ languages. In *Proceedings of the 5th International Conference on Language Resources and Evaluation (LREC'2006)*, pages 2142–2147, Genoa, Italy, May, 24-16.

Andreas Stolcke. 2002. Srilm - an extensible language modeling toolkit. In *Proc. Intl. Conf. Spoken Language Processing*, pages 901–904, Denver, Colorado, September.

Bipin Suresh. 2010. Inclusion of large input corpora in statistical machine translation. Technical report, Stanford University.

Towards a Corpus-based Approach to Modelling Language Production of Foreign Language Learners in Communicative Contexts

Voula Gotsoulia
Research Center for English Language
Faculty of English Studies
National and Kapodistrian University of Athens
vgotsoulia@enl.uoa.gr

Bessie Dendrinos
Department of Language and Linguistics
Faculty of English Studies
National and Kapodistrian University of Athens
vdendrin@enl.uoa.gr

Abstract

This paper discusses linguistic annotation issues, essential to a corpus-based approach to modelling the language use of foreign language learners in various contexts. We focus on learners of English and describe the corpora we use as well as the linguistic approach underlying their development. We present a scheme for describing grammatical choices and meaning components expressed in texts produced by learners. Our goal is to model the associations of corpus-attested linguistic patterns with their contexts, at different levels of language proficiency.

1 Introduction

Learning a foreign language is a complex process involving mastering a range of elements of a non-trivial system of communication and being able to use them appropriately in different social contexts. In a related vein, assessing a learner's ability to use language (i.e. his/her *linguistic competence*) is a significantly complicated task, requiring well-defined criteria for describing the instantiations of the system of language in socially meaningful ways. The *Common European Framework of Reference for Languages* (CEFR) has attempted to provide an objective basis for the explicit description of language proficiency across Europe, aimed to promote the transparency of language courses and 'the mutual recognition of qualifications gained in different contexts'.

CEFR distinguishes among several types of language-related communicative competences (i.e. lexical, grammatical, semantic, phonological, orthographic, orthoepic, sociolinguistic, pragmatic) and gives illustrative *descriptors* for each of these competences across the six-level scale of language proficiency established by the Council of Europe.[1] These descriptors are formulated in a very general way. In practice, incorporating their insight into concrete models of language learning and assessment is an open issue.[2]

In this paper, we address the foundations of a corpus-based approach to modelling the learners' production of language in relation to particular communicative contexts. Such a model can be used to support reliable assessment of language performance across proficiency levels, as well as test and materials development. We focus on English as a Foreign Language (EFL) and, more precisely, on the use of grammatical resources for the production of written texts.

In section 2, we describe the EFL learner corpora we use. Section 3 presents the linguistic framework we essentially draw upon and discusses methodological issues related to the representation of the range of grammatical resources employed by learners when producing written texts. Finally, in section 4 we specify the precise goals that we intend to pursue in the immediate future.

2 EFL Learner Corpora

As a basis for our study, we use the EFL learner corpora available from the KPG examinations, i.e. the Greek State examinations for certification of foreign language proficiency.[3] The KPG exams

[1] This scale comprises the European standard for grading language proficiency and includes the following reference levels: breakthrough or beginner (A1), waystage or elementary (A2), threshold or pre-intermediate (B1), vantage or intermediate (B2), effective operational proficiency or upper intermediate (C1), and mastery or advanced (C2).

[2] The English Profile Project, for instance, is currently working on providing concrete examples of the competences laid out in CEFR. It aims at clearly describing what a learner of English can be expected to know at each level (http://www.englishprofile.org/).

[3] The initials KPG stand for the Greek words 'Kratiko Pistopiitiko Glossomathias' (State Certificate for Language Proficiency): http://www.kpg.minedu.gov.gr/.

(carried out since 2003) currently include six foreign languages (English, French, German, Italian, Spanish, and Turkish) and conform to the European scale of language proficiency.

Research carried out in the KPG project is related to the ongoing development of two databases, a database containing past papers and a database containing the candidates' answers and written texts (*scripts*). These databases are organised and linked to one another in terms of exam dates, languages, language levels, and exam modules. The scripts, in particular, are also classified in grading bands (i.e. fully satisfactory, moderately satisfactory, and unsatisfactory).

Our work will focus on written texts in the KPG script database for the English language. This corpus amounts to 3.5 million words and comprises collections of texts produced by learners of all ages in Module 2 (Written Production and Mediation) of the KPG exam. Module 2 tests a learner's ability to express himself/herself in written form by providing him/her with a *source text* as anchor to a particular communicative context and asking him/her to produce new texts in the target language (*target texts*). There are two types of source texts: one is in English and the other is in the candidate's mother tongue (Greek). In the latter case, the candidate is asked to *mediate* to an English speaker who does not speak Greek and relay the content of the source text, adapting it to a different context or a different communicative purpose.

The notion of *text* as the concrete configuration of discourse is central in the theory of language underlying the KPG exams. Departing from testing approaches emphasising the grammatical well-formedness of utterances, KPG emphasises the use of language as text in specific *contexts of situation* (i.e. communicative contexts). A *text* is defined as an independent unit of language which is meaningful for the context for which it has been produced. Put differently, it is a unit of language closely tied to aspects of a given situation (i.e. who is writing to whom, for what purpose, where the text might appear, etc.)

Both source and target texts stored in the KPG databases are described in terms of a number of parameters capturing information about their situational contexts (Kondyli and Lykou, 2010). These parameters include the text *type* (e.g. article, announcement, report, advertisement, prose excerpt, etc.), the *source* from which a text is taken (e.g. newspaper, magazine, encyclopedia, dictionary, web page, novel, etc.), the communicative *purpose* for which it has been produced (e.g. to inform, announce, convince, warn, invite, advise, protest, evaluate, etc.), the language *process* by means of which the purpose is fulfilled (i.e. description, narration, explanation, argument, instruction), the *domain* to which the text pertains (e.g. environment, travel, entertainment, science, sport, etc.), as well as the author's and addressee's communicative *roles* or identities (journalist, writer, friend, etc.).[4] Combinations of these parameters capture different text *genres*: a newspaper article written by a journalist who aims to inform readers about a scientific breakthrough by describing experiments, explaining goals, and arguing in favour of their importance differs from an article on the same topic published in a scientific journal, written by a scientist who aims to present his work to the academic community describing his experiments, explaining his goals and arguing in favour of the importance of his research.

Across the KPG exam levels, a variety of text genres and situations (ranging from everyday to formal communication) are associated with activities assessing different aspects of a learner's competence in the target language. The activities stored in the KPG databases along with the corresponding texts and their metadata and are managed and viewed via an intuitive web-based interface allowing SQL queries for information retrieval.

3 Corpus Annotation of Grammatical Patterns

The goal of our research is to describe in a systematic fashion the range of grammatical *choices* made by learners of English, using language in different communicative contexts, at different levels of proficiency. Furthermore, we seek to relate corpus-attested linguistic patterns with nonlinguistic properties of the texts in which they appear, so as to model the contextualised use of language.

For this purpose, we also generalise across texts by organising the types of *text sources* currently

[4] *Processes* are defined in accordance with genre model proposed by Knapp and Watkins (2005). This model identifies genres that e.g. '*describe* through the process of ordering things into commonsense of technical frameworks of meaning, *explain* through the process of sequencing phenomena in temporal and/or causal relationships', etc.

specified by KPG in ontological structures. For instance, a novel, a short story, a fairy tale, a myth, a legend, a play script, and a comic strip are classified under a more general category called 'literary prose', which in turn inherits from a category referred to as 'literary text'; the latter is also inherited by 'literary rhythmic text' including poetry and lyrics. A newspaper, a magazine, and a news portal or blog are generally identified as 'news', while a letter, an e-mail, a note or comment, a postcard, and an invitation fall under the rubric 'interpersonal communication text'. In a similar way, text types, domains, and types of authors and addresses are also organised ontologically. This sort of classification can support the study of language use across generalised situational contexts.

The linguistic framework which we adopt for modelling language use is Halliday's Systemic Functional Grammar (SFG) (Halliday, 1976, 1985). Functional linguistics emphasises the continuities between language and social experience (i.e. real-world situations). That is, SFG views language is a system of *semiosis* that cannot be divorced from its context. It describes the resources of this complex system in terms of a compositional structure comprising three distinct layers (*strata*): *phonology*, *lexicogrammar* and *semantics*. Lexicogrammatical resources create meaning in the form of *text*.

3.1 The Annotation Scheme

Annotation of grammatical patterns spans across four types of text units: *sentences*, *clauses*, *phrases*, and *words*. For each text unit, we distinguish two levels of linguistic description: a Grammatical Type (GT) and a Semantic Type (ST) level. The former includes morphological and syntactic information about the unit in question, while the latter describes its semantic *function*, i.e. its function as a building block of textual meaning.

To illustrate the scheme with a concrete example, consider the sentence (1), taken from a B2 level script.

(1) I read in your email that you are thinking to quit school and work as a waitress, because you want to make money and travel all over the world.

The annotation of (1) involves several *annotation sets*. Each one includes combinations of GT and ST labels for a given type of text unit. The set shown in (2) describes the whole sentence.

(2) GT: S.Complex
ST: S.Declarative

Following the insight of Systemic Functional Grammar, we classify sentences in one of the types: Simple, Compound, and Complex. A sentence is an independent utterance with complete meaning. A Simple sentence typically contains a verb and its arguments.[5] A Compound sentence comprises two or more interdependent clauses of equal status (e.g. *[He came to a thicket] and [at that time he heard the faint rustling of leaves]*) (the definition of the clause follows). A Complex sentence includes two or more interdependent clauses of unequal status (e.g. *[When the path reaches the road], [follow the road downhill for about 200 metres]*).[6]

At the semantic level, we classify sentences as *Declarative*, *Interrogative*, *Imperative*, or *Exclamatory*. These categories essentially capture what Halliday (1979) called the *interpersonal* function of language referring to the ways in which meaning is negotiated between participants in a communicative act.

Another annotation set for (1) includes the descriptions in (3), (4), and (5) below, representing the clauses '*I read in your email*', '*that you're thinking to quit school and work as a waitress*', '*because you want to make money and travel all over the world*', respectively. A clause is a dependent utterance with incomplete meaning; it comprises a verb and its subject (at least).

(3) GT: Cfin_act.Main
ST: C.Mental

(4) GT: Cfin_act[that].Dep_Obj
ST: C.Mental

(5) GT: Cfin_act[because].Dep
ST: C.Mental

These representations capture the grammatical properties of the clauses above as well as their semantic functions. The utterance in (1) involves three clauses with finite (*fin*), active voice (*act*) verbs. (3) is the main clause, which introduces the semantic basis of the utterance. The semantics of (4) depends on that of (3) (i.e. it is the Object

[5]Yet an utterance like 'Hello!' or, simply, an exclamation is also considered a Simple sentence.

[6]The examples in parentheses are from Halliday and Matthiessen (2004). The different degrees of interdependency between sentences are referred to with the terms *parataxis* (equal status) and *hypotaxis* (unequal status).

of its verb), while (5) depends on (4). The structural (syntactic) typing of clauses (i.e. Main, Dep, Dep_Subj, Dep_Obj) is recorded at the GT level.

The semantic level comprises a description of the content of each clause. The content is represented in terms of general types of *events* or *processes*, as identified by Halliday (2004), i.e. *Mental, Verbal, Material, Relational, Behavioural, Existential* processes. We define these processes as functions referring to real-world events or situations. For their definitions, we specify sets of properties shared by participants in the designated events or situations. Note that we replace the Material type (whose definition is somewhat vague) with a Causation type (referring to events with causally affected participants) and we include additional types: Intentional Action, Motion, and Possession (see Gotsoulia (2011) for a description of the theoretical approach we adopt for defining broad categories of event semantics).

Similar annotation sets are specified for Verb Phrases (VPs), which also denote events, as exemplified by the representations of the phrases '*to quit school*' (6), and '*travel all over the world*' (7):

(6) GT: VPinf_act[to].Dep_Obj
ST: VP.Intentional_action

(7) GT: VPinf_act[to].Dep_Obj
ST: VP.Intentional_action

As illustrated in the above representations, our scheme emphasises the significance of general events in the creation of textual meaning. The linguistic expression of events is captured across different types of text units (i.e. clauses and phrases). Note that at the phrase level, we also represent Noun Phrases (NPs) (i.e. nominalisations), Adjectival Phrases (ADJPs), or Prepositional Phrases (PPs) denoting events of the sort we are interested in:

(8) $[_{NP}$The announcement of the results] was postponed. (*GT:NP, ST:NP.Verbal*)

(9) He is $[_{ADJP}$interested] $[_{PP}$in working] as a translator. (*GT:ADJP, ST:ADJP.Mental*) (*GT:PPing, ST:PP.Intentional Action*)

4 Future Work

The two-layer annotation scheme presented above encodes systematic associations of criterial lexical functions forming *textual meaning* and grammatical structures expressing each function.

Currently, we are in the process of annotating a portion of the KPG corpora with SFG categories. From the annotated data, we will be able to acquire frequencies of lexicogrammatical patterns in particular communicative contexts, proficiency levels, and grading bands. The novelty of our approach lies exactly at the combined representation of lexical and grammatical components, which (to our knowledge) has not yet been explored in the analysis of learner corpora. For example, the relevant research strands in the English Profile Project (i.e. the morpho-syntactic and the lexico-semantic strand) are unrelated.

While annotation is currently carried out manually, in the immediate future we intend to address semi-automatic tagging of SFG lexicogrammatical categories by using a syntactic and a semantic parser and mapping the output to the designated SFG categories. The proposed representations can ultimately be used to support reliable, semi-automatic assessment of contextualised language use in learners' scripts by computing similarities of graded and novel (not graded) scripts in terms of lexicogrammatical features and their frequencies.

Acknowledgments

Work presented in this paper is part of the project 'Differentiated and graded National Foreign Language Examinations', co-financed by the European Social Fund and National Resources.

References

Buttery, P. 2009. *Using large-scale corpora within the English Profile program; computational methods for constructing reference levels descriptors.* AAAL 2009. Denver, Colorado.

Gotsoulia, V. 2011. *An abstract scheme for representing semantic roles and modelling the syntax-semantics interface.* In Proceedings of the 9th International Conference on Computational Semantics (organised by the ACL Special Interest Group on Computational Semantics). Oxford, United Kingdom.

Halliday, .A.K. and Hasan R. 1976. *Cohesion in English.* London: Longman.

Halliday, M.A.K. and Hasan R. 1985. *Language, Context and Text: Aspects of Language in a Social-semiotic Perspective.* Oxford: Oxford University Press.

Halliday, M.A.K. and Matthiessen C. 1999. *Construing experience through meaning.* London, New York: Continuum.

Halliday, .A.K. and Matthiessen C. 2004. *An Introduction to Functional Grammar. (3rd ed.)* NY: Arnold.

Hawkins, J.A. and Buttery, P. 2009. *Using learner language from corpora to profile levels of proficiency: Insights from the English Profile Programme.* In: Studies in Language Testing: The Social and Educational Impact of Language Assessment. Cambridge University Press.

Knapp, P. and Watkins, M. 2005. *Genre, text, grammar: Technologies for teaching and assessing writing.* Sydney: UNSW press.

Kondyli M. and Lykou C. 2010 *Linguistic Description of the KPG tasks and texts: The text type and lexicogrammar perspective. (in Greek)* Research Periodical: http://rcel.enl.uoa.gr/periodical/article$_e$n.htm

Parsing a Polysynthetic Language

Petr Homola
Codesign, s.r.o.
phomola@codesign.cz

Abstract

We present the results of a project of building a lexical-functional grammar of Aymara, an Amerindian language. There was almost no research on Aymara in computational linguistics to date. The goal of the project is two-fold: First, we want to provide a formal description of the language. Second, NLP resources (lexicon and grammar) are being developed that could be used in machine translation and other NLP tasks. The paper presents formal description of selected properties of Aymara which are uncommon in well-researched Western languages. Furthermore, we present an experimental machine translation system into Spanish and English.

1 Introduction

Aymara is an Amerindian language spoken in Bolivia, Chile and Peru by approx. two million people. It is a polysynthetic language that has many lexical and structural similarities with Quechua but the often suggested genetic relationship between these languages is still disputed.

The only research on Aymara in the field of computational linguistics we know about is the project described in (Beesley, 2006). The presented project uses Lexical-Functional Grammar (LFG) (Kaplan and Bresnan, 1982; Bresnan, 2001) to formally describe the lexicon, morphology and syntax of Aymara in a manner suitable for natural language processing (NLP). The grammar we have implemented is capable of parsing complex sentences with embedded clauses. We have also done experiments with machine translation (MT) into Spanish and English; the results are presented in Section 4.

Aymara is a polysynthetic language with a very complicated system of polypersonal agreement (see Section 2.3 for a brief description). A rare property of words in Aymara is the so-called vowel elision (sometimes called 'subtractive morphology') which is quite hard to describe formally. We show how vowel elision can be dealt with in the lexicon.

The paper is organized as follows: Section 2 presents selected properties of Aymara, many of them absent from well-researched languages such as English, and their formal analysis in LFG. Section 3 introduces a dependency-based abstraction of f-structures which brings formal grammars closer cross-linguistically. Section 4 describes our experiment with MT from Aymara into Spanish and English. Finally, we conclude in Section 5 and give an outlook for further research.

2 Some Properties of Aymara

In this section, we focus on some properties of Aymara at the level of morphology and syntax which are mostly absent from Western languages such as English, and sketch their analysis in LFG. A detailed description of the language can be found in (Hardman et al., 2001; Adelaar and Muysken, 2007; Cerrón-Palomino and Carvajal, 2009; Briggs, 1976).

2.1 Agglutinative Morphology

Aymara has a very rich inflection. Suffixes of various categories can be chained to build up long words that would be expressed by a sentence in languages like English. For example, *alanxarusksmawa* (*ala-ni-xaru-si-ka-sma-wa*) means "I am preparing myself to go and buy it for you".

In concordance with the principle of lexical integrity (Bresnan, 2001), we deal with morphology in the lexicon. Ishikawa (1985) has suggested to use word-internal (sublexical) rules to analyze structurally complex words in agglutinative languages. We have adopted this analysis.

2.2 Vowel elision

Aymara uses vowel elision as morphosyntacic marking, as illustrated in (1) and (2).[1]

(1) *aycha manq'ani*
meat eater
"who eats much meat"

(2) *aych manq'ani*
meat-ELI eat-FUT$_{3\to 3}$
"(s)he will eat meat"

There are three types of vowel elision that interact with each other. *Object elision* marks a noun or pronoun as direct object, such as in (3) (as opposed to (4)).

(3) *khits uñji*
whom-ELI see-NFUT$_{3\to 3}$
"Whom does he/she see?"

(4) *khitis uñji*
who see-NFUT$_{3\to 3}$
"Who does see him/her?"

Noun compound elision occurrs in NPs. The final vowel of noun attributes gets elided if they have three or more syllables, as illustrated in (5) and (6).

(5) *aymar aru*
Aymara-ELI language
"the Aymara language"

(6) *qala uta*
stone house
"stone house"

Complement elision is applied to all words that are arguments or adjuncts of a verb except for the final word of a clause.[2]

Whereas object elision concerns the nucleus of a word (the stem with an optional possessive and/or plural suffix), noun compound and complement elisions concern the final vowel of a word (the vowel of the last suffix or the stem if there are no suffixes). Vowel elision is dealt with in the lexicon. As for noun compound elision, all nouns with more than two syllables get ($\uparrow$ COMPEL) = + if the final vowel of the word nucleus is elided and ($\uparrow$ COMPEL) = − if it is not. Nouns with two vowels do not define this attribute, i.e., it can be unified with both values. The corresponding rule for compound nouns is given in (7).

(7)
$$N' \rightarrow \underset{\substack{(\uparrow \text{MOD}) = \downarrow \\ (\downarrow \text{COMPEL}) = +}}{(N')} \quad \underset{\uparrow=\downarrow}{N}$$

2.3 Polypersonal agreement

Being a polysynthetic language, Aymara has polypersonal conjugation, i.e., the finite verb agrees with the subject and with another argument which may be the object (direct or indirect) or an oblique argument. An example is given in (8).

(8) *Uñjsma*
see-NFUT$_{1\to 2}$
"I see/saw you."

The morpholexical entry for *uñjsma* is given in (9).[3] Note that the PRED value for both subject and object is optional.[4]

(9)
uñjsma V (↑PRED) ='uñjaña⟨(↑SUBJ)(↑OBJ)⟩'
(↑TAM TENSE) = NON-FUT
(↑TAM MOOD) = INDIC
((↑SUBJ PRED) = 'PRO')
(↑SUBJ PERS) = 1
((↑OBJ PRED) = 'PRO')
(↑OBJ PERS) = 2

The verb agrees with the subject and with the most animate argument which may be a patient, addressee or source, e.g., *um churäma*-FUT$_{1\to 2}$ "I will give you water" (addresse), *aych aläma*-FUT$_{1\to 2}$ "I will buy meat from you" (source) etc. However, there are verbal suffixes which can make the verb agree with other arguments, such as the beneficiary, e.g., *aych churarapitäta*-BEN,FUT$_{2\to 1}$ "You will give him/her bread for me" (the verb agrees with the beneficiary instead of the addressee). All these agreement rules are encoded in the lexicon.

2.4 Free Word Order

At the clause level, the word order in Aymara is not restricted although SOV is preferred. There is also no evidence for a VP, thus we assume a flat phrase structure. The rules for matrix clauses are given in (10).[5]

[1] In the glosses, FUT$_{3\to 3}$ means future tense. The numbers express the person of the subject and an additional argument, mostly object.

[2] Object and noun compound elision has the gloss ELI in our examples.

[3] TAM means Tense-Aspect-Mood.

[4] Both arguments can be dropped.

[5] In the functional annotation, κ is either '−' (no case) or a semantic case and GF is the corresponding grammatical function.

(10)

$$\begin{array}{lll} S & \rightarrow & \mathcal{X}^{+} \end{array}$$

$$\text{where } \mathcal{X} \text{ is } \begin{array}{c} \text{V} \\ \uparrow=\downarrow \end{array} \text{ or } \begin{array}{c} \text{NP/CP} \\ (\downarrow \text{CASE}) = \kappa \Rightarrow \\ (\uparrow \text{GF}) = \downarrow \end{array}$$

$$\begin{array}{lllll} \text{CP} & \rightarrow & \underset{\uparrow=\downarrow}{\text{(C)}} & , & \underset{\uparrow=\downarrow}{\text{S}} \end{array}$$

As can be seen, word order in a clause is free with the exception of an optional complementizer (see (11) and (12)) which can be placed at the beginning of the clause or at its end.

(11) *Ukat juti*
then come-NFUT$_{3\rightarrow3}$
"Then (s)he came."

(12) *Jutät ukaxa...*
come-FUT$_{2\rightarrow3}$ if
"If you will come..."

There are no discontinuous constituents and complement clauses can be embedded in the matrix sentence. Since Aymara is not discourse-configurational (see the next subsection), the word order, despite of being free, is usually unmarked (SOV) and if it is different then mostly for stylistic reasons.

2.5 Topic-Focus Articulation

We have adopted the approach proposed by King (1997). Thus we use an i(nformation)-structure to approximate topic-focus articulation (TFA).[6]

A simple example of two sentences which differ only in TFA is given in (13) (the word *qullqirï* is a verbalized noun).

(13) *Jumax qillqirïtawa*
you-SG,TOP be-a-writer-NFUT$_{2\rightarrow3}$,FOC
"You are a writer."

Jumaw qillqirïtaxa
you-SG,FOC be-a-writer-NFUT$_{2\rightarrow3}$,TOP
"It is you who is the writer."

The morpholexical entries for *jumax* and *jupaw* and corresponsing i-structures for the sentences in (13) are given in (14) and (15), respectively.

(14) *jumax* PRON (↑PRED) = 'PRO'
(↑PERS) = 2
(↑PRED FN) ∈ (↑$_i$TOP)

$$\begin{bmatrix} \text{TOP} & \left\{\text{`jumax'}\right\} \\ \text{FOC} & \left\{\text{`qillqiri'}\right\} \end{bmatrix}$$

(15) *jumaw* PRON (↑PRED) = 'PRO'
(↑PERS) = 2
(↑PRED FN) ∈ (↑$_i$FOC)

$$\begin{bmatrix} \text{TOP} & \left\{\text{`qillqiri'}\right\} \\ \text{FOC} & \left\{\text{`jumax'}\right\} \end{bmatrix}$$

The i-structure is very important for correct translation. For example, the sentence *Chachax liwrw liyi* would be translated as "The man read(s) a book" whereas *Chachaw liwrx liyi* would be better translated as "The book is/was read by a man".[7]

3 Lexical Mapping Theory and D-Structures

Although f-structures abstract to some extent from language specific features (such as differential object marking, see (16) where the Spanish dative phrase and the Polish genitive phrase would be in accusative in German), there are still many differences even between relatively closely related languages.[8]

(16) *Ayer visité a Juan*
yesterday visit-PAST,1SG to Juan
"I visited Juan yesterday."

Nie mam samochodu
NEG have-PRES,1SG car-SG,GEN
"I don't have a car."

Wong and Hancox (1998) examine the use of a(rgument)-structures in machine translation

[6]The difference is that we use only two discourse functions, TOP or FOC, with the possibility for words being discourse-unspecified (the term 'discourse-neutral' is used sometimes). This is exactly how morphological marking of TFA works in Aymara.

[7]Unlike some other languages with morphological topic and/or focus markers, such as Japanese (cf. examples from (Kroeger, 2004): *Taroo-wa*-TOP *sono hon-o*-ACC *yondeiru* "Taroo is reading that book." vs. *Sono hon-wa*-TOP *Taroo-ga*-NOM *yondeiru* "That book, Taroo is reading"), Aymara allows their co-occurrence with case suffixes without limitation.

[8]For example, the East Baltic language Latvian has only agent-less passives (i.e., in LFG, it completely lacks OBL$_{ag}$, cf. (Forssman, 2001)), whereas its closest and partially mutually intelligible relative Lithuanian has and frequently uses agents in passives.

(MT). In LFG, a-structures are another level of linguistic representation which provides the lexico-syntactic interface. The mapping between a-structures and f-structures is defined by the so-called Lexical Mapping Theory (LMT; see (Bresnan, 2001)). We will give a brief overview of LMT here.

LFG assumes that there is a prominence hierarchy of semantic roles. We use the hierarchy shown in (17) (proposed by Bresnan (2001)):

(17) agent $\succ$ beneficiary/maleficiary $\succ$ experiencer/goal $\succ$ instrument $\succ$ patient/theme $\succ$ locative

Argument grammatical functions (GF) are assigned features *objective* and *restricted* as in (18). The markedness hierarchy of GFs is given in (19).

(18)

	-r	+r
-o	SUBJ	OBL_θ
+o	OBJ	OBJ_θ

(19) SUBJ $\succ$ OBJ, $OBL_\theta \succ OBJ_\theta$

Verbs in LFG have an a-structure that expresses their valence. The arguments of each verb are ordered according to the hierarchy in (17) and annotated with $-o$, $-r$, $+o$, $+r$. General LMT principles determine how the arguments are mapped onto GFs. The initial role is mapped onto SUBJ if classified with $[-o]$. Otherwise, the leftmost role classified $[-r]$ is mapped onto SUBJ. Other roles are mapped onto the lowest compatible GF according to the hierarchy in (19). There are two other constraints: Every verb must have a SUBJ and each role must be associated with a unique function, and conversely.

Bresnan (2001) argues that LMT allows for natural treatment of passives, ditransitives and other constructions which have been handled by lexical rules in earlier versions of LFG.

We use the information provided by f-structures, i-structures, c-structures and a-structures to create a dependency-based representation of parsed sentences (a tectogrammatical tree in the terminology of Sgall et al. (1986)). The main reason is that we already have a module that generates English and Spanish sentences from (tectogrammatical) syntax trees.

In the following, we will use the term d(ependency)-structure to refer to dependency trees induced by LFG structures. Table 1 gives a brief overview of which information at different levels of linguistic representation in LFG is used in d-structures.

LFG layer	**information in d-structures**
c-structure	original word order
f-structure	dependencies and coreferences
i-structure	topic-focus articulation
a-structure	valence

Table 1: Information provided by LFG layers to d-structures

The skeleton of a d-structure is provided by the f-structure. According to a generally accepted principle of deep syntax (tectogrammatics) only autosemantic (content) word are represented by nodes in d-structures. In LFG, autosemantic words are associated with projections of lexical categories, i.e., f-structures with the PRED attribute (see (Bresnan, 2001) for a detailed discussion of lexical and functional categories and the so-called 'coheads'). Thus a d-structure derived from (20) would have three nodes for the words *dog, chases* and *cat*.

(20)
$$\begin{bmatrix} \text{PRED} & \text{`chase}\langle(\uparrow\text{SUBJ})(\uparrow\text{OBJ})\rangle\text{'} \\ \text{TENSE} & \text{PRES} \\ \text{SUBJ} & \begin{bmatrix} \text{PRED} & \text{`dog'} \\ \text{SPEC} & \begin{bmatrix} \text{DEF} & + \end{bmatrix} \end{bmatrix} \\ \text{OBJ} & \begin{bmatrix} \text{PRED} & \text{`cat'} \\ \text{SPEC} & \begin{bmatrix} \text{DEF} & - \end{bmatrix} \end{bmatrix} \end{bmatrix}$$

The edges are labelled with semantic roles. This is possible due to the bi-uniqueness of the mapping between roles and GFs (see above). However, there is one exception: The initial role is assigned a special label which we call 'actor' (ACT, which is equivalent to what Bresnan (2001) marks $\hat{\theta}$ and calls 'logical subject'). This partially reflects the shifting of actants in tectogrammatics as defined by Sgall et al. (1986).[9]

So far, we have an unordered tree (f-structures are unordered by definition).[10] We define an ordering based on information structure, as proposed

[9]The edge labels are theory specific and somewhat arbitrary. For example, Butt et al. (1999) distinguish between 'semantic' and 'non-semantic' prepositions. As a consequence, the complement in *He relies on the book* is an OBJ and therefore PAT in the corresponding d-structure although *on the book* is not a direct object in the traditional dependency grammar.

[10]Generally, the skeleton rendered by f-structures may contain a cycle, i.e., a node with more than one mother nodes.

for deep syntax by Sgall et al. (1986). Thus we use the i-structure to define a partial ordering on the nodes of the d-structure (TOP $\prec$ 'discourse-unspecified' $\prec$ FOC). The nodes in each of the three topic-focus domains are ordered according to their original ordering in the sentence (which is captured by c-structures).[11]

The resulting d-structure is given in (21).[12]

(21)

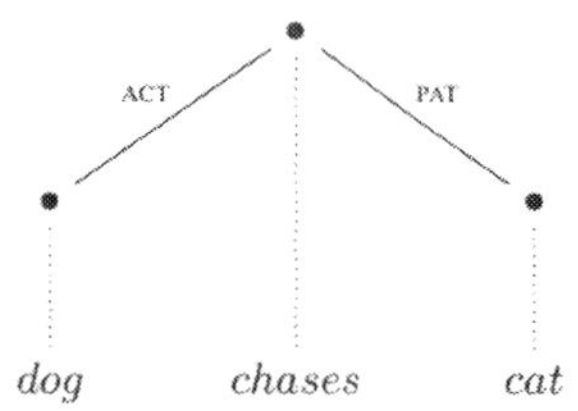

Let us briefly point out some properties of d-structures as defined above. Most of them directly correspond to properties of deep syntax (tectogrammatical) trees.

1. There is a bi-unique mapping between d-structure nodes and autosemantic (content) words. Synsemantic (auxiliary/function) words are represented as attributes of nodes. This is a direct consequence of LFG 'coheads'.

2. 'Dropped' words (e.g., subject and/or object pronouns in so-called pro-drop languages) are re-established in d-structures as a consequence of the LFG Principle of Completeness since PRED attributes are instantiated in the lexicon if needed (cf. (Bresnan, 2001)).

3. Edge labels in d-structures reflect semantic relations rather the GFs which are more language specific.

4. The ordering of d-structure nodes is partially determined by topic-focus articulation.

This is how LFG handles coreferences, such as in the sentence *I want to go home* where the complement clause is an open complement (XCOMP) in the f-structure of 'want' and $(\uparrow \text{SUBJ}) = (\uparrow \text{XCOMP SUBJ})$. To obtain a well-formed tree, we reflect the path of length 1 in the f-structure as an edge and the remaining (conflicting) functional paths as co-references.

[11] In free word-order languages, NPs and PPs usually have more rigid word order than clause arguments and adjuncts, thus in an MT system, the module for syntactic synthesis of the target language would reorder the d-structure according to language specific word-order rules.

[12] The attributes associated with nodes can be obtained from corresponding f-structures (in LFG, all lingustic levels are interlinked).

However, there are several differences. For example, d-structures can be non-projective (tectogrammatical trees are projective by definition (Sgall et al., 1986)) which is a direct consequence of how long-distance dependencies are represented in f-structures. Furthermore, one word can be represented by more than one d-structure nodes (such as in languages with incorporation).

Butt et al. (1999) give a detailed description of the process of parallel grammar development. In our approach, the correspondence between original LFG structures and d-structures poses some (mostly technical) limitations on grammar writers. For example, f-structures of synsemantic words (functional categories) must be 'coheads' of their functional categories (however, this is a general requirement in modern LFG according to Bresnan (2001)). Also, GFs must conform to the strict constraints imposed by LMT.

Table 2 show how many c-structures, f-structures and d-structures are identical (two d-structures are identical if they have the same structure and edge labels) in a parallel Aymara-Spanish corpus of 1,000 sentences.

level	**identical representation**
c-structure	7.8%
f-structure	38.3%
d-structure	69.5%

Table 2: Identical c-, f- and d-structures in a parallel corpus

4 Machine Translation

In this section, we briefly present the results of an MT experiment from Aymara into Spanish and English. All modules of the system were developed in SWI Prolog (Wielemaker, 2003).

It is obvious (cf. Section 2) the there are very few structural similarities between Aymara and Spanish or English, thus a 'direct' or 'shallow' approach to MT, as proposed by Dyvik (1995), would not lead to quality translation. As has been said above, we have developed an LFG grammar for Aymara. Kaplan and Wedekind (2000) have shown that the generation of sentences out of a f-structure according to an LFG grammar yields a context-free language. However an LFG grammar developed for parsing may not be suitable for generation (due to overgeneration). That is why we use d-structures as defined in Section 3.

Evaluation results are given in Table 3.

language pair	WER
Aymara-Spanish	22.3%
Aymara-English	24.8%

Table 3: Evaluation of MT into Spanish and English

While the error rate is not low, it is acceptable given the fact that the source language is structurally very different from the target language. Most translation errors can be tracked to diverging valency of verbs in both languages.

5 Conclusions and Further Research

We have presented a formal grammar for Aymara and pointed out some interesting properties of the language and how they can be dealt with in the LFG framework.

As can be seen, the LFG framework can be easily used to develop formal grammars of polysynthetic languages such as Aymara. While the rules we have developed cover a large part of the Aymara syntax, the lexicon we have now needs to be expaned. Currently, we are focusing on refining sublexical rules.

We have chosen LFG for our grammar because it has a solid formal foundation while providing grammars that can be used directly in NLP. However, we are developing the grammar for use in MT and LFG's f-structures are still relatively language-specific. To overcome this limitation, we have developed a fully automatic procedure which induces d(ependency)-structures (deep syntax trees) that are at a higher level of abstraction. Our d-structures are not only more suitable for cross-lingual NLP tasks such as MT but they also disclose that LFG is, in its core, a dependency-based formalism.

References

Willem Adelaar and Pieter Muysken. 2007. *The Languages of the Andes*. Cambridge University Press.

Kenneth R. Beesley. 2006. Finite-state Morphological Analysis and Generation for Aymara. In *Proceedings of the Global Symposium on Promoting the Multilingual Internet*.

Joan Bresnan. 2001. *Lexical-Functional Syntax*. Blackwell Textbooks in Linguistics, New York.

Lucy Therina Briggs. 1976. *Dialectal Variation in the Aymara Language of Bolivia and Peru*. Ph.D. thesis, University of Florida.

Miriam Butt, Tracy Holloway King, María-Eugenia Niño, and Frédérique Segond. 1999. *A Grammar Writer's Cookbook*. CSLI Publications.

R. Cerrón-Palomino and J. Carvajal Carvajal. 2009. Aimara. In M. Crevels and P. Muysken, editors, *Lenguas de Bolivia*. Plural Editores, La Paz, Bolivia.

Helge Dyvik. 1995. Exploiting Structural Similarities in Machine Translation. *Computers and Humanities*, 28:225–245.

Berthold Forssman. 2001. *Lettische Grammatik*. Verlag J.H. Roell, Dettelbach.

Martha Hardman, J. Vásquez, and J. Yapita de Dios. 2001. *Aymara. Compendio de estructura fonológica y gramatical*. Instituto de Lengua y Cultura Aymara.

Akira Ishikawa. 1985. *Complex Predicates and Lexical Operations in Japanese*. Ph.D. thesis, Stanford University.

Ronald M. Kaplan and Joan Bresnan. 1982. Lexical-Functional Grammar: A formal system for grammatical representation. In Joan Bresnan, editor, *Mental Representation of Grammatical Relations*. MIT Press, Cambridge.

Ronald M. Kaplan and Jürgen Wedekind. 2000. LFG Generation Produces Context-free Languages. In *Proceedings of COLING-2000, Saarbrücken*.

Tracy Holloway King. 1997. Focus Domains and Information Structure. In Miriam Butt and Tracy Holloway King, editors, *Proceedings of the LFG Conference*.

Paul R. Kroeger. 2004. *Analyzing Syntax*. Cambridge University Press.

Petr Sgall, Eva Hajičová, and Jarmila Panevová. 1986. *The Meaning of the Sentence in Its Semantic and Pragmatic Aspects*. D. Reider Publishing Company.

Jan Wielemaker. 2003. An overview of the SWI-Prolog programming environment. In Fred Mesnard and Alexander Serebenik, editors, *Proceedings of the 13th International Workshop on Logic Programming Environments*, pages 1–16, Heverlee, Belgium, december. Katholieke Universiteit Leuven. CW 371.

Shun Ha Sylvia Wong and Peter Hancox. 1998. An Investigation into the Use of Argument Structure and Lexical Mapping Theory for Machine Translation. In *Proceedings of the 12th Pacific Asia Conference on Linguistics, Information and Computation*, Singapore.

An Algorithm of Identifying Semantic Arguments of a Verb from Structured Data

Minhua Huang
Department of Computer Science
Graduate School and University Center
City University of New York
New York, U.S.A
mhuang@gc.cuny.edu

Robert M. Haralick
Department of Computer Science
Graduate School and University Center
City University of New York
New York, U.S.A
haralick@aim.com

Abstract

We discuss a method for identifying semantic arguments of a verb from a sentence. It differs from existing methods by an unique feature that represents all semantic arguments of a verb in a syntactic parse tree. The feature is a path in which at least one of the children of a node is a root of a subtree that associates with a semantic argument. Experiments on WSJ data from Penn TreeBank and PropBank show that our method achieves an average of precision 92.3% and an average of recall 94.2% on identifying semantic arguments of over six hundred verbs.

1 Introduction

Semantic argument identification is one of the subtasks of semantic role labeling (Gildea and Jurafsky, 2002) (Chen and Rambow, 2002) (Hacioglu, 2004b) which classifies a sequence of words associated with a semantic argument of a verb but does not assign its role. It is the most difficult task in semantic role labeling. Moreover, it is one of the core techniques for a machine to understand the semantics of a sentence. For instance, in the sentences *Lisa cut the ribbon with a pair of scissors.* and *The ribbon was cut by Lisa with a pair of scissors*, *cut* is the verb. Semantic arguments of *cut* will be *Lisa, the ribbon, and a pair of scissors*, where *Lisa* is the one who performs the action of cutting, *the ribbon* is the material to be cut by Lisa, and *a pair of scissors* is the tool used for cutting. For semantic role labeling, arguments of cut need to be determined. Then, each argument will be assigned to a label, such as $agent$, $theme$, and $instrument$ in the example. In this report, we presents an algorithm for finding a semantic argument of a verb which is the first task required for assigning a role for the verb.

Over the years, two approaches have been discussed by researchers, such as methods developed based on hierarchical trees (Gildea and Jurafsky, 2002) (Hacioglu, 2004b) (Hacioglu, 2004c) and methods developed based on flat chunks (Hacioglu and Ward, 2003) (Hacioglu, 2004a). In almost all the methods of the first approach, a syntactic tree is transformed into a sequence of constituents. Each semantic argument of a verb is represented by a set of constituents. Each constituent is represented by a set of features. These features are extracted based on linguistic knowledge and local knowledge of the tree structure. Finally, sophisticated classifiers such as support vector machines or maximum entropy modeling classifiers are employed to identify semantic arguments of each verb. In contrast to these methods, our method is based on the idea that if a sentence has a correspondent labeled rooted tree (parser tree), a semantic argument of a verb in the sentence will be associated with a labeled rooted subtree. Hence, all semantic arguments of a verb in the sentence will be represented by a set of labeled rooted subtrees. For each verb node v, there exists a path from node a to node b, from which, all roots of the subtrees will be extracted. Obviously, all semantic arguments of a verb are represented by an unique feature – a path.

We find the path for a verb in a labeled rooted tree associated with a sentence by the probabilistic graphical model discussed in the paper (Huang and Haralick, 2009). This model is fast, uses less memory, and is very effective on text data. We construct the path by starting from a verb node and determining the next node by selecting the node that has the largest probability value among the adjacent nodes which have not been encountered yet. Then, a sibling or a child of a node in the path is identified as a root of a subtree associating with a semantic argument of the verb.

We have tested our method on the WSJ data

the 00 section from Penn TreeBak and PropBank (Weischedel et al., 2007). There are a total of 233 trees associating with about 600 verbs and 2000 semantic arguments. The evaluation metrics we have used are *precision*, *recall*, and *f-measure*. By applying 10-folder cross validation technique, we have obtained an average of precision 92.64%, an average of recall 94.94%, and an average of f-measure 93.81%. Our experiments show that our method is particularly effective for identifying such semantic arguments, which them are associated with a sequence of consecutive words. Our method is less effective for semantic arguments, which they are associated with two or more sequences of consecutive words (separated by other phrases). Details are shown in Section 4. We are doing more experiments on CoNLL-2005 shared task data set to further verify our method.

The paper is organized into six sections. Section two defines a labeled rooted tree and forest; section three discusses the algorithm; section four demonstrates empirical results; section five shows related research and comparisons; and section six gives a conclusion.

2 A Labeled Rooted Tree and a Labeled Rooted Forest

A rooted tree T is a 3-tuple (V, E, r), where V is a finite set of vertices, $E \subseteq V \times V$ is a finite set of edges, and $r \in V$ is the root that all edges of T are directed away from it. The tree-order is the partial ordering on V for any $v, u \in V, u \leq v$ if and only if the unique path from the root r to v passes through u.

In T, the root r is a unique minimal vertex and has level 0. An edge $(x < y)$ in E is an ordered pair $(x, y) \in (V \times V)$ s.t. $x < y$ and there exists no $z \in V$ with $x < z < y$. In this case, x is a parent of y and y is a child of x. If two nodes[1] x, y have the same parent z, x and y are called siblings. Any node y is on the unique path from r to x is called an ancestor of x. In this case, x is a descendant of y. The sub-tree rooted at node x is the tree induced by descendants of x. A node with no children is an external node or a leaf. A node that is not a leaf node is an internal node. The largest depth of a node in T is the *height* of T.

[1]In a rooted tree, a vertex can be also called a node.

2.0.1 Definition of a Labeled Rooted Tree

A labeled rooted tree is a 5-tuple (V, E, r, A, L). It is a rooted tree with additional two elements: a labeling alphabet A and a labeling function $L : V \rightarrow A$ that assigns labels to vertices.

2.0.2 Definition of a Labeled Rooted Forest

A labeled rooted forest is a set of labeled rooted trees, s.t. $F = \{T_i | i = 1 \ldots N\}$ where T_i is a labeled rooted tree.

3 The Method

3.1 Defining the Task

Let $T = (V, E, r, A, L)$ be a labeled rooted tree associated with a sentence, where A is defined by (Weischedel et al., 2007). Let π be a set of labels associated with verbs, s.t. $\pi \subseteq A$. Let $C = \{C_1, C_2\}$ be a set of class categories, where C_1 represents that a path will be extended from the current node to an adjacent node; C_2 represents that a path will not be extended from the current node to an adjacent node.

The task can be stated as follows:

- Form a path $\mathcal{P}(x) = \tau_1, \rightarrow \ldots, \rightarrow \tau_K$, where $x \in V$, $L(x) \in \pi$, and x is not a node in $\mathcal{P}'(y)$, $\mathcal{P}'(y)$ is a path that has been already formed previously. Each $\tau_k \in V$, $k = 1, \ldots, K$
  - find a sequence nodes $< \tau_1, \ldots, \tau_K >$, s.t.

$$\begin{aligned} &< \tau_1, \ldots, \tau_K > \\ = \; & \underset{b_1,\ldots,b_K}{argmax}\, p(c_1, \ldots, c_K, b_1, \ldots, b_K) \end{aligned}$$

  - where $c_k \in C$, b_k is one of adjacent nodes of b_{k-1}, $b_{k-1}, b_k \in V$, $b_{k-1}b_k \in E$.
- Form a set of roots $R(x) = \{r_i | i = 1 \ldots M\}$, where $r_i \leq \tau_k$, $L(r_i) \notin \pi$, and $1 \leq k \leq K$.
- Form a labeled rooted forest $F(x) = \{T_1, \ldots T_M\}$, where each T_i is a labeled rooted tree, rooted as r_i, and induced by the descendants of r_i.
- T_i associates with a semantic argument of x.

Figure 1 illustrates the labeled rooted tree for the sentence *Mrs. Hills said that the U.S. is still concerned about "disturbing developments in*

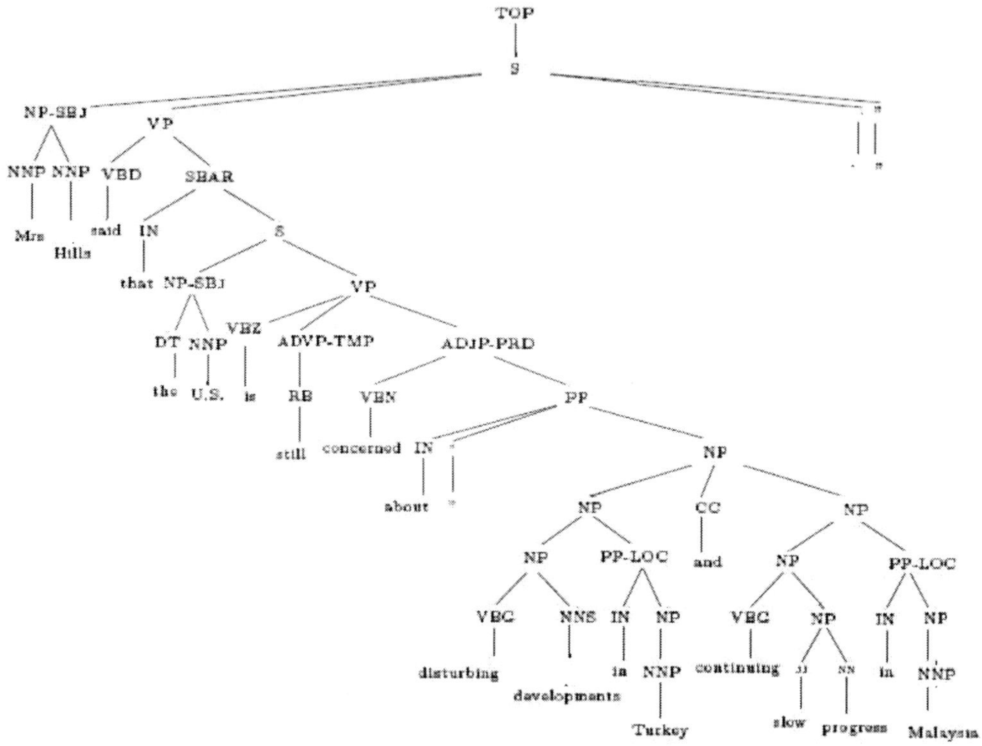

Figure 1: *Mrs. Hills said that the U.S. is still concerned about "disturbing developments in Turkey and continuing slow process in Malaysia".*

Turkey and continuing slow process in Malaysia". $\pi = \{VB, VBN, VBG, VBZ, VBP, VBD\} \subseteq A$.

3.2 The Algorithm

3.2.1 Obtaining $< \tau_1, \ldots, \tau_K >$

We use equation (1) proposed by (Huang and Haralick, 2010b) (Huang and Haralick, 2009) to obtain the probability value of $p(c_1, \ldots, c_K, b_1, \ldots, b_K)$.

$$\begin{aligned} & p(c_1, \ldots, c_K, b_1, \ldots, b_K) \\ = & \prod_{i=1}^{K} p(b_{i-1}|b_i c_i) p(b_{i+1}|b_i, c_i) p(b_i|c_i) p(c_i) \\ = & \prod_{i=1}^{K} P(b_{i-1}, b_i, b_{i+1}, c_i) \end{aligned} \tag{1}$$

We use the equation (2) to find a sequence of optimal nodes $< \tau_1, ..., \tau_K >$ in T, where $\tau_i \neq \tau_j$, $i, j = 1, ..., K$, $\tau_{i-1}\tau_i \in E$ and $\tau_i \tau_{i+1} \in E$ but $\tau_{i-1}\tau_{i+1} \notin E$

$$\begin{aligned} & < \tau_1, ..., \tau_K >= \\ & \underset{c_1 \in C, b_1, b' \in E}{argmax} \{p(b_2|b_1, c_1) p(b_1|c_1) p(c_1)\} \\ & \underset{c_2 \in C, b_2, b' \in E}{argmax} \{p(b_1|s_2, c_2) p(b_3|b_2, c_2) p(b_2|c_2) p(c_2)\} \\ & \ldots \\ & \underset{c_K \in C, b_K, b' \in E}{argmax} \{p(b_{K-1}|b_K, c_K) p(b_K|c_K) p(c_K)\} \end{aligned} \tag{2}$$

Note: b' is a node in a path, $b'b_k \in E$, $k = 1...K$.

3.2.2 Time Complexity

For each node b_k, we need to assign a c_k, s.t.

$$\mathcal{P}_k = max\{P(b_{k-1}, b_k, b_{k+1}, c_k) \mid c_k \in C\}$$

To compute a $P(b_{k-1}, b_k, b_{k+1}, c_k)$, we need to have four multiplications. To obtain the maximum probability value $\mathcal{P}_k$, we need to have $M-1$ comparisons. In the case of a path of N nodes, we have

$$T_c = 4 * N * (M-1) * (L-1) = O(N * M * L)$$

Note: M is the cardinality of C, L is the maximum degree of a node in the tree, and N is the length of the path.

3.2.3 Memory Complexity

Because the global maximum probability is determined by each local maximal probability, for a path of N symbols, we only need to store the information of the current node. That is, we need only store M probability values in order to find the maximal probability value. Therefore,

$$M_c = M = O(M)$$

3.2.4 An Example of a Path

The path $P(x)$, where $L(x)$ =*VBN* (associating with the verb *concern*) in Figure 1 is $VBZ \rightarrow VP \rightarrow ADJP - PRD \rightarrow VBN$ in Figure 2.

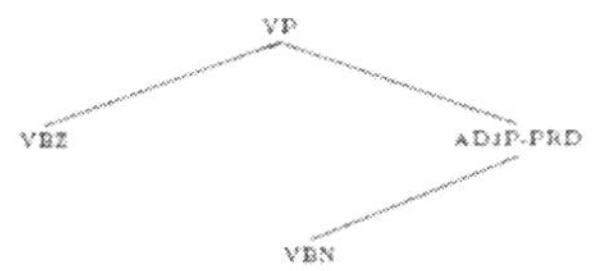

Figure 2: *All the semantic arguments of the verb concern can be extracted from this path.*

3.2.5 Finding a set of roots $r_i \in R(x)$

Let $Q(x)$ denote a set of nodes in path $\mathcal{P}(x)$ and let $R(x)$ denote a set of roots we want to find.

- $R(x) = \phi$, $Q(x) = \{\tau_i | 1 \leq i \leq K\}$
- If $Q(x) \neq \phi$ continue the following procedure:
  1. For each $\tau_i \in Q(x)$
  2. For all siblings of τ_i, find z, s.t. $L(z) \notin \pi$ and $z \notin \{\tau_i | i = 1, \ldots, K\}$, $R(x) \leftarrow R(x) \cup \{z\}$
  3. For all children of τ_i, if none of children z, $L(Z) \in \pi$, GOTO 4. Otherwise, find y, s.t. $L(y) \notin \pi$ *and* $y \notin \{\tau_i | i = 1, \ldots, K\}$, $R(x) \leftarrow R(x) \cup \{y\}$
  4. $Q(x) \leftarrow Q(x) - \{\tau_i\}$
- Otherwise, stop the procedure and return $R(x)$.

3.2.6 Building a Labeled Rooted Forest $F(x)$

Let T be a original labeled rooted tree, $R(x)$ be a set of roots of subtrees that we want to build, and $F(x) = \phi$.

1. For each $r_i \in R(x)$, we assign r_i to the variable α. We initialize T_i with only a vertex r_i. We visit α.
2. For $\{\alpha, \beta\} \in E$, and β has not been visited, we attach $\{\alpha, \beta\}$ to T_i.
3. Assign β to α and visit α. Go to 2.
   - If $\alpha = r_i$, then the labeled rooted tree T_i has been built. $F(x) \leftarrow F(x) \cup T_i$
   - If $\alpha \neq r_i$, backtrack from α to its parent β in T. Then assign β to α and go to 2

Figure 3 illustrates a labeled rooted forest for verb *concern* for the labeled rooted tree corresponds to the sentence *Mrs. Hills said that the U.S. is still concerned about "disturbing developments in Turkey and continuing slow process in Malaysia".*

4 Experiments

We have tested our method on data set developed by (Weischedel et al., 2007), specifically, the WSJ section 00 from Penn Treebank and PropBank. A total of 233 trees associates with 233 sentences and 621 verbs, each verb has an average of three semantic arguments, hence about 2000 semantic arguments are in total. The evaluation metrics we have used are *precision , recall, and f-measure* (F_1). Moreover, we have used 10-fold cross validation technique to obtain the average result.

For each sentence, Treebank provides a corresponding parse tree while PropBank provides corresponding semantic arguments of predicates in the sentence. These trees were generated by a statistic parser from corresponding sentences with an average accuracy 95%. These semantic arguments of predicates in PropBank were generated manually.

From the experiment, among 621 verbs, we found 621 paths in total. By excluding 30 types of paths of which occurs less than 2 times, six types of paths are remained. Among these remaining patterns, 86% paths fall in the first three patterns. Table 1 shows these patterns.

Moreover, a set of labeled rooted subtrees managed by labeled rooted forests are obtained based on the procedure described in Section 3.2.5. The test results are shown in Table 2. Note, the precision (recall or f-measure) is obtained by applying 10-fold cross validation. On the average, each time, among the $\frac{1}{10}$ semantic arguments that have been classified, about 93% semantic arguments are correctly identified and 7% semantic arguments are classified wrong. By checking these classified instances, we found that our method is very effective in the case of a semantic argument being a sequence of consecutive words. However, if a

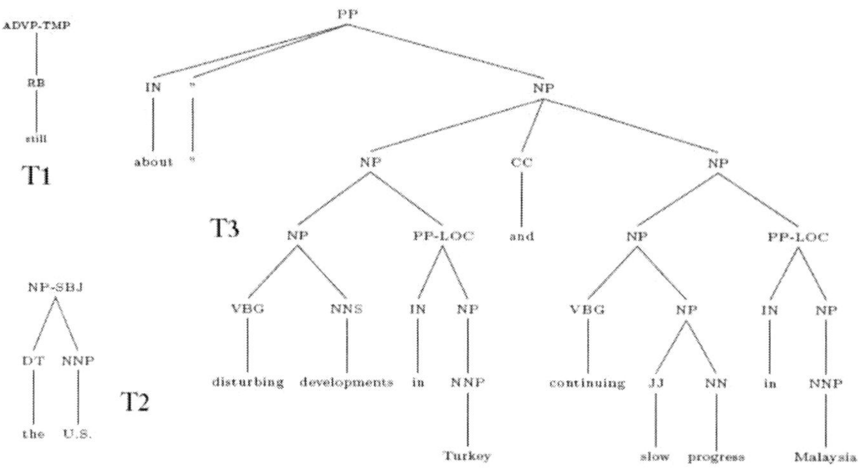

Figure 3: A labeled rooted forest $F = \{T_1, T_2, T_3\}$ for verb *concern* for the sentence *Mrs. Hills said that the U.S. is still concerned about "disturbing developments in Turkey and continuing slow process in Malaysia".*

Table 1: Six Types of Paths .

NO	%	Path
1	62.1	$VBZ(VBD, VBG, VBP, VBN, VB) \to VP$
2	14.2	$MD(TO) \to VP \to VP \to VB$
3	10.1	$VBP(VBZ, VBD) \to VP$ $\to VP \to VBN$
4	4.2	$VBD(VBZ, VBN) \to VP$ $\to RB \to VP \to VB$
5	2.4	$TO \to VP \to VP \to VB \to VP \to VBN$
6	2.2	$MD \to VP \to RB \to VP$ $\to VBP(VB) \to VP \to VBN$

Table 2: testing result on WSJ data

Files	Precision %	Recall %	F-Measure %
WSJ 20,37,49,89			
Average	92.335	94.1675	93.2512
Standard-Deviation	0.6195	0.5174	0.4605

semantic argument consists of two or more word fragments, separated by some phrases, our algorithm is less effective. For example, the sentence: *He wants to see for instance the movie Superman.* Our methods can not distinguish the semantic argument of *want* from the phrase *for instance*. The reason is that this phrase is the part of leaves of the tree induced from one of the roots determined by our algorithm. This suggests us that in order to exclude phrases from a semantic argument, we need to develop a method so that a set of subroots can be found. Each of them corresponds to a fragment of a semantic argument. Then, these fragments must be combined together to obtain the semantic argument. Moreover, other misclassified instances are generated by errors carried in original syntactic trees.

5 Related Researches and Comparisons

Methods for identifying semantic arguments of predicates in a sentence can be divided into two categories with respect to the representation of the sentence, namely tree-related (Gildea and Jurafsky, 2002) (Hacioglu, 2004b) (Hacioglu, 2004c) and chunk-related (Hacioglu and Ward, 2003) (Hacioglu, 2004a) semantic argument identifiers. While systems are built use the first approach are more accurate, systems are build use the second approach are very efficient and robust.

In the first approach, a sentence is represented by a syntactic tree (Gildea and Jurafsky, 2002) or some variants, such as a dependence tree (Hacioglu, 2004c) obtained from a syntactic tree. For each predicate in a tree, a set of syntactic constituents (non-terminals) is extracted. Each constituent is determined by a set of features derived from sentence structure or a linguistic context defined for the constituent. These features may be predicate lemma, path from constituents to the predicate, phrase type, dependency relations between predicates and constituents, position of constituent with respect to it predicate, voice, head word stem, sub-categorization. Classifiers such as support vector machines and maximum entropy models have been employed to identify constituents into one of semantic arguments of predicates.

In the second approach, semantic argument identification is formulated as a chunking task (Hacioglu, 2004a). For each predicate in a sentence, each word in the sentence is classified into three categories which are inside a semantic argument, outside a semantic argument, or begin a new semantic argument by using a set of features defined for the word. These features may be the lexicon of the word, the POS of the word, and the syntactical phrase chunks. Then, a bank of SVM classifiers, a one-versus-all classifier, can be used for each class.

Our method is based on syntactic trees. However, our method differs from others in several ways. Instead of linearly transforming a syntactic tree into a sequence of syntactic constituents, we directly traverse the tree from top to bottom and left to right to find a set roots, each of them corresponds a semantic argument of a verb. Moreover, instead of finding a set of features for each semantic arguments of a verb based on the linguistic knowledge or syntactic structure, we find our feature, a path, by the method proposed by (Huang and Haralick, 2010a). This method is simple, fast, and uses less memory. In contrast with other methods, our feature represents not one semantic argument but all semantic arguments of a verb. Furthermore, instead of finding semantic arguments of a verb by using complex classifiers such as support vector machine or maximum entropy models, we determine the semantic arguments of a verb only by setting simple rules of looking up relatives of each node in our path. We argue that our feature is the most effective, efficient, and simplest feature compared with the existing methods.

6 Conclusion

An algorithm for identifying semantic arguments of a verb in a sentence has been discussed throughout this paper. The method is developed based on the argument that a link must exist from a verb to its all semantic arguments if a sentence is structured syntactically with the root vertex been labeled with S and the leaf vertices been labeled with lexicon of words in the sentence. A semantic argument of a verb in the sentence can be represented as a labeled rooted subtree rooted at an internal node and induced by its all descendants. Therefore, to find semantic arguments of a verb is to find a set of such subtrees, more precisely, a set of roots. In our method, we apply a probabilistic graphical model to extract such a link – a path. Then we determine these roots from the path by a set of predefined rules. Experiments are conducted on WSJ data set from Penn Treebank and PropBank. Results demonstrate that our method is effective.

References

John Chen and Owen Rambow. 2002. Use of deep linguistic features for the recognition and labeling of semantic argument. In *Proceedings of EMNLP-2003*.

Daniel Gildea and Daniel Jurafsky. 2002. Automatic labelling of semantic roles. *Computational Linguistics*, pages 245–288.

Kadri Hacioglu and Wayne Ward. 2003. Target word detection and semantic role chunking using support vector machines. In *Proceedings of HLT/NAACL-03*.

Kadri Hacioglu. 2004a. A lightweight semantic chunking model based on tagging. In *Proceedings of HLT/NAACL-04*.

Kadri Hacioglu. 2004b. A semantic chunking model based on tagging. In *Proceedings of HLT/NACCL-2004*.

Kadri Hacioglu. 2004c. Semantic role labeling using dependency trees. In *Proceedings of Coling 2004*, pages 1273–1276, Geneva, Switzerland, Aug 23–Aug 27. COLING.

Minhua Huang and Robert M. Haralick. 2009. Discovering patterns in texts. In *2009 IEEE International Conference on Semantic Computing*, pages 59–64.

Minhua Huang and Robert M. Haralick. 2010a. Discovering semantics of a word from a sentence. In *2010 International Conference on Artificial Intelligence and Pattern Recognition*, pages 51–57.

Minhua Huang and Robert M. Haralick. 2010b. *Recognizing Patterns in Texts*. River.

Ralph Weischedel, Martha Palmer, Mitchell Marcus, and Eduard Hovy. 2007. Ontonotes release 2.0 with ontonotes db tool v. 0.92 beta and ontoviewer v.0.9 beta. In *http://www.bbn.com/NLP/OntoNotes*.

Construction of an HPSG Grammar for the Arabic Relative Sentences

Ines Zalila
Faculty of Economics and Management of Sfax
ines.zalila@yahoo.fr

Kais Haddar
Sciences Faculty of Sfax
kais.haddar@fss.rnu.tn

Abstract

The paper proposes a treatment of relative sentences within the framework of Head-driven Phrase Structure Grammar (HPSG). Relative sentences are considered as a rather delicate linguistic phenomenon and not explored enough by Arabic researchers. In an attempt to deal with this phenomenon, we propose in this paper a study about different forms of relative clauses and the interaction of relatives with other linguistic phenomena such as ellipsis and coordination. In addition, in this paper we shed light on the recursion in Arabic relative sentences which makes this phenomenon more delicate in its treatment. This study will be used for the construction of an HPSG grammar that can process relative sentences. The HPSG formalism is based on two fundamental components: features and AVM (Attribute-Value-Matrix). In fact, an adaptation of HPSG for the Arabic language is made here in order to integrate features and rules of the Arabic language. The established HPSG grammar is specified in TDL (Type Description Language). This specification is used by the LKB platform (Linguistic Knowledge Building) in order to generate the parser.

1 Introduction

Relative phenomenon has a great importance in all natural languages and in all corpus kinds. That's way researchers in linguistics or in computer sciences pay great attention to this phenomenon (i.e., (Belkacemi, 1998), (Elleuch., 2004) and (Garcia,2006)). Indeed, a phase of parsing of this phenomenon is fundamental for several types of Natural Language Processing (NLP) applications such as grammatical correction and machine translation. Nevertheless, the researches concerning the parsing of relatives, object of this work, have not reached an advanced stage yet. This is due, on the one hand, to the complexity of this phenomenon and, on the other hand, to the interaction with simple and complex linguistics phenomena.

Thus, one of the objectives of this work is to study the various forms of the Arabic relative sentences. This study is based on old grammatical theories (Abdelwahed, 2004), (Belkacemi, 1998) and (Dahdah, 1992), and on discussions with linguists. From the study carried out, we also want to identify all possible syntactic representations of the Arabic relative sentences. The choice of the HPSG is justified by the fact that this formalism has shown great efficiency in several languages such as German.

The elaborated HPSG grammar is specified in TDL (Type Description Language). Based on the elaborated TDL specification, an Arabic parser is generated using the LKB linguistic platform. The generated parser can process complex sentences containing relatives. The originality of this work consists, on the one hand, in the identification of a relative sentences typology, and on the other hand, in the proposition of a HPSG extension detailing under-categorization. This extension is specified in TDL (Type Description Language) (Krieger and Schäfer, 1994), the language supported by LKB platform.

In this paper, we begin with presenting some projects dealing with the relative phenomenon. Then, we give a typology for Arabic relative sentences. After that, we introduce the HPSG formalism and we present modifications made on this formalism to adapt it to the Arabic language. Using this formalism, we elaborate a grammar for the Arabic language which can process relatives and we specify this grammar in TDL. We test this specification by generating a parser in LKB and applying it to a corpus of complex sentences. Finally, we conclude the paper by giving some perspectives of our work.

2 Related works

Researchers on the Arabic Language Processing began in the 1970's. The projects carried out since then and which have proposed parsers based on HPSG are limited.

Most of projects have proposed prototypes of parsers covering some phenomena (i.e., simple sentence, ellipsis). For example, in (Aloulou, 2003) and (Bahou *et al.*, 2003) authors studied the simple Arabic sentences and their representation with HPSG. They proposed some modifications on HPSG to adapt it to the Arabic language. These works are integrated in a multi-agent platform. In (Abdelkader *et al.*, 2006), the elaborated grammar makes it possible to analyze the Arabic nominal sentences. Also, priorities were introduced while applying HPSG schemata.

For the complex Arabic sentences, we take as an example the work presented in (Elleuch, 2004). It allows processing of simple sentences as well as complex ones. This work is based on the use of a large number of production and dynamic rules because the HPSG used version is old. Also, we take the research project presented in (Maaloul *et al*, 2004) which deals with Arabic sentences containing joint components and makes modifications on HPSG to adapt it to coordination. Note that all these works are based on their own parser. The relative phenomenon is also studied in (Belkacemi, 1998). This work shows that conjunctive nouns are not considered as determinants but as modifiers.

Concerning, the projects using the second approach which consists in the use of a tool for generation, we find essentially researchers studying Latin languages. For example, the project proposed in (Garcia, 2005) aims to analyze the Spanish relative subordinate clauses. This analysis is made on the LKB platform and is specified in TDL. In the same way, the project presented in (Tseng, 2006) deals with the French phrase affixes.

3 Arabic Relatives

The relative linguistic phenomenon is frequent in sentences and exists in all languages. In this section, we give an overview on the Arabic relative sentence, and then we explain the various forms that can take and we give some ambiguities in the treatment of Arabic relative sentences.

3.1 Definition

An Arabic relative sentence is a subordinate clause that carries out the various grammatical functions of a noun. It can play the role of a topic (مبتدأ), a predicate (خبر), a subject (فاعل) or object (مفعول به). Relative sentences are introduced by a special class of nouns called conjunctive nouns like 'الذي, who' and are followed by a special clause called relative clause.

Relative sentence (Srel) =
Conjonctive Noun (CN) + relative Clause (Crel)
مركب موصولي = اسم موصول + صلة الموصول

The following example illustrates previous rule that describe relative sentence structure:

[التلميذ [الذي نجح في الامتحان]] سافر الى فرنسا.
[The boy [who succeeded in the examination]] has travelled to France.

In this example, the noun "التلميذ" is modified by the relative sentence Srel "الذي نجح في الامتحان". This relative sentence is composed by the conjunctive noun CN "الذي" followed by verbal clause Crel "نجح في الامتحان".

For Arabic relative sentence, we distinguish those which have an antecedent and others not. The relative ones with antecedent generally make it possible to give information on the antecedent (explanatory relative). In contrast, the relative ones without antecedent are themselves which supplement the means of the sentence (completive relative).

3.2 Relatives Typology

The proposed Arabic relative typology is inspired from the old grammatical theory and the former research tasks. Indeed, it is based on nature of clause which follows the conjunctive noun (Crel). The clause (Crel) can be a verbal phrase (VP), a prepositional phrase (PP) or a nominal phrase (NP). The (Crel) clause nature depends also of conjunctive noun's nature. The categorization of conjunctive nouns (NC) as well as Arabic relative forms is defined in the following sections.

- **Conjunctive noun's nature**

Conjunctive noun's nature plays a role in the categorization of Arabic relative sentences. Indeed, a conjunctive noun (الاسم الموصول) is considered as an indeclined insignificant noun. It occupies the functional head of the sentence and it is semantically co-referent with the antecedent. The conjunctive nouns are categorized as two kinds: Nominal conjunctive (الموصولات الاسمية) and prepositional conjunctive (الموصولات الحرفية). Nominal conjunctive are categorized in two subforms: common conjunctive and special conjunctive. As for the prepositional conjunctive, they are subdivided in two sub-forms: conjunctive ones influencing the verbs and others influencing the nouns.

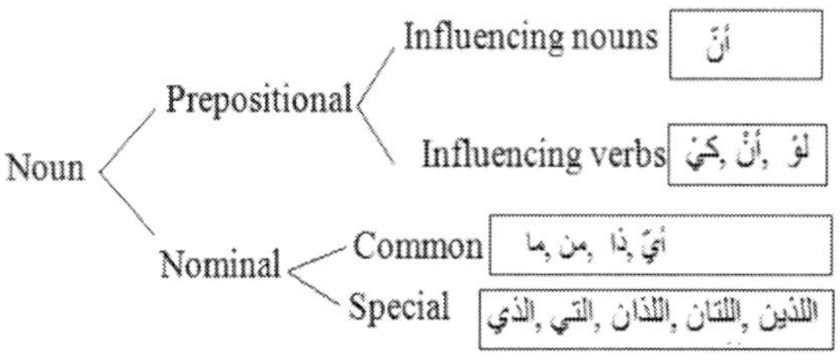

Figure 1: Categorization of conjunctive nouns

Based on elaborated study, explanatory relative is introduced by special conjunctive. All other nature of conjunctive nouns can introduce completive relative. In addition, according to the nature of the relative clause which follows the conjunctive noun, we distinguish two forms.

- **Relative clauses Typology**

The clause (Prel) which follows the conjunctive noun can be a verbal phrase (VP), prepositional phrase (PP) or nominal phrase (NP). According to these criteria, we identify two forms:

First form: Conjunctive noun followed by a verbal phrase (VP) or prepositional phrase (PP)

This form regroups conjunctive nouns which require the existence of a verbal phrase or prepositional one. For this form, we identify three types of relative's nouns: special nominal conjunctives, common nominal conjunctives, except for the conjunctive "أيّ", and prepositional conjunctives influencing the verbs. We define these various natures of conjunctive nouns as follows.

صافح المدير الذي تكلم كثيرا , البنت التي تحصلت على الجائزة

The director, who spoke a lot, greeted the girl who took the award

In the previous example, the conjunctive noun 'الذي' agrees with its antecedent 'المدير' in gender and number. If the number is conserved and the antecedent's gender was modified the conjunctive noun will be replaced by their correspondent one.

For neutral common conjunctives, they are independent from gender or number 'من، ما،أيٌّ،ذا'. Except for 'أيّ', all neutral common conjunctives require a VP or a PP.

قرأ الولد (البنت) [ما كتب الأب في الرسالة]

The boy (the girl) has read what the father wrote in the letter

The example above illustrates the independence of the common conjunctive 'ما' in gender and number. Conjunctive nouns 'ما' and 'من' do not require an agreement with the verb of VP.

Second form: Conjunctive noun followed by a nominal phrase (NP)

The second form covers conjunctive nouns which require the existence of a nominal clause. These conjunctives are represented by the common nominal pronoun 'أيّ' and the prepositional conjunctives influencing nouns. These natures of conjunctive nouns are detailed as follows.

The conjunctive noun 'أيّ' is a declined common conjunctive noun which refers to all what is human. The conjunctive noun 'أيّ' have a various forms according to the function which plays. Following example illustrates this correspondence:

سيكافئ الأستاذ [أيّ مجتهد]

The teacher will reward any diligent

سيفوز [أيٌ مجتهد] بالجائزة

Any diligent will win a prize

Examples above show that the connective noun "أي" can have in a sentence different grammatical functions. In the first example, the connective noun "أي" is a part of the object. So, it is open ending. For the second example, connective noun "أي" is a subject. Then, it is regular.

The prepositional conjunctive noun "أنّ" requires the existence of nominal phrases after this type of conjunctive. The NP must be open ending.

قال الأب [أنّ الولدَ مريض]

The father says [that the child is sick]

As we already mentioned, prepositional conjunctive noun "أنّ" is followed by a nominal phrase "الولدَ مريض". This conjunctive does not require an agreement.

As we already mentioned, the relative phenomenon is complex. This complexity is due to the diversity of possible forms and to the ambiguities founded during the analysis like interaction with other linguistic phenomena as ellipsis and coordination. This interaction increases the complexity degree of this phenomenon. The following example illustrates this interaction.

وجد الولد الكتاب [الذي يريد و يرغب]

The child who took the book [which he wants and desires]

In sentence above, we can note that the phenomenon of ellipsis intervenes on the level of the verbs. Indeed, the objects of these two verbs were elided.

In addition, in Arabic language, relatives can be recursive. Indeed, relative sentence can contain another relative sentence. Recursion can contain different types of relative (completive or explanatory). The example above show that the explanatory relative, whose antecedent is "البنت", containing another " البنت التي تحصلت على الجائزة التي تتكون من عدة كتب".

In order to analyze suitably the relatives, some modifications were made to the HPSG formalism.

In the following paragraph, we develop an adequate HPSG grammar.

4 HPSG for Arabic relatives

HPSG (Head-driven Phrases Grammar Structure) is a grammar of unification which was proposed by (Pollard & Sag, 1994). It is considered among best grammars for the modeling of the universal grammatical principles and a complete representation of the linguistic knowledge. Indeed, it make possible to represent in the lexical entries phonological, morphological, syntactic and semantic information.

In order to implement HPSG for the Arabic language, we adopt the already made modifications in order to integrate the particularities of this language (Boukedi et al., 2007). Figure 2 presents the SAV of a conjunctive noun using the majority of features added to the noun's type.

The example in figure 2 shows that "الذي" is not a significantly declined noun. This information is expressed by the features MAJ and NFORM. As for the feature INDEX, it shows that "الذي" is a singular masculine noun.

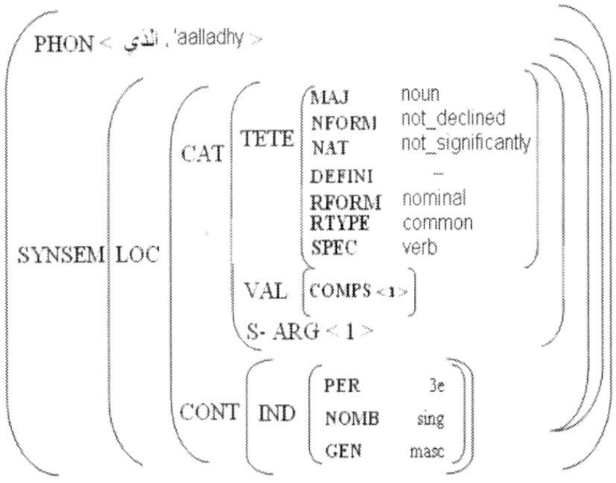

Figure 2: The SAV of the noun "'alladhy الذي"

As it's indicated in previous parts, the immediate dominance (ID) schemata allow the generation of the derivation trees (Pollard and Sag, 1994) and (Blache, 1995). The arabized HPSG formalism must necessarily adapt these schemata in the sense of reading since the Arabic language is written from right to left (Boukedi et al., 2007). As follows, we present the modification of the mark's schemas taking into account the phenomenon of relatives.

Marking schema represents, on the one hand, a son head not having a descent not limited to enclose and on the other hand, a son marker referring HEAD of the marker type. The markers are associated with the feature SYN-SEM | LOC | CAT| MARK. This schema allows generally representing the relative sentences of the Arabic language. Thus, any sentence containing a conjunctive will be represented on this schema.

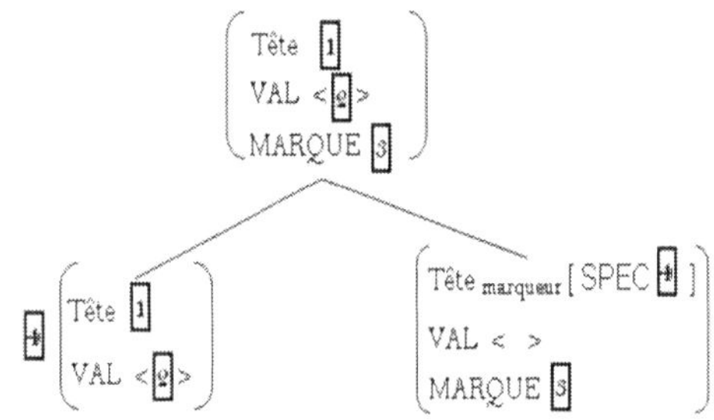

Figure 3: The rule of mark: Modified schema.

For example, the phrase " الذي أكل التفاحة" represents a relative clause whose marker is the conjunctive noun «الذي» followed by a verbal phrase «أكل تفاحة» indexed 4.

Besides the marking rule, we use the modification schema to control the selection of the antecedent by the conjunctive noun. Indeed, the majority of conjunctive noun have an antecedent presented in the form of a noun.

The following phrase represents a relative clause whose modifier is the conjunctive noun « الذي » which modifies its antecedent: the noun « الولد ».

[الولد الذي ...]

[the child who ...]

The figure 4 illustrates the generation of syntax tree for « .... الولد الذي» using the already mentioned rule of modification.

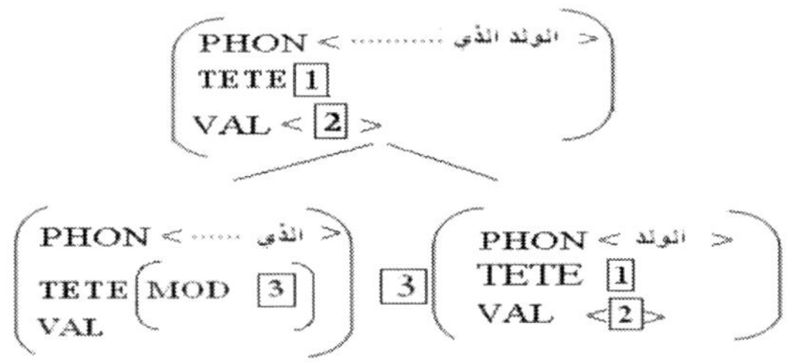

Figure 4: HPSG representation of the phrase " الولد الذي..."

In conclusion, the HPSG grammar designed and adapted to the Arabic language makes possible to analyze relative sentences while applying, amongst other things, the rule of marking and modification previously definite.

The elaborated HPSG grammar will be specified on TDL (Type Description Language). Indeed, TDL language is a language syntactically very similar to the attributes-values structures which are the base of HPSG formalism. In the following paragraph, we give an idea on TDL syntax and specification of the proposed HPSG grammar for Arabic relatives.

5 TDL Specification

TDL specification of the proposed HPSG grammar requires knowledge about its syntax. The TDL language is a language syntactically very similar to the attributes-values structures which are the base of HPSG formalism. Thus, there are several similarities between HPSG and TDL syntax (Krieger and Schäfer, 1994). These similarities can easily specify HPSG grammars in TDL. Indeed, the addition of the constraints on types is done by the symbol "&". Besides, the co-indexations are preceded by the symbol "#". The comments are preceded by the symbol ";". Moreover, a new type definition is done with the assistance of the symbol ":=". As in HPSG, the feature structures are delimited by brackets [ ].

In order to generate with the LKB a parser dealing with relative sentences, it is necessary to translate into TDL a HPSG lexicon, grammatical rules and a type hierarchy. We propose here an example of TDL specification of marking rule:

```
Regle-marque:=regle-bin-t-fin &
    [SS.LOC.CAT [VAL #val,  MARQUE
   #marque], BRS [BRS-NTETE
   <[SS.LOC.CAT[TETE.SPEC #tete,
     MARQUE #marque]]>,
   BR-TETE [SS #tete &
    [LOC.CAT.VAL #val]]]].
```

Once the syntactic rules are implemented in TDL and gathered in a TDL file named "*rsynt.tdl*", we pass to the experimentation of the grammar implemented in TDL.

The specified linguistic resources (proposed type hierarchy, lexicon and syntactic rules) are used as an input to LKB platform in order to experiment the constructed HPSG grammar. In the next paragraph, we give an idea about LKB platform. Then, we experiment and evaluate the established Arabic grammar.

6 Experimentation and evaluation

Linguistic Knowledge Building (LKB) system is a generation tool, proposed by (Copestake, 2002). It is based on two types of files: TDL files and LISP files. The first type represents the grammar's files. In fact, this grammar is based on seven TDL files: lexicon, type, type-lex, type-rules, rsynt, noeuds and roots.

The second type represents files to parameterize LKB system. It is based on five LISP files. Among these files, we can especially mention the file: "script.lsp' which indicates the name and the repertory of each grammar file.

The evaluation of the constructed grammar is based on a corpus of 500 sentences containing essentially relatives. Besides, the test corpus contains other linguistic phenomena such as the elision, the call, the description. The used lexicon contains approximately 3000 words (~2500 verbs, 450 nouns and 50 particles). It is formed mainly of the corpus words.

For the tested sentences, we note that the generated parser could correctly build their syntactic structures in a reasonable time. In addition, 2% of the sentences do not produce derivation trees, 84% of sentences have only one analysis and 14% have at least two derivation trees.

For the remaining sentences, the failure is due to the existence of more than one derivation tree for the same sentence. In fact, this problem was encountered in previous works using LKB system such as (Garcia, 2005) and (Tseng, 2006). In our work, we introduced other constraints more specific, to resolve the encountered problem according to the proposed type hierarchy. Nevertheless, ambiguous cases persist. This is caused mainly by ambiguities found during relative sentences analysis. Figure 5 represents an example of sentence covering ambiguous cases.

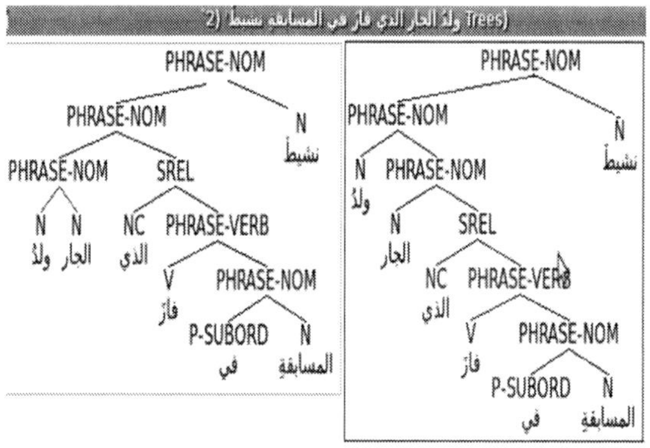

Figure 5: Implementation TDL of "الذي "

Indeed, the relative phrase " ولد الجار الذي فاز في المسابقة نشيط" can refer to the noun or to the nominal group "ولد الجار". This nominal group represents an annexed phrase.

Besides, there is another problem at the level of lexicon. This problem was encountered also in previous projects working on Arabic language such as (Alnajem and Alzhouri, 2008), (Bahou *et al.*, 2003) and (Elleuch., 2004). In our work, we have added an interface written in JAVA which can enrich the file "lexique.tdl" by new words automatically and without knowing TDL syntax. Moreover, this lexicon can easy be extended using tools that we have developed in our laboratory like the translator from LMF toward TDL (Fehri et al, 2006).

7 Conclusion and Perspectives

In this paper, we have constructed an HPSG grammar for Arabic language treating particularly relative sentences. For this reason, we have proposed a type hierarchy categorizing Arabic words in different types. According to the proposed type hierarchy, we brought some modifications to HPSG grammar in order to treat Arabic specificities. The constructed grammar was experimented on LKB platform. Therefore, we specified Arabic HPSG with TDL language. This TDL specification is original, in our work since it integrates some operations and verifies certain concepts such as inheritance, adjunction and recursion. The evaluation phase shows that obtained results are satisfactory.

As perspectives of this work, we aim to test our parser on a larger corpus. We plan also to extend the HPSG description to cover other linguistic phenomena. Also, we plan to extend this work to cover semantic analysis. However, more works should be carried out to cover linguistic ambiguities such as recursion.

References

Abdelkader A., Haddar K. and Ben Hamadou A., « Etude et analyse de la phrase nominale arabe en HPSG », Traitement Automatique des Langue Naturelles, Louvain, UCL Presses de Louvain: 379-388, 2006.

Abdelwahed A., « 'alkalima fy 'attourath 'allisaany 'alaraby , الكلمة في التراث اللساني العربي », Librairie Aladin 1ère édition, Sfax – Tunisie : 1-100, 2004.

Alnajem S. and Alzhouri F., "An HPSG Approach to Arabic Nominal Sentences", Journal of the American society for information Scienceand Technology: 422 – 434, 2008.

Aloulou C., « Analyse syntaxique de l'Arabe: Le système MASPAR », RECITAL, NantesFrance, 2003.

Bahou Y., Hadrich Belguith L., Aloulou C. and Ben Hamedou A.. «Adaptation and implementation of HPSG grammars to parse non-voweled Arabic texts », memory of Master, Faculty of Economics and Management of Sfax.

Belkacemi C., «The relative marker: a definite marker substitute? », ArOr Archiv Orientální, 66/2, 142-148, Based on Arabic dialects, 1998.

Blache P., «Les Grammaires de Propriétés: des contraintes pour le traitement automatique des langues naturelles». Hermès Sciences, Paris, 2001.

Boukedi S., Haddar K. and Abdelwahed A., « Vers une analyse des phrases arabes en HPSG et LKB ». GEI 2008, 8ème Journées Scientifiques des Jeunes Chercheurs en Génie Electrique et Informatique, Sousse, Tunisie : 487- 498, 2008.

Copestake A., « Implementing Typed Feature Structure Grammars ». CSLI Publications, Stanford University, 2002.

Dahdah A.. « معجم قواعد اللغة العربية في جداول و لوحات », Librairie de Nachirun Lebanon, 5ème edition, 1992.

Elleuch S., « Analyse syntaxique de la langue arabe basée sur le formalisme d'unification HPSG ». Mémoire de DEA en Système d'information et Nouvelles Technologies, Tunisie : 55-88, 2004.

Fehri H., Loukil N., Haddar K. and Ben Hamadou A., "Un système de projection du HPSG arabisé vers la plate-forme LMF ». JETALA, Maroc, 1-11, 2006.

Garcia O., « Une introduction à l'implémentation des relatives de l'espagnol en HPSG–LKB », Mémoire de recherche, 2005.

Haddar K. and Ben Hamadou A., « Un système de recouvrement des ellipses de la langue arabe ». Proceedings of VEXTAL, San Servolo V.I.U. 22(11) : 159-167, 1999.

Krieger H. and Schäfer U., « TDL: A Type Description Language for HPSG». Part 1 and Part 2, Research Report, RR-94-37, 1994.

Loukam M. and Laskri M., « Vers la modélisation de la grammaire de l'arabe standard basée sur le formalisme HPSG », Actes JED'2007, Journées de l'Ecole Doctorale, 27(5), Annaba/Algérie, 2007.

Maaloul H., Haddar K. and Ben Hamadou A., «La coordination arabe : étude et analyse en HPSG », MCSEAI 2004, 8ème conférence maghrébine sur le GL et l'IA, Sousse, Tunisie : 487- 498, 2004.

Meurers W. D., «A Web-based Instructional Platform for Constraint-Based Grammar Formalisms and Parsing». In Dragomir Radev and Chris Brew (eds.), Effective Tools and Methodologies for Teaching NLP and CL, New Brunswick, NJ: The Association for Computational Linguistics: 18 – 25, 2002.

Pollard C. and Sag I., «Head-drive phrase structure grammars», CSLI series, Chicago University Press, 1994.

Tseng J., « Implémentation HPSG avec LKB: La Matrix et la Grenouille », Séminaire HPSG-UFRL, Paris 7, 14(12), 2006

Automatically Selected Skip Edges in Conditional Random Fields for Named Entity Recognition

Roman Klinger
Department of Bioinformatics
Fraunhofer Institute for Algorithms and Scientific Computing
Schloss Birlinghoven
53754 Sankt Augustin, Germany
roman.klinger@scai.fraunhofer.de

Abstract

Incorporating distant information via manually selected skip chain templates has been shown to be beneficial for the performance of conditional random field models in contrast to a simple linear chain based structure (Sutton and McCallum, 2007; Galley, 2006; Liu et al., 2010). The set of properties to be captured by a template is typically manually chosen with respect to the application domain.

In this paper, a search strategy to find meaningful skip chains independent from the application domain is proposed. From a huge set of potentially beneficial templates, some can be shown to have a positive impact on the performance. The search for a meaningful graphical structure demonstrates the usefulness of the approach with an increase of nearly 2 % F_1 measure on a publicly available data set (Klinger et al., 2008).

1 Introduction

Many applications in the field of text segmentation, especially named entity recognition, have been addressed with linear chain conditional random fields. Using a linear chain of variables to represent the labeling of text is straight forward, as processing text in a sequential manner suggests itself due to the way it is written and firstly perceived.

While language suggests this linear structure to represent written text, it does not necessarily model all dependencies: Co-referencing a prior entity is an example (while it could be seen as higher order linearity typically pointing back but not forward). Especially in non-scientific texts, information may as well be left out and filled in later to keep a story exciting. Another example is the use of filler words as a trivial case where the meaning of words can be determined by distant tokens.

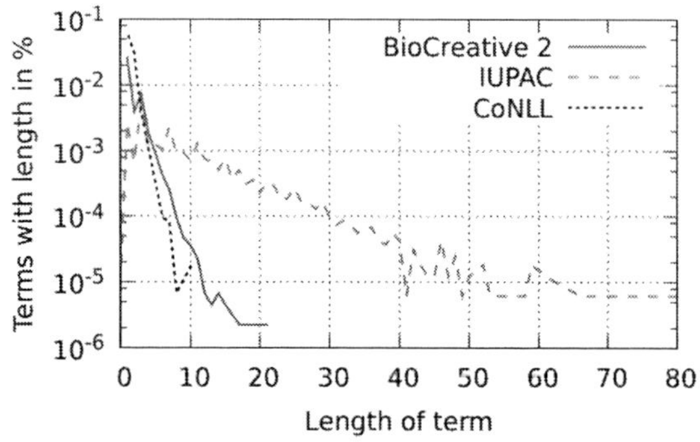

Figure 1: Distribution of the length of three entity classes.

In named entity recognition, typically linear chain structures of conditional random fields are used. The capabilities of a linear chain such structure may be limited in at least two cases: Firstly, relations between distant tokens can have an impact on their meaning. This is a motivation which lead to the previous work presented in the following Section 2. Secondly, long entity classes cannot be captured as a whole, which is especially interesting because a characteristic of named entities in biology and chemistry is their high length with inter-dependencies between tokens of an entity. The distribution of the length of terms in the classes of gene names (BioCreative 2, Smith et al. (2008)), IUPAC names (Klinger et al., 2008) and person names, organizations and places (CoNLL 2005, Sang and De Meulder (2003)) is shown in Figure 1. Gene names and especially IUPAC names are much longer than entities like names, organizations and places. This is the motivation to investigate if a linear-chain structure can be supported by other structures to capture this complexity. The work presented in this paper aims towards an automatic detection of beneficial struc-

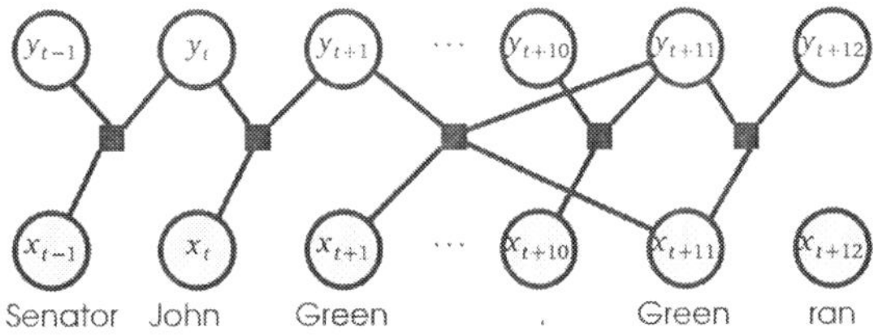

Figure 2: Example of a skip chain CRF structure as used by Sutton and McCallum (2007) (as factor graph depiction). Subsequent labels are connected as well as tokens representing the same string.

tures. The IUPAC domain with its notable long entities is used as an evaluation domain in this paper, presuming that a pure linear chain structure has specific difficulties here (using the training corpus presented by Klinger et al. (2008)).

In the following, the challenge is approached as a search for meaningful skip chain templates (Sutton and McCallum, 2007).

2 Previous Work

The class of CRFs including skip chain edges (unrolled from skip chain templates) has been described by Sutton and McCallum (2007) and Galley (2006) in a named entity recognition scenario. In addition to the linear chain, a template is used to measure the dependencies between same capitalized tokens. This is motivated by the assumption that same words in a sentence or document are likely to have the same label, despite their token distance. An example for such skip chain CRF is shown in Figure 2. As stated by Sutton and McCallum (2007), each pair of nodes can be connected by a skip chain which the developer believes to be similar. They point out that the number of edges unrolled from a template may not be too high as the runtime and memory consumption increases prohibitively. Connecting only capitalized words allows to match most proper names (which is an entity class of interest in their test domain) while they are sparsely distributed.

The work by Liu et al. (2010) enhances that approach by different classes of variables (as special keywords) to be connected. To adapt Sutton's and McCallum's approach to gene and protein names, they introduce three skip chain templates: Firstly, connecting the main parts of gene names (referred to as "keyword" in their work) defined by regular expressions, secondly connecting only similar keywords, only differing to a certain extent, and thirdly connecting typed dependencies like prepositional modifiers or noun compound modifiers. On the BioCreative 2 NER data set (Smith et al., 2008) they show an increase in F_1 measure from 71.73 % with a linear chain to 73.14 % with the best skip chain configuration for a strict evaluation not using the allowed alternatives in the gold data test set. Using the official evaluation with alternatives, they show an increase from 83.29 % to 84.67 % F_1. They argue that the quality of the skip chains is essential for the improvement of the result compared to simple linear chain structures.

In contrast to previous work, this paper addresses the question how to select meaningful skip edges automatically from a set of possibilities. This does not make the domain specific development unnecessary (as the application of feature selection still needs the development of features for a domain), but helps to find templates to improve the results. It can select a specific subset of automatically generated clique templates. This task can be understood as a combinatorial optimization problem: Finding a factor graph with a structure maximizing the performance of the model on a test set.

Several approaches have been published about optimizing the structure of Markov networks or more specifically conditional random fields. They can be divided into methods searching for such structure with a measure to judge the quality of a structure and filtering approaches to decide about the quality of an edge. Beside those, regularization is another way to find a good structure during training.

The work by Schmidt et al. (2008) states to be the first dealing with the structure learning task in discrimatively trained, undirected graphical models. Similarly to Lee et al. (2006) (which is dealing with general Markov networks), L_1 regularization is the incorporated method. While this approach is very elegant due to the joint structure and parameter estimation, it has limitations to deal with large, dynamically generated factor graphs with a lot of features on each factor.

As long as the candidates for the optimal structure have a tractable size, a search in the space of graph structures is feasible. This approach, together with an approximation for the quality measure of each graph is adopted by Parise and Welling (2006). The advantage is that all dependencies in the graph are taken into account, the disadvantage is the complexity of the performed search.

A complementary and fast approach is to measure the quality of an edge with independence tests, as described by Bromberg et al. (2009). The main contribution in their work is to minimize the needed independence tests to find the optimal graph structure.

3 Methods

3.1 Problem Definition

The work described in Section 2 is focusing on graph structures of limited size or on non-conditional Markov graphs. In the following, the problem of finding skip edges is discussed in detail.

A graph structure $G = (V, E)$ is defined via vertexes V and edges $E = V \times V$. Optimizing the structure corresponds to selecting a subset of edges which leads to the maximal performance. A factor graph (Kschischang et al., 2001) is a bipartite graph G between variables and factors defining a probability distribution of a set of output variables $\vec{y}$ conditioned on input variables $\vec{x}$. Each factor Ψ_j computes the so-called score of variables which are neighbors in the graph. It is typically formulated as an exponential function of the weighted sum of features:

$$\Psi_j(\vec{x}, \vec{y}) = \exp\left(\sum_{i=0}^{m} \lambda_i f_i(\vec{x}_j, \vec{y}_j)\right) .$$

A set of factor templates $\Theta = \{\theta_1, \ldots, \theta_n\}$ consists of templates θ_k describing a set of tuples $\{(\vec{x}_k, \vec{y}_k)\}$ on which factors are instantiated for which the property $p_k(\vec{x}_k, \vec{y}_k)$ holds and shares $\vec{\lambda}_k$ and $\vec{f}_k(\cdot)$ between all instantiated factors on the tuples. K_j is the number of parameters of the jth template. The probability distribution on a factor graph with templates Θ becomes

$$P(\vec{y}|\vec{x}) = \frac{1}{Z(\vec{x})} \prod_{\theta_j \in \Theta} \prod_{(\vec{x}_i, \vec{y}_i) \in \theta_j} \exp\left(\sum_{k=1}^{K_j} \lambda_{jk} f_{jk}(\vec{x}_i, \vec{y}_i)\right) .$$

The task of finding meaningful skip chains corresponds to finding a set of templates $\tilde{\Theta}$ describing tuples $(y_u, y_v, \vec{x})$ with a property $p(x_u, x_v)$. A linear chain template θ_{lc} with features $\vec{g}^{\text{lc}}(\vec{x}, j)$ for all possible combinations of label variables is assumed to be present in all configurations. In the following, the set of templates to select from is defined by properties $p_k(x_u, x_v) :=$ holds iff $g_k^{\text{lc}}(\vec{x}, u) = 1$ and $g_k^{\text{lc}}(\vec{x}, v) = 1$ with $k \in \{1, \ldots, |\vec{g}^{\text{lc}}|\}$. Each template holds parameters for features $g_k^{\text{lc}}(\vec{x}, u) \vee g_k^{\text{lc}}(\vec{x}, v)$.[1] In other words, a skip chain factor is added to connect two labeling variables of two tokens if a specified property holds (where we take every occurring feature specified for the linear chain into account, like bag-of-words, prefixes, suffixes of tokens as well as several regular expressions, the full set is given by Klinger et al. (2008)). Each of the skip chain factors has the disjunction of the feature values in the linear chain of the connected tokens.

That definition of the templates to choose from is only for simplicity throughout this paper. A more general formulation does not limit the methods described, though a small set decreases runtime. Especially dependency properties as described by Liu et al. (2010) may be included.

An example of different skip chain factors to choose from is shown in Figure 3. The red property of matching `[.*ine]` seems to be a reasonable skip chain as it connects similar chemical names such that their class can influence the class of the others. The green matching stop words is an example how the size of the factor graph can prohibitively increase what should be avoided. The orange matching of `[,]` could be able to capture enumerations because features which take preceding and succeeding tokens into account may have some importance.

3.2 Best First Search

The most complete approach to find a suitable structure of the graph is a search through the space of all combinations of the skip chain templates. As the complexity is prohibitive even for a small set of templates, the dependencies between possible templates are proposed to be measured via best-first-search (BFS, Russell and Norvig (2003)) on all templates remaining from a heuristic filtering step together with the linear chain factors. Best-first-search is chosen as an exemplary search strategy as it follows only the best

[1] This definition of features on the skip chain factors has been chosen to capture not only shared properties but to measure characteristics of only one participant as well.

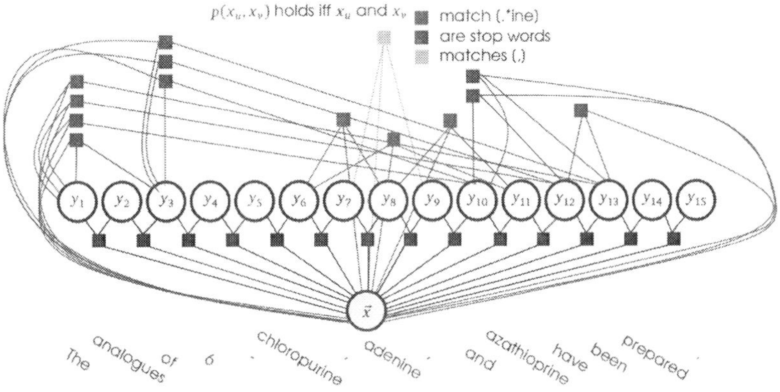

Figure 3: Different skip chain factor templates to choose additionally to the linear chain (example shortened from the abstract by Hasan and Srivastava (1992)).

alternative which limits the performance evaluations needed.

Starting with the linear chain, each template is added respectively, the model is trained and evaluated on a hold-out set. The best template is kept and the prior step is repeated. This process ends if none of the templates can improve the result.

Here, the same inference algorithm is used as for the final model: Loopy belief propagation with tree-based reparameterization for approximate inference (Wainwright et al., 2001). During the steps of BFS, the weights for each template to be kept can be adopted for the next search iteration retraining all parameters. Thereby retraining the model can be performed in a much smaller number of iterations than training from scratch.

4 Experiments and Evaluation

In the following, the feasibility of the basic idea of the proposed approach is evaluated on the IUPAC corpus (Klinger et al. (2008)[2], split into 90 % training and 10 % validation randomly). All templates which occur at least 10 times in the training data were taken into account. These are 5096 templates (from 16710 altogether). Training with and without the skip factors (via maximizing $\log P(\vec{y}|\vec{x})$ with a Gaussian regularization) leads to a ranked list of templates which forms the first layer of the BFS.

This leads to the results depicted in Figure 4 showing the impact of each template. The inference algorithm did not converge for 474 templates. Most of the templates have no or negative impact on the result (3656 templates); 966 have positive impact. The top 10 templates are depicted in Table 1, together with their contribution. The most important template is to add a skip chain between tokens "alpha" with nearly 2 % improvement in comparison to the linear chain only. This term occurs 319 times in the training data and is frequently part of IUPAC names (115) as well as outside of them (204). In a local, linear chain-based setting a feature based on this token can hardly contribute to a decision, but in a distant labeling setting it can. The second best feature to built skip chain factors is "PREFIX2=tr": It occurs 698 times, 284 times in IUPAC names and 414 times outside of them.

Most of the features forming the basis for templates with a positive impact are words occurring close to or in chemical names or are typical chemical pre- or suffixes. These features measure ambiguous characteristics of tokens where the probability of correctly identifying the surrounding terms can be increased by measuring the distant information of them. The context is taken into account by templates based on features of offset conjunction (like `W=alpha@2` measuring the token `alpha` two tokens left of the skip chain connection). The reason is presumably that their common occurrence in a sentence is not labeled differently.

For instance, the term `alpha` is occurring in `alpha-ribofuranosyl` (which is labeled as IUPAC) and in `alpha1-adrenergic` (not labeled as IUPAC). In both examples, `alpha` is occurring multiple times in the text, but not with different labels. Similarly, `tr` can be a prefix of `tributylstannyl` (as IUPAC) or

[2]Statistics of this data set can be found in the original publication and are not cited here due to page limitation.

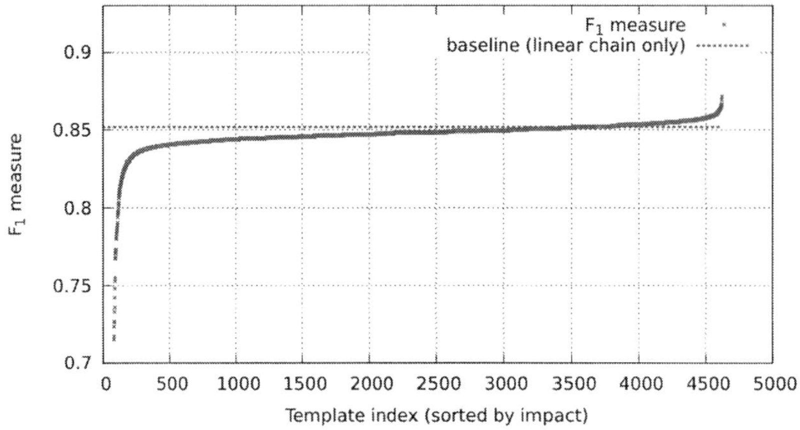

Figure 4: Impact for each proposed templates measured empirically.

`treatment` (as non-IUPAC), but it is not probable that different labels occur in the same text. The feature `W=group@1` is a slightly different case as it does not occur as part of an IUPAC name itself but can occur in the context of chemical names which are difficult to distinguish between IUPAC and not. As an example, `formamidino group` would not be labeled as IUPAC, but `p-methoxybenyl group` is labeled as such. Annotation is quite difficult here, but it is likely that the annotator produced consistent data in one text instance.

Notable is the occurrence of very strict features like `SUFFIX2=31`—it is surprising that obviously some numbers are occurring frequently in IUPAC names and outside of them such that a differentiation with distant information is beneficial.

This discussion illustrates that the found templates are meaningful in the context of the IUPAC example taken for evaluation here. The impact of the automated approach for the first layer of a search shows similar or better possible improvements than the manual approaches by Sutton and McCallum (2007, *cf.* Table 1.2) (0.4 %) or Liu et al. (2010) (1.2 % on BioCreative II data) (this is remarkable although they tested on different data sets).

5 Conclusion and Future Work

This paper presented the principle idea of building skip chain edges to capture distant information for named entity recognition in a similar manner as features to represent tokens are generated. Instead of hand-crafting domain- and problem-specific features, they are generated from the training data; analogously, potentially beneficial skip chain templates are taken into account. It has been shown that this approach is feasible and leads to an improved performance on an example domain.

To be able to apply this methodology in practice, the search complexity for meaningful structures needs to be reduced. Nevertheless, the analysis shows that the idea of automatically selecting distant tokens as a basis for additional factors makes sense. The presented analysis can help in further work and be used as a training set for novel template filtering methods.

Future work includes the analysis how different templates work together for named entity recognition: What is the relation between the linear chain and a skip chain? What characteristics does the linear chain have where skip chains help?

Additionally due to the high complexity of empirically testing all templates, the interaction between different skip chains has not been analyzed.

Another interesting topic is to investigate the impact of specific factors on different evaluation measures. It can be assumed that some support accuracy, whereas some have a special impact on precision or recall.

References

[Bromberg et al.2009] Facundo Bromberg, Dimitris Margaritis, and Vasant Honavar. 2009. Efficient markov network structure discovery using independence tests. *Journal of Artificial Intelligence Research*, 35(1):449–484, May.

[Galley2006] Michel Galley. 2006. A skip-chain conditional random field for ranking meeting utterances

	Template	F_1 measure	to base
1	W=alpha@2	87.15	1.96
2	PREFIX2=tr	86.93	1.74
3	W=liver@1	86.66	1.47
4	W=group@1	86.63	1.44
5	WC=AAA@1	86.59	1.40
6	REFIX2=ox	86.59	1.40
7	PREFIX2=fu@1	86.54	1.35
8	W=rac@1	86.51	1.32
9	W=cis@-1	86.47	1.28
10	SUFFIX2=nt	86.44	1.25
11	SUFFIX2=ro@-2	86.39	1.20
12	W=was@-2	86.39	1.20
13	W=rac@-1	86.39	1.20
14	PREFIX2=hy@1	86.39	1.20
15	PREFIX2=am@1	86.36	1.17
16	SUFFIX2=31	86.32	1.13
17	SUFFIX2=,4	86.32	1.13
18	SUFFIX2=in@2	86.28	1.09
19	SUFFIX2=,4@1	86.28	1.09
20	W=3H@-1	86.28	1.09

Table 1: Top 20 skip chain templates from all proposed templates occurring at least 10 times. ("To base" denotes the difference to the baseline, a linear chain CRF. `W=` denotes exact term match features, `PREFIX2=` the use of the string as prefix of length 2, analogously for `SUFFIX`. `@n` denotes the use of the feature characterizing tokens with an offset of `n` in the token sequence.)

by importance. In *Proceedings of the 2006 Conference on Empirical Methods in Natural Language Processing*, pages 364–372, Sydney, Australia, July. Association for Computational Linguistics.

[Hasan and Srivastava1992] A. Hasan and P. C. Srivastava. 1992. Synthesis and biological studies of unsaturated acyclonucleoside analogues of s-adenosyl-l-homocysteine hydrolase inhibitors. *J Med Chem*, 35(8):1435–1439, Apr.

[Klinger et al.2008] Roman Klinger, Corinna Kolářik, Juliane Fluck, Martin Hofmann-Apitius, and Christoph M. Friedrich. 2008. Detection of IUPAC and IUPAC-like Chemical Names. *Bioinformatics*, 24(13):i268–i276. Proceedings of the International Conference Intelligent Systems for Molecular Biology (ISMB).

[Kschischang et al.2001] Frank Kschischang, Brendan J. Frey, and Hans-Andrea Loeliger. 2001. Factor graphs and the sum-product algorithm. *IEEE Transactions on Information Theory*, 47(2):498–519.

[Lee et al.2006] Su-In Lee, Varun Ganapathi, and Daphne Koller. 2006. Efficient structure learning of markov networks using l1-regularization. In *Advances in Neural Information Processing Systems*.

[Liu et al.2010] Jingchen Liu, Minlie Huang, and Xiaozan Zhu. 2010. Recognizing biomedical named entitities using skip-chain conditional random fields. In *Proceedings of the Workshop on Biomedical Natural Language Processing*.

[Parise and Welling2006] Sridevi Parise and Max Welling. 2006. Structure learning in markov random fields. In *Advances in Neural Information Processing Systems*.

[Russell and Norvig2003] Stuart Russell and Peter Norvig. 2003. *Articifial Intelligence – A Modern Approach*. Prentice Hall.

[Sang and De Meulder2003] Erik F. Tjong Kim Sang and Fien De Meulder. 2003. Introduction to the conll-2003 shared task: Language-independent named entity recognition. In Walter Daelemans and Miles Osborne, editors, *Proceedings of Computational Natural Language Learning (CoNLL)*, pages 142–147. Edmonton, Canada.

[Schmidt et al.2008] Mark Schmidt, Kevin Murphy, Glenn Fung, and R'omer Rosales. 2008. Structure learning in random fields for heart motion abnormality detection. In *Computer Vision and Pattern Recognition*, Anchorage, AK, USA, June. IEEE.

[Smith et al.2008] Larry Smith, Lorraine K. Tanabe, Rie Johnson nee Ando, Cheng-Ju Juo, I-Fang Chung, Chun-Nan Hsu, Yu-Shi Lin, Roman Klinger, Christoph M. Friedrich, Kuzman Ganchev, Manabu Torii, Hongfang Liu, Barry Haddow, Craig A. Struble, Richard J. Povinelli, Andreas Vlachos, William A. Baumgartner Jr., Lawrence Hunter, Bob Carpenter, Richard Tzong-Han Tsai, Hong jie Dai, Feng Liu, Yifei Chen, Chengjie Sun, Sophia Katrenko, Pieter Adriaans, Christian Blaschke, Rafel Torres Perez, Mariana Neves, Preslav Nakov, Anna Divoli, Manuel Mana, Jacinto Mata-Vazquez, and W. John Wilbur. 2008. Overview of biocreative ii gene mention recognition. *Genome Biology*, 9(Suppl 2):S2.2–S2.18, September.

[Sutton and McCallum2007] Charles Sutton and Andrew McCallum. 2007. An introduction to conditional random fields for relational learning. In Lise Getoor and Benjamin Taskar, editors, *Introduction to Statistical Relational Learning*, chapter 4, pages 93–127. MIT Press, November.

[Wainwright et al.2001] Martin J. Wainwright, Tommi Jaakkola, and Alan S. Willsky. 2001. Tree-based reparameterization for approximate inference on loopy graphs. In *Proccedings of the Conference on Neural Information Processing Systems*.

Negation Naive Bayes for Categorization of Product Pages on the Web

Kanako Komiya [1] **Naoto Sato** [1] **Koji Fujimoto** [1,2] **Yoshiyuki Kotani** [1]
Tokyo University of Agriculture and Technology [1]
Tensor Consulting Co.Ltd. [2]
{kkomiya, kotani}@cc.tuat.ac.jp
50009646113@st.tuat.ac.jp
koji.fujimoto@tensor.co.jp

Abstract

We propose the negation naive Bayes (NNB): a new method to categorize product pages on the Web depending on their information. It is a modified version of the naive Bayes (NB) and we got the idea from the complement naive Bayes (CNB). We compared the NNB with the NB and the CNB. Our experiments show that the NNB outperformed the other methods significantly when the product pages were distributed non-uniformly through categories.

1 Introduction

In late years, e-commerce, the services by which users can easily purchase products on the Web without visiting a store, is introduced in many companies. When products are purchased via Internet, the user narrows down the candidate categories of each product in incremental steps. We categorized the products on the Web automatically depending on their information using the method of text classification (Sato et al., 2011).

Many researchers have investigated text classification and the naive Bayes (NB) is one of the most famous methods for it. However when we use the NB classifier to categorize the products, the accuracies were not very high, especially when the data distribution is very skewed.

Hence this paper proposes the negation naive Bayes (NNB): a new method of text classification especially for the product pages on the Web depending on their information. It is a modified version of the NB and we got the idea from the complement naive Bayes (CNB). Our experiments showed that the NNB outperformed the NB and the CNB when the product pages were distributed non-uniformly.

This paper is organized as follows. Section 2 reviews related works on text classifications and the NB classifiers. Section 3 describes the classification methods including our proposal method: the NNB. Section 4 describes the system to categorize the product pages and explains the experimental setting. We describe results in Section 5 and discuss them in Section 6. Finally, we conclude the paper in Section 7.

2 Related Work

Many works on text classification have been accomplished so far. Approaches of Bayes are often used within the area of text classification (Mochihashi, 2006). Izutsu et al. (2005) categorized the html documents and compared the NB classifier with discriminant analysis and the rule-based method. They suggested the simple implementation and the high scalability of the NB classifier. McCallum and Nigam (1998) suggested the difference between multinomial model and multivariate Bernoulli model of the NB classifier in text classification. Lewis (1992) compared the difference of the effect between the types of features used for text classification: words, phrases, clustered words, clustered phrases and indexing terms. W.Church (2000) used a concept called "Adaptation" as the weighting method to the words in substitution for IDF value, and defined the words related to contents but not included a document as "Neighbor". The feature terms were extracted depending on them.

In addition, the method called "Complement Naive Bayes" attracts attention. It estimates parameters of a category using data from all categories except the category which is focused on (J.D.M.Rennie et al., 2003).

On the other hand, there have been the works that used the product information of Internet auctions (Nishimura et al., 2008).These works suggest a method to extract the attribute information from the description of the product pages.

This paper proposes the NNB. Its equation is

derivable from the equation of the NB unlike the CNB but it has the same advantages; it tackles the ununiformity of the texts of each category. We got the classification accuracies that exceed the NB and the CNB significantly when the data distribution is non-uniformly.

3 Classification Method

In this section, we describe the classification methods to categorize the product pages on the Web including our proposal method: the NNB. The distribution of the product pages of each category is very skewed in Internet auctions. Therefore, the classification model which tackles the ununiformity of the data distribution is necessary.

3.1 Naive Bayes Classifier

We used the NB classifier to classify the product pages as a baseline. Let $d = w_1, w_2, \ldots, w_n$ denote the text containing the words and let c denote a category. Here, let $\hat{c}$ denote the category that d belongs to, and $\hat{c}$ is as follows:

$$\hat{c} = \operatorname*{argmax}_c P(c|d) \quad (1)$$

where $P(c)$ and $P(d)$ each represent the prior probability of c and d.

By substituting theorem of conditional probability into the equation, we obtain the following:

$$\begin{aligned}\hat{c} &= \operatorname*{argmax}_c P(c|w_1, w_2, \ldots, w_n) \\ &= \operatorname*{argmax}_c P(w_1, w_2, \ldots, w_n|c)P(c) \quad (2)\end{aligned}$$

We assume that w_i is conditionally independent of every other word. This means that under the above independence assumptions, $P(w_1, w_2, \ldots, w_n|c)$ is approximated by the following:

$$P(w_1, w_2, \ldots, w_n|c) \approx \prod_i P(w_i|c) \quad (3)$$

Finally, the category $\hat{c}$ that d belongs to is determined by following:

$$\hat{c} = \operatorname*{argmax}_c P(c) \prod_i P(w_i|c) \quad (4)$$

When there is the pair of w_i and c where $P(w_i|c) = 0$, the left-hand value of eq. (4) equals 0. Therefore, let N denote the total number of training data, and substitute following eq. (5) for eq. (4) in order to avoid this case.

$$P(w_i|c) = \frac{0.1}{N} \quad (5)$$

3.2 Complement Naive Bayes Classifier

The NB classifier tends to classify documents into the category that contains large number of documents. The CNB classifier is a modification of the NB classifier. This classifier improves classification accuracy by using data from all categories except the category which is focused on. This classifier is also used as a baseline.

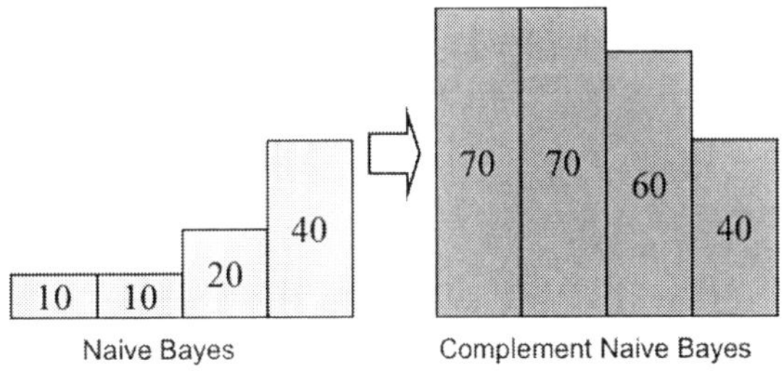

Figure 1: The difference of training data between two methods

Figure 1 shows the difference of the training data between the NB classifier and the CNB classifier. The NB classifier estimates parameters of a category using the data from the category which is focused on. When there are four categories that each contain 10, 10, 20, 40 training data, and the category with the most data has four times data as many as the category with the least data.

On the other hand, the CNB classifier estimates parameters of a category using the data from all categories except the category which is focused on. Therefore, the category with the least data is 40 and the category with the most data is 70. The gap of the number of the training data is less than the NB classifier.

The CNB classifier estimates the likelihood from probability of occurrence of words and decides the category which the product pages are classified into. The CNB estimates $P(w_i|c)$ using data from all categories except c ($\bar{c}$ denote those categories):

$$P(w_i|c) = \prod_{\bar{c}} \frac{1}{P(w_i|\bar{c})} \quad (6)$$

When there is the pair of w_i and $\bar{c}$ where $P(w_i|\bar{c}) = 0$, we used the same the smoothing method as eq. (5).

Finally, the category $\hat{c}$ that d belongs to is determined by following:

$$\hat{c} = \operatorname*{argmax}_c P(c) \prod_{\bar{c}} \frac{1}{P(w_i|\bar{c})} \quad (7)$$

3.3 Negation Naive Bayes Classifier

The CNB is a method that tackles the ununiformity of the data distribution. However we think eq. (7) is not derivable from eq. (1). J.D.M.Rennie et al. (2003) also ignored $P(c)$ assuming it is enough small comparing with $P(w_i|\bar{c})$ but we think $P(c)$ cannot be always ignored and should be calculated especially when the data distributionis very skewed.

Therefore, we propose the NNB, which is derivable from eq. (1) but also have the advantage like the CNB. The derivation of the equation of the NBB is as follows.

First, equ. (8) is obtained from equ. (1) because we would like to find $\hat{c}$: the category which maximaizes the posterior probability $P(c|d)$ here again. Here, we focus on $\bar{c}$: the categories which d is not supposed to belong to, like the CNB.

$$\begin{aligned} \hat{c} &= \operatorname*{argmax}_c (1 - P(\bar{c}|d)) \\ &= \operatorname*{argmin}_c P(\bar{c}|d) \end{aligned} \tag{8}$$

Next, equ. (9) follows from equ. (8) and Bayes' theorem as follows:

$$\begin{aligned} \hat{c} &= \operatorname*{argmin}_c \frac{P(\bar{c})P(d|\bar{c})}{P(d)} \\ &= \operatorname*{argmin}_c (\bar{c})P(d|\bar{c}) \end{aligned} \tag{9}$$

Finally, by substituting theorem of conditional probability like and assuming independence of every other word like , the category $\hat{c}$ that d belongs to is determined by following:

$$\hat{c} = \operatorname*{argmin}_c (\bar{c}) \prod_i P(w_i|\bar{c}) \tag{10}$$

This is an equation of the NNB that we propose. We used the same smoothing method as the CNB.

4 Classification Experiments

In this section, we describe the system to categorize the product pages and explain the setting of the classification experiments.

4.1 Data Set for Experiments

We used the product pages assigned to subordinate category of "Windows desktop PC", "baby products", and "memorial stamps" on Yahoo! auctions[1] as the training and test data. These categories can be narrowed down as follows from top category of Yahoo! auctions.

[1]http://auctions.yahoo.co.jp/

- All products > Computers > Personal computers > Windows > desktop PC
- All products > Baby products
- All products > Antiques or Collections > Stamps or cards > Japanese > Memorial stamps

The left-hand of the mark ">" is the parent category and right-hand is the child category.

We regard the categories assigned by the sellers as the correct labels. In addition, each product belongs to only one category in Yahoo! auctions. Categories are hierarchical and each product is assigned to terminal categories.

We used only one product page by one seller for each category to get rid of bias of notation habits of each seller like (Nishimura et al., 2008). The number of the categories and the product pages before and after removing the product pages of the same sellers is shown in Table 1. In addition, the number of the product pages of Windows desktop PC, baby products, and memorial stamps that we used for classification is each shown in Figure 2, Figure 3, and Figure 4. The categories are sorted by the number of the product pages in these figures. They show the numbers of the product pages are distributed non-uniformly through the categories.

Genre	Before	After	categories
PC	19,849	4,403	21
Baby product	29,477	10,389	62
Stamp	16,543	3,980	53

Table 1: The number of the categories and the product pages before and after removing the product pages of the same sellers

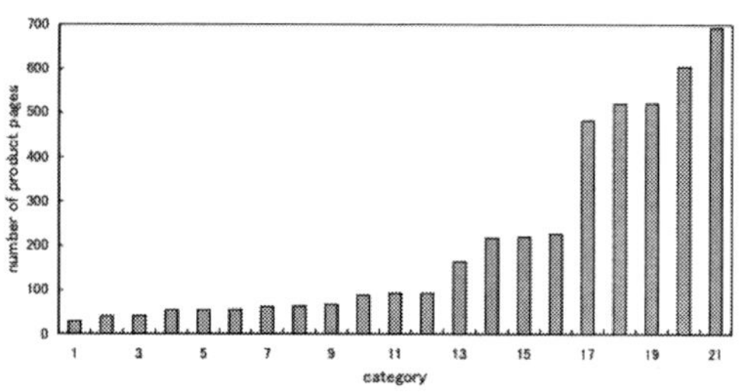

Figure 2: The number of the product pages of Windows desktop PC for each category

The product pages are described in HTML but we removed the HTML tags assuming that they were unnecessary for classification.

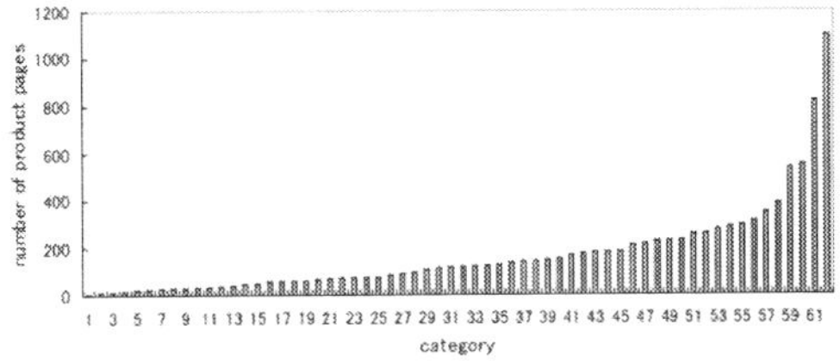

Figure 3: The number of the product pages of baby products for each category

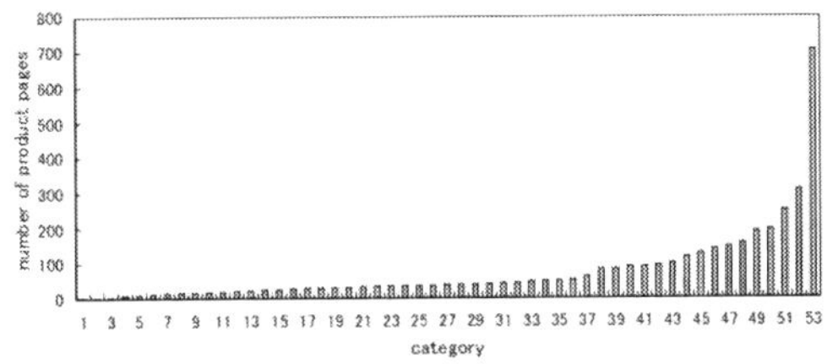

Figure 4: The number of the product pages of memorial stamps for each category

4.2 Features for Classification

The product pages of Yahoo! auctions contain many technical terms and many words which have a very small effect about the classification (e.g. symbols, shipping address, and so on). They also contain itemization and their sentences are short and colloquial. From these properties, we thought that it is not important for classification to see the whole product pages, but to extract words which represent the category of the product. We performed the classification experiments depending on the following four kinds of information.

- All the words in the titles
- The nouns extracted from the titles
- All the words in the titles and the descriptions
- The nouns extracted from the titles and the descriptions

4.3 Procedure of Classification

The procedure of the classification is following.

1. Obtain product pages with the category label which they are classified into.
2. Extract the titles and the description if necessary.
3. Perform morphological analysis on each product pages using Chasen [2].
4. Extract the features for classification.
5. Classify the product pages using the methods shown in Section 3.

[2]http://sourceforge.net/projects/masayu-a/

We used the default settings of Chasen. We used the 5-fold cross validation for the test. The chi-square test was performed to see if the difference is significant or not and its level of significance was 0.05.

5 Results

In this section, we describe the results of the classification experiments. First, we compare the accuracies of classifiers in four settings according to the features to categorize the product pages that we discribed in 4.2 about Windows desktop PC.

Table 2 shows the classification accuracy of the NB, the CNB, and the NNB. The "-" mark in "Descriptions" column means the descriptions of the product pages were not used for classification and the "+" mark means the classification was performed depending of the words from both the title and the description of the product pages. In addition, "Nouns" in "POS" column means only the nouns were used for the features of classification and "all" means all the words were used. Table 2 shows that whatever classifier was used, the accuracies when the titles were used were higher than when the titles and the descriptions were used. The difference was statically significant. Table 2 also shows that product pages can be classified little more correctly depending on only the nouns than all the words, but the difference was not significant.

Descriptions	POS	NB	CNB	NNB
-	all	**0.613**	**0.698**	**0.711**
-	nouns	**0.629**	**0.701**	**0.713**
+	all	0.456	0.623	0.623
+	nouns	0.481	0.641	0.642

Table 2: The classification accuracy using the product pages of Windows desktop PC

Next, we compare the NNB classifier with the NB classifier and the CNB classifier using the data of the following three genres: Windows desktop PC, baby products, and memorial stamps. In view of Table 2, we performed the classification experiments depending on two kinds of features, all the words of the titles and the nouns extracted from them.

Table 3 summarizes classification accuracy of the NB, the CNB, and the NNB using the data of these three grnres. The MFC is an abbreviation for the most frequent category. The "Total" in "Genre" column means the total average of three genres.

Genre	POS	NB	CNB	NNB
PC	all	0.613	0.698	**0.711**
PC	nouns	0.629	0.701	**0.713**
PC	the MFC		0.158	
Baby product	all	0.479	0.445	**0.508**
Baby product	nouns	0.484	0.436	**0.507**
Baby product	the MFC		0.105	
Stamp	all	0.451	0.452	**0.489**
Stamp	nouns	0.436	0.447	**0.490**
Stamp	the MFC		0.177	
Total	all	0.505	0.506	**0.552**
Total	nouns	0.508	0.501	**0.552**
Total	the MFC		0.133	

Table 3: The classification accuracy using the product pages of the three grnres

Table 3 shows that whatever features were used, and the data of whatever genre were used, the accuracies of the NBB classifier were higher than other classifiers. The second best classifier varies depending on the genre of product pages. The difference between the CNB and the NNB of Windows desktop PC, the NB and the CNB of memorial stamps, and the NB and the CNB of the total product pages were not significant. All the other differences were statically significant. Table 3 also shows that sometimes the product pages were classified little more correctly depending on only the nouns than all the words and sometimes not. In addition, all these differences were not significant. Table 2 also shows the accuracies of the three classifiers of the product pages about Windows desktop PC, when the titles and the descriptions were used. The tendency of the results is almost the same as when the titles were used for classification.

Finally, we compare the three methods to classify by three-class classification using the data of the three genres. Here, we classify all the product pages of three genres into three classes: Windows desktop PC, baby products and memorial stamps. Table 4 shows the accuracy of this experiment.

It shows the NB classifier outperformed the other classifiers significantly when all the words

POS	NB	CNB	NNB
all	**0.982**	0.978	0.978
nouns	**0.977**	**0.977**	0.976
the MFC		0.553	

Table 4: The classification accuracy of three class classification

in the title were used for the features of classification, and the NB and the CNB slightly outperformed the NNB when only the nouns on the title were used. When the nouns were used for the features, the difference among the NB, the CNB, and the NNB were not significant. In addition, when the features were compared, the classifier the accuracy when all the nouns were used was higher than when the nouns were used. The difference between the nouns and all the words was significant when the NB classifier was used. All the other differences were not statically significant.

6 Discussion

Table 2 shows that the product pages can be classified more correctly depending on only the titles of the product pages than both the titles and the descriptions of them. It means that the titles of the product pages were better features for classification than the titles and descriptions of them, at least for the product pages about Windows desktop PC. We think that this is because there are lots of words which are unnecessary for classification in the description of the product pages and they obstruct effective classification.

Next, Table 3 shows that whatever features were used, and the data of whatever genre were used, the accuracies of the NNB classifier were higher than the other classifiers. The second best classifier varies depending on the genre of product pages; the CNB was for the texts of Windows desktop PC or memorial stamps and the NB for the texts of baby products. Therefore when the NB classifier and the CNB classifier were compared, it is still unansuwered question that which is the better method to classify these product pages. However, the experiments show that our proposal method, the NNB is always the best method for the classification of the product pages of the three genres. When the total averages were compared, the NNB classifier also outperformed the other NB classifiers significantly.

In the experiments of Table 3, the products that

belong to the categories with a few product pages tended to be classifed into the categories with many product pages when the CNB was used. We think we can see the reason form the equation of the CNB. Here, equ.(10), the equation of the NNB, can be rewritten as the following equ. (11)

$$\hat{c} = \underset{c}{\operatorname{argmax}} \frac{1}{1 - P(c)} \prod_i \frac{1}{P(w_i|\bar{c})} \qquad (11)$$

From the equation of the CNB equ. (7) and equ. (11) , we can see that the difference of the equations between the NNB and the CNB is the usage of the prior probability $P(c)$. We think that the usage of the prior probability $P(c)$ in the equation of the CNB caused this problem.

In addition, Table 4 shows that the NB classifier outperformed the NNB classifier. It means that the NNB is not always the best method to classify the product pages of any genres. We think this is because the uniformity of the data. In this three-class classification, the product pages of each category are 4403, 10389, and 3980 and the distribution is not so non-uniform. The NNB tackles the ununiformity of the text but the advantage does not help in this situation. We think that that is why our proposal method could not classify more correctly than the other classifiers in the three-class classification. The measure of the uniformity of the distribution of texts such as deviation can be considered in the future in order to decide the best classification method for each category.

Finally, the differences between the nouns and all the words are almost always not significant. Only one exception is the difference of the three-class classification when the NB was used. We think this condition is not important comparing with the other conditions.

7 Conclusion

In this paper, we proposed the NNB to categorize product pages on the Web. It is a modified version of the NB and we got the idea from the CNB. Its equation is derivable from the equation of the NB unlike the CNB and it has the same advantage as the CNB: it tackles the ununiformity of the data distribution through categories.

We performed classification experiments using four kinds of features and product pages of three genres to compare three kinds of classification methods: the NB, the CNB, and the NNB. The features are all words in titles of the products pages, nouns extracted from the titles, all words in titles and descriptions of the product pages, and nouns extracted from them. The genres are Windows desktop PC, baby products, and memorial stamps.

The experiments gave us following three observations: (1) The titles of the product pages were better features for classification than the titles and the descriptions of them, at least for the product pages about Windows desktop PC, (2) When the classifiers were developed based on the titles of the product pages, our proposal method the NNB is always the best classification method in the three genres. (3) The NNB is not the best classification of three-class classification of the three genres. Therefore we think that the NNB is good for non-uniformly distributed data but is not so good for uniformly distributed data.

References

Kiyoshi Izutsu, Makoto Yokozawa, and Takeshi Shinohara. 2005. Comparative evaluation and applications of automatic web-based document classification methods. In *IPSJ SIG Notes 2005(32) (In Japanese)*, pages 25–32.

J.D.M.Rennie, L.Shih, J.Teevan, and D.R.Karger. 2003. Tackling the poor assumptions of naive bayes text classification. In *ICML2003*, pages 616–623.

David D. Lewis. 1992. An evaluation of phrasal and clustered representations on a text categorization task. In *15th Annual International ACM SIGIR Conference on Research and Development in Information Retrieval*, pages 37–50.

Andrew McCallum and Kamal Nigam. 1998. A comparison of event models for naive bayes text classification. In *AAAI/ICML-98 Workshop on Learning for Text Categorization*, pages 41–48.

Daichi Mochihashi. 2006. Bayesian approaches in natural language processing. In *IEICE Technical Report. NC, Neurocomputing (In Japanese)*, pages 25–30.

Jun Nishimura, Rintaro Miyazaki, Naoto Maeda, Tatsunori Mori, Shorei O, Yusuke Ishikawa, Hiroyuki Kobayashi, Yuya Tanaka, and Fuyuko Kido. 2008. Attribute-value extraction from description of exhibits for facetted search in net auction system. In *ANLP2008 (In Japanese)*, pages 392–395.

Naoto Sato, Kanako Komiya, Koji Fujimoto, and Yoshiyuki Kotani. 2011. Categorization of product pages depending on information on the web. In *UCSIP2011*, pages 393–398.

Kenneth W.Church. 2000. Empirical estimates of adaptation: The chance of two noriegas is closer to $p/2$ than p^2. In *COLING ' 00*, pages 173–179.

A Hybrid Approach for Event Extraction and Event Actor Identification

Anup Kumar Kolya[1] **Asif Ekbal**[2] **Sivaji Bandyopadhyay**[1]
[1] Computer Science and Engineering Department, Jadavpur University, India
[2] Patna (IITP), India
anup.kolya@gmail.com, asif.ekbal@gmail.com,
sivaji_cse_ju@yahoo.com

Abstract

This paper, we propose an approach for *event extraction* and corresponding *event actor* identification-within the TimeML framework. Firstly, for *event extraction*, we develop SVM based hybrid approach and for *event actor* identification the *baseline* model is developed based on the *subject* information of the dependency-parsed event sentences. Then we develop an unsupervised syntax based model that is based on the relationship of the event verbs with their argument structure extracted from the *head* information of the chunks in the parsed sentences. Evaluation on a collection of TempEval-2 corpus shows the precision, recall and F-measure values for the *baseline* model as 64.31%, 67.74% and 65.98%, respectively and the syntax based model as 69.12%, 66.90% and 67.99%, respectively.

1 Introduction

New sources of textual information, rich in events, grow significantly, such as social networks, blogs, and wikis. They are added to old sources like the informative web sites, emails and forums, which shows the importance to manage these data automatically. One of the important tasks of text analysis clearly requires identifying events described in a text and locating these in time. Event extraction has emerged to be very important in improving complex natural language processing (NLP) applications such as automatic summarization (Daniel et al., 2003) and question answering (QA). TimeML (Pustejovsky et al., 2003) presented a rich specification for annotating events in NL text extending the features of the previous one.

This paper is focused on the TimeML view of events. TimeML defines events as situations that *happen or occur*, or elements describing *states or circumstances* in which something obtains or holds the truth. These events are generally expressed by tensed or un-tensed verbs, nominalizations, adjectives, predicative clauses or prepositional phrases. The 2007 TempEval challenge attempted to address this question (Boguraev et al, 2005). In 2010, TempEval-2, event extraction task was introduced as task B. Let us consider a sentence like,

BAGHDAD, Iraq (AP) _ an American leader of a U.N. weapons inspection team ***resumed work*** *in Iraq Friday, nearly two months after his team was effectively* ***blocked.***

Sentence 1 has three events, namely '***resumed***', '***work***' and '**blocked**'. In this sentence *resumed* and *blocked* can be considered as verbal events but *work* is an nonverbal event. Generally, verbal or non-verbal event are executed by some abstract entities, directly or indirectly. Entities are basically person, organization or location.

2 Event Extraction

Below we present our hybrid approach for event extraction. The system is based on a supervised machine learner, Support Vector Machine (SVM). It makes use of the various features extracted from the TimeML corpus. In order to improve the performance of the system, we incorporate the knowledge of semantic role labeling, WordNet and several heuristics.

2.1 SVM based Approach

Initially, we started with the development of an event extraction method based on SVM. This is used as the *baseline* model. The SVM system is developed based on (Valdimir, 1995), which perform classification by constructing a N-dimensional hyperplane that optimally separates data into two categories. We use *YamCha* toolkit[1], a SVM-based tool for detecting classes in documents and formulating the event extraction

[1] http://chasenorg/~taku/software/yamcha

task as a sequential labeling problem. Here, the *pair wise* multi-class decision method and *polynomial kernel function* are used. We use TinySVM-0.0[2] classifier for classification.

We extract the gold-standard TimeBank features for events in order to train/test the SVM model. We mainly use the various combinations of *part of speech* (PoS), *event tense*, *event aspect*, *event polarity*, *event modality*, *event stem* and *event class* features.

2.2 Use of Semantic Roles for Event Extraction

We use Semantic Role Label (SRL) (Gildea et el, 2002; Sameer et al, 2004) to identify different features of the sentences of a document. These features help us to extract the events from the text. In the present work, we use predicate as an event. Semantic roles can be used to detect the events that are the nominalizations of verbs such as *agreement* for *agree* or *construction* for *construct*. Event nominalisations (or, *deverbal nouns*) are commonly defined as nouns, morphologically derived from verbs, usually by suffixation (Quirk et al., 1985). Let us consider the following example sentence to understand how semantic roles can be used for event extraction.

The output of SRL for this sentence is as follows:

[ARG1 All sites] were [TARGET inspected] to the satisfaction of the inspection team and with full cooperation of Iraqi authorities, [ARG0 Dacey] [TARGET said]

A sentence is scanned as many times as the number of target words in the sentence. In the first traversal, *inspected* is identified as the event. In the second pass, *said* is identified as an event. All the extracted target words are treated as the event words. We observed that many of these target words are identified as the event expressions by the SVM model. But, there exists many nominalised event expressions (i.e., *deverbal nouns*) that are not identified as events by the supervised SVM. These nominalised expressions are correctly identified as events by SRL. We observe performance improvement with the inclusion of this module.

2.3 Use of WordNet for Event Extraction

WorldNet (Miller, 1990) is mainly used to identify *non-deverbal event nouns*. We observed from the outputs of SVM and SRL that the event entities like '*war*', '*attempt*', '*tour*' etc. are not properly identified. These words have noun PoS categories, and the SVM along with SRL can only identify those event words that are verbs. We know from the lexical information of WordNet that the words like '*war*' and '*tour*' are generally used as both *noun* and *verb* forms in the sentence. We design two following rules based on the WordNet:

Rule 1: The word (for example *war*) tokens having noun PoS categories are looked into the WordNet. If it appears in the WordNet with noun and verb senses, then that word token is also considered as an event.

Rule 2: The *stems* of the noun word tokens are looked into WordNet. If one of the WordNet senses is verb then the token will be identified as verb.

We observe significant performance improvement on event extraction with the above mentioned two rules.

2.4 Use of Rules for Event Extraction

We used WordNet to extract the event expressions that appear in the WordNet with both noun and verb senses. Here, we mainly concentrate to identify the specific lexical classes like '*inspection*' and '*resignation*'. These can be identified by the suffixes such as ('*-ción*'), ('*-tion*') or ('*-ion*'), i.e. the morphological markers of deverbal derivations.

Initially, we run the SVM based Stanford Named Entity (NE) tagger[3] on the TempEval-2 test dataset. The output of the system is tagged with *Person*, *Location*, *Organization* and *Other* classes. The words starting with the capital letters are also considered as NEs. Thereafter, we came up with the following rules for event extraction:

Rule-1: The morphologically deverbal nouns are usually identified by the suffixes like '*-tion*', '*-ion*', '*-ing*' and '*-ed*' etc. The non NE nouns but ends with these suffixes are considered as the event words.

Rule-2: After searching verb-noun combination from the test set, non-NE noun words are considered as the events.

Rule- 3: The non-NE nouns occurring after (i) the complements of aspectual PPs headed by prepositions (ii) any time-related verbs (iii) certain expressions are considered as events.

[2](http://cl.aist-nara.ac.jp/~taku ku/software/TinySVM)

[3] http://nlp.stanford.edu/software/CRF-NER.shtml

2.5 Evaluation Results

We use the TempEval-2010 datasets to report the evaluation results. We develop a number of SVM models depending upon the various features included into it. We have a training data in the form (W_i, T_i), where, W_i is the ith pair along with its feature vector and T_i is its corresponding output label (i.e., *Event* or *Other*). Models are built based on the training data and the feature template. We used different feature combinations within the context of previous 3 and next 3 words. The test data had 373 verbal and 125 non-deverbal event nouns. Overall evaluation results are reported in Table 1. The SVM based system shows the precision, recall and F-measure values of 75.8%, 78.5% and 77.13%, respectively. The performance increases by almost 1.59 percentage F-measure points with the use of semantic roles. Table 1 shows very high performance improvement (i.e., 10.98%) with the use of WordNet. The rule-based component also shows the effectiveness with the improvement of 5.37 F-measure percentage points. Finally, the system achieves the precision, recall and F-measure values of 93.00%, 96.00% and 94.47%, respectively. This is actually an improvement of approximately 12% F-measure value over the best reported system.

3 Event Actor Identification

In this section, we detail our method for event actor identification.

3.1 Subject Based Baseline Model

We have preprocessed the TempEval-2 corpus for identifying the actors of the events. We have previously (Kolya et al. 2010a; Kolya et al 2010b) worked on the various problems of event and temporal relation identification such as (i). Event-time and event-documentation creation time (DCT) temporal relation (TE) identification in the same sentence, (ii). Even–event temporal relation identification in two consecutive sentences and (iii). Subevent-subevent temporal relation identification in the same sentence on the Tempeval-1 and Temeval-2 corpus. We have observed from this experience that almost all events are involved with the actors, either active or passive. Actually, event actions are done by someone or somebody is doing this kind of action. Event actions involve with person, organization and sometimes with location also. In the present attempt, we consider the approaches that were conducted for identifying emotion holders (Das and Bandyopadhyay, 2010). Thereafter, we came up with the following heuristics for actor identification, (i) we discard the non-event sentences, i.e. those sentences that don't contain any event entity. (ii) If multiple events exist in any sentence, then all the events will have the same actors. Once an actor is identified for any event, it is assigned to the other event as well. (iii) If there are multiple actors and events, then <event, actor> pairs are formed by considering an event and its closest possible actor in the sentence. All the events may not have an active actor. The actor may be passive also. For example, consider the following sentences:

Table 1. Evaluation results of event extraction

Model	precision	recall	F-measure
SVM	75.80	78.50	77.13
SVM+SRL	77.20	80.30	78.72
SVM+SRL+WordNet	89.30	90.10	89.70
SVM + SRL + WordNet + Rules	93.50	96.70	95.07

1. *This time a <bomb/> at an abortion clinic.*

2. *Plates <recovered/> at the Olympic park bombing <appear/> to <match/> those <found/> at the abortion clinic <bombing/> in Atlanta.*

Corpus Preparation: We did not have any gold standard corpus for event actor identification. We have used the Temeval-2 corpus as a gold standard event actor corpus by manually annotating event actors in each sentence. The gold corpus looks as follows:

<eActor> People </eActor> have <predicted/> his <demise/> so many times , and the <eActor>US<eActor> has <tried/> to <hasten/> it on several occasions .

Here, a *"People"* is the event actor of both events **predicted** and **demise,** and *"US"* is the event actor of the events, **tried** and **hasten.** This corpus has 11 documents, 156 sentences and 459 events.

3.2. Baseline Model based on Dependency Parsing and Subject Extraction

Stanford Parser (de Marneffe et al,2006), a probabilistic lexicalized parser containing 45 different PoS tags of Pen Tree bank is used to get the parsed sentences with dependency relations. The input event sentences are passed through the parser. The dependency relationships extracted from the parsed data are checked for predicates "*nsubj*" and "*xsubj*" so that the *subject* related information in the "*nsubj*" and "*xsubj*" predicate are considered as the probable candidate for identifying the event actor. Other dependency relations are filtered out from the parsed output. The present system is developed based on the filtered subject information only. An example sentence is noted below whose parsed output and dependency relations are shown. Here, the "*nsubj*" relations containing the event word "endures" tags "eActor" as an event actor.

"*Time and again, he* ***endures.***"

```
(ROOT (S  (S   (UCP  (NP (NNP
Time))(CC and)(ADVP (RB again))))(,
,) (NP (PRP he)) (VP (VBZ endures))
(. .)))
```

```
ccomp    (endures-6,    Time-1),advmod
(Time-1, again-3),conj and (Time-1,
again-3),ccomp (endures-6, again-3)
nsubj (endures-6, he-5)
```

This *baseline* model is evaluated on the gold standard holder annotated an emotional sentence that has been extracted from the VerbNet. Total 156 sentences are evaluated and evaluation results are presented in Table 2. So, the next step is to explore the syntactical way for identifying argument structure of the sentences for their corresponding emotional verbs and to capture the emotion holder as a *thematic role* respectively.

3.3. Syntax Based Model

The syntax of a sentence is an important clue to capture the event actor inscribed in text. More specifically, the argument structure or subcategorization information for a verb plays an important role to identify the event actor from an event sentence. A subcategorization frame is a statement of what types of syntactic arguments a verb (or an adjective) takes, such as objects, infinitives, that-clauses, participial clauses, and subcategorized prepositional phrases (Manning et al. 1993). VerbNet (Kipper-Schuler et al, 2005) is the largest online verb lexicon with explicitly stated syntactic and semantic information based on Levin's verb classification (Levin et al 1993). It is a hierarchical domain-independent, broad-coverage verb lexicon with mappings to other lexical resources such as WordNet (Miller et al, 1990), XTAG (2001) and FrameNet (Baker et al, 1998). We use VerbNet throughout this experiment for identifying the event actors. The existing syntax for each event verb is extracted from VerbNet and a separate rule based argument structure acquisition system is developed in the present task for identifying the event actor. The acquired argument structures are compared against the extracted VerbNet frame syntaxes. If the acquired argument structure matches with any of the extracted frame syntaxes, the event actor corresponding to each event verb is tagged with the actor information in the appropriate slot in the sentence.

Syntax Acquisition from VerbNet: VerbNet associates the semantics of a verb with its syntactic frames and combines traditional lexical semantic information such as thematic roles and semantic predicates, with syntactic frames and selectional restrictions. Verb entries in the same VerbNet class share common syntactic frames, and thus they are believed to have the same syntactic behavior. The VerbNet files containing the verbs with their possible subcategorization frames and membership information are stored in XML file format.

<THEMROLES/> <FRAMES>
<FRAME> <DESCRIPTION descriptionNumber="8.1" primary="TO-INF-SC"
secondary="" xtag="0.1"/> .... <EXAMPLE>I loved to write.</EXAMPLE>
<SYNTAX> <NP value="Experiencer">
<SYNRESTRS/> </NP>
<VERB/> <NP value="Theme">
<SEMANTICS> <PRED value="**event_state**">
<ARGS> <ARG type="Event" value="E"/>
<ARG type="**VerbSpecific**"
value="**Event**"/> <ARG type="ThemRole" value="Passive"/> .....
</ARGS> </PRED> </SEMANTICS>
</FRAME>....

The XML files of VerbNet are preprocessed to build up a general list that contains all member verbs and their available syntax information retrieved from VerbNet. This preprocessed list is searched to acquire the syntactical frames for each event verb. One of the main criteria considered for selecting the frames is the presence of "*event_state*" type predicate associated with the frame semantics.

Argument Structure Acquisition Framework: To acquire the argument structure for a sentence, two separate approaches, Methods A and B, have been used, one (Method A) is from the parsed result directly and another (Method B) is from the PoS tagged and chunked sentences accordingly. The parsed event sentences are passed through a rule based *phrasal-head* extraction process to identify the phrase level argument structure of the sentences corresponding to the event verbs. The extracted *head part* of every phrase from the well-structured bracketed parsed data is considered as the component of the argument structure. For example, the *head* parts of the phrases are extracted to make the phrase level pattern or argument structures of the following sentences.

Sentence1: "*Ram killed Shyam with a knife.*"
Parsed Output:
(ROOT (S (**NP** (NNP Ram)) (**VP** (VBD killed) (**NP** (NNS Shyam)) (**PP** (IN **with**) (NP (DT a) (NN knife)))) (. .)))
Acquired Argument Structure: [NP VP NP PP-with]
Simplified Extracted VerbNet Frame Syntax: [<NP value="*Actor*"> <VERB/> <NP *patient*> <PREP value="*with*">]

Event Actor for Event Verbs–The role of Subject and Syntax: It is to be mentioned that the phrases headed by "S" (sentential complement), "PP" (Preposition Phrase), "NP" (Noun Phrase) followed by the event verb phrase contribute in structuring the syntactical argument. One tag conversion routine has been developed to transform the POS information of the system-generated argument structure for comparison with the POS categories of the VerbNet syntax. It has been observed that the phrases that start with ADJP, ADVP (adjective, adverbial phrases) tags generally do not contribute towards valid argument selection strategy. But, the entities in the slots of active frame elements are added if they construct a frame that matches with any of the extracted frames from VerbNet. The *head* part of each phrase with its component attributes (e.g. "*with*" component attribute for "PP" phrase) in the parsed result helps in identifying the maximum matching possibilities. Another alternative way to identify the argument structure from a sentence is carried out based on the PoS tagged and chunked data. The PoS tagged sentences are passed through a Conditional Random Field (CRF) based chunker (Phan et al, 2006) to acquire chunked data where each component of the chunk is marked with *beginning* or *intermediate* or *end* corresponding to the elements slot in that chunk. The POS of the *beginning* part of every chunk are extracted and frames are developed to construct the argument structure of the sentence corresponding to the event verb. The acquired argument structure of a sentence is mapped to all of the extracted VerbNet frames. If a single match is found, the slot devoted for the actor in VerbNet frame is used to tag in the appropriate slot in the acquired frame. For example, the argument structure acquired from the following chunked sentence is "NP-VP-NP".

But, it has been observed that this second system suffers from the inability to recognize arguments from adjuncts as the system blindly captures *beginning* parts as arguments whereas they are adjuncts in real. So, this system is biased to the *b ginning* chunk.

3.4. Evaluation

The evaluation of the baseline system is straightforward. The event actor annotated sentences are extracted from the VerbNet and the sentences are passed through the baseline system to annotate the sentences with their *subject* based actor tag accordingly. Evaluation with 156 sentences is shown in Table 2. It is observed that the *subject* information helps in identifying event actor with high *recall*. But, the actor identification task for passive sentences fails in this *baseline* method and hence there is a fall in *precision* value. Two types of unsupervised rule based methods have been adopted to acquire the argument structure from the event sentences. It has been observed that, the Method-A that acquires argument structure from parsed result directly outperforms the Method-B that acquires these structures from PoS tagged and chunked data. The *recall* value has decreased in Method-B as it fails to distinguish the arguments from the adjuncts. The event actor identification system based on argument structure directly from parsed output gives satisfactory performance.

Table 2. Evaluation results of actor identification

Type	Baseline Model	Syntactic Model	
		Method A	Method B
Precision	64.31	69.12	64.05
Recall	67.74	66.90	65.52
F-measure	65.98	67.99	64.78

4 Conclusion

In this paper, we have reported our work on event extraction under the TempEval -2010 evaluation exercise. Initially, we developed a SVM based supervised system in conjunction with number of techniques based on SRL, WordNet and handcrafted rules for event extraction. We then identify the actors for the events based on the roles associated to *subject* information. The syntactic way of developing the actor extraction module by focusing on the role of arguments of the event verbs improves the result significantly.

Future works include the identification of more precise rules for event identification and multiword events. The actor-annotated corpus preparation from VerbNet especially for event verbs followed by the argument extraction module can be further explored through the help of machine learning approach.

Acknowledgments

The work is partially supported by a grant from English to Indian language Machine Translation(EILMT) funded by Department of Information and Technology (DIT), Government of India.

References

Boguraev, B., Ando, R-K. 2005. *TimeBank-DrivenTimeML Analysis. Annotating, Extracting and Reasoning about Time and Events* 2005.

Baker, C.F., Fillmore, C.J., Lowe, J.B.: *The Berkeley FrameNet project.* COLING/ACL, pp. 86–90 (1998)

Daniel, Naomi, Dragomir Radev, and Timothy Allison.2003. *Sub-event based multi-document summariza-tion.* HLT-NAACL Text summarization workshop, pages 9–16.

Das Dipankar and Sivaji Bandyopadhyay. 2010. Emotion Holder for Emotional Verbs–The role of Subject and Syntax. CICLing- 2010), A. Gelbukh (Ed.), LNCS 6008, pp. 385-393, Romania

De Marneffe, M.-C., MacCartney, B., Manning, C.D.: *Generating Typed Dependency Parses from Phrase Structure Parses.* LREC (2006)

Gildea, D. and D. Jurafsky. 2002. *Automatic Labeling of Semantic Roles.* Computational Linguistics, 28(3):245–288.

Kipper-Schuler, K.: VerbNet: *A broad-coverage, comprehensive verb lexicon.* Ph.D. thesis,Computer and Information Science Dept., University of Pennsylvania, Philadelphia,PA (2005)

Kolya, A., Ekbal, A. and Bandyopadhyay, S. 2010. JU_CSE_TEMP: *A First Step towards Evaluating Events, Time Expressions and Temporal Relations.* SemEval, ACL, July 15-16, Sweden, pp. 345–350.

Kolya, A., Ekbal, A. and Bandyopadhyay, S. (2010a). *Event-Time Relation Identification using Machine Learning and Rules.* In Proceedings of 13th International Conference on Text, Speech and Dialogue, 2010, pp. 114-120.

Kolya, A., Ekbal, A. and Bandyopadhyay, S. (2010b). *Identification of Event-Time Relation:* A CRF based approach. ICCPOL 2010, USA, PP.63-66.

Levin, B.: English Verb Classes and Alternation: *A Preliminary Investigation.* The University of Chicago Press, Chicago (1993)

Manning, C.D.: *Automatic Acquisition of a Large Subcategorization Dictionary from Corpora.*In: 31st Meeting of the ACL, Columbus, Ohio, pp. 235–242 (1993)

Miller, G.A.: WordNet: *An on-line lexical database.* International Journal of Lexicography 3(4), 235–312 (1990)

Pustejovsky, James, Jos´e M. Casta˜no, Robert Ingria,Roser Saur´?, Robert Gaizauskas, Andrea Setzer, andGraham Katz. 2003. *TimeML: Robust Specification of Event and Temporal Expressions in Text.* In IWCS-5.

Phan, X.-H.: CRFChunker: *CRF English Phrase Chunker.* In: PACLIC 2006 (2006)

Quirk, R., S. Greenbaum, G. Leech, and J. Svartvik.1985. *A Comprehensive Grammar of the English Language.* Longman.

Sameer S. Pradhan, Wayne Ward, Kadri Hacioglu, James H. Martin, Daniel Jurafsky, *Shallow Semantic Parsing using Support Vector Machines*. HLT/NAACL-2004, Boston, MA, May 2-7, 2004.

Evaluating Human Correction Quality for Machine Translation from Crowdsourcing

Shasha Liao
Computer Science Department
New York University
liaoss@cs.nyu.edu

Cheng Wu, Juan Huerta
IBM T.J. Watson Research Center
{chengwu,huerta}@us.ibm.com

Abstract

Machine translation (MT) technology is becoming more and more pervasive, yet the quality of MT output is still not ideal. Thus, human corrections are used to edit the output for further studies. However, how to judge the human correction might be tricky when the annotators are not experts. We present a novel way that uses cross-validation to automatically judge the human corrections where each MT output is corrected by more than one annotator. Cross-validation among corrections for the same machine translation, and among corrections from the same annotator are both applied. We get a correlation around 40% in sentence quality for Chinese-English and Spanish-English. We also evaluate the user quality as well. At last, we rank the quality of human corrections from good to bad, which enables us to set a quality threshold to make a trade-off between the scope and the quality of the corrections.

1 Introduction

Human corrections are aimed to give the correct translation by editing the MT output. In this way, they can be used to analyze what kind of mistakes a MT system might make; also, they can be feed back to the MT system to improve the output. Manual human correction is generally thought to be excessively time consuming and expensive and experts are acquired to make sure the quality. However, as the scale of online multi-user communities is increasing, it becomes an easier and faster way to collect a large amount of human corrections. Crowdsourcing is an effective and cost-efficient way to collect human corrected (HC) sentences. However, before feeding back the crowdsourcing data to MT system, there are two challenges (a) how to measure the quality of HC sentences and (b) how to select good quality HC sentences for enhancing the translation models.

If we only have one human correction per sentence, the quality is quite hard to evaluate. However, if each sentence contains more than one human correction, there are much more information we are able to use. In this paper, we used the redundant corrections to apply a cross-validation approach to automatically evaluate the human corrections and rank them.

2 Crowdsourcing Description

Our crowdsourcing is based on enterprise data from employee participation in translation tasks, and conducted inside a worldwide company (Osamuyimen Stewart etc. 2010). This is used to help us with the data collection effort required for improving statistical machine translation algorithms, by harnessing the linguistic skills of worldwide bi-lingual employees for accomplishing the complex translation task that is typically done by professional translators. Participants are presented with text of relevant data e.g., news, technical content, history, etc., in a source language and asked to translate into a target language.

In this paper, we use "benchmark" data in crowdsourcing, where each source sentence contains multiple human corrections from multiple participants. In Benchmark data, for each source sentence, we collect one machine translation sentence, more than two human corrections. Each set is called a *translation set*, and experts are asked to give one reference for each *translation set*[1].

3 Cross-validation for Sentences

In this section, we proposed the cross-validation method. Different features will be examined and

[1] Note that our goal is to evaluate human corrections without reference, and the reference is not used in our

combined to reach the best performance. The basic assumption of cross-validation is that if a correction is similar to other corrections in the same translation set, it implies that other annotators probably agree with this correction; otherwise, it means other annotators has very different opinion on this correction. Thus, if a correction has high similarities to other corrections, it is probably a good correction; otherwise, it is not. By applying this "pseudo-reference" approach, we can judge the sentence level quality more confidently.

As there are many different methods to calculate the similarity, on lexical, syntax, or even semantic levels, we apply these features and evaluate them in the rest of this section. We first apply BLEU, the traditional metric for MT evaluation, and then other features including word similarity, semantic analysis and syntax information, which are widely used in NLP tasks.

Also, based on the special characteristics of the crowdsourcing, we also apply another similarity from the "user" view, where the user quality is used as a special feature.

3.1 Language Model (LM)

Language model are used a lot in machine translation. The basic assumption is that a good translation should be more fluent, and more like the standard sentences.

SRI language model toolkit[2] is used to train the language models from 68,101 English sentences in Crowdsourcing which are translated to other languages, and a 5-gram language models is built. The perplexity score is normalized by the largest perplexity score in the *translation set*.

$$LM^*(s) = \frac{ppl(\max(Set(s))}{ppl(s)}$$

Where *Set(s)* is the translation set containing s, and *max(Set(s))* is the maximal language score in *Set(s)*, *ppl(s)* is the perplexity score for sentence s[3].

3.2 Cross-validated Bleu Score (c-Bleu)

First, we apply a straightforward strategy to see if we can only use BLEU score among different human corrections from the same translation set to give cross-validated score. In this method, only the n-gram among sentences is used, and no linguistic knowledge is needed. Thus, this is a very convenient method, and can apply to evaluation on translation from any language pairs.

3.3 Cross-validated Word Similarity (c-WS)

Instead of using BLEU score, we apply another method of evaluating the translation by calculating the similarity between two sentences. Tokenization is applied before calculation, and the word order is not considered in the normal word similarity. Every sentence is treated as a word vector $Si = (w_{i1}, w_{i2}, \ldots, w_{in})$, and for two sentences S_1 and S_2, the similarity between them is:

$$word\_sim(S_1, S_2) = \frac{\sum_{w_{1i} \in S1, w_{2j} \in S2} sim(w_{1i}, w_{2j})}{\sqrt{|S_1| * |S_2|}}$$

Where $sim(w_{1i}, w_{2j})$ equals 1 if w_{1i} equals w_{2j}, otherwise 0.

3.3.1 Cross-validated Stemmed WS (c-WS1)

Some languages like Chinese don't have plural for example, and translator might translate a Chinese word with single or plural form, which are both correct. This also happens for past form and present form too. As a result, we test another similarity metric that ignores such difference. For example, "attacked" will be stemmed to "attack", and "rules" will be stemmed to "rule". However, as different word forms might predicate different functions in the sentence, for two different words with the same base form, we give them a similarity score of 0.95.

3.3.2 Cross-validated Semantic WS (c-WS2)

Translation can be very different, and people might use different word with the same meaning. For example, "search" and "find" are both good translation for Chinese word "查找". This is also one important reason why evaluation with multiple references is better than that with single reference. In this metric, we involve such information to calculate the similarity between two corrections. In practice, we use WordNet[4] to calculate the semantic similarity between two words (Leacock and Chodorow 1998, Wu and Palmer 1994, Resnik 1995, Lin 1998, and Jiang and Conrath 1997). In our experiment, we use the Information Content (IC) method presented

[2] http://www.speech.sri.com/projects/srilm/

[3] Note that a better sentence will have a lower perplexity score, and we use the inverse of ppl as the language model score.

[4] http://wordnet.princeton.edu/

by Lin (1998), where the IC score ranges from 0.0 to 1.0.

For a sentence, the semantic word similarity between S1 and S2 is calculated by:

```
senscore = 0.0;
For each word w1 in S1
   best_match = 0
   For each word w2 in S2
      score = SimFun(w1,w2)
      If score > best_match
         best_match = score
   if(best_match > threshold)
      senscore += best_match
      remove w1 from S1, remove w2 from S2
senscore = senscore/sqrt(length(S1)*length(S2))
```

Figure1. Procedure of computing semantic similarity for two sentences

3.3.3 Cross-validated Syntax-based WS (c-WS3)

In the above similarity method, the relations between words are not considered, thus no syntax information is provided. In this similarity method, we want to take the dependency tree similarity into consideration. In our experiment, we use the Stanford Dependencies[5] to acquire such syntactic information.

We use the triplets in the dependency tree, which is composed of (relation, governor, dependent). And for every pair of triplets (t1, t2), we calculate its similarity in this way

$$dep\_sim(t1,t2) = sim(relation_{t1}, relation_{t2}) * sim(governor_{t1}, governor_{t2}) * sim(dependent_{t1}, dependent_{t2})$$

where relation will be 1 for exact match, and 0 otherwise. For governor and dependent, we use the semantic similarity mentioned in section 4.3.2. The similarity between two sentences is:

$$dep\_sim(S_1,S_2) = \frac{\sum_{t_{1i}\in T1, t_{2j}\in T2} sim(t_{1i},t_{2j})}{\sqrt{|T_1|*|T_2|}}$$

[5] http://nlp.stanford.edu/software/stanford-dependencies.shtml

However, syntax-based similarity is more sparse than word-based similarity, and we use a parameter α to balance between the two[6]:

$$Sim(S_1,S_2) = \alpha * word\_sim(S1,S2) + (1-\alpha)dep\_sim(S1,S2)$$

3.4 Cross-validated Correction Similarity (c-CS)

As the human correction is derived from machine translation, the difference between the correction and the translation might be more likely to reflect the quality of the corrections. As a result, we calculate the similarity between the corrections (adding and deleting) from machine translation instead of the whole sentence. The difference between sentence similarity and correction similarity is that: for sentence similarity, every sentence is represented by all the words in the sentence, while in correction similarity, we only consider about the words which are inserted or deleted from the machine translation. We also test the correction similarity on stemmed (c-CS1), semantic (c-CS2), and syntax level (c-CS3).

4 Cross-validation for User Evaluation

Above features treat each *translation set* as a whole, and user information are ignored. However, we believe that the user information can also be predictable. If a user's translation skill is good, he should always provide good corrections, while a user with limited translation skill will provide relatively worse corrections. Thus, if we can acquire user quality, we can use it to evaluate the sentence he corrects.

Although the user quality cannot be implicitly evaluated since we do not do any quality test, we can indirectly acquire such information based on the quality of the sentence he translates. As the user quality is judged by all the sentences he corrected, it should be more reliable even the evaluation on sentence is not very confident. The user score is calculated by:

$$US(u) = \frac{\sum_{si\in set(u)} score_{si}}{|set(u)|}$$

where $Set(u)$ is the set of sentence translated by user u,and $score_{si}$ is the sentence score calculated in section 3.3.

After we evaluate each user, we also feed it back as an extra feature for sentence level

[6] In practice, we set α to 0.8.

evaluation. It is another kind of cross-validation, where the quality of a correction is based on other corrections from the same user.

5 Experiment

We use two methods for sentence level evaluation: one is a correlation evaluation that checks the correlation between different features and human assessment; the other is a selection evaluation to see if we can select good human corrections above a threshold to feedback to MT system.

We only use correlation evaluation for user quality evaluation, as we do not want to set a threshold to forbid any user to contribute.

We start with Chinese-English (C-E) and Spanish-English (S-E) MT. In C-E, there are 67 translation sets, with 335 human corrections and 39 people participated; while in S-E, there are 40 translation sets, with 217 human corrections and 38 people participated. Most translations are corrected 3 to 5 times. Users corrected different amount of sentences: some corrected one sentence, while some might correct more than 25 sentences.

5.1 Golden Standard

In this section, we create a key set by human assessment as our gold standard: we mixed up the machine translation, human corrections, and reference for one original sentence and 5 annotators in Chinese-English, and 3 in Spanish-English, were asked to assess the sentences scores from 1 to 5, where 1 corresponds to poor and 5 corresponds to perfect translation.

We calculate the average score of machine translation, reference, and human correction to see how good they are (table 1).

	MT	Ref	HC*	H_HC
Chinese	2.08	4.52	*4.2*	*4.67*
Spanish	2.96	4.3	*3.9*	*4.5*

Table1. Chinese-English overall qualities for machine translation, reference, and human correction[7]

5.2 Correlation Experiments

The basic assumption of correlation experiment is that a good evaluation metric should correlate better to the golden standard. We test the correlation of each feature to the human assessment, and also try to combine the features together to achieve the best performance. As no machine learning involved in this paper, we use simple multiplication to combine scores from different features.

Because we have a reference in benchmark data, we use the correlation between the bleu score between the correction and the reference as our baseline, which is not quite good.

5.2.1 Sentence Evaluation Results

From table2 we can see that language model score correlates worst. This indicates that distinguishing human correction and machine learning might be easier, but distinguishing between corrections is much harder.

Cross validation on BLEU scores works better than bleu score with single reference, but it does not work as well as word similarity method.

Similarity calculation works best, and if more linguistic information is involved, the correlation is better. We try to combine different features together, and only report the ones that improve.

Sentence Correlation / Methods	Chinese	Spanish
Baseline	28.7%	18.7%
c-Bleu	29.7%	24%
LM	17.4%	-0.84%
c-WS	33.7%	31.7%
+Stemmed (c-WS1)	35%	32.8%
+Semantic (c-WS2)	36.3%	30.5%
+Syntax-based (c-WS3)	**37%**	**33.3%**
c-CS	30.7%	36.2%
+Stemmed (c-CS1)	31.8%	**36.6%**
+Semantic (c-CS2)	31.9%	34.3%
+Syntax-based (c-CS3)	**33.1%**	35.2%
c-WS3*c-CS3	**38.8%**	**39.8%**

Table2. Sentence correlation results for different features

5.2.2 User Evaluation Results

The golden standard for each user is judged by the average quality of his corrections, and we test

[7] HC* is the overall HC score, and H_HC represents the best HC from each translation set

the correlation between golden standard and automatic evaluation (table 3).

Methods \ User Correlation	Chinese	Spanish
c-WS3	52.2%	51%
c-CS3	54.6%	64.1%
c-WS3* c-CS3	**57.8%**	**70.5%**

Table3. Results of user quality correlation

Then we added user quality as an extra feature for sentence evaluation. Experiment shows that adding this feature can further improve the correlation by 1.8% for C-E and 1.6% for S-E (table 4).

Methods \ Sentence Correlation	Chinese	Spanish
User_Score (US)	30.6%	28.5%
c-WS3* c-CS3	38.8%	39.8%
c-WS3* c-CS3* US	**40.6%**	**41.4%**

Table4. Results of feedback user quality to sentence quality

5.2.3 Analysis

From the study above, we can see that the similarity score among human corrections performs best, and it can achieve a better result than using bleu score with reference.

N-gram based language model does not help too much, but long distance features, like syntax feature, when combined with word similarity, is helpful.

Language model does not correlate well, especially for Spanish. We checked the data and found that the overall language model score for translated Spanish is better than reference, which means for Spanish, the fluency is not the big problem.

Semantic feature's performance is not stable from different language pairs. For C-E, it improves, but for S-E, it does. The reasons might be that Spanish is more like English, and the use of synonym does not occur much.

Also, experiments show that user information should be kept to make more confident evaluation.

5.3 Selection Experiments

Besides of evaluating the human correction quality by correlation, we also apply another selection experiment to see if there is a way that we can pick up good human corrections and feed them back to machine translation system.

5.3.1 Inner Selection

We use the combined features that perform best in previous experiment, which combines the score of sentence similarity, correction similarity and user quality. From figure 1&2, we can see that if we pick up the human correction with the highest score from each translation set, we can achieve comparable results as the human reference. Most important, the human corrections with score below 3 are total filtered out, which means that the worst human corrections are removed.

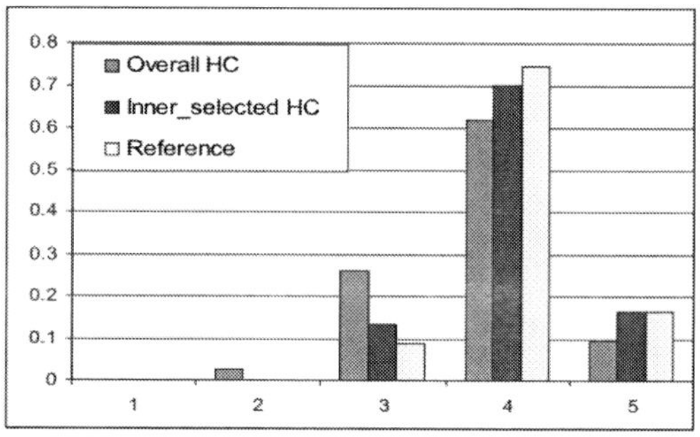

Figure1. Sentence quality distribution

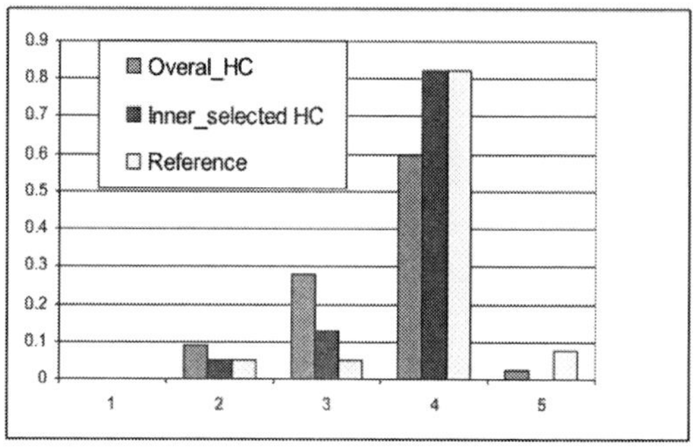

Figure2. Sentence quality distribution

5.3.2 Overall Selection

In this experiment, we only interested in the corrections with a human assessment above 4, which is good enough with the *reference quality*. Figure 3&4 shows that, the less corrections we selected, the more good corrections we get. Thus, we can easily set the threshold to return a subset of crowdsourcing data with higher qualities.

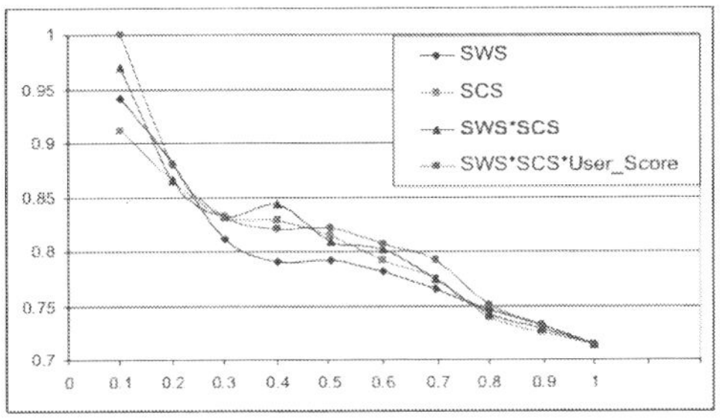

Figure3. Percentages of *reference quality* corrections in Chinese-English

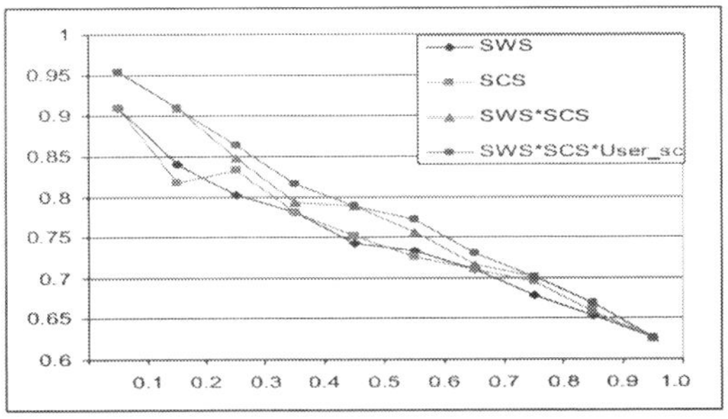

Figure4. Percentages of *reference quality* corrections in Spanish-English

6 Conclusions and Future Work

We evaluated the human correction qualities based on multiple corrections. In this way, we could cross validate the quality of a single correction. We investigated different features and compare their correlation to human assessment. We also tried to rank the quality of human corrections from good to bad, which enabled us to set a threshold to control the qualities of the human corrections.

Acknowledgments

We would like to thank other co-workers from IBM, including Ea-Ee Jan, Sasha Caskey, Hui Wan, Fei Huang and Jia Cui.

References

K. Papineni, et al. BLEU: a method for automatic evaluation of machine translation. *IBM research division technical report, RC22176 (W0109-022), 2001.*

Brabham, D.C. 2008. Crowdsourcing as a model for problem solving: an introduction and cases. *In Convergence: International Journal of Research into New Media Technologies, 14, (1), 75-90*

R Snow, B O'Connor, D Jurafsky, AY. 2008. Cheap and fast---but is it good? evaluating non-expert annotations for natural language tasks. *Proceedings of EMNLP 2008, Honolulu*

C Callison-Burch. 2009. Fast, cheap, and creative: evaluating translation quality using Amazon's Mechanical Turk. *Proceeding of EMNLP 2009, Singapore*

M Marge, S Banerjee, A Rudnicky. 2010. Using the Amazon Mechanical Turk for transcription of spoken language. *Proceeding of ICASSP, March, 2010*

Enrique Amig´o, Jes´us Gim´enez, Julio Gonzalo, and Felisa Verdejo. 2009. The contribution of linguistic features to automatic machine translation evaluation. *In Proceedings of ACL 2009.*

M Gamon, A Aue, M Smets. 2005. Sentence-Level MT evaluation without reference translations: beyond language modeling. *Proceedings of EAMT, 2005*

Quirk, Christopher. 2004. Training a Sentence-Level Machine Translation Confidence Measure. In Proceedings of LREC 2004, pp 525-828.

Alex Kulesza and Stuart M. Shieber. 2004. A Learning Approach to Improving Sentence-Level MT Evaluation. *In Proceedings of the 10th International Conference on Theoretical and Methodological Issues in Machine Translation*

Daniel Cer, Marie-Catherine de Marneffe, Daniel Jurafsky, and Christopher D. Manning. 2010. Parsing to Stanford Dependencies: Trade-offs between speed and accuracy. *In 7th International Conference on Language Resources and Evaluation (LREC 2010)*

D. Lin. 1998. An information-theoretic definition of similarity. *In Proceedings of the International Conference on Machine Learning, Madison, August.*

Jay J. Jiang and David W. Conrath. 1997. Semantic Similarity Based on Corpus Statistics and Lexical Taxonomy. *In Proceedings of International Conference Research on Computational Linguistics (ROCLING X), Taiwan*

P. Resnik. 1995. Using information content to evaluate semantic similarity in a taxonomy. *In Proceedings of the 14th International Joint Conference on Artificial Intelligence, pages 448–453, Montreal, August.*

Radu Soricut, A Echihabi. 2010. TrustRank: Inducing Trust in Automatic Translations via Ranking. *Proceedings of ACL 2010.*

Osamuyimen Stewart, David Lubensky, Juan M. Huerta . 2010. Crowdsourcing participation inequality: a SCOUT model for the enterprise domain *Proceedings of the ACM SIGKDD Workshop on Human Computation*

Multi-Class SVM for Relation Extraction from Clinical Reports

Anne-Lyse Minard[1, 2] **Anne-Laure Ligozat**[1, 3] **Brigitte Grau**[1, 3]
(1) LIMSI-CNRS, BP 133, 91403 Orsay Cedex, France
(2) Université Paris-Sud, 91400 Orsay, France
(3) ENSIIE, 1 square de la résistance, 91000 Évry, France
firstname.lastname@limsi.fr

Abstract

Information extraction in specialized texts raises different problems related to the kind of searched information. In this paper, we are interested in relation identification between some concepts in medical reports, task that was evaluated in the i2b2 2010 challenge. As relations are expressed in natural language with a great variety of forms, we proceeded to sentence analysis by extracting features that enable all together to identify a relation and we modeled this task as a multi-class classification based on an SVM, each type of relation representing a class. We will present the selection of the features used by our system and an error analysis. This approach allowed us to obtain an F-measure of 0.70, classifying the system among the best systems.

1 Introduction

Medical information systems have developed past years, and are used for the storage of the information to facilitate the access to data, to help to search medical information about the patient or to provide decision support to improve the quality of care. The information processed mainly concern medical literature and medical records of patients, such as the clinical reports and the consultation reports which contain a lot of information about the medical follow-up. A large part of this information is in texts. So an important issue is to convert automatically all this information into some structured knowledge as it is the starting point for the development of some semantic interrogation tools and high level processing of this information.

Extraction of medical information raises different problems related to the kind of information sought in texts: i) the recognition of medical terms, ii) related concepts and iii) relations between them. A terminologic analysis of documents lead to build semantic indexes used to search information (Jonquet et al., 2010). Identifying relations between concepts provides a more structured representation. That is useful for precise information retrieval, for example for Question-Answering systems (Tjongkimsang et al., 2005), (Embarek and Ferret, 2010).

In this paper, we present our work[1] on the identification of relations in clinical reports, task of the i2b2 2010 challenge[2]. One of the goals of the challenge was to identify several kinds of relations between concepts (treatment, test and problem). These relations are expressed in the reports by a wide range of wordings. The incompleteness of semantic knowledge bases combined with the difficulty of relating wordings with conceptual representations is an obstacle to the realization of a deep analysis of sentences which would highlight the relations between concepts.

Thus, we considered that a lot of sentence characteristics such as the words used, their syntactic category help to detect the presence of a relation. We realized a shallow analysis of sentences to extract the useful features for the detection of a relation, and we considered relation identification as a multi-class classification task, with each category of relation considered as a class. We will focus on the selection of features, that allowed us to rank 3rd with an F-measure of 0.70.

2 Related work

The first approaches for relation extraction were based on handmade patterns. In the medical domain, the SemRep system (Rindflesch et al., 2000) was developed to identify branching of anatomical relations from reports. It was also applied to detect relations between medical problems and their

[1]This work has been partially supported by OSEO under the Quaero program.

[2]https ://www.i2b2.org/NLP/Relations/

treatments (Srinivasan and Rindflesch, 2002). The MedLEE system extracts relations from radiographic reports, biomolecular interactions (Friedman et al., 2001) and gene-phenotype relations (Chen and Friedman, 2004).

These approaches are not very robust and are mainly effective for precision without broad generalization capacity. So, other approaches are based on supervised machine learning. (Uzuner et al., 2010) use SVM (Support Vector Machines) to class relations between medical problems, tests and treatments in clinical reports. They defined surface features (ordering of the concepts, distance, etc.), lexical features (lexical trigrams, tokens-in-concepts, etc.), and shallow syntactic features (verbs, syntactic bigrams, syntactic link path, etc.). Results show an F-measure from 0.60 to 0.85, but for under-represented relations the classification did not work. (Roberts et al., 2008) also use a SVM to extract relations in the corpus of the Clinical E-Science Framework (CLEF) project that hold between entities (e.g. condition, drug, result) and modifiers (e.g. negation) in clinical records of cancer patients. There are seven classes of relations and each entity pair can be linked by one relation only (except between an investigation and a condition). So the classification task is considered as a binary classification (i.e. the detection of relation) between a type of relation and the non-relation class. The classification is also based on lexical, morpho-syntactic and semantic features.

In the general domain, (Zhou et al., 2005) use SVM to identify relations between people, organizations and places, etc. on the ACE corpus.

Our system also uses SVM to classify fine-grained relations. We make use of classical features as well as features specific to the domain, as the semantic types of the UMLS[3] and medical abbreviation lists, and features specific to the writing style of texts, for handling concept coordination.

3 Corpus

The corpus is made of reports from several medical centers in the USA. It was provided by i2b2 organizers. The texts were manually anonymized and annotated to build the reference. A first corpus was given before the evaluation phase, it consists of 350 documents. We divided this corpus in two parts: training corpus (4515 instances of relations) and test (749 instances of relations). For the final evaluation, i2b2 organizers gave participants a corpus of 477 documents (9070 instances of relations).

[3]Unified Medical Language System (http://www.nlm.nih.gov/research/umls/)

TrIP	Treatment improves medical problem
	<pb> hypertension </pb> was controlled on <treat> hydrochlorothiazide </treat>
TrNAP	Treatment is not administered because of medical problem
	<treat>Relafen</treat> which is contra-indicated because of <pb>ulcers</pb>
TrWP	Treatment worsens medical problem
TrCP	Treatment causes medical problem
TrAP	Treatment is administered for medical problem
TeCP	Test conducted to investigate medical problem
	<test>an VQ scan</test> was performed to investigate <pb>pulmonary embolus</pb>
TeRP	Test reveals medical problem
PIP	Medical problem indicates medical problem
	<pb>Azotemia</pb> presumed secondary to <pb>sepsis</pb>

Table 1: The eight relations to identify

Three types of concepts were manually annotated in the corpora:

- Medical problems defined as the observations made by patients or clinicians about what are thought to be abnormal or caused by a disease.
- Treatments defined as the procedures, interventions, substances and drugs given to the patient to treat a medical problem.
- Tests defined as the procedures and examinations that are done to a patient or body fluid to control or rule out a medical problem.

Between these three kinds of concepts, eight relations can exist. The relations are described in Table 1.

The number of instances of each relation in the corpus is presented Table 2. We also report the inter-annotator agreement (IAA) calculated by the i2b2 organizers. The adjusted IAA was obtained after discussion on problematic cases. We can observe that the IAA is low for TrWP and TrIP relations.

The corpus is made of short sentences (on average 17 words per sentence in the training corpus). Clinical reports are often written using fragments of sentence (1) and enumerations (2).

(1) <pb> C5-6 disc herniation</pb> with <pb>cord compression</pb> and <pb>myelopathy</pb>.

(2) Revealed <pb>icteric sclerae</pb>, <pb>the oropharynx with extensive thrush</pb>, and <pb>an ulcer under his tongue</pb>.

Relation	training	evaluation	IAA	IAA adjusted
TrIP	107	198	0.44	**0.62**
TrWP	56	143	**0.30**	**0.58**
TrCP	296	444	0.50	0.82
TrAP	1423	2487	0.68	0.95
TrNAP	106	191	0.44	0.76
PIP	1239	1986	**0.35**	0.79
TeRP	1734	3033	0.70	0.96
TeCP	303	588	0.43	0.74
All	5264	9070	0.56	0.94

Table 2: Number of each instances of relations and inter-annotator agreement (IAA)

4 Method

4.1 Preprocessing of the corpus

Texts were preprocessed and normalized before the classification process. First, abbreviations were replaced with their meanings, thanks to a list. This list was built for the i2b2 2009[4] challenge by (Deléger et al., 2010) from the biomedical abbreviation list of Berman[5] and examples found in the i2b2 2009 corpus. For example, *h.o.* is converted in *history of* and *p.r.n.* into *as needed.* Then we substituted the anonymized data with the markups *NAME*, *DATE* and *AGE*, and numerical values (mainly proportions) are replaced with the markup *NUM*. Finally texts are part-of-speech (POS) tagged by the TreeTagger (Schmid, 1994) in order to have lemmas and POS categories.

4.2 Classification

The classification makes use of SVM implementation of LIBSVM tool (Chang and Lin, 2001) parametrized for a multi-class classification (*one-versus-one* voting). We chose a RBF kernel, which gave better results than a linear kernel. The parameters are chosen by the script *grid.py* provided with LIBSVM. The *c* parameter was set to 16 and the *gamma* parameter to 0.03125. We also tested a classification by pair of concepts by training a classifier for relations between a test and a medical problem, then between a treatment and a medical problem, and between two medical problems. But results were lower than when we learned with all the relations. The features used for the classification capture surface information, such as the position of the two candidate concepts, lexical information, for example the words which refer to the concepts and the relation, syntactic information as POS tags, and semantic information. The features are automatically computed, if necessary by using tools and external resources. Each feature has an unique identifier, which is set to one if it appears else zero.

[4]https://www.i2b2.org/NLP/Medication/

[5]http://www.julesberman.info/abbtwo.htm

4.2.1 Surface features

Ordering of the candidate concepts: the expression of the relation depends on the position of the test or treatment compared with the problem. In example (3) the test is uttered before the revealed problem, and conversely in example (4) the problem is uttered before the test.

(3) She had <test>a workup</test> by her neurologist and <test>**an MRI**</test> revealed <pb>a C5-6 disc herniation</pb> [...]

(4) The patient was <pb>thrombocytopenic</pb> with <test>**a platelet count**</test> of <NUM> on the <NUM>.

Distance (i.e. number of words[6]) between the candidate concepts: in the training corpus there is never more than 65 words between two related concepts. However two concepts which are not in relation can be separated by a maximum of 205 words. The value of this feature is a number.

Presence of other concepts between the candidate concepts: for 80% of the concept pairs in relation in the training corpus there are no other concepts between them.

4.2.2 Lexical features

In order to provide some structure to the information given in texts, we decompose sentences in three zones: left and right contexts of the two candidate concepts and the between part.

The words and stems[7] which constitute the concepts and the headword[8] of each concept. The stems are used to group inflectional and derivational variations together. The words of concepts can trigger relations. For example in (5) the adjective *recurrent* is the trigger of a TrWP relation (a treatment worsens a problem).

(5) He has had <NUM> week courses of <treat>antibiotics</treat> with <pb>**recurrent** bacteremia</pb>.

The stems of the three words in the left and right context of candidate concepts. After several experiments we chose a window of three words;

[6]The words include also the punctuation signs.

[7]We use the PERL module lingua::stem to obtain the stem of the word.

[8]The headword is the word which precedes a preposition or the last word of the concept (see (Zhou et al., 2005)).

Relation	base	+dist	+conc	+dir	+verb	+prep	+intra	+types
TrIP	0.333	0.333	0.333	0.333	0.235	0.235	0.235	0.235
TrWP	0.000	0.000	0.000	0.000	0.000	0.000	0.000	0.000
TrCP	0.366	0.370	0.405	0.411	0.424	0.441	**0.526**	0.517
TrAP	0.620	0.638	**0.708**	0.721	0.708	0.706	0.737	0.726
TrNAP	0.620	0.620	0.620	0.620	**0.666**	0.666	0.666	0.620
PIP	0.611	0.613	0.664	0.664	0.654	0.671	0.618	**0.659**
TeRP	0.790	0.792	0.833	0.843	0.850	0.848	0.866	0.866
TeCP	0.253	0.253	**0.373**	0.351	0.373	0.351	0.333	0.285
All	0.647	0.652	**0.704**	0.712	0.711	0.713	0.724	**0.727**

Table 3: Variation of the F-measure according to the features (test corpus)

with bigger or smaller windows, precision lightly increases but recall decreases.

The stems of the words between candidate concepts; the most important information for the classification is located here.

The stems of the verbs in the three words at the left and right of candidate concepts and between them. The verb is often the trigger of the relation: for example in (6) the TeRP relation (a test reveals a problem) is expressed by *reveal*.

(6) <test>CT scan</test> was obtained and this **revealed** <pb>free air</pb> and <pb>massive ascites</pb>.

The prepositions between candidate concepts. In (7) the preposition *for* indicates a TrAP relation (a treatment is administered for a problem).

(7) She was treated with <treat>IVF</treat> **for** <pb>her ARF</pb>.

4.2.3 Morpho-syntactic features

The morpho-syntactic tags of the three words at the left and right of candidate concepts.

The presence of a preposition between candidate concepts, regardless of the preposition.

The presence of a punctuation sign between candidate concepts, if it is the only "word". This feature is useful for considering lists.

4.2.4 Semantic features

The semantic type (from the UMLS) of the three words at left and right of candidate concepts. In the example (3) *neurologist* has the semantic type *professional or occupational group*.

The types of candidate concepts (problem, test or treatment): it is the most important feature, because the relations are expressed differently between a test and a problem, a treatment and a problem, and between two problems.

The VerbNet's classes[9] (an expansion of Levin's classes) of the verbs in the three words at the left and right of candidate concepts and between them. For example *reveal* is member of the class *indicate-78-1-1* which contains also the verbs *show*, *prove*, *demonstrate*, etc. In examples (6) and (8) *reveal* and *show* are triggers of the same relation.

(8) <test>Recent chest x-ray</test> **shows** <pb>resolving right lower lobe pneumonia</pb>.

4.2.5 Coordination

Two concepts in relation can be separated by other concepts which do not carry information about the relation. So, we processed sentences before the feature extraction. We deleted other annotated concepts in coordination with candidate concepts, and we added three features: the number of deleted concepts, the coordination words that are the triggers of the deletion (*or*, *and*, a comma), and a feature which indicates that the sentence was reduced. Coordinations are often a sign of the non existence of relation, while they add information that are not useful to type it and even create some noise. In the training corpus the sentences have been reduced for 23% of the pairs of concepts (3819 pairs on 16437). In the example (6) for the pair *CT scan* and *massive ascites*, after reduction the sentence segment is: *CT scan was obtained and this revealed massive ascites*.

4.2.6 Feature relevance

We evaluated the usefulness of each feature with the same method as (Roberts et al., 2008). We observed the performances of the system on the test corpus by adding features class by class. Results are shown in Table 3.

[9] http://verbs.colorado.edu/~mpalmer/projects/verbnet.html

The features are grouped in categories according to the information they describe. The category *base* contains the stems of the words, the morpho-syntactic tags of the three words at the left and right of the concepts, and the stems of the words between the concepts. Then we added the category *dist* (distance between the concepts), *conc* (the other concepts), *dir* (the ordering of the concepts), *verb* (the stems of the verbs and the VerbNet classes), *prep* (the prepositions between the concepts), *intra* (the constituent words and the headword of the concepts) and *types* (semantic types). The results of the last column in the table are the results of the system with all the features. This system corresponds to the system used for the evaluation. In this system we did not use the features about the coordination of concepts. We separately evaluated these features, which increase the F-measure of the final system of 0.002.

5 Evaluation

Table 4 shows the results obtained[10]. We achieved better results over well-represented relations (such as TeRP with an F-measure of 0.852) than over smaller classes of relations (such as TrCP relation with an F-measure of 0.489).

For the i2b2 challenge, we used this system (without the control of the coordination) and we combined it with some patterns to identify the four under-represented relations (patterns have priorities on the classifier). Our system obtains an F-measure of 0.709, and ranked 3rd out of 16 teams. In Table 4 we show the results of the 1st, 2nd and 4th systems and the median. For classification of non-relations, our system obtained a recall of 0.93, a precision of 0.84 and an F-measure of 0.89.

6 Error analysis

For relations occurring between a treatment and a medical problem, we studied the confusion matrice and observed that the misclassified relations are mainly classified in the TrAP category (treatment is administered for medical problem) or as a non-relation. For example 54% of TrIP relations (treatment improves medical problem) are classified as a non-relation and 31% as TrAP relation. It is sometimes difficult to differentiate a TrIP or TrAP relation, because the TrIP relation is a specific TrAP relation. Indeed if a treatment improves

[10]The F-measure for "all relations" is the micro-averaged F-measure that weights each relation by its frequency.

Relation	Recall	Precision	F-measure
TrIP	0.156	0.861	0.264
TrWP	0.000	0.000	0.000
TrCP	0.369	0.725	0.489
TrAP	0.693	0.739	**0.715**
TrNAP	0.057	0.423	0.101
PIP	0.552	0.787	0.649
TeRP	0.835	0.870	**0.852**
TeCP	0.238	0.833	0.370
All relations	**0.628**	**0.803**	**0.705**
Median			0.664
1st system	0.753	0.720	0.736
2nd system	0.693	0.773	0.731
4th system	0.675	0.730	0.701

Table 4: Recall, precision and F-measure obtained on the evaluation corpus

a medical problem so the treatment is administered because of a medical problem. It is the same for TrWP relation which includes cases where the treatment is administered for a medical problem but worsens it.

For relations between two medical problems, we observed that 50% of PIP relations (medical problem indicates medical problem) were not detected. In the training corpus there are enough examples, but the description of the relation might not be precise enough (see IAA in Table 2). In example (9) a PIP relation was annotated between *symptoms* and *anxiety*, but not in the example (10) between *symptoms* and *dry cough*.

(9) She was hooked up with support services in Collot Ln, Dugo, Indiana <NUM> for <treat>further counselling</treat> and given <treat>Xanax</treat> for <pb>**symptoms**</pb> of <pb>**anxiety**</pb>.

(10) Pt was o/w in his USOH until <NUM> weeks ago when he developed <pb>a URI</pb> with <pb>**symptoms**</pb> of <pb>**dry cough;**</pb> no <pb>fever</pb> [...]

By studying sentences of misclassified relations we have found three types of errors:

- The relation is expressed by a verb or an expression, but this construction is not represented in the training corpus. In (11), the system classified the relation between *pulmonary nodules in his RML* and *fu imaging* as TeRP. Indeed *reveal* is a trigger of a TeRP relation, and the trigger of the TeCP relation is *which need*, but this last verb occurs only once in the training corpus.

(11) <test>CTS chest</test> was negative for <pb>PE </pb>, however it did **reveal** <pb>pulmonary nodules in his RML</pb> **which need** <test>fu imaging</test> in <NUM> months.

- The relation cannot be classified without using external resources or more training examples. In (12) the system wrongfully detected a relation, as it would need to know that there is no relation possible between incisions and obesity to correctly classify the relation.

(12) <pb>obese</pb> with <pb>multiple well healed surgical incisions</pb>, positive bowel sounds.

- The annotation of the relation is debatable. In (9) a relation between *symptoms* and *anxiety* has been annotated, but this two terms make reference to the same concept.

To improve the extraction of under-represented relations such as TrWP or TrIP, a bigger corpus is necessary, as these relations are represented by a few number of occurrences in the corpus. However there is no such annotated available corpus.

7 Conclusion

Relation extraction between concepts in clinical reports is a task that helps improve access to information in medical documentation. This task is based on the recognition of the several wordings that the relation can take in the sentences. This variability is very important as for the vocabulary variability as syntactic structures. So, we have taken into account these variabilities by defining different features, which can describe such kinds of sentences. We used features specific to the domain, the type of concepts for instance, features specific to the kind of texts and general domain features. We obtained very good results thanks to the selection of the features and the combination we made. The selected features are general enough that they can be used on corpora in other fields, with an adaptation of the domain dependent features (such as semantic types).

The results are low for not well-represented relations in the corpus. To have more representative instances of these relations, we could operate a reduction of the syntactic variability and a simplification of sentences before the learning stage.

References

Chih-Chung Chang and Chih-Jen Lin, 2001. *LIBSVM: a library for support vector machines.* Software available at http://www.csie.ntu.edu.tw/ cjlin/libsvm.

Lifeng Chen and Carol Friedman. 2004. Extracting phenotypic information from the literature via natural language processing. In *Medinfo 2004: Proceedings Of THe 11th World Congress On Medical Informatics.*

Louise Deléger, Cyril Grouin, and Pierre Zweigenbaum. 2010. Extracting medical information from narrative patient records: the case of medication-related information. *JAMIA*, 17(5):555–558.

Mehdi Embarek and Olivier Ferret. 2010. Can esculape cure the complex of œdipe in the medical domain? In *Adaptivity, Personalization and Fusion of Heterogeneous Information*, RIAO '10.

Carol Friedman, Pauline Kra, Hong Yu, Michael Krauthammer, and Andrey Rzhetsky. 2001. Genies: a natural-language processing system for the extraction of molecular pathways from journal articles. *Bioinformatics*, 17.

Clement Jonquet, Paea LePendu, Sean M. Falconer, Adrien Coulet, Natalya F. Noy, Mark A. Musen, and Nigam H. Shah. 2010. Ncbo resource index: Ontology-based search and mining of biomedical resources. In *Semantic Web Challenge, 9th International Semantic Web Conference, ISWC'10.*

Thomas C. Rindflesch, Carol A. Bean, and Charles A. Sneiderman. 2000. Argument identification for arterial branching predications asserted in cardiac catheterization reports. In *AMIA Annu Symp Proc.*

Angus Roberts, Robert Gaizauskas, and Mark Hepple. 2008. Extracting clinical relationships from patient narratives. In *BioNLP2008: Current Trends in Biomedical Natural Language Processing.*

Helmut Schmid. 1994. Probabilistic part-of-speech tagging using decision trees. In *Proceedings of the International Conference on New Methods in Language Processing*, pages 44–49.

Padmini Srinivasan and Thomas Rindflesch. 2002. Exploring text mining from medline. In *Proc AMIA Symp*, pages 722–726.

Erik Tjongkimsang, Gosse Bouma, and Maarten de Rijke. 2005. Developing Offline Strategies for Answering Medical Questions. In *Proceedings of the AAAI-05 Workshop on Question Answering in Restricted Domains, Pittsburgh, PA, USA.*

Ozlem Uzuner, Jonathan Mailoa, Russell Ryan, and Tawanda Sibanda. 2010. Semantic relations for problem-oriented medical records. *Artificial Intelligence in Medicine*, 50:63–73.

GuoDong Zhou, Jian Su, Jie Zhang, and Min Zhang. 2005. Exploring various knowledge in relation extraction. In *Proceedings of the 43rd Annual Meeting of the ACL*, pages 427–434.

Discovering Coreference Using Image-Grounded Verb Models

Amitabha Mukerjee
Dept. of CS, IITK, India
amit@cse.iitk.ac.in

Kruti Neema
Dept. of CS, IITK, India
krutineema@gmail.com

Sushobhan Nayak
Dept. of EE, IITK, India
snayak@iitk.ac.in

Abstract

Breaking away from traditional attempts at coreference resolution from discourse-only inputs, we try to do the same by constructing rich verb semantics from perceptual data, viz. a 2-D video. Using a bottom-up dynamic attention model and relative-motion-features between agents in the video, transitive verbs, their argument ordering etc. are learned through association with co-occurring adult commentary. This leads to learning of synonymous NP phrases as well as anaphora such as "it","each other" etc. This preliminary demonstration argues for a new approach to developmental NLP, with multi-modal semantics as the basis for computational language learning.

1 Introduction

It is common in discourse to refer to the same object using many phrases. For example, in a shared scene with two square shapes (Figure 1), the larger square may be called "the big box", "the square" or by anaphoric references such as "it", "itself", etc. Resolving the many types of co-reference remains a challenging problem in NLP (Stoyanov et al.(2009)). There are increasing calls for mechanisms with direct semantic interpretation, learned from multimodal input (Roy and Reiter(2005)). This work is posited along such lines; it does not attempt to resolve coreferences, but merely to illustrate how knowledge relating verb argument structure to the visual action schemas may be learned from multi-modal input. The possibility hinted at is that such grounds-up learning driven NLP systems may eventually have a rich enough library of syntacto-semantic structure to handle coreference more fully. Present attempts at analyzing multimodal interfaces (Fang et al.(2009); Steels(2003)) aim to identify the referents in interaction discourse, whereas our objectives are to build a system that can learn the principles of coreference, particularly anaphora. Furthermore, models that consider actions often use prior knowledge for visual parsing of actions (Dominey and Boucher(2005)). With reference to the work on resolving coreference problems, such models typically encode considerable structural knowledge of the linguistic and visual domains. Our work proposes mechanisms whereby these structures may be learned.

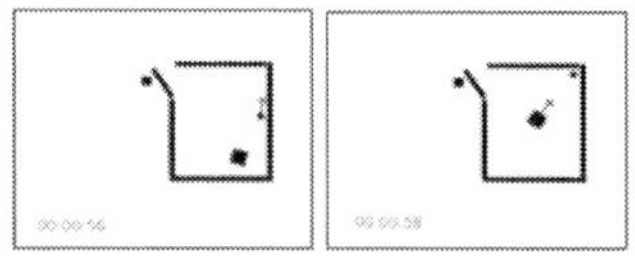

Figure 1: *Multimodal input: 2D video "Chase"*: Three shapes, [big-square], [small-square] and [circle] interact playfully (velocities shown with aroows).

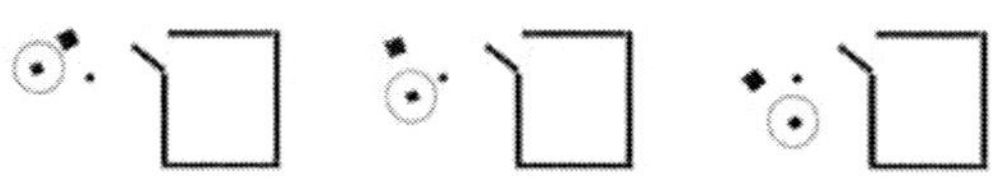

(a) (b) (c)

Figure 2: Computed bottom-up attention during the part of the action [chase(big-square,small-square)].

2 Learning Action Models and Argument Structure

Here we consider how an unsupervised process may acquire action structures from simple videos by clustering frequently observed sequences of motions. The perceptual database in the present model is a single 2-D video (from Heider and Simmel(1944)) (Figure 1). Here, the referent objects (a big square, a small square and a circle) are moving around, interacting with each other, and are easily segmented, as opposed to static referents in game-like contexts used in other multimodal co-reference analysis (Fang et al.(2009)). This presents a mechanism for learning events, which is extremely difficult in general contexts. The linguistic database consists of a co-occuring narrative with 36 descriptions of the video. In the 13 from the original Stanford corpus asked the subjects to discriminate actions in a fine and coarse manner. The subsequent 23 collected by us, also from student subjects, were completely unconstratined. Thus, these narratives exhibit a wide range of linguistic variation both in focus (perspective) and on lexical and construction choice.

We consider two-agent spatial interactions, which correspond to verbs with two arguments. The model uses bottom-up dynamic attention (Figure 2) to identify the objects that are related by attention switches (Satish and Mukerjee(2008)). The system considers pairs of objects attended to within a short timespan, and computes two inner-product features a) *pos·velDiff* $[(\vec{x}_B - \vec{x}_A) \cdot (\vec{v}_B - \vec{v}_A)]$ and b) *pos·velSum* $[(\vec{x}_B - \vec{x}_A) \cdot (\vec{v}_B + \vec{v}_A)]$. The temporal histories of these feature vectors are then clustered using the temporal mining algorithm Merge Neural Gas (Strickert and Hammer(2005)). Four action clusters are discovered, two of which correspond to [come-closer] and [move-away], and two correspond to [chase](Figure 3). Chase has two clusters because it is asymmetric, and the primary attention may be on the chaser (cluster 3) or on the chased (cluster 4). By computing the feature vectors with the referents switched, the system can by itself determine this alternation.

These learned models or *visual schemas* are acquired prior to language, and defined on the perceptual space. The learned models include the agents participating in the action, which constitutes the visual arguments of the action. They will next be related to the linguistic input.

Associating with textual phrases: Next, when our computational learner encounters language, it associates perceptual objects under attention to linguistic units in the co-occurring utterances. For this, it first considers those sentences which overlap temporally with the period when the ac-

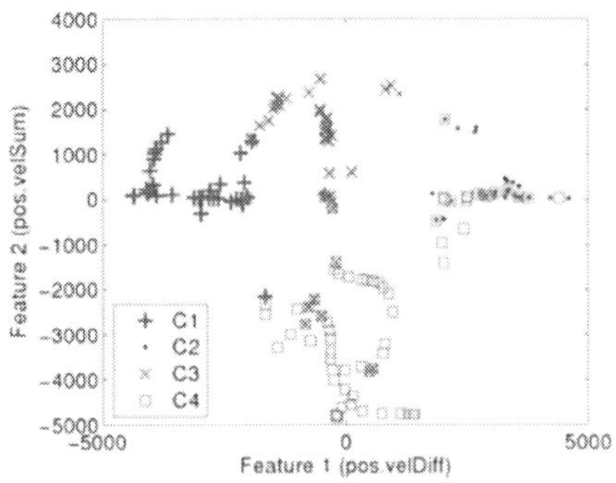

Figure 3: *Feature Vectors of the Four Clusters* : CC: C_1, MA: C_2, Chase(focus is on [chaser]): C_3, Chase(focus is on [chased]): C_4; The clusters reflect the spatio-temporal proximity of the vectors.

tion clusters are active, using an approach similar to (Roy and Reiter(2005)). One can now align sentences with objects in attentive focus to identify the names of objects (nouns) (Yu and Ballard(2004)). At this point, we assume that the learner knows these nouns, which are not considered as labels for verbs. Extremely frequent words (e.g. the, an, etc) are also dropped from consideration for mapping to actions. Using 1-, 2- and 3-word sequences from the text, the strongest associations for the action clusters are shown in Figure 4, and we see that clusters 1 [come-closer] and 2 [move away] have strongest associations with "move toward each" and "move away", but these are not very dominant over other competitors. On the other hand, for clusters 3 and 4 [chase], there is a strong association with the word "chase".

Next, it associates sentences uttered during the cognitive focus and correlates them with these actions. The strongest associations are learned as labels for actions (verbs) (Satish and Mukerjee(2008)).

Linguistic Constructions and Argument Structure mapping: At this stage the system knows the most preferred names for the participants (e.g. "big square"), as well as the label for the action (e.g. "chase"). Among the utterances co-occurrent with the action, it now computes the probability of different orderings for the units (e.g. the ordering of "chase"+grammatical-particle, [chased] and [chaser]). Here [chased], [chaser] are used by us for clarity - the system knows these based as a trajector-object distinction, in terms of visual focus. For cluster C3, the pattern *[chaser] chas* [chased]* dominates with frequency 0.90,

CLUSTER 1 (Come-Close)		CLUSTER 2 (Move-Away)		CLUSTER 3 (Chase)		CLUSTER 4 (Chase)	
ONE WORD LONG LINGUISTIC LABELS(MONOGRAMS)							
corner	0.077	away	0.069	chase	0.671	chase	0.429
move	0.055	move	0.055	other	0.185	after	0.112
attack	0.042	chase	0.049	around	0.183	out	0.033
TWO WORD LONG LINGUISTIC LABELS(BIGRAMS)							
each other	0.086	move away	0.111	chase around	0.306	chase after	0.218
move toward	0.065	go into	0.035	each other	0.227	just chase	0.060
toward each	0.065	into with	0.035	chase each	0.198	chase out	0.058
THREE WORD LONG LINGUISTIC LABELS(TRIGRAMS)							
move toward each	0.182	go into with	0.099	chase each other	0.558	just chase out	0.142
toward each other	0.182	run away out	0.051	start run away	0.132	run away out	0.047
move close together	0.114	scare in corner	0.032	begin to move	0.127	to go after	0.031

Figure 4: Figure showing the strongest association of linguistic lebels and action clusters. Dominant association of [chase] with the word "chase" is evident.

and in C4 its frequency is 0.84. This construction matches sentences such as "The square chased the circle" or "The big square was chasing them". In a minority of cases, it also notes the construction *[chased] chase+particle by [chaser]*. Thus, it determines that with high probability, the construction for the action [chase] in English is *[chaser] chase+particle [chased]*. We assume our computational learner has this level of competence (the input to Algorithm 1) before it attempts to detect substituted arguments and missing arguments in linguistic structures. Now we are ready to address the question of coreference.

3 Synonyms and Anaphora

We propose a plausible approach towards discovering anaphora-mappings in Algorithm 1. For discovering synonymy, the model needs only to relate participants in known events, such as [chase], with the phrases it observes in the sentence before and after the word "chase" (Steps 1 and 2 of the algorithm). Whie attempting to discover synonyms and named entities of the discourse, the system discovers referentially stable mappings for fixed, single referents. But it also discovers several other units whose referents are dynamically determined by the recent discourse. This may be considered as a semantically-driven approach for discovering grammatical structures like 'the word order of arguments', and 'the phenomenon anaphora'.

Pronominal Anaphora ("it"): In Fig. 5, computing the relative motion features between the two objects in attentive focus (Fig. 2, the big square ([BS]) and the small square ([SS]) the learner finds that the motion sequence matches the visual schema for the action [chase], and given the order of the objects in the feature computation, one can say that the visual schema encodes the semantics of the predicate *chase([BS], [SS])*. Note however, that we do not explicitly use any predicates or logical structures; these are implicit in the visual schema. However, we remove some of the topmost frequent words "the" in this analysis where they appear as part of a phrase. If the entire phrase is a common word (e.g. "it", "they"), it is retained.

We now consider several sentences cotemporaneous with the scene of Fig. 5. For example in *large square chases little square*, when we match the arguments with the linguistic construction, we can associate "large square" with [BS] and "little square" with [SS]. Now, "big square" and "little square" are already known as labels for [BS] and [SS], so "large square" is associated with [BS] as a possible synonym map.

Another sentence aligned with the same action, *it is chasing the small box* results in the associations "it":[BS], and "small box":[SS]. Similarly, in *chases little block*, there is no referent at all for [BS], and "little block" is identified as a possible synonym for [SS].

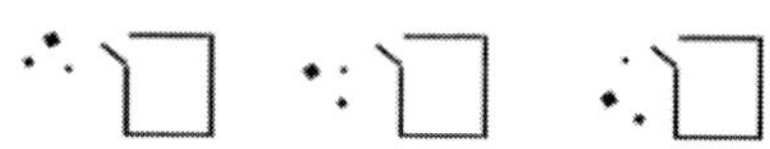

(a) (b) (c)

Figure 5: Frame sequence in video showing predicate *chase(BS,SS)*.Corresponding narrations include *large square chases little square*, *it is chasing the small box* and *chases little square*.

Estimating Probabilities for Action Maps: In obtaining frequency estimates for synonyms, we require these phrases to co-occcur with instances where a known verb appears. However, even with 36 parallel narratives, the perspectival variation among speakers is such that quite often the same scene will not be focused on, and even where it is, completely unknown phrases may be used (e.g. "tries to get" for "chases"). Thus, one is not able to label these phrases. In order to demonstrate the plausibility of this approach, the results reported below are divided into two parts - one mainly based on "chase", and the other making a further (unimplemented) assumption that other verbs such as "hit" and "push" may also be known using mechanisms similar to those used to discover [chase]. The two differing assumptions are:

a. *Chase-only:* Linguistic forms for [move away] and [come closer] are diffuse, so we consider primarily the learned cluster [chase]. We discover that [chase] maps to "follow", and include sentences with "follow" leading to a corpus of 36+9 sentences which is still small with infrequent specific strings.

b. *+Hit+Push:* In the second model, we assume that in addition to [chase], we have action models and linguistic mappings for the actions [hit] and [push], which occur often in the commentary.

The second (stronger) results should be taken as indicative of the plausibility of the approach, and not as a complete implementation of the algorithm.

Discourses Mapping [chase] Only: Of the three classes of actions for which we have acquired visual schemas from the perceptual data, the narratives for [come-closer] and [move-away] have widely varying constructions. Focusing on the action chase, we discover that it maps to two verbs in the linguistic descriptions: "chase", and "follow". Constructions for both have the structure *[chaser] verb+particle [chased]*.

There are only 36 + 9 sentences with "chase" + "follow", so the data for these arguments is rather sparse. After ruling out phrases that have a sample size of one, cases where the conditional probability of the entity given the phrase is 1 (Steps 3 and 4 of the algorithm), is taken as a synonym (names known earlier in italics) — {[BS]: *big square*, square, big box, large square, big block, bigger square}; {[SS]: *little square*, small square, little box};{[C] : *circle*, little circle, ball, small circle}.

Algorithm 1 A plausible approach towards the discovery of anaphora.

Input :

1. Set of timestamped action predicates *Verb(arg1, arg2)*
2. Set of timestamped narrative sentences

Alignment :

1. Align co-occurrent predicates with sentences containing the corresponding verb.
2. Increment the object associations against each language phrases L_i:
   - For linguistic constructs of the form [$\langle L_1 \rangle$ verb $\langle L_2 \rangle$], map L_1 to arg1 and L_2 to arg2
   - For constructs of the form [$\langle L_1 \rangle$ verb by $\langle L_2 \rangle$], map L_1 to arg2 and L_2 to arg1
3. For set of three agents (big and small square, circle), plus pairs (total 6 object-groups), estimate the conditional probability P(object/language phrase).
4. If the probability is close to 1, the language phrase is likely to be a proper synonym of the corresponding object.
5. If some linguistic units are acting as a synonym for multiple objects, their referent may not be fixed, but may depend on some other aspect.

Now, after ruling out synonyms and infrequent phrases (those occurring only once), we are left with three units - "it", "them" and "each other" (Table 1). We were surprised ourselves that all three instances found are anaphora. Noticing that these units don't have a fixed referent, other regularities are searched by which their referents can be identified. This may be the start of a process which leads to the idea of anaphora.

With [hit] + [push] : While we have no computational models for actions such as [hit] and [push], there is considerable evidence that these concepts are typically acquired fairly early, and also reflected in early vocabularies (Clark(2003)). In the analysis next (Table 2), we assume the availability of [hit] and [push] models in addition to [chase], and consider the same analysis as above, but now on the larger set of sentences encoding

Phrase (Ph)	# Ph	BS /Ph	SS /Ph	C /Ph	BSSS /Ph	SSC /Ph
it	10	0.5	0.4	0.1	0	0
them	5	0	0	0	0.2	0.8
each other	3	0	0	0	0.66	0.33
[missing]	15	0.46	0.2	0.33	0	0

Table 1: Conditional probability computation (with values in the column headers) for the non-synonymical arguments in sentences mapping [chase] action.

these actions. A few additional synonyms are learned ("he" for [BS], "small box", "little block" for [SS]). Also the labels "square and circle", and "little circle and square" are associated with the combination [SS&C], sentences mapping multiple predicates where both were involved in a patient role. These results may also be interpreted as a slightly advanced stage for the learner, when it has acquired these additional structures.

Step 5 of Algorithm 1 gives the first indication of phenomena such as anaphora. After synonym matching, words remain that are not assigned to any single entity but as in the [chase]-only case, they can be applied to multiple referents. To the learner, this implies that this aspect, that these phrases can be applied to multiple referents, is stable, and not an artifact related to a single action or context. The learner may now attempt to discover other regularities in how the referents for each of these words is assigned. This requires even greater vocabulary, since the prior referent must also be known.

Phrase (Ph)	# Ph	BS /Ph	SS /Ph	C /Ph	BSSS /Ph	SSC /Ph
it	19	0.63	0.26	0.11		0
each other	10	0	0	0	0.9	0.1
they	6	0	0	0	0.66	0.33
them	5	0	0	0	0.2	0.8
[missing]	29	0.59	0.24	0.17	0	0

Table 2: Conditional probability computation (with values in column headers) for the arguments of [chase], [hit] and [push].

Focusing on the word "it", and assuming a greater inventory of verbs, we can consider sequences of sentences such as *The bigger square just went inside the box / Looks like it is chasing the small square*. The "it" in the second sentence is known to our learner as [BS] based on the video parse, and one notes how the agent in the previous sentence is also [BS]. In another situation we have *The large square was chasing the other square / And it got away*. Here the "it" refers to the most recent antecedent, [SS] (though in other examples, it refers to the parallel antecedent). In the chase-only case, we note that "it" refers to the immediately previous referent in 6/10 situations. Two cases involve plural vs single disambiguation: e.g. *Big square is chasing them / They outrun it*, and one case involves parallel reference, e.g. *Now the big square is hitting the small square / It has hit it again* (in fact, unlike our learner, the reader may have difficulty disambiguate the "it"s here). While the referent identification pattern isn't very clear, the learner realizes that "it" at least refers to some earlier referent in the discourse.

Further, even reciprocal anaphors such as "each other" can be recognized since sentences such as *they hit each other* overlap with multiple predicates with switched arguments (*hit([BS],[SS])* and *hit([SS],[BS])*). Beyond this little domain, as our learner is exposed to thousands of linguistic fragments every day, these regularities are likely to get reinforced.

Finally, considering the cases of missing arguments, there are two cues available to the early learner: a) that the relevant action involves two arguments, but fewer are available in the discourse, and b) that the missing argument refers to an antecedent in the discourse. In English, zero anaphora is a very common phenomenon. Even in our very small corpus, there are 570 agents, of which 99 are zero anaphors. Clearly this is a sufficiently high probability phenomenon which deserves the attention of the early learner. Once the absent argument is observed, it can be associated with the appropriate argument. Note that since this substitution is occurring at the semantic level and not in the syntax, only antecedents matching the activity will be considered. Estimating the probabilities in terms of frequencies even for this very small dataset, reveals that of the 99 zero anaphors, 96 refer to the most recent agent argument, often coming as a series e.g. *big square says "uh uh, don't do that" / pushes little square around / pushes little square around again/ chases little square*. Thus, the most recent argument may emerge as a dominant reference pattern for zero anaphora. Also, we note how considerable knowledge beyond syntax is involved in the remaining situations e.g. *Door is shut/ Went into the corner*.

4 Conclusion

We have outlined how an unsupervised approach correlating prior sensori-motor knowledge with linguistic structures, might be used to eventually learn complex aspects of grammar such as argument structure, and lead to the discovery of phenomena such as anaphora. Also, we highlight many cases of zero anaphora, and show how these may also be inferred, most commonly as the most recent agent in the perceptual input.

However, this work, even though it is different from traditional discourse-only-input-based attempts at anaphora resolution, is clearly just a beginning. We have demonstrated unsupervised learning for only one verb, "chase", and it is by no means clear that other action models needed for other verbs can be similarly learned. Nonetheless, there is considerable work that hints at the infants being able to use perceptual cues to learn the base model of many motion primitives of this nature (Pasek(2006)). But clearly more work is needed to be able to approach verbs that are not directly based on motion. Also, the mapping to language also may not be as straightforward for many other verbs.

This limited demonstration, nonetheless, highlights several points. First, it underscores the role of concept argument structures in aligning with linguistic expressions. It provides some evidence for the position that some aspects of semantics may be ontologically prior to syntax, at least for human-like learning processes. Secondly, it addresses the very vexed question of learning grammar from domain-general capabilities. While a computational demonstration such as this cannot provide full answers, certainly it raises a very plausible mechanism, and attempts to learn some complex grammatical constructs such as anaphora. Finally, it addresses some of the issues related to learning language from shared perception, such as the radical translation argument highlighted by Quine's *gavagai* example (Quine(1960)), and instantiates a possibility that dynamic attention may prune the visual input and align with linguistic focus.

A key aspect underscored by this work is the necessity of creating multimodal databases with video, audio and textual corpora, so that more such learning can take place. This work may be taken merely as a straw model that raises more questions than it answers. It will take considerably more work, and creation of significantly larger resources.

References

Clark, EV. 2003. *First language acquisition*. Cambridge University Press.

Dominey, PF and JD Boucher. 2005. Learning to talk about events from narrated video in a construction grammar framework. *AI* 167(1-2):31–61.

Fang, R., J.Y. Chai, and F. Ferreira. 2009. Between linguistic attention and gaze fixations in multimodal conversational interfaces. In *Proc. of ICMI*. ACM, pages 143–150.

Heider, F. and M.Simmel. 1944. An experimental study of apparent behavior. *American Journal of Psychology* 57:243–259.

Pasek, R ,M.Golinkoff, K Hirsh, editor. 2006. *Action meets word: how children learn verbs*. Oxford University Press US.

Quine, WVO. 1960. *Word and Object*. MIT Press, Cambridge,MA.

Roy, D and E Reiter. 2005. Connecting language to the world. *AI: Special Issue* 167:112.

Satish, G. and A. Mukerjee. 2008. Acquiring linguistic argument structure from multimodal input using attentive focus. pages 43 –48.

Steels, Luc. 2003. Evolving grounded communication for robots. *Trends in Cognitive Sciences* 7(7):308–312.

Stoyanov, V., N. Gilbert, C. Cardie, and E.Riloff. 2009. Conundrums in noun phrase coreference resolution: Making sense of the state-of-the-art. In *Proc. of 47th AMACL and 4th IJCNLP of AFNLP*. ACL, pages 656–664.

Strickert, M and B Hammer. 2005. Merge SOM for temporal data. *Neurocomputing* 64:39–71.

Yu, C. and D.H. Ballard. 2004. A multimodal learning interface for grounding spoken language in sensory perceptions. *ACM TAP(TAP)* 1(1):57–80.

Word and Phrase Learning based on Prior Semantics

Amitabha Mukerjee and **Nikhil Joshi**
Department of Computer Science and Engineering
Indian Institute of Technology,
Kanpur (UP, India) - 208016
{amit,joshins}@cse.iitk.ac.in

Abstract

Based on the evidences of preverbal conceptual development in infants, we adopt semantics-first approach for word-learning. We first cluster several perceptual categories from a complex visual interaction. Using a surveillance traffic video, we a) identify the moving objects by separating these from a static background, and b) group the similar appearances into clusters. The resulting models are found to be noisy approximations of traffic object categories and motion actions. Next, we consider these models along with parallel commentaries that describe the scene in free, unconstrained language. A bottom-up model of dynamic attention is applied to identify objects in perceptual focus, which are mapped to words in co-temporaneous utterances. Using no language-specific knowledge such as syntax, we show the ability to learn words for the object classes and also for the motion actions.

1 Introduction

The problem of word-learning primarily focuses on mapping the linguistic representation of a word to its semantics. In most of the attempts to learn the language to semantics mappings, semantic representations were often limited to the logical representations (Zettlemoyer and Collins, 2005; H Alshawi, 2011). However, the need of much richer semantic representations such as percptual schema (Barsalou, 1999), image schema (Mandler, 1992) is argued for grounding the meanings of words(Harnad, 1990). A number of approaches have tried to construct such term-meaning associations from sensorimotor data (Steels and Kaplan, 2002; Gorniak and Roy, 2004; Roy and Pentland, 2002; Oates et al., 2000). However, these approaches used scenes with simple objects and constrained linguistic descriptions. Also, learning was guided by considerable feedback.

In this work, we consider learning objects and interactions from a complex 3D-scene and mapping them to words and phrases from free, unconstrained language with full sentences describing the scene. The key to handle referential uncertainty (Siskind, 1996) is the visual saliency predicted using a bottom-up attention model. The salient objects are then associated with the co-occurring utterances in the narratives to learn the labels for the visual concepts. Owing to evidences of preverbal conceptual development (Mandler, 1992), we adopt semantics-first approach (Yu and Ballard, 2004) where we learn visual semantics first and then discover appropriate word associated with it

For learning objects and interactions, image sequences from a fixed camera, as typically used in surveillance scenarios, are considered. The stable patterns of background are first learned, and used to extract foreground blobs corresponding to the objects of interest. The object blobs are tracked across the frames and regions of occlusion are identified. Unoccluded object appearances are then projected to a feature space based on the "Pyramidal Histogram of visual Words" (PHOW) approach (Bosch et al., 2007). The resulting PHOW descriptor for the blobs are then classified in an unsupervised manner, resulting in a number of object classes. For every object tracked, a trajectory is modeled using the position and velocity of object blobs in successive frames. These trajectories are then clustered to obtain a number of motion classes. The object and motion classes obtained are evaluated based on the user labels (the *ground-truth*). We note that the resulting models are similar to the *conceptualizer* of (Steels and Kaplan, 2002), but unlike in that work, the model here is learned and not programmed beforehand.

For the word association task, we first compile a set of narratives by asking nine adults to describe objects and activities in free unconstrained language. The transcribed narratives (text) are then aligned with the objects and activities in visual focus, as identified by the bottom-up attention model. We are able to discover the appropriate nouns for four object classes with high visual purity viz. BICYCLE, MOTORCYCLE, TRUCK and CAR. Phrases like "*bAe-N se dAe-N*" and "*geT kI taraf*" are also discovered for the trajectory LEFT-TO-RIGHT and TURN. During association, we remove units that are very frequent in general discourse, assuming these to be non-relevant to this context. However, no linguistic knowledge (pos, syntax or morphology) except the knowledge of word segementation is assumed.

Our unsupervised approach to word learning implies two important scalability advantages. Since we use no knowledge of the camera placement or the types of objects in the scene, the visual analysis is potentially applicable to a wide range of scenes. Also, since we use no knowledge of the syntax of the target language, it is possible to use the approach to other languages as well. Since the terms learned are grounded in the visual domain, it can be flexibly related to new input situations. This is demonstrated in this work via successful queries on novel traffic video.

2 Unsupervised object classification

In recent years, supervised learning for visual object categories has been able to distinguish hundreds of classes of objects with high accuracies (Bosch et al., 2007; Mutch and Lowe, 2006). The critical step in these approaches is to project the images onto a set of patterns, called "words", so that each image is characterized as a distribution on the words. This class of approaches, known as "bag of words" after similar approaches in document analysis, classify novel images based on their similarity to the trained models. In this work, we extend these ideas to unsupervised object classification. Here the object images (foreground blobs from surveillance video) have the advantage that these are relatively tightly cropped around the region of interest. We track salient patches in each blob to identify the same agent across contiguous frames - sample views of some agents are shown in Figure 1. As can be seen, the results are very noisy owing to occlusions, shadows, tracking errors, agent appearance changes etc.

Figure 1: *Agents as sequences of isolated foreground blobs.* Bottom row (agent 130): the sequence is initially tracking a car - but after it exits, it is erroneously mapped to a motorcycle.

The tracking step considers substantially overlapping sequences of blobs. Only where an agent is isolated is the blob considered for modeling its appearance. We use the pyramidal histogram of words (PHOW) approach (Bosch et al., 2007), based on computing the SIFT operator (Lowe, 1999) on a very large number of points (100K) on these blobs. These are clustered to obtain a code-book of 300 "words". Next, each foreground blob in a tracked agent is projected onto these words, and the agent is modeled as a probability distribution on the space of words (estimated by the histogram).

Using a Bhattacharya distance metric, the histograms are clustered using k-means (results reported for $k = 30$). This results in an oversegmentation of the category space, and to evaluate the effectiveness of the clusters, we manually categorize the agents into seven *groundtruth* classes: TEMPO (T), BICYCLE (B), MOTORCYCLE (M), TRUCK (L), HUMAN (H), CAR (C), and also a small category NOISE (N) with object fragments and lighting effects etc. The purity of each cluster is defined as the percentage of its dominant class. We assign the dominant ground-truth category in a cluster as ground-truth of that cluster. The average

Class: # agents	Clusters	Purity
H:52	C1,C2,C4,C10, C11,C12,C14,C21	51/63 (81%)
M:36	C3,C8,C9,C22, C23,C24,C26	35/48 (73%)
B:32	C5,C6,C7,C15, C20,C28	22/25 (88%)
T:21	C0,C16,C17, C18,C25	15/27 (56%)
L:12	C12,C29	11/13 (83%)
C:16	C19	9/10 (90%)
N:8	C27	2/4 (50%)

Table 1: *Clusters from k- means (k = 30).* Clusters are assigned to one of six ground-truth categories. Purity of a cluster = degree to which it is dominated by a single object category.)

purity of the clusters obtained by this process is 76.5%. By training the model with a $N - M$ of agents and testing with the remaining M, we obtain a cross-validation accuracy of 70.8% (for $M = 5$). Table 1 shows the ground-truth distribution for 30 clusters obtained using k-means. Figure 2 shows blobs of agents from some of the clusters formed for k=30.

Some clusters appear to have fine-graded semantic significance - e.g. the class C16 ("passengers getting off from tempo") and C21 ("humans either on some vehicle")in Figure 2.While such classes were not marked in the ground-truth, this finer discrimination may actually help in detecting activities. Some other clusters are less meaningful; e.g. cluster C27 , is mostly noise.

For every agent tracked across the frames, we define its trajectory based on position and velocity of object blobs in ten frames at regular intervals. Positions of an agent are taken relative to its position in the starting frame to avoid locational bias. Based on these features and euclidean distance measure, trajectories are clustered into seven clusters using *k-means* algorithm. For evaluation purpose, we marked the ground-truth of these trajectories as one of the five categories: LEFT-TO-RIGHT (LR), RIGHT-TO-LEFT (RL), TURN (T), CROSS (C) and NOISE (N) with not so meanigful trajectories. The purity of each cluster is calculated in the same way as it is calculated for object clusters. Table 2 shows the distribution of ground-truth categories for each of the seven trajectory clusters discovered. Similarly, many vehicles crossing the road come from left, move towards right and then cross the road resulting in low purity of C5. The very low purity of cluster C6 is mostly because of noisy trajectories of human blobs which move arbitrarily in the scene. Errors in tracking agents also result in noisy trajectories and lead to inaccuracies in the clustering.

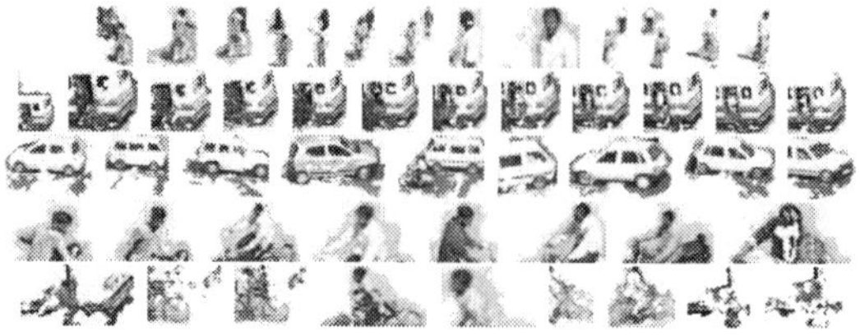

Figure 2: *k-means (k = 30) clusters* Clusters C10, C16, C19, C21, C27. Representative views from all agents in each class are shown. The membership of these clusters can be seen in Table 1. Whereas C10 and C19 are relatively clean classes, C27 has several noise agents

Cluster/GT	LR	RL	T	C	N	Purity
C1 (RL)	0	20	0	0	1	20/21
C2 (LR)	15	0	1	0	1	15/17
C3 (LR)	20	0	2	0	1	20/23
C4 (RL)	0	26	8	1	3	26/38
C5 (LR)	21	2	4	8	4	21/39
C6 (LR)	13	8	4	2	7	13/34
C7 (T)	0	3	14	3	0	14/20

Table 2: *Ground-Truth distribution*: Distribution of ground-truth categories for each of seven trajectory clusters

3 Attention Model

We use attention model to find the most salient part of the scene that humans are likely attend to. The words used in the description are more likely to refer to objects that are in perceptual focus. This resolves the referential uncertainty.

In general, attention combines bottom-up

mechanisms (independent of task) with top-down mechanisms (task dependent). While a number of models are available for bottom-up attention, on both still (Itti and Koch, 2001) and dynamic (Singh et al., 2006) images, top-down attention is far more difficult to model owing to complexities in modeling the task. Also, in our context, commentaries were collected without providing any specific task, so we use a dynamic bottom-up model.

In our work, we have an advantage over traditional dynamic attention models since the objects of attention are already segmented and available as tracked sequences of segmented foreground blobs. These are the scene regions that are competing for attention. Unlike many computational models that consider saliency of pixels in the data, we are in a position to evaluate the saliency of the segmented foreground region directly. Our attention model is based on the findings that a) Objects with higher speed are likely to be more salient, and b) Objects with a larger image size are more likely to be attended (Itti and Koch, 2001). We ignore some other factors such as colour and texture, which are more relevant in still images; for image sequences, motion and size are more significant. In addition to the saliency map based on the above factors, we also need to construct a confidence map, based on how recently was the object attended. Objects which have not been attended for some time tend to decay in their confidence, and thus become more likely to be attended to. We combine all these aspects to define saliency of object blob j as

$$S_j = (1 - e^{-k\Delta t})(w_1 A_j + w_2 v_j)$$

where A_j is the image area (in pixels) and v_j is image speed (in pixels per frame) of the object j. Δt is the time elapsed since the object was last updated. Parameters w_1, w_2 and k capturing relative importance of object size, velocity and confidence are all set to 1.

4 Learning language labels

For the purpose of learning language labels for concepts learned from video, we use human narratives describing the same visual scene. We asked 9 native speakers (college students: all male) to watch the video once, and give their commentary on it the next time around. In the instructions, they were asked to focus on people, vehicles in the scene and their activities. The narratives were broken into segments at sentences boundaries as well as at pauses longer than 1.5s, and transcribed without correcting grammar errors. Also, initial 40 seconds and final 20 seconds of data were discarded since people appeared to be talking more generally at the beginning of the video, and events in the end could not be commented upon. Around 600 sentences with 3398 words were used in the analysis.

Since the subjects were not constrained in their descriptions in any way, the lexical choice and linguistic constructions varied widely. Thus the same event may be described as "gADI dAe.N se bAe.N or gayI" (car went from right to left), "ek sa.NTro gayI"(one Santro went) etc. As perspectives varied tremendously, for the same time interval in the video, different subjects said: "ek kAr aAyI" (One car came), "vah saD.ak krOs kar rahA hai" (He is crossing the road) etc. Even after asking the narrators to focus on the people, vehicles and their activities during instructions, the commentaries collected include considerable peripheral descriptions like "bIch meIn koI DivAiDar nahIn hai" (There is no divider in the middle).

In order to identify the relevant linguistic units, we align segments of the commentary with the most salient objects in the video as identified by the attention model described above. For computational purposes, we assume linguistic units to be contiguous at word-level and associate k-grams (for $k = 1$ to 4) with co-occuring salient concepts in the video. We seek to identify the unit having maximal *conditional probability* given a concept.

4.1 Object-Label associations

Table 3 reports the top two 1-gram at the word level for six ground-truth object classes. The conditional probabilities shown are multiplied by 100. Dominating associations are discovered for four object categories: BICYCLE, MOTORCYCLE, TRUCK and CAR (*sAikal*, *bAik*, *Trak* and *kAr* respectively). Units like *lefT* ("left"), *dAe.N* ("right") indicating the directions of movement are also appearing among top2 *1-word* associations.

Part of the reason for difficulty in learn-

Concept	Word	Cond. Prob
TEMPO	bAik	6.70
	dAe-N	6.46
BICYCLE	sAikal	3.17
	moTarsAikal	1.59
MOTOR-CYCLE	bAik	8.37
	Tempo	8.29
TRUCK	Trak	19.54
	lefT	6.13
HUMAN	dAe-N	10.86
	pe	10.29
CAR	kAr	7.50
	pe	5.00

Table 3: *Association results:* top2 1-word associations for each of object categories

Trajectory	3-gram	Prob
C1	purI KalI hai	1.71
	saD.ak pUrI KalI	1.71
C2	bae-N se dAe-N	3.16
	lAl SirT me-m	2.73
C3	bae-N se dAe-N	4.44
	puch rahA hai	3.96
C4	roD krOs kar	4.62
	krOs kar rahA	4.47
C5	krOs kar rahA	4.67
	roD krOs kar	4.20
C6	kuch log roD	2.20
	dae-N kI taraf	2.18
C7	geT kI taraf	3.57
	Ai Ai TI	3.57

Table 4: *Association results:* top2 3-word associations for each of trajectory clusters

ing labels for other categories can be seen in Table 1, where we see that the average purity for CAR, BICYCLE and TRUCK is quite high whereas that for TEMPO is very poor. Though the purity of HUMAN is moderate. we find that there are many relevant labels in the narratives; e.g. a person with bicycle is described as *sAikalwAlA* (bicyclist) or as *aAdmI* (man). Also, attentional salience is more often on the larger, faster-moving vehicles and not on smaller human blobs. Possibly for these reasons, label for humans is not learned.

4.2 Trajectory-Label association

Table 4 shows top2 3-grams according to conditional probability measures for seven clusters of trajectories. As can be seen, for clusters C2 and C3 representing LEFT-TO-RIGHT (LR), *bAe-N se dAe-N* ("left to right") appears as the strongest 3-gram. Similarly, for clusters C5 and C6 *dAe-N kI taraf* ("towards right") appears third (not reported here). For the cluster C7 representing TURN (T), *geT kI taraf* ("towards the gate") appears as the strongest label as the agents in the cluster C7 are generally turning towards the gate of an institute. For other two clusters, C1 and C4, however, appropriate labels could not be learnt. Perhaps, the event of RIGHT-TO-LEFT may not have been commented as profoundly as the events of LEFT-TO-RIGHT or TURN.

4.3 Testing on Novel scenes

In order to test our semantic model, we used two different videos of the similar scene, and attempted to recognize the three classes of objects with high viusal purity.

Figure 3: *Test videos.* Training video at left. Samples from two test videos, from novel camera positions, at middle and right.

Figure 4: *Test agents from novel videos. Sample blobs from thirteen test agents. Agents on bottom row were not correctly labeled.*

These videos were shot on different days, from different vantage points, and varied considerably in the imaging (Figure 3). Our video query consisted of identifying objects of a given class. For evaluation, we manually identified TRUCK (3), BICYCLE (5), and CAR (5) agents. Sample blobs for each agent shown in Figure 4. The truck query responded with all three agents of TRUCK. The CAR agents did not fare that well, only two out of five were correctly identified; two being labeled as TEMPO (possibly because the class TEMPO was very noisy and had several CARs in it), and one as MOTORCYCLE. One of the cars seen in the novel video is a sedan (leftmost in bottom row, Figure 4), which was not present in the training data. Three of the BICYCLE agents were correctly identified; other two were HUMAN (man standing besides his bicycle) and TEMPO but were misinterpreted as BICYCLE.

As we scale up and include more videos and different vantage points for training, more refined models of object classes are expected to be learned, so that such production or recognition errors would go down.

5 Conclusion & Future Work

In this work we have attempted to learn visual concepts for some object classes and motion trajectories, and map these to Hindi words or phrases, based on a) an unsupervised model that discovers object categories from a fixed-camera video; b) a model of synthetic blob-based attention that identifies the most salient agent among many moving objects; and c) an association between the concepts learnt from the video and the k-grams in the user commentaries. The model has been demonstrated in a video querying task.

Our unsupervised object clustering is able to distinguish among several object categories and also some motion trajectories even from a very short video of around 4.5 minutes. With greater exposure, the models may be refined further. Further, there were only 600 sentences of narrative with which to work. To put it in context, a typical child is exposed to a much larger corpus of co-occurrent text and visual context every *hour*. As NLP searches for richer models of semantics, such multimodal data mining will become more widely used. To help bootstrap this process, both the multimodal corpora and and textual database has been made available.

Given the unsupervised nature and particularly the minimal dependence on linguistic knowledge, we are currently expanding this approach to learn several languages. A larger goal is to integrate models of motion-trajectories with the knowledge of nominals, and begin to attempt to build the kind of defeasible knowledge structures.

References

[Barsalou1999] L Barsalou. 1999. Perceptual symbol systems. *Behavioral and Brain Sciences*, 22(4):577–609.

[Bosch et al.2007] A. Bosch, A. Zisserman, and X. Munoz. 2007. Image classification using random forests and ferns. In *ICCV'07*, pages 1–8.

[Gorniak and Roy2004] P. Gorniak and D. Roy. 2004. Grounded semantic composition for visual scenes. *JAIR*, 21(1):429–470.

[H Alshawi2011] M Ringgaard H Alshawi, P Chang. 2011. Deterministic statistical mapping of sentences to underspecified semantics. In *Proceedings of the Ninth IWCS*, pages 15–24.

[Harnad1990] S Harnad. 1990. The symbol grounding problem. *Physica D: Nonlinear Phenomena*, 42(1-3):335 – 346.

[Itti and Koch2001] L Itti and C Koch. 2001. Computational modeling of visual attention. *Nature Reviews Neuroscience*, 2(3):194–203.

[Lowe1999] D Lowe. 1999. Object recognition from local scale-invariant features. In *ICCV, 1999*, volume 2, pages 1150 –1157.

[Mandler1992] J M Mandler. 1992. How to Build a Baby: II. Conceptual Primitives. *Psychological Review*, 99(4):587–604.

[Mutch and Lowe2006] J. Mutch and D Lowe. 2006. Multiclass object recognition with sparse, localized features. In *IEEE CVPR*, volume 1, pages 11–18.

[Oates et al.2000] T Oates, Z Eyler-walker, and P. Cohen. 2000. Toward natural language interfaces for robotic agents: Grounding linguistic meaning in sensors. In *Proceedings of the 4th ICAA*, pages 227–228.

[Roy and Pentland2002] D Roy and A Pentland. 2002. Learning words from sights and sounds: a computational model. *Cognitive Science*, 26:113–146.

[Singh et al.2006] V K Singh, S Maji, and A Mukerjee. 2006. Confidence based updation of motion conspicuity in dynamic scenes. In *Third Canadian CRV 2006*, page 13.

[Siskind1996] J M Siskind. 1996. A computational study of cross-situational techniques for learning word-to-meaning mappings. *Cognition*, 61(1-2):1–38.

[Steels and Kaplan2002] L. Steels and F. Kaplan. 2002. Bootstrapping grounded word semantics. In *Linguistic Evolution through Language Acquisition: Formal and Computational Models*, chapter 3, pages 53–74. Cambridge University Press.

[Yu and Ballard2004] C. Yu and D.H. Ballard. 2004. A multimodal learning interface for grounding spoken language in sensory perceptions. *ACM Transactions on Applied Perception (TAP)*, 1(1):57–80.

[Zettlemoyer and Collins2005] L S. Zettlemoyer and M Collins. 2005. Learning to map sentences to logical form: Structured classification with probabilistic categorial grammars. In *UAI*, pages 658–666.

Domain-Dependent Identification of Multiword Expressions

István Nagy T.[1], **Veronika Vincze**[2] and **Gábor Berend**[1]
[1]Department of Informatics, University of Szeged
{nistvan,berendg}@inf.u-szeged.hu
[2]Hungarian Academy of Sciences, Research Group on Artificial Intelligence
vinczev@inf.u-szeged.hu

Abstract

The identification of different kinds of multiword expressions require different solutions, on the other hand, there might be domain-related differences in their frequency and typology. In this paper, we show how our methods developed for identifying noun compounds and light verb constructions can be adapted to different domains and different types of texts. Our results indicate that with little effort, existing solutions for detecting multiword expressions can be successfully applied to other domains as well.

1 Introduction

Multiword expressions (MWEs) are lexical units that consist of more than one orthographical word, i.e. a lexical unit that contains spaces (Sag et al., 2002; Calzolari et al., 2002). There are several methods developed for identifying several types of MWEs, however, different kinds of multiword expressions require different solutions. Furthermore, there might be domain-related differences in the frequency of a specific MWE type. In this paper, we show how our methods developed for identifying noun compounds and light verb constructions can be adapted to different domains and different types of texts, namely, Wikipedia articles and texts from various topics. Our results suggest that with simple modifications, competitive results can be achieved on the target domains.

2 Related work

There are several solutions developed for identifying different types of MWEs in different domains. Bonin et al. (2010) use contrastive filtering in order to identify multiword terminology in scientific, Wikipedia and legal texts: term candidates are ranked according to their belonging to the general language or the sublanguage of the domain. The tool `mwetoolkit` (Ramisch et al., 2010a) is designed to identify several types of MWEs in different domains, which is illustrated by identifying English compound nouns in the Genia and Europarl corpora and in general texts (Ramisch et al., 2010b; Ramisch et al., 2010c).

Statistical models are used for the identification of several types of multiword expressions in several languages (e.g. Bouma (2010),Villavicencio et al. (2007)). However, they require (costly) annotated resources on the one hand and they are not able to identify rare MWEs in corpora on the other hand – as Piao et al. (2003) emphasize, about 68% of multiword expressions occur only once or twice in their corpus.

Some hybrid systems make use of both statistical and linguistic information as well, that is, rules based on syntactic or semantic regularities are also incorporated into the system (Bannard, 2007; Cook et al., 2007; Al-Haj and Wintner, 2010). This results in better coverage of multiword expressions. On the other hand, these methods are highly specific because of the amount of linguistic rules encoded, thus, it requires much effort to adapt them to different languages or even to different types of multiword expressions. Thus, the adaptation of linguistics-based models or hybrid models is required for identifying rare MWEs in small corpora from different domains.

3 Experiments

In this paper, we focus on the identification of two types of multiword expressions, namely noun compounds and light verb constructions. A compound is a lexical unit that consists of two or more elements that exist on their own. Light verb constructions are verb and noun combinations in which the verb has lost its meaning to some degree and the noun is used in one of its original senses (e.g. *have a walk*).

We selected noun compounds since they are very frequent in language use (in the Wiki50 corpus (Vincze et al., 2011b) 67.3% of the sentences contain a noun compound on average). On the other hand, they are productive: new noun compounds are being created all the time hence they cannot be exhaustively listed. Light verb constructions are less frequent (8.5% of the sentences contain one), however, they are syntactically flexible: the nominal component and the verb may not be adjacent, which hinders their identification. Their proper treatment is especially important in information (event) extraction, where verbal elements play a central role and extracted events may differ if the verbal and the nominal component are not considered as one complex predicate.

For the automatic identification of noun compounds and light verb constructions, we implemented several rule-based methods, which we describe below in detail.

As opposed to earlier studies (Cook et al., 2007; Bannard, 2007; Tan et al., 2006), we would like to identify light verb constructions in running text without assuming that syntactic information is necessarily available (in line with Vincze et al. (2011a)). Thus, in our investigations, we will pay distinctive attention to the added value of syntactic features on the system's performance.

3.1 Methods for MWE identification

For identifying noun compounds, we made use of a list constructed from the English Wikipedia. Lowercase n-grams which occurred as links were collected from Wikipedia articles and the list was automatically filtered in order to delete non-English terms, named entities and non-nominal compounds etc. In the case of the method 'Match', a noun compound candidate was marked if it occurred in the list.

In the case of 'POS-rules', a noun compound candidate was marked if it occurred in the list and its POS-tag sequence matched one of the previously defined patterns (e.g. `JJ (NN|NNS)`). For light verb constructions, the POS-rule method meant that each n-gram for which the pre-defined patterns (e.g. `VB.? (NN|NNS)`) could be applied was accepted as light verb constructions. For POS-tagging, we used the Stanford POS-tagger (Toutanova and Manning, 2000). Since the methods to follow rely on morphological information (i.e. it is required to know which element is a noun), matching the POS-rules is a prerequisite to apply those methods for identifying MWEs.

The 'Suffix' method exploited the fact that many nominal components in light verb constructions are derived from verbs. Thus, in this case only constructions that matched our POS-rules and contained nouns that end in certain derivational suffixes were allowed.

The 'Most frequent verb' (MFV) method relied on the fact that the most common verbs function typically as light verbs (e.g. *do*, *make*, *take* etc.) Thus, the 12 most frequent verbs typical of light verb constructions were collected and constructions that matched our POS-rules and where the stem of the verbal component was among those of the most frequent ones were accepted.

The 'Stem' method pays attention to the stem of the noun. In the case of light verb constructions, the nominal component is typically one that is derived from a verbal stem (*make a decision*) or coincides with a verb (*have a walk*). In this case, we accepted only candidates that had a nominal component whose stem was of verbal nature, i.e. coincided with a stem of a verb.

Syntactic information can also be exploited in identifying MWEs. Typically, the syntactic relation between the verb and the nominal component in a light verb construction is `dobj` or `partmod` (using Stanford parser (Klein and Manning, 2003)) – if it is a prepositional light verb construction, the relation between the verb and the preposition is `prep`. The 'Syntax' method accepts candidates among whose members the above syntactic relations hold.

We also combined the above methods to identify noun compounds and light verb constructions in our databases (the union of candidates yielded by the methods is denoted by ∪ while the intersection is denoted by ∩ in the respective tables).

3.2 Corpora used for evaluation

For the evaluation of our models, we made use of three corpora. Data on the corpora are shown in Table 1.

First, we used Wiki50 (Vincze et al., 2011b), in which several types of multiword expressions (including nominal compounds and light verb constructions) and named entities were marked. The corpus contains 2929 occurrences of nominal compounds and 368 occurrences of light verb con-

Corpus	Sentence	Token	NC	LVC
Wikipedia	4350	114,570	2929	368
BNC dataset	1000	21,631	368	-
Parallel	14,262	298,948	-	1100

Table 1: Corpora used for evaluation. NC: noun compounds, LVC: light verb constructions.

structions.

Our methods for identifying noun compounds were originally developed for a 1000-sentence dataset from the British National Corpus that contains 368 two-part noun compounds (Nicholson and Baldwin, 2008). The dataset includes texts from various domains such as literary work, essays, newspaper articles etc. These methods were later adapted to the Wikipedia domain.

Light verb constructions were also identified in the English part of a parallel corpus in which we annotated light verb constructions (14,261 sentence alignment units in size containing 1100 occurrences of light verb constructions). The parallel corpus consists of texts from magazines, novels[1], language books and texts on the European Union are also included. The corpus is available under the Creative Commons license at `http://rgai.inf.u-szeged.hu/mwe`.

3.3 Methodology

We first developed our methods for MWE identification for the source corpora. For both noun compounds and light verb constructions, the corpus that is smaller in size and contains simpler annotation was selected as the source domain. It entails that for noun compounds, the BNC dataset functions as the source domain (containing 1000 sentences and only two-part noun compounds) whereas for light verb constructions, the Wikipedia dataset was selected (containing 4350 sentences and not being annotated for subtypes of light verb constructions).

3.3.1 Detecting noun compounds

For identifying noun compounds in the source domain, we applied the methods 'Match' and 'POS-rules'. Results can be seen in the 'Source' column of Table 2. As it can be expected, POS-rules are beneficial as they improve results.

[1]Not all of the literary texts have been annotated for light verb constructions in the corpus, which made us possible to study the characteristics of the domain and the corpus without having access to the test dataset.

The adaptation process involved the development of more fine-tuned and sophisticated methods considering the domain-specific features of the texts and characteristics of the annotations. Thus, in the case of noun compounds, POS-rules were extended in order to identify noun compounds with more than two parts (e.g. *high school teacher*) because there was no restriction on the length of the annotated noun compounds in Wiki50 and about 20% of them consist of at least 3 parts. The method 'Match' was used as described above. We also implemented a new method for identifying longer noun compounds, which involved the merge of two possible noun compounds: if *a b* and *b c* both occurred in the list, *a b c* was also accepted as a noun compound ('Merge'). Finally, we combined the available methods ('Combined').

The **TARGET** column in Table 2 shows results achieved on the target domain when using the original methods whereas the **T+ADAPT** shows those achieved by applying domain-specific methods. The best result can be obtained on the target domain if the three methods are combined, that is, a target-specific method performs best. The process of adaptation is more successful in the case of POS-rules than 'Match', which may be related to the fact that longer units are also identified in Wiki50 and the list we automatically collected from Wikipedia probably contains more noise in the case of longer units. On the other hand, extended POS-rules add to performance.

Another striking fact is that the basic methods (i.e. without any adaptation) perform better on the target domain than on the source domain. The analysis of errors reveals that although it is stated in the BNC paper (Nicholson and Baldwin, 2008) that only sequences of two nouns are annotated, there are in fact longer noun compounds that are also annotated (e.g. *silk jersey halter-neck evening dress*), for which our methods were not prepared. On the other hand, some of the errors are related to annotation errors, for instance, marking noun compounds that contain a proper noun, e.g. *Belfast primary school headmaster*, as simple noun compounds instead of proper nouns (as they should be according to the guidelines), which our system could not identify.

3.3.2 Detecting light verb constructions

Results on the rule-based identification of light verb constructions can be seen in Table 3. In

Method	SOURCE			TARGET			T+ADAPT		
Match	26.93	43.48	33.26	40.45	52.65	45.75	37.7	54.73	44.65
POS-rules	36.91	40.87	38.79	49.04	50.8	49.9	55.56	49.98	52.62
Merge	-	-	-	-	-	-	40.06	57.63	47.26
Combined	-	-	-	-	-	-	59.46	52.48	**55.75**

Table 2: Results of dictionary-based methods for noun compounds in terms of precision, recall and F-measure. SOURCE: source domain, TARGET: target domain without adaptation techniques, T+ADAPT: target domain with adaptation techniques, Match: dictionary match, Merge: merge of two overlapping noun compounds, POS-rules: matching of POS-patterns, Combined: the union of Match, Merge and POS-rules.

the case of the source domain, the 'Most frequent verb' (MFV) feature proves to be the most useful: the verbal component of the light verb construction is lexically much more restricted than the noun, which is exploited by this feature.

Methods developed for the source domain were also evaluated on the target domain without any modification (**TARGET** column). Overall results are lower than those of the source domain, which is especially true for the 'MFV' method: while it performed best on the source domain (41.94%), it considerably declines on the target domain, reaching only 31.18%. The intersection of a verbal and a nominal feature, namely, 'MFV' and 'Stem' yields the best result on the target domain.

Techniques for identifying light verb constructions were also adapted to the other domain. The parallel corpus contained annotation for nominal and participial occurrences of light verb constructions. However, the number of nominal occurrences was negligible (58 out of 1100) hence we aimed at identifying only verbal and participial occurrences in the corpus. For this reason, POS-rules and syntactic rules were extended to treat postmodifiers as well (participial instances of light verb constructions typically occurred as postmodifiers, e.g. *photos taken*).

Since the best method on the Wiki50 corpus (i.e. 'MFV') could not reach such an outstanding result on the parallel corpus, we conducted an analysis of data on the unannotated parts of the parallel corpus. It was revealed that *have* and *go* mostly occurred in non light verb senses in these types of texts. *Have* usually denotes possession as in *have a son* vs. *have a walk* while *go* typically refers to physical movement instead of an abstract change of state (*go home* vs. *go on strike*). The reason for this might be that it is primarily everyday topics that can be found in magazines or novels rather than official or scientific topics, where it is less probable that possession or movement is described. Thus, a new list of typical light verbs was created which did not contain *have* and *go* but included *pay* and *catch* as they seemed to occur quite often in the unannotated parts of the corpus and in this way, an equal number of light verb candidates was used in the different scenarios.

The **T+ADAPT** column of Table 3 shows the results of domain adaptation. As for the individual features, 'MFV' proves to be the most successful on its own, thus, the changes in the verb list are beneficial. Although the features 'Suffix' and 'Stem' were not modified, they perform better after adaptation, which suggests that there might be more deverbal nominal components in the PART class of the target domain. Adaptation techniques add 1.5% to the F-measure on average, however, this value is 6.55% in the case of 'MFV'.

The added value of syntax was also investigated for LVC detection in both the source and the target domains after adaptation. As represented in Table 3, syntax clearly helps in identifying light verb constructions: on average, it adds 2.58% and 2.37% to the F-measure on the source and the target domains, respectively.

4 Discussion

Our adapted methods achieved better results on the target domains than the original ones as regards both noun compounds and light verb constructions. However, the overall results are better for the source domain in the case of light verbs and for the target domain in the case of noun compounds. The latter may be explained by the inconsistent annotation of the BNC dataset – without it, our original methods might have achieved similar results to those on the target domain. As for the former, there is not much difference between

Method	SOURCE			TARGET			T+ADAPT			SOURCE+SYNT			T+ADAPT+SYNT		
POS-rules	7.02	76.63	12.86	5.2	81.47	9.78	5.07	79.4	9.52	9.35	72.55	16.56	6.89	72.97	12.59
Sf	9.62	16.3	12.1	9.7	15.84	12.03	10.5	15.24	12.43	11.52	15.22	13.11	12.81	14.52	13.61
MFV	33.83	55.16	**41.94**	20.59	64.16	31.18	28.81	54.64	37.73	40.21	51.9	**45.31**	34.82	51.19	41.45
St	8.56	50.54	14.64	7.43	62.01	13.26	7.66	61.55	13.62	11.07	47.55	17.96	10.16	56.19	17.2
Sf ∩ MFV	44.05	10.05	16.37	32.13	10.74	16.1	48.31	10.24	16.9	11.42	54.35	18.88	55.03	9.76	16.58
Sf ∪ MFV	19.82	61.41	29.97	15.69	69.26	25.59	19.02	59.64	28.84	23.99	57.88	33.92	23.06	55.95	32.66
Sf ∩ St	10.35	11.14	11.1	10.27	11.41	10.8	11.14	11.07	11.1	12.28	11.14	11.68	14.02	10.59	12.07
Sf ∪ St	8.87	57.61	15.37	7.49	66.44	13.46	7.74	65.71	13.84	11.46	54.35	18.93	10.18	60.12	17.4
MFV ∩ St	39.53	36.96	38.2	27.96	49.4	**35.71**	38.87	43.45	**41.03**	46.55	34.78	39.81	44.04	40.48	**42.18**
MFV ∪ St	10.42	68.75	18.09	7.92	76.78	14.35	8.25	72.74	14.82	13.36	64.67	22.15	10.99	66.9	18.88
Sf ∩ MFV ∩ St	47.37	7.34	12.7	35.09	8.05	13.1	47.41	7.62	13.13	50.0	6.79	11.96	53.98	7.26	12.8
Sf ∪ MFV ∪ St	10.16	72.28	17.82	7.76	78.52	14.13	8.05	74.29	14.53	13.04	68.2	21.89	10.64	68.33	18.49

Table 3: Results of rule-based methods for light verb constructions in terms of precision, recall and F-measure. SOURCE: source domain, TARGET: target domain without adaptation techniques, T+ADAPT: target domain with adaptation techniques, SOURCE+SYNT: source domain with syntactic information, T+ADAPT+SYNT: target domain with adaptation techniques and syntactic information, POS-rules: matching of POS-patterns, Sf: the noun ends in a given suffix, MFV: the verb is among the 12 most frequent light verbs, St: the noun is deverbal.

the performance on the source and the target domains, which might be related to differences in the distribution of (a)typical light verb constructions. However, 'MFV' proves to be the most important feature for both domains, which suggests that with a well-designed domain-specific list of light verb candidates, competitive results can be achieved on any domain, especially if enhanced with syntactic features.

Contrasting the detection of noun compounds and light verb constructions, detecting noun compounds seems to be easier as it achieved better results in terms of F-measure. Indeed, simple features can be successfully applied in identifying noun compounds such as POS-tags and lists because they are syntactically less flexible than light verb constructions on the one hand and a greater part of phrases that match a POS-rule is a noun compound than it is the case for light verb constructions (compare the precision values of the POS-rules method). Thus, the identification of light verb constructions requires morphological, lexical or syntactic features such as the stem of the noun, the lemma of the verb or the dependency relation between the noun and the verb.

The characteristics of the corpora also have an impact on the adaptation process. The smaller the distance between the domains, the easier the adaptation. The topic of the texts were dissimilar in both scenarios (encyclopedia entries in the Wikipedia corpus and miscellaneous topics in the other two corpora) and annotation principles were also quite different in both cases. As our results indicate, the distance is small between the source and the target domain in the case of light verb constructions since similar results can be achieved on the two domains if domain-specific solutions are employed. However, the methods designed for the BNC dataset outperform results on the source domain if evaluated on the target domain, which suggests that the quality of the source data could be improved and thus, no further conclusions can be made on the comparison of the source and target domain in the case of noun compounds.

5 Conclusion

In this paper, we focused on the identification of noun compounds and light verb constructions in different domains, namely, Wikipedia articles and general texts of miscellaneous topics. Our rule-based methods developed for the source domains were adapted to the characteristics of the target domains. Our results indicate that with simple modifications and little effort, our initial methods can be successfully adapted to the target domains as well. For noun compounds, using POS-tagging and lists can lead to acceptable results while a domain-specific list of light verb candidates collected on the basis of sense distribution seems to be essential in detecting light verb constructions.

Obviously, our methods can be further improved. First, the identification of noun compounds relies on an automatically generated list, which can be refined and filtered. Second, stemming of the nominal components of light verb constructions can be enhanced by e.g. wordnet features in order to eliminate false negative matches originating from the stemming principles of the

Porter stemmer (e.g. the stems of *decision* and *decide* do not coincide). Third, the lists of possible light verb candidates can be extended as well. Finally, investigations on other domains and corpora would also be beneficial, which we would like to carry out as future work.

Acknowledgments

This work was supported by the Project "TÁMOP-4.2.1/B-09/1/KONV-2010-0005 – Creating the Center of Excellence at the University of Szeged", supported by the European Union and co-financed by the European Regional Development Fund and by the project BELAMI financed by the National Innovation Office of the Hungarian government.

References

Hassan Al-Haj and Shuly Wintner. 2010. Identifying multi-word expressions by leveraging morphological and syntactic idiosyncrasy. In *Proceedings of Coling 2010*, pages 10–18, Beijing, China, August.

Colin Bannard. 2007. A measure of syntactic flexibility for automatically identifying multiword expressions in corpora. In *Proceedings of the Workshop on a Broader Perspective on Multiword Expressions*, MWE '07, pages 1–8, Morristown, NJ, USA. ACL.

Francesca Bonin, Felice Dell'Orletta, Giulia Venturi, and Simonetta Montemagni. 2010. Contrastive filtering of domain-specific multi-word terms from different types of corpora. In *Proceedings of the 2010 Workshop on Multiword Expressions: from Theory to Applications*, pages 77–80, Beijing, China, August. Coling 2010 Organizing Committee.

Gerlof Bouma. 2010. Collocation extraction beyond the independence assumption. In *Proceedings of the ACL 2010 Conference Short Papers*, pages 109–114, Uppsala, Sweden, July. ACL.

Nicoletta Calzolari, Charles Fillmore, Ralph Grishman, Nancy Ide, Alessandro Lenci, Catherine MacLeod, and Antonio Zampolli. 2002. Towards best practice for multiword expressions in computational lexicons. In *Proceedings of LREC-2002*, pages 1934–1940, Las Palmas.

Paul Cook, Afsaneh Fazly, and Suzanne Stevenson. 2007. Pulling their weight: exploiting syntactic forms for the automatic identification of idiomatic expressions in context. In *Proceedings of the Workshop on a Broader Perspective on Multiword Expressions*, MWE '07, pages 41–48, Morristown, NJ, USA. ACL.

Dan Klein and Christopher D. Manning. 2003. Accurate unlexicalized parsing. In *Proceedings of ACL 2003*, pages 423–430, Stroudsburg, PA, USA. Association for Computational Linguistics.

Jeremy Nicholson and Timothy Baldwin. 2008. Interpreting Compound Nominalisations. In *LREC 2008 Workshop: Towards a Shared Task for Multiword Expressions (MWE 2008)*, pages 43–45, Marrakech, Morocco.

Scott S. L. Piao, Paul Rayson, Dawn Archer, Andrew Wilson, and Tony McEnery. 2003. Extracting multiword expressions with a semantic tagger. In *Proceedings of the ACL 2003 workshop on Multiword expressions: analysis, acquisition and treatment*, pages 49–56, Morristown, NJ, USA. ACL.

Carlos Ramisch, Aline Villavicencio, and Christian Boitet. 2010a. Multiword Expressions in the wild? The mwetoolkit comes in handy. In *Coling 2010: Demonstrations*, pages 57–60, Beijing, China, August.

Carlos Ramisch, Aline Villavicencio, and Christian Boitet. 2010b. mwetoolkit: a framework for multiword expression identification. In *Proceedings of LREC'10*, Valletta, Malta, May. ELRA.

Carlos Ramisch, Aline Villavicencio, and Christian Boitet. 2010c. Web-based and combined language models: a case study on noun compound identification. In *Coling 2010: Posters*, pages 1041–1049, Beijing, China, August.

Ivan A. Sag, Timothy Baldwin, Francis Bond, Ann Copestake, and Dan Flickinger. 2002. Multiword Expressions: A Pain in the Neck for NLP. In *Proceedings of CICLing-2002*, pages 1–15, Mexico City, Mexico.

Yee Fan Tan, Min-Yen Kan, and Hang Cui. 2006. Extending corpus-based identification of light verb constructions using a supervised learning framework. In *Proceedings of the EACL Workshop on Multi-Word Expressions in a Multilingual Contexts*, pages 49–56, Trento, Italy, April. ACL.

Kristina Toutanova and Christopher D. Manning. 2000. Enriching the knowledge sources used in a maximum entropy part-of-speech tagger. In *Proceedings of EMNLP 2000*, pages 63–70, Stroudsburg, PA, USA. ACL.

Aline Villavicencio, Valia Kordoni, Yi Zhang, Marco Idiart, and Carlos Ramisch. 2007. Validation and evaluation of automatically acquired multiword expressions for grammar engineering. In *Proceedings of EMNLP-CoNLL 2007*, pages 1034–1043, Prague, Czech Republic, June. ACL.

Veronika Vincze, István Nagy T., and Gábor Berend. 2011a. Detecting noun compounds and light verb constructions: a contrastive study. In *Proceedings of the Workshop on Multiword Expressions: from Parsing and Generation to the Real World*, pages 116–121, Portland, Oregon, USA, June. ACL.

Veronika Vincze, István Nagy T., and Gábor Berend. 2011b. Multiword expressions and named entities in the Wiki50 corpus. In *Proceedings of RANLP 2011*, Hissar, Bulgaria.

Robust Semantic Analysis for Unseen Data in FrameNet

Alexis Palmer, Afra Alishahi, Caroline Sporleder
Computational Linguistics and Phonetics
Saarland University, Germany
{apalmer,afra,csporled}@coli.uni-saarland.de

Abstract

We present a novel method for FrameNet-based semantic role labeling (SRL), focusing on limitations posed by the limited coverage of available annotated data. Our SRL model is based on Bayesian clustering and has the advantage of being very robust in the face of unseen and incomplete data. Frame labeling and role labeling are modeled in like fashions, allowing cascading classification scenarios. The model is shown to perform especially well on unseen data. In addition, we show that for seen data, predicting semantic types for roles improves role labeling performance.

1 Introduction

The majority of recent work in semantic role labeling (SRL) has been carried out on PropBank-style semantic argument annotations (Palmer et al., 2005), rather than on FrameNet-style annotations (Ruppenhofer et al., 2006). FrameNet differs from PropBank in that FrameNet annotations are more strongly semantically driven. FrameNet generalizes over different parts of speech and can assign the same sense (*frame*) to a noun and a verb as in (1), where both *competition* and *play* are assigned the COMPETITION frame. Also, FrameNet assigns semantic roles not only to syntactic arguments of the target but also to constituents which are not directly syntactically dependent on the target but can be semantically understood as filling a role, e.g., *Wivenhoe Town* in (1a).

(1) a. [Wivenhoe Town]$_{Participant1}$ have never won the **competition**$_{Competition}$.
b. [Olympiakos]$_{Participant1}$ **plays**$_{Competition}$ [against Aris Salonica]$_{Participant1}$ [in Piraeus]$_{Place}$.

A major challenge for FrameNet-style SRL is posed by the limited coverage of available annotated data. The FrameNet lexicographic corpus was annotated on a frame-by-frame basis, selecting individual example sentences for each *lexical unit* (LU), or pairing of lemma and frame. This means that many common lemmas are missing from FrameNet, and for those that *are* included the number of example sentences is often relatively small and not in accordance with distributions found in naturally-occurring texts.

FrameNet's well-known coverage gaps translate directly to drops in labeling performance, motivating the development of systems which are more robust in the face of sparse data. For example, the supervised SRL system Shalmaneser (Erk and Padó, 2006) obtains a frame labeling accuracy of 93% on FrameNet 1.2 (with a 90-10 training-test split), but the same system's performance drops to 47% accuracy when trained on FrameNet 1.3 and tested on texts with full frame-semantic annotations (Palmer and Sporleder, 2010). Similarly, Das et al. (2010) report a 60% frame labeling F-Score on SemEval-07 data, but of 210 unseen lemmas, their system predicts just four frames correctly.[1]

In general the term *unseen* could refer to unseen frames, unseen lemmas, or unseen LUs. As further discussed in Section 4, we are interested in unseen LUs: cases in which the system has not been exposed to a particular pairing of lemma and frame. We propose a novel method for SRL based on Bayesian clustering. The model is well suited to deal with incomplete data, both in terms of missing feature values and in terms of feature-label combinations not seen in the training data.

2 Related Work

While early FrameNet-style SRL systems (Gildea and Jurafsky, 2002; Erk and Padó, 2006, among others) are unable to make predictions for LUs not seen in the training data, several more recent stud-

[1]Under the SemEval-07 partial matching scheme, a majority of the other frame predictions receive partial credit.

ies have addressed the coverage issue. For example, Das et al. (2010) introduce a latent variable ranging over seen targets, allowing them to infer likely frames for unseen words, and the SRL system of Johansson and Nugues (2007) uses WordNet to generalise to unseen lemmas. In a similar vein, Burchardt et al. (2005) propose a system that generalizes over WordNet synsets to guess frames for unknown words. Pennacchiotti et al. (2008) compare WordNet-based and distributional approaches to inferring frames and conclude that a combination of the two leads to the best results, while (Cao et al., 2008) discuss how different distributional models can be utilised. Several approaches have also addressed other coverage problems, e.g., how to automatically expand the number of example sentences for a given lexical unit (Padó et al., 2008; Fürstenau and Lapata, 2009).

Another related approach is that of generalizing over semantic roles. Baldewein et al. (2004) use the FrameNet hierarchy to model the similarity of roles, boosting seldom-seen instances by reusing training data for similar roles, though without significant gains in performance. The most extensive study on role generalization to date (Matsubayashi et al., 2009) compares different ways of grouping roles—exploiting hierarchical relations in FrameNet, generalizing via role names, utilising role types, and using thematic roles from VerbNet—with the best results from using all groups together.

3 Model

We formalize frame and role assignment using an extended version of the construction learning model of Alishahi and Stevenson (2010). The model uses Bayesian clustering for learning argument structure constructions: each construction is a grouping of individual predicate usages which probabilistically share form-meaning associations. These groupings typically correspond to general constructions in the language such as intransitive, transitive, and ditransitive. By detecting similar usages and clustering them into constructions, the model forms probabilistic associations between syntactic positions of arguments with respect to the predicate, and the lexical semantic properties of the predicate and the arguments.

We model frame and role assignment in this fashion, where the most probable values for a missing frame or the semantic roles of arguments are predicted based on the acquired constructions (or clusters), and the extracted features from the corpus. This strategy provides a number of advantages. First, the model can easily deal with incomplete data; that is, input instances for which any number of features are missing can be seamlessly clustered or considered for prediction, based on the similarity of their features with those in the existing clusters. Moreover, a single core prediction mechanism is used for a variety of tasks (e.g. predicting a missing frame label, role, or role type), which can lead to cascading prediction. For example, for a partial (i.e. unannotated) frame instance, the best role type for each argument can be predicted based on the available features, and then argument roles can be predicted based on those features and the predicted role types.

An important characteristic of this model is its generalizability. It uses a full Bayesian prediction model, which takes into account the contribution of *every* cluster to predicting the best value for a missing feature. This way, there is no built-in difference between predicting a frame label or semantic role for *seen* versus *unseen* instances. Naturally, the outcome of prediction will be more accurate if the model has seen several instances similar to a test instance (i.e., from the same lexical unit or lemma). But even for unseen instances, the model is still capable of generalizing the properties of the training instances given that there are similarities between their available features, such as the syntactic pattern and the semantic properties of the predicate and the arguments.

3.1 Clustering Frame Instances

From the FrameNet corpus, we extract for each instance the nine features shown in Table 1. Different subsets of these features are used for the experiments reported in Section 5.

An incremental Bayesian clustering process groups each extracted frame instance with the most similar existing cluster of instances. If no existing cluster has sufficiently high probability for the new frame instance, a new cluster is created.

Adding a frame instance X to a cluster c is formulated as finding the c with the maximum probability given X, where c ranges over the indices of all clusters, with index 0 representing recognition of a new cluster. Using Bayes rule, and dropping $P(X)$ which is constant for all c:

$$P(c|X) = \frac{P(c)P(X|c)}{P(X)} \sim P(c)P(X|c) \quad (2)$$

The prior probability $P(c)$ is given by the relative frequency of the frame instances it contains, over all observed instances. The posterior probability of an instance X is expressed in terms of the individual probabilities of its features, which we assume are independent, thus yielding a simple product of feature probabilities:

$$P(X|c) = \prod_{i \in Features(X)} P(X_i|c) \quad (3)$$

This probability is estimated using smoothed maximum likelihood:

$$P(X_i|c) = \frac{\sum_{X' \in c} \mathrm{match}(X_i, X'_i) + \lambda}{n_c + \alpha_i \lambda} \quad (4)$$

where n_c is the number of instances in cluster c, and α_i and λ are the smoothing factors. For single-valued features (e.g. head word), the function match returns 1 if the two feature values are identical, and 0 otherwise.

For features whose value is a set (semantic properties of the predicate and arguments, word classes), an exact match between two sets is rare. We instead assume that the members of set-valued features are independent of each other, and calculate the probability of displaying a set S_i on feature i in cluster c as:

$$P(S_i|c) = \frac{1}{|S_c \cup S_i|}\left(\prod_{s \in S_i} P(s|c) \times \prod_{s \in S_c - S_i} P(\neg s|c)\right) \quad (5)$$

where S_c is the superset of all the set values of feature i for members in cluster c. Likelihood probabilities $P(s|c)$ and $P(\neg s|c)$ are estimated as in Eqn. (4), by counting members of cluster c whose value for feature f does or does not contains s, respectively. The product is rescaled by the size of the union of the two sets, $S_c \cup S_i$.

3.2 Frame Identification and Role Assignment

For any instance in the test set, both frame identification and role assignment can be modeled as finding the most probable value for a target feature, given other available features.

The probability of an unobserved feature i displaying value X_i given other feature values in an instance X is estimated as:

$$\begin{aligned} P(X_i|X) &= \sum_c P(X_i|c)P(c|X) \quad (6) \\ &= \sum_c P(X_i|c)P(c)P(X|c) \end{aligned}$$

The conditional probabilities $P(X|c)$ and $P(X_i|c)$ are determined as in the learning module. Ranging over the possible values X_i of feature i, the value of an unobserved feature can be predicted by maximizing $P(X_i|X)$:

$$\mathrm{BestValue}(X, i) = \operatorname*{argmax}_{X_i} P(X_i|X) \quad (7)$$

Identifying a frame can be simulated as finding the frame label X_{frame} with the highest $P(X_{frame}|X)$, or estimating $\mathrm{BestValue}(X, \mathrm{frame})$. Similarly, assigning roles or role types to the arguments of an instance X is modeled as estimating $\mathrm{BestValue}(X, \mathrm{role})$ or $\mathrm{BestValue}(X, \mathrm{role\_type})$, respectively.

4 Data

In this work we use the FrameNet 1.3 lexicographic corpus to evaluate the performance of our model on both seen and unseen data. This corpus provides annotated example sentences for each lexical unit (LU; frame-lemma pairing), documenting a range of syntactic and semantic usages, and it consists of 139,439 annotated example sentences distributed over 10,195 LUs. After excluding 4161 sentences due to inconsistencies with FrameNet definitions, we created two data sets: **seen** and **unseen**.

Seen Data. In the seen set-up, we assume that the model has complete information about each instance's lexicographic status. This means that for *frame labeling* the model knows which frames each target lemma can have and, further, has access to the training instances for each of those frames. Frame labeling is thus performed on a lemma-by-lemma basis. For *role labeling* we assume that the frame of the target lemma is known (e.g., has been previously predicted, either automatically or by an oracle), as well as that frame's role inventory, though it is not known which roles are instantiated in the given test instance. Role labeling is thus performed on an LU basis.

To evaluate frame labeling, we split the set of sentences by lemma and perform 5-fold cross-validation. Cross-validation splits for role labeling are done according to LU.

Unseen Data. To evaluate the performance of our system on unseen data,we simulate a situation in which individual LUs are unseen; specifically, we assume that the frame of a given LU has been seen before but not with the target lemma.[2] We also allow the case that a target lemma has been seen with a different frame. Note that while having seen the target frame before will help the model to select the correct frame, having seen the target lemma is not necessarily helpful, as it might lead the system to predict the incorrect seen frame rather than the correct but previously unseen frame.

To simulate the unseen condition for a given LU, all annotated sentences for that LU are removed from the training set and put into the test set. To test our hypothesis that the performance of correctly predicting a frame (and by extension also the roles) for an unseen LU depends on the frequency of the target frame after removing the LU, we computed the *inverse frequency* of each LU, i.e., the frame frequency summed over all other LUs with the same target frame, and sorted the set of LUs into three frequency bands based on their inverse frequency. Each band contains approximately the same number of LUs, subject to the constraint that LUs with the same inverse frequency are grouped together. A test set was then created by randomly selecting 10% of the LUs from each band, making sure that the test set contains each frame only once; the training set consists of all remaining LUs. Because this configuration does not allow proper cross-validation, instead five random training-test splits were created and tested.

5 Experiments

Automatic semantic analysis under the FrameNet approach is generally modeled as a two-part process: frame identification (Section 5.1) and role assignment (Section 5.2). Having a frame label for an instance's target lemma is a prerequisite to role assignment, as there is a distinct inventory of possible role labels for the semantic arguments of any given frame.[3] We evaluate our model independently on the two component tasks and then perform a preliminary evaluation on the complete semantic analysis task, taking a pipeline approach.

Features. The model uses nearly the same feature set for both prediction tasks, with a few exceptions. Table 1 shows which features are used for each task and whether the feature values are gold-standard or predicted.

	FramePred	RolePred	Pipeline
target lemma	G	G	G
target pos	G	G	G
# args	A	G	A
arg head	A	A*	A
arg head POS	A	A*	A
syn pattern	A	G	A
WordNet props	A	A	A
frame label	-	G	M
role types	-	M/G	M

Table 1: Features used for each task. **G**: gold-standard feature values; **A**: automatically-obtained feature values; **A***: automatically-obtained feature values based on gold-standard input; **M**: feature values predicted by our model

Values for automatically-obtained argument-related features are extracted from a metafeature representation produced by the frame assignment component of the Shalmaneser SRL system (Erk and Padó, 2006). The automatic syntactic patterns are then computed by aligning arguments with the text and replacing the arguments with their phrase-level syntactic categories.

WordNet features are extracted for each noun and verb in the lexicon. First, all hypernyms are extracted for the first sense of the word. In addition, one member from each hypernym synset is added to the list of properties for the lexical item.

Baselines and reporting. For each task we calculate an item baseline based on the number of possible outcomes. In the case of frame identification, the baseline reflects the number of frames a target predicate can participate in. If an LU exists in the frame dictionary, the number of possible outcomes is equal to the number of potential frame labels in the dictionary; if it does not, the denominator will be the total number of frame labels observed in the training data. For role labeling, the baseline reflects the number of roles available for labeling a given argument. Again, lemmas appearing in the frame-role dictionary have fewer possible labels. The baselines reported in Table 2 and Table 3 are the respective averages of all item baselines across different data sets.

Because our clustering algorithm is incremental and each training instance is processed only once, the model's performance in each task depends on the order of input items in the training set. In practice, though, no significant difference was observed across different cross-validation folds.

[2] This is in line with previous research on SRL for unseen data; creating or inducing entirely novel frames is beyond the reach of any current SRL system.

[3] Some role names appear in multiple frames, but they cannot necessarily be assumed to be semantically equivalent.

Frame Prediction		
Seen Data	Unseen Data	Baseline
88.32	88.76	87.09

Table 2: Accuracy of frame predictions for seen and unseen data, five-fold cross-validation.

Also, in the case of unseen data sets, no significant difference was observed across different frequency bands. Therefore, in the following sections, the reported results are averaged over all three frequency bands (as well as over all cross-validation folds).

5.1 Frame identification

For frame identification, we assume that the target lemma has been previously identified, and the model's predictions are constrained by a per-lemma frame dictionary built from FrameNet. This dictionary contains *all* LUs defined in FrameNet, so constraining the model with the frame dictionary is not equivalent to constraining the model to the LUs seen in training. This latter constraint is responsible for some of the coverage problems faced by other supervised models, so relaxing this constraint helps our model.

Results. The results for frame prediction on both seen and unseen data appear in Table 2. The high baseline figure reflects the fact that many lemmas in FrameNet appear with only a single frame. In combination with the frame dictionary, then, getting these right is a trivial matter. Nonetheless, our model improves on the baseline for both the seen and the unseen case. The latter is particularly positive as it means that we are able to infer the frame even for unseen LUs.

5.2 Role assignment

In a complete, end-to-end semantic role labeling system, role assignment involves both determining the span of the semantic arguments and assigning role labels to them. As our focus in this paper is the clustering model, we do not evaluate on the argument identification task, but rather assume gold-standard argument spans as input to role assignment. Having perfect argument spans greatly reduces the noisiness of both the argument head features and the syntactic pattern, at the same time improving the quality of the extracted WordNet features. Of course, assuming perfect input to role assignment is unrealistic for any real-world setting; thus we briefly report results on executing the entire SRL pipeline in Section 5.3.

Role Prediction		
	Seen Data	Unseen Data
no types	60.00	46.31
predicted types	67.00	46.29
gold types	74.84	73.65
Baseline	11.95	

Table 3: Accuracy of role assignment for seen and unseen data, five-fold cross-validation, with and without semantic types for roles.

The model's role label predictions are constrained using a frame-role dictionary extracted from FrameNet. For each individual instance, the set of available role labels is restricted to those defined for the frame assigned to the target lemma.

Predicted role types. As an additional feature for role assignment, we use semantic types on role fillers, as given in FrameNet. For example, for the frame COGITATION, the filler of the COGNIZER role must be a *Sentient* entity. Most types correspond to one or more WordNet synsets (Ruppenhofer et al., 2006). Unlike role names, these semantic types are not specific to frames, but rather shared across the lexicon.

In theory, these semantic types should be a powerful feature for assigning role labels. However, gold-standard semantic types are available for only a small part of the frame-specific roles defined in FrameNet. Though some previous work has used these semantic types to generalize over roles (Matsubayashi et al., 2009), no system so far has predicted role types to fill those gaps. To address this particular coverage problem, we first train a model on the available role types, predict values for all role types in the test data, and incorporate the predicted types as a novel feature for role assignment.

Results. Results for role assignment appear in Table 3. All results improve on the baseline. Unsurprisingly, gold standard role types lead to the largest performance gain. However, it can be seen that even when the role types are first predicted automatically, noticeable performance gains can be obtained compared to not using type information at all, at least for seen data. For unseen data automatically inferred type information does not help, possibly because the type prediction for LUs not seen in the training data is too noisy. Predictably, the results are lower for unseen data than for seen LUs, however, the model degenerates gracefully

Complete analysis		
	no types	predict types
Seen Data	41.80	45.76

Table 4: Performance on role prediction as a pipeline task, seen data only, five-fold cross-validation.

and is still able to correctly label almost every second argument for unseen LUs.

5.3 Complete semantic analysis

To evaluate our model's performance on complete semantic analysis, we use a pipeline approach: frame prediction, role type prediction, and role assignment. For all but the first task, predictions from the prior stage of analysis are fed into the model for the next. The only types of oracle information the model has access to are the target lemma and its part of speech tag, and the frame and role dictionaries described above.

Our results on seen data are in the same neighbourhood as the state-of-the-art. For example, the SEMAFOR system (Das et al., 2010) is reported to reach an F1 score of 46.00 for full parsing using oracle targets.

6 Conclusion

We present a Bayesian clustering and prediction model for FrameNet semantic role labeling. The proposed model is capable of generalizing its knowledge of similar frame instances to novel cases and is particularly competent in handling previously unseen data. Our results show that the model performs much better than chance in assigning semantic roles to arguments in an instance of a lexical unit which has not been seen in the training data. Also, the performance of the model for frame prediction on test sets of unseen data is as good as its performance on seen data.

We also propose a novel strategy which significantly improves the accuracy of SRL for seen data: we use all other features from an annotated instance to predict the most probable *role type*, and then use the predicted role type as an additional feature for predicting the semantic role.

Although we do not improve on state of the art results for frame prediction or role assignment, our model offers better coverage than existing models. In the future, we plan to improve the performance of our model by exploring the contribution of additional features (such as word classes and dependency relations between the arguments and the predicate), and to evaluate our model on additional data sets such as SemEval 2007.

Acknowledgments

This research has been funded by the German Research Foundation (DFG) under the MMCI Cluster of Excellence.

References

A. Alishahi, S. Stevenson. 2010. A computational model of learning semantic roles from child-directed language. *Language and Cognitive Processes*, 25(1):50–93.

U. Baldewein, K. Erk, S. Padó, D. Prescher. 2004. Semantic role labelling with similarity-based generalization using em-based clustering. In *Proc of Senseval-04*.

A. Burchardt, K. Erk, A. Frank. 2005. A WordNet detour to FrameNet. In B. Fisseni, H.-C. Schmitz, B. Schröder, P. Wagner, eds., *Sprachtechnologie, mobile Kommunikation und linguistische Ressourcen*, volume 8.

D. D. Cao, D. Croce, M. Pennacchiotti, R. Basili. 2008. Combining word sense and usage for modeling frame semantics. In *Proceedings of STEP-08*.

D. Das, N. Schneider, D. Chen, N. A. Smith. 2010. Probabilistic frame-semantic parsing. In *Proc of NAACL-HLT-10*.

K. Erk, S. Padó. 2006. Shalmaneser – a toolchain for shallow semantic parsing. In *Proc of LREC-06*.

H. Fürstenau, M. Lapata. 2009. Semi-supervised semantic role labeling. In *Proc of EACL-09*.

D. Gildea, D. Jurafsky. 2002. Automatic labeling of semantic roles. *Computational Linguistics*, 28(3):245–288.

R. Johansson, P. Nugues. 2007. Using WordNet to extend FrameNet coverage. In *Proc of the Wkshp on Building Frame-semantic Resources for Scandinavian & Baltic Languages, NODALIDA*.

Y. Matsubayashi, N. Okazaki, J. Tsujii. 2009. A comparative study on generalization of semantic roles in framenet. In *Proc of ACL-09*.

S. Padó, M. Pennacchiotti, C. Sporleder. 2008. Semantic role assignment for event nominalisations by leveraging verbal data. In *Proc of Coling-08*.

A. Palmer, C. Sporleder. 2010. Evaluating FrameNet-style semantic parsing: The role of coverage gaps in FrameNet. In *Proc of COLING-10*.

M. Palmer, D. Gildea, P. Kingsbury. 2005. The Proposition Bank: An Annotated Corpus of Semantic Roles. *Computational Linguistics*, 31(1):71–105.

M. Pennacchiotti, D. D. Cao, R. Basili, D. Croce, M. Roth. 2008. Automatic induction of FrameNet lexical units. In *Proc of EMNLP-08*.

J. Ruppenhofer, M. Ellsworth, M. R. L. Petruck, C. R. Johnson, J. Scheffczyk. 2006. FrameNet II: Extended Theory and Practice.

Studying Translationese at the Character Level

Marius Popescu
University of Bucharest
Department of Computer Science
Academiei 14, Bucharest, Romania
mpopescu@phobos.cs.unibuc.ro

Abstract

This paper presents a set of preliminary experiments which show that identifying translationese is possible with machine learning methods that work at character level, more precisely methods that use string kernels. But caution is necessary because string kernels very easily can introduce confounding factors.

1 Introduction

The term *translationese* designates the specific characteristics of translated texts compared to non translated text, the trace that the translation process leaves on translated texts. The term was introduced by Gellerstam in (1986). In an initial stage various features specific to translated texts, *universal features of translation*, were identified and corpus based approaches were employed to test the statistical significance of these translation universals (Baker, 1993; Laviosa, 2002). Recently, machine learning techniques have started to be used to investigate translationese: to distinguish between translated texts and non-translated ones, to identify the source language of a translated text, etc. (Baroni and Bernardini, 2006; Kurokawa et al., 2008; van Halteren, 2008; Ilisei et al., 2010; Koppel and Ordan, 2011).

These learning systems use a variety of features: (grammatical) words, part of speech tags, sentence length, etc.. By using this kind of features these methods implicitly handle the text at word level or above. Perhaps surprisingly, recent results have proved that methods that handle the text at character level can also be very effective in text analysis tasks. In (Lodhi et al., 2002) string kernels were used for document categorization with very good results. String kernels were also successfully used in authorship identification (Sanderson and Guenter, 2006; Popescu and Dinu, 2007) and plagiarism detection (Grozea et al., 2009).

In this paper we set to investigate if identifying translationese is possible with machine learning methods that work at the character level. More precisely, we will use string kernels in conjunction with different kernel methods in a series of experiments to see what performance can be achieved. Doing this we hope to answer the question if looking at the texts as just sequences of symbols (strings) is enough to identify translationese, and provide a method of identifying translationese that is language independent and theory neutral.

In the next section the related work and how our approach differs from it is discussed. In section 3 we briefly describe the kernel methods we used and string kernels. Section 4 describes the performed experiments and the obtained results, and the last section contains a discussion of these results and suggestions for future work.

2 Related Work

Using words is natural in text analysis tasks like text categorization (by topic), authorship identification and plagiarism detection. Perhaps surprisingly, recent results have proved that methods handling the text at character level can also be very effective in text analysis tasks. In (Lodhi et al., 2002) string kernels were used for document categorization with very good results. Trying to explain why treating documents as symbol sequences and using string kernels led to such good results the authors suppose that: "the [string] kernel is performing something similar to stemming, hence providing semantic links between words that the word kernel must view as distinct". String kernels were also successfully used in authorship identification (Sanderson and Guenter, 2006; Popescu and Dinu, 2007). A possible reason for the success of string kernels in authorship identification is given in (Popescu and Dinu, 2007): "the similarity of two strings as it is measured by string kernels reflects the similarity of the two texts as it is given by the short words (2-5 characters) which usually are function words, but also takes into account other morphemes like suffixes ('ing' for example) which also can be good indicators of the authors style".

Even more interesting is the fact that two methods that obtained very good results for text categorization (by topic) (Lodhi et al., 2002) and authorship identification (Popescu and Dinu, 2007) are essentially the same, both are based on SVM and a string kernel of length 5. How is this possible? Traditionally, the two tasks, text categorization (by topic) and authorship identification are viewed as opposed. When words are used as features, for text categorization the (stemmed) content words are used (the stop words being eliminated), while for authorship identification the function words (stop words) are used as features, the others words (content words) being eliminated. Then, why did the same string kernel (of length 5) work well in both cases? In our opinion the key factor is the kernel-based learning algorithm. The string kernel implicitly embeds the texts in a high dimensional feature space, in our case the space of all (sub)strings of length 5. The kernel-based learning algorithm (SVM or another kernel method), aided by regularization, implicitly assigns a weight to each feature, thus selecting the features that are important for the discrimination task. In this way, in the case of text categorization the learning algorithm (SVM) enhances the features (substrings) representing stems of content words, while in the case of authorship identification the same learning algorithm enhances the features (substrings) representing function words.

Support Vector Machines (SVM) were also used in identifying translationese. Actually it is the dominant approach. In (Baroni and Bernardini, 2006) and (Kurokawa et al., 2008) the learning method used was SVM, In (van Halteren, 2008) and (Ilisei et al., 2010) several learning methods were used, SVM being included among them and reported to be among the top performers. Only in (Koppel and Ordan, 2011) a kernel method was not used. All these approaches use features computed at the word level or above: words, part of speech tags, sentence length, etc.. It might appear, because of the linguistically shallow representation, that these methods are language independent, but they directly or indirectly depend on resources specific to a given language. Most of the methods use part of speech tags (directly as features or indirectly as the proportion of some specific POS tags in text) and this implies the existence of a POS tagger for that language which is not always available. Even a method that uses as features only function words like the one in (Koppel and Ordan, 2011) is not completely language independent because it needs a way to segment a text into words which is not an easy task for some languages, like Chinese.

Using string kernels will make the corresponding learning method completely language independent because the texts will be treated as sequences of symbols (strings). Such a method will also have the advantage of being theory neutral. Methods working at the word level or above very often restrict their feature space according to theoretical or empirical principles. For example, they select only features that reflect *simplification universal* (Ilisei et al., 2010) or only some type of words (function words) (Koppel and Ordan, 2011), etc.. These features prove to be very effective for specific tasks, but other, possibly good features, depending on the particular task, may exist, for example source language specific features (Koppel and Ordan, 2011). String kernels embed the texts in a very large feature space (all substrings of length k) and leave it to the learning algorithm (SVM) to select important features for the specific task, by highly weighting these features.

3 Kernel Methods and String Kernels

Kernel-based learning algorithms work by embedding the data into a feature space (a Hilbert space), and searching for linear relations in that space. The embedding is performed implicitly, that is by specifying the inner product between each pair of points rather than by giving their coordinates explicitly.

Given an input set $\mathcal{X}$ (the space of examples), and an embedding vector space $\mathcal{F}$ (feature space), let $\phi : \mathcal{X} \rightarrow \mathcal{F}$ be an embedding map called feature map.

A *kernel* is a function k, such that for all $x, z \in \mathcal{X}$, $k(x, z) =< \phi(x), \phi(z) >$, where $< ., . >$ denotes the inner product in $\mathcal{F}$.

In the case of binary classification problems, kernel-based learning algorithms look for a discriminant function, a function that assigns $+1$ to examples belonging to one class and -1 to examples belonging to the other class. This function will be a linear function in the space $\mathcal{F}$, that means it will have the form:

$$f(x) = \text{sign}(< w, \phi(x) > +b),$$

for some weight vector w. The kernel can be exploited whenever the weight vector can be expressed as a linear combination of the training points, $\sum_{i=1}^{n} \alpha_i \phi(x_i)$, implying that f can be expressed as follows:

$$f(x) = \text{sign}(\sum_{i=1}^{n} \alpha_i k(x_i, x) + b)$$

.

Various kernel methods differ by the way in which they find the vector w (or equivalently the vector α). Support Vector Machines (SVM) try to find the vector w that defines the hyperplane that maximally separates the images in $\mathcal{F}$ of the training examples belonging to the two classes. Mathematically, SVMs choose the w and the b that satisfy the following optimization criterion:

$$\min_{w,b} \frac{1}{n} \sum_{i=1}^{n} [1 - y_i(< w, \phi(x_i) > +b)]_+ + \nu ||w||^2$$

where y_i is the label ($+1/-1$) of the training example x_i, ν a regularization parameter and $[x]_+ = \max(x, 0)$.

Kernel Fisher Discriminant (KFD) selects the w that gives the direction on which the training examples should be projected in order to obtain a maximum separation between the means of the two classes scaled according to the variances of the two classes in that direction. The optimization criterion is:

$$\max_{w} \frac{(\mu_w^+ - \mu_w^-)^2}{(\sigma_w^+)^2 + (\sigma_w^-)^2 + \lambda ||w||^2}$$

where μ_w^+ is the mean of the projection of positive examples onto the direction w, μ_w^- is the mean for the negative examples, σ_w^+ and σ_w^- are the corresponding standard deviations and λ is a regularization parameter. Details about SVM and KFD can be found in (Taylor and Cristianini, 2004). What is important is that the above optimization problems are solved in such a way that the coordinates of the embedded points are not needed, only their pairwise inner products, which in turn are given by the kernel function k, are required.

The kernel function offers to the kernel methods the power to naturally handle input data that are not in the form of numerical vectors, for example strings. The kernel function captures the intuitive notion of similarity between objects in a specific domain and can be any function defined on the respective domain that is symmetric and positive definite. For strings, many such kernel functions exist with various applications in computational biology and computational linguistics (Taylor and Cristianini, 2004).

Perhaps one of the most natural ways to measure the similarity of two strings is to count how many substrings of length p the two strings have in common. This gives rise to the p-spectrum kernel. Formally, for two strings over an alphabet Σ, $s, t \in \Sigma^*$, the p-spectrum kernel is defined as:

$$k_p(s,t) = \sum_{v \in \Sigma^p} \text{num}_v(s)\text{num}_v(t)$$

where $\text{num}_v(s)$ is the number of occurrences of string v as a substring in s [1]. The feature map defined by this kernel associates to each string a vector of dimension $|\Sigma|^p$ containing the histogram of frequencies of all its substrings of length p. Taking into account all substrings of length less than p, a kernel that is called the *blended spectrum kernel* will be obtained:

$$k_1^p(s,t) = \sum_{q=1}^{p} k_q(s,t)$$

The p-spectrum kernel will be the kernel that we shall be using in conjunction with SVM and KFD in our experiments. More precisely we shall use a normalized version of the kernel to allow a fair comparison of strings of different lengths:

$$\hat{k}_p(s,t) = \frac{k_p(s,t)}{\sqrt{k_p(s,s)k_p(t,t)}}$$

4 Evaluation

4.1 The Corpus

For our experiments we have assembled a corpus of literary works, most of them dating from the nineteenth century, with very few dating from the end of the eighteenth century or the beginning of twentieth century. All of them are book-length, the majority are novels, but also some essays, memoirs or autobiographies are included. In total we

[1]Note that the notion of substring requires contiguity. See (Taylor and Cristianini, 2004) for a discussion about the ambiguity between the terms "substring" and "subsequence" across different traditions: biology, computer science.

have collected 214 books. Half of them, 108, were originally written in English by both American and British authors. The other half of the corpus consists of translated works: 76 from French authors and 30 from German authors. The type of works we collected is very diverse, from classical works (works of Goethe, Balzac, Dickens) to popular fiction of the time (Eugène Sue's The Wandering Jew, the works of Karl May, Reynolds's Mysteries of London).

The source of the books was the Project Gutenberg[2], but in rare cases we also used other sources[3]. The Project Gutenberg policy - "We carry high quality ebooks: Our ebooks were previously published by *bona fide* publishers..." - ensures at least a minimal quality of the translated texts.

There is no space to list here all the titles in our corpus. Instead, in Table 1, we enumerate the authors represented in the corpus and the number of books by each author contained in the corpus.

Group	Authors
French authors	Balzac(10), Paul Bourget(1), Alphonse Daudet(3), Alexandre Dumas père(9), Alexandre Dumas fils(1), Flaubert(6), Anatole France(4), Théophile Gautier(1), Hugo(3), Hector Malot(2), Maupassant(6), Henry Murger(1), Prosper Mérimée(1), George Sand(1), Count Philip de Segur(1), Nahum Slouschz(1), Eugène Sue(1), Alexis de Tocqueville(1), Jules Verne(14), Émile Zola(9)
German authors	Berthold Auerbach(10), Gustav Freytag(1), E. T. A. Hoffmann(2), Goethe(2), Brothers Grimm(1), Friedrich Maximilian von Klinger(1), Karl May(5), Albert Pfister(1), Wilhelm Raabe(1), Leopold von Sacher-Masoch(1), Christoph von Schmid(1), Theodor W. Storm(1), Johann Ludwig Tieck(3)
American authors	James Fenimore Cooper(4), Stephen Crane(2), Nathaniel Hawthorne(4), Henry James(4), Herman Melville(4)
British authors	Jane Austen(5), Emily Brontë(1), Anne Brontë(2), Charlotte Brontë(4), George Bulwer-Lytton(4), Lewis Carroll(3), William Wilkie Collins(3), Joseph Conrad(4), Charles Dickens(13), Sir Arthur Coman Doyle(2), George Eliot(4), H. Rider Haggard(2), Thomas Hardy(5), George Reynolds(2), Sir Walter Scott(23), William Makepeace Thackeray(5), Anthony Trollope(5), H. G. Wells(3)

Table 1: The list of authors and the number of their books contained in the corpus

4.2 Experimental Setup

In all our experiments the objective was to learn a classifier able to distinguish translated texts from non-translated ones, thus obtaining a binary classification problem. The texts in the corpus were labeled as translated (T) if they were works of French and German authors translated into English or were labeled as original English (O) if they were works originally written in English by British or American authors.

Because the string kernels work at the character level, we didn't need to split the texts into words or to do any preprocessing. The only editing done to the texts was the replacing of sequences of consecutive space characters (space, tab new line, etc.) with only one space character. This normalization was needed in order to not artificially increase or decrease the similarity between texts because of different spacing.

In all experiments we have used a p-spectrum normalized kernel of length 5 ($\hat{k}_5$). We chose the length 5 to see if the same kernel that was reported to work well in the case of document categorization (Lodhi et al., 2002) and authorship identification (Popescu and Dinu, 2007) will also work for translationese identification. We did not attempt to optimize the value of the length of the p-spectrum kernel.

In all experiments the results obtained by KFD and SVM were almost identical. Here we reported only the result obtained by SVM.

p-spectrum kernel implicitly embeds the texts in a high dimensional feature space. Because we have a small number of examples (214), in a high dimensional feature space, the data set is separable and the best working SVM is a hard margin SVM that can be obtained setting the C parameter of the SVM to a high value (Taylor and Cristianini, 2004). In all our experiments the value of C was set to 100.

4.3 Experiments and Results

In the first experiment we have performed a cross-validation on the entire corpus. The goal of the cross-validation was not to set or tune any parameter of the learning method (all parameters were set by other criteria, see the previous section). The purpose of the cross-validation was to obtain a first estimation of the accuracy of the classifier learned by SVM based on a p-spectrum kernel of length 5. The 10-fold cross-validation accuracy was 99.53% and the leave one out cross-validation accuracy was 100%. The obtaine results are higher than the ones reported in other studies. In fact, the results were so good they made us suspicious.

In the second experiment we have prepared a much harder setting to test the learning method.

[2]http://www.gutenberg.org

[3]For example, the works of Karl May were taken from: http://www.karl-may-gesellschaft.de

We have used for training all the texts translated from French and the original English texts written by British authors. We have tested the obtained classifier on the texts translated from German and the original English texts written by American authors. This scenario is more difficult because training texts for the class T were translations from some fixed source language (French), while all test texts in T were translations from a different source language (German). Similar cases are discussed in (Koppel and Ordan, 2011). This setting also violates one of the fundamental assumptions in machine learning: that the training and test data are drawn from the same distribution. The accuracy obtained in this setting was 45.83%. This means that nothing was learned and the obtained classifier is a random one.

The great discrepancy between cross-validation accuracy and the accuracy obtained in the second experiment is a clear symptom of over-fitting. Most probable, the learning method found some features (substrings) that can be used to distinguish with very high accuracy between translated and non-translated texts in the case of training data, but failed to do the same thing in the case of test data. Because we have used a kernel method it is hard to examine individual features in order to see their importance within the classification function. But because we know the difference between training data and test data (the different source languages of the translated texts) we can guess what kind of features can act as confounding variables. Most likely these are substrings extracted from foreign proper names. Such substrings that differ from typical English substrings can be very good indicators of translationese. In the case of cross-validation typical French and German substrings can be seen in the training examples and this explains the good results. In the second experiment the learning method sees only French translations and thus fails to recognize German translations as translated texts.

One possible remedy to this problem would be to replace all proper names with a special string or symbol, solution adopted by others (Baroni and Bernardini, 2006) as well. But this would mean that our method treats texts at word level and not at character level. We opted for a more direct approach.

For the third experiment we have collected the French original of all the works of French authors in the corpus. These French texts formed a reference corpus. We modified the p-spectrum kernel so as to exclude all substrings that appear in the reference corpus. More precisely, when the p-spectrum kernel is computed between two texts, if a substring of length p that is common to the two texts is found, it will be counted as a common substring only if it does not appear as a substring of a text in the reference corpus. In this way, the substrings belonging to French proper names in the corpus will be eliminated from the feature space, but, of course, many other substrings will also be eliminated. This procedure was applied when the kernel was computed between any pair of texts from the corpus regardless of the source language (translated from French, translated from German or English original).

When we have repeated the previous experiment, training on texts from French and British authors and testing on texts from German and American authors, with the new kernel, the obtained accuracy was 77.08%. In a similar experiment, training using translated texts from French and testing using translated texts from German, but on a different data set (Europarl corpus), Koppel and Ordan (2011) reported an accuracy of 68.5%.

This third experiment proves that identifying translationese is possible with machine learning methods that work at the character level, using SVM and a modified string kernel.

Finally, we have performed a fourth experiment to see if the fact that we have used for training the works of British authors and for testing the works of American authors had any consequence regarding accuracy. As in the previous experiments we used for training translated texts from French authors and for testing translated texts from German authors. The original English texts, regardless of the nationality of the author, were randomly partitioned into 6 parts, one part being kept for testing and the other 5 being used for training (like in cross-validation, with the difference that the procedure was followed only for original English texts). The average accuracy obtained was 76.88%, being not significantly different from the accuracy obtained in the previous experiment (77.08%).

5 Conclusions and Further Work

In this paper we have performed a set of experiments regarding the identification of translationese using string kernel in conjunction with kernel methods. We have found that identifying translationese is possible with machine learning methods that work at the character level, SVM and string kernels, but caution is necessary because string kernels very easily can introduce confounding factors.

More experiments are needed in order to clarify all aspects of identifying translationese at the character level.

To eliminate the confounding factors introduced by p-spectrum kernel when training examples come from one source language and testing examples from another we used the original version of the translated texts in the training set. This is a strong requirement. Can we use as reference corpus other texts in the source language, not necessarily the original version of the translated texts? We plan to investigate this question.

It is likely that the confounding factors will not appear if a corpus more suited for studying translationese (comparable corpora (Laviosa, 1997)) will be used. We plan to test the method on such corpora (like Europarl).

Acknowledgments

Work supported by the National University Research Council of Romania (the "Ideas" research programme, PN II-IDEI), Contract No. 659/2009.

References

M. Baker. 1993. Corpus linguistics and translation studies, implications and applications. In M. Baker, editor, *Text and Technology, In honour of John Sinclair.* John Benjamins Publishing Company., Philadelphia/Amsterdam.

M. Baroni and S. Bernardini. 2006. A new approach to the study of translationese: Machine-learning the difference between original and translated text. *Literary and Linguistic Computing*, 21(3):259–274.

M. Gellerstam. 1986. Translationese in swedish novels translated from english. In L. Wollin and H. Lindqvist, editors, *Translation studies in Scandinavia*.

C. Grozea, C. Gehl, and M. Popescu. 2009. ENCOPLOT: Pairwise Sequence Matching in Linear Time Applied to Plagiarism Detection. In *3rd PAN WORKSHOP. UNCOVERING PLAGIARISM, AUTHORSHIP AND SOCIAL SOFTWARE MISUSE*, page 10.

I. Ilisei, D. Inkpen, G. Corpas Pastor, and R. Mitkov. 2010. Identification of translationese: A machine learning approach. In A. F. Gelbukh, editor, *CICLing*, volume 6008 of *Lecture Notes in Computer Science*, pages 503–511. Springer.

M. Koppel and N. Ordan. 2011. Translationese and its dialects. In *Proceedings of the 49th Annual Meeting of the Association for Computational Linguistic: Human Language Technologiess*, Portland, Oregon, USA, June. Association for Computational Linguistics.

D. Kurokawa, C. Goutte, and P. Isabelle. 2008. Automatic detection of translated text and its impact on machine translation. In *Proceedings of MT-Summit XII*.

S. Laviosa. 1997. How comparable can 'comparable corpora' be? *Targe*, 9(2):289–320.

S. Laviosa. 2002. *Corpus-based Translation Studies. Theory, Findings, Applications*. Amsterdam & New York: Rodopi.

Huma Lodhi, Craig Saunders, John Shawe-Taylor, Nello Cristianini, and Christopher J. C. H. Watkins. 2002. Text classification using string kernels. *Journal of Machine Learning Research*, 2:419–444.

Marius Popescu and Liviu P. Dinu. 2007. Kernel methods and string kernels for authorship identification: The federalist papers case. In *Proceedings of the International Conference on Recent Advances in Natural Language Processing (RANLP-07)*, Borovets, Bulgaria, September.

Conrad Sanderson and Simon Guenter. 2006. Short text authorship attribution via sequence kernels, markov chains and author unmasking: An investigation. In *Proceedings of the 2006 Conference on Empirical Methods in Natural Language Processing*, pages 482–491, Sydney, Australia, July. Association for Computational Linguistics.

J. S. Taylor and N. Cristianini. 2004. *Kernel Methods for Pattern Analysis*. Cambridge University Press, New York, NY, USA.

H. van Halteren. 2008. Source language markers in EUROPARL translations. In *Proceedings of the 22nd International Conference on Computational Linguistics (Coling 2008)*, pages 937–944, Manchester, UK, August. Coling 2008 Organizing Committee.

Linear Transduction Grammars and Zipper Finite-State Transducers

Markus Saers and **Dekai Wu**
Human Language Technology Center
Dept. of Computer Science and Engineering
Hong Kong University of Science and Technology
Hong Kong
{masaers|dekai}@cs.ust.hk

Abstract

We examine how the recently explored class of linear transductions relates to finite-state models. Linear transductions have been neglected historically, but gained recent interest in statistical machine translation modeling, due to empirical studies demonstrating that their attractive balance of generative capacity and complexity characteristics lead to improved accuracy and speed in learning alignment and translation models. Such work has until now characterized the class of linear transductions in terms of either (a) linear inversion transduction grammars (LITGs) which are linearized restrictions of inversion transduction grammars or (b) linear transduction grammars (LTGs) which are bilingualized generalizations of linear grammars. In this paper, we offer a new alternative characterization of linear transductions, as relating four finite-state languages to each other. We introduce the devices of zipper finite-state automata (ZFSAs) and zipper finite-state transducers (ZFSTs) in order to construct the bridge between linear transductions and finite-state models.

1 Introduction

Linear transductions are a long overlooked class of transductions positioned between finite-state transductions and inversion transductions in terms of complexity. In the Aho–Ullman hierarchy, linear transductions are those that can be generated by SDTGs[1] of rank 1, but that is about all that is said about them.

[1]Syntax-directed transduction grammars or SDTGs (Lewis and Stearns, 1968; Aho and Ullman, 1972) have also been referred to recently in the statistical machine translation subcommunity as synchronous context-free grammars.

Recently, however, linear transduction grammars (LTGs) have been shown to be both effective and efficient for learning word alignments in statistical machine translation models (Saers et al., 2010b; Saers et al., 2010a). LTGs can align words more accurately than FSTs since they allow words to be reordered, and yet alignment and training complexity is two orders of magnitude lower than with ITGs (Wu, 1997).

The added efficiency means that LTGs can be learned directly from parallel corpora rather than relying on external word alignment tools for *a priori* annotation. The added efficiency does, however, come at a price in expressivity, and it is vital to understand the nature of this trade-off. The automaton/transducer perspective of linear transductions described in this paper offers another vector towards understanding the properties of linear transductions.

Thus far, such work has not characterized the class of linear transductions in terms of finite-state models. Saers et al. (2010b) define linear transductions in terms of linear inversion transduction grammars (LITGs), which are inversion transduction grammars with a linear restriction. Alternatively, Saers et al. (2010a) introduce linear transduction grammars (LTGs), which are the natural bilingual generalization of linear grammars, and show that they define the same class of linear transductions as LITGs.

In this paper, we offer a new alternative characterization of linear transductions based on finite-state models. We will start by giving a definition of LTGs, as the principal mechanism for generating linear transductions (Section 2). As an intermediate step, we will note that linear languages (which are related by linear transductions) can be handled by FSTs under some conditions: we treat linear languages as two finite-state languages dependent on each other, by introducing the device of zipper finite-state automata (Section 3). We then general-

$$G = \langle \{S, F\}, \Sigma, \Delta, S, R \rangle \text{ such that}$$
$$\Sigma = \{\text{b, l, sandwich, t, -}\},$$
$$\Delta = \{\text{bacon, bread, lettuce, mayonnaise, tomato}\},$$
$$R = \left\{ \begin{array}{l} S \rightarrow \epsilon/\text{bread } F \text{ sandwich/bread}, \\ F \rightarrow \text{b}/\epsilon \; F \; \epsilon/\text{bacon}, \\ F \rightarrow \text{l/lettuce } F, \\ F \rightarrow \text{t/tomato } F, \\ F \rightarrow \text{-}/\epsilon, \\ F \rightarrow \text{-/mayonnaise} \end{array} \right\}$$

(a) Linear transduction grammar

$$\begin{aligned} S &\underset{G}{\Rightarrow} \epsilon/\text{bread } F \text{ sandwich/bread} \\ &\underset{G}{\Rightarrow} \text{b/bread } F \text{ sandwich/bacon bread} \\ &\underset{G}{\Rightarrow} \text{b l/bread lettuce } F \text{ sandwich/bacon bread} \\ &\underset{G}{\Rightarrow} \text{b l t/bread lettuce tomato } F \text{ sandwich/bacon bread} \\ &\underset{G}{\Rightarrow} \text{b l t - sandwich/bread lettuce tomato mayonnaise bacon bread} \end{aligned}$$

(b) Generation

Figure 1: A linear transduction grammar (a) generating a bistring (b). The transduction defined establishes the concept "BLT-sandwich" and the ordered components of its realization: bacon, lettuce and tomato (with optional mayonnaise) sandwiched between two slices of bread.

ize this to introduce zipper finite-state transducers, treating linear transductions as relating two linear languages to each other (Section 4). Since linear languages relate two finite-state languages to each other, and linear transductions relate two linear languages to each other, linear transductions can be said to relate four finite-state languages to each other.

2 Linear transduction grammars

A linear transduction grammar (LTG) is an inversion transduction grammar (ITG) or syntax-directed transduction grammar (SDTG), of rank 1, which means that any rule may produce at most one nonterminal, eliminating any branching. Figure 1 contains an example of an LTG, and how it generates a bistring.

Definition 1 A linear transduction grammar (LTG) over languages L_1 and L_2 is a tuple:

$$G = \langle N, \Sigma, \Delta, S, R \rangle$$

where N is a finite nonempty set of nonterminal symbols, Σ is a finite nonempty set of L_1 symbols, Δ is a finite nonempty set of L_2 symbols, $S \in N$ is the designated start symbol and R is a finite nonempty set of production rules on the forms:

$$A \rightarrow {}^{a}\!/\!_{x} \, B \, {}^{b}\!/\!_{y}$$
$$A \rightarrow {}^{a}\!/\!_{x}$$

where the nonterminals $A, B \in N$ and the biterminals ${}^{a}\!/\!_{x}, {}^{b}\!/\!_{y} \in \Sigma^* \times \Delta^*$.

Definition 2 The rules in an LTG $G = \langle N, \Sigma, \Delta, S, R \rangle$ define a binary relation $\underset{G}{\Rightarrow}$ over $(\Sigma^* \times \Delta^*)(N \cup (\Sigma^* \times \Delta^*))(\Sigma^* \times \Delta^*)$ such that:

$$\begin{aligned} {}^{a}\!/\!_{w} A \, {}^{d}\!/\!_{z} &\underset{G}{\Rightarrow} {}^{ab}\!/\!_{wx} B \, {}^{cd}\!/\!_{yz} && \text{iff } A \rightarrow {}^{b}\!/\!_{x} B \, {}^{c}\!/\!_{y} \in R \\ {}^{a}\!/\!_{w} A \, {}^{d}\!/\!_{z} &\underset{G}{\Rightarrow} {}^{abd}\!/\!_{wxz} && \text{iff } A \rightarrow {}^{b}\!/\!_{x} \in R \end{aligned}$$

Note that both the biterminal expressions ${}^{a}\!/\!_{w} \, {}^{b}\!/\!_{x}$ and ${}^{ab}\!/\!_{wx}$ can designate the translation between the terminal strings ab and wx. The reflexive transitive closure of this relation can be used to define the transduction generated by an LTG as the set of bistrings that can be generated from the grammar's start symbol.

Definition 3 The transduction generated by the LTG $G = \langle N, \Sigma, \Delta, S, R \rangle$ is:

$$T(G) = \left\{ \langle a, x \rangle \middle| S \overset{*}{\underset{G}{\Rightarrow}} {}^{a}\!/\!_{x} \right\} \cap (\Sigma^* \times \Delta^*)$$

Even though no normal form is given in Aho and Ullman (1972) for LTGs or SDTGs of rank 1, it is useful to have such a normal form. In this work we will adopt the following normal form for LTGs.

Definition 4 An LTG in normal form is an LTG where the rules are constrained to have one of the forms:

$$A \rightarrow {}^{a}\!/\!_{x'}\ B\ {}^{b'}\!/\!_{y'} \qquad A \rightarrow {}^{a'}\!/\!_{x}\ B\ {}^{b'}\!/\!_{y'}$$
$$A \rightarrow {}^{a'}\!/\!_{x'}\ B\ {}^{b}\!/\!_{y'} \qquad A \rightarrow {}^{a'}\!/\!_{x'}\ B\ {}^{b'}\!/\!_{y}$$
$$A \rightarrow {}^{\epsilon}\!/\!_{\epsilon}$$

where $A, B \in N$, $a, b \in \Sigma$, $a', b' \in \Sigma \cup \{\epsilon\}$, $x, y \in \Delta$ and $x', y' \in \Delta \cup \{\epsilon\}$.

That is: only rules where at least one terminal symbol is produced together with a nonterminal symbol, and rules where the empty bistring is produced, are allowed. The "primed" symbols are allowed to be the empty string, whereas the others are not. It is possible to construct an LTG in normal form from an arbitrary LTG in the same way that a linear grammar (LG) is normalized.

Theorem 1. *Grammars of type* LTG *and type* LTG *in normal form generate the same class of transductions.*

Proof. Given an LTG $G = \langle N, \Sigma, \Delta, S, R \rangle$, we can construct an LTG in normal form $G' = \langle N', \Sigma, \Delta, S, R' \rangle$ that generates the same language. For every rule in R we can produce a series of corresponding rules in R'. We start by removing useless nonterminals, rules where one nonterminal rewrites into another nonterminal only. This can be done in the same way as for SDTGs, see Aho and Ullman (1972). The rules can then be recursively shortened until they are in normal form.

If the rule $A \rightarrow {}^{a}\!/\!_{x}\ B\ {}^{c}\!/\!_{z}$ is not in normal form, it can be rephrased as two rules:

$$A \rightarrow {}^{a}\!/\!_{x\,1}\ \bar{B}\ {}^{c}\!/\!_{z\,m}$$
$$\bar{B} \rightarrow {}^{a}\!/\!_{x\,2} \ldots {}^{a}\!/\!_{x\,n}\ B\ {}^{c}\!/\!_{z\,1} \ldots {}^{c}\!/\!_{z\,m-1}$$

where $\bar{B}$ is a newly created unique nonterminal, n is the length of the biterminal ${}^{a}\!/\!_{x}$ and m is the length of the biterminal ${}^{c}\!/\!_{z}$. The first rule is in normal form by definition. The second rule can be subjected to the same procedure until it is in normal form. Having either ${}^{a}\!/\!_{x}$ or ${}^{c}\!/\!_{z}$ be empty does not affect the results of the procedure, and since we started by eliminating useless rules, one of them is guaranteed to be nonempty.

If the rule $A \rightarrow {}^{b}\!/\!_{y}$ is not in normal form (meaning that ${}^{b}\!/\!_{y}$ is nonempty), it can be replaced by two rules:

$$A \rightarrow {}^{b}\!/\!_{y\,1}\ \bar{B}$$
$$\bar{B} \rightarrow {}^{b}\!/\!_{y\,2} \ldots {}^{b}\!/\!_{y\,n}$$

where $\bar{B}$ is a newly created unique nonterminal, and n is the length of the biterminal ${}^{b}\!/\!_{y}$. The set of nonterminals N' is the old set N in union with the set of all nonterminals that were created when R' was constructed.

Whenever there is a production in G such that:

$${}^{a}\!/\!_{w}\ A\ {}^{d}\!/\!_{z} \underset{G}{\Rightarrow} {}^{ab}\!/\!_{wx}\ B\ {}^{cd}\!/\!_{yz}$$

or

$${}^{a}\!/\!_{x}\ A\ {}^{c}\!/\!_{z} \underset{G}{\Rightarrow} {}^{abc}\!/\!_{xyz}$$

There is, by construction, a sequence of productions in G' such that:

$${}^{a}\!/\!_{w}\ A\ {}^{d}\!/\!_{z} \overset{*}{\underset{G'}{\Rightarrow}} {}^{ab}\!/\!_{wx}\ B\ {}^{cd}\!/\!_{yz}$$

or

$${}^{a}\!/\!_{x}\ A\ {}^{c}\!/\!_{z} \overset{*}{\underset{G'}{\Rightarrow}} {}^{abc}\!/\!_{xyz}$$

This means that G' is capable of generating any string that G can generate, giving us the inequality:

$$L(G) \subseteq L(G')$$

Since the normal form constitutes a restriction, we also know that:

$$L(G') \subseteq L(G)$$

Which leads us to conclude that:

$$L(G) = L(G') \qquad \square$$

For statistical machine translation applications, LTGs can be made weighted or stochastic (Saers et al., 2010b; Saers et al., 2010a) in the same way as ITGs Wu (1997).

3 Linear languages revisited

In this section we will take a look at the connection between linear languages (LLs) and FSTs, and leverage the relationship to define a new type of automaton to handle LLs. The new class of automata is referred to as zipper finite-state automata (ZFSAs), which will replace one-turn pushdown automata (Ginsburg and Spanier, 1966, 1-PDAs) and nondeterministic two-tape automata (Rosenberg, 1967, 2-NDAs) as the principal machine for handling linear languages. This is mainly to facilitate the move into the bilingual domain, and offers nothing substantially new.

Ginsburg and Spanier (1966, Theorem 6.1) show that a linear language can be seen as the input to an FST concatenated with the reverse of its output. Rosenberg (1967, Theorems 9 and 10) shows that any linear grammar can be said to generate the concatenation of the first tape from a 2-NDA with the reverse of the second. Instead of giving the original theorems, we will give two lemmas in the spirit of the previous works.

Lemma 2. *For every one-restricted finite-state transducer (1-FST) M there is an LG in normal form that generates the language $\{ab^{\leftarrow} | \langle a, b\rangle \in T(M)\}$.*[2]

Proof. Given that $M = \langle Q, \Sigma, \Delta, q_0, F, \delta\rangle$ is a 1-FST, we can construct an LG in normal form $G = \langle Q, \Sigma \cup \Delta, q_0, R\rangle$ where

$$R = \{q \rightarrow a\ q'\ b | \langle q, a, b, q'\rangle \in \delta\} \cup \{q \rightarrow \epsilon | q \in F\}$$

where $q, q' \in Q$, $a \in \Sigma \cup \{\epsilon\}$ and $b \in \Delta \cup \{\epsilon\}$. Whenever there is a transition sequence with M such that:

$$\begin{aligned}\langle q_0, a, b\rangle &= \langle q_0, a_1 \ldots a_n, b_1 \ldots b_n\rangle \\ &\vdash_M \langle q_1, a_2 \ldots a_n, b_2 \ldots b_n\rangle \\ &\vdash^*_M \langle q_{n-1}, a_n, b_n\rangle \\ &\vdash_M \langle q_n, \epsilon\rangle\end{aligned}$$

where $q_i \in Q$, $a_i \in \Sigma \cup \{\epsilon\}$, $a \in \Sigma^*$, $b_i \in \Delta \cup \{\epsilon\}$ and $b \in \Delta^*$ for all i, and where the state q_n is a member of F, there is, by construction, a derivation with G such that:

$$\begin{aligned}q_0 &\underset{G}{\Rightarrow} a_1 q_1 b_1 \\ &\underset{G}{\overset{*}{\Rightarrow}} a_1 \ldots a_n q_n b_n \ldots b_1 \\ &\underset{G}{\Rightarrow} a_1 \ldots a_n b_n \ldots b_1 = ab^{\leftarrow}\end{aligned}$$

Thus: whenever the bistring $\langle a, b\rangle$ is a member of $T(M)$, the string $ab^{\leftarrow}$ is a member of $L(G)$. By construction, G cannot generate any other strings. We thus conclude that

$$L(G) = \{ab^{\leftarrow} | \langle a, b\rangle \in T(M)\} \qquad \square$$

Lemma 3. *For every LG in normal form (G), there exists a 1-FST (M) such that, for all string $s \in L(G)$, there exists a partition $s = ab^{\leftarrow}$ such that $\langle a, b\rangle \in T(M)$.*

Proof. Given that $G = \langle N, \Sigma, S, R\rangle$ is an LG in normal form, we can construct a 1-FST $M = \langle N, \Sigma, \Sigma, S, F, \delta\rangle$ where:

$$\begin{aligned}F &= \{A | A \rightarrow \epsilon \in R\}, \\ \delta &= \{\langle A, a, b, B\rangle | A \rightarrow a\ B\ b \in R\}\end{aligned}$$

where $A, B \in N$ and $a, b \in \Sigma \cup \{\epsilon\}$. Whenever there is a derivation with G such that:

$$\begin{aligned}S &\underset{G}{\Rightarrow} a_1 X_1 b_1 \\ &\underset{G}{\overset{*}{\Rightarrow}} a_1 \ldots a_n X_n b_n \ldots b_1 \\ &\underset{G}{\Rightarrow} a_1 \ldots a_n b_n \ldots b_1 = ab^{\leftarrow}\end{aligned}$$

there is, by definition, a sequence of transitions with M such that:

$$\begin{aligned}\langle S, a, b\rangle &= \langle S, a_1 \ldots a_n, b_1 \ldots b_n\rangle \\ &\vdash_M \langle X_1, a_2 \ldots a_n, b_2 \ldots b_n\rangle \\ &\vdash^*_M \langle X_{n-1}, a_n, b_n\rangle \\ &\vdash_M \langle X_n, \epsilon, \epsilon\rangle\end{aligned}$$

(where $q_i \in Q$, $a_i \in \Sigma \cup \{\epsilon\}$, $a \in \Sigma^*$, $b_i \in \Delta \cup \{\epsilon\}$ and $b \in \Delta^*$ for all i) and the state X_n is by definition a member of F. Thus: whenever G generates $ab^{\leftarrow}$, M can recognize $\langle a, b\rangle$. By construction, M cannot recognize any other bistrings. We thus conclude that

$$T(M) = \{\langle a, b\rangle | ab^{\leftarrow} \in L(R)\} \qquad \square$$

[2]Where $b^{\leftarrow}$ is used to mean the reverse of b.

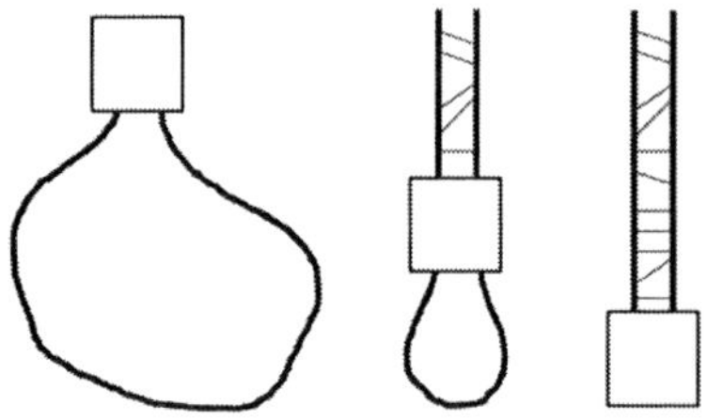

Figure 2: A zipper finite-state automata relates the two parts of a string to each other, and define the partitioning of the string at the same time.

There is a discrepancy between FSTs and linear languages in that every string in the language has to be partitioned into two strings before the FST can process them. Naturally, the number of ways to partition a string is proportional to its length. Naïvely trying all possible partitions would take $\mathcal{O}(n^3)$ time ($\mathcal{O}(n)$ partitions and $\mathcal{O}(n^2)$ time to run the FST on each string pair), which is equal to CFGs. If linear languages are as time-consuming to process as CFLs, we might as well use the more expressive language class. If, however, the partition point could be found as a part of the analysis process rather than conjectured *a priori*, the process would be faster than CFGs.

It is possible to reinterpret the transition relation defined by an FST such that it reads from both tapes, rather than reads from one and writes to the other. We define this relation as:

$$\langle q, a\alpha, \beta b\rangle \vdash_{M,r} \langle q', \alpha, \beta\rangle \quad \text{iff} \quad \langle q, a, b, q'\rangle \in \delta$$

where $q, q' \in Q$, $a \in \Sigma$, $b \in \Delta$, $\alpha \in \Sigma^*$ and $\beta \in \Delta^*$. Using this interpretation of the FST M (designated M' under this reinterpretation) we have that:

$$\langle \alpha, \beta^{\leftarrow}\rangle \in T(M) \quad \text{iff} \quad \langle \alpha, \beta\rangle \in T(M')$$

which, by lemmas 2 and 3, means that the concatenation of α and β over the entire transduction constitutes a linear language. This is the intuition behind zipper finite-state automata. By constructing a string $\gamma \in (\Sigma \cup \Delta)^*$ such that $\gamma = \alpha\beta$, we can rewrite the reinterpreted FST relation as:

$$\langle q, a\gamma b\rangle \vdash_{M',r} \langle q', \gamma\rangle \quad \text{iff} \quad \langle q, a, b, q'\rangle \in \delta$$

which define a linear language over $(\Sigma \cup \Delta)^*$. The partitioning of the string is also implicitly defined since the automaton will end up somewhere in the original string, defining the place of partitioning that makes the two parts related (or concluding that they are not, and that the string is not a member of the language defined by the automaton). The attribute "zipper" comes from the visualization, where the control of the automaton slides down two ends of the tape until it reaches the bottom after having drawn all connections between the two parts of the tape—like a zipper (see Figure 2). Again, this is merely a reinterpretation of previous work. The idea of a dedicated automaton to process a single tape containing strings from a linear language with finite control (as opposed to using a stack as the 1-PDAs do, or partitioning the tapes as 2-NDAs strictly speaking have to do) is not new. Nagy (2008) presents $5' \rightarrow 3'$ sensing Watson-Crick finite automata which are used to process DNA strings, and Loukanova (2007) presents nondeterministic finite automata to handle linear languages. Our reinterpretation is made to facilitate the transition into the bilingual domain.

Definition 5 A zipper finite-state automaton (ZFSA) is a tuple:

$$M = \langle Q, \Sigma, q_0, F, \delta\rangle$$

where Q is a finite nonempty set of states, Σ is a finite set of symbols, $q_0 \in Q$ is the start state, $F \subseteq Q$ is a set of accepting states and $\delta \subseteq Q \times \Sigma^* \times \Sigma^* \times Q$ is a finite set of transitions. Transitions define a binary relation over $Q \times \Sigma^*$ such that:

$$\langle q, \alpha\gamma\beta\rangle \vdash_M \langle q', \gamma\rangle \quad \text{iff} \quad \langle q, \alpha, \beta, q'\rangle \in \delta$$

where $q, q' \in Q$ and $\alpha, \beta, \gamma \in \Sigma^*$.

Lemma 4. *Every* FST *can be expressed as a* ZFSA.

Proof. Let $M = \langle Q, \Sigma, \Delta, q_0, F, \delta\rangle$ be an FST, and let $M' = \langle Q, \Sigma \cup \Delta, q_0, F, \delta\rangle$ be the corresponding ZFSA. The only differences are that M' uses the union of the two alphabets that M transduces between, and that the interpretation of the relation defined by δ is different in M and M'. □

Lemma 5. *Every* ZFSA *can be expressed as an* FST.

Proof. Let $M = \langle Q, \Sigma, q_0, F, \delta\rangle$ be a ZFSA, and let $M' = \langle Q, \Sigma, \Sigma, q_0, F, \delta\rangle$ be the corresponding FST transducing within the same alphabet. The only differences are that M' uses two copies of

$$M = \langle Q, \Sigma, \Delta, q_S, \{q'\}, \delta\rangle \text{ such that}$$
$$Q = \{q_S, q_F, q'\},$$
$$\Sigma = \{\text{b}, \text{l}, \text{sandwich}, \text{t}, \text{-}\},$$
$$\Delta = \{\text{bacon}, \text{bread}, \text{lettuce}, \text{mayonnaise}, \text{tomato}\},$$
$$\delta = \left\{\begin{array}{l} \langle q_S, \epsilon, \text{bread}, \text{sandwich}, \text{bread}, q_F\rangle, \\ \langle q_F, \text{b}, \epsilon, \epsilon, \text{bacon}, q_F\rangle, \\ \langle q_F, \text{l}, \text{lettuce}, \epsilon, \epsilon, q_F\rangle, \\ \langle q_F, \text{t}, \text{tomato}, \epsilon, \epsilon, q_F\rangle, \\ \langle q_F, \text{-}, \epsilon, \epsilon, \epsilon, q'\rangle \\ \langle q_F, \text{-}, \text{mayonnaise}, \epsilon, \epsilon, q'\rangle \end{array}\right\}$$

(a) Zipper finite-state transducer

$$\begin{array}{l} \langle q_S, \text{b l t - sandwich}, \text{bread lettuce tomato mayonnaise bacon bread}\rangle \\ \vdash_M \langle q_F, \text{b l t -}, \text{lettuce tomato mayonnaise bacon}\rangle \\ \vdash_M \langle q_F, \text{l t -}, \text{lettuce tomato mayonnaise}\rangle \\ \vdash_M \langle q_F, \text{t -}, \text{tomato mayonnaise}\rangle \\ \vdash_M \langle q_F, \text{-}, \text{mayonnaise}\rangle \\ \vdash_M \langle q', \epsilon, \epsilon\rangle \end{array}$$

(b) Recognition

Figure 3: A zipper finite-state transducer (a) recognizing a bistring (b). This is the same bistring that was generated in Figure 1.

the same alphabet (Σ), and that the interpretation of the relation defined by δ is different in M and M'. □

Theorem 6. FST*s in recognition mode are equivalent to* ZFSA*s.*

Proof. Follows from Lemmas 4 and 5. □

Theorem 7. *The class of languages recognized by* ZFSA*s is the class of linear languages.*

Proof. From Lemmas 2 and 3 we have that FSTs generate linear languages, and from theorem 6 we have that ZFSAs are equivalent to FSTs. □

To recognize with a ZFSA is as complicated as recognizing with an FST, which can be done in $\mathcal{O}(n^2)$ time. Since we are effectively equating a transduction with a language, it is helpful to instead consider this as "finite-state in two dimensions." For the finite-state transduction, this is easy, since it relates two finite-state languages to each other. For the linear languages it takes a little more to consider them as languages that internally relate one part of every string to the other part of that string. The key point is that they are both relating something that is in some sense finite-state to something else that is also finite-state.

4 Zipper finite-state transducers

Having condensed a finite-state relation down to a language, we can relate two such languages to each other. This is what zipper finite-state transducers (ZFSTs) do. If linear languages relate one part of every string to the other, linear transductions relate these two parts to the two parts of all the strings in another linear language. There are in all four kinds of entities involved, $\langle a, b\rangle \in L_1$ and $\langle x, y\rangle \in L_2$, and linear transduction have to relate them all to each other. We claim that this is what LTGs do, and in this section we will see that the transducer class for linear languages, ZFSTs, is equivalent to LTGs. An example of a ZFST can be found in Figure 3.

Definition 6 A ZFST over languages L_1 and L_2 is a tuple:

$$M = \langle Q, \Sigma, \Delta, q_0, F, \delta\rangle$$

where Q is a finite nonempty set of states, Σ is a finite nonempty set of L_1 symbols, Δ is a finite nonempty set of L_2 symbols, $q_0 \in Q$ is the designated start state, $F \subseteq Q$ is a set of accepting states and:

$$\delta \subseteq Q \times \Sigma^* \times \Delta^* \times \Sigma^* \times \Delta^* \times Q$$

is a finite set of transitions. The transitions define a binary relation over $Q \times \Sigma^* \times \Delta^*$ such that:

$$\langle q, abc, xyz\rangle \vdash_M \langle q', b, y\rangle \quad \text{iff} \quad \langle q, a, x, c, z, q'\rangle \in \delta$$

where $q, q' \in Q$, $a, b, c \in \Sigma^*$ and $x, y, z \in \Delta^*$.

We know that ZFSTs relate linear languages to each other, they are defined to do so, and we conjecture that LTGs relate linear languages to each other. By proving that ZFSTs and LTGs handle the same class of transductions we can assert that LTGs do indeed generate a transduction relation between linear languages.

Lemma 8. *For every* LTG *there is a* ZFST *that recognizes the language generated by the* LTG.

Proof. Let $G = \langle N, \Sigma, \Delta, S, R\rangle$ be an LTG, and let $M = \langle N', \Sigma, \Delta, S, \{S'\}, \delta\rangle$ be the corresponding ZFST where S' is a unique final state, $N' = N \cup \{S'\}$ and:

$$\delta = \{\langle A, a, x, c, z, B\rangle | A \rightarrow {}^{a}\!/\!_{x}\ B\ {}^{c}\!/\!_{z} \in R\} \cup \{\langle A, b, y, \epsilon, \epsilon, S'\rangle | A \rightarrow {}^{b}\!/\!_{y} \in R\}$$

where $A, B \in N$, $a, b, c \in \Sigma^*$ and $x, y, z \in \Delta^*$. Whenever there is a derivation with G such that:

$$\begin{aligned} S &\underset{G}{\Rightarrow} {}^{a_1}\!/\!_{x_1}\ A_1\ {}^{c_1}\!/\!_{z_1} \\ &\overset{*}{\underset{G}{\Rightarrow}} {}^{a_1}\!/\!_{x_1} \cdots {}^{a_n}\!/\!_{x_n}\ A_n\ {}^{c_n}\!/\!_{z_n} \cdots {}^{c_1}\!/\!_{z_1} \\ &\underset{G}{\Rightarrow} {}^{a_1}\!/\!_{x_1} \cdots {}^{a_n}\!/\!_{x_n}\ {}^{b}\!/\!_{y}\ {}^{c_n}\!/\!_{z_n} \cdots {}^{c_1}\!/\!_{z_1} \end{aligned}$$

(where $S, A_i \in N$, $a_i, b_i \in \Sigma^*$ and $x_i, y_i \in \Delta^*$ for all i),[3] we have, by construction, a sequence of transitions in M that takes it from an initial configuration with the generated bistring to an accepting configuration:

$$\begin{aligned} &\langle S, a_1 \ldots a_n b c_n \ldots c_1, x_1 \ldots x_n y z_n \ldots z_1\rangle \\ \vdash_M &\langle A_1, a_2 \ldots a_n b c_n \ldots c_2, x_2 \ldots x_n y z_n \ldots z_2\rangle \\ \vdash_M^* &\langle A_n, b, y\rangle \\ \vdash_M &\langle S', \epsilon, \epsilon\rangle \end{aligned}$$

[3]These i indices are not indicating individual symbols in a string, but different strings.

This means that M can recognize all strings generated by G. By construction, M cannot recognize any other strings. We thus conclude that

$$T(M) = T(G) \qquad \square$$

Lemma 9. *For every* ZFST, *there is an* LTG *that generates the transduction recognized by the* ZFST.

Proof. Let $M = \langle Q, \Sigma, \Delta, q_0, F, \delta\rangle$ be a ZFST, and let $G = \langle Q, \Sigma, \Delta, q_0, R\rangle$ be the corresponding LTG where:

$$R = \{q \rightarrow {}^{a}\!/\!_{x}\ q'\ {}^{b}\!/\!_{y} | \langle q, a, x, b, y, q'\rangle \in \delta\} \cup \{q \rightarrow {}^{\epsilon}\!/\!_{\epsilon} | q \in F\}$$

where $q, q' \in Q$, $a, b, c \in \Sigma^*$ and $x, y, z \in \Delta^*$. For every bistring that M can recognize:

$$\begin{aligned} &\langle q_0, a_1 \ldots a_n b_n \ldots b_1, x_1 \ldots x_n y_n \ldots y_1\rangle \\ \vdash_M &\langle q_1, a_2 \ldots a_n b_n \ldots b_2, x_2 \ldots x_n y_n \ldots y_2\rangle \\ \vdash_M^* &\langle q_n, \epsilon, \epsilon\rangle \end{aligned}$$

(where $q_i \in Q$, $a_i, b_i \in \Sigma^*$ and $x_i, y_i \in \Delta^*$ for all i,[4] and where $q_n \in F$), we have, by construction, a derivation with G that generates that bistring:

$$\begin{aligned} q_0 &\underset{G}{\Rightarrow} {}^{a_1}\!/\!_{x_1}\ q_1\ {}^{b_1}\!/\!_{y_1} \\ &\overset{*}{\underset{G}{\Rightarrow}} {}^{a_1}\!/\!_{x_1} \cdots {}^{a_n}\!/\!_{x_n}\ q_n\ {}^{b_n}\!/\!_{y_n} \cdots {}^{b_1}\!/\!_{y_1} \\ &\underset{G}{\Rightarrow} {}^{a_1}\!/\!_{x_1} \cdots {}^{a_n}\!/\!_{x_n}\ {}^{b_n}\!/\!_{y_n} \cdots {}^{b_1}\!/\!_{y_1} \end{aligned}$$

This means that G can generate all strings that M can recognize. By construction, G cannot generate any other strings. We thus conclude that

$$T(G) = T(M) \qquad \square$$

Theorem 10. *The class of transductions generated by* LTG*s is the same as that recognized by* ZFST*s.*

Proof. Follows from lemmas 8 and 9. $\square$

[4]Again, these indices do not refer to individual symbols in a string, but different strings.

5 Conclusion

We have examined how the class of linear transductions relates to finite-state models. Our analysis complements earlier characterizations of linear transductions in terms of LITGs (linearized restrictions of inversion transduction grammars) and LTGs (bilingualized generalizations of linear grammars). Our new alternative characterization has shown how linear transductions relate four finite-state languages to each other, with the aid of the devices zipper finite-state automata and transducers.

Acknowledgments

This work was funded by the Defense Advanced Research Projects Agency under GALE Contract Nos. HR0011-06-C-0023 and HR0011-06-C-0023, and the Hong Kong Research Grants Council (RGC) under research grants GRF621008, GRF612806, DAG03/04.EG09, RGC6256/00E, and RGC6083/99E. Any opinions, findings and conclusions or recommendations expressed in this material are those of the authors and do not necessarily reflect the views of the Defense Advanced Research Projects Agency. We would also like to thank the four anonymous reviewers, whose feedback made this a better paper.

References

Alfred V. Aho and Jeffrey D. Ullman. 1972. *The Theory of Parsing, Translation, and Compiling*. Prentice-Halll, Englewood Cliffs, NJ.

Seymour Ginsburg and Edwin H. Spanier. 1966. Finite-turn pushdown automata. *Society for Industrial and Applied Mathematics Journal on Control*, 4(3):429–453.

Philip M. Lewis and Richard E. Stearns. 1968. Syntax-directed transduction. *Journal of the Association for Computing Machinery*, 15(3):465–488.

Roussanka Loukanova. 2007. Linear context free languages. In Cliff Jones, Zhiming Liu, and Jim Woodcock, editors, *Theoretical Aspects of Computing – ICTAC 2007*, volume 4711 of *Lecture Notes in Computer Science*, pages 351–365. Springer Berlin/Heidelberg.

Benedek Nagy. 2008. On $5' \rightarrow 3'$ sensing Watson–Crick finite automata. In Max Garzon and Hao Yan, editors, *DNA Computing*, volume 4848 of *Lecture Notes in Computer Science*, pages 256–262. Springer Berlin/Heidelberg.

Arnold L. Rosenberg. 1967. A machine realization of the linear context-free languages. *Information and Control*, 10:175–188.

Markus Saers, Joakim Nivre, and Dekai Wu. 2010a. A systematic comparison between inversion transduction grammar and linear transduction grammar for word alignment. In *Proceedings of the 4th Workshop on Syntax and Structure in Statistical Translation*, pages 10–18, Beijing, China, August. Coling 2010 Organizing Committee.

Markus Saers, Joakim Nivre, and Dekai Wu. 2010b. Word alignment with stochastic bracketing linear inversion transduction grammar. In *Human Language Technologies: The 2010 Annual Conference of the North American Chapter of the Association for Computational Linguistics*, pages 341–344, Los Angeles, California, June. Association for Computational Linguistics.

Dekai Wu. 1997. Stochastic inversion transduction grammars and bilingual parsing of parallel corpora. *Computational Linguistics*, 23(3):377–403.

Finding Negative Key Phrases for Internet Advertising Campaigns using Wikipedia

Martin Scaiano
University of Ottawa
mscai056@uottawa.ca

Diana Inkpen
University of Ottawa
diana@site.uottawa.com

Abstract

In internet advertising, negative key phrases are used in order to exclude the display of an advertisement to non-target audience. We describe a method for automatically identifying negative key phrases. We use Wikipedia as our sense inventory and as an annotated corpus from which we create context vectors and determine negative phrases, which correlate with negative senses of a positive key phrase.

1 Introduction

Online advertisers select and bid on key phrases for which their ads will be displayed. Each time an ad is displayed, it is called an impression. The cost of the advertising campaign may be tied directly or indirectly to the number of impressions: each impression may cost the customer, or pricing maybe based on the rate of response to an advertisement (click through rate). Either way, impressions to those who are not interested in a product can cost the advertiser.

Key phrase advertising attempts to infer the interest of a "searcher" from the key phrases they are searching for. Many key phrases have multiple meanings; thus extra phrases are required to accurately infer meaning. There are two approaches that can be taken to avoid uninterested "searchers": over-specification to exclude all other meanings of ambiguous key phrases; and explicit exclusion of some expressions, called negative key phrases.

Over-specification would simply involve selecting long enough and specific enough key phrases so that all ambiguity is removed. This can lead to an explosion of key phrases, many of which may never occur. Finding all possible specific key phrases could be an exhaustive task. Managing all these key phrases could become cumbersome; but worst of all, interested "searchers" who use the ambiguous terms may not see the advertisement.

Negative key phrases refer to phrases that suggest that a "searcher" is not interested in the product. Thus, in the case of an ambiguous query the advertisement should be shown; but if any negative keywords are present in the query, then the advertisement should not be shown. Negative keywords are a basic function of internet advertising platforms such as Adwords by Google.

There are two types of negative keywords: negative emotions and negative meanings. Negative emotion keywords indicate a "searcher" has negative feelings about the product. Negative meaning refers to unrelated alternate senses of a keyword. Consider for example if you were selling Toyota Corollas (a car). You would likely bid on the word "Corolla" in hopes of attracting a customer. Some negative emotional keywords might be "lemon" or "defects", which suggest the "searcher" has negative sentiments regarding the vehicle. A negative sense keyword might be "flower", which strongly suggests the "searcher" is interested in flower petals (corollas) and not the car.

Our goal is to develop an automated method for selecting negative keywords for an advertising campaign. Automated selection of negative keywords would reduce the effort required to set up such the campaign. In this paper we do not address negative emotion words; we focus solely on identifying negative sense keywords for ambiguous key phrases. It should be noted that negative key phrases are frequently single words, but they can be composed of multiple words.

In section 2 we describe the past research which has guided our work. In Section 3 we describe the method for selecting negative keywords. Section 4 is our evaluation of the method using data from our industrial partner. Section 5 presents our conclusions.

2 Background

Our inspiration for identifying negative keywords comes from word sense disambiguation (WSD) literature (Navigli, 2009). Mihalcea (2007) describes a method for using Wikipedia as a sense inventory and as an annotated corpus for word sense disambiguation. Mihalcea considers each Wikipedia article (or page) as a sense and links as annotated examples of that sense. Each link provides an annotated realization of the sense. In this way, Wikipedia may be considered a partially-labelled corpus and a word sense inventory.

It seems natural to consider the text of an article as related or context words, instead we use the text in the paragraphs containing links to an article as contexts. In other words, instead of using the definition and description as context (Lesk, 1986; Pedersen, 2002), the words around realizations of a sense are used as context.

Wikipedia seems a good choice of sense inventory and corpus for our task, because it is a broad resource covering many topics and specialized domain terms; also it is constantly being updated with modern terms and information, thus already being adapted to new potential advertising topics. Our current Wikipedia index has over 10 million senses and about 50 million annotated examples.

Our system is intended for use with Google Adwords. Google defined negative keywords in the following way[1]:

> Negative keywords are a core component of a successful keyword list. Adding a negative keyword to your ad group or campaign means that your ads won't show for searches containing that term. By filtering out unwanted impressions, negative keywords can help you reach the most appropriate prospects, reduce your cost-per-click (CPC), and increase your ROI [Return on Investment].

Wordstream[2] provides an interactive tool for selecting negative keywords; a user interactively selects a few positive and negative keywords which bootstrap the process. A 2010 US patent Application (20100185661) uses a variety of historic campaign performance information to select negative keywords. Our method is fully automatic and is intended to setup new campaigns (no historic information is required).

[1] http://adwords.google.com/support/aw/bin/answer.py?hl=en&answer=63235

[2] http://www.wordstream.com/negative-keywords

3 Method

The basic concept behind our negative keyword generation system is to create context vectors for all senses of an ambiguous key phrases, then to identify components of the context vectors which correlate highly with negative senses and poorly with the positive sense. This is not complete WSD, since the concern is only explicitly identifying one sense, while all other senses are grouped together as negative senses.

The basic steps of the algorithm are shown in Figure 1, while sections 3.1-3.5 describe each step in more detail.

The method can be applied to a set of positive key phrases or to a single key phrase; most steps only consider a single key phrase at a time, but step 4 is intended to improve processing of sets of key phrases. When processing a set of key phrases steps 1-3 are executed for all key phrases, and then step 4 uses all the resulting information.

3.1 Finding all the senses for a key phrase

Given a positive key phrase, we find all possible senses (Wikipedia articles). To do this, we find all the links containing the key phrase. Then from those links, we collect all the final destination pages, also accounting for redirected pages. The set of destination pages for the key phrase is considered the set of possible senses; each sense includes a frequency metric, that is the number of links to the page that used the given key phrase. To optimize this step, we created an indexed database table of all the links in Wikipedia. We recommend flattening this table by storing not just the link destinations, but, if the destination page is a redirect, the redirected destination page.

Consider the keyword "Corolla"; imagine that the word "Corolla" appears in links on pages A, B, C, D. The links on pages A, B and C go to the Toyota Corolla article, while the links on page D go to flower petals. Thus for Corolla the possible senses are Toyota Corolla and flower petal, with frequencies of 3 and 1 respectively.

3.2 Generating context vectors for each sense

Our context vectors are generated from all unigrams (though larger n-grams can be considered) in all paragraphs containing links to a possible

Figure 1: Algorithm for selecting negative keywords

1. Find all the senses for a key phrase
   (a) Get all pages referred to by links containing the key phrase.
2. Generate context vectors for each sense
   (a) Find all links referring to this sense;
   (b) Create a vector of words appearing in the paragraph containing the referencing link.
3. Identify the intended sense
   (a) If only one sense exists, mark it as the intended sense;
   (b) else use the most frequent sense or context vector comparison to select the intended sense.
4. Create a broad-scope intended-sense list
   (a) Collect all intended senses for a collection of key phrases (usually key phrases are from an ad group or campaign).
5. Find negative key phrases
   (a) Assign tf-idf values to words (components) in the context vector;
   (b) Divide all related senses between two lists: intended and unintended senses;
   (c) Find the words from the context vectors of the unintended senses that have the highest tf-idf and that do not appear in the context vectors of the indented senses.

sense. In other words, for each possible sense we use the database table of all the links to find all the pages referring to a particular sense. We then tokenize each of the paragraphs containing a link to the sense being considered. All the words are recorded and counted as a dimension in the vector.

Continuing our previous example, imagine a Toyota Corolla article also has references on pages X and Y (perhaps the link text is "Toyota small car"); while the flower petal article is referred to on page Z (with link text "flower petals"). We would generate a context vector for Toyota Corolla from pages A, B, C, X, and Y; and a context vector for flower petal from pages D and Z. Generating the context vector simply involves counting the words, in the paragraphs where the links appears.

3.3 Identifying the Intended Sense

There are many ways that the intended sense can be assigned, depending on the resources available. WSD could be applied to an example context if one is available; in our case examples are likely the ads from the advertising campaign.

A simple WSD method that can be used when no examples are available is selecting the most frequent sense of the key phrase; this can be determined using the frequency information from step 1. We found that this method works quite well when multiple key phrases are being processed because step 4 will compensate for a few mislabeled senses. When examples are available, another simple WSD method is to compare the context vectors of a sense to the example contexts (in our case advertisements) and choose the sense with the most similar vector.

3.4 Creating a broad-scope intended-sense list

This step is only relevant if multiple key phrases are being processed. This step requires all intended senses for all key phrases. We collect all the intended senses of all key phrases into what we call the broad scope intended sense list. There are a number of cases where a key phrase may have more than one intended sense, using this method we collect all the intended senses and avoid blocking secondary intended senses.

False positive senses will generate unwanted impressions, which are undesirable, but false negative senses are more problematic because an ad may not be shown to the intended audience. There are often multiple positive key phrases assigned to any single sense and thus, by collecting all the intended senses, we reduce the risk of assigning a false negative sense. We observed that, even if a single key phrase is mislabeled (in our case due to choosing the most frequent sense), the correct label was consistently identified by other keywords.

Furthermore, the collection of these senses could be used with clustering or other techniques that might reveal additional senses that should have been considered. These additional senses may even provide new positive key phrases.

Consider setting up an advertising campaign for Toyota Vehicles. A small selection of key phrases that might be used in this campaign is: "Corolla", "Sienna", "Toyota minivan". If each key phrase was assigned the following senses, respectively, then the broad scope intended sense list would be: "Toyota Corolla", "Sienna Miller", "Toyota Sienna". "Sienna Miller" (an actress) is in fact a mislabeled sense, but due to other keywords, the correct sense has been included in the broad scope intended sense list, thus avoiding a false negative.

3.5 Finding negative key phrases

We divide all senses of a positive key phrase into two sets of senses: the positive set (anything in the broad scope sense list), and the negative set (everything else). We evaluate all components of the context vectors from all senses: first we evaluate the components (unigram, bigram, etc.) using tf-idf (Salton, 1989), where *tf* is simply the frequency from Step 1 and *idf* has been precalculated from the Wikipedia corpus. We then select the N highest valued (tf-idf) components above a minimum threshold, from the negative set, and then confirm that each component either never appears as a component in the positive set, or that the positive set tf-idf is below a choosen threshold.

4 Evaluation

We used existing campaign data from our industrial partner as test data. We generated lists of negative keywords for the key phrases in an existing ad campaign. We could not consider the existing negative keyword lists from the campaign as a gold standard because they were incomplete, for only a few topics; they also contained intentional misspellings (something that this system does not consider); they contained negative keywords that were related to user intention instead of meaning (such as car rentals instead of purchases); and they contained a few emotional negative keywords indicating that the audience had negative sentiments towards the focus of the ad.

Thus, we used a number of ad hoc tests to determine the effectiveness of our system. First, we examined the results for any obvious patterns or flaws. We discuss these impressions and considerations in the subjective evaluation. To empirically and more objectively evaluate the effectiveness of our negative keyword selection, we collected metrics from Google's Adwords evaluation tools; these are discussed in the empirical evaluation. Table 1 summarizes both the empirical and subjective evaluation.

4.1 Subjective Evaluation

In table 1, all of the negative keywords for "Toyota Sienna" are strongly associated with some topic other than "Toyota Sienna", "minivans", etc. Most of them refer to people or groups. This is probably the nature of the word "Sienna", which is normally a proper name. It should be noted that "Miller" does not appear in the list, even though it would be an effective negative keyword removing the sense "Sienna Miller". It would in fact rank higher than our current number 1, but due to an error in the overly simple sense disambiguation method "Sienna Miller" was consider a correct sense, along with "Toyota Sienna".

In table 1, the top ten negative keywords for "Corolla" refer almost entirely to a single topic: the "flower petals". "Corolla" is not a common word and thus this was probably one of the only alternative senses. Neither "Corolla petals" nor "corolla flowers" were frequent enough to be listed in the Google traffic estimator. All our searches for these terms produced "Toyota Corolla" advertisements, even though none of the top articles were about Toyota Corollas.

4.2 Empirical Evaluation

We limited our empirical evaluation to the top 10 negative results for 5 positive keywords. Our first empirical evaluation was against the existing negative keywords from the campaign, but only 2 of the 50 negative keywords existed in the list, though a small number of thematic correlations existed. The choice of words were different, but often words with similar senses were present. The generated negative keyword list provided a number of senses not covered under the original campaign list.

We collected the following metrics from the Google Adwords evaluation tool for each pair of positive and negative key phrases:

1. How many of the top ten search results were related (in any way) to a positive sense. We hoped to evaluate whether the key phrases were in fact highly correlated with a positive or negative sense.

2. What was the estimated monthly search frequency for the combined positive and negative key phrase pairs. This would help determine the effectiveness or utility of the negative key phrases.

3. Were the campaign ads (or very closely related ads) shown or not. This would determine whether these key phrases would be beneficial to the campaign.

Positive	**Negative**	Freq.	Top Ten	Ad
Corolla	petals	0	10	•
Corolla	flowers	260	10	
Corolla	sepals	0	10	•
Corolla	flower	880	10	
Corolla	centimeters	0	9	•
Corolla	stamens	0	10	•
Corolla	species	0	10	
Corolla	flowering	0	10	
Corolla	fruit	0	10	•
Corolla	calochortus	0	10	•
Corolla	erect	0	10	•
Avalon	b0e0e6	0	10	
Avalon	webcomic	58	10	
Avalon	frankie	22200	10	
Avalon	newfoundland	1300	10	
Avalon	ranavalona	0	10	
Avalon	avalonia	0	10	
Avalon	peninsula	1900	10	
Avalon	arthur	2400	10	
Avalon	mists	27100	10	
Avalon	funicello	880	10	
Avalon	laurentia	0	10	
Highlander	league	260	10	
Highlander	baseball	0	10	○
Highlander	sox	0	10	○
Highlander	scottish	2900	10	
Highlander	highlands	390	10	
Highlander	pitcher	0	10	•
Highlander	team	320	10	
Highlander	nyy	0	10	•
Highlander	player	0	10	
Highlander	boston	0	2	•
Highlander	dodgers	0	7	
Sienna	guillory	74000	10	
Sienna	edward	0	7	
Sienna	louis	0	8	
Sienna	france	0	10	
Sienna	emperor	0	10	
Sienna	pope	0	10	
Sienna	burnt	8100	10	
Sienna	samuel	0	10	
Sienna	jackson	110	5	
Sienna	bargagagli	0	7/7	○
Sienna	hollzman	0	10	
Tacoma	he	0	10	•
Tacoma	rainiers	14800	10	
Tacoma	soccer	2900	10	
Tacoma	season	0	10	○
Tacoma	airport	18100	10	○
Tacoma	league	0	10	○
Tacoma	bridge	40500	10	
Tacoma	indoor	0	10	•
Tacoma	mariners	0	10	
Tacoma	dome	33100	10	
Tacoma	seattle	40500	10	

Table 1: Empirical evaluation of results.

The top ten search results for 44 of the 50 evaluated key phrase pairs were entirely about the negative topics. There were only two cases where at least half of the top ten results were related to a positive sense. This suggests that the system generally provides negative key phrases that are not correlated with the positive senses.

21 key phrase pairs had an estimated search frequency of over a hundred times a month. 8 of the 50 pairs were estimated to be searched tens of thousands of times each month. The existing campaign could save over a hundred thousand impressions to uninterested costumers using our negative keyword list. This metric also showed that about half of our keywords were either for infrequent topics or just infrequent terms; perhaps the estimated monthly search frequency should somehow be considered in the Step 5 where negative keywords are selected using tf-idf. It should be noted that negative key phrases do not cost the advertiser and thus adding infrequent key phrases is

not harmful.

12 of the 50 key phrase pairs triggered ads from our campaign and 20 of the 50 had ads closely related to our campaign. Thus, there are situations where an unintended audience is shown the ad. Note that there seems to be an inverse relation between the estimated number of searches per month and the presentation of the ads in negative contexts. We believe Google Adwords has already implemented some form of sense disambiguation for frequently-searched key phrases; it seems that frequently-searched negative senses for ads are already filtered out. Even if Google may have such a system in place, the addition of negative key phrases does not cost a campaign, may be of assistance on other advertising platforms, and safeguards against any failure of Google's system.

Table 1 shows a selection of the raw data from our evaluation. The first column indicates the positive keyword for which the negative keyword was generated. The second column is the generated negative keyword. The third column represents the estimated monthly search frequency. The fourth column indicates how many of the the top search results, when searching for the positive and the negative keywords together, were unrelated to the intended positive topic; a result of 10 indicates the results are completely unrelated to the positive topic. Please note that all the positive topics here refer to automobiles from Toyota. The last column is marked with a bullet (•) if a campaign ad was shown, a circle (○) if a related ad was shown, and left empty if all the ads were unrelated to the positive topic. A bullet means impressions are likely given to the wrong audience, while no bullet is ideal to the advertiser.

5 Conclusions

We conclude that our system for negative key phrase generation using Wikipedia effectively finds negative topics, finds words strongly correlated with negative topics, and can improve internet advertising campaigns. Yet we must again state that it seems Google Adwords does not (at least partially) show unintended ads for frequently searched terms.

While we have mentioned that Wikipedia is a broad sense inventory covering many domains, it still has a number of lexical limitations in very specific domains. We observed that with a few very domain specific acronyms and terms (such as names of US government regulations), there was either no appropriate sense or no realization of a particular key phrase.

This paper presented one component of an automated system for configuring internet advertising campaigns. Other components include key phrase extraction and generation for advertisements, grouping (clustering) of keywords and advertisements, and optimization by automated analysis of historic campaign performance.

Further research could include improving Step 4 to identify additional senses through sense clustering. This effort may be combined with keyword generation (selection of non extractive keywords) another component of our industrial partnership.

Future work may include research into better evaluation methods for negative keyword selection. Ironically, evaluation methods may ascribe an estimated value about the effectiveness of a negative key phrase, and thus the evaluation may in turn be a selection method.

Acknowledgments

This research was a joint project between Apption Software Inc.[3] and the University of Ottawa, funded through Natural Sciences and Engineering Research Council of Canada (NSERC). Thank you to Shahzad Khan, Shane Daniel, and Chris Fournier for their help and discussions on this project.

References

M Lesk. 1986. Automatic sense disambiguation using machine readable dictionaries: how to tell a pine cone from an ice cream cone. *Proceedings of the 5th annual international conference on Systems documentation*, Jan.

R Mihalcea. 2007. Using wikipedia for automatic word sense disambiguation. *Proceedings of NAACL HLT*, Jan.

R Navigli. 2009. Word sense disambiguation: A survey. *ACM Computing Surveys (CSUR)*, Jan.

T Pedersen. 2002. A baseline methodology for word sense disambiguation. *Lecture Notes In Computer Science*, Jan.

G Salton. 1989. Automatic text processing. *Addison-Wesley Longman Publishing Co., Inc. Boston, MA, USA ©1988*, Jan.

[3]http://www.apption.com

Establishing Implementation Priorities in Aiding Writers of Controlled Crisis Management Texts

Irina Temnikova
Research Institute in Information and Language Processing
University of Wolverhampton, UK
irina.temnikova@gmail.com

Abstract

As clarity in the Crisis Management domain is crucial, and there exists an enormous amount of Crisis Management documents, a specific language resource (the Controlled Language for Crisis Management, CLCM) for editing Crisis Management instructions in English has been previously developed. Based on a specially designed controlled language evaluation experiment, we have determined that manual simplification, far from being easy, is an extremely time-consuming process and thus automatization is essential in order to facilitate the writing of clear instructions. This article describes this experiment which also aims to determine which operations should be privileged and are more urgent to be implemented in order to address the most critical issues first.

1 Introduction

Attention paid to the Crisis Management domain has strongly increased in recent years (Schneid and Collins, 2001), due to the urgent need to guarantee safe and efficient management of emergency situations. There exists an enormous amount of already written crisis management documents and new ones are being created with exponentially growing speed. Efficient communication between crisis management teams and local populations is crucial in situations in which there is a very short reaction time (Ogrizek and Guillery, 1999; Winerman, 2009). It is also known that human comprehension under stress is different from the one in normal conditions (Kiwan et al., 1999). For this reason the clarity and conciseness of the information exchanged during emergency situations is crucial. A controlled language (CL) is a very good manual approach for ensuring clarity of crisis management texts. Unfortunately, it has been previously shown (Goyvaerts, 1996; Huijsen, 1998) that manual editing of texts according to controlled language guidelines is a difficult and highly time-consuming process. Natural Language Processing (NLP) techniques are thus a good way to at least partially automatize and thus improve and speed up manual text simplification. This article introduces a controlled language for text simplification in the crisis management domain and its evaluation in terms of time and cognitive efforts for the human simplifiers and draws conclusions about which operations to implement first, in order to speed up and facilitate manual controlled language-based simplification. The article is structured as follows: Section 2 presents the related work in the crisis management domain and in Controlled Languages aids, Section 3 presents the Controlled Language for Crisis Management (CLCM), Section 4 describes the text simplification evaluation experiment, Section 5 discusses the results of the experiment and Section 6 provides some conclusions and future work.

2 Related Work

Although the large recent activity in crisis management, there are not many NLP works in this domain. Roman (2008) has worked on redundancy identification from personal web blogs on emergency topics. Ireson (2009) has worked in Information Extraction in detection and monitoring of emergency events from open discussion forums. During the project EPIC, managed by the University of Colorado at Boulder and the University of California, some work was done in the extraction of important information relevant to mass emergencies signaled in Twitter (Corvey et al., 2010). In medical crisis management, Chapman et al. (2005) have applied NLP approaches to syndromic surveillance in order to obtain free text classification of chief complaints. As the existing NLP approaches deal mainly with emergencies detection, this is the first known attempt to process text simplicity of instructions delivered to the general population during mass emergencies. In terms of controlled languages, CLCM is the first controlled language for English for this domain. The existing NLP tools for controlled language simplification are Controlled Language Editors (CLEs) and Controlled Language Checkers (CLCs). The CLEs are used in order to facilitate writing text according to controlled Language specifications, while the CLCs – to check whether an already created text is written in accordance with the controlled language rules. Compagnon LiSe is an example of a very simple CLE that facilitates writing sentences according to the controlled language rules but does not apply any NLP techniques. It has been developed for the French version of CLCM (Renahy et al., 2010). Two other CLEs have been developed for the machine-oriented controlled languages PENG and ACE (Schwitter, 2008; Kuhn, 2009). Mitamura and Nyberg (2001) have developed the KANT controlled language re-writing system which checks compliance with a machine translation-oriented controlled language. This article aims to assist with the initial design of an NLP-based CLCM Editing Aid, in order to facilitate text simplification in the crisis management domain.

3 The Controlled Language for Crisis Management

The Controlled Language for Crisis Management has been adapted to English on the basis of a controlled language for French (Renahy, 2009) in the context of MESSAGE Project[1]. As a result of MESSAGE, four controlled languages for different European languages have been developed (French, Spanish, Polish and English), together with two prototypes for Modern Greek and Bulgarian (Temnikova and Margova, 2009). CLCM has been developed on the basis of a collected corpus of crisis management documents, amounting to over 2.5 million words and collected from the web.

The existing version of CLCM applies only to instructions for the general public (GP), as these are considered to be the documents which most need simplification, as their audience members are not trained specialists. Although covering different topics, these instructions have high document structure and language similarity, which allowed the development of a specific CL tailored to them. The role of CLCM is two-fold: on one hand to provide rules for the efficient simplification of existing crisis management documents, and on the other hand - to provide rules for writing new crisis management documents. CLCM is easily transferable to other domains' documents, containing instructions.

[1]http://message-project.univ-fcomte.fr/ Accessed 12 May 2011.

In_L_05: Keep preposition and verb together in phrasal verbs.

~~*Switch the lights off.*~~	*Switch off* the lights.

Explanation: Preposition and verb separated by many words create difficulties for both non native speakers and machine translation engines.

Figure 1: Example of a CLCM rule.

The CLCM features thirty pages of over eighty simplification rules, which address different text aspects, starting from general text structure and ending with punctuation, as well as different document elements (titles, conditions, instructions, lists). Below are provided examples of some of the existing rule types and in Figure 1 - a screenshot of a rule taken from the CLCM guidelines:

- General: If there are distinguished situations:
  - Identify the specific situations.
  - Divide the blocks of instructions regarding the specific situations into subsections.
  - Write first the most specific situation.
  - Write the next more general situation.
  - End with the most general situation.
- Formatting: Separate with a new line each block of instructions.
- Lexical: Use only words defined in the dictionary.
- Syntactic: Avoid passive voice
- Punctuation: Avoid any punctuation signs at the end of the titles.

As can be seen from Figure 1, each rule has a reference number which is formed by: the type of document ("In" = "instructions"), a number of rules are document type-specific; the type of rule ("L" = "lexical"); and a standard number. Also below each rule is shown an example of how text should not look according to this rule (stroke through) and how it should look instead. Sometimes below these illustrative examples less important information is provided, as for example an explanation of why the rule is necessary. Previously two experiments have been conducted in order to evaluate CLCM. One experiment evaluated the impact of the controlled language on human translation (Temnikova and Orasan, 2009), while the second experiment evaluated the impact of the controlled language simplification on machine translation (Temnikova and Orasan, 2009; Temnikova, 2010). These experiments have shown that although CLCM was written for human readers, it had a significant impact on and improved the results of both human and machine translation.

4 Description of the Evaluation Experiment

The aim of the experiment carried out was to evaluate the quality of the CLCM guidelines. The experiment consisted in asking six linguists - English advanced and native speakers with a computational linguistics background, to read carefully and familiarise themselves with the CLCM simplification guidelines and to simplify manually four texts of a total of two thousand words according to the simplification rules in these guidelines. In order to direct the participants and simplify their task in remembering over eighty rules, an assisting leaflet was provided. The leaflet contained the thirty most important rules to be consulted during simplification. The rules in the leaflet were classified into three natural language generation-like groups:

1. Rules for discourse structure organisation at text level;
2. Rules for discourse structure organisation at paragraph level;
3. Concrete linguistic realization rules.

The experiment was performed in two stages distributed over two days to avoid the impact of the factor of tiredness. The four texts were taken from the previously collected Crisis Management Corpus and represent instructions for the general population in different emergency situations: precautions to be taken after a flood, instructions how to clean chemicals from clothing, actions to be taken after volcanic eruptions. Time is measured during the first time reading guidelines and during the manual simplification of each text. Table 1 shows the text lengths per text for each day of the experiment calculated in words.

Day	**Text**	**Words**	**Chars**
Day 1	Text 1	166	900
	Text 2	833	5018
Total	**Day 1**	**999**	**5918**
Day 2	Text 3	271	1562
	Text 4	728	4486
Total	**Day 2**	**999**	**6048**
Total	**Day 1 and 2**	**1998**	**11966**

Table 1: Lengths of texts used for the CLCM guidelines evaluation.

As can be seen from the Table 1, the first two columns show which texts were presented to the participants each day while the last two columns provide the text lengths in words and in characters. A text complexity analysis of the four original texts was run, by examining the main text complexity features according to literature. The results of this analysis are provided in Table 2.

Text	**SL**	**WL**	**SM**	**LD**	**WS**
Text 1	12.69	4.24	3.64	0.50	11.48
Text 2	16.76	4.94	4.67	0.42	8.08
Text 3	14.83	4.68	5.62	0.39	7.95
Text 4	14.74	5.03	4.87	0.44	8.86

Table 2: Text Complexity analysis of the four texts.

In Table 2, the first column contains the text reference number, while the following five columns - the text complexity features they have been analysed for, namely:

- SL - average sentence length, measured in number of words;
- WL - average word length, measured in number of letters;
- SM - percentage of subordinating markers;
- LD - lexical diversity, measured as types/tokens ratio;
- WS - average number of word senses per word

In order to do this text complexity analysis, the texts were pre-processed using Connexor parser [2]

[2]www.connexor.eu Accessed 12 May 2011.

and WordNet (Fellbaum, 1998) was used for calculating the average number of senses per word.

At the end of the second day, the participants were asked to fill in a questionnaire asking details regarding the work they had done in the previous two days. The questionnaire collected data in three parts - Part 1 was asking for personal comments in the form of free text, Part 2 was providing a list of rules to be evaluated in terms of how difficult they are to be applied, while Part 3 was suggesting a list of implementations to be rated. The personal comments in the first part of the questionnaire were requested by the following question: "Could you think of what was most difficult for you while simplifying?". The rules, provided in the second part were those thirty most important rules, contained in the assisting leaflet. The participants were asked to write next to each rule whether it was easy or difficult to apply and mark those ones which, if automated, would speed up their work. The suggested implementations in Part 3 were offering preliminary easy-to-implement operations which would result in highlighting different text elements. The text elements to be highlighted ranged from single words to whole paragraphs and were CLCM-specific. The participants were asked to give scores to these operations, according to the following ranking: 1 - Implementing this operation will not help at all; 2 - Implementing this operation will help to a certain extent; 3 - Implementing this operation will help very much.

Additionally, most of the participants provided useful feedback on the design of the experiment and the future implementation, thanks to their NLP background.

5 Results of the Experiment

The analysis of the results of the experiment provided useful information about the internal process of manual simplification of texts according to the CLCM rules and shows that text simplification is not a trivial task, even when precise guidelines are provided. The analysis of the times and speed for reading the guidelines show that the average time for reading the guidelines for the first time was between 30 to 45 minutes. The speeds for simplifying manually the texts are given in Table 3.

The first column of Table 3 indicates the participant, while the next four columns - the four texts. The values in the table are given in characters/minute, in order to take into consideration the different length of texts. Obviously, although the value of Subject 2 is the outlier of the sample. can be clearly seen that the speed ranges between 18.7 to 358.4 characters per minute, depending on the text complexity and the subject. I.e. the speed difference is 20 times. Even if a clear learning effect is visible from the data, it is still clear that simplifying text takes a large amount of time. The table also provides the mean and standard deviation values with and without the outlier. Row "mean 6" provides the mean values of all six participants, together with the outlier, while row "mean 5" - only of the five participants, excluding the outlier. In a similar way, row "st.dev. 6" provides the standard deviation values of all six participants, while row "st.dev. 5" the standard deviations without the outlier. The standard deviation values excluding Subject 2 decreases significantly, for example, for Text 2 from 120.4 to 14.9.

Subject	Text 1	Text 2	Text 3	Text 4
Sub1	21.9	69.7	71.0	203.9
Sub2	75.0	**358.4**	173.6	263.9
Sub3	30.0	47.8	78.1	149.5
Sub4	30.0	83.6	97.6	121.2
Sub5	**18.7**	52.3	33.9	48.2
Sub6	33.3	72.7	67.9	115.0
mean 6	**34.8**	**114.1**	**86.5**	**150.3**
st.dev. 6	**18.7**	**110.0**	**43.0**	**68.7**
mean 5	**26.8**	**65.2**	**69.7**	**127.6**
st.dev. 5	**5.5**	**13.3**	**20.7**	**50.6**

Table 3: Manual simplifying speed per subject and per text, measured in characters per minute.

Another demonstration of the fact that manual simplification is not a trivial task is the results provided by the questionnaire the language experts were asked to fill in at the end of the second day. The aim of this questionnaire was to determine which rules were most difficult to apply and which simplification operations would need to be automatized. As mentioned before, the questionnaire was composed of three parts: Part 1 containing personal comments in free text, Part 2 containing the list of the thirty main rules to be evaluated as "easy"/"difficult" to be manually applied and whether to be implemented or not and Part 3 containing a list of suggested implementations to be ranked as "will not help at all"/"will help to a certain extent"/"will help very much". Surprisingly, most of the subjects have very similar personal comments in answering the question, posed in Part 1 "Could you think of what was most difficult for you while simplifying?". The answers were put in a common table and were given a mark "1" if a Subject has mentioned it in the free comments and "0" if not. The marks were added and averages were obtained. In this way, the top four results were, ordered from the one with the highest score to the one with the lowest score:

- Avoiding negatives/Re-phrasing negative phrases.
- Remembering to remove pronouns/Avoiding pronouns.
- Being mindful of word difficulty/Replacing technical terms.
- Re-organizing and re-grouping the content of the original.

In Part 2, the marks were given different weights in the following way:

- "no answer" or "easy" = 0
- "simplify" = 1
- "moderate" = 1.5
- "difficult" = 2
- "difficult" and "simplify" = 3
- "very difficult" = 4
- "very difficult" and "simplify" = 5

As the participants have used different combinations of marks, the conclusive marks have been given weights in correspondence with the apparent ranks of the different marks. The results of Questionnaire Part 2 were added and averages were obtained. The top twelve results are shown in the Table 4.

Table 4 has two columns, the first one indicating the CLCM rule, while the second one - the average score, obtained after adding the scores, provided by the participants. "N" stands for "noun", while "V" stands for "verb". The top ten results of Part 3 are given in Table 5. The results were again added and averages were ordered from the highest to the lowest one.

Table 5 is composed, like Table 4, by two columns. The first column contains the suggested implementations, while the second column – the average scores, obtained by adding the participant scores and dividing them per number of participants. The top results confirm that the rules found more difficult to apply manually by participants are those which are tackling cognitively hard to process linguistic phenomena (negation, passive, ambiguity). This makes an NLP application a good solution to the aforementioned problems.

Rule	**Score**
Try to avoid negative forms	3
Replace passive with active voice	2.17
Avoid any pronouns (person., poss., demonst.)	2
Avoid ambiguous words	1.83
Replace idiomatic expressions with literal ones	1.83
Replace techn. terms with common synonyms	1.83
Order instructions in logic. and chronol. order	1.67
If 2+ complem. determ. the same N, repeat the N	1.67
Write only one action per line	1.67
If a prep./adj. refers to 2+ N, repeat the prep/adj.	1.67
Use standard word order	1.67
Place conditions before instructions	1.5

Table 4: Questionnaire Part 2 results.

Rule	**Score**
Highlighting the ambiguous lexical terms	2.67
Highlighting the phrasal verbs	2.5
Highlighting the separate thematic situations	2.5
Highlighting the negative phrases	2.33
Highlighting the ambiguous syntact. expressions	2.33
Highlighting the technical terms	2.33
Highlighting the beginning of instructions	2.17
Highlighting the beginning of conditions	2.17
Highlighting the beginning of explanations	2.17
Highlighting the acronyms and abbreviations	2.17

Table 5: Questionnaire Part 3 results.

6 Conclusions and Future Work

The analysis of the results of the experiment shows that human simplifiers employ too much time in simplifying even short texts and thus simplifying is not a trivial task. More particularly, the results collected from the questionnaire show that the simplifiers mostly agreed on the set of difficult rules and on the set of suggested implementations. Future work will include cognitively analysing rules' formulations before proceeding with any NLP implementation. For example the rule "Avoid negative forms" may be difficult to apply, as which negative forms to avoid are not concretely defined in the guidelines. Otherwise NLP techniques may be applied in a way to perform negative forms recognition and suggestion of alternative positive forms. While some of the suggested implementations could be solved by an appropriate training, others, such as "highlight in the text the phrasal verbs in case the main verb and the preposition are split up" cannot and would help to be implemented. On the basis of the conclusions drawn from this very useful experiment, future work will be to apply some of the suggested implementations and to find automatic solutions to the highest ranked manual rules as first steps towards a high-level NLP-based Controlled Language Editing Aid. As "avoiding negatives" was listed as first choice in Part 1 and Part 2 and also had one of the highest scores in Part 3, we choose it as the most urgent issue to be solved and possibly implemented. Negation implementation would include constructing patterns for recognizing negation to avoid in emergency instructions, based on the collected corpus and building a grammar to help supplying the user with positive alternatives to negated phrases. Another candidate for implementation is, of course, "Highlighting the ambiguous lexical terms", which has emerged as the suggested implementation with the highest ranking score (2.67). Future work would also include testing whether more appropriate training of human simplifiers would change the rules considered difficult to apply.

References

Chapman, W.W., et al. (2005) *Classifying free-text triage chief complaints into syndromic categories with natural language processing.* Artif Intell Med. 2005 Jan; 33(1):31-40.

Corvey, W. J., Vieweg, S., Rood, T. and Palmer, M. (2010) *Twitter in Mass Emergency: What NLP Techniques can Contribute.* In Proceedings of the NAACL HLT 2010 Workshop on Computational Linguistics in a World of Social Media (Los Angeles, California, June 2010), 2324.

Fellbaum, C. (1998) *WordNet: an Electronic Lexical Database* MIT Press.

Goyvaerts P. (1996) *Controlled English, curse or blessing? A users perspective.* Proceedings of CLAW 1996.

Huijsen, W.O. (1998) *Controlled Language An Introduction.* Proceedings of the Second International Workshop on Controlled Language Applications. Pitsburgh, Pennsylvania.

Ireson, N. (2009) *Local Community Situation Awareness During an Emergency.* Proceedings of the IEEE International Conference on Digital Ecosystems and Technologies (IEEE-DEST 2009).

Kiwan, D., Ahmed, A. and Pollitt, A. (1999) *The effects of text comprehension and performance in examinations.* Proceedings of BPS London Conference, December, 1999.

Kuhn, T. (2009) *Controlled English for Knowledge Representation. Ph.D. Thesis.* University of Zurich, Switzerland.

Mitamura, T. and Nyberg, E. (2001) *Automatic rewriting for controlled language translation.* Proceedings of the NLPRS-2001 Workshop on Automatic Paraphrasing: Theories and Applications. Tokyo, Japan. Pages 1-12.

Ogrizek, M. and Guillery, J-M. (1999) *Communicating in crisis.* Transaction Publishers.

Quirk, R., Greenbaum, S., Leech, G., Svartvik, J. (1985) *A comprehensive grammar of the English language.* Harlow: Longman. Pp. 1779.

Renahy J. (2009) *Controlled Languages: a Scientific Popularization through the Example of the Controlled Language "LiSe".* ISMTCL Proceedings, International Review Bulag, pp 215-222.

Renahy, J. et al. (2010) *Development and Evaluation of a Controlled Language and of a computerized writing assistant LiSe to improve the quality and safety of medical protocols.* International Forum on Quality and Safety of Health Care. 20-23 April 2010, The Nice Acropolis, Nice, France.

Roman, J.H., et al. (2008) *Reducing information overload in emergencies by detecting themes in Web content.* Proceedings of the 5th International ISCRAM Conference 2008;101-6.

Schneid, T.D. and Collins, L. (2001) *Disaster management and preparedness.* Lewis Publishers.

Schwitter, R. (2008) *A Controlled Natural Language for the Semantic Web.* Journal of Intelligent Systems, 17, pp.125-141.

Temnikova, I. (2010) *A Cognitive Evaluation Approach for a Controlled Language Post-Editing Experiment.* Proceedings of the International Conference "Language Resources and Evaluation" (LREC2010), Valletta, Malta.

Temnikova, I. and Margova, R. (2009) *Towards a Controlled Language in Crisis Management: The Case of Bulgarian.* Proceedings of the International Symposium on Data and Sense Mining, Machine Translation and Controlled Languages (ISMTCL), Besancon, France, July 1-3, 2009.

Temnikova, I. and Orasan, C. (2009) *Post-editing Experiments with MT for a Controlled Language.* Proceedings of the International Symposium on Data and Sense Mining, Machine Translation and Controlled Languages (ISMTCL), Besancon, France, July 1-3, 2009.

Winerman, L. (2009) *Crisis Communication.* Nature, vol. 457, p 376.

TechWatchTool: Innovation and Trend Monitoring

Hong Li **Feiyu Xu** **Hans Uszkoreit**

German Research Center for Artificial Intelligence (DFKI), LT-Lab
Alt-Moabit 91c, 10559 Berlin, Germany
{lihong,feiyu,uszkoreit}@dfki.de
http://www.dfki.de/lt/

Abstract

In this paper we present an information service system that allows users to search for the key players of requested technology areas and for their collaboration networks. This system utilizes information extraction and wrapper technologies for detecting persons, organizations, publications and patents as well as relationships among them. Furthermore, it applies relation extraction to detect statements on the web that indicate innovation trends. Various visualization methods are provided to let users monitor key players, their networks and technology trends in a comfortable way.

1 Introduction

The innovation cycle of technologies is getting shorter and shorter. In recent years, many companies became aware of the potential of advanced information technologies for the efficient discovery and analysis of useful information in large volumes of online data such as business news, business reports, scientific publications and patents. Exploring patents or publications is an important approach to analyzing the trends of technology development. Therefore, several systems emerged recently, which attempt to describe and predict the technology development trend based on the analysis of patents or publications (e.g., (Yoon and Park, 2004), illumin8 system[1], Google Trends[2](Rech, 2007), BlogPulse[3] (Glance et al., 2004) and Collexis[4]). Most available systems are mainly based on a combination of statistical methods and string match. There is still a big potential to apply language technologies to this task.

In this paper, we present a system named TECHWATCHTOOL[5], that has already been successfully tested by corporate users. In daily operation, it now aids companies and analysts in detecting emergent technologies and in identifying associated key players, their cooperative networks and new trends that are relevant for their business sector. TECHWATCHTOOL applies methods from bibliometrics, information wrapping, information extraction and data mining. Language technology plays a central role in the extraction of names and technologies. The system monitors technologies with three modules: 1) a retrieval and extraction module for publications and patents for identification of key players and their relations, 2) a trend identification module and 3) an ontology-based navigation module. Furthermore, TECHWATCHTOOL provides different views of the discovered data, which facilitate understanding and interpretation of the results.

The remainder of the paper is organized as follows: Section 2 explains existing systems for technology and trend monitoring. Section 3 introduces the NLP tools used in TECHWATCHTOOL. Section 4 describes our system architecture and the core modules. Section 5 explains the result visualization and presentation. Finally, Section 6 gives a short conclusion.

2 Related Work

Yoon and Park (2004) present a method to create patent networks with text mining methods to investigate the technology development. Patents are represented as nodes in a graph. Similar patents are connected by edges, which are computed automatically from relevant keywords. The system illumin8 implements a semantic search in patent- and web-documents. For a given keyword, the corresponding ontology concepts are identified in the

[1] http://www.illumin8.com/
[2] http://www.google.de/trends
[3] http://www.blogpulse.com/
[4] http://www.collexis.com/products
[5] http://th-ordo.dfki.de/TechWatch_Smila/login.jsp

documents. The system provides a modeling of various concepts (e.g. products), but the collaboration networks among the concepts are missing. In addition, illumin8 also illustrates the change of the numbers of active persons or organizations in a certain period. Google Trends is not more than a statistical summarization of its search function (Rech, 2007). As a more advanced example, BlogPulse (Glance et al., 2004) is a system for automatic discovery of trends in blogs. It can find new trends as well as visualize the chronological development of specific terms. BlogPulse extracted trends based not only on terms, but also on videos, news and links which are the targets of daily interests. The system Collexis can discover relationships between elements from different content sources. It can aggregate information from multiple content sources and help to discover potential new hypotheses on large amounts of unstructured contents. All these systems rely more and less on information retrieval technologies and are limited in extracting structured information from free texts.

3 NLP Tools

In TECHWATCHTOOL, named entity (NE) recognition and information extraction (IE) tools are applied to extract named entities (persons, organizations, etc.) and to detect relations or mentions of trends. Two tools are integrated in our system:

1. SProUT as named entity recognizer (Drozdzynski et al., 2004) and
2. DARE as relation extractor and trend sentence detector (Xu et al., 2007; Xu, 2007).

3.1 SProUT

SProUT[6] (Shallow Processing with Unification and Typed Feature Structures) is a platform for development of multilingual shallow text processing and information extraction systems. It is a generic rule-based recognizer to extract named entities or concept terms. Users can write corresponding recognition patterns and specify linguistic resources, such as lexicons, gazetteers and tokenizers. The platform provides linguistic processing resources for several languages including English, German, etc. SProUT uses typed feature structures (TFS) as a uniform data structure for representing the input resources and the recognized named entities. In TECHWATCHTOOL, SProUT is utilized to extract named entities (e.g., persons, organizations and journals) from free texts and to deal with name variants. A special heuristics is implemented in our system via the unification method provided by SProUT, in order to find the equivalent classes of persons and organizations. For example if "Eckhard Beyer" and "Prof. E. Beyer" are the authors of publications about the same technology, they might be identified as name variants of the same person by our method.

[6]`http://sprout.dfki.de/index.html`

3.2 DARE

DARE[7] (Domain Adaptive Relation Extraction) is a minimally supervised machine learning framework for extracting relations of various complexity. It consists two major parts: 1) rule learning, 2) relation extraction. Rule learning and relation extraction feed each other in a bootstrapping framework. The bootstrapping starts from so-called "semantic seed" as a search query, which is a small set of instances of the target relation. (Uszkoreit, 2011) and (Li et al., 2011) describe the application and evaluation of DARE on different corpora for different relation extraction tasks. Currently DARE provides linguistic components which process English and German free texts. In TECHWATCHTOOL, DARE is used to learn linguistic patterns to recognize sentences that potentially contain the trend information and also relations between persons and organizations. To learn patterns from trend sentences, we used the corpus offered by the project partner ThyssenKrupp AG, which is annotated with trend sentences and terms by the experts. From the annotation, we acquire examples as seed for DARE to learn patterns, e.g.,

- ("lithium-ion battery", "car", "future")
- ("Gary Mepsted", "lithium-ion battery"")

The following is an example of trend-statement with its pattern:

pattern: *"power:Verb" ([subj:Noun], [obj:"car"], [mod:"future"])*

trend-statement: Lithium batteries power hybrid cars of future[8]

[7]`http://dare.dfki.de`

[8]`http://www.reuters.com/article/2007/06/21/environment-batteries-lithium-saft-dc-idUSL2055095620070621`

To learn patterns for recognizing the relation between persons and their positions in an organization, we use the Penn Treebank as our linguistically annotated corpus and some examples of the following triple:

<person, organization, position>

as start seeds.

4 System Architecture

TECHWATCHTOOL is a web application for multiple users, implemented in Java6. It has three modules dealing with different scenarios:

1. Searching and identification of key players and their collaboration network from patents and publications
2. Identification of trends for an area
3. Ontology-based navigation of a specific domain

4.1 Search and Identification of Key Players

Scientific publications and patents are two important indicators of technology development. Authors, applicants or owners of these two resources are active persons or organizations in their respective areas. Our task is to extract these active persons and institutions, identify their relationships and discover key players among them.

Fig. 1 shows the workflow and components of this module.

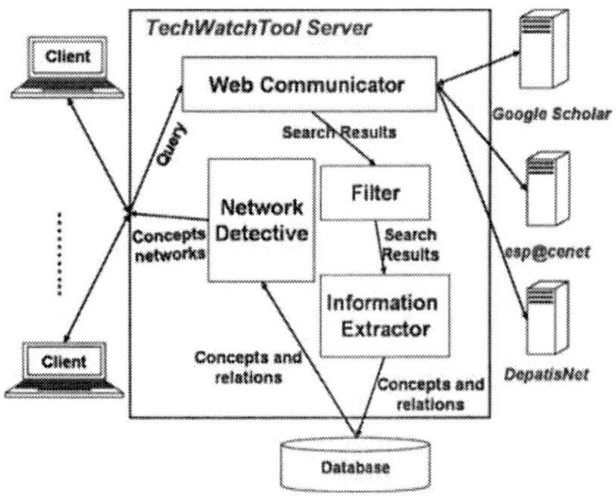

Figure 1: Workflow of search and identification of key players

Given a user query, for example, a technology term (e.g., "laser beam welding") or a company name (e.g. "NISSAN Motor"), the *Web Communicator* will acquire the relevant publications and patents from three resources: Google Scholar[9], esp@cenet[10] and DepatisNet[11]. Three wrappers are implemented to extract relevant concepts such as publication names, publication types, patent names, applicants, owners and author names and their relations by utilizing the named entity recognition tool SProUT.

The ranking of a key player is based on the number of publications or patents published or owned by a person or an organization, the recency of the publications and patents and the connectivity of the person and the organization in their technology community.

$$score(p \in P) = \frac{|P|}{\textit{index of } p \textit{ in } P} \qquad (1)$$

where P is the search result list of patents or publications from the three web resources.

$$\begin{aligned} score(t) = \quad & \alpha \times \textstyle\sum_{pat \in Pat(t)} score(pat) + \\ & (1-\alpha) \times \textstyle\sum_{pub \in Pub(t)} score(pub) \end{aligned} \qquad (2)$$

where t is a player that can be either a person or organization, $Pat(t)$ is the patent set belongs to this player as the inventor or owner and $Pub(t)$ is the corresponding publication set. α is the scoring parameter ranged from 0 to 1. The default value is set to 0.5.

The identified key players' names can be used as new search queries to search for new patents and publications about relevant technologies.

4.2 Identification of Technology Trends

Fig. 2 shows the detailed workflow of this module. The task of technology trend identification is to extract statements indicating the future trends of a specific technology expressed by key players. TECHWATCHTOOL retrieves firstly relevant documents with the Google Custom Search Engines[12], which are defined by the experts of the user company. Linguistic patterns are applied to the documents to recognize sentences that potentially contain the trend information. The linguistic patterns are determined in two ways:

[9] `http://scholar.google.de/`, a search engine for scientific publications

[10] `http://ep.espacenet.com/`, the European patent web server

[11] `http://depatisnet.dpma.de/DepatisNet/`, the German patent web server

[12] `http://www.google.com/cse/`

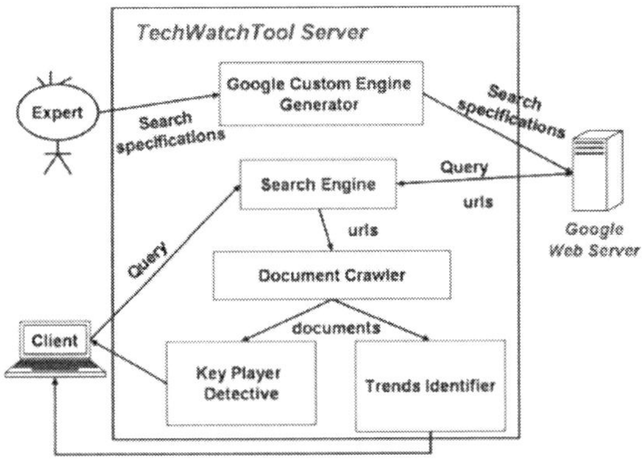

Figure 2: Trend identification

1. the linguistic experts define and evaluate the initial set of patterns in the form of regular expressions;
2. the machine learning system DARE (see Section 3.2) acquires additional patterns by learning rules from the dependency structures.

The regular expressions are designed based on the lexical indicators of the potential trend statements. The domain experts highlight the texts as samples for designing and scoring the patterns. Text statements that match these patterns are considered the indicators of potential trends. In the following, we show an example of the trend patterns and a statement matching them:

pattern1: *future of(.){0,20}car*

pattern2: *in (the)? future*

trend-statement: Mass.-based A123 Systems is now worth nearly \$2 billionindicating huge investor confidence **in the future of electric cars**, plug-in hybrids, and the batteries that make them go.[13]

As described in Section 3.2, we use the DARE system to identify the text statements and trend terms. Compared to the regular expression-based patterns, the rules learned by DARE are more accurate because they consider the syntactic structures and more bigger linguistic contexts. Therefore, the recognition is more precise. Furthermore, DARE is able to correct and update the rules when more queries and more documents are generated through the users. On the other hand, the dependency structures in DARE system are fairly strict, therefore, not as robust as the regular expressions. Therefore, we combine both methods to detect more trend statements without compromising on the accuracy.

Using this module, TECHWATCHTOOL can also identify the key players who are active in a certain domains without identified connections to any publications or patents. Such key players may be large corporations, department leaders or managers. The persons and organizations are evaluated based on their relevance to the given query

$$score(t) = \frac{occurrences\ of\ t\ with\ the\ query\ in\ sentence}{occurrences\ of\ t\ in\ document} \quad (3)$$

The relations between these persons and organizations are detected by patterns acquired by DARE as described in Section 3.2. The following is an example sentence for the given query *machine learning*:

> *One of those bright-eyed children was* ***Christopher Bishop****, now a partner at* ***Microsoft Research*** *in Cambridge and* ***a leading expert*** *in machine learning.*[14]

This module can be connected with the patent and publication search module to find out whether the identified key players are also owners of any publications or patents.

4.3 Interactive Ontology-based Navigation

TECHWATCHTOOL allows users of a specific technology domain to monitor the technology development via a web-based ontology-based navigation user interface. An ontology for a specific technology domain is usually provided by the experts of the user companies. Users can zoom into the ontology and find concepts (named by technology terms) and their subconcepts and obtain information about selected items. The information can contain a description of this concept, recent publications and patents, its new key players and new trends in the area. Fig. 3 displays a screen shot of the web interface.

5 Data Visualization and Result Presentation

It is always a challenge for web applications to present users the results in an intuitive way (Andrews, 1995; Rohrer and Swing, 1997). TECHWATCHTOOL allows users to have at least three

[13] http://www.hybridcars.com/news/investors-embrace-a123-lithium-new-ethanol-26126.html

[14] http://www.theengineer.co.uk/in-depth/interviews/machine-learning-expert-prof-chris-bishop/1008899.article

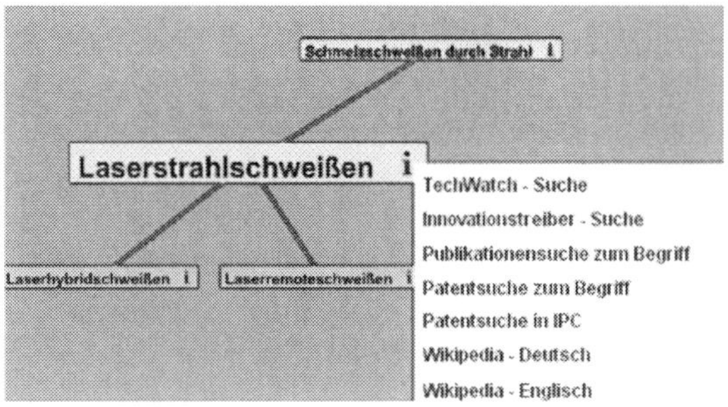

Figure 3: Ontology-based navigation

views onto the results: i) graph view ii) table view iii) diagram and chart view.

The graph view is suited for presenting the collaboration networks among active persons and organizations and their relations to publications and patents. Fig. 4 shows an example of such networks. The advantage of the graph viewer is that

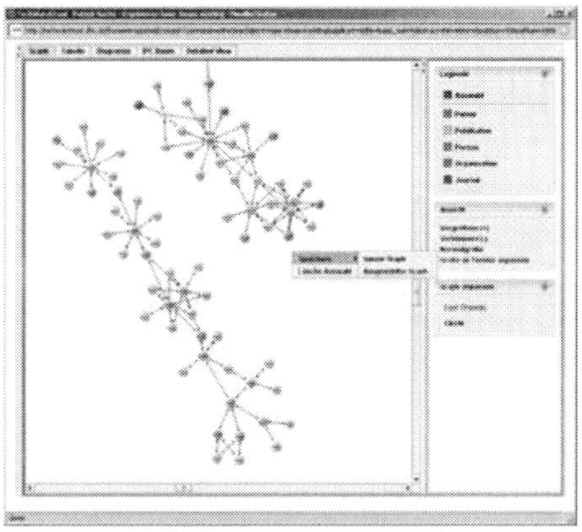

Figure 4: Interactive graph viewer for collaboration networks among persons, organizations, journals, publications and patents

users can monitor and observe new clusters of collaborations in a very straightforward way. Furthermore, the viewer offers to the users various convenient functionalities such as graph layouts, zooming and focusing functions as well as customization of the color scheme.

In order to assist users in finding key players quickly, the table view provides sortable tables containing relevance ranking information about persons or organizations.

For monitoring the technology development in a certain time interval, a diagram viewer is included in TECHWATCHTOOL as depicted in Fig. 6. This diagram viewer provides the total number of publications or patents for each year within the time

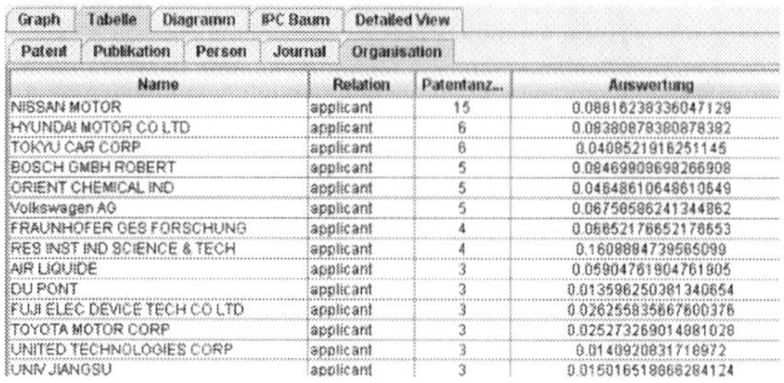
Graph | Tabelle | Diagramm | IPC Baum | Detailed View
Patent | Publikation | Person | Journal | Organisation

Name	Relation	Patentanz...	Auswertung
NISSAN MOTOR	applicant	15	0.08816238336047129
HYUNDAI MOTOR CO LTD	applicant	6	0.08380878380878382
TOKYU CAR CORP	applicant	6	0.04085219816251145
BOSCH GMBH ROBERT	applicant	5	0.08469809698266908
ORIENT CHEMICAL IND	applicant	5	0.04648610648610649
Volkswagen AG	applicant	5	0.06758586241344862
FRAUNHOFER GES FORSCHUNG	applicant	4	0.06652176652176653
RES INST IND SCIENCE & TECH	applicant	4	0.1608884739565099
AIR LIQUIDE	applicant	3	0.05904761904761905
DU PONT	applicant	3	0.013596250381340654
FUJI ELEC DEVICE TECH CO LTD	applicant	3	0.026255835667600376
TOYOTA MOTOR CORP	applicant	3	0.025273269014981028
UNITED TECHNOLOGIES CORP	applicant	3	0.01408920831716972
UNIV JIANGSU	applicant	3	0.015016518666284124

Figure 5: Table view: sortable table

interval and offers users a fairly direct overview of the historic development of the technology. Furthermore, users can also compare the changing proportions between publications and patents (Fig. 7).

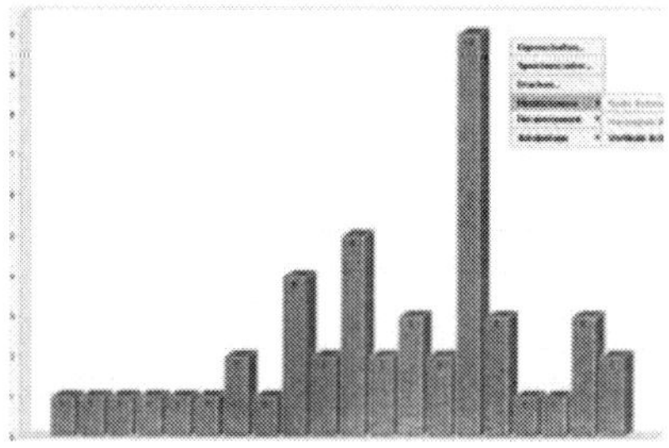

Figure 6: Diagram viewer for publications and patents

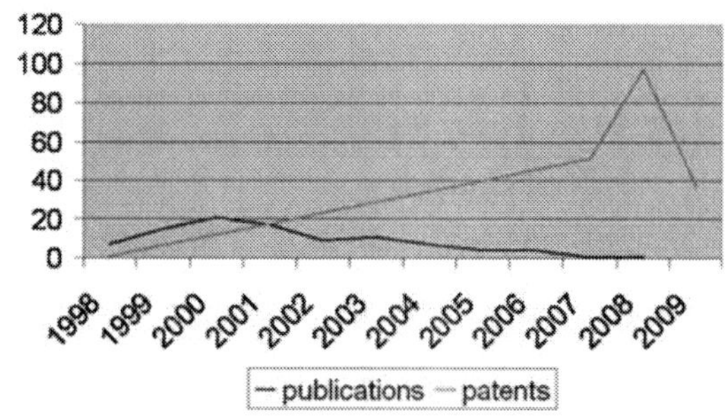

Figure 7: Relationships between publications and patents

Furthermore, TECHWATCHTOOL features many other visualization functions such as tree viewer, html viewer etc. All these visualization tools can export their graphs or tables into files when required. The export function facilitates the further processing of the result information.

6 Conclusion and Future Work

This paper describes and demonstrates a provenly useful application that assists experts in monitoring new technology developments and detecting new technology trends. The system combines information wrapping, information extraction and data mining technologies and provides different views of result presentation. Through these means, users can access and interpret the information in a very convenient way and thus gain valuable new insights.

As described in Section 3, the recognition of concept terms relies on the NLP tools. Therefore, the errors of NLP tools can damage the accuracy of TECHWATCHTOOL analysis. Meanwhile the patent and publication analysis is based on the search results of the web search engines that can neither guarantee precision nor recall. Therefore, avoiding the negative consequences of these factors and evaluating the quality of the TECHWATCHTOOL system proper remains an open challenge. It is also very difficult to automatically assess the extraction and identification results of the trend search module. We plan to evaluate it manually by annotating a small sample of documents. The identification algorithm of the trend search module still needs to be improved. We plan to run the DARE rule-learning system during the application of TECHWATCHTOOL automatically to acquire new patterns and to validate the learned patterns. We also intend to update the ontology by the new technology terms learned from document via the trend search module. Our current method for evaluating the persons and organizations in the trend module still produces errors. It happens that unrelated persons or organizations occasionally occur together with the given query pattern. This over-detection will hopefully be alleviated by NLP tools that utilize the syntactic structures of the sentences, such as DARE does.

Acknowledgments

The research reported in this paper was initialized in the context of industrial projects funded by ThyssenKrupp AG and was further developed in the project Theseus Ordo (funded by the German Federal Ministry of Economics and Technology (BMWi) through the contract 01MQ07016). Many thanks to Peter Seyfried, Ralf Sünkel and Haydar Mecit of ThyssenKrupp for their valuable suggestions, comments and ccoperation.

References

K. Andrews. 1995. Visualizing cyberspace: Information visualization in the Harmony Internet browser. *Proceedings of Information Visualization*, pages 97–104.

Witold Drozdzynski, Hans-Ulrich Krieger, Jakub Piskorski, Ulrich Schäfer, and Feiyu Xu. 2004. Shallow processing with unification and typed feature structures — foundations and applications. *Künstliche Intelligenz*, 1:17–23.

N. Glance, M. Hurst, and T. Tomokiyo. 2004. Blogpulse: Automated trend discovery for weblogs. In *WWW 2004 Workshop on the Weblogging Ecosystem: Aggregation, Analysis and Dynamics*, volume 2004. Citeseer.

Hong Li, Feiyu Xu, and Hans Uszkoreit. 2011. Minimally supervised rule learning for the extraction of biographic information from various social domains. In *Proceedings of RANLP 2011*.

J. Rech. 2007. Discovering trends in software engineering with google trend. *ACM SIGSOFT Software Engineering Notes*, 32(2):1–2.

R.M. Rohrer and E. Swing. 1997. Web-based information visualization. *IEEE Computer Graphics and Applications*, 17(4):52–59.

H. Uszkoreit. 2011. Learning relation extraction grammars with minimal human intervention: strategy, results, insights and plans. *Computational Linguistics and Intelligent Text Processing*, pages 106–126.

Feiyu Xu, Hans Uszkoreit, and Hong Li. 2007. A seed-driven bottom-up machine learning framework for extracting relations of various complexity. In *Proceedings of ACL 2007, 45th Annual Meeting of the Association for Computational Linguistics*, Prague, Czech Republic, 6.

Feiyu Xu. 2007. *Bootstrapping Relation Extraction from Semantic Seeds*. Phd-thesis, Saarland University.

B. Yoon and Y. Park. 2004. A text-mining-based patent network: Analytical tool for high-technology trend. *The Journal of High Technology Management Research*, 15(1):37–50.

”Yes we can?”: Subjectivity Annotation and Tagging for the Health Domain

Muhammad Abdul-Mageed
Department of Linguistics and
School of Library & Info. Science,
Indiana University,
Bloomington
mabdulma@indiana.edu

Mohammed Korayem
School of Informatics
& Computing
Indiana University,
Bloomington
mkorayem@indiana.edu

Ahmed YoussefAgha
Applied Health Science Department
Indiana University,
Bloomington
ahmyouss@indiana.edu

Abstract

The area of *Subjectivity and sentiment analysis (SSA)* has been witnessing a flurry of novel research. However, only few attempts have been made to build SSA systems for the health domain. In the current study, we report efforts to partially bridge this gap. We present a new labeled corpus of professional articles collected from major Websites focused on the Obama health reform plan (OHRP). We introduce a new annotation scheme that incorporates subjectivity as well as topics directly related to the OHRP and describe a highly-successful SSA system that exploits the annotation. In the process, we introduce a number of novel features and a wide-coverage polarity lexicon for the health domain.

1 Introduction

In recent years, searches and processing of data beyond the limiting level of surface words are becoming more important than it used to be (Diab et al., 2009). One of the areas that has been witnessing a swelling interest is that of *Subjectivity and sentiment analysis (SSA)*. *Subjectivity* in natural language refers to aspects of language used to express opinions, feelings, evaluations, and speculations (Banfield, 1982; Wiebe, 1994) and it, thus, incorporates *sentiment*. *Subjectivity classification* refers to the task of classifying texts into either *Objective* (e.g., *The Obama Health Committe submitted a report last week.*) or *Subjective*. Subjective text is further classified with *sentiment* or *polarity*. For sentiment classification, the task refers to identifying whether a subjective text is *positive* (e.g., *Obama's reform plan will solve all our health problems!*), *negative* (e.g., *The proposed ideas will lead to definite failure!*), *neutral* (e.g., *The president may make changes to some of the ideas proposed.*), and, sometimes, *mixed* (e.g., *The plan is bad, but I like Obama.*).

In spite of the great interest in SSA, only few studies have been conducted on the health domain. The quick dissemination of information characteristic of our world today, makes opinions expressed in these media more important than they traditionally used to be, and hence building SSA systems on top of these media is a valuable endeavor. In the current paper, we present a paragraph-level novel annotation scheme for professional articles from the health domain that incorporates customized topic annotation. More specifically, we focus on articles treating the Obama Healthcare Reform Plan (OHRP).

The rest of the paper is organized as follows: In Section 2, we motivate work on the news genre. In Section 3, we introduce data set, summarize subjectivity and topic annotations, and provide examples of categories in our data. In Section 4 we describe our approach. In Section 5, we describe our system. In Section 6 we provide the results and evaluation. Section 7 is the about related work, and Section 8 is the conclusion.

2 Professional Articles

Most SSA work has focused on highly subjective, user-generated genres such as blogs and product or movie reviews where authors express their opinions quite freely (Balahur and Steinberger, 2009). Professional articles (i.e., position articles written by experts) published by major news organizations is a genre that has almost been disregarded in SSA. These articles tend to differ from regular news stories reporting events in that their authors are highly specialized. Although the sentiment expressed in regular news articles is usually subtle professional articles observably have more explicit sentiment that usually differs depending on the specific dimension of the topic under discussion. In this way, the sentiment can easily shift from a paragraph to another. For this specific reason, our annotation is fine-grained (i.e., conducted at the paragraph level).

3 Data set and Annotation

3.1 Corpus

The corpus is collection of news articles crawled from 105 popular online news sites (e.g., ABC News, The Associated Press, Belfast Telegraph)Articles were selected by searching the websites using all possible combinations of the queries "Obama healthcare," "Obama health reform," and "health care reform". Only articles written by professionals treating the specific subject of OHRP that were published between October 2008 and September 2010 were included. Since our unit of analysis is the paragraph, articles were divided into their component paragraphs (making up 1850 paragraphs).

3.2 Subjectivity and Sentiment Annotation

We prepared guidlines for the task of subjectivity and sentiment annotation. In the current paper we summarize some of these guidelines, and cite some of the related literature.

Subjectivity and Sentiment Categories: For each paragraph, each annotator assigned one of 5 possible labels: (1) OBJECTIVE (OBJ), (2) SUBJECTIVE-POSITIVE (S-POS), (3) SUBJECTIVE-NEGATIVE (S-NEG), (4) SUBJECTIVE-NEUTRAL (S-NEUT), and (5) SUBJECTIVE-MIXED (S-MIXED). We followed (Wiebe et al., 1999) in operationalizing the SUBJ vs. OBJ categories. In other words, if the primary goal of a paragraph is perceived to be the objective reporting of information, it was labeled OBJ. Otherwise, the paragraph would be a candidate for one of the four SUBJ classes. Two college-educated native speakers of English annotated the 1850 paragraphs for both subjectivity, with inter-rater agreement at 84%. Our data has 1571 SUBJ and 279 OBJ cases. The SUBJ cases are broken into 237 S-POS, 301 S-NEG, 707 S-NEUT, and 326 S-MIXED cases

3.3 Topic Annotation

The same two colledge-educated native speakers of English who coded the data for SSA also manually assigned each paragraph a domain/topic label. The topic labels are inspired by the Obama administration's focus on three main topics for popularizing the OHRP: (1) stability & security, (2) quality & affordability, and (3) funding. [1]. The set of topic labels is thus as follows: {*STABILITY & SECURITY (297 cases), (2) QUALITY & AFFORDABILITY (380 cases), (3) FUNDING (328 cases), OTHER (845 cases)*}. We did not make further attempts to identify other topics outside the scope of the administration's focus. Topic annotation turned out to be an easier task than subjectivity annotation, which is indicated by inter-annotator agreement for topic label assignment being at 94%. Explanations of each category in our data set are provided in Section 3.4, with some illustrating examples.

3.4 SSA and Topic Examples

Stability & Security: Descriptions of the *Stability & Security* topic/dimension included that the plan (1) ends discrimination against people with pre-existing conditions, (2) prevents insurance companies from dropping coverage when people are sick and need it most, etc.Below, we provide one example labeled with this topic from the OBJ class:[2]

- "I was denied coverage as spinal fractures were misdiagnosed (by the insurer's doctor, who avoided the cost of a CT scan) concluding my 25% spinal misalignment was pre-existing." **(OBJ)**

Quality & Affordability: Descriptions of the *Quality & Affordability* included that the plan (1) creates

[1] www.whitehouse.gov/assets/documents/obama_plan_card.PDF

[2] For limitations of space, we are not able to provide examples belonging to all our SSA categories.

a new insurance marketplace the Exchange that allows people without insurance and small businesses to compare plans and buy insurance at competitive prices, (2) provides new tax credits to help people buy insurance and to help small businesses cover their employees, etc. The following is an example:

- "Massachusetts became the only state to mandate health insurance in 2006. It has passed legal muster and led to 97 percent of residents having some form of coverage, said Alan Sager, director of the Health Reform Program at Boston University's School of Public Health." **(OBJ)**

Funding: Descriptions of the *Funding* dimension included that the plan (1) will not add a dime to the deficit and is paid for upfront, (2) creates an independent commission of doctors and medical experts to identify waste, fraud and abuse in the health care system, etc. Below is an example:

- "The House plan is projected to guarantee coverage for 96 percent of Americans at a cost of more than $1 trillion over the next 10 years, according to the nonpartisan Congressional Budget Office." **(OBJ)**

4 Approach

4.1 Features

The following are the set of features we apply:

TOPIC: We apply a feature indicating the *topic/dimension* of the each paragraph.

UNIQUE: Following Wiebe et al. (2004), to account for the frequency of words' effect, we include a *unique* feature. Namely words that occur in our corpus with a frequency ≤ 3 are replaced with the token "UNIQUE".

N-GRAM: We run experiments with N-grams ≤ 3 and all possible combinations of them. Thus, we employ N-gram combinations, as follows:(1) 1g, (2) 2g, (3) 3g, (4) 1g+2g, (5) 1g+3g, (6) 2g+3g, (7) 1g+2g+3g.

POLARITY_LEX: We apply a binary *has_polar* feature indicating whether or not any of the polarized entries in a polarity lexicon. We compare the performance of a number of polarity lexicons, including a manually labeled lexicon we manually developed i.e., the YouTube Lexicon (YT_LEX). We describe YT_LEX as well as the other lexicons we use below:

- **YT_LEX**: We used Google's YouTube Data API to crawl all comments on 1000 YouTube videos using the query "obama health care". This corpus, which we refer to as *YouTube Health Corpus [YuHC]* is harvested as part of another project we are working on and totals 229,177 comments. After reducing all repeated letters of frequency ¿ 2 to only 2 (e.g., the word *cooool* is reduced to *cool*), we extracted the top 29.991 words[3] and manually labeled them with semantic orientation tags. Each word was given a label of the set {*positive, negative, neutral*}. We refer to this lexicon as the *YT_LEX*.

- **HW_LEX**: This is a list of adjectives comprising all gradable and dynamic adjectives, both manually prepared and automatically extracted, by (Hatzivassiloglou and Wiebe, 2000)[4].

- **SentiWN_LEX**: This lexicon is composed of all positive and negative entries with a score $>$ 0.25 [5] from SentiWordnet 3.0 (Baccianella et al., 2010).

- **SentiWN_Strong_LEX**: This lexicon is composed of all positive and negative entries with a score $>$ 0.50 [6] from Sentiwordnet 3.0.

SOURCE: We apply a "SOURCE" feature to each paragraph vector. This feature indicated the news source (i.e., the news site/organization [e.g., SOURCE_CNN, SOURCE_CNBC]) from which the paragraph's document was collected. This feature is intended to capture any bias with or against the OHRP, or one or more aspect of it, on the part of the news site/organization.

AUTHOR: We apply an "AUTHOR" feature to each paragraph vector. This feature indicated the author of each the document to which the paragraph belongs. Again, this feature is intended to capture

[3]Extracted words were of frequency of 3 or more.

[4]The list is made available by (Hatzivassiloglou and Wiebe, 2000) here: http://www.cs.pitt.edu/ wiebe/pubs/coling00

[5]We averaged the score for repeated entries (i.e., those with more than one sense).

[6]We also averaged the score for entries with more than one sense.

any bias with or against the OHRP, or one or more aspect of it, on the part of the author.

Both the SOURCE and AUTHOR features can be viewed as meta-data features. These two features are novel ones that we introduce to the task of paragraph-level subjectivity analysis. One advantage of these two features is that they are easy to incorporate as a document is pre-processed, and hence do not need any manual tagging.

5 Automatic tagging of Subjectivity

5.1 Method

In this study, we only report experiments for subjectivity classification where attempts are made to tease apart the SUBJ from OBJ cases in our dataset. Since our data set is very biased toward the SUBJ class, we equalize the two classes by making use of all the 279 OBJ cases and randomly sampling 279 SUBJ cases from the corpus. All experiments reported below are hence run on this equalized data sample, with a baseline of 50%.

We use an Support Vector Machine classifier SVM^{light} package (Joachims, 2008). We experiment with various kernels and parameter settings and find that linear kernels yield the best performance for our specific problem. We run experiments with *presence* vectors, i.e. for each sentence vector, the value of each dimension is binary either a 1 (regardless of how many times a feature occurs) or 0.

Experimental Conditions: We run three sets of experiments. We first run experiments using each of the three features *TOPIC (T), SOURCE (S), AUTHOR (A)* separately and then combined across the various *N-GRAM* and *N-GRAM* combinations described earlier. We call this first set of experiments TSA_EXP. Second, we run the UNIQUE_EXP experiments where we apply the "UNIQUE" feature explained earlier with the best-yielding *N-GRAM* or *N-GRAM* combination from TSA_EXP. Third, we run the POLAR_EXP experiments using each of the polarity lexicons separately with the following configurations: (1) the best yielding *N-GRAM* or *N-GRAM* combination from TSA_EXP, (2) the best-yielding feature (i.e., TOPIC, SOURCE, or AUTHOR) or feature combination (TOPIC+SOURCE+AUTHOR) from TSA_EXP, (3) the best yielding setting from UNIQUE_EXP, and (4) the combination of 3 and 4 configurations (i.e., the best-yileding feature or feature combination from TSA_EXP and the best-yielding setting from UNIQUE_EXP).

6 Results and Evaluation

We report results in 10-fold cross validation where we train on 9 folds and test on the 10th and average the results. Results are reported in accuracy A and F-measure (F).

TSA_EXP: As table 1 shows, each of the three features TOPIC, SOURCE, and AUTHOR improves the classification when applied. For the TOPIC feature, whereas the best A is 72.21% and is acquired using unigrams (i.e., 1g), the best F is 73.76% and is achieved with the unigram+bigram (i.e., 1g+2g) combination. Although these results are slightly higher than the results acquired using only the bag-of-words, they are $>$ 20.00% better than the 50.00% majority class baseline. Using the SOURCE feature resuls in 88.51% A and 87.93% F with bigrams, and hence an improvement of 24.24% A and 18.30% F over the results acquired with the bag-of-words with bigrams. Better results are, however, acquired when the AUTHOR feature is applied, with A reaching 95.50% and F reaching 95.51%. Applying the three features TOPIC, SOURCE, and AUTHOR combined results 95.15% A and 94.97% F. In this way, applying the AUTHOR feature alone achieves the best permofrmance.

UNIQUE_EXP: Since the best performance (in both A and F) from TSA_ EXP was with trigrams, we apply the UNIQUE feature with the trigram configuration. As table 2 below shows, we apply the UNIQUE feature with the number of words replaced by the "UNIQUE" token $\leq$ 5 absolute frequency. We acquire the best results when we replace tokens with frequency =3, with 60.43% A and 68.91% F. This is an improvement of 10.43% A and 18.90% F over the baseline.

POLAR_EXP: As stated earlier, POLAR_EXP experiments were run with four different configuration. The four configurations are (1) BASE TRIGRAMS (i.e., only trigrams), (2) BASE TRIGRAMS+UNIQUE3 (i.e., the UNIQUE feature with frequency =3), (3) BASE TRIGRAMS+AUTHOR, and (4) BASE TRI-

N-gram	Bag-of-Words		Topic		Source		Author		Topic+Source+Author	
	A	F	A	F	A	F	A	F	A	F
1g	**70.42**	72.11	**72.21**	73.50	85.82	85.79	86.54	86.80	93.35	93.19
2g	64.27	69.63	68.96	72.74	**88.51**	**87.93**	93.17	93.36	**95.15**	**94.97**
3g	54.66	67.93	63.51	67.99	86.88	86.30	**95.50**	**95.51**	95.15	94.92
1g+2g	70.06	**72.70**	71.48	**73.76**	82.60	82.97	79.37	80.69	89.59	89.71
1g+3g	68.81	71.22	69.51	72.10	82.95	83.28	79.73	81.21	90.12	90.10
2g+3g	60.86	69.07	64.83	70.55	87.44	87.16	89.40	90.33	93.36	93.11
1g+2g+3g	68.44	71.55	70.41	73.59	79.37	80.47	76.33	78.52	86.36	86.77
Baseline	50%		50%		50%		50%		50%	

Table 1: TSA_EXP Results

N-gram	Bag-of-Words		unique1		unique2		unique3		unique4		unique5	
	A	F	A	F	A	F	A	F	A	F	A	F
3g	54.66	67.93	57.35	68.03	59.17	68.09	**60.43**	**68.91**	57.52	66.14	56.64	65.12
Baseline	50%		50%		50%		50%		50%		50%	

Table 2: UNIQUE_EXP Results

GRAMS+UNIQUE3+AUTHOR.

As Table 3 shows, when the HAS_POLAR feature is applied with the BASE TRIGRAMS configuration, the best *A* (i.e., 64.74%) is acquired using GI_LEX and the best *F* (i.e., 70.05%) is acquired when applying SentiWN_LEX. This is an improvement of 14.74% *A* and 20.05% *F* over BASE TRIGRAMS and 10.08% *A* and 2.19% *F*over the majority class baseline. As for the BASE TRIGRAMS+UNIQUE3 configuration, 64.21% *A* (with GI_LEX) and 69.55% *F* (with YT_LEX) are achieved. Although this is an improvement over the baseline, a slight degradation of performance (i.e., 0.53% *A* and 0.50% *F*) occurs as compared to the best results achieved with BASE TRIGRAMS.

Regarding the BASE TRIGRAMS+AUTHOR configuration, the best results of 95.51% *A* and 95.60% *F* are achieved using the YT_LEX. This is 45.51% *A* and 45.56% *A* improvement over the baseline. As Table 3 also shows, applying this configuration also improves over both the BASE TRIGRAMS and the BASE TRIGRAMS+UNIQUE3 configurations. The TRIGRAMS+UNIQUE3+AUTHOR achieves 94.78% *A* and 94.80% *F* with YT_LEX applied, which is a significant improvement over the baseline and a slight improvement (i.e., 0.07% over the *F* of the BASE TRIGRAMS).

From Table 3, it can be concluded that the best results are acquired using the BASE TRIGRAMS+AUTHOR configuration when the YT_LEX is employed. This shows that our manually-created YT_LEX outperforms the number of popular lexicons we test. We deduce that our lexicon is best suited to the health domain.

7 Related Work

A number of datasets have been labeled for SSA. Most relevant to us is work on the news genre. (Wiebe et al., 2005) label a news corpus at the word and phrase level, but neither label data for domain nor use the *Author* and *News source* we introduce here. (Balahur et al., 2009) label quotations from the news involving one person mentioning another entity and maintain that quotations typically contain more sentiment expressions than other parts of news articles. Our work is different from that of (Balahur et al., 2009) in that we label all sentences regardless whether they include quotations or not.

Many subjectivity tagging systems have also been proposed. For example, Wiebe et al. (Wiebe et al., 1999) attempt to classify news data for subjectivity, at the sentence level. useing POS features and lexical features. They report 72.17% accuracy, which is more than 20% points higher than a baseline accu-

	BASE TRIGRAMS		+UNIQUE3		+AUTHOR		+UNIQUE+AUTHOR	
	A	F	A	F	A	F	A	F
-HAS_POLAR	54.66	67.93	60.43	68.91	95.50	95.51	94.78	94.73
+HAS_POLAR **(GI_LEX)**	**64.74**	62.99	**64.21**	66.74	92.27	92.81	91.72	92.20
+HAS_POLAR **(YT_LEX)**	54.66	67.93	61.14	**69.55**	**95.51**	**95.60**	**94.78**	**94.80**
+HAS_POLAR **(HW_LEX)**	58.25	68.51	60.06	67.55	94.43	94.60	94.05	94.11
+HAS_POLAR **(SentiWN_LEX)**	64.73	**70.05**	64.02	67.30	93.34	93.74	92.08	92.43
+HAS_POLAR **(SentiWN_Strong_LEX)**	62.23	63.96	61.49	65.65	93.88	94.16	92.44	92.67
Baseline	50%		50%		50%		50%	

Table 3: POLAR_EXP Results

racy obtained by always choosing the majority class. Bruce & Wiebe (Bruce and Wiebe, 1999) performed a statistical analysis of the assigned classifications in the corpus reported in (Wiebe et al., 1999). The analysis showed that adjectives are statistically significantly and positively correlated with subjective sentences in the corpus.

8 Conclusion

In this paper, we present a corpus of professional articles annotated at the paragraph level for subjectivity and sentiment, as well as topic. We motivate SSA for professional news articles and summarize our annotation scheme. Our approach is unique in that we label the data with topics inspired by the Obama administration as part of its popularization of the OHRP. In addition, we present a subjectivity tagging system that exploits this data, making use of novel and cheap meta-data features (i.e., SOURCE and AUTHOR) that significantly boost system performance. Further, we introduce a wide-coverage polarity lexicon that performs better on the health-domain data as represented by our data set than a number of other popular lexicons. Our system performs very successfuly on the task, with 95.51% accuracy and 95.60% *F*-measure, beating a 50.00% baseline.

References

S. Baccianella, A. Esuli, and F. Sebastiani. 2010. Sentiwordnet 3.0: An enhanced lexical resource for sentiment analysis and opinion mining. In *Seventh conference on International Language Resources and Evaluation, Malta. Retrieved May*, volume 25, page 2010.

A. Balahur and R. Steinberger. 2009. Rethinking Sentiment Analysis in the News: from Theory to Practice and back. *Proceeding of WOMSA*.

A. Balahur, R. Steinberger, E. van der Goot, B. Pouliquen, and M. Kabadjov. 2009. Opinion mining on newspaper quotations. In *2009 IEEE/WIC/ACM International Conference on Web Intelligence and Intelligent Agent Technology*, pages 523–526. IEEE.

A. Banfield. 1982. *Unspeakable Sentences: Narration and Representation in the Language of Fiction*. Routledge Kegan Paul, Boston.

R. Bruce and J. Wiebe. 1999. Recognizing subjectivity. a case study of manual tagging. *Natural Language Engineering*, 5(2).

M.T. Diab, L. Levin, T. Mitamura, O. Rambow, V. Prabhakaran, and W. Guo. 2009. Committed belief annotation and tagging. In *Proceedings of the Third Linguistic Annotation Workshop*, pages 68–73. Association for Computational Linguistics.

V. Hatzivassiloglou and J. Wiebe. 2000. Effects of adjective orientation and gradability on sentence subjectivity. In *International Conference on Computational Linguistics, (COLING-2000)*.

T. Joachims. 2008. Svmlight: Support vector machine. http://svmlight.joachims.org/, Cornell University, 2008.

J. Wiebe, R. Bruce, and T. O'Hara. 1999. Development and use of a gold standard data set for subjectivity classifications. In *Proc. 37th Annual Meeting of the Assoc. for Computational Linguistics (ACL-99)*, pages 246–253, University of Maryland: ACL.

J. Wiebe, T. Wilson, R. Bruce, M. Bell, and M. Martin. 2004. Learning subjective language. *Computational linguistics*, 30(3):277–308.

J. Wiebe, T. Wilson, and C. Cardie. 2005. Annotating expressions of opinions and emotions in language. *Language Resources and Evaluation*, 39(2):165–210.

J. Wiebe. 1994. Tracking point of view in narrative. *Computional Linguistics*, 20(2):233–287.

Wordnets: State of the Art and Perspectives.

Case study: the Romanian Wordnet

Verginica Barbu Mititelu
Romanian Academy
vergi@racai.ro

Abstract

During a quarter of a century of existence and in spite of much criticism, wordnets have thoroughly proved their appropriateness as repositories of linguistic knowledge and their usefulness in various applications. In this paper we present the methodology of creating the Romanian wordnet (RoWN), with special emphasis on the strategies adopted during ten years of ceaseless implementation and which highlight the efforts invested, the way we dealt with the alignment of the RoWN (previously aligned to PWN 2.0) to the PWN 3.0, as well as the future work we envisage for enriching and extending this resource.

1 Generalities on wordnets

Language is a system of signs. This structuralist perspective on language serves extremely well the description of natural languages by both theoretical linguists and specialists in the formal representation of language. Notions like *paradigm* (i.e. class of similar elements), *syntagm* (i.e. a linguistic environment in which the elements of a paradigm can occur), *value* (the distinguishable functional role of an element in a syntagm) are modeled to serve the formal representation of language as a whole.

Among the different knowledge representation formalisms, we focus here on wordnets, a special kind of semantic networks. While semantic networks have words in nodes and the arcs are semantic relations, wordnets are definitely more than that: they are:

- monolingual dictionaries: they contain words with definitions for each of their senses;
- multilingual dictionaries: via the Inter-Lingual Index, ILI, access from one language-specific network to all the others is facilitated; thus, it is possible to compare the organization of the lexical material of various languages, to find examples supporting the thesis of semantic specificity of languages, to introduce the multilingual dimension in various applications relying on wordnets;
- thesauri: lexical information is organized in terms of word meanings, not word forms;
- lexical ontologies: wordnets contain concepts lexicalizations from various domains and the relations between these concepts lexicalizations. There have been more projects enriching wordnet with ontological information: WordNet Domains (Pianta et al. 2002), SUMO (Niles and Pease 2003).

2 Development

There are more ways of creating a wordnet. The most accurate is the manual one. Used for developing the Princeton WordNet, it stands up most criticisms. However, the high costs involved in terms of money and time prevent other teams to undertake a similar enterprise. A rather cheap approach is to automatically extract the synsets and the relations between them from various resources available: such experiments are presented in Aggire et al (2002) for Basque, Barbu and Barbu Mititelu (2005) for Romanian, Fišer and Sagot (2008) for Slovene and French, Isahara et al. (2008) for Japanese. Translation of the PWN synsets and transfer of its structure into the newly created wordnet is a fast way of creating a wordnet: the Finnish (Linden and Carlson 2010) and the Thai (Leenoi et al. 2009) wordnets have been made like this. Many projects used a combined top-down method: a core wordnet was first developed (usually by translation of the English synsets) and then it was enriched in various ways: the EuroWordNet (Vossen et al. 1999), the BalkaNet (Tufiş 2004) projects. All these approaches assume a close conceptual similarity among languages, due to which the PWN structure is tranferable to other wordnets (this is also the assumption behind MultiWordNet, Pianta et al. 2002). Further manual revision is mentioned by most of the authors. Unlike the expand model used in all the above cases, in the merge approach a wordnet is developed for a certain language and then aligned to the PWN; this is the case of the Russian WordNet (Balkova et al. 2004).

The Romanian team undertook a methodology of development from scratch, combining the expand and merge models. Each English synset is considered as part of the lexical network, it is viewed in the system of relations which it enters, it is contrasted with its hypernyms, hyponyms, co-hyponyms, troponyms, etc., so that the lexicographer can understand its exact meaning which needs to be expressed in Romanian. For each English synset, a list of possible Romanian translations is suggested to the lexicographer from an electronic English-Romanian dictionary (of 74000 translation pairs). For each such translation, some sets of synonyms are proposed from an electronic synonyms dictionary (containing around 26000 sets of synonyms). The lexicographer can choose the correct one, can adapt it if necessary, by deleting or adding literals from/to it, can write a different synset, if none of the proposed ones is correct. Each literal is assigned a sense number from the electronic explanatory dictionary (containing around 70000 entries).

More than 400 synsets were added to the RoWN during the BalkaNet project (as well as to the other wordnets created meanwhile), synsets that are considered specific to the culture and civilization of our geographical region. They are not dangling nodes, but were assigned the appropriate relations in the network.

The structure of the RoWN is imported from the PWN. Most of the relations it contains are conceptual, so they are transferable from one language to another. Thus the hierarchy of the PWN is preserved. Nevertheless, this does not contradict the thesis of semantic specificity of languages, since we mark the concepts that lack a Romanian lexicalization with the notation NL (for non-lexicalized). The differences on the horizontal and on the vertical axes are easily found in the wordnets aligned to the ILI.

During our implementation, we noticed that antonymy is transferrable into our network.

A rather sensitive topic is represented by derivational relations. Let e_1 and e_2 be two English literals, and, for instance, r_1 and r_2 their Romanian equivalents; if e_1 is derived from e_2 with a certain affix, it may be the case, but it is not obligatory so, that r_1 is derived from r_2 with an affix. Thus, in English there are *drive* – *driver* and in Romanian *şofa* „drive" – *şofer* „driver"; in English there are *teach* – *teacher* but in Romanian there are *preda* „teach" – *profesor* „teacher"; in Romanian there are *bucătar* – *bucătărie*, while in English there are *cook* – *kitchen* respectively. Such examples can be found for any language pairs. Marking derivational relations is of great help: a base word and all the words derived from it belong to the same semantic field. Relating them can (at least partially) solve the famous "tennis problem" of wordnets (Fellbaum 1998: 10). Thus, derivation proved to be the third relation as importance for obtaining good quality lexical chains, after hypernymy and hyponymy (Novischi and Moldovan 2006). Lexical chains are then used in various tasks: improvement of QA systems (Novischi and Moldovan 2006), summarization (Barzilay and Elhadad 1997), document indexing (Stairmand 1996), detection of malapropism (Hirst and St-Onge 1997) and others.

In PWN some of the derivation relations are already marked (Fellbaum et al. 2009). Due to the lexical nature of these relations (i.e. they establish between two words, not between synsets), they cannot be automatically transferred into other wordnets. However, some other wordnets have derivation relations marked: the Czech one (Pala and Smrz 2004), the Bulgarian (Koeva 2008), the Russian (Azarova 2008) ones.

2.1 Sense numbering

In PWN polysemous words have sense numbers attributed in an artificial manner: the word senses are distributed in a decreasing order of their number of occurrences in tagged corpora.

Specific to the RoWN among all the existent wordnets is the way sense numbers are assigned to literals. Whenever a word is present in the EXPD, its sense number is preserved in the RoWN synset. However, in EXPD the organization of word meanings is hierarchical, highlighting their relatedness: many of them are derived

from other meanings. Here are the meanings of the Romanian word *spart* "broken" in the EXPD:
1.1 Spargere. (En. "breaking into");
1.2 Sfârşit, încheiere a unei activităţi (En. "end of an activity");
1.3 Expresie: *A ajunge la spartul târgului (sau iarmarocului)*; a ajunge undeva prea târziu, când lucrurile sunt lichidate. (En. Expression *a ajunge la spartul târgului* "to arrive too late");
2.1.1 Prefăcut în bucăţi, în cioburi (En. "turned into pieces");
2.1.2 plesnit, crăpat (En. "cracked");
2.1.3 găurit (En. "drilled");
2.2.1. Expresie: *a fi mână spartă*; a fi risipitor (En. Expression *a fi mână spartă* "to be easy money");
2.2.2. Expresie: *A mânca de parc-ar fi spart*; se spune cuiva sau despre cineva care mănâncă foarte mult şi cu lăcomie (En. Expression *A mânca de parc-ar fi spart* "to eat very much and with greed");
2.3. (Despre lemne) Tăiat în bucăţi mici (potrivite pentru a fi arse în sobă) (En. (About woodsticks) to be chopped in small pieces (appropriate for burning in a stove));
2.4. (Despre pământ) Răscolit, plin de gropi (En. (about ground) embowelled);
2.5. (Rar, despre butoaie) Desfundat (En. (rare, about barrels) bilged);
2.6. (figurativ (Despre sunete)) Lipsit de sonoritate, răguşit, dogit (En. (fig. (about sounds)) lacking sonority, hoarse, jangle);
2.7. (Despre ziduri, clădiri) Stricat, dărăpănat, ruinat (En. (about walls, buildings) broken down, decaying);
2.8. (Despre obiecte de încălţăminte, de îmbrăcăminte) Rupt, uzat, tocit (En. (about footwear and clothes) worn out).
On the first hand, there is a clear distinction between homonyms (senses under 1 and senses under 2). On the other hand, senses under 1 are clearly distinguished one from the other, express activities. Senses under 2 express results and are grouped together as follows: those under 2.1 refer to objects, those under 2.2 are senses in expressions, while those under 2.3 to 2.8 refer to various entities that can undergo a disruption, a fracture of their wholeness; these are specific senses.

We decided to maintain these imbricated sense numbers for literals because they can be viewed as an extra "relation" in wordnet, which keeps track of related meanings (and can help in clustering experiments). Linguists can also extract from the semantic network statistics of various kinds of semantic evolutions of word meanings.

A special case is represented by words that have meanings unattested in EXPD. The lexicographer carefully examines the attested ones in order to find the closest one; if it exists, the unattested meaning gets the same sense number as this one with ".x" added at its end. Thus, the hierarchical organization of meanings remains unaltered. If it does not exist, i.e. the meaning under consideration is not close to any of the recorded meanings in EXPD, then the "x" sense "number" is assigned to it, so it is treated as a distinct meaning.

Sometimes, although extremely carefully examining two synsets, lexicographers realize that they simply cannot find any distinction between them. The solution in such a case is to appeal to a native speaker's knowledge of his/her mother tongue. If (s)he also cannot find any motivation for the existence of these two synsets, then we adopted a notation to manage these cases: we add ".c" after the sense number. A suggestive example in this case is the pair of synsets: {eclipse:3} (gloss: "cause an eclipse of; of celestial bodies") and {eclipse:2, occult:1} (gloss: "cause an eclipse of (a celestial body) by intervention"). A further proof of this impossibility to differentiate semantically between the two PWN 2.0 synsets is the fact that in PWN3.0 the two different synsets have been merged into one: the latter. (In other words, the former has been eliminated from the wordnet.) The Romanian synsets corresponding to these two were identical: {eclipsa:1.c}. However, after aligning the RoWN to PWN 3.0, one of these identical synsets disappeared. Thus, the notation ".c" becomes void of significance. It can be automatically removed alongside with other such cases that are easily identified in the wordnet: if there is only one occurrence of a literal with a certain sense number ending in ".c", then we can safely remove this ending without losing any information.

Another case in which this notation proves useful is represented by pairs of synsets such as: {mister:1, Mr:1} (gloss: "a form of address for a man") and {sir:1} (gloss: "term of address for a man"). According to Cambridge Dictionary, the former is a title, although it is also "an informal and often rude form of address for a man whose name you do not know" (http://dictionary.cambridge.org/dictionary/british/mister), while the latter is "used as a formal and polite way of speaking to a man, especially one who you are providing a service to or who is in a position of authority" (http://dictionary.cambridge.org/dictionary/british/sir_1). Their Romanian equivalent is *domn:1.1* ("polite form of address for a man"). It is also used as a title. However, since such a title is used to address a man, there is no semantic reason to postulate the existence of another meaning for *domn*. That is why we implemented these two synsets with two synsets of the form {domn:1.1.c}.

So the sense numbers that literals can have in RoWN have any of the forms covered by the regular expression: \d+(\.\d+)*(\.[xc])?|x

2.2 Tools

Two tools were designed to help the lexicographers develop the synsets of the RoWN: WNBuilder and WNCorrect (Tufiş and Barbu 2004). The former is a configurable graphical interface, language independent (but resources dependent) that assists the lexicographer in the synsets development, imports the relations for the created Romanian synsets from the PWN xml file, performs validation of the created synsets: the lexicographer receives a message about the existent problem(s) and suggestions for solving it/them and generates the xml version of the file.

WNCorrect is designed for the semantic validation of the RoWN. After identifying the synsets with conflicting literals (i.e. synsets in which a literal occurs with the same sense number), their list is given to a lexicographer. Using the WNCorrect, (s)he can visualize the synsets in which each literal occurs and can perform the necessary corrections.

2.3 Valence frames

The syntactic frames in which a verb can occur are registered in PWN in a highly general way, using indefinite pronouns like *somebody*, *something* and indefinite adverbs like *somewhere*. More frames are given for the same synset, in an uneconomical way: for optional arguments a new frame is recorded. For instance, for the verb *inherit* with sense number 1 (gloss: "obtain from someone after their death"), there are two frames: "Somebody ----s something" and "Somebody ----s something from somebody".

RoWN also contains valence frames for some verbs. They are defined at the literal level. That is why, for one synset more than one valence frames can be found. They are the result of an experiment relying on parallel corpora, word alignment and word sense disambiguation technologies through which we imported syntactic-semantic information from one part of the bitext, richly annotated for the respective language, into the other part where the linguistic annotation is scarce or missing.

The resources used in this experiment were: the *1984* corpus (available in Czech and Romanian), the Czech wordnet and the RoWN. The Czech wordnet contains valence frames for many verbs (Pala and Smrž 2004). Via the interlingual equivalence relations among the Czech verbal synsets and Romanian synsets we imported about 600 valence frames. They were manually checked against the BalkaNet test-bed parallel corpus (*1984*) and more than 500 subcategorisation frames were valid as they were imported or minor modifications were operated.

Very similar to the frames used in the FrameNet project (www.icsi.berkeley.edu/~framenet), the valence frames are attached to verbs only in our wordnet (although other words that can be logical predicates can also have such frames) and specify syntactic and semantic restrictions for the arguments of the predicate denoting the meaning of a given synset. They also specify the case roles of the arguments. The nice property of the Czech valence frames is that the semantic restrictions are endogenous, i.e. they are specified in terms of other synsets of the same wordnet. Let us consider, for instance, the verbal synset ENG20-02609765-v (se_afla:3.1, se_găsi:9.1, fi:3.1) with the gloss "be located or situated somewhere; occupy a certain position". Its valence frame is described by the following expression: (nom*AG(ființă:1.1)|nom*PAT(obiect_fizic:1)) = prep-acc*LOC(loc:1), where Ro ființă:1.1 means En being:2, Ro obiect_fizic:1 means En physical_object:1, and Ro loc:1 means En location:1.

The specified meaning of this synset is: an action the logical subject of which is either a *ființă* (sense 1.1) with the AGENT role(AG), or a *obiect_fizic* (sense 1) with the PATIENT role (PAT). The logical subject is realized as a noun/NP in the nominative case (nom). The second argument is a *loc* (sense 1) and it is realized by a prepositional phrase with the noun/NP in the accusative case (prep-acc).

A verbal synset can have two different frames, thus proving that the synonymy between words in the same synset is not very strictly defined in wordnet.

3 Aligning RoWN to PWN 3.0

Wordnets for various languages are useful in multilingual tasks if aligned to the same versionof PWN. We have recently aligned the RoWN to PWN version 3.0 via a mapping from PWN2.0 (to which the RoWN was aligned) to PWN 3.0. The main problems encountered in this process are of three types:

- there were 457 cases in which two or more Romanian synsets were aligned to one PWN 3.0 synset: in this case we had to decide which of the Romanian synsets is the best equivalent of the English one; necessary modifications in the synsets structure and in the gloss were operated;
- there were 56 cases when one Romanian synset aligned to two PWN 3.0 synsets: in their case we decided which of the two PWN 3.0 synsets is the correct equivalent of the Romanian synset and we also implemented an equivalent for the other PWN synset;
- 210 Romanian synsets disappeared through this mapping: their equivalent English synsets were eliminated: this is the case of many participial adjectives, of obsolete, euphemistic and slang meanings; some meanings were merged due to their identity; some compound literals were morphologically reanalyzed in simple words that were already in the network (e.g. *well endowed*), etc.

At present, the Romanian wordnet aligned to the PWN 3.0 contains 51986 literals in 57895 synsets. Its version aligned to the PWN 2.0 contained 52357 literals in 58725 synsets. Around 400 literals and 900 synsets were lost in the mapping process.

4 Conclusions and further work

In spite of the criticism against various aspects of the wordnet (treatment of various relations, sense granularity), there is a worldwide proliferation of the projects in which such a resource is created by various methods, either automatic or manual. To catch up with the PWN, many teams appeal to fast and cheap strategies, such as the automatic translation of the PWN and the import of its structure, sometimes leaving the glosses not translated, thus making it impossible to talk about that wordnet as a monolingual dictionary. However, the richness of relations is aimed by many developers as they can facilitate the extraction of valuable information for various applications. Such efforts are a proof that lexical resources in the form of wordnets are a must for natural languages in the electronic era, although there are still unsettled matters about wordnets. Further proof of their utility can be found in the applications relying on wordnets: summarization, question answering, word sense disambiguation, machine translation, information extraction and so on.

The ongoing development of the RoWN in the last decade followed three directions of research: implementation of new concepts and associated relations in the RoWN, with the aim of attaining a huge coverage of the Romanian lexicon, extensions to the RoWN and its using in applications (Word Sense Disambiguation see Ion and Tufiş 2004, Question Answering see Barbu Mititelu et al. 2009). The extensions to RoWN are the description of literals in terms of paradigmatic morphology (thus offering the great facility of searching for a word by its inflected forms, which is of extreme help in various applications using RoWN, especially as Romanian has a rich inflectional system, see Irimia 2007 for details) and the subjective mark-up of synsets (with the aim of mining opinions in text, see Tufiş 2009).

As other teams of researchers have already started to do, we also envisage the marking of derivational relations between words in RoWN, as well as enrichment of these relations with semantic information about the semantic type of the derived nominal, which could be of great help in various applications in which our wordnet will be used.

Acknowledgments

Part of the work reported here is suported by the Sectorial Operational Programme Human Resources Development (SOP HRD), financed from the European Social Fund and by the Romanian Government under the contract number SOP HRD/89/1.5/S/59758.

References

Eneko Agirre, Olatz Ansa, Xabier Arregi, José Mari Arriola, Arantza Diaz de Ilarraza, Eli Pociello, Larraitz Uria. 2002. Methodological Issues in the building of the Basque WordNet: quantitative and qualitative analysis. *Proceedings of the first International Conference of Global WordNet Association.*

V. Balkova, A. Suhonogov, S.A. Yablonsky. 2004. Russia WordNet. From UML-notation to Internet / Intranet Database Implementation. *Proceedings of the Second International WordNet* Conference:31–38.

Eduard Barbu and Verginica Barbu Mititelu. 2005. Automatic Building of Wordnets. *Proceedings of the International Conference Recent Advances in Natural Language Processing*:99-106

Verginica Barbu Mititelu, Alexandru Ceaușu, Radu Ion, Elena Irimia, Dan Ștefănescu, Dan Tufiș. 2009. Resurse lingvistice pentru un sistem de întrebare-răspuns pentru limba română. *Revista Română de Interacțiune Om-Calculator* 2:1-17.

Regina Barzilay and Michael Elhadad. 1997. Using lexical chains for text summarization. *Proceedings of the Intelligent Scalable Text Summarization Workshop*.

Darja Fišer and Benoît Sagot. 2008. Combining multiple resources to build reliable wordnets. *TSD*.

Christiane Fellbaum (Ed.). 1998. *WordNet: An electronic lexical database*. Cambridge, MA: MIT Press.

Christiane Fellbaum. 2009. Putting Semantics into WordNet's "Morphosemantic" Links. In Z. Vetulani, H. Uszhoreit (Eds.), *Human Language Technology*, Springer:350-358.

Graeme Hirst and D. St-Onge. 1998. Lexical Chains as Representation of Context for Detection and Correction of Malapropisms. In Ch. Fellbaum (Ed.)

Radu Ion and Dan Tufiș. 2004. Multilingual Word Sense Disambiguation Using Aligned Wordnets. *Romanian Journal of Information Science and technology*, vol. 7, no. 1-2:183-200.

Elena Irimia. 2007. ROG - A Paradigmatic Morphological Generator for Romanian. In Z. Vetulani (Ed.), *Proceedings of the 3rd Language & Technology Conference: Human Language Technologies as a Challenge for Computer Science and Linguistics*:408-412.

Hitoshi Isahara, Francis Bond, Kiyotaka Uchimoto, Masao Utiyama, Kyoko Kanzaki. 2008. Development of the Japanese WordNet. *Proceedings of LREC'2008*.

Svetla Koeva. 2008. Derivational and Morpho-Semantic Relations in Bulgarian Wordnet. *Intelligent Information Systems*, XVI: 359-369, Academic Publishing House.

Krister Lindén and Lauri Carlson. 2010. Finn-WordNet - WordNet på finska via översättning. *LexicoNordica - Nordic Journal of Lexicography*, vol 17.

George A. Miller, Richard Beckwith, Christiane Fellbaum, Derek Gross, Katherine Miller. 1993 Introduction to WordNet: An On-line Lexical Database. *Special Issue of the International Journal of Lexicography*, 3 (4), initial version 1990.

Karel Pala and Pavel Smrž. 2004. Building Czech WordNet. *Romanian Journal of Information Science and technology*, vol 7, numbers 1-2:79-88.

Ian Niles and Adam Pease. 2001 Towards a Standard Upper Ontology. *Proceedings of the 2nd International Conference on Formal Ontology in Information* Systems:2-9.

Adrian Novischi and Dan Moldovan. 2006. Question Answering with Lexical Chains Propagating Verb Argument. *ACL*.

Emanuele Pianta, Luisa Bentivogli, Christian Girardi. 2002. MultiWordNet: developing an aligned multilingual database. *Proceedings of the First International Conference on Global WordNet*.

M.A. Stairmand. 1996. *A Computational Analysis of Lexical Cohesion with applications in Information Retrieval*, Ph.D Thesis, UMIST.

Dan Tufiș. 2009. Paradigmatic Morphology and Subjectivity Mark-up in the RO-WordNet Lexical Ontology. In H.N. Teodorescu, J. Watada, L.C. Jains (Eds.), *Intelligent Systems and Technologies – Methods and Applications*, Springer:161-179.

Dan Tufiș and Eduard Barbu. 2004. A Methodology and Associated Tools for Building Interlingual Wordnets. *Proceedings of the 4th International Conference on Language Resources and Evaluation LREC 2004*:1067-1070.

Dan Tufiș, Dan Cristea, Sofia Stamou. 2004. BalkaNet: Aims, Methods, Results and Perspectives. *Special Issue of the Romanian Journal of Information Science and Technology*, vol. 7, no. 1-2:9-43.

Piek Vossen, Wim Peters, Julio Gonzalo. 1999 Towards a universal index of meaning. *Proceedings of the ACL-99 Siglex workshop*:81-90.

Creation and Development of the Romanian Lexical Resources

Elena Boian, Constantin Ciubotaru, Svetlana Cojocaru, Alexandru Colesnicov, Ludmila Malahov, Mircea Petic
Institute of Mathematics and Computer Science,
Chişinău, Moldova
{lena,chebotar,svetlana.cojocaru,kae,mal,mirsha}@math.md

Abstract

This article describes the Romanian lexical resources containing morphological data and dictionaries: synonyms, Romanian-English, and Romanian-Russian.

The inflection process at the creation of morphological resources based on the functional grammar with scattered context is considered. An arbitrary word is inflected knowing only its part of speech, and the gender for nouns.

New words were obtained also by using prefixing and suffixing. The research in automated prefixing and suffixing permitted us to determine some word classes for which this method is applicable, and to implement the corresponding algorithms.

We describe the database structure, and the DB population programming tools.

The article describes an approach to the checking of integrity and correctness of the morphological resources presented as a database mapping Romanian words to their morphological derivatives.

1 Introduction

Creation and development of the lexical resources are important parts of Natural Language Processing (NLP).

One of such resources for the Romanian language are Reusable Resources for the Romanian Language (RRRL).[1]

This article describes how these lexical resources were created and developed, the database structure, and the corresponding programming tools. The morphological and, more specifically, the inflectional aspects are pointed out.

[1]http://www.math.md/elrr/

In Sec. 2, the implemented programs are described that populate the resources by automatic inflection (Boian and Cojocaru, 1996). The starting point for this approach was the book (Lombard and Gâdei, 1981), where most of Romanian productive classes of words (nouns, adjectives and verbs) were classified according to their inflection groups. The classification was made from the linguistic point of view, and, for example, the accents were taken into account. In this case, it is possible to operate only with the graphical representation of the word that equally simplifies and complicates the problem. Nevertheless, this classification was useful and led to the idea to formalize word-forms producing with the special grammar that is presented into Sec. 3. Other parts of speech (numerals, pronouns, articles, conjunctions, prepositions, interjections) were entered into the Database (DB) manually as being not so numerous.

It is shown also how the inflectional model for an arbitrary word can be determined (Sec. 4). Knowing this information it is possible to perform the inflection automatically (Sec. 5).

The proposed solution is not restricted by the Romanian language but could be also applied to other natural languages with inflectional mechanisms similar to these of Romanian.

Another way to populate the DB is affixing. New words were generated by prefixing and suffixing (Cojocaru et al., 2009). The research in the possibilities of automated prefixing and suffixing permitted to determine some word classes for which this method is applicable, and to implement the corresponding algorithms. This led to considerable lexicon extension (Sec. 6).

In Sec. 7, the structure of the DB is described, the relations between the main and auxiliary tables, and some techniques are discussed that were used to check the DB integrity and information correctness in maximally automated mode (Cojocaru et al., 2006).

2 Acquisition of lexical resources

An important direction in NLP is acquisition of lexical resources. The problem of the automation of words inflexion process in Romanian was investigated in (Boian and Cojocaru, 1996). The obtained results permitted to construct an electronic lexicon RRRL containing the lemmas and their word-forms. Lexical resources acquisition is carried out by using static and dynamic methods for words inflexion.

Static methods use the morphological dictionary (Lombard and Gâdei, 1981), where the inflexion groups are indicated explicitly. The algorithm based on static method uses the formalism of the inflexion grammar for a natural language proposed in (Boian and Cojocaru, 1996).

Dynamic methods tried to find the inflexion model analyzing the word structure, and especially its affixes. These affixes were determined by examining of different lexicographic sources. Dynamic method attempts to calculate the inflexion paradigm using some classifications. The inflexion programs created on the base of these methods permit to generate approx. 90% of all Romanian inflexions. Sometimes the user intervention is requested to solve ambiguities.

3 Scattered Context Grammars for Vocabulary Generation

The scattered context grammar rules have the following form:

$$[/] * [\#][N_1]a_1\overline{b_1}a_2 \ldots a_{n-1}\overline{b_{n-1}}a_n \rightarrow a'_1\overline{b_1}a'_2 \ldots a'_{n-1}\overline{b_{n-1}}a'_nN_2,$$

where a_i, a'_i are arbitrary words, and either b_i is nonempty word, or the special symbol $*$ stands instead of b_i, admits arbitrary f_i. Numbers N_j are codes of the ending sets.

The interpretation of this rule is as follows. Let w be the base word to produce word-forms. Every slash / indicates cutting the last letter from w. The word v obtained after this is considered as a root (if N_1 exists) and N_2 is its index in ending set list L. In any case the word v should have the form

$$f_0a_1f_1a_2f_2 \ldots a_{n-1}f_{n-1}a_nf_n,$$

where every f_i is an arbitrary (possible empty) word, not containing (for $i = 1, 2, \ldots, n-1$) the veto sub-word b_i. Veto for b_i is conditioned by the necessity to determine the position of the sub-word a_i to be substituted. If there exists more then one representation of this kind the first one (scanning v from left to the right or vice versa if the sign $\#$ is present) should be selected.

Let us take the example word w ="*frate*" (Eng. "brother") that fits this case: masculine gender, singular number, indefinite form, is inflected using the rule M46 / 5 t→ţ 3. We have two sublists of endings for this word: $T_5 = \{e, e, e, ele, elui, e\}$ and $T_3 = \{i, i, i, ii, ilor, ilor\}$. The rule is interpreted as follows. First of all the last symbol of word w is deleted. It gives the root v_1 ="*frat*" that is concatenated with the set of endings T_5. One part of inflections is formed without alternation. The list of inflected words is: *frate, frate, frate, fratele, fratelui, frate*. Then the alteration of consonants $t \rightarrow$ ţ is performed in the root v_1. The obtained root v_2 is concatenated with the set of endings T_3. The list of the rest inflected words for v_2="*fraţ*" is the following: *fraţi, fraţi, fraţi, fraţii, fraţilor, fraţilor*.

The obtained inflected words for w="*frate*" are: *frate, frate, frate, fratele, fratelui, frate, fraţi, fraţi, fraţi, fraţii, fraţilor, fraţilor*.

Using such grammar rules, the process of creating of the decomposed vocabulary was formalized. The inflexion grammar for Romanian contains 866 rules and 320 ending sets. They were used to obtain a morphological lexicon using dictionary with about 30,000 lemmas (Lombard and Gâdei, 1981).

4 Description of the Inflection Process

Romanian is a highly inflected language. As we mentioned already, open productive parts of speech for Romanian are nouns, adjectives, and verbs. These open classes contain tens of thousands elements, and are characterized by a productive process of inflection, derivation and composition. In this case the problem is complicated not only because it is impossible enumerate the elements existing at the moment, but also because a successful formalism should be able to serve future neologisms that could occur in the language. In the following we operate with the paradigms of inflection, by which we understand the systematic arrangement of all inflection forms of a word.

We work not with the whole words, but with their variable parts, including roots and inflectional morphemes added to them. Below, we mention list of inflectional morphemes as the (inflectional) paradigm.

An incomplete set of rules was shown in papers (Tufiş et al., 1996; Peev et al., 1996; Hristea and Moroianu, 2003). There, concatenation of inflectional morpheme for nouns and adjectives is performed not concerning the problem of the alternations in the root. Therefore, having the aim to achieve the model of inflection, we developed a formalism, which includes two processes: alternation in the root, and concatenation of an inflectional morpheme.

5 Determining the Inflection Group

We use the word spelling only to determine its inflexion group. The grammar rules define, in fact, the inflexion model on the algorithmic level: cutting a given number of symbols at the word ending; obtaining different roots by substitutions (in order to produce vowel and consonant alternation), attaching the corresponding morphemes (endings) to the roots.

This method can be applied only in the case when the inflexion group (inflexion model) is known. Otherwise, the problem appears of inflexion model calculation, knowing the graphical representation of the word. Is it possible to solve algorithmically this problem? The answer is negative. The first obstacle is the determination of part of speech: there are several examples of homonyms, which represent different parts of speech, e.g., *mare* (Eng. big) is an adjective, and *mare* (Eng. sea) is a noun.

Let us restrict the formulation of the problem: is it possible to establish the model of inflection (in the conditions indicated above) knowing the part of speech?

The answer is negative in this case too. For confirmation we can bring a list of examples, which show us that without invoking phonetic or etymological information we cannot determine the model of inflection. Let us illustrate this assertion by analyzing feminine noun *masă*. Following the meaning of furniture object we will form plural *mese*, using the model with vowel alternation $a \rightarrow e$. But if you follow the meaning "compact crowd of people", the plural *mase* should be produced without alternation. The origin of this phenomenon is etymological: in the first case the origin of the word is from Latin *mensa*, but in the second case from the French word *masse*. The problem might be tackled in another way: to establish some criteria which permit, after the analyzing of the word structure, to conclude about the possibility to determine the inflexion model and, if this is possible, to fix the specific model. Otherwise, we will try to formulate the criterion according to which one can affirm that the inflexion process can be performed automatically and denote the corresponding model.

Let we have a word (a lemma) in its graphical representation. We know the part of speech, and the gender in the case of noun. We divide all words into three categories:

irregular, the case being determined from a preset list of words;

absolutely regular, that admitting the automatic inflexion (a unique inflectional model can be calculated);

partially regular, those words which need some additional information except the graphical representation to be inflected, and calculation produces two or more inflectional models.

To simplify, we exclude from the examination the irregular words as their presence or absence does not affect the generality of the algorithm.

In (Cojocaru, 2006), the algorithm had been proposed, which analyses the dictionary of classification into morphological groups with entries of type (w, σ), where w is a word in natural language, and σ – number (label) of inflection group, constructs two groups of sets $A = \{A_1, A_2, \ldots, A_k\}$ and $P = \{P_1, P_2, \ldots P_s\}$, $\cap_{i=1}^{k} A_i = \emptyset, \cap_{i=1}^{s} P_i = \emptyset$. $A_i \cap P_j = \emptyset$.

These sets consisted of sub-words α_j of the words $w = w'\alpha_j$, where $1 \leq |\alpha_j| \leq |w|$. It is shown that for certain categories of words it is possible to construct such sets A_i, that from the fact that $\alpha_j \in A_i$ it results unequivocally that the word w belongs to the single inflection group σ, and these words being named "absolutely regular". With the help of the same algorithm there are constructed also such sets P_i, that from the fact that $\alpha_j \in P_i$ it results that $w = w'\alpha_j$ can belong to several inflection groups $\sigma_1, \ldots, \sigma_m$, and the respective words being named "partially regular".

5.1 Construction of Ending Sets

Let L be the set of all words of a language. We come from the assumption (valid for majority of natural languages) that there is a classification dictionary $D \subseteq L$, so that to any $\omega \in D$ it puts into correspondence an inflectional model ν, where ν is a positive integer. We will present dictionary D as a union of words classified by parts of speech (and gender, for nouns), $D = \cup(C)_{i=1}^{5}$, where C_i is one of the sets of words of open classes: nouns (masculine, feminine, neuter), adjectives and verbs. For each C_i the dictionary D puts into correspondence the finite set of inflectional models $N_i = \{\nu_1, \ldots, \nu_{n_k}\}$, such that for $\forall\omega \in C_i$ there is at least a $\nu \in N_i$. We will separately operate with each of these classes.

Let C be one of these classes. The idea of algorithm to build the sets of endings is the following. For each word $\omega \in C$, to which the inflectional model $\nu_m \in N$ corresponds (N is the set of integers of inflectional models for words in C), the endings were built with decreasing lengths from $|\omega|$ to 1. The pairs (γ_i, ν_m) are formed, where γ_i is a substring of length i of the word ω, $(1 \leq i \leq |\omega|)$. The pairs, constructed thus, are compared and filtered. The filtration process is carried out in the following way.

Out of each two elements (γ_i, ν_m), (η_i, ν_n), we keep only one, if $\gamma_i = \eta_i$ and $\nu_m = \nu_n$, where γ_i is a substring of length i of the word $|\omega|$, and η_i is a substring of length i of the word ψ (i. e. only non-coincident pairs are kept).

If for all the pairs in which $\gamma_i \neq \eta_i$ the equality $\nu_m = \nu_n$ takes place, then the pairs (γ_i, ν_m) and (η_i, ν_n) are elements of the set A of the endings corresponding to absolutely regular words.

If $\gamma_i = \eta_i$ and $\nu_m \neq \nu_n$, then the ending η_i indicates a substring of the word ψ partially regular from the set P, to which several inflectional models $\nu_m, \nu_n, \ldots$ correspond.

We describe the filtration process using the next example. Let $D = \{$ *(grup, 1), (grup, 2), (dulap, 1), (cuvînt, 2), (vînt, 1), (tractor, 3), (muzeu, 41)*$\}$.

Initially $A = \emptyset$, $P = \emptyset$.

We take as C all the words from D, i.e.,

$C = \{$ *grup, dulap, cuvînt, vînt, tractor, muzeu*$\}$ (in English: group, wardrobe, word, wind, tractor, museum).

$L_{max} = 7$; $N = \{1, 2, 3, 41\}$.

We construct the sets of endings of the lengths $7, 6, \ldots, 2, 1$ of words from C, to which the inflectional models N are being put into correspondence.

Sub-words were sorted descendently at their lenghts:

$D = \{$ *(tractor, 3)* $\cup$ *(cuvînt, 2), (ractor, 3)* $\cup$ *(uvînt, 2), (actor, 3), (dulap, 1), (muzeu, 41)* $\cup$ *(grup, 1), (grup, 2), (vînt, 2), (vînt, 1), (ctor, 3), (ulap, 1), (uzeu, 41)* $\cup$ *(rup, 1), (rup, 2), (înt, 2), (înt, 1), (lap, 1), (tor, 3), (zeu, 41)* $\cup$ *(up, 1), (up, 2), (nt, 2), (nt, 1), (ap, 3), (or, 3),(eu, 41)* $\cup$ *(p, 1), (p, 2), (t, 2), (t, 1), (p, 3), (r, 3), (u, 41)* $\}$.

Then we obtain the sets A and P using above mentioned rules with the following components:

$A = \{$*(dulap, 1), (ulap, 1), (lap, 1), (ap, 1), (cuvînt, 2), (uvînt, 2), (tractor, 3), (ractor, 3), (actor, 3), (ctor, 3), (tor, 3), (or, 3), (r, 3), (muzeu, 41), (uzeu, 41), (zeu, 41), (eu, 41), (u, 41)*$\}$.

$P = \{$*(grup,1, 2), (rup,1, 2), (up, 1, 2), (vînt,1, 2), (înt,1, 2), (nt, 1, 2), (p, 1, 2), (t, 1, 2)*$\}$.

5.2 Determination of the Inflection Group

We determine the inflexion group for the word $\psi \in C$.

The algorithm for the inflexion group determination is the following.

The substrings ξ_i $(1 \leq i \leq |\psi|)$ of the endings with decreasing length from $|\psi|$ to 1 of the word ψ are constructed. Initially we look for a completely regular model, comparing the ending ξ_i $(|\xi_i| = i)$ with the elements $(\gamma, \nu_m) \in A$ $(|\gamma_i| = i)$. If $\exists\gamma_i = \xi_i$, then ν_m is the inflection model number.

In case if we did not find an appropriate model in A, we look for it in P. If $\exists\gamma_i = \xi_i$ $(\gamma_i, \nu_{n_1}, \nu_{n_2}, \ldots, \nu_{n_k} \in P)$, the word ψ is partially regular and it has to inflect in correspondence with the inflexion models $\nu_{n_1}, \nu_{n_2}, \ldots, \nu_{n_k}$.

In the case when $\xi_i \neq \gamma_i$ for $\forall\gamma_i$ from A and P the inflection model can not be determined automatically and the intervention of user (the expert in linguistics) is needed.

Reviewing the example of construction of ending sets A and P from the previous section, we can determine the inflectional group for the word *motor* (in English: engine).

We obtain that the word w =*"motor"* is inflected using the inflectional group 3. The substrings ξ_i $(1 \leq i \leq 5)$ of the endings with decreasing length from 5 to 1 of the word w are constructed: *motor, otor, tor, or, r*. Initially we look for a completely regular model, comparing the ending ξ_i $(|\xi_i| = i)$ with the elements $(\gamma, \nu_m) \in A$ $(|\gamma_i| = i)$ and *tor* as substring of word w and *tor* from $(tor, 3) \in A$ coincide, then 3 is the inflection model for w =*"motor"*.

Characteristics	Number
derivatives	15300
roots/stems	6800
prefixes	42
suffixes	433

Table 1: The tables characteristics

6 Prefixing and Suffixing

Existent electronic linguistic resources represent one of the important moment in the process of derivatives generator elaboration. In the case of the lexicons they are not simple repositories only of words, but they need to contain the prefixes and/or suffixes with their descriptions (Carota, 2006; Petic, 2010).

To work with affixing, we take the correspondent information from the electronic variant of derivatives dictionary (S.Constantinescu, 2008) (Tab. 1) and added four tables to the DB: *prefixes, suffixes, roots-stems-derivatives*, and the table which mapes affixes to roots/stems in order to form the derivatives. The last table consists of 3 fields destinated to prefixes and 4 for suffixes, because the electronic variant of derivatives dictionary has derivatives with maximum 2 prefixes, for example, dez/ră/suci (Eng. untwist), pre/în/noi (Eng. restore), or 3 suffixes, for example, loc/al/iza/re (Eng. localization).

With this structure attached to RRRL, it was possible to elaborate some queries that allow:

- derivative extraction by a prefix or suffix;
- lexical family extraction for a root or stem;
- the part of speech establishing of the derivatives and/or roots-stems;
- determining the alternations that are present in the process of derivation.

The lexicon completion can be implemented with the help of automatic tools (Cojocaru et al., 2009). Starting with the derivation rules, an algorithm which forms a set of words corresponding to the derivation constraints is going to be elaborated. This algorithm of derivation is applied to these words and the result is a set of derivatives. Therefore not all the derivatives correspond to the norms of human language. After applying the method of validation, we obtain correct words on the basis

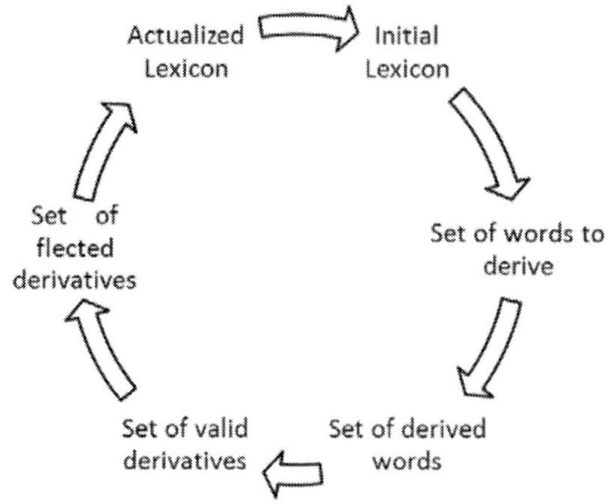

Figure 1: Cycle of the lexicon completion

of language. These words are inflected by means of programs for inflection (Boian and Cojocaru, 1996) that result in a set of inflected words. This veryfied set can complete the initial lexicon, making it actual (Fig. 1).

Nevertheless after a cycle of bringing the lexicon up to date it is possible to apply another similar cycle (Cojocaru et al., 2009). So, after a finite number of cycles it is likely to finish the process of completion, in the end obtaining a "filled" (saturated) lexicon which will be complete from the point of view of derivation.

7 Correctness and Integrity of the DB

Before to make lexical resources widely available we checked their correctness and integrity. We did it in maximally automated mode: using some programs to select suspicious information for ulterior correction by the operator or the expert in philology to make the final decision.

7.1 Structure of the RRRL DB

The Resources DB for RRRL has two main tables and a lot of auxiliary ones. Auxiliary tables contain different codes used in the main tables, e. g., codes of morphological characteristics or languages.

The *words* table contains the part code (part of speech) and field code (domain of the word usage) fields. Numerically encoded word in the flexies table marks the base word of flexies.

The *word_flexies* table contains the flexy word field keeping derivatives of Romanian words. Each derivative is associated with its base word in the *words* table through the integer prim word code field. The integer *morpho_code* field substantiates morphological information (tense, number, case, etc.).

As for auxiliary tables, the *morpho_code* field is substantiated using not one single table but ten auxiliary tables in correspondence to ten Romanian parts of speech: noun, adjective, verb, numeral, adverb, pronoun, preposition, conjunction, article, interjection. The fields in these tables contain codes of Romanian morphologic categories corresponding to the part of speech.

The DB was populated from textual information files.

The DB population program produces a file that shows if words were inserted, word codes, and the result for each operation. Errors are marked and can be easily found. We also see how many words were entered and which words were not entered because they double the existing ones in the DB.

Textual information files were got by a semi-automatic program that generates all word-forms for a given Romanian word (Boian et al., 2005). The program is wizard-like and the input should be done by an expert linguist.

For the *word_flexies* table, each group contains one word-lemma with all its derivatives (word-forms). Encoded morphological information is included with each word-form.

7.2 DB Integrity

The building of a lexical resource is a difficult process. We tried to automate it maximally using specially developed programs. To deal with errors, a set of techniques was developed that are described below.

First of all, it is possible apply formal methods to check validity of the DB content. These methods can be formulated using the semantics and interdependencies of the DB fields and tables. In this purpose, all DB fields are divided in four categories:

1. fields containing textual representation of words;

2. fields containing references that connect different tables, e. g., codes of Romanian word-lemmas that replace words themselves in the *word_flexies* table;

3. fields containing morphological attributes;

4. fields containing textual representation (deciphering) of attributes; these fields only exist in the auxiliary tables.

Depending of the used DB engine, some formal relationships can be supported automatically,

Non-formal checking may be executed by variety of techniques depending on the field category. Foe example, the fields of the category 1 can be checked by usual spell checkers. For Romanian, there exists a spell checker RomSP (Malahova and Colesnicov, 1996). The corresponding list of Romanian words was carefully tested and updated both by developers and users of the product, and can be taken as being quite reliable. Romanian spell checker from MS Office was also used. For Romanian, words that were rejected by both spell checkers were marked as highly suspicious. The analysis show that most of them were erroneous. Other word lists can also be used, e.g., those coming with free spell checkers like ISpell.[2]

A different method of word checking supposes the selection of *n-grams* (word fragments of n letters, $n > 2$) from the given set of words, and calculation of their frequencies. Less frequent n-grams are considered to be suspicious. Words that contain such n-grams should be checked by experts.

7.3 DB Correctness

The next check is search for duplicates. The unique field of the *words* table is prim_ word_ code. The corresponding information consists of the Romanian word in its textual form, its part of speech, and its field of usage. These data are checked for uniqueness during DB population.

We saw that category 3 fields can be formally checked as containing in one of additional tables as the record number. The correspondence between fields of categories 3 and 4 can be checked informally using interval of values for different attributes but this is partial checking only. In any case, additional tables are short and can be checked visually. We can also search for unused codes in them. The correspondence of codes in the morpho. categories table and tables for each part of speech was checked by issuing requests that show in parallel decoded values of each code.

The next category of checks is search for duplicates. Our DB population programs query for existence of the information before its insertion into

[2] http://www.gnu.org/software/ispell/ispell.html

any of tables, therefore, absence of duplicates can be supposed. Meanwhile, search for duplicates can expose some errors in the prepared data for population of the DB, or in the DB population programs themselves.

In the *words* table, the unique field is *prim_word_code*. The corresponding information consists of the Romanian word in its textual form, its part of speech and field of usage. These data are checked for uniqueness during DB population. Non-unique combination found means something wrong with these programs, and we can check their codes visually for this combination.

Moreover, we checked the words table for uniqueness of word's textual form ignoring even its part of speech. In Romanian, adjective can coincide with adverb and noun can coincide with adjective, but such cases are relatively rare. This check permitted to detect several errors also.

Uniqueness of records in the *word_flexies* table is also checked during DB population. The corresponding check can be performed after population to test the DB population programs.

We performed also the following informal semantic checks.

Normally, Romanian words have some standard number of inflective derivatives depending of the part of speech: 12 for nouns, 20 for adjectives, and 35, 39, or 40 for verbs. We queried for the actual number of derivatives for words from the *words* table. For example, the result of the first such test for one of verbs was 160 derivatives. The impossible number of derivatives for some words permitted us to correct some errors. For example, it was found analyzing the case of verbs with more derivatives than necessary that some details of Romanian grammar were misunderstood during the design stage.

Parallel dictionaries are very useful and widely used in computer linguistics. Our DB contains translations of many Romanian words into English and Russian. We could not get sufficient results from the English translations. The Russian translations permitted us to formulate several useful criteria because Russian is a highly inflective language like Romanian. We used endings of Russian translations, that are more or less standard depending of part of speech, for:

- Check for words that are not verbs but Russian translations have "verbal" endings -ти -тись -ть -ться -чь -чься. We found 4119 of them, being mostly OK, but several errors were found.
- Check for words that are not adjectives but Russian translations have "adjectival" endings -ая -ев -ий -ин -ов -ые -ый -ье -ья. No such words were found.
- Check for words that are not adverbs but Russian translations have the corresponding endings -е -о -у -ем -ём -мя -ой -ом -ски. This check was not so successful (18974 words) but we shortened the result by deleting all verbs, adjectives, and nouns, and found several errors more.

As errors were found, they were corrected in the source data files. At a small quantity of corrections, erroneous records were deleted taking into account all interdependencies, and the corresponding part of the data file was entered anew. Having a lot of corrections, we populated anew the whole DB that takes quite acceptable time.

We do not enter specific field of usage for a word where we enter its morphological derivatives. In this case, the corresponding field is always set to 1 ("general"). Therefore, we can check for uniqueness of the combination of a word's textual form and part of speech and analyze the corresponding fields of usage and tables where are used "non-general" words. We created the list of uninflected words that coincide with some inflected pairs of text and part of speech, and the list of "truly" uninflected words.

Conclusions and Results

A computational lexicon for Romanian containing about 1 mil. words (obtained by inflexion of 100,000 lemmas) was constructed. The lexicon was used for different linguistic applications: the spelling checker for Romanian, the data base of linguistic resources, the search algorithm for web pages.

Certain criteria were established for a word that allow to determine which is its inflexion model, analyzing the word structure.

The derivation rules formalization for some Romanian affixes offer the possibility to elaborate algorithms for the lexical resources completion. The process of new derivatives validation is one that raises many questions and it seems that there are solutions though there are some difficulties in this process. Thus, it is impossible to neglect the aspect of source credibility in the process of word validation. In this context the word validation using the existent corpora seems to be the best solution.

The automatic completion cycle model for lexical resources by the derivation and inflectional mechanisms allows the consciousness of the steps in the process of lexicon enrichment.

DB was selected as linguistic information stock because of possibility of quick parallel and distant access, flexibility of possible queries, wide use and availability of the corresponding programming techniques. Other forms of information presentation like, e. g., word lists, can be easily obtained from the DB. Applications can be developed using this DB directly or indirectly.

The information containing in the DB should be thoroughly checked using different techniques. A set of methods was proposed that were found useful in the case. The discussed techniques can be applied at checking of lexical information in other cases.

References

E. Boian and S. Cojocaru. 1996. The inflexion regularities for the Romanian language. *Computer Science Journal of Moldova*, 4(1):40–58.

E. Boian, A. Danilchenco, and L. Topal. 1993. The automation of speech parts inflexion process. *Computer Science Journal of Moldova*, 1(2):14–26.

E. Boian, C. Ciubotaru, S. Cojocaru, A. Colesnicov, V. Demidova, and L. Malahova. 2005. Lexical resources for Romanian. In *Scientific Memories of the Romanian Academy*, volume 26 of *IV*, pages 267–278. Bucharest, România.

S. Cojocaru and E. Boian. 2010. Determination of inflexional group using P systems. *Computer Science Journal of Moldova*, 18(1(52)):70–78.

S. Cojocaru, M. Evstiunin, and V. Ufnarovski. 1993. Detecting and correcting spelling errors for Romanian language. *Computer Science Journal of Moldova*, 1(1):3–22.

S. Cojocaru, A. Colesnicov, and L. Malahova. 2006. Integrity and correctness checking of a lexical database. *Computer Science Journal of Moldova*, 14(1(40)):138–151.

S. Cojocaru, E. Boian, and M. Petic. 2009. Stages in automatic derivational morphology processing. In *Proceedings of the International Conference on Knowledge Engineering, Principles and Techniques KEPT2009*, pages 49–53, Cluj-Napoca (Romania), July 2–4.

F. Carota. 2006. Derivational morphology of Italian: Principles of formalization. *Literary and Linguistic Computing*, 21(Suppl. Issue).

M. Petic. 2010. Developing a derivatives generator. *Computer Science Journal of Moldova*, 18(1(52)):82–96.

D. Tufiş, L. Diaconu, C. Diaconu, and A.M. Barbu. 1996. Morfologia limbii române, o resursă lingvistică reversibilă şi reutilizabilă (Morphology of Romanian, a reversible and reusable linguistic resource). In *Limbaj şi Tehnologie*, pages 59–65. Editura Academiei Române, Bucureşti. (in Romanian).

S. Cojocaru. 2006. The ascertainment of the inflexion models for Romanian. *Computer Science Journal of Moldova*, 14(1(40)):103–112.

1998. *Dicţionarul explicativ al limbii române (The Explanatory Dictionary of the Romanian Language)*. Academia Română, Institutul de Lingvistică "Iorgu Iordan", Editura Univers Enciclopedic. (in Romanian).

T. Hristea and C. Moroianu. 2003. Generarea formelor flexionare substantivale şi adjectivale în limba română (Generation of flexional forms for nouns and adjective in the Romanian language). In F. Hristea and M. Popescu, editors, *Building Awareness in Language Technology*, pages 443–460. Editura Universităţii din Bucureşti, Bucureşti. (in Romanian).

S. Constantinescu. *Dicţionarul de cuvinte derivate*. Editura HERRA, Bucureşti, 2008.

D. Irimia. 2004. *Gramatica limbii române (The Grammar of the Romanian language)*. Polirom, Bucureşti, 2 edition. (in Romanian).

A. Lombard and C. Gâdei. 1981. *Dictionnaire morphologique de la langue roumaine*. Editura Academiei, Bucureşti.

L. Malahova and A. Colesnicov. 1996. Implementation of the Romanian Spelling Pack for Windows. In *The International Conference on Technical Informatics CONTI'96. Proceedings. Computer Science and Engineering*, volume 1, pages 23–28, Timişoara, România.

L. Peev, L. Bibolar, and E. Jodal. 1996. Un model de formalizare a morfologiei limbii române (A formalization model of Romanian morphology). In *Limbaj şi Tehnologie*, pages 67–72. Editura Academiei Române, Bucureşti. (in Romanian).

Analyses Tools for Non-head Structures

Sirine Boukédi
Faculty of Sciences Economy and Management of Sfax
Sirine.boukedi@gmail.com

Kais Haddar
Sciences Faculty of Sfax
Kais.haddar@fss.rnu.tn

Abstract

Syntactic analysis is a fundamental phase in NLP (Natural Language Processing) domain. This phase occurs in several applications and at different levels. Moreover, it wasn't spilled in domain research, especially for Arabic language. In fact, most of researchers working on Arabic language treated simple structures and neglected complicated ones such as relatives, coordination, ellipse and juxtaposition. In this context, the present work lies within the construction of a HPSG (Head-driven Phrase Structure Grammar) grammar treating Arabic coordination. The established grammar is specified on TDL (Type Description Language) and experimented with a parser generated by LKB (Linguistic Knowledge Building) system.

1 Introduction

The study on Arabic language showed that coordination is one of particular structures. It is frequent in different corpus and occurs with many other phenomena. The interaction with the other structures makes the study very delicate. For this reason, it wasn't spilled in research domain.

Based on a large literature, most of existing researchers treated coordination structure for Roman languages except some works such as (Haddar, 2000) and (Maaloul *et al.*, 2004). In fact, Arabic coordination is very complicate. It covers many forms and different structures. Therefore, there is a big problem in the categorization of Arabic coordination.

Moreover the last researchers found a problem in the choice of the adequate formalism representing the different forms of coordination structures. But most of related works used HPSG. The choice of this formalism is justified. In fact, HPSG offers a complete representation for linguistic entries.

Therefore, our work aims to find an adequate typology classifying Arabic coordination structures and to construct a HPSG grammar representing the different forms of coordination. This grammar will be validated on LKB system.

In the present paper, we start by describing some related works treating coordination structure. Then, we adapted HPSG grammar to represent the different forms of our phenomenon, based on a proposed typology. It should be noted that the established grammar treated simple sentences and complex ones representing the different forms of coordination except cases of interaction with ellipse phenomenon. Finally, we validated our grammar on LKB system after specification in TDL. According to the obtained results, we evaluate our grammar and we enclose our work by a conclusion and some perspectives.

2 Previous works

The study on previous works showed that researchers on coordination structure started since 1970, such as (Hudsan, 1976), (Postal, 1974) and (Rau, 1985), for many languages. The different researches used various grammars. Some works used the GCCA (Applicative Categorical Combinatory Grammar), other works used GI (Interactive Grammar) and other ones were based on HPSG Grammar. But most of them, used this last one (HPSG formalism).

For French language, we can mention (Biskri and Desclés, 2006) who studied coordination structure of similar constituents, based on GCCA grammar. Moreover, (Le Roux and Perrier, 2006) studied constituent and non constituent structures based on XMG tools, a compilation tool, and used the GI formalism.

For Portuguese language, (Villavicencio *et al.*, 2005) studied the coordination of nominal phras es. They identified different strategies of analyses based on the HPSG formalism.

For Bulgarian language, we can mention the work of (Osenova and Simov, 2005) who studied the coordination phenomenon and its interaction with ellipse forms based on HPSG grammar. It should be noted that the formalization was encoded in XML.

According to our research, the study showed that most of the related works treated the coordination of Roman language. But, there is some works treating Arabic coordination such as (Haddar, 2000) and (Maaloul *et al.*, 2004). The proposed typology is similar in most of the related works. The difference between them appears in the choice of the grammar and the analysis tools.

For Arabic works, for example, Haddar (2000) studied syntactic analyses of Arabic coordination based on ATN (Augmented Transition Network) and (Maaloul *et al.*, 2004) studied the coordination of Arabic constituent based on HPSG grammar. This grammar was tested and validated on a constructed system, AICOO.

Based on the proposed typology, these related researches working on Arabic coordination didn't treat all forms of this structure. Therefore, the originality of our work is to construct a HPSG grammar covering all the possible forms of coordination and its interaction with the other phenomena such as the ellipse one. In the following paragraph, we present the proposed typology of Arabic coordination that we adopted from the related works.

3 Proposed typology for Arabic coordination

According to some linguists such as (Abdelwahed, 2004) and (Dahdeh, 1992), the coordination phenomenon joins two or several elements with a particle of coordination (conjunction). In Arabic, there exist nine conjunctions (و ، فـ ، ثمّ، حتّى، لكن، أم، أو، لا، بل).

Based on some related works (Haddar, 2000) and (Maaloul *et al.*, 2004), coordination structure in Arabic can be subdivided, like Roman languages, in two categories: coordination of constituent and coordination of non constituent. The first category covers cases when the conjunction joins two or several well formed constituents. These constituents can have similar or different categories. The figure 1 represents the coordination of similar constituents. The figure 2 represents the coordination of different constituents.

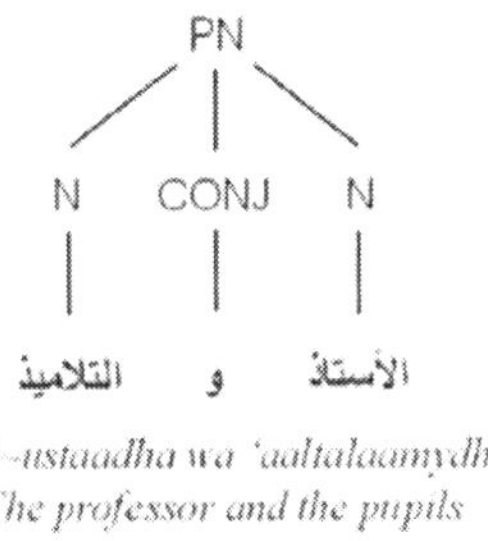

Figure 1. Coordination of constituents having similar categories.

As shown in Figure 1, the conjunction" و, and" joins two compounds having the same category, two defined nouns "الأستاذ, the professor" and "التلاميذ, the pupils".

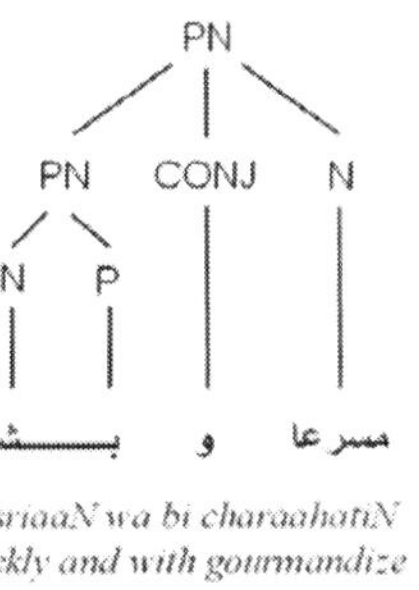

Figure 2. Coordination of constituents having different categories.

However in Figure 2, the same conjunction joins two different compounds. The first one "مسرعا, quickly" is an adverb, the second one ", بشراهة, with gourmandize" is a reduction phrase " مركب بالجر, reduction phrase".

For the second category, coordination of non constituent, the conjunction joins two or several constituents where one of them is incomplete. In fact, it represents the case where there is interaction with the ellipse phenomenon.

According to some references, there exist four forms of ellipse: Right Node Raising, Left Node Raising, Gapping and VP-ellipse. The first form: Right Node Raising, designed the case when the first element that should be at the right of the second compound, is missed.

The second form: the Left Node Raising designed the case when the second element is missed in the left of the second compound of coordination phrase.

For the third form: Gapping, it represented when there exist discontinuities in the second compound of the coordination phrase.

Finally, for the last form, VP-ellipse, it represented the case when the verbal phrase is missed and replaced by a proverb like "كذلك, also".

Based on the proposed typology for the Arabic coordination, we adapted the HPSG grammar. In fact, based on some references such as (Godard, 2006), the coordination phenomenon is a non head structure. Its representation differs from other phenomena. So it necessitates a particular structure. In the following paragraph, we present the HPSG grammar and the different modifications brought to this formalism to represent Arabic language. Then, we present the HPSG structure of Arabic coordination.

4 HPSG for the Arabic language

HPSG is a unification grammar (Pollard and Sag, 1994). It is characterized by a reliable modeling of the universal grammatical principles and a complete representation of linguistic knowledge.

HPSG grammar is based on two essential components: AVMs (Attribute Value Matrix) and a set of immediate domination schemata (DI schemata). An AVM is based on a set of features characterizing a lexical entry. The DI schemata, describe a syntactic phenomenon. It should be noted that to compose the various phrases, a set of principles should be verified (i.e., HFP Head Feature Principle).

HPSG grammar was conceived for Roman languages. To use it for Arabic language, we present in the following paragraph the modifications made to HPSG. These modifications were made on the features and schemata level.

4.1 Arabic features

Referring to previous projects (Elleuch, 2004), (Bahou *et al*, 2005) and (Abdelkader *et al.*, 2006), we have kept some features and have added some others according to the proposed type's hierarchy. As example, we present, in table 1 below, the features characterizing the Arabic particle.

Features	Possible values
PFORM	- Non operative مهمل - Operative عامل
NATP	- elision particle حرف جر - Subjunctive حرف نصب

Table 1. Arabic particle features

Indeed, an Arabic particle can be operative particles or non operative. The coordination particles are classified as non operative particles. In fact, it didn't specify any constraint to the conjoint compounds.

The modifications brought to this formalism cover not only the features but also the different schemata of the HPSG grammar. In the following paragraph, we present as example the conceived schema for Arabic coordination.

4.2 Arabic schemata

HPSG grammar is based on six schemata. In this work, we adapted each schema to represent an Arabic syntactic phenomenon (the simple one). In the context of our work; we present the conceived schema for Arabic coordination.

To represent coordination structure, a complicate phenomenon, we have represented, at first, the simple one. In fact, coordination interacts with different others phenomenon. All other representations were headed structure. However, the coordination has a particular structure. In fact, according to some references, the coordination is a non headed structure. Godard (2003) showed that the conjunction can't be the head of the phrase. In fact, a coordination particle is non operative. Thus, it can't specify conjunct elements.

Therefore, we developed a ternary non headed rule for the coordination phenomenon to obtain the representation below:

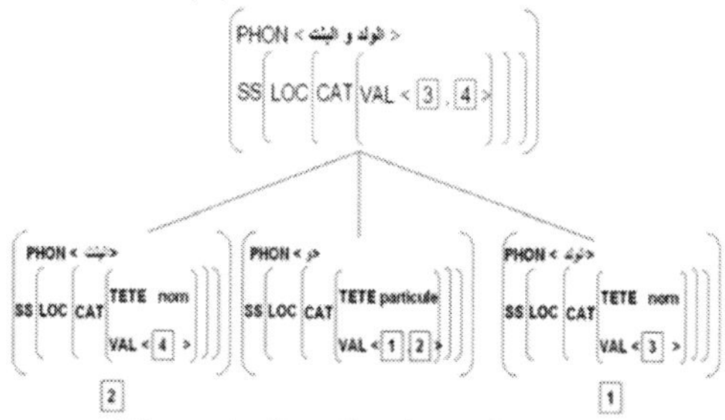

Figure 3. Coordination schema

As represented in figure 3, this structure doesn't contains three non headed daughters: two Fils-conj representing the two compounds of the coordination phrase الولد, (*'aalwaladu, the boy*) and البنت, (*'aalbintu, the girl*) and the Fils-conjonction representing the coordination particle و, (*wa, and*).

To validate our constructed grammar with LKB system, we specified it in TDL (Type Description Language). The choice of LKB platform is justified. In fact, it generates automatically a reliable parser. Some related works such as (Garcia, 2005) used this system and they obtained good results.

In the following paragraph, we give an idea about the specification of the constructed HPSG.

5 TDL specification

According to (Krieger and Schäfer, 1994), the TDL syntax presents an important similitude with the HPSG representation. Therefore, the TDL specification was simple. At the present time, our grammar covers the first category of coordination mentioned in section 3: coordination of constituents.

To specify this grammar, we specified the lexical entries AVMs, the type hierarchy and the syntactic rules representing the different forms of coordination and all possible simple sentences (verbal and nominal).

In the following paragraph, we present an example of TDL specification of an AVM and some schemata.

5.1 TDL specification of an AVM

From a HPSG representation, the TDL specification of an AVM is very simple. We present in the following figure the specification TDL of "هذا, that" (hadha).

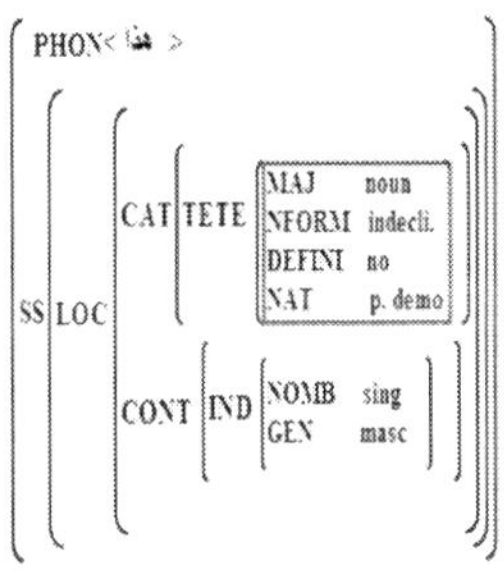


```
hadha:=lex-nom-non-decline &
 [PHON <!«hadha»!>,
 SS[LOC[
 CAT[
   TÊTE
      [MAJ noun,
      NFORM indecli.,
      DEFINI no,
      NAT P.demo]],
 CONT[
      IND[NOMB sing,
          GEN masc]
 ]]].
```

Figure 4. TDL Specification of "that" (hadha, هذا)

In fact, the symbol ":=" designates that "هذا", (*hadha, this*) is an instance of indeclinable nouns. The different constraints are added by the symbol &. The feature structures are delimited by brackets [ ]. Besides, the various attributes values are separated by commas "," and the full stop ". " designates the end of the AVM.

5.2 TDL specification of a schema

To specify the syntactic rule of Arabic coordination, we started by rules representing simple phenomenon. For the coordination structure, we specified two different rules. The first one represents verbal phrases and sentences. The second one represents nominal phrases and sentences. In the following figure we present the TDL specification of the coordination of nominal phrases.

```
regle_coordination_nom := regle-tern-sans-t &
     [SS.LOC[CAT[TETE[DEFINI oui, DEC #dec],
               VAL [TOPIC < >, SPR <#nontete1>,
                     COMPS <#comps1, #comps2>]],
           CONT.IND [NOMB duel]],
     BRS.BRS-NTETE <[SS #nontete1 &
                     [LOC[CAT[TETE nom &[DEC #dec],
                              VAL [COMPS <#comps1>]]]]],
                    [SS #nontete2 &
                    [LOC[CAT[TETE particule_non_operative,
                             VAL [SPR <#nontete1>]]]]],
                    [SS[LOC[CAT[TETE nom & [DEC #dec],
                               VAL [SPR <#nontete2>,
                                    COMPS <#comps2>]]]]]>].
```

Figure 5. TDL Specification of the coordination rule

As represented in this figure, this rule joins nominal phrases. It extends from the type regle-tern-sans-t. This type of rules represents non headed structures. In fact, before implementing this syntactic rule, we specified this type of rules. (Figure 6):

```
regle-tern-sans-t :=
  regle-ternaire &
  [BRS struc-sans-tete &
      [BRS-NTETE < #1, #2, #3 >],
   ARGS < #1, #2, #3 >].
```

Figure 6. TDL Specification of the type rule regle-tern-sans-t

In fact, regle-tern-sans-t is a ternary rule having two non-headed daughters joined with a particle of coordination.

Following the phase of specification TDL, we tested the adapted HPSG grammar with the LKB system. In the next paragraph, we give an idea about this system. Then we describe the experimentation and the evaluation of this grammar.

6 Experimentation and evaluation

LKB system is a parser generation tool, proposed by (Copestake, 2002). This system can run on Windows or on UNIX. But the version on Windows can't support Unicode. In fact, LKB is written in LISP using Motif. Therefore, we have added Trollet (TROndheim LingLab Engineering Tool), a tool for multilingual grammar development. It is easy to extend and can be used only on UNIX system. Therefore we installed Ubunto system. Then we install LKB and Trollet. Thus LKB is embedded in Trollet and invisible for the user. This tool replaced the LKB window.

It should be noted that the LKB is based on two types of files: TDL files and LISP files. The first type represents the grammar's files (i.e., types.tdl, rsynt.tdl, lexique.tdl). The second type represents files to parameterize the LKB system. Among these files, we can especially mention the file: "script.lsp'. It is a very important file. It charges the grammar on LKB. In fact, it indicates the name and the root of each grammar file. In the following paragraph, we describe the stages of syntactic analysis. Then, we present the experimentation of the constructed grammar.

6.1 Stages of syntactic analyses

After charging the constructed grammar on LKB, this system offers a generated parser to analyze a simple sentence or a corpus of sentences. But, it should be noted that this corpus must be segmented in sentences. In fact, LKB system didn't have a module segmenting the tested corpuses.

To analyze a simple phrase, we have to unroll the "parse" menu and choose the "parse input" order. Thus, the LKB system generates a zone of text to type the sentence and as result, a derivation tree appears. The following figure represents the result of a sentence's analysis.

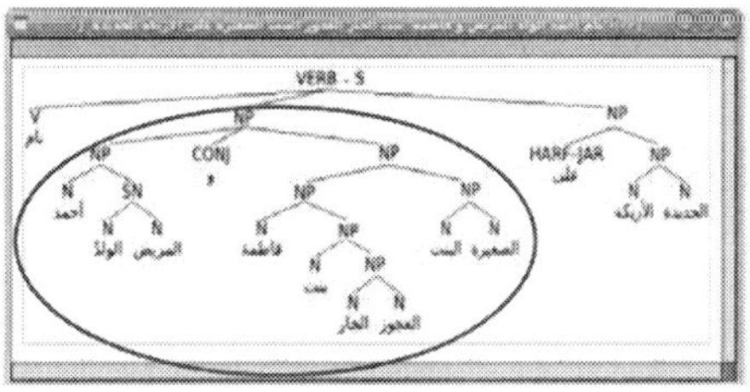

Figure 7. Derivation's tree of a verbal sentence

The derivation's tree in figure 7 is a representation of the following verbal sentence:

نام أحمد الولد المريض و فاطمة بنت الجار العجوز البنت الصغيرة على الأريكة الجديدة

ahmadu the sick boy and fatimatu the girl of the old neighbour, the little girl, are slept on the new couch

As shown in Figure 7, with TROLLET, we resolved the problem of transliteration. Contrary to the LKB on Windows, this system on UNIX can now support Arabic language except that the reading direction of the tree is false. Indeed an Arabic sentence must be read from the right to the left. At the present time, we are looking for a solution for this problem.

The choice of this sentence as example is justified. It represents the interaction of the coordination structure with various syntactic phenomena (i.e. annexing, description). In fact, the subject (circled in red in the figure) is a coordination of constituents joining two nominal phrases.

To analyse a corpus of sentences with LKB, we should specify to it two paths: the path of the file containing the sentences (corpus.txt) composing the corpus, and the path of the file that will contain the results (results.txt). In

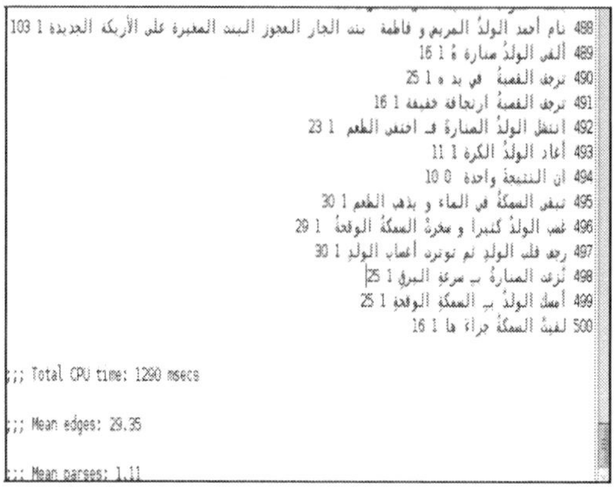

Figure 8. Extract of results.txt

Figure 8 represents our test corpus containing 500 sentences which are extracted from different linguistic resources and containing coordination structures using different particles (و, ثمّ, ف). It should be noted that in "results.txt", LKB represents the total time of analyses and for each example; it represents the number of tree's derivation and the number of nodes in the creation of the derivation's tree.

According to the obtained results, we evaluated our work. This evaluation is described in the following paragraph.

6.2 Evaluation

To test our HPSG grammar, we used a corpus of 500 sentences. This corpus was created from a lexicon of 2000 words. It covers different sentences containing coordination structures using different particles. As we have mentioned before, LKB system or TROLLET didn't have a segmentation module to cut sentences composing the corpus. At the present time, it is done manually. Therefore, we missed much time in this phase. But, we are looking for a segmentation tool toad it to our system.

At the present time, we treated only constituent's cases and we are working on ellipse phenomenon and its interaction with the coordination one. According to the file "results.txt", we obtained the following results.

Number of derivation's trees (n)	Number of sentences having n analysis
0	50
1	420
2	30
	500

Table 2. Obtained results

In fact, 84% of sentences were analyzed correctly. The failure cases (0 analyzes) are due to the absence of rules treating some particular syntactic phenomena (i.e., relative phenomenon, coordination phenomenon). In fact, at the present time we treated constituent structures. We have not yet treating ellipse phenomenon and its interaction of the coordination phenomenon. The ambiguous cases (2 analyzes) are due to a no precise specification of the constraints specification of some syntactic rules.

7 Conclusion and perspectives

In this article, we proposed a typology for coordination structure in Arabic language. Based on this hierarchy, we adapted the HPSG grammar. In fact, we defined a particular structure for this phenomenon. Then we specified syntactic rules treating simple sentences and coordination structures. The specified grammar was validated with the LKB system. The experimentation was done on a corpus of 500 sentences. According to the obtained results, we evaluated our grammar.

As perspectives, we are going to treat ellipse phenomenon and its interaction with coordination structures. Then, we will treat other particular phenomena and specify more constraints to eliminate the ambiguous cases. Moreover we consider developing lexical rules to make our lexicon extensional. Furthermore, we aim to construct a converter permitting to convert the lexical entries of XML in TDL in order to facilitate the development of the lexicon.

References

Abdelkader A., Haddar K., and Ben Hamadou A. 2006, *study and analyses of nominal sentences in HPSG*, TALN, Louvain, 379-388.

Abdelwahed A. 2004, *'alkalima fy 'attourath 'allisaany 'alaraby* , *الكلمة في التراث اللساني العربي*, Aladin library, Sfax – Tunisie, 1-100.

Bahou Y., Hadrich Belguith L., Aloulou C. and Ben Hamedou A. 2005, *Adaptation and implementation of HPSG grammars to parse non-voweled Arabic texts*, Faculty of Economics and Management of Sfax.

Blache P. 2001, *Propriety grammar : constraints for NL*, Hermès Sciences, Paris.

Biskri I., Desclés J., 2006, *coordination of different categories in French*, Quebec university, Canada.

Bourigault D.and Fabre C. 2000, *Linguistic approach for syntactic analyse of corpuses*, Sémantisue et corpus, 131-151.

Copestake A. 2002, *Implementing Typed Feature Structure Grammars*, CSLI Publications, Stanford University.

Dahdah A. 1992, *معجم قواعد اللغة العربية في جداول و لوحات*, Librairie de Nachirun ebanon, 5ème edition.

Elleuch S. 2004, *syntactic analyse of arabic language based on HPSG formalism*, DEA memory on Information system and new technology, 55-88.

Garcia O. 2005, *Une introduction à l'implémentation des relatives de l'espagnol en HPSG–LKB*, Research memory.

Godard D. 2003, *Syntacyic problems of coordination and recent propositions in syntagmatic grammars*, study journey in the university of Paris 7.

Haddar K. 2000, *Formel caracterization of Arabic ellipse and recouvrement processus in Arabic language*, University of Tunis II – Sciences Faculty of Tunis.

Hudson R. 1976, *Conjunction Reduction, gapping and right-node raising*, 535-562.

Krieger H. and Schäfer U. 1994, *TDL: A Type Description Language for HPSG,* Part 1 and Part 2, Research Report, RR, 94-37.

Le Roux J., Perrier G. 2006, *coordination modelisation in Interactive grammars*, TAL, Volume 47, n° 3, 89-113.

Maaloul H., Haddar K., and Ben Hamadou A. 2004, *Arabic coordination: HPS analyse*, MCSEAI 2004, 8th maghrébine conference on GL and IA, Sousse, Tunisie : 487- 498.

Osenova P. and Simov K., *Special Linguistic phenomena in the Bulgarian HPSG_based Treebank*, BulTreeBank Project, Linguistic modelling laboratory, IPP, Bulgarian Academy of Sciences.

Pollard C. and Sag I. 1994, *Head-drive phrase structure grammars*, CSLI series, Chicago University Press.

Postal P. 1974, *On raising*, MIT Press, Cambridge/MA.

Rau F. L. 1985, *the understanding and generation of ellipses in a natural language system*, Berkeley Artificial Intelligence Research project.

Villavicencio A., Sadler L. and Arnold D. 2005, *An HPSG account of closest conjunct Agreement in NP Coordination in Portuguese*, Proceedings of the HPSG05 conference, Department of Informations, University of Lisbon.

Visualization for Coreference Annotation

Andre Burkovski and **Gunther Heidemann**
Intelligent Systems Group
Institute for Visualization and Interactive Systems
University of Stuttgart
{firstname.lastname}@vis.uni-stuttgart.de

Abstract

The annotation of documents with linguistic information requires time-consuming and therefore expensive manual annotation. Especially, a complex task, like coreference resolution, needs large data sets for the training of supervised machine learning methods. We present a tool which combines visualization techniques and unsupervised machine learning to support the annotation of documents with coreference information. Self-organizing Maps are used to cluster similar data and visualize the feature space. For link visualization, precise annotation, and error correction a matrix-based coreference visualization is used which exploits the transitive property of the coreference relation.

1 Introduction

The task of finding noun phrases which refer to the same discourse entity in a plain text is called coreference resolution. Many applications in information retrieval (Nicolov et al., 2008), machine translation, and text summarization (Mitkov et al., 2007) use coreference resolution to improve the results. Currently, the popular Jeopardy! winner machine "Watson" uses a coreference resolution module among other modules for question answering (Ferruci et al., 2010).

In many cases, coreference is resolved using supervised machine learning methods. These methods need large amounts of training samples. Yet, particularly for languages other than English, such data sets are rare and they mostly contain relatively few samples. Another problem is that supervised methods which are trained on a specific domain, such as news articles, may degrade on texts from other domains, like books or reports. E.g. Bakkenson and Soroka (2010) report on how the genre influences pronominal anaphora resolution.

The manual annotation of a document with coreference information is time consuming, because it depends not only on the background knowledge of the annotator, but also requires a high level of concentration to avoid annotation errors. Most annotation tools use text-based visualizations to show and highlight the noun phrases for coreference annotation. However, using only text-based visualizations tools has a major drawback. Annotators are prone to annotation errors because they often need to repeatedly read passages in a text for every new unlabeled noun phrase. Mitkov et al. (2000) introduce some strategies for annotators to reduce errors and to accelerate the annotation speed, but the annotation of large data sets still is a problem. Rule-based or unsupervised machine learning methods may be used to highlight probable coreference pairs and chains and to support the annotators in identifying coreferences. Such an approach further reduces the time spent on the search of suitable coreference candidates.

In our approach we address the annotation efficiency from the visualization and interaction point of view. We propose a combination of unsupervised machine learning method and visualizations for annotation purposes. We use the Self-organizing Map (SOM) to visualize gropus of similar links of noun-phrases. These groups are further visualized with a coreference matrix, which takes advantage of the equivalence relation property of the coreference relationship. In such a way annotators are able to quickly identify conflicting annotations and to correct them.

2 Related Work

Generally, coreference annotation tools, like CorefDraw (Harabagiu et al., 2001), GATE (Cunningham et al., 2002), PALinkA (Orăsan, 2003), MMAX2 (Müller and Strube, 2006), or BART (Versley et al., 2008) provide only a text-based visualization of coreference information. The recently introduced Reconcile tool (Stoyanov et al., 2009), which provide resources for developing a coreference resolution system, also uses plain text for presentation of coreference information.

All text-based visualizations present coreference information via a color scheme, link identification by indices, or visual edges between noun phrases. This does not show the the feature space or the similarity between links. Such visualizations are also limited by the size and the number of lines/colors a user can distinguish. This makes it difficult to analyze large chains, inter-document coreference or many links at once.

Advanced visualizations for coreference resolution exist. Witte and Tang (2007) present a graph-based visualization of coreferences. The framework manage coreferences as topic maps. The views used in the framework provide a good overview about the relationship of noun phrases in a link. The authors address the problem that the visualization of coreferences consists solely of highlighted plain text, possibly including edges for marking a coreference relation. We agree with them that textual visualization slows down the user and also makes cross document annotation difficult. Nonetheless, their representation only serves to visualize and navigate the space of already annotated coreferences. Another visualization created by Zeldes et al. (2009) add parse trees to plain text visualization to support annotation decisions. Still, visualization of coreference information is somewhat rare.

In contrast, we aim to visualize the actual coreferences as well as the coreference feature space and provide interaction methods for annotation in both visualizations. The basic idea is to use SOMs for clustering similar data and allow a fast and structured approach to annotation. Bekel et al. (2005) and Moehrmann et al. (2011) successfully applied this technique for image annotation. Instead of images we use pairs of noun phrases (links) as input. We extend the work of (Burkovski et al., 2011), where SOMs are used to create feature space visualizations of links and focus on methods for coreference annotation. We augment the SOM visualization with annotation information and additional matrix-based coreference visualization for a more precise annotation and annotation error detection supported by a visualization for links in a text-based manner. All visualizations are linked together via multiple coordinated views (Roberts, 2007). Such an approach allows annotators to independently cycle through different representations of the data and systematically annotate different sets of links.

3 Coreference and Annotation

Coreference resolution is an active research area. Elango (2005) provide a detailed survey and Ng (2010) summarizes challenges and recent machine learning advances. In this work we use a pairwise model for coreferences: two noun phrases are considered to be coreferent if by replacing each other they do not change the meaning of a sentence. These two noun phrases form a link. The coreference relationship is reflexive, symmetric and transitive and therefore an equivalence relation. This property is used to automatically deduce and create additional annotations as well as to perform error detection of the manual annotation. A set of noun phrases which all refer to the same entity is called a chain. In a coreference chain every phrase is coreferent to every other phrase in that chain due to the transitive and symmetry property.

The main purpose of annotated data is to be used as a training and test set in supervised machine learning methods. One can argue, that it is enough to annotate only coreferent links to form coreference chains as one can create non-coreferent samples by creating links between disjunct chains. Such an approach would neglect the presence of non-referential noun phrases in a text, such as idioms, duration phrases, and others. Yet, links of these non-referential noun phrases are useful samples for supervised learning. Therefore, it is beneficial to annotate such links as well. Although a non-coreferent link does not guarantee that a noun phrase in the link is non-referential, it reduces the annotation errors. An erroneous annotation of a noun phrase as a non-referential would result in many false negative samples in the training set.

4 Visualization Methods

Visualization is an important tool to understand the underlying data (Shneiderman, 1996; Roberts, 2007; Keim et al., 2010) and in our case allow a systematic approach to annotation. Mitkov et al. (2000) developed systematic rules for annotators and the idea is to support this manual work with visualizations. First, we use a SOM to cluster similar links (Figure 1). We extract features from links of a pairwise coreference model and let the SOM create groups of similar links. SOMs are easy to visualize and are rather intuitive. Second, the links in the selected clusters are visualized using the coreference matrix (Figure 2). The coreference matrix allows easy and systematic interaction for annotation. It shows annotations which contradict the transitive property of the coreference relationship and allows annotators to identify and resolve annotation errors. The visualizations are additionally supported by a traditional text-based visualization of links (not shown here).

4.1 Self-organizing Maps

A SOM is an unsupervised machine learning method where artificial neurons are connected to each other by a low dimensional topology (Kohonen, 1990). This topology is applied to the high-dimensional data and the SOM learning algorithm tries to create a suitable projection of high-dimensional data. Thus, similar feature vectors in the feature space will be close in the projection space. Such coherence between the low dimensional map and high dimensional data allows creation of intuitive visualizations. The most popular visualization is the U-Matrix (Ultsch and Siemon, 1990) and its variants. The U-Matrix shows the low-dimensional grid with nodes and edges and color-codes them based on their distance in the high-dimensional feature space. Further, for a systematic annotation we use the component planes visualization introduced by Vesanto (1999). Component planes visualize the influence of one or more features to cluster formation.

To train the SOM, we use feature vectors created from pairs of noun phrases. We used a subset of features inspired by the popular feature set of Ng and Cardie (2002). Although using basic features, the SOM already clusters the data in a way, that annotators may annotate whole clusters with a low error rate. However, the SOM **does not** perform unsupervised coreference resolution. Instead, the SOM and its visualization provides methods to systematically select nodes and clusters with similar properties. For example, using component planes for string matching and Wordnet distance annotators are able to select areas of the SOM where links match in their head words and also are semantically close to each other. Interaction allows to annotate whole clusters as well as to show the actual links in selected clusters. For the visualization of links we use the coreference matrix.

4.2 Coreference Matrix

Transitive relations can be easily visualized in a matrix. Since coreference is symmetric, for annotation purposes we only need to show the upper triangular matrix. Each element of the matrix represents a link between the phrase in the row and the phrase in the column. Rows and columns are ordered by the text position of a phrase. Annotators can systematically cycle through the matrix entries and annotate the links accordingly. The contents of the links are visualized by displaying the surrounding text in another coordinated text-based visualization (not shown here). However, the key to an efficient annotation is an intelligent interaction technique. Annotators do not need to explore all entries in the matrix, but only entries in the upper triangular matrix close to the main diagonal, because of the transitive property.

For example, let i, j, k, l be phrases in the according column/row ordered by their position in the text. Let every link $(i, j), (i, k), (i, l), (j, k), (j, l), (k, l)$ be coreferent. To annotate the links, the annotator only has to visit and label the cells $(i, j), (j, k)$, and (k, l). Due to the transitive property, the annotation for the remaining links can be done automatically.

Another feature of the coreference matrix is to show annotation errors. The coreference matrix is able to highlight links that violate the transitive property. Such errors are created by a contradicting annotation by the annotator. A phrase a cannot be coreferent to a phrase b and non-coreferent to a phrase c when both phrases b and c are coreferent. In such cases, annotators are able to correct the links and modify the annotation accordingly.

The coreference matrix allow further strategy to annotate the links. Beginning with a row in the trace (diagonal) of the matrix annotators traverse the cells to the right until they find and annotate a coreferent noun phrase. Along the way, they annotate the cells between two noun phrases as non-coreferent. Now annotators follow either the chain, thereby jumping to the row of the next noun phrase in the current chain, or switch to the annotation of the next row, possibly creating a new coreference chain. The first interaction strategy allows a fast annotation of a single chain. It helps to create many coreferent samples (deduced from

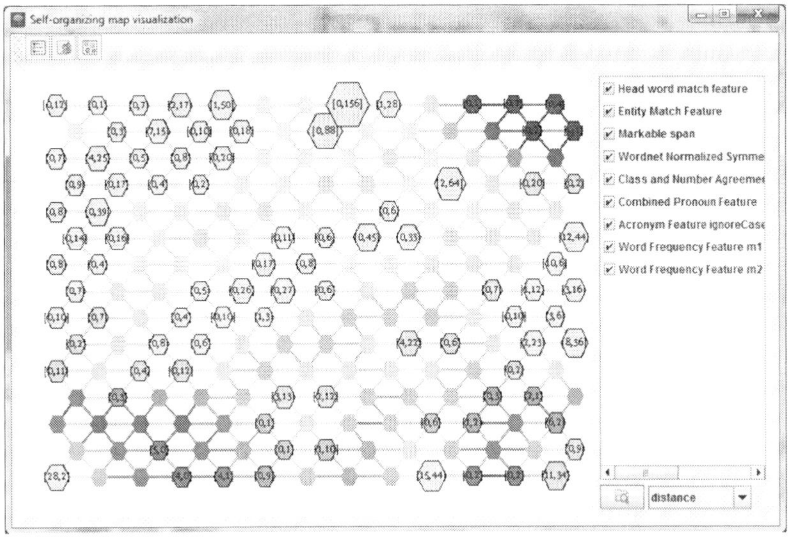

Figure 1: Self-organizing Map visualization of coreference feature space for links extracted from Ontonotes corpus (Pradhan et al., 2007). The feature vectors of links are assigned to nodes in the SOM (black border). The size of the nodes is a hint for the amount of links that are assigned to a node. The label indicates the number of links which are annotated coreferent and non-coreferent separated by a comma. Additional labels are possible e.g. the number of links with no annotation or the proportion of coreferent and non-coreferent links in a node. Annotators are able to select individual features (component planes) to show their influence in the SOM. By selecting individual nodes or group of nodes annotators select the contents in the nodes (links) and enabling the to these links. Additionally, the links are highlighted in the coreference matrix for further inspection and error correction.

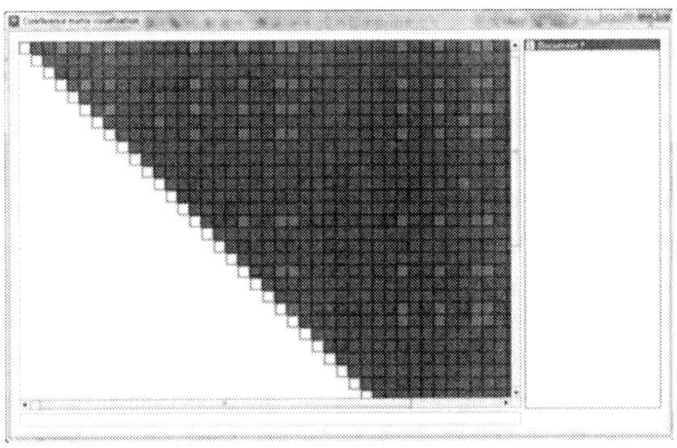

(a) Annotation Overview

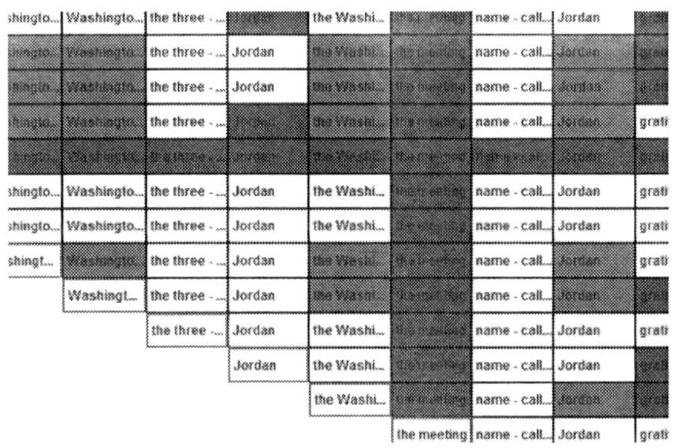

(b) Zoom and Details

Figure 2: Visualization of links and their annotations in the coreference matrix. Figure 2b shows enlarged details of the coreference matrix. Each cell represents a link between the noun phrase in the row and the noun phrase in the column. Annotators are able to select individual cells and annotate them as coreferent or non-coreferent. Cells colored green contain links annotated as coreferent and cells colored red have a non-coreferent annotation. White cells represent links which has currently no annotation. Cells/links where the annotations are in conflict with other annotations due to the transitive property of the coreference relation are highlighted with the magenta color. After every annotation the transitive property is checked and additionally deduced coreferent links are added. Figure 2a shows a zoomed out and fully annotated version of the coreference matrix for a single document in the Ontonotes corpus. Links selected from a node of the SOM are highlighted with blue border.

the transitive property) and non-coreferent annotations to that chain in a single pass. The second interaction strategy allows the creation of multiple chains. From multiple chains non-coreferent samples are deduced by creating links with phrases from disjunct chains.

5 Annotation Strategies using Visualizations

The proposed visualizations allow additional annotation strategies to the guidelines presented by Mitkov et al. (2000).

SOMs can be trained for nominal to nominal noun phrase annotation only. In that case, clusters of similar noun phrases, as defined by the features, can lead to faster recognition of coreferent and non-coreferent links in matrix-based and text-based visualizations. After the annotation of nominal phrases, the SOM can be trained on nominal to pronominal links. By annotating a pronoun to a noun phrase in a chain, an annotation for all noun phrases in the chain is created automatically. Alternatively, the SOM can be trained with all kinds of noun phrases and additional features. Annotators are then able to use the component planes of the SOM to systematically investigate different combinations of noun phrases as shown by Burkovski et al. (2011).

Using the coreference matrix, annotators can follow two different strategies. First, annotators can use the SOM to select nodes with good indicators for coreferent or non-coreferent links. Such indicators depend of the features used. E.g. the head match feature is a good indicator for coreference. Annotators can easily identify regions with interesting features by using component planes of the SOM. Subsequently, by selecting the SOM nodes, the links are highlighted in the matrix and annotators are able to annotate them. In many cases most links are annotated automatically due to the transitive property. Second, starting with the first noun phrase, annotators can use the matrix to annotate some links in advance. The annotations will be reflected in the SOM, and allow annotators to see potentially coreferent and non-coreferent regions in the SOM. Also, using the SOM for general, and probably erroneous annotation the annotators will discover conflicts in the annotation. With the coreference matrix visualization it is easier to resolve conflicts in annotation than to annotate all links correctly in one single pass.

6 Conclusion

In this work we presented a visualization approach to coreference annotation. Instead of using traditional text-based visualization only, we propose Self-organizing Maps (SOM) and a matrix-based visualization of links in addition to text-based visualizations. SOM visualizes the feature space of the links where annotators may systematically choose regions with interesting links by utilizing component planes for feature space navigation. The matrix-based link visualization with interaction techniques allows a detailed and precise annotation of links. The coreference matrix exploits the transitive property of the coreference relation to detect and highlight annotation errors made in the process. Using visualizations as multiple coordinated views, annotators are able to systematically create coreference annotations. Our vision is that the next generation of annotation tools will employ more visualization techniques for a more efficient annotation of the data[1].

Future work includes additional coreference resolution methods (other classifiers or rule-based systems) for the links in a SOM node which may provide confidence values. This can easily be visualized in the matrix or in the SOM by using a color gradient. For such links, annotators are able to quickly navigate to the matrix entries and inspect the proposed automatic annotation. Additional interaction techniques and graph-based visualizations will be investigated which may further improve and support a systematic annotation. In the future, we plan to show the efficiency of the tool by conducting a long term user study.

References

Michael Bakkenson and Barry I. Soroka. 2010. Importance of genre in pronominal anaphora resolution. In *International Conference on Artificial Intelligence*, pages 900–906.

Holger Bekel, Gunther Heidemann, and Helge Ritter. 2005. Interactive image data labeling using self-organizing maps in an augmented reality scenario. *Neural Networks*, 18(5–6):566–574.

Andre Burkovski, Wiltrud Kessler, Gunther Heidemann, Hamidreza Kobdani, and Hinrich Schütze. 2011. Self Organizing Maps in NLP: Exploration of Coreference Feature Space. In *Workshop on Self-Organizing Maps*, pages 228–237.

[1]The tool will be available at the project page: `www.vis.uni-stuttgart.de/suekre/`

Hammish Cunningham, Diana Maynard, Kalina Bontcheva, and Valentin Tablan. 2002. GATE: A Framework and Graphical Development Environment for Robust NLP Tools and Applications. In *Proceedings of the 40th Anniversary Meeting of the Association for Computational Linguistics*, pages 168–175.

Pradheep Elango. 2005. Coreference resolution: A survey. Technical report, Unversity of Wisconsin Madison.

David Ferruci, Eric Brown, Jennifer Chu-Caroll, James Fan, David Gondek, Aditya A. Kalyanpur, Adam Lally, J. William Murdock, John Prager, Nico Schlaefer, and Chris Welty. 2010. Building Watson: An Overview of the DeepQA Project. *AI Magazine, Association for the Advancement of Artificial Intelligence*, 31(3):59–79.

Sanda M. Harabagiu, Razvan C. Bunescu, and Stefan Trausan-Matum. 2001. Corefdraw: A tool for annotation and visualization of coreference data. In *Proceedings of the 13th IEEE International Conference on Tools with Artificial Intelligence*, pages 273–279, Los Alamitos, CA, USA. IEEE Computer Society.

Daniel A. Keim, Joern Kohlhammer, Geoffrey Ellis, and Florian Mansmann, editors. 2010. *Mastering The Information Age - Solving Problems with Visual Analytics*. Eurographics, to appear.

Teuvo Kohonen. 1990. The self-organizing map. *Proceedings of the IEEE*, 78(9):1464–1480.

Ruslan Mitkov, Richard Evans, Constantin Orăsan, Catalina Barbu, Lisa Jones, and Violeta Sotirova. 2000. Coreference and anaphora: developing annotating tools, annotated resources and annotation strategies. In *Proceedings of the Discourse, Anaphora and Reference Resolution Conference*, pages 49–58.

Ruslan Mitkov, Richard Evans, Constantin Orăsan, Le An Ha, and Viktor Pekar. 2007. Anaphora Resolution: To What Extent Does It Help NLP Applications? *Anaphora: Analysis, Algorithms and Applications*, 29:179 – 190.

Julia Moehrmann, Stefan Bernstein, Thomas Schlegel, Günter Werner, and Gunther Heidemann. 2011. Improving the Usability of Hierarchical Representations for Interactively Labeling Large Image Data Sets. In *HCI International*, pages 618–627.

Christoph Müller and Michael Strube. 2006. Multilevel annotation of linguistic data with MMAX2. In *Corpus Technology and Language Pedagogy: New Resources, New Tools, New Methods*, pages 197–214. Peter Lang.

Vincent Ng and Claire Cardie. 2002. Improving machine learning approaches to coreference resolution. In *Proceedings of the 40th Annual Meeting of the Association for Computational Linguistics*, pages 104–111.

Vincent Ng. 2010. Supervised noun phrase coreference research: the first fifteen years. In *Proceedings of the 48th Annual Meeting of the Association for Computational Linguistics*, pages 1396–1411, Stroudsburg, PA, USA. Association for Computational Linguistics.

Nicolas Nicolov, Franco Salvetti, and Steliana Ivanova. 2008. Sentiment Analysis: Does Coreference Matter? In *In Proceedings of the Symposium on Affective Language in Human and Machine*, pages 37–40.

Constantin Orăsan. 2003. PALinkA: A highly customisable tool for discourse annotation. In *4th SIGdial Workshop on Discourse and Dialogue*, pages 39 – 43.

Sameer S. Pradhan, Eduard Hovy, Mitch Marcus, Martha Palmer, Lance Ramshaw, and Ralph Weischedel. 2007. Ontonotes: A unified relational semantic representation. In *International Conference on Semantic Computing*, pages 517–526.

Jonathan C. Roberts. 2007. State of the art: Coordinated multiple views in exploratory visualization. In *Coordinated and Multiple Views in Exploratory Visualization, 2007. Fifth International Conference on Coordinated & Multiple Views.*, pages 61–71.

Ben Shneiderman. 1996. The eyes have it: a task by data type taxonomy for information visualizations. In *IEEE Symposium on Visual Languages, 1996. Proceedings.*, pages 336–343.

Veselin Stoyanov, Claire Cardie, Nathan Gilbert, Ellen Riloff, David Buttler, and David Bysom. 2009. Reconcile: A coreference resolution research platform. Technical report, Lawrence Livermore National Laboratory.

Alfred Ultsch and H.P. Siemon. 1990. Kohonen's self organizing feature maps for exploratory data analysis. In *Proceedings of International Neural Networks Conference*, pages 305–308.

Yannick Versley, Simone Paolo Ponzetto, Massimo Poesio, Vladimir Eidelman, Alan Jern, Jason Smith, Xiaofeng Yang, and Alessandro Moschitti. 2008. Bart: a modular toolkit for coreference resolution. In *HLT '08: Proceedings of the 46th Annual Meeting of the Association for Computational Linguistics on Human Language Technologies*, pages 9–12, Morristown, NJ, USA. Association for Computational Linguistics.

Juha Vesanto. 1999. SOM-Based data visualization methods. *Intelligent Data Analysis*, 3:111–126.

René Witte and Ting Tang. 2007. Task-Dependent Visualization of Coreference Resolution Results. In *International Conference on Recent Advances in Natural Language Processing*.

Amir Zeldes, Julia Ritz, Anke Lüdeling, and Christian Chiarcos. 2009. ANNIS: a search tool for multilayer annotated corpora. In *Proceedings of Corpus Linguistics*.

The RST Spanish Treebank On-line Interface

Iria da Cunha
Instituto Universitario de Lingüística Aplicada (UPF)
iria.dacunha@upf.edu

Juan-Manuel Torres-Moreno
Laboratoire Informatique d'Avignon, Universidad Nacional Autónoma de México, École Polytechnique de Montréal
juan-manuel.torres@univ-avignon.fr

Gerardo Sierra
Universidad Nacional Autónoma de México
gsierram@iingen.unam.mx

Luis-Adrián Cabrera-Diego
Universidad Nacional Autónoma de México
LCabreraD@iingen.unam.mx

Brenda-Gabriela Castro-Rolón
Universidad Nacional Autónoma de México
BCastroR@iingen.unam.mx

Juan-Miguel Rolland-Bartilotti
Universidad Nacional Autónoma de México
jrollandb@iingen.unam.mx

Abstract

In this article, we present the on-line interface that we have developed for the RST Spanish Treebank, the first corpus including Spanish texts annotated with rhetorical relations. This interface allows users to consult or download the texts and their corresponding annotations. In addition, it allows carrying out several tasks over a selected subcorpus: searching statistics in terms of words, rhetorical relations and Elementary Discourse Units (EDUs), and extracting information, in terms of texts passages marked with rhetorical relations (ex. Result, Cause or Background), which users may select.

1 Introduction

According to Hovy (2010), there are 7 core questions in corpus' design: selecting a corpus, instantiating the theory, designing the interface, selecting and training the annotators, designing and managing the annotation procedure, validating results, and delivering and maintaining the product. All these points are really relevant when compiling a corpus. However, we consider that usually one of them is underestimated: the interface design. When Hovy (2010) mentions this aspect, he mainly refers to the annotation interface. We think that the annotation interface is important but, as well, that, if there is an available annotation interface suitable for the purposes of a corpus project, it can be used. Nevertheless, we consider that an interface allowing users to consult or download the corpus' texts, and even carrying out searches (both statistics and linguistics) over a selected subcorpus, is really useful and necessary.

Compiling and annotating an adequate corpus is not a trivial task; it implies lots of people, resources, time and effort. Thus, we consider that it is important to develop a friendly and useful interface to be able to exploit the created corpus, and transform it into a most accessible resource. Therefore, in this article, we present the on-line interface that we have developed in order to include the RST Spanish Treebank (da Cunha et al., 2011). The RST Spanish Treebank is the first corpus including Spanish texts annotated with rhetorical relations of the Rhetorical Structure Theory (RST) by Mann and Thompson (1988). It contains texts from nine specialized domains (Astrophysics, Earthquake Engineering, Economy, Law, Linguistics, Mathematics, Medicine, Psychology and Sexuality). It includes 52,746 words, 267 texts, 2,256 sentences and 3,349 discourse segments. The segmentation criteria are similar to those employed by da Cunha et al. (2011). Each text was tagged by 1 person, from a team of 10 RST expert annotators. There is a 31% of the corpus double-annotated. The corpus is not annotated with syntactic structure, although we are conscious this would be interesting. The corpus will be useful for the development of a rhetorical parser for this language and several other applications related to computational linguistics (automatic translation, automatic summarization, information extraction, etc.). In addition, this corpus will be helpful for researchers and students interested on the analysis of rhetorical relations. Thus, before the search interface design, we wondered which kind of information they would need for their discourse studies. We considered that they would like to know the quantity of discourse segments included in a corpus (for example, to compare the discourse complexity among languages), the number of rhetorical relations of each type (for example, to try to characterize the discourse of a genre, a domain or a language, in the same line of Iruskieta and da Cunha, 2011), or to extract text passages corresponding to some rhetorical relations (for example, to determine how these relations are explicit in the text and if they are marked with discourse connectors). With these possible needs in mind, we have developed some search tools and we have included them in the interface. Thus, the interface allows users to consult or download the texts and their corresponding annotations and, in addition, it allows carrying out several statistical and linguistic searches over a selected subcorpus. The interface is available in: http://www.corpus.unam.mx/rst/.

In Section 2, we present some previous work. In Section 3, we explain the development of the interface: the website, the annotated texts selection and downloading interface, the search tools (statistical and linguistic), the annotated texts uploading interface and the administrator interface. In Section 4, we establish some conclusions and future work.

2 Previous Work

Nowadays, there are lots of corpora containing texts annotated at different levels (morphological, syntactic, semantic, etc.), for the majority of the most used languages. Despite this fact, there are not so many corpora annotated with rhetorical relations. The most used rhetorical framework for this task is the RST, an independent language theory departing from the idea that a text can be segmented into Elementary Discourse Units (EDUs) linked by means of nucleus-satellite or multinuclear rhetorical relations. In the first case, the satellite gives additional information about the other one, the nucleus, on which it depends. Some examples are the relations of Antithesis, Background, Cause, Reformulation or Result. In the second case, several elements, all nuclei, are connected at the same level, that is, there are no elements dependent on others and they all have the same importance with regard to the intentions of the author of the text. They are the relations of Contrast, List, Joint or Sequence, among others.

Until now, there were RST corpora only for three languages: English (Carlson et al., 2002; Taboada and Renkema, 2008), German (Stede, 2004) and Portuguese (Pardo et al., 2008; Pardo and Seno, 2005). These RST corpora suppose an important step on the RST research and they have been very useful to develop several applications, like information extraction, text generation, automatic summarization, etc. Each one has some advantages and disadvantages, related to the number of included texts and words, the annotation systematicity, the texts' domain heterogeneity, the amount of double-annotated texts (to measure the agreement between annotators), etc. (see da Cunha et al., 2011) Nevertheless, we consider that there is one limitation shared by almost all these corpora: the lack of a free on-line corpus interface, to consult the corpus and to carry out searches over it. Most of these corpora offer a folder containing all the annotated texts individually into the format of the annotation interface RSTtool (O'Donnell, 2000). The only one offering a search tool (allowing to users to search at different linguistic levels) is the German Potsdam Commentary Corpus (Stede, 2004), although, to our knowledge, this tool is not available on-line.

3 Developing the Interface

In this section, we explain all the aspects regarding the developing of the interface.

3.1 The Website

The RST Spanish Treebank is free for research purposes and it can be consulted or downloaded by means of the on-line interface we have developed for it. Ide and Pustejovsky (2010) mention several different kinds of documentation which a corpus project must provide. Following these guideliness, the website including the RST Spanish Treebank contains a high level description of the resource for non-specialist public, annotation guidelines, information on the theoretical framework, project documentation (location, personnel, contact, etc.), corpus documentation, among other information.

The RST Spanish Treebank interface and all the related information are written in Spanish, although they will be also in English soon.

3.2 Annotated Texts Selection and Downloading Interface

The RST Spanish Treebank interface allows the visualization and downloading of all the original documents in plain text format (txt), with their corresponding annotated trees in RSTtool format (rs3), as well as in image format (png). Each text includes its title, its reference, its web link (if it is an on-line text) and its number of words.

The copyright of the texts included in a corpus is a polemical subject. Usually, written authorization to the authors of the texts must be requested in order to include the texts in a corpus. However, as Sierra (2008) explains, there are exceptions or limits in some cases. One of them is the case of non-profit research projects, where only passages of texts (not complete texts) are provided and their origin and corresponding bibliographic reference are stated. This is precisely the case of the RST Spanish Treebank, since it is a non-profit research project which provides the corpus through an interface that includes only passages of the original texts (for example, abstracts of scientific articles, sections of webpages, thesis introductions, etc.) and the bibliographic references (and links, in the cases of electronic publications) of all the documents.

The interface shows texts by areas and allows the user to select a subcorpus (including individual files and/or folders containing several files). The selection of the subcorpus can be saved on local disk (generating an xml file including the IDs of the selected texts) for future analyses.

As the RST Spanish Treebank is a growing corpus, our interface is dynamic too, in order to be able to do changes (for example, to include new domains categories) without modifying the interface code. To solve this challenge, we have developed an in-house program that recursively reads the entire corpus' directory and creates a general xml with the information of each document (as location, number of words, etc.). As well, at the same time, this program creates an individual xml for each file, which contains its bibliographic reference, origin, among other data.

Appendix A includes a screenshot of the texts selection and downloading interface.

3.3 Search Tools

Until now, we have developed four search tools, which are included in the RST Spanish Treebank interface. Three of them are statistical; the other one is linguistic. The four tools are developed in Perl and can be applied over the total corpus or over a subcorpus selected by the user.

3.3.1 Statistic Tools

Firstly, users can know the number of words of the selected subcorpus automatically and in real time. This tool is simple but it is important, because it allows the user to increase or decrease his subcorpus easily regarding his research aims.

Secondly, users may obtain the number of EDUs of the selected corpus, using the tool RST_stats_EDUs. This tool analyses automatically the rs3 archives of the selected subcorpus and it calculates the amount of EDUs present into these texts. This tool is useful to have an idea of the discourse "potential" of a corpus.

Thirdly, the interface includes a statistical tool that allows obtaining statistics of rhetorical relations in a subcorpus selected by the user. It is called RST_stats_Rel. We consider that this is the most useful tool, because the user may carry out statistical researches about the rhetorical relations existing into the texts of the studied corpus, which usually are performed by hand. The RSTtool also offers this option but it can be only used for one text at time. We consider that it is more useful for the user to obtain statistics from various texts, so as to get significant statistical results. As the RSTtool, our tool allows to count the multinuclear relations in two ways: a) one unit for each detected multinuclear relation, and b) one unit for each detected nucleus. For example, Figure 1 shows a RST tree containing a multinuclear relation of Contrast. If we select the strategy a), the tool will count 1, and if we select the strategy b), the tool will count 2.

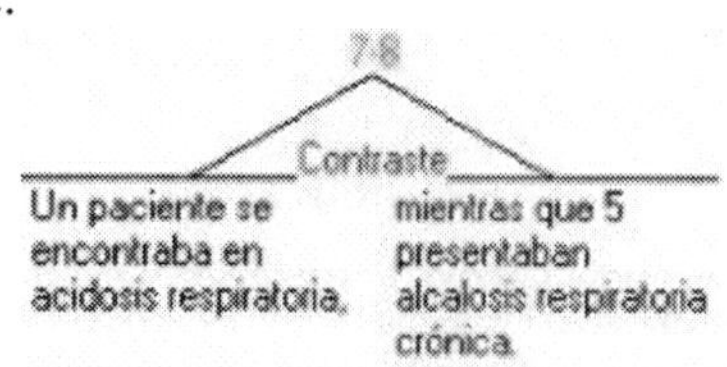

English translation: One patient was found in breathing acidosis, whereas 5 presented chronic breathing alkalosis.

Figure 1: Example of multinuclear Contrast relation

Table 1 contains the list of the nucleus-satellite relations of the RST Spanish Treebank, with the number and percentage of rhetorical relations, calculated by RST_stats_Rel.

Relation	Quantity	
	N°	%
Elaboration	765	24.56
Preparation	475	15.25
Background	204	6.55
Result	193	6.20
Means	175	5.62
Circumstance	140	4.49
Purpose	122	3.92
Interpretation	88	2.83
Antithesis	80	2.57
Cause	77	2.47
Evidence	59	1.89
Condition	53	1.70
Concession	50	1.61
Justification	39	1.25
Solution	32	1.03
Motivation	28	0.90
Reformulation	22	0.71
Otherwise	3	0.10
Evaluation	11	0.35
Summary	8	0.26
Enablement	5	0.16
Unless	2	0.06

Table 1: Amount of nucleus-satellite rhetorical relations in the RST Spanish Treebank

Table 2 includes the list of multinuclear relations of the corpus, using strategies a) and b). As it can be observed, using b), the amount of detected relations is higher than using a).

Relation	Quantity			
	Strategy a		Strategy b	
	N°	%	N°	%
List	172	5.52	864	19.09
Joint	160	5.14	537	11.86
Sequence	74	2.38	289	6.39
Contrast	58	1.86	153	3.38
Conjunction	11	0.35	28	0.62
Disjunction	9	0.29	24	0.53

Table 2: Amount of multinuclear rhetorical relations in the RST Spanish Treebank

3.3.2 Linguistic Tool

The RST_extract is a tool aimed to extract information from the annotated texts. This tool allows the user to select a subcorpus and to extract from it the EDUs corresponding to the rhetorical relation selected, like a multidocument specialized summarizer guided by user's interests. This tool might be useful, for example, to elaborate a compendium of results of diverse medical articles about a certain topic (selecting the relation of Result) or to compile a state of the art about one topic (selecting the relation of Background). At present some monodocument summarizers based on RST exist for some languages (Marcu 2000; Pardo and Rino, 2001; da Cunha et al., 2007, among others), but, at our knowledge, no multidocument specialized RST summarizers exist. We can mention here the works about multidocument summarization for Portuguese based on the Cross-document Structure Theory (CSS) (Radev, 2000), a theory derived from RST (Jorge and Pardo, 2010). Figure 2 contains a passage of the output of the RST_extract, applying it over the subcorpus of Sexuality and selecting the rhetorical relation of Result (the English tranlation is ours). We show 3 of the 20 extracted Result satellites.

```
se00028.rs3: La hipertrofia del epitelio produce acantosis y la aparición de papiloma de 3 meses a 2 años después del inicio de la infección.
    The epithelium hypertrophy causes acanthosis and the occurrence of papilloma from 3 months to 2 years after the beginning of the infection.
se00032.rs3: Las complicaciones más graves de la enfermedad inflamatoria pélvica son la esterilidad y embarazo ectópico secundario.
    The most severe complications of the pelvic inflammatory illness are the sterility and the secondary ectopic pregnancy.
se00032.rs3: La infección puede ascender y dar como resultado salpingitis, abscesos tubo-ováricos y enfermedad inflamatoria pélvica.
    The infection can rise and to give as result salpingitis, tube-ovarian abscesses and pelvic inflammatory illness.
```

Figure 2: Example of the output of RST_extract

RST_extract uses as input the rs3 files from RSTTool. Due to the complexity of this kind of format, for the moment, our tool only extracts satellites of nucleus-satellite relations, being simple EDUs (not SPANs).

3.4 Annotated Texts Uploading Interface

The RST Spanish Treebank interface also includes a screen that permits the users to send comments, suggestions, and also to send their own annotated texts. Our aim is for the RST Spanish Treebank to become a dynamic corpus, in constant evolution, increasing with texts annotated by users. This has a double advantage since, on the one hand, the corpus will grow and, on the other hand, users will profit from the interface's applications, using their own subcorpora. The only requirement is to use the relations and the segmentation and annotation criteria of our project. Once the texts are sent, the RST Spanish Treebank data manager will verify if the annotation corresponds to these criteria.

3.5 Administrator Interface

The sustainability of a language resource is a crucial aspect. As Ide and Pustejovsky (2010) assess, "means for resource preservation and maintenance should be established prior to publication to ensure continued availability [...]. In the case where resources are distributed via the web [...], ensured sustainability is the reponsibility of the resource developer". Having this requirement in mind, we have a data manager who is the responsible for the administration of the RST Spanish Treebank and its interface. This manager is the person in charge of the new texts and information that will be included in the corpus (both texts from users and texts selected by our research team). Data manager work is important because, although a part of the task is automatic (texts uploading), the texts data (ID, title, bibliographic reference and link) are included semi-automatically.

The administrator interface is divided in two parts. The first one is a program that connects to the server through Secure Shell Protocol; using this application, the data manager can upload all the files to be added at the corpus and set their location. The second part of the administrator interface is an on-line template that includes four fixed fields (text ID, title, reference and link). Once the documents are uploaded and their templates are filled, the data manager can press an update button. This button brings up to date the general xml of the corpus and the individual xml of each file, and executes the first statistical tool to count the number of words of each new file at the server.

4 Conclusions

In this paper, we have presented the RST Spanish Treebank interface that we have developed in order to include the RST Spanish Treebank, the first corpus containing Spanish texts annotated with RST relations. As we have shown, this interface allows users to consult or download the texts and their corresponding annotations freely and on-line. Moreover, it allows carrying out several statistical and linguistic searches over a selected subcorpus. We consider this interface is necessary and useful to exploit all the data contained in a corpus, which in this case will be in continuous growth.

We think that this work means an important step for the RST research in Spanish. Additionally, the RST Spanish Treebank and its interface will be useful to carry out diverse researches about RST in this language. These researches can be developed both from a descriptive point of view (contrastive analysis among specialized texts from different domains, analysis of genres, analysis of discourse markers, etc.) and an applied point of view (development of discourse parsers, development of natural language processing applications, like automatic summarization, automatic translation, information extraction, etc.). In addition, we consider that this interface would be useful to contain and analyze automatically RST corpora for other languages, because the interface architecture would allow it without too much adaptation effort.

As future work, we would like to insert a sentence segmentator (in order to count sentences automatically) and to optimize the RST_extract tool (in order to extract satellites and nuclei being SPANs, not only EDUs).

Acknowledgments

This research was supported by the research project CONACyT (Mexico), n. 82050; and the Spanish projects RICOTERM (FFI2010-21365-C03-01) and APLE (FFI2009-12188-C05-01).

References

Lynn Carlson, Daniel Marcu, and Mary Ellen Okurowski. 2002. RST Discourse Treebank. Pennsylvania: Linguistic Data Consortium.

Iria da Cunha, Juan-Manuel Torres-Moreno, and Gerardo Sierra. 2011. On the Development of the RST Spanish Treebank. In Proc. of the 5th Linguistic Annotation Workshop. 49th Annual Meeting of the ACL. 1-10.

Iria da Cunha, Eric SanJuan, Juan-Manuel Torres-Moreno, Marina Lloberes, and Irene Castellón. 2011. DiSeg 1.0: The First System for Spanish Discourse Segmentation. Expert Systems with Applications.

Iria da Cunha, Leo Wanner, and María Teresa Cabré. 2007. Summarization of specialized discourse: The case of medical articles in Spanish. Terminology, 13(2):249-286.

Mikel Iruskieta and Iria da Cunha. 2010. El potencial de las relaciones retóricas para la discriminación de textos especializados de diferentes dominios en euskera-español. Calidoscópio, 8(3):181-202.

Maria Lucía del Rosario Castro Jorge and Thiago Alexandre Salgueiro Pardo. 2010. Experiments with CST-based Multidocument Summarization. In Proc. of the ACL Work. TextGraphs-5: Graph-based Methods for NLP. 74-82.

Eduard Hovy. 2010. Annotation. A Tutorial. Presented at the 48th Annual Meeting of ACL.

Nancy Ide and James Pustejovsky. 2010. What Does Interoperability Mean, anyway? Toward an Operational Definition of Interoperability. In Proc. of the 2° Int. Conf. on Global Interoperability for Language Resources.

William C. Mann and Sandra A. Thompson. 1988. Rhetorical structure theory: Toward a functional theory of text organization. Text, 8(3):243-281.

Daniel Marcu. 2000. The Theory and Practice of Discourse Parsing Summarization. Massachusetts: Institute of Technology.

Michael O'Donnell. 2000. RSTTOOL 2.4 – A markup tool for rhetorical structure theory. In Proc. of Int. Natural Lang. Generation Conf.. 253-256.

Dragomir R. Radev. 2000. A common theory of information fusion from multiple text sources, step one: Cross-document structure. In Proc. of the 1st ACL SIGDIAL Work. on Discourse and Dialogue.

Thiago Alexandre Salgueiro Pardo and Eloize Rossi Marques Seno. 2005. Rhetalho: um corpus de referência anotado retoricamente. In Anais do V Encontro de Corpora. São Carlos-SP, Brasil.

Gerardo Sierra. 2008. Diseño de corpus textuales para fines lingüísticos. In Proc. of the IX Encuentro Inter. de Lingüística en el Noroeste 2. 445-462.

Manfred Stede. 2004. The Potsdam commentary corpus. In Proc. of the Workshop on Discourse Annotation. 42nd Meeting of ACL.

Maite Taboada and Jan Renkema. 2008. Discourse Relations Reference Corpus. Simon Fraser University and Tilburg University. http://www.sfu.ca/rst/06tools/discourse_relations_corpus.html.

Appendix A. Screenshot of the interface with an annotated text

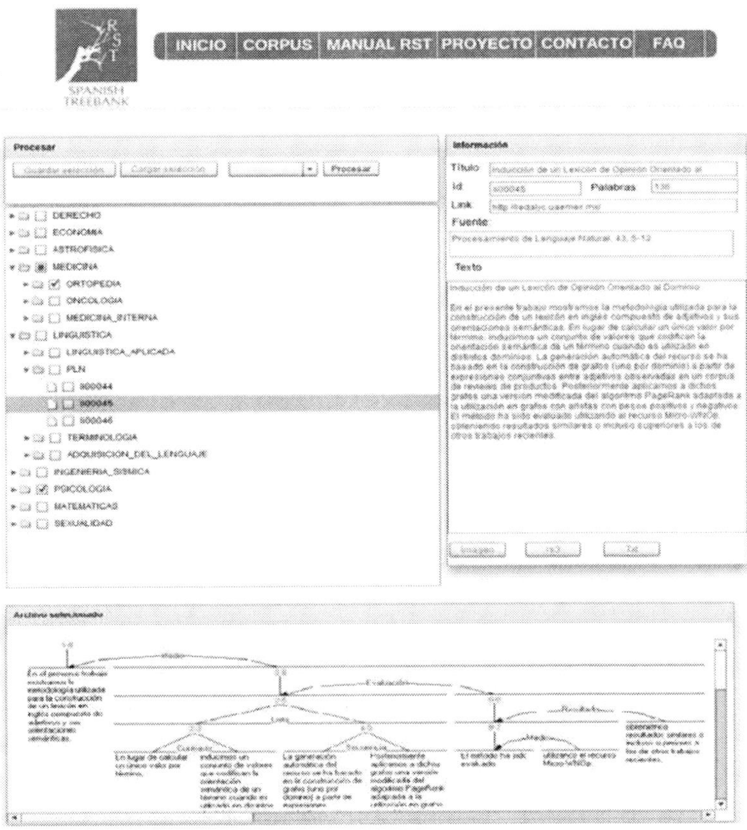

Lexical Generalisation for Word-level Matching in Plagiarism Detection

Miranda Chong
University of Wolverhampton
Miranda.Chong@wlv.ac.uk

Lucia Specia
University of Wolverhampton
L.Specia@wlv.ac.uk

Abstract

Plagiarism has always been a concern in many sectors, particularly in education. With the sharp rise in the number of electronic resources available online, an increasing number of plagiarism cases has been observed in recent years. As the amount of source materials is vast, the use of plagiarism detection tools has become the norm to aid the investigation of possible plagiarism cases. This paper describes an approach to improve plagiarism detection by incorporating a lexical generalisation technique. The goal is to identify plagiarised texts even if they are paraphrased using different words. Experiments performed on a subset of the PAN'10 corpus show that the matching approach involving lexical generalisation yields promising results, as compared to standard n-gram matching strategies.

1 Introduction

Plagiarism is a growing challenge in modern society. In an attempt to maintain academic integrity, the use of plagiarism detection tools has become the norm in many higher education institutions. However, the methods used in these tools are mostly limited to comparisons of suspicious plagiarised texts and potential source texts at the string level. If the texts have not been copied verbatim, these tools are not able to identify the obfuscated texts effectively. Therefore, the accuracy of these methods is yet to reach a satisfactory level.

This paper investigates the use of pre-processing, morphological and lexical semantics techniques from Natural Language Processing (NLP) in automatic plagiarism detection. The hypothesis is that by enhancing standard string matching approaches with linguistic information it is possible to improve the accuracy of plagiarism identification at the document level. More specifically, the goal is to generalise the text comparison to include morphological and lexical variations (synonyms). Different from previous work, instead of restricting the expansion of words in the documents to synonyms with the same *sense*, we use a simpler approach that considers all possible expansions. This approach does not require word sense disambiguation and is therefore less prone to common errors due to incorrect disambiguation.

This paper is organised as follows: in Section 2 we describe related work in the plagiarism detection field using NLP; in Section 3 we outline the experimental settings; in Section 4 we present the results of our experiments; in Section 5 we discuss the findings; and in Section 6 we conclude and suggest future work.

2 Related Work

Our focus is on external monolingual plagiarism detection of English documents. External detection refers to cases where potential source texts are available for comparison against suspicious plagiarised texts. Following the standard terminology in the field, we name *suspicious document* a potentially plagiarised text, and *source document* the possible origin of the plagiarised material.

Current studies in this area have suggested the use of approaches such as n-gram matching between suspicious and potential source documents. NLP has only recently started to be exploited for this problem. However, most approaches focus on shallow techniques or the processing of very small corpora.

The PAN workshop series "Uncovering Plagiarism, Authorship, and Social Software Misuse" has been organised in recent years to provide a common ground for developing and testing plagiarism detection systems. Each year, the workshop provides a corpus for large-scale detection experiments (Barrón-Cedeno and Rosso, 2010). Reports from the 1st and 2nd competition (PAN'09 and PAN'10) have shown that most competitors used n-gram-based hashed-indexing approach, but little or no effort was made to use NLP techniques. Although some levels of shallow NLP techniques such as stemming were used to generalise string matching (Costa-jussà et al., 2010; Pereira et al., 2010; Torrejón and Ramos, 2010), the reports did not specify whether the application of these techniques contributed to the detection accuracy. Due to the very short time given to participants to process the corpus for the official competitions, little effort has been made in these competitions to further explore NLP techniques.

Outside of these competitions, lexical resources with synonymy information have been used in a few approaches. Similar to our work, the idea is to generalise the words in the texts by considering synonyms when searching for lexical matching between suspicious and source texts, in addition to exact matching of words.

The use of a lexical thesaurus such as WordNet (Fellbaum, 1998) was investigated by Nahnsen et al. (2005). The paper described the use of lexical resources in text similarity detection, which involved the use of cosine similarity on n-grams of lexical chains, with word sense disambiguation applied to nouns, verbs and adjectives. They computed *tf-idf* of the disambiguated words as a similarity measure but if the WSD process is not accurate, it would affect the similarity scores.

Another research by Chen et al. (2010) has concluded that using WordNet to perform synonym recognition can help determine whether a sentence pair contains similar words. They measure the similarity by comparing the synonyms within each synsets, ie. they compare the synonyms in synset 1 for suspicious document word A and synonyms in synset 1 for source document word B, however, this method would not return any similarity scores if the synonyms are in different synsets even if they belonged to the same word. In comparison, the use of WordNet in Ceska (2009)'s experiment did not show significant improvement over the other shallow text-processing methods. Ceska performed synonymy recognition with word sense disambiguation and it was said using the *ad hoc* rule to choose the "first synset" or word sense disambiguation techniques to choose the "most suitable synset" were not effective.

In previous work we performed experiments on a small-scale manually created corpus to incorporate shallow text pre-processing, morphological, lexical and syntactic information (Chong et al, 2010). The results suggested NLP techniques can help to improve the identification of plagiarised documents. However, besides being small, the corpus contained easily detectable short cases of induced plagiarism. In this paper we concentrate on the subset of linguistic processing techniques identified as the most promising in our previous work and apply it to the much larger PAN'10 corpus. More specifically, we evaluate the use of lexical generalisation in this large-scale scenario, without the need of word sense disambiguation. Since word sense disambiguation is a complex task on its own, we can avoid mistakes resulting from incorrect disambiguation. Syntactic processing was not used here due to the nature of the corpus: a large proportion of the plagiarised cases are artificially created by random text operations including automatically replacing, adding and removing words and changing sentence structure, resulting in text that is not always grammatical.

3 Experimental Settings

3.1 Corpus

The corpus used in the experiment is the PAN'10 [1] corpus. It consists of a total of 11,147 source and 15,925 suspicious documents. Plagiarism cases refer to segments in suspicious documents, annotated in terms of character offsets. Of all the plagiarism cases, 40% are verbatim copies from multiple sources (no obfuscation). Other 40% of cases contain artificially inserted passages with two levels, low or high, of automatic obfuscations such as modifying sentence structures and replacing words with their synonyms. A small proportion of cases (6%) are simulated plagiarism cases where texts were manually rewritten with different wordings using the *Amazon Mechanical Turks*. The remaining cases consisted of translated plagiarism texts, that is, suspicious texts produced from automatically translating source documents using a machine translation system. The length of plagiarism segments in a suspicious document range from a minimum of 50 words to a maximum of 5,000 words, and the segments can come from 1 to more than 50 sources. 50% of the suspicious and source documents contain 1 to 10 pages, 35% contain 10 to 100 pages, and 15% contain 100-1000 pages. The corpus contains both external and intrinsic plagiarism cases, that is, cases where plagiarism is to be identified

[1] 2nd International Workshop on Uncovering Plagiarism, Authorship, and Social Software Misuse PAN-10 http://pan.webis.de/

within the actual suspicious document, without referring to a source document.

For practical reasons, in this paper we selected a subset of the PAN corpus: the first 1,000 suspicious documents, along with all 11,147 source documents. Since our goal is to investigate external plagiarism of English texts, all intrinsic and translated plagiarism cases were excluded from the dataset. We therefore removed 186 cases from the subset of 1,000 suspicious documents and 731 non-English cases from the source documents. The experiments presented here are thus based on 814 suspicious documents and 10,416 source documents, which gives a total of 8,478,624 possible pairwise comparisons.

The method used in this paper is a binary classification of documents, that is, we classify each suspicious-source document pair as *plagiarised* or *not plagiarised*. Although in the PAN competition plagiarised cases are expected to be reported at the segment level, in this paper cases are treated at document level, where a pair of documents is considered as *plagiarised* whenever at least one segment within the suspicious document is plagiarised from the source document. Given that NLP techniques are much more computationally expensive than simple string matching techniques, document level processing is a more realistic scenario for this feasibility study. Moreover, flagging plagiarised documents can be a helpful aid for humans checking potential plagiarism cases by filtering out a very large amout of documents from the process.

3.2 Processing Techniques

We follow the standard 2-phase methodology in plagiarism detection. The first phase is *candidate document selection*, that is, filtering documents in order to narrow down the search space to document pairs that can contain plagiarised segments. The second phase is a detailed analysis of the remaining candidate document pairs.

In order to generalise the texts for subsequent similarity comparisons, both source and suspicious documents were processed using the following pre-processing and morphological processing techniques as available in NLTK[2] (Bird et al., 2010).

Tokenisation: determine token (words, punctuation symbols) boundaries in sentences.

Lowercasing: substitute every uppercase letter with their lowercase form.

Punctuation removal: remove all punctuation symbols.

Stemming: morphological analysis to transform words into their stems by removal of derivational affixes, for example: 'computational', 'computing' and 'compute' will be returned to the base form 'comput'. Stemming is used as a common pre-processing method in plagiarism detection task and we have followed this approach.

For the experiment with lexical generalisation, functional words (**stop words**) were removed and all remaining (content) words were generalised using their **WordNet synsets**, that is, groups of synonym words. In other words, we expanded the source and suspicious documents by replacing each of its content word by the words in all of its synsets from WordNet. It is important to notice that WordNet performs morphological generalisation by lemmatising words, that is, converting them into their basic form, for example: 'operative', 'operational' and 'operation' into 'operate'.

3.3 Similarity Metrics

Based on the corpus processed with the techniques described above, the next step is to measure the similarity between source-suspicious document pairs. As shown in Table 1, we differentiate between the proposed approach (Dataset (II)) and a baseline using the same pre-processing steps, but having stemming as a morphological generalization technique, as opposed to the use of WordNet for morphological and lexical generalization (Dataset (I)). We propose a synset overlap metric and compare it against a standard 5-gram overlap metric for our baseline dataset.

Data set	Techniques	Similarity Metric
(I)	Tokenisation Lowercasing Punctuation Removal Stemming	5-gram overlap
(II)	Tokenisation Lowercasing Punctuation Removal Stopwords Removal WordNet All Synsets	Synset overlap

Table 1: Similarity metrics applied to the baseline and proposed approaches

[2] http://www.nltk.org/

The use of overlapping n-grams is a common practise in the PAN competitions; the use of hashed 5-grams was one of the techniques contributing to the top-ranked approaches (Kasprzak and Brandejs, 2010; Zou et al., 2010). Therefore, in this experiment the overlap of chunks of 5-grams was used as our baseline. More specifically, we used the overlap coefficient, a common n-gram similarity metric (Clough and Stevenson, 2009).

$$Sim_{Overlap}(A,B) = \frac{|S(A,n) \cap S(B,n)|}{min(|S(A,n)|,|S(B,n)|)} \quad (1)$$

where $S(A,n)$ and $S(B,n)$ are the unique 5-grams contained in the suspicious and source documents, respectively. The number of common 5-grams in both sets is normalized by the smaller of $S(A,n)$ or $S(B,n)$ to account for differences in the sizes of suspicious and source documents.

For the version of the corpus expanded with WordNet synsets, the matching is performed based on unigrams of synsets. In other words, the number of common synsets of the source $S(A)$ and suspicious $S(B)$ documents is computed and then normalised by the total number of synsets in both suspicious and source documents, using the *Jaccard coefficient*:

$$Sim_{WordNet}(A,B) = \frac{|S(A) \cap S(B)|}{|S(A) \cup S(B)|} \quad (2)$$

3.4 Filtering

In plagiarism detection tasks, it is essential to perform initial filtering with superficial techniques to reduce the number of potential source documents, and therefore the number of document pairs to be processed in the next stage. The use of progressive filtering makes the application of deeper NLP techniques more feasible in the remaining document pairs. The filtering stage is referred to as the *candidate document selection* and the suspicious-source documents selected for further processing are referred to as *candidate documents*.

In this paper, the filtering strategy is based on empirical observation and consists in applying the following steps to all document pairs in the dataset processed with superficial techniques and 5-gram overlap coefficient (Dataset (I) in Table 1):

1. Rank the documents pairs in descending order according to their similarity scores.
2. For each suspicious document, select the top 10 potential source doc. This resulted in 8,140 document pairs.
3. Remove document pairs that do not have at least 10 common 5-grams or with an overlap coefficient score (Equation 1) of less than 0.01. This resulted in 1,534 candidate document pairs in Dataset I.

The 1,534 candidate document pairs are then processed for lexical generalisation using WordNet (resulting in Dataset II). We then compare and evaluate both datasets using the 1,534 document pairs.

4 Results

We treat the detection problem as a binary classification task where the documents are said to be *plagiarised* when their similarity score is above a certain threshold, or *not plagiarised* if the similarity score is below that threshold. Therefore, standard evaluation metrics of precision, recall and F-score can be employed to measure detection performance. The number of correctly classified plagiarised documents - True Positives (TP), correctly classified non-plagiarised documents - True Negatives (TN), non-plagiarised documents incorrectly classified as plagiarised - False Positives (FP), and the plagiarised documents incorrectly classified as non-plagiarised - False Negatives (FN) are used for the standard calculation of precision, recall, and F-score.

The similarity scores are tested with various thresholds to investigate the trade-off between precision and recall. Ideally, a detection approach should make sure that all potential plagiarised documents are flagged (high recall), but also make sure that non-plagiarised documents are not flagged (high precision), to save humans' time when manually analysing the flagged documents. However, as in most classification tasks, a high recall may come at the price of a low precision, and vice-versa. Therefore, depending on the detection task, it may be more important to favour one metric or another. For this reason, instead of fixing a threshold, we show, in Figures 1, the precision and recall at different thresholds.

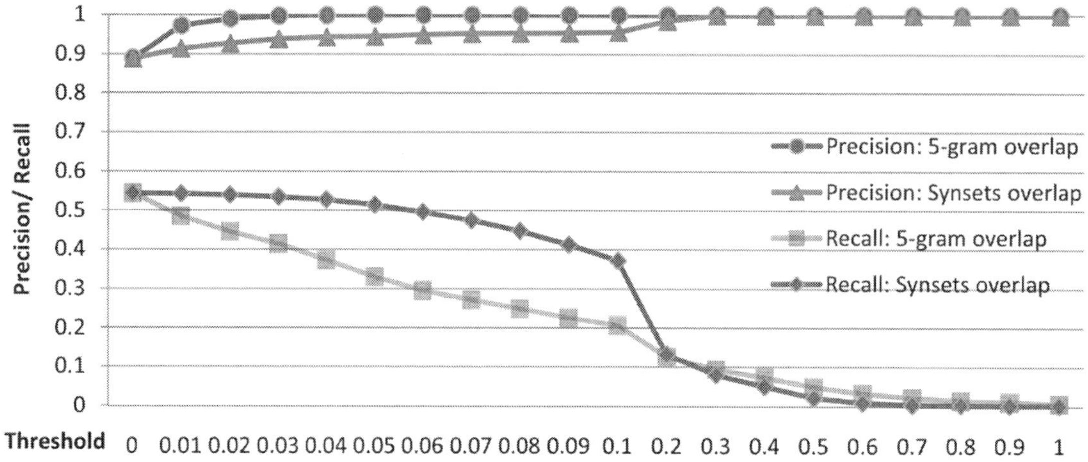

Figure 1: Precision and Recall for several thresholds in the similarity metrics. Statistically significant differences were observed according to pair-wise *t*-test (p-value < 0.05) between the baseline 5-gram overlap (Dataset I) and proposed approach Synsets overlap (Dataset II).

5 Discussion

As we can see in Figure 1, the WordNet-based similarity metric shows improvement over the baseline, achieving similar precision and a significantly higher recall for lower thresholds. The high recall figure indicates that using all synsets in the similarity metric can help reduce the number of false negative cases. However, the slightly lower precision indicates that using all synsets may be too lenient. This suggests that the use of WordNet may be more appropriate to investigate a subset of highly suspicious plagiarism cases after filtering by using other methods.

Upon further analysis based on individual levels of obfuscation, that is, the four levels of plagiarism annotation in the PAN'10 corpus (manual paraphrase, low artificial obfuscation, high artificial obfuscation, and no obfuscation), we noticed that the use of WordNet synsets matching is more effective than the 5-gram overlap baseline in all obfuscation levels. Although the baseline is effective in detecting direct verbatim copies, the WordNet synsets matching is capable of achieving better results regardless of how the plagiarised texts have been produced. In particular, this strategy has identified significantly more simulated and obfuscated plagiarism cases than the baseline.

For example, Table 2 shows the the recall of both approaches on different levels of obfuscation, based on a threshold of 0.03.

Obfuscation level	Dataset (I)	Dataset (II)
None	0.48	0.62
Artificial - low	0.42	0.54
Artificial - high	0.35	0.46
Simulated	0.27	0.37

Table 2: Recall obtained by the of 5-gram overlap baseline and the synset-based similarity matching for different obfuscation levels

Although this initial experiment is based on a subset of the corpus, we believe that by using a combination of 5-gram overlap and WordNet-based similarity metrics, a more accurate detection performance could be achieved. Further experiments need to be performed on this direction.

6 Further Work and Conclusions

In this paper we proposed using lexical generalisation to improve the performance of string-based matching plagiarism detection approaches. The experiments were performed with a subset of the PAN'10 corpus, but a similar performance is expected with larger datasets. The results have shown the influence of lexical generalisation on plagiarism detection performance in terms of precision and recall. Different levels of threshold have different effects on precision, recall and F-score. Therefore, the threshold needs to be set in accordance to the detection task requirement. A future direction is to use machine learning algorithms to set this threshold. Machine learning algorithms will also allow a principled way of classifying documents based on a combination of similarity scores generated from different metrics, such as scores from 5-gram overlap and WordNet synsets.

Further investigation is needed to seek for better filtering strategies to optimise the detection performance, as well as better similarity metrics to account for other linguistic variations. Areas such as Recognising Textual Entailment (RTE) and stylistic approaches used in authorship attribution may provide additional improvements. Semantic parsing by using tools such as semantic role labellers can provide deeper analysis in terms of the semantic structure of texts. It is expected that such rich features will be more effective in identifying simulated plagiarism cases.

Last but not least, future experiments using the PAN corpus will be performed on passage level instead of document level in order to allow comparative evaluation to be performed using the standard PAN evaluation measures.

References

Barrón-Cedeno, A. and Rosso, P. (2010). Towards the 2nd International Competition on Plagiarism Detection and Beyond. Proceedings for the 4th International Plagiarism Conference. Newcastle, UK.

Bird, S., Klein, E. and Loper, E. (2010). Natural Language Processing with Python--- Analyzing Text with the Natural Language Toolkit.

Ceska, Z. (2009). Automatic Plagiarism Detection Based on Latent Semantic Analysis. Doctoral Thesis. University of West Bohemia, CR.

Chen, C.-Y., Yeh, J.-Y. and Ke, H.-R. (2010). Plagiarism Detection using ROUGE and WordNet.

Chong, M., Specia, L. and Mitkov, R. (2010). Using Natural Language Processing for Automatic Detection of Plagiarism. Proceedings of the 4th International Plagiarism Conference. Newcastle, UK.

Clough, P. and Stevenson, M. (2009). Developing a Corpus of Plagiarised Short Answers. Language Resources and Evaluation, 1–20. Springer.

Costa-jussà, M. R., Banchs, R. E., Grivolla, J. and Codina, J. (2010). Plagiarism Detection Using Information Retrieval and Similarity Measures Based on Image Processing Techniques. Proceedings of the Uncovering Plagiarism, Authorship, and Social Software Misuse (PAN) 2010 Workshop. Padua, Italy.

Fellbaum, C. (1998, ed.). WordNet: An Electronic Lexical Database. Cambridge, MA: MIT Press.

Kasprzak, J. and Brandejs, M. (2010). Improving the Reliability of the Plagiarism Detection System Lab Report for PAN at CLEF 2010. Proceedings of the Uncovering Plagiarism, Authorship, and Social Software Misuse (PAN) 2010 Workshop. Padua, Italy.

Nahnsen, T., Uzuner, O. and Katz, B. (2005). Lexical chains and sliding locality windows in content-based text similarity detection. CSAIL Memo.

Pereira, R. C., Moreira, V. P. and Galante, R. (2010). UFRGS @ PAN2010 : Detecting External Plagiarism Lab Report for Pan at CLEF 2010. Proceedings of the Uncovering Plagiarism, Authorship, and Social Software Misuse (PAN) 2010 Workshop. Padua, Italy.

Torrejón, D. A. R. and Ramos, J. M. M. (2010). CoReMo System (Contextual Reference Monotony) Lab Report for PAN at CLEF 2010. Proceedings of the Uncovering Plagiarism, Authorship, and Social Software Misuse (PAN) 2010 Workshop. Padua, Italy.

Zou, D., Long, W.J., and Ling, Z. (2010). A Cluster-Based Plagiarism Detection Method. Proceedings of the Uncovering Plagiarism, Authorship, and Social Software Misuse (PAN) 2010 Workshop. Padua, Italy.

Multiple Evidence for Term Extraction in Broad Domains

Boris Dobrov
Research Computing Center of Lomonosov
Moscow State University,
Moscow, Russia
dobroff@mail.cir.ru

Natalia Loukachevitch
Research Computing Center of Lomonosov
Moscow State University,
Moscow, Russia
louk_nat@mail.cir.ru

Abstract

The paper describes the method of extraction of two-word domain terms combining their features. The features are computed from three sources: the occurrence statistics in a domain-specific text collection, the statistics of global search engines, and a domain-specific thesaurus. The evaluation of the approach is based on manually created thesauri. We show that the use of multiple features considerably improves the automatic extraction of domain-specific terms. We compare the quality of the proposed method in two different domains.

1 Introduction

The important stage of domain specific knowledge acquisition is recognition of terms, representing domain concepts in documents. Automatic extraction of domain terms from texts is a subject of constant interest in automatic document processing. The special difficulty is the automatic extraction of multiword terms (Zhang et. al. 2008; Wong et. al. 2008).

Contemporary information systems usually contain documents related to broad domains, which requires development of large terminological resources. Term extraction to develop such resources should be based on processing of large amount of documents. Besides, existing terminological resources need periodic updates.

For many years, researchers tried to find the best statistical feature for term extraction. Now machine learning methods allow for the combination of many features (Vivaldi et.al, 2001, Pecina and Schlesinger, 2008, Foo and Merkel, 2010).

In (Vivaldi et. al., 2001) features for extraction of medical terms are combined using boosting algorithm. The features include information from EuroWordNet, Greek and Latin word forms, statistical measures. Some of the features are rather domain-dependent. (Foo and Merkel, 2010) study applicacability of rule-based machine-learning algorithm Ripper for term extraction from patent texts.

In (Pecina and Schlesinger, 2008) the combination of statistical characteristics of phrases, based on the Czech text collection, is used to extract several types of collocations (such as phrasal verbs, idioms, terms). The authors used over 80 features and obtained 20% improvement compared with the best individual feature. But the authors of this paper indicate that efficiency of different features is very variable and depends on a collection, types of expressions and so on.

In this paper we describe an experiment to extract two-word terms (noun groups) based on a combination of three types of features: features based on a domain-specific text collection, features obtained from an Internet search engine, features obtained from a domain-specific thesaurus.

Working with a thesaurus, we simulate the situation when the thesaurus partially exists. We want to study its potential to recognise new terms. The important point of our research is to study the stability of the term extraction model among different domains.

2 Description of Experiment: Data and Evaluation

We conduct our study in two domains. The first domain is the very broad domain of natural sciences and technologies. The second one is domain of banking and bank regulation. For both domains we have Russian thesauri, developed manually, which we use as a basis for evaluation of term extraction methods (see section 2.1).

Besides, there are Russian domain-specific text collections used for development of these thesauri. From the text collections, we have extracted single words and multiword expressions. Two-word expressions belong to two types of noun groups: *Adjective+Noun* and *Noun+Noun_in_Genitive*.

The extracted expressions were initially ordered in descending order of their frequencies. Terminologists usually work with these term candidate lists paying more attention to expressions with high frequencies. However it was noted that the important terms could have medium or low frequencies because of the unbalance of text collections. So the aim of our new term extraction method is to reorder the extracted expressions to get more approved terms in the top of the candidate list. We experimented with five thousands of the most frequent two-word expressions from these lists.

2.1 Terminological Resources Used for Evaluation

Ontology on Natural Sciences and Technologies comprises Russian terminology in a very broad domain of natural sciences including mathematics, physics, chemistry, geology and elementary biology. It was created for automatic text processing of scientific documents such as automatic conceptual indexing, search results visualization, search query expansion, automatic text categorization, text summarization etc. The wide scope of the ontology is intended to support interdisciplinary research, to serve as a general source of terminology described in a formalized way. The current volume of Ontology on Natural Sciences is more than 140 thousand terms (Dobrov and Loukachevitch, 2006).

Banking thesaurus was created during a state contract with the Central Bank of the Russian Federation. It comprises the terminology related to activity of the Central Bank, including such issues as banking activity, banking regulation, monetary politics, macroeconomics. Now it includes about 15 thousand terms.

In structure, both terminological resources are similar to classical information-retrieval thesauri (ISO 2788), having descriptors, corresponding to concepts of the domain; synonyms and term variants attached to the descriptors; relations between the descriptors.

At the same time, the resources are intended to be used in automatic text processing (in contrast to classical information-retrieval thesauri for manual indexing) and therefore they have considerable coverage of their domains, in particular, including a lot of term variants, occurred in real texts of the domain. This feature of our resources facilitates evaluation of term extraction methods (Nazarenko and Zargayouna, 2009). So we suppose that all term variants have been already described in our gold standards.

2.2 Measure for Evaluation of Term Extraction Performance

The evaluation of term candidates extracted from texts is a complicated procedure, because of, for example, subjectivity of domain experts, variativity of terms (Nazarenko and Zargayouna, 2009).

We suppose that term extraction is needed for a broad domain with thousands of terms and term variants. A term extraction procedure is based on processing of large domain-specific text collections consisting of hundreds and thousands megabytes of texts. From these texts a ranked list of term candidates is generated. The real domain terms should be situated mainly in the top of the list to facilitate expert work or automatic exploitation of such a list. So we want to evaluate reordering performance of various methods of term recognition

To evaluate the reordering performance of methods we use the measure of average precision adopted from information retrieval (Manning et. al., 2009). Average precision AvP in the task of term extraction is calculated as follows.

Suppose that in an ordered list of expressions there are k terms, and pos (i) – the position of the i-th term from the beginning of the list. Then the precision on the level of the i-th terminological expression $PrecTerm_i$ in an ordered list is PrecTerm (pos (i)), that is the value of precision $PrecTerm_i$ is calculated at the time of inclusion to the list of i-th term and is equal to the percentage of terms in the list from 1 to pos (i) positions.

Average precision for the given ordered list is equal to the average value of $PrecTerm_i$:

$$AvP=\frac{1}{k}\sum_{1}^{k} PrecTerm_i$$

3 Features for Term Candidate Reordering

For extracted phrases we compute features of three types:

- features based on a domain-specific text collection,

- features obtained from an Internet search engine,
- features obtained from a domain-specific thesaurus.

Each type of features allows us to model different aspects of domain terms.

3.1 Features Based on Domain Specific Collection

We use several features calculated on the basis of a domain-specific text collection. The chosen features reveal different properties of domain terms.

Frequency in the collection (Freq). This feature is often used in term extraction methods because it is known that terms have to be frequent in domain-specific texts and the most frequent phrases of a domain include large share of domain terms.

Mutual information (MI). The feature is also very popular in extraction of terms and is calculated as follows:

$$MI(ab) = log\left(\frac{N \cdot freq(ab)}{freq(a) \cdot freq(b)}\right)$$

where ab – is a two-word phrase, $freq\,()$ is the frequency of phrases or words in the collection, N – number of words in the collection. The feature indicates difference between real co-occurrences of a phrase and independent occurrences of phrase components.

Cubical Mutual Information (MI_3). This feature is a modification of MI feature. In corpora research it was shown that this feature better orders low frequent phrases (Daille et. al., 1998):

$$MI_3(ab) = log\left(\frac{N \cdot freq^3(ab)}{freq(a) \cdot freq(b)}\right)$$

Insideness. Insideness is calculated as the inverse ratio between the phrase frequency and the maximal frequency of a three-word expression comprising the given phrase.

$$Inside(ab) = \frac{freq(*ab*)}{freq(ab)}$$

This feature is intended to reveal truncated word sequences – parts of real terms. The similar phenomenon is modeled by C-value feature, described in (Maynard and Ananiadou, 2000).

3.2 Features Based on Internet Search

An important characteristic of a domain term is "termhood" that is relevance to the domain *(*Kageura and Umino, 1996*)*. The known way to estimate "termhood" is comparative analysis of a given text collection with a contrast text collection. The huge collection of Internet texts can serve as such a contrast collection.

In previous research the Web was used for developing domain specific corpora (Penas et.al., 2001; Baroni and Bernardini, 2004). (Turney, 2003) exploits the Web to obtain the most important domain terms using so called coherence feature, ranking higher term candidates that co-occur with other candidates in Web documents.

In our study we extract several phrase features from the Web and combine them with other types of features (collection-based and thesaurus-based). We obtain Internet-based features using xml-interface of Russian Search Engine Yandex on the basis of specially formulated queries. For our experiments we utilised so-called search snippets - short fragments of texts explaining search results.

Use of Internet search is important for the following reasons. First, a text collection of a broad domain is often not sufficient because a lot of fairly significant terms may have relatively low frequencies in it. Involvement of the Internet helps us get additional information on such terms. Secondly, the use of information from the Internet allows us to find out if a given phrase is rigidly connected with the domain.

To calculate the Internet-based features, 100 snippets from search results were utilised. The snippets from the same query were merged into one document and processed by a morphological processor. As a result, for each set of snippets, lemmas (words in a dictionary form) were extracted and their frequencies of occurrence were calculated.

So, for every query we obtain a vector of lemmas with corresponding frequencies. Snippets were generated for the whole phrases and their constituent words. We denote S_{ab} – a vector of lemma frequencies derived from phrase snippets, S_a, S_b - vectors of lemmas from constituent word snippets. Using such vectors, the following types of features were calculated.

Scalar Features: $\mathbf{Scalar_1}$, $\mathbf{Scalar_2}$, $\mathbf{Boolean_1}$, $\mathbf{Boolean_2}$. The first group of Internet-based features are scalar products of snippet vectors: $<S_{ab}, S_a>$ **($\mathbf{Scalar_1}$)**, $<S_{ab}, S_b>$ **($\mathbf{Scalar_2}$)**. Many domain-specific terms have specificity of their meanings, which can not be deduced from their components (so-called non-compositionality). This specificity usually can be revealed using comparison of contexts of a phrase and its component words. The usual way to do this is to find scalar products between vectors of contexts. Also we calculated scalar products of boolean variants of snippet vectors (vector elements are from {0, 1}) : $<Sb_{ab}, Sb_a>$ **(Boolean$_1$)**, $<Sb_{ab}, Sb_b>$ **(Boolean$_2$).**

Features of semantically specific context (SnipFreq$_0$, SnipFreq$_1$, SnipFreq$_2$). Another way to find specificity of a phrase is to find a single lemma that is very frequent in phrase snippets and absent (or rarely mentioned) in component snippets.

Let lemma L occur f_{ab} times in phrase snippets and occur f_a, f_b times in snippets of components. Then we calculate SnipFreq$_0$ feature as follows:

$$SnipFreq_0 = \max_L \cdot \left(f_{ab-a-b} \cdot \log\left(\frac{N - dlcol}{dlcol}\right)\right)$$

where $f_{ab-a-b} = max\ (f_{ab} - f_a - f_b,\ 0)$, $dlcol$ is the lemma frequency in documents of a contrast collection, N – is the number of documents in the contrast collection. Factor $\log\left(\frac{N - dlcol}{dlcol}\right)$ is so-called idf-factor known from information retrieval research (Manning et. al., 2009); it helps to diminish influence of frequent general words. The contrast collection is the collection of Belorussian Internet documents distributed in the framework of Russian Information Retrieval Evaluatopn Seminar (www.romip.ru/en/index.html).

Features **SnipFreq1** and **SnipFreq2** are calculated in a similar way excluding words in a window of 1 (2) words near every occurrence of phrase *ab*. These variants of SnipFreq feature are intended to remove partial fragments of longer terms from consideration. For example, for such macroeconomic terms as *negative cash flow* and *negative cash balance* lemmas *flow* and *balance* will be very frequent in snippets of phrase *negative cash* and will be situated immediately after phrase *negative cash,* but this phrase is not a real term.

The frequency of a phrase in its own snippets (FreqBySnip). We supposed that if the value of this feature is significantly greater than 100 (sometimes this feature reached 250-300 occurrences in 100 snippets), it means that there are many contexts in which this phrase is explained in detail, is the theme of the fragment, and, most likely, this phrase denotes an important concept or a specific entity, as, for example, phrase *internal debt* in the following snippet: *The first distinction to be made is between an internal debt and an external debt. An internal debt is owed by a nation.*

Number of definitional words in snippets (NearDefWords). This feature calculates overall frequency of so called definitional words in phrase snippets. These words (as *type, class, define* etc.) are often used in dictionary definitions. Therefore their presence in snippets can mean that a snippet contains a definition of this phrase or the phrase is used in definition of other term. **NearDefWords** feature is equal to the number of these definitional words that appeared immediately adjacent (left or right) with the original phrase in snippets.

Number of marker words in snippets (Markers). This feature denotes number of five-ten the most important words of the domain in snippets of the phrase. For the natural science domain these words were as follows: *mathematics, mathematical, physics, physical, chemisry, chemical, geology, geological, biology, biological.*

Number of Internet page titles (SnipTitle). We calculated number of Internet page titles coinciding with a given phrase, because we supposed that the use of the phrase as the title of an Internet page stresses significance of the phrase.

3.3 Features Based on Terms of Domain-Specific Thesaurus

In many domains there are well-known terms and even information-retrieval thesauri. The third type of our features is based on the assumption that the known terms can help to predict unknown terms. For the experiments in two domains, we used the relevant thesauri. If a phrase was a thesaurus term, then it was excluded from the terminological basis for feature generation. We considered the following features obtained from a domain-specific thesaurus.

Synonym to Thesaurus Term (SynTerm). Domain documents can contain a lot of variants of the same term (Nenadic et. al., 2004). Therefore we can suppose that a phrase similar to a thesaurus term is also a term. Let *a* and *b* be components of phrase *ab*. We consider phrase *cd* as a synonym of phrase *ab* if every component word of phrase *cd* is either equal to a component word of *ab* either is a synonym of a component word of *ab*. The order of components in the phrases is unimportant.

Synonym to Non-Term (SynNotTerm). We also fix a feature of similarity to a phrase not included to the thesaurus.

Completeness of Description (Completeness). It is possible that component words *a* and/or *b* of phrase *ab* have been already described in a domain thesaurus. For example, *a* is related to thesaurus descriptor $D_{a,}$ and *b* is related to thesaurus descriptor D_b.Descriptor D_a has s_a synonyms and r_a relations to other descriptors. Descriptor D_b has s_b synonyms and r_b relations to other descriptors. **Completeness** feature is a sum of thesaurus relations of component terms that is:

$$Completeness = s_a + s_b + r_a + r_b$$

If a component of a phrase is not included to the thesaurus then its s_a and r_a are equal to 0.

4 Results of Experiments

We experimented in two domains: the banking domain and the domain of natural sciences. In all experiments 5 thousand most frequent two-word expressions extracted from the corresponding text collections were used. For these expressions, all above-mentioned features were calculated. To obtain the best combination of features for term extraction, we used machine learning methods implemented in programming package RapidMiner (www.rapidminer.com). The quality of reordering was evaluated with AvP measure. The training set was three-quarters of the phrase list, the testing set was a remaining part. As basic minimal levels of AvP we used the alphabet order and the decreasing frequency order.

To find the best combination of features for phrase reordering we tested various machine learning methods from RapidMiner package. Every time logistic regression achieved maximal level of AvP. Therefore we took this method as a basic machine learning method for our experiments on term extraction.

Table 1 shows AvP values for single features and their combination obtained with logistic regression. SynTerm and SynNotTerm features are Boolean and can not be evaluated with AvP. We concluded that SynTerm feature is highly informative: if *SynTerm* (*ab*) =1 then phrase *ab* is a domain term with probability more than 80%.

Feature	AvP (Banking) %	AvP (Natural Sciences)%
Alphabet	40%	57%
Frequency	57%	66%
MI	43%	64%
MI3	45%	67%
Inside	55%	75%
FreqBySnip	53%	69%
NearDefWords	49%	73%
$Scalar_1$	42%	61%
$Scalar_2$	45%	60%
$Boolean_1$	49%	64%
$Boolean_2$	48%	62%
$SnipFreq_0$	34%	66%
$SnipFreq_1$	38%	67%
$SnipFreq_2$	38%	67%
Markers	40%	65%
Completeness	52%	69%
SnipTitle	50%	-
Logistic Regression	**79% (+38.6% from Freq)**	**83% (+25.8% from Freq)**

Table 1. Average Precision (AvP) for single features and logistic regression. Feature SnipTitle was not extracted for phrases in science domain

From the table we can see that in both cases the same set of features and using of machine learning methods lead to much higher values of average precision. However there are significant distinctions in ratios between AvP of features between domains. For example, in the banking domain AvP of the frequency feature has the highest value, features with high average precision in the science domain have relatively low values in the banking domain.

We explain this phenomenon with relative narrowness of the banking domain. Banking documents contain a lot of terminology of neighbour domains such as economy or politics. So among extracted expressions, there are many real terms having all specific qualities of "unithood", but not related to the banking activity. In the scientific text collection the share of terms from other domains is much lower.

Also we can see relative failure of $SnipFreq_i$ features in banking domain. The reason of this phenomenon, in our opinion, is as follows: the banking domain is subject to legal regulation, therefore documents of the domain contain a lot of citations from legal acts which leads to false large values of $SnipFreq_i$.

To evaluate the significance of proposed features we fulfilled a feature selection procedure. For science domain the selected features were $Boolean_1$, **Completeness, FreqBySnip, Inside,**

MI, Neardefwords, SynTerm (AvP – 82%). For banking domain the selected features were **Completeness, FreqBySnip, MI, NearDefWords,** $Scalar_1$, $SnipFreq_0$, **SynTerm** (AvP – 78%). Selected features repeated for both domains are highlighted. We can see that in both cases all three types of features are represented in the short list of features.

5 Conclusion

In this paper we proposed to use three types of features for extraction of two-word terms and showed that all these types of features are useful for term extraction. The set of features includes new features such as features extracted from the existing domain-specific thesauri and features based on Internet search results.

We showed that the combination of several types of features considerably enhances the quality of the term extraction procedure. The developed system of term extraction reorders terms in a list of candidates much better than the basic-line ordering by decreasing frequency.

We studied the set of features for term extraction in two different domains. We found that for developing term extraction models in a specific domain, it is important to take into account such properties of the domain as broad scope or narrow scope (science vs. banking) and connection with the socio-political domain, which is regulated with legal acts. We suppose that it is possible to find the main types of domains for term extraction, to select the best feature sets and special machine learning models for every type of domains.

References

M. Baroni, S. Bernardini. 2004. BootCaT: Bootstrapping Corpora and Terms from the Web. In *Proc. of LREC- 2004*: 1313-1316.

B. Daille, E. Gaussier, J. Lang. 1998. An evaluation of statistics scores for word association. In *Proc. of Tbilisi Symposium on Logic, Language and Computation*. CSLI Publications: 177-188.

B. Dobrov and N. Loukachevitch. 2006. Development of Linguistic Ontology on Natural Sciences and Technology. In *Proc. of LREC-2006*.

J. Foo and M. Merkel. 2010. Using machine learning to perform automatic term recognition. In *Proc. of LREC2010 Aquisition Workshop*.

ISO-2788. 1986. Documentation -- Guidelines for the establishment and development of monolingual thesauri.

K. Kageura and B. Umino. 1996. Methods of automatic term recognition: a review. *Terminology, 3(2):259–289.*

Ch. Manning, P. Raghavan and H. Shutze. 2008. Introduction to Information Retrieval. Cambridge *University Press*.

D. Maynard and S. Ananiadou. 2000. Identifying Terms by their Family and Friends. In *Proc. of 18th International Conference on Computational Linguistics COLING-2000.*

A. Nazarenko and H. Zargayouna. 2009. Evaluation Term Extraction. In *Proc. of RANLP-2009*.

G. Nenadic, S. Ananiadou, J. McNaught. 2004. Enhancing automatic term recognition through recognition of variation. In *Proc. of International Conference on Computational Linguistics COLING-2004*: 604-610.

P. Pecina and P. Schlesinger. 2006. Combining association measures for collocation extraction. In *Proc. of Annual Meeting of the Association for Computational Linguistics ACL-2006*.

A. Peñas, F. Verdejo and J. Gonzalo. 2001. Corpus-Based Terminology Extraction Applied to Information Access. In *Proc. of Corpus Linguistics-2001*, Lancaster University.

S. Sato and Y. Sasaki. 2003. Automatic Collection of Related Terms from the Web. *The Companion Volume to the Proceedings of 41st Annual Meeting of the ACL*, Sapporo, Japan, 2003: 121–124.

P. D. Turney. 2003. Coherent Keyphrase Extraction via Web Mining. In *Proc. the 18th International Joint Conference on Artificial Intelligence IJCAI-03*: 434–439.

J.Vivaldi, L. Marquez and H. Rodriguez. 2001. Improving Term Extraction by System Combination Using Boosting. In *Proc. of ICML* 2001, LNCS, V2167: 515-526.

W. Wong, W. Liu. and M. Mennamoun. 2008. Determination of Unithood and Termhood for Term Recognition. In *Proc.: M.Song and Y.Wu. (eds) Handbook of Research on Text and Web Mining Technologies*, IGI Global.

Z. Zhang, J. Iria, Ch. Brewster and F. Ciravegna. 2008. A Comparative Evaluation of Term Recognition Algorithms. In *Proc. Language Resources and Evaluation Conference of LREC-2008*.

Language Modeling for Document Selection in Question Answering

Nicolas Foucault, Gilles Adda, Sophie Rosset
LIMSI - CNRS
firstname.lastname@limsi.fr

Abstract

Usually, in the Question Answering domain, for a question in natural language, precise answers to the question are extracted from documents according only to the context of the question. In this work, we complemented this approach by adding a filtering process on top of the document retrieval. This way, the system re-evaluates the documents it has originally selected during the information retrieval step before the answer extraction and scoring. Such re-evaluation aims at filtering out documents considered unusable for the search. Based on statistical language modeling, the filtering process firstly determines the intrinsic relevancy of a document and then decides whether this document is *a priori* relevant for finding answers. Evaluation on factoid questions and a collection of 500k web documents has shown our approach properly supports the Question Answering task.

1 Introduction

Question-Answering (QA) systems can be seen as an extension of the Information Retrieval (IR) engines. In IR systems a user is able to search for information using a set of keywords. The search result is a set of documents or links to documents the user needs to peruse to find the precise information he asked for. In contrast, the QA task consists of providing short, relevant answers to natural language questions which can be textual or spoken. For instance, looking for the main actors playing in the "Titanic" movie directed by James Cameron, a possible question to a QA system would be: *Who did play the main roles in the Titanic movie directed by James Cameron?*. In return, the system might reply: *Leonardo DiCaprio and Kate Winslet.*

Question-Answering systems usually follow a standard strategy. They start by preprocessing the documents before their indexation.

The indexation for subsequent retrieval is done by a classical (e.g. Lucene[1]) or specific search engine (Rosset et al., 2008) developped on purpose to best fit the system needs.

Following these steps which predates any retrieval, the work turns towards the questions. The question analysis aims at providing information from the question that has to be found in the documents. The second part of the analysis aims to predict what type of answers the question expects (Pardino et al., 2008), usually a named entity category (such as person, location, etc.) and also to predict what the question class is, so as to constrain the system to search for specific answer types.

The results of these analysis are given to the search engine which retrieves whole documents or snippets, based on the indexation, in order the system finally rank candidates answers it extracted from them.

In this paper, we describe a method which first determines the intrinsic relevancy of a document using a language model and then decides whether this document is relevant for searching answers to any question. In the following section we present related work. Section 3 presents the proposed method. Section 4 shows experiments conducted for its evaluation. Finally, in section 5 we conclude and gives future perspectives about our work.

2 Related Work

In QA the document selection is done given a specific question. As far as we know, no work addressed the problem of selecting documents independently to the question, using only a document

[1] http://www.lucene.apache.org

quality evaluation. Such a method involves assessing whether a document is intrinsically relevant or not, and is totally compliant with previous and further analysis in the standard QA strategy.

Statistical language modeling (SLM) seems suitable for such a task. SLM (Jelinek et al., 1990; Rosenfeld, 2000) provides an easy way to cope with the complexity of natural language by expressing various language phenomena in terms of simple parameters in a statistical model. If SLMs have not been used extensively in pure QA, although they have shown promizing results e.g. to evaluate the intrinsic relevancy of documents estimated for ranking passages (Ganesh and Varma, 2009), they are classically used to help solving tasks closely related to the QA one, especially when topic modeling is worth e.g. entity linking and guided summarization [2] (Varma et al., 2010).

3 Document evaluation method

3.1 Overview

The document evaluation method applied to a given d document is 2-twofold: firstly, d is scored using a language model (LM) in order to estimate its intrinsic relevancy. Then, a Gaussian Mixture Model (GMM) predicts whether d is relevant, given a model of *a priori* relevant documents (which are the documents included in the development set, DEV) and the LM. In other words, d is considered as relevant only if d is close enough both to the documents used to build the LM and to the DEV documents.

The LM is built on a very large collection of journalistic articles to define a model with a broad scope. Preliminary experiments have shown that the *perplexity* (PPX) and the *out of vocabulary words* (OOV) ratio were the most suitable parameters to characterize the document relevancy. PPX is defined as:

$$PPX(d) = P_{LM}(d)^{-\frac{1}{|d|}} \quad (1)$$

where $P_{LM}(d)$ is the document estimated probability, given the LM, and $|d|$ is the number of word in d. PPX might be seen as a distance between d and the documents known by the LM. OOV ratio is defined as:

$$OOV(d) = \frac{|\overline{d \cap LM}|}{|d|} \quad (2)$$

[2]for details about such tasks see the KBP/GS tracks at http://www.nist.gov.tac

where $d \cap LM$ are the words in d which belong to the LM vocabulary, and conversely $\overline{d \cap LM}$ are the words in d unknown by the LM. OOV is a ratio, corresponding to the number of words unknown by the LM divided by the total number of words in d.

3.2 Methods

The first step is to build a 3-gram LM based on a 500k words dictionary obtained from a large corpus of French newspapers articles. Then, OOV and PPX scores are calculated to each DEV documents using the LM and we estimate the distribution (assuming they are Gaussian) related to each parameter by calculation of the mean and standard deviation. Finally, we define a GMM which combines the OOV and PPX distributions. The GMM acts as a binary classifier able to predict whether any new web page is *relevant* or *irrelevant*.

As the DEV set is noisy, and contains some errors or marginal documents i.e. the *outliers* documents, we introduced a variant to estimate the distributions in our method and remove the outliers from the DEV set. In order to find them, we used the OOV and PPX parameter mean values estimated based on the DEV documents. Any of the DEV documents having a PPX and/or an OOV score either too high or too low, given the mean values is considered as an outlier.

The approach using the variant is named the *restricted* method, as oppsed to the *normal* method, which was first described. For each method, we give the mean and deviation values used to build the GMMs in Table 1. As we can see in this table, removing outliers affects largely both PPX and OOV distributions.

We defined 3 ways to combine the OOV and PPX distributions estimated during the GMM creation: OOV+PPX, OOV alone and PPX alone. The F filtering function of our GMM is defined as:

$$F = Mp + c \times SDp \quad (3)$$

where $p \in \{OOV{+}PPX, OOV, PPX\}$ Mp and SDp corresponds to the mean and standard deviation related to p. Relying on some preliminary experiments, we chose $c \in \{0, 0.5, 1, 1.5, 2, 2.5, 3\}$ and forces the standard deviation to variate. Bigger is c or larger is SDp and more documents will be conserved by the GMMs. Conversely, smaller is c or tighter is SDp and more documents will be filtered out by the GMMs. Based on the overall c and p values, plus the two ways of creating GMMs, we built a total of 42 GMMs.

	normal		restricted	
	M	SD	M	SD
OOV	1.74	1.98	1.46	1.12
PPX	210.2	252.9	187.6	106.1

Table 1: Mean (M) and standard deviation (SD) estimated for the OOV and PPX parameters and the *normal* vs. *restricted* methods.

3.2.1 Data

The data used in our work is split in 3 corpora: the documents collection used in the LM creation, the DEV documents set used to generate the GMMs and the corpus of documents (french5G) used to test our filtering method during the experiments.

The first corpora is about 2G words. It is composed of French news articles in journalistic style. 85% of them come from newspapers e.g. Le Monde, AFP, and web newspapers e.g. Google news, Yahoo!.

The second corpora counts 509 documents. This corpora has been released behind the previous QA evaluation campaign we participated in (Quintard et al., 2010). It gathers documents containing only adjudicated answers to the evaluation questions found by the systems participant. As a control, we verified that the GMMs we build have rejected less than 10% of the DEV documents.

The last corpora count 499734 French web pages, provided by the Quaero project.

4 Evaluation

4.1 Experimental setup

4.1.1 Ritel-qa

The QA system used in our experiments is presented in details in (Rosset et al., 2008).

The same complete and multilevel analysis is carried out on both questions and documents. The analysis identifies about 300 different types of entities.

From the question analysis, the system build a search descriptor that contains the important elements of the question, the question class predicted from them, and the possible answer types with associated weights. This search descriptor is used by our IR engine to retrieve documents and snippets (Rosset et al., 2008). Then answer extractions and validation procedures are applied (Bernard et al., 2009).

4.1.2 List selection

We submitted to each GMM induced in Section 3 the entire french5G corpus and obtained 42 different lists of a-priori relevant documents used during our experiments. Table 2 shows the quantity of documents composing these lists according to each GMM, as a ratio of the total number of documents in the corpus. We also created the *full-list*, which is composed of all french5G documents.

All the lists were used to feed a filter we plugged in our QA chain to refine the original documents selection made by the system during the IR step. To reduce the number of eligible documents for searching answers we intersect the list of documents retrieved by the system during the IR step with one of the 43 lists. The objective of this filter is to help the QA system to choose the best documents given an estimation of their quality and the question.

For the tuning of answer selection parameters of our QA system, we use a set of 722 *factoid* questions and answers references (Quintard et al., 2010) as well as the 43 document lists provided by the filtering module. For all the possible configurations of parameters, the system provides results for the complete QA chain. These results after tuning serve as a basis for selecting the best document lists.

We defined two different list selection methodologies. In the first one (methodology-1), each question class is associated to the same list: the list for which the QA system obtains the best global success rate. In the second one (methodology-2), the best per-class list is selected, for each of the most frequent question class found throughout the training set. In this case, based on the different success rates obtained per class after tuning, the filtering module automatically determines how to associate question class and document list.

4.2 Results

We evaluated the performance of the different document lists on a test set of 309 *factoid* questions (Quintard et al., 2010) independant from the training set.

For each document list selection methodology, we give in table 3 the results obtained by the system using the best lists according to the tuning (best-1,2) as well as the results it obtained

method	normal							restricted						
c	0	0.5	1	1.5	2	2.5	3	0	0.5	1	1.5	2	2.5	3
OOV+PPX	27.0	49.5	65.3	75.4	81.8	86.0	88.7	21.0	33.9	45.3	54.7	62.7	69.1	74.0
OOV	39.1	58.7	72.8	81.8	87.4	91.0	93.3	32.9	45.4	56.3	65.2	72.6	78.2	82.5
PPX	47.3	71.9	82.2	87.2	90.1	91.8	93.0	39.9	55.5	66.2	73.1	78.0	81.6	84.2

Table 2: Quantity of a-priori relevant documents per lists, as a ratio of the French Quaero corpus french5G, for each of the 42 GMMs obtained with different distribution combination of LM parameters (OOV, PPX, OOV+PPX), c value ($c \in [0-3]$) and method (normal vs. restricted).

using the *full-list* (baseline). For instance, for methodology-1, the best document list (o+p2.5n) has been generated based on the GMM merging OOV and PPX information with a c value of 2.5 following the *normal* approach for its creation (see section 3.2). The *baseline* system does not use our approach for document filtering. The lines 2 to 4 and 5 to 7 of table 3 shows the results obtained with methodology-1 and -2, respectively.

Results are measured given the classical QA evaluation metrics: precision (or top-1), mean reciproqual rank and recall (or top-10).

S	L	Qc	P	MRR	R	#q
baseline	full	all	31.7	39.5	53.4	309
best-1	o+p2.5n	all	33.0	40.6	55.0	309
best-qc	p2.5n	loc	57.6	64.5	75.8	66
best-1	o+p2.5n	loc	54.5	62.8	75.8	66
best-2	-	all	31.1	39.4	54.7	309
-	p1.5r	time	29.2	38.5	56.2	48
-	p2n	loc	54.5	63.2	75.8	66

Table 3: Results on the test data following methodology-1 (top) and methodology-2 (bottom). **S**: system; **L**: document list selection mode; **Qc**: question class; **P**: precision; **MRR**: mean reciprocal rank; **R**: recall; **#q**: number of questions.

According to the best-1 line, using a document filtering improves the overall results: all the metrics are improved by ~1% absolute. In methodology-1 one single list is chosen for all question classes, which could be sub-optimal locally, i.e. given a specific question class. This is shown in the first part of the Table 3 with the oracle results (best-qc) associated to the *localization* class. If the system had used this list instead of the general best list, the results could have been improved on this question class by almost 3% of precision. The other methodology (choosing the best list for each question class) seemed then to be more optimal. Although, using methodology-2 we observed a significant gain on tuning data, this gain was not preserved with new data (best-2). This is due to an insufficient amount of training data for each question class.

We see also that normal lists give better results than the restricted ones. This shows that, given the small number of DEV documents used to generate the GMMs, the filtering should aim only at removing unarguably bad documents where the system would not be able to extract any correct answers. If a more decent number of developement documents would have been available, more precise filtering techniques could have been more successful.

S	L	Qc	P	MRR	R	#q
best-1	o+p2.5n	all	33.0	40.6	55.0	309
baseline	full	all	31.7	39.5	53.4	309
random	-	all	31.4	39.2	53.4	309
*09*best-1	p3r	all	28.2	34.2	45.6	309
*09*baseline	full	all	24.6	31.6	45.6	309

Table 4: Results on the test data using methodology-1 (best-1, *09*best-1, baseline and *09*baseline) and choosing one among the 42 lists for each question class (random). *09* point out results obtained on our 2009 QA chain. **S**: system; **L**: document list; **Qc**: question class; **P**: precision; **MRR**: mean reciprocal rank; **R**: recall; **#q**: number of questions.

In order to validate our approach we did two controls. First, we compared the results obtained with the QA system using our document filtering with the best system obtained following methodology-1 (best-1) against a system using a random document lists selection (random). Then, we reproduced the experiments following the same methodology on our 2009 QA chain completed with filtering. As we can see in table 4, the random selection is worse than methodology-1 and the older version of our system using the filtering method (*09*best-1) outperforms the corresponding baseline system (*09*baseline). Thereby, we confirmed our documents selection method is usefull for a QA system.

5 Conclusion and perspectives

We have presented a method to evaluate the intrinsic quality of web pages to be used in a question-answering system. The approach is twofold: first the intrinsic relevancy of a document is determined using a n-gram language model and then a GMM-based classifier decides whether this document may be considered as relevant for searching answers to any question. The GMMs are built based on the perplexity, the out-of-vocabulary ratio and a combination of these two informations. For this purpose, we completed the classical QA model with a filtering on top of the document retrieval, before the extraction of answers.

The results show that the a-priori document filtering approach provides a significant improvement of the QA system, for all measures.

We observed the best lists are not the most filtering ones but those which kept 80%-90% of the documents. We also observed the best results obtained on the tuning using a per-class decision about the lists were not confirmed on the test data, showing the amount of training data is insufficient to leverage the question classification at this point.

The parameters used in our experiments are very primitive. They are able to filter out only extremely irrelevant documents. In addition to the intrinsic relevancy, we plan testing extra features to support the filtering process. Given the nature of the QA task, we think semantic features like document topics (extracted from URL) could be very useful.

We also think it would be interesting to investigate in the direction of creating specialized classifiers (based on SLMs or other) to support the documents classification according to outputs of linguistics analyzers.

Size and content of web documents are extremely variable. Reducing this variability should help Web-oriented QA. Thus, we plan to segment the documents prior to filtering.

Acknowledgments

This work has been partially financed by OSEO under the Quaero program.

References

G. Bernard, S. Rosset, O. Galibert, E. Bilinski, and G. Adda. 2009. The limsi participation in the qast 2009 track: experimentating on answer scoring. In *CLEF 2009*, Corfu, Grece, September.

Surya Ganesh and Vasudeva Varma. 2009. Exploiting the use of prior probabilities for passage retrieval in question answering. In *RANLP-2009*, pages 99–102, Borovets, Bulgaria, September. Association for Computational Linguistics.

F. Jelinek, B. Merialdo, S. Roukos, and M. Strauss I, 1990. *Readings in Speech Recognition*, chapter Self-organized language modeling for speech recognition, pages 450–506. Morgan Kaufmann.

M. Pardino, J.M. Gómez, H. Llorens, R. Múnoz-Terol, B. Navarro-Colorado a nd E. Saquete, P. Martínez-Barco, P. Moreda, and M. Palomar. 2008. Adapting ibqas to work with text transcriptions in qast task: Ibqast. In *CLEF 2008*, Aarhus, Denmark, September.

Ludovic Quintard, Olivier Galibert, Gilles Adda, Brigitte Grau, Dominique Laurent, Véronique Moriceau, Sophie Rosset, Xavier Tannier, and Anne Vilnat. 2010. Question answering on web data: The qa evaluation in quæro. In *LREC'10*, Valletta, Malta, may.

Ronald Rosenfeld. 2000. Two decades of statistical language modeling: Where do we go from here. *Proceedings of the IEEE*, 88(8):1270–1278.

S. Rosset, O. Galibert, G. Bernard, E. Bilinski, and G. Adda. 2008. The limsi participation to the qast track. In *Working Notes of CLEF 2008 Workshop*, Aarhus, Denmark, September.

V. Varma, P. Bysani, K. Reddy, V.B. Reddy, S. Kovelamudi, S.R. Vaddepally, R. Nanduri, K. Kumar N, S. Gsk, and P. Pingali. 2010. Iiit hyderabad in guided summarization and knowledge based population. In *TAC 2010*, Gaithersburg, Maryland USA, November.

Evaluating Various Linguistic Features on Semantic Relation Extraction

Marcos Garcia
Center for Research in
Information Technologies (CITIUS)
University of Santiago de Compostela
marcos.garcia.gonzalez@usc.es

Pablo Gamallo
Center for Research in
Information Technologies (CITIUS)
University of Santiago de Compostela
pablo.gamallo@usc.es

Abstract

Machine learning approaches for Information Extraction use different types of features to acquire semantically related terms from free text. These features may contain several kinds of linguistic knowledge: from orthographic or lexical to more complex features, like PoS-tags or syntactic dependencies. In this paper we select four main types of linguistic features and evaluate their performance in a systematic way. Despite the combination of some types of features allows us to improve the f-score of the extraction, we observed that by adjusting the positive and negative ratio of the training examples, we can build high quality classifiers with just a single type of linguistic feature, based on generic lexico-syntactic patterns. Experiments were performed on the Portuguese version of Wikipedia.

1 Introduction

With the exponential growth of data, the interest in learning semantic information related to named entities has been increased. For instance, from the sentence *Ernest Hemingway (July 21, 1899 - July 2, 1961) was an American author*, a system may learn various properties about Hemingway (his birth and death dates, his origin as well as his occupation).

Many techniques employ Machine Learning (ML) algorithms for the extraction task. They arrange into a set of features the contexts or sentences in which pairs of related entities occur. These features are then used to train a classifier. The starting point is a number of labeled training examples ("Ernest Hemingway - author"), as well as a corpus-based strategy to identify and represent as features those sentences (contexts) in which the training examples occur. These techniques may have different degrees of supervision, from manually constructed corpora to weakly supervised on unsupervised methods. Moreover, it must be pointed out that features can be represented at different levels of generality, according to different types of knowledge. However, there are no much work on the importance of knowing what linguistic information is actually useful in order to increase the performance of these systems.

In this article, we evaluate and compare the impact of different types of linguistic features for Relation Extraction (RE). We built and tested a distant supervision system with different types of linguistic features: bags of lemmas and PoS-tags, lexico-syntactic patterns and syntactic dependencies. We evaluated the performance of these types of features individually and in several combinations. Preliminary results in Portuguese data show that, usually, the combination of some types of linguistic features allows us to increase recall without losing precision. Furthermore, we also observed that a deep analysis of the positive/negative (P/N) ratio of the training examples improves the f-score of the classifiers.

Sect. 2 introduces some related work. Then, 3 shows the method for obtaining the data and Sect. 4 presents the features. In Sect. 5 we show the results. Finally, Sect. 6 draws the conclusions of our work.

2 Related Work

Since the work of Hearst (1992), many approaches have been implemented in order to obtain patterns for extracting related terms, such as Brin (1998).

More recent works (Mann, 2002; Fleischman et al., 2003; Agichtein, 2005) use different features (words, lemmas, PoS-tags, etc.) for training ML systems with several algorithms. Other works (Snow et al., 2005; Bunescu and Mooney, 2005) created statistical models using the results of syntactic parsing. Despite that some preliminary results show that the use of deep linguistic knowledge is better for RE, Bunescu and Mooney (2005) warn of the importance of knowing what of this information is actually useful to increase the performance of an IE system.

In this sense, some works must be cited: Kambhatla (2004) and Zhou *et al.* (2005), which evaluate the effectiveness of diverse lexical, syntactic, and semantic information on RE, and Zhao and Grishman (2005), which use a more complex kernel-based strategy to combine features of different linguistic levels. However, their work differs from ours in a key point: the linguistic feature space is not the same, in particular they do not make use of lexico-syntactic patterns. Moreover, our evaluation concerns other languages than English as well as a deep analysis of the impact of negative examples on the training data (see Garcia and Gamallo (2011) for some other evaluations in Spanish).

Finally, Wu and Weld (2010) present *woe*, an Open Information Extraction method based on data obtained from Wikipedia semi-structured resources.

3 Method Overview

In order to easily evaluate the performance of various types of features, we use the following distant supervision method (Mintz et al., 2009):

We get a large set of entity pairs of a desired relation from (semi)structured resources, such as Wikipedia infoboxes. For instance, for the *Occupation* relation we get pairs such as "Michel Tournier - writer", "Edgar Snow - journalist", etc. (with about 95% precision). We use these pairs to select from the unstructured text of Wikipedia sentences that contain both a named entity and an occupation, so no bootstrapping is required. If the two terms match a known pair of the initial list, the example is annotated as positive. Otherwise, it is annotated as negative. Then, we lemmatize, PoS-tag and recognize the proper names with FreeLing (Padró et al., 2010; Garcia and Gamallo, 2010). Syntactic dependencies are identified by a robust, partial, and rule-based dependency parser (Gamallo and González, 2011).

The two target entities are replaced by both **X** and **Y** (standing for the first and the second entities of the pair, respectively) and put labels to mark the left, middle, and right contexts.

All the process is performed without human revision. Let us note this method may lead us to automatically annotate *false positives* ("*Linus Torvalds* discussed with a *software engineer* in Italy", **true**) or *false negatives* ("*Fernando Pessoa* was a *literary critic*", **false**, since this attribute does not appear in the infobox). The manual revision of the test set showed that this method has a precision of about 80%. This issue will be addressed by using ML algorithms that are tolerant to noise by minimizing the effect of the false samples.

4 Feature Space and Types of Features

Each selected, tagged, and parsed sentence represents a *linguistic structure* containing all the relevant information required by the systems. Linguistic structures can be conceived as knowledge-rich spaces incorporating several levels of linguistic information. These spaces should be as complete as possible in the sense that all features potentially useful for RE are included. A linguistic structure contains the surrounding context of the related entities: **X** stands for the named entity and **Y** for the occupation name. We include within a linguistic structure the left context of the first entity, the middle context, and the right context of the second entity. Left and right contexts have a maximum size of 3 tokens (from *pos* -1 to -3 and +1 to +3), while middle context may contain 12 tokens (from *pos* 1 to 12). The window size was empirically set to 3 and 12 after having tested different values in preliminary experiments. We will distinguish experiments taking into account all contexts (left, right, and middle) from those considering only the middle one.

In Figure 1, columns 1, 2, 3, and 4 respectively stands for position, token, lemma, and PoS-tag. The structure also contains the syntactic dependencies identified by the parser: Column 5 identifies the head position of the current token, while the label of the dependency is shown by column 6. Since we use

Sentence: Amancio Ortega Gaona is a Spanish fashion entrepreneur.

Structure:

pos	token	lemma	tag	head	label
0	**X**	**X**	NP	1	subj
1	is	be	V	0	-
2	a	a	DI	5	spec
3	Spanish	spanish	ADJ	5	modif
4	fashion	fashion	N	5	modif
5	**Y**	**Y**	N	1	attr

Figure 1: Example of a linguistic structure.

a partial parser, not all possible word dependencies are identified. These linguistic structures are used to extract the different types of features needed by our classifiers. We use 4 main different types of linguistic features in order to build the RE systems:

Basic Patterns: The first type of feature uses all the explicit information contained in the linguistic structures except two elements: dependency relations and some lemmas. We only take into account lemmas of verbs, common nouns and prepositions. We have observed in preliminary experiments that the performance of classifiers decreased when either these types of lemmas were removed or all lemmas including grammatical words (stop words), adjectives and proper names were retained. It follows that verbs, common nouns and prepositions are critical pieces of information to define the lexico-syntactic contexts of the target terms. An example of basic patterns associated to the relation "Occupation" is the following (for the same sentence as in Figure 1):

Pattern: <**X** be_V DI ADJ fashion_N **Y**>

(where V means verb, DI indefinite article, ADJ adjective, and N noun). We have to note that this kind of approach requires a huge training corpus, due to the lack of flexibility of the patterns. With this type of feature, the problem of sparse data is crucial.

Pattern Generalization: To minimize the sparse data problem, we apply an algorithm based on similarity between basic patterns, generalizing them and thus increasing the coverage of the model. In order to generalize two patterns, we check first if they are similar and then we remove all those units that they do not share. After computing the similarity between two patterns p_1 and p_2, the longest common string (*lcs*) is extracted if and only if p_2 is the most similar pattern of p_1 and the similarity score is higher than a particular threshold. The *lcs* of two patterns is considered as their generalized pattern.

Bags of Lemmas and Tags: Instead of using a set of entire patterns as features, a common method that allows us to increase the coverage of the extractor is the utilization of smaller items, such as lemmas with PoS annotation. In this case, the example sentence (Figure 1) would generate the following features (notice again that for some categories only the tag is retained): <be_V>, <DI>, <ADJ> and <fashion_N>.

Syntactic Dependencies: We consider a subset of all the syntactic dependencies derived from the full linguistic structures. Given a sentence, two types of dependencies are retained: (i) dependencies between the two target terms (**X** or **Y**), and (ii) dependencies between one of the two target terms and one entity of the (left, middle, or right) context.

For instance, from the previous example sentence the selected dependencies would be the following: <subj;**X**;be_V>, <attr;be_V;**Y**>, <spec;**Y**;DI>, <modif;**Y**;ADJ> and <modif;**Y**;fashion_N>.

Each feature is a triple constituted by the dependency label, the head, and the dependent token. Only dependencies with at least one term (**X** or **Y**) were selected from the linguistic structure. The selected information, thus, corresponds to the local dependency context around the related terms. Finally, labels of dependencies (e.g., modifier, subject, etc.) are also taken into account to define the features.

Note that the analysis is very partial. In many cases, the parser is not able to complete the dependency path between the two terms. Grammars for other languages than English are often not complete or they are not freely available.

5 Experiments

We evaluated both the performance of the features individually as well as the best combinations of them. We also examined the effect of limited training input on the learning process by incrementally adding examples to the training data. Furthermore, we also performed some experiments concerning the ratio of positive and negative examples in the training set. The experiments were performed with WEKA (Witten and Frank, 2005), using its implementation of the SMO algorithm. This choice was made because in preliminary experiments (using Naive Bayes, Decision Trees as well as SMO algorithms), SMO scored the best.

The training examples were obtained from the Portuguese Wikipedia with the method showed in Section 3. We focused on examples of the semantic relation "Occupation", which is a kind of *is_a* relation. We first selected about 50, 000 relation pairs from infoboxes. Then, we identified near 500, 000 sentences containing a named entity and an occupation noun, which were automatically classified as positive or negative. Finally, we randomly selected an initial set of 2000 sentences for training, 50% of them being positive examples. For testing, we randomly extracted and manually revised a set of 700 sentences (different than those used for training).

5.1 Results

The evaluated classifiers were built with the types of features explained in Section 4:

pattern-all and *pattern-mid* use the basic patterns as features. The former was trained with all contexts (left, right, and middle), while the latter was only trained with the middle context.

pattern_gen-mid uses as features the generalized patterns and the middle context.

bow-all and *bow-mid* were built with the bag of lemmas and tags technique.

dep-all and *dep-mid* are the dependency-based models described in the previous section.

Precision is the number of correct positive decisions divided by the number of positive decisions (true and false positives). Recall here refers to the number of correct positive decisions divided by the total number of positive examples in the test set.

Single Types of Features: Our first experiment consists of the evaluation of seven classifiers built with the individual types of features, extracted from the training set. Table 1 let us observe that the best features are those based on lexico-syntactic patterns with middle contexts: *pattern_gen-mid* and *pattern-mid*, with f-score values between 72%/77%. The score reached by *pattern-all* is much lower because of very poor recall values. This is due to the fact that, in this case, both left and right contexts tend to be too sparse. By contrast, *bow* and *dep* classifiers improved their performance using *all* contexts.

Model	Prec.	Rec.	f-score
pattern-all	91.66%	2.65%	5.16%
pattern-mid	**94.9%**	58.45%	72.34%
pattern_gen-mid	93.26%	66.9%	**77.9%**
bow-all	74.14%	**67.87%**	70.87%
bow-mid	74.13%	31.15%	43.87%
dep-all	79.21%	48.79%	60.38%
dep-mid	76.92%	41.06%	53.54%

Table 1: Precision, Recall and f-score of 7 classifiers based on different types of linguistic features.

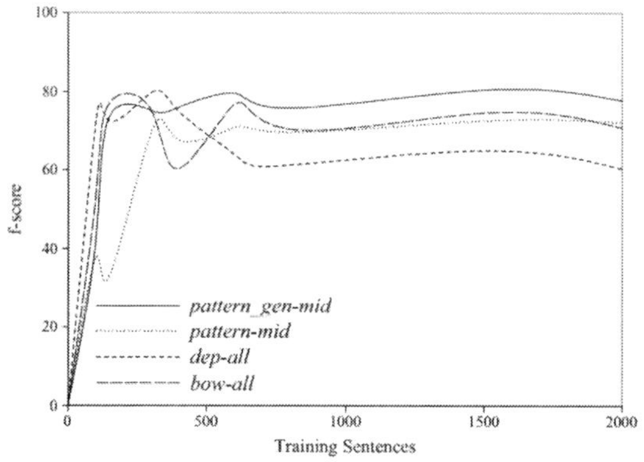

Figure 2: F-score vs training size (0 – 2000 sentences) of the 4 best features for each linguistic type.

Learning Curves: Figure 2, shows the f-score of the best individual features (for each of the main types) in different partitions. It can be observed that the curve stabilizes when the training corpus is constituted by about 1000 sentences. So, no more training corpus is required to improve results. We can also observe that, except for *pattern-mid*, f-score slightly decreases with more than 1500 examples.

The results of these tests allow us to know the performance of the classifiers based on individual types of features. In the next experiment we evaluate several combinations of individual types of features.

Similarity and Combination of Models: When analyzing the differences between the feature models, we compute the Dice similarity coefficient to

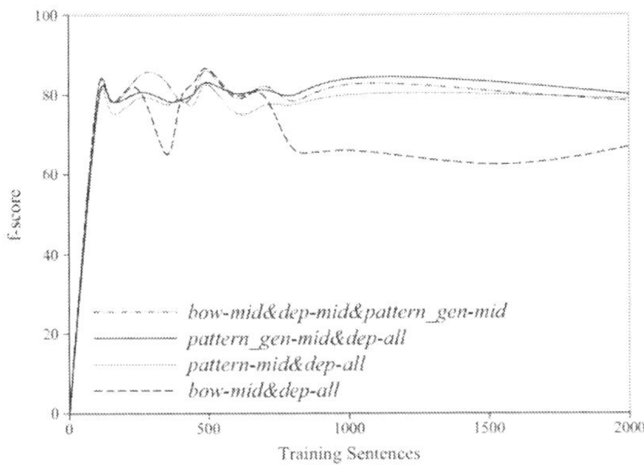

Figure 3: F-score vs training size (0 – 2000 sentences) of the 4 best combinations of features.

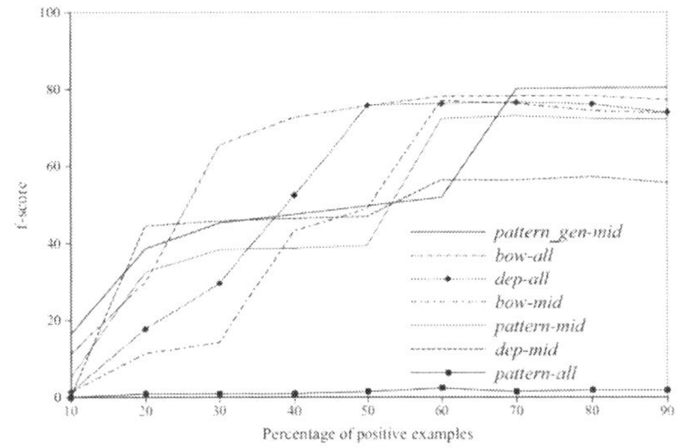

Figure 4: F-score vs P/N ratio of 7 classifiers. Training sets are 9 partitions of 500 sentences with different ratio of P/N examples (from 10%/90% to 90%/10%).

Model	Prec.	Rec.	f-score	Diff.	P/N
p-all	81.3%	3.1%	6.1%	+0.9	90%
p-mid	**91%**	68.4%	78.1%	+5.7	90%
p_gen-m.	90.1%	76.6%	**82.8%**	+4.9	90%
bow-all	67.9%	**87.2%**	76.3%	+5.4	70%
bow-mid	76.3%	78.5%	77.4%	+33.5	60%
dep-all	73.4%	84.1%	78.4%	+18.0	70%
dep-mid	63.5%	54.4%	57.4%	+3.9	90%

Table 2: Precision, Recall and f-score of 7 classifiers. The distribution of P/N examples in the training was adjusted for each classifier (*p* models are the *pattern* models).

find whether the decisions taken by two models are or not on the same instances. In general, a high Dice coefficient may imply that there are few correct decisions taken on different instances and, conversely, a low Dice coefficient means that there are many correct decisions taken on different instances. Only pairs of models with low Dice coefficient were combined since they are likely to be complementary.

Figure 3 shows the results of combining the best individual features. The results of several combinations based on a similarity analysis show that these classifiers may help to achieve a trade-off between precision and recall. Furthermore, the best combined classifiers also improve the general f-score of the best single type of feature, *pattern_gen-mid*.

5.2 On-Going Experiments

We are evaluating the impact of negative examples in the training corpus, taking into account that the initial set of 2000 sentences had a 50%/50% ratio of positive and negative examples. In order to know the best P/N distribution, we collected several sets of sentences differing in the P/N ratio they have. Note that this kind of evaluation also deals with the amount of positive or negative instances, and not only with the P/N ratio. So, in order to avoid this effect, we performed two major experiments: (i) we automatically collected 9 sets of 500 sentences differing in the P/N ratio: from 10%/90% to 90%/10% (positive/negative) and (ii) we did the same distributional partitions from a larger corpus (sets of 2000 sentences). Finally, we analyzed how the learning process is influenced by the P/N ratio as well as by the number of positive and negative examples.

Figure 4 shows the f-score values of each model according to the P/N examples distribution. In most cases, the peak of the f-score curve is reached when the training sentences contain between 60% and 70% of positive examples, except for pattern-based features, whose performance gradually improves with more positive samples. This tendency occurs in both experiments (500 and 2000 sentences), so we can infer the best P/N ratio for each type of feature.

The results from the previous experiment provide us information to train new models with the P/N distribution adjusted to each model. So, we built classifiers based on the same individual types of features described above. We randomly selected seven sets of 2000 sentences, each one with a distribution of positive and negative examples adjusted to the needs of each type of feature, and test them on the test set. Table 2 shows that by adjusting the P/N ratio in the training involves several differences in the performance of the models. We observed that the precision values present some decrease (namely in *pattern-all*, *bow-all* and *dep-mid*). However, since all the systems show dramatically recall improvements, the f-score of the seven classifiers increase. Column 5 in Table 2 shows the f-score differences compared to those classifiers trained with a 50%/50% P/N ratio. Column 6 shows the percentage of positive training samples for each classifier.

We have to note that with this adjustment in the P/N ratio, the performance of the best classifiers based on individual features (*pattern_gen-mid*, with 82.77% f-score) scored similar to the best combinations of features (*pattern_gen-mid & dep-all*, reaching maximum values of 83.2%).

6 Conclusions and Further Work

This paper analyzes the impact of various linguistic features in a distant-supervision system for extracting semantic relations from unstructured text.

Experiments performed in Portuguese data show that features based on lexico-syntactic patterns achieve higher precision values than those with bags of lemmas and tags or syntactic dependencies. Pattern-based models performed better with *middle* contexts than with *all* contexts, but in case of *dep* models, *all* contexts behave better. Models based on bags of lemmas and tags tend to be more unstable.

Moreover, the combination of some types of features helps to achieve a trade-off between precision and recall, improving the performance of the single features. However, we observed that the adjustment of the positive and negative examples ratio in the training set involves dramatically increases in recall.

Further experiments will analyze the performance of combinations of the single features with an adjusted training set. Moreover, we will test these classifiers with different text genres, as well as with other relations and languages.

Acknowledgments

This work has been supported by the MICINN, within the project with reference FFI2010-14986.

References

Agichtein, Y. E. 2005. *Extracting Relations from Large Text Collections*. Ph.D. thesis, Columbia University.

Brin, S. 1998. Extracting patterns and relations from the world wide web. *WebDB Workshop at EDBT'98*: 172–183.

Bunescu, R. C. and Mooney, R. J. 2005. A Shortest Path Dependency Kernel for Relation Extraction. *Proceedings of HLT/EMNLP'05*: 724–731. ACL, Vancouver.

Fleischman, M., Hovy, E., and Echihabi, A. 2003. Offline strategies for online question answering: Answering questions before they are asked. *Proceedings of ACL'03*: 1–7.

Gamallo, P. and González, I. 2011. A Grammatical Formalism based on Patterns of Part-of-Speech Tags. *Journal of Corpus Linguistics* 16(1): 45–71.

Garcia, M. and Gamallo, P. 2010. Análise Morfossintáctica para Português Europeu e Galego: Problemas, Soluções e Avaliação. *Linguamática. Revista para o Processamento Automático das Línguas Ibéricas* 2 (2): 59–67.

Garcia, M. and Gamallo, P. 2011. An Exploration of the Linguistic Knowledge for Semantic Relation Extraction in Spanish. *Proceedings of Joint Workshop FAM-LbR/KRAQ'11* at IJCAI 2011. Barcelona.

Hearst, M. A. 1992. Automatic acquisition of hyponyms from large text corpora. *Proceedings of COLING'92*, 2: 539–545.

Kambhatla, N. 2004. Combining lexical, syntactic and semantic features with Maximum Entropy models for extracting relations. *Proceedings of ACL'04*.

Mann, G. S. 2002. Fine-Grained Proper Noun Ontologies for Question Answering. *SemaNet'02: Building and Using Semantic Networks*. Taipei, Taiwan.

Mintz, M., Bills, S., Snow, R. and Jurafsky, D. 2009. Distant supervision for relation extraction without labeled data. *Proceedings of the ACL/IJCNLP*, 2.

Padró, Ll., Collado, M., Reese, S., Lloberes, M. and Castellón, I. 2010. FreeLing 2.1: Five Years of Open-Source Language Processing Tools. In *Proceedings of LREC'10*, ELRA. La Valletta, Malta.

Snow, R., Jurafsky, D. and Ng, A. Y. 2005. Learning Syntactic Patterns for Automatic Hypernym Discovery. *Advances in Neural Information Processing Systems* 17: 1297–1304.

Witten, I. H. and Frank, E. 2005. *Data mining: practical machine learning tools and techniques with java implementations*. Elsevier Inc., San Francisco.

Wu, F. and Weld, D. S. 2010. Open information extraction using Wikipedia. In *Proceedings of ACL'10*: 118–127.

Zhao, S. and R. Grishman 2005. Extracting Relations with Integrated Information Using Kernel Methods *Proceedings of ACL'05*: 419–426.

Zhou, G., Su, J., Zhang, J., and Zhang, M. 2005. Exploring Various Knowledge in Relation Extraction *Proceedings of ACL'05*: 427–434.

Automatic titling of Articles Using Position and Statistical Information

Cédric Lopez, Violaine Prince, and Mathieu Roche
LIRMM - CNRS - University of Montpellier 2, France
{lopez, prince, mroche}@lirmm.fr

Abstract

This paper describes a system facilitating information retrieval in a set of textual documents by tackling the automatic titling and subtitling issue. Automatic titling here consists in extracting relevant noun phrases from texts as candidate titles. An original approach combining statistical criteria and noun phrases positions in the text helps collecting relevant titles and subtitles. So, the user may benefit from an outline of all the subjects evoked in a mass of documents, and easily find the information he/she is looking for. An evaluation on real data shows that the solutions given by this automatic titling approach are relevant.

1 Introduction

Web pages contain a multitude of information concerning many domains. Very often, the user has to supply heavy cognitive efforts to find the information he/she is looking for. For handicapped persons, while the access to Internet is a tremendous vector of integration in society, the localization of information remains complex. One of the key domains of web pages accessibility, such as defined by a standard proposed by handicap associations (W3C standard), concerns the titling (and subtitling) of web pages. The main goal is to increase the legibility of pages obtained from a search engine, where the relevance of results is often weak, disheartening readers, or to improve pages indexing, in order to obtain a better search. Besides, automatic titling can be integrated into diverse applications. For instance, it might help the editorial staff, proposing to the author of a given text, a segmented version, according to the issue tackled by (Akrifed, 2000; Prince and Labadié, 2007) and automatically titled. So, a new industrial application, based on automatic titling, would include the automatic generation of contents, saving time.

One of the major benefits of the system described in this paper, is to help the user in assimilating the semantic contents of a set of textual document. Another is to allow him/her to quickly find the relevant information. Applied to textual resources, the proposed approach consists in providing texts subjects by using the automatically generated titles, and so to facilitate information communication and localization. Titles determination requires to know titles morphosyntactic structure, as well as their associated subtitles. From some statistical studies, performed on data described in section 3, concerning morphosyntactic characteristics, we propose a two-stages process. The main idea is to extract, from a given text, the most relevant noun phrase and use it as title. The first stage consists in extracting all noun phrases existing in the text (section 4.1). The second stage determines the most relevant phrase among those previously extracted (section 4.2). An evaluation, performed by human judgment on real data, is presented (section 5) and discussed. Experiments have been run on French data, but could be easily transposed to several Western languages, which share with French a rather common set of linguistic features (i.e., most Indo-European languages).

2 Previous Works

It seems that no scientific study leading to an automatic titling application was published. However, the title issue is studied in numerous works. Titling is a process aiming at relevantly representing the contents of documents. It might use metaphors, humor or emphasis, thus separating a titling task from a summarization process, proving the importance of rhetorical status in both tasks (Teufel and Moens, 1998). Titles have been studied as textual objects focusing on fonts, sizes, colors, (Ho-Dac et al., 2004). Also, since a title suggests an outline of the associated document topic, it is endowed with a semantic contents that has three functions: Interest and captivate the reader, inform the reader, introduce the topic of the text.

A title is not exactly the smallest possible abstract. While a summary, the most condensed form of a text, has to give an outline of the text contents that respects the text structure, a title indicates the treated subject in the text without revealing all the content (Wang et al., 2009). Summarization might rely on titles, such as in (Goldsteiny et al., 1999) where titles are systematically used to create the summary. This method stresses out the title role, but also the necessity to know the title to obtain a good summary. Text compression could be interesting for titling if a strong compression could be undertaken, resulting in a single relevant word group. Compression texts methods (e.g. (Yousfi-Monod and Prince, 2008)) could be used to choose a word group obeying to titles constraints. However, one has to largely prune compression results to select the relevant group (Teufel and Moens, 1998).

A title is not an index : A title does not necessarily contain key words (and indexes are key words), and might present a partial or total reformulation of the text (what an index is not).

Finally, a title is a full entity, has its own functions, and titling has to be sharply distinguished from summarizing and indexing.

It was noticed that elements appearing in the title are often present in the body of the text (Zajic et al., 2002). (Baxendale, 1958) has showed that the first and last sentences of paragraphs are considered important. The recent work of (Belhaoues, 2009) (Jacques and Rebeyrolle, 2004) (Zhou and Hovy, 2003) supports this idea and shows that the covering rate of those words present in titles, is very high in the first sentences of a text. (Vinet, 1993) notices that very often, a definition is given in the first sentences following the title, especially in informative or academic texts, meaning that relevant words tend to appear in the beginning since definitions introduce the text subject while exhibiting its complex terms. The latter indicate relevant semantic entities and constitute a better representation of the semantic document contents (Mitra et al., 1997).

Therefore, this article will first describe a statistical analysis of the corpus titles, for each category (e.g., coverage rate, words number, presence of common nouns, verbs, and so forth). The provided corpus is a bunch of articles which have been titled by their authors. The specific features are studied in order to shape a titling process methodology, mostly relying on statistics and lexical selection.

3 Coverage Rate of Titles Words

To analyze the behavior of human-based titles and subtitles, a corpus of journalistic articles, using the Factiva database (http://factiva.com/), was built. It lists, among others, newspapers articles. The studied corpus contains articles stemming from three French newspapers: *Le Monde*, *Le Figaro*, *Les Echos*. This choice was dependent on the presence of subtitles in articles. The corpus contains 300 articles, that is, 300 titles, covering varied domains (politics, sport, society, sciences). Subtitles are about 354. The corpus admits a total of $169,796$ words.

We were interested in the coverage rate of titles and subtitle words. The **coverage rate** is based on the presence, and frequency, of a title word within the titled text. In this calculation, functional words were not taken into account (i.e. determiners, prepositions,...), nor was punctuation. These statistics were obtained after texts and titles tagging with TreeTagger (Schmid, 1994), where the basic named entities are tagged with the proper nouns label (NAM in TreeTagger). The results indicate that in our corpus, 66 % of the words contained in the titles are present in the text (idem for subtitles). For titles and subtitles, the coverage rate strictly decreases the further the text is processed, with an exception concerning the last part of the text that increases slightly (See Figure 1 and 2). We can thus consider that, at least for those journalistic articles in our corpus, the relevant terms for the titling and subtitling are present at the beginning of the text. Besides, statistics have also pointed out a heavy presence of common nouns and named entities with regard to verbs. Therefore, the main idea is to determine the most relevant **noun phrase** of the text, and use it as title. Thus, the method first stage consisted in extracting a set of candidate noun phrases for titling.

4 The Automatic Titling Approach

The automatic titling process of a given set of textual data, is performed in two stages presented in

Newspapers	Le Monde	Le Figaro	Les Echos	Average
Length of titles (avg.)	6.3	4.5	5.5	5.3
Verbs (%)	55	52	68	58
Common Nouns (%)	99	98	99	99
Nammed Entities (%)	75	70	72	72
Covery Rate (%)	66	65	68	66

Table 1: Features of journalistic titles

Newspapers	Le Monde	Le Figaro	Les Echos	Average
Length of titles (avg.)	2.7	2.5	2.4	2.5
Verbs (%)	5	7	10	8
Common Nouns (%)	99	98	100	99
Nammed Entities (%)	7	16	12	12
Covering Rate (%)	55	82	74	70

Table 2: Features of journalistic subtitles

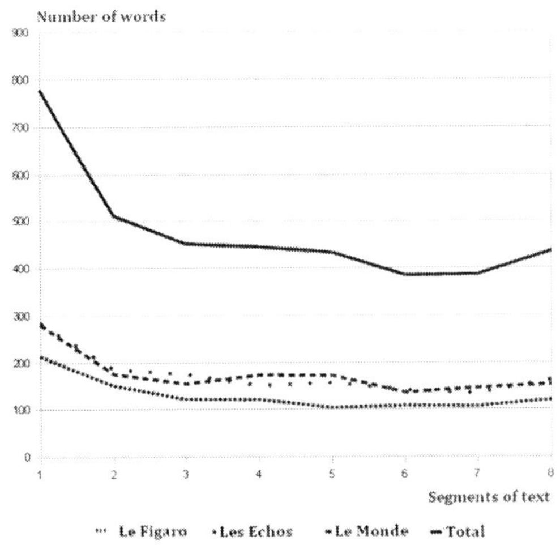

Figure 1: Curves presenting the distribution of title words in the text.

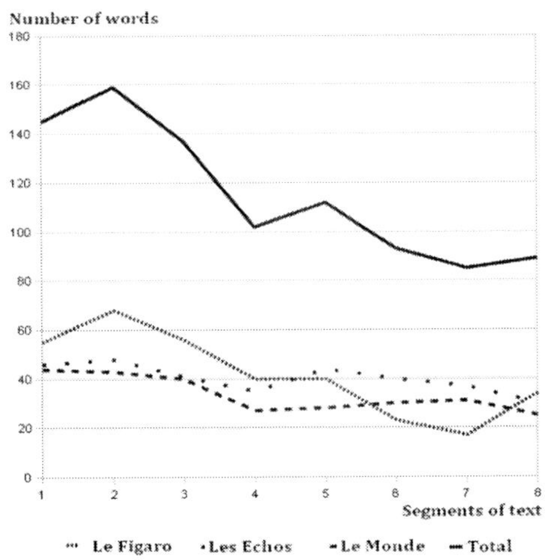

Figure 2: Curves presenting the distribution of subtitle words in the text.

the following subsections: Extracting of the candidate noun phrases; Determining the most relevant title.

4.1 Extracting Noun Phrases (NP)

Extracting all noun phrases (NP) of the text is motivated by the assumption that each noun phrase potentially represents a title. TreeTagger is used, producing a POS (part-of-speech) text tagging. (Daille, 1996) has deeply focused on noun phrase (NP) syntactic patterns, and her patterns have inspired the chosen extraction patterns, which mostly rely on the following POS tags: Common noun, Adjective, Proper Noun, Determiner, Punctuation, Preposition ... NP patterns combine those tags and the filtered NP constitute a list of candidates for the titling process.

4.2 Determining (best) Title(s)

Since a title has to be representative and informative of the text contents, a basic intuitive line leads to select the most "frequent" NP in the text, with a sensible definition of frequency. For that, using TF-IDF (Salton and Buckley, 1988) to compute the score of every extracted noun phrase from the text, and then ranking NPs according to this score, has seemed to be a reasonable way of implementing the representativity requirement. However, if a new article is inserted into the corpus, TF-IDF has to be computed again. A first score, NP_{TF-IDF} is computed for each NP. It is the sum of each term TF-IDF, present in the NP (except functional words) [1].

$$NP_{TF-IDF} = \sum_{term=1}^{n} (TF * IDF)_{term} \quad (1)$$

The main inconvenience of this score is that it does not take into account the NP position in the text, thus neglecting a precious information provided by literature as well as the data statistical analysis (sections 2 and 3). So, if two noun phrases, $NP1$, found at the beginning of a text and $NP2$, anywhere in the middle, obtain an identical score, they will be considered as having the same degree of relevance, which disagrees with the idea that first sentences (and sometimes the last ones) are the most promising areas to mine for relevant titles. Thus, this score is corrected by considering the NP position information in the text (NP_{POS}). The statistical study showed that the

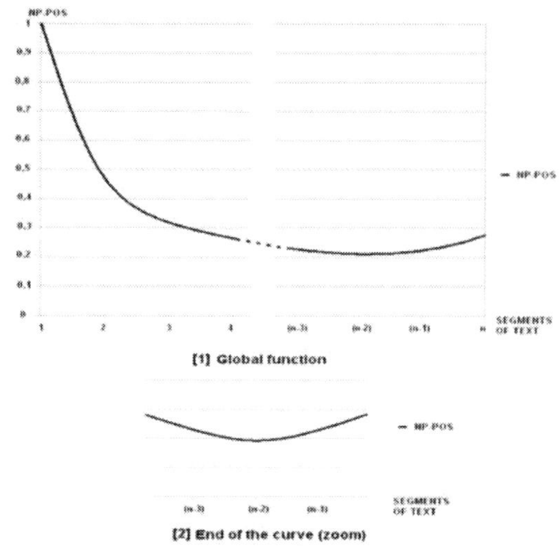

Figure 3: Function $NP_{POS}(P)$

presence of the words of human-defined titles decreases the further the text is processed (Zajic et al., 2002), except for the end of the text where it regains some of its previous importance. So the method incorporates a **position score** NP_{POS}. It takes into account the position of the NP in the text. Computing it goes as following: The text is divided into several segments of equal sizes (considering the number of words). n is the number of segments of the text and P is the part of the text where appear the noun phrases ($P \in [1, n]$). Since the same study showed that the maximal coverage rate (CR) is obtained at the beginning of the text, then the score needs to decrease in the same proportion. Furthermore, CR decreases abruptly in the first two parts of the text, then moderately until last but one part. This phenomenon is well formalized with an exponential function (see Figure 3)[2]

$$NP_{POS}(P) = \begin{cases} e^{1-P} & if\ P \in [1, n-2] \\ e^{2-n} & if\ P = n-1 \\ e^{3-n} & if\ P = n \end{cases} \quad (2)$$

Finally, NP_{POS} [2] formula faithfully translates the global aspect of the coverage rate, which weakens until $n-2$ and modestly grows from $n-2$ on. Locally, this function offers a hyperbolic curve centered around $n - 2$ [1]. The information about the NP position is translated by the score NP_{POS} that enables to correct the score computed by the TF-IDF (NP_{TF-IDF}). The coefficient λ variation balances the position score as well as the T-F.IDF score -[3]. The optimal value of $\lambda \in [0, 1]$ for our corpus is discussed in the section 5.1.

$$NP_{score}(P) = \lambda \times NP_{POS} + (1-\lambda) \times NP_{TF-IDF} \quad (3)$$

5 Evaluation

The purpose of the evaluation presented in this section, is double. First, the 'on-surface evaluation' consists in estimating the automatically determined candidate titles relevance on a set of various texts. It can be associated with a 'deep evaluation' tackling the choice of the 'best' NP(s) among all the extracted NPs. The conclusion of these evaluations points at an optimal value for λ. In this study, we define $n = 8$, i.e.,each text is segmented in 8 parts of identical size. This figure has been empirically obtained from corpora features (manual) observation.

5.1 On-surface Evaluation

The first evaluation is performed on 90 French journalistic articles extracted from our corpus (30 articles of each of the three presented newspapers). Articles retained for this evaluation are the thirty first ones published (from September 11th to September 15th 2010) in *Le Monde*, *Les Echos*, and *Le Figaro*, with the requirement that they present at least one subtitle. The variation of λ between 0 and 1 determines the value adapted to the corpus. All in all, 270 titles were manually estimated (30 articles, so 30 titles according to 9 values for λ). For each title, an expert attributed one of the two following labels, "relevant title" or "irrelevant title". Many candidates for representing a title are acceptable. A **relevant title** is a well formed word group giving a relevant outline of the text contents. The results indicate that for $\lambda = 0$, 25 articles were titled in a relevant way, against only 8 for $\lambda = 1$. The best results of automatic titling are obtained with $0.4 \leq \lambda \leq 0.6$. It thus seems that, for the given corpus, *relevance* (i.e. NP_{TF-IDF}) and *position* (i.e. NP_{POS}) are equally important. So, by defining $\lambda = 0.5$, our method attributes a relevant title to two articles over three (58 relevant titles for 90 articles). Several titles (thus several NPs) could be relevant for the same article. So, it is necessary to

[1]for which $NP_{POS}(n-3) = NP_{POS}(n-1)$ and $NP_{POS}(n-4) = NP_{POS}(n)$

study the relevance of the chosen NPs among all the extracted NPs.

5.2 In-depth evaluation

This evaluation has been performed on three journalistic articles (one from each newspaper), amounting $1,681$ words. All extracted NPs were manually estimated. Many candidates can be juged as relevant for a same article. The evaluating protocol rationale is more to get a fine grained appraisal, than to have a quantitative score. Table 3 presents the in-depth evaluation values for precision, recall, and F-measure with $\lambda \in [0, 1]$. The threshold, between 5% and 40% (beyond 40%, the results are similar), corresponds to the number of NPs found by the automatic method, with regard to the total number of NP extracted by the proposed syntactical filters. It is interesting to study the presence of relevant titles found by our method according to the threshold, knowing that several relevant titles can appear in the list of NPs. For instance, if 260 NPs are extracted from the text, a threshold of 10% indicates that the best 26 NPs (with the highest NP_{Score}) extracted by our method, are proposed to the user. A good quality system will propose the best relevant titles at the top of the classification. The results in Table 1 indicate that the most relevant titles are obtained for $0.30 \leq \lambda \leq 0.90$ (F-measure = 59,74%) with a threshold of 5%. Finally, the most relevant titles are among the first NPs, ranked by (NP_{score}), from the highest to the lowest. Let us notice that with λ between 0.30 and 0.90, the recall reaches 100% with a threshold of 10%. In other words, in a more general way, our method gathers all the relevant NPs to serve as titles, at the top of its classification.

T	λ	0	0.10	0.20	0.30	0.40	0.50	0.60	0.70	0.80	0.90	1
5%	Precision	3	22	28	44	44	44	44	44	44	44	15
	Recall	0	56	76	93	93	93	93	93	93	93	17
	F-measure	**0**	**31.59**	**40.92**	**59.74**	**59.74**	**59.74**	**59.74**	**59.74**	**59.74**	**59.74**	**15.94**
10%	Precision	4	17	21	24	24	24	24	24	24	24	21
	Recall	20	93	93	100	100	100	100	100	100	100	83
	F-measure	**6.67**	**28.75**	**34.26**	**38.71**	**38.71**	**38.71**	**38.71**	**38.71**	**38.71**	**38.71**	**33.52**
20%	Precision	12	13	12	12	12	12	12	12	12	12	11
	Recall	100	100	100	100	100	100	100	100	100	100	100
	F-measure	**21.43**	**23.01**	**21.43**	**21.43**	**21.43**	**21.43**	**21.43**	**21.43**	**21.43**	**21.43**	**19.82**
40%	Precision	6	6	6	6	6	6	6	6	6	6	6
	Recall	100	100	100	100	100	100	100	100	100	100	100
	F-measure	**11.32**	**11.32**	**11.32**	**11.32**	**11.32**	**11.32**	**11.32**	**11.32**	**11.32**	**11.32**	**11.32**

Table 3: Evaluation of journalistic titles (%). T: Threshold.

6 Conclusion

In this paper, we have tried to sketch a method that automatically extracts and ranks noun phrases (NPs) from untitled texts, to be used as possible titles. Titling web pages and texts has appeared to be a requirement for Web content accessibility, thus pushing researchers to contemplate this task as a useful tool for users. Headlines, or titles, are required to be much shorter than most 'summaries', as well as syntactically well-formed (which disqualified pure lexical approaches) and semantically representative, thus needing a frequency measure. This has led us to choose small syntactic patterns for candidate titles, and corpus observation has highlighted the role of NPs as a good choice. Choosing the most relevant NP for the role of a headline, or at least ranking NPs according to criteria accounting for that relevance, determined the importance of two particular items: The NP *position* in the text, and the *TF-IDF* score of its meaningful components. They helped extracting relevant NPs for titling, among all the NPs extracted by syntactical patterns. Evaluation has shown that relevant titles were provided for French journalistic articles with a satisfactory estimation. Among the pending questions, two appear as the most urgent to tackle: First, has the corpus style (e.g. journalistic, scientific , e-commerce or information web sites...) an influence on the method? On which particular criteria does it impact the method: Nature of the patterns; Value of the λ coefficient; Modification of the threshold value? Those are possible tracks to deal with. The second most urgent deals with the first of these, e.g., in addressing verb phrases within the syntactical patterns, and extracting new types or possibly longer titles (as it happens in scientific articles). Further, automatic generation could be contemplated for titling, to produce titles with reformulation or metaphoric features.

References

F. Akrifed. 2000. Segmentation automatique des textes, l'exemple du logiciel tropes: Bilan et perspectives= automatic texts segmentation, example of tropes software: assessment and prospects. In *Colloque international francophone sur l'écrit et le document*, pages 373–382.

B. Baxendale. 1958. Man-made index for technical literature - an experiment. *IBM Journal of Research and Development.*, pages 354–361.

M. Belhaoues. 2009. Titrage automatique de pages web. *Master Thesis, University Montpellier II, France.*

B. Daille. 1996. Study and implementation of combined techniques for automatic extraction of terminology. *The Balancing Act : Combining Symbolic and Statistical Approaches to language.*, pages 29–36.

J. Goldsteiny, M. Kantrowitz, V. Mittal, and J. Carbonelly. 1999. Summarizing text documents: Sentence selection and evaluation metrics. pages 121–128.

L-M. Ho-Dac, M-P. Jacques, and J. Rebeyrolle. 2004. Sur la fonction discursive des titres. *S. Porhiel and D. Klingler (Eds). L'unité texte, Pleyben, Perspectives.*, pages 125–152.

MP. Jacques and J. Rebeyrolle. 2004. Titres et structuration des documents. *Actes International Symposium: Discourse and Document.*, pages 125–152.

M. Mitra, C. Buckley, A. Singhal, and C. Cardi. 1997. An analysis of statistical and syntactic phrases. In *RIAO'1997*.

V. Prince and A. Labadié. 2007. Text segmentation based on document understanding for information retrieval. *Natural Language Processing and Information Systems*, pages 295–304.

G. Salton and C. Buckley. 1988. Term-weighting approaches in automatic text retrieval. *Information Processing and Management 24*, page 513 523.

H. Schmid. 1994. Probabilistic part-of-speech tagging using decision trees. In *International Conference on New Methods in Language Processing*, pages 44–49.

S. Teufel and M. Moens. 1998. Sentence extraction and rhetorical classification for flexible abstracts. In *AAAI Spring Symposium on Intelligent Text Summarisation*, pages 16–25.

M.T. Vinet. 1993. L'aspet et la copule vide dans la grammaire des titres. *Persee*, 100:83–101.

D. Wang, S. Zhu, T. Li, and Y. Gong. 2009. Multi-document summarization using sentence-based topic models. In *ACL-IJCNLP '09: Joint conference of the 47th Annual Meeting of the Association for Computational Linguistics and the 4th International Joint Conference on Natural Language Processing of the Asian Federation of Natural Language Processing*, pages 297–300.

M. Yousfi-Monod and V. Prince. 2008. Sentence compression as a step in summarization or an alternative path in text shortening. In *Coling'08: International Conference on Computational Linguistics, Manchester, UK.*, pages 139–142.

D. Zajic, B. Door, and R. Schwarz. 2002. Automatic headline generation for newspaper stories. *Workshop on Text Summarization (ACL 2002 and DUC 2002 meeting on Text Summarization). Philadelphia.*

L. Zhou and E. Hovy. 2003. Headline summarization at isi. In *Document Understanding Conference (DUC-2003), Edmonton, Alberta, Canada.*

Unsupervised Domain Adaptation based on Text Relatedness

Georgios Petasis
Software and Knowledge Engineering Laboratory,
Institute of Informatics and Telecommunications,
National Centre for Scientific Research "Demokritos",
Athens, Greece
petasis@iit.demokritos.gr

Abstract

In this paper an unsupervised approach to domain adaptation is presented, which exploits external knowledge sources in order to port a classification model into a new thematic domain. Our approach extracts a new feature set from documents of the target domain, and tries to align the new features to the original ones, by exploiting text relatedness from external knowledge sources, such as WordNet. The approach has been evaluated on the task of document classification, involving the classification of newsgroup postings into 20 news groups.

1 Introduction

The portability of natural language processing (NLP) systems to new thematic domains is still a research area that attracts a significant research interest. During the last two decades, the use of machine learning has greatly improved the adaptability to new domains, or even languages. However, the vast majority of machine learning algorithms operate under a basic assumption: both the training and test data should use the same feature space, and follow the same distribution, suggesting that both should originate from the same thematic domain. When the distribution changes, the models must be re-generated from newly collected data. The adaptation can be separated into three large categories, according to the available data from the new domain. In supervised approaches, there is an adequate number of labelled data to train the model from scratch, on the new domain. When a limited number of labelled data are available, usually too few to train a model with satisfactory performance, along with unlabeled ones, the adaptation process is characterised as semi-supervised. Finally, unsupervised approaches must adapt their model to a new domain by learning solely from unlabelled examples.

Transfer learning or *knowledge transfer* is a research area, which tries to extract knowledge from previous experience and apply it on new learning tasks. Based on the idea that prior knowledge (i.e. identifying oranges) can be used on new tasks (i.e. identifying lemons), transfer learning researches three main central problems (Zhang and Shakya, 2009): 1) how to extract the prior knowledge that is related, 2) how to represent the knowledge, and 3) how to apply the knowledge in the new learning task. *Domain adaptation* is a sub-category of transfer learning, where (Pan and Yang, 2010):

1. The source and target domains are different, but related.
2. The source and target tasks are the same (i.e. classification or regression).
3. Labelled examples are available for the source domain.
4. Only unlabeled examples are available for the target domain.

In this paper, we propose a novel approach for the task of domain adaptation. Our method concentrates on the *feature space*, by trying to expand the features of the source domain with features that appear only in the target domain. Features that originate from the two different domains are aligned or linked to each other, through text relatedness. Text relatedness can take many forms, but we have opted for a simple relatedness measure, based on WordNet (Miller, 1995) synonymity.

The rest of the paper is organized as follows: in section 2 related work is presented, where our method is compared to existing approaches. In section 3 our approach to model adaptation based on text relatedness is presented, while section 4 presents evaluation on the 20-newsgroup corpus (Lang, 1995). Finally, section 5 concludes this paper and presents some future directions.

2 Related work

The task of transfer learning can be defined as follows: given a source domain D_S, a source task T_S, a target domain $D_T \neq D_S$, and a target task T_T, transfer learning aims in learning a function f_T that accomplishes task T_T, by exploiting knowledge derived from D_S and T_S. A fairly recent overview of the area of transfer learning is given in the survey of (Pan and Yang, 2010), including the definition of transfer learning, its relation to traditional machine learning, a categorisation of transfer learning approaches, and practical applications of transfer learning. More recent approaches that target the task of domain adaptation can be found on the ACL 2010 Workshop on Domain Adaptation for Natural Language Processing (DANLP 2010) (Daumé III et al., 2010).

A lot of approaches exist that perform model adaptation in a fully supervised way (i.e. requiring labelled examples for both the source and target domains). For example, EASYADAPT (Daumé III, 2007) augments the source domain feature space using features extracted from labelled data in target domain. Prior work on semi-supervised approaches to domain adaptation also exists in literature. Recent work in domain adaptation has focused on approaches such as *self-training* and *structural correspondence learning* (SCL). The former approach involves adding self-labelled data from the target domain produced by a model trained in-domain (McClosky, Charniak and Johnson, 2006). The latter approach focuses on ways of generating shared source-target representations based on good pivot features (Blitzer, McDonald and Pereira, 2006); (Ando, 2004); (Daumé III, Kumar and Saha, 2010).

However, the approach presented in this paper follows an *unsupervised* approach, thus requiring no labelled examples from the target domain. Unsupervised approaches try to exploit knowledge either from external knowledge sources, like our approach and (Gabrilovich and Markovitch, 2005), or from the distribution followed by the target domain (Thrun and Pratt, 1998); (Dai et al., 2007). The work presented in this paper can be categorised as an "unsupervised feature construction" approach, according to (Pan and Yang, 2010). Thus, approaches that try to extend a feature set through the unsupervised extraction of new features share some common ground with our approach. In (Gabrilovich and Markovitch, 2005) an approach that extracts new features by exploiting world knowledge is presented. World knowledge is represented through publically available ontologies, such as the Open Directory Project (ODP), where features from the source domain are mapped to appropriate ontology concepts, and "is-a" relations are exploited in order to acquire new features that augment the original feature set. Finally, the most appropriate features are selected through a feature selection phase. The work presented in (Zhang and Shakya, 2009) is also closely related to our approach: *feature correlation* is used in order to group features into *correlated groups*. For example, words like "orange", "lemon", "apple" and "pear" may often appear together in documents: aggregating them into a new correlated group "fruits", creates a new feature. If enough evidence exists in a document from the target domain (i.e. some of the features of the correlated group appear in the document), the feature that corresponds to the correlated group may help the task T_T in the target domain. In a sense, both approaches exploit information that can be characterised as "text relatedness" (or "feature relatedness"), as both "is-a" relations and correlation can be viewed as a relatedness measure between features. However, our method has also some important differences with these two methods. Our text relatedness measure is based on synonymity, as provided by an electronic dictionary such as WordNet. An electronic dictionary may be an easier resource to find than an ontology or hierarchy, thus our approach may have a small advantage in initial requirements when compared to (Gabrilovich and Markovitch, 2005). On the other hand, the calculation of feature correlation has no initial requirements in resources, but requires a corpus of adequate size, in order to extract the correlated groups. In addition, mining correlated groups may be computationally intensive if the feature set from the source domain is large enough (a problem tackled by limiting the source domain feature set to 2000 features, selected through mutual information, as reported in (Zhang and Shakya, 2009)). Finally, synonymity is a slightly more restricted text relatedness measure, compared to "is-a" relations (that can have many levels in the concept hierarchy) or correlation (which can relate possible unrelated features). Being a slightly more accurate text relatedness metric, it constitutes the need for feature selection, after the expansion of the source feature set, less important. In fact, our approach does not have a feature selection phase at all, in contrary to the two related approaches.

3 Domain adaptation based on text relatedness

The proposed methodology assumes a source domain D_S, a target domain $D_T \neq D_S$, a task T common for both domains, a feature space for the source domain $\mathcal{X}_S$, a label space $\mathcal{L}$ common for both domains, and a set of labelled examples originating from the source domain $L_S = \{X_1, \cdots, X_n\}$, where $X_i = \{x_1, \cdots, x_n, l_i\}$, $x_i \in \mathcal{X}_S$, $l_i \in \mathcal{L}$. In addition, our approach assumes a binary function $r(x_\alpha, x_\beta) \in \{0, 1\}$, $x_\alpha, x_\beta \in \mathcal{X}_S, \mathcal{X}_T$, which decides if two features are related, according to a text relatedness metric. Finally, a function $f_{\mathcal{X}_T}$ is assumed, that can extract a feature space $\mathcal{X}_T$ from the target domain D_T. The function $f_{\mathcal{X}_T}$ can be even a naive one, i.e. a function that returns all words in a corpus from the target domain D_T.

3.1 Text relatedness based on synonymity

Our approach assumes a binary relatedness function $r(x_\alpha, x_\beta)$, that can compare two features (either from the source or from the target feature spaces), and return whether the two features are related or not. Although many relatedness metrics can be devised and used, we have opted for a simple one, based on synonymity. Assuming an electronic dictionary, which contains synonyms, our text relatedness that is based on synonymity can be described with the following algorithm:

- If x_α and x_β are the same, return 1.
- Let S_α be the set of synonyms of x_α, and S_β the set of synonyms of x_β, according to the dictionary.
- If $x_\beta \in S_\alpha$ or $x_\alpha \in S_\beta$, return 1.
- If $S_\alpha \cap S_\beta \neq \emptyset$, return 1.
- Else, return 0.

In simple words, our synonymity relatedness metric returns true, if the two features are synonyms, or when they have at least one common synonym. The electronic dictionary that has been chosen is WordNet (Miller, 1995), as has already been mentioned. It should be noted that all synonyms for all senses are treated equally, without performing any kind of word sense disambiguation (Navigli, 2009), as is performed for example in the approach described in (Gabrilovich and Markovitch, 2005).

3.2 Extracting features from the target domain

Our approach assumes that there is a function $f_{\mathcal{X}_T}$, which can extract features from the target domain D_T. Since no further requirements are assumed about this function, the function can be as naive or complex as the task T requires. We have considered two feature extraction procedures, one naive, and one slightly more complex. The naive feature extraction (the aim of which is to be applied on the target domain D_T) simply extracts all the words that can be found on a corpus from D_T, minus the words that are considered as "stop words", and are filtered by using a stop word list. For the purposes of the experiments that will be presented in subsequent sections, the stop word filtering facilities offered by the Ellogon (Petasis et al., 2002) language engineering platform have been used.

A second feature extraction procedure has been additionally devised, aiming to be applied on the source domain D_S, in case such a need arises. This procedure examines all documents of a corpus, and calculates the TF-IDF score for every word of the document. "Stop words" are also rejected, and the rest of the remaining words are sorted according to their TF-IDF score, in a descending list. Then, an amount of the best scoring words, specified through a parameter θ (interpreted as a percent of the total words in a document), is extracted from each document, and added to the feature space that will be returned as the result.

3.3 Extracting new features

Once we have a method for extracting possible new features from the target domain D_T, through the function $f_{\mathcal{X}_T}$, and a text relatedness metric $r(x_\alpha, x_\beta)$, we can apply these two functions in order to acquire a feature set from the target domain:

- Let $\mathcal{X}_T^{\text{Initial}}$ be the feature space, as extracted from the target domain D_T by the function $f_{\mathcal{X}_T}$.
- Each feature $x_s \in \mathcal{X}_S$ from the source feature set is compared to each feature $x_T \in \mathcal{X}_T^{\text{Initial}}$ in the extracted from the target domain feature set. The function $r(x_\alpha, x_\beta)$ is used for comparing the pair of features.
- Features from the $\mathcal{X}_T^{\text{Initial}}$ that are not related to any feature in $\mathcal{X}_S$, are eliminated

from $\mathcal{X}_T^{\text{Initial}}$, leading to a new feature space $\mathcal{X}_T^{\text{Related}}$.

- As a final step, all features $x_T \in \mathcal{X}_T^{\text{Related}}$ are examined: every feature x_T that is related to more than one features in $\mathcal{X}_S$, is removed from $\mathcal{X}_T^{\text{Related}}$, leading to the final feature space that relates to the target domain $\mathcal{X}_T^{\text{Final}}$.

The result of this procedure, the final feature space that should be used for performing task T on the target domain D_T is the union of the two feature spaces: $\mathcal{X} = \mathcal{X}_S \cup \mathcal{X}_T^{Final}$.

3.4 Representing the extracted knowledge

The augmented feature space $\mathcal{X}$ that has been extracted as described in the previous subsection, contains all features of the source domain D_S, and new features from the target domain, each of which is unambiguously related to a single feature from D_S. The only unsolved issue is how this augmented feature space is going to be represented as vectors, which can be used with a machine learning algorithm. Although this decision may rely on the particular machine learning algorithm that will be used, empirical evaluation suggested that the best alternative is to form "groups of features", where each old feature is replaced by two features: the original one, plus the related one from the target feature space, if one exists. This representation has been proved beneficial, at least for the task we have chosen to evaluate our approach (document classification), the chosen representation (bag-of-words) and the chosen classifier (kNN with $k = 1$ and cosine similarity as the distance metric).

4 Empirical evaluation

This section will present an empirical evaluation of the proposed approach for domain adaptation based on text relatedness, with the help of the 20-newsgroup dataset (Lang, 1995): the 20-newsgroup dataset is a collection of approximately 20000 newsgroup documents, partitioned (nearly) evenly across 20 different newsgroups, and is a standard evaluation corpus in many works related to domain adaptation or transfer learning. The task chosen for the empirical evaluation is document classification.

4.1 The 20-newsgroup corpus

The 20-newsgroup corpus is preconfigured in training and testing material. Despite the fact that it is a popular evaluation corpus for domain adaptation approaches, it is unclear to us if all works that report results on the corpus use the same train/test partitioning, as different results are reported even for the base cases, as in (Pan and Yang, 2010) for example. In order to ease comparison with other approaches we opted in using the predefined train/test segmentation of the corpus, as it is distributed. Regarding the task, we will limit evaluation to the three more popular evaluation pairs: "rec vs talk", "rec vs sci", "sci vs talk".

The main idea behind the separation of these pairs, is that newsgroup posts from relevant but different newsgroups are put in the source/target domains. The "rec vs talk" class for example, may contain posts from the newsgroups "talk.politics.misc", "talk.politics.guns", "rec. motorcycles", and "rec.sport.hockey" as training material representing the source domain, while the test data (representing the target domain) may comprise from posts of the following newsgroups: "talk.politics.mideast", "talk.religion. misc", "rec.autos" and "rec.sport.baseball".

All posts in the three pairs of interest were pre-processed, in order for words to be recognised. A feature space from the posts constituting the training material was extracted, using the second method described in subsection 3.2, the one that extracts the top scoring words according to their TF-IDF weights, the number of which is controlled through a percentage of the total words of each post. This parameter was set to 0.003%, as it was found to roughly correspond to about one word from each post, leading for example to 4564 features for "rec vs sci", whose training material contains 4762 newsgroup posts. The reason behind this choice was to avoid possible over-fitting in the presence of too many features, and to provide our domain adaptation approach a chance to discover a large number of features from the target domain. As a measure of comparison, in (Zhang and Shakya, 2009) an initial feature space of 2000 features was selected.

Another point of interest is the choice of the machine learning algorithm, which will be used in order to learn from vectors. Support Vector Machines (SVMs) are quite popular as a base case in model adaptation problems, since prior studies found SVMs to offer the best performance, at least for document classification using a bag-of-words representation (Dumais et al., 1998); (Yang and Liu, 1999). However, since our approach expands the feature space, we wanted to evaluate the effect of the augmented feature

Pair	Source Domain Posts	Target Domain Posts	kNN (k = 1, cosine similarity)			SVM (LIBLINEAR)		
			Precision	Recall	F_1	Precision	Recall	F_1
rec vs sci	4762	3169	83.00%	41.90%	55.69%	83.62%	42.22%	56.11%
rec vs talk	4341	2891	83.35%	51.61%	55.51%	87.04%	53.89%	66.57%
sci vs talk	4325	2880	78.98%	41.63%	54.52%	82.67%	43.58%	57.07%

Table 1: Corpus characteristics and base case evaluation for the 20-newsgroup corpus.

Domain adaptation based on text relatedness						
Pair	kNN (k = 1, cosine similarity)			SVM (LIBLINEAR)		
	Precision	Recall	F_1	Precision	Recall	F_1
rec vs sci	64.88%	50.02% (+8.12)	56.49%	65.75%	50.69% (+8.47)	57.25%
rec vs talk	61.17%	55.44% (+3.83)	58.17%	65.11%	59.01% (+5.12)	61.91%
sci vs talk	59.60%	49.70% (+8.07)	54.20%	63.18%	52.69% (+9.11)	57.46%
(Shi, Fan and Ren, 2008)						
Pair	Recall (base/SVM)	Recall (TrAdaBoost)	Recall (AcTraK)			
rec vs sci	59.1%	67.4% (+8.3)	70.6% (+11.5)			
rec vs talk	60.2%	72.3% (+12.1)	75.4% (+15.2)			
sci vs talk	57.6%	71.3% (+13.7)	75.1% (+17.5)			

Table 2: Evaluation results on domain adaptation for the 20-newsgroup corpus. Results from (Shi, Fan and Ren, 2008) are also shown for comparison purposes (evaluated on different data partitioning).

space with the least possible intervention from the chosen machine learning algorithm. Thus, we selected one of the simplest machine learning algorithms available, the k-nearest neighbour algorithm (kNN). kNN does not have a training phase, it just classifies test instances using a similarity metric to measure distances from the training instances. In all experiments reported in this work, a kNN implementation was used with k=1, and cosine similarity as the distance metric.

The bag-of-words representation was used for all experiments in this paper. Under this representation, each document (newsgroup post) is represented with a single vector, which has the same dimension as the feature namespace in use. The value for each feature is binary: 1 represents that this feature exists in the document, 0 represents that this feature does not exist in the document. The characteristics of the 20-newsgroup corpus, as well as evaluation results for the base classifier are shown in Table 1. Despite the fact that kNN is the chosen classifier due to reasons already discussed, we have also applied an SVM algorithm with linear kernel, as implemented by the LIBLINEAR library (Fan et al., 2008). LIBLINEAR has been applied in order to ease comparisons with other approaches employing SVMs for classification.

The evaluation results of our approach are shown in Table 2. The upper part of Table 2 contains the evaluation results of our approach. The rows correspond to the examined pairs of newsgroups, while columns include information about the performance of both the kNN and LIBLINEAR classifiers, in terms of precision, recall and F-measure (F_1). In table columns concerning recall, the improvement from the base case is also displayed, as difference between percentages. The lower part of Table 2 contains evaluation results from (Shi, Fan and Ren, 2008), where two model adaptation approaches were evaluated and compared with SVMs, used as a base case. While experiments in (Shi, Fan and Ren, 2008) use a different partitioning of the corpus as training and testing data, suggesting that the performance of these approaches are not directly comparable to our approach, the improvement in performance provides a good indication of the contribution of the approaches, and can be compared to the improvement achieved by our approach.

As we can see from Table 2, the kNN classifier is able to provide answers for a much larger number of documents after the feature space has been augmented with features from the target domain. This is evident by the increase in recall. However, another aspect of feature space expansion should be noted: the classifier is able to provide an answer for a much larger number of newsgroup posts, even if the answer is not correct. For example, only 1600 (out of 3169) posts of the target domain contained features from the feature space of the source domain, in the case of the "rec vs sci" pair. However, after our approach expands the feature space with features from the target domain, 2289 posts of the target domain contained at least one feature from the augmented feature space, offering the possibility for classifying a larger number of posts.

The increase in performance achieved by our approach ranges from 4% (for "rec vs talk") to 8% (for "rec vs sci"). In comparison, the algorithm TrAdaBoost (Dai et al., 2007) achieved an increase ranging from 8% to 14%. The algorithm TrAdaBoost employs boosting in a semi-supervised approach, which exploits a small set of labelled data from the target domain, in addition to a large labelled data set from the source domain., in order to minimise the importance of labelled data from source domain (through weighting) whose distribution does not match the one of the target domain. Considering the fact that our approach employs a simple classification algorithm (kNN, $k = 1$, binary features), along with a fairly simple text relatedness similarity (synonymity), our approach performed surprisingly well. AcTraK (Shi, Fan and Ren, 2008) achieves an additional improved of about 4% compared to TrAdaBoost, with the help of active learning in a semi-supervised approach, where labelled data may be asked when necessary.

4.2 Representing the augmented feature space

Given the specific choices we have done regarding the task of document classification for the representation and the machine learning algorithm in use, we have performed an empirical evaluation in order to examine the effect of different ways in representing the acquired knowledge. We have examined three cases, concerning the incorporation of the augmented features in $\mathcal{X}_{\mathrm{T}}^{\mathrm{Final}}$ to the vectorial representation:

Expanding training vectors: under this scenario, the new features are also represented in the vectors, increasing the dimensionality of the vectors. A new dimension is created for each feature in the $\mathcal{X}_{\mathrm{T}}^{\mathrm{Final}}$ feature space. The value for each new feature is the value of its related, original feature in this vector.

Expanding and duplicating vectors: this case is very similar to the previous one regarding dimensionality: the dimensionality also increases, identical to the previous case. However, there is a difference in how the values of new features are set: instead of placing the value 1 to the original training vector, if the linked original feature is also 1, the original vector is duplicated, and the value 1 is set in the copy, for the new feature. As a result, each original vector is duplicated as many times as there are augmented features whose value should be 1 for this vector. Each copy differs from the original one only at the value of one feature.

Grouping features: under this scenario, the dimensionality of the vectors is not increased. Instead some of the features become "grouped features": they occupy a single dimension in vectors, but they represent different words, when matched in documents. This case was used in the evaluation presented in the previous subsection.

The evaluation has been performed only for the "rec vs sci" pair of newsgroups, using the same classifier as in subsection 4.1. The results are shown in Table 3. Our approach managed to achieve an improvement in accuracy (recall) in all three cases. However, the improvement was significantly better for case 3, while case 2 performed worse than the other two methods. The reason for the worst improvement can be attributed to the fact that the number of vectors that were added was not enough to cover all possible permutations. Assuming N augmented features whose value must be 1 (as there are also N original features whose value is 1), $2N^2 - 1$ vectors must be inserted, in order to cover all possible permutations. However, adding so many vectors can quickly lead to an intractable problem. Instead our approach followed a more conservative path, adding only $N - 1$ vectors to the original training set, covering unfortunately only a part of possible cases, and not fully exploiting the potential of the augmented features.

	Precision	Recall	F_1
Case 1	79.26%	45.69%	57.96%
Case 2	76.79%	44.27%	56.16%
Case 3	64.88%	50.02%	56.94%
Base case	83.00%	41.90%	55.69%

Table 3: Evaluation results for various representations of the augmented feature space.

Case 1 was not too far from case 2. The reason for this behaviour can be attributed to the classification algorithm we have used. Cosine similarity depends on the number of common features with value 1 between the two vectors, divided by the magnitude of the two vectors. We can easily image a case where in a post, some of the original features without augmented ones exist in the post, but from the related features, only some of the augmented features exists, and none of the original related features exists. Trying to match such a test vector to a training one that has the augmented, but also their original related features set to 1, may be misclassified in favour of a vector with less magnitude, and possibly with no related features (both original and augmented) set to one. Thus, also this case is unable to fully exploit the augmented features, as it may favour classifying test vectors with augmented features into training vectors without augmented features.

5 Conclusions and future work

In this paper, a domain adaptation approach was presented, that exploits text relatedness in the form of WordNet synonymity, in order to augment an initial feature space, derived from the source domain, with new features from the target domain. The proposed approached was empirically evaluated with the help of a manually annotated corpus. Evaluation results suggest that our approach can achieve an improvement comparable to other approaches that can be found in the bibliography, despite the fact that it employs kNN as its classifier to the task of document classification.

Since our current implementation of text relatedness is quite simple, based on WordNet synonymity, trying out more complex relatedness functions would be an interesting future direction to explore. A particularly interesting text relatedness function is Omiotis (Tsatsaronis, Varlamis and Vazirgiannis, 2010), which exploits many knowledge sources in order to estimate the relatedness between two words.

Acknowledgments

The author would like to acknowledge partial support of this work from the European Community Seventh Framework Programme, as part of the FP7 – 231854 SYNC3 project.

References

Ando, R.K. (2004) 'Exploiting unannotated corpora for tagging and chunking', Proceedings of the ACL 2004 on Interactive poster and demonstration sessions (ACLdemo '04), Stroudsburg, PA, USA.

Blitzer, J., McDonald, R. and Pereira, F. (2006) 'Domain Adaptation with Structural Correspondence Learning', Proceedings of the Conference on Empirical Methods in Natural Language Processing (EMNLP '06), Sydney, Australia, 120--128.

Dai, W., Yang, Q., Xue, G.-R. and Yu, Y. (2007) 'Boosting for transfer learning', Proceedings of the Twenty-Fourth International Conference (ICML 2007), Corvalis, Oregon, USA, 193-200.

Daumé III, H. (2007) 'Frustratingly Easy Domain Adaptation', Proceedings of the 45th Annual Meeting of the Association of Computational Linguistics, Prague, Czech Republic, 256--263.

Daumé III, H., Deoskar, T., McClosky, D., Plank, B. and Tiedemann, J. (2010) Proceedings of the 2010 Workshop on Domain Adaptation for Natural Language Processing, Uppsala, Sweden: Association for Computational Linguistics.

Daumé III, H., Kumar, A. and Saha, A. (2010) 'Frustratingly Easy Semi-Supervised Domain Adaptation', Proceedings of the 2010 Workshop on Domain Adaptation for Natural Language Processing (DANLP 2010), Uppsala, Sweden, 53--59.

Dumais, S., Platt, J., Sahami, M. and Heckerman, D. (1998) 'Inductive Learning Algorithms and Representations for Text Categorization', CIKM'98, 148--155.

Fan, R.-E., Chang, K.-W., Hsieh, C.-J., Wang, X.-R. and Lin, C.-J. (2008) 'LIBLINEAR: A Library for Large Linear Classification', Journal of Machine Learning Research, vol. 9, Aug, pp. 1871--1874.

Gabrilovich, E. and Markovitch, S. (2005) 'Feature Generation for Text Categorization Using World Knowledge', Proceedings of The Nineteenth International Joint Conference for Artificial Intelligence, Edinburgh, Scotland, 1048--1053.

Lang, K. (1995) 'NewsWeeder: Learning to filter netnews', Proceedings of the Twelfth International Conference on Machine Learning, 331-339.

McClosky, D., Charniak, E. and Johnson, M. (2006) 'Reranking and self-training for parser adaptation', Proceedings of ACL-COLING, Sydney, Australia, 337--344.

Miller, G.A. (1995) 'WordNet: a lexical database for English', Commun. ACM, vol. 38, no. 11, November, pp. 39--41, Available: 0001-0782.

Navigli, R. (2009) 'Word sense disambiguation: A survey', ACM Comput. Surv., vol. 41, no. 2, February, pp. 10:1--10:69, Available: 0360-0300.

Pan, S.J. and Yang, Q. (2010) 'A Survey on Transfer Learning ', IEEE Transactions on Knowledge and Data Engineering, vol. 22, no. 10, October, pp. 1345 - 1359.

Petasis, G., Karkaletsis, V., Paliouras, G., Androutsopoulos, I. and Spyropoulos, C.D. (2002) 'Ellogon: A New Text Engineering Platform', LREC 2002, Canary Islands, 72--78.

Shi, X., Fan, W. and Ren, J. (2008) 'Actively Transfer Domain Knowledge', Proceedings of the European conference on Machine Learning and Knowledge Discovery in Databases (ECML PKDD '08) - Part II, Berlin, Heidelberg, 342--357.

Thrun, S. and Pratt, L. (1998) Learning To Learn, Kluwer Academic Publishers.

Tsatsaronis, G., Varlamis, I. and Vazirgiannis, M. (2010) 'Text Relatedness Based on a Word Thesaurus', Journal of Artificial Intelligence Research, vol. 37, pp. 1--39.

Yang, Y. and Liu, X. (1999) 'A Re-Examination of Text Categorization Methods', SIGIR'99, 42--49.

Zhang, J. and Shakya, S.S. (2009) 'Knowledge Transfer for Feature Generation in Document Classification', Proceedings of the 2009 International Conference on Machine Learning and Applications (ICMLA '09), Washington, DC, USA, 255--260.

Bilingual Experiments with an Arabic-English Corpus for Opinion Mining

Mohammed Rushdi-Saleh
SINAI research group
University of Jaén
msaleh@ujaen.es

M. Teresa Martín-Valdivia
SINAI research group
University of Jaén
maite@ujaen.es

L. Alfonso Ureña-López
SINAI research group
University of Jaén
laurena@ujaen.es

José M. Perea-Ortega
SINAI research group
University of Jaén
jmperea@ujaen.es

Abstract

Recently, Opinion Mining (OM) is receiving more attention due to the abundance of forums, blogs, e-commerce web sites, news reports and additional web sources where people tend to express their opinions. There are a number of works about Sentiment Analysis (SA) studying the task of identifying the polarity, whether the opinion expressed in a text is positive or negative about a given topic. However, most of research is focused on English texts and there are very few resources for other languages. In this work we present an Opinion Corpus for Arabic (OCA) composed of Arabic reviews extracted from specialized web pages related to movies and films using this language. Moreover, we have translated the OCA corpus into English, generating the EVOCA corpus (English Version of OCA). In the experiments carried out in this work we have used different machine learning algorithms to classify the polarity in these corpora showing that, although the experiments with EVOCA are worse than OCA, the results are comparable with other English experiments, since the loss of precision due to the translation is very slight.

1. Introduction

Nowadays, the interest in Opinion Mining (OM) has grown significantly due to different factors. On the one hand, the rapid evolution of the World Wide Web has changed our view of the Internet. It has turned into a collaborative framework where technological and social trends come together, resulting in the over exploited term Web 2.0. On the other hand, the tremendous use of e-commerce services has been accompanied by an increase in freely available online reviews and opinions about products and services. A customer who wants to buy a product usually searches information on the Internet trying to find other consumer analyses. In fact, web sites such as Amazon[1], Epinions[2] or IMDb[3], can affect the customer decision. Moreover, the automatic Sentiment Analysis (SA) is useful not only for individual customer but also for any company or institution. However, the huge amount of information makes necessary to accomplish new methods and strategies to tackle the problem.

Thus, SA is becoming one of the main research areas that combines Natural Language Processing (NLP) and Text Mining (TM). This new discipline attempts to identify and analyze opinions and emotions. It includes several subtasks such as subjectivity detection, polarity classification, review summarization, humor detection, emotion classification, sentiment transfer, and so on [9]. However, most of works related to OM are oriented to use English language. Perhaps due to the novelty of the task, there are very few papers analyzing the opinions using other languages different to English. In this paper, we present the experiments accomplished with an Opinion Corpus for Arabic (OCA) collected from different web pages with comments about movies. In addition, we have used automatic machine translation tools to translate OCA corpus into English. We have generated different classifiers using Support Vector Machine and Naïve Bayes in order to determinate the polarity of the opinions. The experiments carried out with the English Version of OCA (EVOCA) show that, although we lost precision in the translation, the results are comparable to other works using English texts. So, we can use this procedure in order to determine the polarity of an Arabic corpus by using English translation. This is important because most of resources are in English and we can take advantage of this situation.

The paper is organized as following: Next section presents some papers about OM using non-English language. Section 3 and Section 4 describe the OCA

[1] http://www.amazon.com
[2] http://www.epinions.com
[3] http://www.imdb.com

corpus and its English version (EVOCA), respectively. In Section 5, accomplished experiments are showed and results are analyzed. Finally, conclusion and future work is presented.

2. Related works

Although opinions and comments in the Internet are expressed in any language, most of research in OM is focused on English texts. However, languages such as Chinese, Spanish or Arabic, are ever more present on the web[4]. Thus, it is important to develop resources for helping researcher to work with these languages.

There are some interesting papers that have studied the problem using non-English collections. For example, Denecke [5] worked on German comments collected from Amazon. These reviews were translated into English using standard machine translation software. Then the translated reviews were classified as positive or negative, using three different classifiers: LingPipe7, SentiWordNet [6] with classification rule, and SentiWordNet with machine learning.

Zhang et al. [12] applied Chinese sentiment analysis on two datasets. In the first one euthanasia reviews were collected from different web sites, while the second dataset was about six product categories collected from Amazon (Chinese reviews).

Ghorbel and Jacot [7] used a corpus with movie reviews in French. They applied a supervised classification combined with SentiWordNet in order to determinate the polarity of the reviews.

Agić et al. [2] presented a manually annotated corpus with news on the financial market in Croatia.

Boldrini et al. [4] aimed to build up a corpus with a fine-gained annotation scheme for the detection of subjective elements. The data were collected manually from 300 blogs in three different languages: Spanish, Italian and English.

Regarding opinion mining for Arabic language, Ahmad et al. [3] performed a local grammar approach for three languages: Arabic, Chinese and English using financial news. They selected and compared the distribution of words in a domain-specific document to the distribution of words in a general corpus.

Finally, Abbasi et al. [1] accomplished a study for sentiment classification on English and Arabic inappropriate content. Specifically, they applied their methodologies on a U.S. supremacist forum for English and a Middle Eastern extremist group for Arabic language.

3. OCA: Opinion Corpus for Arabic

Despite the importance of the Arabic language on the Internet, there are very few web pages which specialize in Arabic reviews. The most common Arabic opinion sites in the Internet are related to movies and films, although these blogs also present several obstacles to their being used in sentiment analysis tasks. Some of these difficulties are stated below:

- **Nonsense and non related comments**. Many reviews in different web pages are not related to the topic. People attempt to comment on anything, even with unrelated words or nonsense. For instance, instead of comment an item, the user just types a word:

  Thaaaaaaanks= مشكووووور

- **Romanization of Arabic**. Many comments use the Roman alphabet. Each phoneme in Arabic can be replaced by its counterpart in the Roman alphabet. This can be due to non-use of Arabic keyboards for people who comment on Arabic topics from abroad. For instance, Table 1 shows a fragment explaining the problem of commenting on a topic using the Roman alphabet. There are also possible variants in the case of Romanization of Arabic for the above example, taking into account the diacritics in the Arabic language. However, a native speaker could still understand this sentence.

Table 1. Different variants of Roman alphabet transcriptions

English	*Qatar is a great country*
Arabic	قطر دولة عظيمة
Roman alphabet 1	*Qatar dawla athema*
Roman alphabet2	*Qatr dawlah 3athema*
Roman alphabet3	*9atar dawlah 3athemah*

- **Comments in different languages.** It is also possible to find international languages in Arabic web pages, so you could read comments in English, Spanish or French mixed with Arabic sentences.

In order to generate the Opinion Corpus for Arabic we have extracted the reviews from different web pages about movies. OCA consists of 500 reviews in Arabic, of which 250 are considered as positive reviews and the other 250 as negative opinions. This process has consisted of collecting reviews from several Arabic blog sites and web pages. Table 2 presents the number of reviews according to negative or positive classification from each web page, the name of the web page and the highest score used in the rating system.

[4] http://www.internetworldstats.com

Table 2. Distribution of reviews crawled from different web pages

	Name	web page	Rating system	PR	NR
1	Cinema Al Rasid	http://cinema.al-rasid.com	10	36	1
2	Film Reader	http://filmreader.blogspot.com	5	0	92
3	Hot Movie Reviews	http://hotmoviews.blogspot.com	5	45	4
4	Elcinema	http://www.elcinema.com	10	0	56
5	Grind House	http://grindh.com	10	38	0
6	Mzyon-dubai	http://www.mzyondubai.com	10	0	15
7	Aflamee	http://aflamee.com	5	0	1
8	Grind Film	http://grindfilm.blogspot.com	10	0	8
9	Cinema Gate	http://www.cingate.net	bad/good	0	1
10	Emad Ozery Blog	http://emadozery.blogspot.com	10	0	1
11	Fil Fan	http://www.filfan.com	5	81	20
12	Sport4Ever	http://sport4ever.maktoob.com	10	0	1
13	DVD4ArabPos	http://dvd4arab.maktoob.com	10	11	0
14	Gamraii	http://www.gamraii.com	10	39	0
15	Shadows and Phantoms	http://shadowsandphantoms.blogspot.com	10	0	50
			Total	250	250

We have removed HTML tags and special characters as well as spelling mistakes were corrected manually. Next, a processing of each review was carried out which consisted of tokenizing, removing Arabic stop words, stemming and filtering those tokens whose length was less than two characters. Figure 1 shows the different steps followed in our approach in order to generate the OCA corpus and Table 3 shows some statistics on such corpus.

On the other hand, there are important issues that must be taken into account in these blogs:

- **Rating system**. We found that there is no common system of rating among these blogs. Some of them use a rating scale of 10 points, so reviews with less than five points are classified as negative while those with a rating between five and 10 points are classified as positive. Other blogs use a 5-rating scale. In these cases, we considered the movies with three, four and five points as positive, while those with less than three points were classified as negative. This classification was based on a deep study of the reviews which were rated as neutral. Finally, we also found binary classifications such as *good* or *bad*.

Table 3. Statistics on the OCA opinion corpus

	Negative	Positive
Total **documents**	250	250
Total **tokens**	94,556	121,392
Total **sentences**	4,881	3,137

- **Cultural and political emotions**. Culture in Arabic countries can also affect the behavior of the reviewers. For instance, an "Antichrist" movie is rated with 1 point from 10 in one of the Arabic blogs, while the same movie on IMDb is rated at 6.7 out of 10.

- **Movie and actor names in English**. There are different ways of naming movies and actors in the reviews. In some cases, the names are translated into Arabic, while others keep the names in English and the reviews in Arabic.

4. EVOCA: English Version of OCA

In order to compare the experiment for Arabic and English, we have translated OCA into English using an automatic Machine Translation (MT) tool freely available. Specifically, we have used the online translator provided by PROMT[5].

The processing followed to carry out the translation consisted of splitting the text of the reviews in blocks of 500 characters to fit with the maximum length allowed by the online translator. Secondly, after the translation, extra UTF-8 invalid characters were removed and, finally, the translated reviews were generated from the blocks belonging to each of them. Figure 2 summarizes the processing followed to generate the EVOCA corpus.

The new corpus EVOCA contains the same number of positive and negative reviews that OCA corpus, with a total of 500 reviews. Table 4 shows some statistics for the EVOCA corpus.

Table 4. Statistics on the EVOCA opinion corpus

	Negative	Positive
Total **documents**	250	250
Total **tokens**	122,135	153,581
Avg. tokens per review	488.54	614.32
Total **sentences**	5,030	3,483
Avg. sentences per review	20.12	13.93

[5] Available at http://translation2.paralink.com

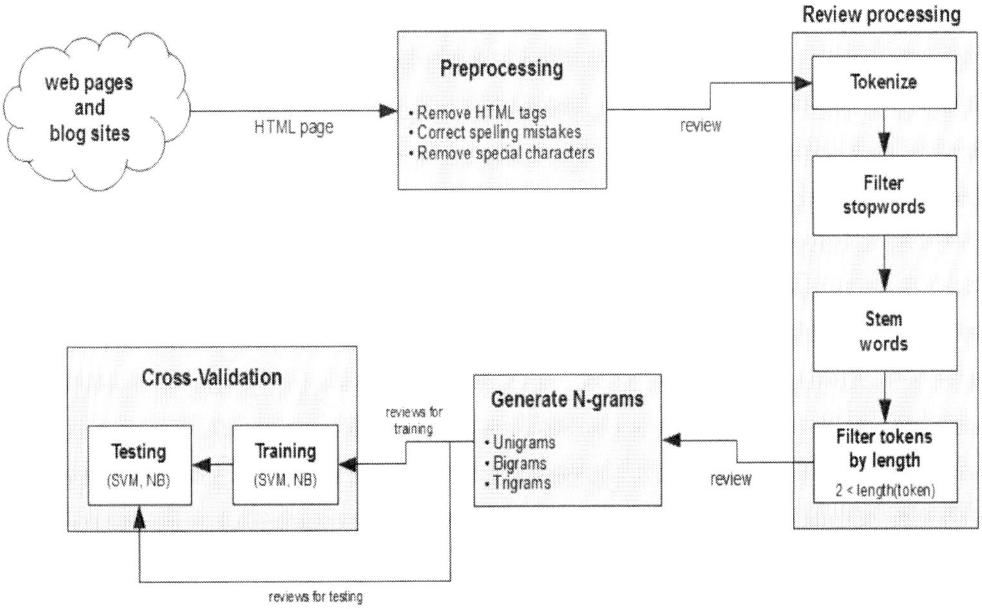

Figure 1. Steps followed in the generation and validation of the OCA corpus

5. Experiments and Results

For the experiments, we have used the Rapid Miner[6] software with its text mining plug-in which contains different tools designed to assist in the preparation of text documents for mining tasks (tokenization, stop word removal and stemming, among others). Rapid Miner is an environment for machine learning and data mining processes.

We have applied two of the most used classifiers: Support Vector Machines (SVM) and Naïve Bayes (NB).

SVM [11] is based on the structural risk minimization principle from the computational learning theory, and seek a decision surface to separate the training data points into two classes and makes decisions based on the support vectors that are selected as the only effective elements in the training set.

On the other hand, NB algorithm [8] is based on the Bayes theorem. Due to its complex calculation, the algorithm has to make two main assumptions: first, it considers the Bayes denominator invariant, and second, it assumes that the input variables are conditional independence.

In our experiments, the 10-fold cross-validation has been used in order to evaluate the classifier. This evaluation has been carried out on three main measures: precision (P), recall (R) and F1 measure [10].

Moreover, for each machine learning algorithm, we have analyzed how the use of stemmer affects the experiments. TF·IDF has been used as weighting scheme. We have also accomplished several experiments using different n-grams models. However, the obtained results with bi-grams and trigrams were very similar to unigrams. For this reason we have only shown the best results obtained with unigrams. Results for SVM and NB are shown in Table 5 and Table 6, respectively.

As we can see, taking into account the F1 measure, all the experiments with OCA overcome EVOCA except when we use SVM and stemmer. In fact, this is the only case where stemmer obtains a better result although the improvement is very slight (+1.54%). Anyway, the best result is achieved using SVM without stemmer over the OCA corpus with 0.9073 of F1 measure.

[6] http://rapid-i.com

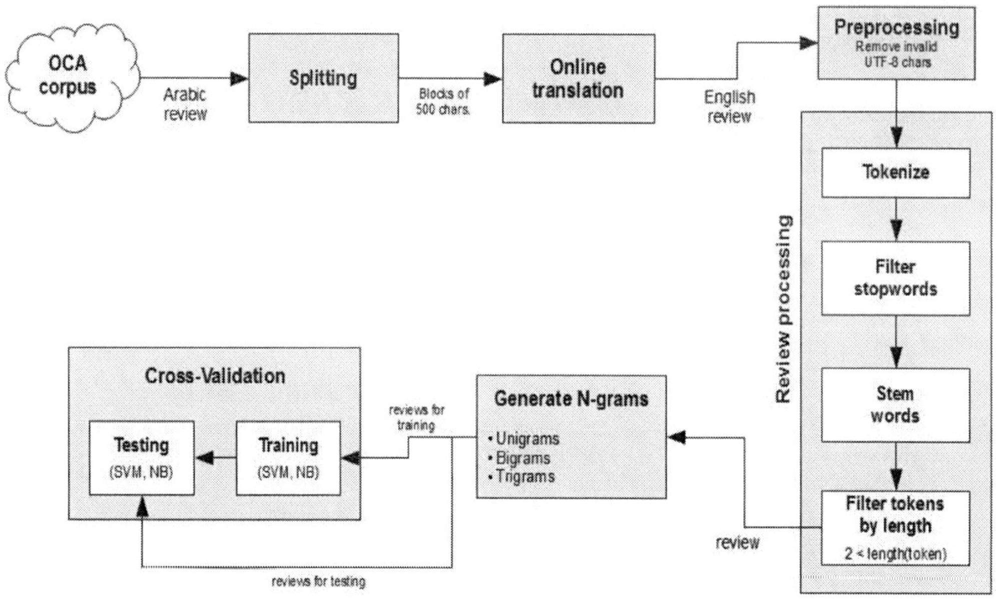

Figure 2. Processing followed to generate and validate the EVOCA corpus

However, it is interesting to note that, in the SVM experiments, the loss of precision due to the translation is very little. The highest difference is 4.31% when we do not apply stemmer, while it is 1.54% when the stemmer is applied. In general, the results with EVOCA, near to 90%, are very good comparing them with other works using SVM and English corpora [9].

Table 5. Results with SVM

	Stem	P	R	F1
OCA	Yes	0.8614	0.8800	0.8706
	No	0.8699	0.9480	**0.9073**
EVOCA	Yes	0.9007	0.8680	0.8840
	No	0.8561	0.8840	0.8698

Table 6. Results with NB

	Stem	P	R	F1
OCA	Yes	0.8106	0.8880	0.8475
	No	0.8274	0.9520	**0.8853**
EVOCA	Yes	0.7100	0.8320	0.7662
	No	0.7323	0.8640	0.7927

As regard the machine learning algorithm, it is clear that SVM works better in all cases. Taking into account the best results on the OCA corpus, SVM improves 2.49% the result obtained with NB (both without applying stemmer). On the EVOCA corpus the difference is higher for SVM +15.37% and +9.73%, using stemmer and without using it, respectively. Although the differences between SVM and NB over the OCA corpus are small, when they are applied over EVOCA, NB loses too much precision. In this case, the translation is affecting highly the results.

Finally, we have analyzed the impact of the stemmer in the experiments. As can be observed in both Table 5 and Table 6, in all cases the stemming process gets worse results except when we use SVM on the EVOCA corpus (+1.63% for stemming). For the OCA corpus, not use the stemmer always improves the results when we apply it (+4.22% using SVM and +4.46% using NB), while we obtain an improvement of 3.46% on the EVOCA corpus using NB.

6. Conclusion

In this paper we have presented an Arabic corpus for opinion mining along with its English translation. OCA and EVOCA corpora are freely available for the research community[7]. The OCA corpus is composed of Arabic reviews obtained from specialized Arabic web pages related to movies and films. Then, we have generated the EVOCA corpus, which is the English translation of the OCA corpus using an automatic machine translation tool. Both corpora include a total of 500 reviews, 250 positives and 250 negatives. In

[7] OCA and EVOCA corpora are freely available at http://sinai.ujaen.es/wiki/index.php/Recursos

addition, we have accomplished several experiments over the corpora using two different machine learning algorithms (SVM and Naïve Bayes) and applying a stemming process. The results obtained show that, although the precision with the EVOCA are lower, they are comparable with other sentiment analysis researches using English texts. This loss of precision due to the translation is very slight (-4.31% when stemmer is not applied) and therefore it is very interesting for the future because we could apply English resources for opinion mining such as SentiWorNet in order to improve the results. On the other hand, we have shown that the use of the stemming process is not recommended to work with these corpora.

7. Acknowledgments

This work has been partially supported by a grant from the Fondo Europeo de Desarrollo Regional (FEDER), project TEXT-COOL 2.0 (TIN2009-13391-C04-02) from the Spanish Government, a grant from the Andalusian Government, project GeOasis (P08-TIC-41999), and a grant from the Instituto de Estudios Giennenses, project Geocaching Urbano (RFC/IEG2010). Also, another part of this project was funded by Agencia Española de Cooperación Internacional para el Desarrollo MAEC-AECID.

8. References

[1] Abbasi, A., Chen, H., & Salem, A. (2008). Sentiment analysis in multiple languages: Feature selection for opinion classification in Web forums. ACM Trans. Inf. Syst. 26 (3).

[2] Agić, Z., Ljubešić, N., & Tadić, M. (2010). Towards Sentiment Analysis of Financial Texts in Croatian. In N. Calzolari, K. Choukri, B. Maegaard, J. Mariani, J. Odijk, S. Piperidis, M. Rosner & D. Tapias (Eds.), Language Resources and Evaluation (LREC). European Language Resources Association.

[3] Ahmad, K., Cheng, D., & Almas, Y. (2006). Multilingual sentiment analysis of financial news streams. Proceedings of Science (GRID2006).

[4] Boldrini, E., Balahur, A., Martínez-Barco, P., & Montoyo, A. (2009). Emotiblog: an annotation scheme for emotion detection and analysis in non-traditional textual genres. In R. Stahlbock, S.F. Crone & S. Lessmann (Eds.), DMIN (pp. 491-497). CSREA Press.

[5] Denecke, K. (2008). Using SentiWordNet for multilingual sentiment analysis. ICDE Workshops (pp. 507–512). IEEE Computer Society.

[6] Esuli, A., & Sebastiani, F. (2006). SentiWordNet: A Publicly Available Lexical Resource for Opinion Mining. Proceedings of the 5th Conference on Language Resources and Evaluation (LREC) (pp. 417-422).

[7] Ghorbel, H., & Jacot, D. (2010). Sentiment analysis of French movie reviews. Proceedings of the 4th international Workshop on Distributed Agent-based Retrieval Tools (DART 2010). Geneva, Italy.

[8] Mitchell, T. (1997). Machine Learning. McGraw-Hill.

[9] Pang, B., & Lee, L. (2008). Opinion mining and sentiment analysis. Foundations and Trends in Information Retrieval 2 (1-2) (pp. 1-135).

[10] Sebastiani, F. (2002). Machine Learning in Automated Text Categorization. ACM Computing Surveys, 34(1), 1.

[11] Vapnik, V. (1995). The Nature of Statistical Learning Theory. Springer-Verlag, New York.

[12] Zhang, C., Zeng, D., Li, J., Wang, F.-Y., & Zuo, W. (2009). Sentiment analysis of Chinese documents: From sentence to document level. Journal of the American Society for Information Science and Technology (JASIST), 60(12), 2474–2487.

Experiments on Term Extraction using Noun Phrase Subclassifications

Merley S. Conrado
Walter Koza
Universidad de São Paulo
merleyc@icmc.usp.br
kozawalter@opendeusto.es

Josuka Díaz-Labrador
Joseba Abaitua
Solange O. Rezende
Universidad Nacional de Rosario
josuka@deusto.es
joseba.abaitua@deusto.es
solange@icmc.usp.br

Thiago A. S. Pardo
Zulema Solana
Universidad de Deusto
taspardo@icmc.usp.br
zsolana@arnet.com.ar

Abstract

In this paper we describe and compare three approaches for the automatic extraction of medical terms using noun phrases (NPs) previously recognized on medical text corpus in Spanish. In the first approach, as baseline, we extracted all NPs, while for the second and third ones the extraction process is directed to "specific NPs" that are determined on the basis of the syntactic and positional criteria, among others. As contributions (i) we showed that it is possible to extract medical terms using "specific NPs", (ii) new terms were added in the software dictionary, and (iii) terms that were not in the reference lists were extracted. For the third contribution, we used the SNOMED CT® terms lists, aiming at improving the IULA reference lists.

1 Introduction

According to Moreno-Sandoval (2009), generally, noun phrases (NPs) correspond to specific terms of a particular domain. The terms can be formed by only a head or a head and complements. Then, the automatic term extraction task was mainly based on the recognition of this kind of phrases.

In this paper, automatic extraction experiments for medical term extraction using noun phrases (NPs) previously recognized on medical text corpus in Spanish are described and compared. For this task, in a first stage, as baseline, all identified NPs are considered as term candidates, while in the other stages the extraction is directed to "specific NPs" that are determined on the basis of syntactic and positional criteria, among others. The novelty of this work is that we are not using pure noun phrases, like many works utilize. In fact, we are using specific NPs, is to say, a subclassification of phrases. We use the IULA corpus (Bach et al., 1997) of medical texts in Spanish and results are compared with reference lists of unigrams, bigrams and trigrams.

According to the results, (i) we showed that it is possible to extract medical terms using "specific NPs", (ii) the software dictionary was improved with 2,445 new terms, and (iii) other terms that were not in the reference lists were extracted. For the third contribution we used the SNOMED CT® term lists aiming at improving the IULA reference lists. However, it should be mentioned that we detected other expressions that were neither in the reference lists nor in SNOMED CT®, although they could be considered medical terms. In this case, we have to say that new terms are added almost on a daily basis, and it is practically impossible to manually update the terms lists.

2 Term extraction in medicine

There are different works about term extraction that may be applied for different domains, sometimes adaptations are necessary for each of them. For the medical domain, we may mention the contributions of Névéol and Ozdowska (2005) and Bessagnet et al. (2010) for the French; Hao-Min et al. (2008), for the Chinese, and the Lopes et al. (2009), for Portuguese. For the English, we cite the Krauthammer and Nenadic (2004) work, which makes a detailed description of automatic term recognition (ATR) systems in the medical field. Those systems are based either on internal characteristics of specific classes or on external clues that can support the recognition of word sequences that represent specific domain concepts. Different types of features are used, such as orthographic (capital letters, digits, Greek letters) and morphological clues (specific affixes, POS tags), or syntactic information from shallow parsing. Also, different statistical measures are suggested for "promoting" term candidates into terms.

In our work, the term extraction is applied in

the medical domain in Spanish. So here, we mention the main works in this area. We may mention the ONCOTERM Project (Bilingual System of Information and Cancer Resources), the Describe® System, the Vivaldi and Rodríguez works, the Castro et al. works, and the large terminology developed by the SNOMED CT® Project.

ONCOTERM (López Rodríguez et al., 2006) is a Project whose goal is to develop a information system for the oncology domain, in which the concepts are linked to an ontology. The authors worked from Spanish texts to create a terminology database, with correspondences in English and German.

The Describe® system (Sierra et al., 2009), meanwhile, applies a Defining Contexts Extractor (Alarcón, 2009) for the search, classification, and grouping of medical definitions from the web.

Vivaldi and Rodríguez (2010) created a term extraction system that uses Wikipedia (WP) semantic information. It was tested in a medical corpus, and, according to its results, WP was considered a good resource for tasks of medical term extraction.

Castro et al. (2010) work presents a semantic annotation of clinical notes and an application of an automatic tool for medical concept recognition on the SNOMED CT® ontology. Furthermore, a tool test is presented in 100 clinical notes, and, according to the authors, the results are quite good.

SNOMED CT®[1] is a big medical terminology and is the result of the fusion between SNOMED RT and the Clinical Terms Version 3, a terminology previously known as Read Codes, created by the National Health Service (NHS) in England.

3 Term extraction methodology

With the objective of indentifying medical terms, we have developed rules for "specific" NPs recognition. They were used for extracting terms and, as baseline, we consider the term extraction usually performed with NP. We applied it to Spanish, but it may be adapted to others languages, adjusting the linguistic informations of parsers used.

According to Figure 1, the term extraction, carried out this work, starts with the delimitation of the domain and the **corpus**. Afterwards, it is necessary to perform an **orthographic normalization**, changing the corpus file codification to UTF-8. Also, line changes are removed to prevent problems with the tools for the morphological analysis. In the sequence, the **tokenization and morphological analysis** is carried out aiming at tagging words and punctuation marks.

This way, we developed NPs recognition rules (e.g., article + noun = " NP") to shape the NPs to be worked with. Phrase recognition allows the **extraction** of term candidates. At this stage, stopwords are removed of these candidates.

After cleaning the candidates, they are separated into lists of unigrams, bigrams, trigrams and higher than trigrams to allow evaluation.

3.1 Experiments

For the experiments we used the IULA-UPF technical corpus[2] that belongs to the health and medical domains. This corpus is composed of 12 texts in Spanish and the average of words per document is 8,207. With it, the IULA-UPF has also provided three reference term lists, containing a total of 697 unigrams (e.g. "*alergia*" - allergy), 665 bigrams consisting of a name plus an adjective (e.g. "*ácido benzoico*" - benzoic acid) and 82 trigrams formed by a name plus the preposition "de" plus another name (e.g. "*grupo de riesgo*").

From the corpus, we had to recognize noun phrases (NPs), prepositional phrases (PP), and nucleus verbal phrase (nvp).

The term extraction is detailed in Figure 1. The morphological analysis of corpus words was carried out using the SMORPH program (Aït-Mokhtar, 1998), that is a finite-state part of speech tagger that Infosur[3] Group has adapted to Spanish. As an example, for the fragment "*Pruebas de provocación bronquial con ejercicio y con histamina en niños asmáticos.*" (Bronchial provocation tests with exercise and with histamine in asthmatic children.), the test result of SMORPH[4]

[1]SNOMED CT® - `http://www.nlm.nih.gov/research/umls/Snomed/snomed_main.html` - *"This material includes SNOMED Clinical Terms® (SNOMED CT®), which is used with permission of the International Health Terminology Standards Development Organisation (IHTSDO). All rights reserved. SNOMED CT® was originally created by The College of American Pathologists. "SNOMED" and "SNOMED CT" are registered trademarks of the IHTSDO."*

[2]IULA-UPF technical corpus - *"Data belonging to the TECHNICAL CORPUS from Institut Universitari de Lingüística Aplicada de la Universitat Pompeu Fabra (http://bwananet.iula.upf.edu/) in December 2010."*

[3]Infosur - http://www.infosurrevista.com.ar

[4]References: EMS: morphosyntactic tag; nom: noun; GEN: genre; fem: female; NUM: number; PL: plural; v: verb; ind: indicative; PERS: person; 2a: second, TPO: time; pres: present; TR: type of regularity; irr: irregular; TC: type

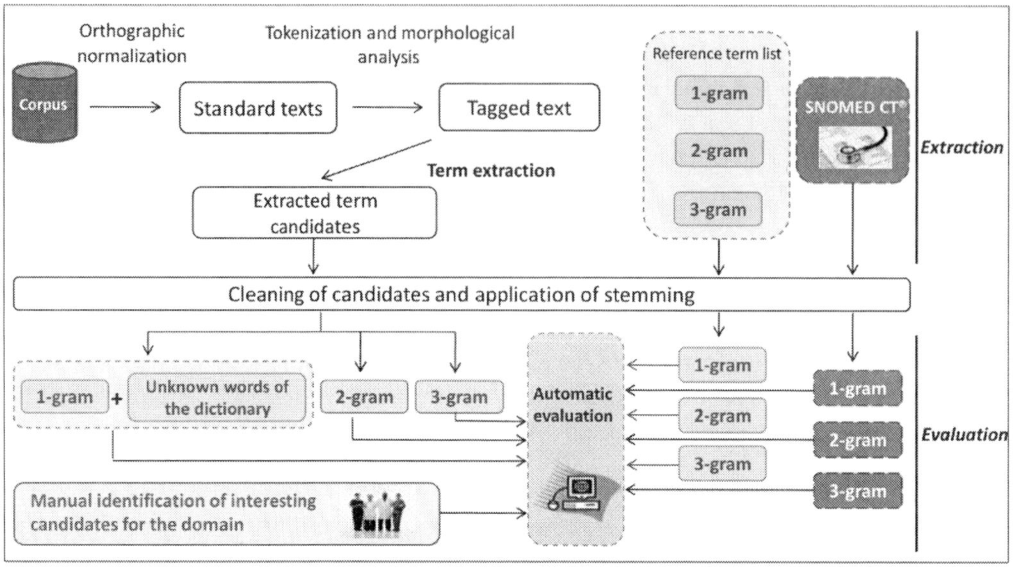

Figure 1: Term extraction and evaluation methodology.

is showed in Table 1. A total of 2,445 words of this corpus were not identified by the parser. This way, they were manually analyzed and added to the original dictionary of the program.

'Pruebas'.
['prueba', 'EMS','nom', 'GEN','fem', 'NUM','pl'].
['probar', 'EMS','v', 'EMS','ind', 'PERS','2a', 'NUM', 'sg', 'TPO','pres', 'TR','irr', 'TC','c1', 'TDIAL','est'].
'de'. ['de', 'EMS','prde'].
'provocación'.
['provocación', 'EMS','nom', 'GEN','fem', 'NUM','sg'].
'bronquial'.
['bronquial', 'EMS','adj', 'GEN','_', 'NUM','sg'].
'con'. ['con', 'EMS','prep'].
'ejercicio'.
['ejercicio', 'EMS','nom', 'GEN','masc', 'NUM','sg'].
'y'. ['y', 'EMS','cop'].
'con'. ['con', 'EMS','prep'].
'histamina'.
['histamina', 'EMS','nom', 'GEN','fem', 'NUM','sg'].
'en'. ['en', 'EMS','prep'].
'niños'.
['niño', 'EMS','nom', 'GEN','masc', 'NUM','pl'].
'asmáticos'.
['asmático', 'EMS','adj', 'GEN','masc', 'NUM','pl'].
'.' ['linsig', 'EMS','pun'].

Table 1: Morphological analysis SMORPH.

In the sequence, noun phrase recognition rules were developed. These rules are loaded into the MPS syntactic parser (Abbaci, 1999) that receives the SMORPH output as input.

Three different experiments were performed considering the noun phrase sub-classification.

For the first experiment (**Exp. NP**), all expressions previously tagged as NPs were considered as term candidates. For the second one (**Exp. S_NP**), after manual observations about the terms, some NP that could be relevant were subclassified. This subclassification considered the possibility that:

- the NP could be a verbal argument (NP_VARG): "*detectó la bronconeumonía*" (He *detects bronchopneumonia*). For it, the rule corresponding to the structure *NP + svn = NP_VARG* was created.

- the NP could be an antecedent of a non-defining clause (NP_NONDEF): "*el asma, que se traduce...*" (asthma, which means). Here we took several rules and an example of them is *NP + coma + relative + svn = NP_NONDEF*. Rules for non-defining clause recognition were created. For this work, we only considered that expression from the NP-antecedent until verb clause.

- the NP could be an item from an enumeration (NP_ENUM): "*dolor de garganta, fiebre y tos*" (headache, fever, and cough). An example of enumeration rule is *NP + coma + NP + conjunction + NP = NOM_COMP_ENUM* (Nominal complete enumeration).

- the NP could be in parentheses (NP_PARENT): *(fenoterol)*. The rule corresponding to the structure *parentheses*

of conjugation; c1: first conjugation; TDIAL: type of dialectal variety; est: standard; prde: preposition "*de*"; prep: preposition; masc: male; cop: copulative; sg: singular, linsing: next line; pun: dot.

+ NP + parentheses = NP_PARENT was created.

- the NP could be at the beginning of the clause (NP_INIC): "*...en los últimos años.* `El mecanismo inmunológico` *es...*" (...in recent years. `The immunological mechanism` is...). In this case, for the construction of the rule, the endpoint of the previous sentence was considered: *endpoint + NP = NP_INIC*. NP that appears at the beginning of clause was regarded as a candidate, because the candidate of this sentence position could be the subject or it could be a topicalized element. This rule considered that subjects and topicalized elements are relevant to the terminology extraction.

- the NP could be a argument of a prepositional phrase (PP) at the beginning of the clause (NP_PPINIC): "*...infección bacteriana.* `Para el diagnóstico`*...*" (...bacterial infection. `For diagnosis`...). In the same way as in the previous case, the endpoint of the sentence was considered: endpoint + preposition + NP = NP_PPINIC.

In the third experiment (**Exp. S_NP2**), we used the subclassification of *Exp. S_NP* and the NPs that are PP arguments were added: "*en estudios epidemiológicos*" (in epidemiological studies).

In all experiments, the **cleaning** of the extracted terms was carried out aiming at removing the numerals. This cleaning consists of discarding of candidates composed only of one letter, stopwords from the extremities of the candidates, and candidates that fully corresponded to stopwords. We used the stoplist available in the Snowball Project[5] and we added verb conjugations *poder* and *deber* and some words such as *año* (year), *días* (days), *algún* (any), etc., totaling 733 stopwords.

Also, in the case of NP_VERB, the right extremities *svn* were removed. For example, in the NP_VERB "*se detectan 636 asmáticos*" - (636 asthmatics were detected), after removing "se detectan" and cleaning this example, the candidate was reduced to: "*asmáticos*" (asthmatics).

Subsequently, in order to allow further evaluation, term candidates were separated into term lists of unigrams, bigrams, trigrams.

[5]Snowball Project - `http://snowball.tartarus.org/algorithms/spanish/stop.txt`

3.2 Results and evaluation of experiments

The number of extracted candidates is showed in Table 2.

	Unigrams	Bigrams	Trigrams
Experiment NP	1744	2684	1999
Experiment S_NP	856	1172	824
Experiment S_NP2	1188	1913	1419

Table 2: Number of extracted candidates.

Two automatic tests were carried out (Figure 1). In the first one, IULA **reference lists** were used to verify the quality of extracted candidates.

First of all, it was necessary to apply **stemming** techniques (PreTexT II tool (Soares et al., 2008)) to the extracted terms and reference term list, due to morphological variations in the words. Subsequently, it was possible to compare the extracted terms and the reference term list.

The accuracy and coverage for all three experiments (NP, S_NP and S_NP2) are showed in Figures 2, 3, and 4, respectively, for unigrams, bigrams, and trigrams. The figures are modified from Vivaldi and Rodríguez (2010) because they used the same corpus in their experiments, so, we also present a comparison between our and their results. In their work, *EWN* corresponds to the group of extracted terms using the YATE method (Vivaldi, 2001). The other terms were extracted with the Wikipedia categories (WP) having "Medicina" as domain name and varying the calculation of the domain coefficient. In *WP.lc*, the number of simple steps given in Wikipedia is considered; *WP.lmc* takes into consideration the mean number of paths in Wikipedia; *WP.nc* takes into consideration the number of paths in Wikipedia. It is important to notice that the extraction proposal of Vivaldi and Rodríguez only considered patterns with the following structures: (i) *noun* (for unigrams), (ii) *noun + adjective* (for bigrams), and (iii) *noun + the "de" preposition + noun* (for trigrams). This highly contrasts with our extraction that considers all possible combinations.

For the second test, the quality of the candidates was verified according to the SNOMED CT® list, which has 1,060,632 Spanish terms. Subsequently, the candidates that could be interesting for the medical domain were manually identified and, afterwards, we checked if those candidates were present or not in the SNOMED CT® list. The verification was done separately for each experiment (Exp. NP, Exp. S_NP, and Exp. S_NP2) and the results were separated into unigrams, bi-

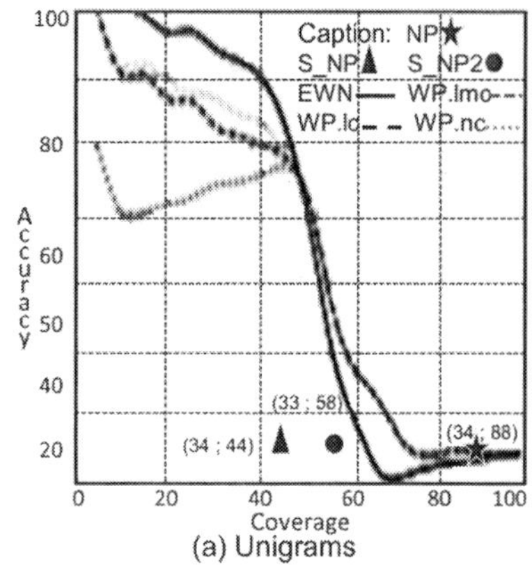

Figure 2: Accuracy and coverage values obtained for unigrams.

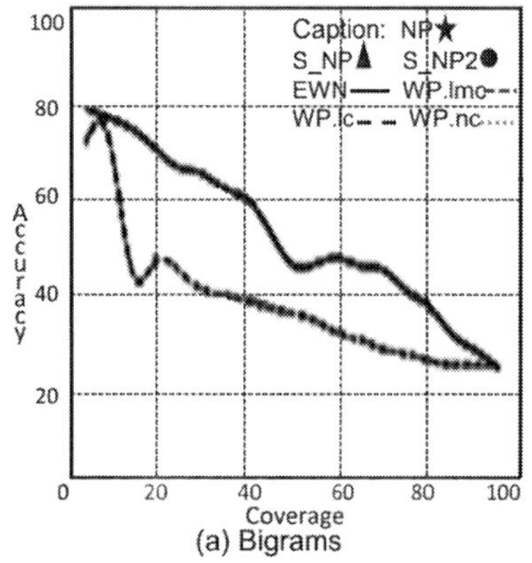

Figure 3: Accuracy and coverage values obtained for bigrams.

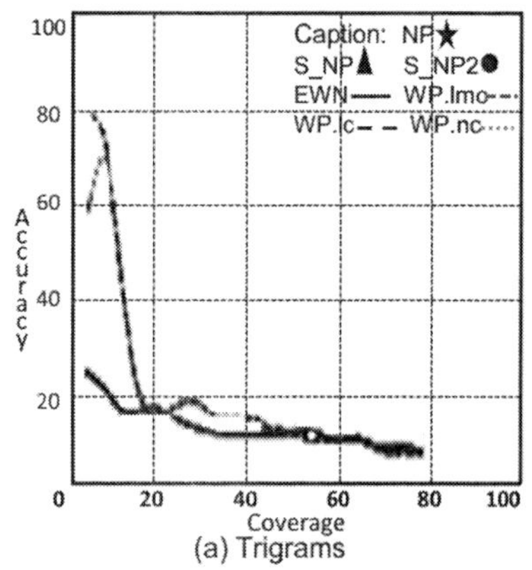

Figure 4: Accuracy and coverage values obtained for trigrams.

grams, and trigrams. The candidates that could represent terms according to the SNOMED CT® list are showed in Figure 5.

It is quite difficult to get a constant and immedi-

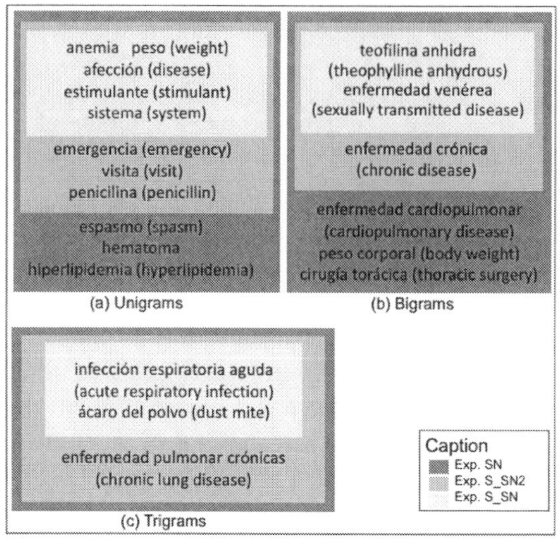

Figure 5: Extra terms obtained.

ate updating on medical terminology (Krauthammer and Nenadic, 2004). This fact motivated us to perform a **manual identification of candidates that are interesting for the medical domain**. These candidates were not present in the reference lists nor in SNOMED CT®, although they seem to be important for this specific domain. Here we present some examples: "*insuficiencia ventilatoria obstructiva*" (obstructive ventilatory failure), "*paciente asmático atópico*" (atopic asthmatic patient), (respiratory atopic diseases), "*traumatismo encéfalo craneano*" (traumatic brain injury), etc.

4 Conclusions

If we compare the three experiments carried out (NP, S_NP, and S_NP2), little accuracy variations are found for unigrams, bigrams, and trigrams, although the coverage varies in each case. We were able to obtain the best coverage in the first experiments, in which we took all NPs as term candidates. Nevertheless, we expected those results because most of the candidates are obtained when all NPs are extracted, and it allows for a large coverage. However, we expected better accuracy rates for the cases with "specific NPs".

In the comparison, we may see that the results obtained were similar to those of Vivaldi and Rodríguez in the case of unigrams, although they were able to obtain better results for bigrams and trigrams. Regarding this fact, we observed that the best accuracy rate was achieved with the experiments in which the NPs were part of an enumeration. Also, we emphasize the simplicity of our extraction method, which does not require external knowledge and was able to work well using the SMORPH dictionary and MPS recognition rules, also not considering only reference list patterns but all possibilities. In addition, better accuracy is expected by new and more specific MPS rules.

According to the results, we obtained three interesting contributions: (i) we were able to show the possibility of extracting medical terms from recognition of "specific NPs", even that it is necessary improvements in the method; (ii) the SMORPH dictionary was improved with 2,445 new terms. Thus, we expect to have better experiments in the medical domain with this tool; (iii) other terms that were not present in the reference lists were also extracted. Those terms were tested with the SNOMED CT® and we obtained terms that could be added to the IULA reference lists, which means an improvement of these lists. At the same time, we observed that there were other terms with a different structure from "noun + the 'de' preposition + noun". This evidences the fact that there exists important trigrams that do not necessarily fit to that pattern.

As future work, we intend to improvethe accuracy with new filtering rules, to increase the SMORPH dictionary, and to test the extraction rules in larger corpora and other domains.

Acknowledgments

Thanks to Erasmus Mundus, CNPq, FAPESP y CONICET for financial support and to Vivaldi y Rodríguez for making available the dataset.

References

F Abbaci. 1999. Développment du module post-smorph. In *Memória del DEA de Linguistique et Informatique*. Groupe de Recherche dans les Industries de la Langue - Universidad Blaise-Pascal - Clermont-Ferrand.

Rodrigo Alarcón. 2009. *Extracción automática de contextos definitorios en corpus especializados*. Ph.D. thesis, Universidad Pompeu Fabra, Barcelona.

S Aït-Mokhtar. 1998. *L'analyse présintaxique en une seule étape*. Ph.D. thesis, Groupe de Recherche dans les Industries de la Langue - Universidad Blaise-Pascal - Clermont-Ferrand.

Carme Bach, Roser Saurí Colomer, Jordi Vivaldi, and M. Teresa Cabré Castellví. 1997. El corpus de l'IULA: descripció. Technical Report 17, Universitat Pompeu Fabra – Institut Universitari de Lingüística Aplicada, Barcelona - Spain.

Marie-Noëlle Bessagnet, Eric Kergosien, and Mauro Gaio. 2010. Extraction de termes, reconnaissance et labellisation de relations dans un thésaurus. *CoRR*, abs/1002.0215.

Elena Castro, Ana Iglesias, Paloma Martínez, and Leonardo Castaño. 2010. Automatic identification of biomedical concepts in spanish-language unstructured clinical texts. In *Proceedings of the 1st ACM International Health Informatics Symposium*, pages 751–757, New York, NY, USA. ACM.

Li Hao-Min, Ying Li, Hui-Long Duan, and Xu-Dong Lv. 2008. Term extraction and negation detection method in chinese clinical document. *Chinese Journal of Biomedical Engineering*, 27(5).

Michael Krauthammer and Goran Nenadic. 2004. Term identification in the biomedical literature. *J. of Biomedical Informatics*, 37:512–526, December.

Lucelene Lopes, Renata Vieira, Maria Finatto, Daniel Martins, Adriano Zanette, and Luiz Ribeiro Jr. 2009. Extração automática de termos compostos para construção de ontologias: um experimento na área da saúde - doi: 10.3395/reciis.v3i1.244pt. *Revista Eletrônica de Comunicação, Informação e Inovação em Saúde*, 3(1).

Clara Inés López Rodríguez, Maribel Tercedor, and Pamela Faber. 2006. Gestión terminológica basada en el conocimiento y generación de recursos de información sobre el cáncer: el proyecto Oncoterm. *Revista E Salud*, 2(8).

A. Moreno-Sandoval. 2009. Terminología y Sociedad del conocimiento. pages 99–116. Peter Lang.

Aurélie Névéol and Sylwia Ozdowska. 2005. Extraction bilingue de termes médicaux dans un corpus parallèle anglais/français. In *EGC*, pages 655–666.

Gerardo Sierra, Rodrigo Alarcon, Alejandro Molina, and Edwin Aldana. 2009. Web exploitation for Definition extraction. In *Proceedings of the 2009 Latin American Web Congress*, pages 217–223, Washington, DC, USA. IEEE Computer Society.

M. V. B. Soares, R. C. Prati, and M. C. Monard. 2008. Pretext II: Descrição da reestruturacão da ferramenta de pré-processamento de textos. Technical Report 333, Instituto de Ciências Matemáticas e de Computação (ICMC) - USP - São Carlos, São Carlos - SP.

Jorge Vivaldi and Horacio Rodríguez. 2010. Using wikipedia for term extraction in the biomedical domain: first experiences. *Procesamiento del Lenguaje Natural*, 45:251–254.

Jorge Vivaldi. 2001. *Extracción de candidatos a término mediante combinación de estrategias heterogéneas*. Ph.D. thesis, Universitat Politécnica de Catalunya, Barcelona, Spain.

Adaptive Feedback Message Generation for Second Language Learners of Arabic

Khaled Shaalan
The British University in Dubai,
PO Box 345015 Dubai, UAE
khaled.shaalan@buid.ac.ae

Marwa Magdy
Faculty of Computers & Information,
Cairo University, 12613 Egypt
m.magdy@fci-cu.edu.eg

Abstract

This paper addresses issues related to generating feedback messages to errors related to Arabic verbs made by second language learners (SLLs). The proposed approach allows for individualization. When a SLL of Arabic writes a wrong verb, it performs analysis of the input and distinguishes between different lexical error types. The proposed system issues the intelligent feedback that conforms to the learner's proficiency level for each class of error. The proposed system has been effectively evaluated using real test data and achieved satisfactory results.

1 Introduction

Second language acquisition is a difficult task. There are various methods to acquire a new language and all of them require some form of feedback, a reaction to what has been said or written. The recent trend is to automate the feedback through Intelligent Language Tutoring System (ILTS).

The current trend concentrates on NLP tools and techniques geared towards the diagnosis of errors produced by SLLs and identifying the cause of their errors rather than providing the correct version directly.

This paper is about the generation of feedback message based on individual proficiency levels. The proficiency level measure is based on the progression in the learner answers. In particular, when a SLL of Arabic writes a wrong verb, it distinguishes between this set of lexical error types: *lexical category selection, pattern selection, tense selection, mood selection, subject-verb agreement, verb conjugation, connected pronouns* and/or *consonant,* and *vowel letters.* Nevertheless, it provides the intelligent feedback that conforms to the learner's expertise for each class of error. There are three learning levels for each concept covered: *beginner, intermediate* and *advanced.* A learner who generally has mastered an Arabic concept might receive a hint just indicating the *class of error.* Whereas, the learner who generally knows the concept but still needs practice in its application the feedback is the *type of the error.* For the beginner learning level, the feedback is as specific as possible, the exact *source of the error* is provided.

The edit distance technique is employed to analyze the erroneous Arabic verb. The deep analysis of the learner input helps in accurately detecting the lexical errors and issuing the appropriate feedback to the learner.

To the best of our knowledge, very few researches has considered true diagnosis and issuing feedback of Arabic lexical errors. For example, Shaalan (2005a; 2005b) has developed an ILTS system for Arabic learners which just embed specific morphological analysis rules to provide feedback. In addition, there exist some systems that are designed for SLLs of other languages than Arabic which still keep the behavior of spell checkers (Faltin et al., 2005; Faltin, 2003; Rimrott, 2003; Hsieh et al., 2002).

The rest of this paper is structured as follows. Section 2 introduces an analysis of Arabic lexical errors. Section 3 describes the proposed model. Section 4 discusses the results. Section 5 gives concluding remarks.

2 Arabic Lexical Error Typology

To decide on the set of errors handled, we investigated the literature which defined the most frequent types of errors made by Arabic SLLs (cf. Ali 1998; Abd Alghaniy 1998; Jassem 2000). These errors can be classified into: *Errors in word formation, Errors in semantic or word choice* and *Errors at the interface of lexical and grammar.* Tables 1 through 4 provide details of lexical errors.

Error Type	Source of Error
Verb pattern Acronym: VP	Incorrect usage of root pattern. Wrong: أتوصل*/Âa-tawaS~al/[1] (I-arrive). Correct: أواصل /Âu-wASil/ (I-continue)

Table 1: Semantic or Word Choice Errors

Error Type	Source of Error
Connected pronouns Acronym: CP	Incorrect usage of pronouns with respect to verb tense. Wrong: يجئت* /ya-jiŷ.-tu/ (I-he-came) Correct: جئت /jiŷ.-tu/ (I-came)
Verb conjugation Acronym: VC	Incorrect conjugation of Arabic weak verbs. wrong: نجو* /najaw/ correct: نجا /najA/ (he escaped)

Table 2: Word Formation Errors due to Morphology

Error Type	Source of Error
Consonant letters Acronym: CL	Incorrect usage of letters with a closely related pronunciation. Wrong: أصتطيع* /Âa-S.taTiyς/ Correct: أستطيع /Âa-s.taTiyς / (I-am-able).
Vowel letters Acronym: VL	Making short vowel a long one. Wrong: أصباحت* /ÂaS.bAH-at/. Correct: أصبحت /ÂaS.baH-at / (be-came)
	Making long vowel a short one. Wrong: تزرين* /ta-zuri-yna/. Correct: تزورين /ta-zwri-yna/ (you-visit)

Table 3: Word Formation Errors due to Phonology

3 System Overview

The proposed system is specially designed for individualized SLL of Arabic. The objective test method is used such that the expected learner's answer is relatively short and well-focused[2]. The system contains the following components:

The *lexical error checker* is an NLP component that analyzes the learner's answer and detects possible source of errors. It gets the initial error detection assumptions about each word in the learner answer from the word analyzer module such as the one explained in (Shaalan et al., 2010a; Shaalan et al., 2011).

Error Type	Source of Error
Lexical category Acronym: LC	Switching a conjugated verb with its infinitive, e.g. Wrong: الصلاة* /AlSalAah/ (the-praying) Correct: أصلي /Âu-Sal~iy/ (I-pray)
	Switching an infinitive with its conjugated verb, e.g. Wrong word: بعت* /biς.-tu/ (I-sold) Correct word: البيع /Albay. ς/ (the-selling)
Verb tense Acronym: VT	Using incorrect verb tense, e.g. Wrong word: نريد* /nu-riyd/ (we-want) Correct word: أرادنا /ÂarAda-nA/ (we-wanted)
Disagreement of a connected pronoun with the subject Acronym: SVD	The disagreement may be in gender, number and person disagreement, e.g. Wrong word: ليؤدي* /liyu-ŵad~iy/ (to-pray-he) Correct word: لأودي /liÂu-ŵad~iy/ (to-pray-I)
Verb mood Acronym: VM	Using incorrect verb mood, e.g. Wrong: يأتي* /ya-Â.tiy/ (he-come [indicative]) Correct: يأت /ya-Â.t/ (he-come [jussive])

Table 4: Errors at the Interface of Lexical and Grammar

This module generates all possible word analyses for each ill-formed input. It uses constraint relaxation and edit-distance techniques to split each erroneous word into three possible segments: *prefix+stem+suffix*. Then the lexical error checker proceeds to detect source of errors using edit distance techniques. *Tutoring module* is responsible for initialization of the student model and issuing appropriate error specific feedback message suited to the learner's expertise level. The proposed system keeps a record of the learner's performance history. This information is held in the *student model*. The *item banking* component contains different types of questions to be issued to the learner.

[1] Habash et al. (2007) Arabic transliteration is used here to Romanize Arabic examples.

[2] There is only one possible correct answer

3.1 Item Banking

The item banking is a database of test items. It includes different types of questions like Dictation, Word order, Build a sentence, Transform a sentence category, Word formation practice and Fill in blank.

Each question is accompanied by an associated list of concepts to test how well the learner has mastered them. Furthermore, each question has some parameters that help the system to diagnose errors. The parameter list is a list of *feature structures* (FSs) for all Arabic words in the correct answer. They include features: *correct word without diacritics, correct word with diacritics, root, pattern, type of verb, prefix string, suffix string, lexical category, tense, voice, mood, subject, object gender, number* and *person.*

3.2 Student Model

The student model used here contains only information about the proficiency level of the student. The *perturbation error* model is used to represent this knowledge. In this model, there exist one or more misconceptions for each concept in an introductory course for teaching Arabic weak verbs. For example, the *vowel letters* concept has two associated misconceptions: *make short vowel long one* and the vice versa.

For each concept along with its associated bug, the student model keeps a frequency of this error, to each student, which falls in the range of one of the three learning levels. The frequency of the bug is expressed by a number pair [*S*, *T*]; where the variable *S* represents how many times the student has made this error and the variable T represents the total number of times in which the student has met this concept.

3.3 Lexical Error Checker

This module gets its input from the word analyzer module. The input presents all possible initial analyses for each erroneous word in the learner answer. These analyses consist of five elements: prefix, stem, suffix, FS that describes the analyzed word, and an initial error indication. The later is a list that denotes: the required editing operation (e.g., insert) to the affix string, the actual character and the position where the operation should take place. For example, if the learner writes the wrong verb قالتو* /qAl.-tw/ (told-I). The input of the lexical error checker in this case is as follows:

Prefix: Null, **Stem:** "قال", **Suffix:** "ت", **FS:** first person singular perfect verb, **Error indication:** [insert('و',5)]

The objective of the lexical error checker is to detect errors in the stem string and to confirm errors in affixes given from the word analyzer module. It contains the following components: error analysis, error classification, filtering module.

3.3.1 Error Analysis Module

This module proceeds with the analysis of all words in the learner's answer. It receives a list containing all possible word analyses from word analyzer module and all possible analyses that have the same root as the correct answer from the morphological analyzer module. And then generate the final analysis of the input words. The following shows how this module works:

Example 1: Write a sentence using the following Arabic roots. ق-و-ل، ح-ق، د-و-م /q-w-l, H-q, d-w-m/.

Assume the following two answers; where (a) includes a wrong conjugation of a Hollow (middle weak) verb, and (b) is the correct answer.

a. **قالتو*** الحق دائما /qAl.-tw AlHaq~ dAŷimAã/ (I always told the-truth).

b. **أقول** الحق دائما /Âa-quwl AlHaq~ dAŷimAã/ (I always tell the-truth).

Step1: the morphological analyzer does not result in any solution that has the same root as correct answer ق-و-ل /q-w-l/. However, applying the word analyzer module on the word قالتو* /qAl.-tw/ (I-told) results in only one solution, '*first person singular perfect verb active voice with extra Waw in the affix*', which becomes the output of step 1.

Step2: The input solution list could be minimized by a number of factors: learner's answer, question parameters, and error categories handled by the system. We derived a set of heuristic rules to discard irrelevant solutions. An example of these rules is given in Table 5.

Step3: For every solution in the list, the system morphologically generates a well-formed stem. A shallow morphological generator is developed that is based on the notion of a Morphological Form Hierarchy (MFH) or tree (Cavalli et al., 2000). The input of this module is a FS.

The transformation rules attached to each leaf node of the MFH effects the desired morphological transformations for that node. The output of the transformation is the *transformed stem* string from the root string. Figure 1 shows an example of a rule attached to a node in the MFH.

Rule (1): Description
IF the **affix string** in the learner answer **matches** the **correct** affix string *AND* the **FS** of the **correct answer** does not **match** with the FS of the **learner answer** *THEN* discard this solution.
Example: if the learner writes the word قالت /qAl.-tu/ (I-told) instead of قلت /qul-tu/ (I-told), the system will extract **four** suffixes that have the same orthographic form but differ in their meaning. All these suffixes except 1st singular suffix are discarded

Table 5: An example of a filtering rule

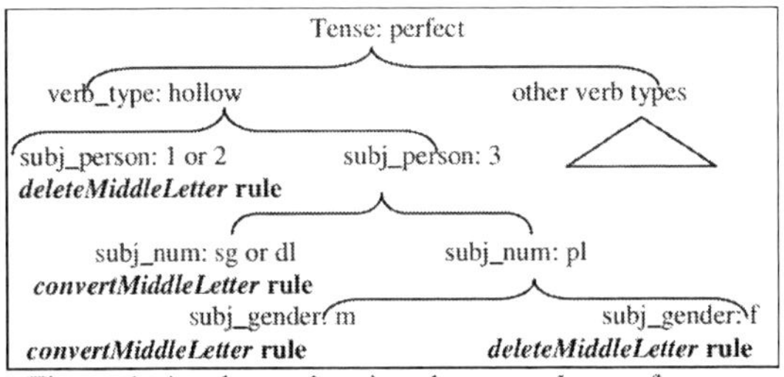

Figure 1: A subtree showing the stem change for perfect verbs of pattern فعل/faEala/

The rationale behind this module is that the specified FS is matched against the features defining each subtree until a leaf is reached. At that point, the transformation rule attached to the leaf node is tried. If no rule is found or none of the clauses of the applicable rule match, it returns the value of *root* unchanged. After applying this step on Example 1, it produces the stem قل /qul/

Step4: In this step, the system matches the generated stem with the extracted (analyzed) one using *three-way-match* method (Elmi and Evens 1998). The inserted and deleted characters are only constraints to be weak letters[3]. Also, the converted characters should only be performed with another one that has similar pronunciation. The matching process works as follows: partition the two words according to the following patterns the generated stem pattern = x*u*z and extracted stem pattern = x*v*z. Where *x* is the initial segment, *z* is the tail segment; *u* and *v* are the error segments. First, the initial segment is selected. The tail segment is processed likewise. Finally, the error segments are the remaining characters of the two words.

[3] This is because the learner may have a problem in either verb conjugation or vowel letters.

Applying this step on Example 1, the extracted stem is قال /qAl/ while the generated one is قل /qul/. The matched initial segment is {ق} and the matched tail segment is {ل}. The error segment for the extracted stem is {ا} whereas it is empty for the generated stem. Therefore, the system concludes that there is some extra character ا /A/. This extra character does not match the diacritic sign of the generated word at this position (i.e. the added character is ا while the diacritic sign at second position is ضمة /u/).

Step5: Ambiguity is a standard problem in any NLP application. In ILTS, relaxing the constraints of the language in order to be able to analyze learner's answer generally produces more interpretations than systems designed for only well-formed input. The ambiguity problem mentioned here is discussed and partially solved in (Shaalan et al., 2010b).

3.3.2 Error Classification Module

This module will recognize different error types from word analysis structure. It contains a set of *if-then* rules to recognize different error types. Examples of these rules are given below.

```
Rule Make Short Vowel long one Error:
IF there is an inserted character in
the affix OR (there is an inserted
character in the stem AND this char-
acter matches with the diacritic sign
at this position of the correct word)
THEN the error in vowel letters. The
parameter of this error is ["short",
"long"]
```

Notice that the learner might make multiple errors in his input. So, this module exhaustively tests *all* IF-statements to detect all possible error types the learner has made.

Applying this module on the input word قالتو /qAl.-tw/ (I-told), it detects that the learner has made three errors: 1) *Verb tense* error since the correct word tense is *imperfect* while the analyzed one is *perfect,* 2) *Make short vowel long one* since there is an extra character in affix, and 3) *Verb conjugation* error since there is an extra character at position 2 in the stem and this character does not match the correct diacritic sign.

3.3.3 Filtering Module

This module accommodates multiple errors, instructional feedback messages need to be prioritized by the system and displayed one at a time to the student to avoid multiple error reports.

The system maintains an error priority queue to rank feedback with respect to the dependency of errors, e.g. verb tense error has higher priority than verb conjugation error.

3.4 Tutoring Module

This module is responsible for initializing the student model for each new registered student and issuing appropriate error specific feedback message suited to the learner's level. The initialization process is to set the frequency of all bugs in the student model to `[0, 0]`.

The feedback system is responsible for generating feedback messages that conform to the learner's expertise. It includes *error database* and *feedback message generator*. The error database contains a specification of all different errors categories handled by the system.

The feedback message generator module receives a number that defines proficiency level according to this error- beginner or intermediate or advanced. In addition, it receives the error type along with its parameters. Then, it proceeds as follows: for the advanced learning level, the feedback is to provide a hint to the class of the error. For the intermediate, it provides the type of error. For the beginner, the feedback refers to the exact source of the error. For example, the advanced learner will get the following message "error at the interface of lexical and grammar". While the intermediate will get "verb tense error". The beginner message is "incorrect use of perfect verb instead of imperfect"

4 System Evaluation

We conducted an experiment that measures how successfully the proposed model diagnoses errors and provides correct error specific feedback that conforms to the learning level. The *quantitative* measures are used. These measures rely on collecting different test sets written by real SLLs in a typical teaching/learning environment. It was necessary that these learners have different backgrounds (i.e., differ in their first language) to test if the system is general enough and not aimed to a specific sort of learners. The different types of errors and the exact source of errors in the test set are *subjectively* identified by a human specialist to produce the reference set. The test set is then fed into the system and the detected and undetected errors are reported. The recall rate for each error type is calculated.

The above mentioned methodology is applied on a real test set that consists of 116 real Arabic sentences. Table 6 summarizes the evaluation results. The first column in this table describes the different error types while the second column presents the total number of occurrences of each error type in the test set. The rest of columns present the recall rate of fully diagnosed errors, partially-diagnosed, and general error indication, respectively.

Error Type	N	*fully Diagnosed*		Partially diagnosed		General Error indication	
		N	%	N	%	N	%
CL	8	8	100	0	0	0	0
VL	24	19	79.2	0	0	5	20.8
VC	21	14	66.7	1	4.8	6	28.6
CP	7	6	85.7	0	0	1	14.3
VP	14	8	57.1	3	21.4	3	21.4
LC	16	14	87.5	0	0	2	12.5
VT	17	11	64.7	0	0	6	35.3
SVD	24	17	70.8	5	20.8	2	8.3
VM	2	2	100	0	0	0	0
Total	133	99	74.4	9	6.8	25	18.8

Table 6: Evaluation Results

Notice, however, the error specific feedback message produced by the system in cases of partially diagnosed errors is the same for both the beginner and intermediate learning level. This is because the source of error was not detected by the system. While the feedback message in cases of general error indication is a catch-all error message for all learning levels.

The highly recall rate is for *consonant letters* and *verb mood* (100%). While the less recall rate is for *verb pattern* (57.1%). This is because of the ambiguity problem. The system has no direct knowledge of what the student meant to express. For example, if the learner writes the word علمت instead of تعلمت /ta-çal~am-tu/ (I-study). It is not clear whether the learner meant علمت /çalim-tu/ (I-knew) by using the pattern فعل /façil/ or علّمت /çal~am-tu/ (I-taught) by using the pattern فعّل /façal/. The system successfully detects that the error type is *verb pattern* but fails to identify the exact wrong pattern. Therefore the feedback message for both beginner and intermediate learner in this case is the same "incorrect use of verb pattern".

5 Conclusion

Learning Arabic language is a challenge because of its complex linguistic structure which poses a difficulty to SLLs. They not only make errors done by native speakers but also others that arise due to competence issues. Our study indicated that using methods and tools designed for a native speaker spell checking is certain to be inadequate, especially for highly derivational and inflectional languages such as Arabic. Therefore, we adopted methods and tools that meet the SLLs of Arabic needs. Moreover, those learners want to improve their language skills in order not to fall in the same mistakes very often. Therefore, it was appropriate that we developed a diagnosis system, letting the learners find out the correct solution for themselves. Error messages point the learner to the right direction for correction.

In order to evaluate our approach, we acquired a test data set from a real educational SLLs environment. In the absence of a complete computationally erroneous Arabic corpus, either for research or commercial purposes, we only could manually collect a relatively small test set. Fortunately, it was sufficient to show that approach and techniques employed in this paper have successfully analyzed ill-formed verbs written by SLLs of Arabic. Nevertheless, it shows the capability of issuing an intelligent feedback message that conforms to the learner proficiency level allowing the system to perform individualization in the teaching process.

The approach and techniques described in this research can be used with other Semitic languages which share similar morphological features of Arabic to provide appropriate feedback to their SLLs.

References

Abd Alghaniy, K. E. 1998. Arabic and Malaysian Languages from Phonological and Morphological Perspective: A Contrastive Analysis Approach. Master Thesis, Cairo University, Egypt, 1998.

Ali, M. B. 1998. Linguistic Analysis of Mistakes by Students at the University of Malaya: An Error Analysis Approach. Master Thesis, Cairo University, Egypt, 1998.

Cavalli-Sforza, V., Soudi, A. and Mitamura, T. 2000. Arabic Morphology Generation Using a Concatenative Strategy. In Proceedings of the 1st Conference, NAACL 00. Seattle, Washington, pp: 86-93.

Elmi, M. A. and Evens, M. 1998. Spelling Correction Using Context. In Proceedings of 36th ACL 98, Montreal, Canada, pp: 360-364.

Faltin, A. V., L'haire, S. and Ndiaye, M. 2005. A Spell Checker for Language Learners of French and a Learner Corpus. In Proceedings of EUROCALL 05. Cracow, Poland.

Faltin, A. V. 2003. Syntactic Error Diagnosis in the Context of Computer Assisted Language Learning. PhD Thesis, University of Geneva, Switzerland, 2003.

Habash, N., Soudi, A., and Buckwalter, T. 2007. On Arabic Transliteration. In Arabic Computational Morphology: Knowledge-based and Empirical Methods. Soudi, Abdelhadi; van den Bosch, Antal; Neumann, Günter (Eds.), 2007. ISBN: 978-1-4020-6045-8

Hsieh, C.-C., Tsai, T.-H., Wible, D. and Hsu, W.-L. 2002. Exploiting Knowledge Representation in an Intelligent Tutoring System for English Lexical Errors. In Proceedings of ICCE 2002, Auckland, New Zealand, pp: 115-116.

Jassem, J. A. 2000. Study on Second Language Learners of Arabic: An Error Analysis Approach. Kuala Lumpur (Malaysia): A.S. Noordeen. ISBN 983-065-093-6.

Rimrott, A. 2003. SANTY: A Spell Checking Algorithm for Treating Predictable Verb Inflection Mistakes Made by Non-Native Writers of German. Term Paper for LING 807 – Computational Linguistics at Simon Fraser University (Burnaby, Canada).

Shaalan, K., Magdy, M., Fahmy, A. 2011. Morphological analysis of ill formed Arabic verbs for second language learners. In McCarthy, P.M & Boonthum, C. (ed.), Applied Natural Language Processing and content analysis: Identification, Investigation, and Resolution (In Press).

Shaalan, K., Magdy, M., Fahmy, A. 2010a. Morphological Analysis of Ill-formed Arabic Verbs in Intelligent Language Tutoring Framework. In the Proceedings of FLAIRS-23, Applied Natural Language Processing Track, Florida, USA, 2010.

Shaalan, K., Samy, D. and Magdy, M. 2010b. Towards Resolving Morphological Ambiguity in Arabic Intelligent Language Tutoring Framework. In Proceedings of International Workshop on Supporting e-Learning with Language Resources and Semantic Data (LREC 2010), Valletta, Malta

Shaalan K. 2005a. An Intelligent Computer Assisted Language Learning System for Arabic Learners, in Computer Assisted Language Learning: An International Journal, Taylor & Francis Group Ltd., 18(1 & 2): 81-108.

Shaalan K. 2005b. Arabic GramCheck: A Grammar Checker for Arabic, Software Practice and Experience, John Wiley & sons Ltd., UK, 35(7):643-665.

Building a Patient-based Ontology for User-written Web Messages

Marina Sokolova
Faculty of Medicine,
University of Ottawa
and
Electronic Health Information Lab,
CHEO Research Institute
sokolova@uottawa.ca

David Schramm
Faculty of Medicine,
University of Ottawa
and
Children's Hospital of Eastern Ontario
The Ottawa Hospital
dschramm@toh.on.ca

Abstract

We introduce an ontology that is representative of health discussions and vocabulary used by the general public. The ontology structure is built upon general categories of information that patients use when describing their health in clinical encounters. The pilot study shows that the general structure makes the ontology useful in text mining of social networking web sites.

1 Introduction

Recent studies have shown that public health surveillance benefits from information posted by users on the Web (Carneiro and Mylonakis, 2009; Ginsberg et al, 2008). Health-related messages can be found on Web forums hosting social networks (e.g., www.PatientsLikeMe.com) or individual blogs (e.g., http://www.jackslemonade.com).

For medical professionals, the user-written health information assists in prediction of public attitude towards health policies. In user messages, patient-based information prevails over biomedical information. Patient-based information is brought forth when a user views himself as a potential or real patient of a health care provider. This information reveals details of one's health that are usually discussed during visits to a health care provider. Patient-based information is often identified as evidence-based, whereas the biomedical information is viewed as knowledge-based (Hersh, 2009).

Development of social media has prompted refocusing of text analysis from biomedical to patient-based health information mining. Several academic groups actively work on health information studies (Angelova, 2010; Chapman, 2010; Chanlekha and Collier, 2010). These groups work on methods for the analysis of academic and professional articles in medical journals and traditional news media, as well as hospital documentation.

At present, user-written health information is the subject of studies by data mining where the analysis primarily relies on statistical methods (Lampos and Christianini, 2010) and public health informatics which usually addresses specific questions, e.g., injury discussions by military servicemen (Konovalov et al, 2010).

A prevalent trend in health-related text analysis is to solve a particular task which is closely associated with a particular data source, e.g., identifying involuntary childlessness terminology on a dedicated web site (Himmel et al., 2009) or finding new terms used on a patient social networking site (Doing-Harris and Zeng-Treiler, 2011). The specific focus makes the accumulated knowledge inherently individualized towards the task and the data. It permits high accuracy on the original data, whereas shifting to other data sets is likely to experience performance set-back.

Our goal is to build a patient-based resource organized as an ontology, a repository of health-related terms assigned into a hierarchical structure of semantic categories. The general categories are durable and able to withstand the rapidly evolving environment of the Web. In an empirical setting, we show that the ontology content is representative of health-related topics and vocabulary used by the general public on the Web.

2 Motivation

Major health concerns, related events and issues, and behavioural trends can be identified from what people post on social networks. The importance of this analysis became more pronounced during the H1N1 pandemic as recent research demonstrates (Lampos and Christianini, 2010).

User-written health information extraction can be challenging in a two-fold way:

Twitter
11: i can't cos i haven't slept yet and it's 9:43am. i'm having some serious insomnia. i'm trying to sleep but i keep checking mail. 12: the doctor came, examined me and told me i had early tonsilitis. will look it up on the net. i'm in my mom's room while my room aerates.
20 News groups
I sometimes see OTC preparations for muscle aches/back aches that combine aspirin with a diuretic. The idea seems to be to reduce inflammation by getting rid of fluid. Does this actually work?
MySpace
i thouroughly understand ur point though, my grandmother has lung cancer so i cant stand smoking, its all a personal choice; you cant change someones mind if they choose not to listen. . . .
Amazon.com
Just purchased this blender & am returning it immediately. It has a number of terrible features: it's very difficult to remove the cover if you have carpal tunnel, arthritis, or weak hands.

Figure 1: Examples of user messages.

i various web sites host texts written in different styles (Figure 1 lists samples from four web sites); thus, a site-specific method has an application range limited to the site;

ii existing text mining tools focus on biomedical and professional terminology that may be absent in social media (Casoto et al, 2010); as a result, these tools need a considerable readjustment before application to user-written text.

Standardized classification of diseases and other health-related problems is critical for epidemiologic and health management purposes. At the same time, there are few publications dedicated to user-written health information. In one study (Doing-Harris and Zeng-Treiler, 2011), the authors looked for new health-related terms in messages posted on `PatientsLikeMe.com`. User requests posted on an involuntary childlessness message board were studied in (Himmel et al., 2009). Blogs written by military servicemen were studied by (Konovalov et al, 2010). The researchers sought terms that described clinically relevant combat exposure. All the three listed studies have a restricted appeal: each was carried out on one data set only and was not applied or reproduced on other data sets.

Biomedical information extraction and text classification have a successful history of method and tool development, including deployed information retrieval systems (Hersh, 2009), knowledge resources and ontologies (Cohen et al, 2010; Yu, 2006). Exponential increase in bio-, bioinformatics and medical publications has caused a rapid development of ontologies that help to recognize and categorize research and professional vocabulary (Yu, 2006). We discuss here a few examples.

GENIA[1] is built for the microbiology domain. Categories include DNA-metabolism, Protein-metabolism, and Cellular process. *Medical Subjects Heading (MeSH)* is a controlled vocabulary thesaurus, produced by the National Library of Medicine[2]. Its terms are informative to experts but might not be in use by the general public (e.g., Work Schedule Tolerance at the top level and Motor Cortex, Trypanosoma cruzi at the bottom level). The *Medical Entities Dictionary (MED)*[3] is an ontology containing approximately $60,000$ concepts, $208,000$ synonyms, and $84,000$ hierarchies. This powerful lexical and knowledge resource is designed with medical research vocabulary in mind. *Unified Medical Language System (UMLS)* has 135 semantic types and 54 relations that include organisms, anatomical structures, biological functions, chemicals, etc.

Another internationally recognized classification scheme is the Systematized Nomenclature of Medicine Clinical Terms (*SNOMED CT*) maintained by the International Health Terminology Standards Development Organization.[4] Although *SNOWMED CT* is considered to be the most comprehensive clinical health care terminology classification system, it is primarily used to permit standardization of electronic medical records rather than to mine user-written health-related content. A public health ontology *BioCaster*[5] is built for surveillance of traditional media. It helps to find disease outbreaks and predict possible epidemic threats.

[1] `http://www-tsujii.is.s.u-tokyo.ac.jp/-genia/topics/Corpus/genia-ontology.html`

[2] `http://www.nlm.nih.gov/mesh/`

[3] `http://med.dmi.columbia.edu/`

[4] `http://www.nlm.nih.gov/research/umls/Snomed/snomed$\_$faq.html` Accessed 18/07/2011

[5] `http://born.nii.ac.jp/?page=ontology`

All these sources would require considerable modification before they could be used for analysis of messages posted on public Web forums.

3 Methodology

Adequate patient treatment depends on a correct understanding of what people say about their health and cross-referencing of the terms they use (Aspden et al., 2003). We began by building a set of semantic categories that a patient would use when discussing personal health in a clinical setting.

There are several internationally accepted interrelated disease and health-related problems classification schemes:

- The International Statistical Classification of Diseases and Related Health Problems (ICD-10) developed by The World Health Organization is the internationally recognized standard diagnostic classification system (ICD–10, 2004).

- The International Classification of Procedures in Medicine (ICPM) categorizes medical and surgical procedures (ICPM, 1978).

- The International Classification of Functioning, Disability and Health (ICF) categorizes and qualifies disability, physiological functioning of body systems and their impairment, anatomical parts of the body and their impairment, activities of an individual and their limitations, participation in life situations and their restrictions, and health-related environmental factors (ICF, 2001).

We amalgamated and streamlined these international health related classification scheme taxonomies to facilitate the classification of user-written health-related content on the web. Extensive clinical experience of one of the authors was applied to empirically adapt the classification scheme to users' description of their health on various social networking web sites. Figure 2 shows the ontology structure.

We populate the categories with terms found in sources that provide patient-friendly terminology.[6] Many of the terms utilized in the International Classification of Functioning, Disability and Health (ICF) and International Statistical Classification of Diseases and Related Health Problems (ICD-10) nomenclature are typical of the vocabulary that individuals may use to describe their health related states (adapted for Diseases and Symptoms subcategories).

We used Merriam-Webster Visual Dictionary to add the Person terms and Webster's New World Medical Dictionary to the Procedures subcategory. Provider and Setting terms were adapted from lists of certified medical doctor boards [7] and associations of other health occupations[8].

- Person
  - Anatomical parts of the body
  - Physiological functioning of body
- Diseases and Health-Related Problems
  - Diseases
  - Symptoms
- Health Care System
  - Health Care Providers
    * Physician
    * Nurse
    * Physiotherapist
    * Psychologist
    * Other Health Care Provider
  - Health Care Setting
    * Hospital
    * Ambulatory surgery center
    * Physician Office
    * Community Health Care Clinic
    * Other Health Care Setting
  - Health Care Procedures
    * Diagnostic
    * Therapeutic
- Health-Related Environmental Factors
  - Physical
  - Social
  - Attitudinal

Figure 2: The structure of the ontology.

[6] The ontology is posted on http://www.ehealthinformation.ca/ap0/opendata.asp.

[7] http://www.certificationmatters.org/about-board-certified-doctors/

[8] http://www.ama-assn.org/ama/pub/

4 Data

To assess the ontology usefulness, we used publicly available data sets *20 News Groups*[9], *Twitter* and *MySpace* [10], and *Amazon.com*[11].

20 News groups has $20,000$ texts divided into 20 groups, including a group of medical texts. The medical group consists of 990 messages gathered from Web chat boards. In these messages, users discuss their health problems, ask questions pertaining to health, give advice and share relevant experience. The set has $239,120$ words, an average length of a message is 242 words, including partial citations of previous messages when applicable. Full grammatical constructs and a rich lexicon make the messages reminiscent of a more traditional, pre-Internet writing.

Twitter is a micro-blogging service, with instant message postings. It is organized as a social network of Twitter users. A user can post short messages, no longer than 140 characters, that are publicly visible by default. Other users can subscribe to these tweets (i.e., become followers) and respond with their messages. A user can group his messages by topic or types and make them accessible only to followers. URL shortening is common, e.g., *goo.gl* for *www.google.com*. Other condensing happens through shorthand (e.g., "LOL" (laugh out loud),"DWT" (driving while texting), "4gt"(forgot)) and emoticons (e.g., `;-)`).

We worked with $30,164$ threads of consequent tweets. The treads are split into two subsets, $3,754,668$ and $15,199,470$ words. An average length of a thread is 560 words, albeit some words can be very short (e.g., "u","4").

MySpace (aka My___, Myspace) has been a leading social network in 2006 – 2008, when 95 million unique users visited the web site in a year. Friends can leave their comments in the user's "Friends Space"; it is left to the user's discretion to keep or delete those comments or mandate to approve them before posting. Users can assign emoticons to posts (e.g., `:-O`, `:-()`. Ability to reach all friends simultaneously is given through bulletins, messages posted on the bulletin board and remaining there for 10 days. Profiles have enhanced blogging that promotes longer posts. However, a typical post may exhibit the Internetspeak features, such as the the shorthand and simplified grammar (e.g., "l8r" (later), "c u" (see you)).

We analyzed $18,178$ posts split into four subsets of $218,628$, $1,219,730$, $1,987,495$ and $9,403,345$ words respectively. An average length of a post available to us is 167 words.

Amazon.com posts user reviews of consumer products. In the reviews, users share their experience and opinion about the products. Those comments are often accompanied or illustrated by a narrative of real life events included health-related problems. Messages are organized according to the types of the assessed goods.

We worked with $8,000$ reviews, evenly split along four topics: books ($349,530$ words) , DVD ($337,473$ words), electronics ($222,862$ words), and kitchen&houseware ($188,137$ words). An average length of reviews is counted in words: books – 175, DVD – 169, Electronics – 111, Kitchen – 99. The grammatical structure and vocabulary are rich enough to provide meaningful communication and lexical information.

5 Empirical Results

We built N-gram word models ($N = 1,2,3,4$). The N-gram models estimate the probability of a word sequence $w_1 \ldots w_n$ appearing in the data. The estimate is computed as a conditional probability of the word w_n appearing after the sequence of words $w_1 \ldots w_{n-1}$:

$$P(w_n|w_1^{n-1}) \approx P(w_n|w_{n-N+1}^{n-1})s \qquad (1)$$

We searched all four data sets for the presence of the ontology terms. In each data set, we concentrated on terms with occurrence ≥ 10. These words are more likely to be representative across many users, but not indicative of individual preferences. Representativeness of the ontology categories varied in coverage and support. Within the data sets, *Body* and *Symptoms* were represented by $80\% - 90\%$ of their terms, a larger proportion than other categories. Although only $30\% - 50\%$ of *Doctor* terms were extracted from every data set, the found terms were among the most frequent in every corpora (e.g., *doctor, physician*).

The term disambiguation was especially important for non-professional terms which could have

education-careers

[9]http://kdd.ics.uci.edu/databases/20newsgroups/20newsgroups.html

[10]http://caw2.barcelonamedia.org/node/7

[11]http://www.cs.jhu.edu/~mdredze/datasets/sentiment/

Relevance	Data	Post
Relevant	Twitter	thinkin there's a doctor's appointment in my future. tired of being sick. need to get back to taking care of my family before christmas.
	MySpace	my best friend stephanie's brother mike's best friend paolo was just diagnosed with a.l.l. leukemia.
Irrelevant	MySpace	to ensure the protection of military and civilian personnel in the department of defense from an influenza pandemic, including an avian influenza pandemic.
	Amazon	With one hand, pull the superoposterior part of the pinna in a superoposterior direction while inserting the earphone with the other. This straightens the ear canal and makes it easier to insert the earphone. (Your doctor uses the same maneuver when he/she examines you with an otoscope.).

Table 1: Examples of posts extracted with the health ontology.

Category	20 New groups	Twitter	MySpace	Amazon.com
Doctors	doctor, physician, radiologist	cardiologist, dermatologist, doctor, gynecologist, pediatrician	cardiologist, doctor, gynecologist, neurologist, pathologist	cardiologist, gynecologist, pediatrician, physician
Procedures	diet, circumcision, needles, ultrasound	diet, ecg, homeopathy, massage, pacemaker	abort, colonoscopy, ct, diet	diet, massage, pacemaker, scan, shots

Table 2: The least ambiguous ontology categories and examples of their terms.

several non-medical meanings (e.g., *head*, *leg*, *assistant*, *lab*). For terms with multiple meanings, corresponding personal pronouns were strong indicators of a reference to individuals (e.g., *my neck* vs. *attachable neck*, *our doctor* vs. *spin doctor*). Tri- and quadri-grams were useful in finding idiomatic expressions that use ontology terms figuratively (e.g., *technophobes won't have a heart-attack*).

To validate our term choice, we manually examined the use of frequent terms in posts. For each term, we randomly selected 3–6 posts in each data set. We then classified the posts as relevant or irrelevant to person's health information. The examined *20 NewsGroups, Twitter, MySpace* posts were relevant, albeit one was an official document on influenza prevention in military. *Amazon.com* presented an example of a difficult data, where many posts were "false positive", i.e., they used health-related terms in a different context. Table 1 lists the post examples. *Doctors* and *Procedures* terms are the least ambiguous and the most effective in identifying patient-oriented information (Table 2).

6 Discussion

We have addressed an important issue of tracking health-related information posted by users on the Web. This information is in demand by health care policy-makers, population and community health organizations and medical practitioners.

Information retrieval/extraction and text mining are popular topics in Health Informatics. The field, however, only recently started to investigate health information in user-written texts. Relationship between self-disclosure and stigmatized health conditions in medical information search have been analyzed (Buchanan et al, 2007). Health information disseminated through medical and military blogs have been studied (Lagu et al, 2008; Konovalov et al, 2010).

Topic classification of user-written health messages has been a focus of research (Frank and Bouckaert, 2006). The study aimed to discriminate between messages with different health topics. Our goal is to extract health-related information from messages. When text data mining systems are deployed to analyze health information they often process institutional documents (Angelova, 2010; Cohen et al, 2010; Chapman, 2010; Ware et al, 2009). We instead work with health-related information.

7 Conclusions

Our goal is to assist medical practitioners and researchers in the analysis of Web-based social media. For example, medical professionals may wish to follow the understanding in the general population of a common medical condition such as otitis media and the indications for surgical intervention. We designed a set of semantic categories based on international classification schemes and extensive clinical experience of one of the authors. The categories are representative of notions and concepts that patients invoke in presentation of their health in clinical settings. To find adequate terms, we directly accessed clinical resources used by health care practitioners.

The evidence of ontology usefulness has been obtained from social networking sites. The ontology can be further used for detection of posted confidential health information; aggregation of user health concerns within a certain geographic area; survey of public awareness about particular issues. Additionally, the ontology can be used by tools that analyze health information on electronic media other than the Web (El Emam et al, 2010).

Acknowledgements

This work is in part funded by a NSERC Discovery grant available to the first author and The Ottawa Hospital Academic Medical Organization – to the second author.

References

Angelova, G. Use of Domain Knowledge in the Automatic Extraction of Structured Representations from Patient-Related Texts. *Procedings of ICCS 2010*, p.p. 14–27

Aspden, P., J. Corrigan, J. Wolcott, S. Erickson (Eds) *Patient Safety: Achieving a New Standard for Care.* Board on Health Care Services, Institute of Medicine, 2003.

Buchanan, T., A. Joinson, C. Paine, U.-D. Reips. "Looking for medical information on the Internet: self-disclosure, privacy and trust", *He@lth Information on the Internet*, **58**: 8–9, 2007.

Carneiro, H. and E. Mylonakis. "Google trends: a web-based tool for real-time surveillance of disease outbreaks", *Clinical Infectious Diseases*, **49**(10), 1557–1564 , Oxford, 2009.

Casoto, P., A. Dattolo, P. Omero, N. Pudota, C. Tasso. "Accessing, Analysing, and Extracting Information from User Generated Contents", in *Handbook of Research on Web 2.0, 3.0, and X.0*, S. Murugesan (ed.), p.p. 312–328, IGI Global, 2010.

Chanlekha, H. and Collier, N. Analysis of syntactic and semantic features for fine-grained event-spatial understanding in outbreak news reports, *Journal of Biomedical Semantics*, **1**(3), 2010.

Chapman, W. A Hybrid Information Model to Represent Clinical and Linguistic Data Extracted from Clinical Narrative Documents. *Proceeding of American Medical Informatics Association*, 2010.

Cohen, K., C. Roeder, W. Baumgartner Jr., L. Hunter, and K. Verspoor Test suite design for biomedical ontology concept recognition systems. *Language Resources and Evaluation Conference*, pp. 441–446, 2010.

Doing-Harris K, Zeng-Treiler Q. Computer-Assisted Update of a Consumer Health Vocabulary Through Mining of Social Network Data. *Journal of Medical Internet Research*, 2011; 13(2):e37.

El Emam, K., Neri, E., Jonker, E., Sokolova, M., Peyton, L, Neisa, A., and Scassa, T.. "The Inadvertent Disclosure of Personal Health Information through Peer-to-peer File Sharing Programs", JAMIA, **17**: 148–158, 2010.

Frank, E., and Bouckaert, R. Naive bayes for text classication with unbalanced classes. *Proceedings of PKDD 2006*, 503–510, 2006.

Ginsberg, J., M. Mohebbi, R. Patel, L. Brammer, M. Smolinski, L. Brilliant. Detecting influenza epidemic using search engine query data. *Nature*, **457** (7232), 1012–1014, 2008.

Hersh W., *Information retrieval: a health and biomedical perspective*, 3rd ed., 2009: Springer.

Himmel W, Reincke U, Michelmann H. Text Mining and Natural Language Processing Approaches for Automatic Categorization of Lay Requests to Web-Based Expert Forums. *Journal of Medical Internet Research*, 2009; 11(3):e25.

ICD-10: International Statistical Classification of Diseases and Related Health Problems: tenth revision, 2nd ed., World Health Organization, 2004.

International Classification of Functioning, Disability and Health (ICF), World Health Organization, 2001.

International Classification of Procedures in Medicine (ICPM), **1–2**, World Health Organization, 1978.

Konovalov S, M. Scotch, L. Post, C. Brandt. Biomedical Informatics Techniques for Processing and Analyzing Web Blogs of Military Service Members, *Journal of Medical Internet Research*, **12**(4), 2010.

Lagu, T., E. Kaufman, D. Asch, and K. Armstrong. 2008. Content of Weblogs Written by Health Professionals. *Journal of General Internal Medicine*, **23** (10): 1642–1646, 2008.

Lampos, V. and N. Christianini. "Tracking the flu pandemic by monitoring the social web". *2nd Workshop on Cognitive Information Processing*, 2010.

Ware, H., C. Mullett, and V. Jagannathan. Natural Language Processing (NLP) Framework to Assess Clinical Conditions. *JAMIA*,**16**:585–589, 2009.

Yu, A. Methods in biomedical ontology. *Journal of Biomedical Informatics*, **39**, 252–266, 2006.

Recognition and Classification of Numerical Entities in Basque

Ander Soraluze, Iñaki Alegria, Olatz Ansa, Olatz Arregi and Xabier Arregi
IXA Group. University of the Basque Country
ander.soraluze@ehu.es, i.alegria@ehu.es, olatz.ansa@ehu.es,
olatz.arregi@ehu.es, xabier.arregi@ehu.es

Abstract

This paper presents a system based on Finite State Technology that recognises and classifies numerical entities in texts written in Basque. The system deals with a wide range of entities, such as temporal expressions, numbers related to units of measurement, or those that refer to common nouns. The system obtains 86.96% F-measure score following MUC evaluation and 78.82% using IREX and CONLL simple scoring protocol.

1 Introduction

Named Entity Recognition and Classification (NERC) has become an important sub-task in the Natural Language Processing area. It is known that an effective treatment of Named Entities can benefit the performance of applications like Machine Translation (MT), Information Extraction (IE), Information Retrieval (IR) or Question Answering (QA). In the early stages, NERC systems identified a few types of entities, namely person, organisation and location names. Over time, numerical and temporal expressions have been also considered as identifiable types of entities.

Concerning to Basque, there is a NERC system called *Eihera* (Alegria et al., 2003) that recognises and classifies person, organisation and location names, but it does not deal with numerical entities up to date. The Numerical Entity Recogniser and Classifier for Basque (NuERCB) presented here aims to address this lack.

NuERCB identifies the numbers of the text and decides whether they express date or time, or are associated with units of measurement or, otherwise, just refer to common nouns. When numbers are linked to units or symbols of measurement, NuERCB determines which specific property maps with each of them. For instance, units like "square meter", "meter per second squared", "second" or "Celsius" are associated with properties like "area", "acceleration", "time" and "temperature" respectively.

Since numerical expressions, particularly those related to units of measurement, are very common in technical texts, we have used in this work the *ZT* corpus, a Basque corpus specialized in science and technology (Areta et al., 2007). In this dataset numerical expressions are more likely to appear, so it allows us to test the system on a wide variety of cases.

This paper is structured as follows. After reviewing related work, section 3 describes the linguistic features related to numerical expressions in Basque texts. Sections 4 and 5 show the methods for number detection and classification. Section 6 presents the main experimental results, which are analysed in section 7. Finally, the conclusions and future work are mentioned.

2 Related Work

The set of categories used to classify Named Entities has enriched over the time. As defined in the Message Understanding Conference (MUC) (Chinchor, 1998), Named Entity recognition consists on the identification and categorization of three types of specializations: "ENAMEX" for person, organisation and location, "TIMEX" for time and date, and "NUMEX" for money and percent. Furthermore, TIMEX2 (Ferro et al., 2003), which extends MUC definition of the TIMEX category, was used in Time Expression Recognition and Normalization evaluation (TERN 2004). Nowadays, rich hierarchies of Named Entity types have been proposed in the literature. For instance, the set of BBN[1] categories consists of 29 NE types and 64 subtypes used for Question Answering, and (Sekine and Nobata, 2004) currently gathers a hierarchy of 200 categories[2]. Temporal and numerical expressions are included in these sets.

Systems that deal with temporal and numerical expressions can be distinguished depending on the applied techniques. On the one hand, systems like LTG (Mikheev et al., 1998), MUSE (Maynard et al.,

[1] http://www.ldc.upenn.edu/Catalog/docs/LDC2005T33/
[2] http://nlp.cs.nyu.edu/ene/version7_1_0Beng.html

2001), HNERC (Farmakiotou et al., 2002), OAK (Sekine and Nobata, 2004), (Magnini et al., 2002) and (Arora et al., 2009) use pattern-based rules. On the other hand, it is worth mentioning approaches based on Hidden Markov Model (HMM) like Nymble (Bikel et al., 1997) and (Zhou and Su, 2002). A comparison between them shows that hand-crafted rule-based systems normally obtain better precision than systems based on statistical models, but the recall is lower and they require much manual work. On the contrary, statistical NERC systems require a large amount of manually annotated training data. Therefore, factors like the specificity of the domain and the availability of big training data are determinant in order to decide which method to use.

It is remarkable that systems that work on less-resourced languages normally choose a rule-based approach, as (Arora et al., 2009) for Hindi or (Farmakiotou et al., 2002) for Greek.

3 Numbers in Basque

Numbers appear in many different ways in Basque written texts. Due to Basque is an agglutinative language, a given lemma makes different word forms and this occurs even with numbers. For example, the same number can appear in different ways such as *15, 15ek, 15engana* "15, the 15, to the 15", depending on the role that it plays in the sentence.

In order to determine the different types of numerical entities we analysed the *ZT* Corpus. This corpus is a tagged collection of specialised texts in Basque. It is composed of a 1.6 million-word part, whose annotation has been revised by hand, and another automatically tagged 6 million-word part.

Numerical entities can express a wide range of information such as percentages, magnitudes, dates, times, etc. Although most of the numbers follow a simple pattern (digit and unit of measurement or category) the difficulty lies in some compound structures such as percentages or pairs of numbers with a conjunction between them. In general the patterns where the categories and the numbers are far from each other are difficult to treat. Moreover, special attention must be paid to the order of the words in the phrase. Occasionally the number can appear after the category, like in *2 lagun, lagun 2* "2 friends".

4 Number Detection

The input of NuERCB is the result of the Basque shallow syntactic analyser (Aduriz and Díaz de Ilarraza, 2003) developed in IXA[3] group. The analyser identifies and tags numbers according to six predefined types:

ZEN: Non declined numbers written with digits; cardinals *22*, percentages *% 4,5*, times *23:30*, etc.

ZEN_DEK: Declined numbers; cardinals *22k, 45i, 5ek*, percentages *% 45ean*, times *23:30etan* "at 23:30", etc.

HAUL_ZNB: Multiword numbers; *98_milioi* "98 million".

HAUL_DATA: Multiword date structure; *martxoaren_19an* "on March 19".

ERROM: Roman numerals; *VI*.

DET_DZH: Numbers written in characters; *hamaika* "eleven".

We have evaluated the accuracy of the numbers detection carried out by the syntactic analyser, so that we can know the error rate in the input of NuERCB. We took 200 numbers randomly and we compared the analyser's tags with the actual ones. The obtained accuracy was 92,5%.

Observing the result, we concluded that the detection of numbers by the syntactic analyser was satisfactory as a starting point of our work. Nevertheless, some of the errors produced by the syntactic analyser have been handled by NuERCB to improve the overall performance.

5 Number Classification

In this section, we first introduce the kinds of categories used in NuERCB, and then describe the system itself.

5.1 Numerical entities

The range of categories for numerical entities is wide. On the one hand, there are categories associated with specific properties such as area, density, length, temperature, time, etc. that are represented by units or symbols: metre (m), kilogram (kg), second (s), etc. We identified 41 different properties, 2006 units and 1986 symbols. These categories are denoted as closed. On the other hand, each common noun or concept can be considered as an open category.

In the case of the closed categories, our goal is to mark numerical entities along with the property they refer to and the unit or symbol which is used for it. For example, in the sentence *Hegazkinak 2000 km/h-ko abiaduran mugi daitezke* "The airplanes can fly at 2000 km/h", 2000 is labeled with a couple of

[3]http://ixa.si.ehu.es/Ixa

tags: the symbol of measurement is "km/h" and the associated property is "speed".

In the case of the open categories, we distinguish between the percent expressions like *hazkundea % 10ekoa izan da* "the growth has been 10 %", and the simple numbers or amounts like *1250 biztanle* "1250 inhabitants". In these cases the system determines which common noun refers to the numerical entity: *% 10* is linked to *hazkundea* "the growth" and *1250* is linked to *biztanle* "inhabitants". It must be underlined that in general other systems do not classify these open categories, and in the case of percents they only tag the number followed by the percent symbol, but not the common noun that the number refers to.

5.2 System overview

NuERCB is conceived to be used in diverse applications where the response time is a critical factor. Therefore, we need NuERCB to have a high processing speed using low memory capacity. So we have chosen the Finite State Technology to implement NuERCB because of its mathematical and computational simplicity and its high performance.

NuERCB compiles a set of hand-crafted rules which have been implemented in Finite State Transducers (FST). We defined 34 FSTs to classify closed categories and 2 more for open categories that correspond to common nouns. They were defined using Foma (Hulden, 2009), an open source platform for finite-state automata and transducers. In total, the FSTs set is composed by 2095 hand-crafted rules which are able to identify 41 properties, 2006 units and 1986 symbols.

The tagging process is divided into three main phases. Firstly, the properties associated with units or symbols and boundaries of the numerical entities are tagged. Afterwards, the units or symbols of the properties that have been detected in the previous step are marked. Also, ellipsis cases of units or symbols are detected. And finally, percents, some multiword and date structures and open categories are tagged.

The input of the system is a syntactically analysed text. The format of this analysed text has been adapted to be used for the FST set, and vice versa the tagged output of the FSTs is returned to its original format.

The architecture of the system is shown in Figure 1.

To illustrate the application of the method we focus on the following examples: *21 ordu 5 minutu eta 12 segundoko* ... "... of 21 hours 5 minutes and 12 seconds" and *azalera osoaren % 8,38* "the % 8.38 of the total area". The first one is a typical composed time

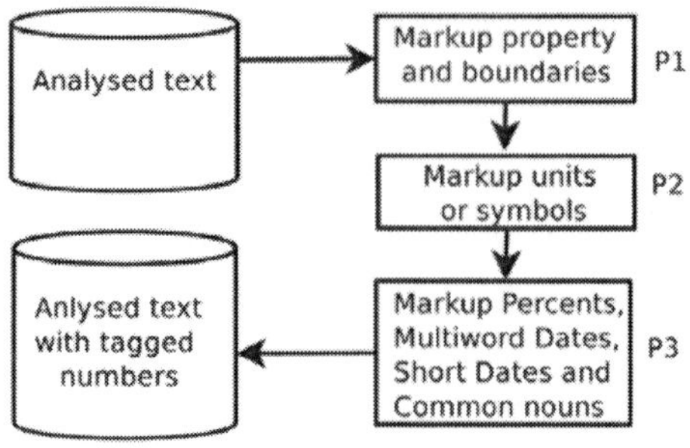

Figure 1: Architecture of NuERCB.

structure and it will be detected in the first phase (P1) and completed in the second one (P2). The second example shows a percent with a common noun category which will be detected in the third phase (P3).

P1. In this phase only the property and boundaries of the first example are detected and marked: *<TIME>21 ordu 5 minutu eta 12 segundoko</TIME>*. In Figure 2, R1[4] recognises the structure boundaries of the time property.

P2. Here units and symbols associated with each number in the structure are detected and marked: *<TIME><HOUR> 21 <MINUTE> 5 and <SECOND> 12 </TIME>*. R2 defined in Figure 2 is able to tag the *second* unit based on the *<TIME>* and *</TIME>* tags added by the previous rule (R1).

P3. Finally, the numerical entity of the second example is detected and marked. R3 in Figure 3 detects that an adjective can appear between a common noun and a percent number. Firstly the rule adds CN (Common Noun) to the tag *<PERCENT-CN> %8,38*, then a postprocess is carried out in order to replace CN by the category that corresponds. The final result is *<PERCENT-AREA> %8,38*. As we can observe the percent number is tagged correctly with the correspondent category (*azalera* "area") instead of the adjective (*osoa* "total").

6 Experimental Results

To evaluate the system we have taken 255 numerical entities and their context from the *ZT* Corpus.

The evaluation was carried out using two well known methods, the MUC evaluation system and the Exact-match evaluation which is used in IREX and CONLL.

[4]Syntax for regular expressions in Foma can be consulted in http://foma.sf.net/dokuwiki

```
define TimeStruct Number [ TimeUnit |TimeSymbol ];
define R1  TimeStruct ([(",") TimeStruct]* Conjunction TimeStruct)
                                                @-> "<TIME>" ... "</TIME>";
define SecondPost [ SecondUnit | SecondSymbol];
define R2  Number @-> "<SECOND>" ... ||"<TIME>" ?* _ SecondPost ?* "</TIME>";
```

Figure 2: Simplified rules to recognise temporal structures.

```
define R3   Number @-> "<PERCENT_CN>" ... "</PERCENT_CN>"
                                  ||CommonNoun Adjective PercentSymbol _ ;
```

Figure 3: Simplified rule to recognise percent structures.

In MUC evaluations (Grishman and Sundheim, 1996) a system is scored in two axes: its ability to find the correct type (TYPE) of the entity and its ability to find the correct text (TEXT). A correct type is credited if the entity type is assigned correctly. A correct TEXT is credited if the boundaries of the entity are marked correctly. The TYPE and TEXT are credited independently, regardless if one of them is incorrect (Nadeau and Sekine, 2007).

We use a slightly changed version of MUC evaluation. Besides the TYPE and TEXT we include SUBTYPE, which is used in the closed categories. The SUBTYPE is credited when a unit or symbol that expresses a property is marked correctly. So when we detect a numerical entity associated with a property, TYPE is credited if the property is assigned correctly, SUBTYPE is credited if the unit or symbol is marked correctly and TEXT is credited if the boundaries of the numerical entity are identified properly.

For TYPE, SUBTYPE and TEXT three measures are kept: the number of correct answers (COR), the number of actual answers that the system guesses (ACT) and the number of possible entities in the answer (POS).

In MUC, precision is calculated as COR / ACT and the recall is COR / POS. The final score is the Micro-Averaged F-measure (MAF).

IREX and CONLL share a simple scoring protocol called "Exact-Match evaluation". Systems are evaluated based on the Micro-Averaged F-measure (MAF). The precision is the percentage of named entities found by the system that are correct and the recall is the percentage of named entities present in the dataset that are found by the system. A proposed named entity is correct only if it is an exact match of the corresponding entity in the text.

In Table 1 there is a comparison between both evaluation methods taking into account two outputs. In this example, *5 metro eta 50 zentimetro* "5 metres and 50 centimetres", the MUC evaluation for the first output credits 4 points in COR and ACT: 1 point for identifying properly the structure boundaries, 1 for detecting correctly the property (*length*) and 2 more for tagging the unit of each number (*m* and *cm*). The second output is credited as follows: 3 points in COR (*length, m, cm*) and 6 points in ACT (2 boundaries, 2 times the length property and 1 point for each unit). However, Exact-Match evaluation only credits 1 point for identifying correctly all the features mentioned above in the first output.

Example	5 metres and 50 centimetres		
Correct tagging	<L> <M> 5 and <CM> 50 </L>	MUC	Exact-match
System output 1	<L> <M> 5 and <CM> 50 </L>	COR = 4 ACT = 4 POS = 1	COR = 1 ACT = 1 POS = 1
System output 2	<L> <M> 5 </L> and <L> <CM> 50 </L>	COR = 3 ACT = 6 POS = 4	COR = 0 ACT = 2 POS = 1

Table 1: Comparison of MUC and Exact-match evaluation methods.

The Precision, Recall and F-measure values obtained by NuERCB according to the two scoring protocols mentioned above are shown in Table 2. The first row shows scores for closed categories and the second one shows results for open categories. The last row summarizes the total values.

	MUC			CONLL-IREX
	P	R	F_1	F_1
CLOSED	89.59	86,95	88.25	83.70
OPEN	86.29	83.59	84.92	73.33
TOTAL	88.32	85.65	86.96	78.82

Table 2: NuERCB scores for closed and open categories.

Table 3 shows scores of the most frequent closed categories (date, time, length, weight and money), along with a specific row for percents as they have been particularly dealt among the open categories.

	MUC			CONLL-IREX
	P	R	F_1	F_1
DATE	87.18	85.00	86.08	80.00
TIME	97.73	97.73	97.73	93.10
LENGTH	90.79	92.00	91.39	92.00
WEIGHT	97.14	94.44	95.77	91.67
MONEY	92.31	88.90	90.57	88.89
PERCENT	72.73	60.38	65.98	36.84

Table 3: NuERCB scores for main closed and open categories.

The comparison of our system with other similar ones is shown in Table 4. Although systems used different category-sets, we present those that can be considered comparable.

7 Discussion

According to MUC evaluation method NuERCB obtains a 86.96% F-measure score and in conformity with Exact-Match scoring it reaches 78.82% for the total of the categories.

Analysing separately the scores for closed and open categories (see Table 2), we realize that our system's performance is better classifying closed categories (MUC: 88.25%, Exact-match: 83.70%) than open ones (MUC: 84.92%, Exact-match: 73.33%). With respect to closed categories most of the errors were due to the fact that units or symbols had not been defined in the hierarchy. As a consequence the system was not able to identify and classify these entities correctly. The problem of open categories is that sometimes the category is not near the number.

Focusing on Table 3 we notice that NuERCB gets good scores for the main categories. The lowest score are obtained in DATE and percent structure cases.

	F_1				
	1	2	3	4	5
DATE	86.08	86.98	91.9	96.59	93.73
TIME	97.73	—	92.4	92.89	87.07
WEIGHT	95.77	75.00	—	—	—
MONEY	90.57	96.47	94.83	95.54	95.47
PERCENT	65.98	—	—	94.61	98.47

Table 4: Comparison of scores among systems. 1=NuERCB, 2=OAK (Sekine and Nobata, 2004), 3=(Arora et al., 2009), 4=(Magnini et al., 2002), 5=LTG (Mikheev et al., 1998)

In DATE cases some numbers referring to date has no context clues that help in their classification. For example, the number 1963 may be a year but if there is not contextual evidence it is difficult to determine whether it is a date or not.

In the case of percent structures the task is more complex than in usual MUC systems. It is remarkable that other systems only classify simple percent structures like 20% that is a number followed by a percent symbol (%). In our case the task of identifying a percent numerical entity requires also to find the common noun that the percent number refers to. In percent structures the common noun and the percent number appear often far from each other, even in different sentences. This makes very difficult to identify correctly the category using only hand-crafted rules. Suppose that we have this example, *Emakumezkoak unibertsitateetako irakasle titularren % 13-18 soilik dira, Finlandia, Frantzia eta Espainian; Herberehetan, Alemanian eta Danimarkan % 6,5 baino gutxiago dira* "In Finland, France and Spain, women are only 13-18% of university lecturers; in Holland, Germany and Denmark are less than % 6.5." Obviously it is very complicated to tag 6.5 % with its correct category (*emakume* "woman") using just rules.

To finish the analysis of the results we compare NuERCB with other systems (see Table 4). In most of the categories our scores are similar to the others, in some cases better (TIME and WEIGHT) and in others lower (DATE and MONEY). Clearly the most significant difference is in percents as we mentioned above.

Finally, it is important to underline that some errors of the syntactic analyser, such as incorrect multiword detection or tokenizing and stemming errors, have affected our system's performance.

8 Conclusions and Future Work

We have presented the first system for Basque that addresses the recognition and classification of numerical entities. The system has a wide coverage and deals with numerical entities in a general way taking into account the diversity of phenomena in written texts. We have predefined thousands of units and symbols that allow to capture lots of properties, and we have treated common nouns as an open set of categories.

The use of Finite State Technology makes possible to process large dataset with high processing speed using low memory. We have compiled a set of 2095 hand-crafted rules in Foma. This platform facilitates the use and integration of NuERCB in information processing applications.

Although Basque is a less-resourced language and the set of categories is not limited, evaluation scores of our system are comparable to those obtained by other systems.

In the future we aim to tackle the improvement of the performance of NuERCB in some weak points. Mainly, in what respect to percentage structures, we are considering to apply some anaphora resolution methods. In general, it will be interesting to apply machine-learning techniques like is proposed in (Erro et al., 2004) in order to correct mistakes. Using machine-learning techniques could increase the coverage of the system without rebuilding the linguistic resources.

We also aim to apply the NuERCB system in information recovery tasks, namely in an existing Question Answering system for Basque (Ansa et al., 2009). We have already integrated the NuERCB module into the QA system and nowadays we are facing its evaluation in an application-oriented way.

Acknowledgments

This work has been supported by Ander Soraluze's PhD grant from the University of the Basque Country (UPV/EHU), KNOW2 (TIN2009-14715-C04-01) and Berbatek (IE09-262) projects. Thanks to Mans Hulden for his help in defining the transducers using *foma*.

References

Aduriz, I. and Díaz de Ilarraza, A. (2003). Morphosyntactic disambiguation ands shallow parsing in Computational Processing of Basque.

Alegria, I., Ezeiza, N., Fernandez, I., and Urizar, R. (2003). Named Entity Recognition and Classification for texts in Basque. In *II Jornadas de Tratamiento y Recuperación de Información, JOTRI, Madrid. 2003. ISBN 84-89315-33-7.*

Ansa, O., Arregi, X., Otegi, A., and Soraluze, A. (2009). Ihardetsi: A Basque Question Answering System at QA@CLEF 2008. In *Evaluating Systems for Multilingual and Multimodal Information Access, 9th Workshop of CLEF, 2008. LNCS, Vol. 5706/2009, pp. 369-376. Springer Berlin / Heidelberg. ISSN 0302-9743.*

Areta, N., Gurrutxaga, A., Leturia, I., Alegria, I., Artola, X., Díaz de Ilarraza, A., Ezeiza, N., and Sologaistoa, A. (2007). ZT Corpus: Annotation and tools for Basque corpora. In *Copus Linguistics. Birminghan.*

Arora, S., Tyagi, R., and Arora, K. K. (2009). A Tool for Identification of Numeric, Temporal and Web Expressions in Hindi Text. In *Proceedings of ASCNT*, pages 51–57, India.

Bikel, D. M., Miller, S., Schwartz, R., and Weischedel, R. (1997). Nymble: a High-Performance Learning Name-finder. In *Proceedings of the fifth conference on Applied natural language processing*, pages 194–201, Morristown, NJ, USA. Association for Computational Linguistics.

Chinchor, N. A. (1998). Overview of MUC-7/MET-2. In *Proceedings of the 7th Message Understanding Conference (MUC-7).*

Erro, L. E., Solorio, T., and Computacionales, C. D. C. (2004). Improvement of Named Entity Tagging by Machine Learning. Technical report, Coordinacin de Ciencias Computacionales.

Farmakiotou, D., Karkaletsis, V., Samaritakis, G., Petasis, G., and Spyropoulos, C. D. (2002). Named entity recognition in Greek web pages. In *In Proceedings of the 2nd Panhellenic Conference on Artificial Intelligence*, pages 91–102.

Ferro, L., Gerber, L., Mani, I., Sundheim, B., and Wilson, G. (2003). *TIDES 2003 Standard for the Annotation of Temporal Expressions*. MITRE corporation.

Grishman, R. and Sundheim, B. (1996). Message understanding conference - 6: A brief history. In *Proceedings of the International Conference on Computational Linguistics.*

Hulden, M. (2009). Foma: a Finite-State Compiler and Library. In *EACL (Demos)*, pages 29–32.

Magnini, B., Negri, M., Prevete, R., and Tanev, H. (2002). A WordNet-based approach to Named Entities recognition. In *COLING-02 on SEMANET*, pages 1–7, Morristown, NJ, USA. Association for Computational Linguistics.

Maynard, D., Tablan, V., Ursu, C., Cunningham, H., and Wilks, Y. (2001). Named Entity Recognition from Diverse Text Types. In *In Recent Advances in Natural Language Processing 2001 Conference, Tzigov Chark.*

Mikheev, A., Grover, C., and Moens, M. (1998). Description of The LTG System Used for MUC-7. In *Proceedings of the 7th Message Understanding Conference (MUC-7).*

Nadeau, D. and Sekine, S. (2007). A survey of named entity recognition and classification. *Linguisticae Investigationes*, pages 3–26. Publisher: John Benjamins Publishing Company.

Sekine, S. and Nobata, C. (2004). Definition, dictionaries and tagger for Extended Named Entity Hierarchy. In *Conference on Language Resources and Evaluation.*

Zhou, G. and Su, J. (2002). Named Entity Recognition using an HMM-based Chunk Tagger. In *Proc. 40th Annual Meeting of the Association for Computational Linguistics (ACL 2002).*

Multilingual Entity-Centered Sentiment Analysis Evaluated by Parallel Corpora

Josef Steinberger and **Polina Lenkova** and **Mijail Kabadjov**
Ralf Steinberger and **Erik van der Goot**
EC Joint Research Centre
21027, Ispra (VA), Italy
Josef.Steinberger, Polina.Lenkova, Ralf.Steinberger
Mijail.Kabadjov, Erik.van-der-Goot
@jrc.ec.europa.eu

Abstract

We propose the creation and use of a multilingual parallel news corpus annotated with opinion towards entities, produced by projecting sentiment annotation from one language to several others. The objective is to save annotation time for development and evaluation purposes, and to guarantee comparability of opinion mining evaluation results across languages. By creating this resource, we answered the question whether sentiment is consistently translated across languages so that projection can actually be an option. We describe our approach to multilingual sentiment analysis and show its performance in 7 languages of the parallel corpus.

1 Introduction

In sentiment analysis the goal is to detect and classify subjective content of a text. The text can be classified as a whole such as in product reviews, in which an overall judgment is assigned to the product. If we move to the news domain, the overall sentiment score of an article can be used for detecting bad or good news. It can be used also for detecting the changes in sentiment in a particular topic. However, if the goal is to detect sentiment expressed towards entities, the aggregated sentiment of the articles, in which the entity appears, need not to correspond to opinions expressed towards the entity. The entity can be mentioned positively in a very negative article. We have to go down and analyze each entity mention based on the surrounding context.

Solving the problem in multilingual environment and gathering large amounts of articles from many sources give advantage to detect news opinions expressed in different countries towards same persons. Also, it eliminates the biased news. However, multilinguality brings another challenge. For instance, it is not easy to develop NLP tools like parsers or taggers in many languages, also using them can cause computational problems when applied on large amounts of articles every day. Another difficulty comes with resources. Sentiment-annotated data are not usually available for other types of texts then reviews, or they are almost exclusively available for English. Sentiment dictionaries are also mostly available for English only or, if they exist for other languages, they are not comparable, in the sense that they have been developed for different purposes, have different sizes, are based on different definitions of what sentiment or opinion means.

We addressed the resource bottleneck for sentiment dictionaries, by developing highly multilingual and comparable sentiment dictionaries having similar sizes and based on a common specification (Steinberger et al., 2011).

Our sentiment system is simply based on counting subjective terms around entity mentions (mainly persons and organizations). Evaluating its performance in more languages would multiply the annotation efforts. In this paper we propose using parallel corpora to automatically project annotations from English. We study the subjectivity of the entity-centered sentiment annotation and evaluate our sentiment system in seven languages (English, Spanish, French, German, Czech, Italian and Hungarian). As a side effect this evaluation serves as a task-based evaluation of the quality of the sentiment dictionaries.

Firstly, we discuss related work in Section 2. Next, we shortly mention the development of sentiment dictionaries and briefly discuss our sentiment system (Section 3). Then we focus on the annotation of the parallel corpus in Section 4. We show the figures of inter-annotator agreement. Before we conclude all, we discuss evaluation results of our system run on the parallel corpus (Section 5).

2 Related work

The substantial growth in subjective information on the world wide web in the past years has made sentiment analysis a task on which constantly growing efforts have been concentrated. Subjectivity in natural language refers to aspects of language used to express opinions, evaluations, and speculations (Wiebe et al., 2005). To classify statements (as traditionally to positive, neutral (objective) and negative) is not a trivial task, as many expressions carry in themselves a certain subjectivity and many expressions are used both in a subjective (even both positive and negative), as well as objective manner.

Sentiment analysis has been done at a document level, the most often for review texts, starting from the assumption that each document focuses on a single object and contains opinion from a single opinion holder. There were numerous approaches dealing with document level sentiment classification (Pang et al., 2002; Dave et al., 2003). The approaches are usually evaluated by comparing the outcome of the analysis against the number of stars given to the review.

The document level assumptions do not hold for newspaper articles or blog posts where each sentence expresses one single opinion (sentence level approaches) about a target. (Hatzivassiloglou and Wiebe, 2000; Wiebe and Mihalcea, 2006; Wilson et al., 2004) use subjectivity analysis to detect sentences from which patterns can be deduced for sentiment analysis, based on a subjectivity lexicon. Kim and Hovy (2004) try to find, given a certain topic, the positive, negative and neutral sentiments express on it and the source of opinions (the opinion holder). The authors computed the sentiment of the sentence in a window of different sizes around target.

Most of the work in obtaining subjectivity lexicons was done for English. However, there were some authors who developed methods for the mapping of subjectivity lexicons to other languages. Kim and Hovy (2006) use a machine translation system and subsequently use a subjectivity analysis system that was developed for English. Mihalcea et al. (2007) propose a method to learn multilingual subjective language via cross-language projections. Another approaches in obtaining subjectivity lexicons for other languages than English were explored in Banea et al. (2008) or Wan (2008).

In the effort to guarantee comparability of results across languages, various authors have suggested using multilingual parallel corpora. For instance, Koehn (2002) used the multilingual parallel corpus EuroParl to evaluate Machine Translation performance across language pairs. Zaanen et al. (2004) propose to use a multilingual parallel parsed corpus as the best and fairest gold standard for grammatical inference evaluation, because parallel documents can be assumed to have the same degree of language complexity. Turchi et al. (2010) use parallel corpora for the evaluation of multilingual multi-document summarisation, in which the annotation is very expensive. It also makes the evaluation results across languages directly comparable.

3 Method for multilingual sentiment analysis

The objective of this paper is to focus on the creation and use of the sentiment-annotated parallel corpus. Our sentiment analysis tools will therefore only be described briefly. Any other sentiment analysis tool could be applied to this parallel corpus instead.

Our objective is to detect positive or negative opinions expressed towards entities in the news across different languages and to follow trends over time. Entities of interest are mostly persons and organisations, but also concepts such as the '7th Framework Program' or 'European Constitution'. Entities can be mentioned positively in negative news context, and vice versa, so that document level analysis is not sufficient (Balahur et al., 2010), but opinions expressed towards the specific entity mention must be detected. As we do not have access to parsers or even part-of-speech taggers for the range of languages we intend to analyse, we chose to use an extremely simple method that does not require language-specific tools besides NER software and language-specific sentiment dictionaries: we add up positive and negative sentiment scores in six-word windows around the entities, distinguishing two positive and two negative levels of sentiment words (having values of -4, -2, 2 and 4 points, respectively). Enhancers and diminishers add or remove 1 point, negation inverts the value, except for negated high positive ('not very good' is not equivalent to 'very bad').

The sentiment dictionaries – currently available in 15 languages – were created using a triangulation method, which was described in detail in (Steinberger et al., 2011). In a nutshell: carefully elaborated English and Spanish sentiment word lists were translated into third languages. The introduction of errors through word sense ambiguity was limited by taking the intersection of both target language word lists. According to our evaluation, approximately 90% of these intersection words were correct, while only about 50% of those words were correct that were translations from either English or Spanish, but not from both. For Arabic, Czech, French, German, Italian and Russian, these word lists were manually checked and enhanced, while for Bulgarian, Dutch, Hungarian, Polish, Portuguese, Slovak and Turkish we simply used the intersecting word list. For a subset of languages (Czech, English and Russian), wild cards were manually added to the sentiment word lists in order to capture morphological variants. For the other languages, the same will be done in the future. The results in section 5 differ heavily depending on whether morphological variants are dealt with.

4 Building a sentiment-annotated parallel corpus

In this section we give details about the parallel corpus, sentiment annotation and inter-annotator agreement.

4.1 Named entity-annotated parallel corpus

We worked with data from Workshops on Statistical Machine Translation (2008, 2009, 2010)[1] which provide parallel corpora of news stories in 7 European languages: English, Spanish, French, German, Czech, Italian (only 2009) and Hungarian (only 2008 and 2009). Putting together the data from the three years resulted in 7 065 parallel sentences in five languages, and a subset in Italian and Hungarian. We ran our in-house entity recognition on the data. Only known entities (entities present in our database) were marked in the data. It gave us enough samples to run sentiment experiments although guessing other entities (and considering coreference mentions) would considerably increase the pool of samples. For English we received 1 274 entity mentions, resulting in the same number of sentence-target (S-T) pairs for testing sentiment analysis. We built golden standard annotations and projected them to other languages. Because of different performance of entity recognition we obtained fewer S-T pairs in other languages than in English.

[1]http://www.statmt.org/wmt10/translation-task.html.

4.2 Sentiment annotation and inter-annotator agreement

Annotating sentiment in news is clearly a subjective task. Even the same person can assign different values to the same entity mention when reviewing it in a different time. Also, we were not sure whether there is the same sentiment in all language variants of the same sentence. If so we could project it automatically after annotating the S-T pairs only in one language. We had two annotators to judge the cases. The first one, native Russian speaker with advanced knowledge of English and Italian, and the second one, a native Czech speaker with advanced knowledge of English. Each of the annotators were asked to judge randomly-ordered S-T pairs. The first annotator in both English and Italian languages and the second one in both English and Czech languages. We could thus measure the agreement on how the same annotator judged the same sentences in different languages at a different time. Also, we could see the agreement between the annotators. The results in Table 1 show that there were cases considered differently by the same annotator while reviewing them in different languages. When analyzing the disagreed cases we have not found any example in which the reason of attaching different polarity would be that the sentiment was not correctly translated with the sentence. The agreement was 87%, resp. 90%, far above random agreement which results in high Kappa. We measured 80% agreement between annotators with fair Kappa (0.65). The first annotator assigned POS to 16% of the cases, NEG to 17% and NEUT to 67%. The second one assigned non-neutral polarity more often: POS – 26%, NEG – 24% and NEUT – 50%.

Because we wanted to obtain golden standard annotations the disagreed cases were judged by the third (super-)annotator.

Many controversial cases are related to the sentences where both positive and negative sentiments are expressed. Below we present three different examples (target is in bold) of such cases and our suggestions on how to deal with them.

1st annot.	A1-English	A2-English	A1-English
2nd annot.	**A1-Italian**	**A2-Czech**	**A2-English**
ALL	0.87	0.90	0.80
POS	0.78	0.81	0.78
NEUT	0.91	0.94	0.86
NEG	0.78	0.87	0.79
POS/NEG	0.78	0.83	0.78
Random	0.54	0.48	0.42
Kappa	0.72	0.81	0.65

Table 1: Inter-annotator agreement. A1/A2 = Annotator 1/2.

1. Positive and negative aspects of an event/entity

   Britain's building societies could face a bill of more than 80m after the rescue of the ***Bradford & Bingley bank****.*

   The above statement seems to be quite balanced, in the sense it presents both negative and positive characteristics, which do not contradict one another. Following our guidelines, POS/NEG cases are considered to be neutral.

2. Polarized opinions about the same entity:

   According to Russian observers, the reasons for this are the welfare and stability in the country led by ***Alexander Lukashenko****, while Organization for Security and Co-operation in Europe (OSCE) explains it as vote counting frauds.*

   This sentence might seem a bit more controversial than the previous one, as the author presents two different opinions, and we could expect that he supports one of them. By examining this sentence in isolation, we cannot say which side the journalist takes. Therefore we mark it as a neutral statement.

3. One sentiment value is stronger than the other. As an illustration consider the following example:

   It's almost funny to see how ***Barack Obama****, reputedly the wisest president, is trying so hard in the matter of the Afghan war to repeat the strategy of his predecessor, having himself considered him to be the most foolish.*

   In this sentence, we have a reference to Barack Obama as the wisest president, which is obviously a positive statement about him. On the other hand, the journalist claims that the president tries to follow his predecessor, whom he strongly criticizes, which reveals a stark inconsistency in the president's policy. Therefore the overall sentiment about him is negative.

4. Sometimes, sentiment towards one entity implicates the same sentiment towards another entity

   "We are satisfied with what we have reached during the night and we highly appreciate the efforts of the two parties in order to stabilize our financial markets and protect our economy", declared ***Tony Fratto, spokesman of the White House****.*

   The sentence describes an achievement reached in the White House, which positively characterizes the entity, but also its speaker Tony Fratto, as being representative of the White House.

   In the example below, there is a positive sentiment expressed towards Krugman, and since this positive sentiment is linked to the fact that he is a leader writer of New York Times, we conclude that New York Times as well bears positive characteristics.

   55 year old Krugman is a neo-Keynesian that teaches at Princeton University and he is a well-known leader writer of the ***New York Times****.*

5. Another, probably less obvious example of the sentiment transferred from one entity to another:

   A new case of positive testing during the last ***Tour de France****: it is the Austrian Bernhard Kohl, of the team Gerolsteiner, third in classification and winner of the best grimpeur shirt.*

   It is evident that positive testing characterizes negatively Bernhard Kohl, but also brings a bad reputation to the Tour de France, which has been affected by a few cases of positive testing.

6. There are also cases where we are unable to correctly detect sentiment without using world knowledge:

*However, in spite of all these arguments, the winning trumf for the Democrats is **George Bush**.*

The sentence sounds positively, however, cosidering the fact that George Bush is Republican inverts the polarity.

5 Evaluation

We projected the sentiment polarities in golden standard data to other languages and we ran the sentiment system. Table 2 compares the system results for each language with Random baseline. Another baseline is when all cases are attached to the most frequent neutral class (All NEUT), even if this baseline is not that valuable (no sentiment analysis at all). We can see that the overall agreement with golden standard was from 66% (Italian) to 74% (English and Czech). The best two performing languages are the ones with all steps of dictionary creation finished. In all languages the system performed better than the Random baseline and on the same level as the ALL NEUT baseline. Kappa shows the difference to random agreement. It uncovers the poorest performing language - Hungarian, for which we currently have only raw triangulated dictionaries. Thus this evaluation can serve as a task-based evaluation of the quality of sentiment dictionaries: best performing English and Czech (the most advanced dictionaries) are followed by French, Italian, German and Spanish, in which the lack of all morphological variants results in lower recall, with Hungarian at the end of the list. The cases on which the system fails to capture the right polarity can be found in the previous section. Consider the subjective terms like *rescue*, *positive testing* or *winning trumf*.

Another observation is that the system performs better on negative statements than on positive ones. We think that the reason is that the gap between the negative and the neutral class is larger than the gap between the positive and the neutral class.

The per-case sentiment assignment works at the 70% level. However, it goes down if we do not consider the neutral cases - around 50%. And this is exactly what we are interested in and these are the cases that we are going to summarise and show in the news monitoring system. The question is: Is this performance good enough to assess sentiment expressed in news towards an entity? We try to answer it by the following experiment. We gathered all mentions of an entity in the corpus, emulating the time period. We computed how many times the entity was mentioned positively and negative in the golden standard. The difference would be its aggregated score (e.g. -2 means there were two more negative mentions than positive). We do the same with the system annotations. If both the golden standard and the system attached the same polarity to the entity we consider it as a correct answer. Because we process large amounts of articles every day, precision is more important than recall. Also, aggregated values close to zero are the most dangerous. One mistake in polarity assignment can invert the polarity of the whole entity within the time period. Thus, we experimented with different thresholds. For example threshold 2 means that we need the aggregated value to be at least 2 to consider the entity positive, resp. -2 to consider it negative. We report only the cases in which both the system the golden standard reported a non-neutral value to remove the borderline unreliable cases (Table 3). We can observe that with the basic threshold (1) we correctly classified 78% entities and by lifting the threshold up to 2 the system reached the performance of 93%. The only wrongly classified entity for English was *al-Qaeda*. While annotators assigned to this entity clearly negative overall sentiment (-5), many difficult cases led the system to a positive overall sentiment (+2). We did not find any wrong case in which the system did not agree on polarity with the golden standard with threshold 3. Testing higher thresholds would require analyzing a larger set.

Threshold	1	2	3
English	0.80 (102)	0.88 (8)	1.00 (3)
Spanish	0.58 (26)	0.75 (4)	1.00 (1)
French	0.85 (41)	1.00 (5)	1.00 (2)
German	0.75 (32)	1.00 (4)	—
Czech	0.88 (24)	1.00 (3)	1.00 (1)
Italian	0.76 (21)	1.00 (2)	1.00 (2)
Hungarian	0.75 (12)	1.00 (1)	—
Total	0.78 (258)	0.93 (27)	1.00 (9)

Table 3: Precision of aggregated sentiment for each entity across the corpus for three different thresholds which divide POS/NEG sentiment from NEUT. *precision (No. of entities)*

6 Conclusion

We presented the extensive evaluation of our multilingual sentiment analysis system. We con-

Language	English	Spanish	French	German	Czech	Italian	Hungarian
ALL	0.74	0.71	0.72	0.70	0.74	0.66	0.68
POS	0.44 / 0.32	0.31 / 0.08	0.43 / 0.12	0.32 / 0.10	0.48 / 0.12	0.34 / 0.18	0.38 / 0.07
NEUT	0.79 / 0.90	0.73 / 0.96	0.74 / 0.96	0.72 / 0.96	0.76 / 0.95	0.70 / 0.90	0.70 / 0.96
NEG	0.58 / 0.31	0.57 / 0.10	0.62 / 0.18	0.70 / 0.10	0.57 / 0.23	0.56 / 0.19	0.36 / 0.06
POS/NEG	0.50 / 0.31	0.43 / 0.09	0.53 / 0.15	0.45 / 0.10	0.53 / 0.18	0.44 / 0.18	0.37 / 0.06
ALL NEUT	0.72	0.71	0.71	0.70	0.73	0.66	0.69
Random	0.62	0.67	0.66	0.66	0.68	0.59	0.66
Kappa	0.31	0.11	0.17	0.12	0.20	0.17	0.05

Table 2: System's results on the parallel corpus. The cells that correspond to POS, NEUT, NEG and POS/NEG rows contain precision/recall figures.

tributed to resources of the sentiment community by building the multilingual sentiment dictionaries and annotating the parallel corpus. Working on parallel data enabled to evaluate such a system in many languages with a little annotation effort and, also, the results are comparable across the languages. The evaluation also serves as a task-based evaluation for sentiment dictionaries.

Our system is language-independent, although it needs to be fed by sentiment dictionaries for each language. So far, we created dictionaries for 15 languages with varied quality, however, we have capabilities to further improve the resources. The final goal is to feed the output of the sentiment analysis into the news monitoring system in all the 50 languages it supports.

Even if discovering the right polarity of sentiment towards an entity in a sentence is a difficult task and the system's results for non-neutral cases are modest, per-entity sentiment aggregation leads to precise conclusions when used carefully.

References

A. Balahur, R. Steinberger, M. Kabadjov, V. Zavarella, E. van der Goot, M. Halkia, B. Pouliquen, and J. Belyaeva. 2010. Sentiment analysis in the news. In *Proceedings of LREC*.

C. Banea, R. Mihalcea, and J. Wiebe. 2008. A bootstrapping method for building subjectivity lexicons for languages with scarce resources. In *Proceedings of LREC*.

K. Dave, S. Lawrence, and D. Pennock. 2003. Mining the peanut gallery: Opinion extraction and semantic classification of product reviews. In *Proceeding of WWW*.

V. Hatzivassiloglou and J. Wiebe. 2000. Effects of adjective orientation and gradability on sentence subjectivity. In *Proceedings of COLING*.

S.M. Kim and E. Hovy. 2004. Determining the sentiment of opinions. In *Proceedings of COLING*.

S.M. Kim and E. Hovy. 2006. Extracting opinions, opinion holders, and topics expressed in online news media text. In *Proceedings of the ACL Workshop on Sentiment and Subjectivity in Text*.

P. Koehn. 2002. Europarl: A multilingual corpus for evaluation of machine translation. In *Unpublished draft*.

R. Mihalcea, C. Banea, and J. Wiebe. 2007. Learning multilingual subjective language via cross-lingual projections. In *Proceedings of ACL*.

B. Pang, L. Lee, and S. Vaithyanathan. 2002. Thumbs up? sentiment classification using machine learning techniques. In *Proceeding of EMNLP*.

J. Steinberger, P. Lenkova, M. Ebrahim, M. Ehrman, A. Hurriyetoglu, M. Kabadjov, R. Steinberger, H. Tanev, V. Zavarella, and S. Vazquez. 2011. Creating sentiment dictionaries via triangulation. In *Proceedings of the ACL's WASSA Workshop*.

M. Turchi, J. Steinberger, M. Kabadjov, and R. Steinberger. 2010. Using parallel corpora for multilingual (multi-document) summarisation evaluation. In *Proceedings of CLEF*.

X. Wan. 2008. Co-training for cross-lingual sentiment classification. In *Proceedings of ACL*.

J. Wiebe and R. Mihalcea. 2006. Word sense and subjectivity. In *Proceedings of COLING-ACL*.

J. Wiebe, T. Wilson, and C. Cardie. 2005. Annotating expressions of opinions and emotions in language. *Language Resources and Evaluation*, 39(2-3).

T. Wilson, J. Wiebe, and R. Hwa. 2004. Just how mad are you? finding strong and weak opinion clauses. In *Proceeding of AI*.

M. Van Zaanen, A. Roberts, and E. Atwell. 2004. A multilingual parallel parsed corpus as gold standard for grammatical inference evaluation. In *Proceedings of The Amazing Utility of Parallel and Comparable Corpora Workshop*.

Term Validation for Vocabulary Construction and Key Term Extraction

Alexander Ulanov
Hewlett-Packard Labs
alexander.ulanov@hp.com

Andrey Simanovsky
Hewlett-Packard Labs
andrey.simanovsky@hp.com

Abstract

We extract new terminology from a text by term validation in a dictionary. Our approach is based on estimating probabilities for previously unseen terms, i.e. not present in a dictionary. To do this we apply several probabilistic models previously not used for term recognition and propose a new one. We apply restriction of domain similarity on terms used for probability estimation and vary the parameters of the models. Performance of our approach is demonstrated using Wikipedia titles vocabulary.

1 Introduction

Keyphrase extraction or automatic term recognition is an important task in the area of information retrieval. It is used for annotating text articles, tagging documents, etc. Keyphrases facilitate easier searching, browsing documents, detecting topics, classification, adding contextual advertisement, and so on.

Current methods of term extraction rely either on statistics of terms inside documents or on external dictionaries. These approaches work relatively well with large texts and with specialized vocabularies. The problem arrives when a text contains a lot of cross-domain terms which are essential and vocabulary does not cover them. One option is to use several vocabularies: a very broad one, like Wikipedia or WordNet, and another one very specific, like Burton's legal thesaurus. Even in this case two types of terms will not be identified: new terms and term collocations. New terms appear in emerging areas, and established thesauri will not catch them. Term collocation means a specific term used in conjunction with a broad-sense term. Usually it is hard to automatically identify if collocation is a new term or not.

This paper addresses the problem of detecting new terms in a text that are missing in the dictionary in order to enrich it, or to create a new, domain-specific one.

2 State of the art

A comprehensive overview and comparison of automatic term recognition (ATR) methods is presented in (Zhang et al., 2008).

The generic approach includes chunking or POS-tagging, stop-word removal, and restricting candidate terms to phrases, usually noun-based (Frantzi and Ananiadou, 1999), (Wermter and Hahn, 2005). These candidates are ranked using word statistics or mappings to external dictionaries. Word statistics is used to calculate termhood and unithood. Termhood is a measure of term relevancy to the subject domain. Unithood is a measure of words cohesion in a term. Termhood is usually frequency-based, computed using plain TF or TF-IDF (Medelyan and Witten, 2006). Other approaches to termhood computation use a notion of weirdness (Ahmad et al., 2000), which is based on the term frequency in a different domain compared to the subject domain. It is extended to the notions of domain pertinence in (Sclano et al., 2007). In the work of (Wartena et al., 2010) term distributions are compared to background corpus as a measure of descriptiveness.

Dictionaries are used to verify that candidate terms cannot be split and POS tags are correct (Aubin and Hamon , 2006). Statistics across corpus can be combined with the values from the dictionary. Several measures of association strength (word cohesion) in bi-grams are inspected in this way (Fahmi et al., 2007). Mukherjea et al. (2004) use external dictionaries such as UMLS to learn typical term suffixes and affixes. Then they are used in patterns for terms extraction. The number of relations between found terms derived from thesauri is proposed to be used together with the term frequency as a ranking function in (Gazendam et al., 2010). Common terms dictionary is used in (OpenCalais, 2011) for term extraction.

The advantage of our approach is that it does not rely on terms frequency in a text. Instead it uses probabilistic model of a dictionary. The approach is beneficial when texts are rather small and where is the need to enrich a given dictionary. Our approach is more accurate comparing with the present works in which either patterns for finding terms are collected (Mukherjea et al., 2004) or any collocation with a dictionary term is considered as a new term (OpenCalais, 2011).

3 Proposed approach

We propose to detect new terminology with the use of models build on top of vocabularies. The question is how to do this since new terms are not present in vocabularies. We use language modeling approach and treat phrases as n-grams or sequences of tokens. We use bi-grams as approximation for phrases of other length for the sake of simplicity. All possible decompositions of phrases into two parts are considered.

There are several ways how to estimate the probability of unseen n-grams to be in a vocabulary. A straightforward way is redistribution of the probability mass via lower level conditional distributions:

$$P_{BO}(w_m/w_1^{m-1}) = \begin{cases} d_{w_1^m}\frac{c(w_1^m)}{c(w_1^{m-1})} & \text{if } c \geq k; \\ \alpha P_{BO}(w_m/w_1^{m-2}) & \text{otherwise} \end{cases},$$

where w_1^m is m-gram, c is the number of occurences (0 in our case), α is a normalizing constant, d is a probability discounting. In the back-off part this model doesn't address association strength between phrase tokens. This happens since it uses lower level conditional probabilities. This estimation is quite rough, at least for bi-grams. It happens because two words encountered separately may have extremely different meanings and frequencies as compared to when whey stand next to each other in a phrase. To cope with this problem, back-off model is updated with the notions of association strength and similarity restriction. The following smoothing model for bi-grams was proposed by Essen and Steinbiss (1992):

$$P_{SE}(w_2/w_1) = \sum_{w_1',w_2'} P(w_2/w_1')P(w_1'/w_2')P(w_2'/w_1),$$

where w_1 and w_1' are the first tokens, and w_2 and w_2' are the second tokens of bi-grams w_1w_2 and $w_1'w_2'$.

We also use the similarity model for bi-grams (Dagan et al., 1994):

$$P_{SD}(w_2/w_1) = \sum_{w_1' \in S(w_1)} P(w_2/w_1')\frac{W(w_1',w_1)}{\sum_{w_1' \in S(w_1)} W(w_1',w_1)},$$

where $W(w_1', w_1)$ is the weight that determines similarity between tokens w_1' and w_1.

In order to use both similarity and collocation strength we propose the following estimation for unobserved bi-grams in addition to the mentioned models (we will refer to it as "*C-Similarity*"):

$$P_{BS}(w_2/w_1) = \sum_{w_1',w_2'} P(w_2/w_1')P(w_2'/w_1), \quad S(w_1w_2', w_1'w_2) \geq S_{max}.$$

where S is the similarity function between bi-grams. The trivia behind this model is to find pairs of bi-grams that share common parts in the same places with unobserved ones. According to the similarity constraint, these bi-grams must be from the same domain.

4 Experiments

As we mentioned in the Introduction we believe that our model is preferrable among others in the case of short texts. The experimental setup was designed to test that hypothesis. We considered the extreme artificial scenario of texts composed of single phrases that should be either recognized as a term or not. We considered Wikipedia titles and their reversals as such collection of texts. Since Wikipedia editors aim at comprehensive coverage of all notable topics and are partial about including alternave lexical representations for them we can assume that if some reversal of a Wikipedia title is a term it should be present among Wikipedia titles. Thus, the titles and reversals collection could be correctly classified into terms and not terms by lookup into Wikipedia titles dictionary. We used that classification as a gold standard. The testing methodology included splitting the collection into training and test sets and measuring precision and recall of the models compared to the gold standard.

The mentioned term validation models were benchmarked using the discussed texts collection. We extracted all articles titles from the Wikipedia dump dated May 2010. Their total number is 8521847. Among them, there are 1567357 single word titles, 2928330 2-gram titles, and 1836494 3-gram titles. We filter out only 2-grams and 3-grams for the sake of simplicity [1].

The four above-mentioned models were used: back-off, smoothing, similarity, and co-similarity. For the similarity model we employed 2 different distance functions to compute W. The first is Kullback-Leibler distance D:

$$D(w_1 \| w_1') = \sum_{w_2} P(w_2/w_1) \log \frac{P(w_2/w_1)}{P(w_2/w_1')}.$$

This model is referred as "*Similarity-KL*". We also used:

$$W(w_1/w_1') = \sum_{w_2} P(w_2/w_1), w_2 : \exists w_2' S(w_1 w_2', w_1' w_2) \geq S_{max}.$$

This model is referred as "*Similarity-S*".

Wikipedia category structure is employed to measure similarities S between terms. For each term we extracted a subset of 27 Wikipedia main topic categories (categories from "Category:Main Topic Classifications"). A certain category was assigned to a term if it was reachable from this category by browsing the category tree down looking in at most 8 intermediate categories. Similarity between two terms was measured as Jaccard coefficient between corresponding category sets:

$$S(term_1, term_2) = \frac{|Categories_1 \bigcap Categories_2|}{|Categories_1 \bigcup Categories_2|}.$$

This function is too rough for determining semantic similarity on the given set of categories. However it is a good and fast approximation for the domain similarity.

We conduct experiments to measure precision and recall of each term validation model. Wikipedia was split into two parts of equal size using modulo 2 for articles *id*'s. Such splitting can be considered pseudo-random because article *id*'s roughly correspond to the order in which articles were added to Wikipedia. One part was treated as a set of observed n-grams and was used to train the models. The other part was used as a gold standard.

[1]We treat n-grams as bi-grams/tri-grams. All possible decompositions of n-grams into two parts are considered.

We required a set on which the gold standard would be a good approximation of the desired behavior of the system. Namely, we needed a set that would be considerably larger than the set of Wikipedia titles, and at the same time contain phrases that are unlikely to become Wikipedia titles. We created such a set by uniting the gold standard 2-grams and 3-grams with their reversals. We rely on an assumption that the editors deliberately decide to include either both or just one of the terms "X Y" and "Y X" into Wikipedia. Thus, we were able to estimate how good the golden standard can be predicted by the model and how precise it is. Precision (P) was computed in the following way:

$$P = \frac{N_{G \cap V}}{N_V},$$

where $N_{G \cap V}$ is the number of validated n-grams from the golden standard and N_V is the number of n-grams validated by the model.

Recall (R) was computed as:

$$R = \frac{N_{G \cap V}}{N_G},$$

where N_G is the number of n-grams in the golden standard.

In our tests, n-grams were validated by our model if their probability estimation exceeded a particular threshold. It was chosen as a minimum non-null probability estimation for an unobserved n-gram.

The results of the experiments are represented in Table 1. Back-off stands for back-off model (P_{BO}). Smoothing stands for Essen and Steinbiss model ($P_S E$). Similarity-KL and Similarity-S are the variations of similarity model which we described earlier. C-Similarity stands for the proposed original model. In brief, incorporating semantic similarity into the model allows the extraction to perform significantly better. As one can see from the table, the back-off model is very volatile with respect to Wikipedia titles. For 2-grams its unigram setting provides too relaxed assumptions, while for 3-trams it starts to lack statistics. Smoothing removes volatility, but appears to be too restrictive. The reason is that it relies on observation of connecting $w_1\prime w_2\prime$ 2-gram (we refer here to the 2-gram case). If the observation probability is replaced with an arbitrary weight $0 \leq W(w_1\prime w_2\prime) \leq 1$, we will obtain generalization of Smoothing and C-Similarity (for

C-Similarity W gets the values of 0 and 1 depending on the similarity between the q-grams). The similarity that was used is less restrictive as a smoothing factor than the observation probability. It is reflected by C-Similarity having smaller precision and greater recall than Smoothing. To compare C-Similarity with the previous similarity model we considered two weighting schemes. Similarity-KL uses a common approach with Kullback-Leibler divergence. Lack of semantics similarity resulted in Similarity-KL performing worse than C-Similarity. In Similarity-S we incorporated semantic similarity knowledge into the previous similarity model. As one can see from the results, our C-Similarity and Similarity-S demonstrate comparable quality, Similarity-S working better with 2-grams and C-Similarity outperforming on 3-grams.

Table 1: Term validation experiments results.

	2-grams		**3-grams**	
Model	**P**	**R**	**P**	**R**
Back-off	0.51	0.69	0.93	0.44
Smoothing	**0.78**	0.28	**0.95**	0.28
Similarity-KL	0.58	0.68	0.81	0.54
Similarity-S	0.58	**0.79**	0.82	0.65
C-Similarity	0.62	0.67	0.83	**0.66**

5 Conclusion

We applied a range of probabilistic models for estimating probability of previously unseen terms to be a part of a dictionary. They use dictionary statistics as compared to current approaches that use corpus. We proposed an additional model. All these models have not been applied before in the field of term recognition. Our experiments showed their applicability in the task of finding new terminology.

Our plans are to conduct more experiments and to use n-grams of any size for validation of a particular n-gram (not only with the same number of words). Further work is connected with exploring various model restrictions that may allow raising recall. For example, we will use various similarity functions. We plan to incorporate term validation with keyphrase extraction techniques as well. Another interesting direction is to iteratively find new terms and update dictionaries.

Our ultimate goal is to build domain-specific dictionaries and determine the meaning of newly discovered terms.

Compiling comparable corpora might be another area of application of the proposed model.

Acknowledgments

The authors would like to thank Dr. Pankaj Mehra for valuable and inspiring discussions.

References

Khurshid Ahmad, Lee Gillam, and Lena Tostevin. 2000. Weirdness Indexing for Logical Document Extrapolation and Retrieval (WILDER) In (Eds.) E.M. Voorhees and D.K. Harman. *The 8th Text Retrieval Conference (TREC-8)*: 717-724.

Sophie Aubin and Thierry Hamon. 2006. Improving Term Extraction with Terminological Resources. *In Advances in Natural Language Processing (5th International Conference on NLP, FinTAL 2006)*: 380-387.

Ido Dagan, Fernando Pereira, and Lillian Lee. 1994. Similarity-based estimation of word cooccurrence probabilities. *Proceedings of the 32nd annual meeting on Association for Computational Linguistics*: 272-278.

Ute Essen and Volker Steinbiss. 1992. Cooccurrence smoothing for stochastic language modeling. *IEEE International Conference on Acoustics, Speech, and Signal Processing*, 1:161-164.

Ismail Fahmi, Gosse Bouma, and Lonneke vd. Plas. 2007. Using Known Terms for Automatic Term Extraction. *Computational Linguistics in Nederland (CLIN)*.

Katerina T. Frantzi and Sophia Ananiadou. 1999. The c/nc value domain independent method for multiword term extraction. *Journal of Natural Language Processing*.

Luit Gazendam, Christian Wartena, and Rogier Brussee. 2010. Thesaurus Based Term Ranking for Keyword Extraction. *In 7th International Workshop on Text-based Information Retrieval*.

Slava M. Katz. 1987. Estimation of probabilities from sparse data for the language model component of a speech recognizer. *IEEE Transactions on Acoustics, Speech, and Signal Processing*, 35(3):400-401.

Olena Medelyan and Ian H. Witten. 2006. Thesaurus based automatic keyphrase indexing. *Proceedings of the 6th ACMIEEECS joint conference on Digital libraries JCDL 06*.

Sougata Mukherjea, L. Venkata Subramaniam, Gaurav Chanda, Sriram Sankararaman, Ravi Kothari, Vishal S. Batra, Deo N. Bhardwaj, and Biplav Srivastava.

2004. Enhancing a biomedical information extraction system with dictionary mining and context disambiguation. *IBM Journal of Research and Development*, 48(5-6): 693-702.

Reuters Thomson OpenCalais. 2011. `www.opencalais.com`.

Francesco Sclano and Paola Velardi. 2007. Termextractor: a web application to learn the shared terminology of emergent web communities. *In Proceedings of the 3rd International Conference on Interoperability for Enterprise Software andApplications (I-ESA 2007).*

Christian Wartena, Rogier Brussee, and Wout Slakhorst. 2010. Keyword Extraction using Word Co-occurrence. *In 7th International Workshop on Text-based Information Retrieval.*

Joachim Wermter and Udo Hahn. 2005. Finding new terminology in very large corpora. *Proceedings of the 3rd International Conference on Knowledge Capture (K-CAP 2005)*, 137-144.

Ziqi Zhang, Jose Iria, Christopher Brewster, and Fabio Ciravegna. A Comparative Evaluation of Term Recognition Algorithms. *In The sixth international conference on Language Resources and Evaluation, (LREC 2008).*

Agreement: How to Reach it?
Defining Language Features Leading to Agreement in Dialogue

Tatiana Zidraşco
Technical University of Moldova
tzidrashco@yahoo.com

Victoria Bobicev
Technical University of Moldova
victoria.bobicev@rol.md

Shun Shiramatsu
Nagoya Institute of Technolo
siramatu@toralab.ics.nitech.ac.jp

Tadachika Ozono
Nagoya Institute of Technology
ozono@toralab.ics.nitech.ac.jp

Toramatsu Shintani
Nagoya Institute of Technology
tora@toralab.ics.nitech.ac.jp

Abstract

Consensus is the desired result in many argumentative discourses such as negotiations, public debates, and goal-oriented forums. However, due to the fact that usually people are poor arguers, a support of argumentation is necessary. Web-2 provides means for the online discussions which have their characteristic features. In our paper we study the features of discourse which lead to agreement. We use an argumentative corpus of Wikipedia discussions in order to investigate the influence of discourse structure and language on the final agreement. The corpus had been annotated with rhetorical relations and rhetorical structures leading to successful and unsuccessful discussions were analyzed. We also investigated language patterns extracted from the corpus in order to discover which ones are indicators of the following agreement. The results of our study can be used in system designing, whose purpose is to assist on-line interlocutors in consensus building.

1 Introduction

The issue of consensus building within discourse has become more substantial since the computer and web technologies offer vast opportunities for public debates, collaborative discussions, negotiations etc. In computational linguistics there have been numerous studies dedicated to discourse analysis, modelling and analysis of collaboration (Chu-Carroll and Carbery, 1998; Sidner 1994), negotiations (Sokolova et.al. 2004) and agreement process (Di Eugenio et al., 2000).

Two important components of discourse studies are representation of discourse structure and language. We investigated discourse structure in an attempt to find out how it can reflect successful or unsuccessful result of a web-discussion. Our aim was to determine structures of discourse representation that lead to consensus at the end of the discussion and structures that do not lead to consensus. We think these types of structures could help for better understanding of position and intentions of participants during agreement process. We performed our study using web-discussions (Wikipedia Talk pages, English language), where participants had as their goal to agree upon the editing policy of Wikipedia articles.

To build up the discourse structure we used Rhetorical Structure Theory (RST) relations (Mann and Thomson, 1987). We then applied statistical analysis to our corpus of discussions annotated with 918 relations.

As mentioned before, another important component of discourse analysis is language cue or better said those words and phrases used by the participants to directly indicate the structure of the argument to the other participants. After preliminary determination of some rhetorical structures that could lead to consensus, we, as well, investigated how language reflects success or failure in our web-discussions.

2 Related works

There have been a number of approaches of modelling and analyzing negotiation and agreement process in computational linguistics.

In (Sidner 1994) multiagent collaborative planning discourse is analyzed and an artificial language is formulated for modeling such discourse. Multiagent collaborative planning process is represented in artificial language as one agent making a proposal to the other agents, and the other agents either accept or reject this proposal. Modeling is done using proposal/acceptance and proposal/rejection sequences. Propose-Evaluation-Modify framework for collaboration is proposed in (Chu-Carroll and Carbery, 1998). They focus on identifying strategies for content selection, when 1) the system initiates information-sharing to gather further information in order to make an informed decision about whether to accept a proposal from the user, and 2) the system initiates collaborative negotiation to negotiate with the user to resolve a detected conflict in the user's proposal. A slightly different approach to the problem of modeling of agreement process is described in (Di Eugenio et al., 2000). They propose specific instantiations of the agreement process attuned to the characteristics of task oriented dialogues. They model their participant's collaborative behavior according to Balance-Propose-Dispose agreement process and they focus on how information is exchanged in order to arrive to a proposal and what constitutes a proposal and it acceptance or rejection and discover that the notion of commitment is more useful to model the agreement process. We proposed to build discourse structure using RST and based on empirical analysis, to determine which types of discourse structures are leading to final consensus.

In (Sokolova et.al. 2004) the preliminary study investigates how language reflects success or failure of electronic negotiations. They seek text characteristics which can help in prediction of negotiations success or failure. Using NLP and ML techniques they show how language differs in successful and failed negotiations. Thus we have also analyzed the discussion language in order to identify language features that influence the outcome in argumentative discourse.

3 Discourse structure

We collected a corpus of discussions from Wikipedia free encyclopedia Talk pages. The purpose of Wikipedia talk page is to provide space for editors to discuss changes to associated article or project page. We stopped at Wikipedia discussions for two reasons: 1) these are web-mediated discussions; 2) these are task-oriented discussion - the purpose is to reach consensus when discussing subtopics related to the final version of Wikipedia article. Each subtopic was discussed by two or more participants (editors). We considered a discussion to be successful when most of the participants agreed on the solution of the problem given within the subtopic at the time given.

As mentioned above, we aimed to represent argumentative discourse structure so, that it would be possible to analyze the consensus building process within the discourse. To build up the structure of the discourse we address Rhetorical Structure Theory; we use rhetorical relations, which are well-known tagging schemes for annotating both monologue texts and dialogues (Toboada and Mann, 2005). The kinds of intentional relations we borrowed from RST include *evidence, justification* (original *justify*), *background, concession* etc. We, as well, introduced additional rhetorical relations that helped to reflect the structure of argumentative discussions. For example, in such discussions, it is important for question-answer pairs to identify the question intention. So we added *require evidence, require detail, require yes/no* rhetorical relations. We obtained 27 rhetorical relations that can be divided into 7 groups that have some common rhetorical meaning: *Answer, Argumentation, Consensus, Question, Action Request, Dialogue Act, and Conclusion.* For example, *Consensus* includes *agreement* and *disagreement* relations. In Table 1 we present the example of organization of our annotation tag set.

For the cases when the relation definition is not covered with any of the rhetorical relations from our tag set, we introduce relation tag unknown.

Next issue, following the definition of the tag set was determination of annotation elementary unit. Since one user's statement might contain different types of information; we segmented statements into units corresponding to speech acts. According to the definition, speech act is a term that refers to the act of successful communicating an intended understanding to the listener. Each speech act within one user's statement has a separate speech function like asking question, explaining, etc. Thus, in this study, speech act became the elementary unit for annotation.

Answer	Action Request
Affirmation	Request to do
Negation	Suggestion
Argumentation	*Dialogue Act*
Evidence	Apology
Justification	Accusation
Elaboration	Gratitude
Explanation	Ironic_comment
Background	Offence
Example	Solution
Consensus	Warning
Agreement	*Conclusion*
Disagreement	Concession
Question	Summary
Require evidence	Unknown
Require detail	Response
Require yes/no	Addition

Table 1: Annotation tag set

Once, the elementary units have been determined, text segments were connected through rhetorical relations, building discourse structure. For each unit one or more relations were allowed. For example, the sample below,

A: (1) I think you should stop smoking
B: (2) Why should i?
A: (3) For example, me, stopped smoking two years ago.

was annotated in the following way: (1) ← (2) was tagged as *require evidence,* (2) ← (3) as *response*, (1) ← (3) was labeled as *example.*

The annotation was done with the help of the tool for visualizing the discussion structure. The tool allowed to segment participants' statements into units and provided annotator with the list of the rhetorical relations.

4 Rhetorical structure analysis

To investigate the influence of rhetorical structures on agreement we model our discourse as a directed graph with nodes representing statements and arcs representing rhetorical relations that hold between statements. We first investigated the frequency of rhetorical relations. The most frequent relations are listed in Table 2. As it can be seen, the most frequent rhetorical relations were *evidence, agreement, disagreement.*

We assumed that successful or unsuccessful tendency of argumentative discourse can be determined through patterns of rhetorical structures that hold between the discourse units.

Relation	Frequency	Percentage
Explanation	151	16.4%
Agreement	150	16.3%
Disagreement	135	14.7%
Suggestion	96	10.5%
Evidence	55	6.0%
Justification	42	4.6%
Require evidence	41	4.5%
Gratitude	29	3.2%
Answer	29	3.2%
Ironic_comment	27	2.9%
Other rhetorical relations	96	10.5%
Total	918	100%

Table 2: Frequent rhetorical relations

For example, we presumed that the discourse sub – graph structures *require evidence – evidence* or *evidence – agreement* have tendency to create a successful discussion. In addition, we made a supposition, that in successful discussions the number of pairs such as *evidence – agreement* will be bigger compared to the *evidence – disagreement* or *suggestion – agreement.*

To verify the assumptions, we firstly, analyzed our corpus performing so called sequence-based analysis. We counted frequencies of bigrams of rhetorical relations (r1, r2), where let r1 be a preceding relation and r2 be a succeeding relation that follows r1. We calculated frequency of rhetorical relations bigrams for *agreement* (*disagreement*) pairs and calculated priori

$$P(r2|r1)=C(r1,r2)/C(r1) \quad (1)$$

and posterior

$$P(r1|r2)=C(r1,r2)/C(r2) \quad (2)$$

probabilities, where, C(r) and C(r1,r2) denote frequencies of a rhetorical relation r and relation bigram (r1,r2), respectively. Here, C(r) and C(r1,r2) denote frequencies of a rhetorical relation r and relation bigram (r1,r2), respectively. These calculations allow us to identify rhetorical relations that precede *agreement* and *disagreement*. The results are presented in Table 3 and Table 4.

We sorted data by posteriori probability of preceding relation when the following relation is agreement/disagreement, because it can be regarded as a contribution of preceding rhetorical relation for consensus building. The results showed that, most frequently, agreement relation was preceded by evidence.

Relation r_1	$P(r_2$=Agreement$\|r_1)$		$P(r_1\|r_2$= Agreement)	
Evidence	0.176	(12/68)	0.072	(12/166)
Suggestion	0.170	(19/112)	0.114	(19/ 166)
Disagreement	0.133	(22/166)	0.133	(22/ 166)
Agreement	0.120	(20/166)	0.120	(20/ 166)
Answer	0.138	(4 / 29)	0.024	(4 / 166)
Explanation	0.107	(18 /169)	0.108	(18/ 166)
Require evidence	0.082	(4 / 49)	0.024	(4 / 166)
Justification	0.021	(1 / 47)	0.006	(1 / 166)

Table 3: Priori and posteriori probability for most frequent agreement pairs

Relation r_1	$P(r_2$=Disagreement$\|r_1)$		$P(r_1\|r_2$=Disagreement)	
Evidence	0.221	(15/68)	0.090	(1 / 166)
Suggestion	0.277	(31/112)	0.187	(31/ 166)
Disagreement	0.127	(21/166)	0.127	(21/ 166)
Agreement	0.024	(4/166)	0.024	(4 / 166)
Answer	0.034	(1/29)	0.006	(1 / 166)
Explanation	0.077	(13/169)	0.078	(13/ 166)
Require evidence	0	(0/49)	0	(0 / 166)
Justification	0.064	(3/ 47)	0.018	(3 / 166)

Table 4: Priori and posteriori probability for most frequent disagreement pairs

After that, we applied Evidence-based analysis to investigate the influence of contribution (on this stage it is evidence) relation on final agreement. The contribution relation r1 is a target relation for analyzing its influence on final consensus relation. The consensus relation r2 corresponds to agreement or disagreement. Here we concentrated on evidence as the contribution relation. There is a probability that usually when evidence is given, it will be rather followed by agreement. We calculated the probability of the bigram (r1, r2) to see the probability that agreement would come after the evidence.

We considered the following two possibilities: when r2 is agreement (disagreement), while r1 is Evidence and when r2 is agreement (disagreement), while r1 is any other rhetorical relation. We compared ratios of appearing of agreement and disagreement in evidenced and non-evidenced pairs and observed the following inequations from our corpus

$$(r2 = Agr|r1 = Ev) > P(r2 = Agr|r1 \neq Ev) \quad (3)$$

and

$$P(r2 = Agr|r1 = Ev) > P(r2 = Disagr|r1 = Ev) \quad (4).$$

Fisher's exact test for (3) showed that (3) is statistically significant in 1% level because p-value was 0.0047 (<0.01). Hence, the two 95% confidence intervals for

$$P(r2 = Agr|r1 = Ev)$$

and

$$P(r2 = Agr|r1 \neq Ev)$$

do not overlap. Fisher's exact test for (4) showed that observation of (4) didn't have enough statistical significance because p-value was 0.146 (>0.01). That is, the results indicated partial validity of our assumption about *evidence* being the first relation followed by *agreement*, which allowed us to say that evidenced structures tend to lead to success in discussions.

5 Language patterns investigation

We also made another assumption, that language used in discussions has an impact on consensus building. Thus, we decided to analyze word unigrams, bigrams and trigrams in different types of statements. (Sokolova et al., 2004) proved that there were characteristic words for successful and unsuccessful negotiations called 'indicative words'.

We made an attempt to make similar analysis for our corpus. The corpus consisted of 320 files of Wikipedia discussion pages, total number of word tokens was 148948 and number of word types was 11545.

In (Sokolova et al., 2004) analysis of negotiations were based on the final result: success or failure of the negotiation; thus all discussion was considered as successful or unsuccessful. In our dialogue there was no final result; we concentrated on each message as one unit with its rhetorical relation. Firstly, we made frequency dictionaries of words, word bigrams and word trigrams for all messages annotated with the same rhetorical relations. Quick analysis of these dictionaries revealed 'indicative words' for the relations. For example, *disagreement* is indicated with the higher rate of negations 'not', 'i don't', 'there is no', 'it is not', etc. *agreement* on the contrary, had clear indicators: 'I agree with', 'have to agree'. However, not all relations could be detected so easily; for example, *justification, explanation, suggestion* had less specific words and much more content words referring to the discussed topic. As 'indicative words' for these relations could be mentioned:

- *justification* – adverbs 'reasonably', 'rather', 'as well';

- *explanation* – verbs 'want to', 'could be', 'I feel';
- *suggestion* – 'I think', 'should be', 'we should'.

Actually, the investigation of 'indicative words' for different type of relations should be a more extensive study which we plan for the future. In this paper we concentrated on the connections between relations, particularly on the relations which preceded *agreement* and *disagreement* messages.

We selected all relations pairs r1, r2, where r2 is agreement or disagreement and r1 is the message which precedes r2. We create the unigram, bigram and trigram frequency dictionaries for r1 messages which preceded agreement or disagreement respectively and calculated log-likelihood statistics as was described in (Sokolova et al., 2004). The next step was the comparison of words for one type of messages which preceded agreement and disagreement respectively in order to reveal which words are indicative for the following agreement. In Table 5 the most frequent pairs of relations are presented, their indicative words and some comments are added.

In general, we observed that bigrams and trigrams of words which are indicative for agreement do not depend on relation. For all relations we investigated, specific features for agreement are gentle, polite phrases. Also, to our surprise, pronouns have the great impact on following agreement: 'we' is good indicator of agreement, while 'you' indicate opposition, especially in phrases 'you have', and 'you should'. We did not find verbs to be indicative words. Adverbs also have less impact on the result.

6 Conclusion

In the paper we attempted to investigate two important components of the discourse: representation of the discourse structure and linguistic cues. We proposed to represent discourse structure using Rhetorical Structure Theory and based on empirical analysis, to determine what types of rhetorical structures in the discourse do lead to final consensus. We collected a corpus of web-mediated discussions from Wikipedia and annotated it with our tag set of rhetorical relations. Our corpus contained 1764 statements with the total number of 506 participants and 918 rhetorical relations labels that connected statements. We made an assumption that successful or unsuccessful tendency of argumentative discourse can be determined through patterns of rhetorical structures that hold between the discourse units. To verify the assumptions, we applied two types of statistical analysis: *sequence-based* and *Evidence-based* which allowed us to detect the existence of rhetorical structures patterns that could influence consensus building in collaborative discussion.

Relation bigram		indicative words	comments
r_1	r_2		
Suggestion	Agreement	i think, we have, could be, kinds of, think we should, we could	use of pronoun 'we' predominate, which indicate that people are rather colleagues than opponents
Suggestion	Disagreement	highly, quite, rather, reason is quite, should be, would be, better to	suggestions are more categorical and are formulated as from superior to inferior which provoke negation
Explanation	Agreement	if i'm wrong, maybe, correct me if, we should, why should, i feel	a mild language, less personal, more text on topic, the pronoun 'we' is used again
Explanation	Disagreement	will not admit, you can, no good	the phrases used are categorical and the authors form opposition
Evidence	Agreement	we, if, a few, a certain, for the purposes, deem that, can cite some	less indicative words, more text about the topic, the language is more concrete and more gentle
Evidence	Disagreement	you due to, you need a, you will need, you'd have to	an aggressive language with many combinations of 'you have', 'you should', etc.

Table 5: The most frequent pairs of rhetorical relations, their indicative words and comments

The obtained results partially confirm our assumptions about existence of discourse structures that can indicate tendency to consensus. It should be mentioned in this respect, that in order to obtain more extensive and reliable results, it would also be desirable to investigate which relations are significantly more often appearing before *agreement* and *disagreement,* rather than only focus on the evidence analysis. Also other criteria, as for example, participants ID of statements and considering relationship between participants during the analysis, would be important factors for the consensus building.

Investigation of the indicative words unigrams, bigrams and trigrams showed that specific features of language which led to *agreement* or *disagreement* were similar indifferent which type of rhetorical relation preceded *agreement* or *disagreement* respectively. Actually, one of the most natural extensions of the study of language in discussion is more sophisticated statistical method application but our corpus is comparatively small and data is rather sparse. Thus we leave this study for the future when we obtain more annotated texts

The results we obtained could be used for consensus facilitating function design in an argumentation support system.

References

Ann Macintosh, Thomas F. Gordon, and Alastair Renton.2009 *Providing Argument Support for E- Participation.* Journal of Information Technology & Politics, 6(1):43-59.

Amanda Stent. 2000. *Rhetorical Structure in Dialog.* Proc. 1st Int. Conf. on Natural Language Generation (INLG'2000), Mitzpe Ramon, Israel, pp. 247-252.

Barbara Di Eugenio, Richmond. H. Thomason, Pamela W. Jordan, Johanna D. Moore. 2000 *The Agreement Process: an Empirical Investigation of Human-Human Computer-Mediated Collaborative Dialogues.* International Journal of Human Computer Studies 53(6):1017-1076.

Bart Verheij. 2001. *Artificial Argument Assistants for Defeasible Argumentation.* Artificial Intelligence: 150 (1-2):291-324.

Candace L. Sidner. 1995. *An Artificial Discourse Language for Collaborative Negotiation.* In Proc. 12th Nat. Conf. on Artificial Intelligence, pp. 814-819.

Chris Reed, Glen Rowe. 2004. *Araucaria: Software for Argument Analysis, Diagramming and Representation.* International Journal of AI Tools, 14, pp. 961-980.

Chu-Carroll, Jennifer and Sandra Carberry. 1998. *Collaborative Response Generation in Planning Dialogues.* Computational Linguistics 24(3):355-400.

Johanna D. Moore, C. L. Paris. 1993. *Planning text for advisory dialogues: Capturing Intentional and Rhetorical Information.* In Computational linguistics - Association for Computational Linguistics, MIT Press, Cambridge, MA, ETATS-UNIS, pp. 651-694.

K. Hashida. 2007. *Semantic Authoring and Semantic Computing.* In Artificial Intelligence: Joint Proc. of the 17th and 18th An. Conf. of the Japanese Society for Artificial Intelligence, eds . A. Sakurai, K. Hashida, K. Nitta Vol. 3609 of Lecture Notes in Computer Science, Springer, pp. 137-149.

Lynn Carlson, Daniel Marcu, Mary Elen Okurowski. 2003. *Building a Discourse-Tagged Corpus in the Framework o Rhetorical Structure Theory.* In Current Directions in Discourse and Dialogue, eds. j. van Kuppevelt and R. Smith, Kluwer Academic Publishers, pp 85-112.

Marina Sokolova, Vivi Nastase, Stan Szpakowicz. 2004. Language in Electronic Negotiations: Patterns in Completed and Uncompleted Negotiations, Natural Language Processing (Proceedings of ICON'2004), pp.142-151.

Maite Taboada, William C. Mann. 2005. Applications of Rhetorical Structure Theory, Discourse Studies 8 (4):567—588.

Natasa Jovanovic, Rieks op den Akker, Anton Nijholt. 2006. A Corpus for Studying Addressing Behaviour in Multi-Party Dialogues, Springer Science + Business Media B.V.

O. Scheuer, F. Loll, N. Pinkwart, B. M. McLaren. 2010. *Computer-supported argumentation: A review of the state of the art, International Society of the Learning Sciences.* In: International Journal of Computer-Supported Collaborative Learning (IJCSCL), 5(1): 43-102.

R. Tokuhisa, R. Terashima. 2006. *Relationship between Utterances and "Enthusiasm" in Non-task-oriented Conversational Dialogue.* In Proc. 7th SIGDIAL Workshop on Discourse and Dialogue, Sydney, pp. 161-167.

Thanasis, Daradoumis, 1996. *Towards a Representation of the Rhetorical structure of Interrupted Exchanges, Trends in Natural Language Generation: An Artificial Intelligence Perspective.* Springer, Berlin, pp. 106-124.

William C. Mann, Sandra A. Thompson. 1987. Rhetorical Structure Theory: A Theory of Text Organization, ISI: Information Sciences Institute, Los Angeles, CA, ISI/RS-87-190, 1-81. Reprinted from *The Structure of Discourse, L. Polanyi, ed.*

Author Index

Association for Computational Linguistics
209 N. Eighth Street
Stroudsburg, Pennsylvania 18360